CRIMINAL PRACTICE

BLACKSTONE'S

CRIMINAL PRACTICE

2016

RULES AND GUIDELINES

GENERAL EDITORS

DAVID ORMEROD QC (HON)

LAW COMMISSIONER, BARRISTER, BENCHER OF MIDDLE TEMPLE, PROFESSOR OF CRIMINAL JUSTICE, UNIVERSITY COLLEGE LONDON

DAVID PERRY QC

BARRISTER, 6KBW COLLEGE HILL

FOUNDING EDITOR

HHJ PETER MURPHY

CONSULTANT EDITOR

HHJ JOHN PHILLIPS CBE

CONTRIBUTORS

DUNCAN ATKINSON, ALEX BAILIN QC, DIANE BIRCH OBE, ED CAPE, HHJ JOHANNAH CUTTS QC, ANAND DOOBAY, ANTHONY EDWARDS, RUDI FORTSON QC, MICHAEL HIRST, LAURA C. H. HOYANO, PETER HUNGERFORD-WELCH, PAUL JARVIS, ADRIAN KEANE, MICHAEL LEREGO QC, RICHARD MCMAHON QC, VALSAMIS MITSILEGAS, TIM MOLONEY QC, STEPHEN PARKINSON, AMANDA PINTO QC, EDWARD REES QC, HHJ PETER ROOK QC, RICHARD D. TAYLOR, MARK TOPPING, CLARE WADE, MARTIN WASIK CBE

OXFORD
UNIVERSITY PRESS

OXFORD
UNIVERSITY PRESS

Great Clarendon Street, Oxford, OX2 6DP,
United Kingdom

Oxford University Press is a department of the University of Oxford.
It furthers the University's objective of excellence in research, scholarship,
and education by publishing worldwide. Oxford is a registered trade mark of
Oxford University Press in the UK and in certain other countries

First Edition published in 2016
Impression: 1

Published in the United States of America by Oxford University Press
198 Madison Avenue, New York, NY 10016, United States of America

British Library Cataloguing in Publication Data
Data available

ISBN 978–0–19–876640–7

Printed and bound in Great Britain by
Ashford Colour Press Ltd, Gosport, Hampshire

Introduction

Blackstone's Rules and Guidelines contains the complete text of the Criminal Procedure Rules 2015, the Criminal Practice Directions, and the Sentencing Guidelines, as at 1 February 2016.

In 2013 the Practice Direction was restructured and revised to make it more accessible and useful to practitioners. A key part of that change was to rearrange the Practice Direction so that it corresponded as far as practicable with the related parts of the Criminal Procedure Rules.

In this book, to assist practitioners further, the Criminal Procedure Rules and the relevant Practice Directions are presented as a single integrated document.

Please visit the *Blackstone's Criminal Practice 2016* companion website at www.oup.com/blackstones/criminal for free online monthly updates and other digital products. You may also register to receive the *Blackstone's Criminal Practice Update*, a free quarterly newsletter. If you have any queries, please contact blackstonescriminal@oup.com.

Contents

Table of Cases

Table of Statutes

Table of Statutory Instruments

Table of Practice Directions

Table of Codes of Conduct

Table of Guidelines

Table of Protocols and Circulars

Table of International Treaties and Conventions and other Legal Instruments

Table of European Legislation

CRIMINAL PROCEDURE RULES 2015 AND CRIMINAL PRACTICE DIRECTIONS

Criminal Procedure Rules 2015 (SI 2015 No. 1490) and Criminal Practice Directions

The following text reproduces the Criminal Procedure Rules 2015 and the Criminal Practice Directions which are in force from 5 October 2015. The objective of the restructuring and revision of the Practice Direction in 2013 was to make it more accessible and useful to practitioners and a key part of that is arranging the Practice Direction so as to correspond so far as practicable with the related parts of the Criminal Procedure Rules. We have integrated the texts of the Rules and the Practice Direction so far as possible. The text of the Rules is displayed in black text and is accompanied by a number (e.g., **R-36**) in addition to the numbering in the rules themselves. The text of the Practice Direction is displayed in grey boxes and follows the relevant text of the Rules (save where this is impracticable) and is accompanied by a number (e.g., **PD-18**) in addition to the number used in the Practice Direction itself.

Criminal Practice Directions General Matters

CPD I General matters A **PD-1**

A.1 The Lord Chief Justice has power, including power under section 74 of the Courts Act 2003 and Part 1 of Schedule 2 to the Constitutional Reform Act 2005, to make directions as to the practice and procedure of the criminal courts. The following directions are given accordingly.

A.2 These Practice Directions replace the Criminal Practice Directions given on 7th October 2013 [2013] EWCA Crim 1631; [2013] 1 WLR 3164 as amended by the Directions given on (i) 10th December, 2013 [2013] EWCA Crim 2328; [2014] 1 WLR 35, (ii) 23rd July, 2014 [2014] EWCA Crim 1569; [2014] 1 WLR 3001, (iii) 18th March, 2015 [2015] EWCA Crim 430; [2015] 1 WLR 1643 and (iv) 16th July, 2015 [2015] EWCA Crim 1253.

A.3 Annexes D and E to the Consolidated Criminal Practice Direction of 8th July, 2002, [2002] 1 WLR 2870; [2002] 2 Cr App R 35, as amended, which set out forms for use in connection with the Criminal Procedure Rules, remain in force. See also paragraph I 5A of these Practice Directions.

A.4 These Practice Directions supplement many, but not all, Parts of the Criminal Procedure Rules, and include other directions about practice and procedure in the courts to which they apply. They are to be known as the Criminal Practice Directions 2015. They come into force on 5th October, 2015. They apply to all cases in all the criminal courts of England and Wales from that date.

A.5 Consequent on the rearrangement of the Criminal Procedure Rules in the Criminal Procedure Rules 2015, SI 2015/1490:

(a) the content of these Practice Directions is arranged to correspond. Within each division of these Directions the paragraphs are numbered to correspond with the associated Part of the Criminal Procedure Rules 2015. Compared with the Criminal Practice Directions given in 2013, as amended, the numbering and content of some divisions is amended consequentially, as shown in this table:

Derivations	
Divisions of 2015 Directions	***Divisions of 2013 Directions***
I General matters	I General matters;
II Preliminary proceedings	II Preliminary proceedings 16A — C II Preliminary proceedings 9A, 10A, 14A — B
III Custody and bail	III Custody and bail
IV Disclosure	IV Disclosure
V Evidence	V Evidence
VI Trial	VI Trial
VII Sentencing	VII Sentencing
VIII Confiscation and related proceedings [empty]	VIII Confiscation and related proceedings [empty]
IX Appeal	X Appeal
X Costs [Criminal Costs Practice Direction]	XI Costs [Criminal Costs Practice Direction]
XI Other proceedings	II Preliminary proceedings 6A, 17A — F; IX Contempt of court
XII General application	XII General application
XIII Listing	XIII Listing

(b) the text of these Practice Directions is amended:
   (i) to bring up to date the cross-references to the Criminal Procedure Rules and to other paragraphs of these Directions which that text contains, and
   (ii) to adopt the abbreviation of references to the Criminal Procedure Rules ('CrimPR') for which rule 2.3(2) of the Criminal Procedure Rules 2015 provides.

A.6 In all other respects, the content of the Criminal Practice Directions 2015 reproduces that of the Criminal Practice Directions 2013, as amended.

CRIMINAL PROCEDURE RULES PART 1 THE OVERRIDING OBJECTIVE

R-1 **The overriding objective**

1.1 (1) The overriding objective of this procedural code is that criminal cases be dealt with justly.
(2) Dealing with a criminal case justly includes—
   (a) acquitting the innocent and convicting the guilty;
   (b) dealing with the prosecution and the defence fairly;
   (c) recognising the rights of a defendant, particularly those under Article 6 of the European Convention on Human Rights;
   (d) respecting the interests of witnesses, victims and jurors and keeping them informed of the progress of the case;
   (e) dealing with the case efficiently and expeditiously;
   (f) ensuring that appropriate information is available to the court when bail and sentence are considered; and
   (g) dealing with the case in ways that take into account—
      (i) the gravity of the offence alleged,
      (ii) the complexity of what is in issue,
      (iii) the severity of the consequences for the defendant and others affected, and
      (iv) the needs of other cases.

R-2 **The duty of the participants in a criminal case**

1.2 (1) Each participant, in the conduct of each case, must—
   (a) prepare and conduct the case in accordance with the overriding objective;
   (b) comply with these Rules, practice directions and directions made by the court; and
   (c) at once inform the court and all parties of any significant failure (whether or not that participant is responsible for that failure) to take any procedural step required by these Rules, any practice direction or any direction of the court. A failure is significant if it might hinder the court in furthering the overriding objective.
(2) Anyone involved in any way with a criminal case is a participant in its conduct for the purposes of this rule.

R-3 **The application by the court of the overriding objective**

1.3 The court must further the overriding objective in particular when—
   (a) exercising any power given to it by legislation (including these Rules);
   (b) applying any practice direction; or
   (c) interpreting any rule or practice direction.

CRIMINAL PRACTICE DIRECTIONS PART 1 THE OVERRIDING OBJECTIVE

PD-2 **CPD I General matters 1A: The Overriding Objective**

1A.1 The presumption of innocence and an adversarial process are essential features of English and Welsh legal tradition and of the defendant's right to a fair trial. But it is no part of a fair trial that questions of guilt and innocence should be determined by procedural manoeuvres. On the contrary, fairness is best served when the issues between the parties are identified as early and as clearly as possible. As Lord Justice Auld noted, a criminal trial is not a game under which a guilty defendant should be provided with a sporting chance. It is a search for truth in accordance with the twin principles that the prosecution must prove its case and that a defendant is not obliged to inculpate himself, the object being to convict the guilty and acquit the innocent.

1A.2 Further, it is not just for a party to obstruct or delay the preparation of a case for trial in order to secure some perceived procedural advantage, or to take unfair advantage of a mistake by someone else. If courts allow that to happen it damages public confidence in criminal justice. The Rules and the Practice Direction, taken together, make it clear that courts must not allow it to happen.

Criminal Procedure Rules Part 2 Understanding and Applying the Rules

When the Rules apply R-4

2.1 (1) In general, the Criminal Procedure Rules apply—
(a) in all criminal cases in magistrates' courts and in the Crown Court;
(b) in extradition cases in the High Court; and
(c) in all cases in the criminal division of the Court of Appeal.
(2) If a rule applies only in one or some of those courts, the rule makes that clear.
(3) These Rules apply on and after 5th October, 2015, but—
(a) unless the court otherwise directs, they do not affect a right or duty existing under the Criminal Procedure Rules 2014; and
(b) unless the High Court otherwise directs, Section 3 of Part 50 (Extradition — appeal to the High Court) does not apply to a case in which notice of an appeal was given before 6th October, 2014.
(4) In a case in which a request for extradition was received by a relevant authority in the United Kingdom on or before 31st December, 2003—
(a) the rules in Part 50 (Extradition) do not apply; and
(b) the rules in Part 17 of the Criminal Procedure Rules 2012 (Extradition) continue to apply as if those rules had not been revoked.

Definitions R-5

2.2 (1) In these Rules, unless the context makes it clear that something different is meant:
'advocate' means a person who is entitled to exercise a right of audience in the court under section 13 of the Legal Services Act 2007;
'business day' means any day except Saturday, Sunday, Christmas Day, Boxing Day, Good Friday, Easter Monday or a bank holiday;
'court' means a tribunal with jurisdiction over criminal cases. It includes a judge, recorder, District Judge (Magistrates' Court), lay justice and, when exercising their judicial powers, the Registrar of Criminal Appeals, a justices' clerk or assistant clerk;
'court officer' means the appropriate member of the staff of a court;
'justices' legal adviser' means a justices' clerk or an assistant to a justices' clerk;
'legal representative' means:
(i) the person for the time being named as a party's representative in any legal aid representation order made under section 16 of the Legal Aid, Sentencing and Punishment of Offenders Act 2012, or
(ii) subject to that, the person named as a party's representative in any notice for the time being given under rule 46.2 (Notice of appointment or change of legal representative), provided that person is entitled to conduct litigation in the court under section 13 of the Legal Services Act 2007;
'live link' means an arrangement by which a person can see and hear, and be seen and heard by, the court when that person is not in court;
'Practice Direction' means the Lord Chief Justice's Criminal Practice Directions, as amended, and 'Criminal Costs Practice Direction' means the Lord Chief Justice's Practice Direction (Costs in Criminal Proceedings), as amended;
'public interest ruling' means a ruling about whether it is in the public interest to disclose prosecution material under sections 3(6), 7A(8) or 8(5) of the Criminal Procedure and Investigations Act 1996; and
'Registrar' means the Registrar of Criminal Appeals or a court officer acting with the Registrar's authority.
(2) Definitions of some other expressions are in the rules in which they apply.

References to legislation, including these Rules R-6

2.3 (1) In these Rules, where a rule refers to an Act of Parliament or to subordinate legislation by title and year, subsequent references to that Act or to that legislation in the rule are shortened: so, for example, after a reference to the Criminal Procedure and Investigations Act 1996 that Act is called 'the 1996 Act'; and after a reference to the Criminal Procedure and Investigations Act 1996 (Defence Disclosure Time Limits) Regulations 2011 those Regulations are called 'the 2011 Regulations'.
(2) In the courts to which these Rules apply—
(a) unless the context makes it clear that something different is meant, a reference to the Criminal Procedure Rules, without reference to a year, is a reference to the Criminal Procedure Rules in force at the date on which the event concerned occurs or occurred;

(b) a reference to the Criminal Procedure Rules may be abbreviated to 'CrimPR'; and
(c) a reference to a Part or rule in the Criminal Procedure Rules may be abbreviated to, for example, 'CrimPR Part 3' or 'CrimPR 3.5'.

Criminal Procedure Rules Part 3 Case Management

General rules

R-7 When this Part applies

3.1 (1) Rules 3.1 to 3.12 apply to the management of each case in a magistrates' court and in the Crown Court (including an appeal to the Crown Court) until the conclusion of that case.
(2) Rules 3.13 to 3.26 apply where—
(a) the defendant is sent to the Crown Court for trial;
(b) a High Court or Crown Court judge gives permission to serve a draft indictment; or
(c) the Court of Appeal orders a retrial.

R-8 The duty of the court

3.2 (1) The court must further the overriding objective by actively managing the case.
(2) Active case management includes—
(a) the early identification of the real issues;
(b) the early identification of the needs of witnesses;
(c) achieving certainty as to what must be done, by whom, and when, in particular by the early setting of a timetable for the progress of the case;
(d) monitoring the progress of the case and compliance with directions;
(e) ensuring that evidence, whether disputed or not, is presented in the shortest and clearest way;
(f) discouraging delay, dealing with as many aspects of the case as possible on the same occasion, and avoiding unnecessary hearings;
(g) encouraging the participants to co-operate in the progression of the case; and
(h) making use of technology.
(3) The court must actively manage the case by giving any direction appropriate to the needs of that case as early as possible.

R-9 The duty of the parties

3.3 (1) Each party must—
(a) actively assist the court in fulfilling its duty under rule 3.2, without or if necessary with a direction; and
(b) apply for a direction if needed to further the overriding objective.
(2) Active assistance for the purposes of this rule includes—
(a) at the beginning of the case, communication between the prosecutor and the defendant at the first available opportunity and in any event no later than the beginning of the day of the first hearing;
(b) after that, communication between the parties and with the court officer until the conclusion of the case;
(c) by such communication establishing, among other things—
(i) whether the defendant is likely to plead guilty or not guilty,
(ii) what is agreed and what is likely to be disputed,
(iii) what information, or other material, is required by one party of another, and why, and
(iv) what is to be done, by whom, and when (without or if necessary with a direction); and
(d) reporting on that communication to the court—
(i) at the first hearing, and
(ii) after that, as directed by the court.

R-10 Case progression officers and their duties

3.4 (1) At the beginning of the case each party must, unless the court otherwise directs—
(a) nominate someone responsible for progressing that case; and
(b) tell other parties and the court who that is and how to contact that person.

(2) In fulfilling its duty under rule 3.2, the court must where appropriate—
(a) nominate a court officer responsible for progressing the case; and
(b) make sure the parties know who that is and how to contact that court officer.
(3) In this Part a person nominated under this rule is called a case progression officer.
(4) A case progression officer must—
(a) monitor compliance with directions;
(b) make sure that the court is kept informed of events that may affect the progress of that case;
(c) make sure that he or she can be contacted promptly about the case during ordinary business hours;
(d) act promptly and reasonably in response to communications about the case; and
(e) if he or she will be unavailable, appoint a substitute to fulfil his or her duties and inform the other case progression officers.

The court's case management powers R-11

3.5 (1) In fulfilling its duty under rule 3.2 the court may give any direction and take any step actively to manage a case unless that direction or step would be inconsistent with legislation, including these Rules.
(2) In particular, the court may—
(a) nominate a judge, magistrate or justices' legal adviser to manage the case;
(b) give a direction on its own initiative or on application by a party;
(c) ask or allow a party to propose a direction;
(d) for the purpose of giving directions, receive applications and representations by letter, by telephone or by any other means of electronic communication, and conduct a hearing by such means;
(e) give a direction—
(i) at a hearing, in public or in private, or
(ii) without a hearing;
(f) fix, postpone, bring forward, extend, cancel or adjourn a hearing;
(g) shorten or extend (even after it has expired) a time limit fixed by a direction;
(h) require that issues in the case should be—
(i) identified in writing,
(ii) determined separately, and decide in what order they will be determined; and
(i) specify the consequences of failing to comply with a direction.
(3) A magistrates' court may give a direction that will apply in the Crown Court if the case is to continue there.
(4) The Crown Court may give a direction that will apply in a magistrates' court if the case is to continue there.
(5) Any power to give a direction under this Part includes a power to vary or revoke that direction.
(6) If a party fails to comply with a rule or a direction, the court may—
(a) fix, postpone, bring forward, extend, cancel or adjourn a hearing;
(b) exercise its powers to make a costs order; and
(c) impose such other sanction as may be appropriate.

Application to vary a direction R-12

3.6 (1) A party may apply to vary a direction if—
(a) the court gave it without a hearing;
(b) the court gave it at a hearing in that party's absence; or
(c) circumstances have changed.
(2) A party who applies to vary a direction must—
(a) apply as soon as practicable after becoming aware of the grounds for doing so; and
(b) give as much notice to the other parties as the nature and urgency of the application permits.

Agreement to vary a time limit fixed by a direction R-13

3.7 (1) The parties may agree to vary a time limit fixed by a direction, but only if—
(a) the variation will not—
(i) affect the date of any hearing that has been fixed, or
(ii) significantly affect the progress of the case in any other way;

(b) the court has not prohibited variation by agreement; and
(c) the court's case progression officer is promptly informed.

(2) The court's case progression officer must refer the agreement to the court if in doubt that the condition in paragraph (1)(a) is satisfied.

R-14 **Court's power to vary requirements under this Part**

3.8 (1) The court may—
(a) shorten or extend (even after it has expired) a time limit set by this Part; and
(b) allow an application or representations to be made orally.

(2) A person who wants an extension of time must—
(a) apply when serving the application or representations for which it is needed; and
(b) explain the delay.

R-15 **Case preparation and progression**

3.9 (1) At every hearing, if a case cannot be concluded there and then the court must give directions so that it can be concluded at the next hearing or as soon as possible after that.

(2) At every hearing the court must, where relevant—
(a) if the defendant is absent, decide whether to proceed nonetheless;
(b) take the defendant's plea (unless already done) or if no plea can be taken then find out whether the defendant is likely to plead guilty or not guilty;
(c) set, follow or revise a timetable for the progress of the case, which may include a timetable for any hearing including the trial or (in the Crown Court) the appeal;
(d) in giving directions, ensure continuity in relation to the court and to the parties' representatives where that is appropriate and practicable; and
(e) where a direction has not been complied with, find out why, identify who was responsible, and take appropriate action.

(3) In order to prepare for the trial, the court must take every reasonable step—
(a) to encourage and to facilitate the attendance of witnesses when they are needed; and
(b) to facilitate the participation of any person, including the defendant.

(4) Facilitating the participation of the defendant includes finding out whether the defendant needs interpretation because—
(a) the defendant does not speak or understand English; or
(b) the defendant has a hearing or speech impediment.

(5) Where the defendant needs interpretation—
(a) the court officer must arrange for interpretation to be provided at every hearing which the defendant is due to attend;
(b) interpretation may be by an intermediary where the defendant has a speech impediment, without the need for a defendant's evidence direction;
(c) on application or on its own initiative, the court may require a written translation to be provided for the defendant of any document or part of a document, unless—
(i) translation of that document, or part, is not needed to explain the case against the defendant, or
(ii) the defendant agrees to do without and the court is satisfied that the agreement is clear and voluntary and that the defendant has had legal advice or otherwise understands the consequences;
(d) on application by the defendant, the court must give any direction which the court thinks appropriate, including a direction for interpretation by a different interpreter, where —
(i) no interpretation is provided,
(ii) no translation is ordered or provided in response to a previous application by the defendant, or
(iii) the defendant complains about the quality of interpretation or of any translation.

(6) Facilitating the participation of any person includes giving directions for the appropriate treatment and questioning of a witness or the defendant, especially where the court directs that such questioning is to be conducted through an intermediary.

(7) Where directions for appropriate treatment and questioning are required, the court must—
(a) invite representations by the parties and by any intermediary; and
(b) set ground rules for the conduct of the questioning, which rules may include—
(i) a direction relieving a party of any duty to put that party's case to a witness or a defendant in its entirety,
(ii) directions about the manner of questioning,

(iii) directions about the duration of questioning,
(iv) if necessary, directions about the questions that may or may not be asked,
(v) where there is more than one defendant, the allocation among them of the topics about which a witness may be asked, and
(vi) directions about the use of models, plans, body maps or similar aids to help communicate a question or an answer.

Readiness for trial or appeal R-16

3.10 (1) This rule applies to a party's preparation for trial or appeal, and in this rule and rule 3.11 'trial' includes any hearing at which evidence will be introduced.
(2) In fulfilling the duty under rule 3.3, each party must—
(a) comply with directions given by the court;
(b) take every reasonable step to make sure that party's witnesses will attend when they are needed;
(c) make appropriate arrangements to present any written or other material; and
(d) promptly inform the court and the other parties of anything that may—
(i) affect the date or duration of the trial or appeal, or
(ii) significantly affect the progress of the case in any other way.
(3) The court may require a party to give a certificate of readiness.

Conduct of a trial or an appeal R-17

3.11 In order to manage the trial or an appeal, the court—
(a) must establish, with the active assistance of the parties, what are the disputed issues;
(b) must consider setting a timetable that—
(i) takes account of those issues and any timetable proposed by a party, and
(ii) may limit the duration of any stage of the hearing;
(c) may require a party to identify—
(i) which witnesses that party wants to give evidence in person,
(ii) the order in which that party wants those witnesses to give their evidence,
(iii) whether that party requires an order compelling the attendance of a witness,
(iv) what arrangements are desirable to facilitate the giving of evidence by a witness,
(v) what arrangements are desirable to facilitate the participation of any other person, including the defendant,
(vi) what written evidence that party intends to introduce,
(vii) what other material, if any, that person intends to make available to the court in the presentation of the case, and
(viii) whether that party intends to raise any point of law that could affect the conduct of the trial or appeal; and
(d) may limit—
(i) the examination, cross-examination or re-examination of a witness, and
(ii) the duration of any stage of the hearing.

Duty of court officer R-18

3.12 The court officer must—
(a) where a person is entitled or required to attend a hearing, give as much notice as reasonably practicable to—
(i) that person, and
(ii) that person's custodian (if any);
(b) where the court gives directions, promptly make a record available to the parties.

Preparation for trial in the Crown Court

Pre-trial hearings: general rules R-19

3.13 (1) The Crown Court—
(a) may, and in some cases must, conduct a preparatory hearing where rule 3.14 applies;
(b) must conduct a plea and trial preparation hearing;
(c) may conduct a further pre-trial case management hearing (and if necessary more than one such hearing) only where—
(i) the court anticipates a guilty plea,
(ii) it is necessary to conduct such a hearing in order to give directions for an effective trial, or
(iii) such a hearing is required to set ground rules for the conduct of the questioning of a witness or defendant.

(2) A pre-trial case management hearing—
(a) must be in public, as a general rule, but all or part of the hearing may be in private if the court so directs; and
(b) must be recorded, in accordance with rule 5.5 (Recording and transcription of proceedings in the Crown Court).
(3) Where the court determines a pre-trial application in private, it must announce its decision in public.

R-20 Preparatory hearing

3.14 (1) This rule applies where the Crown Court—
(a) can order a preparatory hearing, under—
(i) section 7 of the Criminal Justice Act 1987 (cases of serious or complex fraud), or
(ii) section 29 of the Criminal Procedure and Investigations Act 1996 (other complex, serious or lengthy cases);
(b) must order such a hearing, to determine an application for a trial without a jury, under—
(i) section 44 of the Criminal Justice Act 2003 (danger of jury tampering), or
(ii) section 17 of the Domestic Violence, Crime and Victims Act 2004 (trial of sample counts by jury, and others by judge alone);
(c) must order such a hearing, under section 29 of the 1996 Act, where section 29(1B) or (1C) applies (cases in which a terrorism offence is charged, or other serious cases with a terrorist connection).
(2) The court may decide whether to order a preparatory hearing—
(a) on an application or on its own initiative;
(b) at a hearing (in public or in private), or without a hearing;
(c) in a party's absence, if that party—
(i) applied for the order, or
(ii) has had at least 14 days in which to make representations.

R-21 Application for preparatory hearing

3.15 (1) A party who wants the court to order a preparatory hearing must—
(a) apply in writing—
(i) as soon as reasonably practicable, and in any event
(ii) not more than 14 days after the defendant pleads not guilty;
(b) serve the application on—
(i) the court officer, and
(ii) each other party.
(2) The applicant must—
(a) if relevant, explain what legislation requires the court to order a preparatory hearing;
(b) otherwise, explain—
(i) what makes the case complex or serious, or makes the trial likely to be long,
(ii) why a substantial benefit will accrue from a preparatory hearing, and
(iii) why the court's ordinary powers of case management are not adequate.
(3) A prosecutor who wants the court to order a trial without a jury must explain—
(a) where the prosecutor alleges a danger of jury tampering—
(i) what evidence there is of a real and present danger that jury tampering would take place,
(ii) what steps, if any, reasonably might be taken to prevent jury tampering, and
(iii) why, notwithstanding such steps, the likelihood of jury tampering is so substantial as to make it necessary in the interests of justice to order such a trial; or
(b) where the prosecutor proposes trial without a jury on some counts on the indictment—
(i) why a trial by jury involving all the counts would be impracticable,
(ii) how the counts proposed for jury trial can be regarded as samples of the others, and
(iii) why it would be in the interests of justice to order such a trial.

R-22 Application for non-jury trial containing information withheld from a defendant

3.16 (1) This rule applies where—
(a) the prosecutor applies for an order for a trial without a jury because of a danger of jury tampering; and
(b) the application includes information that the prosecutor thinks ought not be revealed to a defendant.

(2) The prosecutor must—
(a) omit that information from the part of the application that is served on that defendant;
(b) mark the other part to show that, unless the court otherwise directs, it is only for the court; and
(c) in that other part, explain why the prosecutor has withheld that information from that defendant.
(3) The hearing of an application to which this rule applies—
(a) must be in private, unless the court otherwise directs; and
(b) if the court so directs, may be, wholly or in part, in the absence of a defendant from whom information has been withheld.
(4) At the hearing of an application to which this rule applies—
(a) the general rule is that the court will receive, in the following sequence—
(i) representations first by the prosecutor and then by each defendant, in all the parties' presence, and then
(ii) further representations by the prosecutor, in the absence of a defendant from whom information has been withheld; but
(b) the court may direct other arrangements for the hearing.
(5) Where, on an application to which this rule applies, the court orders a trial without a jury—
(a) the general rule is that the trial will be before a judge other than the judge who made the order; but
(b) the court may direct other arrangements.

Representations in response to application for preparatory hearing R-23

3.17 (1) This rule applies where a party wants to make representations about—
(a) an application for a preparatory hearing;
(b) an application for a trial without a jury.
(2) Such a party must—
(a) serve the representations on—
(i) the court officer, and
(ii) each other party;
(b) do so not more than 14 days after service of the application;
(c) ask for a hearing, if that party wants one, and explain why it is needed.
(3) Where representations include information that the person making them thinks ought not be revealed to another party, that person must—
(a) omit that information from the representations served on that other party;
(b) mark the information to show that, unless the court otherwise directs, it is only for the court; and
(c) with that information include an explanation of why it has been withheld from that other party.
(4) Representations against an application for an order must explain why the conditions for making it are not met.

Commencement of preparatory hearing R-24

3.18 At the beginning of a preparatory hearing, the court must—
(a) announce that it is such a hearing; and
(b) take the defendant's plea under rule 3.24 (Arraigning the defendant on the indictment), unless already done.

Defence trial advocate R-25

3.19 (1) The defendant must notify the court officer of the identity of the intended defence trial advocate—
(a) as soon as practicable, and in any event no later than the day of the plea and trial preparation hearing;
(b) in writing, or orally at that hearing.
(2) The defendant must notify the court officer in writing of any change in the identity of the intended defence trial advocate as soon as practicable, and in any event not more than 5 business days after that change.

Application to stay case for abuse of process R-26

3.20 (1) This rule applies where a defendant wants the Crown Court to stay the case on the grounds that the proceedings are an abuse of the court, or otherwise unfair.

(2) Such a defendant must—
(a) apply in writing—
(i) as soon as practicable after becoming aware of the grounds for doing so,
(ii) at a pre-trial hearing, unless the grounds for the application do not arise until trial, and
(iii) in any event, before the defendant pleads guilty or the jury (if there is one) retires to consider its verdict at trial;
(b) serve the application on—
(i) the court officer, and
(ii) each other party; and
(c) in the application—
(i) explain the grounds on which it is made,
(ii) include, attach or identify all supporting material,
(iii) specify relevant events, dates and propositions of law, and
(iv) identify any witness the applicant wants to call to give evidence in person.
(3) A party who wants to make representations in response to the application must serve the representations on—
(a) the court officer; and
(b) each other party,
not more than 14 days after service of the application.

R-27 **Application for joint or separate trials, etc.**

3.21 (1) This rule applies where a party wants the Crown Court to order—
(a) the joint trial of—
(i) offences charged by separate indictments, or
(ii) defendants charged in separate indictments;
(b) separate trials of offences charged by the same indictment;
(c) separate trials of defendants charged in the same indictment; or
(d) the deletion of a count from an indictment.
(2) Such a party must—
(a) apply in writing—
(i) as soon as practicable after becoming aware of the grounds for doing so, and
(ii) before the trial begins, unless the grounds for the application do not arise until trial;
(b) serve the application on—
(i) the court officer, and
(ii) each other party; and
(c) in the application—
(i) specify the order proposed, and
(ii) explain why it should be made.
(3) A party who wants to make representations in response to the application must serve the representations on—
(a) the court officer; and
(b) each other party,
not more than 14 days after service of the application.

R-28 **Order for joint or separate trials, or amendment of the indictment**

3.22 (1) This rule applies where the Crown Court makes an order—
(a) on an application under rule 3.21 applies (Application for joint or separate trials, etc.); or
(b) amending an indictment in any other respect.
(2) Unless the court otherwise directs, the court officer must endorse any paper copy of each affected indictment made for the court with—
(a) a note of the court's order; and
(b) the date of that order.

R-29 **Application for indication of sentence**

3.23 (1) This rule applies where a defendant wants the Crown Court to give an indication of the maximum sentence that would be passed if a guilty plea were entered when the indication is sought.
(2) Such a defendant must—
(a) apply in writing as soon as practicable; and
(b) serve the application on—
(i) the court officer, and
(ii) the prosecutor.

(3) The application must—
(a) specify—
(i) the offence or offences to which it would be a guilty plea, and
(ii) the facts on the basis of which that plea would be entered; and
(b) include the prosecutor's agreement to, or representations on, that proposed basis of plea.
(4) The prosecutor must—
(a) provide information relevant to sentence, including—
(i) any previous conviction of the defendant, and the circumstances where relevant,
(ii) any statement of the effect of the offence on the victim, the victim's family or others; and
(b) identify any other matter relevant to sentence, including—
(i) the legislation applicable,
(ii) any sentencing guidelines, or guideline cases, and
(iii) aggravating and mitigating factors.
(5) The hearing of the application—
(a) may take place in the absence of any other defendant;
(b) must be attended by—
(i) the applicant defendant's legal representatives (if any), and
(ii) the prosecution advocate.

Arraigning the defendant on the indictment R-30

3.24 (1) In order to take the defendant's plea, the Crown Court must—
(a) ensure that the defendant is correctly identified by the indictment;
(b) in respect of each count in the indictment—
(i) read the count aloud to the defendant, or arrange for it to be read aloud or placed before the defendant in writing,
(ii) ask whether the defendant pleads guilty or not guilty to the offence charged by that count, and
(iii) take the defendant's plea.
(2) Where a count is read which is substantially the same as one already read aloud, then only the materially different details need be read aloud.
(3) Where a count is placed before the defendant in writing, the court must summarise its gist aloud.
(4) In respect of each count in the indictment—
(a) if the defendant declines to enter a plea, the court must treat that as a not guilty plea unless rule 25.10 applies (Defendant unfit to plead);
(b) if the defendant pleads not guilty to the offence charged by that count but guilty to another offence of which the court could convict on that count—
(i) if the prosecutor and the court accept that plea, the court must treat the plea as one of guilty of that other offence, but
(ii) otherwise, the court must treat the plea as one of not guilty;
(c) if the defendant pleads a previous acquittal or conviction of the offence charged by that count—
(i) the defendant must identify that acquittal or conviction in writing, explaining the basis of that plea, and
(ii) the court must exercise its power to decide whether that plea disposes of that count.

Place of trial R-31

3.25 (1) Unless the court otherwise directs, the court officer must arrange for the trial to take place in a courtroom provided by the Lord Chancellor.
(2) The court officer must arrange for the court and the jury (if there is one) to view any place required by the court.

Use of Welsh language at trial R-32

3.26 Where the trial will take place in Wales and a participant wishes to use the Welsh language—
(a) that participant must serve notice on the court officer, or arrange for such a notice to be served on that participant's behalf—
(i) at or before the plea and trial preparation hearing, or
(ii) in accordance with any direction given by the court; and
(b) if such a notice is served, the court officer must arrange for an interpreter to attend.

Criminal Practice Directions Part 3 Case Management

PD-3 **CPD I General matters 3A: Case Management**

3A.1 CrimPR 1.1(2)(e) requires that cases be dealt with efficiently and expeditiously. CrimPR 3.2 requires the court to further the overriding objective by actively managing the case, for example:

a) When dealing with an offence which is triable only on indictment the court must ask the defendant whether he or she intends to plead guilty at the Crown Court (CrimPR 9.7(5));
b) On a guilty plea, the court must pass sentence at the earliest opportunity, in accordance with CrimPR 24.11(9)(a) (magistrates' courts) and 25.16(7)(a) (the Crown Court).

3A.2 Given these duties, magistrates' courts and the Crown Court therefore will proceed as described in paragraphs 3A.3 to 3A.28 below. The parties will be expected to have prepared in accordance with CrimPR 3.3(1) to avoid unnecessary and wasted hearings. They will be expected to have communicated with each other by the time of the first hearing; to report to the court on that communication at the first hearing; and to continue thereafter to communicate with each other and with the court officer, in accordance with CrimPR 3.3(2).

3A.3 There is a Preparation for Effective Trial form for use in the magistrates' courts, and a Plea and Trial Preparation Hearing form for use in the Crown Court, each of which must be used as appropriate in connection with CrimPR Part 3: see paragraph 5A.2 of these Practice Directions. Versions of those forms in pdf and Word, together with guidance notes, are available on the Criminal Procedure Rules pages of the Ministry of Justice website.

Case progression and trial preparation in magistrates' courts

3A.4 CrimPR 8.3 applies in all cases and requires the prosecutor to serve:

i. a summary of the circumstances of the offence;
ii. any account given by the defendant in interview, whether contained in that summary or in another document;
iii. any written witness statement or exhibit that the prosecutor then has available and considers material to plea or to the allocation of the case for trial or sentence;
iv. a list of the defendant's criminal record, if any; and
v. any available statement of the effect of the offence on a victim, a victim's family or others.

The details must include sufficient information to allow the defendant and the court at the first hearing to take an informed view:

i. on plea;
ii. on venue for trial (if applicable);
iii. for the purposes of case management; or
iv. for the purposes of sentencing (including committal for sentence, if applicable).

Defendant in custody

3A.5 If the defendant has been detained in custody after being charged with an offence which is indictable only or triable either way, at the first hearing a magistrates' court will proceed at once with the allocation of the case for trial, where appropriate, and, if so required, with the sending of the defendant to the Crown Court for trial. The court will be expected to ask for and record any indication of plea and issues for trial to assist the Crown Court.

3A.6 If the offence charged is triable only summarily, or if at that hearing the case is allocated for summary trial, the court will forthwith give such directions as are necessary, either (on a guilty plea) to prepare for sentencing, or for a trial.

Defendant on bail

3A.7 If the defendant has been released on bail after being charged, the case must be listed for the first hearing 14 days after charge, or the next available court date thereafter when the prosecutor anticipates a guilty plea which is likely to be sentenced in the magistrates' court. In cases where there is an anticipated not guilty plea or the case is likely to be sent or committed to the Crown Court for either trial or sentence, then it must be listed for the first hearing 28 days after charge or the next available court date thereafter.

Guilty plea in the magistrates' courts

3A.8 Where a defendant pleads guilty or indicates a guilty plea in a magistrates' court the court should consider whether a pre-sentence report — a stand down report if possible — is necessary.

Guilty plea in the Crown Court

3A.9 Where a magistrates' court is considering committal for sentence or the defendant has indicated an intention to plead guilty in a matter which is to be sent to the Crown Court, the magistrates' court should request the preparation of a pre-sentence report for the Crown Court's use if the magistrates' court considers that:

(a) there is a realistic alternative to a custodial sentence; or
(b) the defendant may satisfy the criteria for classification as a dangerous offender; or
(c) there is some other appropriate reason for doing so.

3A.10 When a magistrates' court sends a case to the Crown Court for trial and the defendant indicates an intention to plead guilty at the Crown Court, then that magistrates' court must set a date for a Plea and Trial Preparation Hearing at the Crown Court, in accordance with CrimPR 9.7(5)(a)(i).

Case sent for Crown Court trial: no indication of guilty plea

3A.11 In any case sent to the Crown Court for trial, other than one in which the defendant indicates an intention to plead guilty, the magistrates' court must set a date for a Plea and Trial Preparation Hearing, in accordance with CrimPR 9.7(5)(a)(ii). The Plea and Trial Preparation Hearing must be held within 28 days of sending, unless the standard directions of the Presiding Judges of the circuit direct otherwise. Paragraph 3A.16 below additionally applies to the arrangements for such hearings. A magistrates' court may give other directions appropriate to the needs of the case, in accordance with CrimPR 3.5(3), and in accordance with any standard directions issued by the Presiding Judges of the circuit.

Defendant on bail: anticipated not guilty plea

3A.12 Where the defendant has been released on bail after being charged, and where the prosecutor does not anticipate a guilty plea at the first hearing in a magistrates' court, then it is essential that the initial details of the prosecution case that are provided for that first hearing are sufficient to assist the court, in order to identify the real issues and to give appropriate directions for an effective trial (regardless of whether the trial is to be heard in the magistrates' court or the Crown Court). In these circumstances, unless there is good reason not to do so, the prosecution should make available the following material in advance of the first hearing in the magistrates' court:

(a) A summary of the circumstances of the offence(s) including a summary of any account given by the defendant in interview;
(b) Statements and exhibits that the prosecution has identified as being of importance for the purpose of plea or initial case management, including any relevant CCTV that would be relied upon at trial and any Streamlined Forensic Report;
(c) Details of witness availability, as far as they are known at that hearing;
(d) Defendant's criminal record;
(e) Victim Personal Statements if provided;
(f) An indication of any medical or other expert evidence that the prosecution is likely to adduce in relation to a victim or the defendant;
(g) Any information as to special measures, bad character or hearsay, where applicable.

3A.13 In addition to the material required by CrimPR Part 8, the information required by the Preparation for Effective Trial form must be available to be submitted at the first hearing, and the parties must complete that form, in accordance with the guidance published with it. Where there is to be a contested trial in a magistrates' court, that form includes directions and a timetable that will apply in every case unless the court otherwise orders.

3A.14 Nothing in paragraph 3A.12-3A.13 shall preclude the court from taking a plea pursuant to CrimPR 3.9(2)(b) at the first hearing and for the court to case manage as far as practicable under Part 3 CrimPR.

Exercise of magistrates' court's powers

3A.15 In accordance with CrimPR 9.1, sections 49, 51(13) and 51A(11) of the Crime and Disorder Act 1998, and sections 17E, 18(5) and 24D of the Magistrates' Courts Act 1980 a single justice can:

a) allocate and send for trial;
b) take an indication of a guilty plea (but not pass sentence);
c) take a not guilty plea and give directions for the preparation of trial including:
   i. timetable for the proceedings;
   ii. the attendance of the parties;
   iii. the service of documents;
   iv. the manner in which evidence is to be given.

Case progression and trial preparation in the Crown Court

Plea and Trial Preparation Hearing

3A.16 In a case in which a magistrates' court has directed a Plea and Trial Preparation Hearing, the period which elapses between sending for trial and the date of that hearing must be consistent within each circuit. In every case, the time allowed for the conduct of the Plea and Trial Preparation Hearing must be sufficient for effective trial preparation. It is expected in every case that an indictment will be lodged at least 7 days in advance of the hearing. Please see the Note to the Practice Direction.

3A.17 In a case in which the defendant, not having done so before, indicates an intention to plead guilty to his representative after being sent for trial but before the Plea and Trial Preparation Hearing, the defence representative will notify the Crown Court and the prosecution forthwith. The court will ensure there is sufficient time at the Plea and Trial Preparation Hearing for sentence and a Judge should at once request the preparation of a pre-sentence report if it appears to the court that either:

(a) there is a realistic alternative to a custodial sentence; or
(b) the defendant may satisfy the criteria for classification as a dangerous offender; or
(c) there is some other appropriate reason for doing so.

3A.18 If at the Plea and Trial Preparation Hearing the defendant pleads guilty and no pre-sentence report has been prepared, if possible the court should obtain a stand down report.

3A.19 Where the defendant was remanded in custody after being charged and was sent for trial without initial details of the prosecution case having been served, then at least 7 days before the Plea and Trial Preparation Hearing the prosecutor should serve, as a minimum, the material identified in paragraph 3A.12 above. If at the Plea and Trial Preparation Hearing the defendant does not plead guilty, the court will be expected to identify the issues in the case and give appropriate directions for an effective trial. Please see the Note to the Practice Direction.

3A.20 At the Plea and Trial Preparation Hearing, in addition to the material required by paragraph 3A.12 above, the prosecutor must serve sufficient evidence to enable the court to case manage effectively without the need for a further case management hearing, unless the case falls within paragraph 3A.21. In addition, the information required by the Plea and Trial Preparation Hearing form must be available to the court at that hearing, and it must have been discussed between the parties in advance. The prosecutor must provide details of the availability of likely prosecution witnesses so that a trial date can immediately be arranged if the defendant does not plead guilty.

Further case management hearing

3A.21 In accordance with CrimPR 3.13(1)(c), after the Plea and Trial Preparation Hearing there will be no further case management hearing before the trial unless:

(i) a condition listed in that rule is met; and
(ii) the court so directs, in order to further the overriding objective.

The directions to be given at the Plea and Trial Preparation Hearing therefore may include a direction for a further case management hearing, but usually will do so only in one of the following cases:

(a) Class 1 cases;
(b) Class 2 cases which carry a maximum penalty of 10 years or more;
(c) cases involving death by driving (whether dangerous or careless), or death in the workplace;
(d) cases involving a vulnerable witness;
(e) cases in which the defendant is a child or otherwise under a disability, or requires special assistance;
(f) cases in which there is a corporate or unrepresented defendant;
(g) cases in which the expected trial length is such that a further case management hearing is desirable and any case in which the trial is likely to last longer than four weeks;
(h) cases in which expert evidence is to be introduced;
(i) cases in which a party requests a hearing to enter a plea;
(j) cases in which an application to dismiss or stay has been made;
(k) cases in which arraignment has not taken place, whether because of an issue relating to fitness to plead, or abuse of process or sufficiency of evidence, or for any other reason;
(l) cases in which there are likely to be linked criminal and care directions in accordance with the 2013 Protocol.

3A.22 If a further case management hearing is directed, a defendant in custody will not usually be expected to attend in person, unless the court otherwise directs.

Compliance hearing

3A.23 If a party fails to comply with a case management direction, that party may be required to attend the court to explain the failure. Unless the court otherwise directs a defendant in custody will not usually be expected to attend. See paragraph 3A.26-3A.28 below.

Conduct of case progression hearings

3A.24 As far as possible, case progression should be managed without a hearing in the courtroom, using electronic communication in accordance with CrimPR 3.5(2)(d). Court staff should be nominated to conduct case progression as part of their role, in accordance with CrimPR 3.4(2). To aid effective communication the prosecution and defence representative should notify the court and provide details of who shall be dealing with the case at the earliest opportunity.

Completion of Effective Trial Monitoring form

3A.25 It is imperative that the Effective Trial Monitoring form (as devised and issued by Her Majesty's Courts and Tribunals Service) is accurately completed by the parties for all cases that have been listed for trial. Advocates must engage with the process by providing the relevant details and completing the form.

Compliance courts

3A.26 To ensure effective compliance with directions of the courts made in accordance with the Criminal Procedure Rules and the overriding objective, courts should maintain a record whenever a party to the proceedings has failed to comply with a direction made by the court. The parties may have to attend a hearing to explain any lack of compliance.

3A.27 These hearings may be conducted by live link facilities or via other electronic means, as the court may direct.

3A.28 It will be for the Presiding Judges, Resident Judge and Justices' Clerks to decide locally how often compliance courts should be held, depending on the scale and nature of the problem at each court centre.

CPD I General matters 3B: Pagination and Indexing of Served Evidence PD-4

3B.1 The following directions apply to matters before the Crown Court, where

(a) there is an application to prefer a bill of indictment in relation to the case;

(b) a person is sent for trial under section 51 of the Crime and Disorder Act 1998 (sending cases to the Crown Court), to the service of copies of the documents containing the evidence on which the charge or charges are based under Paragraph 1 of Schedule 3 to that Act; or

(c) a defendant wishes to serve evidence.

3B.2 A party who serves documentary evidence in the Crown Court should:

(a) paginate each page in any bundle of statements and exhibits sequentially;

(b) provide an index to each bundle of statements produced including the following information:
   i. the name of the case;
   ii. the author of each statement;
   iii. the start page number of the witness statement;
   iv. the end page number of the witness statement.

(c) provide an index to each bundle of documentary and pictorial exhibits produced, including the following information:
   i. the name of the case
   ii. the exhibit reference;
   iii. a short description of the exhibit;
   iv. the start page number of the exhibit;
   v. the end page number of the exhibit;
   vi. where possible, the name of the person producing the exhibit should be added.

3B.3 Where additional documentary evidence is served, a party should paginate following on from the last page of the previous bundle or in a logical and sequential manner. A party should also provide notification of service of any amended index.

3B.4 The prosecution must ensure that the running total of the pages of prosecution evidence is easily identifiable on the most recent served bundle of prosecution evidence.

3B.5 For the purposes of these directions, the number of pages of prosecution evidence served on the court includes all

(a) witness statements;

(b) documentary and pictorial exhibits;

(c) records of interviews with the defendant; and

(d) records of interviews with other defendants which form part of the served prosecution documents or which are included in any notice of additional evidence,

but does not include any document provided on CD-ROM or by other means of electronic communication.

PD-5 **CPD I General matters 3C: Abuse of Process Stay Applications**

3C.1 In all cases where a defendant in the Crown Court proposes to make an application to stay an indictment on the grounds of abuse of process, written notice of such application must be given to the prosecuting authority and to any co-defendant as soon as practicable after the defendant becomes aware of the grounds for doing so and not later than 14 days before the date fixed or warned for trial ('the relevant date'). Such notice must:

(a) give the name of the case and the indictment number;
(b) state the fixed date or the warned date as appropriate;
(c) specify the nature of the application;
(d) set out in numbered sub-paragraphs the grounds upon which the application is to be made;
(e) be copied to the chief listing officer at the court centre where the case is due to be heard.

3C.2 Any co-defendant who wishes to make a like application must give a like notice not later than seven days before the relevant date, setting out any additional grounds relied upon.

3C.3 In relation to such applications, the following automatic directions shall apply:

(a) the advocate for the applicant(s) must lodge with the court and serve on all other parties a skeleton argument in support of the application, at least five clear working days before the relevant date. If reference is to be made to any document not in the existing trial documents, a paginated and indexed bundle of such documents is to be provided with the skeleton argument;
(b) the advocate for the prosecution must lodge with the court and serve on all other parties a responsive skeleton argument at least two clear working days before the relevant date, together with a supplementary bundle if appropriate.

3C.4 All skeleton arguments must specify any propositions of law to be advanced (together with the authorities relied upon in support, with paragraph references to passages relied upon) and, where appropriate, include a chronology of events and a list of dramatis personae. In all instances where reference is made to a document, the reference in the trial documents or supplementary bundle is to be given.

3C.5 The above time limits are minimum time limits. In appropriate cases, the court will order longer lead times. To this end, in all cases where defence advocates are, at the time of the preliminary hearing or as soon as practicable after the case has been sent, considering the possibility of an abuse of process application, this must be raised with the judge dealing with the matter, who will order a different timetable if appropriate, and may wish, in any event, to give additional directions about the conduct of the application. If the trial judge has not been identified, the matter should be raised with the Resident Judge.

PD-6 **CPD I General matters 3D: Vulnerable People in the Courts**

3D.1 In respect of eligibility for special measures, 'vulnerable' and 'intimidated' witnesses are defined in sections 16 and 17 of the Youth Justice and Criminal Evidence Act 1999 (as amended by the Coroners and Justice Act 2009); 'vulnerable' includes those under 18 years of age and people with a mental disorder or learning disability; a physical disorder or disability; or who are likely to suffer fear or distress in giving evidence because of their own circumstances or those relating to the case.

3D.2 However, many other people giving evidence in a criminal case, whether as a witness or defendant, may require assistance: the court is required to take 'every reasonable step' to encourage and facilitate the attendance of witnesses and to facilitate the participation of any person, including the defendant (CrimPR 3.9(3)(a) and (b)). This includes enabling a witness or defendant to give their best evidence, and enabling a defendant to comprehend the proceedings and engage fully with his or her defence. The pre-trial and trial process should, so far as necessary, be adapted to meet those ends. Regard should be had to the welfare of a young defendant as required by section 44 of the Children and Young Persons Act 1933, and generally to Parts 1 and 3 of the Criminal Procedure Rules (the overriding objective and the court's powers of case management).

3D.3 Under Part 3 of the Rules, the court must identify the needs of witnesses at an early stage (CrimPR 3.2(2)(b)) and may require the parties to identify arrangements to facilitate the giving of evidence and participation in the trial (CrimPR 3.11(c)(iv) and (v)). There are various statutory special measures that the court may utilise to assist a witness in giving evidence. CrimPR Part 18 gives the procedures to be followed. Courts should note the 'primary rule' which requires the court to give a direction for a special measure to assist a child witness or qualifying witness and that in such cases an application to the court is not required (CrimPR 18.9).

3D.4 Court of Appeal decisions on this subject include a judgment from the Lord Chief Justice, Lord Judge in *R v Cox* [2012] EWCA Crim 549, [2012] 2 Cr App R 6; *R v Wills* [2011] EWCA Crim 1938, [2012] 1 Cr App R 2; and *R v E* [2011] EWCA Crim 3028, [2012] Crim LR 563.

3D.5 In *R v Wills*, the Court endorsed the approach taken by the report of the Advocacy Training Council (ATC) 'Raising the Bar: the Handling of Vulnerable Witnesses, Victims and Defendants in Court' (2011). The report includes and recommends the use of 'toolkits' to assist advocates as they prepare to question vulnerable people at court: http://www.advocacytrainingcouncil.org/vulnerable-witnesses/raising-the-bar

3D.6 Further toolkits are available through the Advocate's Gateway which is managed by the ATC's Management Committee: http://www.theadvocatesgateway.org/

3D.7 These toolkits represent best practice. Advocates should consult and follow the relevant guidance whenever they prepare to question a young or otherwise vulnerable witness or defendant. Judges may find it helpful to refer advocates to this material and to use the toolkits in case management.

3D.8 'Achieving Best Evidence in Criminal Proceedings' (Ministry of Justice 2011) describes best practice in preparation for the investigative interview and trial: http://www.cps.gov.uk/publications/docs/best_evidence_in_criminal_proceedings.pdf

CPD I General matters 3E: Ground Rules Hearings to Plan the Questioning of a Vulnerable Witness or Defendant PD-7

3E.1 The judiciary is responsible for controlling questioning. Over-rigorous or repetitive cross-examination of a child or vulnerable witness should be stopped. Intervention by the judge, magistrates or intermediary (if any) is minimised if questioning, taking account of the individual's communication needs, is discussed in advance and ground rules are agreed and adhered to.

3E.2 Discussion of ground rules is required in all intermediary trials where they must be discussed between the judge or magistrates, advocates and intermediary before the witness gives evidence. The intermediary must be present but is not required to take the oath (the intermediary's declaration is made just before the witness gives evidence).

3E.3 Discussion of ground rules is good practice, even if no intermediary is used, in all young witness cases and in other cases where a witness or defendant has communication needs. Discussion before the day of trial is preferable to give advocates time to adapt their questions to the witness's needs. It may be helpful for a trial practice note of boundaries to be created at the end of the discussion. The judge may use such a document in ensuring that the agreed ground rules are complied with.

3E.4 All witnesses, including the defendant and defence witnesses, should be enabled to give the best evidence they can. In relation to young and/or vulnerable people, this may mean departing radically from traditional cross-examination. The form and extent of appropriate cross-examination will vary from case to case. For adult non vulnerable witnesses an advocate will usually put his case so that the witness will have the opportunity of commenting upon it and/or answering it. When the witness is young or otherwise vulnerable, the court may dispense with the normal practice and impose restrictions on the advocate 'putting his case' where there is a risk of a young or otherwise vulnerable witness failing to understand, becoming distressed or acquiescing to leading questions. Where limitations on questioning are necessary and appropriate, they must be clearly defined. The judge has a duty to ensure that they are complied with and should explain them to the jury and the reasons for them. If the advocate fails to comply with the limitations, the judge should give relevant directions to the jury when that occurs and prevent further questioning that does not comply with the ground rules settled upon in advance. Instead of commenting on inconsistencies during cross-examination, following discussion between the judge and the advocates, the advocate or judge may point out important inconsistencies after (instead of during) the witness's evidence. The judge should also remind the jury of these during summing up. The judge should be alert to alleged inconsistencies that are not in fact inconsistent, or are trivial.

3E.5 If there is more than one defendant, the judge should not permit each advocate to repeat the questioning of a vulnerable witness. In advance of the trial, the advocates should divide the topics between them, with the advocate for the first defendant leading the questioning, and the advocate(s) for the other defendant(s) asking only ancillary questions relevant to their client's case, without repeating the questioning that has already taken place on behalf of the other defendant(s).

3E.6 In particular in a trial of a sexual offence, 'body maps' should be provided for the witness' use. If the witness needs to indicate a part of the body, the advocate should ask the witness to point to the relevant part on the body map. In sex cases, judges should not permit advocates to ask the witness to point to a part of the witness' own body. Similarly, photographs of the witness' body should not be shown around the court while the witness is giving evidence.

PD-8 **CPD I General matters 3F: Intermediaries**

3F.1 Intermediaries are communication specialists (not supporters or expert witnesses) whose role is to facilitate communication between the witness and the court, including the advocates. Intermediaries are independent of the parties and owe their duty to the court (see Registered Intermediaries Procedural Guidance Manual, Ministry of Justice, 2012): http://www.cps.gov.uk/publications/docs/RI_ProceduralGuidanceManual_2012.pdf

3F.2 Intermediaries for witnesses, with the exception of defendants, are one of the special measures available under the Youth Justice and Criminal Evidence Act 1999 and Part 18 of the Criminal Procedure Rules.

3F.3 There is currently no statutory provision in force for intermediaries for defendants. Section 104 of the Coroners and Justice Act 2009 (not yet implemented) creates a new section 33BA of the Youth Justice and Criminal Evidence Act 1999. This will provide an intermediary to an eligible defendant only while giving evidence. A court may use its inherent powers to appoint an intermediary to assist the defendant's communication at trial (either solely when giving evidence or throughout the trial) and, where necessary, in preparation for trial: *R (AS) v Great Yarmouth Youth Court* [2011] EWHC 2059 (Admin), [2012] Crim LR 478; *R v H* [2003] EWCA Crim 1208, Times, April 15, 2003; *R (C) v Sevenoaks Youth Court* [2009] EWHC 3088 (Admin), [2010] 1 All ER 735; *R (D) v Camberwell Green Youth Court*, [2005] UKHL 4, [2005] 1 WLR 393, [2005] 2 Cr App R 1; *R (TP) v West London Youth Court* [2005] EWHC 2583 (Admin), [2006] 1 WLR 1219, [2006] 1 Cr App R 25.

3F.4 Ministry of Justice regulation only applies to Registered Intermediaries appointed for prosecution and defence witnesses through its Witness Intermediary Scheme. All defendant intermediaries — professionally qualified or otherwise — are 'non-registered' in this context, even though they may be a Registered Intermediary in respect of witnesses. Even where a judge concludes he has a common law power to direct the provision of an intermediary, the direction will be ineffective if no intermediary can be identified for whom funding would be available.

3F.5 Assessment should be considered if a child or young person under 18 seems unlikely to be able to recognise a problematic question or, even if able to do so, may be reluctant to say so to a questioner in a position of authority. Studies suggest that the majority of young witnesses, across all age groups, fall into one or other of these categories. For children aged 11 years and under in particular, there should be a presumption that an intermediary assessment is appropriate. Once the child's individual requirements are known and discussed at the ground rules hearing, the intermediary may agree that his or her presence is not needed for the trial.

3F.6 In the absence of an intermediary for the defendant, trials should not be stayed where an asserted unfairness can be met by the trial judge adapting the trial process with appropriate and necessary caution (*R v Cox* [2012] EWCA Crim 549, [2012] 2 Cr App R 6). This includes setting ground rules for all witness testimony to help the defendant follow proceedings; for example, directing that all witness evidence be adduced by simple questions, with witnesses asked to answer in short sentences; and short periods of evidence, followed by breaks to enable the defendant to relax and for counsel to summarise the evidence for him and to take further instructions.

Photographs of court facilities

3F.7 Resident Judges in the Crown Court or the Chief Clerk or other responsible person in the magistrates' courts should, in consultation with HMCTS managers responsible for court security matters, develop a policy to govern under what circumstances photographs or other visual recordings may be made of court facilities, such as a live link room, to assist vulnerable or child witnesses to familiarise themselves with the setting, so as to be enabled to give their best evidence. For example, a photograph may provide a helpful reminder to a witness whose court visit has taken place sometime earlier. Resident Judges should tend to permit photographs to be taken for this purpose by intermediaries or supporters, subject to whatever restrictions the Resident Judge or responsible person considers to be appropriate, having regard to the security requirements of the court.

PD-9 **CPD I General matters 3G: Vulnerable Defendants**

Before the trial, sentencing or appeal

3G.1 If a vulnerable defendant, especially one who is young, is to be tried jointly with one who is not, the court should consider at the plea and case management hearing, or at a case management hearing in a magistrates' court, whether the vulnerable defendant should be tried on his own, but should only so order if satisfied that a fair trial cannot be achieved by use of appropriate special measures or other support for the defendant. If a vulnerable defendant is tried jointly with one who is not, the court should consider whether any of the modifications set out in this direction should apply in the circumstances of the joint trial and, so far as practicable, make orders to give effect to any such modifications.

3G.2 It may be appropriate to arrange that a vulnerable defendant should visit, out of court hours and before the trial, sentencing or appeal hearing, the courtroom in which that hearing is to take place so that he or she can familiarise him or herself with it.

3G.3 Where an intermediary is being used to help the defendant to communicate at court, the intermediary should accompany the defendant on his or her pre-trial visit. The visit will enable the defendant to familiarise him or herself with the layout of the court, and may include matters such as: where the defendant will sit, either in the dock or otherwise; court officials (what their roles are and where they sit); who else might be in the court, for example those in the public gallery and press box; the location of the witness box; basic court procedure; and the facilities available in the court.

3G.4 If the defendant's use of the live link is being considered, he or she should have an opportunity to have a practice session.

3G.5 If any case against a vulnerable defendant has attracted or may attract widespread public or media interest, the assistance of the police should be enlisted to try and ensure that the defendant is not, when attending the court, exposed to intimidation, vilification or abuse. Section 41 of the Criminal Justice Act 1925 prohibits the taking of photographs of defendants and witnesses (among others) in the court building or in its precincts, or when entering or leaving those precincts. A direction reminding media representatives of the prohibition may be appropriate. The court should also be ready at this stage, if it has not already done so, where relevant to make a reporting restriction under section 39 of the Children and Young Persons Act 1933 or, on an appeal to the Crown Court from a youth court, to remind media representatives of the application of section 49 of that Act.

3G.6 The provisions of the Practice Direction accompanying Part 6 should be followed.

The trial, sentencing or appeal hearing

3G.7 Subject to the need for appropriate security arrangements, the proceedings should, if practicable, be held in a courtroom in which all the participants are on the same or almost the same level.

3G.8 Subject again to the need for appropriate security arrangements, a vulnerable defendant, especially if he is young, should normally, if he wishes, be free to sit with members of his family or others in a like relationship, and with some other suitable supporting adult such as a social worker, and in a place which permits easy, informal communication with his legal representatives. The court should ensure that a suitable supporting adult is available throughout the course of the proceedings.

3G.9 It is essential that at the beginning of the proceedings, the court should ensure that what is to take place has been explained to a vulnerable defendant in terms he or she can understand and, at trial in the Crown Court, it should ensure in particular that the role of the jury has been explained. It should remind those representing the vulnerable defendant and the supporting adult of their responsibility to explain each step as it takes place and, at trial, explain the possible consequences of a guilty verdict and credit for a guilty plea. The court should also remind any intermediary of the responsibility to ensure that the vulnerable defendant has understood the explanations given to him/her. Throughout the trial the court should continue to ensure, by any appropriate means, that the defendant understands what is happening and what has been said by those on the bench, the advocates and witnesses.

3G.10 A trial should be conducted according to a timetable which takes full account of a vulnerable defendant's ability to concentrate. Frequent and regular breaks will often be appropriate. The court should ensure, so far as practicable, that the whole trial is conducted in clear language that the defendant can understand and that evidence in chief and cross-examination are conducted using questions that are short and clear. The conclusions of the 'ground rules' hearing should be followed, and advocates should use and follow the 'toolkits' as discussed above.

3G.11 A vulnerable defendant who wishes to give evidence by live link, in accordance with section 33A of the Youth Justice and Criminal Evidence Act 1999, may apply for a direction to that effect; the procedure in CrimPR 18.14 to 18.17 should be followed. Before making such a direction, the court must be satisfied that it is in the interests of justice to do so and that the use of a live link would enable the defendant to participate more effectively as a witness in the proceedings. The direction will need to deal with the practical arrangements to be made, including the identity of the person or persons who will accompany him or her.

3G.12 In the Crown Court, the judge should consider whether robes and wigs should be worn, and should take account of the wishes of both a vulnerable defendant and any vulnerable witness. It is generally desirable that those responsible for the security of a vulnerable defendant who is in custody, especially if he or she is young, should not be in uniform, and that there should be no recognisable police presence in the courtroom save for good reason.

3G.13 The court should be prepared to restrict attendance by members of the public in the courtroom to a small number, perhaps limited to those with an immediate and direct interest in the outcome. The court should rule on any challenged claim to attend. However, facilities for reporting the proceedings (subject to any restrictions under section 39 or 49 of the Children and Young Persons Act 1933) must be provided. The court may restrict the number of reporters attending in the courtroom to such number as is judged practicable and desirable. In ruling on any challenged claim to attend in the courtroom for the purpose of reporting, the court should be mindful of the public's general right to be informed about the administration of justice.

3G.14 Where it has been decided to limit access to the courtroom, whether by reporters or generally, arrangements should be made for the proceedings to be relayed, audibly and if possible visually, to another room in the same court complex to which the media and the public have access if it appears that there will be a need for such additional facilities. Those making use of such a facility should be reminded that it is to be treated as an extension of the courtroom and that they are required to conduct themselves accordingly.

PD-10 **CPD I General matters 3H: Wales and the Welsh Language: Devolution Issues**

3H.1 These are the subject of Practice Direction: (Supreme Court) (Devolution Issues) [1999] 1 WLR 1592; [1999] 3 All ER 466; [1999] 2 Cr App R 486, to which reference should be made.

PD-11 **CPD I General matters 3J: Wales and the Welsh Language: Applications for Evidence to be Given in Welsh**

3J.1 If a defendant in a court in England asks to give or call evidence in the Welsh language, the case should not be transferred to Wales. In ordinary circumstances, interpreters can be provided on request.

PD-12 **CPD I General matters 3K: Wales and the Welsh Language: Use of the Welsh Language in Courts in Wales**

3K.1 The purpose of this direction is to reflect the principle of the Welsh Language Act 1993 that, in the administration of justice in Wales, the English and Welsh languages should be treated on a basis of equality.

General

3K.2 It is the responsibility of the legal representatives in every case in which the Welsh language may be used by any witness or party, or in any document which may be placed before the court, to inform the court of that fact, so that appropriate arrangements can be made for the listing of the case.

3K.3 Any party or witness is entitled to use Welsh in a magistrates' court in Wales without giving prior notice. Arrangements will be made for hearing such cases in accordance with the 'Magistrates' Courts' Protocol for Listing Cases where the Welsh Language is used' (January 2008) which is available on the Judiciary's website: http://www.judiciary.gov.uk/NR/exeres/57AD4763-F265-47B9-8A35-0442E08160E6. See also CrimPR 24.14.

3K.4 If the possible use of the Welsh language is known at the time of sending or appeal to the Crown Court, the court should be informed immediately after sending or when the notice of appeal is lodged. Otherwise, the court should be informed as soon as the possible use of the Welsh language becomes known.

3K.5 If costs are incurred as a result of failure to comply with these directions, a wasted costs order may be made against the defaulting party and / or his legal representatives.

3K.6 The law does not permit the selection of jurors in a manner which enables the court to discover whether a juror does or does not speak Welsh, or to secure a jury whose members are bilingual, to try a case in which the Welsh language may be used.

Preliminary and plea and case management hearings

3K.7 An advocate in a case in which the Welsh language may be used must raise that matter at the preliminary and/or the plea and case management hearing and endorse details of it on the advocates' questionnaire, so that appropriate directions may be given for the progress of the case.

Listing

3K.8 The listing officer, in consultation with the resident judge, should ensure that a case in which the Welsh language may be used is listed

(a) wherever practicable before a Welsh speaking judge, and
(b) in a court in Wales with simultaneous translation facilities.

Interpreters

3K.9 Whenever an interpreter is needed to translate evidence from English into Welsh or from Welsh into English, the court listing officer in whose court the case is to be heard shall contact the Welsh Language Unit who will ensure the attendance of an accredited interpreter.

Jurors

3K.10 The jury bailiff, when addressing the jurors at the start of their period of jury service, shall inform them that each juror may take an oath or affirm in Welsh or English as he wishes.

3K.11 After the jury has been selected to try a case, and before it is sworn, the court officer swearing in the jury shall inform the jurors in open court that each juror may take an oath or affirm in Welsh or English as he wishes. A juror who takes the oath or affirms in Welsh should not be asked to repeat it in English.

3K.12 Where Welsh is used by any party or witness in a trial, an accredited interpreter will provide simultaneous translation from Welsh to English for the jurors who do not speak Welsh. There is no provision for the translation of evidence from English to Welsh for a Welsh speaking juror.

3K.13 The jury's deliberations must be conducted in private with no other person present and therefore no interpreter may be provided to translate the discussion for the benefit of one or more of the jurors.

Witnesses

3K.14 When each witness is called, the court officer administering the oath or affirmation shall inform the witness that he may be sworn or affirm in Welsh or English, as he wishes. A witness who takes the oath or affirms in Welsh should not be asked to repeat it in English.

Opening / closing of Crown Courts

3K.15 Unless it is not reasonably practicable to do so, the opening and closing of the court should be performed in Welsh and English.

Role of Liaison Judge

3K.16 If any question or problem arises concerning the implementation of these directions, contact should in the first place be made with the Liaison Judge for the Welsh language through the Wales Circuit Office:

HMCTS WALES / GLITEM CYMRU
3rd Floor, Churchill House / 3ydd Llawr Tŷ Churchill
Churchill Way / Ffordd Churchill
Cardiff / Caerdydd
CF10 2HH
029 2067 8300

CPD I General Matters 3L: Security of Prisoners at Court PD-13

3L.1 High-risk prisoners identified to the court as presenting a significant risk of escape, violence in court or danger to those in the court and its environs, and to the public at large, will as far as possible, have administrative and remand appearances listed for disposal by way of live link. They will have priority for the use of video equipment.

3L.2 In all other proceedings that require the appearance in person of a high-risk prisoner, the proceedings will be listed at an appropriately secure court building and in a court with a secure (enclosed or ceiling-high) dock.

3L.3 Where a secure dock or live link is not available the court will be asked to consider an application for additional security measures, which may include:

(a) the use of approved restraints (but see below at 3L.6);
(b) the deployment of additional escort staff;
(c) securing the court room for all or part of the proceedings;
(d) in exceptional circumstances, moving the hearing to a prison.

3L.4 National Offender Management Service (NOMS) will be responsible for providing the assessment of the prisoner and it is accepted that this may change at short notice. NOMS must provide notification to the listing officer of all Category A prisoners, those on the Escape-list and Restricted Status prisoners or other prisoners who have otherwise been assessed as presenting a significant risk of violence or harm. There is a presumption that all prisoners notified as high-risk will be allocated a hearing by live link and/or secure dock facilities. Where the court cannot provide a secure listing, the reasons should be provided to the establishment so that alternative arrangements can be considered.

Applications for use of approved restraints

3L.5 It is the duty of the court to decide whether a prisoner who appears before them should appear in restraints or not. Their decision must comply with the requirements of the European Convention on Human Rights, particularly Article 3, which prohibits degrading treatment, see *Ranniman v Finland* (1997) 26 EHRR 56.

3L.6 No prisoner should be handcuffed in court unless there are reasonable grounds for apprehending that he will be violent or will attempt to escape. If an application is made, it must be entertained by the court and a ruling must be given. The defence should be given the opportunity to respond to the application: proceeding in the absence of the defendant or his representative may give rise to an issue under Article 6(1) of the European Convention on Human Rights: *R v Rollinson* (1996) 161 JP 107, CA. If an application is to be made ex parte then that application should be made inter partes and the defence should be given an opportunity to respond.

Additional security measures

3L.7 It may be in some cases that additional dock officers are deployed to mitigate the risk that a prisoner presents. When the nature of the risk is so serious that increased deployment will be insufficient or would in itself be so obtrusive as to prejudice a fair trial, then the court may be required to consider the following measures:

(a) reconsider the case for a live link hearing, including transferring the case to a court where the live link is available;
(b) transfer the case to an appropriately secure court;
(c) the use of approved restraints on the prisoner for all or part of the proceedings;
(d) securing the court room for all or part of the proceedings; and
(e) the use of (armed) police in the court building.

3L.8 The establishment seeking the additional security measures will submit a Court Management Directions Form setting out the evidence of the prisoners identified risk of escape or violence and requesting the courts approval of security measures to mitigate that risk. This must be sent to the listing officer along with current, specific and credible evidence that the security measures are both necessary and proportionate to the identified risk and that the risk cannot be managed in any other way.

3L.9 If the court is asked to consider transfer of the case, then this must be in accordance with the Listing and Allocation Practice Direction XIII F.11-F.13 post. The listing officer will liaise with the establishment, prosecution and the defence to ensure the needs of the witnesses are taken into account.

3L.10 The Judge who has conduct of the case must deal with any application for the use of restraints or any other security measure and will hear representations from the Crown Prosecution Service and the defence before proceeding. The application will only be granted if:

(a) there are good grounds for believing that the prisoner poses a significant risk of trying to escape from the court (beyond the assumed motivation of all prisoners to escape) and/or risk of serious harm towards those persons in court or the public generally should an escape attempt be successful; and
(b) where there is no other viable means of preventing escape or serious harm.

High-risk prisoners giving evidence from the witness box

3L.11 High-risk prisoners giving evidence from the witness box may pose a significant security risk. In circumstances where such prisoners are required to move from a secure dock to an insecure witness box, an application may be made for the court to consider the use of additional security measures including:

(a) the use of approved restraints;
(b) the deployment of additional escort staff or police in the courtroom or armed police in the building. The decision to deploy an armed escort is for the Chief Inspector of the relevant borough: the decision to allow the armed escort in or around the court room is for the Senior Presiding Judge (see below);
(c) securing the courtroom for all or part of the proceedings;
(d) giving evidence from the secure dock; and
(e) use of live link if the prisoner is not the defendant.

PD-14 **CPD I General Matters 3M: Procedure for Application for Armed Police Presence in Crown Courts and Magistrates' Court Buildings**

3M.1 This Practice Direction sets out the procedure for the making and handling of applications for authorisation for the presence of armed police officers within the precincts of any Crown Court and magistrates' court building at any time. It applies to an application to authorise the carriage of firearms or tasers in court. It does not apply to officers who are carrying CS spray or PAVA incapacitant spray, which is included in the standard equipment issued to officers in some forces and therefore no separate authorisation is required for its carriage in court.

3M.2 This Practice Direction applies to all cases in England and Wales in which a police unit intends to request authorisation for the presence of armed police officers in the Crown Court or in the magistrates' court buildings at any time and including during the delivery of prisoners to court.

Emergency situations

3M.3 This Practice Direction does not apply in an emergency situation. In such circumstances, the police must be able to respond in a way in which their professional judgment deems most appropriate.

Designated court centres

3M.4 Applications may only be made for armed police presence in the designated Crown Court and magistrates' court centres (see below). This list may be revised from time to time in consultation with the Association of Chief Police Officers (ACPO) and HMCTS. It will be reviewed at least every five years in consultation with ACPO armed police secretariat and the Presiding Judges.

3M.5 The Crown Court centres designated for firearms deployment are:

(a) Northern Circuit: Carlisle, Chester, Liverpool, Preston, Manchester Crown Square & Manchester Minshull Street.
(b) North Eastern Circuit: Bradford, Leeds, Newcastle upon Tyne, Sheffield, Teesside and Kingston-upon-Hull.
(c) Western Circuit: Bristol, Winchester and Exeter.
(d) South Eastern Circuit (not including London): Canterbury, Chelmsford, Ipswich, Luton, Maidstone, Norwich, Reading and St Albans.
(e) South Eastern Circuit (London only): Central Criminal Court, Woolwich, Kingston and Snaresbrook.
(f) Midland Circuit: Birmingham, Northampton, Nottingham and Leicester.
(g) Wales Circuit: Cardiff, Swansea and Caernarfon.

3M.6 The magistrates' courts designated for firearms deployment are:

(a) South Eastern Circuit (London only): Westminster Magistrates' Court and Belmarsh Magistrates' Court.

Preparatory work prior to applications in all cases

3M.7 Prior to the making of any application for armed transport of prisoners or the presence of armed police officers in the court building, consideration must be given to making use of prison video link equipment to avoid the necessity of prisoners' attendance at court for the hearing in respect of which the application is to be made.

3M.8 Notwithstanding their designation, each requesting officer will attend the relevant court before an application is made to ensure that there have been no changes to the premises and that there are no circumstances that might affect security arrangements.

Applying to the Crown Court

3M.9 All applications should be sent to the Cluster Manager and should be sent by email if possible and must be on the standard form.

3M.10 The Cluster Manager will notify the Presiding Judge on the circuit and the Resident Judge by email, providing a copy of the form and any supporting evidence. The Presiding Judge may ask to see the senior police officer concerned.

3M.11 The Presiding Judge will consider the application. If it is refused the application fails and the police must be informed.

3M.12 If the Presiding Judge approves the application it should be forwarded to the secretary in the Senior Presiding Judge's Office. The Senior Presiding Judge will make the final decision. The Presiding Judge will receive written confirmation of that decision.

3M.13 The Presiding Judge will notify the Cluster Manager and the Resident Judge of the decision. The Cluster Manager will immediately inform the police of the decision by telephone. The decision must then be confirmed in writing to the police.

Urgent applications to the Crown Court

3M.14 If the temporary deployment of armed police arises as an urgent issue and a case would otherwise have to be adjourned; or if the trial judge is satisfied that there is a serious risk to public safety, then the Resident Judge will have a discretion to agree such deployment without having obtained the consent of a Presiding Judge or the Senior Presiding Judge. In such a case:

(a) the Resident Judge should assess the facts and agree the proposed solution with a police officer of at least Superintendent level. That officer should agree the approach with the Firearms Division of the police.

(b) if the proposed solution involves the use of armed police officers, the Resident Judge must try to contact the Presiding Judge and/or the Senior Presiding Judge by email and telephone. The Cluster Manager should be informed of the situation.

(c) if the Resident Judge cannot obtain a response from the Presiding Judge or the Senior Presiding Judge, the Resident Judge may grant the application if satisfied:

(i) that the application is necessary;

(ii) that without such deployment there would be a significant risk to public safety; and

(iii) that the case would have to be adjourned at significant difficulty or inconvenience.

3M.15 The Resident Judge must keep the position under continual review, to ensure that it remains appropriate and necessary. The Resident Judge must make continued efforts to contact the Presiding Judge and the Senior Presiding Judge to notify them of the full circumstances of the authorisation.

Applying to the magistrates' courts

3M.16 All applications should be directed, by email if possible, to the Office of the Chief Magistrate, at Westminster Magistrates' Court and must be on the standard form.

3M.17 The Chief Magistrate should consider the application and, if approved, it should be forwarded to the Senior Presiding Judge's office. The Senior Presiding Judge will make the final decision. The Chief Magistrate will receive written confirmation of that decision and will then notify the requesting police officer and, where authorisation is given, the affected magistrates' court of the decision.

Urgent applications in the magistrates' courts

3M.18 If the temporary deployment of armed police arises as an urgent issue and a case would otherwise have to be adjourned; or if the Chief Magistrate is satisfied that there is a serious risk to public safety, then the Chief Magistrate will have a discretion to agree such deployment without having obtained the consent of the Senior Presiding Judge. In such a case:

(a) the Chief Magistrate should assess the facts and agree the proposed solution with a police officer of at least Superintendent level. That officer should agree the approach with the Firearms Division of the police.

(b) if the proposed solution involves the use of armed police officers, the Chief Magistrate must try to contact the Senior Presiding Judge by email and telephone. The Cluster Manager should be informed of the situation.

(c) if the Chief Magistrate cannot obtain a response from the Senior Presiding Judge, the Chief Magistrate may grant the application if satisfied:

(i) that the application is necessary;

(ii) that without such deployment there would be a significant risk to public safety; and

(iii) that the case would have to be adjourned at significant difficulty or inconvenience.

3M.19 The Chief Magistrate must keep the position under continual review, to ensure that it remains appropriate and necessary. The Chief Magistrate must make continued efforts to contact the Senior Presiding Judge to notify him of the full circumstances of the authorisation.

Criminal Procedure Rules Part 4 Service of Documents

R-33 **When this Part applies**

4.1 (1) The rules in this Part apply—

(a) to the service of every document in a case to which these Rules apply; and

(b) for the purposes of section 12 of the Road Traffic Offenders Act 1988, to the service of a requirement to which that section applies.

(2) The rules apply subject to any special rules in other legislation (including other Parts of these Rules) or in the Practice Direction.

Methods of service R-34

4.2 (1) A document may be served by any of the methods described in rules 4.3 to 4.6 (subject to rule 4.7 and 4.10), or in rule 4.8.

(2) Where a document may be served by electronic means under rule 4.6, the general rule is that the person serving it must use that method.

Service by handing over a document R-35

4.3 (1) A document may be served on—

(a) an individual by handing it to him or her;

(b) a corporation by handing it to a person holding a senior position in that corporation;

(c) an individual or corporation who is legally represented in the case by handing it to that legal representative;

(d) the prosecution by handing it to the prosecutor or to the prosecution representative;

(e) the court officer by handing it to a court officer with authority to accept it at the relevant court office; and

(f) the Registrar of Criminal Appeals by handing it to a court officer with authority to accept it at the Criminal Appeal Office.

(2) If an individual is under 18, a copy of a document served under paragraph (1)(a) must be handed to his or her parent, or another appropriate adult, unless no such person is readily available.

(3) Unless the court otherwise directs, for the purposes of paragraph (1)(c) or (d) (service by handing a document to a party's representative) 'representative' includes an advocate appearing for that party at a hearing.

(4) In this rule, 'the relevant court office' means—

(a) in relation to a case in a magistrates' court or in the Crown Court, the office at which that court's business is administered by court staff;

(b) in relation to an extradition appeal case in the High Court, the Administrative Court Office of the Queen's Bench Division of the High Court.

Service by leaving or posting a document R-36

4.4 (1) A document may be served by addressing it to the person to be served and leaving it at the appropriate address for service under this rule, or by sending it to that address by first class post or by the equivalent of first class post.

(2) The address for service under this rule on—

(a) an individual is an address where it is reasonably believed that he or she will receive it;

(b) a corporation is its principal office, and if there is no readily identifiable principal office then any place where it carries on its activities or business;

(c) an individual or corporation who is legally represented in the case is that legal representative's office;

(d) the prosecution is the prosecutor's office;

(e) the court officer is the relevant court office; and

(f) the Registrar of Criminal Appeals is the Criminal Appeal Office, Royal Courts of Justice, Strand, London WC2A 2LL.

(3) In this rule, 'the relevant court office' means—

(a) in relation to a case in a magistrates' court or in the Crown Court, the office at which that court's business is administered by court staff;

(b) in relation to an extradition appeal case in the High Court, the Administrative Court Office, Royal Courts of Justice, Strand, London WC2A 2LL.

Service by document exchange R-37

4.5 (1) This rule applies where—

(a) the person to be served—

(i) has given a document exchange (DX) box number, and

(ii) has not refused to accept service by DX; or

(b) the person to be served is legally represented in the case and the legal representative has given a DX box number.

(2) A document may be served by—

(a) addressing it to that person or legal representative, as appropriate, at that DX box number; and

(b) leaving it at—

(i) the document exchange at which the addressee has that DX box number, or

(ii) a document exchange at which the person serving it has a DX box number.

R-38 **Service by electronic means**

4.6 (1) This rule applies where—
(a) the person to be served—
(i) has given an electronic address and has not refused to accept service at that address, or
(ii) is given access to an electronic address at which a document may be deposited and has not refused to accept service by the deposit of a document at that address; or
(b) the person to be served is legally represented in the case and the legal representative—
(i) has given an electronic address, or
(ii) is given access to an electronic address at which a document may be deposited.
(2) A document may be served—
(a) by sending it by electronic means to the address which the recipient has given; or
(b) by depositing it at an address to which the recipient has been given access and—
(i) in every case, making it possible for the recipient to read the document, or view or listen to its content, as the case may be,
(ii) unless the court otherwise directs, making it possible for the recipient to make and keep an electronic copy of the document, and
(iii) notifying the recipient of the deposit of the document (which notice may be given by electronic means).
(3) Where a document is served under this rule the person serving it need not provide a paper copy as well.

R-39 **Documents that must be served by specified methods**

4.7 (1) An application or written statement, and notice, under rule 48.9 alleging contempt of court may be served—
(a) on an individual, only under rule 4.3(1)(a) (by handing it to him or her);
(b) on a corporation, only under rule 4.3(1)(b) (by handing it to a person holding a senior position in that corporation).
(2) For the purposes of section 12 of the Road Traffic Offenders Act 1988, a notice of a requirement under section 172 of the Road Traffic Act 1988 or under section 112 of the Road Traffic Regulation Act 1984 to identify the driver of a vehicle may be served—
(a) on an individual, only by post under rule 4.4(1) and (2)(a);
(b) on a corporation, only by post under rule 4.4(1) and (2)(b).

R-40 **Service by person in custody**

4.8 (1) A person in custody may serve a document by handing it to the custodian addressed to the person to be served.
(2) The custodian must—
(a) endorse it with the time and date of receipt;
(b) record its receipt; and
(c) forward it promptly to the addressee.

R-41 **Service by another method**

4.9 (1) The court may allow service of a document by a method—
(a) other than those described in rules 4.3 to 4.6 and in rule 4.8;
(b) other than one specified by rule 4.7, where that rule applies.
(2) An order allowing service by another method must specify—
(a) the method to be used; and
(b) the date on which the document will be served.

R-42 **Documents that may not be served on a legal representative**

4.10 Unless the court otherwise directs, service on a party's legal representative of any of the following documents is not service of that document on that party—
(a) a summons, requisition, single justice procedure notice or witness summons;
(b) notice of an order under section 25 of the Road Traffic Offenders Act 1988;
(c) a notice of registration under section 71(6) of that Act;
(d) notice of a hearing to review the postponement of the issue of a warrant of detention or imprisonment under section 77(6) of the Magistrates' Courts Act 1980;
(e) notice under section 86 of that Act of a revised date to attend a means inquiry;
(f) any notice or document served under Part 14 (Bail and custody time limits);
(g) notice under rule 24.16(a) of when and where an adjourned hearing will resume;
(h) notice under rule 28.5(3) of an application to vary or discharge a compensation order;

(i) notice under rule 28.10(2)(c) of the location of the sentencing or enforcing court;
(j) a collection order, or notice requiring payment, served under rule 30.2(a); or
(k) an application or written statement, and notice, under rule 48.9 alleging contempt of court.

Date of service R-43

4.11 (1) A document served under rule 4.3 or rule 4.8 is served on the day it is handed over.
(2) Unless something different is shown, a document served on a person by any other method is served—
(a) in the case of a document left at an address, on the next business day after the day on which it was left;
(b) in the case of a document sent by first class post or by the equivalent of first class post, on the second business day after the day on which it was posted or despatched;
(c) in the case of a document served by document exchange, on the second business day after the day on which it was left at a document exchange allowed by rule 4.5;
(d) in the case of a document served by electronic means—
(i) on the day on which it is sent under rule 4.6(2)(a), if that day is a business day and if it is sent by no later than 2.30pm that day,
(ii) on the day on which notice of its deposit is given under rule 4.6(2)(b), if that day is a business day and if that notice is given by no later than 2.30pm that day, or
(iii) otherwise, on the next business day after it was sent or such notice was given; and
(e) in any case, on the day on which the addressee responds to it, if that is earlier.
(3) Unless something different is shown, a document produced by a computer system for dispatch by post is to be taken as having been sent by first class post, or by the equivalent of first class post, to the addressee on the business day after the day on which it was produced.
(4) Where a document is served on or by the court officer, 'business day' does not include a day on which the court office is closed.

Proof of service R-44

4.12 The person who serves a document may prove that by signing a certificate explaining how and when it was served.

Court's power to give directions about service R-45

4.13 (1) The court may specify the time as well as the date by which a document must be—
(a) served under rule 4.3 (Service by handing over a document) or rule 4.8 (Service by person in custody); or
(b) sent or deposited by electronic means, if it is served under rule 4.6.
(2) The court may treat a document as served if the addressee responds to it even if it was not served in accordance with the rules in this Part.

Criminal Procedure Rules Part 5 Forms and Court Records

Forms

Applications, etc. by forms or electronic means R-46

5.1 (1) This rule applies where a rule, a practice direction or the court requires a person to—
(a) make an application or give a notice;
(b) supply information for the purposes of case management by the court; or
(c) supply information needed for other purposes by the court.
(2) Unless the court otherwise directs, such a person must—
(a) use such electronic arrangements as the court officer may make for that purpose, in accordance with those arrangements; or
(b) if no such arrangements have been made, use the appropriate form set out in the Practice Direction or the Criminal Costs Practice Direction, in accordance with those Directions.

Forms in Welsh R-47

5.2 (1) Any Welsh language form set out in the Practice Direction, or in the Criminal Costs Practice Direction, is for use in connection with proceedings in courts in Wales.
(2) Both a Welsh form and an English form may be contained in the same document.
(3) Where only a Welsh form, or only the corresponding English form, is served—
(a) the following words in Welsh and English must be added:
'Darperir y ddogfen hon yn Gymraeg / Saesneg os bydd arnoch ei heisiau. Dylech wneud cais yn ddi-oed i (swyddog y llys) (rhodder yma'r cyfeiriad)

This document will be provided in Welsh / English if you require it. You should apply immediately to (the court officer) (address)'; and
(b) the court officer, or the person who served the form, must, on request, supply the corresponding form in the other language to the person served.

R-48 Signature of forms

5.3 (1) This rule applies where a form provides for its signature.
(2) Unless other legislation otherwise requires, or the court otherwise directs, signature may be by any written or electronic authentication of the form by, or with the authority of, the signatory.

Court records

R-49 Duty to make records

5.4 (1) For each case, as appropriate, the court officer must record, by such means as the Lord Chancellor directs—
(a) each charge or indictment against the defendant;
(b) the defendant's plea to each charge or count;
(c) each acquittal, conviction, sentence, determination, direction or order;
(d) each decision about bail;
(e) the power exercised where the court commits or adjourns the case to another court—
(i) for sentence, or
(ii) for the defendant to be dealt with for breach of a community order, a deferred sentence, a conditional discharge, or a suspended sentence of imprisonment, imposed by that other court;
(f) the court's reasons for a decision, where legislation requires those reasons to be recorded;
(g) any appeal;
(h) each party's presence or absence at each hearing;
(i) any consent that legislation requires before the court can proceed with the case, or proceed to a decision;
(j) in a magistrates' court—
(i) any indication of sentence given in connection with the allocation of a case for trial, and
(ii) the registration of a fixed penalty notice for enforcement as a fine, and any related endorsement on a driving record;
(k) in the Crown Court, any request for assistance or other communication about the case received from a juror;
(l) the identity of—
(i) the prosecutor,
(ii) the defendant,
(iii) any other applicant to whom these Rules apply,
(iv) any interpreter or intermediary,
(v) the parties' legal representatives, if any, and
(vi) the judge, magistrate or magistrates, justices' legal adviser or other person who made each recorded decision;
(m) where a defendant is entitled to attend a hearing, any agreement by the defendant to waive that right; and
(n) where interpretation is required for a defendant, any agreement by that defendant to do without the written translation of a document.
(2) Such records must include—
(a) each party's and representative's address, including any electronic address and telephone number available;
(b) the defendant's date of birth, if available; and
(c) the date of each event and decision recorded.

R-50 Recording and transcription of proceedings in the Crown Court

5.5 (1) Where someone may appeal to the Court of Appeal, the court officer must—
(a) arrange for the recording of the proceedings in the Crown Court, unless the court otherwise directs; and
(b) arrange for the transcription of such a recording if—
(i) the Registrar wants such a transcript, or
(ii) anyone else wants such a transcript (but that is subject to the restrictions in paragraph (2)).

(2) Unless the court otherwise directs, a person who transcribes a recording of proceedings under such arrangements—
(a) must not supply anyone other than the Registrar with a transcript of a recording of—
(i) a hearing in private, or
(ii) information to which reporting restrictions apply;
(b) subject to that, must supply any person with any transcript for which that person asks—
(i) in accordance with the transcription arrangements made by the court officer, and
(ii) on payment by that person of any fee prescribed.
(3) A party who wants to hear a recording of proceedings must—
(a) apply—
(i) in writing to the Registrar, if an appeal notice has been served where Part 36 applies (Appeal to the Court of Appeal: general rules), or
(ii) orally or in writing to the Crown Court officer;
(b) explain the reasons for the request; and
(c) pay any fee prescribed.
(4) If the Crown Court or the Registrar so directs, the Crown Court officer must allow that party to hear a recording of—
(a) a hearing in public;
(b) a hearing in private, if the applicant was present at that hearing.

Custody of case materials R-51

5.6 Unless the court otherwise directs, in respect of each case the court officer may—
(a) keep any evidence, application, representation or other material served by the parties; or
(b) arrange for the whole or any part to be kept by some other appropriate person, subject to—
(i) any condition imposed by the court, and
(ii) the rules in Part 34 (Appeal to the Crown Court) and Part 36 (Appeal to the Court of Appeal: General Rules) about keeping exhibits pending any appeal.

Supply to a party of information or documents from records or case materials R-52

5.7 (1) This rule applies where—
(a) a party wants information, or a copy of a document, from records or case materials kept by the court officer (for example, in case of loss, or to establish what is retained); or
(b) a person affected by an order made, or warrant issued, by the court wants such information or such a copy.
(2) Such a party or person must—
(a) apply to the court officer;
(b) specify the information or document required; and
(c) pay any fee prescribed.
(3) The application—
(a) may be made orally, giving no reasons, if paragraph (4) requires the court officer to supply the information or document requested;
(b) must be in writing, unless the court otherwise permits, and must explain for what purpose the information is required, in any other case.
(4) The court officer must supply to the applicant party or person —
(a) a copy of any document served by, or on, that party or person (but not of any document not so served);
(b) by word of mouth, or in writing, as requested—
(i) information that was received from that party or person in the first place,
(ii) information about the terms of any direction or order directed to that party or person, or made on an application by that party or person, or at a hearing in public,
(iii) information about the outcome of the case.
(5) If the court so directs, the court officer must supply to the applicant party or person, by word of mouth or in writing, as requested, information that paragraph (4) does not require the court officer to supply.
(6) Where the information requested is about the grounds on which an order was made, or a warrant was issued, in the absence of the party or person applying for that information—
(a) that party or person must also serve the request on the person who applied for the order or warrant;
(b) if the person who applied for the order or warrant objects to the supply of the information requested, that objector must—
(i) give notice of the objection not more than 14 days after service of the request (or within any longer period allowed by the court),

(ii) serve that notice on the court officer and on the party or person requesting the information, and
(iii) if the objector wants a hearing, explain why one is needed;
(c) the court may determine the application for information at a hearing (which must be in private unless the court otherwise directs), or without a hearing;
(d) the court must not permit the information requested to be supplied unless the person who applied for the order or warrant has had at least 14 days (or any longer period allowed by the court) in which to make representations.

(7) A notice of objection under paragraph (6) must explain—
(a) whether the objection is to the supply of any part of the information requested, or only to the supply of a specified part, or parts, of it;
(b) whether the objection is to the supply of the information at any time, or only to its supply before a date or event specified by the objector; and
(c) the grounds of the objection.

(8) Where a notice of objection under paragraph (6) includes material that the objector thinks ought not be revealed to the party or person applying for information, the objector must—
(a) omit that material from the notice served on that party or person;
(b) mark the material to show that it is only for the court; and
(c) with that material include an explanation of why it has been withheld.

(9) Where paragraph (8) applies—
(a) a hearing of the application may take place, wholly or in part, in the absence of the party or person applying for information;
(b) at any such hearing, the general rule is that the court must consider, in the following sequence—
(i) representations first by the party or person applying for information and then by the objector, in the presence of both, and then
(ii) further representations by the objector, in the absence of that party or person

but the court may direct other arrangements for the hearing.

R-53 Supply to the public, including reporters, of information about cases

5.8 (1) This rule—
(a) applies where a member of the public, including a reporter, wants information about a case from the court officer;
(b) requires the court officer to publish information about cases due to be heard.

(2) A person who wants information about a case from the court officer must—
(a) apply to the court officer;
(b) specify the information requested; and
(c) pay any fee prescribed.

(3) The application—
(a) may be made orally, giving no reasons, if paragraph (4) requires the court officer to supply the information requested;
(b) must be in writing, unless the court otherwise permits, and must explain for what purpose the information is required, in any other case.

(4) The court officer must supply to the applicant—
(a) any information listed in paragraph (6), if—
(i) the information is available to the court officer,
(ii) the supply of the information is not prohibited by a reporting restriction, and
(iii) the trial has not yet concluded, or the verdict was not more than 6 months ago; and
(b) details of any reporting or access restriction ordered by the court.

(5) The court officer must supply that information—
(a) by word of mouth; or
(b) by such other arrangements as the Lord Chancellor directs.

(6) The information that paragraph (4) requires the court officer to supply is—
(a) the date of any hearing in public, unless any party has yet to be notified of that date;
(b) each alleged offence and any plea entered;
(c) the court's decision at any hearing in public, including any decision about—
(i) bail, or
(ii) the committal, sending or transfer of the case to another court;
(d) whether the case is under appeal;

(e) the outcome of any trial and any appeal; and
(f) the identity of—
(i) the prosecutor,
(ii) the defendant,
(iii) the parties' representatives, including their addresses, and
(iv) the judge, magistrate or magistrates, or justices' legal adviser by whom a decision at a hearing in public was made.

(7) If the court so directs, the court officer must—
(a) supply to the applicant, by word of mouth, other information about the case; or
(b) allow the applicant to inspect or copy a document, or part of a document, containing information about the case.

(8) The court may determine an application to which paragraph (7) applies—
(a) at a hearing, in public or in private; or
(b) without a hearing.

(9) The court officer must publish the information listed in paragraph (11) if—
(a) the information is available to the court officer;
(b) the hearing to which the information relates is due to take place in public; and
(c) the publication of the information is not prohibited by a reporting restriction.

(10) The court officer must publish that information—
(a) by notice displayed somewhere prominent in the vicinity of the court room in which the hearing is due to take place;
(b) by such other arrangements as the Lord Chancellor directs, including arrangements for publication by electronic means; and
(c) for no longer than 2 business days.

(11) The information that paragraph (9) requires the court officer to publish is—
(a) the date, time and place of the hearing;
(b) the identity of the defendant; and
(c) such other information as it may be practicable to publish concerning—
(i) the type of hearing,
(ii) the identity of the court,
(iii) the offence or offences alleged, and
(iv) whether any reporting restriction applies.

Supply of written certificate or extract from records R-54

5.9 (1) This rule applies where legislation—
(a) allows a certificate of conviction or acquittal, or an extract from records kept by the court officer, to be introduced in evidence in criminal proceedings; or
(b) requires such a certificate or extract to be supplied by the court officer to a specified person for a specified purpose.

(2) A person who wants such a certificate or extract must—
(a) apply in writing to the court officer;
(b) specify the certificate or extract required;
(c) explain under what legislation and for what purpose it is required; and
(d) pay any fee prescribed.

(3) If the application satisfies the requirements of that legislation, the court officer must supply the certificate or extract requested—
(a) to a party;
(b) unless the court otherwise directs, to any other applicant.

Criminal Practice Directions Part 5 Forms and Court Records

CPD I General matters 5A: Forms PD-15

5A.1 The forms at Annex D to the Consolidated Criminal Practice Direction of 8th July, 2002, [2002] 1 WLR, 2870; [2002] 2 Cr App R 35, or forms to that effect, are to be used in the criminal courts, in accordance with CrimPR 5.1.

5A.2 The forms at Annex E to that Practice Direction, the case management forms, must be used in the criminal courts, in accordance with that rule.

5A.3 The table at the beginning of each section of each of those Annexes lists the forms and:
(a) shows the Rule in connection with which each applies;
(b) describes each form.

5A.4 The forms may be amended or withdrawn from time to time, or new forms added, under the authority of the Lord Chief Justice.

PD-16 **CPD I General matters 5B: Access to Information Held by the Court**

5B.1 Open justice, as Lord Justice Toulson recently re-iterated in the case of *R (Guardian News and Media Ltd) v City of Westminster Magistrates' Court* [2012] EWCA Civ 420, [2013] QB 618, is a 'principle at the heart of our system of justice and vital to the rule of law.' There are exceptions but these 'have to be justified by some even more important principle.' However, the practical application of that undisputed principle, and the proper balancing of conflicting rights and principles, call for careful judgments to be made. The following is intended to provide some assistance to courts making decisions when asked to provide the public, including journalists, with access to or copies of information and documents held by the court. It is not a prescriptive list, as the court will have to consider all the circumstances of each individual case.

5B.2 It remains the responsibility of the recipient of information or documents to ensure that they comply with any and all restrictions such as reporting restrictions (see Part 6 and the accompanying Practice Direction).

5B.3 For the purposes of this direction, the word document includes images in photographic, digital including DVD format, video, CCTV or any other form.

5B.4 Certain information can and should be provided to the public on request, unless there are restrictions, such as reporting restrictions, imposed in that particular case. CrimPR 5.8(4) and 5.8(6) read together specify the information that the court officer will supply to the public; an oral application is acceptable and no reason need be given for the request. There is no requirement for the court officer to consider the non-disclosure provisions of the Data Protection Act 1998 as the exemption under section 35 applies to all disclosure made under 'any enactment. . .or by the order of a court', which includes under the Criminal Procedure Rules.

5B.5 If the information sought is not listed at CrimPR 5.8(6), rule 5.8(7) will apply, and the provision of information is at the discretion of the court. The following guidance is intended to assist the court in exercising that discretion.

5B.6 A request for access to documents used in a criminal case should first be addressed to the party who presented them to the court. Prosecuting authorities are subject to the Freedom of Information Act 2000 and the Data Protection Act 1998 and their decisions are susceptible to review.

5B.7 If the request is from a journalist or media organisation, note that there is a protocol between ACPO, the CPS and the media entitled 'Publicity and the Criminal Justice System': http://www.cps.gov.uk/publications/agencies/mediaprotocol.html

There is additionally a protocol made under Rule 5.8(5) (b) between the media and HMCTS: http://www.newspapersoc.org.uk/sites/default/files/Docs/Protocol-for-Sharing-Court-Registers-and-Court-Lists-with-Local-Newspapers_September-2011.doc

This Practice Direction does not affect the operation of those protocols. Material should generally be sought under the relevant protocol before an application is made to the court.

5B.8 An application to which CrimPR 5.8(7) applies must be made in accordance with rule 5.8; it must be in writing, unless the court permits otherwise, and 'must explain for what purpose the information is required.' A clear, detailed application, specifying the name and contact details of the applicant, whether or not he or she represents a media organisation, and setting out the reasons for the application and to what use the information will be put, will be of most assistance to the court. Applicants should state if they have requested the information under a protocol and include any reasons given for the refusal. Before considering such an application, the court will expect the applicant to have given notice of the request to the parties.

5B.9 The court will consider each application on its own merits. The burden of justifying a request for access rests on the applicant. Considerations to be taken into account will include:

i. whether or not the request is for the purpose of contemporaneous reporting; a request after the conclusion of the proceedings will require careful scrutiny by the court;
ii. the nature of the information or documents being sought;
iii. the purpose for which they are required;
iv. the stage of the proceedings at the time when the application is made;
v. the value of the documents in advancing the open justice principle, including enabling the media to discharge its role, which has been described as a 'public watchdog', by reporting the proceedings effectively;
vi. any risk of harm which access to them may cause to the legitimate interests of others; and
vii. any reasons given by the parties for refusing to provide the material requested and any other representations received from the parties.

Further, all of the principles below are subject to any specific restrictions in the case. Courts should be aware that the risk of providing a document may reduce after a particular point in the proceedings, and when the material requested may be made available.

Documents read aloud in their entirety

5B.10 If a document has been read aloud to the court in its entirety, it should usually be provided on request, unless to do so would be disruptive to the court proceedings or place an undue burden on the court, the advocates or others. It may be appropriate and convenient for material to be provided electronically, if this can be done securely.

5B.11 Documents likely to fall into this category are:

i. Opening notes;
ii. Statements agreed under section 9 of the Criminal Justice Act 1967, including experts' reports, if read in their entirety;
iii. Admissions made under section 10 of the Criminal Justice Act 1967.

Documents treated as read aloud in their entirety

5B.12 A document treated by the court as if it had been read aloud in public, though in fact it has been neither read nor summarised aloud, should generally be made available on request. The burden on the court, the advocates or others in providing the material should be considered, but the presumption in favour of providing the material is greater when the material has only been treated as having been read aloud. Again, subject to security considerations, it may be convenient for the material to be provided electronically.

5B.13 Documents likely to fall into this category include:

i. Skeleton arguments;
ii. Written submissions.

Documents read aloud in part or summarised aloud

5B.14 Open justice requires only access to the part of the document that has been read aloud. If a member of the public requests a copy of such a document, the court should consider whether it is proportionate to order one of the parties to produce a suitably redacted version. If not, access to the document is unlikely to be granted; however open justice will generally have been satisfied by the document having been read out in court.

5B.15 If the request comes from an accredited member of the press (see *Access by reporters* below), there may be circumstances in which the court orders that a copy of the whole document be shown to the reporter, or provided, subject to the condition that those matters that had not been read out to the court may not be used or reported. A breach of such an order would be treated as a contempt of court.

5B.16 Documents in this category are likely to include:

i. Section 9 statements that are edited.

Jury bundles and exhibits (including video footage shown to the jury)

5B.17 The court should consider:

i. whether access to the specific document is necessary to understand or effectively to report the case;
ii. the privacy of third parties, such as the victim (in some cases, the reporting restriction imposed by section 1 of the Judicial Proceedings (Regulation of Reports) Act 1926 will apply (indecent or medical matter));
iii. whether the reporting of anything in the document may be prejudicial to a fair trial in this or another case, in which case whether it may be necessary to make an order under section 4(2) of the Contempt of Court Act 1981.

The court may order one of the parties to provide a copy of certain pages (or parts of the footage), but these should not be provided electronically.

Statements of witnesses who give oral evidence

5B.18 A witness statement does not become evidence unless it is agreed under section 9 of the Criminal Justice Act 1967 and presented to the court. Therefore the statements of witnesses who give oral evidence, including ABE interview and transcripts and experts' reports, should not usually be provided. Open justice is generally satisfied by public access to the court.

Confidential documents

5B.19 A document the content of which, though relied upon by the court, has not been communicated to the public or reporters, nor treated as if it had been, is likely to have been supplied in confidence and should be treated accordingly. This will apply even if the court has made reference to the document or quoted from the document. There is most unlikely to be a sufficient reason to displace the expectation of confidentiality ordinarily attaching to a document in this category, and it would be exceptional to permit the inspection or copying by a member of the public or of the media of such a document. The rights and legitimate interests of others are likely to outweigh the interests of open justice with respect these documents.

5B.20 Documents in this category are likely to include:
- i. Pre-sentence reports;
- ii. Medical reports;
- iii. Victim Personal Statements;
- iv. Reports and summaries for confiscation.

Prohibitions against the provision of information

5B.21 Statutory provisions may impose specific prohibitions against the provision of information. Those most likely to be encountered are listed in the note to CrimPR 5.8 and include the Rehabilitation of Offenders Act 1974, section 18 of the Criminal Procedure and Investigations Act 1996 ('unused material' disclosed by the prosecution), sections 33, 34 and 35 of the Legal Aid, Sentencing and Punishment of Offenders Act 2012 ('LASPO Act 2012') (privileged information furnished to the Legal Aid Agency) and reporting restrictions generally.

5B.22 Reports of allocation or sending proceedings are restricted by section 52A of the Crime and Disorder Act 1998, so that only limited information, as specified in the statute, may be reported, whether it is referred to in the court room or not. The magistrates' court has power to order that the restriction shall not apply; if any defendant objects the court must apply the interests of justice test as specified in section 52A. The restriction ceases to apply either after all defendants indicate a plea of guilty, or after the conclusion of the trial of the last defendant to be tried. If the case does not result in a guilty plea, a finding of guilt or an acquittal, the restriction does not lift automatically and an application must be made to the court.

5B.23 Extradition proceedings have some features in common with committal proceedings, but no automatic reporting restrictions apply.

5B.24 Public Interest Immunity and the rights of a defendant, witnesses and victims under Article 6 and 8 of the European Convention on Human Rights may also restrict the power to release material to third parties.

Other documents

5B.25 The following table indicates the considerations likely to arise on an application to inspect or copy other documents.

Document	Considerations
Charge sheet Indictment	The alleged offence(s) will have been read aloud in court, and their terms must be supplied under CrimPR 5.8(4)
Material disclosed under CPIA 1996	To the extent that the content is deployed at trial, it becomes public at that hearing. Otherwise, it is a criminal offence for it to be disclosed: section 18 of the 1996 Act.
Written notices, applications, replies (including any application for representation)	To the extent that evidence is introduced, or measures taken, at trial, the content becomes public at that hearing. A statutory prohibition against disclosure applies to an application for representation: sections 33, 34 and 35 of the LASPO Act 2012.
Sentencing remarks	Sentencing remarks should usually be provided to the accredited Press, if the judge was reading from a prepared script which was handed out immediately afterwards; if not, then permission for a member of the accredited Press to obtain a transcript should usually be given (see also paragraphs 26 and 29 below).
Official recordings Transcript	See CrimPR 5.5. See CrimPR 5.5.

Access by reporters

5B.26 Under CrimPR Part 5, the same procedure applies to applications for access to information by reporters as to other members of the public. However, if the application is made by legal representatives instructed by the media, or by an accredited member of the media, who is able to produce in support of the application a valid Press Card (http://www.ukpresscardauthority.co.uk/) then there is a greater presumption in favour of providing the requested material, in recognition of the press' role as 'public watch dog' in a democratic society (*Observer and Guardian v United Kingdom* (1992) 14 EHRR 153, Times November 27, 1991). The general principle in those circumstances is that the court should supply documents and information unless there is a good reason not to in order to protect the rights or legitimate interests of others and the request will not place an undue burden on the court *R* (*Guardian News and Media Ltd*) at [87]. Subject to that, the paragraphs above relating to types of documents should be followed.

5B.27 Court staff should usually verify the authenticity of cards, checking the expiry date on the card and where necessary may consider telephoning the number on the reverse of the card to verify the card holder. Court staff may additionally request sight of other identification if necessary to ensure that the card holder has been correctly identified. The supply of information under CrimPR 5.8(7) is at the discretion of the court, and court staff must ensure that they have received a clear direction from the court before providing any information or material under rule 5.8(7) to a member of the public, including to the accredited media or their legal representatives.

5B.28 Opening notes and skeleton arguments or written submissions, once they have been placed before the court, should usually be provided to the media. If there is no opening note, permission for the media to obtain a transcript of the prosecution opening should usually be given (see below). It may be convenient for copies to be provided electronically by counsel, provided that the documents are kept suitably secure. The media are expected to be aware of the limitations on the use to which such material can be put, for example that legal argument held in the absence of the jury must not be reported before the conclusion of the trial.

5B.29 The media should also be able to obtain transcripts of hearings held in open court directly from the transcription service provider, on payment of any required fee. The service providers commonly require the judge's authorisation before they will provide a transcript, as an additional verification to ensure that the correct material is released and reporting restrictions are noted. However, responsibility for compliance with any restriction always rests with the person receiving the information or material: see CPD I General Matters 6B beneath.

5B.30 It is not for the judge to exercise an editorial judgment about 'the adequacy of the material already available to the paper for its journalistic purpose' (*Guardian* at 82) but the responsibility for complying with the Contempt of Court Act 1981 and any and all restrictions on the use of the material rests with the recipient.

CPD I General matters 5C: Issue of Medical Certificates **PD-17**

5C.1 Doctors will be aware that medical notes are normally submitted by defendants in criminal proceedings as justification for not answering bail. Medical notes may also be submitted by witnesses who are due to give evidence and jurors.

5C.2 If a medical certificate is accepted by the court, this will result in cases (including contested hearings and trials) being adjourned rather than the court issuing a warrant for the defendant's arrest without bail. Medical certificates will also provide the defendant with sufficient evidence to defend a charge of failure to surrender to bail.

5C.3 However, a court is not absolutely bound by a medical certificate. The medical practitioner providing the certificate may be required by the court to give evidence. Alternatively the court may exercise its discretion to disregard a certificate which it finds unsatisfactory: *R v Ealing Magistrates' Court ex parte Burgess* [2001] 165 JP 82.

5C.4 Circumstances where the court may find a medical certificate unsatisfactory include:

(a) where the certificate indicates that the defendant is unfit to attend work (rather than to attend court);
(b) where the nature of the defendant's ailment (e.g. a broken arm) does not appear to be capable of preventing his attendance at court;
(c) where the defendant is certified as suffering from stress/anxiety/depression and there is no indication of the defendant recovering within a realistic timescale.

5C.5 It therefore follows that the minimum standards a medical certificate should set out are:

(a) the date on which the medical practitioner examined the defendant;
(b) the exact nature of the defendant's ailments;
(c) if it is not self-evident, why the ailment prevents the defendant attending court;

(d) an indication as to when the defendant is likely to be able to attend court, or a date when the current certificate expires.

5C.6 Medical practitioners should be aware that when issuing a certificate to a defendant in criminal proceedings they make themselves liable to being summonsed to court to give evidence about the content of the certificate, and they may be asked to justify their statements.

CRIMINAL PROCEDURE RULES PART 6 REPORTING, ETC. RESTRICTIONS

General rules

R-55 **When this Part applies**

6.1 (1) This Part applies where the court can—
(a) impose a restriction on—
(i) reporting what takes place at a public hearing, or
(ii) public access to what otherwise would be a public hearing;
(b) vary or remove a reporting or access restriction that is imposed by legislation;
(c) withhold information from the public during a public hearing;
(d) order a trial in private;
(e) allow there to take place during a hearing—
(i) sound recording, or
(ii) communication by electronic means.
(2) This Part does not apply to arrangements required by legislation, or directed by the court, in connection with—
(a) sound recording during a hearing, or the transcription of such a recording; or
(b) measures to assist a witness or defendant to give evidence.

R-56 **Exercise of court's powers to which this Part applies**

6.2 (1) When exercising a power to which this Part applies, as well as furthering the overriding objective, in accordance with rule 1.3, the court must have regard to the importance of—
(a) dealing with criminal cases in public; and
(b) allowing a public hearing to be reported to the public.
(2) The court may determine an application or appeal under this Part—
(a) at a hearing, in public or in private; or
(b) without a hearing.
(3) But the court must not exercise a power to which this Part applies unless each party and any other person directly affected—
(a) is present; or
(b) has had an opportunity—
(i) to attend, or
(ii) to make representations.

R-57 **Court's power to vary requirements under this Part**

6.3 (1) The court may—
(a) shorten or extend (even after it has expired) a time limit under this Part;
(b) require an application to be made in writing instead of orally;
(c) consider an application or representations made orally instead of in writing;
(d) dispense with a requirement to—
(i) give notice, or
(ii) serve a written application.
(2) Someone who wants an extension of time must—
(a) apply when making the application or representations for which it is needed; and
(b) explain the delay.

Reporting and access restrictions

R-58 **Reporting and access restrictions**

6.4 (1) This rule applies where the court can—
(a) impose a restriction on—
(i) reporting what takes place at a public hearing, or
(ii) public access to what otherwise would be a public hearing;
(b) withhold information from the public during a public hearing.

(2) Unless other legislation otherwise provides, the court may do so—
(a) on application by a party; or
(b) on its own initiative.
(3) A party who wants the court to do so must—
(a) apply as soon as reasonably practicable;
(b) notify—
(i) each other party, and
(ii) such other person (if any) as the court directs;
(c) specify the proposed terms of the order, and for how long it should last;
(d) explain—
(i) what power the court has to make the order, and
(ii) why an order in the terms proposed is necessary;
(e) where the application is for a reporting direction under section 45A of the Youth Justice and Criminal Evidence Act 1999 (Power to restrict reporting of criminal proceedings for lifetime of witnesses and victims under 18), explain—
(i) how the circumstances of the person whose identity is concerned meet the conditions prescribed by that section, having regard to the factors which that section lists; and
(ii) why such a reporting direction would be likely to improve the quality of any evidence given by that person, or the level of co-operation given by that person to any party in connection with the preparation of that party's case, taking into account the factors listed in that section;
(f) where the application is for a reporting direction under section 46 of the Youth Justice and Criminal Evidence Act 1999 (Power to restrict reports about certain adult witnesses in criminal proceedings), explain—
(i) how the witness is eligible for assistance, having regard to the factors listed in that section, and
(ii) why such a reporting direction would be likely to improve the quality of the witness' evidence, or the level of co-operation given by the witness to the applicant in connection with the preparation of the applicant's case, taking into account the factors which that section lists.

Varying or removing restrictions R-59

6.5 (1) This rule applies where the court can vary or remove a reporting or access restriction.
(2) Unless other legislation otherwise provides, the court may do so—
(a) on application by a party or person directly affected; or
(b) on its own initiative.
(3) A party or person who wants the court to do so must—
(a) apply as soon as reasonably practicable;
(b) notify—
(i) each other party, and
(ii) such other person (if any) as the court directs;
(c) specify the restriction;
(d) explain, as appropriate, why it should be varied or removed.
(4) A person who wants to appeal to the Crown Court under section 141F of the Education Act 2002 must—
(a) serve an appeal notice on—
(i) the Crown Court officer, and
(ii) each other party;
(b) serve on the Crown Court officer, with the appeal notice, a copy of the application to the magistrates' court;
(c) serve the appeal notice not more than 21 days after the magistrates' court's decision against which the appellant wants to appeal; and
(d) in the appeal notice, explain, as appropriate, why the restriction should be maintained, varied or removed.
(5) Rule 34.11 (Constitution of the Crown Court) applies on such an appeal.

Trial in private R-60

6.6 (1) This rule applies where the court can order a trial in private.
(2) A party who wants the court to do so must—
(a) apply in writing not less than 5 business days before the trial is due to begin; and

(b) serve the application on—
(i) the court officer, and
(ii) each other party.

(3) The applicant must explain—
(a) the reasons for the application;
(b) how much of the trial the applicant proposes should be in private; and
(c) why no measures other than trial in private will suffice, such as—
(i) reporting restrictions,
(ii) an admission of facts,
(iii) the introduction of hearsay evidence,
(iv) a direction for a special measure under section 19 of the Youth Justice and Criminal Evidence Act 1999,
(v) a witness anonymity order under section 86 of the Coroners and Justice Act 2009, or
(vi) arrangements for the protection of a witness.

(4) Where the application includes information that the applicant thinks ought not be revealed to another party, the applicant must—
(a) omit that information from the part of the application that is served on that other party;
(b) mark the other part to show that, unless the court otherwise directs, it is only for the court; and
(c) in that other part, explain why the applicant has withheld that information from that other party.

(5) The court officer must at once—
(a) display notice of the application somewhere prominent in the vicinity of the courtroom; and
(b) give notice of the application to reporters by such other arrangements as the Lord Chancellor directs.

(6) The application must be determined at a hearing which—
(a) must be in private, unless the court otherwise directs;
(b) if the court so directs, may be, wholly or in part, in the absence of a party from whom information has been withheld; and
(c) in the Crown Court, must be after the defendant is arraigned but before the jury is sworn.

(7) At the hearing of the application—
(a) the general rule is that the court must consider, in the following sequence—
(i) representations first by the applicant and then by each other party, in all the parties' presence, and then
(ii) further representations by the applicant, in the absence of a party from whom information has been withheld; but
(b) the court may direct other arrangements for the hearing.

(8) The court must not hear a trial in private until—
(a) the business day after the day on which it orders such a trial, or
(b) the disposal of any appeal against, or review of, any such order, if later.

R-61 Representations in response

6.7 (1) This rule applies where a party, or person directly affected, wants to make representations about an application or appeal.

(2) Such a party or person must—
(a) serve the representations on—
(i) the court officer,
(ii) the applicant,
(iii) each other party, and
(iv) such other person (if any) as the court directs;
(b) do so as soon as reasonably practicable after notice of the application; and
(c) ask for a hearing, if that party or person wants one, and explain why it is needed.

(3) Representations must—
(a) explain the reasons for any objection;
(b) specify any alternative terms proposed.

R-62 Order about restriction or trial in private

6.8 (1) This rule applies where the court—
(a) orders, varies or removes a reporting or access restriction; or
(b) orders a trial in private.

(2) The court officer must—
(a) record the court's reasons for the decision; and
(b) as soon as reasonably practicable, arrange for notice of the decision to be—
(i) displayed somewhere prominent in the vicinity of the courtroom, and
(ii) communicated to reporters by such other arrangements as the Lord Chancellor directs.

Sound recording and electronic communication

Sound recording and electronic communication R-63

6.9 (1) This rule applies where the court can give permission to—
(a) bring into a hearing for use, or use during a hearing, a device for—
(i) recording sound, or
(ii) communicating by electronic means; or
(b) publish a sound recording made during a hearing.
(2) The court may give such permission—
(a) on application; or
(b) on its own initiative.
(3) A person who wants the court to give such permission must—
(a) apply as soon as reasonably practicable;
(b) notify—
(i) each party, and
(ii) such other person (if any) as the court directs; and
(c) explain why the court should permit the use or publication proposed.
(4) As a condition of the applicant using such a device, the court may direct arrangements to minimise the risk of its use—
(a) contravening a reporting restriction;
(b) disrupting the hearing; or
(c) compromising the fairness of the hearing, for example by affecting—
(i) the evidence to be given by a witness, or
(ii) the verdict of a jury.
(5) Such a direction may require that the device is used only—
(a) in a specified part of the courtroom;
(b) for a specified purpose;
(c) for a purpose connected with the applicant's activity as a member of a specified group, for example representatives of news-gathering or reporting organisations;
(d) at a specified time, or in a specified way.

Forfeiture of unauthorised sound recording R-64

6.10 (1) This rule applies where someone without the court's permission—
(a) uses a device for recording sound during a hearing; or
(b) publishes a sound recording made during a hearing.
(2) The court may exercise its power to forfeit the device or recording—
(a) on application by a party, or on its own initiative;
(b) provisionally, despite rule 6.2(3), to allow time for representations.
(3) A party who wants the court to forfeit a device or recording must—
(a) apply as soon as reasonably practicable;
(b) notify—
(i) as appropriate, the person who used the device, or who published the recording, and
(ii) each other party; and
(c) explain why the court should exercise that power.

Criminal Practice Directions Part 6 Reporting, etc. Restrictions

CPD II Preliminary proceedings 6A: Unofficial Sound Recording of Proceedings PD-18

6A.1 Section 9 of the Contempt of Court Act 1981 contains provisions governing the unofficial use of equipment for recording sound in court.
Section 9(1) provides that it is a contempt of court:
(a) to use in court, or bring into court for use, any tape recorder or other instrument for recording sound, except with the permission of the court;
(b) to publish a recording of legal proceedings made by means of any such instrument, or any recording derived directly or indirectly from it, by playing it in the hearing of the public or any

section of the public, or to dispose of it or any recording so derived, with a view to such publication;

(c) to use any such recording in contravention of any conditions of leave granted under paragraph (a).

These provisions do not apply to the making or use of sound recordings for purposes of official transcripts of the proceedings, upon which the Act imposes no restriction whatever.

6A.2 The discretion given to the court to grant, withhold or withdraw leave to use equipment for recording sound or to impose conditions as to the use of the recording is unlimited, but the following factors may be relevant to its exercise:

(a) the existence of any reasonable need on the part of the applicant for leave, whether a litigant or a person connected with the press or broadcasting, for the recording to be made;

(b) the risk that the recording could be used for the purpose of briefing witnesses out of court;

(c) any possibility that the use of the recorder would disturb the proceedings or distract or worry any witnesses or other participants.

6A.3 Consideration should always be given whether conditions as to the use of a recording made pursuant to leave should be imposed. The identity and role of the applicant for leave and the nature of the subject matter of the proceedings may be relevant to this.

6A.4 The particular restriction imposed by section 9(1) (b) applies in every case, but may not be present in the mind of every applicant to whom leave is given. It may therefore be desirable on occasion for this provision to be drawn to the attention of those to whom leave is given.

6A.5 The transcript of a permitted recording is intended for the use of the person given leave to make it and is not intended to be used as, or to compete with, the official transcript mentioned in section 9(4).

6A.6 Where a contravention of section 9(1) is alleged, the procedure in section 2 of Part 48 of the Rules should be followed. Section 9(3) of the 1981 Act permits the court to 'order the instrument, or any recording made with it, or both, to be forfeited'. The procedure at CrimPR 6.10 should be followed.

PD-19 **CPD II Preliminary proceedings 6B: Restrictions on Reporting Proceedings**

6B.1 Open justice is an essential principle in the criminal courts but the principle is subject to some statutory restrictions. These restrictions are either automatic or discretionary. Guidance is provided in the joint publication, *Reporting Restrictions in the Criminal Courts* issued by the Judicial College, the Newspaper Society, the Society of Editors and the Media Lawyers Association. The current version is the fourth edition and has been updated to be effective from May 2015.

6B.2 Where a restriction is automatic no order can or should be made in relation to matters falling within the relevant provisions. However, the court may, if it considers it appropriate to do so, give a reminder of the existence of the automatic restriction. The court may also discuss the scope of the restriction and any particular risks in the specific case in open court with representatives of the press present. Such judicial observations cannot constitute an order binding on the editor or the reporter although it is anticipated that a responsible editor would consider them carefully before deciding what should be published. It remains the responsibility of those reporting a case to ensure that restrictions are not breached.

6B.3 Before exercising its discretion to impose a restriction the court must follow precisely the statutory provisions under which the order is to be made, paying particular regard to what has to be established, by whom and to what standard.

6B.4 Without prejudice to the above paragraph, certain general principles apply to the exercise of the court's discretion:

(a) The court must have regard to CrimPR Parts 6 and 18.

(b) The court must keep in mind the fact that every order is a departure from the general principle that proceedings shall be open and freely reported.

(c) Before making any order the court must be satisfied that the purpose of the proposed order cannot be achieved by some lesser measure e.g., the grant of special measures, screens or the clearing of the public gallery (usually subject to a representative(s) of the media remaining).

(d) The terms of the order must be proportionate so as to comply with Article 10 ECHR (freedom of expression).

(e) No order should be made without giving other parties to the proceedings and any other interested party, including any representative of the media, an opportunity to make representations.

(f) Any order should provide for any interested party who has not been present or represented at the time of the making of the order to have permission to apply within a limited period e.g., 24 hours.

(g) The wording of the order is the responsibility of the judge or Bench making the order: it must be in precise terms and, if practicable, agreed with the advocates.
(h) The order must be in writing and must state:
  (i) the power under which it is made;
  (ii) its precise scope and purpose; and
  (iii) the time at which it shall cease to have effect, if appropriate.
(i) The order must specify, in every case, whether or not the making or terms of the order may be reported or whether this itself is prohibited. Such a report could cause the very mischief which the order was intended to prevent.

6B.5 A series of template orders have been prepared by the Judicial College and are available as an appendix to the Crown Court Bench Book Companion; these template orders should generally be used.

6B.6 A copy of the order should be provided to any person known to have an interest in reporting the proceedings and to any local or national media who regularly report proceedings in the court.

6B.7 Court staff should be prepared to answer any enquiry about a specific case; but it is and will remain the responsibility of anyone reporting a case to ensure that no breach of any order occurs and the onus rests on such person to make enquiry in case of doubt.

CPD I General Matters 6C: Use of live text-based forms of communication (including *Twitter*) from court for the purposes of fair and accurate reporting **PD-20**

6C.1 This part clarifies the use which may be made of live text-based communications, such as mobile email, social media (including *Twitter*) and internet-enabled laptops in and from courts throughout England and Wales. For the purpose of this part these means of communication are referred to, compendiously, as 'live text-based communications'. It is consistent with the legislative structure which:
(a) prohibits:
  (i) the taking of photographs in court (section 41 of the Criminal Justice Act 1925);
  (ii) the use of sound recording equipment in court unless the leave of the judge has first been obtained (section 9 of the Contempt of Court Act 1981); and
(b) requires compliance with the strict prohibition rules created by sections 1, 2 and 4 of the Contempt of Court Act 1981 in relation to the reporting of court proceedings.

General Principles

6C.2 The judge has an overriding responsibility to ensure that proceedings are conducted consistently, with the proper administration of justice, and to avoid any improper interference with its processes.

6C.3 A fundamental aspect of the proper administration of justice is the principle of open justice. Fair and accurate reporting of court proceedings forms part of that principle. The principle is, however, subject to well-known statutory and discretionary exceptions. Two such exceptions are the prohibitions, set out in paragraph 6C.1(a), on photography in court and on making sound recordings of court proceedings.

6C.4 The statutory prohibition on photography in court, by any means, is absolute. There is no judicial discretion to suspend or dispense with it. Any equipment which has photographic capability must not have that function activated.

6C.5 Sound recordings are also prohibited unless, in the exercise of its discretion, the court permits such equipment to be used. In criminal proceedings, some of the factors relevant to the exercise of that discretion are contained in paragraph 6A.2. The same factors are likely to be relevant when consideration is being given to the exercise of this discretion in civil or family proceedings.

Use of Live Text-based Communications: General Considerations

6C.6 The normal, indeed almost invariable, rule has been that mobile phones must be turned off in court. There is however no statutory prohibition on the use of live text-based communications in open court.

6C.7 Where a member of the public, who is in court, wishes to use live text-based communications during court proceedings an application for permission to activate and use, in silent mode, a mobile phone, small laptop or similar piece of equipment, solely in order to make live text-based communications of the proceedings will need to be made. The application may be made formally or informally (for instance by communicating a request to the judge through court staff).

6C.8 It is presumed that a representative of the media or a legal commentator using live text-based communications from court does not pose a danger of interference to the proper administration of justice in the individual case. This is because the most obvious purpose of permitting the use of live text-based communications would be to enable the media to produce fair and accurate reports of the proceedings. As such, a representative of the media or a legal commentator who wishes to use live text-based communications from court may do so without making an application to the court.

6C.9 When considering, either generally on its own motion, or following a formal application or informal request by a member of the public, whether to permit live text-based communications, and if so by whom, the paramount question for the judge will be whether the application may interfere with the proper administration of justice.

6C.10 In considering the question of permission, the factors listed in paragraph 6A.2 are likely to be relevant.

6C.11 Without being exhaustive, the danger to the administration of justice is likely to be at its most acute in the context of criminal trials e.g., where witnesses who are out of court may be informed of what has already happened in court and so coached or briefed before they then give evidence, or where information posted on, for instance, *Twitter* about inadmissible evidence may influence members of the jury. However, the danger is not confined to criminal proceedings; in civil and sometimes family proceedings, simultaneous reporting from the courtroom may create pressure on witnesses, by distracting or worrying them.

6C.12 It may be necessary for the judge to limit live text-based communications to representatives of the media for journalistic purposes but to disallow its use by the wider public in court. That may arise if it is necessary, for example, to limit the number of mobile electronic devices in use at any given time because of the potential for electronic interference with the court's own sound recording equipment, or because the widespread use of such devices in court may cause a distraction in the proceedings.

6C.13 Subject to these considerations, the use of an unobtrusive, hand-held, silent piece of modern equipment, for the purposes of simultaneous reporting of proceedings to the outside world as they unfold in court, is generally unlikely to interfere with the proper administration of justice.

6C.14 Permission to use live text-based communications from court may be withdrawn by the court at any time.

Criminal Procedure Rules Part 7 Starting a Prosecution in a Magistrates' Court

R-65 **When this Part applies**

7.1 (1) This Part applies in a magistrates' court where—
(a) a prosecutor wants the court to issue a summons or warrant under section 1 of the Magistrates' Courts Act 1980;
(b) a prosecutor with the power to do so issues—
(i) a written charge and requisition, or
(ii) a written charge and single justice procedure notice under section 29 of the Criminal Justice Act 2003; or
(c) a person who is in custody is charged with an offence.
(2) In this Part, 'authorised prosecutor' means a prosecutor authorised under section 29 of the Criminal Justice Act 2003 to issue a written charge and requisition or single justice procedure notice.

R-66 **Information and written charge**

7.2 (1) A prosecutor who wants the court to issue a summons must—
(a) serve an information in writing on the court officer; or
(b) unless other legislation prohibits this, present an information orally to the court, with a written record of the allegation that it contains.
(2) A prosecutor who wants the court to issue a warrant must—
(a) serve on the court officer—
(i) an information in writing, or
(ii) a copy of a written charge that has been issued; or
(b) present to the court either of those documents.
(3) An authorised prosecutor who issues a written charge must notify the court officer immediately.
(4) A single document may contain—
(a) more than one information; or
(b) more than one written charge.
(5) Where an offence can be tried only in a magistrates' court, then unless other legislation otherwise provides—
(a) a prosecutor must serve an information on the court officer or present it to the court; or
(b) an authorised prosecutor must issue a written charge,
not more than 6 months after the offence alleged.

(6) Where an offence can be tried in the Crown Court then—
(a) a prosecutor must serve an information on the court officer or present it to the court; or
(b) an authorised prosecutor must issue a written charge,
within any time limit that applies to that offence.

Allegation of offence in information or charge R-67

7.3 (1) An allegation of an offence in an information or charge must contain—
(a) a statement of the offence that—
(i) describes the offence in ordinary language, and
(ii) identifies any legislation that creates it; and
(b) such particulars of the conduct constituting the commission of the offence as to make clear what the prosecutor alleges against the defendant.
(2) More than one incident of the commission of the offence may be included in the allegation if those incidents taken together amount to a course of conduct having regard to the time, place or purpose of commission.

Summons, warrant and requisition R-68

7.4 (1) The court may issue or withdraw a summons or warrant—
(a) without giving the parties an opportunity to make representations; and
(b) without a hearing, or at a hearing in public or in private.
(2) A summons, warrant or requisition may be issued in respect of more than one offence.
(3) A summons or requisition must—
(a) contain notice of when and where the defendant is required to attend the court;
(b) specify each offence in respect of which it is issued;
(c) in the case of a summons, identify—
(i) the court that issued it, unless that is otherwise recorded by the court officer, and
(ii) the court office for the court that issued it; and
(d) in the case of a requisition, identify the person under whose authority it is issued.
(4) A summons may be contained in the same document as an information.
(5) A requisition may be contained in the same document as a written charge.
(6) Where the court issues a summons—
(a) the prosecutor must—
(i) serve it on the defendant, and
(ii) notify the court officer; or
(b) the court officer must—
(i) serve it on the defendant, and
(ii) notify the prosecutor.
(7) Where an authorised prosecutor issues a requisition that prosecutor must—
(a) serve on the defendant—
(i) the requisition, and
(ii) the written charge; and
(b) serve a copy of each on the court officer.
(8) Unless it would be inconsistent with other legislation, a replacement summons or requisition may be issued without a fresh information or written charge where the one replaced—
(a) was served by leaving or posting it under rule 4.7 (documents that must be served only by handing them over, leaving or posting them); but
(b) is shown not to have been received by the addressee.
(9) A summons or requisition issued to a defendant under 18 may require that defendant's parent or guardian to attend the court with the defendant, or a separate summons or requisition may be issued for that purpose.

Criminal Procedure Rules Part 8 Initial Details of the Prosecution Case

When this Part applies R-69

8.1 This Part applies in a magistrates' court,.

Providing initial details of the prosecution case R-70

8.2 (1) The prosecutor must serve initial details of the prosecution case on the court officer—
(a) as soon as practicable; and
(b) in any event, no later than the beginning of the day of the first hearing.

(2) Where a defendant requests those details, the prosecutor must serve them on the defendant—
(a) as soon as practicable; and
(b) in any event, no later than the beginning of the day of the first hearing.
(3) Where a defendant does not request those details, the prosecutor must make them available to the defendant at, or before, the beginning of the day of the first hearing.

R-71 **Content of initial details**

8.3 Initial details of the prosecution case must include—
(a) where, immediately before the first hearing in the magistrates' court, the defendant was in police custody for the offence charged—
(i) a summary of the circumstances of the offence, and
(ii) the defendant's criminal record, if any;
(b) where paragraph (a) does not apply—
(i) a summary of the circumstances of the offence,
(ii) any account given by the defendant in interview, whether contained in that summary or in another document,
(iii) any written witness statement or exhibit that the prosecutor then has available and considers material to plea, or to the allocation of the case for trial, or to sentence,
(iv) the defendant's criminal record, if any, and
(v) any available statement of the effect of the offence on a victim, a victim's family or others.

CRIMINAL PRACTICE DIRECTIONS PART 8 INITIAL DETAILS OF THE PROSECUTION CASE

PD-21 **CPD II Preliminary proceedings 8A: Defendant's Record**

Copies of record

8A.1 The defendant's record (previous convictions, cautions, reprimands, etc) may be taken into account when the court decides not only on sentence but also, for example, about bail, or when allocating a case for trial. It is therefore important that up to date and accurate information is available. Previous convictions must be provided as part of the initial details of the prosecution case under CrimPR Part 8.

8A.2 The record should usually be provided in the following format:

Personal details and summary of convictions and cautions—Police National Computer ['PNC'] Court/Defence/Probation Summary Sheet;

Previous convictions — PNC Court/Defence/Probation printout, supplemented by Form MG16 if the police force holds convictions not shown on PNC;

Recorded cautions—PNC Court/Defence/Probation printout, supplemented by Form MG17 if the police force holds cautions not shown on PNC.

8A.3 The defence representative should take instructions on the defendant's record and if the defence wish to raise any objection to the record, this should be made known to the prosecutor immediately.

8A.4 It is the responsibility of the prosecutor to ensure that a copy of the defendant's record has been provided to the Probation Service.

8A.5 Where following conviction a custodial order is made, the court must ensure that a copy is attached to the order sent to the prison.

Additional information

8A.6 In the Crown Court, the police should also provide brief details of the circumstances of the last three similar convictions and/or of convictions likely to be of interest to the court, the latter being judged on a case-by-case basis.

8A.7 Where the current alleged offence could constitute a breach of an existing sentence such as a suspended sentence, community order or conditional discharge, and it is known that that sentence is still in force then details of the circumstances of the offence leading to the sentence should be included in the antecedents. The detail should be brief and include the date of the offence.

8A.8 On occasions the PNC printout provided may not be fully up to date. It is the responsibility of the prosecutor to ensure that all of the necessary information is available to the court and the Probation Service and provided to the defence. Oral updates at the hearing will sometimes be necessary, but it is preferable if this information is available in advance.

Criminal Procedure Rules Part 9 Allocation and Sending for Trial

General rules

When this Part applies **R-72**

9.1 (1) This Part applies to the allocation and sending of cases for trial under—
(a) sections 17A to 26 of the Magistrates' Courts Act 1980; and
(b) sections 50A to 52 of the Crime and Disorder Act 1998.
(2) Rules 9.6 and 9.7 apply in a magistrates' court where the court must, or can, send a defendant to the Crown Court for trial, without allocating the case for trial there.
(3) Rules 9.8 to 9.14 apply in a magistrates' court where the court must allocate the case to a magistrates' court or to the Crown Court for trial.
(4) Rules 9.15 and 9.16 apply in the Crown Court, where a defendant is sent for trial there.

Exercise of magistrates' court's powers **R-73**

9.2 (1) This rule applies to the exercise of the powers to which rules 9.6 to 9.14 apply.
(2) The general rule is that the court must exercise its powers at a hearing in public, but it may exercise any power it has to—
(a) withhold information from the public; or
(b) order a hearing in private.
(3) The general rule is that the court must exercise its powers in the defendant's presence, but it may exercise the powers to which the following rules apply in the defendant's absence on the conditions specified—
(a) where rule 9.8 (Adult defendant: request for plea), rule 9.9 (Adult defendant: guilty plea) or rule 9.13 (Young defendant) applies, if—
(i) the defendant is represented, and
(ii) the defendant's disorderly conduct makes his or her presence in the courtroom impracticable;
(b) where rule 9.10 (Adult defendant: not guilty plea) or rule 9.11 (Adult defendant: allocation for magistrates' court trial) applies, if—
(i) the defendant is represented and waives the right to be present, or
(ii) the defendant's disorderly conduct makes his or her presence in the courtroom impracticable.
(4) The court may exercise its power to adjourn—
(a) if either party asks; or
(b) on its own initiative.
(5) Where the court on the same occasion deals with two or more offences alleged against the same defendant, the court must deal with those offences in the following sequence—
(a) any to which rule 9.6 applies (Prosecutor's notice requiring Crown Court trial);
(b) any to which rule 9.7 applies (sending for Crown Court trial, without allocation there), in this sequence—
(i) any the court must send for trial, then
(ii) any the court can send for trial; and
(c) any to which rule 9.14 applies (Allocation and sending for Crown Court trial).
(6) Where the court on the same occasion deals with two or more defendants charged jointly with an offence that can be tried in the Crown Court then in the following sequence—
(a) the court must explain, in terms each defendant can understand (with help, if necessary), that if the court sends one of them to the Crown Court for trial then the court must send for trial in the Crown Court, too, any other of them—
(i) who is charged with the same offence as the defendant sent for trial, or with an offence which the court decides is related to that offence,
(ii) who does not wish to plead guilty to each offence with which he or she is charged, and
(iii) (if that other defendant is under 18, and the court would not otherwise have sent him or her for Crown Court trial) where the court decides that sending is necessary in the interests of justice

even if the court by then has decided to allocate that other defendant for magistrates' court trial; and
(b) the court may ask the defendants questions to help it decide in what order to deal with them.
(7) After following paragraph (5), if it applies, where the court on the same occasion—
(a) deals with two or more defendants charged jointly with an offence that can be tried in the Crown Court;

(b) allocates any of them to a magistrates' court for trial; and
(c) then sends another one of them to the Crown Court for trial,

the court must deal again with each one whom, on that occasion, it has allocated for magistrates' court trial.

R-74 Matters to be specified on sending for trial

9.3 (1) Where the court sends a defendant to the Crown Court for trial, it must specify—
(a) each offence to be tried;
(b) in respect of each, the power exercised to send the defendant for trial for that offence; and
(c) the Crown Court centre at which the trial will take place.

(2) In a case in which the prosecutor serves a notice to which rule 9.6(1)(a) applies (notice requiring Crown Court trial in a case of serious or complex fraud), the court must specify the Crown Court centre identified by that notice.

(3) In any other case, in deciding the Crown Court centre at which the trial will take place, the court must take into account—
(a) the convenience of the parties and witnesses;
(b) how soon a suitable courtroom will be available; and
(c) the directions on the allocation of Crown Court business contained in the Practice Direction.

R-75 Duty of justices' legal adviser

9.4 (1) This rule applies—
(a) only in a magistrates' court; and
(b) unless the court—
(i) includes a District Judge (Magistrates' Courts), and
(ii) otherwise directs.

(2) On the court's behalf, a justices' legal adviser may—
(a) read the allegation of the offence to the defendant;
(b) give any explanation and ask any question required by the rules in this Part;
(c) make any announcement required by the rules in this Part, other than an announcement of—
(i) the court's decisions about allocation and sending,
(ii) any indication by the court of likely sentence, or
(iii) sentence.

(3) A justices' legal adviser must—
(a) assist an unrepresented defendant;
(b) give the court such advice as is required to enable it to exercise its powers;
(c) if required, attend the members of the court outside the courtroom to give such advice, but inform the parties of any advice so given.

R-76 Duty of magistrates' court officer

9.5 (1) The magistrates' court officer must—
(a) serve notice of a sending for Crown Court trial on—
(i) the Crown Court officer, and
(ii) the parties;
(b) in that notice record—
(i) the matters specified by the court under rule 9.3 (Matters to be specified on sending for trial),
(ii) any indication of intended guilty plea given by the defendant under rule 9.7 (Sending for Crown Court trial),
(iii) any decision by the defendant to decline magistrates' court trial under rule 9.11 (Adult defendant: allocation to magistrates' court for trial), and
(iv) the date on which any custody time limit will expire;
(c) record any indication of likely sentence to which rule 9.11 applies; and
(d) give the court such other assistance as it requires.

(2) The magistrates' court officer must include with the notice served on the Crown Court officer—
(a) the initial details of the prosecution case served by the prosecutor under rule 8.2;
(b) a record of any—
(i) listing or case management direction affecting the Crown Court,
(ii) direction about reporting restrictions,
(iii) decision about bail, for the purposes of section 5 of the Bail Act 1976,

(iv) recognizance given by a surety, or
(v) representation order; and

(c) if relevant, any available details of any—
(i) interpreter,
(ii) intermediary, or
(iii) other supporting adult, where the defendant is assisted by such a person.

Sending without allocation for Crown Court trial

Prosecutor's notice requiring Crown Court trial **R-77**

9.6 (1) This rule applies where a prosecutor with power to do so requires a magistrates' court to send for trial in the Crown Court—
(a) a case of serious or complex fraud; or
(b) a case which will involve a child witness.

(2) The prosecutor must serve written notice of that requirement—
(a) on the magistrates' court officer and on the defendant; and
(b) before trial in a magistrates' court begins under Part 24 (Trial and sentence in a magistrates' court).

(3) The notice must identify—
(a) the power on which the prosecutor relies; and
(b) the Crown Court centre at which the prosecutor wants the trial to take place.

(4) The prosecutor—
(a) must, when choosing a Crown Court centre, take into account the matters listed in rule 9.3(3) (court deciding to which Crown Court centre to send a case); and
(b) may change the centre identified before the case is sent for trial.

Sending for Crown Court trial **R-78**

9.7 (1) This rule applies where a magistrates' court must, or can, send a defendant to the Crown Court for trial without first allocating the case for trial there.

(2) The court must read the allegation of the offence to the defendant.

(3) The court must explain, in terms the defendant can understand (with help, if necessary)—
(a) the allegation, unless it is self-explanatory;
(b) that the offence is one for which the court, as appropriate—
(i) must send the defendant to the Crown Court for trial because the offence is one which can only be tried there or because the court for some other reason is required to send that offence for trial,
(ii) may send the defendant to the Crown Court for trial if the magistrates' court decides that the offence is related to one already sent for trial there; or
(iii) (where the offence is low-value shoplifting and the defendant is 18 or over) must send the defendant to the Crown Court for trial if the defendant wants to be tried there;
(c) that reporting restrictions apply, which the defendant may ask the court to vary or remove.

(4) In the following sequence, the court must then—
(a) invite the prosecutor to—
(i) identify the court's power to send the defendant to the Crown Court for trial for the offence, and
(ii) make representations about any ancillary matters, including bail and directions for the management of the case in the Crown Court;
(b) invite the defendant to make representations about—
(i) the court's power to send the defendant to the Crown Court, and
(ii) any ancillary matters;
(c) (where the offence is low-value shoplifting and the defendant is 18 or over) offer the defendant the opportunity to require trial in the Crown Court; and
(d) decide whether or not to send the defendant to the Crown Court for trial.

(5) If the court sends the defendant to the Crown Court for trial, it must—
(a) ask whether the defendant intends to plead guilty in the Crown Court and—
(i) if the answer is 'yes', make arrangements for the Crown Court to take the defendant's plea as soon as possible, or
(ii) if the defendant does not answer, or the answer is 'no', make arrangements for a case management hearing in the Crown Court; and
(b) give any other ancillary directions.

Allocation for magistrates' court or Crown Court trial

R-79 Adult defendant: request for plea

9.8 (1) This rule applies where—
(a) the defendant is 18 or over; and
(b) the court must decide whether a case is more suitable for trial in a magistrates' court or in the Crown Court.
(2) The court must read the allegation of the offence to the defendant.
(3) The court must explain, in terms the defendant can understand (with help, if necessary)—
(a) the allegation, unless it is self-explanatory;
(b) that the offence is one which can be tried in a magistrates' court or in the Crown Court;
(c) that the court is about to ask whether the defendant intends to plead guilty;
(d) that if the answer is 'yes', then the court must treat that as a guilty plea and must sentence the defendant, or commit the defendant to the Crown Court for sentence;
(e) that if the defendant does not answer, or the answer is 'no', then—
(i) the court must decide whether to allocate the case to a magistrates' court or to the Crown Court for trial,
(ii) the value involved may require the court to order trial in a magistrates' court (where the offence is one to which section 22 of the Magistrates' Courts Act 1980 applies), and
(iii) if the court allocates the case to a magistrates' court for trial, the defendant can nonetheless require trial in the Crown Court (unless the offence is one to which section 22 of the Magistrates' Courts Act 1980 applies and the value involved requires magistrates' court trial); and
(f) that reporting restrictions apply, which the defendant may ask the court to vary or remove.
(4) The court must then ask whether the defendant intends to plead guilty.

R-80 Adult defendant: guilty plea

9.9 (1) This rule applies where—
(a) rule 9.8 applies; and
(b) the defendant indicates an intention to plead guilty.
(2) The court must exercise its power to deal with the case—
(a) as if the defendant had just pleaded guilty at a trial in a magistrates' court; and
(b) in accordance with rule 24.11 (Procedure if the court convicts).

R-81 Adult defendant: not guilty plea

9.10 (1) This rule applies where—
(a) rule 9.8 applies; and
(b) the defendant—
(i) indicates an intention to plead not guilty, or
(ii) gives no indication of intended plea.
(2) In the following sequence, the court must then—
(a) where the offence is one to which section 22 of the Magistrates' Courts Act 1980 applies, explain in terms the defendant can understand (with help, if necessary) that—
(i) if the court decides that the value involved clearly is less than £5,000, the court must order trial in a magistrates' court,
(ii) if the court decides that it is not clear whether that value is more or less than £5,000, then the court will ask whether the defendant agrees to be tried in a magistrates' court, and
(iii) if the answer to that question is 'yes', then the court must order such a trial and if the defendant is convicted then the maximum sentence is limited;
(b) invite the prosecutor to—
(i) identify any previous convictions of which it can take account, and
(ii) make representations about how the court should allocate the case for trial, including representations about the value involved, if relevant;
(c) invite the defendant to make such representations;
(d) where the offence is one to which section 22 of the Magistrates' Courts Act 1980 applies—
(i) if it is not clear whether the value involved is more or less than £5,000, ask whether the defendant agrees to be tried in a magistrates' court,
(ii) if the defendant's answer to that question is 'yes', or if that value clearly is less than £5,000, order a trial in a magistrates' court,
(iii) if the defendant does not answer that question, or the answer is 'no', or if that value clearly is more than £5,000, apply paragraph (2)(e);

(e) exercise its power to allocate the case for trial, taking into account—
(i) the adequacy of a magistrates' court's sentencing powers,
(ii) any representations by the parties, and
(iii) any allocation guidelines issued by the Sentencing Council.

Adult defendant: allocation for magistrates' court trial R-82

9.11 (1) This rule applies where—
(a) rule 9.10 applies; and
(b) the court allocates the case to a magistrates' court for trial.
(2) The court must explain, in terms the defendant can understand (with help, if necessary) that—
(a) the court considers the case more suitable for trial in a magistrates' court than in the Crown Court;
(b) if the defendant is convicted at a magistrates' court trial, then in some circumstances the court may commit the defendant to the Crown Court for sentence;
(c) if the defendant does not agree to a magistrates' court trial, then the court must send the defendant to the Crown Court for trial; and
(d) before deciding whether to accept magistrates' court trial, the defendant may ask the court for an indication of whether a custodial or non-custodial sentence is more likely in the event of a guilty plea at such a trial, but the court need not give such an indication.
(3) If the defendant asks for such an indication of sentence and the court gives such an indication—
(a) the court must then ask again whether the defendant intends to plead guilty;
(b) if, in answer to that question, the defendant indicates an intention to plead guilty, then the court must exercise its power to deal with the case—
(i) as if the defendant had just pleaded guilty to an offence that can be tried only in a magistrates' court, and
(ii) in accordance with rule 24.11 (Procedure if the court convicts);
(c) if, in answer to that question, the defendant indicates an intention to plead not guilty, or gives no indication of intended plea, in the following sequence the court must then—
(i) ask whether the defendant agrees to trial in a magistrates' court,
(ii) if the defendant's answer to that question is 'yes', order such a trial,
(iii) if the defendant does not answer that question, or the answer is 'no', apply rule 9.14.
(4) If the defendant asks for an indication of sentence but the court gives none, or if the defendant does not ask for such an indication, in the following sequence the court must then—
(a) ask whether the defendant agrees to trial in a magistrates' court;
(b) if the defendant's answer to that question is 'yes', order such a trial;
(c) if the defendant does not answer that question, or the answer is 'no', apply rule 9.14.

Adult defendant: prosecutor's application for Crown Court trial R-83

9.12 (1) This rule applies where—
(a) rule 9.11 applies;
(b) the defendant agrees to trial in a magistrates' court; but
(c) the prosecutor wants the court to exercise its power to send the defendant to the Crown Court for trial instead.
(2) The prosecutor must—
(a) apply before trial in a magistrates' court begins under Part 24 (Trial and sentence in a magistrates' court); and
(b) notify—
(i) the defendant, and
(ii) the magistrates' court officer.
(3) The court must determine an application to which this rule applies before it deals with any other pre-trial application.

Young defendant R-84

9.13 (1) This rule applies where—
(a) the defendant is under 18; and
(b) the court must decide whether to send the defendant for Crown Court trial instead of ordering trial in a youth court.
(2) The court must read the allegation of the offence to the defendant.
(3) The court must explain, in terms the defendant can understand (with help, if necessary)—
(a) the allegation, unless it is self-explanatory;

(b) that the offence is one which can be tried in the Crown Court instead of in a youth court;
(c) that the court is about to ask whether the defendant intends to plead guilty;
(d) that if the answer is 'yes', then the court must treat that as a guilty plea and must sentence the defendant, or commit the defendant to the Crown Court for sentence;
(e) that if the defendant does not answer, or the answer is 'no', then the court must decide whether to send the defendant for Crown Court trial instead of ordering trial in a youth court; and
(f) that reporting restrictions apply, which the defendant may ask the court to vary or remove.

(4) The court must then ask whether the defendant intends to plead guilty.
(5) If the defendant's answer to that question is 'yes', the court must exercise its power to deal with the case—
(a) as if the defendant had just pleaded guilty at a trial in a youth court; and
(b) in accordance with rule 24.11 (Procedure if the court convicts).
(6) If the defendant does not answer that question, or the answer is 'no', in the following sequence the court must then—
(a) invite the prosecutor to make representations about whether Crown Court or youth court trial is more appropriate;
(b) invite the defendant to make such representations;
(c) exercise its power to allocate the case for trial, taking into account—
(i) the offence and the circumstances of the offence,
(ii) the suitability of a youth court's sentencing powers,
(iii) where the defendant is jointly charged with an adult, whether it is necessary in the interests of justice for them to be tried together in the Crown Court, and
(iv) any representations by the parties.

R-85 Allocation and sending for Crown Court trial

9.14 (1) This rule applies where—
(a) under rule 9.10 or rule 9.13, the court allocates the case to the Crown Court for trial;
(b) under rule 9.11, the defendant does not agree to trial in a magistrates' court; or
(c) under rule 9.12, the court grants the prosecutor's application for Crown Court trial.
(2) In the following sequence, the court must—
(a) invite the prosecutor to make representations about any ancillary matters, including bail and directions for the management of the case in the Crown Court;
(b) invite the defendant to make any such representations; and
(c) exercise its powers to—
(i) send the defendant to the Crown Court for trial, and
(ii) give any ancillary directions.

Crown Court initial procedure after sending for trial

R-86 Service of prosecution evidence

9.15 (1) This rule applies where—
(a) a magistrates' court sends the defendant to the Crown Court for trial; and
(b) the prosecutor serves on the defendant copies of the documents containing the evidence on which the prosecution case relies.
(2) The prosecutor must at the same time serve copies of those documents on the Crown Court officer.

R-87 Application to dismiss offence sent for Crown Court trial

9.16 (1) This rule applies where a defendant wants the Crown Court to dismiss an offence sent for trial there.
(2) The defendant must—
(a) apply in writing—
(i) not more than 28 days after service of the prosecution evidence, and
(ii) before the defendant's arraignment;
(b) serve the application on—
(i) the Crown Court officer, and
(ii) each other party;
(c) in the application—
(i) explain why the prosecution evidence would not be sufficient for the defendant to be properly convicted,
(ii) ask for a hearing, if the defendant wants one, and explain why it is needed,

(iii) identify any witness whom the defendant wants to call to give evidence in person, with an indication of what evidence the witness can give,
(iv) identify any material already served that the defendant thinks the court will need to determine the application, and
(v) include any material not already served on which the defendant relies.

(3) A prosecutor who opposes the application must—
(a) serve notice of opposition, not more than 14 days after service of the defendant's notice, on—
(i) the Crown Court officer, and
(ii) each other party;
(b) in the notice of opposition—
(i) explain the grounds of opposition,
(ii) ask for a hearing, if the prosecutor wants one, and explain why it is needed,
(iii) identify any witness whom the prosecutor wants to call to give evidence in person, with an indication of what evidence the witness can give,
(iv) identify any material already served that the prosecutor thinks the court will need to determine the application, and
(v) include any material not already served on which the prosecutor relies.

(4) The court may determine an application under this rule—
(a) at a hearing, in public or in private, or without a hearing;
(b) in the absence of—
(i) the defendant who made the application,
(ii) the prosecutor, if the prosecutor has had at least 14 days in which to serve notice opposing the application.

(5) The court may—
(a) shorten or extend (even after it has expired) a time limit under this rule;
(b) allow a witness to give evidence in person even if that witness was not identified in the defendant's application or in the prosecutor's notice.

Criminal Practice Directions Part 9 Allocation and Sending for Trial

CPD II Preliminary proceedings 9A: Allocation (Mode of Trial) PD-22

9A.1 Courts must follow the Sentencing Council's guideline on Allocation (mode of trial) when deciding whether or not to send defendants charged with 'either way' offences for trial in the Crown Court under section 51(1) of the Crime and Disorder Act 1998. The guideline refers to the factors to which a court must have regard in accordance with section 19 of the Magistrates' Courts Act 1980. Section 19(2) (a) permits reference to previous convictions of the defendant.

9A.2 The Allocation guideline lists four factors, a) to d), that the court must also have regard to. No examples or guidance are given, however, the following could be a consideration when applying the factors: that where cases involve complex questions of fact or difficult questions of law, including difficult issues of disclosure of sensitive material, the court should consider sending for trial.

9A.3 Certain general observations can also be made:
(a) the court should never make its decision on the grounds of convenience or expedition; and
(b) the fact that the offences are alleged to be specimens is a relevant consideration (although it has to be borne in mind that difficulties can arise in sentencing in relation to specimen counts: see *R v Clark* [1996] 2 Cr App R 282, [1996] 2 Cr App R (S) 351; *R v Canavan and others* [1998] 1 WLR 604, [1998] 1 Cr App R 79, [1998] 1 Cr App R (S) 243 and *R v Oakes* [2012] EWCA Crim 2435, [2013] 2 Cr App R (S) 22 (see case of *R v Restivo*)); the fact that the defendant will be asking for other offences to be taken into consideration, if convicted, is not.

Criminal Procedure Rules Part 10 The Indictment

Service of indictment R-88

10.1 (1) The prosecutor must serve a draft indictment on the Crown Court officer not more than 28 days after—
(a) service on the defendant and on the Crown Court officer of copies of the documents containing the evidence on which the charge or charges are based, in a case where the defendant is sent for trial;
(b) a High Court judge gives permission to serve a draft indictment;
(c) the Court of Appeal orders a retrial.

(2) The Crown Court may extend the time limit, even after it has expired.

(3) Unless the Crown Court otherwise directs, the court officer must—
 (a) endorse any paper copy of the indictment made for the court with—
  (i) a note to identify it as the indictment served under this rule, and
  (ii) the date on which the draft indictment was served on the court officer; and
 (b) serve a copy of the indictment on all parties.

R-89 **Form and content of indictment**

10.2 (1) An indictment must be in one of the forms set out in the Practice Direction and must contain, in a paragraph called a 'count'—
 (a) a statement of the offence charged that—
  (i) describes the offence in ordinary language, and
  (ii) identifies any legislation that creates it; and
 (b) such particulars of the conduct constituting the commission of the offence as to make clear what the prosecutor alleges against the defendant.
(2) More than one incident of the commission of the offence may be included in a count if those incidents taken together amount to a course of conduct having regard to the time, place or purpose of commission.
(3) An indictment may contain more than one count if all the offences charged—
 (a) are founded on the same facts; or
 (b) form or are a part of a series of offences of the same or a similar character.
(4) The counts must be numbered consecutively.
(5) An indictment may contain—
 (a) any count charging substantially the same offence as one specified in the notice of the offence or offences for which the defendant was sent for trial; and
 (b) any other count based on the prosecution evidence already served which the Crown Court may try.

Criminal Practice Directions Part 10 The Indictment

PD-23 **CPD II Preliminary proceedings 10A: Settling the Indictment**

10A.1 CrimPR 10.1 requires the prosecutor to serve a draft indictment not more than 28 days after service of the evidence in a case sent for trial, after the sending of the defendant for trial, or after one of the other events listed in that rule. CrimPR 10.2(5) provides that an indictment may contain any count charging substantially the same offence as one sent for trial and any other count based on the prosecution evidence already served which the Crown Court has jurisdiction to try. Where the prosecutor intends to include in the draft indictment counts which differ materially from, or are additional to, those on which the defendant was sent for trial then the defendant should be given as much notice as possible, usually by service of a draft indictment, or a provisional draft indictment, at the earliest possible opportunity.

10A.2 There is no rule of law or practice which prohibits two indictments being in existence at the same time for the same offence against the same person and on the same facts. But the court will not allow the prosecution to proceed on both indictments. They cannot be tried together and the court will require the prosecution to elect the one on which the trial will proceed. Where different defendants have been separately sent for trial for offences which can lawfully be charged in the same indictment, then it is permissible to join in one indictment counts based on the separate sendings for trial even if an indictment based on one of them already has been signed. Where necessary the court should be invited to exercise its powers of amendment under section 5 of the Indictments Act 1915.

10A.3 Save in the special circumstances described in the following paragraphs of this Practice Direction, it is undesirable that a large number of counts should be contained in one indictment. Where defendants on trial have a variety of offences alleged against them then, in the interests of effective case management, it is the court's responsibility to exercise its powers in accordance with the overriding objective set out in CrimPR Part 1. The prosecution may be required to identify a selection of counts on which the trial should proceed, leaving a decision to be taken later whether to try any of the remainder. Where an indictment contains substantive counts and one or more related conspiracy counts, the court will expect the prosecution to justify the joinder. Failing justification, the prosecution should be required to choose whether to proceed on the substantive counts or on the conspiracy counts. In any event, if there is a conviction on any counts that are tried, then those that have been postponed can remain on the file marked 'not to be proceeded with without the leave of the court or the Court of Appeal'. In the event that a conviction is later quashed on appeal, the remaining counts can be tried. Where necessary the court has power to order that an indictment be severed.

Multiple offending: trial by jury and then by judge alone

10A.4 Under sections 17 to 21 of the Domestic Violence, Crime and Victims Act 2004, the court may order that the trial of certain counts will be by jury in the usual way and, if the jury convicts, that other associated counts will be tried by judge alone. The use of this power is likely to be appropriate where justice cannot be done without charging a large number of separate offences and the allegations against the defendant appear to fall into distinct groups by reference to the identity of the victim, by reference to the dates of the offences, or by some other distinction in the nature of the offending conduct alleged.

10A.5 In such a case, it is essential to make clear from the outset the association asserted by the prosecutor between those counts to be tried by a jury and those counts which it is proposed should be tried by judge alone, if the jury convict on the former. A special form of indictment is prescribed for this purpose.

10A.6 An order for such a trial may be made only at a preparatory hearing. It follows that where the prosecutor intends to invite the court to order such a trial it will normally be appropriate to proceed as follows. The draft indictment served under CrimPR 10.1 should be in the form appropriate to such a trial. It should be accompanied by an application under CrimPR 3.5 for a preparatory hearing. This will ensure that the defendant is aware at the earliest possible opportunity of what the prosecution propose and of the proposed association of counts in the indictment. It is undesirable for a draft indictment in the usual form to be served where the prosecutor expects to apply for a two stage trial and hence, of necessity, for permission to amend the indictment at a later stage in order that it may be in the special form.

10A.7 On receipt of a draft two part indictment, a Crown Court officer should sign it at the end of Part Two. At the start of the preparatory hearing, the defendant should be arraigned on all counts in Part One of the indictment. Arraignment on Part Two need not take place until after there has been either a guilty plea to, or finding of guilt on, an associated count in Part One of the indictment.

10A.8 If the prosecution application is successful, the prosecutor should prepare an abstract of the indictment, containing the counts from Part One only, for use in the jury trial. Preparation of such an abstract does not involve 'amendment' of the indictment. It is akin to where a defendant pleads guilty to certain counts in an indictment and is put in the charge of the jury on the remaining counts only.

10A.9 If the prosecution application for a two stage trial is unsuccessful, the prosecutor may apply to amend the indictment to remove from it any counts in Part Two which would make jury trial on the whole indictment impracticable and to revert to a standard form of indictment. It will be a matter for the court whether arraignment on outstanding counts takes place at the preparatory hearing, or at a future date.

Multiple offending: count charging more than one incident

10A.10 CrimPR 10.2(2) allows a single count to allege more than one incident of the commission of an offence in certain circumstances. Each incident must be of the same offence. The circumstances in which such a count may be appropriate include, but are not limited to, the following:

(a) the victim on each occasion was the same, or there was no identifiable individual victim as, for example, in a case of the unlawful importation of controlled drugs or of money laundering;
(b) the alleged incidents involved a marked degree of repetition in the method employed or in their location, or both;
(c) the alleged incidents took place over a clearly defined period, typically (but not necessarily) no more than about a year;
(d) in any event, the defence is such as to apply to every alleged incident without differentiation. Where what is in issue differs between different incidents, a single 'multiple incidents' count will not be appropriate, though it may be appropriate to use two or more such counts according to the circumstances and to the issues raised by the defence.

10A.11 Even in circumstances such as those set out above, there may be occasions on which a prosecutor chooses not to use such a count, in order to bring the case within section 75(3) (a) of the Proceeds of Crime Act 2002 (criminal lifestyle established by conviction of three or more offences in the same proceedings): for example, because section 75(2) (c) of that Act does not apply (criminal lifestyle established by an offence committed over a period of at least six months). Where the prosecutor proposes such a course, it is unlikely that CrimPR Part 1 (the overriding objective) will require an indictment to contain a single 'multiple incidents' count in place of a larger number of counts, subject to the general principles set out at paragraph 10A.3.

10A.12 For some offences, particularly sexual offences, the penalty for the offence may have changed during the period over which the alleged incidents took place. In such a case, additional 'multiple incidents' counts should be used so that each count only alleges incidents to which the same maximum penalty applies.

10A.13 In other cases, such as sexual or physical abuse, a complainant may be in a position only to give evidence of a series of similar incidents without being able to specify when or the precise circumstances in which they occurred. In these cases, a 'multiple incidents' count may be desirable. If on the other hand, the complainant is able to identify particular incidents of the offence by reference to a date or other specific event, but alleges that in addition there were other incidents which the complainant is unable to specify, then it may be desirable to include separate counts for the identified incidents and a 'multiple incidents' count or counts alleging that incidents of the same offence occurred 'many' times. Using a 'multiple incidents' count may be an appropriate alternative to using 'specimen' counts in some cases where repeated sexual or physical abuse is alleged. The choice of count will depend on the particular circumstances of the case and should be determined bearing in mind the implications for sentencing set out in *R v Canavan; R v Kidd; R v Shaw* [1998] 1 WLR 604, [1998] 1 Cr App R 79, [1998] 1 Cr App R (S) 243.

PD-24 **CPD II Preliminary proceedings 10B: Voluntary Bills of Indictment**

10B.1 Section 2(2) (b) of the Administration of Justice (Miscellaneous Provisions) Act 1933 and paragraph 2(6) of Schedule 3 to the Crime and Disorder Act 1998 allow the preferment of a bill of indictment by the direction or with the consent of a judge of the High Court. Bills so preferred are known as 'voluntary bills'.

10B.2 Applications for such consent must not only comply with each paragraph of the Indictments (Procedure) Rules 1971, SI 1971/2084, but must also be accompanied by:

(a) a copy of any charges on which the defendant has been sent for trial;

(b) a copy of any charges on which his or her sending for trial was refused by the magistrates' court;

(c) a copy of any existing indictment which has been preferred in consequence of his or her sending for trial;

(d) a summary of the evidence or other document which;

(i) identifies the counts in the proposed indictment on which he or she has been sent for trial (or which are substantially the same as charges on which he or she has been so sent), and

(ii) in relation to each other count in the proposed indictment, identifies the pages in the accompanying statements and exhibits where the essential evidence said to support that count is to be found.

10B.3 These requirements should be complied with in relation to each defendant named in the indictment for which consent is sought, whether or not it is proposed to prefer any new count against him or her.

10B.4 The preferment of a voluntary bill is an exceptional procedure. Consent should only be granted where good reason to depart from the normal procedure is clearly shown and only where the interests of justice, rather than considerations of administrative convenience, require it.

10B.5 Neither the 1933 Act, the 1998 Act nor the 1971 Rules expressly require a prosecuting authority applying for consent to the preferment of a voluntary bill to give notice of the application to the prospective defendant, nor to serve on him or her a copy of documents delivered to the judge; nor is it expressly required that the prospective defendant have any opportunity to make any submissions to the judge, whether in writing or orally.

10B.6 However, the Attorney-General previously issued guidance to prosecutors on the procedures to be adopted in seeking judicial consent to the preferment of voluntary bills. Those procedures remain applicable and prosecutors should:

(a) on making an application for consent to preferment of a voluntary bill, give notice to the prospective defendant that such application has been made;

(b) at about the same time, serve on the prospective defendant a copy of all the documents delivered to the judge (save to the extent that these have already been served on him or her);

(c) inform the prospective defendant that he or she may make submissions in writing to the judge, provided that he or she does so within nine working days of the giving of notice under (a) above.

10B.7 Prosecutors must follow these procedures unless there are good reasons for not doing so, in which case prosecutors must inform the judge that the procedures have not been followed and seek leave to dispense with all or any of them. Judges should not give leave to dispense unless good reasons are shown.

10B.8 A judge to whom application for consent to the preferment of a voluntary bill is made will, of course, wish to consider carefully the documents submitted by the prosecutor and any written submissions made by the prospective defendant, and may properly seek any necessary amplification. The judge may invite oral submissions from either party, or accede to a request for an opportunity to make oral submissions, if the judge considers it necessary or desirable to receive oral submissions in order to make a sound and fair decision on the application. Any such oral submissions should be made on notice to the other party and in open court.

Criminal Procedure Rules Part 11 Deferred Prosecution Agreements

When this Part applies R-90

11.1 (1) This Part applies to proceedings in the Crown Court under Schedule 17 to the Crime and Courts Act 2013.

(2) In this Part—

(a) 'agreement' means a deferred prosecution agreement under paragraph 1 of that Schedule;
(b) 'prosecutor' means a prosecutor designated by or under paragraph 3 of that Schedule; and
(c) 'defendant' means the corporation, partnership or association with whom the prosecutor proposes to enter, or enters, an agreement.

Exercise of court's powers R-91

11.2 (1) The court must determine an application to which this Part applies at a hearing, which—

(a) must be in private, under rule 11.3 (Application to approve a proposal to enter an agreement);
(b) may be in public or private, under rule 11.4 (Application to approve the terms of an agreement), rule 11.6 (Application to approve a variation of the terms of an agreement) or rule 11.9 (Application to postpone the publication of information by the prosecutor);
(c) must be in public, under rule 11.5 (Application on breach of agreement) or rule 11.7 (Application to lift suspension of prosecution), unless the court otherwise directs.

(2) If at a hearing in private to which rule 11.4 or rule 11.6 applies the court approves the agreement or the variation proposed, the court must announce its decision and reasons at a hearing in public.

(3) The court must not determine an application under rule 11.3, rule 11.4 or rule 11.6 unless—

(a) both parties are present;
(b) the prosecutor provides the court with a written declaration that, for the purposes of the application—
 (i) the investigator enquiring into the alleged offence or offences has certified that no information has been supplied which the investigator knows to be inaccurate, misleading or incomplete, and
 (ii) the prosecutor has complied with the prosecution obligation to disclose material to the defendant; and
(c) the defendant provides the court with a written declaration that, for the purposes of the application—
 (i) the defendant has not supplied any information which the defendant knows to be inaccurate, misleading or incomplete, and
 (ii) the individual through whom the defendant makes the declaration has made reasonable enquiries and believes the defendant's declaration to be true.

(4) The court must not determine an application under rule 11.5 or rule 11.7—

(a) in the prosecutor's absence; or
(b) in the absence of the defendant, unless the defendant has had at least 28 days in which to make representations.

(5) If the court approves a proposal to enter an agreement—

(a) the general rule is that any further application to which this Part applies must be made to the same judge; but
(b) the court may direct other arrangements.

(6) The court may adjourn a hearing—

(a) if either party asks, or on its own initiative;
(b) in particular, if the court requires more information about—
 (i) the facts of an alleged offence,
 (ii) the terms of a proposal to enter an agreement, or of a proposed agreement or variation of an agreement, or

(iii) the circumstances in which the prosecutor wants the court to decide whether the defendant has failed to comply with the terms of an agreement.

(7) The court may—

(a) hear an application under rule 11.4 immediately after an application under rule 11.3, if the court approves a proposal to enter an agreement;

(b) hear an application under rule 11.7 immediately after an application under rule 11.5, if the court terminates an agreement.

R-92 **Application to approve a proposal to enter an agreement**

11.3 (1) This rule applies where a prosecutor wants the court to approve a proposal to enter an agreement.

(2) The prosecutor must—

(a) apply in writing after the commencement of negotiations between the parties but before the terms of agreement have been settled; and

(b) serve the application on—

(i) the court officer, and

(ii) the defendant.

(3) The application must—

(a) identify the parties to the proposed agreement;

(b) attach a proposed indictment setting out such of the offences listed in Part 2 of Schedule 17 to the Crime and Courts Act 2013 as the prosecutor is considering;

(c) include or attach a statement of facts proposed for inclusion in the agreement, which must give full particulars of each alleged offence, including details of any alleged financial gain or loss;

(d) include any information about the defendant that would be relevant to sentence in the event of conviction for the offence or offences;

(e) specify the proposed expiry date of the agreement;

(f) describe the proposed terms of the agreement, including details of any—

(i) monetary penalty to be paid by the defendant, and the time within which any such penalty is to be paid,

(ii) compensation, reparation or donation to be made by the defendant, the identity of the recipient of any such payment and the time within which any such payment is to be made,

(iii) surrender of profits or other financial benefit by the defendant, and the time within which any such sum is to be surrendered,

(iv) arrangement to be made in relation to the management or conduct of the defendant's business,

(v) co-operation required of the defendant in any investigation related to the offence or offences,

(vi) other action required of the defendant,

(vii) arrangement to monitor the defendant's compliance with a term,

(viii) consequence of the defendant's failure to comply with a term, and

(ix) prosecution costs to be paid by the defendant, and the time within which any such costs are to be paid;

(g) in relation to those terms, explain how they comply with—

(i) the requirements of the code issued under paragraph 6 of Schedule 17 to the Crime and Courts Act 2013, and

(ii) any sentencing guidelines or guideline cases which apply;

(h) contain or attach the defendant's written consent to the proposal; and

(i) explain why—

(i) entering into an agreement is likely to be in the interests of justice, and

(ii) the proposed terms of the agreement are fair, reasonable and proportionate.

(4) If the proposed statement of facts includes assertions that the defendant does not admit, the application must—

(a) specify the facts that are not admitted; and

(b) explain why that is immaterial for the purposes of the proposal to enter an agreement.

R-93 **Application to approve the terms of an agreement**

11.4 (1) This rule applies where—

(a) the court has approved a proposal to enter an agreement on an application under rule 11.3; and

(b) the prosecutor wants the court to approve the terms of the agreement.

(2) The prosecutor must—
(a) apply in writing as soon as practicable after the parties have settled the terms; and
(b) serve the application on—
(i) the court officer, and
(ii) the defendant.
(3) The application must—
(a) attach the agreement;
(b) indicate in what respect, if any, the terms of the agreement differ from those proposed in the application under rule 11.3;
(c) contain or attach the defendant's written consent to the agreement;
(d) explain why—
(i) the agreement is in the interests of justice, and
(ii) the terms of the agreement are fair, reasonable and proportionate;
(e) attach a draft indictment, charging the defendant with the offence or offences the subject of the agreement; and
(f) include any application for the hearing to be in private.
(4) If the court approves the agreement and the draft indictment, the court officer must—
(a) endorse any paper copy of the indictment made for the court with—
(i) a note to identify it as the indictment approved by the court, and
(ii) the date of the court's approval; and
(b) treat the case as if it had been suspended by order of the court.

Application on breach of agreement R-94

11.5 (1) This rule applies where—
(a) the prosecutor believes that the defendant has failed to comply with the terms of an agreement; and
(b) the prosecutor wants the court to decide—
(i) whether the defendant has failed to comply, and
(ii) if so, whether to terminate the agreement, or to invite the parties to agree proposals to remedy that failure.
(2) The prosecutor must—
(a) apply in writing, as soon as practicable after becoming aware of the grounds for doing so; and
(b) serve the application on—
(i) the court officer, and
(ii) the defendant.
(3) The application must—
(a) specify each respect in which the prosecutor believes the defendant has failed to comply with the terms of the agreement, and explain the reasons for the prosecutor's belief; and
(b) attach a copy of any document containing evidence on which the prosecutor relies.
(4) A defendant who wants to make representations in response to the application must serve the representations on—
(a) the court officer; and
(b) the prosecutor,
not more than 28 days after service of the application.

Application to approve a variation of the terms of an agreement R-95

11.6 (1) This rule applies where the parties have agreed to vary the terms of an agreement because—
(a) on an application under rule 11.5 (Application on breach of agreement), the court has invited them to do so; or
(b) variation of the agreement is necessary to avoid a failure by the defendant to comply with its terms in circumstances that were not, and could not have been, foreseen by either party at the time the agreement was made.
(2) The prosecutor must—
(a) apply in writing, as soon as practicable after the parties have settled the terms of the variation; and
(b) serve the application on—
(i) the court officer, and
(ii) the defendant.
(3) The application must—
(a) specify each variation proposed;

(b) contain or attach the defendant's written consent to the variation;
(c) explain why—
(i) the variation is in the interests of justice, and
(ii) the terms of the agreement as varied are fair, reasonable and proportionate; and
(d) include any application for the hearing to be in private.

R-96 Application to lift suspension of prosecution

11.7 (1) This rule applies where—
(a) the court terminates an agreement before its expiry date; and
(b) the prosecutor wants the court to lift the suspension of the prosecution that applied when the court approved the terms of the agreement.
(2) The prosecutor must—
(a) apply in writing, as soon as practicable after the termination of the agreement; and
(b) serve the application on—
(i) the court officer, and
(ii) the defendant.
(3) A defendant who wants to make representations in response to the application must serve the representations on—
(a) the court officer; and
(b) the prosecutor,
not more than 28 days after service of the application.

R-97 Notice to discontinue prosecution

11.8 (1) This rule applies where an agreement expires—
(a) on its expiry date, or on a date treated as its expiry date; and
(b) without having been terminated by the court.
(2) The prosecutor must—
(a) as soon as practicable give notice in writing discontinuing the prosecution on the indictment approved by the court under rule 11.4 (Application to approve the terms of an agreement); and
(b) serve the notice on—
(i) the court officer, and
(ii) the defendant.

R-98 Application to postpone the publication of information by the prosecutor

11.9 (1) This rule applies where the prosecutor—
(a) makes an application under rule 11.4 (Application to approve the terms of an agreement), rule 11.5 (Application on breach of agreement) or rule 11.6 (Application to approve a variation of the terms of an agreement);
(b) decides not to make an application under rule 11.5, despite believing that the defendant has failed to comply with the terms of the agreement; or
(c) gives a notice under rule 11.8 (Notice to discontinue prosecution).
(2) A party who wants the court to order that the publication of information by the prosecutor about the court's or the prosecutor's decision should be postponed must—
(a) apply in writing, as soon as practicable and in any event before such publication occurs;
(b) serve the application on—
(i) the court officer, and
(ii) the other party; and
(c) in the application—
(i) specify the proposed terms of the order, and for how long it should last, and
(ii) explain why an order in the terms proposed is necessary.

R-99 Duty of court officer, etc.

11.10 (1) Unless the court otherwise directs, the court officer must—
(a) arrange for the recording of proceedings on an application to which this Part applies;
(b) arrange for the transcription of such a recording if—
(i) a party wants such a transcript, or
(ii) anyone else wants such a transcript (but that is subject to the restrictions in paragraph (2)).
(2) Unless the court otherwise directs, a person who transcribes a recording of proceedings under such arrangements—
(a) must not supply anyone other than a party with a transcript of a recording of—

(i) a hearing in private, or
(ii) a hearing in public to which reporting restrictions apply;
(b) subject to that, must supply any person with any transcript for which that person asks—
(i) in accordance with the transcription arrangements made by the court officer, and
(ii) on payment by that person of any fee prescribed.
(3) The court officer must not identify either party to a hearing in private under rule 11.3 (Application to approve a proposal to enter an agreement) or rule 11.4 (Application to approve the terms of an agreement)—
(a) in any notice displayed in the vicinity of the courtroom; or
(b) in any other information published by the court officer.

Court's power to vary requirements under this Part R-100

11.11 (1) The court may—
(a) shorten or extend (even after it has expired) a time limit under this Part;
(b) allow there to be made orally—
(i) an application under rule 11.4 (Application to approve the terms of an agreement), or
(ii) an application under rule 11.7 (Application to lift suspension of prosecution)
where the court exercises its power under rule 11.2(7) to hear one application immediately after another.
(2) A party who wants an extension of time must—
(a) apply when serving the application or notice for which it is needed; and
(b) explain the delay.

Criminal Procedure Rules Part 12 Discontinuing a Prosecution

When this Part applies R-101

12.1 (1) This Part applies where—
(a) the Director of Public Prosecutions can discontinue a case in a magistrates' court, under section 23 of the Prosecution of Offences Act 1985;
(b) the Director of Public Prosecutions, or another public prosecutor, can discontinue a case sent for trial in the Crown Court, under section 23A of the Prosecution of Offences Act 1985.
(2) In this Part, 'prosecutor' means one of those authorities.

Discontinuing a case R-102

12.2 (1) A prosecutor exercising a power to which this Part applies must serve notice on—
(a) the court officer;
(b) the defendant; and
(c) any custodian of the defendant.
(2) Such a notice must—
(a) identify—
(i) the defendant and each offence to which the notice relates,
(ii) the person serving the notice, and
(iii) the power that that person is exercising;
(b) explain—
(i) in the copy of the notice served on the court officer, the reasons for discontinuing the case,
(ii) that the notice brings the case to an end,
(iii) if the defendant is in custody for any offence to which the notice relates, that the defendant must be released from that custody, and
(iv) if the notice is under section 23 of the 1985 Act, that the defendant has a right to require the case to continue.
(3) Where the defendant is on bail, the court officer must notify—
(a) any surety; and
(b) any person responsible for monitoring or securing the defendant's compliance with a condition of bail.

Defendant's notice to continue R-103

12.3 (1) This rule applies where a prosecutor serves a notice to discontinue under section 23 of the 1985 Act.

(2) A defendant who wants the case to continue must serve notice—
(a) on the court officer; and
(b) not more than 35 days after service of the notice to discontinue.
(3) If the defendant serves such a notice, the court officer must—
(a) notify the prosecutor; and
(b) refer the case to the court.

Criminal Procedure Rules Part 13 Warrants for Arrest, Detention or Imprisonment

R-104 **When this Part applies**

13.1 (1) This Part applies where the court can issue a warrant for arrest, detention or imprisonment.
(2) In this Part, 'defendant' means anyone against whom such a warrant is issued.

R-105 **Terms of a warrant for arrest**

13.2 A warrant for arrest must require each person to whom it is directed to arrest the defendant and—
(a) bring the defendant to a court—
(i) specified in the warrant, or
(ii) required or allowed by law; or
(b) release the defendant on bail (with conditions or without) to attend court at a date, time and place—
(i) specified in the warrant, or
(ii) to be notified by the court.

R-106 **Terms of a warrant for detention or imprisonment**

13.3 (1) A warrant for detention or imprisonment must—
(a) require each person to whom it is directed to detain the defendant and—
(i) take the defendant to any place specified in the warrant or required or allowed by law, and
(ii) deliver the defendant to the custodian of that place; and
(b) require that custodian to detain the defendant, as ordered by the court, until in accordance with the law—
(i) the defendant is delivered to the appropriate court or place, or
(ii) the defendant is released.
(2) Where a magistrates' court remands a defendant to police detention under section 128(7) or section 136 of the Magistrates' Courts Act 1980, or to customs detention under section 152 of the Criminal Justice Act 1988, the warrant it issues must—
(a) be directed, as appropriate, to—
(i) a constable, or
(ii) an officer of Her Majesty's Revenue and Customs; and
(b) require that constable or officer to detain the defendant—
(i) for a period (not exceeding the maximum permissible) specified in the warrant, or
(ii) until in accordance with the law the defendant is delivered to the appropriate court or place.

R-107 **Information to be included in a warrant**

13.4 (1) A warrant must identify—
(a) each person to whom it is directed;
(b) the defendant against whom it was issued;
(c) the reason for its issue;
(d) the court that issued it, unless that is otherwise recorded by the court officer; and
(e) the court office for the court that issued it.
(2) A warrant for detention or imprisonment must contain a record of any decision by the court under—
(a) section 91 of the Legal Aid, Sentencing and Punishment of Offenders Act 2012 (remands of children otherwise than on bail), including in particular—
(i) whether the defendant must be detained in local authority accommodation or youth detention accommodation,
(ii) the local authority designated by the court,
(iii) any requirement imposed by the court on that authority,

(iv) any condition imposed by the court on the defendant, and
(v) the reason for any such requirement or condition;
(b) section 80 of the Magistrates' Courts Act 1980 (application of money found on defaulter to satisfy sum adjudged); or
(c) section 82(1) or (4) of the 1980 Act (conditions for issue of a warrant).

(3) A warrant that contains an error is not invalid, as long as—
(a) it was issued in respect of a lawful decision by the court; and
(b) it contains enough information to identify that decision.

Execution of a warrant R-108

13.5 (1) A warrant may be executed—
(a) by any person to whom it is directed; or
(b) if the warrant was issued by a magistrates' court, by anyone authorised to do so by section 125 (warrants), 125A (civilian enforcement officers) or 125B (execution by approved enforcement agency) of the Magistrates' Courts Act 1980.

(2) The person who executes a warrant must—
(a) explain, in terms the defendant can understand, what the warrant requires, and why;
(b) show the defendant the warrant, if that person has it; and
(c) if the defendant asks—
(i) arrange for the defendant to see the warrant, if that person does not have it, and
(ii) show the defendant any written statement of that person's authority required by section 125A or 125B of the 1980 Act.

(3) The person who executes a warrant of arrest that requires the defendant to be released on bail must—
(a) make a record of—
(i) the defendant's name,
(ii) the reason for the arrest,
(iii) the defendant's release on bail, and
(iv) when and where the warrant requires the defendant to attend court; and
(b) serve the record on—
(i) the defendant, and
(ii) the court officer.

(4) The person who executes a warrant of detention or imprisonment must—
(a) take the defendant—
(i) to any place specified in the warrant, or
(ii) if that is not immediately practicable, to any other place at which the defendant may be lawfully detained (and the warrant then has effect as if it specified that place);
(b) obtain a receipt from the custodian; and
(c) notify the court officer that the defendant has been taken to that place.

Warrants that cease to have effect on payment R-109

13.6 (1) This rule applies to a warrant issued by a magistrates' court under any of the following provisions of the Magistrates' Courts Act 1980—
(a) section 76 (enforcement of sums adjudged to be paid);
(b) section 83 (process for securing attendance of offender);
(c) section 86 (power of magistrates' court to fix day for appearance of offender at means inquiry, etc.);
(d) section 136 (committal to custody overnight at police station for non-payment of sum adjudged by conviction).

(2) The warrant no longer has effect if—
(a) the sum in respect of which the warrant was issued is paid to the person executing it;
(b) that sum is offered to, but refused by, that person; or
(c) that person is shown a receipt for that sum given by—
(i) the court officer, or
(ii) the authority to which that sum is due.

Warrant issued when the court office is closed R-110

13.7 (1) This rule applies where the court issues a warrant when the court office is closed.

(2) The applicant for the warrant must, not more than 72 hours later, serve on the court officer—
(a) a copy of the warrant; and
(b) any written material that was submitted to the court.

Section 1: general rules

R-111 **When this Part applies**

14.1 (1) This Part applies where—
(a) a magistrates' court or the Crown Court can—
(i) grant or withhold bail, or impose or vary a condition of bail, and
(ii) where bail has been withheld, extend a custody time limit;
(b) a magistrates' court can monitor and enforce compliance with a supervision measure imposed in another European Union member State.
(2) In this Part, 'defendant' includes a person who has been granted bail by a police officer.

R-112 **Exercise of court's powers to which this Part applies**

14.2 (1) The court must not make a decision to which this Part applies unless—
(a) each party to the decision and any surety directly affected by the decision—
(i) is present, in person or by live link, or
(ii) has had an opportunity to make representations;
(b) on an application for bail by a defendant who is absent and in custody, the court is satisfied that the defendant—
(i) has waived the right to attend, or
(ii) was present when a court withheld bail in the case on a previous occasion and has been in custody continuously since then;
(c) on a prosecutor's appeal against a grant of bail, application to extend a custody time limit or appeal against a refusal to extend such a time limit—
(i) the court is satisfied that a defendant who is absent has waived the right to attend, or
(ii) the court is satisfied that it would be just to proceed even though the defendant is absent.
(2) The court may make a decision to which this Part applies at a hearing, in public or in private.
(3) The court may determine without a hearing an application to vary a condition of bail if—
(a) the parties to the application have agreed the terms of the variation proposed; or
(b) on an application by a defendant, the court determines the application no sooner than the fifth business day after the application was served.
(4) The court may adjourn a determination to which this Part applies, if that is necessary to obtain information sufficient to allow the court to make the decision required.
(5) At any hearing at which the court makes one of the following decisions, the court must announce in terms the defendant can understand (with help, if necessary) its reasons for—
(a) withholding bail, or imposing or varying a bail condition;
(b) granting bail, where the prosecutor opposed the grant; or
(c) where the defendant is under 18—
(i) imposing or varying a bail condition when ordering the defendant to be detained in local authority accommodation, or
(ii) ordering the defendant to be detained in youth detention accommodation.
(6) At any hearing at which the court grants bail, the court must—
(a) tell the defendant where and when to surrender to custody; or
(b) arrange for the court officer to give the defendant, as soon as practicable, notice of where and when to surrender to custody.

R-113 **Duty of justices' legal adviser**

14.3 (1) This rule applies—
(a) only in a magistrates' court; and
(b) unless the court—
(i) includes a District Judge (Magistrates' Courts), and
(ii) otherwise directs.
(2) A justices' legal adviser must—
(a) assist an unrepresented defendant;
(b) give the court such advice as is required to enable it to exercise its powers;
(c) if required, attend the members of the court outside the courtroom to give such advice, but inform the parties of any advice so given.

General duties of court officer R-114

14.4 (1) The court officer must arrange for a note or other record to be made of—
(a) the parties' representations about bail; and
(b) the court's reasons for a decision—
(i) to withhold bail, or to impose or vary a bail condition, or
(ii) to grant bail, where the prosecutor opposed the grant.
(2) The court officer must serve notice of a decision about bail on—
(a) the defendant (but, in the Crown Court, only where the defendant's legal representative asks for such a notice, or where the defendant has no legal representative);
(b) the prosecutor (but only where the court granted bail, the prosecutor opposed the grant, and the prosecutor asks for such a notice);
(c) a party to the decision who was absent when it was made;
(d) a surety who is directly affected by the decision;
(e) the defendant's custodian, where the defendant is in custody and the decision requires the custodian—
(i) to release the defendant (or will do so, if a requirement ordered by the court is met), or
(ii) to transfer the defendant to the custody of another custodian;
(f) the court officer for any other court at which the defendant is required by that decision to surrender to custody.
(3) Where the court postpones the date on which a defendant who is on bail must surrender to custody, the court officer must serve notice of the postponed date on—
(a) the defendant; and
(b) any surety.
(4) Where a magistrates' court withholds bail in a case to which section 5(6A) of the Bail Act 1976 applies (remand in custody after hearing full argument on an application for bail), the court officer must serve on the defendant a certificate that the court heard full argument.

Section 2: bail

Prosecutor's representations about bail R-115

14.5 (1) This rule applies whenever the court can grant or withhold bail.
(2) The prosecutor must provide the court with all the information in the prosecutor's possession which is material to what the court must decide.
(3) A prosecutor who opposes the grant of bail must specify—
(a) each exception to the general right to bail on which the prosecutor relies; and
(b) each consideration that the prosecutor thinks relevant.
(4) A prosecutor who wants the court to impose a condition on any grant of bail must—
(a) specify each condition proposed; and
(b) explain what purpose would be served by such a condition.

Reconsideration of police bail by magistrates' court R-116

14.6 (1) This rule applies where a party wants a magistrates' court to reconsider a bail decision by a police officer.
(2) An application under this rule must be made to—
(a) the magistrates' court to whose custody the defendant is under a duty to surrender, if any; or
(b) any magistrates' court acting for the police officer's local justice area, in any other case.
(3) The applicant party must—
(a) apply in writing; and
(b) serve the application on—
(i) the court officer,
(ii) the other party, and
(iii) any surety affected or proposed.
(4) The application must—
(a) specify—
(i) the decision that the applicant wants the court to make,
(ii) each offence charged, or for which the defendant was arrested, and
(iii) the police bail decision to be reconsidered and the reasons given for it;
(b) explain, as appropriate—
(i) why the court should grant bail itself, or withdraw it, or impose or vary a condition, and

(ii) if the applicant is the prosecutor, what material information has become available since the police bail decision was made;

(c) propose the terms of any suggested condition of bail; and

(d) if the applicant wants an earlier hearing than paragraph (7) requires, ask for that, and explain why it is needed.

(5) A prosecutor who applies under this rule must serve on the defendant, with the application, notice that the court has power to withdraw bail and, if the defendant is absent when the court makes its decision, order the defendant's arrest.

(6) A party who opposes an application must—

(a) so notify the court officer and the applicant at once; and

(b) serve on each notice of the reasons for opposition.

(7) Unless the court otherwise directs, the court officer must arrange for the court to hear the application as soon as practicable and in any event—

(a) if it is an application to withdraw bail, no later than the second business day after it was served;

(b) in any other case, no later than the fifth business day after it was served.

(8) The court may—

(a) vary or waive a time limit under this rule;

(b) allow an application to be in a different form to one set out in the Practice Direction;

(c) if rule 14.2 allows, determine without a hearing an application to vary a condition.

R-117 **Notice of application to consider bail**

14.7 (1) This rule applies where—

(a) in a magistrates' court—

(i) a prosecutor wants the court to withdraw bail granted by the court, or to impose or vary a condition of such bail, or

(ii) a defendant wants the court to reconsider such bail before the next hearing in the case;

(b) in the Crown Court,

(i) a party wants the court to grant bail that has been withheld, or to withdraw bail that has been granted, or to impose a new bail condition or to vary a present one, or

(ii) a prosecutor wants the court to consider whether to grant or withhold bail, or impose or vary a condition of bail, under section 88 or section 89 of the Criminal Justice Act 2003 (bail and custody in connection with an intended application to the Court of Appeal to which Part 27 (Retrial after acquittal) applies).

(2) Such a party must—

(a) apply in writing;

(b) serve the application on—

(i) the court officer,

(ii) the other party, and

(iii) any surety affected or proposed; and

(c) serve the application not less than 2 business days before any hearing in the case at which the applicant wants the court to consider it, if such a hearing is already due.

(3) The application must—

(a) specify—

(i) the decision that the applicant wants the court to make,

(ii) each offence charged, and

(iii) each relevant previous bail decision and the reasons given for each;

(b) if the applicant is a defendant, explain—

(i) as appropriate, why the court should not withhold bail, or why it should vary a condition, and

(ii) what further information or legal argument, if any, has become available since the most recent previous bail decision was made;

(c) if the applicant is the prosecutor, explain—

(i) as appropriate, why the court should withdraw bail, or impose or vary a condition, and

(ii) what material information has become available since the most recent previous bail decision was made;

(d) propose the terms of any suggested condition of bail; and

(e) if the applicant wants an earlier hearing than paragraph (6) requires, ask for that, and explain why it is needed.

(4) A prosecutor who applies under this rule must serve on the defendant, with the application, notice that the court has power to withdraw bail and, if the defendant is absent when the court makes its decision, order the defendant's arrest.
(5) A party who opposes an application must—
(a) so notify the court officer and the applicant at once; and
(b) serve on each notice of the reasons for opposition.
(6) Unless the court otherwise directs, the court officer must arrange for the court to hear the application as soon as practicable and in any event—
(a) if it is an application to grant or withdraw bail, no later than the second business day after it was served;
(b) if it is an application to impose or vary a condition, no later than the fifth business day after it was served.
(7) The court may—
(a) vary or waive a time limit under this rule;
(b) allow an application to be in a different form to one set out in the Practice Direction, or to be made orally;
(c) if rule 14.2 allows, determine without a hearing an application to vary a condition.

Defendant's application or appeal to the Crown Court after magistrates' court bail decision **R-118**

14.8 (1) This rule applies where a defendant wants to—
(a) apply to the Crown Court for bail after a magistrates' court has withheld bail; or
(b) appeal to the Crown Court after a magistrates' court has refused to vary a bail condition as the defendant wants.
(2) The defendant must—
(a) apply to the Crown Court in writing as soon as practicable after the magistrates' court's decision; and
(b) serve the application on—
(i) the Crown Court officer,
(ii) the magistrates' court officer,
(iii) the prosecutor, and
(iv) any surety affected or proposed.
(3) The application must—
(a) specify—
(i) the decision that the applicant wants the Crown Court to make, and
(ii) each offence charged;
(b) explain—
(i) as appropriate, why the Crown Court should not withhold bail, or why it should vary the condition under appeal, and
(ii) what further information or legal argument, if any, has become available since the magistrates' court's decision;
(c) propose the terms of any suggested condition of bail;
(d) if the applicant wants an earlier hearing than paragraph (6) requires, ask for that, and explain why it is needed; and
(e) on an application for bail, attach a copy of the certificate of full argument served on the defendant under rule 14.4(4).
(4) The magistrates' court officer must as soon as practicable serve on the Crown Court officer—
(a) a copy of the note or record made under rule 14.4(1) in connection with the magistrates' court's decision; and
(b) the date of the next hearing, if any, in the magistrates' court.
(5) A prosecutor who opposes the application must—
(a) so notify the Crown Court officer and the defendant at once; and
(b) serve on each notice of the reasons for opposition.
(6) Unless the Crown Court otherwise directs, the court officer must arrange for the court to hear the application or appeal as soon as practicable and in any event no later than the business day after it was served.
(7) The Crown Court may vary a time limit under this rule.

Prosecutor's appeal against grant of bail **R-119**

14.9 (1) This rule applies where a prosecutor wants to appeal—
(a) to the Crown Court against a grant of bail by a magistrates' court, in a case in which the defendant has been charged with, or convicted of, an offence punishable with imprisonment; or

(b) to the High Court against a grant of bail—
(i) by a magistrates' court, in an extradition case, or
(ii) by the Crown Court, in a case in which the defendant has been charged with, or convicted of, an offence punishable with imprisonment (but not in a case in which the Crown Court granted bail on an appeal to which paragraph (1)(a) applies).

(2) The prosecutor must tell the court which has granted bail of the decision to appeal—
(a) at the end of the hearing during which the court granted bail; and
(b) before the defendant is released on bail.

(3) The court which has granted bail must exercise its power to remand the defendant in custody pending determination of the appeal.

(4) The prosecutor must serve an appeal notice—
(a) on the court officer for the court which has granted bail and on the defendant;
(b) not more than 2 hours after telling that court of the decision to appeal.

(5) The appeal notice must specify—
(a) each offence with which the defendant is charged;
(b) the decision under appeal;
(c) the reasons given for the grant of bail; and
(d) the grounds of appeal.

(6) On an appeal to the Crown Court, the magistrates' court officer must, as soon as practicable, serve on the Crown Court officer—
(a) the appeal notice;
(b) a copy of the note or record made under rule 14.4(1) (record of bail decision); and
(c) notice of the date of the next hearing in the court which has granted bail.

(7) If the Crown Court so directs, the Crown Court officer must arrange for the defendant to be assisted by the Official Solicitor in a case in which the defendant—
(a) has no legal representative; and
(b) asks for such assistance.

(8) On an appeal to the Crown Court, the Crown Court officer must arrange for the court to hear the appeal as soon as practicable and in any event no later than the second business day after the appeal notice was served.

(9) The prosecutor—
(a) may abandon an appeal to the Crown Court without the court's permission, by serving a notice of abandonment, signed by or on behalf of the prosecutor, on—
(i) the defendant,
(ii) the Crown Court officer, and
(iii) the magistrates' court officer
before the hearing of the appeal begins; but
(b) after the hearing of the appeal begins, may only abandon the appeal with the Crown Court's permission.

(10) The court officer for the court which has granted bail must instruct the defendant's custodian to release the defendant on the bail granted by that court, subject to any condition or conditions of bail imposed, if—
(a) the prosecutor fails to serve an appeal notice within the time to which paragraph (4) refers; or
(b) the prosecutor serves a notice of abandonment under paragraph (9).

R-120 Consideration of bail in a murder case

14.10 (1) This rule applies in a case in which—
(a) the defendant is charged with murder; and
(b) the Crown Court has not yet considered bail.

(2) The magistrates' court officer must arrange with the Crown Court officer for the Crown Court to consider bail as soon as practicable and in any event no later than the second business day after—
(a) a magistrates' court sends the defendant to the Crown Court for trial; or
(b) the first hearing in the magistrates' court, if the defendant is not at once sent for trial.

R-121 Condition of residence

14.11 (1) The defendant must notify the prosecutor of the address at which the defendant will live and sleep if released on bail with a condition of residence—

(a) as soon as practicable after the institution of proceedings, unless already done; and
(b) as soon as practicable after any change of that address.

(2) The prosecutor must help the court to assess the suitability of an address proposed as a condition of residence.

Electronic monitoring requirements **R-122**

14.12 (1) This rule applies where the court imposes electronic monitoring requirements, where available, as a condition of bail.

(2) The court officer must—
(a) inform the person responsible for the monitoring ('the monitor') of—
(i) the defendant's name, and telephone number if available,
(ii) each offence with which the defendant is charged,
(iii) details of the place at which the defendant's presence must be monitored,
(iv) the period or periods during which the defendant's presence at that place must be monitored, and
(v) if fixed, the date on which the defendant must surrender to custody;
(b) inform the defendant and, where the defendant is under 16, an appropriate adult, of the monitor's identity and the means by which the monitor may be contacted; and
(c) notify the monitor of any subsequent—
(i) variation or termination of the electronic monitoring requirements, or
(ii) fixing or variation of the date on which the defendant must surrender to custody.

Accommodation or support requirements **R-123**

14.13 (1) This rule applies where the court imposes as a condition of bail a requirement, where available, that the defendant must—
(a) reside in accommodation provided for that purpose by, or on behalf of, a public authority;
(b) receive bail support provided by, or on behalf of, a public authority.

(2) The court officer must—
(a) inform the person responsible for the provision of any such accommodation or support ('the service provider') of—
(i) the defendant's name, and telephone number if available,
(ii) each offence with which the defendant is charged,
(iii) details of the requirement,
(iv) any other bail condition, and
(v) if fixed, the date on which the defendant must surrender to custody;
(b) inform the defendant and, where the defendant is under 16, an appropriate adult, of—
(i) the service provider's identity and the means by which the service provider may be contacted, and
(ii) the address of any accommodation in which the defendant must live and sleep; and
(c) notify the service provider of any subsequent—
(i) variation or termination of the requirement,
(ii) variation or termination of any other bail condition, and
(iii) fixing or variation of the date on which the defendant must surrender to custody.

Requirement for a surety or payment, etc. **R-124**

14.14 (1) This rule applies where the court imposes as a condition of bail a requirement for—
(a) a surety;
(b) a payment;
(c) the surrender of a document or thing.

(2) The court may direct how such a condition must be met.

(3) Unless the court otherwise directs, if any such condition or direction requires a surety to enter into a recognizance—
(a) the recognizance must specify—
(i) the amount that the surety will be required to pay if the purpose for which the recognizance is entered is not fulfilled, and
(ii) the date, or the event, upon which the recognizance will expire;
(b) the surety must enter into the recognizance in the presence of—
(i) the court officer,
(ii) the defendant's custodian, where the defendant is in custody, or
(iii) someone acting with the authority of either; and

(c) the person before whom the surety enters into the recognizance must at once serve a copy on—
(i) the surety, and
(ii) as appropriate, the court officer and the defendant's custodian.

(4) Unless the court otherwise directs, if any such condition or direction requires someone to make a payment, or surrender a document or thing—
(a) that payment, document or thing must be made or surrendered to—
(i) the court officer,
(ii) the defendant's custodian, where the defendant is in custody, or
(iii) someone acting with the authority of either; and
(b) the court officer or the custodian, as appropriate, must serve immediately on the other a statement that the payment, document or thing has been made or surrendered.

(5) The custodian must release the defendant when each requirement ordered by the court has been met.

R-125 **Forfeiture of a recognizance given by a surety**

14.15 (1) This rule applies where the court imposes as a condition of bail a requirement that a surety enter into a recognizance and, after the defendant is released on bail,—
(a) the defendant fails to surrender to custody as required, or
(b) it appears to the court that the surety has failed to comply with a condition or direction.

(2) The court officer must serve notice on—
(a) the surety; and
(b) each party to the decision to grant bail,
of the hearing at which the court will consider the forfeiture of the recognizance.

(3) The court must not forfeit the recognizance less than 5 business days after service of notice under paragraph (2).

R-126 **Bail condition to be enforced in another European Union member State**

14.16 (1) This rule applies where the court can impose as a condition of bail pending trial a requirement—
(a) with which the defendant must comply while in another European Union member State; and
(b) which that other member State can monitor and enforce.

(2) The court—
(a) must not exercise its power to impose such a requirement until the court has decided what, if any, condition or conditions of bail to impose while the defendant is in England and Wales;
(b) subject to that, may exercise its power to make a request for the other member State to monitor and enforce that requirement.

(3) Where the court makes such a request, the court officer must—
(a) issue a certificate requesting the monitoring and enforcement of the defendant's compliance with that requirement, in the form required by EU Council Framework Decision 2009/829/JHA;
(b) serve on the relevant authority of the other member State—
(i) the court's decision or a certified copy of that decision,
(ii) the certificate, and
(iii) a copy of the certificate translated into an official language of the other member State, unless English is such a language or the other member State has declared that it will accept a certificate in English; and
(c) report to the court—
(i) any request for further information returned by the competent authority in the other member State, and
(ii) that authority's decision.

(4) Where the competent authority in the other member State agrees to monitor and enforce the requirement—
(a) the court—
(i) may exercise its power to withdraw the request (where it can), but
(ii) whether or not it does so, must continue to exercise the powers to which this Part applies in accordance with the rules in this Part;
(b) the court officer must immediately serve notice on that authority if—
(i) legal proceedings are brought in relation to the requirement being monitored and enforced

(ii) the court decides to vary or revoke that requirement, or to issue a warrant for the defendant's arrest; and

(c) the court officer must promptly report to the court any information and any request received from that authority.

Enforcement of measure imposed in another European Union member State R-127

14.17 (1) This rule applies where the Lord Chancellor serves on the court officer a certificate requesting the monitoring and enforcement of a defendant's compliance with a supervision measure imposed by an authority in another European Union member State.

(2) The court officer must arrange for the court to consider the request—

(a) as a general rule—

(i) within 20 business days of the date on which the Lord Chancellor received it from the requesting authority, or

(ii) within 40 business days of that date, if legal proceedings in relation to the supervision measure are brought within the first 20 business days;

(b) exceptionally, later than that, but in such a case the court officer must immediately serve on the requesting authority—

(i) an explanation for the delay, and

(ii) an indication of when the court's decision is expected.

(3) On consideration of the request by the court, the court officer must—

(a) without delay serve on the requesting authority—

(i) notice of any further information required by the court, and

(ii) subject to any such requirement and any response, notice of the court's decision; and

(b) where the court agrees to monitor the supervision measure, serve notice of the court's decision on any supervisor specified by the court.

(4) Where the court agrees to monitor the supervision measure—

(a) the court officer must immediately serve notice on the requesting authority if there is reported to the court—

(i) a breach of the measure, or

(ii) any other event that might cause the requesting authority to review its decision;

(b) the court officer must without delay serve notice on the requesting authority if—

(i) legal proceedings are brought in relation to the decision to monitor compliance with the bail condition,

(ii) there is reported to the court a change of the defendant's residence, or

(iii) the court decides (where it can) to stop monitoring the defendant's compliance with the measure.

Section 3: custody time limits

Application to extend a custody time limit R-128

14.18 (1) This rule applies where the prosecutor gives notice of application to extend a custody time limit.

(2) The court officer must arrange for the court to hear that application as soon as practicable after the expiry of—

(a) 5 days from the giving of notice, in the Crown Court; or

(b) 2 days from the giving of notice, in a magistrates' court.

(3) The court may shorten a time limit under this rule.

Appeal against custody time limit decision R-129

14.19 (1) This rule applies where—

(a) a defendant wants to appeal to the Crown Court against a decision by a magistrates' court to extend a custody time limit;

(b) a prosecutor wants to appeal to the Crown Court against a decision by a magistrates' court to refuse to extend a custody time limit.

(2) The appellant must serve an appeal notice—

(a) on—

(i) the other party to the decision,

(ii) the Crown Court officer, and

(iii) the magistrates' court officer;

(b) in a defendant's appeal, as soon as practicable after the decision under appeal;

(c) in a prosecutor's appeal—
(i) as soon as practicable after the decision under appeal, and
(ii) before the relevant custody time limit expires.
(3) The appeal notice must specify—
(a) each offence with which the defendant is charged;
(b) the decision under appeal;
(c) the date on which the relevant custody time limit will expire;
(d) on a defendant's appeal, the date on which the relevant custody time limit would have expired but for the decision under appeal; and
(e) the grounds of appeal.
(4) The Crown Court officer must arrange for the Crown Court to hear the appeal as soon as practicable and in any event no later than the second business day after the appeal notice was served.
(5) The appellant—
(a) may abandon an appeal without the Crown Court's permission, by serving a notice of abandonment, signed by or on behalf of the appellant, on—
(i) the other party,
(ii) the Crown Court officer, and
(iii) the magistrates' court officer
before the hearing of the appeal begins; but
(b) after the hearing of the appeal begins, may only abandon the appeal with the Crown Court's permission.

Criminal Practice Directions Part 14 Bail and Custody Time Limits

PD-25 **CPD III Custody and bail 14A: Bail Before Sending for Trial**

14A.1 Before the Crown Court can deal with an application under CrimPR 14.8 by a defendant after a magistrates' court has withheld bail, it must be satisfied that the magistrates' court has issued a certificate, under section 5(6A) of the Bail Act 1976, that it heard full argument on the application for bail before it refused the application. The certificate of full argument is produced by the magistrates' court's computer system, Libra, as part of the GENORD (General Form of Order). Two hard copies are produced, one for the defence and one for the prosecution. (Some magistrates' courts may also produce a manual certificate which will usually be available from the justices' legal adviser at the conclusion of the hearing; the GENORD may not be produced until the following day.) Under CrimPR 14.4(4), the magistrates' court officer will provide the defendant with a certificate that the court heard full argument. However, it is the responsibility of the defence, as the applicant in the Crown Court, to ensure that a copy of the certificate of full argument is provided to the Crown Court as part of the application (CrimPR 14.8(3)(e)). The applicant's solicitors should attach a copy of the certificate to the bail application form. If the certificate is not enclosed with the application form, it will be difficult to avoid some delay in listing.

Venue

14A.2 Applications should be made to the court to which the defendant will be, or would have been, sent for trial. In the event of an application in a purely summary case, it should be made to the Crown Court centre which normally receives Class 3 work. The hearing will be listed as a chambers matter, unless a judge has directed otherwise.

PD-26 **CPD III Custody and bail 14B: Bail: Failure to Surrender and Trials in Absence**

14B.1 The failure of defendants to comply with the terms of their bail by not surrendering, or not doing so at the appointed time, undermines the administration of justice and disrupts proceedings. The resulting delays impact on victims, witnesses and other court users and also waste costs. A defendant's failure to surrender affects not only the case with which he or she is concerned, but also the court's ability to administer justice more generally, by damaging the confidence of victims, witnesses and the public in the effectiveness of the court system and the judiciary. It is, therefore, most important that defendants who are granted bail appreciate the significance of the obligation to surrender to custody in accordance with the terms of their bail and that courts take appropriate action, if they fail to do so.

14B.2 A defendant who will be unable for medical reasons to attend court in accordance with his or her bail must obtain a certificate from his or her general practitioner or another appropriate medical practitioner such as the doctor with care of the defendant at a hospital. This should be obtained in advance of the hearing and conveyed to the court through the defendant's legal representative. In order to minimise the disruption to the court and to others, particularly witnesses if the case is listed for trial, the defendant should notify the court through his legal representative as soon as his inability to attend court becomes known.

14B.3 Guidance has been produced by the British Medical Association and the Crown Prosecution Service on the roles and responsibilities of medical practitioners when issuing medical certificates in criminal proceedings. Judges and magistrates should seek to ensure that this guidance is followed. However, it is a matter for each individual court to decide whether, in any particular case, the issued certificate should be accepted. Without a medical certificate or if an unsatisfactory certificate is provided, the court is likely to consider that the defendant has failed to surrender to bail.

14B.4 If a defendant fails to surrender to his or her bail there are at least four courses of action for the courts to consider taking:

(a) imposing penalties for the failure to surrender;
(b) revoking bail or imposing more stringent conditions;
(c) conducting trials in the absence of the defendant; and
(d) ordering that some or all of any sums of money lodged with the court as a security or pledged by a surety as a condition on the grant of bail be forfeit.

The relevant sentencing guideline is the Definitive Guideline Fail to Surrender to Bail. Under section 125(1) of the Coroners and Justice Act 2009, for offences committed on or after 6 April 2010, the court must follow the relevant guideline unless it would be contrary to the interests of justice to do so. The guideline can be obtained from the Sentencing Council's website: http://sentencingcouncil.judiciary.gov.uk/guidelines/guidelines-to-download.htm/

CPD III Custody and bail 14C: Penalties for Failure to Surrender PD-27

Initiating Proceedings — Bail granted by a police officer

14C.1 When a person has been granted bail by a police officer to attend court and subsequently fails to surrender to custody, the decision whether to initiate proceedings for a section 6(1) or section 6(2) offence will be for the police/prosecutor and proceedings are commenced in the usual way.

14C.2 The offence in this form is a summary offence although section 6(10) to (14) of the Bail Act 1976, inserted by section 15(3) of the Criminal Justice Act 2003, disapplies section 127 of the Magistrates' Courts Act 1980 and provides for alternative time limits for the commencement of proceedings. The offence should be dealt with on the first appearance after arrest, unless an adjournment is necessary, as it will be relevant in considering whether to grant bail again.

Initiating Proceedings — Bail granted by a court

14C.3 Where a person has been granted bail by a court and subsequently fails to surrender to custody, on arrest that person should normally be brought as soon as appropriate before the court at which the proceedings in respect of which bail was granted are to be heard. (There is no requirement to lay an information within the time limit for a Bail Act offence where bail was granted by the court).

14C.4 Given that bail was granted by a court, it is more appropriate that the court itself should initiate the proceedings by its own motion although the prosecutor may invite the court to take proceedings, if the prosecutor considers proceedings are appropriate.

Timing of disposal

14C.5 Courts should not, without good reason, adjourn the disposal of a section 6(1) or section 6(2) Bail Act 1976 offence (failure to surrender) until the conclusion of the proceedings in respect of which bail was granted but should deal with defendants as soon as is practicable. In deciding what is practicable, the court must take into account when the proceedings in respect of which bail was granted are expected to conclude, the seriousness of the offence for which the defendant is already being prosecuted, the type of penalty that might be imposed for the Bail Act offence and the original offence, as well as any other relevant circumstances.

14C.6 If the Bail Act offence is adjourned alongside the substantive proceedings, then it is still necessary to consider imposing a separate penalty at the trial. In addition, bail should usually be revoked in the meantime. Trial in the absence of the defendant is not a penalty for the Bail Act offence and a separate penalty may be imposed for the Bail Act offence.

Conduct of Proceedings

14C.7 Proceedings under section 6 of the Bail Act 1976 may be conducted either as a summary offence or as a criminal contempt of court. Where proceedings are commenced by the police or prosecutor, the prosecutor will conduct the proceedings and, if the matter is contested, call the evidence. Where the court initiates proceedings, with or without an invitation from the prosecutor, the court may expect the assistance of the prosecutor, such as in cross-examining the defendant, if required.

14C.8 The burden of proof is on the defendant to prove that he had reasonable cause for his failure to surrender to custody (section 6(3) of the Bail Act 1976).

Sentencing for a Bail Act offence

14C.9 A defendant who commits an offence under section 6(1) or section 6(2) of the Bail Act 1976 commits an offence that stands apart from the proceedings in respect of which bail was granted. The seriousness of the offence can be reflected by an appropriate and generally separate penalty being imposed for the Bail Act offence.

14C.10 As noted above, there is a sentencing guideline on sentencing offenders for Bail Act offences and this must be followed unless it would be contrary to the interests of justice to do so. Where the appropriate penalty is a custodial sentence, consecutive sentences should be imposed unless there are circumstances that make this inappropriate.

PD-28 CPD III Custody and bail 14D: Relationship between the Bail Act Offence and Further Remands on Bail or in Custody

14D.1 The court at which the defendant is produced should, where practicable and legally permissible, arrange to have all outstanding cases brought before it (including those from different courts) for the purpose of progressing matters and dealing with the question of bail. This is likely to be practicable in the magistrates' court where cases can easily be transferred from one magistrates' court to another. Practice is likely to vary in the Crown Court. If the defendant appears before a different court, for example because he is charged with offences committed in another area, and it is not practicable for all matters to be concluded by that court then the defendant may be remanded on bail or in custody, if appropriate, to appear before the first court for the outstanding offences to be dealt with.

14D.2 When a defendant has been convicted of a Bail Act offence, the court should review the remand status of the defendant, including the conditions of that bail, in respect of all outstanding proceedings against the defendant.

14D.3 Failure by the defendant to surrender or a conviction for failing to surrender to bail in connection with the main proceedings will be significant factors weighing against the re-granting of bail.

14D.4 Whether or not an immediate custodial sentence has been imposed for the Bail Act offence, the court may, having reviewed the defendant's remand status, also remand the defendant in custody in the main proceedings.

PD-29 CPD III Custody and bail 14E: Trials in Absence

14E.1 A defendant has a right, in general, to be present and to be represented at his trial. However, a defendant may choose not to exercise those rights, such as by voluntarily absenting himself and failing to instruct his lawyers adequately so that they can represent him.

14E.2 The court has a discretion as to whether a trial should take place or continue in the defendant's absence and must exercise its discretion with due regard for the interests of justice. The overriding concern must be to ensure that such a trial is as fair as circumstances permit and leads to a just outcome. If the defendant's absence is due to involuntary illness or incapacity it would very rarely, if ever, be right to exercise the discretion in favour of commencing or continuing the trial.

Trials on Indictment

14E.3 Proceeding in the absence of a defendant is a step which ought normally to be taken only if it is unavoidable. The court must exercise its discretion as to whether a trial should take place or continue in the defendant's absence with the utmost care and caution. Due regard should be had to the judgment of Lord Bingham in *R v Jones* [2002] UKHL 5, [2003] 1 AC 1, [2002] 2 Cr App R 9. Circumstances to be taken into account before proceeding include:

i) the conduct of the defendant;
ii) the disadvantage to the defendant;
iii) the public interest, taking account of the inconvenience and hardship to witnesses, and especially to any complainant, of a delay; if the witnesses have attended court and are ready to give evidence, that will weigh in favour of continuing with the trial;
iv) the effect of any delay;
v) whether the attendance of the defendant could be secured at a later hearing; and
vii) the likely outcome if the defendant is found guilty.

Even if the defendant is voluntarily absent, it is still generally desirable that he or she is represented.

Trials in the Magistrates' Courts

14E.4 Section 11 of the Magistrates' Courts Act 1980 applies. If either party is absent, the court should follow the procedure at CrimPR 24.12. Subject to the provisions of the statute, the principles outlined above are applicable. Benches and legal advisers will note that the presumption at rule 24.12(3) (a) does not apply if the defendant is under 18 years of age.

CPD III Custody and bail 14F: Forfeiture of Monies Lodged as Security or Pledged by a Surety/ Estreatment of Recognisances **PD-30**

14F.1 A surety undertakes to forfeit a sum of money if the defendant fails to surrender as required. Considerable care must be taken to explain that obligation and the consequences before a surety is taken. This system, in one form or another, has great antiquity. It is immensely valuable. A court concerned that a defendant will fail to surrender will not normally know that defendant personally, nor indeed much about him. When members of the community who do know the defendant say they trust him to surrender and are prepared to stake their own money on that trust, that can have a powerful influence on the decision of the court as to whether or not to grant bail. There are two important side-effects. The first is that the surety will keep an eye on the defendant, and report to the authorities if there is a concern that he will abscond. In those circumstances, the surety can withdraw. The second is that a defendant will be deterred from absconding by the knowledge that if he does so then his family or friends who provided the surety will lose their money. In the experience of the courts, it is comparatively rare for a defendant to fail to surrender when meaningful sureties are in place.

14F.2 Any surety should have the opportunity to make representations to the defendant to surrender himself, in accordance with their obligations.

14F.3 The court should not wait or adjourn a decision on estreatment of sureties or securities until such time, if any, that the bailed defendant appears before the court. It is possible that any defendant who apparently absconds may have a defence of reasonable cause to the allegation of failure to surrender. If that happens, then any surety or security estreated would be returned. The reason for proceeding is that the defendant may never surrender, or may not surrender for many years. The court should still consider the sureties' obligations if that happens. Moreover, the longer the matter is delayed the more probable it is that the personal circumstances of the sureties will change.

14F.4 The court should follow the procedure at CrimPR 14.15. Before the court makes a decision, it should give the sureties the opportunity to make representations, either in person, through counsel or by statement.

14F.5 The court has discretion to forfeit the whole sum, part only of the sum, or to remit the sum. The starting point is that the surety is forfeited in full. It would be unfortunate if this valuable method of allowing a defendant to remain at liberty were undermined. Courts would have less confidence in the efficacy of sureties. It is also important to note that a defendant who absconds without in any way forewarning his sureties does not thereby release them from any or all of their responsibilities. Even if a surety does his best, he remains liable for the full amount, except at the discretion of the court. However, all factors should be taken into account and the following are noted for guidance only:

i) The presence or absence of culpability is a factor, but is not in itself a reason to reduce or set aside the obligations entered into by the surety.
ii) The means of a surety, and in particular changed means, are relevant.

iii) The court should forfeit no more than is necessary, in public policy, to maintain the integrity and confidence of the system of taking sureties.

PD-31 **CPD III Custody and bail 14G: Bail During Trial**

14G.1 The following should be read subject to the Bail Act 1976.

14G.2 Once a trial has begun the further grant of bail, whether during the short adjournment or overnight, is in the discretion of the trial judge or trial Bench. It may be a proper exercise of this discretion to refuse bail during the short adjournment if the accused cannot otherwise be segregated from witnesses and jurors.

14G.3 An accused who was on bail while on remand should not be refused bail during the trial unless, in the opinion of the court, there are positive reasons to justify this refusal. Such reasons might include:

(a) that a point has been reached where there is a real danger that the accused will abscond, either because the case is going badly for him, or for any other reason;

(b) that there is a real danger that he may interfere with witnesses, jurors or co-defendants.

14G.4 Once the jury has returned a guilty verdict or a finding of guilt has been made, a further renewal of bail should be decided in the light of the gravity of the offence, any friction between co-defendants and the likely sentence to be passed in all the circumstances of the case.

PD-32 **CPD III Custody and bail 14H: Crown Court Judge's Certification of Fitness to Appeal and Applications to the Crown Court for Bail Pending Appeal**

14H.1 The trial or sentencing judge may grant a certificate of fitness for appeal (see, for example, sections 1(2) (b) and 11(1A) of the Criminal Appeal Act 1968); the judge in the Crown Court should only certify cases in exceptional circumstances. The Crown Court judge should use the Criminal Appeal Office Form C (Crown Court Judge's Certificate of fitness for appeal) which is available to court staff on the HMCTS intranet.

14H.2 The judge may well think it right to encourage the defendant's advocate to submit to the court, and serve on the prosecutor, before the hearing of the application, a draft of the grounds of appeal which he will ask the judge to certify on Form C.

14H.3 The first question for the judge is then whether there exists a particular and cogent ground of appeal. If there is no such ground, there can be no certificate; and if there is no certificate there can be no bail. A judge should not grant a certificate with regard to sentence merely in the light of mitigation to which he has, in his opinion, given due weight, nor in regard to conviction on a ground where he considers the chance of a successful appeal is not substantial. The judge should bear in mind that, where a certificate is refused, application may be made to the Court of Appeal for leave to appeal and for bail; it is expected that certificates will only be granted in exceptional circumstances.

14H.4 Defence advocates should note that the effect of a grant of a certificate is to remove the need for leave to appeal to be granted by the Court of Appeal. It does not in itself commence the appeal. The completed Form C will be sent by the Crown Court to the Criminal Appeal Office; it is not copied to the parties. The procedures in CrimPR Part 39 should be followed.

14H.5 Bail pending appeal to the Court of Appeal (Criminal Division) may be granted by the trial or sentencing judge if they have certified the case as fit for appeal (see sections 81(1)(f) and 81(1B) of the Senior Courts Act 1981). Bail can only be granted in the Crown Court within 28 days of the conviction or sentence which is to be the subject of the appeal and may not be granted if an application for bail has already been made to the Court of Appeal. The procedure for bail to be granted by a judge of the Crown Court pending an appeal is governed by CrimPR Part 14. The Crown Court judge should use the Criminal Appeal Office Form BC (Crown Court Judge's Order granting bail) which is available to court staff on the HMCTS intranet.

14H.6 The length of the period which might elapse before the hearing of any appeal is not relevant to the grant of a certificate; but, if the judge does decide to grant a certificate, it may be one factor in the decision whether or not to grant bail. If bail is granted, the judge should consider imposing a condition of residence in line with the practice in the Court of Appeal (Criminal Division).

Criminal Procedure Rules Part 15 Disclosure

When this Part applies R-130

15.1 This Part applies—
(a) in a magistrates' court and in the Crown Court;
(b) where Parts I and II of the Criminal Procedure and Investigations Act 1996 apply.

Prosecution disclosure R-131

15.2 (1) This rule applies in the Crown Court where, under section 3 of the Criminal Procedure and Investigations Act 1996, the prosecutor—
(a) discloses prosecution material to the defendant; or
(b) serves on the defendant a written statement that there is no such material to disclose.
(2) The prosecutor must at the same time so inform the court officer.

Prosecutor's application for public interest ruling R-132

15.3 (1) This rule applies where—
(a) without a court order, the prosecutor would have to disclose material; and
(b) the prosecutor wants the court to decide whether it would be in the public interest to disclose it.
(2) The prosecutor must—
(a) apply in writing for such a decision; and
(b) serve the application on—
(i) the court officer,
(ii) any person who the prosecutor thinks would be directly affected by disclosure of the material, and
(iii) the defendant, but only to the extent that serving it on the defendant would not disclose what the prosecutor thinks ought not be disclosed.
(3) The application must—
(a) describe the material, and explain why the prosecutor thinks that—
(i) it is material that the prosecutor would have to disclose,
(ii) it would not be in the public interest to disclose that material, and
(iii) no measure such as the prosecutor's admission of any fact, or disclosure by summary, extract or edited copy, adequately would protect both the public interest and the defendant's right to a fair trial;
(b) omit from any part of the application that is served on the defendant anything that would disclose what the prosecutor thinks ought not be disclosed (in which case, paragraph (4) of this rule applies); and
(c) explain why, if no part of the application is served on the defendant.
(4) Where the prosecutor serves only part of the application on the defendant, the prosecutor must—
(a) mark the other part, to show that it is only for the court; and
(b) in that other part, explain why the prosecutor has withheld it from the defendant.
(5) Unless already done, the court may direct the prosecutor to serve an application on—
(a) the defendant;
(b) any other person who the court considers would be directly affected by the disclosure of the material.
(6) The court must determine the application at a hearing which—
(a) must be in private, unless the court otherwise directs; and
(b) if the court so directs, may take place, wholly or in part, in the defendant's absence.
(7) At a hearing at which the defendant is present—
(a) the general rule is that the court must consider, in the following sequence—
(i) representations first by the prosecutor and any other person served with the application, and then by the defendant, in the presence of them all, and then
(ii) further representations by the prosecutor and any such other person in the defendant's absence; but
(b) the court may direct other arrangements for the hearing.
(8) The court may only determine the application if satisfied that it has been able to take adequate account of—
(a) such rights of confidentiality as apply to the material; and
(b) the defendant's right to a fair trial.

(9) Unless the court otherwise directs, the court officer—
(a) must not give notice to anyone other than the prosecutor—
(i) of the hearing of an application under this rule, unless the prosecutor served the application on that person, or
(ii) of the court's decision on the application;
(b) may—
(i) keep a written application or representations, or
(ii) arrange for the whole or any part to be kept by some other appropriate person, subject to any conditions that the court may impose.

R-133 Defence disclosure

15.4 (1) This rule applies where—
(a) under section 5 or 6 of the Criminal Procedure and Investigations Act 1996, the defendant gives a defence statement;
(b) under section 6C of the 1996 Act, the defendant gives a defence witness notice.
(2) The defendant must serve such a statement or notice on—
(a) the court officer; and
(b) the prosecutor.

R-134 Defendant's application for prosecution disclosure

15.5 (1) This rule applies where the defendant—
(a) has served a defence statement given under the Criminal Procedure and Investigations Act 1996; and
(b) wants the court to require the prosecutor to disclose material.
(2) The defendant must serve an application on—
(a) the court officer; and
(b) the prosecutor.
(3) The application must—
(a) describe the material that the defendant wants the prosecutor to disclose;
(b) explain why the defendant thinks there is reasonable cause to believe that—
(i) the prosecutor has that material, and
(ii) it is material that the Criminal Procedure and Investigations Act 1996 requires the prosecutor to disclose; and
(c) ask for a hearing, if the defendant wants one, and explain why it is needed.
(4) The court may determine an application under this rule—
(a) at a hearing, in public or in private; or
(b) without a hearing.
(5) The court must not require the prosecutor to disclose material unless the prosecutor—
(a) is present; or
(b) has had at least 14 days in which to make representations.

R-135 Review of public interest ruling

15.6 (1) This rule applies where the court has ordered that it is not in the public interest to disclose material that the prosecutor otherwise would have to disclose, and—
(a) the defendant wants the court to review that decision; or
(b) the Crown Court reviews that decision on its own initiative.
(2) Where the defendant wants the court to review that decision, the defendant must—
(a) serve an application on—
(i) the court officer, and
(ii) the prosecutor; and
(b) in the application—
(i) describe the material that the defendant wants the prosecutor to disclose, and
(ii) explain why the defendant thinks it is no longer in the public interest for the prosecutor not to disclose it.
(3) The prosecutor must serve any such application on any person who the prosecutor thinks would be directly affected if that material were disclosed.
(4) The prosecutor, and any such person, must serve any representations on—
(a) the court officer; and
(b) the defendant, unless to do so would in effect reveal something that either thinks ought not be disclosed.

(5) The court may direct—
(a) the prosecutor to serve any such application on any person who the court considers would be directly affected if that material were disclosed;
(b) the prosecutor and any such person to serve any representations on the defendant.
(6) The court must review a decision to which this rule applies at a hearing which—
(a) must be in private, unless the court otherwise directs; and
(b) if the court so directs, may take place, wholly or in part, in the defendant's absence.
(7) At a hearing at which the defendant is present—
(a) the general rule is that the court must consider, in the following sequence—
(i) representations first by the defendant, and then by the prosecutor and any other person served with the application, in the presence of them all, and then
(ii) further representations by the prosecutor and any such other person in the defendant's absence; but
(b) the court may direct other arrangements for the hearing.
(8) The court may only conclude a review if satisfied that it has been able to take adequate account of—
(a) such rights of confidentiality as apply to the material; and
(b) the defendant's right to a fair trial.

Defendant's application to use disclosed material R-136

15.7 (1) This rule applies where a defendant wants the court's permission to use disclosed prosecution material—
(a) otherwise than in connection with the case in which it was disclosed; or
(b) beyond the extent to which it was displayed or communicated publicly at a hearing.
(2) The defendant must serve an application on—
(a) the court officer; and
(b) the prosecutor.
(3) The application must—
(a) specify what the defendant wants to use or disclose; and
(b) explain why.
(4) The court may determine an application under this rule—
(a) at a hearing, in public or in private; or
(b) without a hearing.
(5) The court must not permit the use of such material unless—
(a) the prosecutor has had at least 28 days in which to make representations; and
(b) the court is satisfied that it has been able to take adequate account of any rights of confidentiality that may apply to the material.

Unauthorised use of disclosed material R-137

15.8 (1) This rule applies where a person is accused of using disclosed prosecution material in contravention of section 17 of the Criminal Procedure and Investigations Act 1996.
(2) A party who wants the court to exercise its power to punish that person for contempt of court must comply with the rules in Part 48 (Contempt of court).
(3) The court must not exercise its power to forfeit material used in contempt of court unless—
(a) the prosecutor; and
(b) any other person directly affected by the disclosure of the material.
is present, or has had at least 14 days in which to make representations.

Court's power to vary requirements under this Part R-138

15.9 The court may—
(a) shorten or extend (even after it has expired) a time limit under this Part;
(b) allow a defence statement, or a defence witness notice, to be in a different written form to one set out in the Practice Direction, as long as it contains what the Criminal Procedure and Investigations Act 1996 requires;
(c) allow an application under this Part to be in a different form to one set out in the Practice Direction, or to be presented orally; and
(d) specify the period within which—
(i) any application under this Part must be made, or
(ii) any material must be disclosed, on an application to which rule 15.5 applies (Defendant's application for prosecution disclosure).

Criminal Practice Directions Part 15 Disclosure

PD-33 **CPD IV Disclosure 15A: Disclosure of Unused Material**

15A.1 Disclosure is a vital part of the preparation for trial, both in the magistrates' courts and in the Crown Court. All parties must be familiar with their obligations, in particular under the Criminal Procedure and Investigations Act 1996 as amended and the Code issued under that Act, and must comply with the relevant judicial protocol and guidelines from the Attorney-General. These documents have recently been revised and the new guidance will be issued shortly as *Judicial Protocol on the Disclosure of Unused Material in Criminal Cases* and the *Attorney-General's Guidelines on Disclosure*. The new documents should be read together as complementary, comprehensive guidance. They will be available electronically on the respective websites.

15A.2 In addition, certain procedures are prescribed under CrimPR Part 15 and these should be followed. The notes to Part 15 contain a useful summary of the requirements of the CPIA 1996 as amended.

Criminal Procedure Rules Part 16 Written Witness Statements

R-139 **When this Part applies**

16.1 This Part applies where a party wants to introduce a written witness statement in evidence under section 9 of the Criminal Justice Act 1967.

R-140 **Content of written witness statement**

16.2 The statement must contain—
(a) at the beginning—
(i) the witness' name, and
(ii) the witness' age, if under 18;
(b) a declaration by the witness that—
(i) it is true to the best of the witness' knowledge and belief, and
(ii) the witness knows that if it is introduced in evidence, then it would be an offence wilfully to have stated in it anything that the witness knew to be false or did not believe to be true;
(c) if the witness cannot read the statement, a signed declaration by someone else that that person read it to the witness; and
(d) the witness' signature.

R-141 **Reference to exhibit**

16.3 Where the statement refers to a document or object as an exhibit—
(a) the statement must contain such a description of that exhibit as to identify it clearly; and
(b) the exhibit must be labelled or marked correspondingly, and the label or mark signed by the maker of the statement.

R-142 **Written witness statement in evidence**

16.4 (1) A party who wants to introduce in evidence a written witness statement must—
(a) before the hearing at which that party wants to introduce it, serve a copy of the statement on—
(i) the court officer, and
(ii) each other party; and
(b) at or before that hearing, serve on the court officer the statement or an authenticated copy.
(2) If that party relies on only part of the statement, that party must mark the copy in such a way as to make that clear.
(3) A prosecutor must serve on a defendant, with the copy of the statement, a notice—
(a) of the right to object to the introduction of the statement in evidence instead of the witness giving evidence in person;
(b) of the time limit for objecting under this rule; and
(c) that if the defendant does not object in time, the court—
(i) can nonetheless require the witness to give evidence in person, but
(ii) may decide not to do so.
(4) A party served with a written witness statement who objects to its introduction in evidence must—
(a) serve notice of the objection on—
(i) the party who served it, and
(ii) the court officer; and

(b) serve the notice of objection not more than 7 days after service of the statement unless—
  (i) the court extends that time limit, before or after the statement was served,
  (ii) rule 24.8 (Written guilty plea: special rules) applies, in which case the time limit is the later of 7 days after service of the statement or 7 days before the hearing date, or
  (iii) rule 24.9 (Single justice procedure: special rules) applies, in which case the time limit is 21 days after service of the statement.

(5) The court may exercise its power to require the witness to give evidence in person—
(a) on application by any party; or
(b) on its own initiative.

(6) A party entitled to receive a copy of a statement may waive that entitlement by so informing—
(a) the party who would have served it; and
(b) the court.

CRIMINAL PRACTICE DIRECTIONS PART 16 WRITTEN WITNESS STATEMENTS

CPD V Evidence 16A: Evidence by Written Statement PD-34

16A.1 Where the prosecution proposes to tender written statements in evidence under section 9 of the Criminal Justice Act 1967, it will frequently be necessary for certain statements to be edited. This will occur either because a witness has made more than one statement whose contents should conveniently be reduced into a single, comprehensive statement, or where a statement contains inadmissible, prejudicial or irrelevant material. Editing of statements must be done by a Crown Prosecutor (or by a legal representative, if any, of the prosecutor if the case is not being conducted by the Crown Prosecution Service) and not by a police officer.

Composite statements

16A.2 A composite statement giving the combined effect of two or more earlier statements must be prepared in compliance with the requirements of section 9 of the 1967 Act; and must then be signed by the witness.

Editing single statements

16A.3 There are two acceptable methods of editing single statements. They are:

(a) By marking copies of the statement in a way which indicates the passages on which the prosecution will not rely. This merely indicates that the prosecution will not seek to adduce the evidence so marked. The original signed statement to be tendered to the court is not marked in any way.
The marking on the copy statement is done by lightly striking out the passages to be edited, so that what appears beneath can still be read, or by bracketing, or by a combination of both. It is not permissible to produce a photocopy with the deleted material obliterated, since this would be contrary to the requirement that the defence and the court should be served with copies of the signed original statement.
Whenever the striking out/bracketing method is used, it will assist if the following words appear at the foot of the frontispiece or index to any bundle of copy statements to be tendered: '*The prosecution does not propose to adduce evidence of those passages of the attached copy statements which have been struck out and/or bracketed (nor will it seek to do so at the trial unless a notice of further evidence is served)*'.

(b) By obtaining a fresh statement, signed by the witness, which omits the offending material, applying the procedure for composite statements above.

16A.4 In most cases where a single statement is to be edited, the striking out/bracketing method will be the more appropriate, but the taking of a fresh statement is preferable in the following circumstances:

(a) When a police (or other investigating) officer's statement contains details of interviews with more suspects than are eventually charged, a fresh statement should be prepared and signed, omitting all details of interview with those not charged except, insofar as it is relevant, for the bald fact that a certain named person was interviewed at a particular time, date and place.

(b) When a suspect is interviewed about more offences than are eventually made the subject of charges, a fresh statement should be prepared and signed, omitting all questions and answers about the uncharged offences unless either they might appropriately be taken into consideration, or evidence about those offences is admissible on the charges preferred. It may, however, be desirable to replace the omitted questions and answers with a phrase such as: '*After referring to some other matters, I then said,* "........"', so as to make it clear that part of the interview has been omitted.

(c) A fresh statement should normally be prepared and signed if the only part of the original on which the prosecution is relying is only a small proportion of the whole, although it remains desirable to use the alternative method if there is reason to believe that the defence might itself wish to rely, in mitigation or for any other purpose, on at least some of those parts which the prosecution does not propose to adduce.

(d) When the passages contain material which the prosecution is entitled to withhold from disclosure to the defence.

16A.5 Prosecutors should also be aware that, where statements are to be tendered under section 9 of the 1967 Act in the course of summary proceedings, there will be a need to prepare fresh statements excluding inadmissible or prejudicial material, rather than using the striking out or bracketing method.

16A.6 Whenever a fresh statement is taken from a witness and served in evidence, the earlier, unedited statement(s) becomes unused material and should be scheduled and reviewed for disclosure to the defence in the usual way.

PD-35 **CPD V Evidence 16B: Video Recorded Evidence in Chief**

16B.1 The procedure for making an application for leave to admit into evidence video recorded evidence in chief under section 27 of the Youth Justice and Criminal Evidence Act 1999 is given in CrimPR Part 18.

16B.2 Where a court, on application by a party to the proceedings or of its own motion, grants leave to admit a video recording in evidence under section 27(1) of the 1999 Act, it may direct that any part of the recording be excluded (section 27(2) and (3)). When such direction is given, the party who made the application to admit the video recording must edit the recording in accordance with the judge's directions and send a copy of the edited recording to the appropriate officer of the Crown Court and to every other party to the proceedings.

16B.3 Where a video recording is to be adduced during proceedings before the Crown Court, it should be produced and proved by the interviewer, or any other person who was present at the interview with the witness at which the recording was made. The applicant should ensure that such a person will be available for this purpose, unless the parties have agreed to accept a written statement in lieu of attendance by that person.

16B.4 Once a trial has begun, if, by reason of faulty or inadequate preparation or for some other cause, the procedures set out above have not been properly complied with and an application is made to edit the video recording, thereby necessitating an adjournment for the work to be carried out, the court may, at its discretion, make an appropriate award of costs.

PD-36 **CPD V Evidence 16C: Evidence of Audio and Video Recorded Interviews**

16C.1 The interrogation of suspects is primarily governed by Code C, one of the Codes of Practice under the Police and Criminal Evidence Act 1984 ('PACE'). Under that Code, interviews must normally be contemporaneously recorded. Under PACE Code E, interviews conducted at a police station concerning an indictable offence must normally be audio-recorded. In practice, most interviews are audio-recorded under Code E, or video-recorded under Code F, and it is best practice to do so. The questioning of terrorism suspects is governed separately by Code H. The Codes are available electronically on the Home Office website.

16C.2 Where a record of the interview is to be prepared, this should be in accordance with the current national guidelines, as envisaged by Note 5A of Code E.

16C.3 If the prosecution wishes to rely on the defendant's interview in evidence, the prosecution should seek to agree the record with the defence. Both parties should have received a copy of the audio or video recording, and can check the record against the recording. The record should be edited (see below) if inadmissible matters are included within it and, in particular if the interview is lengthy, the prosecution should seek to shorten it by editing or summary.

16C.4 If the record is agreed there is usually no need for the audio or video recording to be played in court. It is a matter for the discretion of the trial judge, but usual practice is for edited copies of the record to be provided to the court, and to the jury if there is one, and for the prosecution advocate to read the interview with the interviewing officer or the officer in the case, as part of the officer's evidence in chief, the officer reading the interviewer and the advocate reading the defendant and defence representative. In the magistrates' court, the Bench sometimes retire to read the interview themselves, and the document is treated as if it had been read aloud in court. This is permissible, but CrimPR 24.5 should be followed.

16C.5 Where the prosecution intends to adduce the interview in evidence, and agreement between the parties has not been reached about the record, sufficient notice must be given to allow consideration of any amendment to the record, or the preparation of any transcript of the interview, or any editing of a recording for the purpose of playing it in court. To that end, the following practice should be followed:

(a) Where the defence is unable to agree a record of interview or transcript (where one is already available) the prosecution should be notified at latest at the Plea and Case Management Hearing ('PCMH'), with a view to securing agreement to amend. The notice should specify the part to which objection is taken, or the part omitted which the defence consider should be included. A copy of the notice should be supplied to the court within the period specified above. The PCMH form inquires about the admissibility of the defendant's interview and shortening by editing or summarising for trial.

(b) If agreement is not reached and it is proposed that the audio or video recording or part of it be played in court, notice should be given to the prosecution by the defence as ordered at the PCMH, in order that the advocates for the parties may agree those parts of the audio or video recording that should not be adduced and that arrangements may be made, by editing or in some other way, to exclude that material. A copy of the notice should be supplied to the court.

(c) Notice of any agreement reached should be supplied to the court by the prosecution, as soon as is practicable.

16C.6 Alternatively, if, the prosecution advocate proposes to play the audio or video recording or part of it, the prosecution should at latest at the PCMH, notify the defence and the court. The defence should notify the prosecution and the court within 14 days of receiving the notice, if they object to the production of the audio or video recording on the basis that a part of it should be excluded. If the objections raised by the defence are accepted, the prosecution should prepare an edited recording, or make other arrangements to exclude the material part; and should notify the court of the arrangements made.

16C.7 If the defendant wishes to have the audio or video recording or any part of it played to the court, the defence should provide notice to the prosecution and the court at latest at the PCMH. The defence should also, at that time, notify the prosecution of any proposals to edit the recording and seek the prosecution's agreement to those amendments.

16C.8 Whenever editing or amendment of a record of interview or of an audio or video recording or of a transcript takes place, the following general principles should be followed:

(i) Where a defendant has made a statement which includes an admission of one or more other offences, the portion relating to other offences should be omitted unless it is or becomes admissible in evidence;

(ii) Where the statement of one defendant contains a portion which exculpates him or her and partly implicates a co-defendant in the trial, the defendant making the statement has the right to insist that everything relevant which is exculpatory goes before the jury. In such a case the judge must be consulted about how best to protect the position of the co-defendant.

16C.9 If it becomes necessary for either party to access the master copy of the audio or video recording, they should give notice to the other party and follow the procedure in PACE Code E at section 6.

16C.10 If there is a challenge to the integrity of the master recording, notice and particulars should be given to the court and to the prosecution by the defence as soon as is practicable. The court may then, at its discretion, order a case management hearing or give such other directions as may be appropriate.

16C.11 If an audio or video recording is to be adduced during proceedings before the Crown Court, it should be produced and proved in a witness statement by the interviewing officer or any other officer who was present at the interview at which the recording was made. The prosecution should ensure that the witness is available to attend court if required by the defence in the usual way.

16C.12 It is the responsibility of the prosecution to ensure that there is a person available to operate any audio or video equipment needed during the course of the proceedings. Subject to their other responsibilities, the court staff may be able to assist.

16C.13 If either party wishes to present audio or video evidence, that party must ensure, in advance of the hearing, that the evidence is in a format that is compatible with the court's equipment, and that the material to be used does in fact function properly in the relevant court room.

16C.14 In order to avoid the necessity for the court to listen to or watch lengthy or irrelevant material before the relevant part of a recording is reached, counsel shall indicate to the equipment operator those parts of a recording which it may be necessary to play. Such an indication should, so far as possible, be expressed in terms of the time track or other identifying process used by the interviewing police force and should be given in time for the operator to have located those parts by the appropriate point in the trial.

16C.15 Once a trial has begun, if, by reason of faulty preparation or for some other cause, the procedures above have not been properly complied with, and an application is made to amend the record of interview or transcript or to edit the recording, as the case may be, thereby making necessary an adjournment for the work to be carried out, the court may make at its discretion an appropriate award of costs.

16C.16 Where a case is listed for hearing on a date which falls within the time limits set out above, it is the responsibility of the parties to ensure that all the necessary steps are taken to comply with this Practice Direction within such shorter period as is available.

Criminal Procedure Rules Part 17 Witness Summonses, Warrants and Orders

R-143 **When this Part applies**

17.1 (1) This Part applies in magistrates' courts and in the Crown Court where—
(a) a party wants the court to issue a witness summons, warrant or order under—
(i) section 97 of the Magistrates' Courts Act 1980,
(ii) paragraph 4 of Schedule 3 to the Crime and Disorder Act 1998,
(iii) section 2 of the Criminal Procedure (Attendance of Witnesses) Act 1965, or
(iv) section 7 of the Bankers' Books Evidence Act 1879;
(b) the court considers the issue of such a summons, warrant or order on its own initiative as if a party had applied; or
(c) one of those listed in rule 17.7 wants the court to withdraw such a summons, warrant or order.
(2) A reference to a 'witness' in this Part is a reference to a person to whom such a summons, warrant or order is directed.

R-144 **Issue etc. of summons, warrant or order with or without a hearing**

17.2 (1) The court may issue or withdraw a witness summons, warrant or order with or without a hearing.
(2) A hearing under this Part must be in private unless the court otherwise directs.

R-145 **Application for summons, warrant or order: general rules**

17.3 (1) A party who wants the court to issue a witness summons, warrant or order must apply as soon as practicable after becoming aware of the grounds for doing so.
(2) The party applying must—
(a) identify the proposed witness;
(b) explain—
(i) what evidence the proposed witness can give or produce,
(ii) why it is likely to be material evidence, and
(iii) why it would be in the interests of justice to issue a summons, order or warrant as appropriate.
(3) The application may be made orally unless—
(a) rule 17.5 applies; or
(b) the court otherwise directs.

R-146 **Written application: form and service**

17.4 (1) An application in writing under rule 17.3 must be in the form set out in the Practice Direction, containing the same declaration of truth as a witness statement.
(2) The party applying must serve the application—
(a) in every case, on the court officer and as directed by the court; and
(b) as required by rule 17.5, if that rule applies.

R-147 **Application for summons to produce a document, etc.: special rules**

17.5 (1) This rule applies to an application under rule 17.3 for a witness summons requiring the proposed witness—
(a) to produce in evidence a document or thing; or
(b) to give evidence about information apparently held in confidence, that relates to another person.
(2) The application must be in writing in the form required by rule 17.4.
(3) The party applying must serve the application—
(a) on the proposed witness, unless the court otherwise directs; and

(b) on one or more of the following, if the court so directs—
(i) a person to whom the proposed evidence relates,
(ii) another party.
(4) The court must not issue a witness summons where this rule applies unless—
(a) everyone served with the application has had at least 14 days in which to make representations, including representations about whether there should be a hearing of the application before the summons is issued; and
(b) the court is satisfied that it has been able to take adequate account of the duties and rights, including rights of confidentiality, of the proposed witness and of any person to whom the proposed evidence relates.
(5) This rule does not apply to an application for an order to produce in evidence a copy of an entry in a banker's book.

Application for summons to produce a document, etc.: court's assessment of relevance and confidentiality **R-148**

17.6 (1) This rule applies where a person served with an application for a witness summons requiring the proposed witness to produce in evidence a document or thing objects to its production on the ground that—
(a) it is not likely to be material evidence; or
(b) even if it is likely to be material evidence, the duties or rights, including rights of confidentiality, of the proposed witness or of any person to whom the document or thing relates, outweigh the reasons for issuing a summons.
(2) The court may require the proposed witness to make the document or thing available for the objection to be assessed.
(3) The court may invite—
(a) the proposed witness or any representative of the proposed witness; or
(b) a person to whom the document or thing relates or any representative of such a person, to help the court assess the objection.

Application to withdraw a summons, warrant or order **R-149**

17.7 (1) The court may withdraw a witness summons, warrant or order if one of the following applies for it to be withdrawn—
(a) the party who applied for it, on the ground that it no longer is needed;
(b) the witness, on the grounds that—
(i) he was not aware of any application for it, and
(ii) he cannot give or produce evidence likely to be material evidence, or
(iii) even if he can, his duties or rights, including rights of confidentiality, or those of any person to whom the evidence relates, outweigh the reasons for the issue of the summons, warrant or order; or
(c) any person to whom the proposed evidence relates, on the grounds that—
(i) he was not aware of any application for it, and
(ii) that evidence is not likely to be material evidence, or
(iii) even if it is, his duties or rights, including rights of confidentiality, or those of the witness, outweigh the reasons for the issue of the summons, warrant or order.
(2) A person applying under the rule must—
(a) apply in writing as soon as practicable after becoming aware of the grounds for doing so, explaining why he wants the summons, warrant or order to be withdrawn; and
(b) serve the application on the court officer and as appropriate on—
(i) the witness,
(ii) the party who applied for the summons, warrant or order, and
(iii) any other person who he knows was served with the application for the summons, warrant or order.
(3) Rule 17.6 applies to an application under this rule that concerns a document or thing to be produced in evidence.

Court's power to vary requirements under this Part **R-150**

17.8 (1) The court may—
(a) shorten or extend (even after it has expired) a time limit under this Part; and
(b) where a rule or direction requires an application under this Part to be in writing, allow that application to be made orally instead.

(2) Someone who wants the court to allow an application to be made orally under paragraph (1)(b) of this rule must—
(a) give as much notice as the urgency of his application permits to those on whom he would otherwise have served an application in writing; and
(b) in doing so explain the reasons for the application and for wanting the court to consider it orally.

Criminal Practice Directions Part 17 Witness Summonses, Warrants and Orders

PD-37 **CPD V Evidence 17A: Wards of Court and Children Subject to Current Family Proceedings**

17A.1 Where police wish to interview a child who is subject to current family proceedings, leave of the Family Court is only required where such an interview may lead to a child disclosing information confidential to those proceedings and not otherwise available to the police under Working Together to Safeguard Children (March 2013), a guide to inter-agency working to safeguard and promote the welfare of children: www.workingtogetheronline.co.uk/chapters/contents.html

17A.2 Where exceptionally the child to be interviewed or called as a witness in criminal proceedings is a Ward of Court then the leave of the court which made the wardship order will be required.

17A.3 Any application for leave in respect of any such child must be made to the court in which the relevant family proceedings are continuing and must be made on notice to the parents, any actual carer (e.g., relative or foster parent) and, in care proceedings, to the local authority and the guardian. In private proceedings the Family Court Reporter (if appointed) should be notified.

17A.4 If the police need to interview the child without the knowledge of another party (usually a parent or carer), they may make the application for leave without giving notice to that party.

17A.5 Where leave is given the order should ordinarily give leave for any number of interviews that may be required. However, anything beyond that actually authorised will require a further application.

17A.6 Exceptionally the police may have to deal with complaints by or allegations against such a child immediately without obtaining the leave of the court as, for example:
(a) a serious offence against a child (like rape) where immediate medical examination and collection of evidence is required; or
(b) where the child is to be interviewed as a suspect.

When any such action is necessary, the police should, in respect of each and every interview, notify the parents and other carer (if any) and the Family Court Reporter (if appointed). In care proceedings the local authority and guardian should be notified. The police must comply with all relevant Codes of Practice when conducting any such interview.

17A.7 The Family Court should be appraised of the position at the earliest reasonable opportunity by one of the notified parties and should thereafter be kept informed of any criminal proceedings.

17A.8 No evidence or document in the family proceedings or information about the proceedings should be disclosed into criminal proceedings without the leave of the Family Court.

Criminal Procedure Rules Part 18 Measures to Assist a Witness or Defendant to Give Evidence

General rules

R-151 **When this Part applies**

18.1 This Part applies—
(a) where the court can give a direction (a 'special measures direction'), under section 19 of the Youth Justice and Criminal Evidence Act 1999, on an application or on its own initiative, for any of the following measures—
(i) preventing a witness from seeing the defendant (section 23 of the 1999 Act),
(ii) allowing a witness to give evidence by live link (section 24 of the 1999 Act),
(iii) hearing a witness' evidence in private (section 25 of the 1999 Act),
(iv) dispensing with the wearing of wigs and gowns (section 26 of the 1999 Act),
(v) admitting video recorded evidence (sections 27 and 28 of the 1999 Act),
(vi) questioning a witness through an intermediary (section 29 of the 1999 Act),
(vii) using a device to help a witness communicate (section 30 of the 1999 Act);
(b) where the court can vary or discharge such a direction, under section 20 of the 1999 Act;
(c) where the court can give, vary or discharge a direction (a 'defendant's evidence direction') for a defendant to give evidence—
(i) by live link, under section 33A of the 1999 Act, or
(ii) through an intermediary, under sections 33BA and 33BB of the 1999 Act;

(d) where the court can—
   (i) make a witness anonymity order, under section 86 of the Coroners and Justice Act 2009, or
   (ii) vary or discharge such an order, under section 91, 92 or 93 of the 2009 Act;
(e) where the court can give or discharge a direction (a 'live link direction'), on an application or on its own initiative, for a witness to give evidence by live link under—
   (i) section 32 of the Criminal Justice Act 1988, or
   (ii) sections 51 and 52 of the Criminal Justice Act 2003;
(f) where the court can exercise any other power it has to give, vary or discharge a direction for a measure to help a witness give evidence.

Meaning of 'witness' R-152

18.2 In this Part, 'witness' means anyone (other than a defendant) for whose benefit an application, direction or order is made.

Making an application for a direction or order R-153

18.3 A party who wants the court to exercise its power to give or make a direction or order must—
(a) apply in writing as soon as reasonably practicable, and in any event not more than—
   (i) 28 days after the defendant pleads not guilty, in a magistrates' court, or
   (ii) 14 days after the defendant pleads not guilty, in the Crown Court; and
(b) serve the application on—
   (i) the court officer, and
   (ii) each other party.

Decisions and reasons R-154

18.4 (1) A party who wants to introduce the evidence of a witness who is the subject of an application, direction or order must—
   (a) inform the witness of the court's decision as soon as reasonably practicable; and
   (b) explain to the witness the arrangements that as a result will be made for him or her to give evidence.
(2) The court must announce, at a hearing in public before the witness gives evidence, the reasons for a decision—
   (a) to give, make, vary or discharge a direction or order; or
   (b) to refuse to do so.

Court's power to vary requirements under this Part R-155

18.5 (1) The court may—
   (a) shorten or extend (even after it has expired) a time limit under this Part; and
   (b) allow an application or representations to be made in a different form to one set out in the Practice Direction, or to be made orally.
(2) A person who wants an extension of time must—
   (a) apply when serving the application or representations for which it is needed; and
   (b) explain the delay.

Custody of documents R-156

18.6 Unless the court otherwise directs, the court officer may—
(a) keep a written application or representations; or
(b) arrange for the whole or any part to be kept by some other appropriate person, subject to any conditions that the court may impose.

Declaration by intermediary R-157

18.7 (1) This rule applies where—
   (a) a video recorded interview with a witness is conducted through an intermediary;
   (b) the court directs the examination of a witness or defendant through an intermediary.
(2) An intermediary must make a declaration—
   (a) before such an interview begins;
   (b) before the examination begins (even if such an interview with the witness was conducted through the same intermediary).
(3) The declaration must be in these terms—
'I solemnly, sincerely and truly declare [*or* I swear by Almighty God] that I will well and faithfully communicate questions and answers and make true explanation of all matters and things as shall be required of me according to the best of my skill and understanding.'

Special measures directions

R-158 **Exercise of court's powers**

18.8 The court may decide whether to give, vary or discharge a special measures direction—
(a) at a hearing, in public or in private, or without a hearing;
(b) in a party's absence, if that party—
(i) applied for the direction, variation or discharge, or
(ii) has had at least 14 days in which to make representations.

R-159 **Special measures direction for a young witness**

18.9 (1) This rule applies where, under section 21 or section 22 of the Youth Justice and Criminal Evidence Act 1999, the primary rule requires the court to give a direction for a special measure to assist a child witness or a qualifying witness—
(a) on an application, if one is made; or
(b) on the court's own initiative, in any other case.
(2) A party who wants to introduce the evidence of such a witness must as soon as reasonably practicable—
(a) notify the court that the witness is eligible for assistance;
(b) provide the court with any information that the court may need to assess the witness' views, if the witness does not want the primary rule to apply; and
(c) serve any video recorded evidence on—
(i) the court officer, and
(ii) each other party.

R-160 **Content of application for a special measures direction**

18.10 An applicant for a special measures direction must—
(a) explain how the witness is eligible for assistance;
(b) explain why special measures would be likely to improve the quality of the witness' evidence;
(c) propose the measure or measures that in the applicant's opinion would be likely to maximise, so far as practicable, the quality of that evidence;
(d) report any views that the witness has expressed about—
(i) his or her eligibility for assistance,
(ii) the likelihood that special measures would improve the quality of his or her evidence, and
(iii) the measure or measures proposed by the applicant;
(e) in a case in which a child witness or a qualifying witness does not want the primary rule to apply, provide any information that the court may need to assess the witness' views;
(f) in a case in which the applicant proposes that the witness should give evidence by live link—
(i) identify someone to accompany the witness while the witness gives evidence,
(ii) name that person, if possible, and
(iii) explain why that person would be an appropriate companion for the witness, including the witness' own views;
(g) in a case in which the applicant proposes the admission of video recorded evidence, identify—
(i) the date and duration of the recording,
(ii) which part the applicant wants the court to admit as evidence, if the applicant does not want the court to admit all of it;
(h) attach any other material on which the applicant relies; and
(i) if the applicant wants a hearing, ask for one, and explain why it is needed.

R-161 **Application to vary or discharge a special measures direction**

18.11 (1) A party who wants the court to vary or discharge a special measures direction must—
(a) apply in writing, as soon as reasonably practicable after becoming aware of the grounds for doing so; and
(b) serve the application on—
(i) the court officer, and
(ii) each other party.
(2) The applicant must—
(a) explain what material circumstances have changed since the direction was given (or last varied, if applicable);

(b) explain why the direction should be varied or discharged; and
(c) ask for a hearing, if the applicant wants one, and explain why it is needed.

Application containing information withheld from another party **R-162**

18.12 (1) This rule applies where—
(a) an applicant serves an application for a special measures direction, or for its variation or discharge; and
(b) the application includes information that the applicant thinks ought not be revealed to another party.

(2) The applicant must—
(a) omit that information from the part of the application that is served on that other party;
(b) mark the other part to show that, unless the court otherwise directs, it is only for the court; and
(c) in that other part, explain why the applicant has withheld that information from that other party.

(3) Any hearing of an application to which this rule applies—
(a) must be in private, unless the court otherwise directs; and
(b) if the court so directs, may be, wholly or in part, in the absence of a party from whom information has been withheld.

(4) At any hearing of an application to which this rule applies—
(a) the general rule is that the court must consider, in the following sequence—
(i) representations first by the applicant and then by each other party, in all the parties' presence, and then
(ii) further representations by the applicant, in the absence of a party from whom information has been withheld; but
(b) the court may direct other arrangements for the hearing.

Representations in response **R-163**

18.13 (1) This rule applies where a party wants to make representations about—
(a) an application for a special measures direction;
(b) an application for the variation or discharge of such a direction; or
(c) a direction, variation or discharge that the court proposes on its own initiative.

(2) Such a party must—
(a) serve the representations on—
(i) the court officer, and
(ii) each other party;
(b) do so not more than 14 days after, as applicable—
(i) service of the application, or
(ii) notice of the direction, variation or discharge that the court proposes; and
(c) ask for a hearing, if that party wants one, and explain why it is needed.

(3) Where representations include information that the person making them thinks ought not be revealed to another party, that person must—
(a) omit that information from the representations served on that other party;
(b) mark the information to show that, unless the court otherwise directs, it is only for the court; and
(c) with that information include an explanation of why it has been withheld from that other party.

(4) Representations against a special measures direction must explain, as appropriate—
(a) why the witness is not eligible for assistance; or
(b) if the witness is eligible for assistance, why—
(i) no special measure would be likely to improve the quality of the witness' evidence,
(ii) the proposed measure or measures would not be likely to maximise, so far as practicable, the quality of the witness' evidence, or
(iii) the proposed measure or measures might tend to inhibit the effective testing of that evidence;
(c) in a case in which the admission of video recorded evidence is proposed, why it would not be in the interests of justice for the recording, or part of it, to be admitted as evidence.

(5) Representations against the variation or discharge of a special measures direction must explain why it should not be varied or discharged.

Defendant's evidence directions

R-164 Exercise of court's powers

18.14 The court may decide whether to give, vary or discharge a defendant's evidence direction—
(a) at a hearing, in public or in private, or without a hearing;
(b) in a party's absence, if that party—
(i) applied for the direction, variation or discharge, or
(ii) has had at least 14 days in which to make representations.

R-165 Content of application for a defendant's evidence direction

18.15 An applicant for a defendant's evidence direction must—
(a) explain how the proposed direction meets the conditions prescribed by the Youth Justice and Criminal Evidence Act 1999;
(b) in a case in which the applicant proposes that the defendant give evidence by live link—
(i) identify a person to accompany the defendant while the defendant gives evidence, and
(ii) explain why that person is appropriate;
(c) ask for a hearing, if the applicant wants one, and explain why it is needed.

R-166 Application to vary or discharge a defendant's evidence direction

18.16 (1) A party who wants the court to vary or discharge a defendant's evidence direction must—
(a) apply in writing, as soon as reasonably practicable after becoming aware of the grounds for doing so; and
(b) serve the application on—
(i) the court officer, and
(ii) each other party.
(2) The applicant must—
(a) on an application to discharge a live link direction, explain why it is in the interests of justice to do so;
(b) on an application to discharge a direction for an intermediary, explain why it is no longer necessary in order to ensure that the defendant receives a fair trial;
(c) on an application to vary a direction for an intermediary, explain why it is necessary for the direction to be varied in order to ensure that the defendant receives a fair trial; and
(d) ask for a hearing, if the applicant wants one, and explain why it is needed.

R-167 Representations in response

18.17 (1) This rule applies where a party wants to make representations about—
(a) an application for a defendant's evidence direction;
(b) an application for the variation or discharge of such a direction; or
(c) a direction, variation or discharge that the court proposes on its own initiative.
(2) Such a party must—
(a) serve the representations on—
(i) the court officer, and
(ii) each other party;
(b) do so not more than 14 days after, as applicable—
(i) service of the application, or
(ii) notice of the direction, variation or discharge that the court proposes; and
(c) ask for a hearing, if that party wants one, and explain why it is needed.
(3) Representations against a direction, variation or discharge must explain why the conditions prescribed by the Youth Justice and Criminal Evidence Act 1999 are not met.

Witness anonymity orders

R-168 Exercise of court's powers

18.18 (1) The court may decide whether to make, vary or discharge a witness anonymity order—
(a) at a hearing (which must be in private, unless the court otherwise directs), or without a hearing (unless any party asks for one);
(b) in the absence of a defendant.
(2) The court must not exercise its power to make, vary or discharge a witness anonymity order, or to refuse to do so—
(a) before or during the trial, unless each party has had an opportunity to make representations;
(b) on an appeal by the defendant to which applies Part 34 (Appeal to the Crown Court) or Part 39 (Appeal to the Court of Appeal about conviction or sentence), unless in each party's case—
(i) that party has had an opportunity to make representations, or

(ii) the appeal court is satisfied that it is not reasonably practicable to communicate with that party;

(c) after the trial and any such appeal are over, unless in the case of each party and the witness—

(i) each has had an opportunity to make representations, or

(ii) the court is satisfied that it is not reasonably practicable to communicate with that party or witness.

Content and conduct of application for a witness anonymity order R-169

18.19 (1) An applicant for a witness anonymity order must—

(a) include in the application nothing that might reveal the witness' identity;

(b) describe the measures proposed by the applicant;

(c) explain how the proposed order meets the conditions prescribed by section 88 of the Coroners and Justice Act 2009;

(d) explain why no measures other than those proposed will suffice, such as—

(i) an admission of the facts that would be proved by the witness,

(ii) an order restricting public access to the trial,

(iii) reporting restrictions, in particular under sections 45, 45A or 46 of the Youth Justice and Criminal Evidence Act 1999,

(iv) a direction for a special measure under section 19 of the Youth Justice and Criminal Evidence Act 1999,

(v) introduction of the witness' written statement as hearsay evidence, under section 116 of the Criminal Justice Act 2003, or

(vi) arrangements for the protection of the witness;

(e) attach to the application—

(i) a witness statement setting out the proposed evidence, edited in such a way as not to reveal the witness' identity,

(ii) where the prosecutor is the applicant, any further prosecution evidence to be served, and any further prosecution material to be disclosed under the Criminal Procedure and Investigations Act 1996, similarly edited, and

(iii) any defence statement that has been served, or as much information as may be available to the applicant that gives particulars of the defence; and

(f) ask for a hearing, if the applicant wants one.

(2) At any hearing of the application, the applicant must—

(a) identify the witness to the court, unless at the prosecutor's request the court otherwise directs; and

(b) present to the court, unless it otherwise directs—

(i) the unedited witness statement from which the edited version has been prepared,

(ii) where the prosecutor is the applicant, the unedited version of any further prosecution evidence or material from which an edited version has been prepared, and

(iii) such further material as the applicant relies on to establish that the proposed order meets the conditions prescribed by section 88 of the 2009 Act.

(3) At any such hearing—

(a) the general rule is that the court must consider, in the following sequence—

(i) representations first by the applicant and then by each other party, in all the parties' presence, and then

(ii) information withheld from a defendant, and further representations by the applicant, in the absence of any (or any other) defendant; but

(b) the court may direct other arrangements for the hearing.

(4) Before the witness gives evidence, the applicant must identify the witness to the court—

(a) if not already done;

(b) without revealing the witness' identity to any other party or person; and

(c) unless at the prosecutor's request the court otherwise directs.

Duty of court officer to notify the Director of Public Prosecutions R-170

18.20 The court officer must notify the Director of Public Prosecutions of an application, unless the prosecutor is, or acts on behalf of, a public authority.

Application to vary or discharge a witness anonymity order R-171

18.21 (1) A party who wants the court to vary or discharge a witness anonymity order, or a witness who wants the court to do so when the case is over, must—

(a) apply in writing, as soon as reasonably practicable after becoming aware of the grounds for doing so; and

(b) serve the application on—
(i) the court officer, and
(ii) each other party.
(2) The applicant must—
(a) explain what material circumstances have changed since the order was made (or last varied, if applicable);
(b) explain why the order should be varied or discharged, taking account of the conditions for making an order; and
(c) ask for a hearing, if the applicant wants one.
(3) Where an application includes information that the applicant thinks might reveal the witness' identity, the applicant must—
(a) omit that information from the application that is served on a defendant;
(b) mark the information to show that it is only for the court and the prosecutor (if the prosecutor is not the applicant); and
(c) with that information include an explanation of why it has been withheld.
(4) Where a party applies to vary or discharge a witness anonymity order after the trial and any appeal are over, the party who introduced the witness' evidence must serve the application on the witness.

R-172 **Representations in response**

18.22 (1) This rule applies where a party or, where the case is over, a witness, wants to make representations about—
(a) an application for a witness anonymity order;
(b) an application for the variation or discharge of such an order; or
(c) a variation or discharge that the court proposes on its own initiative.
(2) Such a party or witness must—
(a) serve the representations on—
(i) the court officer, and
(ii) each other party;
(b) do so not more than 14 days after, as applicable—
(i) service of the application, or
(ii) notice of the variation or discharge that the court proposes; and
(c) ask for a hearing, if that party or witness wants one.
(3) Where representations include information that the person making them thinks might reveal the witness' identity, that person must—
(a) omit that information from the representations served on a defendant;
(b) mark the information to show that it is only for the court (and for the prosecutor, if relevant); and
(c) with that information include an explanation of why it has been withheld.
(4) Representations against a witness anonymity order must explain why the conditions for making the order are not met.
(5) Representations against the variation or discharge of such an order must explain why it would not be appropriate to vary or discharge it, taking account of the conditions for making an order.
(6) A prosecutor's representations in response to an application by a defendant must include all information available to the prosecutor that is relevant to the conditions and considerations specified by sections 88 and 89 of the Coroners and Justice Act 2009.

Live link directions

R-173 **Exercise of court's powers**

18.23 The court may decide whether to give or discharge a live link direction—
(a) at a hearing, in public or in private, or without a hearing;
(b) in a party's absence, if that party—
(i) applied for the direction or discharge, or
(ii) has had at least 14 days in which to make representations in response to an application by another party.

R-174 **Content of application for a live link direction**

18.24 An applicant for a live link direction must—
(a) unless the court otherwise directs, identify the place from which the witness will give evidence;
(b) if that place is in the United Kingdom, explain why it would be in the interests of the efficient or effective administration of justice for the witness to give evidence by live link;

(c) if the applicant wants the witness to be accompanied by another person while giving evidence—
(i) name that person, if possible, and
(ii) explain why it is appropriate for the witness to be accompanied;
(d) ask for a hearing, if the applicant wants one, and explain why it is needed.

Application to discharge a live link direction R-175

18.25 (1) A party who wants the court to discharge a live link direction must—
(a) apply in writing, as soon as reasonably practicable after becoming aware of the grounds for doing so; and
(b) serve the application on—
(i) the court officer, and
(ii) each other party.
(2) The applicant must—
(a) explain what material circumstances have changed since the direction was given;
(b) explain why it is in the interests of justice to discharge the direction; and
(c) ask for a hearing, if the applicant wants one, and explain why it is needed.

Representations in response R-176

18.26 (1) This rule applies where a party wants to make representations about an application for a live link direction or for the discharge of such a direction.
(2) Such a party must—
(a) serve the representations on—
(i) the court officer, and
(ii) each other party;
(b) do so not more than 14 days after service of the application; and—
(c) ask for a hearing, if that party wants one, and explain why it is needed.
(3) Representations against a direction or discharge must explain, as applicable, why the conditions prescribed by the Criminal Justice Act 1988 or the Criminal Justice Act 2003 are not met.

Criminal Practice Directions Part 18 Measures to Assist a Witness or Defendant to Give Evidence

CPD V Evidence 18A: Measures to Assist a Witness or Defendant to give Evidence PD-38

18A.1 For special measures applications, the procedures at CrimPR Part 18 should be followed. However, assisting a vulnerable witness to give evidence is not merely a matter of ordering the appropriate measure. Further directions about vulnerable people in the courts, ground rules hearings and intermediaries are given in paragraphs I 3D to 3G.

18A.2 Special measures need not be considered or ordered in isolation. The needs of the individual witness should be ascertained, and a combination of special measures may be appropriate. For example, if a witness who is to give evidence by live link wishes, screens can be used to shield the live link screen from the defendant and the public, as would occur if screens were being used for a witness giving evidence in the court room.

CPD V Evidence 18B: Witnesses giving Evidence by Live Link PD-39

18B.1 A special measures direction for the witness to give evidence by live link may also provide for a specified person to accompany the witness (CrimPR 18.10(f)). In determining who this should be, the court must have regard to the wishes of the witness. The presence of a supporter is designed to provide emotional support to the witness, helping reduce the witness's anxiety and stress and contributing to the ability to give best evidence. It is preferable for the direction to be made well before the trial begins and to ensure that the designated person is available on the day of the witness's testimony so as to provide certainty for the witness.

18B.2 An increased degree of flexibility is appropriate as to who can act as supporter. This can be anyone known to and trusted by the witness who is not a party to the proceedings and has no detailed knowledge of the evidence in the case. The supporter may be a member of the Witness Service but need not be an usher or court official. Someone else may be appropriate.

18B.3 The usher should continue to be available both to assist the witness and the witness supporter, and to ensure that the court's requirements are properly complied with in the live link room.

18B.4 In order to be able to express an informed view about special measures, the witness is entitled to practise speaking using the live link (and to see screens in place). Simply being shown the room and equipment is inadequate for this purpose.

18B.5 If, with the agreement of the court, the witness has chosen not to give evidence by live link but to do so in the court room, it may still be appropriate for a witness supporter to be selected in the same way, and for the supporter to sit alongside the witness while the witness is giving evidence.

PD-40 **CPD V Evidence 18C: Visually Recorded Interviews: Memory Refreshing and Watching at a Different Time from the Jury**

18C.1 Witnesses are entitled to refresh their memory from their statement or visually recorded interview. The court should enquire at the PTPH or other case management hearing about arrangements for memory refreshing. The witness's first viewing of the visually recorded interview can be distressing or distracting. It should not be seen for the first time immediately before giving evidence. Depending upon the age and vulnerability of the witness several competing issues have to be considered and it may be that the assistance of the intermediary is needed to establish exactly how memory refreshing should be managed.

18C.2 If the interview is ruled inadmissible, the court must decide what constitutes an acceptable alternative method of memory refreshing.

18C.3 Decisions about how, when and where refreshing should take place should be court-led and made on a case-by-case basis in respect of each witness. General principles to be addressed include:

i. the venue for viewing. The delicate balance between combining the court familiarisation visit and watching the DVD, and having them on two separate occasions, needs to be considered in respect of each witness as combining the two may lead to 'information overload'. Refreshing need not necessarily take place within the court building but may be done, for example, at the police ABE suite;
ii. requiring that any viewing is monitored by a person (usually the officer in the case) who will report to the court about anything said by the witness;
iii. whether it is necessary for the witness to see the DVD more than once for the purpose of refreshing. The court will need to ask the advice of the intermediary, if any, with respect to this;
iv. arrangements, if the witness will not watch the DVD at the same time as the trial bench or judge and jury, for the witness to watch it before attending to be cross examined, (depending upon their ability to retain information this may be the day before).

18C.4 There is no legal requirement that the witness should watch the interview at the same time as the trial bench or jury. Increasingly, this is arranged to occur at a different time, with the advantages that breaks can be taken as needed without disrupting the trial, and cross-examination starts while the witness is fresh. An intermediary may be present to facilitate communication but should not act as the independent person designated to take a note and report to the court if anything is said. Where the viewing takes place at a different time from that of the jury, the witness is sworn just before cross-examination, asked if he or she has watched the interview and if its contents are 'true' (or other words tailored to the witness's understanding).

PD-41 **CPD V Evidence 18D: Witness Anonymity Orders**

18D.1 This direction supplements CrimPR 18.18 to 18.22, which governs the procedure to be followed on an application for a witness anonymity order. The court's power to make such an order is conferred by the Coroners and Justice Act 2009 (in this section, 'the Act'); section 87 of the Act provides specific relevant powers and obligations.

18D.2 As the Court of Appeal stated in *R v Mayers and Others* [2008] EWCA Crim 2989, [2009] 1 WLR 1915, [2009] 1 Cr App R 30 and emphasised again in *R v Donovan and Kafunda* [2012] EWCA Crim 2749, unreported, 'a witness anonymity order is to be regarded as a special measure of the last practicable resort': Lord Chief Justice, Lord Judge. In making such an application, the prosecution's obligations of disclosure 'go much further than the ordinary duties of disclosure' (*R v Mayers*); reference should be made to the Judicial Protocol on Disclosure, see paragraph IV 15A.1.

Case management

18D.3 Where such an application is proposed, with the parties' active assistance the court should set a realistic timetable, in accordance with the duties imposed by CrimPR 3.2 and 3.3. Where possible, the trial judge should determine the application, and any hearing should be attended by the parties' trial advocates.

Service of evidence and disclosure of prosecution material pending an application

18D.4 Where the prosecutor proposes an application for a witness anonymity order, it is not necessary for that application to have been determined before the proposed evidence is served. In most cases, an early indication of what that evidence will be if an order is made will be consistent with a party's duties under CrimPR 1.2 and 3.3. The prosecutor should serve with the other prosecution evidence a witness statement setting out the proposed evidence, redacted in such a way as to prevent disclosure of the witness' identity, as permitted by section 87(4) of the Act. Likewise the prosecutor should serve with other prosecution material disclosed under the Criminal Procedure and Investigations Act 1996 any such material appertaining to the witness, similarly redacted.

The application

18D.5 An application for a witness anonymity order should be made as early as possible and within the period for which CrimPR 18.3 provides. The application, and any hearing of it, must comply with the requirements of that rule and with those of rule 18.19. In accordance with CrimPR 1.2 and 3.3, the applicant must provide the court with all available information relevant to the considerations to which the Act requires a court to have regard.

Response to the application

18D.6 A party upon whom an application for a witness anonymity order is served must serve a response in accordance with CrimPR 18.22. That period may be extended or shortened in the court's discretion: CrimPR 18.5.

18D.7 To avoid the risk of injustice, a respondent, whether the Prosecution or a defendant, must actively assist the court. If not already done, a respondent defendant should serve a defence statement under section 5 or 6 of the Criminal Procedure and Investigations Act 1996, so that the court is fully informed of what is in issue. When a defendant makes an application for a witness anonymity order the prosecutor should consider the continuing duty to disclose material under section 7A of the Criminal Procedure and Investigations Act 1996; therefore a prosecutor's response should include confirmation that that duty has been considered. Great care should be taken to ensure that nothing disclosed contains anything that might reveal the witness' identity. A respondent prosecutor should provide the court with all available information relevant to the considerations to which the Act requires a court to have regard, whether or not that information falls to be disclosed under the 1996 Act.

Determination of the application

18D.8 All parties must have an opportunity to make oral representations to the court on an application for a witness anonymity order: section 87(6) of the Act. However, a hearing may not be needed if none is sought: CrimPR 18.18(1) (a). Where, for example, the witness is an investigator who is recognisable by the defendant but known only by an assumed name, and there is no likelihood that the witness' credibility will be in issue, then the court may indicate a provisional decision and invite representations within a defined period, usually 14 days, including representations about whether there should be a hearing. In such a case, where the parties do not object the court may make an order without a hearing. Or where the court provisionally considers an application to be misconceived, an applicant may choose to withdraw it without requiring a hearing. Where the court directs a hearing of the application then it should allow adequate time for service of the representations in response.

18D.9 The hearing of an application for a witness anonymity order usually should be in private: CrimPR 18.18(1)(a). The court has power to hear a party in the absence of a defendant and that defendant's representatives: section 87(7) of the Act and rule 18.18(1)(b). In the Crown Court, a recording of the proceedings will be made, in accordance with CrimPR 5.5. The Crown Court officer must treat such a recording in the same way as the recording of an application for a public interest ruling. It must be kept in secure conditions, and the arrangements made by the Crown Court officer for any transcription must impose restrictions that correspond with those under CrimPR 5.5(2).

18D.10 Where confidential supporting information is presented to the court before the last stage of the hearing, the court may prefer not to read that information until that last stage.

18D.11 The court may adjourn the hearing at any stage, and should do so if its duty under CrimPR 3.2 so requires.

18D.12 On a prosecutor's application, the court is likely to be assisted by the attendance of a senior investigator or other person of comparable authority who is familiar with the case.

18D.13 During the last stage of the hearing it is essential that the court test thoroughly the information supplied in confidence in order to satisfy itself that the conditions prescribed by the Act are met. At that stage, if the court concludes that this is the only way in which it can satisfy itself as to a relevant condition or consideration, exceptionally it may invite the applicant to present the proposed witness to be questioned by the court. Any such questioning should be carried out at such a time, and the witness brought to the court in such a way, as to prevent disclosure of his or her identity.

18D.14 The court may ask the Attorney General to appoint special counsel to assist. However, it must be kept in mind that, 'Such an appointment will always be exceptional, never automatic; a course of last and never first resort. It should not be ordered unless and until the trial judge is satisfied that no other course will adequately meet the overriding requirement of fairness to the defendant': *R v H* [2004] UKHL 3, [2004] 2 AC 134 (at paragraph 22), [2004] 2 Cr App R 10. Whether to accede to such a request is a matter for the Attorney General, and adequate time should be allowed for the consideration of such a request.

18D.15 The Court of Appeal in *R v Mayers* 'emphasise[d] that all three conditions, A, B and C, must be met before the jurisdiction to make a witness anonymity order arises. Each is mandatory. Each is distinct.' The Court also noted that if there is more than one anonymous witness in a case any link, and the nature of any link, between the witnesses should be investigated: 'questions of possible improper collusion between them, or cross-contamination of one another, should be addressed.'

18D.16 Following a hearing the court should announce its decision on an application for a witness anonymity order in the parties' presence and in public: CrimPR 18.4(2). The court should give such reasons as it is possible to give without revealing the witness' identity. In the Crown Court, the court will be conscious that reasons given in public may be reported and reach the jury. Consequently, the court should ensure that nothing in its decision or its reasons could undermine any warning it may give jurors under section 90(2) of the Act. A record of the reasons must be kept. In the Crown Court, the announcement of those reasons will be recorded.

Order

18D.17 Where the court makes a witness anonymity order, it is essential that the measures to be taken are clearly specified in a written record of that order approved by the court and issued on its behalf. An order made in a magistrates' court must be recorded in the court register, in accordance with CrimPR 5.4.

18D.18 Self-evidently, the written record of the order must not disclose the identity of the witness to whom it applies. However, it is essential that there be maintained some means of establishing a clear correlation between witness and order, and especially where in the same proceedings witness anonymity orders are made in respect of more than one witness, specifying different measures in respect of each. Careful preservation of the application for the order, including the confidential part, ordinarily will suffice for this purpose.

Discharge or variation of the order

18D.19 Section 91 of the Act allows the court to discharge or vary a witness anonymity order: on application, if there has been a material change of circumstances since the order was made or since any previous variation of it; or on its own initiative. CrimPR 18.21 allows the parties to apply for the variation of a pre-trial direction where circumstances have changed.

18D.20 The court should keep under review the question of whether the conditions for making an order are met. In addition, consistently with the parties' duties under CrimPR 1.2 and 3.3, it is incumbent on each, and in particular on the applicant for the order, to keep the need for it under review.

18D.21 Where the court considers the discharge or variation of an order, the procedure that it adopts should be appropriate to the circumstances. As a general rule, that procedure should approximate to the procedure for determining an application for an order. The court may need to hear further representations by the applicant for the order in the absence of a respondent defendant and that defendant's representatives.

Retention of confidential material

18D.22 If retained by the court, confidential material must be stored in secure conditions by the court officer. Alternatively, subject to such directions as the court may give, such material may be committed to the safe keeping of the applicant or any other appropriate person in exercise of the powers conferred by CrimPR 18.6. If the material is released to any such person, the court should ensure that it will be available to the court at trial.

Criminal Procedure Rules Part 19 Expert Evidence

R-177 **When this Part applies**

19.1 (1) This Part applies where a party wants to introduce expert opinion evidence.

(2) A reference to an 'expert' in this Part is a reference to a person who is required to give or prepare expert evidence for the purpose of criminal proceedings, including evidence required to determine fitness to plead or for the purpose of sentencing.

Expert's duty to the court R-178

19.2 (1) An expert must help the court to achieve the overriding objective—

(a) by giving opinion which is—

(i) objective and unbiased, and

(ii) within the expert's area or areas of expertise; and

(b) by actively assisting the court in fulfilling its duty of case management under rule 3.2, in particular by—

(i) complying with directions made by the court, and

(iii) at once informing the court of any significant failure (by the expert or another) to take any step required by such a direction.

(2) This duty overrides any obligation to the person from whom the expert receives instructions or by whom the expert is paid.

(3) This duty includes obligations—

(a) to define the expert's area or areas of expertise—

(i) in the expert's report, and

(ii) when giving evidence in person;

(b) when giving evidence in person, to draw the court's attention to any question to which the answer would be outside the expert's area or areas of expertise; and

(c) inform all parties and the court if the expert's opinion changes from that contained in a report served as evidence or given in a statement.

Introduction of expert evidence R-179

19.3 (1) A party who wants another party to admit as fact a summary of an expert's conclusions must serve that summary—

(a) on the court officer and on each party from whom that admission is sought;

(b) as soon as practicable after the defendant whom it affects pleads not guilty.

(2) A party on whom such a summary is served must—

(a) serve a response stating—

(i) which, if any, of the expert's conclusions are admitted as fact, and

(ii) where a conclusion is not admitted, what are the disputed issues concerning that conclusion; and

(b) serve the response—

(i) on the court officer and on the party who served the summary,

(ii) as soon as practicable, and in any event not more than 14 days after service of the summary.

(3) A party who wants to introduce expert evidence otherwise than as admitted fact must—

(a) serve a report by the expert which complies with rule 19.4 (Content of expert's report) on—

(i) the court officer, and

(ii) each other party;

(b) serve the report as soon as practicable, and in any event with any application in support of which that party relies on that evidence;

(c) serve with the report notice of anything of which the party serving it is aware which might reasonably be thought capable of detracting substantially from the credibility of that expert;

(d) if another party so requires, give that party a copy of, or a reasonable opportunity to inspect—

(i) a record of any examination, measurement, test or experiment on which the expert's findings and opinion are based, or that were carried out in the course of reaching those findings and opinion, and

(ii) anything on which any such examination, measurement, test or experiment was carried out.

(4) Unless the parties otherwise agree or the court directs, a party may not—

(a) introduce expert evidence if that party has not complied with paragraph (3);

(b) introduce in evidence an expert report if the expert does not give evidence in person.

Content of expert's report R-180

19.4 (1) Where rule 19.3(3) applies, an expert's report must—

(a) give details of the expert's qualifications, relevant experience and accreditation;

(b) give details of any literature or other information which the expert has relied on in making the report;

(c) contain a statement setting out the substance of all facts given to the expert which are material to the opinions expressed in the report, or upon which those opinions are based;
(d) make clear which of the facts stated in the report are within the expert's own knowledge;
(e) say who carried out any examination, measurement, test or experiment which the expert has used for the report and—
(i) give the qualifications, relevant experience and accreditation of that person,
(ii) say whether or not the examination, measurement, test or experiment was carried out under the expert's supervision, and
(iii) summarise the findings on which the expert relies;
(f) where there is a range of opinion on the matters dealt with in the report—
(i) summarise the range of opinion, and
(ii) give reasons for the expert's own opinion;
(g) if the expert is not able to give an opinion without qualification, state the qualification;
(h) include such information as the court may need to decide whether the expert's opinion is sufficiently reliable to be admissible as evidence;
(i) contain a summary of the conclusions reached;
(j) contain a statement that the expert understands an expert's duty to the court, and has complied and will continue to comply with that duty; and
(k) contain the same declaration of truth as a witness statement.

R-181 **Expert to be informed of service of report**

19.5 A party who serves on another party or on the court a report by an expert must, at once, inform that expert of that fact.

R-182 **Pre-hearing discussion of expert evidence**

19.6 (1) This rule applies where more than one party wants to introduce expert evidence.
(2) The court may direct the experts to—
(a) discuss the expert issues in the proceedings; and
(b) prepare a statement for the court of the matters on which they agree and disagree, giving their reasons.
(3) Except for that statement, the content of that discussion must not be referred to without the court's permission.
(4) A party may not introduce expert evidence without the court's permission if the expert has not complied with a direction under this rule.

R-183 **Court's power to direct that evidence is to be given by a single joint expert**

19.7 (1) Where more than one defendant wants to introduce expert evidence on an issue at trial, the court may direct that the evidence on that issue is to be given by one expert only.
(2) Where the co-defendants cannot agree who should be the expert, the court may—
(a) select the expert from a list prepared or identified by them; or
(b) direct that the expert be selected in another way.

R-184 **Instructions to a single joint expert**

19.8 (1) Where the court gives a direction under rule 19.7 for a single joint expert to be used, each of the co-defendants may give instructions to the expert.
(2) A co-defendant who gives instructions to the expert must, at the same time, send a copy of the instructions to each other co-defendant.
(3) The court may give directions about—
(a) the payment of the expert's fees and expenses; and
(b) any examination, measurement, test or experiment which the expert wishes to carry out.
(4) The court may, before an expert is instructed, limit the amount that can be paid by way of fees and expenses to the expert.
(5) Unless the court otherwise directs, the instructing co-defendants are jointly and severally liable for the payment of the expert's fees and expenses.

R-185 **Court's power to vary requirements under this Part**

19.9 (1) The court may extend (even after it has expired) a time limit under this Part.
(2) A party who wants an extension of time must—
(a) apply when serving the report, summary or notice for which it is required; and
(b) explain the delay.

Criminal Practice Directions Part 19 Expert Evidence

CPD V Evidence 19A: Expert Evidence **PD-42**

19A.1 Expert opinion evidence is admissible in criminal proceedings at common law if, in summary, (i) it is relevant to a matter in issue in the proceedings; (ii) it is needed to provide the court with information likely to be outside the court's own knowledge and experience; and (iii) the witness is competent to give that opinion.

19A.2 Legislation relevant to the introduction and admissibility of such evidence includes section 30 of the Criminal Justice Act 1988, which provides that an expert report shall be admissible as evidence in criminal proceedings whether or not the person making it gives oral evidence, but that if he or she does not give oral evidence then the report is admissible only with the leave of the court; and CrimPR Part 19, which in exercise of the powers conferred by section 81 of the Police and Criminal Evidence Act 1984 and section 20 of the Criminal Procedure and Investigations Act 1996 requires the service of expert evidence in advance of trial in the terms required by those rules.

19A.3 In the Law Commission report entitled 'Expert Evidence in Criminal Proceedings in England and Wales', report number 325, published in March, 2011, the Commission recommended a statutory test for the admissibility of expert evidence. However, in its response the government declined to legislate. The common law, therefore, remains the source of the criteria by reference to which the court must assess the admissibility and weight of such evidence; and CrimPR 19.4 lists those matters with which an expert's report must deal, so that the court can conduct an adequate such assessment.

19A.4 In its judgment in *R v Dlugosz and Others* [2013] EWCA Crim 2, the Court of Appeal observed (at paragraph 11): 'It is essential to recall the principle which is applicable, namely in determining the issue of admissibility, the court must be satisfied that there is a sufficiently reliable scientific basis for the evidence to be admitted. If there is then the court leaves the opposing views to be tested before the jury.' Nothing at common law precludes assessment by the court of the reliability of an expert opinion by reference to substantially similar factors to those the Law Commission recommended as conditions of admissibility, and courts are encouraged actively to enquire into such factors.

19A.5 Therefore factors which the court may take into account in determining the reliability of expert opinion, and especially of expert scientific opinion, include:

(a) the extent and quality of the data on which the expert's opinion is based, and the validity of the methods by which they were obtained;

(b) if the expert's opinion relies on an inference from any findings, whether the opinion properly explains how safe or unsafe the inference is (whether by reference to statistical significance or in other appropriate terms);

(c) if the expert's opinion relies on the results of the use of any method (for instance, a test, measurement or survey), whether the opinion takes proper account of matters, such as the degree of precision or margin of uncertainty, affecting the accuracy or reliability of those results;

(d) the extent to which any material upon which the expert's opinion is based has been reviewed by others with relevant expertise (for instance, in peer-reviewed publications), and the views of those others on that material;

(e) the extent to which the expert's opinion is based on material falling outside the expert's own field of expertise;

(f) the completeness of the information which was available to the expert, and whether the expert took account of all relevant information in arriving at the opinion (including information as to the context of any facts to which the opinion relates);

(g) if there is a range of expert opinion on the matter in question, where in the range the expert's own opinion lies and whether the expert's preference has been properly explained; and

(h) whether the expert's methods followed established practice in the field and, if they did not, whether the reason for the divergence has been properly explained.

19A.6 In addition, in considering reliability, and especially the reliability of expert scientific opinion, the court should be astute to identify potential flaws in such opinion which detract from its reliability, such as:

(a) being based on a hypothesis which has not been subjected to sufficient scrutiny (including, where appropriate, experimental or other testing), or which has failed to stand up to scrutiny;

(b) being based on an unjustifiable assumption;

(c) being based on flawed data;

(d) relying on an examination, technique, method or process which was not properly carried out or applied, or was not appropriate for use in the particular case; or

(e) relying on an inference or conclusion which has not been properly reached.

R-186 **When this Part applies**

20.1 This Part applies—

(a) in a magistrates' court and in the Crown Court;
(b) where a party wants to introduce hearsay evidence, within the meaning of section 114 of the Criminal Justice Act 2003.

R-187 **Notice to introduce hearsay evidence**

20.2 (1) This rule applies where a party wants to introduce hearsay evidence for admission under any of the following sections of the Criminal Justice Act 2003—

(a) section 114(1)(d) (evidence admissible in the interests of justice);
(b) section 116 (evidence where a witness is unavailable);
(c) section 117(1)(c) (evidence in a statement prepared for the purposes of criminal proceedings);
(d) section 121 (multiple hearsay).

(2) That party must—

(a) serve notice on—
(i) the court officer, and
(ii) each other party;
(b) in the notice—
(i) identify the evidence that is hearsay,
(ii) set out any facts on which that party relies to make the evidence admissible,
(iii) explain how that party will prove those facts if another party disputes them, and
(iv) explain why the evidence is admissible; and
(c) attach to the notice any statement or other document containing the evidence that has not already been served.

(3) A prosecutor who wants to introduce such evidence must serve the notice not more than—

(a) 28 days after the defendant pleads not guilty, in a magistrates' court; or
(b) 14 days after the defendant pleads not guilty, in the Crown Court.

(4) A defendant who wants to introduce such evidence must serve the notice as soon as reasonably practicable.

(5) A party entitled to receive a notice under this rule may waive that entitlement by so informing—

(a) the party who would have served it; and
(b) the court.

R-188 **Opposing the introduction of hearsay evidence**

20.3 (1) This rule applies where a party objects to the introduction of hearsay evidence.

(2) That party must—

(a) apply to the court to determine the objection;
(b) serve the application on—
(i) the court officer, and
(ii) each other party;
(c) serve the application as soon as reasonably practicable, and in any event not more than 14 days after—
(i) service of notice to introduce the evidence under rule 20.2,
(ii) service of the evidence to which that party objects, if no notice is required by that rule, or
(iii) the defendant pleads not guilty
whichever of those events happens last; and
(d) in the application, explain—
(i) which, if any, facts set out in a notice under rule 20.2 that party disputes,
(ii) why the evidence is not admissible, and
(iii) any other objection to the evidence.

(3) The court—

(a) may determine an application—
(i) at a hearing, in public or in private, or
(ii) without a hearing;
(b) must not determine the application unless the party who served the notice—
(i) is present, or
(ii) has had a reasonable opportunity to respond;
(c) may adjourn the application; and

(d) may discharge or vary a determination where it can do so under—
(i) section 8B of the Magistrates' Courts Act 1980 (ruling at pre-trial hearing in a magistrates' court), or
(ii) section 9 of the Criminal Justice Act 1987, or section 31 or 40 of the Criminal Procedure and Investigations Act 1996 (ruling at preparatory or other pre-trial hearing in the Crown Court).

Unopposed hearsay evidence R-189

20.4 (1) This rule applies where—
(a) a party has served notice to introduce hearsay evidence under rule 20.2; and
(b) no other party has applied to the court to determine an objection to the introduction of the evidence.
(2) The court must treat the evidence as if it were admissible by agreement.

Court's power to vary requirements under this Part R-190

20.5 (1) The court may—
(a) shorten or extend (even after it has expired) a time limit under this Part;
(b) allow an application or notice to be given in a different form to one set out in the Practice Direction, or to be made or given orally;
(c) dispense with the requirement for notice to introduce hearsay evidence.
(2) A party who wants an extension of time must—
(a) apply when serving the application or notice for which it is needed; and
(b) explain the delay.

Criminal Procedure Rules Part 21 Evidence of Bad Character

When this Part applies R-191

21.1 This Part applies—
(a) in a magistrates' court and in the Crown Court;
(b) where a party wants to introduce evidence of bad character, within the meaning of section 98 of the Criminal Justice Act 2003.

Content of application or notice R-192

21.2 (1) A party who wants to introduce evidence of bad character must—
(a) make an application under rule 21.3, where it is evidence of a non-defendant's bad character;
(b) give notice under rule 21.4, where it is evidence of a defendant's bad character.
(2) An application or notice must—
(a) set out the facts of the misconduct on which that party relies,
(b) explain how that party will prove those facts (whether by certificate of conviction, other official record, or other evidence), if another party disputes them, and
(c) explain why the evidence is admissible.

Application to introduce evidence of a non-defendant's bad character R-193

21.3 (1) This rule applies where a party wants to introduce evidence of the bad character of a person other than the defendant.
(2) That party must serve an application to do so on—
(a) the court officer; and
(b) each other party.
(3) The applicant must serve the application—
(a) as soon as reasonably practicable; and in any event
(b) not more than 14 days after the prosecutor discloses material on which the application is based (if the prosecutor is not the applicant).
(4) A party who objects to the introduction of the evidence must—
(a) serve notice on—
(i) the court officer, and
(ii) each other party
not more than 14 days after service of the application; and
(b) in the notice explain, as applicable—
(i) which, if any, facts of the misconduct set out in the application that party disputes,
(ii) what, if any, facts of the misconduct that party admits instead,
(iii) why the evidence is not admissible, and
(iv) any other objection to the application.

(5) The court—
(a) may determine an application—
(i) at a hearing, in public or in private, or
(ii) without a hearing;
(b) must not determine the application unless each party other than the applicant—
(i) is present, or
(ii) has had at least 14 days in which to serve a notice of objection;
(c) may adjourn the application; and
(d) may discharge or vary a determination where it can do so under—
(i) section 8B of the Magistrates' Courts Act 1980 (ruling at pre-trial hearing in a magistrates' court), or
(ii) section 9 of the Criminal Justice Act 1987, or section 31 or 40 of the Criminal Procedure and Investigations Act 1996 (ruling at preparatory or other pre-trial hearing in the Crown Court).

R-194 **Notice to introduce evidence of a defendant's bad character**

21.4 (1) This rule applies where a party wants to introduce evidence of a defendant's bad character.
(2) That party must serve notice on—
(a) the court officer; and
(b) each other party.
(3) A prosecutor who wants to introduce such evidence must serve the notice not more than—
(a) 28 days after the defendant pleads not guilty, in a magistrates' court; or
(b) 14 days after the defendant pleads not guilty, in the Crown Court.
(4) A co-defendant who wants to introduce such evidence must serve the notice—
(a) as soon as reasonably practicable; and in any event
(b) not more than 14 days after the prosecutor discloses material on which the notice is based.
(5) A party who objects to the introduction of the evidence must—
(a) apply to the court to determine the objection;
(b) serve the application on—
(i) the court officer, and
(ii) each other party
not more than 14 days after service of the notice; and
(c) in the application explain, as applicable—
(i) which, if any, facts of the misconduct set out in the notice that party disputes,
(ii) what, if any, facts of the misconduct that party admits instead,
(iii) why the evidence is not admissible,
(iv) why it would be unfair to admit the evidence, and
(v) any other objection to the notice.
(6) The court—
(a) may determine an application—
(i) at a hearing, in public or in private, or
(ii) without a hearing;
(b) must not determine the application unless the party who served the notice—
(i) is present, or
(ii) has had a reasonable opportunity to respond;
(c) may adjourn the application; and
(d) may discharge or vary a determination where it can do so under—
(i) section 8B of the Magistrates' Courts Act 1980 (ruling at pre-trial hearing in a magistrates' court), or
(ii) section 9 of the Criminal Justice Act 1987, or section 31 or 40 of the Criminal Procedure and Investigations Act 1996 (ruling at preparatory or other pre-trial hearing in the Crown Court).
(7) A party entitled to receive a notice may waive that entitlement by so informing—
(a) the party who would have served it; and
(b) the court.

R-195 **Reasons for decisions**

21.5 The court must announce at a hearing in public (but in the absence of the jury, if there is one) the reasons for a decision—
(a) to admit evidence as evidence of bad character, or to refuse to do so; or
(b) to direct an acquittal or a retrial under section 107 of the Criminal Justice Act 2003.

Court's power to vary requirements under this Part R-196

21.6 (1) The court may—
(a) shorten or extend (even after it has expired) a time limit under this Part;
(b) allow an application or notice to be in a different form to one set out in the Practice Direction, or to be made or given orally;
(c) dispense with a requirement for notice to introduce evidence of a defendant's bad character.
(2) A party who wants an extension of time must—
(a) apply when serving the application or notice for which it is needed; and
(b) explain the delay.

Criminal Practice Directions Part 21 Evidence of Bad Character

CPD V Evidence 21A: Spent Convictions PD-43

21A.1 The effect of section 4(1) of the Rehabilitation of Offenders Act 1974 is that a person who has become a rehabilitated person for the purpose of the Act in respect of a conviction (known as a 'spent' conviction) shall be treated for all purposes in law as a person who has not committed, or been charged with or prosecuted for, or convicted of or sentenced for, the offence or offences which were the subject of that conviction.

21A.2 Section 4(1) of the 1974 Act does not apply, however, to evidence given in criminal proceedings: section 7(2)(a). During the trial of a criminal charge, reference to previous convictions (and therefore to spent convictions) can arise in a number of ways. The most common is when a bad character application is made under the Criminal Justice Act 2003. When considering bad character applications under the 2003 Act, regard should always be had to the general principles of the Rehabilitation of Offenders Act 1974.

21A.3 On conviction, the court must be provided with a statement of the defendant's record for the purposes of sentence. The record supplied should contain all previous convictions, but those which are spent should, so far as practicable, be marked as such. No one should refer in open court to a spent conviction without the authority of the judge, which authority should not be given unless the interests of justice so require. When passing sentence the judge should make no reference to a spent conviction unless it is necessary to do so for the purpose of explaining the sentence to be passed.

Criminal Procedure Rules Part 22 Evidence of a Complainant's Previous Sexual Behaviour

When this Part applies R-197

22.1 This Part applies in magistrates' courts and in the Crown Court where a defendant wants to—
(a) introduce evidence; or
(b) cross-examine a witness

about a complainant's sexual behaviour despite the prohibition in section 41 of the Youth Justice and Criminal Evidence Act 1999.

Application for permission to introduce evidence or cross-examine R-198

22.2 The defendant must apply for permission to do so—
(a) in writing; and
(b) not more than 28 days after the prosecutor has complied or purported to comply with section 3 of the Criminal Procedure and Investigations Act 1996 (disclosure by prosecutor).

Content of application R-199

22.3 The application must—
(a) identify the issue to which the defendant says the complainant's sexual behaviour is relevant;
(b) give particulars of—
(i) any evidence that the defendant wants to introduce, and
(ii) any questions that the defendant wants to ask;
(c) identify the exception to the prohibition in section 41 of the Youth Justice and Criminal Evidence Act 1999 on which the defendant relies; and
(d) give the name and date of birth of any witness whose evidence about the complainant's sexual behaviour the defendant wants to introduce.

Service of application R-200

22.4 The defendant must serve the application on the court officer and all other parties.

R-201 **Reply to application**

22.5 A party who wants to make representations about an application under rule 22.2 must—
(a) do so in writing not more than 14 days after receiving it; and
(b) serve those representations on the court officer and all other parties.

R-202 **Application for special measures**

22.6 If the court allows an application under rule 22.2 then—
(a) a party may apply not more than 14 days later for a special measures direction or for the variation of an existing special measures direction; and
(b) the court may shorten the time for opposing that application.

R-203 **Court's power to vary requirements under this Part**

22.7 The court may shorten or extend (even after it has expired) a time limit under this Part.

Criminal Procedure Rules Part 23 Restriction on Cross-Examination by a Defendant

General rules

R-204 **When this Part applies**

23.1 This Part applies where—
(a) a defendant may not cross-examine in person a witness because of section 34 or section 35 of the Youth Justice and Criminal Evidence Act 1999 (Complainants in proceedings for sexual offences; Child complainants and other child witnesses);
(b) the court can prohibit a defendant from cross-examining in person a witness under section 36 of that Act (Direction prohibiting accused from cross-examining particular witness).

R-205 **Appointment of advocate to cross-examine witness**

23.2 (1) This rule applies where a defendant may not cross-examine in person a witness in consequence of—
(a) the prohibition imposed by section 34 or section 35 of the Youth Justice and Criminal Evidence Act 1999; or
(b) a prohibition imposed by the court under section 36 of the 1999 Act.

(2) The court must, as soon as practicable, explain in terms the defendant can understand (with help, if necessary)—
(a) the prohibition and its effect;
(b) that the defendant is entitled to arrange for a lawyer with a right of audience in the court to cross-examine the witness on his or her behalf;
(c) that the defendant must notify the court officer of the identity of any such lawyer, with details of how to contact that person, by no later than a date set by the court;
(d) that if the defendant does not want to make such arrangements, or if the defendant gives no such notice by that date, then—
(i) the court must decide whether it is necessary in the interests of justice to appoint such a lawyer to cross-examine the witness for the defendant, and
(ii) if the court decides that that is necessary, the court will appoint a lawyer chosen by the court.

(3) Having given those explanations, the court must—
(a) ask whether the defendant wants to arrange for a lawyer to cross-examine the witness, and set a date by when the defendant must notify the court officer of the identity of that lawyer if the answer to that question is 'yes';
(b) if the answer to that question is 'no', or if by the date set the defendant has given no such notice—
(i) decide whether it is necessary in the interests of justice for the witness to be cross-examined by an advocate appointed to represent the defendant's interests, and
(ii) if the court decides that that is necessary, give directions for the appointment of such an advocate.

(4) Where an advocate is appointed by the court—
(a) the directions that the court gives under paragraph (3)(b)(ii) must provide for the material to be supplied to that advocate, including by whom and when it must be supplied; and
(b) the appointment terminates at the conclusion of the cross-examination of the witness.

(5) The court may give the explanations and ask the questions required by this rule—
(a) at a hearing, in public or in private; or
(b) without a hearing, by written notice to the defendant.
(6) The court may extend (even after it has expired) the time limit that it sets under paragraph (3)(a)—
(a) on application by the defendant; or
(b) on its own initiative.

Application to prohibit cross-examination

Exercise of court's powers R-206

23.3 (1) The court may decide whether to impose or discharge a prohibition against cross-examination under section 36 of the Youth Justice and Criminal Evidence Act 1999—
(a) at a hearing, in public or in private, or without a hearing;
(b) in a party's absence, if that party—
(i) applied for the prohibition or discharge, or
(ii) has had at least 14 days in which to make representations.
(2) The court must announce, at a hearing in public before the witness gives evidence, the reasons for a decision—
(a) to impose or discharge such a prohibition; or
(b) to refuse to do so.

Application to prohibit cross-examination R-207

23.4 (1) This rule applies where under section 36 of the Youth Justice and Criminal Evidence Act 1999 the prosecutor wants the court to prohibit the cross-examination of a witness by a defendant in person.
(2) The prosecutor must—
(a) apply in writing, as soon as reasonably practicable after becoming aware of the grounds for doing so; and
(b) serve the application on—
(i) the court officer,
(ii) the defendant who is the subject of the application, and
(iii) any other defendant, unless the court otherwise directs.
(3) The application must—
(a) report any views that the witness has expressed about whether he or she is content to be cross-examined by the defendant in person;
(b) identify—
(i) the nature of the questions likely to be asked, having regard to the issues in the case,
(ii) any relevant behaviour of the defendant at any stage of the case, generally and in relation to the witness,
(iii) any relationship, of any nature, between the witness and the defendant,
(iv) any other defendant in the case who is subject to such a prohibition in respect of the witness, and
(v) any special measures direction made in respect of the witness, or for which an application has been made;
(c) explain why the quality of evidence given by the witness on cross-examination—
(i) is likely to be diminished if no such prohibition is imposed, and
(ii) would be likely to be improved if it were imposed; and
(d) explain why it would not be contrary to the interests of justice to impose the prohibition.

Application to discharge prohibition imposed by the court R-208

23.5 (1) A party who wants the court to discharge a prohibition against cross-examination which the court imposed under section 36 of the Youth Justice and Criminal Evidence Act 1999 must—
(a) apply in writing, as soon as reasonably practicable after becoming aware of the grounds for doing so; and
(b) serve the application on—
(i) the court officer, and
(ii) each other party.
(2) The applicant must—
(a) explain what material circumstances have changed since the prohibition was imposed; and
(b) ask for a hearing, if the applicant wants one, and explain why it is needed.

R-209 Application containing information withheld from another party

23.6 (1) This rule applies where—
(a) an applicant serves an application for the court to impose a prohibition against cross-examination, or for the discharge of such a prohibition; and
(b) the application includes information that the applicant thinks ought not be revealed to another party.
(2) The applicant must—
(a) omit that information from the part of the application that is served on that other party;
(b) mark the other part to show that, unless the court otherwise directs, it is only for the court; and
(c) in that other part, explain why the applicant has withheld that information from that other party.
(3) Any hearing of an application to which this rule applies—
(a) must be in private, unless the court otherwise directs; and
(b) if the court so directs, may be, wholly or in part, in the absence of a party from whom information has been withheld.
(4) At any hearing of an application to which this rule applies—
(a) the general rule is that the court must consider, in the following sequence—
(i) representations first by the applicant and then by each other party, in all the parties' presence, and then
(ii) further representations by the applicant, in the absence of a party from whom information has been withheld; but
(b) the court may direct other arrangements for the hearing.

R-210 Representations in response

23.7 (1) This rule applies where a party wants to make representations about—
(a) an application under rule 23.4 for a prohibition against cross-examination;
(b) an application under rule 23.5 for the discharge of such a prohibition; or
(c) a prohibition or discharge that the court proposes on its own initiative.
(2) Such a party must—
(a) serve the representations on—
(i) the court officer, and
(ii) each other party;
(b) do so not more than 14 days after, as applicable—
(i) service of the application, or
(ii) notice of the prohibition or discharge that the court proposes; and
(c) ask for a hearing, if that party wants one, and explain why it is needed.
(3) Representations against a prohibition must explain in what respect the conditions for imposing it are not met.
(4) Representations against the discharge of a prohibition must explain why it should not be discharged.
(5) Where representations include information that the person making them thinks ought not be revealed to another party, that person must—
(a) omit that information from the representations served on that other party;
(b) mark the information to show that, unless the court otherwise directs, it is only for the court; and
(c) with that information include an explanation of why it has been withheld from that other party.

R-211 Court's power to vary requirements

23.8 (1) The court may—
(a) shorten or extend (even after it has expired) a time limit under rule 23.4 (Application to prohibit cross-examination), rule 23.5 (Application to discharge prohibition imposed by the court) or rule 23.7 (Representations in response); and
(b) allow an application or representations required by any of those rules to be made in a different form to one set out in the Practice Direction, or to be made orally.
(2) A person who wants an extension of time must—
(a) apply when serving the application or representations for which it is needed; and
(b) explain the delay.

Criminal Procedure Rules Part 24 Trial and Sentence in a Magistrates' Court

When this Part applies R-212

24.1 (1) This Part applies in a magistrates' court where—
(a) the court tries a case;
(b) the defendant pleads guilty;
(c) under section 14 or 16E of the Magistrates' Courts Act 1980, the defendant makes a statutory declaration of not having found out about the case until after the trial began;
(d) under section 142 of the 1980 Act, the court can—
(i) set aside a conviction, or
(ii) vary or rescind a costs order, or an order to which Part 31 applies (Behaviour orders).
(2) Where the defendant is under 18, in this Part—
(a) a reference to convicting the defendant includes a reference to finding the defendant guilty of an offence; and
(b) a reference to sentence includes a reference to an order made on a finding of guilt.

General rules R-213

24.2 (1) Where this Part applies—
(a) the general rule is that the hearing must be in public; but
(b) the court may exercise any power it has to—
(i) impose reporting restrictions,
(ii) withhold information from the public, or
(iii) order a hearing in private; and
(c) unless the court otherwise directs, only the following may attend a hearing in a youth court—
(i) the parties and their legal representatives,
(ii) a defendant's parents, guardian or other supporting adult,
(iii) a witness,
(iv) anyone else directly concerned in the case, and
(v) a representative of a news-gathering or reporting organisation.
(2) Unless already done, the justices' legal adviser or the court must—
(a) read the allegation of the offence to the defendant;
(b) explain, in terms the defendant can understand (with help, if necessary)—
(i) the allegation, and
(ii) what the procedure at the hearing will be;
(c) ask whether the defendant has been advised about the potential effect on sentence of a guilty plea;
(d) ask whether the defendant pleads guilty or not guilty; and
(e) take the defendant's plea.
(3) The court may adjourn the hearing—
(a) at any stage, to the same or to another magistrates' court; or
(b) to a youth court, where the court is not itself a youth court and the defendant is under 18.
(4) Paragraphs (1) and (2) of this rule do not apply where the court tries a case under rule 24.9 (Single justice procedure: special rules).

Procedure on plea of not guilty R-214

24.3 (1) This rule applies—
(a) if the defendant has—
(i) entered a plea of not guilty, or
(ii) not entered a plea; or
(b) if, in either case, it appears to the court that there may be grounds for making a hospital order without convicting the defendant.
(2) If a not guilty plea was taken on a previous occasion, the justices' legal adviser or the court must ask the defendant to confirm that plea.
(3) In the following sequence—
(a) the prosecutor may summarise the prosecution case, identifying the relevant law and facts;
(b) the prosecutor must introduce the evidence on which the prosecution case relies;

(c) at the conclusion of the prosecution case, on the defendant's application or on its own initiative, the court—
  (i) may acquit on the ground that the prosecution evidence is insufficient for any reasonable court properly to convict, but
  (ii) must not do so unless the prosecutor has had an opportunity to make representations;
(d) the justices' legal adviser or the court must explain, in terms the defendant can understand (with help, if necessary)—
  (i) the right to give evidence, and
  (ii) the potential effect of not doing so at all, or of refusing to answer a question while doing so;
(e) the defendant may introduce evidence;
(f) a party may introduce further evidence if it is then admissible (for example, because it is in rebuttal of evidence already introduced);
(g) the prosecutor may make final representations in support of the prosecution case, where—
  (i) the defendant is represented by a legal representative, or
  (ii) whether represented or not, the defendant has introduced evidence other than his or her own; and
(h) the defendant may make final representations in support of the defence case.

(4) Where a party wants to introduce evidence or make representations after that party's opportunity to do so under paragraph (3), the court—
(a) may refuse to receive any such evidence or representations; and
(b) must not receive any such evidence or representations after it has announced its verdict.

(5) If the court—
(a) convicts the defendant; or
(b) makes a hospital order instead of doing so,
it must give sufficient reasons to explain its decision.

(6) If the court acquits the defendant, it may—
(a) give an explanation of its decision; and
(b) exercise any power it has to make—
  (i) a behaviour order,
  (ii) a costs order.

R-215 **Evidence of a witness in person**

24.4 (1) This rule applies where a party wants to introduce evidence by calling a witness to give that evidence in person.

(2) Unless the court otherwise directs—
(a) a witness waiting to give evidence must not wait inside the courtroom, unless that witness is—
  (i) a party, or
  (ii) an expert witness;
(b) a witness who gives evidence in the courtroom must do so from the place provided for that purpose; and
(c) a witness' address must not be announced unless it is relevant to an issue in the case.

(3) Unless other legislation otherwise provides, before giving evidence a witness must take an oath or affirm.

(4) In the following sequence—
(a) the party who calls a witness must ask questions in examination-in-chief;
(b) every other party may ask questions in cross-examination;
(c) the party who called the witness may ask questions in re-examination.

(5) If other legislation so permits, at any time while giving evidence a witness may refer to a record of that witness' recollection of events.

(6) The justices' legal adviser or the court may—
(a) ask a witness questions; and in particular
(b) where the defendant is not represented, ask any question necessary in the defendant's interests.

R-216 **Evidence of a witness in writing**

24.5 (1) This rule applies where a party wants to introduce in evidence the written statement of a witness to which applies—
(a) Part 16 (Written witness statements);
(b) Part 19 (Expert evidence); or
(c) Part 20 (Hearsay evidence).

(2) If the court admits such evidence—
(a) the court must read the statement; and
(b) unless the court otherwise directs, if any member of the public, including any reporter, is present, each relevant part of the statement must be read or summarised aloud.

Evidence by admission R-217

24.6 (1) This rule applies where—
(a) a party introduces in evidence a fact admitted by another party; or
(b) parties jointly admit a fact.
(2) Unless the court otherwise directs, a written record must be made of the admission.

Procedure on plea of guilty R-218

24.7 (1) This rule applies if—
(a) the defendant pleads guilty; and
(b) the court is satisfied that the plea represents a clear acknowledgement of guilt.
(2) The court may convict the defendant without receiving evidence.

Written guilty plea: special rules R-219

24.8 (1) This rule applies where—
(a) the offence alleged—
(i) can be tried only in a magistrates' court, and
(ii) is not one specified under section 12(1)(a) of the Magistrates' Courts Act 1980;
(b) the defendant is at least 16 years old;
(c) the prosecutor has served on the defendant—
(i) the summons or requisition,
(ii) the material listed in paragraph (2) on which the prosecutor relies to set out the facts of the offence,
(iii) the material listed in paragraph (3) on which the prosecutor relies to provide the court with information relevant to sentence,
(iv) a notice that the procedure set out in this rule applies, and
(v) a notice for the defendant's use if the defendant wants to plead guilty without attending court; and
(d) the prosecutor has served on the court officer—
(i) copies of those documents, and
(ii) a certificate of service of those documents on the defendant.
(2) The material that the prosecutor must serve to set out the facts of the offence is—
(a) a summary of the evidence on which the prosecution case is based;
(b) any—
(i) written witness statement to which Part 16 (Written witness statements) applies, or
(ii) document or extract setting out facts; or
(c) any combination of such a summary, statement, document or extract.
(3) The material that the prosecutor must serve to provide information relevant to sentence is—
(a) details of any previous conviction of the defendant which the prosecutor considers relevant, other than any conviction listed in the defendant's driving record;
(b) if applicable, a notice that the defendant's driving record will be made available to the court;
(c) a notice containing or describing any other information about the defendant, relevant to sentence, which will be made available to the court.
(4) A defendant who wants to plead guilty without attending court must, before the hearing date specified in the summons or requisition—
(a) serve a notice of guilty plea on the court officer; and
(b) include with that notice—
(i) any representations that the defendant wants the court to consider, and
(ii) a statement of the defendant's assets and other financial circumstances.
(5) A defendant who wants to withdraw such a notice must notify the court officer in writing before the hearing date.
(6) If the defendant does not withdraw the notice before the hearing date, then on or after that date—
(a) to establish the facts of the offence and other information about the defendant relevant to sentence, the court may take account only of—
(i) information contained in a document served by the prosecutor under paragraph (1),
(ii) any previous conviction listed in the defendant's driving record, where the offence is under the Road Traffic Regulation Act 1984, the Road Traffic Act 1988, the Road

Traffic (Consequential Provisions) Act 1988 or the Road Traffic (Driver Licensing and Information Systems) Act 1989,
(iii) any other information about the defendant, relevant to sentence, of which the prosecutor served notice under paragraph (1), and
(iv) any representations and any other information served by the defendant under paragraph (4)

and rule 24.11(3) to (9) inclusive must be read accordingly;
(b) unless the court otherwise directs, the prosecutor need not attend; and
(c) the court may accept such a guilty plea and pass sentence in the defendant's absence.

(7) With the defendant's agreement, the court may deal with the case in the same way as under paragraph (6) where the defendant is present and—
(a) has served a notice of guilty plea under paragraph (4); or
(b) pleads guilty there and then.

R-220 Single justice procedure: special rules

24.9 (1) This rule applies where—
(a) the offence alleged—
(i) can be tried only in a magistrates' court, and
(ii) is not one punishable with imprisonment;
(b) the defendant is at least 18 years old;
(c) the prosecutor has served on the defendant—
(i) a written charge,
(ii) the material listed in paragraph (2) on which the prosecutor relies to set out the facts of the offence,
(iii) the material listed in paragraph (3) on which the prosecutor relies to provide the court with information relevant to sentence,
(iv) a notice that the procedure set out in this rule applies,
(v) a notice for the defendant's use if the defendant wants to plead guilty,
(vi) a notice for the defendant's use if the defendant wants to plead guilty but wants the case dealt with at a hearing by a court comprising more than one justice, and
(vii) a notice for the defendant's use if the defendant wants to plead not guilty; and
(d) the prosecutor has served on the court officer—
(i) copies of those documents, and
(ii) a certificate of service of those documents on the defendant.

(2) The material that the prosecutor must serve to set out the facts of the offence is—
(a) a summary of the evidence on which the prosecution case is based;
(b) any—
(i) written witness statement to which Part 16 (Written witness statements) applies, or
(ii) document or extract setting out facts; or
(c) any combination of such a summary, statement, document or extract.

(3) The material that the prosecutor must serve to provide information relevant to sentence is—
(a) details of any previous conviction of the defendant which the prosecutor considers relevant, other than any conviction listed in the defendant's driving record;
(b) if applicable, a notice that the defendant's driving record will be made available to the court;
(c) a notice containing or describing any other information about the defendant, relevant to sentence, which will be made available to the court.

(4) Not more than 21 days after service on the defendant of the documents listed in paragraph (1)(c)—
(a) a defendant who wants to plead guilty must serve a notice to that effect on the court officer and include with that notice—
(i) any representations that the defendant wants the court to consider, and
(ii) a statement of the defendant's assets and other financial circumstances;
(b) a defendant who wants to plead guilty but wants the case dealt with at a hearing by a court comprising more than one justice must serve a notice to that effect on the court officer;
(c) a defendant who wants to plead not guilty must serve a notice to that effect on the court officer.

(5) If within 21 days of service on the defendant of the documents listed in paragraph (1)(c) the defendant serves a notice to plead guilty under paragraph (4)(a)—
(a) the court officer must arrange for the court to deal with the case in accordance with that notice; and
(b) the time for service of any other notice under paragraph (4) expires at once.

(6) If within 21 days of service on the defendant of the documents listed in paragraph (1)(c) the defendant wants to withdraw a notice which he or she has served under paragraph (4)(b) (notice to plead guilty at a hearing) or under paragraph (4)(c) (notice to plead not guilty), the defendant must—
(a) serve notice of that withdrawal on the court officer; and
(b) serve any substitute notice under paragraph (4).
(7) Paragraph (8) applies where by the date of trial the defendant has not—
(a) served notice under paragraph (4)(b) or (c) of wanting to plead guilty at a hearing, or wanting to plead not guilty; or
(b) given notice to that effect under section 16B(2) of the Magistrates' Courts Act 1980.
(8) Where this paragraph applies—
(a) the court may try the case in the parties' absence and without a hearing;
(b) the court may accept any guilty plea of which the defendant has given notice under paragraph (4)(a);
(c) to establish the facts of the offence and other information about the defendant relevant to sentence, the court may take account only of—
(i) information contained in a document served by the prosecutor under paragraph (1),
(ii) any previous conviction listed in the defendant's driving record, where the offence is under the Road Traffic Regulation Act 1984, the Road Traffic Act 1988, the Road Traffic (Consequential Provisions) Act 1988 or the Road Traffic (Driver Licensing and Information Systems) Act 1989,
(iii) any other information about the defendant, relevant to sentence, of which the prosecutor served notice under paragraph (1), and
(iv) any representations and any other information served by the defendant under paragraph (4)(a)
and rule 24.11(3) to (9) inclusive must be read accordingly.
(9) Paragraph (10) applies where—
(a) the defendant serves on the court officer a notice under paragraph (4)(b) or (c); or
(b) the court which tries the defendant under paragraph (8) adjourns the trial for the defendant to attend a hearing by a court comprising more than one justice.
(10) Where this paragraph applies, the court must exercise its power to issue a summons and—
(a) the rules in Part 7 apply (Starting a prosecution in a magistrates' court) as if the prosecutor had just served an information in the same terms as the written charge;
(b) the rules in Part 8 (Initial details of the prosecution case) apply as if the documents served by the prosecutor under paragraph (1) had been served under that Part;
(c) except for rule 24.8 (Written guilty plea: special rules) and this rule, the rules in this Part apply.

Application to withdraw a guilty plea R-221

24.10 (1) This rule applies where the defendant wants to withdraw a guilty plea.
(2) The defendant must apply to do so—
(a) as soon as practicable after becoming aware of the reasons for doing so; and
(b) before sentence.
(3) Unless the court otherwise directs, the application must be in writing and the defendant must serve it on—
(a) the court officer; and
(b) the prosecutor.
(4) The application must—
(a) explain why it would be unjust not to allow the defendant to withdraw the guilty plea;
(b) identify—
(i) any witness that the defendant wants to call, and
(ii) any other proposed evidence; and
(c) say whether the defendant waives legal professional privilege, giving any relevant name and date.

Procedure if the court convicts R-222

24.11 (1) This rule applies if the court convicts the defendant.
(2) The court—
(a) may exercise its power to require—
(i) a statement of the defendant's financial circumstances,
(ii) a pre-sentence report; and

(b) may (and in some circumstances must) remit the defendant to a youth court for sentence where—
(i) the defendant is under 18, and
(ii) the convicting court is not itself a youth court.

(3) The prosecutor must—
(a) summarise the prosecution case, if the sentencing court has not heard evidence;
(b) identify any offence to be taken into consideration in sentencing;
(c) provide information relevant to sentence, including any statement of the effect of the offence on the victim, the victim's family and others; and
(d) where it is likely to assist the court, identify any other matter relevant to sentence, including—
(i) the legislation applicable,
(ii) any sentencing guidelines, or guideline cases,
(iii) aggravating and mitigating features affecting the defendant's culpability and the harm which the offence caused, was intended to cause or might forseeably have caused, and
(iv) the effect of such of the information listed in paragraph (2)(a) as the court may need to take into account.

(4) The defendant must provide details of financial circumstances—
(a) in any form required by the court officer;
(b) by any date directed by the court or by the court officer.

(5) Where the defendant pleads guilty but wants to be sentenced on a different basis to that disclosed by the prosecution case—
(a) the defendant must set out that basis in writing, identifying what is in dispute;
(b) the court may invite the parties to make representations about whether the dispute is material to sentence; and
(c) if the court decides that it is a material dispute, the court must—
(i) invite such further representations or evidence as it may require, and
(ii) decide the dispute.

(6) Where the court has power to order the endorsement of the defendant's driving record, or power to order the defendant to be disqualified from driving—
(a) if other legislation so permits, a defendant who wants the court not to exercise that power must introduce the evidence or information on which the defendant relies;
(b) the prosecutor may introduce evidence; and
(c) the parties may make representations about that evidence or information.

(7) Before the court passes sentence—
(a) the court must—
(i) give the defendant an opportunity to make representations and introduce evidence relevant to sentence, and
(ii) where the defendant is under 18, give the defendant's parents, guardian or other supporting adult, if present, such an opportunity as well; and
(b) the justices' legal adviser or the court must elicit any further information relevant to sentence that the court may require.

(8) If the court requires more information, it may exercise its power to adjourn the hearing for not more than—
(a) 3 weeks at a time, if the defendant will be in custody; or
(b) 4 weeks at a time.

(9) When the court has taken into account all the evidence, information and any report available, the court must—
(a) as a general rule, pass sentence there and then;
(b) when passing sentence, explain the reasons for deciding on that sentence, unless neither the defendant nor any member of the public, including any reporter, is present;
(c) when passing sentence, explain to the defendant its effect, the consequences of failing to comply with any order or pay any fine, and any power that the court has to vary or review the sentence, unless—
(i) the defendant is absent, or
(ii) the defendant's ill-health or disorderly conduct makes such an explanation impracticable;
(d) give any such explanation in terms the defendant, if present, can understand (with help, if necessary); and
(e) consider exercising any power it has to make a costs or other order.

(10) Despite the general rule—
(a) the court must adjourn the hearing if the defendant is absent, the case started with a summons, requisition or single justice procedure notice, and either—
(i) the court considers passing a custodial sentence (where it can do so), or
(ii) the court considers imposing a disqualification (unless it has already adjourned the hearing to give the defendant an opportunity to attend);
(b) the court may exercise any power it has to—
(i) commit the defendant to the Crown Court for sentence (and in some cases it must do so), or
(ii) defer sentence for up to 6 months.

Procedure where a party is absent R-223

24.12 (1) This rule—
(a) applies where a party is absent; but
(b) does not apply where—
(i) the defendant has served a notice of guilty plea under rule 24.8 (Written guilty plea: special rules), or
(ii) the court tries a case under rule 24.9 (Single justice procedure: special rules).
(2) Where the prosecutor is absent, the court may—
(a) if it has received evidence, deal with the case as if the prosecutor were present; and
(b) in any other case—
(i) enquire into the reasons for the prosecutor's absence, and
(ii) if satisfied there is no good reason, exercise its power to dismiss the allegation.
(3) Where the defendant is absent—
(a) the general rule is that the court must proceed as if the defendant—
(i) were present, and
(ii) had pleaded not guilty (unless a plea already has been taken)
and the court must give reasons if it does not do so; but
(b) the general rule does not apply if the defendant is under 18;
(c) the general rule is subject to the court being satisfied that—
(i) any summons or requisition was served on the defendant a reasonable time before the hearing, or
(ii) in a case in which the hearing has been adjourned, the defendant had reasonable notice of where and when it would resume;
(d) the general rule is subject also to rule 24.11(10)(a) (restrictions on passing sentence in the defendant's absence).
(4) Where the defendant is absent, the court—
(a) must exercise its power to issue a warrant for the defendant's arrest, if it passes a custodial sentence; and
(b) may exercise its power to do so in any other case, if it does not apply the general rule in paragraph (3)(a) of this rule about proceeding in the defendant's absence.

Provision of documents for the court R-224

24.13 (1) A party who introduces a document in evidence, or who otherwise uses a document in presenting that party's case, must provide a copy for—
(a) each other party;
(b) any witness that party wants to refer to that document;
(c) the court; and
(d) the justices' legal adviser.
(2) Unless the court otherwise directs, on application or on its own initiative, the court officer must provide for the court—
(a) any copy received under paragraph (1) before the hearing begins; and
(b) a copy of the court officer's record of—
(i) information supplied by each party for the purposes of case management, including any revision of information previously supplied,
(ii) each pre-trial direction for the management of the case,
(iii) any pre-trial decision to admit evidence,
(iv) any pre-trial direction about the giving of evidence, and
(v) any admission to which rule 24.6 applies.
(3) Where rule 24.8 (Written guilty plea: special rules) applies, the court officer must provide for the court—
(a) each document served by the prosecutor under rule 24.8(1)(d);

(b) the defendant's driving record, where the offence is under the Road Traffic Regulation Act 1984, the Road Traffic Act 1988, the Road Traffic (Consequential Provisions) Act 1988 or the Road Traffic (Driver Licensing and Information Systems) Act 1989);
(c) any other information about the defendant, relevant to sentence, of which the prosecutor served notice under rule 24.8(1); and
(d) the notice of guilty plea and any representations and other information served by the defendant under rule 24.8(4).

(4) Where the court tries a case under rule 24.9 (Single justice procedure: special rules), the court officer must provide for the court—
(a) each document served by the prosecutor under rule 24.9(1)(d);
(b) the defendant's driving record, where the offence is under the Road Traffic Regulation Act 1984, the Road Traffic Act 1988, the Road Traffic (Consequential Provisions) Act 1988 or the Road Traffic (Driver Licensing and Information Systems) Act 1989;
(c) any other information about the defendant, relevant to sentence, of which the prosecutor served notice under rule 24.9(1); and
(d) any notice, representations and other information served by the defendant under rule 29.9(4)(a).

R-225 Place of trial

24.14 (1) The hearing must take place in a courtroom provided by the Lord Chancellor, unless—
(a) the court otherwise directs; or
(b) the court tries a case under rule 24.9 (Single justice procedure: special rules).

(2) Where the hearing takes place in Wales—
(a) any party or witness may use the Welsh language; and
(b) if practicable, at least one member of the court must be Welsh-speaking.

R-226 Duty of justices' legal adviser

24.15 (1) A justices' legal adviser must attend the court and carry out the duties listed in this rule, as applicable, unless the court—
(a) includes a District Judge (Magistrates' Courts); and
(b) otherwise directs.

(2) A justices' legal adviser must—
(a) before the hearing begins, by reference to what is provided for the court under rule 24.13 (Provision of documents for the court) draw the court's attention to—
(i) what the prosecutor alleges,
(ii) what the parties say is agreed,
(iii) what the parties say is in dispute, and
(iv) what the parties say about how each expects to present the case, especially where that may affect its duration and timetabling;
(b) whenever necessary, give the court legal advice and—
(i) if necessary, attend the members of the court outside the courtroom to give such advice, but
(ii) inform the parties (if present) of any such advice given outside the courtroom; and
(c) assist the court, where appropriate, in the formulation of its reasons and the recording of those reasons.

(3) A justices' legal adviser must—
(a) assist an unrepresented defendant;
(b) assist the court by—
(i) making a note of the substance of any oral evidence or representations, to help the court recall that information,
(ii) if the court rules inadmissible part of a written statement introduced in evidence, marking that statement in such a way as to make that clear,
(iii) ensuring that an adequate record is kept of the court's decisions and the reasons for them, and
(iv) making any announcement, other than of the verdict or sentence.

(4) Where the defendant has served a notice of guilty plea to which rule 24.8 (Written guilty plea: special rules) applies, a justices' legal adviser must—
(a) unless the court otherwise directs, if any member of the public, including any reporter, is present, read aloud to the court—
(i) the material on which the prosecutor relies to set out the facts of the offence and to provide information relevant to sentence (or summarise any written statement included in that material, if the court so directs), and
(ii) any written representations by the defendant;

(b) otherwise, draw the court's attention to—
(i) what the prosecutor alleges, and any significant features of the material listed in paragraph (4)(a)(i), and
(ii) any written representations by the defendant.

(5) Where the court tries a case under rule 24.9 (Single justice procedure: special rules), a justices' legal adviser must draw the court's attention to—
(a) what the prosecutor alleges, and any significant features of the material on which the prosecutor relies to prove the alleged offence and to provide information relevant to sentence; and
(b) any representations served by the defendant.

Duty of court officer R-227

24.16 The court officer must—
(a) serve on each party notice of where and when an adjourned hearing will resume, unless—
(i) the party was present when that was arranged,
(ii) the defendant has served a notice of guilty plea to which rule 24.8 (Written guilty plea: special rules) applies, and the adjournment is for not more than 4 weeks, or
(iii) the court tries a case under rule 24.9 (Single justice procedure: special rules), and the adjourned trial will resume under that rule;
(b) if the reason for the adjournment was to postpone sentence, include that reason in any such notice to the defendant;
(c) unless the court otherwise directs, make available to the parties any written report to which rule 24.11 (Procedure if the court convicts) applies;
(d) where the court has ordered a defendant to provide information under section 25 of the Road Traffic Offenders Act 1988, serve on the defendant notice of that order unless the defendant was present when it was made;
(e) serve on the prosecutor—
(i) any notice of guilty plea to which rule 24.8 (Written guilty plea: special rules) applies, and
(ii) any declaration served under rule 24.17 (Statutory declaration of ignorance of proceedings) that the defendant did not know about the case;
(f) serve on the prosecutor notice of any hearing date arranged in consequence of such a declaration, unless—
(i) the prosecutor was present when that was arranged, or
(ii) the court otherwise directs;
(g) serve on the prosecutor—
(i) notice of any hearing date arranged in consequence of the issue of a summons under rule 24.9 (Single justice procedure: special rules), and in that event
(ii) any notice served by the defendant under rule 24.9(2)(b) or (c);
(h) record the court's reasons for not proceeding in the defendant's absence where rule 24.12(3)(a) applies; and
(i) give the court such other assistance as it requires.

Statutory declaration of ignorance of proceedings R-228

24.17 (1) This rule applies where—
(a) the case started with—
(i) an information and summons,
(ii) a written charge and requisition, or
(iii) a written charge and single justice procedure notice; and
(b) under section 14 or 16E of the Magistrates' Courts Act 1980, the defendant makes a statutory declaration of not having found out about the case until after the trial began.

(2) The defendant must—
(a) serve such a declaration on the court officer—
(i) not more than 21 days after the date of finding out about the case; or
(ii) with an explanation for the delay, if serving it more than 21 days after that date;
(b) serve with the declaration one of the following, as appropriate, if the case began with a written charge and single justice procedure notice—
(i) a notice under rule 24.9(4)(a) (notice of guilty plea), with any representations that the defendant wants the court to consider and a statement of the defendant's assets and other financial circumstances, as required by that rule,

(ii) a notice under rule 24.9(4)(b) (notice of intention to plead guilty at a hearing before a court comprising more than one justice), or
(iii) a notice under rule 24.9(4)(c) (notice of intention to plead not guilty).

(3) The court may extend that time limit, even after it has expired—
(a) at a hearing, in public or in private; or
(b) without a hearing.

(4) Where the defendant serves such a declaration, in time or with an extension of time in which to do so, and the case began with a summons or requisition—
(a) the court must treat the summons or requisition and all subsequent proceedings as void (but not the information or written charge with which the case began);
(b) if the defendant is present when the declaration is served, the rules in this Part apply as if the defendant had been required to attend the court on that occasion;
(c) if the defendant is absent when the declaration is served—
(i) the rules in Part 7 apply (Starting a prosecution in a magistrates' court) as if the prosecutor had just served an information in the same terms as the original information or written charge;
(ii) the court may exercise its power to issue a summons in accordance with those rules; and
(iii) except for rule 24.8 (Written guilty plea: special rules), the rules in this Part then apply.

(5) Where the defendant serves such a declaration, in time or with an extension of time in which to do so, and the case began with a single justice procedure notice—
(a) the court must treat the single justice procedure notice and all subsequent proceedings as void (but not the written charge with which the case began);
(b) rule 24.9 (Single justice procedure: special rules) applies as if the defendant had served the notice required by paragraph (2)(b) of this rule within the time allowed by rule 24.9(4); and
(c) where that notice is under rule 24.9(4)(b) (notice of intention to plead guilty at a hearing before a court comprising more than one justice) or under rule 24.9(4)(c) (notice of intention to plead not guilty), then—
(i) if the defendant is present when the declaration is served, the rules in this Part apply as if the defendant had been required to attend the court on that occasion,
(ii) if the defendant is absent when the declaration is served, paragraph (6) of this rule applies.

(6) Where this paragraph applies, the court must exercise its power to issue a summons and—
(a) the rules in Part 7 apply (Starting a prosecution in a magistrates' court) as if the prosecutor had just served an information in the same terms as the written charge;
(b) except for rule 24.8 (Written guilty plea: special rules) and rule 24.9 (Single justice procedure: special rules), the rules in this Part apply.

R-229 Setting aside a conviction or varying a costs etc. order

24.18 (1) This rule applies where under section 142 of the Magistrates' Courts Act 1980, the court can—
(a) set aside a conviction, or
(b) vary or rescind—
(i) a costs order, or
(ii) an order to which Part 31 applies (Behaviour orders).

(2) The court may exercise its power—
(a) on application by a party, or on its own initiative;
(b) at a hearing, in public or in private, or without a hearing.

(3) The court must not exercise its power in a party's absence unless—
(a) the court makes a decision proposed by that party;
(b) the court makes a decision to which that party has agreed in writing; or
(c) that party has had an opportunity to make representations at a hearing (whether or not that party in fact attends).

(4) A party who wants the court to exercise its power must—
(a) apply in writing as soon as reasonably practicable after the conviction or order that that party wants the court to set aside, vary or rescind;
(b) serve the application on—
(i) the court officer, and
(ii) each other party; and
(c) in the application—
(i) explain why, as appropriate, the conviction should be set aside, or the order varied or rescinded,
(ii) specify any variation of the order that the applicant proposes,

(iii) identify any witness that the defendant wants to call, and any other proposed evidence,
(iv) say whether the defendant waives legal professional privilege, giving any relevant name and date, and
(v) if the application is late, explain why.

(5) The court may—
(a) extend (even after it has expired) the time limit under paragraph (4), unless the court's power to set aside the conviction, or vary the order, can no longer be exercised;
(b) allow an application to be made orally.

Criminal Practice Directions Part 24 Trial and Sentence in a Magistrates' Court

CPD VI Trial 24A: Role of the Justices' Clerk/Legal Adviser PD-44

24A.1 The role of the justices' clerk/legal adviser is a unique one, which carries with it independence from direction when undertaking a judicial function and when advising magistrates. These functions must be carried out in accordance with the Bangalore Principles of Judicial Conduct (judicial independence, impartiality, integrity, propriety, ensuring fair treatment and competence and diligence). More specifically, duties must be discharged in accordance with the relevant professional Code of Conduct and the Legal Adviser Competence Framework.

24A.2 A justices' clerk is responsible for:
(a) the legal advice tendered to the justices within the area;
(b) the performance of any of the functions set out below by any member of his staff acting as justices' legal adviser;
(c) ensuring that competent advice is available to justices when the justices' clerk is not personally present in court; and
(d) ensuring that advice given at all stages of proceedings and powers exercised (including those delegated to justices' legal advisers) take into account the court's duty to deal with cases justly and actively to manage the case.

24A.3 Where a person other than the justices' clerk (a justices' legal adviser), who is authorised to do so, performs any of the functions referred to in this direction, he or she will have the same duties, powers and responsibilities as the justices' clerk. The justices' legal adviser may consult the justices' clerk, or other person authorised by the justices' clerk for that purpose, before tendering advice to the bench. If the justices' clerk or that person gives any advice directly to the bench, he or she should give the parties or their advocates an opportunity of repeating any relevant submissions, prior to the advice being given.

24A.4 When exercising judicial powers, a justices' clerk or legal adviser is acting in exactly the same capacity as a magistrate. The justices' clerk may delegate powers to a justices' legal adviser in accordance with the relevant statutory authority. The scheme of delegation must be clear and in writing, so that all justices' legal advisers are certain of the extent of their powers. Once a power is delegated, judicial discretion in an individual case lies with the justices' legal adviser exercising the power. When exercise of a power does not require the consent of the parties, a justices' clerk or legal adviser may deal with and decide a contested issue or may refer that issue to the court.

24A.5 It shall be the responsibility of the justices' clerk or legal adviser to provide the justices with any advice they require to perform their functions justly, whether or not the advice has been requested, on:
(a) questions of law;
(b) questions of mixed law and fact;
(c) matters of practice and procedure;
(d) the process to be followed at sentence and the matters to be taken into account, together with the range of penalties and ancillary orders available, in accordance with the relevant sentencing guidelines;
(e) any relevant decisions of the superior courts or other guidelines;
(f) the appropriate decision-making structure to be applied in any given case; and
(g) other issues relevant to the matter before the court.

24A.6 In addition to advising the justices, it shall be the justices' legal adviser's responsibility to assist the court, where appropriate, as to the formulation of reasons and the recording of those reasons.

24A.7 The justices' legal adviser has a duty to assist an unrepresented defendant, see CrimPR 9.4(3)(a), 14.3(2)(a) and 24.15(3)(a), in particular when the court is making a decision on allocation, bail, at trial and on sentence.

24A.8 Where the court must determine allocation, the legal adviser may deal with any aspect of the allocation hearing save for the decision on allocation, indication of sentence and sentence.

24A.9 When a defendant acting in person indicates a guilty plea, the legal adviser must explain the procedure and inform the defendant of their right to address the court on the facts and to provide details of their personal circumstances in order that the court can decide the appropriate sentence.

24A.10 When a defendant indicates a not guilty plea but has not completed the relevant sections of the Magistrates' Courts Trial Preparation Form, the legal adviser must either ensure that the Form is completed or, in appropriate cases, assist the court to obtain and record the essential information on the form.

24A.11 Immediately prior to the commencement of a trial, the legal adviser must summarise for the court the agreed and disputed issues, together with the way in which the parties propose to present their cases. If this is done by way of pre-court briefing, it should be confirmed in court or agreed with the parties.

24A.12 A justices' clerk or legal adviser must not play any part in making findings of fact, but may assist the bench by reminding them of the evidence, using any notes of the proceedings for this purpose, and clarifying the issues which are agreed and those which are to be determined.

24A.13 A justices' clerk or legal adviser may ask questions of witnesses and the parties in order to clarify the evidence and any issues in the case. A legal adviser has a duty to ensure that every case is conducted justly.

24A.14 When advising the justices, the justices' clerk or legal adviser, whether or not previously in court, should:

(a) ensure that he is aware of the relevant facts; and
(b) provide the parties with an opportunity to respond to any advice given.

24A.15 At any time, justices are entitled to receive advice to assist them in discharging their responsibilities. If they are in any doubt as to the evidence which has been given, they should seek the aid of their legal adviser, referring to his notes as appropriate. This should ordinarily be done in open court. Where the justices request their adviser to join them in the retiring room, this request should be made in the presence of the parties in court. Any legal advice given to the justices other than in open court should be clearly stated to be provisional; and the adviser should subsequently repeat the substance of the advice in open court and give the parties the opportunity to make any representations they wish on that provisional advice. The legal adviser should then state in open court whether the provisional advice is confirmed or, if it is varied, the nature of the variation.

24A.16 The legal adviser is under a duty to assist unrepresented parties, whether defendants or not, to present their case, but must do so without appearing to become an advocate for the party concerned. The legal adviser should also ensure that members of the court are aware of obligations under the Victims' Code.

24A.17 The role of legal advisers in fine default proceedings, or any other proceedings for the enforcement of financial orders, obligations or penalties, is to assist the court. They must not act in an adversarial or partisan manner, such as by attempting to establish wilful refusal or neglect or any other type of culpable behaviour, to offer an opinion on the facts, or to urge a particular course of action upon the justices. The expectation is that a legal adviser will ask questions of the defaulter to elicit information which the justices will require to make an adjudication, such as the explanation for the default. A legal adviser may also advise the justices as to the options open to them in dealing with the case.

24A.18 The performance of a legal adviser is subject to regular appraisal. For that purpose the appraiser may be present in the justices' retiring room. The content of the appraisal is confidential, but the fact that an appraisal has taken place, and the presence of the appraiser in the retiring room, should be briefly explained in open court.

Criminal Procedure Rules Part 25 Trial and Sentence in the Crown Court

R-230 **When this Part applies**

25.1 This Part applies in the Crown Court where—
(a) the court tries a case; or
(b) the defendant pleads guilty.

R-231 **General powers and requirements**

25.2 (1) Where this Part applies, the general rule is that—
(a) the trial must be in public, but that is subject to the court's power to—
(i) impose a restriction on reporting what takes place at a public hearing, or public access to what otherwise would be a public hearing,

(ii) withhold information from the public during a public hearing, or
(iii) order a trial in private;
(b) the court must not proceed if the defendant is absent, unless the court is satisfied that—
(i) the defendant has waived the right to attend, and
(ii) the trial will be fair despite the defendant's absence;
(c) the court must not sentence the defendant to imprisonment or detention unless—
(i) the defendant has a legal representative,
(ii) the defendant has been sentenced to imprisonment or detention on a previous occasion in the United Kingdom, or
(iii) the defendant could have been represented under legal aid but is not because section 83(3) of the Powers of Criminal Courts (Sentencing) Act 2000 applies to him or her.
(2) The court may adjourn the trial at any stage.

Application for ruling on procedure, evidence or other question of law **R-232**

25.3 (1) This rule applies to an application—
(a) about—
(i) case management, or any other question of procedure, or
(ii) the introduction or admissibility of evidence, or any other question of law;
(b) that has not been determined before the trial begins.
(2) The application is subject to any other rule that applies to it (for example, as to the time and form in which the application must be made).
(3) Unless the court otherwise directs, the application must be made, and the court's decision announced, in the absence of the jury (if there is one).

Procedure on plea of guilty **R-233**

25.4 (1) This rule applies if—
(a) the defendant pleads guilty to an offence; and
(b) the court is satisfied that the plea represents a clear acknowledgement of guilt.
(2) The court need not receive evidence unless rule 25.16(4) applies (determination of facts for sentencing).

Application to vacate a guilty plea **R-234**

25.5 (1) This rule applies where a party wants the court to vacate a guilty plea.
(2) Such a party must—
(a) apply in writing—
(i) as soon as practicable after becoming aware of the grounds for doing so, and
(ii) in any event, before the final disposal of the case, by sentence or otherwise; and
(b) serve the application on—
(i) the court officer, and
(ii) the prosecutor.
(3) Unless the court otherwise directs, the application must—
(a) explain why it would be unjust for the guilty plea to remain unchanged;
(b) indicate what, if any, evidence the applicant wishes to call;
(c) identify any proposed witness; and
(d) indicate whether legal professional privilege is waived, specifying any material name and date.

Selecting the jury **R-235**

25.6 (1) This rule—
(a) applies where—
(i) the defendant pleads not guilty,
(ii) the defendant declines to enter a plea and the court treats that as a not guilty plea, or
(iii) the court determines that the defendant is not fit to be tried;
(b) does not apply where—
(i) the court orders a trial without a jury because of a danger of jury tampering or where jury tampering appears to have taken place, or
(ii) the court tries without a jury counts on an indictment after a trial of sample counts with a jury.
(2) The court must select a jury to try the case from the panel, or part of the panel, of jurors summoned by the Lord Chancellor to attend at that time and place.

(3) Where it appears that too few jurors to constitute a jury will be available from among those so summoned, the court—
(a) may exercise its own power to summon others in the court room, or in the vicinity, up to the number likely to be required, and add their names to the panel summoned by the Lord Chancellor; but
(b) must inform the parties, if they are absent when the court exercises that power.
(4) The court must select the jury by drawing at random each juror's name from among those so summoned and—
(a) announcing each name so drawn; or
(b) announcing an identifying number assigned by the court officer to that person, where the court is satisfied that that is necessary.
(5) If too few jurors to constitute a jury are available from the panel after all their names have been drawn, the court may—
(a) exercise its own power to summon others in the court room, or in the vicinity, up to the number required; and
(b) announce—
(i) the name of each person so summoned, or
(ii) an identifying number assigned by the court officer to that person, where the court is satisfied that that is necessary.
(6) The jury the court selects—
(a) must comprise no fewer than 12 jurors;
(b) may comprise as many as 14 jurors to begin with, where the court expects the trial to last for more than 4 weeks.
(7) Where the court selects a jury comprising more than 12 jurors, the court must explain to them that—
(a) the purpose of selecting more than 12 jurors to begin with is to fill any vacancy or vacancies caused by the discharge of any of the first 12 before the prosecution evidence begins;
(b) any such vacancy or vacancies will be filled by the extra jurors in order of their selection from the panel;
(c) the court will discharge any extra juror or jurors remaining by no later than the beginning of the prosecution evidence; and
(d) any juror who is discharged for that reason then will be available to be selected for service on another jury, during the period for which that juror has been summoned.
(8) Each of the 12 or more jurors the court selects—
(a) must take an oath or affirm; and
(b) becomes a full jury member until discharged.
(9) The oath or affirmation must be in these terms, or in any corresponding terms that the juror declares to be binding on him or her—
'I swear by Almighty God [*or* I do solemnly, sincerely and truly declare and affirm] that I will faithfully try the defendant and give a true verdict according to the evidence.'

R-236 Discharging jurors

25.7 (1) The court may exercise its power to discharge a juror at any time—
(a) after the juror completes the oath or affirmation; and
(b) before the court discharges the jury.
(2) No later than the beginning of the prosecution evidence, if the jury then comprises more than 12 jurors the court must discharge any in excess of 12 in reverse order of their selection from the panel.
(3) The court may exercise its power to discharge the jury at any time—
(a) after each juror has completed the oath or affirmation; and
(b) before the jury has delivered its verdict on each offence charged in the indictment.
(4) The court must exercise its power to discharge the jury when, in respect of each offence charged in the indictment, either—
(a) the jury has delivered its verdict on that offence; or
(b) the court has discharged the jury from reaching a verdict.

R-237 Objecting to jurors

25.8 (1) A party who objects to the panel of jurors must serve notice explaining the objection on the court officer and on the other party before the first juror's name or number is drawn.

(2) A party who objects to the selection of an individual juror must—
(a) tell the court of the objection—
(i) after the juror's name or number is announced, and
(ii) before the juror completes the oath or affirmation; and
(b) explain the objection.
(3) A prosecutor who exercises the prosecution right without giving reasons to prevent the court selecting an individual juror must announce the exercise of that right before the juror completes the oath or affirmation.
(4) The court must determine an objection under paragraph (1) or (2)—
(a) at a hearing, in public or in private; and
(b) in the absence of the jurors, unless the court otherwise directs.

Procedure on plea of not guilty **R-238**

25.9 (1) This rule applies where—
(a) the defendant pleads not guilty; or
(b) the defendant declines to enter a plea and the court treats that as a not guilty plea.
(2) In the following sequence—
(a) where there is a jury, the court must—
(i) inform the jurors of each offence charged in the indictment to which the defendant pleads not guilty, and
(ii) explain to the jurors that it is their duty, after hearing the evidence, to decide whether the defendant is guilty or not guilty of each offence;
(b) the prosecutor may summarise the prosecution case;
(c) the prosecutor must introduce the evidence on which the prosecution case relies;
(d) subject to paragraph (3), at the end of the prosecution evidence, on the defendant's application or on its own initiative, the court—
(i) may direct the jury (if there is one) to acquit on the ground that the prosecution evidence is insufficient for any reasonable court properly to convict, but
(ii) must not do so unless the prosecutor has had an opportunity to make representations;
(e) subject to paragraph (4), at the end of the prosecution evidence, the court must ask whether the defendant intends to give evidence in person and, if the answer is 'no', then the court must satisfy itself that there has been explained to the defendant, in terms the defendant can understand (with help, if necessary)—
(i) the right to give evidence in person, and
(ii) that if the defendant does not give evidence in person, or refuses to answer a question while giving evidence, the court may draw such inferences as seem proper;
(f) the defendant may summarise the defence case, if he or she intends to call at least one witness other than him or herself to give evidence in person about the facts of the case;
(g) in this order (or in a different order, if the court so directs) the defendant may—
(i) give evidence in person,
(ii) call another witness, or witnesses, to give evidence in person, and
(iii) introduce any other evidence;
(h) a party may introduce further evidence if it is then admissible (for example, because it is in rebuttal of evidence already introduced);
(i) the prosecutor may make final representations, where—
(i) the defendant has a legal representative,
(ii) the defendant has called at least one witness, other than the defendant him or herself, to give evidence in person about the facts of the case, or
(iii) the court so permits; and
(j) the defendant may make final representations.
(3) Paragraph (2)(d) does not apply in relation to a charge of murder, manslaughter, attempted murder, or causing harm contrary to section 18 or 20 of the Offences against the Person Act 1861 until the court has heard all the evidence (including any defence evidence), where the defendant is charged with—
(a) any of those offences; and
(b) an offence of causing or allowing a child or vulnerable adult to die or to suffer serious physical harm, contrary to section 5 of the Domestic Violence, Crime and Victims Act 2004.
(4) Paragraph (2)(e) does not apply where it appears to the court that, taking account of all the circumstances, the defendant's physical or mental condition makes it undesirable for the defendant to give evidence in person.

(5) Where there is more than one defendant, this rule applies to each in the order their names appear in the indictment, or in an order directed by the court.

(6) Unless the jury (if there is one) has retired to consider its verdict, the court may allow a party to introduce evidence, or make representations, after that party's opportunity to do so under paragraph (2).

(7) Unless the jury has already reached a verdict on a count, the court may exercise its power to—
(a) discharge the jury from reaching a verdict on that count;
(b) direct the jury to acquit the defendant on that count; or
(c) invite the jury to convict the defendant, if the defendant pleads guilty to the offence charged by that count.

R-239 Defendant unfit to plead

25.10 (1) This rule applies where—
(a) it appears to the court, on application or on its own initiative, that the defendant may not be fit to be tried; and
(b) the defendant has not by then been acquitted of each offence charged by the indictment.

(2) The court—
(a) must exercise its power to decide, without a jury, whether the defendant is fit to be tried;
(b) may postpone the exercise of that power until immediately before the opening of the defence case.

(3) Where the court determines that the defendant is not fit to be tried—
(a) the court must exercise its power to appoint a person to put the case for the defence, taking account of all the circumstances and in particular—
(i) the willingness and suitability (including the qualifications and experience) of that person,
(ii) the nature and complexity of the case,
(iii) any advantage of continuity of representation, and
(iv) the defendant's wishes and needs;
(b) the court must select a jury, if none has been selected yet; and
(c) rule 25.9 (Procedure on plea of not guilty) applies, if the steps it lists have not already been taken, except that—
(i) everything which that rule requires to be done by the defendant may be done instead by the person appointed to put the case for the defence,
(ii) under rule 25.9(2)(a), the court must explain to the jurors that their duty is to decide whether or not the defendant did the act or made the omission charged as an offence, not whether the defendant is guilty of that offence, and
(iii) rule 25.9(2)(e) does not apply (warning of consequences of defendant not giving evidence).

R-240 Evidence of a witness in person

25.11 (1) This rule applies where a party wants to introduce evidence by calling a witness to give that evidence in person.

(2) Unless the court otherwise directs—
(a) a witness waiting to give evidence must not wait inside the courtroom, unless that witness is—
(i) a party, or
(ii) an expert witness;
(b) a witness who gives evidence in the courtroom must do so from the place provided for that purpose; and
(c) a witness' address—
(i) must not be given in public unless the address is relevant to an issue in the case,
(ii) may be given in writing to the court, parties and jury.

(3) Unless other legislation otherwise provides, before giving evidence a witness must take an oath or affirm.

(4) In the following sequence—
(a) the party who calls a witness may ask questions in examination-in-chief;
(b) if the witness gives evidence for the prosecution—
(i) the defendant, if there is only one, may ask questions in cross-examination, or
(ii) subject to the court's directions, each defendant, if there is more than one, may ask such questions, in the order their names appear in the indictment or as directed by the court;

(c) if the witness gives evidence for a defendant—
   (i) subject to the court's directions, each other defendant, if there is more than one, may ask questions in cross-examination, in the order their names appear in the indictment or as directed by the court, and
   (ii) the prosecutor may ask such questions;
(d) the party who called the witness may ask questions in re-examination arising out of any cross-examination.

(5) If other legislation so permits, at any time while giving evidence a witness may refer to a record of that witness' recollection of events.

(6) The court may—
(a) ask a witness questions; and in particular
(b) where the defendant is not represented, ask a witness any question necessary in the defendant's interests.

Evidence of a witness in writing R-241

25.12 (1) This rule applies where a party wants to introduce in evidence the written statement of a witness to which applies—
(a) Part 16 (Written witness statements);
(b) Part 19 (Expert evidence); or
(c) Part 20 (Hearsay evidence).

(2) If the court admits such evidence—
(a) the court and the jury (if there is one) must read the statement;
(b) the gist of the statement must be summarised aloud; and
(c) unless the court otherwise directs, if any member of the public, including any reporter, is present, each relevant part of the statement must be read or summarised aloud.

Evidence by admission R-242

25.13 (1) This rule applies where—
(a) a party introduces in evidence a fact admitted by another party; or
(b) parties jointly admit a fact.

(2) Unless the court otherwise directs, a written record must be made of the admission.

Directions to the jury and taking the verdict R-243

25.14 (1) This rule applies where there is a jury.

(2) The court must give the jury directions about the relevant law at any time at which to do so will assist jurors to evaluate the evidence.

(3) After following the sequence in rule 25.9 (Procedure on plea of not guilty), the court must—
(a) summarise for the jury, to such extent as is necessary, the evidence relevant to the issues they must decide;
(b) give the jury such questions, if any, as the court invites jurors to answer in coming to a verdict;
(c) direct the jury to retire to consider its verdict;
(d) if necessary, recall the jury to answer jurors' questions;
(e) if appropriate, recall the jury to give directions for a verdict by a majority; and
(f) recall the jury when it informs the court that it has reached a verdict.

(4) The court may give the jury directions, questions or other assistance in writing.

(5) When the court recalls the jury to deliver its verdict, the court must ask the foreman chosen by the jury, in respect of each count—
(a) whether the jury has reached a verdict on which all the jurors agree;
(b) if so, whether that verdict is guilty or not guilty;
(c) if not, where the jury has deliberated for at least 2 hours and if the court decides to invite a majority verdict, then—
   (i) whether at least 10 (of 11 or 12 jurors), or 9 (of 10 jurors), agreed on a verdict,
   (ii) if so, is that verdict guilty or not guilty, and
   (iii) if (and only if) such a verdict is guilty, how many jurors agreed to that verdict and how many disagreed.

(6) Where evidence has been given that the defendant was insane, so as not to be responsible for the act or omission charged as the offence, then under paragraph (4)(b) the court must ask whether the jury's verdict is guilty, not guilty, or not guilty by reason of insanity.

R-244 **Conviction or acquittal without a jury**

25.15 (1) This rule applies where—
(a) the court tries the case without a jury; and
(b) after following the sequence in rule 25.9 (Procedure on plea of not guilty).
(2) In respect of each count, the court must give reasons for its decision to convict or acquit.

R-245 **Procedure if the court convicts**

25.16 (1) This rule applies where, in respect of any count in the indictment—
(a) the defendant pleads guilty; or
(b) the court convicts the defendant.
(2) The court may exercise its power—
(a) if the defendant is an individual—
(i) to require a pre-sentence report,
(ii) to request a medical report,
(iii) to require a statement of the defendant's assets and other financial circumstances;
(b) if the defendant is a corporation, to require such information as the court directs about the defendant's corporate structure and financial resources;
(c) to adjourn sentence pending—
(i) receipt of any such report, statement or information,
(ii) the verdict in a related case.
(3) The prosecutor must—
(a) summarise the prosecution case, if the sentencing court has not heard evidence;
(b) identify in writing any offence that the prosecutor proposes should be taken into consideration in sentencing;
(c) provide information relevant to sentence, including—
(i) any previous conviction of the defendant, and the circumstances where relevant,
(ii) any statement of the effect of the offence on the victim, the victim's family or others; and
(d) identify any other matter relevant to sentence, including—
(i) the legislation applicable,
(ii) any sentencing guidelines, or guideline cases,
(iii) aggravating and mitigating features affecting the defendant's culpability and the harm which the offence caused, was intended to cause or might forseeably have caused, and
(iv) the effect of such of the information listed in paragraph (2) as the court may need to take into account.
(4) Where the defendant pleads guilty, the court may give directions for determining the facts on the basis of which sentence must be passed if—
(a) the defendant wants to be sentenced on a basis agreed with the prosecutor; or
(b) in the absence of such agreement, the defendant wants to be sentenced on the basis of different facts to those disclosed by the prosecution case.
(5) Where the court has power to order the endorsement of the defendant's driving record, or power to order the defendant to be disqualified from driving—
(a) if other legislation so permits, a defendant who wants the court not to exercise that power must introduce the evidence or information on which the defendant relies;
(b) the prosecutor may introduce evidence; and
(c) the parties may make representations about that evidence or information.
(6) Before passing sentence—
(a) the court must give the defendant an opportunity to make representations and introduce evidence relevant to sentence;
(b) where the defendant is under 18, the court may give the defendant's parents, guardian or other supporting adult, if present, such an opportunity as well; and
(c) if the court requires more information, it may exercise its power to adjourn the hearing.
(7) When the court has taken into account all the evidence, information and any report available, the court must—
(a) as a general rule, pass sentence at the earliest opportunity;
(b) when passing sentence—
(i) explain the reasons,
(ii) explain to the defendant its effect, the consequences of failing to comply with any order or pay any fine, and any power that the court has to vary or review the sentence,

unless the defendant is absent or the defendant's ill-health or disorderly conduct makes such an explanation impracticable, and
(iii) give any such explanation in terms the defendant, if present, can understand (with help, if necessary); and
(c) deal with confiscation, costs and any behaviour order.
(8) The general rule is subject to the court's power to defer sentence for up to 6 months.

Provision of documents for the court R-246

25.17 (1) Unless the court otherwise directs, a party who introduces a document in evidence, or who otherwise uses a document in presenting that party's case, must provide a copy for—
(a) each other party;
(b) any witness that party wants to refer to the document; and
(c) the court.
(2) If the court so directs, a party who introduces or uses a document for such a purpose must provide a copy for the jury.
(3) Unless the court otherwise directs, on application or on its own initiative, the court officer must provide for the court—
(a) any copy received under paragraph (1) before the trial begins; and
(b) a copy of the court officer's record of—
(i) information supplied by each party for the purposes of case management, including any revision of information previously supplied,
(ii) each pre-trial direction for the management of the case,
(iii) any pre-trial decision to admit evidence,
(iv) any pre-trial direction about the giving of evidence, and
(v) any admission to which rule 25.13 (Evidence by admission) applies; and
(c) any other document served on the court officer for the use of the court.

Duty of court officer R-247

25.18 The court officer must—
(a) serve on each party notice of where and when an adjourned hearing will resume, unless that party was present when that was arranged;
(b) if the reason for the adjournment was to postpone sentence, include that reason in any such notice to the defendant;
(c) unless the court otherwise directs, make available to the parties any written report to which rule 25.16(2) applies (pre-sentence and medical reports);
(d) where the court has ordered a defendant to provide information under section 25 of the Road Traffic Offenders Act 1988, serve on the defendant notice of that order unless the defendant was present when it was made;
(e) give the court such other assistance as it requires, including—
(i) selecting jurors from the panel summoned by the Lord Chancellor, under rule 25.6 (Selecting the jury),
(ii) taking the oaths or affirmations of jurors and witnesses, under rules 25.6 and 25.11 (Evidence of a witness in person),
(iii) informing the jurors of the offence or offences charged in the indictment, and of their duty, under rule 25.9 (Procedure on plea of not guilty),
(iv) recording the date and time at which the court gives the jury oral directions under rule 25.14(2) (directions about the law),
(v) recording the date and time at which the court gives the jury any written directions, questions or other assistance under rule 25.14(4), and
(vi) asking the jury foreman to deliver the verdict, under rule 25.14(5).

Criminal Procedure Rules Part 26 Jurors

Appeal against officer's refusal to excuse or postpone jury service R-248

26.1 (1) This rule applies where a person summoned for jury service in the Crown Court, the High Court or the county court wants to appeal against a refusal by an officer on the Lord Chancellor's behalf—
(a) to excuse that person from such service; or
(b) to postpone the date on which that person is required to attend for such service.
(2) The appellant must appeal to the court to which the appellant has been summoned.

(3) The appellant must—
(a) apply in writing, as soon as reasonably practicable; and
(b) serve the application on the court officer.

(4) The application must—
(a) attach a copy of—
(i) the jury summons, and
(ii) the refusal to excuse or postpone which is under appeal; and
(b) explain why the court should excuse the appellant from jury service, or postpone its date, as appropriate.

(5) The court to which the appeal is made—
(a) may extend the time for appealing, and may allow the appeal to be made orally;
(b) may determine the appeal at a hearing in public or in private, or without a hearing;
(c) may adjourn any hearing of the appeal;
(d) must not determine an appeal unless the appellant has had a reasonable opportunity to make representations in person.

R-249 Excusal from jury service by court

26.2 At any time before a juror completes the oath or affirmation, the court may exercise its power to excuse him or her from jury service for lack of capacity to act effectively as a juror because of an insufficient understanding of English—
(a) on the court's own initiative, or where the court officer refers the juror to the court; and
(b) after enquiry of the juror.

R-250 Provision of information for jurors

26.3 The court officer must arrange for each juror to receive—
(a) by such means as the Lord Chancellor directs, general information about jury service and about a juror's responsibilities;
(b) written notice of the prohibitions against—
(i) research by a juror into the case,
(ii) disclosure by a juror of any such research to another juror during the trial,
(iii) conduct by a juror which suggests that that juror intends to try the case otherwise than on the evidence,
(iv) disclosure by a juror of the deliberations of the jury;
(c) written warning that breach of those prohibitions is an offence, for which the penalty is imprisonment or a fine or both, and may be a contempt of court.

R-251 Assessment of juror's availability for long trial, etc.

26.4 (1) The court may invite each member of a panel of jurors to provide such information, by such means and at such a time as the court directs, about—
(a) that juror's availability to try a case expected to last for longer than the juror had expected to serve;
(b) any association of that juror with, or any knowledge by that juror of—
(i) a party or witness, or
(ii) any other person, or any place, of significance to the case.

(2) Where jurors provide information under this rule, the court may postpone the selection of the jury to try a case to allow each juror an opportunity to review and amend that information before that selection.

(3) Using that information, the court may exercise its power to excuse a juror from selection as a member of the jury to try a case, but the court must not—
(a) excuse a juror without allowing the parties an opportunity to make representations; or
(b) refuse to excuse a juror without allowing that juror such an opportunity.

R-252 Surrender of electronic communication devices by jurors

26.5 (1) This rule applies where the court can order the members of a jury to surrender for a specified period any electronic communication devices that they possess.

(2) The court may make such an order—
(a) on application; or
(b) on its own initiative.

(3) A party who wants the court to make such an order must—
(a) apply as soon as reasonably practicable;
(b) notify each other party;
(c) specify for what period any device should be surrendered; and

(d) explain why—
 (i) the proposed order is necessary or expedient in the interest of justice, and
 (ii) the terms of the proposed order are a proportionate means of safeguarding those interests.

Criminal Practice Directions Part 26 Jurors

CPD VI Trial 26A: Juries: introduction PD-45

26A.1 Jury service is an important public duty which individual members of the public are chosen at random to undertake. As the Court has acknowledged: 'Jury service is not easy; it never has been. It involves a major civic responsibility' (*R v Thompson* [2010] EWCA Crim 1623, [9] per Lord Judge CJ, [2011] 1 WLR 200, [2010] 2 Cr App R 27).

Provision of information to prospective jurors

26A.2 HMCTS provide every person summoned as a juror with information about the role and responsibilities of a juror. Prospective jurors are provided with a pamphlet, 'Your Guide to Jury Service', and may also view the film 'Your Role as a Juror' online at anytime on the Ministry of Justice YouTube site www.youtube.com/watch?v=JP7slp-X9Pc There is also information at https://www.gov.uk/jury-service/overview

CPD VI Trial 26B: Juries: Preliminary Matters Arising before Jury Service Commences PD-46

26B.1 The effect of section 321 of the Criminal Justice Act 2003 was to remove certain categories of persons from those previously ineligible for jury service (the judiciary and others concerned with the administration of justice) and certain other categories ceased to be eligible for excusal as of right, (such as members of Parliament and medical professionals). The normal presumption is that everyone, unless ineligible or disqualified, will be required to serve when summoned to do so.

Excusal and deferral

26B.2 The jury summoning officer is empowered to defer or excuse individuals in appropriate circumstances and in accordance with the HMCTS *Guidance for summoning officers when considering deferral and excusal applications* (2009): http://www.official-documents.gov.uk/document/other/9780108508400/9780108508400.pdf

Appeals from officer's refusal to excuse or postpone jury service

26B.3 CrimPR 26.1 governs the procedure for a person's appeal against a summoning officer's decision in relation to excusal or deferral of jury service.

Provision of information at court

26B.4 The court officer is expected to provide relevant further information to jurors on their arrival in the court centre.

CPD VI Trial 26C: Juries: Eligibility PD-47

English language ability

26C.1 Under the Juries Act 1974 section 10, a person summoned for jury service who applies for excusal on the grounds of insufficient understanding of English may, where necessary, be brought before the judge.

26C.2 The court may exercise its power to excuse any person from jury service for lack of capacity to act effectively as a juror because of an insufficient understanding of English.

26C.3 The judge has the discretion to stand down jurors who are not competent to serve by reason of a personal disability: *R v Mason* [1981] QB 881, (1980) 71 Cr App R 157; *R v Jalil* [2008] EWCA Crim 2910, [2009] 2 Cr App R (S.) 40.

Jurors with professional and public service commitments

26C.4 The legislative change in the Criminal Justice Act 2003 means that more individuals are eligible to serve as jurors, including those previously excused as of right or ineligible. Judges need to be vigilant to the need to exercise their discretion to adjourn a trial, excuse or discharge a juror should the need arise.

26C.5 Whether or not an application has already been made to the jury summoning officer for deferral or excusal, it is also open to the person summoned to apply to the court to be excused. Such applications must be considered with common sense and according to the interests of justice. An explanation should be required for an application being much later than necessary.

Serving police officers, prison officers or employees of prosecuting agencies

26C.6 A judge should always be made aware at the stage of jury selection if any juror in waiting is in these categories. The juror summons warns jurors in these categories that they will need to alert court staff.

26C.7 In the case of police officers an inquiry by the judge will have to be made to assess whether a police officer may serve as a juror. Regard should be had to: whether evidence from the police is in dispute in the case and the extent to which that dispute involves allegations made against the police; whether the potential juror knows or has worked with the officers involved in the case; whether the potential juror has served or continues to serve in the same police units within the force as those dealing with the investigation of the case or is likely to have a shared local service background with police witnesses in a trial.

26C.8 In the case of a serving prison officer summoned to a court, the judge will need to inquire whether the individual is employed at a prison linked to that court or is likely to have special knowledge of any person involved in a trial.

26C.9 The judge will need to ensure that employees of prosecuting authorities do not serve on a trial prosecuted by the prosecuting authority by which they are employed. They can serve on a trial prosecuted by another prosecuting authority: *R v Abdroikov* [2007] UKHL 37, [2007] 1 WLR 2679, [2008] 1 Cr App R 21; *Hanif v UK* [2011] ECHR 2247, (2012) 55 EHRR 16; *R v L* [2011] EWCA Crim 65, [2011] 1 Cr App R 27. Similarly, a serving police officer can serve where there is no particular link between the court and the station where the police officer serves.

26C.10 Potential jurors falling into these categories should be excused from jury service unless there is a suitable alternative court/trial to which they can be transferred.

PD-48 **CPD VI Trial 26D: Juries: Precautionary Measures before Swearing**

26D.1 There should be a consultation with the advocates as to the questions, if any, it may be appropriate to ask potential jurors. Topics to be considered include:

a. the availability of jurors for the duration of a trial that is likely to run beyond the usual period for which jurors are summoned;
b. whether any juror knows the defendant or parties to the case;
c. whether potential jurors are so familiar with any locations that feature in the case that they may have, or come to have, access to information not in evidence;
d. in cases where there has been any significant local or national publicity, whether any questions should be asked of potential jurors.

26D.2 Judges should however exercise caution. At common law a judge has a residual discretion to discharge a particular juror who ought not to be serving, but this discretion can only be exercised to prevent an individual juror who is not competent from serving. It does not include a discretion to discharge a jury drawn from particular sections of the community or otherwise to influence the overall composition of the jury. However, if there is a risk that there is widespread local knowledge of the defendant or a witness in a particular case, the judge may, after hearing submissions from the advocates, decide to exclude jurors from particular areas to avoid the risk of jurors having or acquiring personal knowledge of the defendant or a witness.

Length of trial

26D.3 Where the length of the trial is estimated to be significantly longer than the normal period of jury service, it is good practice for the trial judge to enquire whether the potential jurors on the jury panel foresee any difficulties with the length and if the judge is satisfied that the jurors' concerns are justified, he may say that they are not required for that particular jury. This does not mean that the judge must excuse the juror from sitting at that court altogether, as it may well be possible for the juror to sit on a shorter trial at the same court.

Juror with potential connection to the case or parties

26D.4 Where a juror appears on a jury panel, it will be appropriate for a judge to excuse the juror from that particular case where the potential juror is personally concerned with the facts of the particular case, or is closely connected with a prospective witness. Judges need to exercise due caution as noted above.

PD-49 **CPD VI Trial 26E: Juries: Swearing in Jurors**

Swearing Jury for trial

26E.1 All jurors shall be sworn or affirm. All jurors shall take the oath or affirmation in open court in the presence of one another. If, as a result of the juror's delivery of the oath or affirmation, a judge has concerns that a juror has such difficulties with language comprehension or reading ability that might affect that juror's capacity to undertake his or her duties, bearing in mind the likely evidence in the trial, the judge should make appropriate inquiry of that juror.

Form of oath or affirmation

26E.2 Each juror should have the opportunity to indicate to the court the Holy Book on which he or she wishes to swear. The precise wording will depend on his or her faith as indicated to the court.

26E.3 Any person who prefers to affirm shall be permitted to make a solemn affirmation instead. The wording of the affirmation is: 'I do solemnly, sincerely and truly declare and affirm that I will faithfully try the defendant and give a true verdict according to the evidence'.

CPD VI Trial 26F: Juries: Ensuring an effective jury panel **PD-50**

Adequacy of numbers

26F.1 By section 6 of the Juries Act 1974, if it appears to the court that a jury to try any issue before the court will be, or probably will be, incomplete, the court may, if the court thinks fit, require any persons who are in, or in the vicinity of, the court, to be summoned (without any written notice) for jury service up to the number needed (after allowing for any who may not be qualified under section 1 of the Act, and for excusals and challenges) to make up a full jury.

CPD VI Trial 26G: Juries: Preliminary Instructions to Jurors **PD-51**

26G.1 After the jury has been sworn and the defendant has been put in charge the judge will want to give directions to the jury on a number of matters.

26G.2 Jurors can be expected to follow the instructions diligently. As the Privy Council stated in *Taylor* [2013] UKPC 8, [2013] 1 WLR 1144:

> The assumption must be that the jury understood and followed the direction that they were given: ... the experience of trial judges is that juries perform their duty according to law. ... [T]he law proceeds on the footing that the jury, acting in accordance with the instructions given to them by the trial judge, will render a true verdict in accordance with the evidence. To conclude otherwise would be to underrate the integrity of the system of trial by jury and the effect on the jury of the instructions by the trial judge.

At the start of the trial

26G.3 Trial judges should instruct the jury on general matters which will include the time estimate for the trial and normal sitting hours. The jury will always need clear guidance on the following:

i. The need to try the case only on the evidence and remain faithful to their oath or affirmation;
ii. The prohibition on internet searches for matters related to the trial, issues arising or the parties;
iii. The importance of not discussing any aspect of the case with anyone outside their own number or allowing anyone to talk to them about it, whether directly, by telephone, through internet facilities such as Facebook or Twitter or in any other way;
iv. The importance of taking no account of any media reports about the case;
v. The collective responsibility of the jury. As the Lord Chief Justice made clear in *R v Thompson and Others* [2010] EWCA Crim 1623, [2011] 1 WLR 200, [2010] 2 Cr App R 27:

> [T]here is a collective responsibility for ensuring that the conduct of each member is consistent with the jury oath and that the directions of the trial judge about the discharge of their responsibilities are followed. ... The collective responsibility of the jury for its own conduct must be regarded as an integral part of the trial itself.

vi. The need to bring any concerns, including concerns about the conduct of other jurors, to the attention of the judge at the time, and not to wait until the case is concluded. The point should be made that, unless that is done while the case is continuing, it may not be possible to deal with the problem at all.

Subsequent reminder of the jury instructions

26G.4 Judges should consider reminding jurors of these instructions as appropriate at the end of each day and in particular when they separate after retirement.

CPD VI Trial 26H: Juries: Discharge of a juror for personal reasons **PD-52**

26H.1 Where a juror unexpectedly finds him or herself in difficult professional or personal circumstances during the course of the trial, the juror should be encouraged to raise such problems with the trial judge. This might apply, for example, to a parent whose childcare arrangements unexpectedly fail, or a worker who is engaged in the provision of services the need for which can be critical, or a Member of Parliament who has deferred their jury service to an apparently more convenient time, but is unexpectedly called back to work for a very important reason. Such difficulties would normally be raised through a jury note in the normal manner.

26H.2 In such circumstances, the judge must exercise his or her discretion according to the interests of justice and the requirements of each individual case. The judge must decide for him or herself whether the juror has presented a sufficient reason to interfere with the course of the trial. If the juror has presented a sufficient reason, in longer trials it may well be possible to adjourn for a short period in order to allow the juror to overcome the difficulty.

26H.3 In shorter cases, it may be more appropriate to discharge the juror and to continue the trial with a reduced number of jurors. The power to do this is implicit in section 16(1) of the Juries Act 1974. In unusual cases (such as an unexpected emergency arising overnight) a juror need not be discharged in open court. The good administration of justice depends on the co-operation of jurors, who perform an essential public service. All such applications should be dealt with sensitively and sympathetically and the trial judge should always seek to meet the interests of justice without unduly inconveniencing any juror.

PD-53 **CPD VI Trial 26J: Juries: Views**

26J.1 In each case in which it is necessary for the jury to view a location, the judge should produce ground rules for the view, after discussion with the advocates. The rules should contain details of what the jury will be shown and in what order and who, if anyone, will be permitted to speak and what will be said. The rules should also make provision for the jury to ask questions and receive a response from the judge, following submissions from the advocates, while the view is taking place.

PD-54 **CPD VI Trial 26K: Juries: Directions to jury before retirement**

26K.1 At the conclusion of the summing up, a number of directions are required. In particular it is important that judges direct the jury:

i. That their verdict must be unanimous in respect of each count and each defendant.
ii. Not to think about 'majority verdicts' unless and until given further directions.
iii. That they will need to select one of their number to chair their discussions and speak on their behalf.

PD-55 **CPD VI Trial 26L: Juries: Jury access to exhibits and evidence in retirement**

26L.1 At the end of the summing up it is also important that the judge informs the jury that any exhibits they wish to have will be made available to them.

26L.2 Judges should invite submissions from the advocates as to what material the jury should retire with and what material before them should be removed, such as the transcript of an ABE interview (which should usually be removed from the jury as soon as the recording has been played.)

26L.3 Judges will also need to inform the jury of the opportunity to view certain audio, DVD or CCTV evidence that has been played (excluding, for example ABE interviews). If possible, it may be appropriate for the jury to be able to view any such material in the jury room alone, such as on a sterile laptop, so that they can discuss it freely; this will be a matter for the judge's discretion, following discussion with counsel.

PD-56 **CPD VI Trial 26M: Juries: Jury Irregularities**

26M.1 This practice direction replaces the protocol regarding jury irregularities issued by the President of the Queen's Bench Division in November 2012, and the subsequent practice direction, in light of sections 20A to 20D of the Juries Act 1974 and the associated repeal of section 8 of the Contempt of Court Act 1981 (confidentiality of jury's deliberations).

It applies to juries sworn on or after 13 April 2015.

26M.2 A jury irregularity is anything that may prevent one or more jurors from remaining faithful to their oath or affirmation to 'faithfully try the defendant and give a true verdict according to the evidence.' Jury irregularities take many forms. Some are clear-cut such as a juror conducting research about the case or an attempt to suborn or intimidate a juror. Others are less clear-cut — for example, when there is potential bias or friction between jurors.

26M.3 A jury irregularity may involve contempt of court and / or the commission of an offence by or in relation to a juror.

26M.4 Under the previous version of this practice direction, the Crown Court required approval from the Vice-President of the Court of Appeal (Criminal Division) (CACD) prior to providing a juror's details to the police for the purposes of an investigation into a jury irregularity. Such approval is no longer required. Provision of a juror's details to the police is now a matter for the Crown Court.

Jury Irregularity During Trial

26M.5 A jury irregularity that comes to light during a trial may impact on the conduct of the trial. It may also involve contempt of court and / or the commission of an offence by or in relation to a juror. **The primary concern of the judge should be the impact on the trial.**

26M.6 A jury irregularity should be drawn to the attention of the judge in the absence of the jury as soon as it becomes known.

26M.7 **When the judge becomes aware of a jury irregularity, the judge should follow the procedure set out below:**

STEP 1: Consider isolating juror(s)
STEP 2: Consult with advocates
STEP 3: Consider appropriate provisional measures (which may include surrender / seizure of electronic communications devices and taking defendant into custody)
STEP 4: Seek to establish basic facts of jury irregularity
STEP 5: Further consult with advocates
STEP 6: Decide what to do in relation to conduct of trial
STEP 7: Consider ancillary matters (contempt in face of court and / or commission of criminal offence)

STEP 1: Consider isolating juror(*s*)

26M.8 The judge should consider whether the juror(s) concerned should be isolated from the rest of the jury, particularly if the juror(s) may have conducted research about the case.

26M.9 If two or more jurors are concerned, the judge should consider whether they should also be isolated from each other, particularly if one juror has made an accusation against another.

STEP 2: Consult with advocates

26M.10 The judge should consult with the advocates and invite submissions about appropriate provisional measures (Step 3) and how to go about establishing the basic facts of the jury irregularity (Step 4).

26M.11 The consultation should be conducted
— in open court;
— in the presence of the defendant; and
— with all parties represented
unless there is good reason not to do so.

26M.12 If the jury irregularity involves a suspicion about the conduct of the defendant or another party, there may be good reason for the consultation to take place in the absence of the defendant or the other party. There may also be good reason for it to take place in private. If so, the proper location is in the court room, with DARTS recording, rather than in the judge's room.

26M.13 If the jury irregularity relates to the jury's deliberations, the judge should warn all those present that it is an offence to disclose, solicit or obtain information about a jury's deliberations (section 20D(1) of the Juries Act 1974 — see 26M.35 to 26M.38 regarding the offence and exceptions). This would include disclosing information about the jury's deliberations divulged in court during consultation with the advocates (Step 2 and Step 5) or when seeking to establish the basic facts of the jury irregularity (Step 4). The judge should emphasise that the advocates, court staff and those in the public gallery would commit the offence by explaining to another what is said in court about the jury's deliberations.

STEP 3: Consider appropriate provisional measures

26M.14 **The judge should consider appropriate provisional measures which may include surrender / seizure of electronic communications devices and taking the defendant into custody.**

Surrender / seizure of electronic communications devices

26M.15 The judge should consider whether to make an order under section 15A(1) of the Juries Act 1974 requiring the juror(s) concerned to surrender electronic communications devices, such as mobile telephones or smart phones.

26M.16 Having made an order for surrender, the judge may require a court security officer to search a juror to determine whether the juror has complied with the order. Section 54A of the Courts Act 2003 contains the court security officer's powers of search and seizure.

26M.17 Section 15A(5) of the Juries Act 1974 provides that it is contempt of court for a juror to fail to surrender an electronic communications device in accordance with an order for surrender (see paragraphs 26M.29 to 26M.30 regarding the procedure for dealing with such a contempt).

26M.18 Any electronic communications device surrendered or seized under these provisions should be kept safe by the court until returned to the juror or handed to the police as evidence.

Taking defendant into custody

26M.19 If the defendant is on bail, and the jury irregularity involves a suspicion about the defendant's conduct, the judge should consider taking the defendant into custody. If that suspicion involves an attempt to suborn or intimidate a juror, the defendant should be taken into custody.

STEP 4: Seek to establish basic facts of jury irregularity

26M.20 The judge should seek to establish the basic facts of the jury irregularity for the purpose of determining how to proceed in relation to the conduct of the trial. The judge's enquiries may involve having the juror(s) concerned write a note of explanation and / or questioning the juror(s). The judge may enquire whether the juror(s) feel able to continue and remain faithful to their oath or affirmation. If there is questioning, each juror should be questioned separately, in the absence of the rest of the jury, unless there is good reason not to do so.

26M.21 In accordance with paragraphs 26M.10 to 26M.13, the enquiries should be conducted in open court; in the presence of the defendant; and with all parties represented unless there is good reason not to do so.

STEP 5: Further consult with advocates

26M.22 The judge should further consult with the advocates and invite submissions about how to proceed in relation to the conduct of the trial and what should be said to the jury (Step 6).

26M.23 In accordance with paragraphs 26M.10 to 26M.13, the consultation should be conducted in open court; in the presence of the defendant; and with all parties represented unless there is good reason not to do so.

STEP 6: Decide what to do in relation to conduct of trial

26M.24 When deciding how to proceed, the judge may take time to reflect.

26M.25 Considerations may include the stage the trial has reached. The judge should be alert to attempts by the defendant or others to thwart the trial. In cases of potential bias, the judge should consider whether a fair minded and informed observer would conclude that there was a real possibility that the juror(s) or jury would be biased (*Porter v Magill* [2001] UKHL 67, [2002] 2 AC 357).

26M.26 In relation to the conduct of the trial, there are three possibilities:

1. **Take no action and continue with the trial**

   If so, the judge should consider what, if anything, to say to the jury. For example, the judge may reassure the jury nothing untoward has happened or remind them their verdict is a decision of the whole jury and that they should try to work together. Anything said should be tailored to the circumstances of the case.

2. ***Discharge the juror(s) concerned and continue with the trial***

   If so, the judge should consider what to say to the discharged juror(s) and the jurors who remain. All jurors should be warned not to discuss what has happened.

3. ***Discharge the whole jury***

   If so, the judge should consider what to say to the jury and they should be warned not to discuss what has happened.

   If the judge is satisfied that jury tampering has taken place, depending on the circumstances, the judge may continue the trial without a jury (section 46(3) of the Criminal Justice Act 2003) or order a new trial without a jury (section 46(5) of the Criminal Justice Act 2003). Alternatively, the judge may re-list the trial. If there is a real and present danger of jury tampering in the new trial, the prosecution may apply for a trial without a jury (section 44 of the Criminal Justice Act 2003).

STEP 7: Consider ancillary matters

26M.27 **A jury irregularity may also involve contempt in the face of the court and / or the commission of a criminal offence. The possibilities include the following:**

— Contempt in the face of the court by a juror

— An offence by a juror or a non-juror under the Juries Act 1974

Offences that may be committed by jurors are researching the case, sharing research, engaging in prohibited conduct or disclosing information about the jury's deliberations (sections 20A to 20D of the Juries Act 1974). Non-jurors may commit the offence of disclosing, soliciting or obtaining information about the jury's deliberations (section 20D of the Juries Act 1974).

- **An offence by juror or a non-juror other than under the Juries Act 1974** A juror may commit an offence such as assault or theft. A non-juror may commit an offence in relation to a juror such as attempting to pervert the course of justice — for example, if the defendant or another attempts to suborn or intimidate a juror.

Contempt in the face of the court by a juror

26M.28 If a juror commits contempt in the face of the court, the juror's conduct may also constitute an offence. If so, the judge should decide whether to deal with the juror summarily under the procedure for contempt in the face of the court or refer the matter to the Attorney General's Office or the police (see paragraphs 26M.31 and 26M.33).

26M.29 In the case of a *minor and clear* contempt in the face of the court, the judge may deal with the juror summarily. The judge should follow the procedure in CrimPR 48.5 to 48.8. The judge should also have regard to the practice direction regarding contempt of court issued in March 2015 (Practice Direction: Committal for Contempt of Court — Open Court), which emphasises the principle of open justice in relation to proceedings for contempt before all courts.

26M.30 If a juror fails to comply with an order for surrender of an electronic communications device (see paragraphs 26M.15 to 26M.18), the judge should deal with the juror summarily following the procedure for contempt in the face of the court.

Offence by a juror or non-juror under the Juries Act 1974

26M.31 If it appears that an offence under the Juries Act 1974 may have been committed by a juror or non-juror (and the matter has not been dealt with summarily under the procedure for contempt in the face of the court), **the judge** should contact the Attorney General's Office to consider a police investigation, setting out the position neutrally. The officer in the case should not be asked to investigate.

Contact details for the Attorney General's Office are set out at the end of this practice direction.

26M.32 If relevant to an investigation, any electronic communications device surrendered or seized pursuant to an order for surrender should be passed to the police as soon as practicable.

Offence by a juror or non-juror other than under the Juries Act 1974

26M.33 If it appears that an offence, other than an offence under the Juries Act 1974, may have been committed by a juror or non-juror (and the matter has not been dealt with summarily under the procedure for contempt in the face of the court), **the judge or a member of court staff** should contact the police setting out the position neutrally. The officer in the case should not be asked to investigate.

26M.34 If relevant to an investigation, any electronic communications device surrendered or seized pursuant to an order for surrender should be passed to the police as soon as practicable.

Other matters to consider

Jury deliberations

26M.35 **In light of the offence of disclosing, soliciting or obtaining information about a jury's deliberations (section 20D(1) of the Juries Act 1974), great care is required if a jury irregularity relates to the jury's deliberations.**

26M.36 *During the trial,* there are exceptions to this offence that enable the judge (and only the judge) to:

- Seek to establish the basic facts of a jury irregularity involving the jury's deliberations (Step 4); and
- Disclose information about the jury's deliberations to the Attorney General's Office if it appears that an offence may have been committed (Step 7).

26M.37 With regard to seeking to establish the basic facts of a jury irregularity involving the jury's deliberations (Step 4), it is to be noted that during the trial it is not an offence for the judge to disclose, solicit or obtain information about the jury's deliberations for the purposes of dealing with the case (sections 20E(2)(a) and 20G(1) of the Juries Act 1974).

26M.38 With regard to disclosing information about the jury's deliberations to the Attorney General's Office if it appears that an offence may have been committed (Step 7), it is to be noted that during the trial:

- It is not an offence for the judge to disclose information about the jury's deliberations for the purposes of an investigation by a relevant investigator into whether an offence or contempt of court has been committed by or in relation to a juror (section 20E(2)(b) of the Juries Act 1974); and
- A relevant investigator means a police force or the Attorney General (section 20E(5) of the Juries Act 1974).

Minimum number of jurors

26M.39 If it is decided to discharge one or more jurors (Step 6), a minimum of nine jurors must remain if the trial is to continue (section 16(1) of the Juries Act 1974).

Preparation of statement by judge

26M.40 If a jury irregularity occurs, and the trial continues, the judge should have regard to the remarks of Lord Hope in *R v Connors and Mirza* [2004] UKHL 2 at [127] and [128], [2004] 1 AC 1118, [2004] 2 Cr App R 8 and consider whether to prepare a statement that could be used in an application for leave to appeal or an appeal relating to the jury irregularity.

Jury Irregularity After Jury Discharged

26M.41 A jury irregularity that comes to light after the jury has been discharged may involve the commission of an offence by or in relation to a juror. It may also provide a ground of appeal.

26M.42 **A jury irregularity after the jury has been discharged may come to the attention of the:**
- **Trial judge or court**
- **Registrar of Criminal Appeals (the Registrar)**
- **Prosecution**
- **Defence**

Role of the trial judge or court

26M.43 The judge has no jurisdiction in relation to a jury irregularity that comes to light after the jury has been discharged (*R v Thompson and others* [2010] EWCA Crim 1623, [2011] 1 WLR 200, [2010] 2 Cr App R 27A). The jury will be deemed to have been discharged when all verdicts on all defendants have been delivered or when the jury has been discharged from giving all verdicts on all defendants.

26M.44 The judge will be *functus officio* in relation to a jury irregularity that comes to light during an adjournment between verdict and sentence. The judge should proceed to sentence unless there is good reason not to do so.

26M.45 In practice, a jury irregularity often comes to light when the judge or court receives a communication from a former juror.

26M.46 If a jury irregularity comes to the attention of a judge or court after the jury has been discharged, and regardless of the result of the trial, the judge or a member of court staff should contact the Registrar setting out the position neutrally. Any communication from a former juror should be forwarded to the Registrar.

Contact details for the Registrar are set out at the end of this practice direction.

Role of the Registrar

26M.47 If a jury irregularity comes to the attention of the Registrar after the jury has been discharged, and regardless of the result of the trial, the Registrar should consider if it appears that an offence may have been committed by or in relation to a juror. The Registrar should also consider if there may be a ground of appeal.

26M.48 When deciding how to proceed, particularly in relation to a communication from a former juror, the Registrar may seek the direction of the Vice-President of the Court of Appeal (Criminal Division) (CACD) or another judge of the CACD in accordance with instructions from the Vice-President.

26M.49 If it appears that an offence may have been committed by or in relation to a juror, the Registrar should contact the Private Office of the Director of Public Prosecutions to consider a police investigation.

26M.50 If there may be a ground of appeal, the Registrar should inform the defence.

26M.51 If a communication from a former juror is not of legal significance, the Registrar should respond explaining that no action is required. An example of such a communication is if it is restricted to a general complaint about the verdict from a dissenting juror or an expression of doubt or second thoughts.

Role of the prosecution

26M.52 If a jury irregularity comes to the attention of the prosecution after the jury has been discharged, which may provide a ground of appeal, they should notify the defence in accordance with their duties to act fairly and assist in the administration of justice (*R v Makin* [2004] EWCA Crim 1607, 148 SJLB 821).

Role of the defence

26M.53 If a jury irregularity comes to the attention of the defence after the jury has been discharged, which provides an arguable ground of appeal, an application for leave to appeal may be made.

Other matters to consider

Jury deliberations

26M.54 **In light of the offence of disclosing, soliciting or obtaining information about a jury's deliberations (section 20D(1) of the Juries Act 1974), great care is required if a jury irregularity relates to the jury's deliberations.**

26M.55 *After the jury has been discharged*, there are exceptions to this offence that enable a judge, a member of court staff, the Registrar, the prosecution and the defence to disclose information about the jury's deliberations if it appears that an offence may have been committed by or in relation to a juror or if there may be a ground of appeal.

26M.56 For example, it is to be noted that:

— After the jury has been discharged, it is not an offence for a person to disclose information about the jury's deliberations to defined persons if the person reasonably believes that an offence or contempt of court may have been committed by or in relation to a juror or the conduct of a juror may provide grounds of appeal (section 20F(1) (2) of the Juries Act 1974).

— The defined persons to whom such information may be disclosed are a member of a police force, a judge of the CACD, the Registrar of Criminal Appeals (the Registrar), a judge where the trial took place or a member of court staff where the trial took place who would reasonably be expected to disclose the information only to one of the aforementioned defined persons (section 20F(2) of the Juries Act 1974).

— After the jury has been discharged, it is not an offence for a judge of the CACD or the Registrar to disclose information about the jury's deliberations for the purposes of an investigation by a relevant investigator into whether an offence or contempt of court has been committed by or in relation to a juror or the conduct of a juror may provide grounds of appeal (section 20F(4) of the Juries Act 1974).

— A relevant investigator means a police force, the Attorney General, the Criminal Cases Review Commission (CCRC) or the Crown Prosecution Service (section 20F(10) of the Juries Act 1974).

Investigation by the Criminal Cases Review Commission (CCRC)

26M.57 If an application for leave to appeal, or an appeal, includes a ground of appeal relating to a jury irregularity, the Registrar may refer the case to the Full Court to decide whether to direct the CCRC to conduct an investigation under section 23A of the Criminal Appeal Act 1968.

26M.58 If the Court directs the CCRC to conduct an investigation, directions should be given as to the scope of the investigation.

Contact Details

Attorney General's Office
Contempt.SharedMailbox@attorneygeneral.gsi.gov.uk
Telephone: 020 7271 2492

The Registrar
penny.donnelly@hmcts.x.gsi.gov.uk (Secretary) or
criminalappealoffice.generaloffice@hmcts.gsi.gov.uk
Telephone: 020 7947 6103 (Secretary) or 020 7947 6011

CPD VI Trial 26N: Open Justice **PD-57**

26N.1 There must be freedom of access between advocate and judge. Any discussion must, however, be between the judge and the advocates on both sides. If an advocate is instructed by a solicitor who is in court, he or she, too, should be allowed to attend the discussion. This freedom of access is important because there may be matters calling for communication or discussion of such a nature that the advocate cannot, in the client's interest, mention them in open court, e.g. the advocate, by way of mitigation, may wish to tell the judge that reliable medical evidence shows that the defendant is suffering from a terminal illness and may not have long to live. It is imperative that, so far as possible, justice must be administered in open court. Advocates should, therefore, only ask to see the judge when it is felt to be really necessary. The judge must be careful only to treat such communications as private where, in the interests of justice, this is necessary. Where any such discussion takes place it should be recorded, preferably by audio recording.

PD-58 **CPD VI Trial 26P: Defendant's Right to Give or Not to Give Evidence**

26P.1 At the conclusion of the evidence for the prosecution, section 35(2) of the Criminal Justice and Public Order Act 1994 requires the court to satisfy itself that the defendant is aware that the stage has been reached at which evidence can be given for the defence and that the defendant's failure to give evidence, or if he does so his failure to answer questions, without a good reason, may lead to inferences being drawn against him.

If the defendant is legally represented

26P.2 After the close of the prosecution case, if the defendant's representative requests a brief adjournment to advise his client on this issue the request should, ordinarily, be granted. When appropriate the judge should, in the presence of the jury, inquire of the representative in these terms:

'*Have you advised your client that the stage has now been reached at which he may give evidence and, if he chooses not to do so or, having been sworn, without good cause refuses to answer any question, the jury may draw such inferences as appear proper from his failure to do so?*'

26P.3 If the representative replies to the judge that the defendant has been so advised, then the case shall proceed. If counsel replies that the defendant has not been so advised, then the judge shall direct the representative to advise his client of the consequences and should adjourn briefly for this purpose, before proceeding further.

If the defendant is not legally represented

26P.4 If the defendant is not represented, the judge shall, at the conclusion of the evidence for the prosecution, in the absence of the jury, indicate what he will say to him in the presence of the jury and ask if he understands and whether he would like a brief adjournment to consider his position.

26P.5 When appropriate, and in the presence of the jury, the judge should say to the defendant:

'*You have heard the evidence against you. Now is the time for you to make your defence. You may give evidence on oath, and be cross-examined like any other witness. If you do not give evidence or, having been sworn, without good cause refuse to answer any question, the jury may draw such inferences as appear proper. That means they may hold it against you. You may also call any witness or witnesses whom you have arranged to attend court or lead any agreed evidence. Afterwards you may also, if you wish, address the jury. But you cannot at that stage give evidence. Do you now intend to give evidence?*'

PD-59 **CPD VI Trial 26Q: Majority Verdicts**

26Q.1 It is very important that all those trying indictable offences should, so far as possible, adopt a uniform practice when complying with section 17 of the Juries Act 1974, both in directing the jury in summing-up and also in receiving the verdict or giving further directions after retirement. So far as the summing-up is concerned, it is inadvisable for the judge, and indeed for advocates, to attempt an explanation of the section for fear that the jury will be confused.

Before the jury retires, however, the judge should direct the jury in some such words as the following:

'*As you may know, the law permits me, in certain circumstances, to accept a verdict which is not the verdict of you all. Those circumstances have not as yet arisen, so that when you retire I must ask you to reach a verdict upon which each one of you is agreed. Should, however, the time come when it is possible for me to accept a majority verdict, I will give you a further direction.*'

26Q.2 Thereafter, the practice should be as follows:

Should the jury return before two hours and ten minutes has elapsed since the last member of the jury left the jury box to go to the jury room (or such longer time as the judge thinks reasonable) (see section 17(4)), they should be asked:

(a) "Have you reached a verdict upon which you are all agreed? Please answer 'Yes' or 'No'.";
(b) (i) If unanimous, "What is your verdict?";
    (ii) If not unanimous, the jury should be sent out again for further deliberation, with a further direction to arrive if possible at a unanimous verdict.

26Q.3 Should the jury return (whether for the first time or subsequently) or be sent for after the two hours and ten minutes (or the longer period) has elapsed, questions (a) and (b)(i) in the paragraph above should be put to them and, if it appears that they are not unanimous, they should be asked to retire once more and told they should continue to endeavour to reach a unanimous verdict but that, if they cannot, the judge will accept a majority verdict as in section 17(1).

26Q.4 When the jury finally return, they should be asked:

(a) "Have at least ten (or nine as the case may be) of you agreed on your verdict?";
(b) If "Yes", "What is your verdict? Please only answer 'Guilty' or 'Not Guilty'.";
(c) (i) If "Not Guilty", accept the verdict without more ado;
 (ii) If "Guilty", "Is that the verdict of you all, or by a majority?";
(d) If "Guilty" by a majority, "How many of you agreed to the verdict and how many dissented?"

26Q.5 At whatever stage the jury return, before question (a) is asked, the senior officer of the court present shall state in open court, for each period when the jury was out of court for the purpose of considering their verdict(s), the time at which the last member of the jury left the jury box to go to the jury room and the time of their return to the jury box; and will additionally state in open court the total of such periods.

26Q.6 The reason why section 17(3) is confined to a majority verdict of 'Guilty', and for the somewhat complicated procedure set out above, is to prevent it being known that a verdict of 'Not Guilty' is a majority verdict. If the final direction continues to require the jury to arrive, if possible, at a unanimous verdict and the verdict is received as specified, it will not be known for certain that the acquittal is not unanimous.

26Q.7 Where there are several counts (or alternative verdicts) left to the jury the above practice will, of course, need to be adapted to the circumstances. The procedure will have to be repeated in respect of each count (or alternative verdict), the verdict being accepted in those cases where the jury are unanimous and the further direction being given in cases in which they are not unanimous.

26Q.8 Should the jury in the end be unable to agree on a verdict by the required majority, the judge in his discretion will either ask them to deliberate further, or discharge them.

26Q.9 Section 17 will, of course, apply also to verdicts other than 'Guilty' or 'Not Guilty', e.g. to special verdicts under the Criminal Procedure (Insanity) Act 1964, following a finding by the judge that the defendant is unfit to be tried, and special verdicts on findings of fact. Accordingly, in such cases the questions to jurors will have to be suitably adjusted.

Criminal Procedure Rules Part 27 Retrial After Acquittal

General

When this Part applies R-253

27.1 (1) Rule 27.2 applies where, under section 54 of the Criminal Procedure and Investigations Act 1996, the Crown Court or a magistrates' court can certify for the High Court that interference or intimidation has been involved in proceedings leading to an acquittal.

(2) Rules 27.3 to 27.7 apply where, under section 77 of the Criminal Justice Act 2003, the Court of Appeal can—

(a) quash an acquittal for a serious offence and order a defendant to be retried; or
(b) order that an acquittal outside the United Kingdom is no bar to the defendant being tried in England and Wales,

if there is new and compelling evidence and it is in the interests of justice to make the order.

Application for certificate to allow order for retrial

Application for certificate R-254

27.2 (1) This rule applies where—

(a) a defendant has been acquitted of an offence;
(b) a person has been convicted of one of the following offences involving interference with or intimidation of a juror or a witness (or potential witness) in any proceedings which led to the defendant's acquittal—
 (i) perverting the course of justice,
 (ii) intimidation etc. of witnesses, jurors and others under section 51(1) of the Criminal Justice and Public Order Act 1994, or
 (iii) aiding, abetting, counselling, procuring, suborning or inciting another person to commit an offence under section 1 of the Perjury Act 1911; and
(c) the prosecutor wants the court by which that person was convicted to certify for the High Court that there is a real possibility that, but for the interference or intimidation, the defendant would not have been acquitted.

(2) The prosecutor must—
(a) apply in writing as soon as practicable after that person's conviction; and
(b) serve the application on—
(i) the court officer, and
(ii) the defendant who was acquitted, if the court so directs.
(3) The application must—
(a) give details, with relevant facts and dates, of—
(i) the conviction for interference or intimidation, and
(ii) the defendant's acquittal; and
(b) explain—
(i) why there is a real possibility that, but for the interference or intimidation, the defendant would not have been acquitted, and
(ii) why it would not be contrary to the interests of justice to prosecute the defendant again for the offence of which he or she was acquitted, despite any lapse of time or other reason.
(4) The court may—
(a) extend the time limit under paragraph (2);
(b) allow an application to be in a different form to one set out in the Practice Direction, or to be made orally;
(c) determine an application under this rule—
(i) at a hearing, in private or in public; or
(ii) without a hearing.
(5) If the court gives a certificate, the court officer must serve it on—
(a) the prosecutor; and
(b) the defendant who was acquitted.

Application to Court of Appeal to quash acquittal and order retrial

R-255 Application for reporting restriction pending application for order for retrial

27.3 (1) This rule applies where—
(a) no application has been made under rule 27.4 (Application for order for retrial);
(b) an investigation by officers has begun into an offence with a view to an application under that rule; and
(c) the Director of Public Prosecutions wants the Court of Appeal to make, vary or remove an order for a reporting restriction under section 82 of the Criminal Justice Act 2003 (Restrictions on publication in the interests of justice).
(2) The Director must—
(a) apply in writing;
(b) serve the application on—
(i) the Registrar, and
(ii) the defendant, unless the court otherwise directs.
(3) The application must, as appropriate—
(a) explain why the Director wants the court to direct that it need not be served on the defendant until the application under rule 27.4 is served;
(b) specify the proposed terms of the order, and for how long it should last;
(c) explain why an order in the terms proposed is necessary;
(d) explain why an order should be varied or removed.

R-256 Application for order for retrial

27.4 (1) This rule applies where—
(a) a defendant has been acquitted—
(i) in the Crown Court, or on appeal from the Crown Court, of an offence listed in Part 1 of Schedule 5 to the Criminal Justice Act 2003 (qualifying offences),
(ii) in proceedings elsewhere than in the United Kingdom of an offence under the law of that place, if what was alleged would have amounted to or included one of those listed offences;
(b) with the Director of Public Prosecutions' written consent, a prosecutor wants the Court of Appeal to make an order, as the case may be—
(i) quashing the acquittal in the Crown Court and ordering the defendant to be retried for the offence, or
(ii) declaring whether the acquittal outside the United Kingdom is a bar to the defendant's trial in England and Wales and, if it is, whether that acquittal shall not be such a bar.

(2) Such a prosecutor must—
(a) apply in writing;
(b) serve the application on the Registrar;
(c) not more than 2 business days later serve on the defendant who was acquitted—
(i) the application, and
(ii) a notice charging the defendant with the offence, unless the defendant has already been arrested and charged under section 87 of the Criminal Justice Act 2003 (arrest, under warrant or otherwise, and charge).
(3) The application must—
(a) give details, with relevant facts and dates, of the defendant's acquittal;
(b) explain—
(i) what new and compelling evidence there is against the defendant, and
(ii) why in all the circumstances it would be in the interests of justice for the court to make the order sought;
(c) include or attach any application for the following, with reasons—
(i) an order under section 80(6) of the Criminal Justice Act 2003 (Procedure and evidence) for the production of any document, exhibit or other thing which in the prosecutor's opinion is necessary for the determination of the application,
(ii) an order under that section for the attendance before the court of any witness who would be a compellable witness at the trial the prosecutor wants the court to order,
(iii) an order for a reporting restriction under section 82 of the Criminal Justice Act 2003 (Restrictions on publication in the interests of justice); and
(d) attach—
(i) written witness statements of the evidence on which the prosecutor relies as new and compelling evidence against the defendant,
(ii) relevant documents from the trial at which the defendant was acquitted, including a record of the offence or offences charged and of the evidence given, and
(iii) any other document or thing that the prosecutor thinks the court will need to decide the application.

Respondent's notice R-257

27.5 (1) A defendant on whom a prosecutor serves an application may serve a respondent's notice, and must do so if the defendant wants to make representations to the court.
(2) Such a defendant must serve the respondent's notice on—
(a) the Registrar; and
(b) the prosecutor,
not more than 28 days after service of the application.
(3) The respondent's notice must—
(a) give the date on which the respondent was served with the prosecutor's application;
(b) summarise any relevant facts not contained in that application;
(c) explain the defendant's grounds for opposing that application;
(d) include or attach any application for the following, with reasons—
(i) an extension of time within which to serve the respondent's notice,
(ii) bail pending the hearing of the prosecutor's application, if the defendant is in custody,
(iii) a direction to attend in person any hearing that the defendant could attend by live link, if the defendant is in custody,
(iv) an order under section 80(6) of the Criminal Justice Act 2003 (Procedure and evidence) for the production of any document, exhibit or other thing which in the defendant's opinion is necessary for the determination of the prosecutor's application,
(v) an order under that section for the attendance before the court of any witness who would be a compellable witness at the trial the prosecutor wants the court to order; and
(e) attach or identify any other document or thing that the defendant thinks the court will need to decide the application.

Application to Crown Court for summons or warrant R-258

27.6 (1) This rule applies where—
(a) the prosecutor has served on the Registrar an application under rule 27.4 (Application for order for retrial);
(b) the defendant is not in custody as a result of arrest under section 88 of the Criminal Justice Act 2003 (Bail and custody before application); and

(c) the prosecutor wants the Crown Court to issue—
(i) a summons requiring the defendant to appear before the Court of Appeal at the hearing of the prosecutor's application, or
(ii) a warrant for the defendant's arrest
under section 89 of the 2003 Act (Bail and custody before hearing).

(2) The prosecutor must—
(a) apply in writing; and
(b) serve the application on the Crown Court officer.

(3) The application must—
(a) explain what the case is about, including a brief description of the defendant's acquittal, the new evidence and the stage that the application to the Court of Appeal has reached;
(b) specify—
(i) the decision that the prosecutor wants the Crown Court to make,
(ii) each offence charged, and
(iii) any relevant previous bail decision and the reasons given for it;
(c) propose the terms of any suggested condition of bail.

R-259 **Application of other rules about procedure in the Court of Appeal**

27.7 On an application under rule 27.4 (Application for order for retrial)—
(a) the rules in Part 36 (Appeal to the Court of Appeal: general rules) apply with the necessary modifications;
(b) rules 39.8, 39.9 and 39.10 (bail and bail conditions in the Court of Appeal) apply as if the references in those rules to appeal included references to an application under rule 27.4; and
(c) rule 39.14 (Renewal or setting aside of order for retrial) applies as if the reference to section 7 of the Criminal Appeal Act 1968 were a reference to section 84 of the Criminal Justice Act 2003 (Retrial).

CRIMINAL PRACTICE DIRECTIONS: SENTENCING

PD-60 **CPD VII Sentencing A: Pleas of Guilty in the Crown Court**

A.1 Prosecutors and Prosecution Advocates should be familiar with and follow the Attorney-General's Guidelines on the Acceptance of Pleas and the Prosecutor's Role in the Sentencing Exercise.

PD-61 **CPD VII Sentencing B: Determining the Factual Basis of Sentence**

'Where a guilty plea is offered to less than the whole indictment and the prosecution is minded to accept pleas tendered to some counts or to lesser alternative counts.'

B.1 In some cases, defendants wishing to plead guilty will simply plead guilty to all charges on the basis of the facts as alleged and opened by the prosecution, with no dispute as to the factual basis or the extent of offending. Alternatively a defendant may plead guilty to some of the charges brought; in such a case, the judge will consider whether that plea represents a proper plea on the basis of the facts set out by the papers.

B.2 Where the prosecution advocate is considering whether to accept a plea to a lesser charge, the advocate may invite the judge to approve the proposed course of action. In such circumstances, the advocate must abide by the decision of the judge.

B.3 If the prosecution advocate does not invite the judge to approve the acceptance by the prosecution of a lesser charge, it is open to the judge to express his or her dissent with the course proposed and invite the advocate to reconsider the matter with those instructing him or her.

B.4 In any proceedings where the judge is of the opinion that the course proposed by the advocate may lead to serious injustice, the proceedings may be adjourned to allow the following procedure to be followed:
(a) as a preliminary step, the prosecution advocate must discuss the judge's observations with the Chief Crown Prosecutor or the senior prosecutor of the relevant prosecuting authority as appropriate, in an attempt to resolve the issue;
(b) where the issue remains unresolved, the Director of Public Prosecutions or the Director of the relevant prosecuting authority should be consulted;
(c) in extreme circumstances the judge may decline to proceed with the case until the prosecuting authority has consulted with the Attorney General, as may be appropriate.

B.5 Prior to entering a plea of guilty, a defendant may seek an indication of sentence under the procedure set out in *R v Goodyear* [2005] EWCA Crim 888, [2005] 1 WLR 2532, [2005] 2 Cr App R 20; see below.

Where a guilty plea is offered on a limited basis

B.6 A defendant may put forward a plea of guilty without accepting all of the facts as alleged by the prosecution. The basis of plea offered may seek to limit the facts or the extent of the offending for which the defendant is to be sentenced. Depending on the view taken by the prosecution, and the content of the offered basis, the case will fall into one of the following categories:

(a) a plea of guilty upon a basis of plea agreed by the prosecution and defence;
(b) a plea of guilty on a basis signed by the defendant but in respect of which there is no or only partial agreement by the prosecution;
(c) a plea of guilty on a basis that contains within it matters that are purely mitigation and which do not amount to a contradiction of the prosecution case; or
(d) in cases involving serious or complex fraud, a plea of guilty upon a basis of plea agreed by the prosecution and defence accompanied by joint submissions as to sentence.

(a) A plea of guilty upon a basis of plea agreed by the prosecution and defence

B.7 The prosecution may reach an agreement with the defendant as to the factual basis on which the defendant will plead guilty, often known as an 'agreed basis of plea'. It is always subject to the approval of the court, which will consider whether it adequately and appropriately reflects the evidence as disclosed on the papers, whether it is fair and whether it is in the interests of justice.

B.8 *R v Underwood* [2004] EWCA Crim 2256, [2005] 1 Cr App R 13, [2005] 1 Cr App R (S) 90 outlines the principles to be applied where the defendant admits that he or she is guilty, but disputes the basis of offending alleged by the prosecution:

(a) The prosecution may accept and agree the defendant's account of the disputed facts or reject it in its entirety, or in part. If the prosecution accepts the defendant's basis of plea, it must ensure that the basis of plea is factually accurate and enables the sentencing judge to impose a sentence appropriate to reflect the justice of the case;
(b) In resolving any disputed factual matters, the prosecution must consider its primary duty to the court and must not agree with or acquiesce in an agreement which contains material factual disputes;
(c) If the prosecution does accept the defendant's basis of plea, it must be reduced to writing, be signed by advocates for both sides, and made available to the judge prior to the prosecution's opening;
(d) An agreed basis of plea that has been reached between the parties should not contain matters which are in dispute and any aspects upon which there is not agreement should be clearly identified;
(e) On occasion, the prosecution may lack the evidence positively to dispute the defendant's account, for example, where the defendant asserts a matter outside the knowledge of the prosecution. Simply because the prosecution does not have evidence to contradict the defendant's assertions does not mean those assertions should be agreed. In such a case, the prosecution should test the defendant's evidence and submissions by requesting a *Newton* hearing (*R v Newton* (1982) 77 Cr App R 13, (1982) 4 Cr App R (S) 388), following the procedure set out below;
(f) If it is not possible for the parties to resolve a factual dispute when attempting to reach a plea agreement under this part, it is the responsibility of the prosecution to consider whether the matter should proceed to trial, or to invite the court to hold a *Newton* hearing as necessary.

B.9 *R v Underwood* emphasises that, whether or not pleas have been 'agreed', the judge is not bound by any such agreement and is entitled of his or her own motion to insist that any evidence relevant to the facts in dispute (or upon which the judge requires further evidence for whatever reason) should be called. Any view formed by the prosecution on a proposed basis of plea is deemed to be conditional on the judge's acceptance of the basis of plea.

B.10 A judge is not entitled to reject a defendant's basis of plea absent a *Newton* hearing unless it is determined by the court that the basis is manifestly false and as such does not merit examination by way of the calling of evidence or alternatively the defendant declines the opportunity to engage in the process of the *Newton* hearing whether by giving evidence on his own behalf or otherwise.

(b) A plea of guilty on a basis signed by the defendant but in respect of which there is no or only partial agreement by the prosecution

B.11 Where the defendant pleads guilty, but disputes the basis of offending alleged by the prosecution and agreement as to that has not been reached, the following procedure should be followed:

(a) The defendant's basis of plea must be set out in writing, identifying what is in dispute and must be signed by the defendant;

(b) The prosecution must respond in writing setting out their alternative contentions and indicating whether or not they submit that a *Newton* hearing is necessary;
(c) The court may invite the parties to make representations about whether the dispute is material to sentence; and
(d) If the court decides that it is a material dispute, the court will invite such further representations or evidence as it may require and resolve the dispute in accordance with the principles set out in *R v Newton*.

B.12 Where the disputed issue arises from facts which are within the exclusive knowledge of the defendant and the defendant is willing to give evidence in support of his case, the defence advocate should be prepared to call the defendant. If the defendant is not willing to testify, and subject to any explanation which may be given, the judge may draw such inferences as appear appropriate.

B.13 The decision whether or not a *Newton* hearing is required is one for the judge. Once the decision has been taken that there will be a *Newton* hearing, evidence is called by the parties in the usual way and the criminal burden and standard of proof applies. Whatever view has been taken by the prosecution, the prosecutor should not leave the questioning to the judge, but should assist the court by exploring the issues which the court wishes to have explored. The rules of evidence should be followed as during a trial, and the judge should direct himself appropriately as the tribunal of fact. Paragraphs 6 to 10 of *Underwood* provide additional guidance regarding the *Newton* hearing procedure.

(c) A plea of guilty on a basis that contains within it matters that are purely mitigation and which do not amount to a contradiction of the prosecution case

B.14 A basis of plea should not normally set out matters of mitigation but there may be circumstances where it is convenient and sensible for the document outlining a basis to deal with facts closely aligned to the circumstances of the offending which amount to mitigation and which may need to be resolved prior to sentence. The resolution of these matters does not amount to a *Newton* hearing properly so defined and in so far as facts fall to be established the defence will have to discharge the civil burden in order to do so. The scope of the evidence required to resolve issues that are purely matters of mitigation is for the court to determine.

(d) Cases involving serious fraud — a plea of guilty upon a basis of plea agreed by the prosecution and defence accompanied by joint submissions as to sentence

B.15 This section applies when the prosecution and the defendant(s) to a matter before the Crown Court involving allegations of serious or complex fraud have agreed a basis of plea and seek to make submissions to the court regarding sentence.

B.16 Guidance for prosecutors regarding the operation of this procedure is set out in the 'Attorney General's Guidelines on Plea Discussions in Cases of Serious or Complex Fraud', which came into force on 5 May 2009 and is referred to in this direction as the 'Attorney General's Plea Discussion Guidelines'.

B.17 In this part —

(a) 'a plea agreement' means a written basis of plea agreed between the prosecution and defendant(s) in accordance with the principles set out in *R v Underwood*, supported by admissible documentary evidence or admissions under section 10 of the Criminal Justice Act 1967;
(b) 'a sentencing submission' means sentencing submissions made jointly by the prosecution and defence as to the appropriate sentencing authorities and applicable sentencing range in the relevant sentencing guideline relating to the plea agreement;
(c) 'serious or complex fraud' includes, but is not limited to, allegations of fraud where two or more of the following are present:
 (i) the amount obtained or intended to be obtained exceeded £500,000;
 (ii) there is a significant international dimension;
 (iii) the case requires specialised knowledge of financial, commercial, fiscal or regulatory matters such as the operation of markets, banking systems, trusts or tax regimes;
 (iv) the case involves allegations of fraudulent activity against numerous victims;
 (v) the case involves an allegation of substantial and significant fraud on a public body;
 (vi) the case is likely to be of widespread public concern;
 (vii) the alleged misconduct endangered the economic well-being of the United Kingdom, for example by undermining confidence in financial markets.

Procedure

B.18 The procedure regarding agreed bases of plea outlined above, applies with equal rigour to the acceptance of pleas under this procedure. However, because under this procedure the parties will have been discussing the plea agreement and the charges from a much earlier stage, it is vital that the judge is fully informed of all relevant background to the discussions, charges and the eventual basis of plea.

B.19 Where the defendant has not yet appeared before the Crown Court, the prosecutor must send full details of the plea agreement and sentencing submission(s) to the court, at least 7 days in advance of the defendant's first appearance. Where the defendant has already appeared before the Crown Court, the prosecutor must notify the court as soon as is reasonably practicable that a plea agreement and sentencing submissions under the Attorney General's Plea Discussion Guidelines are to be submitted. The court should set a date for the matter to be heard, and the prosecutor must send full details of the plea agreement and sentencing submission(s) to the court as soon as practicable, or in accordance with the directions of the court.

B.20 The provision to the judge of full details of the plea agreement requires sufficient information to be provided to allow the judge to understand the facts of the case and the history of the plea discussions, to assess whether the plea agreement is fair and in the interests of justice, and to decide the appropriate sentence. This will include, but is not limited to:

(i) the plea agreement;
(ii) the sentencing submission(s);
(iii) all of the material provided by the prosecution to the defendant in the course of the plea discussions;
(iv) relevant material provided by the defendant, for example documents relating to personal mitigation; and
(v) the minutes of any meetings between the parties and any correspondence generated in the plea discussions.

The parties should be prepared to provide additional material at the request of the court.

B.21 The court should at all times have regard to the length of time that has elapsed since the date of the occurrence of the events giving rise to the plea discussions, the time taken to interview the defendant, the date of charge and the prospective trial date (if the matter were to proceed to trial) so as to ensure that its consideration of the plea agreement and sentencing submissions does not cause any unnecessary further delay.

Status of plea agreement and joint sentencing submissions

B.22 Where a plea agreement and joint sentencing submissions are submitted, it remains entirely a matter for the court to decide how to deal with the case. The judge retains the absolute discretion to refuse to accept the plea agreement and to sentence otherwise than in accordance with the sentencing submissions made under the Attorney General's Plea Discussion Guidelines.

B.23 Sentencing submissions should draw the court's attention to any applicable range in any relevant guideline, and to any ancillary orders that may be applicable. Sentencing submissions should not include a specific sentence or agreed range other than the ranges set out in sentencing guidelines or authorities.

B.24 Prior to pleading guilty in accordance with the plea agreement, the defendant(s) may apply to the court for an indication of the likely maximum sentence under the procedure set out below (a '*Goodyear* indication').

B.25 In the event that the judge indicates a sentence or passes a sentence which is not within the submissions made on sentencing, the plea agreement remains binding.

B.26 If the defendant does not plead guilty in accordance with the plea agreement, or if a defendant who has pleaded guilty in accordance with a plea agreement, successfully applies to withdraw his plea under CrimPR 25.5, the signed plea agreement may be treated as confession evidence, and may be used against the defendant at a later stage in these or any other proceedings. Any credit for a timely guilty plea may be lost. The court may exercise its discretion under section 78 of the Police and Criminal Evidence Act 1984 to exclude any such evidence if it appears to the court that, having regard to all the circumstances, including the circumstances in which the evidence was obtained, the admission of the evidence would have such an adverse effect on the fairness of the proceedings that the court ought not to admit it.

B.27 Where a defendant has failed to plead guilty in accordance with a plea agreement, the case is unlikely to be ready for trial immediately. The prosecution may have been commenced earlier than it otherwise would have been, in reliance upon the defendant's agreement to plead guilty. This is likely to be a relevant consideration for the court in deciding whether or not to grant an application to adjourn or stay the proceedings to allow the matter to be prepared for trial in accordance with the protocol on the 'Control and Management of Heavy Fraud and other Complex Criminal Cases', or as required.

PD-62 **CPD VII Sentencing C: Indications of Sentence: *R v Goodyear***

C.1 Prior to pleading guilty, it is open to a defendant in the Crown Court to request from the judge an indication of the maximum sentence that would be imposed if a guilty plea were to be tendered at that stage in the proceedings, in accordance with the guidance in *R v Goodyear* [2005] EWCA Crim 888, [2005] 1 WLR 2532, [2005] 2 Cr App R 20. The defence should notify the court and the prosecution of the intention to seek an indication in advance of any hearing.

C.2 Attention is drawn to the guidance set out in paragraphs 53 and following of *R v Goodyear*. The objective of the *Goodyear* guidelines is to safeguard against the creation or appearance of judicial pressure on a defendant. Any advance indication given should be the maximum sentence if a guilty plea were to be tendered at that stage of the proceedings only; the judge should not indicate the maximum possible sentence following conviction by a jury after trial. The judge should only give a *Goodyear* indication if one is requested by the defendant, although the judge can, in an appropriate case, remind the defence advocate of the defendant's entitlement to seek an advance indication of sentence.

C.3 Whether to give a *Goodyear* indication, and whether to give reasons for a refusal, is a matter for the discretion of the judge, to be exercised in accordance with the principles outlined by the Court of Appeal in that case. Such indications should normally not be given if there is a dispute as to the basis of plea unless the judge concludes that he or she can properly deal with the case without the need for a *Newton* hearing. If there is a basis of plea agreed by the prosecution and defence, it must be reduced into writing and a copy provided to the judge. As always, any basis of plea will be subject to the approval of the court. In cases where a dispute arises, the procedure in *R v Underwood* should be followed prior to the court considering a sentence indication further, as set out above. The judge should not become involved in negotiations about the acceptance of pleas or any agreed basis of plea, nor should a request be made for an indication of the different sentences that might be imposed if various different pleas were to be offered.

C.4 There should be no prosecution opening nor should the judge hear mitigation. However, during the sentence indication process the prosecution advocate is expected to assist the court by ensuring that the court has received all of the prosecution evidence, any statement from the victim about the impact of the offence, and any relevant previous convictions. Further, where appropriate, the prosecution should provide references to the relevant statutory powers of the court, relevant sentencing guidelines and authorities, and such other assistance as the court requires.

C.5 Attention is drawn to paragraph 70(d) of *Goodyear* which emphasises that the prosecution 'should not say anything which may create the impression that the sentence indication has the support or approval of the Crown.' This prohibition against the Crown indicating its approval of a particular sentence applies in all circumstances when a defendant is being sentenced, including when joint sentencing submissions are made.

C.6 An indication, once given, is, save in exceptional circumstances (such as arose in *R v Newman* [2010] EWCA Crim 1566, [2011] 1 Cr App R (S) 68), binding on the judge who gave it, and any other judge, subject to overriding statutory obligations such as those following a finding of 'dangerousness'. In circumstances where a judge proposes to depart from a *Goodyear* indication this must only be done in a way that does not give rise to unfairness (see *Newman*). However, if the defendant does not plead guilty, the indication will not thereafter bind the court.

C.7 If the offence is a specified offence such that the defendant might be liable to an assessment of 'dangerousness' in accordance with the Criminal Justice Act 2003 it is unlikely that the necessary material for such an assessment will be available. The court can still proceed to give an indication of sentence, but should state clearly the limitations of the indication that can be given.

C.8 A *Goodyear* indication should be given in open court in the presence of the defendant but any reference to the hearing is not admissible in any subsequent trial; and reporting restrictions should normally be imposed.

PD-63 **CPD VII Sentencing D: Facts to be Stated on Pleas of Guilty**

D.1 To enable the press and the public to know the circumstances of an offence of which an accused has been convicted and for which he is to be sentenced, in relation to each offence to which an accused has pleaded guilty the prosecution shall state those facts in open court, before sentence is imposed.

PD-64 **CPD VII Sentencing E: Concurrent and Consecutive Sentences**

E.1 Where a court passes on a defendant more than one term of imprisonment, the court should state in the presence of the defendant whether the terms are to be concurrent or consecutive. Should this not be done, the court clerk should ask the court, before the defendant leaves court, to do so.

E.2 If a defendant is, at the time of sentence, already serving two or more consecutive terms of imprisonment and the court intends to increase the total period of imprisonment, it should use the expression 'consecutive to the total period of imprisonment to which you are already subject' rather than 'at the expiration of the term of imprisonment you are now serving', as the defendant may not then be serving the last of the terms to which he is already subject.

E.3 The Sentencing Council has issued a definitive guideline on Totality which should be consulted. Under section 125(1) of the Coroners and Justice Act 2009, for offences committed after 6 April 2010, the guideline must be followed unless it would be contrary to the interests of justice to do so.

CPD VII Sentencing F: Victim Personal Statements PD-65

F.1 Victims of crime are invited to make a statement, known as a Victim Personal Statement ('VPS'). The statement gives victims a formal opportunity to say how a crime has affected them. It may help to identify whether they have a particular need for information, support and protection. The court will take the statement into account when determining sentence. In some circumstances, it may be appropriate for relatives of a victim to make a VPS, for example where the victim has died as a result of the relevant criminal conduct. The revised Code of Practice for Victims of Crime, published on 29 October 2013 gives further information about victims' entitlements within the criminal justice system, and the duties placed on criminal justice agencies when dealing with victims of crime.

F.2 When a police officer takes a statement from a victim, the victim should be told about the scheme and given the chance to make a VPS. The decision about whether or not to make a VPS is entirely a matter for the victim; no pressure should be brought to bear on their decision, and no conclusion should be drawn if they choose not to make such a statement. A VPS or a further VPS may be made (in proper s.9 form, see below) at any time prior to the disposal of the case. It will not normally be appropriate for a VPS to be made after the disposal of the case; there may be rare occasions between sentence and appeal when a further VPS may be necessary, for example, when the victim was injured and the final prognosis was not available at the date of sentence. However, VPS after disposal should be confined to presenting up to date factual material, such as medical information, and should be used sparingly.

F.3 If the court is presented with a VPS the following approach, subject to the further guidance given by the Court of Appeal in *R v Perkins; Bennett; Hall* [2013] EWCA Crim 323, [2013] Crim LR 533, should be adopted:

a) The VPS and any evidence in support should be considered and taken into account by the court, prior to passing sentence.

b) Evidence of the effects of an offence on the victim contained in the VPS or other statement, must be in proper form, that is a witness statement made under section 9 of the Criminal Justice Act 1967 or an expert's report; and served in good time upon the defendant's solicitor or the defendant, if he or she is not represented. Except where inferences can properly be drawn from the nature of or circumstances surrounding the offence, a sentencing court must not make assumptions unsupported by evidence about the effects of an offence on the victim. The maker of a VPS may be cross-examined on its content.

c) At the discretion of the court, the VPS may also be read aloud or played in open court, in whole or in part, or it may be summarised. If the VPS is to be read aloud, the court should also determine who should do so. In making these decisions, the court should take account of the victim's preferences, and follow them unless there is good reason not to do so; examples of this include the inadmissibility of the content or the potentially harmful consequences for the victim or others. Court hearings should not be adjourned solely to allow the victim to attend court to read the VPS. For the purposes of CPD I General matters 5B: Access to information held by the court, a VPS that is read aloud or played in open court in whole or in part should be considered as such, and no longer treated as a confidential document.

d) In all cases it will be appropriate for a VPS to be referred to in the course of the sentencing hearing and/or in the sentencing remarks.

e) The court must pass what it judges to be the appropriate sentence having regard to the circumstances of the offence and of the offender, taking into account, so far as the court considers it appropriate, the impact on the victim. The opinions of the victim or the victim's close relatives as to what the sentence should be are therefore not relevant, unlike the consequences of the offence on them. Victims should be advised of this. If, despite the advice, opinions as to sentence are included in the statement, the court should pay no attention to them.

CPD VII Sentencing G: Families Bereaved by Homicide and other Criminal Conduct PD-66

G.1 In cases in which the victim has died as a result of the relevant criminal conduct, the victim's family is not a party to the proceedings, but does have an interest in the case. Bereaved families have particular entitlements under the Code of Practice for Victims of Crime. All parties should have regard to the needs of the victim's family and ensure that the trial process does not expose bereaved families to avoidable intimidation, humiliation or distress.

G.2 In so far as it is compatible with family members' roles as witnesses, the court should consider the following measures:

a) Practical arrangements being discussed with the family and made in good time before the trial, such as seating for family members in the courtroom; if appropriate, in an alternative area, away from the public gallery;
b) Warning being given to families if the evidence on a certain day is expected to be particularly distressing;
c) Ensuring that appropriate use is made of the scheme for Victim Personal Statements, in accordance with the paragraphs above.

G.3 The sentencer should consider providing a written copy of the sentencing remarks to the family after sentence has been passed. Sentencers should tend in favour of providing such a copy, unless there is good reason not to do so, and the copy should be provided as soon as is reasonably practicable after the sentencing hearing.

PD-67 **CPD VII Sentencing H: Community Impact Statements**

H.1 A community impact statement may be prepared by the police to make the court aware of particular crime trends in the local area and the impact of these on the local community.

H.2 Such statements must be in proper form, that is a witness statement made under section 9 of the Criminal Justice Act 1967 or an expert's report; and served in good time upon the defendant's solicitor or the defendant, if he is not represented.

H.3 The community impact statement and any evidence in support should be considered and taken into account by the court, prior to passing sentence. The statement should be referred to in the course of the sentencing hearing and/or in the sentencing remarks. Subject to the court's discretion, the contents of the statement may be summarised or read out in open court.

H.4 The court must pass what it judges to be the appropriate sentence having regard to the circumstances of the offence and of the offender, taking into account, so far as the court considers it appropriate, the impact on the local community. Opinions as to what the sentence should be are therefore not relevant. If, despite the advice, opinions as to sentence are included in the statement, the court should pay no attention to them.

H.5 Except where inferences can properly be drawn from the nature of or circumstances surrounding the offence, a sentencing court must not make assumptions unsupported by evidence about the effects of an offence on the local community.

H.6 It will not be appropriate for a Community Impact Statement to be made after disposal of the case but before an appeal.

PD-68 **CPD VII Sentencing I: Impact Statements for Businesses**

I.1 Individual victims of crime are invited to make a statement, known as a Victim Personal Statement ('VPS'), see CPD VII Sentencing F. If the victim, or one of the victims, is a business or enterprise (including charities but excluding public sector bodies), of any size, a nominated representative may make an Impact Statement for Business ('ISB'). The ISB gives a formal opportunity for the court to be informed how a crime has affected a business. The court will take the statement into account when determining sentence. This does not prevent individual employees from making a VPS about the impact of the same crime on them as individuals. Indeed the ISB should be about the impact on the business exclusively, and the impact on any individual included within a VPS.

I.2 When a police officer takes statements about the alleged offence, he or she should also inform the business about the scheme. An ISB may be made to the police at that time, or the ISB template may be downloaded from www.police.uk, completed and emailed or posted to the relevant police contact. Guidance on how to complete the form is available on www.police.uk and on the CPS website. There is no obligation on any business to make an ISB.

I.3 An ISB or an updated ISB may be made (in proper s.9 form, see below) at any time prior to the disposal of the case. It will not be appropriate for an ISB to be made after disposal of the case but before an appeal.

I.4 A business wishing to make an ISB should consider carefully who to nominate as the representative to make the statement on its behalf. A person making an ISB on behalf of a business, the nominated representative, must be authorised to do so on behalf of the business, either by nature of their position within the business, such as a director or owner, or by having been suitably authorised, such as by the owner or Board of Directors. The nominated representative must also be in a position to give admissible evidence about the impact of the crime on the business. This will usually be through first hand personal knowledge, or using business documents (as defined in section 117 of the Criminal Justice Act 2003). The most appropriate person will vary depending on the nature of the crime, and the size and structure of the business and may for example include a manager, director, chief executive or shop owner.

I.5 If the nominated representative leaves the business before the case comes to court, he or she will usually remain the representative, as the ISB made by him or her will still provide the best evidence of the impact of the crime, and he or she could still be asked to attend court. Nominated representatives should be made aware of the on-going nature of the role at the time of making the ISB.

I.6 If necessary a further ISB may be provided to the police if there is a change in circumstances. This could be made by an alternative nominated representative. However, the new ISB will usually supplement, not replace, the original ISB and again must contain admissible evidence. The prosecutor will decide which ISB to serve on the defence as evidence, and any ISB that is not served in evidence will be included in the unused material and considered for disclosure to the defence.

I.7 The ISB must be made in proper form, that is as a witness statement made under section 9 of the Criminal Justice Act 1967 or an expert's report; and served in good time upon the defendant's solicitor or the defendant, if he or she is not represented. The maker of an ISB can be cross-examined on its content.

I.8 The ISB and any evidence in support should be considered and taken into account by the court, prior to passing sentence. The statement should be referred to in the course of the sentencing hearing and/or in the sentencing remarks. Subject to the court's discretion, the contents of the statement may be summarised or read out in open court; the views of the business should be taken into account in reaching a decision.

I.9 The court must pass what it judges to be the appropriate sentence having regard to the circumstances of the offence and of the offender, taking into account, so far as the court considers it appropriate, the impact on the victims, including any business victim. Opinions as to what the sentence should be are therefore not relevant. If, despite the advice, opinions as to sentence are included in the statement, the court should pay no attention to them.

I.10 Except where inferences can properly be drawn from the nature of or circumstances surrounding the offence, a sentencing court must not make assumptions unsupported by evidence about the effects of an offence on a business.

CPD VII Sentencing J: Binding Over Orders and Conditional Discharges PD-69

J.1 This direction takes into account the judgments of the European Court of Human Rights in *Steel v United Kingdom* (1999) 28 EHRR 603, [1998] Crim LR 893 and in *Hashman and Harrup v United Kingdom* (2000) 30 EHRR 241, [2000] Crim LR 185. Its purpose is to give practical guidance, in the light of those two judgments, on the practice of imposing binding over orders. The direction applies to orders made under the court's common law powers, under the Justices of the Peace Act 1361, under section 1(7) of the Justices of the Peace Act 1968 and under section 115 of the Magistrates' Courts Act 1980. This direction also gives guidance concerning the court's power to bind over parents or guardians under section 150 of the Powers of Criminal Courts (Sentencing) Act 2000 and the Crown Court's power to bind over to come up for judgment. The court's power to impose a conditional discharge under section 12 of the Powers of Criminal Courts (Sentencing) Act 2000 is also covered by this direction.

Binding over to keep the peace

J.2 Before imposing a binding over order, the court must be satisfied so that it is sure that a breach of the peace involving violence, or an imminent threat of violence, has occurred or that there is a real risk of violence in the future. Such violence may be perpetrated by the individual who will be subject to the order or by a third party as a natural consequence of the individual's conduct.

J.3 In light of the judgment in *Hashman*, courts should no longer bind an individual over 'to be of good behaviour'. Rather than binding an individual over to 'keep the peace' in general terms, the court should identify the specific conduct or activity from which the individual must refrain.

Written order

J.4 When making an order binding an individual over to refrain from specified types of conduct or activities, the details of that conduct or those activities should be specified by the court in a written order, served on all relevant parties. The court should state its reasons for the making of the order, its length and the amount of the recognisance. The length of the order should be proportionate to the harm sought to be avoided and should not generally exceed 12 months.

Evidence

J.5 Sections 51 to 57 of the Magistrates' Courts Act 1980 set out the jurisdiction of the magistrates' court to hear an application made on complaint and the procedure which is to be followed. This includes a requirement under section 53 to hear evidence and the parties, before making any order. This practice should be applied to all cases in the magistrates' court and the Crown Court where the court is considering imposing a binding over order. The court should give the individual who would be subject to the order and the prosecutor the opportunity to make representations, both as to the making of the order and as to its terms. The court should also hear any admissible evidence the parties wish to call and which has not already been heard in the proceedings. Particularly careful consideration may be required where the individual who would be subject to the order is a witness in the proceedings.

J.6 Where there is an admission which is sufficient to found the making of a binding over order and/or the individual consents to the making of the order, the court should nevertheless hear sufficient representations and, if appropriate, evidence, to satisfy itself that an order is appropriate in all the circumstances and to be clear about the terms of the order.

J.7 Where there is an allegation of breach of a binding over order and this is contested, the court should hear representations and evidence, including oral evidence, from the parties before making a finding. If unrepresented and no opportunity has been given previously the court should give a reasonable period for the person said to have breached the binding over order to find representation.

Burden and standard of proof

J.8 The court should be satisfied so that it is sure of the matters complained of before a binding over order may be imposed. Where the procedure has been commenced on complaint, the burden of proof rests on the complainant. In all other circumstances, the burden of proof rests upon the prosecution.

J.9 Where there is an allegation of breach of a binding over order, the court should be satisfied on the balance of probabilities that the defendant is in breach before making any order for forfeiture of a recognisance. The burden of proof shall rest on the prosecution.

Recognisance

J.10 The court must be satisfied on the merits of the case that an order for binding over is appropriate and should announce that decision before considering the amount of the recognisance. If unrepresented, the individual who is made subject to the binding over order should be told he has a right of appeal from the decision.

J.11 When fixing the amount of recognisance, courts should have regard to the individual's financial resources and should hear representations from the individual or his legal representatives regarding finances.

J.12 A recognisance is made in the form of a bond giving rise to a civil debt on breach of the order.

Refusal to enter into a recognisance

J.13 If there is any possibility that an individual will refuse to enter a recognisance, the court should consider whether there are any appropriate alternatives to a binding over order (for example, continuing with a prosecution). Where there are no appropriate alternatives and the individual continues to refuse to enter into the recognisance, the court may commit the individual to custody. In the magistrates' court, the power to do so will derive from section 1(7) of the Justices of the Peace Act 1968 or, more rarely, from section 115(3) of the Magistrates' Courts Act 1980, and the court should state which power it is acting under; in the Crown Court, this is a common law power.

J.14 Before the court exercises a power to commit the individual to custody, the individual should be given the opportunity to see a duty solicitor or another legal representative and be represented in proceedings if the individual so wishes. Public funding should generally be granted to cover representation. In the Crown Court this rests with the Judge who may grant a Representation Order.

J.15 In the event that the individual does not take the opportunity to seek legal advice, the court shall give the individual a final opportunity to comply with the request and shall explain the consequences of a failure to do so.

Antecedents

J.16 Courts are reminded of the provisions of section 7(5) of the Rehabilitation of Offenders Act 1974 which excludes from a person's antecedents any order of the court 'with respect to any person otherwise than on a conviction'.

Binding over to come up for judgment

J.17 If the Crown Court is considering binding over an individual to come up for judgment, the court should specify any conditions with which the individual is to comply in the meantime and not specify that the individual is to be of good behaviour.

J.18 The Crown Court should, if the individual is unrepresented, explain the consequences of a breach of the binding over order in these circumstances.

Binding over of parent or guardian

J.19 Where a court is considering binding over a parent or guardian under section 150 of the Powers of Criminal Courts (Sentencing) Act 2000 to enter into a recognisance to take proper care of and exercise proper control over a child or young person, the court should specify the actions which the parent or guardian is to take.

Security for good behaviour

J.20 Where a court is imposing a conditional discharge under section 12 of the Powers of Criminal Courts (Sentencing) Act 2000, it has the power, under section 12(6) to make an order that a person who consents to do so give security for the good behaviour of the offender. When making such an order, the court should specify the type of conduct from which the offender is to refrain.

CPD VII Sentencing K: Committal for Sentence PD-70

K.1 CrimPR 28.10 applies when a case is committed to the Crown Court for sentence and specifies the information and documentation that must be provided by the magistrates' court. On a committal for sentence any reasons given by the magistrates for their decision should be included with the documents. All of these documents should be made available to the judge in the Crown Court if the judge requires them, in order to decide before the hearing questions of listing or representation or the like. They will also be available to the court during the hearing if it becomes necessary or desirable for the court to see what happened in the lower court.

CPD VII Sentencing L: Imposition of Life Sentences PD-71

L.1 Section 82A of the Powers of Criminal Courts (Sentencing) Act 2000 empowers a judge when passing a sentence of life imprisonment, where such a sentence is not fixed by law, to specify by order such part of the sentence ('the relevant part') as shall be served before the prisoner may require the Secretary of State to refer his case to the Parole Board. This is applicable to defendants under the age of 18 years as well as to adult defendants.

L.2 Thus the life sentence falls into two parts:

(a) the relevant part, which consists of the period of detention imposed for punishment and deterrence, taking into account the seriousness of the offence; and

(b) the remaining part of the sentence, during which the prisoner's detention will be governed by consideration of risk to the public.

L.3 The judge is not obliged by statute to make use of the provisions of section 82A when passing a life sentence. However, the judge should do so, save in the very exceptional case where the judge considers that the offence is so serious that detention for life is justified by the seriousness of the offence alone, irrespective of the risk to the public. In such a case, the judge should state this in open court when passing sentence.

L.4 In cases where the judge is to specify the relevant part of the sentence under section 82A, the judge should permit the advocate for the defendant to address the court as to the appropriate length of the relevant part. Where no relevant part is to be specified, the advocate for the defendant should be permitted to address the court as to the appropriateness of this course of action.

L.5 In specifying the relevant part of the sentence, the judge should have regard to the specific terms of section 82A and should indicate the reasons for reaching his decision as to the length of the relevant part.

CPD VII Sentencing M: Mandatory Life Sentences PD-72

M.1 The purpose of this section is to give practical guidance as to the procedure for passing a mandatory life sentence under section 269 and schedule 21 of the Criminal Justice Act 2003 ('the Act'). This direction also gives guidance as to the transitional arrangements under section 276 and schedule 22 of the Act. It clarifies the correct approach to looking at the practice of the Secretary of State prior to December 2002 for the purposes of schedule 22 of the Act, in the light of the judgment in *R v Sullivan, Gibbs, Elener and Elener* [2004] EWCA Crim 1762, [2005] 1 Cr App R 3, [2005] 1 Cr App R (S) 67.

M.2 Section 269 came into force on 18 December 2003. Under section 269, all courts passing a mandatory life sentence must either announce in open court the minimum term the prisoner must serve before the

Parole Board can consider release on licence under the provisions of section 28 of the Crime (Sentences) Act 1997 (as amended by section 275 of the Act), or announce that the seriousness of the offence is so exceptionally high that the early release provisions should not apply at all (a 'whole life order').

M.3 In setting the minimum term, the court must set the term it considers appropriate taking into account the seriousness of the offence. In considering the seriousness of the offence, the court must have regard to the general principles set out in Schedule 21 of the Act as amended and any guidelines relating to offences in general which are relevant to the case and not incompatible with the provisions of Schedule 21. Although it is necessary to have regard to such guidance, it is always permissible not to apply the guidance if a judge considers there are reasons for not following it. It is always necessary to have regard to the need to do justice in the particular case. However, if a court departs from any of the starting points given in Schedule 21, the court is under a duty to state its reasons for doing so (section 270(2)(b) of the Act).

M.4 Schedule 21 states that the first step is to choose one of five starting points: 'whole life', 30 years, 25 years, 15 years or 12 years. Where the 15 year starting point has been chosen, judges should have in mind that this starting point encompasses a very broad range of murders. At paragraph 35 of *Sullivan*, the court found it should not be assumed that Parliament intended to raise all minimum terms that would previously have had a lower starting point, to 15 years.

M.5 Where the offender was 21 or over at the time of the offence, and the court takes the view that the murder is so grave that the offender ought to spend the rest of his life in prison, the appropriate starting point is a 'whole life order' (paragraph 4(1) of Schedule 21). The effect of such an order is that the early release provisions in section 28 of the Crime (Sentences) Act 1997 will not apply. Such an order should only be specified where the court considers that the seriousness of the offence (or the combination of the offence and one or more other offences associated with it) is exceptionally high. Paragraph 4(2) sets out examples of cases where it would normally be appropriate to take the 'whole life order' as the appropriate starting point.

M.6 Where the offender is aged 18 to 20 and commits a murder that is so serious that it would require a whole life order if committed by an offender aged 21 or over, the appropriate starting point will be 30 years. (Paragraph 5(2)(h) of Schedule 21).

M.7 Where a case is not so serious as to require a 'whole life order' but where the seriousness of the offence is particularly high and the offender was aged 18 or over when he committed the offence, the appropriate starting point is 30 years (paragraph 5(1) of Schedule 21). Paragraph 5(2) sets out examples of cases where a 30 year starting point would normally be appropriate (if they do not require a 'whole life order').

M.8 Where the offender was aged 18 or over when he committed the offence, took a knife or other weapon to the scene intending to commit any offence or have it available to use as a weapon, and used it in committing the murder, the offence is normally to be regarded as sufficiently serious for an appropriate starting point of 25 years (paragraph 5A of Schedule 21).

M.9 Where the offender was aged 18 or over when he committed the offence and the case does not fall within paragraph 4(1), 5(1) or 5A(1) of Schedule 21, the appropriate starting point is 15 years (see paragraph 6).

M.10 18 to 20 year olds are only the subject of the 30-year, 25-year and 15-year starting points.

M.11 The appropriate starting point when setting a sentence of detention during Her Majesty's pleasure for offenders aged under 18 when they committed the offence is always 12 years (paragraph 7 of Schedule 21).

M.12 The second step after choosing a starting point is to take account of any aggravating or mitigating factors which would justify a departure from the starting point. Additional aggravating factors (other than those specified in paragraphs 4(2), 5(2) and 5A) are listed at paragraph 10 of Schedule 21. Examples of mitigating factors are listed at paragraph 11 of Schedule 21. Taking into account the aggravating and mitigating features, the court may add to or subtract from the starting point to arrive at the appropriate punitive period.

M.13 The third step is that the court should consider the effect of section 143(2) of the Act in relation to previous convictions; section 143(3) of the Act where the offence was committed whilst the offender was on bail; and section 144 of the Act where the offender has pleaded guilty (paragraph 12 of Schedule 21). The court should then take into account what credit the offender would have received for a remand in custody under section 240 or 240ZA of the Act and/or for a remand on bail subject to a qualifying curfew condition under section 240A, but for the fact that the mandatory sentence is one of life imprisonment. Where the offender has been thus remanded in connection with the offence or a related offence, the court should have in mind that no credit will otherwise be given for this time when the prisoner is considered for early release. The appropriate time to take it into account is when setting the minimum term. The court should make any appropriate subtraction from the punitive period it would otherwise impose, in order to reach the minimum term.

M.14 Following these calculations, the court should have arrived at the appropriate minimum term to be announced in open court. As paragraph 9 of Schedule 21 makes clear, the judge retains ultimate discretion and the court may arrive at any minimum term from any starting point. The minimum term is subject to appeal by the offender under section 271 of the Act and subject to review on a reference by the Attorney-General under section 272 of the Act.

CPD VII Sentencing N: Transitional Arrangements for Sentences where the Offence was Committed before 18 December 2003 **PD-73**

N.1 Where the court is passing a sentence of mandatory life imprisonment for an offence committed before 18 December 2003, the court should take a fourth step in determining the minimum term in accordance with section 276 and Schedule 22 of the Act.

N.2 The purpose of those provisions is to ensure that the sentence does not breach the principle of non-retroactivity, by ensuring that a lower minimum term would not have been imposed for the offence when it was committed. Before setting the minimum term, the court must check whether the proposed term is greater than that which the Secretary of State would probably have notified under the practice followed by the Secretary of State before December 2002.

N.3 The decision in *Sullivan, Gibbs, Elener and Elener* [2004] EWCA Crim 1762, [2005] 1 Cr App R 3, [2005] 1 Cr App R (S) 67 gives detailed guidance as to the correct approach to this practice and judges passing mandatory life sentences where the murder was committed prior to 18 December 2003 are well advised to read that judgment before proceeding.

N.4 The practical result of that judgment is that in sentences where the murder was committed before 31 May 2002, the best guide to what would have been the practice of the Secretary of State is the letter sent to judges by Lord Bingham CJ on 10th February 1997, the relevant parts of which are set out below.

N.5 The practice of Lord Bingham, as set out in his letter of 10 February 1997, was to take 14 years as the period actually to be served for the 'average', 'normal' or 'unexceptional' murder. Examples of factors he outlined as capable, in appropriate cases, of mitigating the normal penalty were:

(1) Youth;
(2) Age (where relevant to physical capacity on release or the likelihood of the defendant dying in prison);
(3) [Intellectual disability or mental disorder];
(4) Provocation (in a non-technical sense), or an excessive response to a personal threat;
(5) The absence of an intention to kill;
(6) Spontaneity and lack of premeditation (beyond that necessary to constitute the offence: e.g., a sudden response to family pressure or to prolonged and eventually insupportable stress);
(7) Mercy killing;
(8) A plea of guilty, or hard evidence of remorse or contrition.

N.6 Lord Bingham then listed the following factors as likely to call for a sentence more severe than the norm:

(1) Evidence of planned, professional, revenge or contract killing;
(2) The killing of a child or a very old or otherwise vulnerable victim;
(3) Evidence of sadism, gratuitous violence, or sexual maltreatment, humiliation or degradation before the killing;
(4) Killing for gain (in the course of burglary, robbery, blackmail, insurance fraud, etc.);
(5) Multiple killings;
(6) The killing of a witness, or potential witness, to defeat the ends of justice;
(7) The killing of those doing their public duty (policemen, prison officers, postmasters, firemen, judges, etc.);
(8) Terrorist or politically motivated killings;
(9) The use of firearms or other dangerous weapons, whether carried for defensive or offensive reasons;
(10) A substantial record of serious violence;
(11) Macabre attempts to dismember or conceal the body.

N.7 Lord Bingham further stated that the fact that a defendant was under the influence of drink or drugs at the time of the killing is so common he would be inclined to treat it as neutral. But in the not unfamiliar case in which a couple, inflamed by drink, indulge in a violent quarrel in which one dies, often against a background of longstanding drunken violence, then he would tend to recommend a term somewhat below the norm.

N.8 Lord Bingham went on to say that given the intent necessary for proof of murder, the consequences of taking life and the understandable reaction of relatives to the deceased, a substantial term will almost always be called for, save perhaps in a truly venial case of mercy killing. While a recommendation of a punitive term longer than, say, 30 years will be very rare indeed, there should not be any upper limit. Some crimes will certainly call for terms very well in excess of the norm.

N.9 For the purposes of sentences where the murder was committed after 31 May 2002 and before 18 December 2003, the judge should apply the Practice Statement handed down on 31 May 2002 reproduced at paragraphs N.10 to N.20 below.

N.10 This Statement replaces the previous single normal tariff of 14 years by substituting a higher and a normal starting point of respectively 16 (comparable to 32 years) and 12 years (comparable to 24 years). These starting points have then to be increased or reduced because of aggravating or mitigating factors such as those referred to below. It is emphasised that they are no more than starting points.

The normal starting point of 12 years

N.11 Cases falling within this starting point will normally involve the killing of an adult victim, arising from a quarrel or loss of temper between two people known to each other. It will not have the characteristics referred to in paragraph N.13. Exceptionally, the starting point may be reduced because of the sort of circumstances described in the next paragraph.

N.12 The normal starting point can be reduced because the murder is one where the offender's culpability is significantly reduced, for example, because:

(a) the case came close to the borderline between murder and manslaughter; or
(b) the offender suffered from mental disorder, or from a mental disability which lowered the degree of his criminal responsibility for the killing, although not affording a defence of diminished responsibility; or
(c) the offender was provoked (in a non-technical sense) such as by prolonged and eventually unsupportable stress; or
(d) the case involved an over-reaction in self-defence; or
(e) the offence was a mercy killing.

These factors could justify a reduction to 8/9 years (equivalent to 16/18 years).

The higher starting point of 15/16 years

N.13 The higher starting point will apply to cases where the offender's culpability was exceptionally high, or the victim was in a particularly vulnerable position. Such cases will be characterised by a feature which makes the crime especially serious, such as:

(a) the killing was 'professional' or a contract killing;
(b) the killing was politically motivated;
(c) the killing was done for gain (in the course of a burglary, robbery etc.);
(d) the killing was intended to defeat the ends of justice (as in the killing of a witness or potential witness);
(e) the victim was providing a public service;
(f) the victim was a child or was otherwise vulnerable;
(g) the killing was racially aggravated;
(h) the victim was deliberately targeted because of his or her religion or sexual orientation;
(i) there was evidence of sadism, gratuitous violence or sexual maltreatment, humiliation or degradation of the victim before the killing;
(j) extensive and/or multiple injuries were inflicted on the victim before death;
(k) the offender committed multiple murders.

Variation of the starting point

N.14 Whichever starting point is selected in a particular case, it may be appropriate for the trial judge to vary the starting point upwards or downwards, to take account of aggravating or mitigating factors, which relate to either the offence or the offender, in the particular case.

N.15 Aggravating factors relating to the offence can include:

(a) the fact that the killing was planned;
(b) the use of a firearm;
(c) arming with a weapon in advance;
(d) concealment of the body, destruction of the crime scene and/or dismemberment of the body;

(e) particularly in domestic violence cases, the fact that the murder was the culmination of cruel and violent behaviour by the offender over a period of time.

N.16 Aggravating factors relating to the offender will include the offender's previous record and failures to respond to previous sentences, to the extent that this is relevant to culpability rather than to risk.

N.17 Mitigating factors relating to the offence will include:

(a) an intention to cause grievous bodily harm, rather than to kill;
(b) spontaneity and lack of pre-meditation.

N.18 Mitigating factors relating to the offender may include:

(a) the offender's age;
(b) clear evidence of remorse or contrition;
(c) a timely plea of guilty.

Very serious cases

N.19 A substantial upward adjustment may be appropriate in the most serious cases, for example, those involving a substantial number of murders, or if there are several factors identified as attracting the higher starting point present. In suitable cases, the result might even be a minimum term of 30 years (equivalent to 60 years) which would offer little or no hope of the offender's eventual release. In cases of exceptional gravity, the judge, rather than setting a whole life minimum term, can state that there is no minimum period which could properly be set in that particular case.

N.20 Among the categories of case referred to in paragraph N.13, some offences may be especially grave. These include cases in which the victim was performing his duties as a prison officer at the time of the crime, or the offence was a terrorist or sexual or sadistic murder, or involved a young child. In such a case, a term of 20 years and upwards could be appropriate.

N.21 In following this guidance, judges should bear in mind the conclusion of the Court in *Sullivan* that the general effect of both these statements is the same. While Lord Bingham does not identify as many starting points, it is open to the judge to come to exactly the same decision irrespective of which was followed. Both pieces of guidance give the judge a considerable degree of discretion.

CPD VII Sentencing P: Procedure for Announcing the Minimum Term in Open Court PD-74

P.1 Having gone through the three or four steps outlined above, the court is then under a duty, under section 270 of the Act, to state in open court, in ordinary language, its reasons for deciding on the minimum term or for passing a whole life order.

P.2 In order to comply with this duty, the court should state clearly the minimum term it has determined. In doing so, it should state which of the starting points it has chosen and its reasons for doing so. Where the court has departed from that starting point due to mitigating or aggravating features, it must state the reasons for that departure and any aggravating or mitigating features which have led to that departure. At that point, the court should also declare how much, if any, time is being deducted for time spent in custody and/or on bail subject to a qualifying curfew condition. The court must then explain that the minimum term is the minimum amount of time the prisoner will spend in prison, from the date of sentence, before the Parole Board can order early release. If it remains necessary for the protection of the public, the prisoner will continue to be detained after that date. The court should also state that where the prisoner has served the minimum term and the Parole Board has decided to direct release, the prisoner will remain on licence for the rest of his life and may be recalled to prison at any time.

P.3 Where the offender was 21 or over when he committed the offence and the court considers that the seriousness of the offence is so exceptionally high that a 'whole life order' is appropriate, the court should state clearly its reasons for reaching this conclusion. It should also explain that the early release provisions will not apply.

CPD VII Sentencing Q: Financial, Etc. Information Required for Sentencing PD-75

Q.1 These directions supplement CrimPR 24.11 and 25.16, which set out the procedure to be followed where a defendant pleads guilty, or is convicted, and is to be sentenced. They are not concerned exclusively with corporate defendants, or with offences of an environmental, public health, health and safety or other regulatory character, but the guidance which they contain is likely to be of particular significance in such cases.

Q.2 The rules set out the prosecutor's responsibilities in all cases. Where the offence is of a character, or is against a prohibition, with which the sentencing court is unlikely to be familiar, those responsibilities are commensurately more onerous. The court is entitled to the greatest possible assistance in identifying information relevant to sentencing.

Q.3 In such a case, save where the circumstances are very straightforward, it is likely that justice will best be served by the submission of the required information in writing: see *R v Friskies Petcare (UK) Ltd* [2000] 2 Cr App R (S) 401. Though it is the prosecutor's responsibility to the court to prepare any such document, if the defendant pleads guilty, or indicates a guilty plea, then it is very highly desirable that such sentencing information should be agreed between the parties and jointly submitted. If agreement cannot be reached in all particulars, then the nature and extent of the disagreement should be indicated. If the court concludes that what is in issue is material to sentence, then it will give directions for resolution of the dispute, whether by hearing oral evidence or by other means. In every case, when passing sentence the sentencing court must make clear on what basis sentence is passed: in fairness to the defendant, and for the information of any other person, or court, who needs or wishes to understand the reasons for sentence.

Q.4 If so directed by or on behalf of the court, a defendant must supply accurate information about financial circumstances. In fixing the amount of any fine the court must take into account, amongst other considerations, the financial circumstances of the offender (whether an individual or other person) as they are known or as they appear to be. Before fixing the amount of fine when the defendant is an individual, the court must inquire into his financial circumstances. Where the defendant is an individual the court may make a financial circumstances order in respect of him. This means an order in which the court requires an individual to provide a statement as to his financial means, within a specified time. It is an offence, punishable with imprisonment, to fail to comply with such an order or for knowingly/recklessly furnishing a false statement or knowingly failing to disclose a material fact. The provisions of section 20A Criminal Justice Act 1991 apply to any person (thereby including a corporate organisation) and place the offender under a statutory duty to provide the court with a statement as to his financial means in response to an official request. There are offences for non-compliance, false statements or non-disclosure. It is for the court to decide how much information is required, having regard to relevant sentencing guidelines or guideline cases. However, by reference to those same guidelines and cases the parties should anticipate what the court will require, and prepare accordingly. In complex cases, and in cases involving a corporate defendant, the information required will be more extensive than in others. In the case of a corporate defendant, that information usually will include details of the defendant's corporate structure; annual profit and loss accounts, or extracts; annual balance sheets, or extracts; details of shareholders' receipts; and details of the remuneration of directors or other officers.

Q.5 In *R v F Howe and Son (Engineers) Ltd* [1999] 2 Cr App R (S) 37 the Court of Appeal observed:

> 'If a defendant company wishes to make any submission to the court about its ability to pay a fine it should supply copies of its accounts and any other financial information on which it intends to rely in good time before the hearing both to the court and to the prosecution. This will give the prosecution the opportunity to assist the court should the court wish it. Usually accounts need to be considered with some care to avoid reaching a superficial and perhaps erroneous conclusion. Where accounts or other financial information are deliberately not supplied the court will be entitled to conclude that the company is in a position to pay any financial penalty it is minded to impose. Where the relevant information is provided late it may be desirable for sentence to be adjourned, if necessary at the defendant's expense, so as to avoid the risk of the court taking what it is told at face value and imposing an inadequate penalty.'

Q.6 In the case of an individual, the court is likewise entitled to conclude that the defendant is able to pay any fine imposed unless the defendant has supplied financial information to the contrary. It is the defendant's responsibility to disclose to the court such information relevant to his or her financial position as will enable it to assess what he or she reasonably can afford to pay. If necessary, the court may compel the disclosure of an individual defendant's financial circumstances. In the absence of such disclosure, or where the court is not satisfied that it has been given sufficient reliable information, the court will be entitled to draw reasonable inferences as to the offender's means from evidence it has heard and from all the circumstances of the case.

Criminal Procedure Rules Part 28 Sentencing Procedures in Special Cases

R-260 **Reasons for not following usual sentencing requirements**

28.1 (1) This rule applies where the court decides—
- (a) not to follow a relevant sentencing guideline;
- (b) not to make, where it could—
  - (i) a reparation order (unless it passes a custodial or community sentence),
  - (ii) a compensation order,
  - (iii) a slavery and trafficking reparation order, or
  - (iv) a travel restriction order;

(c) not to order, where it could—
(i) that a suspended sentence of imprisonment is to take effect,
(ii) the endorsement of the defendant's driving record, or
(iii) the defendant's disqualification from driving, for the usual minimum period or at all;
(d) to pass a lesser sentence than it otherwise would have passed because the defendant has assisted, or has agreed to assist, an investigator or prosecutor in relation to an offence.
(2) The court must explain why it has so decided, when it explains the sentence that it has passed.
(3) Where paragraph (1)(d) applies, the court must arrange for such an explanation to be given to the defendant and to the prosecutor in writing, if the court thinks that it would not be in the public interest to explain in public.

Notice of requirements of suspended sentence and community, etc. orders **R-261**

28.2 (1) This rule applies where the court—
(a) makes a suspended sentence order;
(b) imposes a requirement under—
(i) a community order,
(ii) a youth rehabilitation order, or
(iii) a suspended sentence order; or
(c) orders the defendant to attend meetings with a supervisor.
(2) The court officer must notify—
(a) the defendant of—
(i) the length of the sentence suspended by a suspended sentence order, and
(ii) the period of the suspension;
(b) the defendant and, where the defendant is under 14, an appropriate adult, of—
(i) any requirement or requirements imposed, and
(ii) the identity of any responsible officer or supervisor, and the means by which that person may be contacted;
(c) any responsible officer or supervisor, and, where the defendant is under 14, the appropriate qualifying officer (if that is not the responsible officer), of—
(i) the defendant's name, address and telephone number (if available),
(ii) the offence or offences of which the defendant was convicted, and
(iii) the requirement or requirements imposed; and
(d) the person affected, where the court imposes a requirement—
(i) for the protection of that person from the defendant, or
(ii) requiring the defendant to reside with that person.
(3) If the court imposes an electronic monitoring requirement, the monitor of which is not the responsible officer, the court officer must—
(a) notify the defendant and, where the defendant is under 16, an appropriate adult, of the monitor's name, and the means by which the monitor may be contacted; and
(b) notify the monitor of—
(i) the defendant's name, address and telephone number (if available),
(ii) the offence or offences of which the defendant was convicted,
(iii) the place or places at which the defendant's presence must be monitored,
(iv) the period or periods during which the defendant's presence there must be monitored, and
(v) the identity of the responsible officer, and the means by which that officer may be contacted.

Notification requirements **R-262**

28.3 (1) This rule applies where, on a conviction, sentence or order, legislation requires the defendant—
(a) to notify information to the police; or
(b) to be included in a barred list.
(2) The court must tell the defendant that such requirements apply, and under what legislation.

Variation of sentence **R-263**

28.4 (1) This rule—
(a) applies where a magistrates' court or the Crown Court can vary or rescind a sentence or order, other than an order to which rule 24.18 applies (Setting aside a conviction or varying a costs etc. order); and
(b) authorises the Crown Court, in addition to its other powers, to do so within the period of 56 days beginning with another defendant's acquittal or sentencing where—
(i) defendants are tried separately in the Crown Court on the same or related facts alleged in one or more indictments, and
(ii) one is sentenced before another is acquitted or sentenced.

(2) The court may exercise its power—
(a) on application by a party, or on its own initiative;
(b) at a hearing, in public or in private, or without a hearing.
(3) A party who wants the court to exercise that power must—
(a) apply in writing as soon as reasonably practicable after—
(i) the sentence or order that that party wants the court to vary or rescind, or
(ii) where paragraph (1)(b) applies, the other defendant's acquittal or sentencing;
(b) serve the application on—
(i) the court officer, and
(ii) each other party; and
(c) in the application—
(i) explain why the sentence should be varied or rescinded,
(ii) specify the variation that the applicant proposes, and
(iii) if the application is late, explain why.
(4) The court must not exercise its power in the defendant's absence unless—
(a) the court makes a variation—
(i) which is proposed by the defendant, or
(ii) the effect of which is that the defendant is no more severely dealt with under the sentence as varied than before; or
(b) the defendant has had an opportunity to make representations at a hearing (whether or not the defendant in fact attends).
(5) The court may—
(a) extend (even after it has expired) the time limit under paragraph (3), unless the court's power to vary or rescind the sentence cannot be exercised;
(b) allow an application to be made orally.

R-264 **Application to vary or discharge a compensation, etc. order**

28.5 (1) This rule applies where on application by the defendant a magistrates' court can vary or discharge—
(a) a compensation order; or
(b) a slavery and trafficking reparation order.
(2) A defendant who wants the court to exercise that power must—
(a) apply in writing as soon as practicable after becoming aware of the grounds for doing so;
(b) serve the application on the magistrates' court officer;
(c) where the order was made in the Crown Court, serve a copy of the application on the Crown Court officer; and
(d) in the application, specify the order that the defendant wants the court to vary or discharge and explain (as applicable)—
(i) what civil court finding shows that the injury, loss or damage was less than it had appeared to be when the order was made,
(ii) in what circumstances the person for whose benefit the order was made has recovered the property for the loss of which it was made,
(iii) why a confiscation order, unlawful profit order or slavery and trafficking reparation order makes the defendant now unable to pay compensation or reparation in full, or
(iv) in what circumstances the defendant's means have been reduced substantially and unexpectedly, and why they seem unlikely to increase for a considerable period.
(3) The court officer must serve a copy of the application on the person for whose benefit the order was made.
(4) The court must not vary or discharge the order unless—
(a) the defendant, and the person for whose benefit it was made, each has had an opportunity to make representations at a hearing (whether or not either in fact attends); and
(b) where the order was made in the Crown Court, the Crown Court has notified its consent.

R-265 **Application to remove, revoke or suspend a disqualification or restriction**

28.6 (1) This rule applies where, on application by the defendant, the court can remove, revoke or suspend a disqualification or restriction included in a sentence (except a disqualification from driving).
(2) A defendant who wants the court to exercise such a power must—
(a) apply in writing, no earlier than the date on which the court can exercise the power;
(b) serve the application on the court officer; and

(c) in the application—
(i) specify the disqualification or restriction, and
(ii) explain why the defendant wants the court to remove, revoke or suspend it.
(3) The court officer must serve a copy of the application on the chief officer of police for the local justice area.

Application for a restitution order by the victim of a theft R-266

28.7 (1) This rule applies where, on application by the victim of a theft, the court can order a defendant to give that person goods obtained with the proceeds of goods stolen in that theft.
(2) A person who wants the court to exercise that power if the defendant is convicted must—
(a) apply in writing as soon as practicable (without waiting for the verdict);
(b) serve the application on the court officer; and
(c) in the application—
(i) identify the goods, and
(ii) explain why the applicant is entitled to them.
(3) The court officer must serve a copy of the application on each party.
(4) The court must not determine the application unless the applicant and each party has had an opportunity to make representations at a hearing (whether or not each in fact attends).
(5) The court may—
(a) extend (even after it has expired) the time limit under paragraph (2); and
(b) allow an application to be made orally.

Requests for medical reports, etc. R-267

28.8 (1) This rule applies where the court—
(a) requests a medical examination of the defendant and a report; or
(b) requires information about the arrangements that could be made for the defendant where the court is considering—
(i) a hospital order, or
(ii) a guardianship order.
(2) Unless the court otherwise directs, the court officer must, as soon as practicable, serve on each person from whom a report or information is sought a note that—
(a) specifies the power exercised by the court;
(b) explains why the court seeks a report or information from that person; and
(c) sets out or summarises any relevant information available to the court.

Information to be supplied on admission to hospital or guardianship R-268

28.9 (1) This rule applies where the court—
(a) orders the defendant's detention and treatment in hospital; or
(b) makes a guardianship order.
(2) Unless the court otherwise directs, the court officer must, as soon as practicable, serve on (as applicable) the hospital or the guardian—
(a) a record of the court's order;
(b) such information as the court has received that appears likely to assist in treating or otherwise dealing with the defendant, including information about—
(i) the defendant's mental condition,
(ii) the defendant's other circumstances, and
(iii) the circumstances of the offence.

Information to be supplied on committal for sentence, etc. R-269

28.10 (1) This rule applies where a magistrates' court or the Crown Court convicts the defendant and—
(a) commits or adjourns the case to another court—
(i) for sentence, or
(ii) for the defendant to be dealt with for breach of a deferred sentence, a conditional discharge, or a suspended sentence of imprisonment, imposed by that other court;
(b) deals with a deferred sentence, a conditional discharge, or a suspended sentence of imprisonment, imposed by another court; or
(c) makes an order that another court is, or may be, required to enforce.
(2) Unless the convicting court otherwise directs, the court officer must, as soon as practicable—
(a) where paragraph (1)(a) applies, arrange the transmission from the convicting to the other court of a record of any relevant—
(i) certificate of conviction,

(ii) magistrates' court register entry,
(iii) decision about bail, for the purposes of section 5 of the Bail Act 1976,
(iv) note of evidence,
(v) statement or other document introduced in evidence,
(vi) medical or other report,
(vii) representation order or application for such order, and
(viii) interim driving disqualification;

(b) where paragraph (1)(b) or (c) applies, arrange—
(i) the transmission from the convicting to the other court of notice of the convicting court's order, and
(ii) the recording of that order at the other court;

(c) in every case, notify the defendant and, where the defendant is under 14, an appropriate adult, of the location of the other court.

R-270 Application to review sentence because of assistance given or withheld

28.11 (1) This rule applies where the Crown Court can reduce or increase a sentence on application by a prosecutor in a case in which—
(a) since being sentenced, the defendant has assisted, or has agreed to assist, an investigator or prosecutor in relation to an offence; or
(b) since receiving a reduced sentence for agreeing to give such assistance, the defendant has failed to do so.

(2) A prosecutor who wants the court to exercise that power must—
(a) apply in writing as soon as practicable after becoming aware of the grounds for doing so;
(b) serve the application on—
(i) the court officer, and
(ii) the defendant; and
(c) in the application—
(i) explain why the sentence should be reduced, or increased, as appropriate, and
(ii) identify any other matter relevant to the court's decision, including any sentencing guideline or guideline case.

(3) The general rule is that the application must be determined by the judge who passed the sentence, unless that judge is unavailable.

(4) The court must not determine the application in the defendant's absence unless the defendant has had an opportunity to make representations at a hearing (whether or not the defendant in fact attends).

Criminal Procedure Rules Part 29 Road Traffic Penalties

R-271 Representations about obligatory disqualification or endorsement

29.1 (1) This rule applies—
(a) where the court—
(i) convicts the defendant of an offence involving obligatory disqualification from driving and section 34(1) of the Road Traffic Offenders Act 1988 (Disqualification for certain offences) applies,
(ii) convicts the defendant of an offence where section 35 of the 1988 Act (Disqualification for repeated offences) applies, or
(iii) convicts the defendant of an offence involving obligatory endorsement of the defendant's driving record and section 44 of the 1988 Act (Orders for endorsement) applies;
(b) unless the defendant is absent.

(2) The court must explain, in terms the defendant can understand (with help, if necessary)—
(a) where paragraph (1)(a)(i) applies (obligatory disqualification under section 34)—
(i) that the court must order the defendant to be disqualified from driving for a minimum of 12 months (or 2 or 3 years, as the case may be, according to the offence and the defendant's driving record), unless the court decides that there are special reasons to order disqualification for a shorter period, or not to order disqualification at all, and
(ii) if applicable, that the period of disqualification will be reduced by at least 3 months if, by no later than 2 months before the end of the reduced period, the defendant completes an approved driving course;
(b) where paragraph (1)(a)(ii) applies (disqualification under section 35)—
(i) that the court must order the defendant to be disqualified from driving for a minimum of 6 months (or 1 or 2 years, as the case may be, according to the defendant's

driving record), unless, having regard to all the circumstances, the court decides to order disqualification for a shorter period, or not to order disqualification at all, and
(ii) that circumstances of which the court cannot take account in making its decision are any that make the offence not a serious one; hardship (other than exceptional hardship); and any that during the last 3 years already have been taken into account by a court when ordering disqualification for less than the usual minimum period, or not at all, for repeated driving offences;
(c) where paragraph (1)(a)(iii) applies (obligatory endorsement), that the court must order the endorsement of the defendant's driving record unless the court decides that there are special reasons not to do so;
(d) in every case, as applicable—
(i) that the court already has received representations from the defendant about whether any such special reasons or mitigating circumstances apply and will take account of them, or
(ii) that the defendant may make such representations now, on oath or affirmation.
(3) Unless the court already has received such representations from the defendant, before it applies rule 24.11 (magistrates' court procedure if the court convicts) or rule 25.16 (Crown Court procedure if the court convicts), as the case may be, the court must—
(a) ask whether the defendant wants to make any such representations; and
(b) if the answer to that question is 'yes', require the defendant to take an oath or affirm and make them.

Application to remove a disqualification from driving **R-272**

29.2 (1) This rule applies where, on application by the defendant, the court can remove a disqualification from driving.
(2) A defendant who wants the court to exercise that power must—
(a) apply in writing, no earlier than the date on which the court can exercise the power;
(b) serve the application on the court officer; and
(c) in the application—
(i) specify the disqualification,and
(ii) explain why the defendant wants the court to remove it.
(3) The court officer must serve a copy of the application on the chief officer of police for the local justice area.

Information to be supplied on order for endorsement of driving record, etc. **R-273**

29.3 (1) This rule applies where the court—
(a) convicts the defendant of an offence involving obligatory endorsement, and orders there to be endorsed on the defendant's driving record (and on any counterpart licence, if other legislation requires)—
(i) particulars of the conviction,
(ii) particulars of any disqualification from driving that the court imposes, and
(iii) the penalty points to be attributed to the offence;
(b) disqualifies the defendant from driving for any other offence; or
(c) suspends or removes a disqualification from driving.
(2) The court officer must, as soon as practicable, serve on the Secretary of State notice that includes details of—
(a) where paragraph (1)(a) applies—
(i) the local justice area in which the court is acting,
(ii) the dates of conviction and sentence,
(iii) the offence, and the date on which it was committed,
(iv) the sentence, and
(v) the date of birth, and sex, of the defendant, where those details are available;
(b) where paragraph (1)(b) applies—
(i) the date and period of the disqualification,
(ii) the power exercised by the court;
(c) where paragraph (1)(c) applies—
(i) the date and period of the disqualification,
(ii) the date and terms of the order for its suspension or removal,
(iii) the power exercised by the court, and
(iv) where the court suspends the disqualification pending appeal, the court to which the defendant has appealed.

R-274 **Statutory declaration to avoid fine after fixed penalty notice**

29.4 (1) This rule applies where—
(a) a chief officer of police, or the Secretary of State, serves on the magistrates' court officer a certificate registering, for enforcement as a fine, a sum payable by a defendant after failure to comply with a fixed penalty notice;
(b) the court officer notifies the defendant of the registration; and
(c) the defendant makes a statutory declaration with the effect that there become void—
(i) the fixed penalty notice, or any associated notice sent to the defendant as owner of the vehicle concerned, and
(ii) the registration and any enforcement proceedings
(2) The defendant must serve that statutory declaration not more than 21 days after service of notice of the registration, unless the court extends that time limit.
(3) The court officer must—
(a) serve a copy of the statutory declaration on the person by whom the certificate was registered;
(b) cancel any endorsement on the defendant's driving record (and on any counterpart licence, if other legislation requires); and
(c) notify the Secretary of State of any such cancellation.

R-275 **Application for declaration about a course or programme certificate decision**

29.5 (1) This rule applies where the court can declare unjustified—
(a) a course provider's failure or refusal to give a certificate of the defendant's satisfactory completion of an approved course; or
(b) a programme provider's giving of a certificate of the defendant's failure fully to participate in an approved programme.
(2) A defendant who wants the court to exercise that power must—
(a) apply in writing, not more than 28 days after—
(i) the date by which the defendant was required to complete the course, or
(ii) the giving of the certificate of failure fully to participate in the programme;
(b) serve the application on the court officer; and
(c) in the application, specify the course or programme and explain (as applicable)—
(i) that the course provider has failed to give a certificate,
(ii) where the course provider has refused to give a certificate, why the defendant disagrees with the reasons for that decision, or
(iii) where the programme provider has given a certificate, why the defendant disagrees with the reasons for that decision.
(3) The court officer must serve a copy of the application on the course or programme provider.
(4) The court must not determine the application unless the defendant, and the course or programme provider, each has had an opportunity to make representations at a hearing (whether or not either in fact attends).

R-276 **Appeal against recognition of foreign driving disqualification**

29.6 (1) This rule applies where—
(a) a Minister gives a disqualification notice under section 57 of the Crime (International Co-operation) Act 2003; and
(b) the person to whom it is given wants to appeal under section 59 of the Act to a magistrates' court.
(2) That person ('the appellant') must serve an appeal notice on—
(a) the court officer, at a magistrates' court in the local justice area in which the appellant lives; and
(b) the Minister, at the address given in the disqualification notice.
(3) The appellant must serve the appeal notice within the period for which section 59 of the 2003 Act provides.
(4) The appeal notice must—
(a) attach a copy of the disqualification notice;
(b) explain which of the conditions in section 56 of the 2003 Act is not met, and why section 57 of the Act therefore does not apply; and
(c) include any application to suspend the disqualification, under section 60 of the Act.
(5) The Minister may serve a respondent's notice, and must do so if—
(a) the Minister wants to make representations to the court; or
(b) the court so directs.

(6) The Minister must—
(a) unless the court otherwise directs, serve any such respondent's notice not more than 14 days after—
(i) the appellant serves the appeal notice, or
(ii) a direction to do so;
(b) in any such respondent's notice—
(i) identify the grounds of opposition on which the Minister relies,
(ii) summarise any relevant facts not already included in the disqualification and appeal notices, and
(iii) identify any other document that the Minister thinks the court will need to decide the appeal (and serve any such document with the notice).
(7) Where the court determines an appeal, the general rule is that it must do so at a hearing (which must be in public, unless the court otherwise directs).
(8) The court officer must serve on the Minister—
(a) notice of the outcome of the appeal;
(b) notice of any suspension of the disqualification; and
(c) the appellant's driving licence, if surrendered to the court officer.

Criminal Procedure Rules Part 30 Enforcement of Fines and Other Orders for Payment

When this Part applies R-277

30.1 (1) This Part applies where a magistrates' court can enforce payment of—
(a) a fine, or a sum that legislation requires the court to treat as a fine; or
(b) any other sum that a court has ordered to be paid—
(i) on a conviction, or
(ii) on the forfeiture of a surety.
(2) Rules 30.7 to 30.9 apply where the court, or a fines officer, issues a warrant for an enforcement agent to take control of a defendant's goods and sell them, using the procedure in Schedule 12 to the Tribunals, Courts and Enforcement Act 2007.
(3) In this Part—
(a) 'defendant' means anyone liable to pay a sum to which this Part applies;
(b) 'payment terms' means by when, and by what (if any) instalments, such a sum must be paid.

Exercise of court's powers R-278

30.2 The court must not exercise its enforcement powers unless—
(a) the court officer has served on the defendant any collection order or other notice of—
(i) the obligation to pay,
(ii) the payment terms, and
(iii) how and where the defendant must pay; and
(b) the defendant has failed to comply with the payment terms.

Duty to give receipt R-279

30.3 (1) This rule applies where the defendant makes a payment to—
(a) the court officer specified in an order or notice served under rule 30.2;
(b) another court officer;
(c) any—
(i) custodian of the defendant,
(ii) supervisor appointed to encourage the defendant to pay, or
(iii) responsible officer appointed under a community sentence or a suspended sentence of imprisonment; or
(d) a person executing a warrant to which rule 13.6 (warrants for arrest, detention or imprisonment that cease to have effect on payment) or this Part applies.
(2) The person receiving the payment must—
(a) give the defendant a receipt; and
(b) as soon as practicable transmit the payment to the court officer specified in an order or notice served under rule 30.2, if the recipient is not that court officer.

Appeal against decision of fines officer R-280

30.4 (1) This rule applies where—
(a) a collection order is in force;

(b) a fines officer makes a decision under one of these paragraphs of Schedule 5 to the Courts Act 2003—
(i) paragraph 22 (Application to fines officer for variation of order or attachment of earnings order, etc.),
(ii) paragraph 31 (Application to fines officer for variation of reserve terms), or
(iii) paragraph 37 (Functions of fines officer in relation to defaulters: referral or further steps notice); and
(c) the defendant wants to appeal against that decision.

(2) Unless the court otherwise directs, the defendant must—
(a) appeal in writing not more than 10 business days after the decision;
(b) serve the appeal on the court officer; and
(c) in the appeal—
(i) explain why a different decision should be made, and
(ii) specify the decision that the defendant proposes.

(3) Where the court determines an appeal the general rule is that it must do so at a hearing.

R-281 **Application to reduce a fine, vary payment terms or remit a courts charge**

30.5 (1) This rule applies where—
(a) no collection order is in force; and the defendant wants the court to—
(i) reduce the amount of a fine, or
(ii) vary payment terms;
(b) the defendant, a fines officer or an enforcement agent wants the court to remit a criminal courts charge.

(2) Unless the court otherwise directs, such a defendant, fines officer or enforcement agent must—
(a) apply in writing;
(b) serve the application on the court officer;
(c) if the application is to reduce a fine or vary payment terms, explain—
(i) what relevant circumstances have not yet been considered by the court, and
(ii) why the fine should be reduced, or the payment terms varied;
(d) if the application is to remit a criminal courts charge, explain—
(i) how the circumstances meet the time limits and other conditions in section 21E of the Prosecution of Offences Act 1985, and
(ii) why the charge should be remitted.

(3) The court may determine an application—
(a) at a hearing, which may be in public or in private; or
(b) without a hearing.

R-282 **Claim to avoid fine after penalty notice**

30.6 (1) This rule applies where—
(a) a chief officer of police serves on the magistrates' court officer a certificate registering, for enforcement as a fine, a sum payable by a defendant after failure to comply with a penalty notice; and
(b) the court or a fines officer enforces the fine.

(2) A defendant who claims not to be the person to whom the penalty notice was issued must, unless the court otherwise directs—
(a) make that claim in writing; and
(b) serve it on the court officer.

(3) The court officer must—
(a) notify the chief officer of police by whom the certificate was registered; and
(b) refer the case to the court.

(4) Where such a claim is made—
(a) the general rule is that the court must adjourn the enforcement for 28 days and fix a hearing; but
(b) the court may make a different order.

(5) At any such hearing, the chief officer of police must introduce any evidence to contradict the defendant's claim.

R-283 **Information to be included in a warrant of control**

30.7 (1) A warrant must identify—
(a) each person to whom it is directed;
(b) the defendant against whom it was issued;

(c) the sum for which it was issued and the reason that sum is owed;
(d) the court or fines officer who issued it, unless that is otherwise recorded by the court officer; and
(e) the court office for the court or fines officer who issued it.

(2) A person to whom a warrant is directed must record on it the date and time at which it is received.

(3) A warrant that contains an error is not invalid, as long as—
(a) it was issued in respect of a lawful decision by the court or fines officer; and
(b) it contains enough information to identify that decision.

Warrant of control: application by enforcement agent for extension of time, etc. **R-284**

30.8 (1) This rule applies where an enforcement agent wants the court to exercise a power under Schedule 12 to the Tribunals, Courts and Enforcement Act 2007, or under regulations made under that Schedule, to—
(a) shorten or extend a time limit;
(b) give the agent authority to—
(i) enter premises which the agent would not otherwise have authority to enter,
(ii) enter or remain on premises at a time at which the agent would not otherwise have authority to be there,
(iii) use reasonable force, in circumstances in which the agent would not otherwise have authority to use such force,
(iv) sell goods by a method which the agent would not otherwise have authority to use, or
(v) recover disbursements which the agent would not otherwise have authority to recover;
(c) specify the manner in which goods which have not been sold must be disposed of.

(2) Such an enforcement agent must—
(a) apply in writing;
(b) serve the application on the court officer; and
(c) pay any fee prescribed.

(3) The application must—
(a) identify the power that the agent wants the court to exercise;
(b) explain how the conditions for the exercise of that power are satisfied, including any condition that requires the agent to give another person notice of the application;
(c) specify those persons, if any, to whom the agent has given notice in accordance with such a condition; and
(d) propose the terms of the order that the agent wants the court to make.

(4) A person to whom the enforcement agent has given notice of an application and who wants to make representations to the court must—
(a) serve the representations on—
(i) the court officer,
(ii) the enforcement agent, and
(iii) any other person to whom the enforcement agent gave notice;
(b) do so as soon as reasonably practicable and in any event within such period as the court directs; and
(c) in the representations, propose the terms of the order that that person wants the court to make, and explain why.

(5) The court—
(a) must not determine an application unless any person to whom the enforcement agent gave notice—
(i) is present, or
(ii) has had a reasonable opportunity to respond;
(b) subject to that, may determine an application—
(i) at a hearing, which must be in private unless the court otherwise directs, or
(ii) without a hearing.

Warrant of control: application to resolve dispute **R-285**

30.9 (1) This rule applies where a defendant's goods are sold using the procedure in Schedule 12 to the Tribunals, Courts and Enforcement Act 2007 and there is a dispute about—
(a) what share of the proceeds of those goods should be paid by the enforcement agent to a co-owner; or
(b) the fees or disbursements sought or recovered by the enforcement agent out of the proceeds.

(2) An enforcement agent, a defendant or a co-owner who wants the court to resolve the dispute must—
(a) apply in writing as soon as practicable after becoming aware of the grounds for doing so;
(b) serve the application on—
(i) the court officer,
(ii) each other party to the dispute, and
(iii) any other co-owner; and
(c) pay any fee prescribed.
(3) The application must—
(a) identify the warrant of control;
(b) specify the goods sold, the proceeds, and the fees and disbursements sought or recovered by the enforcement agent;
(c) identify the power that the applicant wants the court to exercise;
(d) specify the persons served with the application;
(e) explain the circumstances of the dispute; and
(f) propose the terms of the order that the applicant wants the court to make.
(4) A person served with an application who wants to make representations to the court must—
(a) serve the representations on—
(i) the court officer,
(ii) the applicant, and
(iii) any other person on whom the application was served;
(b) do so as soon as reasonably practicable and in any event within such period as the court directs; and
(c) in the representations, propose the terms of the order that that person wants the court to make, and explain why.
(5) The court—
(a) must determine an application at a hearing, which must be in private unless the court otherwise directs;
(b) must not determine an application unless each party—
(i) is present, or
(ii) has had a reasonable opportunity to attend.

R-286 **Financial penalties imposed in other European Union member States**

30.10 (1) This rule applies where the Lord Chancellor gives the court officer a request to enforce a financial penalty imposed in another European Union member State.
(2) The court officer must serve on the defendant—
(a) notice of the request for enforcement, and of its effect;
(b) a copy of—
(i) the certificate requesting enforcement, and
(ii) the decision requiring payment to which that certificate relates; and
(c) notice that the procedure set out in this rule applies.
(3) A defendant who wants the court to refuse enforcement must—
(a) serve notice of objection on the court officer;
(b) unless the court otherwise directs, serve that notice not more than 14 days after service of notice of the request; and
(c) in the notice of objection—
(i) identify each ground for refusal on which the defendant relies,
(ii) summarise any relevant facts not already included in the certificate and decision served with the notice of the request, and
(iii) identify any other document that the defendant thinks the court will need to determine the request (and serve any such document with the notice).
(4) The court—
(a) may determine a request for enforcement—
(i) at a hearing, which must be in public unless the court otherwise directs, or
(ii) without a hearing; but
(b) must not allow enforcement unless the defendant has had at least 14 days in which to serve notice of objection.
(5) Paragraphs (2) and (3) do not apply if, on receipt of the request, the court decides that a ground for refusal applies.
(6) The court officer must serve on the Lord Chancellor notice of the court's decision.

Criminal Procedure Rules Part 31 Behaviour Orders

When this Part applies R-287

31.1 (1) This Part applies where—
(a) a magistrates' court or the Crown Court can make, vary or revoke a civil order—
(i) as well as, or instead of, passing a sentence, or in any other circumstances in which other legislation allows the court to make such an order, and
(ii) that requires someone to do, or not do, something;
(b) a magistrates' court or the Crown Court can make a European protection order;
(c) a magistrates' court can give effect to a European protection order made in another European Union member State.
(2) A reference to a 'behaviour order' in this Part is a reference to any such order.
(3) A reference to 'hearsay evidence' in this Part is a reference to evidence consisting of hearsay within the meaning of section 1(2) of the Civil Evidence Act 1995.

Behaviour orders: general rules R-288

31.2 (1) The court must not make a behaviour order unless the person to whom it is directed has had an opportunity—
(a) to consider—
(i) what order is proposed and why, and
(ii) the evidence in support; and
(b) to make representations at a hearing (whether or not that person in fact attends).
(2) That restriction does not apply to making—
(a) an interim behaviour order, but unless other legislation otherwise provides such an order has no effect unless the person to whom it is directed—
(i) is present when it is made, or
(ii) is handed a document recording the order not more than 7 days after it is made;
(b) a restraining order that gives effect to a European protection order, where rule 31.10 applies (Giving effect to a European protection order made in another EU member State).
(3) Where the court decides not to make, where it could—
(a) a football banning order; or
(b) a parenting order, after a person under 16 is convicted of an offence,
the court must announce, at a hearing in public, the reasons for its decision.
(4) Where the court makes an order which imposes one or more of the prohibitions or restrictions listed in rule 31.9(1), the court must arrange for someone to explain to the person who benefits from that protection—
(a) that person may apply for a European protection order, if he or she decides to reside or stay in another European Union member State;
(b) the basic conditions for making such an application; and
(c) that it is advisable to make any such application before leaving the United Kingdom.

Application for behaviour order and notice of terms of proposed order: special rules R-289

31.3 (1) This rule applies where—
(a) a prosecutor wants the court to make—
(i) an anti-social behaviour order (but this rule does not apply to an application for an interim anti-social behaviour order),
(ii) a serious crime prevention order, or
(iii) a criminal behaviour order; or
(b) a prosecutor proposes, on the prosecutor's initiative or at the court's request a sexual harm prevention order,
if the defendant is convicted.
(2) Where paragraph (1)(a) applies, the prosecutor must serve a notice of intention to apply for such an order on—
(a) the court officer;
(b) the defendant against whom the prosecutor wants the court to make the order; and
(c) any person on whom the order would be likely to have a significant adverse effect, as soon as practicable (without waiting for the verdict).
(3) A notice under paragraph (2) must—
(a) summarise the relevant facts;
(b) identify the evidence on which the prosecutor relies in support;

(c) attach any written statement that the prosecutor has not already served; and
(d) specify the order that the prosecutor wants the court to make.

(4) A defendant served with a notice under paragraph (2) must—
(a) serve written notice of any evidence on which the defendant relies on—
(i) the court officer, and
(ii) the prosecutor,
as soon as practicable (without waiting for the verdict); and
(b) in the notice, identify that evidence and attach any written statement that has not already been served.

(5) Where paragraph (1)(b) applies, the prosecutor must—
(a) serve a draft order on the court officer and on the defendant not less than 2 business days before the hearing at which the order may be made;
(b) in a case in which a sexual harm prevention order is proposed, in the draft order specify those prohibitions which the prosecutor proposes as necessary for the purpose of—
(i) protecting the public or any particular members of the public from sexual harm from the defendant, or
(ii) protecting children or vulnerable adults generally, or any particular children or vulnerable adults, from sexual harm from the defendant outside the United Kingdom.

(6) Where the prosecutor wants the court to make an anti-social behaviour order or a criminal behaviour order, the rules about special measures directions in Part 18 (Measures to assist a witness or defendant to give evidence) apply, but—
(a) the prosecutor must apply when serving a notice under paragraph (2); and
(b) the time limits in rule 18.3(a) do not apply.

R-290 **Evidence to assist the court: special rules**

31.4 (1) This rule applies where the court can make on its own initiative—
(a) a football banning order;
(b) a restraining order; or
(c) an anti-social behaviour order.

(2) A party who wants the court to take account of evidence not already introduced must—
(a) serve notice in writing on—
(i) the court officer, and
(ii) every other party,
as soon as practicable (without waiting for the verdict); and
(b) in the notice, identify that evidence; and
(c) attach any written statement containing such evidence.

R-291 **Application to vary or revoke behaviour order**

31.5 (1) The court may vary or revoke a behaviour order if—
(a) the legislation under which it is made allows the court to do so; and
(b) one of the following applies—
(i) the prosecutor,
(ii) the person to whom the order is directed,
(iii) any other person protected or affected by the order,
(iv) the relevant authority or responsible officer,
(v) the relevant Chief Officer of Police,
(vi) the Director of Public Prosecutions, or
(vii) the Director of the Serious Fraud Office.

(2) A person applying under this rule must—
(a) apply in writing as soon as practicable after becoming aware of the grounds for doing so, explaining—
(i) what material circumstances have changed since the order was made, and
(ii) why the order should be varied or revoked as a result; and
(b) serve the application on—
(i) the court officer,
(ii) as appropriate, the prosecutor or defendant, and
(iii) any other person listed in paragraph (1)(b), if the court so directs.

(3) A party who wants the court to take account of any particular evidence before making its decision must, as soon as practicable—
(a) serve notice in writing on—
(i) the court officer,

(ii) as appropriate, the prosecutor or defendant, and
(iii) any other person listed in paragraph (1)(b) on whom the court directed the application to be served; and
(b) in that notice identify the evidence and attach any written statement that has not already been served.
(4) The court may decide an application under this rule with or without a hearing.
(5) But the court must not—
(a) dismiss an application under this rule unless the applicant has had an opportunity to make representations at a hearing (whether or not the applicant in fact attends); or
(b) allow an application under this rule unless everyone required to be served, by this rule or by the court, has had at least 14 days in which to make representations, including representations about whether there should be a hearing.
(6) The court officer must—
(a) serve the application on any person, if the court so directs; and
(b) give notice of any hearing to—
(i) the applicant, and
(ii) any person required to be served, by this rule or by the court.

Notice of hearsay evidence R-292

31.6 (1) A party who wants to introduce hearsay evidence must—
(a) serve notice in writing on—
(i) the court officer, and
(ii) every other party directly affected; and
(b) in that notice—
(i) explain that it is a notice of hearsay evidence,
(ii) identify that evidence,
(iii) identify the person who made the statement which is hearsay, or explain why if that person is not identified, and
(iv) explain why that person will not be called to give oral evidence.
(2) A party may serve one notice under this rule in respect of more than one notice and more than one witness.

Cross-examination of maker of hearsay statement R-293

31.7 (1) This rule applies where a party wants the court's permission to cross-examine a person who made a statement which another party wants to introduce as hearsay.
(2) The party who wants to cross-examine that person must—
(a) apply in writing, with reasons, not more than 7 days after service of the notice of hearsay evidence; and
(b) serve the application on—
(i) the court officer,
(ii) the party who served the hearsay evidence notice, and
(iii) every party on whom the hearsay evidence notice was served.
(3) The court may decide an application under this rule with or without a hearing.
(4) But the court must not—
(a) dismiss an application under this rule unless the applicant has had an opportunity to make representations at a hearing (whether or not the applicant in fact attends); or
(b) allow an application under this rule unless everyone served with the application has had at least 7 days in which to make representations, including representations about whether there should be a hearing.

Credibility and consistency of maker of hearsay statement R-294

31.8 (1) This rule applies where a party wants to challenge the credibility or consistency of a person who made a statement which another party wants to introduce as hearsay.
(2) The party who wants to challenge the credibility or consistency of that person must—
(a) serve a written notice of intention to do so on—
(i) the court officer, and
(ii) the party who served the notice of hearsay evidence
not more than 7 days after service of that hearsay evidence notice; and
(b) in the notice, identify any statement or other material on which that party relies.
(3) The party who served the hearsay notice—
(a) may call that person to give oral evidence instead; and
(b) if so, must serve a notice of intention to do so on—

(i) the court officer, and
(ii) every party on whom the hearsay notice was served

not more than 7 days after service of the notice under paragraph (2).

R-295 European protection order to be given effect in another EU member State

31.9 (1) This rule applies where—

(a) a person benefits from the protection of one or more of the following prohibitions or restrictions imposed on another person by an order of a court in England and Wales when dealing with a criminal cause or matter—

(i) a prohibition from entering certain localities, places or defined areas where the protected person resides or visits,
(ii) a prohibition or restriction of contact with the protected person by any means (including by telephone, post, facsimile transmission or electronic mail),
(iii) a prohibition or restriction preventing the other person from approaching the protected person whether at all or to within a particular distance; and either

(b) that protected person wants the Crown Court or a magistrates' court to make a European protection order to supplement such an order; or
(c) the court varies or revokes such a prohibition or restriction in such an order and correspondingly amends or revokes a European protection order already made.

(2) Such a protected person—

(a) may apply orally or in writing to the Crown Court at the hearing at which the order imposing the prohibition or restriction is made by that court; or
(b) in any other case, must apply in writing to a magistrates' court and serve the application on the court officer.

(3) The application must—

(a) identify the prohibition or restriction that the European protection order would supplement;
(b) identify the date, if any, on which that prohibition or restriction will expire;
(c) specify the European Union member State in which the applicant has decided to reside or stay, or in which he or she already is residing or staying;
(d) indicate the length of the period for which the applicant intends to reside or stay in that member State;
(e) explain why the applicant needs the protection of that measure while residing or staying in that member State; and
(f) include any other information of which the applicant wants the court to take account.

(4) Where the court makes or amends a European protection order, the court officer must—

(a) issue an order in the form required by Directive 2011/99/EU;
(b) serve on the competent authority of the European Union member State in which the protected person has decided to reside or stay—

(i) a copy of that form, and
(ii) a copy of the form translated into an official language of that member State, or into an official language of the European Union if that member State has declared that it will accept a translation in that language.

(5) Where the court revokes a European protection order, the court officer must without delay so inform that authority.

(6) Where the court refuses to make a European protection order, the court officer must arrange for the protected person to be informed of any available avenue of appeal or review against the court's decision.

R-296 Giving effect to a European protection order made in another EU member State

31.10 (1) This rule applies where the Lord Chancellor serves on the court officer—

(a) a request by an authority in another European Union member State to give effect to a European protection order;
(b) a request by such an authority to give effect to a variation of such an order; or
(c) notice by such an authority of the revocation or withdrawal of such an order.

(2) In the case of a request to which paragraph (1) refers, the court officer must, without undue delay—

(a) arrange for the court to consider the request;
(b) serve on the requesting authority—

(i) notice of any further information required by the court, and
(ii) subject to any such requirement and any response, notice of the court's decision;

(c) where the court gives effect to the European protection order—
(i) include in the notice served on the requesting authority the terms of the restraining order made by the court,
(ii) serve notice of those terms, and of the potential legal consequences of breaching them, on the person restrained by the order made by the court and on the person protected by that order, and
(iii) serve notice on the Lord Chancellor of any breach of the restraining order which is reported to the court;
(d) where the court refuses to give effect to the European protection order—
(i) include in the notice served on the requesting authority the grounds for the refusal,
(ii) where appropriate, inform the protected person, or any representative or guardian of that person, of the possibility of applying for a comparable order under the law of England and Wales, and
(iii) arrange for that person, representative or guardian to be informed of any available avenue of appeal or review against the court's decision.

(3) In the case of a notice to which paragraph (1) refers, the court officer must, as soon as possible, arrange for the court to act on that notice.

(4) Unless the court otherwise directs, the court officer must omit from any notice served on a person against whom a restraining order may be, or has been, made the address or contact details of the person who is the object of the European protection order.

Court's power to vary requirements under this Part R-297

31.11 Unless other legislation otherwise provides, the court may—
(a) shorten a time limit or extend it (even after it has expired);
(b) allow a notice or application to be given in a different form, or presented orally.

Criminal Procedure Rules Part 32 Breach, Revocation and Amendment of Community and Other Orders

When this Part applies R-298

32.1 This Part applies where—
(a) the person responsible for a defendant's compliance with an order to which applies—
(i) Schedule 3, 5, 7 or 8 to the Powers of Criminal Courts (Sentencing) Act 2000,
(ii) Schedule 8 or 12 to the Criminal Justice Act 2003,
(iii) Schedule 2 to the Criminal Justice and Immigration Act 2008, or
(iv) the Schedule to the Street Offences Act 1959
wants the court to deal with that defendant for failure to comply;
(b) one of the following wants the court to exercise any power it has to revoke or amend such an order—
(i) the responsible officer or supervisor,
(ii) the defendant, or
(iii) where the legislation allows, a person affected by the order; or
(c) the court considers exercising on its own initiative any power it has to revoke or amend such an order.

Application by responsible officer or supervisor R-299

32.2 (1) This rule applies where—
(a) the responsible officer wants the court to—
(i) deal with a defendant for failure to comply with an order to which this Part applies, or
(ii) revoke or amend such an order; or
(b) the court considers exercising on its own initiative any power it has to—
(i) revoke or amend such an order, and
(ii) summon the defendant to attend for that purpose.

(2) Rules 7.2 to 7.4, which deal, among other things, with starting a prosecution in a magistrates' court by information and summons, apply—
(a) as if—
(i) a reference in those rules to an allegation of an offence included a reference to an allegation of failure to comply with an order to which this Part applies, and
(ii) a reference to the prosecutor included a reference to the responsible officer or supervisor; and
(b) with the necessary consequential modifications.

R-300 **Application by defendant or person affected**

32.3 (1) This rule applies where—
(a) the defendant wants the court to exercise any power it has to revoke or amend an order to which this Part applies; or
(b) where the legislation allows, a person affected by such an order wants the court to exercise any such power.
(2) That defendant, or person affected, must—
(a) apply in writing, explaining why the order should be revoked or amended; and
(b) serve the application on—
(i) the court officer,
(ii) the responsible officer or supervisor, and
(iii) as appropriate, the defendant or the person affected.

R-301 **Procedure on application by responsible officer or supervisor**

32.4 (1) Except for rules 24.8 (Written guilty plea; special rules) and 24.9 (Single justice procedure: special rules), the rules in Part 24, which deal with the procedure at a trial in a magistrates' court, apply—
(a) as if—
(i) a reference in those rules to an allegation of an offence included a reference to an allegation of failure to comply with an order to which this Part applies,
(ii) a reference to the court's verdict included a reference to the court's decision to revoke or amend such an order, or to exercise any other power it has to deal with the defendant, and
(iii) a reference to the court's sentence included a reference to the exercise of any such power; and
(b) with the necessary consequential modifications.
(2) The court officer must serve on each party any order revoking or amending an order to which this Part applies.

Criminal Procedure Rules Part 33 Confiscation and Related Proceedings

General rules

R-302 **Interpretation**

33.1 In this Part:
'document' means anything in which information of any description is recorded;
'hearsay evidence' means evidence consisting of hearsay within the meaning of section 1(2) of the Civil Evidence Act 1995;
'restraint proceedings' means proceedings under sections 42 and 58(2) and (3) of the Proceeds of Crime Act 2002;
'receivership proceedings' means proceedings under sections 48, 49, 50, 51, 54(4), 59(2) and (3), 62 and 63 of the 2002 Act;
'witness statement' means a written statement signed by a person which contains the evidence, and only that evidence, which that person would be allowed to give orally; and
words and expressions used have the same meaning as in Part 2 of the 2002 Act.

R-303 **Calculation of time**

33.2 (1) This rule shows how to calculate any period of time for doing any act which is specified by this Part for the purposes of any proceedings under Part 2 of the Proceeds of Crime Act 2002 or by an order of the Crown Court in restraint proceedings or receivership proceedings.
(2) A period of time expressed as a number of days shall be computed as clear days.
(3) In this rule 'clear days' means that in computing the number of days—
(a) the day on which the period begins; and
(b) if the end of the period is defined by reference to an event, the day on which that event occurs,
are not included.
(4) Where the specified period is 5 days or less and includes a day which is not a business day that day does not count.

R-304 **Court office closed**

33.3 When the period specified by this Part, or by an order of the Crown Court under Part 2 of the Proceeds of Crime Act 2002, for doing any act at the court office falls on a day on which the office is closed, that act shall be in time if done on the next day on which the court office is open.

Application for registration of Scottish or Northern Ireland Order R-305

33.4 (1) This rule applies to an application for registration of an order under article 6 of the Proceeds of Crime Act 2002 (Enforcement in different parts of the United Kingdom) Order 2002.
(2) The application may be made without notice.
(3) The application must be in writing and may be supported by a witness statement which must—
(a) exhibit the order or a certified copy of the order; and
(b) to the best of the witness's ability, give full details of the realisable property located in England and Wales in respect of which the order was made and specify the person holding that realisable property.
(4) If the court registers the order, the applicant must serve notice of the registration on—
(a) any person who holds realisable property to which the order applies; and
(b) any other person whom the applicant knows to be affected by the order.
(5) The permission of the Crown Court under rule 33.10 is not required to serve the notice outside England and Wales.

Application to vary or set aside registration R-306

33.5 (1) An application to vary or set aside registration of an order under article 6 of the Proceeds of Crime Act 2002 (Enforcement in different parts of the United Kingdom) Order 2002 may be made to the Crown Court by—
(a) any person who holds realisable property to which the order applies; and
(b) any other person affected by the order.
(2) The application must be in writing and may be supported by a witness statement.
(3) The application and any witness statement must be lodged with the Crown Court.
(4) The application must be served on the person who applied for registration at least 7 days before the date fixed by the court for hearing the application, unless the Crown Court specifies a shorter period.
(5) No property in England and Wales may be realised in pursuance of the order before the Crown Court has decided the application.

Register of orders R-307

33.6 (1) The Crown Court must keep, under the direction of the Lord Chancellor, a register of the orders registered under article 6 of the Proceeds of Crime Act 2002 (Enforcement in different parts of the United Kingdom) Order 2002.
(2) The register must include details of any variation or setting aside of a registration under rule 33.5 and of any execution issued on a registered order.
(3) If the person who applied for registration of an order which is subsequently registered notifies the Crown Court that the court which made the order has varied or discharged the order, details of the variation or discharge, as the case may be, must be entered in the register.

Statements of truth R-308

33.7 (1) Any witness statement required to be served by this Part must be verified by a statement of truth contained in the witness statement.
(2) A statement of truth is a declaration by the person making the witness statement to the effect that the witness statement is true to the best of his knowledge and belief and that he made the statement knowing that, if it were tendered in evidence, he would be liable to prosecution if he wilfully stated in it anything which he knew to be false or did not believe to be true.
(3) The statement of truth must be signed by the person making the witness statement.
(4) If the person making the witness statement fails to verify the witness statement by a statement of truth, the Crown Court may direct that it shall not be admissible as evidence.

Use of witness statements for other purposes R-309

33.8 (1) Except as provided by this rule, a witness statement served in proceedings under Part 2 of the Proceeds of Crime Act 2002 may be used only for the purpose of the proceedings in which it is served.
(2) Paragraph (1) does not apply if and to the extent that—
(a) the witness gives consent in writing to some other use of it;
(b) the Crown Court gives permission for some other use; or
(c) the witness statement has been put in evidence at a hearing held in public.

Service of documents R-310

33.9 (1) Rule 49.1 (Notice required to accompany process served outside the United Kingdom and translations) shall not apply in restraint proceedings and receivership proceedings.

(2) An order made in restraint proceedings or receivership proceedings may be enforced against the defendant or any other person affected by it notwithstanding that service of a copy of the order has not been effected in accordance with Part 4 if the Crown Court is satisfied that the person had notice of the order by being present when the order was made.

R-311 **Service outside the jurisdiction**

33.10 (1) Where this Part requires a document to be served on someone who is outside England and Wales, it may be served outside England and Wales with the permission of the Crown Court.

(2) Where a document is to be served outside England and Wales it may be served by any method permitted by the law of the country in which it is to be served.

(3) Nothing in this rule or in any court order shall authorise or require any person to do anything in the country where the document is to be served which is against the law of that country.

(4) Where this Part requires a document to be served a certain period of time before the date of a hearing and the recipient does not appear at the hearing, the hearing must not take place unless the Crown Court is satisfied that the document has been duly served.

R-312 **Certificates of service**

33.11 (1) Where this Part requires that the applicant for an order in restraint proceedings or receivership proceedings serve a document on another person, the applicant must lodge a certificate of service with the Crown Court within 7 days of service of the document.

(2) The certificate must state—

(a) the method of service;

(b) the date of service; and

(c) if the document is served under rule 4.9 (Service by another method), such other information as the court may require when making the order permitting service by that method.

(3) Where a document is to be served by the Crown Court in restraint proceedings and receivership proceedings and the court is unable to serve it, the court must send a notice of non-service stating the method attempted to the party who requested service.

R-313 **External requests and orders**

33.12 (1) The rules in this Part and in Part 42 (Appeal to the Court of Appeal in confiscation and related proceedings) apply with the necessary modifications to proceedings under the Proceeds of Crime Act 2002 (External Requests and Orders) Order 2005 in the same way that they apply to corresponding proceedings under Part 2 of the Proceeds of Crime Act 2002.

(2) This table shows how provisions of the 2005 Order correspond with provisions of the 2002 Act.

Article of the Proceeds of Crime Act 2002 (External Requests and Orders) Order 2005	*Section of the Proceeds of Crime Act 2002*
8	41
9	42
10	43
11	44
15	48
16	49
17	58
23	31
27	50
28	51
41	62
42	63
44	65
45	66

Confiscation proceedings

Statements in connection with confiscation orders R-314

33.13 (1) This rule applies where—

(a) the court can make a confiscation order; and

(b) the prosecutor asks the court to make such an order, or the court decides to make such an order on its own initiative.

(2) Within such periods as the court directs—

(a) if the court so orders, the defendant must give such information, in such manner, as the court directs;

(b) the prosecutor must serve a statement of information relevant to confiscation on the court officer and the defendant;

(c) if the court so directs—

(i) the defendant must serve a response notice on the court officer and the prosecutor, and

(ii) the parties must identify what is in dispute.

(3) Where it appears to the court that a person other than the defendant holds, or may hold, an interest in property held by the defendant which property is likely to be realised or otherwise used to satisfy a confiscation order—

(a) the court must not determine the extent of the defendant's interest in that property unless that other person has had a reasonable opportunity to make representations; and

(b) the court may order that other person to give such information, in such manner and within such a period, as the court directs.

(4) The court may—

(a) shorten or extend a time limit which it has set;

(b) vary, discharge or supplement an order which it has made;

(c) postpone confiscation proceedings without a hearing.

(5) A prosecutor's statement of information must—

(a) identify the maker of the statement and show its date;

(b) identify the defendant in respect of whom it is served;

(c) specify the conviction which gives the court power to make the confiscation order, or each conviction if more than one;

(d) if the prosecutor believes the defendant to have a criminal lifestyle, include such matters as the prosecutor believes to be relevant in connection with deciding—

(i) whether the defendant has such a lifestyle,

(ii) whether the defendant has benefited from his or her general criminal conduct,

(iii) the defendant's benefit from that conduct, and

(iv) whether the court should or should not make such assumptions about the defendant's property as legislation permits;

(e) if the prosecutor does not believe the defendant to have a criminal lifestyle, include such matters as the prosecutor believes to be relevant in connection with deciding—

(i) whether the defendant has benefited from his or her particular criminal conduct, and

(ii) the defendant's benefit from that conduct;

(f) in any case, include such matters as the prosecutor believes to be relevant in connection with deciding—

(i) whether to make a determination about the extent of the defendant's interest in property in which another person holds, or may hold, an interest, and

(ii) what determination to make, if the court decides to make one.

(6) A defendant's response notice must—

(a) indicate the extent to which the defendant accepts the allegations made in the prosecutor's statement of information; and

(b) so far as the defendant does not accept an allegation, give particulars of any matters on which the defendant relies,

in any manner directed by the court.

(7) The court must satisfy itself that there has been explained to the defendant, in terms the defendant can understand (with help, if necessary)—

(a) that if the defendant accepts to any extent an allegation in a prosecutor's statement of information, then the court may treat that as conclusive for the purposes of deciding whether the defendant has benefited from general or particular criminal conduct, and if so by how much;

(b) that if the defendant fails in any respect to comply with a direction to serve a response notice, then the court may treat that as acceptance of each allegation to which the defendant has not replied, except the allegation that the defendant has benefited from general or particular criminal conduct; and

(c) that if the defendant fails without reasonable excuse to comply with an order to give information, then the court may draw such inference as it believes is appropriate.

R-315 **Application for compliance order**

33.14 (1) This rule applies where—

(a) the prosecutor wants the court to make a compliance order after a confiscation order has been made;

(b) the prosecutor or a person affected by a compliance order wants the court to vary or discharge the order.

(2) Such a prosecutor or person must—

(a) apply in writing; and

(b) serve the application on—

(i) the court officer, and

(ii) as appropriate, the prosecutor and any person who is affected by the compliance order (or who would be affected if it were made), unless the court otherwise directs.

(3) The application must—

(a) specify—

(i) the confiscation order,

(ii) the compliance order, if it is an application to vary or discharge that order;

(b) if it is an application for a compliance order—

(i) specify each measure that the prosecutor proposes to ensure that the confiscation order is effective, including in particular any restriction or prohibition on the defendant's travel outside the United Kingdom, and

(ii) explain why each such measure is appropriate;

(c) if it is an application to vary or discharge a compliance order, as appropriate—

(i) specify any proposed variation, and

(ii) explain why it is appropriate for the order to be varied or discharged;

(d) attach any material on which the applicant relies;

(e) propose the terms of the order; and

(f) ask for a hearing, if the applicant wants one, and explain why it is needed.

(4) A person who wants to make representations about the application must—

(a) serve the representations on—

(i) the court officer, and

(ii) the applicant;

(b) do so as soon as reasonably practicable after service of the application;

(c) attach any material on which that person relies; and

(d) ask for a hearing, if that person wants one, and explain why it is needed.

(5) The court—

(a) may determine the application at a hearing (which must be in private unless the court otherwise directs), or without a hearing;

(b) may dispense with service on any person of a prosecutor's application for a compliance order if, in particular—

(i) the application is urgent, or

(ii) there are reasonable grounds for believing that to give notice of the application would cause the dissipation of property that otherwise would be available to satisfy the confiscation order.

R-316 **Application for reconsideration**

33.15 (1) This rule applies where the prosecutor wants the court, in view of fresh evidence—

(a) to consider making a confiscation order where the defendant was convicted but no such order was considered;

(b) to reconsider a decision that the defendant had not benefited from criminal conduct;

(c) to reconsider a decision about the amount of the defendant's benefit.

(2) The application must be in writing and give details of—

(a) the name of the defendant;

(b) the date on which and the place where any relevant conviction occurred;

(c) the date on which and the place where any relevant confiscation order was made or varied;

(d) any slavery and trafficking reparation order made by virtue of any relevant confiscation order;
(e) the grounds for the application; and
(f) an indication of the evidence available to support the application.

(3) The application must be served on the court officer.

(4) The application must be served on the defendant at least 7 days before the date fixed by the court for hearing the application, unless the court specifies a shorter period.

Application for new calculation of available amount **R-317**

33.16 (1) This rule applies where the prosecutor or a receiver wants the court to make a new calculation of the amount available for confiscation.

(2) The application—
(a) must be in writing and may be supported by a witness statement; and
(b) must identify any slavery and trafficking reparation order made by virtue of the confiscation order.

(3) The application and any witness statement must be served on the court officer.

(4) The application and any witness statement must be served on—
(a) the defendant;
(b) the receiver, if the prosecutor is making the application and a receiver has been appointed; and
(c) the prosecutor, if the receiver is making the application,

at least 7 days before the date fixed by the court for hearing the application, unless the court specifies a shorter period.

Variation of confiscation order due to inadequacy of available amount **R-318**

33.17 (1) This rule applies where the defendant, the prosecutor or a receiver wants the court to vary a confiscation order because the amount available is inadequate.

(2) The application—
(a) must be in writing and may be supported by a witness statement; and
(b) must identify any slavery and trafficking reparation order made by virtue of the confiscation order.

(3) The application and any witness statement must be served on the court officer.

(4) The application and any witness statement must be served on—
(a) the prosecutor;
(b) the defendant, if the receiver is making the application; and
(c) the receiver, if the defendant is making the application and a receiver has been appointed,

at least 7 days before the date fixed by the court for hearing the application, unless the court specifies a shorter period.

Application by magistrates' court officer to discharge confiscation order **R-319**

33.18 (1) This rule applies where a magistrates' court officer wants the court to discharge a confiscation order because the amount available is inadequate or the sum outstanding is very small.

(2) The application must be in writing and give details of—
(a) the confiscation order;
(b) any slavery and trafficking reparation order made by virtue of the confiscation order;
(c) the amount outstanding under the order; and
(d) the grounds for the application.

(3) The application must be served on—
(a) the defendant;
(b) the prosecutor; and
(c) any receiver.

(4) The court may determine the application without a hearing unless a person listed in paragraph (3) indicates, within 7 days after the application was served, that he or she would like to make representations.

(5) If the court makes an order discharging the confiscation order, the court officer must, at once, send a copy of the order to—
(a) the magistrates' court officer who applied for the order;
(b) the defendant;
(c) the prosecutor; and
(d) any receiver.

R-320 **Application for variation of confiscation order made against an absconder**

33.19 (1) This rule applies where the defendant wants the court to vary a confiscation order made while the defendant was an absconder.

(2) The application must be in writing and supported by a witness statement which must give details of—

(a) the confiscation order;

(b) any slavery and trafficking reparation order made by virtue of the confiscation order;

(c) the circumstances in which the defendant ceased to be an absconder;

(d) the defendant's conviction of the offence or offences concerned; and

(e) the reason why the defendant believes the amount required to be paid under the confiscation order was too large.

(3) The application and witness statement must be served on the court officer.

(4) The application and witness statement must be served on the prosecutor at least 7 days before the date fixed by the court for hearing the application, unless the court specifies a shorter period.

R-321 **Application for discharge of confiscation order made against an absconder**

33.20 (1) This rule applies where the defendant wants the court to discharge a confiscation order made while the defendant was an absconder and—

(a) the defendant since has been tried and acquitted of each offence concerned; or

(b) the prosecution has not concluded or is not to proceed.

(2) The application must be in writing and supported by a witness statement which must give details of—

(a) the confiscation order;

(b) the date on which the defendant ceased to be an absconder;

(c) the acquittal of the defendant if he or she has been acquitted of the offence concerned; and

(d) if the defendant has not been acquitted of the offence concerned—

(i) the date on which the defendant ceased to be an absconder,

(ii) the date on which the proceedings taken against the defendant were instituted and a summary of steps taken in the proceedings since then, and

(iii) any indication that the prosecutor does not intend to proceed against the defendant.

(3) The application and witness statement must be served on the court officer.

(4) The application and witness statement must be served on the prosecutor at least 7 days before the date fixed by the court for hearing the application, unless the court specifies a shorter period.

(5) If the court orders the discharge of the confiscation order, the court officer must serve notice on any other court responsible for enforcing the order.

R-322 **Application for increase in term of imprisonment in default**

33.21 (1) This rule applies where —

(a) a court varies a confiscation order; and

(b) the prosecutor wants the court in consequence to increase the term of imprisonment to be served in default of payment.

(2) The application must be made in writing and give details of—

(a) the name and address of the defendant;

(b) the confiscation order;

(c) the grounds for the application; and

(d) the enforcement measures taken, if any.

(3) On receipt of the application, the court officer must—

(a) at once, send to the defendant and any other court responsible for enforcing the order, a copy of the application; and

(b) fix a time, date and place for the hearing and notify the applicant and the defendant of that time, date and place.

(4) If the court makes an order increasing the term of imprisonment in default, the court officer must, at once, send a copy of the order to—

(a) the applicant;

(b) the defendant;

(c) where the defendant is in custody at the time of the making of the order, the person having custody of the defendant; and

(d) any other court responsible for enforcing the order.

Compensation—general R-323

33.22 (1) This rule applies where a person who held realisable property wants the court to award compensation for loss suffered in consequence of anything done in relation to that property in connection with confiscation proceedings.

(2) The application must be in writing and may be supported by a witness statement.

(3) The application and any witness statement must be served on the court officer.

(4) The application and any witness statement must be served on—

(a) the person alleged to be in default; and

(b) the person or authority by whom the compensation would be payable,

at least 7 days before the date fixed by the court for hearing the application, unless the court directs otherwise.

Compensation—confiscation order made against absconder R-324

33.23 (1) This rule applies where—

(a) the court varies or discharges a confiscation order made against an absconder;

(b) a person who held realisable property suffered loss as a result of the making of that confiscation order; and

(c) that person wants the court to award compensation for that loss.

(2) The application must be in writing and supported by a witness statement which must give details of—

(a) the confiscation order;

(b) the variation or discharge of the confiscation order;

(c) the realisable property to which the application relates; and

(d) the loss suffered by the applicant as a result of the confiscation order.

(3) The application and witness statement must be served on the court officer.

(4) The application and witness statement must be served on the prosecutor at least 7 days before the date fixed by the court for hearing the application, unless the court specifies a shorter period.

Payment of money in bank or building society account in satisfaction of confiscation order R-325

33.24 (1) An order under section 67 of the Proceeds of Crime Act 2002 requiring a bank or building society to pay money to a magistrates' court officer ('a payment order') shall—

(a) be directed to the bank or building society in respect of which the payment order is made;

(b) name the person against whom the confiscation order has been made;

(c) state the amount which remains to be paid under the confiscation order;

(d) state the name and address of the branch at which the account in which the money ordered to be paid is held and the sort code of that branch, if the sort code is known;

(e) state the name in which the account in which the money ordered to be paid is held and the account number of that account, if the account number is known;

(f) state the amount which the bank or building society is required to pay to the court officer under the payment order;

(g) give the name and address of the court officer to whom payment is to be made; and

(h) require the bank or building society to make payment within a period of 7 days beginning on the day on which the payment order is made, unless it appears to the court that a longer or shorter period would be appropriate in the particular circumstances.

(2) In this rule 'confiscation order' has the meaning given to it by section 88(6) of the Proceeds of Crime Act 2002.

Application to realise seized property R-326

33.25 (1) This rule applies where—

(a) property is held by a defendant against whom a confiscation order has been made;

(b) the property has been seized by or produced to an officer; and

(c) an officer who is entitled to apply wants a magistrates' court—

(i) to make an order under section 67A of the Proceeds of Crime Act 2002 authorising the realisation of the property towards satisfaction of the confiscation order, or

(ii) to determine any storage, insurance or realisation costs in respect of the property which may be recovered under section 67B of the 2002 Act.

(2) Such an officer must—

(a) apply in writing; and

(b) serve the application on—

(i) the court officer, and

(ii) any person whom the applicant believes would be affected by an order.

(3) The application must—
(a) specify the property;
(b) explain—
(i) the applicant's entitlement to apply,
(ii) how the proposed realisation meets the conditions prescribed by section 67A of the 2002 Act, and
(iii) how any storage, etc. costs have been calculated;
(c) attach any material on which the applicant relies; and
(d) propose the terms of the order.
(4) The court may—
(a) determine the application at a hearing, or without a hearing;
(b) consider an application made orally instead of in writing;
(c) consider an application which has not been served on a person likely to be affected by an order.
(5) If the court authorises the realisation of the property, the applicant must—
(a) notify any person affected by the order who was absent when it was made; and
(b) serve on the court officer a list of those so notified.

R-327 Appeal about decision on application to realise seized property

33.26 (1) This rule applies where on an application under rule 33.25 for an order authorising the realisation of property—
(a) a magistrates' court decides not to make such an order and an officer who is entitled to apply wants to appeal against that decision to the Crown Court, under section 67C(1) of the Proceeds of Crime Act 2002;
(b) a magistrates' court makes such an order and a person who is affected by that decision, other than the defendant against whom the confiscation order was made, wants to appeal against it to the Crown Court, under section 67C(2) of the 2002 Act;
(c) a magistrates' court makes a decision about storage, etc. costs and an officer who is entitled to apply wants to appeal against that decision to the Crown Court, under section 67C(4) of the 2002 Act.
(2) The appellant must serve an appeal notice—
(a) on the Crown Court officer and on any other party;
(b) not more than 21 days after the magistrates' court's decision, or, if applicable, service of notice under rule 33.25(5).
(3) The appeal notice must—
(a) specify the decision under appeal;
(b) where paragraph (1)(a) applies, explain why the property should be realised;
(c) in any other case, propose the order that the appellant wants the court to make, and explain why.
(4) Rule 34.11 (Constitution of the Crown Court) applies on such an appeal.

R-328 Application for direction about surplus proceeds

33.27 (1) This rule applies where—
(a) on an application under rule 33.25, a magistrates' court has made an order authorising an officer to realise property;
(b) an officer so authorised holds proceeds of that realisation;
(c) the confiscation order has been fully paid; and
(d) the officer, or a person who had or has an interest in the property represented by the proceeds, wants a magistrates' court or the Crown Court to determine under section 67D of the Proceeds of Crime Act 2002—
(i) to whom the remaining proceeds should be paid, and
(ii) in what amount or amounts.
(2) Such a person must—
(a) apply in writing; and
(b) serve the application on—
(i) the court officer, and
(ii) as appropriate, the officer holding the proceeds, or any person to whom such proceeds might be paid.
(3) The application must—
(a) specify the property which was realised;
(b) explain the applicant's entitlement to apply;

(c) describe the distribution proposed by the applicant and explain why that is proposed;
(d) attach any material on which the applicant relies; and
(e) ask for a hearing, if the applicant wants one, and explain why it is needed.

(4) A person who wants to make representations about the application must—
(a) serve the representations on—
(i) the court officer,
(ii) the applicant, and
(iii) any other person to whom proceeds might be paid;
(b) do so as soon as reasonably practicable after service of the application;
(c) attach any material on which that person relies; and
(d) ask for a hearing, if that person wants one, and explain why it is needed.

(5) The court—
(a) must not determine the application unless the applicant and each person on whom it was served—
(i) is present, or
(ii) has had an opportunity to attend or to make representations;
(b) subject to that, may determine the application–
(i) at a hearing (which must be in private unless the court otherwise directs), or without a hearing,
(ii) in the absence of any party to the application.

Seizure and detention proceedings

Application for approval to seize property or to search R-329

33.28 (1) This rule applies where an officer who is entitled to apply wants the approval of a magistrates' court, under section 47G of the Proceeds of Crime Act 2002—
(a) to seize property, under section 47C of that Act;
(b) to search premises or a person or vehicle for property to be seized, under section 47D, 47E or 47F of that Act.

(2) Such an officer must—
(a) apply in writing; and
(b) serve the application on the court officer.

(3) The application must—
(a) explain—
(i) the applicant's entitlement to apply, and
(ii) how the proposed seizure meets the conditions prescribed by sections 47B, 47C and, if applicable, 47D, 47E or 47F of the 2002 Act;
(b) if applicable, specify any premises, person or vehicle to be searched;
(c) attach any material on which the applicant relies; and
(d) propose the terms in which the applicant wants the court to give its approval.

(4) The court—
(a) must determine the application—
(i) at a hearing, which must be in private unless the court otherwise directs, and
(ii) in the applicant's presence;
(b) may consider an application made orally instead of in writing.

Application to extend detention period R-330

33.29 (1) This rule applies where an officer who is entitled to apply, or the prosecutor, wants a magistrates' court to make an order, under section 47M of the Proceeds of Crime Act 2002, extending the period for which seized property may be detained.

(2) Such an officer or prosecutor must—
(a) apply in writing; and
(b) serve the application on—
(i) the court officer, and
(ii) any person whom the applicant believes would be affected by an order.

(3) The application must—
(a) specify—
(i) the property to be detained, and
(ii) whether the applicant wants it to be detained for a specified period or indefinitely;
(b) explain—
(i) the applicant's entitlement to apply, and
(ii) how the proposed detention meets the conditions prescribed by section 47M of the 2002 Act;

(c) attach any material on which the applicant relies; and
(d) propose the terms of the order.

(4) The court—
(a) must determine the application—
(i) at a hearing, which must be in private unless the court otherwise directs, and
(ii) in the applicant's presence;
(b) may—
(i) consider an application made orally instead of in writing,
(ii) require service of the application on the court officer after it has been heard, instead of before.

(5) If the court extends the period for which the property may be detained, the applicant must—
(a) notify any person affected by the order who was absent when it was made; and
(b) serve on the court officer a list of those so notified.

R-331 **Application to vary or discharge order for extended detention**

33.30 (1) This rule applies where an officer who is entitled to apply, the prosecutor, or a person affected by an order to which rule 33.29 applies, wants a magistrates' court to vary or discharge that order, under section 47N of the Proceeds of Crime Act 2002.

(2) Such a person must—
(a) apply in writing; and
(b) serve the application on—
(i) the court officer, and
(ii) as appropriate, the applicant for the order, or any person affected by the order.

(3) The application must—
(a) specify the order and the property detained;
(b) explain—
(i) the applicant's entitlement to apply,
(ii) why it is appropriate for the order to be varied or discharged,
(iii) if applicable, on what grounds the court must discharge the order;
(c) attach any material on which the applicant relies;
(d) if applicable, propose the terms of any variation; and
(e) ask for a hearing, if the applicant wants one, and explain why it is needed.

(4) A person who wants to make representations about the application must—
(a) serve the representations on—
(i) the court officer, and
(ii) the applicant;
(b) do so as soon as reasonably practicable after service of the application;
(c) attach any material on which that person relies;
(d) ask for a hearing, if that person wants one, and explain why it is needed.

(5) The court—
(a) must not determine the application unless the applicant and each person on whom it was served—
(i) is present, or
(ii) has had an opportunity to attend or to make representations;
(b) subject to that, may determine the application—
(i) at a hearing (which must be in private unless the court otherwise directs), or without a hearing,
(ii) in the absence of any party to the application.

R-332 **Appeal about property detention decision**

33.31 (1) This rule applies where—
(a) on an application under rule 33.29 for an order extending the period for which property may be detained—
(i) a magistrates' court decides not to make such an order, and
(ii) an officer who is entitled to apply for such an order, or the prosecutor, wants to appeal against that decision to the Crown Court under section 47O(1) of the Proceeds of Crime Act 2002;
(b) on an application under rule 33.30 to vary or discharge an order under rule 33.29—
(i) a magistrates' court determines the application, and
(ii) a person who is entitled to apply under that rule wants to appeal against that decision to the Crown Court under section 47O(2) of the 2002 Act.

(2) The appellant must serve an appeal notice—
(a) on the Crown Court officer and on any other party;
(b) not more than 21 days after the magistrates' court's decision, or, if applicable, service of notice under rule 33.29(5).
(3) The appeal notice must—
(a) specify the decision under appeal;
(b) where paragraph (1)(a) applies, explain why the detention period should be extended;
(c) where paragraph (1)(b) applies, propose the order that the appellant wants the court to make, and explain why.
(4) Rule 34.11 (Constitution of the Crown Court) applies on such an appeal.

Restraint and receivership proceedings: rules that apply generally

Taking control of goods and forfeiture R-333

33.32 (1) This rule applies to applications under sections 58(2) and (3) and 59(2) and (3) of the Proceeds of Crime Act 2002 for leave of the Crown Court to take control of goods or levy distress against property, or to exercise a right of forfeiture by peaceable re-entry in relation to a tenancy, in circumstances where the property or tenancy is the subject of a restraint order or a receiver has been appointed in respect of the property or tenancy.
(2) The application must be made in writing to the Crown Court.
(3) The application must be served on—
(a) the person who applied for the restraint order or the order appointing the receiver; and
(b) any receiver appointed in respect of the property or tenancy,
at least 7 days before the date fixed by the court for hearing the application, unless the Crown Court specifies a shorter period.

Joining of applications R-334

33.33 An application for the appointment of a management receiver or enforcement receiver under rule 33.56 may be joined with—
(a) an application for a restraint order under rule 33.51; and
(b) an application for the conferral of powers on the receiver under rule 33.57.

Applications to be dealt with in writing R-335

33.34 Applications in restraint proceedings and receivership proceedings are to be dealt with without a hearing, unless the Crown Court orders otherwise.

Business in chambers R-336

33.35 Restraint proceedings and receivership proceedings may be heard in chambers.

Power of court to control evidence R-337

33.36 (1) When hearing restraint proceedings and receivership proceedings, the Crown Court may control the evidence by giving directions as to—
(a) the issues on which it requires evidence;
(b) the nature of the evidence which it requires to decide those issues; and
(c) the way in which the evidence is to be placed before the court.
(2) The court may use its power under this rule to exclude evidence that would otherwise be admissible.
(3) The court may limit cross-examination in restraint proceedings and receivership proceedings.

Evidence of witnesses R-338

33.37 (1) The general rule is that, unless the Crown Court orders otherwise, any fact which needs to be proved in restraint proceedings or receivership proceedings by the evidence of a witness is to be proved by their evidence in writing.
(2) Where evidence is to be given in writing under this rule, any party may apply to the Crown Court for permission to cross-examine the person giving the evidence.
(3) If the Crown Court gives permission under paragraph (2) but the person in question does not attend as required by the order, his evidence may not be used unless the court gives permission.

Witness summons R-339

33.38 (1) Any party to restraint proceedings or receivership proceedings may apply to the Crown Court to issue a witness summons requiring a witness to—
(a) attend court to give evidence; or
(b) produce documents to the court.

(2) Rule 17.3 (Application for summons, warrant or order: general rules) applies to an application under this rule as it applies to an application under section 2 of the Criminal Procedure (Attendance of Witnesses) Act 1965.

R-340 **Hearsay evidence**

33.39 Section 2(1) of the Civil Evidence Act 1995 (duty to give notice of intention to rely on hearsay evidence) does not apply to evidence in restraint proceedings and receivership proceedings.

R-341 **Disclosure and inspection of documents**

33.40 (1) This rule applies where, in the course of restraint proceedings or receivership proceedings, an issue arises as to whether property is realisable property.

(2) The Crown Court may make an order for disclosure of documents.

(3) Part 31 of the Civil Procedure Rules 1998 as amended from time to time shall have effect as if the proceedings were proceedings in the High Court.

R-342 **Court documents**

33.41 (1) Any order which the Crown Court issues in restraint proceedings or receivership proceedings must—

(a) state the name and judicial title of the person who made it;

(b) bear the date on which it is made; and

(c) be sealed by the Crown Court.

(2) The Crown Court may place the seal on the order—

(a) by hand; or

(b) by printing a facsimile of the seal on the order whether electronically or otherwise.

(3) A document purporting to bear the court's seal shall be admissible in evidence without further proof.

R-343 **Consent orders**

33.42 (1) This rule applies where all the parties to restraint proceedings or receivership proceedings agree the terms in which an order should be made.

(2) Any party may apply for a judgment or order in the terms agreed.

(3) The Crown Court may deal with an application under paragraph (2) without a hearing.

(4) Where this rule applies—

(a) the order which is agreed by the parties must be drawn up in the terms agreed;

(b) it must be expressed as being 'By Consent'; and

(c) it must be signed by the legal representative acting for each of the parties to whom the order relates or by the party if he is a litigant in person.

(5) Where an application is made under this rule, then the requirements of any other rule as to the procedure for making an application do not apply.

R-344 **Slips and omissions**

33.43 (1) The Crown Court may at any time correct an accidental slip or omission in an order made in restraint proceedings or receivership proceedings.

(2) A party may apply for a correction without notice.

R-345 **Supply of documents from court records**

33.44 (1) No document relating to restraint proceedings or receivership proceedings may be supplied from the records of the Crown Court for any person to inspect or copy unless the Crown Court grants permission.

(2) An application for permission under paragraph (1) must be made on notice to the parties to the proceedings.

R-346 **Disclosure of documents in criminal proceedings**

33.45 (1) This rule applies where—

(a) proceedings for an offence have been started in the Crown Court and the defendant has not been either convicted or acquitted on all counts; and

(b) an application for a restraint order under section 42(1) of the Proceeds of Crime Act 2002 has been made.

(2) The judge presiding at the proceedings for the offence may be supplied from the records of the Crown Court with documents relating to restraint proceedings and any receivership proceedings.

(3) Such documents must not otherwise be disclosed in the proceedings for the offence.

Preparation of documents R-347

33.46 (1) Every order in restraint proceedings or receivership proceedings must be drawn up by the Crown Court unless—
(a) the Crown Court orders a party to draw it up;
(b) a party, with the permission of the Crown Court, agrees to draw it up; or
(c) the order is made by consent under rule 33.42.
(2) The Crown Court may direct that—
(a) an order drawn up by a party must be checked by the Crown Court before it is sealed; or
(b) before an order is drawn up by the Crown Court, the parties must lodge an agreed statement of its terms.
(3) Where an order is to be drawn up by a party—
(a) he must lodge it with the Crown Court no later than 7 days after the date on which the court ordered or permitted him to draw it up so that it can be sealed by the Crown Court; and
(b) if he fails to lodge it within that period, any other party may draw it up and lodge it.
(4) Nothing in this rule shall require the Crown Court to accept a document which is illegible, has not been duly authorised, or is unsatisfactory for some other similar reason.

Order for costs R-348

33.47 (1) This rule applies where the Crown Court is deciding whether to make an order for costs in restraint proceedings or receivership proceedings.
(2) The court has discretion as to—
(a) whether costs are payable by one party to another;
(b) the amount of those costs; and
(c) when they are to be paid.
(3) If the court decides to make an order about costs—
(a) the general rule is that the unsuccessful party must be ordered to pay the costs of the successful party; but
(b) the court may make a different order.
(4) In deciding what order (if any) to make about costs, the court must have regard to all of the circumstances, including—
(a) the conduct of all the parties; and
(b) whether a party has succeeded on part of an application, even if he has not been wholly successful.
(5) The orders which the court may make include an order that a party must pay—
(a) a proportion of another party's costs;
(b) a stated amount in respect of another party's costs;
(c) costs from or until a certain date only;
(d) costs incurred before proceedings have begun;
(e) costs relating to particular steps taken in the proceedings;
(f) costs relating only to a distinct part of the proceedings; and
(g) interest on costs from or until a certain date, including a date before the making of an order.
(6) Where the court would otherwise consider making an order under paragraph (5)(f), it must instead, if practicable, make an order under paragraph (5)(a) or (c).
(7) Where the court has ordered a party to pay costs, it may order an amount to be paid on account before the costs are assessed.

Assessment of costs R-349

33.48 (1) Where the Crown Court has made an order for costs in restraint proceedings or receivership proceedings it may either—
(a) make an assessment of the costs itself; or
(b) order assessment of the costs under rule 45.11.
(2) In either case, the Crown Court or the assessing authority, as the case may be, must—
(a) only allow costs which are proportionate to the matters in issue; and
(b) resolve any doubt which it may have as to whether the costs were reasonably incurred or reasonable and proportionate in favour of the paying party.
(3) The Crown Court or the assessing authority, as the case may be, is to have regard to all the circumstances in deciding whether costs were proportionately or reasonably incurred or proportionate and reasonable in amount.
(4) In particular, the Crown Court or the assessing authority must give effect to any orders which have already been made.

(5) The Crown Court or the assessing authority must also have regard to—
(a) the conduct of all the parties, including in particular, conduct before, as well as during, the proceedings;
(b) the amount or value of the property involved;
(c) the importance of the matter to all the parties;
(d) the particular complexity of the matter or the difficulty or novelty of the questions raised;
(e) the skill, effort, specialised knowledge and responsibility involved;
(f) the time spent on the application; and
(g) the place where and the circumstances in which work or any part of it was done.

R-350 Time for complying with an order for costs

33.49 A party to restraint proceedings or receivership proceedings must comply with an order for the payment of costs within 14 days of—
(a) the date of the order if it states the amount of those costs;
(b) if the amount of those costs is decided later under rule 45.11, the date of the assessing authority's decision; or
(c) in either case, such later date as the Crown Court may specify.

R-351 Application of costs rules

33.50 Rules 33.47, 33.48 and 33.49 do not apply to the assessment of costs in proceedings to the extent that section 11 of the Access to Justice Act 1999 applies and provisions made under that Act make different provision.

Restraint proceedings

R-352 Application for restraint order or ancillary order

33.51 (1) This rule applies where the prosecutor, or an accredited financial investigator, makes an application under section 42 of the Proceeds of Crime Act 2002 for—
(a) a restraint order, under section 41(1) of the 2002 Act; or
(b) an ancillary order, under section 41(7) of that Act, for the purpose of ensuring that a restraint order is effective.
(2) The application may be made without notice if the application is urgent or if there are reasonable grounds for believing that giving notice would cause the dissipation of realisable property which is the subject of the application.
(3) An application for a restraint order must be in writing and supported by a witness statement which must—
(a) give the grounds for the application;
(b) to the best of the witness's ability, give full details of the realisable property in respect of which the applicant is seeking the order and specify the person holding that realisable property;
(c) include the proposed terms of the order.
(4) An application for an ancillary order must be in writing and supported by a witness statement which must—
(a) give the grounds for, and full details of, the application;
(b) include, if appropriate—
(i) any request for an order for disclosure of documents to which rule 33.40 applies (Disclosure and inspection of documents),
(ii) the identity of any person whom the applicant wants the court to examine about the extent or whereabouts of realisable property,
(iii) a list of the main questions that the applicant wants to ask any such person, and
(iv) a list of any documents to which the applicant wants to refer such a person; and
(c) include the proposed terms of the order.
(5) An application for a restraint order and an application for an ancillary order may (but need not) be made at the same time and contained in the same documents.
(6) An application by an accredited financial investigator must include a statement that, under section 68 of the 2002 Act, the applicant has authority to apply.

R-353 Restraint and ancillary orders

33.52 (1) The Crown Court may make a restraint order subject to exceptions, including, but not limited to, exceptions for reasonable living expenses and reasonable legal expenses, and for the purpose of enabling any person to carry on any trade, business or occupation.

(2) But the Crown Court must not make an exception for legal expenses where this is prohibited by section 41(4) of the Proceeds of Crime Act 2002.

(3) An exception to a restraint order may be made subject to conditions.

(4) The Crown Court must not require the applicant for a restraint order to give any undertaking relating to damages sustained as a result of the restraint order by a person who is prohibited from dealing with realisable property by the restraint order.

(5) The Crown Court may require the applicant for a restraint order to give an undertaking to pay the reasonable expenses of any person, other than a person who is prohibited from dealing with realisable property by the restraint order, which are incurred in complying with the restraint order.

(6) An order must include a statement that disobedience of the order, either by a person to whom the order is addressed, or by another person, may be contempt of court and the order must include details of the possible consequences of being held in contempt of court.

(7) Unless the Crown Court otherwise directs, an order made without notice has effect until the court makes an order varying or discharging it.

(8) The applicant for an order must—

(a) serve copies of the order and of the witness statement made in support of the application on the defendant and any person who is prohibited by the order from dealing with realisable property; and

(b) notify any person whom the applicant knows to be affected by the order of its terms.

Application for discharge or variation of restraint or ancillary order by a person affected by the order R-354

33.53 (1) This rule applies where a person affected by a restraint order makes an application to the Crown Court under section 42(3) of the Proceeds of Crime Act 2002 to discharge or vary the restraint order or any ancillary order made under section 41(7) of the Act.

(2) The application must be in writing and may be supported by a witness statement.

(3) The application and any witness statement must be lodged with the Crown Court.

(4) The application and any witness statement must be served on the person who applied for the restraint order and any person who is prohibited from dealing with realisable property by the restraint order (if he is not the person making the application) at least 2 days before the date fixed by the court for hearing the application, unless the Crown Court specifies a shorter period.

Application for variation of restraint or ancillary order by the person who applied for the order R-355

33.54 (1) This rule applies where the applicant for a restraint order makes an application under section 42(3) of the Proceeds of Crime Act 2002 to the Crown Court to vary the restraint order or any ancillary order made under section 41(7) of the 2002 Act (including where the court has already made a restraint order and the applicant is seeking to vary the order in order to restrain further realisable property).

(2) The application may be made without notice if the application is urgent or if there are reasonable grounds for believing that giving notice would cause the dissipation of realisable property which is the subject of the application.

(3) The application must be in writing and must be supported by a witness statement which must—

(a) give the grounds for the application;

(b) where the application is for the inclusion of further realisable property in a restraint order give full details, to the best of the witness's ability, of the realisable property in respect of which the applicant is seeking the order and specify the person holding that realisable property;

(c) where the application is to vary an ancillary order, include, if appropriate—

(i) any request for an order for disclosure of documents to which rule 33.40 applies (Disclosure and inspection of documents),

(ii) the identity of any person whom the applicant wants the court to examine about the extent or whereabouts of realisable property,

(iii) a list of the main questions that the applicant wants to ask any such person, and

(iv) a list of any documents to which the applicant wants to refer such a person; and

(d) include the proposed terms of the variation.

(4) An application by an accredited financial investigator must include a statement that, under section 68 of the 2002 Act, the applicant has authority to apply.

(5) The application and witness statement must be lodged with the Crown Court.

(6) Except where, under paragraph (2), notice of the application is not required to be served, the application and witness statement must be served on any person who is prohibited from

dealing with realisable property by the restraint order at least 2 days before the date fixed by the court for hearing the application, unless the Crown Court specifies a shorter period.

(7) If the court makes an order for the variation of a restraint or ancillary order, the applicant must serve copies of the order and of the witness statement made in support of the application on—

(a) the defendant;

(b) any person who is prohibited from dealing with realisable property by the restraint order (whether before or after the variation); and

(c) any other person whom the applicant knows to be affected by the order.

R-356 Application for discharge of restraint or ancillary order by the person who applied for the order

33.55 (1) This rule applies where the applicant for a restraint order makes an application under section 42(3) of the Proceeds of Crime Act 2002 to discharge the order or any ancillary order made under section 41(7) of the 2002 Act.

(2) The application may be made without notice.

(3) The application must be in writing and must state the grounds for the application.

(4) If the court makes an order for the discharge of a restraint or ancillary order, the applicant must serve copies of the order on—

(a) the defendant;

(b) any person who is prohibited from dealing with realisable property by the restraint order (whether before or after the discharge); and

(c) any other person whom the applicant knows to be affected by the order.

Receivership proceedings

R-357 Application for appointment of a management or an enforcement receiver

33.56 (1) This rule applies to an application for the appointment of a management receiver under section 48(1) of the Proceeds of Crime Act 2002 and an application for the appointment of an enforcement receiver under section 50(1) of the 2002 Act.

(2) The application may be made without notice if—

(a) the application is joined with an application for a restraint order under rule 35.51 (Application for restraint order or ancillary order);

(b) the application is urgent; or

(c) there are reasonable grounds for believing that giving notice would cause the dissipation of realisable property which is the subject of the application.

(3) The application must be in writing and must be supported by a witness statement which must—

(a) give the grounds for the application;

(b) give full details of the proposed receiver;

(c) to the best of the witness's ability, give full details of the realisable property in respect of which the applicant is seeking the order and specify the person holding that realisable property;

(d) where the application is made by an accredited financial investigator, include a statement that, under section 68 of the 2002 Act, the applicant has authority to apply; and

(e) if the proposed receiver is not a person falling within section 55(8) of the 2002 Act and the applicant is asking the court to allow the receiver to act—

(i) without giving security, or

(ii) before he has given security or satisfied the court that he has security in place,

explain the reasons why that is necessary.

(4) Where the application is for the appointment of an enforcement receiver, the applicant must provide the Crown Court with a copy of the confiscation order made against the defendant.

(5) The application and witness statement must be lodged with the Crown Court.

(6) Except where, under paragraph (2), notice of the application is not required to be served, the application and witness statement must be lodged with the Crown Court and served on—

(a) the defendant;

(b) any person who holds realisable property to which the application relates; and

(c) any other person whom the applicant knows to be affected by the application,

at least 7 days before the date fixed by the court for hearing the application, unless the Crown Court specifies a shorter period.

(7) If the court makes an order for the appointment of a receiver, the applicant must serve copies of the order and of the witness statement made in support of the application on—

(a) the defendant;

(b) any person who holds realisable property to which the order applies; and

(c) any other person whom the applicant knows to be affected by the order.

Application for conferral of powers on a management receiver or an enforcement receiver **R-358**

33.57 (1) This rule applies to an application for the conferral of powers on a management receiver under section 49(1) of the Proceeds of Crime Act 2002 or an enforcement receiver under section 51(1) of the 2002 Act.

(2) The application may be made without notice if the application is to give the receiver power to take possession of property and—
(a) the application is joined with an application for a restraint order under rule 33.51 (Application for restraint order or ancillary order);
(b) the application is urgent; or
(c) there are reasonable grounds for believing that giving notice would cause the dissipation of the property which is the subject of the application.

(3) The application must be made in writing and supported by a witness statement which must—
(a) give the grounds for the application;
(b) give full details of the realisable property in respect of which the applicant is seeking the order and specify the person holding that realisable property;
(c) where the application is made by an accredited financial investigator, include a statement that, under section 68 of the 2002 Act, the applicant has authority to apply; and
(d) where the application is for power to start, carry on or defend legal proceedings in respect of the property, explain—
(i) what proceedings are concerned, in what court, and
(ii) what powers the receiver will ask that court to exercise.

(4) Where the application is for the conferral of powers on an enforcement receiver, the applicant must provide the Crown Court with a copy of the confiscation order made against the defendant.

(5) The application and witness statement must be lodged with the Crown Court.

(6) Except where, under paragraph (2), notice of the application is not required to be served, the application and witness statement must be served on—
(a) the defendant;
(b) any person who holds realisable property in respect of which a receiver has been appointed or in respect of which an application for a receiver has been made;
(c) any other person whom the applicant knows to be affected by the application; and
(d) the receiver (if one has already been appointed),
at least 7 days before the date fixed by the court for hearing the application, unless the Crown Court specifies a shorter period.

(7) If the court makes an order for the conferral of powers on a receiver, the applicant must serve copies of the order on—
(a) the defendant;
(b) any person who holds realisable property in respect of which the receiver has been appointed; and
(c) any other person whom the applicant knows to be affected by the order.

Applications for discharge or variation of receivership orders, and applications for other orders **R-359**

33.58 (1) This rule applies to applications under section 62(3) of the Proceeds of Crime Act 2002 for orders (by persons affected by the action of receivers) and applications under section 63(1) of the 2002 Act for the discharge or variation of orders relating to receivers.

(2) The application must be made in writing and lodged with the Crown Court.

(3) The application must be served on the following persons (except where they are the person making the application)—
(a) the person who applied for appointment of the receiver;
(b) the defendant;
(c) any person who holds realisable property in respect of which the receiver has been appointed;
(d) the receiver; and
(e) any other person whom the applicant knows to be affected by the application,
at least 7 days before the date fixed by the court for hearing the application, unless the Crown Court specifies a shorter period.

(4) If the court makes an order for the discharge or variation of an order relating to a receiver under section 63(2) of the 2002 Act, the applicant must serve copies of the order on any persons whom he knows to be affected by the order.

R-360 **Sums in the hands of receivers**

33.59 (1) This rule applies where the amount payable under a confiscation order has been fully paid and any sums remain in the hands of an enforcement receiver.

(2) The receiver must make an application to the Crown Court for directions as to the distribution of the sums in his hands.

(3) The application and any evidence which the receiver intends to rely on in support of the application must be served on—

(a) the defendant; and

(b) any other person who held (or holds) interests in any property realised by the receiver,

at least 7 days before the date fixed by the court for hearing the application, unless the Crown Court specifies a shorter period.

(4) If any of the provisions listed in paragraph (5) (provisions as to the vesting of funds in a trustee in bankruptcy) apply, then the Crown Court must make a declaration to that effect.

(5) These are the provisions—

(a) section 31B of the Bankruptcy (Scotland) Act 1985;

(b) section 306B of the Insolvency Act 1986; and

(c) article 279B of the Insolvency (Northern Ireland) Order 1989.

R-361 **Security**

33.60 (1) This rule applies where the Crown Court appoints a receiver under section 48 or 50 of the Proceeds of Crime Act 2002 and the receiver is not a person falling within section 55(8) of the 2002 Act (and it is immaterial whether the receiver is a permanent or temporary member of staff or on secondment from elsewhere).

(2) The Crown Court may direct that before the receiver begins to act, or within a specified time, he must either—

(a) give such security as the Crown Court may determine; or

(b) file with the Crown Court and serve on all parties to any receivership proceedings evidence that he already has in force sufficient security,

to cover his liability for his acts and omissions as a receiver.

(3) The Crown Court may terminate the appointment of a receiver if he fails to—

(a) give the security; or

(b) satisfy the court as to the security he has in force,

by the date specified.

R-362 **Remuneration**

33.61 (1) This rule applies where the Crown Court appoints a receiver under section 48 or 50 of the Proceeds of Crime Act 2002 and the receiver is not a person falling within section 55(8) of the 2002 Act (and it is immaterial whether the receiver is a permanent or temporary member of staff or on secondment from elsewhere).

(2) The receiver may only charge for his services if the Crown Court—

(a) so directs; and

(b) specifies the basis on which the receiver is to be remunerated.

(3) Unless the Crown Court orders otherwise, in determining the remuneration of the receiver, the Crown Court shall award such sum as is reasonable and proportionate in all the circumstances and which takes into account—

(a) the time properly given by him and his staff to the receivership;

(b) the complexity of the receivership;

(c) any responsibility of an exceptional kind or degree which falls on the receiver in consequence of the receivership;

(d) the effectiveness with which the receiver appears to be carrying out, or to have carried out, his duties; and

(e) the value and nature of the subject matter of the receivership.

(4) The Crown Court may refer the determination of a receiver's remuneration to be ascertained by the taxing authority of the Crown Court and rules 45.11 (Assessment and re-assessment) to 45.14 (Application for an extension of time) shall have effect as if the taxing authority was ascertaining costs.

(5) A receiver appointed under section 48 of the 2002 Act is to receive his remuneration by realising property in respect of which he is appointed, in accordance with section 49(2)(d) of the 2002 Act.

(6) A receiver appointed under section 50 of the 2002 Act is to receive his remuneration by applying to the magistrates' court officer for payment under section 55(4)(b) of the 2002 Act.

Accounts **R-363**

33.62 (1) The Crown Court may order a receiver appointed under section 48 or 50 of the Proceeds of Crime Act 2002 to prepare and serve accounts.

(2) A party to receivership proceedings served with such accounts may apply for an order permitting him to inspect any document in the possession of the receiver relevant to those accounts.

(3) Any party to receivership proceedings may, within 14 days of being served with the accounts, serve notice on the receiver—

(a) specifying any item in the accounts to which he objects;

(b) giving the reason for such objection; and

(c) requiring the receiver within 14 days of receipt of the notice, either—

(i) to notify all the parties who were served with the accounts that he accepts the objection, or

(ii) if he does not accept the objection, to apply for an examination of the accounts in relation to the contested item.

(4) When the receiver applies for the examination of the accounts he must at the same time lodge with the Crown Court—

(a) the accounts; and

(b) a copy of the notice served on him under this section of the rule.

(5) If the receiver fails to comply with paragraph (3)(c) of this rule, any party to receivership proceedings may apply to the Crown Court for an examination of the accounts in relation to the contested item.

(6) At the conclusion of its examination of the accounts the court must certify the result.

Non-compliance by receiver **R-364**

33.63 (1) If a receiver appointed under section 48 or 50 of the Proceeds of Crime Act 2002 fails to comply with any rule, practice direction or direction of the Crown Court, the Crown Court may order him to attend a hearing to explain his non-compliance.

(2) At the hearing, the Crown Court may make any order it considers appropriate, including—

(a) terminating the appointment of the receiver;

(b) reducing the receiver's remuneration or disallowing it altogether; and

(c) ordering the receiver to pay the costs of any party.

Proceedings under the Criminal Justice Act 1988 and the Drug Trafficking Act 1994

Statements, etc. relevant to making confiscation orders **R-365**

33.64 (1) Where a prosecutor or defendant—

(a) serves on the magistrates' court officer any statement or other document under section 73 of the Criminal Justice Act 1988 in any proceedings in respect of an offence listed in Schedule 4 to that Act; or

(b) serves on the Crown Court officer any statement or other document under section 11 of the Drug Trafficking Act 1994 or section 73 of the 1988 Act in any proceedings in respect of a drug trafficking offence or in respect of an offence to which Part VI of the 1988 Act applies,

that party must serve a copy as soon as practicable on the defendant or the prosecutor, as the case may be.

(2) Any statement tendered by the prosecutor to the magistrates' court under section 73 of the 1988 Act or to the Crown Court under section 11(1) of the 1994 Act or section 73(1A) of the 1988 Act must include the following particulars—

(a) the name of the defendant;

(b) the name of the person by whom the statement is made and the date on which it was made;

(c) where the statement is not tendered immediately after the defendant has been convicted, the date on which and the place where the relevant conviction occurred; and

(d) such information known to the prosecutor as is relevant to the determination as to whether or not the defendant has benefited from drug trafficking or relevant criminal conduct and to the assessment of the value of any proceeds of drug trafficking or, as the case may be, benefit from relevant criminal conduct.

(3) Where, in accordance with section 11(7) of the 1994 Act or section 73(1C) of the 1988 Act, the defendant indicates in writing the extent to which he or she accepts any allegation contained within the prosecutor's statement, the defendant must serve a copy of that reply on the court officer.

(4) Expressions used in this rule shall have the same meanings as in the 1994 Act or, where appropriate, the 1988 Act.

R-366 Postponed determinations

33.65 (1) Where an application is made by the defendant or the prosecutor—

(a) to a magistrates' court under section 72A(5)(a) of the Criminal Justice Act 1988 asking the court to exercise its powers under section 72A(4) of that Act; or

(b) to the Crown Court under section 3(5)(a) of the Drug Trafficking Act 1994 asking the Court to exercise its powers under section 3(4) of that Act, or under section 72A(5)(a) of the 1988 Act asking the court to exercise its powers under section 72A(4) of the 1988 Act,

the application must be made in writing and the applicant must serve a copy on the prosecutor or the defendant, as the case may be.

(2) A party served with a copy of an application under paragraph (1) must, within 28 days of the date of service, notify the applicant and the court officer, in writing, whether or not that party opposes the application, giving his reasons for any opposition.

(3) After the expiry of the period referred to in paragraph (2), the court may determine an application under paragraph (1) —

(a) without a hearing; or

(b) at a hearing at which the parties may be represented.

R-367 Confiscation orders—revised assessments

33.66 (1) Where the prosecutor makes an application under section 13, 14 or 15 of the Drug Trafficking Act 1994 or section 74A, 74B or 74C of the Criminal Justice Act 1988, the application must be in writing and a copy must be served on the defendant.

(2) The application must include the following particulars—

(a) the name of the defendant;

(b) the date on which and the place where any relevant conviction occurred;

(c) the date on which and the place where any relevant confiscation order was made or, as the case may be, varied;

(d) the grounds on which the application is made; and

(e) an indication of the evidence available to support the application.

R-368 Application to the Crown Court to discharge or vary order to make material available

33.67 (1) Where an order under section 93H of the Criminal Justice Act 1988 (order to make material available) or section 55 of the Drug Trafficking Act 1994 (order to make material available) has been made by the Crown Court, any person affected by it may apply in writing to the court officer for the order to be discharged or varied, and on hearing such an application the court may discharge the order or make such variations to it as the court thinks fit.

(2) Subject to paragraph (3), where a person proposes to make an application under paragraph (1) for the discharge or variation of an order, that person shall give a copy of the application, not later than 48 hours before the making of the application—

(a) to a constable at the police station specified in the order; or

(b) to the office of the appropriate officer who made the application, as specified in the order,

in either case together with a notice indicating the time and place at which the application for discharge or variation is to be made.

(3) The court may direct that paragraph (2) need not be complied with if satisfied that the person making the application has good reason to seek a discharge or variation of the order as soon as possible and it is not practicable to comply with that paragraph.

(4) In this rule:

'constable' includes a person commissioned by the Commissioners for Her Majesty's Revenue and Customs;

'police station' includes a place for the time being occupied by Her Majesty's Revenue and Customs.

R-369 Application to the Crown Court for increase in term of imprisonment in default of payment

33.68 (1) This rule applies to applications made, or that have effect as made, to the Crown Court under section 10 of the Drug Trafficking Act 1994 and section 75A of the Criminal Justice Act 1988 (interest on sums unpaid under confiscation orders).

(2) Notice of an application to which this rule applies to increase the term of imprisonment or detention fixed in default of payment of a confiscation order by a person ('the defendant') shall be made by the prosecutor in writing to the court officer.

(3) A notice under paragraph (2) shall—

(a) state the name and address of the defendant;

(b) specify the grounds for the application;

(c) give details of the enforcement measures taken, if any; and
(d) include a copy of the confiscation order.

(4) On receiving a notice under paragraph (2), the court officer must—
(a) forthwith send to the defendant and the magistrates' court required to enforce payment of the confiscation order under section 140(1) of the Powers of Criminal Courts (Sentencing) Act 2000, a copy of the said notice; and
(b) notify in writing the applicant and the defendant of the date, time and place appointed for the hearing of the application.

(5) Where the Crown Court makes an order pursuant to an application mentioned in paragraph (1) above, the court officer shall send forthwith a copy of the order—
(a) to the applicant;
(b) to the defendant;
(c) where the defendant is at the time of the making of the order in custody, to the person having custody of him or her; and
(d) to the magistrates' court mentioned in paragraph (4)(a).

Drug trafficking—compensation on acquittal in the Crown Court R-370

33.69 Where the Crown Court cancels a confiscation order under section 22(2) of the Drug Trafficking Act 1994, the Crown Court officer must serve notice to that effect on the High Court officer and on the court officer of the magistrates' court which has responsibility for enforcing the order.

Contempt proceedings

Application to punish for contempt of court R-371

33.70 (1) This rule applies where a person is accused of disobeying—
(a) a compliance order made for the purpose of ensuring that a confiscation order is effective;
(b) a restraint order; or
(c) an ancillary order made for the purpose of ensuring that a restraint order is effective.

(2) An applicant who wants the Crown Court to exercise its power to punish that person for contempt of court must comply with the rules in Part 48 (Contempt of court).

Criminal Procedure Rules Part 34 Appeal to the Crown Court

When this Part applies R-372

34.1 (1) This part applies where—
(a) a defendant wants to appeal under—
(i) section 108 of the Magistrates' Courts Act 1980,
(ii) section 45 of the Mental Health Act 1983,
(iii) paragraph 10 of Schedule 3 to the Powers of Criminal Courts (Sentencing) Act 2000, or paragraphs 9(8) or 13(5) of Schedule 8 to the Criminal Justice Act 2003,
(iv) section 42 of the Counter Terrorism Act 2008;
(b) the Criminal Cases Review Commission refers a defendant's case to the Crown Court under section 11 of the Criminal Appeal Act 1995;
(c) a prosecutor wants to appeal under—
(i) section 14A(5A) of the Football Spectators Act 1989, or
(ii) section 147(3) of the Customs and Excise Management Act 1979; or
(d) a person wants to appeal under—
(i) section 1 of the Magistrates' Courts (Appeals from Binding Over Orders) Act 1956,
(ii) section 12(5) of the Contempt of Court Act 1981,
(iii) regulation 3C or 3H of the Costs in Criminal Cases (General) Regulations 1986,
(iv) section 22 of the Football Spectators Act 1989,
(v) section 10(4) or (5) of the Crime and Disorder Act 1998.

(2) A reference to an 'appellant' in this part is a reference to such a party or person.

Service of appeal notice R-373

34.2 (1) An appellant must serve an appeal notice on—
(a) the magistrates' court officer; and
(b) every other party.

(2) The appellant must serve the appeal notice—
(a) as soon after the decision appealed against as the appellant wants; but
(b) not more than 21 days after—
(i) sentence or the date sentence is deferred, whichever is earlier, if the appeal is against conviction or against a finding of guilt,

(ii) sentence, if the appeal is against sentence, or
(iii) the order or failure to make an order about which the appellant wants to appeal, in any other case.

(3) The appellant must serve with the appeal notice any application for the following, with reasons—
(a) an extension of the time limit under this rule, if the appeal notice is late;
(b) bail pending appeal, if the appellant is in custody;
(c) the suspension of any disqualification imposed in the case, where the magistrates' court or the Crown Court can order such a suspension pending appeal.

(4) Where both the magistrates' court and the Crown Court can suspend a disqualification pending appeal, an application for its suspension must indicate by which court the appellant wants the application determined.

R-374 Form of appeal notice

34.3 The appeal notice must be in writing and must—
(a) specify—
(i) the conviction or finding of guilt,
(ii) the sentence, or
(iii) the order, or the failure to make an order
about which the appellant wants to appeal;
(b) summarise the issues;
(c) in an appeal against conviction—
(i) identify the prosecution witnesses whom the appellant will want to question if they are called to give oral evidence, and
(ii) say how long the trial lasted in the magistrates' court and how long the appeal is likely to last in the Crown Court;
(d) in an appeal against a finding that the appellant insulted someone or interrupted proceedings in the magistrates' court, attach—
(i) the magistrates' court's written findings of fact, and
(ii) the appellant's response to those findings;
(e) say whether the appellant has asked the magistrates' court to reconsider the case; and
(f) include a list of those on whom the appellant has served the appeal notice.

R-375 Duty of magistrates' court officer

34.4 The magistrates' court officer must—
(a) as soon as practicable serve on the Crown Court officer—
(i) the appeal notice and any accompanying application served by the appellant,
(ii) details of the parties including their addresses,
(iii) a copy of each magistrates' court register entry relating to the decision under appeal and to any application for bail pending appeal, and
(iv) any report received for the purposes of sentencing;
(b) keep any document or object exhibited in the proceedings in the magistrates' court, or arrange for it to be kept by some other appropriate person, until—
(i) 6 weeks after the conclusion of those proceedings, or
(ii) the conclusion of any proceedings in the Crown Court that begin within that 6 weeks;
(c) provide the Crown Court with any document, object or information for which the Crown Court officer asks, within such period as the Crown Court officer may require; and
(d) arrange for the magistrates' court to hear as soon as practicable any application to that court under rule 34.2(3)(c) (suspension of disqualification pending appeal).

R-376 Duty of person keeping exhibit

34.5 A person who, under arrangements made by the magistrates' court officer, keeps a document or object exhibited in the proceedings in the magistrates' court must—
(a) keep that exhibit until—
(i) 6 weeks after the conclusion of those proceedings, or
(ii) the conclusion of any proceedings in the Crown Court that begin within that 6 weeks,
unless the magistrates' court or the Crown Court otherwise directs; and
(b) provide the Crown Court with any such document or object for which the Crown Court officer asks, within such period as the Crown Court officer may require.

R-377 Reference by the Criminal Cases Review Commission

34.6 (1) The Crown Court officer must, as soon as practicable, serve a reference by the Criminal Cases Review Commission on—
(a) the appellant;

(b) every other party; and
(c) the magistrates' court officer.
(2) The appellant may serve an appeal notice on—
(a) the Crown Court officer; and
(b) every other party,
not more than 21 days later.
(3) The Crown Court must treat the reference as the appeal notice if the appellant does not serve an appeal notice.

Application to introduce further evidence R-378

34.7 (1) This rule applies where—
(a) a party wants to introduce evidence that was not introduced by either party in the magistrates' court; and
(b) one of these Parts applies—
(i) Part 18 (Measures to assist a witness or defendant to give evidence),
(ii) Part 20 (Hearsay evidence),
(iii) Part 21 (Evidence of bad character), or
(iv) Part 22 (Evidence of a complainant's previous sexual behaviour).
(2) Such a party must serve the notice or application to introduce evidence required by that Part not more than 14 days after service of the appeal notice.

Hearings and decisions R-379

34.8 (1) The Crown Court as a general rule must hear in public an appeal or reference to which this part applies, but—
(a) may order any hearing to be in private; and
(b) where a hearing is about a public interest ruling, must hold that hearing in private.
(2) The Crown Court officer must give as much notice as reasonably practicable of every hearing to—
(a) the parties;
(b) any party's custodian; and
(c) any other person whom the Crown Court requires to be notified.
(3) The Crown Court officer must serve every decision on—
(a) the parties;
(b) any other person whom the Crown Court requires to be served; and
(c) the magistrates' court officer and any party's custodian, where the decision determines an appeal.
(4) But where a hearing or decision is about a public interest ruling, the Crown Court officer must not—
(a) give notice of that hearing to; or
(b) serve that decision on,
anyone other than the prosecutor who applied for that ruling, unless the court otherwise directs.

Abandoning an appeal R-380

34.9 (1) The appellant—
(a) may abandon an appeal without the Crown Court's permission, by serving a notice of abandonment on—
(i) the magistrates' court officer,
(ii) the Crown Court officer, and
(iii) every other party
before the hearing of the appeal begins; but
(b) after the hearing of the appeal begins, may only abandon the appeal with the Crown Court's permission.
(2) A notice of abandonment must be signed by or on behalf of the appellant.
(3) Where an appellant who is on bail pending appeal abandons an appeal—
(a) the appellant must surrender to custody as directed by the magistrates' court officer; and
(b) any conditions of bail apply until then.

Court's power to vary requirements under this Part R-381

34.10 The Crown Court may—
(a) shorten or extend (even after it has expired) a time limit under this Part;
(b) allow an appellant to vary an appeal notice that that appellant has served;

(c) direct that an appeal notice be served on any person;
(d) allow an appeal notice or a notice of abandonment to be in a different form to one set out in the Practice Direction, or to be presented orally.

R-382 Constitution of the Crown Court

34.11 On the hearing of an appeal—
(a) the general rule is that the Crown Court must comprise—
(i) a judge of the High Court, a Circuit judge, a Recorder or a qualifying judge advocate, and
(ii) no less than two and no more than four justices of the peace, none of whom took part in the decision under appeal; and
(b) if the appeal is from a youth court—
(i) each justice of the peace must be qualified to sit as a member of a youth court, and
(ii) the Crown Court must include a man and a woman; but
(c) the Crown Court may include only one justice of the peace and need not include both a man and a woman if—
(i) the presiding judge decides that otherwise the start of the appeal hearing will be delayed unreasonably, or
(ii) one or more of the justices of the peace who started hearing the appeal is absent.

Criminal Practice Directions Part 34 Appeal to the Crown Court

PD-76 CPD IX Appeal 34A: Appeals to the Crown Court

34A.1 CrimPR 34.4 applies when a defendant appeals to the Crown Court against conviction or sentence and specifies the information and documentation that must be provided by the magistrates' court.

34A.2 On an appeal against conviction, the reasons given by the magistrates for their decision should not be included with the documents; the appeal hearing is not a review of the magistrates' court's decision but a re-hearing.

34A.3 On an appeal against sentence, the magistrates' court's reasons and factual finding leading to the finding of guilt should be included, but any reasons for the sentence imposed should be omitted as the Crown Court will be conducting a fresh sentencing exercise.

Criminal Procedure Rules Part 35 Appeal to the High Court by Case Stated

R-383 When this Part applies

35.1 This Part applies where a person wants to appeal to the High Court by case stated—
(a) under section 111 of the Magistrates' Courts Act 1980, against a decision of a magistrates' court; or
(b) under section 28 of the Senior Courts Act 1981, against a decision of the Crown Court.

R-384 Application to state a case

35.2 (1) A party who wants the court to state a case for the opinion of the High Court must—
(a) apply in writing, not more than 21 days after the decision against which the applicant wants to appeal; and
(b) serve the application on—
(i) the court officer, and
(ii) each other party.
(2) The application must—
(a) specify the decision in issue;
(b) specify the proposed question or questions of law or jurisdiction on which the opinion of the High Court will be asked;
(c) indicate the proposed grounds of appeal; and
(d) include or attach any application for the following, with reasons—
(i) if the application is to the Crown Court, an extension of time within which to apply to state a case,
(ii) bail pending appeal,
(iii) the suspension of any disqualification imposed in the case, where the court can order such a suspension pending appeal.

(3) A party who wants to make representations about the application must—
(a) serve the representations on—
(i) the court officer, and
(ii) each other party; and
(b) do so not more than 14 days after service of the application.
(4) The court may determine the application without a hearing.
(5) If the court decides not to state a case, the court officer must serve on each party—
(a) notice of that decision; and
(b) the court's written reasons for that decision, if not more than 21 days later the applicant asks for those reasons.

Preparation of case stated R-385

35.3 (1) This rule applies where the court decides to state a case for the opinion of the High Court.
(2) The court officer must serve on each party notice of—
(a) the decision to state a case, and
(b) any recognizance ordered by the court.
(3) Unless the court otherwise directs, not more than 21 days after the court's decision to state a case—
(a) in a magistrates court, the court officer must serve a draft case on each party;
(b) in the Crown Court, the applicant must serve a draft case on the court officer and each other party.
(4) The draft case must—
(a) specify the decision in issue;
(b) specify the question(s) of law or jurisdiction on which the opinion of the High Court will be asked;
(c) include a succinct summary of—
(i) the nature and history of the proceedings,
(ii) the court's relevant findings of fact, and
(iii) the relevant contentions of the parties;
(d) if a question is whether there was sufficient evidence on which the court reasonably could reach a finding of fact—
(i) specify that finding, and
(ii) include a summary of the evidence on which the court reached that finding.
(5) Except to the extent that paragraph (4)(d) requires, the draft case must not include an account of the evidence received by the court.
(6) A party who wants to make representations about the content of the draft case, or to propose a revised draft, must—
(a) serve the representations, or revised draft, on—
(i) the court officer, and
(ii) each other party; and
(b) do so not more than 21 days after service of the draft case.
(7) The court must state the case not more than 21 days after the time for service of representations under paragraph (6) has expired.
(8) A case stated for the opinion of the High Court must—
(a) comply with paragraphs (4) and (5); and
(b) identify—
(i) the court that stated it, and
(ii) the court office for that court.
(9) The court officer must serve the case stated on each party.

Duty of justices' legal adviser R-386

35.4 (1) This rule applies—
(a) only in a magistrates' court; and
(b) unless the court—
(i) includes a District Judge (Magistrates' Courts), and
(ii) otherwise directs.
(2) A justices' legal adviser must—
(a) give the court legal advice; and

(b) if the court so requires, assist it by—
(i) preparing and amending the draft case, and
(ii) completing the case stated.

R-387 **Court's power to vary requirements under this Part**

35.5 (1) The court may shorten or extend (even after it has expired) a time limit under this Part.
(2) A person who wants an extension of time must—
(a) apply when serving the application, representations or draft case for which it is needed; and
(b) explain the delay.

CRIMINAL PROCEDURE RULES PART 36 APPEAL TO THE COURT OF APPEAL: GENERAL RULES

R-388 **When this Part applies**

36.1 (1) This Part applies to all applications, appeals and references to the Court of Appeal to which Parts 37, 38, 39, 40, 41 and 43 apply.
(2) In this Part and in those, unless the context makes it clear that something different is meant, 'court' means the Court of Appeal or any judge of that court.

R-389 **Case management in the Court of Appeal**

36.2 (1) The court and the parties have the same duties and powers as under Part 3 (Case management).
(2) The Registrar—
(a) must fulfil the duty of active case management under rule 3.2; and
(b) in fulfilling that duty may exercise any of the powers of case management under—
(i) rule 3.5 (the court's general powers of case management),
(ii) rule 3.10(3) (requiring a certificate of readiness), and
(iii) rule 3.11 (requiring a party to identify intentions and anticipated requirements) subject to the directions of the court.
(3) The Registrar must nominate a case progression officer under rule 3.4.

R-390 **Power to vary requirements**

36.3 The court or the Registrar may—
(a) shorten a time limit or extend it (even after it has expired) unless that is inconsistent with other legislation;
(b) allow a party to vary any notice that that party has served;
(c) direct that a notice or application be served on any person;
(d) allow a notice or application to be in a different form, or presented orally.

R-391 **Application for extension of time**

36.4 A person who wants an extension of time within which to serve a notice or make an application must—
(a) apply for that extension of time when serving that notice or making that application; and
(b) give the reasons for the application for an extension of time.

R-392 **Renewing an application refused by a judge or the Registrar**

36.5 (1) This rule applies where a party with the right to do so wants to renew—
(a) to a judge of the Court of Appeal an application refused by the Registrar; or
(b) to the Court of Appeal an application refused by a judge of that court.
(2) That party must—
(a) renew the application in the form set out in the Practice Direction, signed by or on behalf of the applicant;
(b) serve the renewed application on the Registrar not more than 14 days after—
(i) the refusal of the application that the applicant wants to renew; or
(ii) the Registrar serves that refusal on the applicant, if the applicant was not present in person or by live link when the original application was refused.

R-393 **Hearings**

36.6 (1) The general rule is that the Court of Appeal must hear in public—
(a) an application, including an application for permission to appeal; and
(b) an appeal or reference,
but it may order any hearing to be in private.

(2) Where a hearing is about a public interest ruling, that hearing must be in private unless the court otherwise directs.

(3) Where the appellant wants to appeal against an order restricting public access to a trial, the court—

(a) may decide without a hearing—

(i) an application, including an application for permission to appeal, and

(ii) an appeal; but

(b) must announce its decision on such an appeal at a hearing in public.

(4) Where the appellant wants to appeal or to refer a case to the Supreme Court, the court—

(a) may decide without a hearing an application—

(i) for permission to appeal or to refer a sentencing case, or

(ii) to refer a point of law; but

(b) must announce its decision on such an application at a hearing in public.

(5) A judge of the Court of Appeal and the Registrar may exercise any of their powers—

(a) at a hearing in public or in private; or

(b) without a hearing.

Notice of hearings and decisions **R-394**

36.7 (1) The Registrar must give as much notice as reasonably practicable of every hearing to—

(a) the parties;

(b) any party's custodian;

(c) any other person whom the court requires to be notified; and

(d) the Crown Court officer, where Parts 37, 38 or 40 apply.

(2) The Registrar must serve every decision on—

(a) the parties;

(b) any other person whom the court requires to be served; and

(c) the Crown Court officer and any party's custodian, where the decision determines an appeal or application for permission to appeal.

(3) But where a hearing or decision is about a public interest ruling, the Registrar must not—

(a) give notice of that hearing to; or

(b) serve that decision on,

anyone other than the prosecutor who applied for that ruling, unless the court otherwise directs.

Duty of Crown Court officer **R-395**

36.8 (1) The Crown Court officer must provide the Registrar with any document, object or information for which the Registrar asks, within such period as the Registrar may require.

(2) Where someone may appeal to the Court of Appeal, the Crown Court officer must keep any document or object exhibited in the proceedings in the Crown Court, or arrange for it to be kept by some other appropriate person, until—

(a) 6 weeks after the conclusion of those proceedings; or

(b) the conclusion of any appeal proceedings that begin within that 6 weeks,

unless the court, the Registrar or the Crown Court otherwise directs.

(3) Where Part 37 applies (Appeal to the Court of Appeal against ruling at preparatory hearing), the Crown Court officer must as soon as practicable serve on the appellant a transcript or note of—

(a) each order or ruling against which the appellant wants to appeal; and

(b) the decision by the Crown Court judge on any application for permission to appeal.

(4) Where Part 38 applies (Appeal to the Court of Appeal against ruling adverse to prosecution), the Crown Court officer must as soon as practicable serve on the appellant a transcript or note of—

(a) each ruling against which the appellant wants to appeal;

(b) the decision by the Crown Court judge on any application for permission to appeal; and

(c) the decision by the Crown Court judge on any request to expedite the appeal.

(5) Where Part 39 applies (Appeal to the Court of Appeal about conviction or sentence), the Crown Court officer must as soon as practicable serve on the Registrar—

(a) the appeal notice and any accompanying application that the appellant serves on the Crown Court officer;

(b) any Crown Court judge's certificate that the case is fit for appeal;

(c) the decision on any application at the Crown Court centre for bail pending appeal;

(d) such of the Crown Court case papers as the Registrar requires; and
(e) such transcript of the Crown Court proceedings as the Registrar requires.

(6) Where Part 40 applies (Appeal to the Court of Appeal about reporting or public access) and an order is made restricting public access to a trial, the Crown Court officer must—
(a) immediately notify the Registrar of that order, if the appellant has given advance notice of intention to appeal; and
(b) as soon as practicable provide the applicant for that order with a transcript or note of the application.

R-396 **Duty of person transcribing proceedings in the Crown Court**

36.9 A person who transcribes a recording of proceedings in the Crown Court under arrangements made by the Crown Court officer must provide the Registrar with any transcript for which the Registrar asks, within such period as the Registrar may require.

R-397 **Duty of person keeping exhibit**

36.10 A person who under arrangements made by the Crown Court officer keeps a document or object exhibited in the proceedings in the Crown Court must—
(a) keep that exhibit until—
(i) 6 weeks after the conclusion of the Crown Court proceedings, or
(ii) the conclusion of any appeal proceedings that begin within that 6 weeks,
unless the court, the Registrar or the Crown Court otherwise directs; and
(b) provide the Registrar with any such document or object for which the Registrar asks, within such period as the Registrar may require.

R-398 **Registrar's duty to provide copy documents for appeal or reference**

36.11 Unless the court otherwise directs, for the purposes of an appeal or reference—
(a) the Registrar must—
(i) provide a party with a copy of any document or transcript held by the Registrar for such purposes, or
(ii) allow a party to inspect such a document or transcript,
on payment by that party of any charge fixed by the Treasury; but
(b) the Registrar must not provide a copy or allow the inspection of—
(i) a document provided only for the court and the Registrar, or
(ii) a transcript of a public interest ruling or of an application for such a ruling.

R-399 **Declaration of incompatibility with a Convention right**

36.12 (1) This rule applies where a party—
(a) wants the court to make a declaration of incompatibility with a Convention right under section 4 of the Human Rights Act 1998; or
(b) raises an issue that the Registrar thinks may lead the court to make such a declaration.

(2) The Registrar must serve notice on—
(a) the relevant person named in the list published under section 17(1) of the Crown Proceedings Act 1947; or
(b) the Treasury Solicitor, if it is not clear who is the relevant person.

(3) That notice must include or attach details of—
(a) the legislation affected and the Convention right concerned;
(b) the parties to the appeal; and
(c) any other information or document that the Registrar thinks relevant.

(4) A person who has a right under the 1998 Act to become a party to the appeal must—
(a) serve notice on—
(i) the Registrar, and
(ii) the other parties,
if that person wants to exercise that right; and
(b) in that notice—
(i) indicate the conclusion that that person invites the court to reach on the question of incompatibility, and
(ii) identify each ground for that invitation, concisely outlining the arguments in support.

(5) The court must not make a declaration of incompatibility—
(a) less than 21 days after the Registrar serves notice under paragraph (2); and
(b) without giving any person who serves a notice under paragraph (4) an opportunity to make representations at a hearing.

Abandoning an appeal R-400

36.13 (1) This rule applies where an appellant wants to—
(a) abandon—
(i) an application to the court for permission to appeal, or
(ii) an appeal; or
(b) reinstate such an application or appeal after abandoning it.
(2) The appellant—
(a) may abandon such an application or appeal without the court's permission by serving a notice of abandonment on—
(i) the Registrar, and
(ii) any respondent
before any hearing of the application or appeal; but
(b) at any such hearing, may only abandon that application or appeal with the court's permission.
(3) A notice of abandonment must be in the form set out in the Practice Direction, signed by or on behalf of the appellant.
(4) On receiving a notice of abandonment the Registrar must—
(a) date it;
(b) serve a dated copy on—
(i) the appellant,
(ii) the appellant's custodian, if any,
(iii) the Crown Court officer, and
(iv) any other person on whom the appellant or the Registrar served the appeal notice; and
(c) treat the application or appeal as if it had been refused or dismissed by the Court of Appeal.
(5) An appellant who wants to reinstate an application or appeal after abandoning it must—
(a) apply in writing, with reasons; and
(b) serve the application on the Registrar.

Abandoning a ground of appeal or opposition R-401

36.14 (1) This rule applies where a party wants to abandon—
(a) a ground of appeal identified in an appeal notice; or
(b) a ground of opposition identified in a respondent's notice.
(2) Such a party must give written notice to—
(a) the Registrar; and
(b) every other party,
before any hearing at which that ground will be considered by the court.

Criminal Procedure Rules Part 37 Appeal to the Court of Appeal against Ruling at Preparatory Hearing

When this Part applies R-402

37.1 (1) This Part applies where a party wants to appeal under—
(a) section 9(11) of the Criminal Justice Act 1987 or section 35(1) of the Criminal Procedure and Investigations Act 1996; or
(b) section 47(1) of the Criminal Justice Act 2003.
(2) A reference to an 'appellant' in this Part is a reference to such a party.

Service of appeal notice R-403

37.2 (1) An appellant must serve an appeal notice on—
(a) the Crown Court officer;
(b) the Registrar; and
(c) every party directly affected by the order or ruling against which the appellant wants to appeal.
(2) The appellant must serve the appeal notice not more than 5 business days after—
(a) the order or ruling against which the appellant wants to appeal; or
(b) the Crown Court judge gives or refuses permission to appeal.

Form of appeal notice R-404

37.3 (1) An appeal notice must be in the form set out in the Practice Direction.
(2) The appeal notice must—
(a) specify each order or ruling against which the appellant wants to appeal;

(b) identify each ground of appeal on which the appellant relies, numbering them consecutively (if there is more than one) and concisely outlining each argument in support;
(c) summarise the relevant facts;
(d) identify any relevant authorities;
(e) include or attach any application for the following, with reasons—
 (i) permission to appeal, if the appellant needs the court's permission,
 (ii) an extension of time within which to serve the appeal notice,
 (iii) a direction to attend in person a hearing that the appellant could attend by live link, if the appellant is in custody;
(f) include a list of those on whom the appellant has served the appeal notice; and
(g) attach—
 (i) a transcript or note of each order or ruling against which the appellant wants to appeal,
 (ii) all relevant skeleton arguments considered by the Crown Court judge,
 (iii) any written application for permission to appeal that the appellant made to the Crown Court judge,
 (iv) a transcript or note of the decision by the Crown Court judge on any application for permission to appeal, and
 (v) any other document or thing that the appellant thinks the court will need to decide the appeal.

R-405 Crown Court judge's permission to appeal

37.4 (1) An appellant who wants the Crown Court judge to give permission to appeal must—
(a) apply orally, with reasons, immediately after the order or ruling against which the appellant wants to appeal; or
(b) apply in writing and serve the application on—
 (i) the Crown Court officer, and
 (ii) every party directly affected by the order or ruling

not more than 2 business days after that order or ruling.

(2) A written application must include the same information (with the necessary adaptations) as an appeal notice.

R-406 Respondent's notice

37.5 (1) A party on whom an appellant serves an appeal notice may serve a respondent's notice, and must do so if—
(a) that party wants to make representations to the court; or
(b) the court so directs.

(2) Such a party must serve the respondent's notice on—
(a) the appellant;
(b) the Crown Court officer;
(c) the Registrar; and
(d) any other party on whom the appellant served the appeal notice.

(3) Such a party must serve the respondent's notice not more than 5 business days after—
(a) the appellant serves the appeal notice; or
(b) a direction to do so.

(4) The respondent's notice must be in the form set out in the Practice Direction.

(5) The respondent's notice must—
(a) give the date on which the respondent was served with the appeal notice;
(b) identify each ground of opposition on which the respondent relies, numbering them consecutively (if there is more than one), concisely outlining each argument in support and identifying the ground of appeal to which each relates;
(c) summarise any relevant facts not already summarised in the appeal notice;
(d) identify any relevant authorities;
(e) include or attach any application for the following, with reasons—
 (i) an extension of time within which to serve the respondent's notice,
 (ii) a direction to attend in person any hearing that the respondent could attend by live link, if the respondent is in custody;
(f) identify any other document or thing that the respondent thinks the court will need to decide the appeal.

Powers of Court of Appeal judge R-407

37.6 A judge of the Court of Appeal may give permission to appeal as well as exercising the powers given by other legislation (including these Rules).

Renewing applications R-408

37.7 Rule 36.5 (Renewing an application refused by a judge or the Registrar) applies with a time limit of 5 business days.

Right to attend hearing R-409

37.8 (1) A party who is in custody has a right to attend a hearing in public.
(2) The court or the Registrar may direct that such a party is to attend a hearing by live link.

Criminal Procedure Rules Part 38 Appeal to the Court of Appeal against Ruling Adverse to Prosecution

When this Part applies R-410

38.1 (1) This Part applies where a prosecutor wants to appeal under section 58(2) of the Criminal Justice Act 2003.
(2) A reference to an 'appellant' in this Part is a reference to such a prosecutor.

Decision to appeal R-411

38.2 (1) An appellant must tell the Crown Court judge of any decision to appeal—
(a) immediately after the ruling against which the appellant wants to appeal; or
(b) on the expiry of the time to decide whether to appeal allowed under paragraph (2).
(2) If an appellant wants time to decide whether to appeal—
(a) the appellant must ask the Crown Court judge immediately after the ruling; and
(b) the general rule is that the judge must not require the appellant to decide there and then but instead must allow until the next business day.

Service of appeal notice R-412

38.3 (1) An appellant must serve an appeal notice on—
(a) the Crown Court officer;
(b) the Registrar; and
(c) every defendant directly affected by the ruling against which the appellant wants to appeal.
(2) The appellant must serve the appeal notice not later than—
(a) the next business day after telling the Crown Court judge of the decision to appeal, if the judge expedites the appeal; or
(b) 5 business days after telling the Crown Court judge of that decision, if the judge does not expedite the appeal.

Form of appeal notice R-413

38.4 (1) An appeal notice must be in the form set out in the Practice Direction.
(2) The appeal notice must—
(a) specify each ruling against which the appellant wants to appeal;
(b) identify each ground of appeal on which the appellant relies, numbering them consecutively (if there is more than one) and concisely outlining each argument in support;
(c) summarise the relevant facts;
(d) identify any relevant authorities;
(e) include or attach any application for the following, with reasons—
(i) permission to appeal, if the appellant needs the court's permission,
(ii) an extension of time within which to serve the appeal notice,
(iii) expedition of the appeal, or revocation of a direction expediting the appeal;
(f) include a list of those on whom the appellant has served the appeal notice;
(g) attach—
(i) a transcript or note of each ruling against which the appellant wants to appeal,
(ii) all relevant skeleton arguments considered by the Crown Court judge,
(iii) any written application for permission to appeal that the appellant made to the Crown Court judge,
(iv) a transcript or note of the decision by the Crown Court judge on any application for permission to appeal,

(v) a transcript or note of the decision by the Crown Court judge on any request to expedite the appeal, and
(vi) any other document or thing that the appellant thinks the court will need to decide the appeal; and

(h) attach a form of respondent's notice for any defendant served with the appeal notice to complete if that defendant wants to do so.

R-414 **Crown Court judge's permission to appeal**

38.5 (1) An appellant who wants the Crown Court judge to give permission to appeal must—
(a) apply orally, with reasons, immediately after the ruling against which the appellant wants to appeal; or
(b) apply in writing and serve the application on—
(i) the Crown Court officer, and
(ii) every defendant directly affected by the ruling
on the expiry of the time allowed under rule 67.2 to decide whether to appeal.

(2) A written application must include the same information (with the necessary adaptations) as an appeal notice.

(3) The Crown Court judge must allow every defendant directly affected by the ruling an opportunity to make representations.

(4) The general rule is that the Crown Court judge must decide whether or not to give permission to appeal on the day that the application for permission is made.

R-415 **Expediting an appeal**

38.6 (1) An appellant who wants the Crown Court judge to expedite an appeal must ask, giving reasons, on telling the judge of the decision to appeal.

(2) The Crown Court judge must allow every defendant directly affected by the ruling an opportunity to make representations.

(3) The Crown Court judge may revoke a direction expediting the appeal unless the appellant has served the appeal notice.

R-416 **Respondent's notice**

38.7 (1) A defendant on whom an appellant serves an appeal notice may serve a respondent's notice, and must do so if—
(a) the defendant wants to make representations to the court; or
(b) the court so directs.

(2) Such a defendant must serve the respondent's notice on—
(a) the appellant;
(b) the Crown Court officer;
(c) the Registrar; and
(d) any other defendant on whom the appellant served the appeal notice.

(3) Such a defendant must serve the respondent's notice—
(a) not later than the next business day after—
(i) the appellant serves the appeal notice, or
(ii) a direction to do so
if the Crown Court judge expedites the appeal; or
(b) not more than 5 business days after—
(i) the appellant serves the appeal notice, or
(ii) a direction to do so
if the Crown Court judge does not expedite the appeal.

(4) The respondent's notice must be in the form set out in the Practice Direction.

(5) The respondent's notice must—
(a) give the date on which the respondent was served with the appeal notice;
(b) identify each ground of opposition on which the respondent relies, numbering them consecutively (if there is more than one), concisely outlining each argument in support and identifying the ground of appeal to which each relates;
(c) summarise any relevant facts not already summarised in the appeal notice;
(d) identify any relevant authorities;
(e) include or attach any application for the following, with reasons—
(i) an extension of time within which to serve the respondent's notice,
(ii) a direction to attend in person any hearing that the respondent could attend by live link, if the respondent is in custody;

(f) identify any other document or thing that the respondent thinks the court will need to decide the appeal.

Public interest ruling R-417

38.8 (1) This rule applies where the appellant wants to appeal against a public interest ruling.
(2) The appellant must not serve on any defendant directly affected by the ruling—
(a) any written application to the Crown Court judge for permission to appeal; or
(b) an appeal notice,
if the appellant thinks that to do so in effect would reveal something that the appellant thinks ought not be disclosed.
(3) The appellant must not include in an appeal notice—
(a) the material that was the subject of the ruling; or
(b) any indication of what sort of material it is,
if the appellant thinks that to do so in effect would reveal something that the appellant thinks ought not be disclosed.
(4) The appellant must serve on the Registrar with the appeal notice an annex—
(a) marked to show that its contents are only for the court and the Registrar;
(b) containing whatever the appellant has omitted from the appeal notice, with reasons; and
(c) if relevant, explaining why the appellant has not served the appeal notice.
(5) Rules 38.5(3) and 38.6(2) do not apply.

Powers of Court of Appeal judge R-418

38.9 A judge of the Court of Appeal may—
(a) give permission to appeal;
(b) revoke a Crown Court judge's direction expediting an appeal; and
(c) where an appellant abandons an appeal, order a defendant's acquittal, his release from custody and the payment of his costs,
as well as exercising the powers given by other legislation (including these Rules).

Renewing applications R-419

38.10 Rule 36.5 (Renewing an application refused by a judge or the Registrar) applies with a time limit of 5 business days.

Right to attend hearing R-420

38.11 (1) A respondent who is in custody has a right to attend a hearing in public.
(2) The court or the Registrar may direct that such a respondent is to attend a hearing by live link.

Criminal Procedure Rules Part 39 Appeal to the Court of Appeal about Conviction or Sentence

When this Part applies R-421

39.1 (1) This Part applies where—
(a) a defendant wants to appeal under—
(i) Part 1 of the Criminal Appeal Act 1968,
(ii) section 274(3) of the Criminal Justice Act 2003,
(iii) paragraph 14 of Schedule 22 to the Criminal Justice Act 2003, or
(iv) section 42 of the Counter-Terrorism Act 2008;
(b) the Criminal Cases Review Commission refers a case to the Court of Appeal under section 9 of the Criminal Appeal Act 1995;
(c) a prosecutor wants to appeal to the Court of Appeal under section 14A(5A) of the Football Spectators Act 1989;
(d) a party wants to appeal under section 74(8) of the Serious Organised Crime and Police Act 2005;
(e) a person found to be in contempt of court wants to appeal under section 13 of the Administration of Justice Act 1960 and section 18A of the Criminal Appeal Act 1968; or
(f) a person wants to appeal to the Court of Appeal under—
(i) section 24 of the Serious Crime Act 2007, or
(ii) regulation 3C or 3H of the Costs in Criminal Cases (General) Regulations 1986.
(2) A reference to an 'appellant' in this Part is a reference to such a party or person.

R-422 Service of appeal notice

39.2 (1) The general rule is that an appellant must serve an appeal notice—

(a) on the Crown Court officer at the Crown Court centre where there occurred—

(i) the conviction, verdict, or finding,

(ii) the sentence, or

(iii) the order, or the failure to make an order

about which the appellant wants to appeal; and

(b) not more than—

(i) 28 days after that occurred, or

(ii) 21 days after the order, in a case in which the appellant appeals against a wasted or third party costs order.

(2) But an appellant must serve an appeal notice—

(a) on the Registrar instead where—

(i) the appeal is against a minimum term review decision under section 274(3) of, or paragraph 14 of Schedule 22 to, the Criminal Justice Act 2003, or

(ii) the Criminal Cases Review Commission refers the case to the court; and

(b) not more than 28 days after—

(i) the minimum term review decision about which the appellant wants to appeal, or

(ii) the Registrar serves notice that the Commission has referred a conviction.

R-423 Form of appeal notice

39.3 (1) An appeal notice must be in the form set out in the Practice Direction.

(2) The appeal notice must—

(a) specify—

(i) the conviction, verdict, or finding,

(ii) the sentence, or

(iii) the order, or the failure to make an order

about which the appellant wants to appeal;

(b) identify each ground of appeal on which the appellant relies, numbering them consecutively (if there is more than one) and concisely outlining each argument in support;

(c) identify the transcript that the appellant thinks the court will need, if the appellant wants to appeal against a conviction;

(d) identify the relevant sentencing powers of the Crown Court, if sentence is in issue;

(e) where the Criminal Cases Review Commission refers a case to the court, explain how each ground of appeal relates (if it does) to the reasons for the reference;

(f) summarise the relevant facts;

(g) identify any relevant authorities;

(h) include or attach any application for the following, with reasons—

(i) permission to appeal, if the appellant needs the court's permission,

(ii) an extension of time within which to serve the appeal notice,

(iii) bail pending appeal,

(iv) a direction to attend in person a hearing that the appellant could attend by live link, if the appellant is in custody,

(v) the introduction of evidence, including hearsay evidence and evidence of bad character,

(vi) an order requiring a witness to attend court,

(vii) a direction for special measures for a witness,

(viii) a direction for special measures for the giving of evidence by the appellant;

(i) identify any other document or thing that the appellant thinks the court will need to decide the appeal.

R-424 Crown Court judge's certificate that case is fit for appeal

39.4 (1) An appellant who wants the Crown Court judge to certify that a case is fit for appeal must—

(a) apply orally, with reasons, immediately after there occurs—

(i) the conviction, verdict, or finding,

(ii) the sentence, or

(iii) the order, or the failure to make an order

about which the appellant wants to appeal; or

(b) apply in writing and serve the application on the Crown Court officer not more than 14 days after that occurred.

(2) A written application must include the same information (with the necessary adaptations) as an appeal notice.

Reference by Criminal Cases Review Commission R-425

39.5 (1) The Registrar must serve on the appellant a reference by the Criminal Cases Review Commission.

(2) The court must treat that reference as the appeal notice if the appellant does not serve such a notice under rule 39.2.

Respondent's notice R-426

39.6 (1) The Registrar—

(a) may serve an appeal notice on any party directly affected by the appeal; and

(b) must do so if the Criminal Cases Review Commission refers a conviction, verdict, finding or sentence to the court.

(2) Such a party may serve a respondent's notice, and must do so if—

(a) that party wants to make representations to the court; or

(b) the court or the Registrar so directs.

(3) Such a party must serve the respondent's notice on—

(a) the appellant;

(b) the Registrar; and

(c) any other party on whom the Registrar served the appeal notice.

(4) Such a party must serve the respondent's notice—

(a) not more than 14 days after the Registrar serves—

(i) the appeal notice, or

(ii) a direction to do so; or

(b) not more than 28 days after the Registrar serves notice that the Commission has referred a conviction.

(5) The respondent's notice must be in the form set out in the Practice Direction.

(6) The respondent's notice must—

(a) give the date on which the respondent was served with the appeal notice;

(b) identify each ground of opposition on which the respondent relies, numbering them consecutively (if there is more than one), concisely outlining each argument in support and identifying the ground of appeal to which each relates;

(c) identify the relevant sentencing powers of the Crown Court, if sentence is in issue;

(d) summarise any relevant facts not already summarised in the appeal notice;

(e) identify any relevant authorities;

(f) include or attach any application for the following, with reasons—

(i) an extension of time within which to serve the respondent's notice,

(ii) bail pending appeal,

(iii) a direction to attend in person a hearing that the respondent could attend by live link, if the respondent is in custody,

(iv) the introduction of evidence, including hearsay evidence and evidence of bad character,

(v) an order requiring a witness to attend court,

(vi) a direction for special measures for a witness; and

(g) identify any other document or thing that the respondent thinks the court will need to decide the appeal.

Adaptation of rules about introducing evidence R-427

39.7 (1) The following Parts apply with such adaptations as the court or the Registrar may direct—

(a) Part 18 (Measures to assist a witness or defendant to give evidence);

(b) Part 20 (Hearsay evidence);

(c) Part 21 (Evidence of bad character); and

(d) Part 22 (Evidence of a complainant's previous sexual behaviour).

(2) But the general rule is that—

(a) a respondent who opposes an appellant's application to which one of those Parts applies must do so in the respondent's notice, with reasons;

(b) an appellant who opposes a respondent's application to which one of those Parts applies must serve notice, with reasons, on—

(i) the Registrar, and

(ii) the respondent

not more than 14 days after service of the respondent's notice; and

(c) the court or the Registrar may give directions with or without a hearing.

R-428 Application for bail pending appeal or retrial

39.8 (1) This rule applies where a party wants to make an application to the court about bail pending appeal or retrial.

(2) That party must serve an application in the form set out in the Practice Direction on—
(a) the Registrar, unless the application is with the appeal notice; and
(b) the other party.

(3) The court must not decide such an application without giving the other party an opportunity to make representations, including representations about any condition or surety proposed by the applicant.

(4) This rule and rule 14.16 (Bail condition to be enforced in another European Union member State) apply where the court can impose as a condition of bail pending retrial a requirement—
(a) with which a defendant must comply while in another European Union member State; and
(b) which that other member State can monitor and enforce.

R-429 Conditions of bail pending appeal or retrial

39.9 (1) This rule applies where the court grants a party bail pending appeal or retrial subject to any condition that must be met before that party is released.

(2) The court may direct how such a condition must be met.

(3) The Registrar must serve a certificate in the form set out in the Practice Direction recording any such condition and direction on—
(a) that party;
(b) that party's custodian; and
(c) any other person directly affected by any such direction.

(4) A person directly affected by any such direction need not comply with it until the Registrar serves that person with that certificate.

(5) Unless the court otherwise directs, if any such condition or direction requires someone to enter into a recognizance it must be—
(a) in the form set out in the Practice Direction and signed before—
(i) the Registrar,
(ii) the custodian, or
(iii) someone acting with the authority of the Registrar or custodian;
(b) copied immediately to the person who enters into it; and
(c) served immediately by the Registrar on the appellant's custodian or vice versa, as appropriate.

(6) Unless the court otherwise directs, if any such condition or direction requires someone to make a payment, surrender a document or take some other step—
(a) that payment, document or step must be made, surrendered or taken to or before—
(i) the Registrar,
(ii) the custodian, or
(iii) someone acting with the authority of the Registrar or custodian;
(b) the Registrar or the custodian, as appropriate, must serve immediately on the other a statement that the payment, document or step has been made, surrendered or taken, as appropriate.

(7) The custodian must release the appellant where it appears that any condition ordered by the court has been met.

(8) For the purposes of section 5 of the Bail Act 1976 (record of decision about bail), the Registrar must keep a copy of—
(a) any certificate served under paragraph (3);
(b) a notice of hearing given under rule 36.7(1); and
(c) a notice of the court's decision served under rule 36.7(2).

(9) Where the court grants bail pending retrial the Registrar must serve on the Crown Court officer copies of the documents kept under paragraph (8).

R-430 Forfeiture of a recognizance given as a condition of bail

39.10 (1) This rule applies where—
(a) the court grants a party bail pending appeal or retrial; and
(b) the bail is subject to a condition that that party provides a surety to guarantee that he will surrender to custody as required; but
(c) that party does not surrender to custody as required.

(2) The Registrar must serve notice on—
(a) the surety; and
(b) the prosecutor,
of the hearing at which the court may order the forfeiture of the recognizance given by that surety.
(3) The court must not forfeit a surety's recognizance—
(a) less than 7 days after the Registrar serves notice under paragraph (2); and
(b) without giving the surety an opportunity to make representations at a hearing.

Right to attend hearing R-431

39.11 A party who is in custody has a right to attend a hearing in public unless—
(a) it is a hearing preliminary or incidental to an appeal, including the hearing of an application for permission to appeal; or
(b) that party is in custody in consequence of—
(i) a verdict of not guilty by reason of insanity, or
(ii) a finding of disability.

Power to vary determination of appeal against sentence R-432

39.12 (1) This rule applies where the court decides an appeal affecting sentence in a party's absence.
(2) The court may vary such a decision if it did not take account of something relevant because that party was absent.
(3) A party who wants the court to vary such a decision must—
(a) apply in writing, with reasons;
(b) serve the application on the Registrar not more than 7 days after—
(i) the decision, if that party was represented at the appeal hearing, or
(ii) the Registrar serves the decision, if that party was not represented at that hearing.

Directions about re-admission to hospital on dismissal of appeal R-433

39.13 (1) This rule applies where—
(a) an appellant subject to—
(i) an order under section 37(1) of the Mental Health Act 1983 (detention in hospital on conviction), or
(ii) an order under section 5(2) of the Criminal Procedure (Insanity) Act 1964 (detention in hospital on finding of insanity or disability)
has been released on bail pending appeal; and
(b) the court—
(i) refuses permission to appeal,
(ii) dismisses the appeal, or
(iii) affirms the order under appeal.
(2) The court must give appropriate directions for the appellant's—
(a) re-admission to hospital; and
(b) if necessary, temporary detention pending re-admission.

Renewal or setting aside of order for retrial R-434

39.14 (1) This rule applies where—
(a) a prosecutor wants a defendant to be arraigned more than 2 months after the court ordered a retrial under section 7 of the Criminal Appeal Act 1968; or
(b) a defendant wants such an order set aside after 2 months have passed since it was made.
(2) That party must apply in writing, with reasons, and serve the application on—
(a) the Registrar;
(b) the other party.

Criminal Practice Directions Part 39 Appeal to the Court of Appeal about Conviction or Sentence

CPD IX Appeal 39A: Appeals Against Conviction and Sentence — The Provision of Notice to the Prosecution PD-77

39A.1 When an appeal notice served under CrimPR 39.2 is received by the Registrar of Criminal Appeals, the Registrar will notify the relevant prosecution authority, giving the case name, reference number and the trial or sentencing court.

39A.2 If the court or the Registrar directs, or invites, the prosecution authority to serve a respondent's notice under CrimPR 39.6, prior to the consideration of leave, the Registrar will also at that time serve on the prosecution authority the appeal notice containing the grounds of appeal and the transcripts, if available. If the prosecution authority is not directed or invited to serve a respondent's notice but wishes to do so, the authority should request the grounds of appeal and any existing transcript from the Criminal Appeal Office. Any respondent's notice received prior to the consideration of leave will be made available to the single judge.

39A.3 The Registrar of Criminal Appeals will notify the relevant prosecution authority in the event that:

(a) leave to appeal against conviction or sentence is granted by the single Judge; or
(b) the single Judge or the Registrar refers an application for leave to appeal against conviction or sentence to the Full Court for determination; or
(c) there is to be a renewed application for leave to appeal against sentence only.

If the prosecution authority has not yet been served with the appeal notice and transcript, the Registrar will serve these with the notification, and if leave is granted, the Registrar will also serve the authority with the comments of the single judge.

39A.4 The prosecution should notify the Registrar without delay if they wish to be represented at the hearing. The prosecution should note that the Registrar will not delay listing to await a response from the Prosecution as to whether they wish to attend. Prosecutors should note that occasionally, for example, where the single Judge fixes a hearing date at short notice, the case may be listed very quickly.

39A.5 If the prosecution wishes to be represented at any hearing, the notification should include details of Counsel instructed and a time estimate. An application by the prosecution to remove a case from the list for Counsel's convenience, or to allow further preparation time, will rarely be granted.

39A.6 There may be occasions when the Court of Appeal Criminal Division will grant leave to appeal to an unrepresented applicant and proceed forthwith with the appeal in the absence of the appellant and Counsel. The prosecution should not attend any hearing at which the appellant is unrepresented. *Nasteska v The former Yugoslav Republic of Macedonia (Application No.23152/05)* As a Court of Review, the Court of Appeal Criminal Division would expect the prosecution to have raised any specific matters of relevance with the sentencing Judge in the first instance.

PD-78 **CPD IX Appeal 39B: Listing of Appeals against Conviction and Sentence in the Court of Appeal Criminal Division (CACD)**

39B.1 Arrangements for the fixing of dates for the hearing of appeals will be made by the Criminal Appeal Office Listing Officer, under the superintendence of the Registrar of Criminal Appeals who may give such directions as he deems necessary.

39B.2 Where possible, regard will be had to an advocate's existing commitments. However, in relation to the listing of appeals, the Court of Appeal takes precedence over all lower courts, including the Crown Court. Wherever practicable, a lower court will have regard to this principle when making arrangements to release an advocate to appear in the Court of Appeal. In case of difficulty the lower court should communicate with the Registrar. In general an advocate's commitment in a lower court will not be regarded as a good reason for failing to accept a date proposed for a hearing in the Court of Appeal.

39B.3 Similarly when the Registrar directs that an appellant should appear by video link, the prison must give precedence to video-links to the Court of Appeal over video-links to the lower courts, including the Crown Court.

39B.4 The copy of the Criminal Appeal Office summary provided to advocates will contain the summary writer's time estimate for the whole hearing including delivery of judgment. It will also contain a time estimate for the judges' reading time of the core material. The Listing Officer will rely on those estimates, unless the advocate for the appellant or the Crown provides different time estimates to the Listing Officer, in writing, within 7 days of the receipt of the summary by the advocate. Where the time estimates are considered by an advocate to be inadequate, or where the estimates have been altered because, for example, a ground of appeal has been abandoned, it is the duty of the advocate to inform the Court promptly, in which event the Registrar will reconsider the time estimates and inform the parties accordingly.

39B.5 The following target times are set for the hearing of appeals. Target times will run from the receipt of the appeal by the Listing Officer, as being ready for hearing.

39B.6

Nature of Appeal:	*From Receipt by Listing Officer to Fixing of Hearing Date:*	*From Fixing of Hearing Date to Hearing:*	*Total Time From Receipt by Listing Officer to Hearing:*
Sentence Appeal	14 days	14 days	28 days
Conviction Appeal	21 days	42 days	63 days
Conviction Appeal where witness to attend	28 days	52 days	80 days

39B.7 Where legal vacations impinge, these periods may be extended. Where expedition is required, the Registrar may direct that these periods be abridged.

39B.8 'Appeal' includes an application for leave to appeal which requires an oral hearing.

CPD IX Appeal 39C: Appeal Notices Containing Grounds of Appeal PD-79

39C.1 The requirements for the service of notices of appeal and the time limits for doing so are as set out in Part 39 of the Criminal Procedure Rules. The Court must be provided with an appeal notice as a single document which sets out the grounds of appeal. Advocates should not provide the Court with an advice addressed to lay or professional clients. Any appeal notice or grounds of appeal served on the Court will usually be provided to the respondent.

39C.2 Advocates should not settle grounds unless they consider that they are properly arguable. Grounds should be carefully drafted; the Court is not assisted by grounds of appeal which are not properly set out and particularised. Should leave to amend the grounds be granted, it is most unlikely that further grounds will be entertained.

CPD IX Appeal 39D: Respondents' Notices PD-80

39D.1 The requirements for the service of respondents' notices and the time limits for doing so are as set out in Part 39 of the Criminal Procedure Rules. Any respondent's notice served should be in accordance with Rule 39.6. The Court does not require a response to the respondent's notice.

CPD IX Appeal 39E: Loss of Time PD-81

39E.1 Both the Court and the single judge have power, in their discretion, under the Criminal Appeal Act 1968 sections 29 and 31, to direct that part of the time during which an applicant is in custody after lodging his notice of application for leave to appeal should not count towards sentence. Those contemplating an appeal should seek advice and should remember that a notice of appeal without grounds is ineffective and that grounds should be substantial and particularised and not a mere formula. When leave to appeal has been refused by the single judge, it is often of assistance to consider the reasons given by the single judge before making a decision whether to renew the application. Where an application devoid of merit has been refused by the single judge he may indicate that the Full Court should consider making a direction for loss of time on renewal of the application. However the Full Court may make such a direction whether or not such an indication has been given by the single judge.

39E.2 Applicants and counsel are reminded of the warning given by the Court of Appeal in *R v Hart and Others* [2006] EWCA Crim 3239, [2007] 1 Cr App R 31, [2007] 2 Cr App R (S) 34 and should 'heed the fact that this court is prepared to exercise its power. . .The mere fact that counsel has advised that there are grounds of appeal will not always be a sufficient answer to the question as to whether or not an application has indeed been brought which was totally without merit.'

CPD IX Appeal 39F: Skeleton Arguments PD-82

39F.1 Advocates should always ensure that the Court, and any other party as appropriate, has a single document containing all of the points that are to be argued. The appeal notice must comply with the requirements of Part 68. In cases of an appeal against conviction, advocates must serve a skeleton argument when the appeal notice does not sufficiently outline the grounds of the appeal, particularly in cases where a complex or novel point of law has been raised. In an appeal against sentence it may be helpful for an advocate to serve a skeleton argument when a complex issue is raised.

39F.2 The appellant's skeleton argument, if any, must be served no later than 21 days before the hearing date, and the respondent's skeleton argument, if any, no later than 14 days before the hearing date, unless otherwise directed by the Court.

39F.3 A skeleton argument, if provided, should contain a numbered list of the points the advocate intends to argue, grouped under each ground of appeal, and stated in no more than one or two sentences. It should be as succinct as possible. Advocates should ensure that the correct Criminal Appeal Office number appears at the beginning of any document and that their names are at the end.

PD-83 **CPD IX Appeal 39G: Criminal Appeal Office Summaries**

39G.1 To assist the Court, the Criminal Appeal Office prepares summaries of the cases coming before it. These are entirely objective and do not contain any advice about how the Court should deal with the case or any view about its merits. They consist of two Parts.

39G.2 Part I, which is provided to all of the advocates in the case, generally contains:

(a) particulars of the proceedings in the Crown Court, including representation and details of any co-accused;
(b) particulars of the proceedings in the Court of Appeal (Criminal Division);
(c) the facts of the case, as drawn from the transcripts, appeal notice, respondent's notice, witness statements and/or the exhibits;
(d) the submissions and rulings, summing up and sentencing remarks.

39G.3 The contents of the summary are a matter for the professional judgment of the writer, but an advocate wishing to suggest any significant alteration to Part I should write to the Registrar of Criminal Appeals. If the Registrar does not agree, the summary and the letter will be put to the Court for decision. The Court will not generally be willing to hear oral argument about the content of the summary.

39G.4 Advocates may show Part I of the summary to their professional or lay clients (but to no one else) if they believe it would help to check facts or formulate arguments, but summaries are not to be copied or reproduced without the permission of the Criminal Appeal Office; permission for this will not normally be given in cases involving children, or sexual offences, or where the Crown Court has made an order restricting reporting.

39G.5 Unless a judge of the High Court or the Registrar of Criminal Appeals gives a direction to the contrary, in any particular case involving material of an explicitly salacious or sadistic nature, Part I will also be supplied to appellants who seek to represent themselves before the Full Court, or who renew to the full court their applications for leave to appeal against conviction or sentence.

39G.6 Part II, which is supplied to the Court alone, contains:

(a) a summary of the grounds of appeal; and
(b) in appeals against sentence (and applications for such leave), summaries of the antecedent histories of the parties and of any relevant pre-sentence, medical or other reports.

39G.7 All of the source material is provided to the Court and advocates are able to draw attention to anything in it which may be of particular relevance.

Criminal Procedure Rules Part 40 Appeal to the Court of Appeal about Reporting or Public Access Restriction

R-435 **When this Part applies**

40.1 (1) This Part applies where a person directly affected by an order to which section 159(1) of the Criminal Justice Act 1988 applies wants to appeal against that order.
(2) A reference to an 'appellant' in this Part is a reference to such a party.

R-436 **Service of appeal notice**

40.2 (1) An appellant must serve an appeal notice on—
(a) the Crown Court officer;
(b) the Registrar;
(c) the parties; and
(d) any other person directly affected by the order against which the appellant wants to appeal.
(2) The appellant must serve the appeal notice not later than—
(a) the next business day after an order restricting public access to the trial;
(b) 10 business days after an order restricting reporting of the trial.

R-437 **Form of appeal notice**

40.3 (1) An appeal notice must be in the form set out in the Practice Direction.
(2) The appeal notice must—
(a) specify the order against which the appellant wants to appeal;
(b) identify each ground of appeal on which the appellant relies, numbering them consecutively (if there is more than one) and concisely outlining each argument in support;
(c) summarise the relevant facts;

(d) identify any relevant authorities;
(e) include or attach, with reasons—
(i) an application for permission to appeal,
(ii) any application for an extension of time within which to serve the appeal notice,
(iii) any application for a direction to attend in person a hearing that the appellant could attend by live link, if the appellant is in custody,
(iv) any application for permission to introduce evidence, and
(v) a list of those on whom the appellant has served the appeal notice; and
(f) attach any document or thing that the appellant thinks the court will need to decide the appeal.

Advance notice of appeal against order restricting public access R-438

40.4 (1) This rule applies where the appellant wants to appeal against an order restricting public access to a trial.
(2) The appellant may serve advance written notice of intention to appeal against any such order that may be made.
(3) The appellant must serve any such advance notice—
(a) on—
(i) the Crown Court officer,
(ii) the Registrar,
(iii) the parties, and
(iv) any other person who will be directly affected by the order against which the appellant intends to appeal, if it is made; and
(b) not more than 5 business days after the Crown Court officer displays notice of the application for the order.
(4) The advance notice must include the same information (with the necessary adaptations) as an appeal notice.
(5) The court must treat that advance notice as the appeal notice if the order is made.

Duty of applicant for order restricting public access R-439

40.5 (1) This rule applies where the appellant wants to appeal against an order restricting public access to a trial.
(2) The party who applied for the order must serve on the Registrar—
(a) a transcript or note of the application for the order; and
(b) any other document or thing that that party thinks the court will need to decide the appeal.
(3) That party must serve that transcript or note and any such other document or thing as soon as practicable after—
(a) the appellant serves the appeal notice; or
(b) the order, where the appellant served advance notice of intention to appeal.

Respondent's notice on appeal against reporting restriction R-440

40.6 (1) This rule applies where the appellant wants to appeal against an order restricting the reporting of a trial.
(2) A person on whom an appellant serves an appeal notice may serve a respondent's notice, and must do so if—
(a) that person wants to make representations to the court; or
(b) the court so directs.
(3) Such a person must serve the respondent's notice on—
(a) the appellant;
(b) the Crown Court officer;
(c) the Registrar;
(d) the parties; and
(e) any other person on whom the appellant served the appeal notice.
(4) Such a person must serve the respondent's notice not more than 3 business days after—
(a) the appellant serves the appeal notice; or
(b) a direction to do so.
(5) The respondent's notice must be in the form set out in the Practice Direction.
(6) The respondent's notice must—
(a) give the date on which the respondent was served with the appeal notice;
(b) identify each ground of opposition on which the respondent relies, numbering them consecutively (if there is more than one), concisely outlining each argument in support and identifying the ground of appeal to which each relates;

(c) summarise any relevant facts not already summarised in the appeal notice;
(d) identify any relevant authorities;
(e) include or attach any application for the following, with reasons—
(i) an extension of time within which to serve the respondent's notice,
(ii) a direction to attend in person any hearing that the respondent could attend by live link, if the respondent is in custody,
(iii) permission to introduce evidence; and
(f) identify any other document or thing that the respondent thinks the court will need to decide the appeal.

R-441 Renewing applications

40.7 Rule 36.5 (Renewing an application refused by a judge or the Registrar) applies with a time limit of 5 business days.

R-442 Right to introduce evidence

40.8 No person may introduce evidence without the court's permission.

R-443 Right to attend hearing

40.9 (1) A party who is in custody has a right to attend a hearing in public of an appeal against an order restricting the reporting of a trial.
(2) The court or the Registrar may direct that such a party is to attend a hearing by live link.

Criminal Procedure Rules Part 41 Reference to the Court of Appeal of Point of Law or Unduly Lenient Sentencing

R-444 When this Part applies

41.1 This Part applies where the Attorney General wants to—
(a) refer a point of law to the Court of Appeal under section 36 of the Criminal Justice Act 1972; or
(b) refer a sentencing case to the Court of Appeal under section 36 of the Criminal Justice Act 1988.

R-445 Service of notice of reference and application for permission

41.2 (1) The Attorney General must—
(a) serve on the Registrar—
(i) any notice of reference, and
(ii) any application for permission to refer a sentencing case; and
(b) with a notice of reference of a point of law, give the Registrar details of—
(i) the defendant affected,
(ii) the date and place of the relevant Crown Court decision, and
(iii) the relevant verdict and sentencing.
(2) The Attorney General must serve an application for permission to refer a sentencing case not more than 28 days after the last of the sentences in that case.

R-446 Form of notice of reference and application for permission

41.3 (1) A notice of reference and an application for permission to refer a sentencing case must be in the appropriate form set out in the Practice Direction, giving the year and number.
(2) A notice of reference of a point of law must—
(a) specify the point of law in issue and indicate the opinion that the Attorney General invites the court to give;
(b) identify each ground for that invitation, numbering them consecutively (if there is more than one) and concisely outlining each argument in support;
(c) exclude any reference to the defendant's name and any other reference that may identify the defendant;
(d) summarise the relevant facts; and
(e) identify any relevant authorities.
(3) An application for permission to refer a sentencing case must—
(a) give details of—
(i) the defendant affected,
(ii) the date and place of the relevant Crown Court decision, and
(iii) the relevant verdict and sentencing;

(b) explain why that sentencing appears to the Attorney General unduly lenient, concisely outlining each argument in support; and
(c) include the application for permission to refer the case to the court.

(4) A notice of reference of a sentencing case must—
(a) include the same details and explanation as the application for permission to refer the case;
(b) summarise the relevant facts; and
(c) identify any relevant authorities.

(5) Where the court gives the Attorney General permission to refer a sentencing case, it may treat the application for permission as the notice of reference.

Registrar's notice to defendant **R-447**

41.4 (1) The Registrar must serve on the defendant—
(a) a notice of reference;
(b) an application for permission to refer a sentencing case.

(2) Where the Attorney General refers a point of law, the Registrar must give the defendant notice that—
(a) the outcome of the reference will not make any difference to the outcome of the trial; and
(b) the defendant may serve a respondent's notice.

(3) Where the Attorney General applies for permission to refer a sentencing case, the Registrar must give the defendant notice that—
(a) the outcome of the reference may make a difference to that sentencing, and in particular may result in a more severe sentence; and
(b) the defendant may serve a respondent's notice.

Respondent's notice **R-448**

41.5 (1) A defendant on whom the Registrar serves a reference or an application for permission to refer a sentencing case may serve a respondent's notice, and must do so if—
(a) the defendant wants to make representations to the court; or
(b) the court so directs.

(2) Such a defendant must serve the respondent's notice on—
(a) the Attorney General; and
(b) the Registrar.

(3) Such a defendant must serve the respondent's notice—
(a) where the Attorney General refers a point of law, not more than 28 days after—
(i) the Registrar serves the reference, or
(ii) a direction to do so;
(b) where the Attorney General applies for permission to refer a sentencing case, not more than 14 days after—
(i) the Registrar serves the application, or
(ii) a direction to do so.

(4) Where the Attorney General refers a point of law, the respondent's notice must—
(a) identify each ground of opposition on which the respondent relies, numbering them consecutively (if there is more than one), concisely outlining each argument in support and identifying the Attorney General's ground or reason to which each relates;
(b) summarise any relevant facts not already summarised in the reference;
(c) identify any relevant authorities; and
(d) include or attach any application for the following, with reasons—
(i) an extension of time within which to serve the respondent's notice,
(ii) permission to attend a hearing that the respondent does not have a right to attend,
(iii) a direction to attend in person a hearing that the respondent could attend by live link, if the respondent is in custody.

(5) Where the Attorney General applies for permission to refer a sentencing case, the respondent's notice must—
(a) say if the respondent wants to make representations at the hearing of the application or reference; and
(b) include or attach any application for the following, with reasons—
(i) an extension of time within which to serve the respondent's notice,
(ii) permission to attend a hearing that the respondent does not have a right to attend,
(iii) a direction to attend in person a hearing that the respondent could attend by live link, if the respondent is in custody.

R-449 **Variation or withdrawal of notice of reference or application for permission**

41.6 (1) This rule applies where the Attorney General wants to vary or withdraw—
(a) a notice of reference; or
(b) an application for permission to refer a sentencing case.
(2) The Attorney General—
(a) may vary or withdraw the notice or application without the court's permission by serving notice on—
(i) the Registrar, and
(ii) the defendant
before any hearing of the reference or application; but
(b) at any such hearing, may only vary or withdraw that notice or application with the court's permission.

R-450 **Right to attend hearing**

41.7 (1) A respondent who is in custody has a right to attend a hearing in public unless it is a hearing preliminary or incidental to a reference, including the hearing of an application for permission to refer a sentencing case.
(2) The court or the Registrar may direct that such a respondent is to attend a hearing by live link.

R-451 **Anonymity of defendant on reference of point of law**

41.8 Where the Attorney General refers a point of law, the court must not allow anyone to identify the defendant during the proceedings unless the defendant gives permission.

Criminal Procedure Rules Part 42 Appeal to the Court of Appeal in Confiscation and Related Proceedings

General rules

R-452 **Extension of time**

42.1 (1) An application to extend the time limit for giving notice of application for permission to appeal under Part 2 of the Proceeds of Crime Act 2002 must—
(a) be included in the notice of appeal; and
(b) state the grounds for the application.
(2) The parties may not agree to extend any date or time limit set by this Part or by the Proceeds of Crime Act 2002 (Appeals under Part 2) Order 2003.

R-453 **Other applications**

42.2 Rules 39.3(2)(h) (Form of appeal notice) applies in relation to an application—
(a) by a party to an appeal under Part 2 of the Proceeds of Crime Act 2002 that, under article 7 of the Proceeds of Crime Act 2002 (Appeals under Part 2) Order 2003, a witness be ordered to attend or that the evidence of a witness be received by the Court of Appeal; or
(b) by the defendant to be given permission by the court to be present at proceedings for which permission is required under article 6 of the 2003 Order,
as it applies in relation to applications under Part I of the Criminal Appeal Act 1968 and the form in which rules 39.3 requires notice to be given may be modified as necessary.

R-454 **Examination of witness by court**

42.3 Rule 36.7 (Notice of hearings and decisions) shall apply in relation to an order of the court under article 7 of the Proceeds of Crime Act 2002 (Appeals under Part 2) Order 2003 to require a person to attend for examination as it applies in relation to such an order of the court under Part I of the Criminal Appeal Act 1968.

R-455 **Supply of documentary and other exhibits**

42.4 Rule 36.11 (Registrar's duty to provide copy documents for appeal or reference) applies in relation to an appellant or respondent under Part 2 of the Proceeds of Crime Act 2002 as it applies in relation to an appellant and respondent under Part I of the Criminal Appeal Act 1968.

R-456 **Registrar's power to require information from court of trial**

42.5 The Registrar may require the Crown Court to provide the Court of Appeal with any assistance or information which it requires for the purposes of exercising its jurisdiction under Part 2 of the Proceeds of Crime Act 2002, the Proceeds of Crime Act 2002 (Appeals under Part 2) Order 2003 or this Part.

Hearing by single judge R-457

42.6 Rule 36.6(5) (Hearings) applies in relation to a judge exercising any of the powers referred to in article 8 of the Proceeds of Crime Act 2002 (Appeals under Part 2) Order 2003 or the powers in rules 42.12(3) and (4) (Respondent's notice), 42.15(2) (Notice of appeal) and 42.16(6) (Respondent's notice), as it applies in relation to a judge exercising the powers referred to in section 31(2) of the Criminal Appeal Act 1968.

Determination by full court R-458

42.7 Rule 36.5 (Renewing an application refused by a single judge or the Registrar) applies where a single judge has refused an application by a party to exercise in that party's favour any of the powers listed in article 8 of the Proceeds of Crime Act 2002 (Appeals under Part 2) Order 2003, or the power in rule 42.12(3) or (4) as it applies where the judge has refused to exercise the powers referred to in section 31(2) of the Criminal Appeal Act 1968.

Notice of determination R-459

42.8 (1) This rule applies where a single judge or the Court of Appeal has determined an application or appeal under the Proceeds of Crime Act 2002 (Appeals under Part 2) Order 2003 or under Part 2 of the Proceeds of Crime Act 2002.

(2) The Registrar must, as soon as practicable, serve notice of the determination on all of the parties to the proceedings.

(3) Where a single judge or the Court of Appeal has disposed of an application for permission to appeal or an appeal under section 31 of the 2002 Act, the Registrar must also, as soon as practicable, serve the order on a court officer of the court of trial and any magistrates' court responsible for enforcing any confiscation order which the Crown Court has made.

Record of proceedings and transcripts R-460

42.9 Rule 5.5 (Recording and transcription of proceedings in the Crown Court) and rule 36.9 (Duty of person transcribing proceedings in the Crown Court) apply in relation to proceedings in respect of which an appeal lies to the Court of Appeal under Part 2 of the Proceeds of Crime Act 2002 as they apply in relation to proceedings in respect of which an appeal lies to the Court of Appeal under Part I of the Criminal Appeal Act 1968.

Appeal to the Supreme Court R-461

42.10 (1) An application to the Court of Appeal for permission to appeal to the Supreme Court under Part 2 of the Proceeds of Crime Act 2002 must be made—

(a) orally after the decision of the Court of Appeal from which an appeal lies to the Supreme Court; or

(b) in the form set out in the Practice Direction, in accordance with article 12 of the Proceeds of Crime Act 2002 (Appeals under Part 2) Order 2003 and served on the Registrar.

(2) The application may be abandoned at any time before it is heard by the Court of Appeal by serving notice in writing on the Registrar.

(3) Rule 36.6(5) (Hearings) applies in relation to a single judge exercising any of the powers referred to in article 15 of the 2003 Order, as it applies in relation to a single judge exercising the powers referred to in section 31(2) of the Criminal Appeal Act 1968.

(4) Rules 36.5 (Renewing an application refused by a judge or the Registrar) applies where a single judge has refused an application by a party to exercise in that party's favour any of the powers listed in article 15 of the 2003 Order as they apply where the judge has refused to exercise the powers referred to in section 31(2) of the 1968 Act.

(5) The form in which rule 36.5(2) requires an application to be made may be modified as necessary.

Confiscation: appeal by prosecutor or by person with interest in property

Notice of appeal R-462

42.11 (1) Where an appellant wishes to apply to the Court of Appeal for permission to appeal under section 31 of the Proceeds of Crime Act 2002, the appellant must serve a notice of appeal in the form set out in the Practice Direction on—

(a) the Crown Court officer; and

(b) the defendant.

(2) When the notice of a prosecutor's appeal about a confiscation order is served on the defendant, it must be accompanied by a respondent's notice in the form set out in the Practice Direction for the defendant to complete and a notice which—

(a) informs the defendant that the result of an appeal could be that the Court of Appeal would increase a confiscation order already imposed, make a confiscation order itself or direct the Crown Court to hold another confiscation hearing;

(b) informs the defendant of any right under article 6 of the Proceeds of Crime Act 2002 (Appeals under Part 2) Order 2003 to be present at the hearing of the appeal, although in custody;
(c) invites the defendant to serve any notice on the Registrar —
(i) to apply to the Court of Appeal for permission to be present at proceedings for which such permission is required under article 6 of the 2003 Order, or
(ii) to present any argument to the Court of Appeal on the hearing of the application or, if permission is given, the appeal, and whether the defendant wishes to present it in person or by means of a legal representative;
(d) draws to the defendant's attention the effect of rule 42.4 (Supply of documentary and other exhibits); and
(e) advises the defendant to consult a solicitor as soon as possible.
(3) The appellant must provide a Crown Court officer with a certificate of service stating that the appellant has served the notice of appeal on the defendant in accordance with paragraph (1) or explaining why it has not been possible to do so.

R-463 Respondent's notice

42.12 (1) This rule applies where a defendant is served with a notice of appeal under rule 42.11.
(2) If the defendant wishes to oppose the application for permission to appeal, the defendant must, not later than 14 days after service of the notice of appeal, serve on the Registrar and on the appellant a notice in the form set out in the Practice Direction—
(a) stating the date on which the notice of appeal was served;
(b) summarising the defendant's response to the arguments of the appellant; and
(c) specifying the authorities which the defendant intends to cite.
(3) The time for giving notice under this rule may be extended by the Registrar, a single judge or by the Court of Appeal.
(4) Where the Registrar refuses an application under paragraph (3) for the extension of time, the defendant is entitled to have the application determined by a single judge.
(5) Where a single judge refuses an application under paragraph (3) or (4) for the extension of time, the defendant is entitled to have the application determined by the Court of Appeal.

R-464 Amendment and abandonment of appeal

42.13 (1) The appellant may amend a notice of appeal served under rule 42.11 or abandon an appeal under section 31 of the Proceeds of Crime Act 2002—
(a) without the permission of the court at any time before the Court of Appeal has begun hearing the appeal; and
(b) with the permission of the court after the Court of Appeal has begun hearing the appeal,

by serving notice in writing on the Registrar.
(2) Where the appellant serves a notice abandoning an appeal under paragraph (1), the appellant must send a copy of it to—
(a) the defendant;
(b) a court officer of the court of trial; and
(c) the magistrates' court responsible for enforcing any confiscation order which the Crown Court has made.
(3) Where the appellant serves a notice amending a notice of appeal under paragraph (1), the appellant must send a copy of it to the defendant.
(4) Where an appeal is abandoned under paragraph (1), the application for permission to appeal or appeal must be treated, for the purposes of section 85 of the 2002 Act (Conclusion of proceedings), as having been refused or dismissed by the Court of Appeal.

Appeal about compliance, restraint or receivership order

R-465 Permission to appeal

42.14 (1) Permission to appeal to the Court of Appeal under section 13B, section 43 or section 65 of the Proceeds of Crime Act 2002 may only be given where—
(a) the Court of Appeal considers that the appeal would have a real prospect of success; or
(b) there is some other compelling reason why the appeal should be heard.
(2) An order giving permission to appeal may limit the issues to be heard and be made subject to conditions.

Notice of appeal R-466

42.15 (1) Where an appellant wishes to apply to the Court of Appeal for permission to appeal under section 13B, 43 or 65 of the Proceeds of Crime Act 2002 Act, the appellant must serve a notice of appeal in the form set out in the Practice Direction on the Crown Court officer.

(2) Unless the Registrar, a single judge or the Court of Appeal directs otherwise, the appellant must serve the notice of appeal, accompanied by a respondent's notice in the form set out in the Practice Direction for the respondent to complete, on—

(a) each respondent;

(b) any person who holds realisable property to which the appeal relates; and

(c) any other person affected by the appeal

as soon as practicable and in any event not later than 5 business days after the notice of appeal is served on the Crown Court officer.

(3) The appellant must serve the following documents with the notice of appeal—

(a) four additional copies of the notice of appeal for the Court of Appeal;

(b) four copies of any skeleton argument;

(c) one sealed copy and four unsealed copies of any order being appealed;

(d) four copies of any witness statement or affidavit in support of the application for permission to appeal;

(e) four copies of a suitable record of the reasons for judgment of the Crown Court; and

(f) four copies of the bundle of documents used in the Crown Court proceedings from which the appeal lies.

(4) Where it is not possible to serve all of the documents referred to in paragraph (3), the appellant must indicate which documents have not yet been served and the reasons why they are not currently available.

(5) The appellant must provide a Crown Court officer with a certificate of service stating that the notice of appeal has been served on each respondent in accordance with paragraph (2) and including full details of each respondent or explaining why it has not been possible to effect service.

Respondent's notice R-467

42.16 (1) This rule applies to an appeal under section 13B, 43 or 65 of the Proceeds of Crime Act 2002.

(2) A respondent may serve a respondent's notice on the Registrar.

(3) A respondent who—

(a) is seeking permission to appeal from the Court of Appeal; or

(b) wishes to ask the Court of Appeal to uphold the decision of the Crown Court for reasons different from or additional to those given by the Crown Court,

must serve a respondent's notice on the Registrar.

(4) A respondent's notice must be in the form set out in the Practice Direction and where the respondent seeks permission to appeal to the Court of Appeal it must be requested in the respondent's notice.

(5) A respondent's notice must be served on the Registrar not later than 14 days after—

(a) the date the respondent is served with notification that the Court of Appeal has given the appellant permission to appeal; or

(b) the date the respondent is served with notification that the application for permission to appeal and the appeal itself are to be heard together.

(6) Unless the Registrar, a single judge or the Court of Appeal directs otherwise, the respondent serving a respondent's notice must serve the notice on the appellant and any other respondent—

(a) as soon as practicable; and

(b) in any event not later than 5 business days,

after it is served on the Registrar.

Amendment and abandonment of appeal R-468

42.17 (1) The appellant may amend a notice of appeal served under rule 42.15 or abandon an appeal under section 13B, 43 or 65 of the Proceeds of Crime Act 2002—

(a) without the permission of the court at any time before the Court of Appeal has begun hearing the appeal; and

(b) with the permission of the court after the Court of Appeal has begun hearing the appeal, by serving notice in writing on the Registrar.

(2) Where the appellant serves a notice under paragraph (1), the appellant must send a copy of it to each respondent.

R-469 **Stay**

42.18 Unless the Court of Appeal or the Crown Court orders otherwise, an appeal under section 13B, 43 or 65 of the Proceeds of Crime Act 2002 does not operate as a stay of any order or decision of the Crown Court.

R-470 **Striking out appeal notices and setting aside or imposing conditions on permission to appeal**

42.19 (1) The Court of Appeal may—
(a) strike out the whole or part of a notice of appeal served under rule 42.15; or
(b) impose or vary conditions upon which an appeal under section 13B, 43 or 65 of the Proceeds of Crime Act 2002 may be brought.
(2) The Court of Appeal will only exercise its powers under paragraph (1) where there is a compelling reason for doing so.
(3) Where a party is present at the hearing at which permission to appeal was given, that party may not subsequently apply for an order that the Court of Appeal exercise its powers under paragraph (1)(b).

R-471 **Hearing of appeals**

42.20 (1) This rule applies to appeals under section 13B, 43 or 65 of the Proceeds of Crime Act 2002.
(2) Every appeal must be limited to a review of the decision of the Crown Court unless the Court of Appeal considers that in the circumstances of an individual appeal it would be in the interests of justice to hold a re-hearing.
(3) The Court of Appeal may allow an appeal where the decision of the Crown Court was—
(a) wrong; or
(b) unjust because of a serious procedural or other irregularity in the proceedings in the Crown Court.
(4) The Court of Appeal may draw any inference of fact which it considers justified on the evidence.
(5) At the hearing of the appeal a party may not rely on a matter not contained in that party's notice of appeal unless the Court of Appeal gives permission.

Criminal Procedure Rules Part 43 Appeal or Reference to the Supreme Court

R-472 **When this Part applies**

43.1 (1) This Part applies where—
(a) a party wants to appeal to the Supreme Court after—
(i) an application to the Court of Appeal to which Part 27 applies (Retrial following acquittal), or
(ii) an appeal to the Court of Appeal to which applies Part 37 (Appeal to the Court of Appeal against ruling at preparatory hearing), Part 38 (Appeal to the Court of Appeal against ruling adverse to prosecution), or Part 39 (Appeal to the Court of Appeal about conviction or sentence); or
(b) a party wants to refer a case to the Supreme Court after a reference to the Court of Appeal to which Part 41 applies (Reference to the Court of Appeal of point of law or unduly lenient sentencing).
(2) A reference to an 'appellant' in this Part is a reference to such a party.

R-473 **Application for permission or reference**

43.2 (1) An appellant must—
(a) apply orally to the Court of Appeal—
(i) for permission to appeal or to refer a sentencing case, or
(ii) to refer a point of law
immediately after the court gives the reasons for its decision; or
(b) apply in writing and serve the application on the Registrar and every other party not more than—
(i) 14 days after the court gives the reasons for its decision if that decision was on a sentencing reference to which Part 70 applies (Attorney General's reference of sentencing case), or
(ii) 28 days after the court gives those reasons in any other case.
(2) An application for permission to appeal or to refer a sentencing case must—
(a) identify the point of law of general public importance that the appellant wants the court to certify is involved in the decision; and

(b) give reasons why—
(i) that point of law ought to be considered by the Supreme Court, and
(ii) the court ought to give permission to appeal.

(3) An application to refer a point of law must give reasons why that point ought to be considered by the Supreme Court.

(4) An application must include or attach any application for the following, with reasons—
(a) an extension of time within which to make the application for permission or for a reference;
(b) bail pending appeal;
(c) permission to attend any hearing in the Supreme Court, if the appellant is in custody.

(5) A written application must be in the form set out in the Practice Direction.

Determination of detention pending appeal, etc. R-474

43.3 On an application for permission to appeal, the Court of Appeal must—
(a) decide whether to order the detention of a defendant who would have been liable to be detained but for the decision of the court; and
(b) determine any application for—
(i) bail pending appeal,
(ii) permission to attend any hearing in the Supreme Court, or
(iii) a representation order.

Bail pending appeal R-475

43.4 Rules 39.8 (Application for bail pending appeal or retrial), 39.9 (Conditions of bail pending appeal or re-trial) and 39.10 (Forfeiture of a recognizance given as a condition of bail) apply.

Criminal Procedure Rules Part 44 Request to the European Court for a Preliminary Ruling

When this Part applies R-476

44.1 This Part applies where the court can request the Court of Justice of the European Union ('the European Court') to give a preliminary ruling, under Article 267 of the Treaty on the Functioning of the European Union.

Preparation of request R-477

44.2 (1) The court may—
(a) make an order for the submission of a request—
(i) on application by a party, or
(ii) on its own initiative;
(b) give directions for the preparation of the terms of such a request.

(2) The court must—
(a) include in such a request—
(i) the identity of the court making the request,
(ii) the parties' identities,
(iii) a statement of whether a party is in custody,
(iv) a succinct statement of the question on which the court seeks the ruling of the European Court,
(v) a succinct statement of any opinion on the answer that the court may have expressed in any judgment that it has delivered,
(vi) a summary of the nature and history of the proceedings, including the salient facts and an indication of whether those facts are proved, admitted or assumed,
(vii) the relevant rules of national law,
(viii) a summary of the relevant contentions of the parties,
(ix) an indication of the provisions of European Union law that the European Court is asked to interpret, and
(x) an explanation of why a ruling of the European Court is requested;
(b) express the request in terms that can be translated readily into other languages; and
(c) set out the request in a schedule to the order.

Submission of request R-478

44.3 (1) The court officer must serve the order for the submission of the request on the Senior Master of the Queen's Bench Division of the High Court.

(2) The Senior Master must—

(a) submit the request to the European Court; but

(b) unless the court otherwise directs, postpone the submission of the request until—

(i) the time for any appeal against the order has expired, and

(ii) any appeal against the order has been determined.

Criminal Practice Directions Part 44 Request to the European Court for a Preliminary Ruling

PD-84 **CPD IX Appeal 44 A: References to the European Court of Justice**

44A.1 Further to rule 44.3 of the Criminal Procedure Rules, the order containing the reference shall be filed with the Senior Master of the Queen's Bench Division of the High Court for onward transmission to the Court of Justice of the European Union. The order should be marked for the attention of Mrs Isaac and sent to the Senior Master:

c/o Queen's Bench Division Associates Dept
Room WG03
Royal Courts of Justice
Strand
London
WC2A 2LL

44A.2 There is no longer a requirement that the relevant court file be sent to the Senior Master. The parties should ensure that all appropriate documentation is sent directly to the European Court at the following address:

The Registrar
Court of Justice of the European Union
Kirchberg
L-2925 Luxemburg

44A.3 There is no prescribed form for use but the following details must be included in the back sheet to the order:

i. Solicitor's full address;
ii. Solicitor's and Court references;
iii. Solicitor's e-mail address.

44A.4 The European Court of Justice regularly updates its Recommendation to national courts and tribunals in relation to the initiation of preliminary ruling proceedings. The current Recommendation is 2012/C 338/01: http://eur-lex.europa.eu/legal-content/EN/TXT/PDF/?uri=CELEX:32012H1106(01)&qid=1440325685329&from=EN

44A.5 The referring court may request the Court of Justice of the European Union to apply its urgent preliminary ruling procedure where the referring court's proceedings relate to a person in custody. For further information see Council Decision 2008/79/EC [2008] OJ L24/42: http://eur-lex.europa.eu/legal-content/EN/TXT/?qid=1440325784497&uri=CELEX:32008L0079

44A.6 Any such request must be made in a document separate from the order or in a covering letter and must set out:

iv. The matters of fact and law which establish the urgency;
v. The reasons why the urgent preliminary ruling procedure applies; and
vi. In so far as possible, the court's view on the answer to the question referred to the Court of Justice of the European Union for a preliminary ruling.

44A.7 Any request to apply the urgent preliminary ruling procedure should be filed with the Senior Master as described above.

Criminal Procedure Rules Part 45 Costs

General rules

R-479 **When this Part applies**

45.1 (1) This Part applies where the court can make an order about costs under—

(a) Part II of the Prosecution of Offences Act 1985 and Part II, IIA or IIB of The Costs in Criminal Cases (General) Regulations 1986;

(b) section 109 of the Magistrates' Courts Act 1980;
(c) section 52 of the Senior Courts Act 1981 and rule 76.6 or rule 76.7;
(d) section 8 of the Bankers Books Evidence Act 1879;
(e) section 2C(8) of the Criminal Procedure (Attendance of Witnesses) Act 1965;
(f) section 36(5) of the Criminal Justice Act 1972;
(g) section 159(5) and Schedule 3, paragraph 11, of the Criminal Justice Act 1988;
(h) section 14H(5) of the Football Spectators Act 1989;
(i) section 4(7) of the Dangerous Dogs Act 1991;
(j) Part 3 of The Serious Crime Act 2007 (Appeals under Section 24) Order 2008; or
(k) Part 1 or 2 of the Extradition Act 2003.

(2) In this Part, 'costs' means—
(a) the fees payable to a legal representative;
(b) the disbursements paid by a legal representative; and
(c) any other expenses incurred in connection with the case.

Costs orders: general rules R-480

45.2 (1) The court must not make an order about costs unless each party and any other person directly affected—
(a) is present; or
(b) has had an opportunity—
(i) to attend, or
(ii) to make representations.

(2) The court may make an order about costs—
(a) at a hearing in public or in private; or
(b) without a hearing.

(3) In deciding what order, if any, to make about costs, the court must have regard to all the circumstances, including—
(a) the conduct of all the parties; and
(b) any costs order already made.

(4) If the court makes an order about costs, it must—
(a) specify who must, or must not, pay what, to whom; and
(b) identify the legislation under which the order is made, where there is a choice of powers.

(5) The court must give reasons if it—
(a) refuses an application for a costs order; or
(b) rejects representations opposing a costs order.

(6) If the court makes an order for the payment of costs—
(a) the general rule is that it must be for an amount that is sufficient reasonably to compensate the recipient for costs—
(i) actually, reasonably and properly incurred, and
(ii) reasonable in amount; but
(b) the court may order the payment of—
(i) a proportion of that amount,
(ii) a stated amount less than that amount,
(iii) costs from or until a certain date only,
(iv) costs relating only to particular steps taken, or
(v) costs relating only to a distinct part of the case.

(7) On an assessment of the amount of costs, relevant factors include—
(a) the conduct of all the parties;
(b) the particular complexity of the matter or the difficulty or novelty of the questions raised;
(c) the skill, effort, specialised knowledge and responsibility involved;
(d) the time spent on the case;
(e) the place where and the circumstances in which work or any part of it was done; and
(f) any direction or observations by the court that made the costs order.

(8) If the court orders a party to pay costs to be assessed under rule 45.11, it may order that party to pay an amount on account.

(9) An order for the payment of costs takes effect when the amount is assessed, unless the court exercises any power it has to order otherwise.

Court's power to vary requirements R-481

45.3 (1) The court may—
(a) extend a time limit for serving an application or representations under rules 45.4 to 45.10, even after it has expired; and

(b) consider an application or representations—
(i) made in a different form to one set out in the Practice Direction, or
(ii) made orally instead of in writing.
(2) A person who wants an extension of time must—
(a) apply when serving the application or representations for which it is needed; and
(b) explain the delay.

Costs out of central funds

R-482 **Costs out of central funds**

45.4 (1) This rule applies where the court can order the payment of costs out of central funds.
(2) In this rule, costs—
(a) include—
(i) on an appeal, costs incurred in the court that made the decision under appeal, and
(ii) at a retrial, costs incurred at the initial trial and on any appeal; but
(b) do not include costs met by legal aid.
(3) The court may make an order—
(a) on application by the person who incurred the costs; or
(b) on its own initiative.
(4) Where a person wants the court to make an order that person must—
(a) apply as soon as practicable; and
(b) outline the type of costs and the amount claimed, if that person wants the court to direct an assessment; or
(c) specify the amount claimed, if that person wants the court to assess the amount itself.
(5) The general rule is that the court must make an order, but—
(a) the court may decline to make a defendant's costs order if, for example—
(i) the defendant is convicted of at least one offence, or
(ii) the defendant's conduct led the prosecutor reasonably to think the prosecution case stronger than it was; and
(b) the court may decline to make a prosecutor's costs order if, for example, the prosecution was started or continued unreasonably.
(6) If the court makes an order—
(a) the court may direct an assessment under, as applicable—
(i) Part III of the Costs in Criminal Cases (General) Regulations 1986, or
(ii) Part 3 of The Serious Crime Act 2007 (Appeals under Section 24) Order 2008;
(b) the court may assess the amount itself in a case in which either—
(i) the recipient agrees the amount, or
(ii) the court decides to allow a lesser sum than that which is reasonably sufficient to compensate the recipient for expenses properly incurred in the proceedings;
(c) an order for the payment of a defendant's costs which includes an amount in respect of fees payable to a legal representative, or disbursements paid by a legal representative, must include a statement to that effect.
(7) If the court directs an assessment, the order must specify any restriction on the amount to be paid that the court considers appropriate.
(8) If the court assesses the amount itself, it must do so subject to any restriction on the amount to be paid that is imposed by regulations made by the Lord Chancellor.

Payment of costs by one party to another

R-483 **Costs on conviction and sentence, etc.**

45.5 (1) This rule applies where the court can order a defendant to pay the prosecutor's costs if the defendant is—
(a) convicted or found guilty;
(b) dealt with in the Crown Court after committal for sentence there;
(c) dealt with for breach of a sentence; or
(d) in an extradition case—
(i) ordered to be extradited, under Part 1 of the Extradition Act 2003,
(ii) sent for extradition to the Secretary of State, under Part 2 of that Act, or
(iii) unsuccessful on an appeal by the defendant to the High Court, or on an application by the defendant for permission to appeal from the High Court to the Supreme Court.
(2) The court may make an order—
(a) on application by the prosecutor; or
(b) on its own initiative.

(3) Where the prosecutor wants the court to make an order—
(a) the prosecutor must—
(i) apply as soon as practicable, and
(ii) specify the amount claimed; and
(b) the general rule is that the court must make an order if it is satisfied that the defendant can pay;
(4) A defendant who wants to oppose an order must make representations as soon as practicable.
(5) If the court makes an order, it must assess the amount itself.

Costs on appeal **R-484**

45.6 (1) This rule—
(a) applies where a magistrates' court, the Crown Court or the Court of Appeal can order a party to pay another person's costs on an appeal, or an application for permission to appeal;
(b) authorises the Crown Court, in addition to its other powers, to order a party to pay another party's costs on an appeal to that court, except on an appeal under—
(i) section 108 of the Magistrates' Courts Act 1980, or
(ii) section 45 of the Mental Health Act 1983.
(2) In this rule, costs include—
(a) costs incurred in the court that made the decision under appeal; and
(b) costs met by legal aid.
(3) The court may make an order—
(a) on application by the person who incurred the costs; or
(b) on its own initiative.
(4) A person who wants the court to make an order must—
(a) apply as soon as practicable;
(b) notify each other party;
(c) specify—
(i) the amount claimed, and
(ii) against whom; and
(d) where an appellant abandons an appeal to the Crown Court by serving a notice of abandonment—
(i) apply in writing not more than 14 days later, and
(ii) serve the application on the appellant and on the Crown Court officer.
(5) A party who wants to oppose an order must—
(a) make representations as soon as practicable; and
(b) where the application was under paragraph (4)(d), serve written representations on the applicant, and on the Crown Court officer, not more than 7 days after it was served.
(6) Where the application was under paragraph (4)(d), the Crown Court officer may—
(a) submit it to the Crown Court; or
(b) serve it on the magistrates' court officer, for submission to the magistrates' court.
(7) If the court makes an order, it may direct an assessment under rule 45.11, or assess the amount itself where—
(a) the appellant abandons an appeal to the Crown Court;
(b) the Crown Court decides an appeal, except an appeal under—
(i) section 108 of the Magistrates' Courts Act 1980, or
(ii) section 45 of the Mental Health Act 1983; or
(c) the Court of Appeal decides an appeal to which Part 40 applies (Appeal to the Court of Appeal about reporting or public access restriction).
(8) If the court makes an order in any other case, it must assess the amount itself.

Costs on an application **R-485**

45.7 (1) This rule—
(a) applies where the court can order a party to pay another person's costs in a case in which—
(i) the court decides an application for the production in evidence of a copy of a bank record,
(ii) a magistrates' court or the Crown Court decides an application to terminate a football banning order,
(iii) a magistrates' court or the Crown Court decides an application to terminate a disqualification for having custody of a dog,
(iv) the Crown Court allows an application to withdraw a witness summons, or

(v) the Crown Court decides an application relating to a deferred prosecution agreement under rule 11.5 (breach), rule 11.6 (variation) or rule 11.7 (lifting suspension of prosecution);

(b) authorises the Crown Court, in addition to its other powers, to order a party to pay another party's costs on an application to that court under rule 11.5, 11.6 or 11.7.

(2) The court may make an order—

(a) on application by the person who incurred the costs; or

(b) on its own initiative.

(3) A person who wants the court to make an order must—

(a) apply as soon as practicable;

(b) notify each other party; and

(c) specify—

(i) the amount claimed, and

(ii) against whom.

(4) A party who wants to oppose an order must make representations as soon as practicable.

(5) If the court makes an order, it may direct an assessment under rule 45.11, or assess the amount itself.

R-486 **Costs resulting from unnecessary or improper act, etc.**

45.8 (1) This rule applies where the court can order a party to pay another party's costs incurred as a result of an unnecessary or improper act or omission by or on behalf of the first party.

(2) In this rule, costs include costs met by legal aid.

(3) The court may make an order—

(a) on application by the party who incurred such costs; or

(b) on its own initiative.

(4) A party who wants the court to make an order must—

(a) apply in writing as soon as practicable after becoming aware of the grounds for doing so;

(b) serve the application on—

(i) the court officer (or, in the Court of Appeal, the Registrar), and

(ii) each other party;

(c) in that application specify—

(i) the party by whom costs should be paid,

(ii) the relevant act or omission,

(iii) the reasons why that act or omission meets the criteria for making an order,

(iv) the amount claimed, and

(v) those on whom the application has been served.

(5) Where the court considers making an order on its own initiative, it must—

(a) identify the party against whom it proposes making the order; and

(b) specify—

(i) the relevant act or omission,

(ii) the reasons why that act or omission meets the criteria for making an order, and

(iii) with the assistance of the party who incurred the costs, the amount involved.

(6) A party who wants to oppose an order must—

(a) make representations as soon as practicable; and

(b) in reply to an application, serve written representations on the applicant and on the court officer (or Registrar) not more than 7 days after it was served.

(7) If the court makes an order, it must assess the amount itself.

Other costs orders

R-487 **Costs against a legal representative**

45.9 (1) This rule applies where—

(a) a party has incurred costs—

(i) as a result of an improper, unreasonable or negligent act or omission by a legal or other representative or representative's employee, or

(ii) which it has become unreasonable for that party to have to pay because of such an act or omission occurring after those costs were incurred; and

(b) the court can—

(i) order the representative responsible to pay such costs, or

(ii) prohibit the payment of costs to that representative.

(2) In this rule, costs include costs met by legal aid.

(3) The court may make an order—
(a) on application by the party who incurred such costs; or
(b) on its own initiative.
(4) A party who wants the court to make an order must—
(a) apply in writing as soon as practicable after becoming aware of the grounds for doing so;
(b) serve the application on—
(i) the court officer (or, in the Court of Appeal, the Registrar),
(ii) the representative responsible,
(iii) each other party, and
(iv) any other person directly affected;
(c) in that application specify—
(i) the representative responsible,
(ii) the relevant act or omission,
(iii) the reasons why that act or omission meets the criteria for making an order,
(iv) the amount claimed, and
(v) those on whom the application has been served.
(5) Where the court considers making an order on its own initiative, it must—
(a) identify the representative against whom it proposes making that order; and
(b) specify—
(i) the relevant act or omission,
(ii) the reasons why that act or omission meets the criteria for making an order, and
(iii) with the assistance of the party who incurred the costs, the amount involved.
(6) A representative who wants to oppose an order must—
(a) make representations as soon as practicable; and
(b) in reply to an application, serve written representations on the applicant and on the court officer (or Registrar) not more than 7 days after it was served.
(7) If the court makes an order—
(a) the general rule is that it must do so without waiting until the end of the case, but it may postpone making the order; and
(b) it must assess the amount itself.
(8) Instead of making an order, the court may make adverse observations about the representative's conduct for use in an assessment where—
(a) a party's costs are—
(i) to be met by legal aid, or
(ii) to be paid out of central funds; or
(b) there is to be an assessment under rule 45.11.

Costs against a third party R-488

45.10 (1) This rule applies where—
(a) there has been serious misconduct by a person who is not a party; and
(b) the court can order that person to pay a party's costs.
(2) In this rule, costs include costs met by legal aid.
(3) The court may make an order—
(a) on application by the party who incurred the costs; or
(b) on its own initiative.
(4) A party who wants the court to make an order must—
(a) apply in writing as soon as practicable after becoming aware of the grounds for doing so;
(b) serve the application on—
(i) the court officer (or, in the Court of Appeal, the Registrar),
(ii) the person responsible,
(iii) each other party, and
(iv) any other person directly affected;
(c) in that application specify—
(i) the person responsible,
(ii) the relevant misconduct,
(iii) the reasons why the criteria for making an order are met,
(iv) the amount claimed, and
(v) those on whom the application has been served.
(5) Where the court considers making an order on its own initiative, it must—
(a) identify the person against whom it proposes making that order; and

(b) specify—
(i) the relevant misconduct,
(ii) the reasons why the criteria for making an order are met, and
(iii) with the assistance of the party who incurred the costs, the amount involved.

(6) A person who wants to oppose an order must—
(a) make representations as soon as practicable; and
(b) in reply to an application, serve written representations on the applicant and on the court officer (or Registrar) not more than 7 days after it was served.

(7) If the court makes an order—
(a) the general rule is that it must do so at the end of the case, but it may do so earlier; and
(b) it must assess the amount itself.

Assessment of costs

R-489 **Assessment and re-assessment**

45.11 (1) This rule applies where the court directs an assessment under—
(a) rule 33.48 (Confiscation and related proceedings—restraint and receivership proceedings; rules that apply generally — assessment of costs);
(b) rule 45.6 (Costs on appeal); or
(c) rule 45.7 (Costs on an application).

(2) The assessment must be carried out by the relevant assessing authority, namely—
(a) the Lord Chancellor, where the direction was given by a magistrates' court or by the Crown Court; or
(b) the Registrar, where the direction was given by the Court of Appeal.

(3) The party in whose favour the court made the costs order ('the applicant') must—
(a) apply for an assessment—
(i) in writing, in any form required by the assessing authority, and
(ii) not more than 3 months after the costs order; and
(b) serve the application on—
(i) the assessing authority, and
(ii) the party against whom the court made the costs order ('the respondent').

(4) The applicant must—
(a) summarise the work done;
(b) specify—
(i) each item of work done, giving the date, time taken and amount claimed,
(ii) any disbursements or expenses, including the fees of any advocate, and
(iii) any circumstances of which the applicant wants the assessing authority to take particular account; and
(c) supply—
(i) receipts or other evidence of the amount claimed, and
(ii) any other information or document for which the assessing authority asks, within such period as that authority may require.

(5) A respondent who wants to make representations about the amount claimed must—
(a) do so in writing; and
(b) serve the representations on the assessing authority, and on the applicant, not more than 21 days after service of the application.

(6) The assessing authority must—
(a) if it seems likely to help with the assessment, obtain any other information or document;
(b) resolve in favour of the respondent any doubt about what should be allowed; and
(c) serve the assessment on the parties.

(7) Where either party wants the amount allowed re-assessed—
(a) that party must—
(i) apply to the assessing authority, in writing and in any form required by that authority,
(ii) serve the application on the assessing authority, and on the other party, not more than 21 days after service of the assessment,
(iii) explain the objections to the assessment,
(iv) supply any additional supporting information or document, and
(v) ask for a hearing, if that party wants one; and

(b) a party who wants to make representations about an application for re-assessment must—
(i) do so in writing,
(ii) serve the representations on the assessing authority, and on the other party, not more than 21 days after service of the application, and
(iii) ask for a hearing, if that party wants one;
(c) the assessing authority—
(i) must arrange a hearing, in public or in private, if either party asks for one,
(ii) subject to that, may re-assess the amount allowed with or without a hearing,
(iii) must re-assess the amount allowed on the initial assessment, taking into account the reasons for disagreement with that amount and any other representations,
(iv) may maintain, increase or decrease the amount allowed on the assessment,
(v) must serve the re-assessment on the parties, and
(vi) must serve written reasons on the parties, if not more than 21 days later either party asks for such reasons.
(8) A time limit under this rule may be extended even after it has expired—
(a) by the assessing authority, or
(b) by the Senior Costs Judge, if the assessing authority declines to do so.

Appeal to a costs judge **R-490**

45.12 (1) This rule applies where—
(a) the assessing authority has re-assessed the amount allowed under rule 45.11; and
(b) either party wants to appeal against that amount.
(2) That party must—
(a) serve an appeal notice on—
(i) the Senior Costs Judge,
(ii) the other party, and
(iii) the assessing authority
not more than 21 days after service of the written reasons for the re-assessment;
(b) explain the objections to the re-assessment;
(c) serve on the Senior Costs Judge with the appeal notice—
(i) the applications for assessment and re-assessment,
(ii) any other information or document considered by the assessing authority,
(iii) the assessing authority's written reasons for the re-assessment, and
(iv) any other information or document for which a costs judge asks, within such period as the judge may require; and
(d) ask for a hearing, if that party wants one.
(3) A party who wants to make representations about an appeal must—
(a) serve representations in writing on—
(i) the Senior Costs Judge, and
(ii) the applicant
not more than 21 days after service of the appeal notice; and
(b) ask for a hearing, if that party wants one.
(4) Unless a costs judge otherwise directs, the parties may rely only on—
(a) the objections to the amount allowed on the initial assessment; and
(b) any other representations and material considered by the assessing authority.
(5) A costs judge—
(a) must arrange a hearing, in public or in private, if either party asks for one;
(b) subject to that, may determine an appeal with or without a hearing;
(c) may—
(i) consult the assessing authority,
(ii) consult the court which made the costs order, and
(iii) obtain any other information or document;
(d) must reconsider the amount allowed by the assessing authority, taking into account the objections to the re-assessment and any other representations;
(e) may maintain, increase or decrease the amount allowed on the re-assessment;
(f) may provide for the costs incurred by either party to the appeal; and
(g) must serve reasons for the decision on—
(i) the parties, and
(ii) the assessing authority.
(6) A costs judge may extend a time limit under this rule, even after it has expired.

R-491 **Appeal to a High Court judge**

45.13 (1) This rule applies where—
(a) a costs judge has determined an appeal under rule 45.12; and
(b) either party wants to appeal against the amount allowed.

(2) A party who wants to appeal—
(a) may do so only if a costs judge certifies that a point of principle of general importance was involved in the decision on the review; and
(b) must apply in writing for such a certificate and serve the application on—
(i) the costs judge,
(ii) the other party

not more than 21 days after service of the decision on the review.

(3) That party must—
(a) appeal to a judge of the High Court attached to the Queen's Bench Division as if it were an appeal from the decision of a master under Part 52 of the Civil Procedure Rules 1998; and
(b) serve the appeal not more than 21 days after service of the costs judge's certificate under paragraph (2).

(4) A High Court judge—
(a) may extend a time limit under this rule even after it has expired;
(b) has the same powers and duties as a costs judge under rule 45.12; and
(c) may hear the appeal with one or more assessors.

R-492 **Application for an extension of time**

45.14 A party who wants an extension of time under rule 45.11, 45.12 or 45.13 must—
(a) apply in writing;
(b) explain the delay; and
(c) attach the application, representations or appeal for which the extension of time is needed.

Criminal Practice Directions Part 45 Costs

PD-85 **CPD X CrimPR Part 45 Costs**

Reference should be made to the Practice Direction (Costs in Criminal Proceedings) 2015.

Criminal Procedure Rules Part 46 Representatives

R-493 **Functions of representatives and supporters**

46.1 (1) Under these Rules, anything that a party may or must do may be done—
(a) by a legal representative on that party's behalf;
(b) by a person with the corporation's written authority, where that corporation is a defendant;
(c) with the help of a parent, guardian or other suitable supporting adult where that party is a defendant—
(i) who is under 18, or
(ii) whose understanding of what the case involves is limited

unless other legislation (including a rule) otherwise requires.

(2) A member, officer or employee of a prosecutor may, on the prosecutor's behalf—
(a) serve on the magistrates' court officer, or present to a magistrates' court, an information under section 1 of the Magistrates' Courts Act 1980; or
(b) issue a written charge and requisition, or single justice procedure notice, under section 29 of the Criminal Justice Act 2003.

R-494 **Notice of appointment, etc. of legal representative: general rules**

46.2 (1) This rule applies—
(a) in relation to a party who does not have legal aid for the purposes of a case;
(b) where such a party—
(i) appoints a legal representative for the purposes of the case, or
(ii) dismisses such a representative, with or without appointing another;
(c) where a legal representative for such a party withdraws from the case.

(2) Where paragraph (1)(b) applies, that party must give notice of the appointment or dismissal to—
(a) the court officer;

(b) each other party; and
(c) where applicable, the legal representative who has been dismissed,
as soon as practicable and in any event within 5 business days.

(3) Where paragraph (1)(c) applies, that legal representative must, as soon as practicable, give notice to—
(a) the court officer;
(b) the party whom he or she has represented; and
(c) each other party.

(4) Any such notice—
(a) may be given orally, but only if—
(i) it is given at a hearing, and
(ii) it specifies no restriction under paragraph (5)(b) (restricted scope of appointment);
(b) otherwise, must be in writing.

(5) A notice of the appointment of a legal representative—
(a) must identify—
(i) the legal representative who has been appointed, with details of how to contact that representative, and
(ii) all those to whom the notice is given;
(b) may specify a restriction, or restrictions, on the purpose or duration of the appointment; and
(c) if it specifies any such restriction, may nonetheless provide that documents may continue to be served on the represented party at the representative's address until—
(i) further notice is given under this rule, or
(ii) that party obtains legal aid for the purposes of the case.

(6) A legal representative who is dismissed by a party or who withdraws from representing a party must, as soon as practicable, make available to that party such documents in the representative's possession as have been served on that party.

Application to change legal representative: legal aid **R-495**

46.3 (1) This rule applies—
(a) in relation to a party who has legal aid for the purposes of a case;
(b) where such a party wants to select a legal representative in place of the representative named in the legal aid representation order.

(2) Such a party must—
(a) apply in writing as soon as practicable after becoming aware of the grounds for doing so; and
(b) serve the application on—
(i) the court officer, and
(ii) the legal representative named in the legal aid representation order.

(3) The application must—
(a) explain what the case is about, including what offences are alleged, what stage it has reached and what is likely to be in issue at trial;
(b) explain how and why the applicant chose the legal representative named in the legal aid representation order;
(c) if an advocate other than that representative has been instructed for the applicant, explain whether the applicant wishes to replace that advocate;
(d) explain, giving relevant facts and dates—
(i) in what way, in the applicant's opinion, there has been a breakdown in the relationship between the applicant and the current representative such that neither the individual representing the applicant nor any colleague of his or hers any longer can provide effective representation, or
(ii) what other compelling reason, in the applicant's opinion, means that neither the individual representing the applicant nor any colleague of his or hers any longer can provide effective representation;
(e) give details of any previous application by the applicant to replace the legal representative named in the legal aid representation order;
(f) state whether the applicant—
(i) waives the legal professional privilege attaching to the applicant's communications with the current representative, to the extent required to allow that representative to respond to the matters set out in the application, or

(ii) declines to waive that privilege and acknowledges that the court may draw such inferences as it thinks fit in consequence;

(g) explain how and why the applicant has chosen the proposed new representative;

(h) include or attach a statement by the proposed new representative which—

(i) confirms that that representative is eligible and willing to conduct the case for the applicant,

(ii) confirms that that representative can and will meet the current timetable for the case, including any hearing date or dates that have been set, if the application succeeds,

(iii) explains what, if any, dealings that representative has had with the applicant before the present case; and

(i) ask for a hearing, if the applicant wants one, and explain why it is needed.

(4) The legal representative named in the legal aid representation order must—

(a) respond in writing no more than 5 business days after service of the application; and

(b) serve the response on—

(i) the court officer,

(ii) the applicant, and

(iii) the proposed new representative.

(5) The response must—

(a) explain which, if any, of the matters set out in the application the current representative disputes;

(b) explain, as appropriate, giving relevant facts and dates—

(i) whether, and if so in what way, in the current representative's opinion, there has been a breakdown in the relationship with the applicant such that neither the individual representing the applicant nor any colleague of his or hers any longer can provide effective representation,

(ii) whether, in the current representative's opinion, there is some other compelling reason why neither the individual representing the applicant nor any colleague of his or hers any longer can provide effective representation, and if so what reason,

(iii) whether the current representative considers there to be a duty to withdraw from the case in accordance with professional rules of conduct, and if so the nature of that duty, and

(iv) whether the current representative no longer is able to represent the applicant through circumstances outside the representative's control, and if so the particular circumstances that render the representative unable to do so;

(c) explain what, if any, dealings the current representative had had with the applicant before the present case; and

(d) ask for a hearing, if the current representative wants one, and explain why it is needed.

(6) The court may determine the application—

(a) without a hearing, as a general rule; or

(b) at a hearing, which must be in private unless the court otherwise directs.

(7) Unless the court otherwise directs, any hearing must be in the absence of each other party and each other party's representative and advocate (if any).

(8) If the court allows the application, as soon as practicable—

(a) the current representative must make available to the new representative such documents in the current representative's possession as have been served on the applicant party; and

(b) the new representative must serve notice of appointment on each other party.

(9) Paragraph (10) applies where—

(a) the court refuses the application;

(b) in response to that decision—

(i) the applicant declines further representation by the current representative or asks for legal aid to be withdrawn, or

(ii) the current representative declines further to represent the applicant; and

(c) the court in consequence withdraws the applicant's legal aid.

(10) The court officer must serve notice of the withdrawal of legal aid on—

(a) the applicant; and

(b) the current representative.

Criminal Procedure Rules Part 47 Investigation Orders and Warrants

Section 1: understanding and applying this Part

When this Part applies R-496

47.1 (1) Sections 2 and 3 of this Part apply where, for the purposes of a terrorist investigation—
(a) a Circuit judge can make, vary or discharge—
(i) an order for the production of, or for giving access to, material, or for a statement of its location, under paragraphs 5 and 10 of Schedule 5 to the Terrorism Act 2000,
(ii) an explanation order, under paragraphs 10 and 13 of Schedule 5 to the 2000 Act,
(iii) a customer information order, under paragraphs 1 and 4 of Schedule 6 to the 2000 Act;
(b) a Circuit judge can make, and the Crown Court can vary or discharge, an account monitoring order, under paragraphs 2 and 4 of Schedule 6A to the 2000 Act.
(2) Sections 2 and 4 of this Part apply where, for the purposes of an investigation to which Part 8 of the Proceeds of Crime Act 2002 or the Proceeds of Crime Act 2002 (External Investigations) Order 2014 applies, a Crown Court judge can make, and the Crown Court can vary or discharge—
(a) a production order, under sections 345 and 351 of the 2002 Act or under articles 6 and 12 of the 2014 Order;
(b) an order to grant entry, under sections 347 and 351 of the 2002 Act or under articles 8 and 12 of the 2014 Order;
(c) a disclosure order, under sections 357 and 362 of the 2002 Act or under articles 16 and 21 of the 2014 Order;
(d) a customer information order, under sections 363 and 369 of the 2002 Act or under articles 22 and 28 of the 2014 Order;
(e) an account monitoring order, under sections 370, 373 and 375 of the 2002 Act or under articles 29, 32 and 34 of the 2014 Order.
(3) Rule 47.5 and Section 5 of this Part apply where—
(a) a justice of the peace can make or discharge an investigation anonymity order, under sections 76 and 80(1) of the Coroners and Justice Act 2009;
(b) a Crown Court judge can determine an appeal against—
(i) a refusal of such an order, under section 79 of the 2009 Act,
(ii) a decision on an application to discharge such an order, under section 80(6) of the 2009 Act.
(4) Sections 2 and 6 of this Part apply where a justice of the peace can make an order approving—
(a) the grant or renewal of an authorisation, or the giving or renewal of a notice, under section 23A of the Regulation of Investigatory Powers Act 2000;
(b) the grant or renewal of an authorisation under section 32A of the 2000 Act.
(5) Rule 47.5 and Section 7 of this Part apply where a justice of the peace can issue a warrant under—
(a) section 8 of the Police and Criminal Evidence Act 1984;
(b) section 2 of the Criminal Justice Act 1987;
(c) other powers to which sections 15 and 16 of the Police and Criminal Evidence Act 1984 apply.
(6) Rules 47.4 and 47.5 and Section 8 of this Part apply where—
(a) a District Judge (Magistrates' Court) can make an order under—
(i) section 63F(7) or 63R(6) of the Police and Criminal Evidence Act 1984, or
(ii) paragraph 20B(5) or 20G(6) of Schedule 8 to the Terrorism Act 2000;
(b) the Crown Court can determine an appeal under—
(i) section 63F(10) of the Police and Criminal Evidence Act 1984, or
(ii) paragraph 20B(8) of Schedule 8 to the Terrorism Act 2000.

Meaning of 'court', 'applicant' and 'respondent' R-497

47.2 In this Part—
(a) a reference to the 'court' includes a reference to any justice of the peace or judge who can exercise a power to which this Part applies;
(b) 'applicant' means any person who, or an authority which, can apply for an order or warrant to which this Part applies; and

(c) 'respondent' means any person—
(i) against whom such an order is sought or made, or
(ii) on whom an application for such an order is served.

Section 2: general rules

R-498 Exercise of court's powers

47.3 (1) Subject to paragraphs (2) and (3), the court may determine an application for an order, or to vary or discharge an order—
(a) at a hearing (which must be in private unless the court otherwise directs), or without a hearing; and
(b) in the absence of—
(i) the applicant,
(ii) the respondent (if any),
(iii) any other person affected by the order.
(2) The court must not determine such an application in the applicant's absence if—
(a) the applicant asks for a hearing; or
(b) it appears to the court that—
(i) the proposed order may infringe legal privilege, within the meaning of section 10 of the Police and Criminal Evidence Act 1984 or of section 348 or 361 of the Proceeds of Crime Act 2002,
(ii) the proposed order may require the production of excluded material, within the meaning of section 11 of the 1984 Act, or
(iii) for any other reason the application is so complex or serious as to require the court to hear the applicant.
(3) The court must not determine such an application in the absence of any respondent or other person affected, unless—
(a) the absentee has had at least 2 business days in which to make representations; or
(b) the court is satisfied that—
(i) the applicant cannot identify or contact the absentee,
(ii) it would prejudice the investigation if the absentee were present,
(iii) it would prejudice the investigation to adjourn or postpone the application so as to allow the absentee to attend, or
(iv) the absentee has waived the opportunity to attend.
(4) The court must not make, vary or discharge an order unless the applicant states, in writing or orally, that to the best of the applicant's knowledge and belief—
(a) the application discloses all the information that is material to what the court must decide; and
(b) the content of the application is true.
(5) Where the statement required by paragraph (4) is made orally—
(a) the statement must be on oath or affirmation, unless the court otherwise directs; and
(b) the court must arrange for a record of the making of the statement.

R-499 Court's power to vary requirements under this Part

47.4 (1) The court may—
(a) shorten or extend (even after it has expired) a time limit under this Part;
(b) dispense with a requirement for service under this Part (even after service was required); and
(c) consider an application made orally instead of in writing.
(2) A person who wants an extension of time must—
(a) apply when serving the application for which it is needed; and
(b) explain the delay.

R-500 Documents served on the court officer

47.5 (1) Unless the court otherwise directs, the court officer may—
(a) keep a written application; or
(b) arrange for the whole or any part to be kept by some other appropriate person, subject to any conditions that the court may impose.
(2) Where the court makes an order when the court office is closed, the applicant must, not more than 72 hours later, serve on the court officer—
(a) a copy of the order; and
(b) any written material that was submitted to the court.

(3) Where the court issues a warrant—
(a) the applicant must return it to the court officer as soon as practicable after it has been executed, and in any event not more than 3 months after it was issued (unless other legislation otherwise provides); and
(b) the court officer must—
(i) keep the warrant for 12 months after its return, and
(ii) during that period, make it available for inspection by the occupier of the premises to which it relates, if that occupier asks to inspect it.

Section 3: orders under the Terrorism Act 2000

Application for an order under the Terrorism Act 2000 R-501

47.6 (1) This rule applies where an applicant wants the court to make one of the orders listed in rule 47.1(1).
(2) The applicant must—
(a) apply in writing;
(b) serve the application on—
(i) the court officer, and
(ii) the respondent (unless the court otherwise directs);
(c) identify the respondent;
(d) give the information required by whichever of rules 47.7 to 47.10 applies; and
(e) serve any order made on the respondent.

Content of application for a production etc. order R-502

47.7 As well as complying with rule 47.6, an applicant who wants the court to make an order for the production of, or access to, material, or for a statement of its location, must—
(a) describe that material;
(b) explain why the applicant thinks the material is—
(i) in the respondent's possession, custody or power, or
(ii) likely to be so within 28 days of the order;
(c) explain how the material constitutes or contains excluded material or special procedure material;
(d) confirm that none of the material is expected to be subject to legal privilege;
(e) explain why the material is likely to be of substantial value to the investigation;
(f) explain why it is in the public interest for the material to be produced, or for the applicant to be given access to it, having regard to—
(i) the benefit likely to accrue to the investigation if it is obtained, and
(ii) the circumstances in which the respondent has the material, or is expected to have it; and
(g) propose—
(i) the terms of the order, and
(ii) the period within which it should take effect.

Content of application for an explanation order R-503

47.8 As well as complying with rule 47.6, an applicant who wants the court to make an explanation order must—
(a) identify the material that the applicant wants the respondent to explain;
(b) confirm that the explanation is not expected to infringe legal privilege; and
(c) propose—
(i) the terms of the order, and
(ii) the period within which it should take effect, if 7 days from the date of the order would not be appropriate.

Content of application for a customer information order R-504

47.9 As well as complying with rule 47.6, an applicant who wants the court to make a customer information order must—
(a) explain why it is desirable for the purposes of the investigation to trace property said to be terrorist property within the meaning of the Terrorism Act 2000;
(b) explain why the order will enhance the effectiveness of the investigation; and
(c) propose the terms of the order.

Content of application for an account monitoring order R-505

47.10 As well as complying with rule 47.6, an applicant who wants the court to make an account monitoring order must—
(a) specify—
(i) the information sought,

(ii) the period during which the applicant wants the respondent to provide that information (to a maximum of 90 days), and
(iii) where, when and in what manner the applicant wants the respondent to provide that information;
(b) explain why it is desirable for the purposes of the investigation to trace property said to be terrorist property within the meaning of the Terrorism Act 2000;
(c) explain why the order will enhance the effectiveness of the investigation; and
(d) propose the terms of the order.

R-506 **Application to vary or discharge an order**

47.11 (1) This rule applies where one of the following wants the court to vary or discharge an order listed in rule 47.1(1)—
(a) an applicant;
(b) the respondent; or
(c) a person affected by the order.
(2) That applicant, respondent or person affected must—
(a) apply in writing as soon as practicable after becoming aware of the grounds for doing so;
(b) serve the application on—
(i) the court officer, and
(ii) the respondent, applicant, or any person known to be affected, as applicable;
(c) explain why it is appropriate for the order to be varied or discharged;
(d) propose the terms of any variation; and
(e) ask for a hearing, if one is wanted, and explain why it is needed.

R-507 **Application containing information withheld from a respondent or other person**

47.12 (1) This rule applies where—
(a) an applicant serves on a respondent or other person an application for one of the orders listed in rule 47.1(1), or for the variation or discharge of such an order; and
(b) the application includes information that the applicant thinks ought not be revealed to that recipient.
(2) The applicant must—
(a) omit that information from the part of the application that is served on the respondent or other person;
(b) mark the other part, to show that it is only for the court; and
(c) in that other part, explain why the applicant has withheld it.
(3) A hearing of an application to which this rule applies may take place, wholly or in part, in the absence of the respondent and any other person.
(4) At a hearing of an application to which this rule applies—
(a) the general rule is that the court must consider, in the following sequence—
(i) representations first by the applicant and then by the respondent and any other person, in the presence of them all, and then
(ii) further representations by the applicant, in the others' absence; but
(b) the court may direct other arrangements for the hearing.

R-508 **Application to punish for contempt of court**

47.13 (1) This rule applies where a person is accused of disobeying—
(a) a production etc. order made under paragraph 5 of Schedule 5 to the Terrorism Act 2000;
(b) an explanation order made under paragraph 13 of that Schedule; or
(c) an account monitoring order made under paragraph 2 of Schedule 6A to that Act.
(2) An applicant who wants the court to exercise its power to punish that person for contempt of court must comply with the rules in Part 48 (Contempt of court).

Section 4: orders under the Proceeds of Crime Act 2002 etc.

R-509 **Application for an order under the Proceeds of Crime Act 2002 etc.**

47.14 (1) This rule applies where an applicant wants the court to make one of the orders listed in rule 47.1(2).
(2) The applicant must—
(a) apply in writing;
(b) serve the application on—
(i) the court officer, and
(ii) the respondent (unless the court otherwise directs);

(c) identify—
(i) the respondent, and
(ii) the person or property the subject of the investigation;
(d) in the case of an investigation in the United Kingdom, explain why the applicant thinks that—
(i) the person under investigation has benefited from criminal conduct, in the case of a confiscation investigation, or committed a money laundering offence, in the case of a money laundering investigation, or
(ii) the cash involved is property obtained through unlawful conduct, or is intended to be used in unlawful conduct, in the case of a detained cash investigation;
(e) in the case of an investigation outside the United Kingdom, explain why the applicant thinks that—
(i) there is an investigation by an overseas authority which relates to a criminal investigation or to criminal proceedings (including proceedings to remove the benefit of a person's criminal conduct following that person's conviction), and
(ii) the investigation is into whether property has been obtained as a result of or in connection with criminal conduct, or into the extent or whereabouts of such property;
(f) give the additional information required by whichever of rules 47.15 to 47.19 applies; and
(g) serve any order made on each respondent.

Content of application for a production order R-510

47.15 As well as complying with rule 47.14, an applicant who wants the court to make an order for the production of, or access to, material, must—
(a) describe that material;
(b) explain why the applicant thinks the material is in the respondent's possession or control;
(c) confirm that none of the material is—
(i) expected to be subject to legal privilege, or
(ii) excluded material;
(d) explain why the material is likely to be of substantial value to the investigation;
(e) explain why it is in the public interest for the material to be produced, or for the applicant to be given access to it, having regard to—
(i) the benefit likely to accrue to the investigation if it is obtained, and
(ii) the circumstances in which the respondent has the material; and
(f) propose—
(i) the terms of the order, and
(ii) the period within which it should take effect, if 7 days from the date of the order would not be appropriate.

Content of application for an order to grant entry R-511

47.16 An applicant who wants the court to make an order to grant entry in aid of a production order must—
(a) specify the premises to which entry is sought;
(b) explain why the order is needed; and
(c) propose the terms of the order.

Content of application for a disclosure order R-512

47.17 As well as complying with rule 47.14, an applicant who wants the court to make a disclosure order must—
(a) describe in general terms the information that the applicant wants the respondent to provide;
(b) confirm that none of the information is—
(i) expected to be subject to legal privilege, or
(ii) excluded material;
(c) explain why the information is likely to be of substantial value to the investigation;
(d) explain why it is in the public interest for the information to be provided, having regard to the benefit likely to accrue to the investigation if it is obtained; and
(e) propose the terms of the order.

Content of application for a customer information order R-513

47.18 As well as complying with rule 47.14, an applicant who wants the court to make a customer information order must—
(a) explain why customer information about the person under investigation is likely to be of substantial value to that investigation;

(b) explain why it is in the public interest for the information to be provided, having regard to the benefit likely to accrue to the investigation if it is obtained; and
(c) propose the terms of the order.

R-514 **Content of application for an account monitoring order**

47.19 As well as complying with rule 47.14, an applicant who wants the court to make an account monitoring order for the provision of account information must—
(a) specify—
(i) the information sought,
(ii) the period during which the applicant wants the respondent to provide that information (to a maximum of 90 days), and
(iii) when and in what manner the applicant wants the respondent to provide that information;
(b) explain why the information is likely to be of substantial value to the investigation;
(c) explain why it is in the public interest for the information to be provided, having regard to the benefit likely to accrue to the investigation if it is obtained; and
(d) propose the terms of the order.

R-515 **Application to vary or discharge an order**

47.20 (1) This rule applies where one of the following wants the court to vary or discharge an order listed in rule 47.1(2)—
(a) an applicant;
(b) the respondent; or
(c) a person affected by the order.
(2) That applicant, respondent or person affected must—
(a) apply in writing as soon as practicable after becoming aware of the grounds for doing so;
(b) serve the application on—
(i) the court officer, and
(ii) the respondent, applicant, or any person known to be affected, as applicable;
(c) explain why it is appropriate for the order to be varied or discharged;
(d) propose the terms of any variation; and
(e) ask for a hearing, if one is wanted, and explain why it is needed.

R-516 **Application containing information withheld from a respondent or other person**

47.21 (1) This rule applies where—
(a) an applicant serves on a respondent or other person an application for one of the orders listed in rule 47.1(2), or for the variation or discharge of such an order; and
(b) the application includes information that the applicant thinks ought not be revealed to that recipient.
(2) The applicant must—
(a) omit that information from the part of the application that is served on the respondent or other person;
(b) mark the other part, to show that it is only for the court; and
(c) in that other part, explain why the applicant has withheld it.
(3) A hearing of an application to which this rule applies may take place, wholly or in part, in the absence of the respondent and any other person.
(4) At a hearing of an application to which this rule applies—
(a) the general rule is that the court must consider, in the following sequence—
(i) representations first by the applicant and then by the respondent and any other person, in the presence of them all, and then
(ii) further representations by the applicant, in the others' absence; but
(b) the court may direct other arrangements for the hearing.

R-517 **Application to punish for contempt of court**

47.22 (1) This rule applies where a person is accused of disobeying—
(a) a production order made under section 345 of the Proceeds of Crime Act 2002 or article 6 of the Proceeds of Crime Act 2002 (External Investigations) Order 2014; or
(b) an account monitoring order made under section 370 of the 2002 Act or article 29 of the 2014 Order.
(2) An applicant who wants the court to exercise its power to punish that person for contempt of court must comply with the rules in Part 48 (Contempt of court).

Section 5: orders under the Coroners and Justice Act 2009

Exercise of court's powers R-518

47.23 (1) The court may determine an application for an investigation anonymity order, and any appeal against the refusal of such an order—
(a) at a hearing (which must be in private unless the court otherwise directs); or
(b) without a hearing.
(2) The court must determine an application to discharge an investigation anonymity order, and any appeal against the decision on such an application—
(a) at a hearing (which must be in private unless the court otherwise directs); and
(b) in the presence of the person specified in the order, unless—
(i) that person applied for the discharge of the order,
(ii) that person has had an opportunity to make representations, or
(iii) the court is satisfied that it is not reasonably practicable to communicate with that person.
(3) The court may consider an application or an appeal made orally instead of in writing.

Application for an investigation anonymity order R-519

47.24 (1) This rule applies where an applicant wants a magistrates' court to make an investigation anonymity order.
(2) The applicant must—
(a) apply in writing;
(b) serve the application on the court officer;
(c) identify the person to be specified in the order, unless—
(i) the applicant wants the court to determine the application at a hearing, or
(ii) the court otherwise directs;
(d) explain how the proposed order meets the conditions prescribed by section 78 of the Coroners and Justice Act 2009;
(e) say if the applicant intends to appeal should the court refuse the order;
(f) attach any material on which the applicant relies; and
(g) propose the terms of the order.
(3) At any hearing of the application, the applicant must—
(a) identify to the court the person to be specified in the order, unless—
(i) the applicant has done so already, or
(ii) the court otherwise directs; and
(b) unless the applicant has done so already, inform the court if the applicant intends to appeal should the court refuse the order.

Application to discharge an investigation anonymity order R-520

47.25 (1) This rule applies where one of the following wants a magistrates' court to discharge an investigation anonymity order—
(a) an applicant; or
(b) the person specified in the order.
(2) That applicant or the specified person must—
(a) apply in writing as soon as practicable after becoming aware of the grounds for doing so;
(b) serve the application on—
(i) the court officer, and as applicable
(ii) the applicant for the order, and
(iii) the specified person;
(c) explain—
(i) what material circumstances have changed since the order was made, or since any previous application was made to discharge it, and
(ii) why it is appropriate for the order to be discharged; and
(d) attach—
(i) a copy of the order, and
(ii) any material on which the applicant relies.
(3) A party must inform the court if that party intends to appeal should the court discharge the order.

Appeal R-521

47.26 (1) This rule applies where one of the following ('the appellant') wants to appeal to the Crown Court—
(a) the applicant for an investigation anonymity order, where a magistrates' court has refused to make the order;

(b) a party to an application to discharge such an order, where a magistrates' court has decided that application.

(2) The appellant must—

(a) serve on the Crown Court officer a copy of the application to the magistrates' court; and

(b) where the appeal concerns a discharge decision, notify each other party,

not more than 21 days after the decision against which the appellant wants to appeal.

(3) The Crown Court must hear the appeal without justices of the peace.

Section 6: orders under the Regulation of Investigatory Powers Act 2000

R-522 **Application for approval for authorisation or notice**

47.27 (1) This rule applies where an applicant wants a magistrates' court to make an order approving—

(a) under sections 23A and 23B of the Regulation of Investigatory Powers Act 2000—

(i) an authorisation to obtain or disclose communications data, under section 22(3) of the 2000 Act, or

(ii) a notice that requires a postal or telecommunications operator if need be to obtain, and in any case to disclose, communications data, under section 22(4) of the 2000 Act;

(b) under sections 32A and 32B of the Regulation of Investigatory Powers Act 2000, an authorisation for—

(i) the carrying out of directed surveillance, under section 28 of the 2000 Act, or

(ii) the conduct or use of a covert human intelligence source, under section 29 of the 2000 Act.

(2) The applicant must—

(a) apply in writing and serve the application on the court officer;

(b) attach the authorisation or notice which the applicant wants the court to approve;

(c) attach such other material (if any) on which the applicant relies to satisfy the court—

(i) as required by section 23A(3) and (4) of the 2000 Act, in relation to communications data,

(ii) as required by section 32A(3) and (4) of the 2000 Act, in relation to directed surveillance, or

(iii) as required by section 32A(5) and (6), and, if relevant, section 43(6A), of the 2000 Act, in relation to a covert human intelligence source; and

(d) propose the terms of the order.

R-523 **Exercise of court's power to quash an authorisation or notice**

47.28 (1) This rule applies where, under section 23A or 32A of the Regulation of Investigatory Powers Act 2000, a magistrates' court refuses to approve the grant, giving or renewal of an authorisation or notice.

(2) The court must not exercise its power to quash that authorisation or notice unless the applicant has had at least 2 business days from the date of the refusal in which to make representations.

Section 7: search warrants

R-524 **Exercise of court's powers**

47.29 (1) The court must determine an application for a warrant—

(a) at a hearing, which must be in private unless the court otherwise directs;

(b) in the presence of the applicant; and

(c) in the absence of any person affected by the warrant, including any person in occupation or control of premises which the applicant wants to search.

(2) If the court so directs, the applicant may attend the hearing by live link.

(3) The court must not determine an application unless satisfied that sufficient time has been allowed for it.

(4) The court must not determine an application unless the applicant confirms, on oath or affirmation, that to the best of the applicant's knowledge and belief—

(a) the application discloses all the information that is material to what the court must decide, including any circumstances that might reasonably be considered capable of undermining any of the grounds of the application; and

(b) the content of the application is true.

(5) If the court requires the applicant to answer a question about an application—

(a) the applicant's answer must be on oath or affirmation;

(b) the court must arrange for a record of the gist of the question and reply; and

(c) if the applicant cannot answer to the court's satisfaction, the court may—
(i) specify the information the court requires, and
(ii) give directions for the presentation of any renewed application.

(6) Unless to do so would be inconsistent with other legislation, on an application the court may issue—
(a) a warrant in respect of specified premises;
(b) a warrant in respect of all premises occupied or controlled by a specified person;
(c) a warrant in respect of all premises occupied or controlled by a specified person which specifies some of those premises; or
(d) more than one warrant—
(i) each one in respect of premises specified in the warrant,
(ii) each one in respect of all premises occupied or controlled by a person specified in the warrant (whether or not such a warrant also specifies any of those premises), or
(iii) at least one in respect of specified premises and at least one in respect of all premises occupied or controlled by a specified person (whether or not such a warrant also specifies any of those premises).

Application for warrant under section 8 of the Police and Criminal Evidence Act 1984 R-525

47.30 (1) This rule applies where an applicant wants a magistrates' court to issue a warrant or warrants under section 8 of the Police and Criminal Evidence Act 1984.

(2) The applicant must—
(a) apply in writing;
(b) serve the application on—
(i) the court officer, or
(ii) if the court office is closed, the court;
(c) give the court an estimate of how long the court should allow—
(i) to read and prepare for the application, and
(ii) for the hearing of the application; and
(d) tell the court when the applicant expects any warrant issued to be executed.

(3) The application must—
(a) specify the offence under investigation (and see paragraph (4));
(b) so far as practicable, identify the material sought (and see paragraph (5));
(c) specify the premises to be searched (and see paragraphs (6) and (7));
(d) state whether the applicant wants the premises to be searched on more than one occasion (and see paragraph (8)); and
(e) state whether the applicant wants other persons to accompany the officers executing the warrant or warrants (and see paragraph (9)).

(4) In relation to the offence under investigation, the application must—
(a) state whether that offence is—
(i) an indictable offence, or
(ii) a relevant offence as defined in section 28D of the Immigration Act 1971; and
(b) explain the grounds for believing that the offence has been committed.

(5) In relation to the material sought, the application must explain the grounds for believing that that material—
(a) is likely to be of substantial value to the investigation (whether by itself, or together with other material);
(b) is likely to be admissible evidence at trial for the offence under investigation; and
(c) does not consist of or include items subject to legal privilege, excluded material or special procedure material.

(6) In relation to premises which the applicant wants to be searched and can specify, the application must—
(a) specify each set of premises;
(b) in respect of each set of premises, explain the grounds for believing that material sought is on those premises; and
(c) in respect of each set of premises, explain the grounds for believing that—
(i) it is not practicable to communicate with any person entitled to grant entry to the premises,
(ii) it is practicable to communicate with such a person but it is not practicable to communicate with any person entitled to grant access to the material sought,
(iii) entry to the premises will not be granted unless a warrant is produced, or
(iv) the purpose of a search may be frustrated or seriously prejudiced unless a constable arriving at the premises can secure immediate entry to them.

(7) In relation to premises which the applicant wants to be searched but at least some of which the applicant cannot specify, the application must—
(a) explain the grounds for believing that—
(i) because of the particulars of the offence under investigation it is necessary to search any premises occupied or controlled by a specified person, and
(ii) it is not reasonably practicable to specify all the premises which that person occupies or controls which might need to be searched;
(b) specify as many sets of premises as is reasonably practicable;
(c) in respect of each set of premises, whether specified or not, explain the grounds for believing that material sought is on those premises; and
(d) in respect of each specified set of premises, explain the grounds for believing that—
(i) it is not practicable to communicate with any person entitled to grant entry to the premises,
(ii) it is practicable to communicate with such a person but it is not practicable to communicate with any person entitled to grant access to the material sought,
(iii) entry to the premises will not be granted unless a warrant is produced, or
(iv) the purpose of a search may be frustrated or seriously prejudiced unless a constable arriving at the premises can secure immediate entry to them.
(8) In relation to any set of premises which the applicant wants to be searched on more than one occasion, the application must—
(a) explain why it is necessary to search on more than one occasion in order to achieve the purpose for which the applicant wants the court to issue the warrant; and
(b) specify any proposed maximum number of occasions.
(9) In relation to any set of premises which the applicant wants to be searched by the officers executing the warrant with other persons authorised by the court, the application must—
(a) identify those other persons, by function or description; and
(b) explain why those persons are required.
(10) The application must disclose anything known or reported to the applicant that might reasonably be considered capable of undermining any of the grounds of the application.
(11) Where the application includes information that the applicant thinks should be supplied only to the court, the applicant may—
(a) set out that information in a separate document, marked accordingly; and
(b) in that document, explain why the applicant thinks that that information ought not to be supplied to anyone other than the court.
(12) The application must include—
(a) a declaration by the applicant that to the best of the applicant's knowledge and belief—
(i) the application discloses all the information that is material to what the court must decide, including anything that might reasonably be considered capable of undermining any of the grounds of the application, and
(ii) the content of the application is true; and
(b) a declaration by an officer senior to the applicant that the senior officer has reviewed and authorised the application.
(13) The application must attach a draft warrant or warrants in the terms proposed by the applicant.

R-526 Application for warrant under section 2 of the Criminal Justice Act 1987

47.31 (1) This rule applies where an applicant wants a magistrates' court to issue a warrant or warrants under section 2 of the Criminal Justice Act 1987.
(2) The applicant must—
(a) apply in writing;
(b) serve the application on—
(i) the court officer, or
(ii) if the court office is closed, the court;
(c) give the court an estimate of how long the court should allow—
(i) to read and prepare for the application, and
(ii) for the hearing of the application; and
(d) tell the court when the applicant expects any warrant issued to be executed.
(3) The application must—
(a) describe the investigation being conducted by the Director of the Serious Fraud Office and include—
(i) an explanation of what is alleged and why, and
(ii) a chronology of relevant events;

(b) specify the document, documents or description of documents sought by the applicant (and see paragraphs (4) and (5)); and
(c) specify the premises which the applicant wants to be searched (and see paragraph (6)).
(4) In relation to each document or description of documents sought, the application must—
(a) explain the grounds for believing that each such document—
(i) relates to a matter relevant to the investigation, and
(ii) could not be withheld from disclosure or production on grounds of legal professional privilege; and
(b) explain the grounds for believing that—
(i) a person has failed to comply with a notice by the Director to produce the document or documents,
(ii) it is not practicable to serve such a notice, or
(iii) the service of such a notice might seriously impede the investigation.
(5) In relation to any document or description of documents which the applicant wants to be preserved but not seized under a warrant, the application must—
(a) specify the steps for which the applicant wants the court's authority in order to preserve and prevent interference with the document or documents; and
(b) explain why such steps are necessary.
(6) In respect of each set of premises which the applicant wants to be searched, the application must explain the grounds for believing that a document or description of documents sought by the applicant is on those premises.
(7) If the court so directs, the applicant must make available to the court material on which is based the information given under paragraph (3).
(8) The application must disclose anything known or reported to the applicant that might reasonably be considered capable of undermining any of the grounds of the application.
(9) Where the application includes information that the applicant thinks should be supplied only to the court, the applicant may—
(a) set out that information in a separate document, marked accordingly; and
(b) in that document, explain why the applicant thinks that that information ought not to be supplied to anyone other than the court.
(10) The application must include—
(a) a declaration by the applicant that to the best of the applicant's knowledge and belief—
(i) the application discloses all the information that is material to what the court must decide, including anything that might reasonably be considered capable of undermining any of the grounds of the application, and
(ii) the content of the application is true; and
(b) a declaration by an officer senior to the applicant that the senior officer has reviewed and authorised the application.
(11) The application must attach a draft warrant or warrants in the terms proposed by the applicant.

Application for warrant under another power to which sections 15 and 16 of the Police and Criminal Evidence Act 1984 apply R-527

47.32 (1) This rule applies where—
(a) an applicant wants a magistrates' court to issue a warrant or warrants under a power to which sections 15 and 16 of the Police and Criminal Evidence Act 1984 apply; and
(b) neither rule 47.30 nor rule 47.31 applies.
(2) The applicant must—
(a) apply in writing;
(b) serve the application on—
(i) the court officer, or
(ii) if the court office is closed, the court;
(c) give the court an estimate of how long the court should allow—
(i) to read and prepare for the application, and
(ii) for the hearing of the application; and
(d) tell the court when the applicant expects any warrant issued to be executed.
(3) The application must—
(a) state the legislation which allows the court to issue the warrant (in this rule, described as 'the main search power'; and see paragraph (4));
(b) so far as practicable, identify the articles or persons sought (and see paragraph (5));
(c) specify the premises to be searched (and see paragraphs (6) and (7));

(d) state whether the applicant wants the premises to be searched on more than one occasion (and see paragraph (8)); and
(e) state whether the applicant wants other persons to accompany the officers executing the warrant or warrants (and see paragraph (9)).

(4) The application must—
(a) include or attach the terms of the main search power; and
(b) explain how the circumstances satisfy any criteria prescribed by the main search power for making the application.

(5) In relation to the articles or persons sought, the application must explain how they satisfy any criteria prescribed by the main search power about such articles or persons.

(6) In relation to premises which the applicant wants to be searched and can specify, the application must—
(a) specify each set of premises; and
(b) in respect of each, explain how the circumstances satisfy any criteria prescribed by the main search power—
(i) for thinking that the articles or persons sought are on those premises, and
(ii) for asserting that the court can exercise its power to authorise the search of those premises.

(7) In relation to premises which the applicant wants to be searched but at least some of which the applicant cannot specify, the application must—
(a) explain how the main search power allows the court to authorise such searching;
(b) specify the person who occupies or controls such premises;
(c) specify as many sets of such premises as is reasonably practicable;
(d) explain why—
(i) it is necessary to search more premises than those specified, and
(ii) it is not reasonably practicable to specify all the premises which the applicant wants to be searched;
(e) in respect of each set of premises, whether specified or not, explain how the circumstances satisfy any criteria prescribed by the main search power for thinking that the articles or persons sought are on those premises; and
(f) in respect of each specified set of premises, explain how the circumstances satisfy any criteria prescribed by the main search power for asserting that the court can exercise its power to authorise the search of those premises.

(8) In relation to any set of premises which the applicant wants to be searched on more than one occasion, the application must—
(a) explain how the main search power allows the court to authorise such searching;
(b) explain why the applicant wants the premises to be searched more than once; and
(c) specify any proposed maximum number of occasions.

(9) In relation to any set of premises which the applicant wants to be searched by the officers executing the warrant with other persons authorised by the court, the application must—
(a) identify those other persons, by function or description; and
(b) explain why those persons are required.

(10) The application must disclose anything known or reported to the applicant that might reasonably be considered capable of undermining any of the grounds of the application.

(11) Where the application includes information that the applicant thinks should be supplied only to the court, the applicant may—
(a) set out that information in a separate document, marked accordingly; and
(b) in that document, explain why the applicant thinks that that information ought not to be supplied to anyone other than the court.

(12) The application must include—
(a) a declaration by the applicant that to the best of the applicant's knowledge and belief—
(i) the application discloses all the information that is material to what the court must decide, including anything that might reasonably be considered capable of undermining any of the grounds of the application, and
(ii) the content of the application is true; and
(b) a declaration by an officer senior to the applicant that the senior officer has reviewed and authorised the application.

(13) The application must attach a draft warrant or warrants in the terms proposed by the applicant.

Information to be included in a warrant R-528

47.33 (1) A warrant must identify—
(a) the person or description of persons by whom it may be executed;
(b) any person who may accompany a person executing the warrant;
(c) so far as practicable, the material, documents, articles or persons to be sought;
(d) the legislation under which it was issued;
(e) the name of the applicant;
(f) the court that issued it, unless that is otherwise recorded by the court officer;
(g) the court office for the court that issued it; and
(h) the date on which it was issued.
(2) A warrant must specify—
(a) the premises to be searched, where the application specified premises;
(b) the person in occupation or control of premises to be searched, where the application specified such a person; and
(c) the number of occasions on which specified premises may be searched, if more than one.
(3) A warrant must include, by signature, initial, or otherwise, an indication that it has been approved by the court that issued it.
(4) Where a warrant comprises more than a single page, each page must include such an indication.
(5) A copy of a warrant must include a prominent certificate that it is such a copy.

Section 8: orders for the retention of fingerprints, etc.

Exercise of court's powers R-529

47.34 (1) The court must determine an application under rule 47.35, and an appeal under rule 47.36—
(a) at a hearing, which must be in private unless the court otherwise directs; and
(b) in the presence of the applicant or appellant.
(2) The court must not determine such an application or appeal unless any person served under those rules—
(a) is present; or
(b) has had an opportunity—
(i) to attend, or
(ii) to make representations.

Application to extend retention period R-530

47.35 (1) This rule applies where a magistrates' court can make an order extending the period for which there may be retained material consisting of—
(a) fingerprints taken from a person—
(i) under a power conferred by Part V of the Police and Criminal Evidence Act 1984,
(ii) with that person's consent, in connection with the investigation of an offence by the police, or
(iii) under a power conferred by Schedule 8 to the Terrorism Act 2000 in relation to a person detained under section 41 of that Act;
(b) a DNA profile derived from a DNA sample so taken; or
(c) a sample so taken.
(2) A chief officer of police who wants the court to make such an order must—
(a) apply in writing—
(i) within the period of 3 months ending on the last day of the retention period, where the application relates to fingerprints or a DNA profile, or
(ii) before the expiry of the retention period, where the application relates to a sample;
(b) in the application—
(i) identify the material,
(ii) state when the retention period expires,
(iii) give details of any previous such application relating to the material, and
(iv) outline the circumstances in which the material was acquired;
(c) serve the application on the court officer, in every case; and
(d) serve the application on the person from whom the material was taken, where—
(i) the application relates to fingerprints or a DNA profile, or
(ii) the application is for the renewal of an order extending the retention period for a sample.

(3) An application to extend the retention period for fingerprints or a DNA profile must explain why that period should be extended.

(4) An application to extend the retention period for a sample must explain why, having regard to the nature and complexity of other material that is evidence in relation to the offence, the sample is likely to be needed in any proceedings for the offence for the purposes of—

(a) disclosure to, or use by, a defendant; or

(b) responding to any challenge by a defendant in respect of the admissibility of material that is evidence on which the prosecution proposes to rely.

(5) On an application to extend the retention period for fingerprints or a DNA profile, the applicant must serve notice of the court's decision on any respondent where—

(a) the court makes the order sought; and

(b) the respondent was absent when it was made.

R-531 **Appeal**

47.36 (1) This rule applies where, under rule 47.35, a magistrates' court determines an application relating to fingerprints or a DNA profile and—

(a) the person from whom the material was taken wants to appeal to the Crown Court against an order extending the retention period; or

(b) a chief officer of police wants to appeal to the Crown Court against a refusal to make such an order.

(2) The appellant must—

(a) serve an appeal notice—

(i) on the Crown Court officer and on the other party, and

(ii) not more than 21 days after the magistrates' court's decision, or, if applicable, service of notice under rule 47.35(5); and

(b) in the appeal notice, explain, as appropriate, why the retention period should, or should not, be extended.

(3) Rule 34.11 (Constitution of the Crown Court) applies on such an appeal.

CRIMINAL PRACTICE DIRECTIONS PART 47 INVESTIGATION ORDERS AND WARRANTS

PD-86 **CPD XI Other Proceedings 47A: Investigation Orders and Warrants**

47A.1 Powers of entry, search and seizure, and powers to obtain banking and other confidential information, are among the most intrusive that investigators can exercise. Every application must be carefully scrutinised with close attention paid to what the relevant statutory provision requires of the applicant and to what it permits. CrimPR Part 47 must be followed, and the accompanying forms must be used. These are designed to prompt applicants, and the courts, to deal with all of the relevant criteria.

47A.2 The issuing of a warrant or the making of such an order is never to be treated as a formality and it is therefore essential that the judge or magistrate considering the application is given, and must take, sufficient time for the purpose. The prescribed forms require the applicant to provide a time estimate, and listing officers and justices' legal advisers should take account of these.

47A.3 Applicants for orders and warrants owe the court duties of candour and truthfulness. On any application made without notice to the respondent, and so on all applications for search warrants, the duty of frank and complete disclosure is especially onerous. The applicant must draw the court's attention to any information that is unfavourable to the application. The existence of unfavourable information will not necessarily lead to the application being refused; it will be a matter for the court what weight to place on each piece of information.

47A.4 Where an applicant supplements an application with additional oral or written information, on questioning by the court or otherwise, it is essential that the court keeps an adequate record. What is needed will depend upon the circumstances. The Rules require that a record of the 'gist' be retained. The purpose of such a record is to allow the sufficiency of the court's reasons for its decision subsequently to be assessed. The gravity of such decisions requires that their exercise should be susceptible to scrutiny and to explanation by reference to all of the information that was taken into account.

47A.5 The forms that accompany CrimPR Part 47 of the Rules provide for the most frequently encountered applications. However, there are some hundreds of powers of entry, search and seizure, supplied by a corresponding number of legislative provisions. In any criminal matter, if there is no form designed for the particular warrant or order sought, the forms should still be used, as far as is practicable, and adapted as necessary. The applicant should pay particular attention to the specific legislative requirements for the granting of such an application to ensure that the court has all of the necessary information, and, if the court might be unfamiliar with the legislation, should provide a copy of the relevant provisions. Applicants must comply with the duties of candour and truthfulness, and include in their application the declarations required by the Rules and must make disclosure of any unfavourable information to the court.

Criminal Procedure Rules Part 48 Contempt of Court

General rules

When this Part applies R-532

48.1 (1) This Part applies where the court can deal with a person for conduct—
(a) in contempt of court; or
(b) in contravention of the legislation to which rules 48.5 and 48.9 refer.
(2) In this Part, 'respondent' means any such person.

Exercise of court's power to deal with contempt of court R-533

48.2 (1) The court must determine at a hearing—
(a) an enquiry under rule 48.8;
(b) an allegation under rule 48.9.
(2) The court must not proceed in the respondent's absence unless—
(a) the respondent's behaviour makes it impracticable to proceed otherwise; or
(b) the respondent has had at least 14 days' notice of the hearing, or was present when it was arranged.
(3) If the court hears part of an enquiry or allegation in private, it must announce at a hearing in public—
(a) the respondent's name;
(b) in general terms, the nature of any conduct that the respondent admits, or the court finds proved; and
(c) any punishment imposed.

Notice of suspension of imprisonment by Court of Appeal or Crown Court R-534

48.3 (1) This rule applies where—
(a) the Court of Appeal or the Crown Court suspends an order of imprisonment for contempt of court; and
(b) the respondent is absent when the court does so.
(2) The respondent must be served with notice of the terms of the court's order—
(a) by any applicant under rule 48.9; or
(b) by the court officer, in any other case.

Application to discharge an order for imprisonment R-535

48.4 (1) This rule applies where the court can discharge an order for a respondent's imprisonment for contempt of court.
(2) A respondent who wants the court to discharge such an order must—
(a) apply in writing, unless the court otherwise directs, and serve any written application on—
(i) the court officer, and
(ii) any applicant under rule 48.9 on whose application the respondent was imprisoned;
(b) in the application—
(i) explain why it is appropriate for the order for imprisonment to be discharged, and
(ii) give details of any appeal, and its outcome; and
(c) ask for a hearing, if the respondent wants one.

Contempt of court by obstruction, disruption, etc.

Initial procedure on obstruction, disruption etc. R-536

48.5 (1) This rule applies where the court observes, or someone reports to the court—
(a) in the Court of Appeal or the Crown Court, obstructive, disruptive, insulting or intimidating conduct, in the courtroom or in its vicinity, or otherwise immediately affecting the proceedings;
(b) in the Crown Court, a contravention of—
(i) section 3 of the Criminal Procedure (Attendance of Witnesses) Act 1965 (disobeying a witness summons);

(ii) section 20 of the Juries Act 1974 (disobeying a jury summons);
(iii) section 8 of the Contempt of Court Act 1981 (obtaining details of a jury's deliberations, etc.);
(c) in a magistrates' court, a contravention of—
(i) section 97(4) of the Magistrates' Courts Act 1980 (refusing to give evidence), or
(ii) section 12 of the Contempt of Court Act 1981 (insulting or interrupting the court, etc.);
(d) a contravention of section 9 of the Contempt of Court Act 1981 (without the court's permission, recording the proceedings, etc.);
(e) any other conduct with which the court can deal as, or as if it were, a criminal contempt of court, except failure to surrender to bail under section 6 of the Bail Act 1976.
(2) Unless the respondent's behaviour makes it impracticable to do so, the court must—
(a) explain, in terms the respondent can understand (with help, if necessary)—
(i) the conduct that is in question,
(ii) that the court can impose imprisonment, or a fine, or both, for such conduct,
(iii) (where relevant) that the court has power to order the respondent's immediate temporary detention, if in the court's opinion that is required,
(iv) that the respondent may explain the conduct,
(v) that the respondent may apologise, if he or she so wishes, and that this may persuade the court to take no further action, and
(vi) that the respondent may take legal advice; and
(b) allow the respondent a reasonable opportunity to reflect, take advice, explain and, if he or she so wishes, apologise.
(3) The court may then—
(a) take no further action in respect of that conduct;
(b) enquire into the conduct there and then; or
(c) postpone that enquiry (if a magistrates' court, only until later the same day).

R-537 Review after temporary detention

48.6 (1) This rule applies in a case in which the court has ordered the respondent's immediate temporary detention for conduct to which rule 48.5 applies.
(2) The court must review the case—
(a) if a magistrates' court, later the same day;
(b) in the Court of Appeal or the Crown Court, no later than the next business day.
(3) On the review, the court must—
(a) unless the respondent is absent, repeat the explanations required by rule 48.5(2)(a); and
(b) allow the respondent a reasonable opportunity to reflect, take advice, explain and, if he or she so wishes, apologise.
(4) The court may then—
(a) take no further action in respect of the conduct;
(b) if a magistrates' court, enquire into the conduct there and then; or
(c) if the Court of Appeal or the Crown Court—
(i) enquire into the conduct there and then, or
(ii) postpone the enquiry, and order the respondent's release from such detention in the meantime.

R-538 Postponement of enquiry

48.7 (1) This rule applies where the Court of Appeal or the Crown Court postpones the enquiry.
(2) The court must arrange for the preparation of a written statement containing such particulars of the conduct in question as to make clear what the respondent appears to have done.
(3) The court officer must serve on the respondent—
(a) that written statement;
(b) notice of where and when the postponed enquiry will take place; and
(c) a notice that—
(i) reminds the respondent that the court can impose imprisonment, or a fine, or both, for contempt of court, and
(ii) warns the respondent that the court may pursue the postponed enquiry in the respondent's absence, if the respondent does not attend.

R-539 Procedure on enquiry

48.8 (1) At an enquiry, the court must—
(a) ensure that the respondent understands (with help, if necessary) what is alleged, if the enquiry has been postponed from a previous occasion;

(b) explain what the procedure at the enquiry will be; and
(c) ask whether the respondent admits the conduct in question.
(2) If the respondent admits the conduct, the court need not receive evidence.
(3) If the respondent does not admit the conduct, the court must consider—
(a) any statement served under rule 48.7;
(b) any other evidence of the conduct;
(c) any evidence introduced by the respondent; and
(d) any representations by the respondent about the conduct.
(4) If the respondent admits the conduct, or the court finds it proved, the court must—
(a) before imposing any punishment for contempt of court, give the respondent an opportunity to make representations relevant to punishment;
(b) explain, in terms the respondent can understand (with help, if necessary)—
(i) the reasons for its decision, including its findings of fact, and
(ii) the punishment it imposes, and its effect; and
(c) if a magistrates' court, arrange for the preparation of a written record of those findings.
(5) The court that conducts an enquiry—
(a) need not include the same member or members as the court that observed the conduct; but
(b) may do so, unless that would be unfair to the respondent.

Contempt of court by failure to comply with court order, etc.

Initial procedure on failure to comply with court order, etc. R-540

48.9 (1) This rule applies where—
(a) a party, or other person directly affected, alleges—
(i) in the Crown Court, a failure to comply with an order to which applies rule 33.70 (compliance order, restraint order or ancillary order), 47.13 (certain investigation orders under the Terrorism Act 2000), or rule 47.22 (certain investigation orders under the Proceeds of Crime Act 2002),
(ii) in the Court of Appeal or the Crown Court, any other conduct with which that court can deal as a civil contempt of court, or
(iii) in the Crown Court or a magistrates' court, unauthorised use of disclosed prosecution material under section 17 of the Criminal Procedure and Investigations Act 1996;
(b) the court deals on its own initiative with conduct to which paragraph (1)(a) applies.
(2) Such a party or person must—
(a) apply in writing and serve the application on the court officer; and
(b) serve on the respondent—
(i) the application, and
(ii) notice of where and when the court will consider the allegation (not less than 14 days after service).
(3) The application must—
(a) identify the respondent;
(b) explain that it is an application for the respondent to be dealt with for contempt of court;
(c) contain such particulars of the conduct in question as to make clear what is alleged against the respondent; and
(d) include a notice warning the respondent that the court—
(i) can impose imprisonment, or a fine, or both, for contempt of court, and
(ii) may deal with the application in the respondent's absence, if the respondent does not attend the hearing.
(4) A court which acts on its own initiative under paragraph (1)(b) must—
(a) arrange for the preparation of a written statement containing the same information as an application; and
(b) arrange for the service on the respondent of—
(i) that written statement, and
(ii) notice of where and when the court will consider the allegation (not less than 14 days after service).

Procedure on hearing R-541

48.10 (1) At the hearing of an allegation under rule 48.9, the court must—
(a) ensure that the respondent understands (with help, if necessary) what is alleged;
(b) explain what the procedure at the hearing will be; and
(c) ask whether the respondent admits the conduct in question.
(2) If the respondent admits the conduct, the court need not receive evidence.

(3) If the respondent does not admit the conduct, the court must consider—
(a) the application or written statement served under rule 48.9;
(b) any other evidence of the conduct;
(c) any evidence introduced by the respondent; and
(d) any representations by the respondent about the conduct.
(4) If the respondent admits the conduct, or the court finds it proved, the court must—
(a) before imposing any punishment for contempt of court, give the respondent an opportunity to make representations relevant to punishment;
(b) explain, in terms the respondent can understand (with help, if necessary)—
(i) the reasons for its decision, including its findings of fact, and
(ii) the punishment it imposes, and its effect; and
(c) in a magistrates' court, arrange for the preparation of a written record of those findings.

R-542 **Introduction of written witness statement or other hearsay**

48.11 (1) Where rule 48.9 applies, an applicant or respondent who wants to introduce in evidence the written statement of a witness, or other hearsay, must—
(a) serve a copy of the statement, or notice of other hearsay, on—
(i) the court officer, and
(ii) the other party; and
(b) serve the copy or notice—
(i) when serving the application under rule 48.9, in the case of an applicant, or
(ii) not more than 7 days after service of that application or of the court's written statement, in the case of the respondent.
(2) Such service is notice of that party's intention to introduce in evidence that written witness statement, or other hearsay, unless that party otherwise indicates when serving it.
(3) A party entitled to receive such notice may waive that entitlement.

R-543 **Content of written witness statement**

48.12 (1) This rule applies to a written witness statement served under rule 48.11.
(2) Such a written witness statement must contain a declaration by the person making it that it is true to the best of that person's knowledge and belief.

R-544 **Content of notice of other hearsay**

48.13 (1) This rule applies to a notice of hearsay, other than a written witness statement, served under rule 48.11.
(2) Such a notice must—
(a) set out the evidence, or attach the document that contains it; and
(b) identify the person who made the statement that is hearsay.

R-545 **Cross-examination of maker of written witness statement or other hearsay**

48.14 (1) This rule applies where a party wants the court's permission to cross-examine a person who made a statement which another person wants to introduce as hearsay.
(2) The party who wants to cross-examine that person must—
(a) apply in writing, with reasons; and
(b) serve the application on—
(i) the court officer, and
(ii) the party who served the hearsay.
(3) A respondent who wants to cross-examine such a person must apply to do so not more than 7 days after service of the hearsay by the applicant.
(4) An applicant who wants to cross-examine such a person must apply to do so not more than 3 days after service of the hearsay by the respondent.
(5) The court—
(a) may decide an application under this rule without a hearing; but
(b) must not dismiss such an application unless the person making it has had an opportunity to make representations at a hearing.

R-546 **Credibility and consistency of maker of written witness statement or other hearsay**

48.15 (1) This rule applies where a party wants to challenge the credibility or consistency of a person who made a statement which another party wants to introduce as hearsay.
(2) The party who wants to challenge the credibility or consistency of that person must—
(a) serve a written notice of intention to do so on—
(i) the court officer, and
(ii) the party who served the hearsay; and
(b) in it, identify any statement or other material on which that party relies.

(3) A respondent who wants to challenge such a person's credibility or consistency must serve such a notice not more than 7 days after service of the hearsay by the applicant.
(4) An applicant who wants to challenge such a person's credibility or consistency must serve such a notice not more than 3 days after service of the hearsay by the respondent.
(5) The party who served the hearsay—
(a) may call that person to give oral evidence instead; and
(b) if so, must serve a notice of intention to do so on—
(i) the court officer, and
(ii) the other party
as soon as practicable after service of the notice under paragraph (2).

Magistrates' courts' powers to adjourn, etc. R-547

48.16 (1) This rule applies where a magistrates' court deals with unauthorised disclosure of prosecution material under sections 17 and 18 of the Criminal Procedure and Investigations Act 1996.
(2) The sections of the Magistrates' Courts Act 1980 listed in paragraph (3) apply as if in those sections—
(a) 'complaint' and 'summons' each referred to an application or written statement under rule 48.9;
(b) 'complainant' meant an applicant; and
(c) 'defendant' meant the respondent.
(3) Those sections are—
(a) section 51 (issue of summons on complaint);
(b) section 54 (adjournment);
(c) section 55 (non-appearance of defendant);
(d) section 97(1) (summons to witness);
(e) section 121(1) (constitution and place of sitting of court);
(f) section 123 (defect in process).
(4) Section 127 of the 1980 Act (limitation of time) does not apply.

Court's power to vary requirements R-548

48.17 (1) The court may shorten or extend (even after it has expired) a time limit under rule 48.11, 48.14 or 48.15.
(2) A person who wants an extension of time must—
(a) apply when serving the statement, notice or application for which it is needed; and
(b) explain the delay.

Criminal Practice Directions Part 48 Contempt of Court

CPD XI Other proceedings 48A: Contempt in the Face of the Magistrates' Court PD-87

General

48A.1 The procedure to be followed in cases of contempt of court is given in CrimPR Part 48. The magistrates' courts' power to deal with contempt in the face of the court is contained within section 12 of the Contempt of Court Act 1981. Magistrates' courts also have the power to punish a witness who refuses to be sworn or give evidence under section 97(4) of the Magistrates' Courts Act 1980.

Contempt consisting of wilfully insulting anyone specified in section 12 or interrupting proceedings

48A.2 In the majority of cases, an apology and a promise as to future conduct should be sufficient for the court to order a person's release. However, there are likely to be certain cases where the nature and seriousness of the misconduct requires the court to consider using its powers, under section 12(2) of the Contempt of Court Act 1981, either to fine or to order the person's committal to custody.

Imposing a penalty for contempt

48A.3 The court should allow the person a further opportunity to apologise for his or her contempt, and should follow the procedure at CrimPR 48.8(4). The court should consider whether it is appropriate to release the person or whether it must exercise its powers to fine the person or to commit the person to custody under section 12(2) of the 1981 Act. In deciding how to deal with the person, the court should have regard to the period for which he or she has been detained, whether the conduct was admitted and the seriousness of the contempt. Any period of committal to custody should be for the shortest period of time commensurate with the interests of preserving good order in the administration of justice.

R-549 **Notice required to accompany process served outside the United Kingdom and translations**

49.1 (1) The notice which by virtue of section 3(4)(b) of the Crime (International Co-operation) Act 2003 (general requirements for service of process) must accompany any process served outside the United Kingdom must give the information specified in paragraphs (2) and (4) below.

(2) The notice must—

(a) state that the person required by the process to appear as a party or attend as a witness can obtain information about his rights in connection therewith from the relevant authority; and

(b) give the particulars specified in paragraph (4) about that authority.

(3) The relevant authority where the process is served—

(a) at the request of the prosecuting authority, is that authority; or

(b) at the request of the defendant or the prosecutor in the case of a private prosecution, is the court by which the process is served.

(4) The particulars referred to in paragraph (2) are—

(a) the name and address of the relevant authority, together with its telephone and fax numbers and e-mail address; and

(b) the name of a person at the relevant authority who can provide the information referred to in paragraph (2)(a), together with his telephone and fax numbers and e-mail address.

(5) The justices' clerk or Crown Court officer must send, together with any process served outside the United Kingdom—

(a) any translation which is provided under section 3(3)(b) of the 2003 Act; and

(b) any translation of the information required to be given by this rule which is provided to him.

(6) In this rule 'process' has the same meaning as in section 51(3) of the 2003 Act.

R-550 **Proof of service outside the United Kingdom**

49.2 (1) A statement in a certificate given by or on behalf of the Secretary of State—

(a) that process has been served on any person under section 4(1) of the Crime (International Co-operation) Act 2003 (service of process otherwise than by post);

(b) of the manner in which service was effected; and

(c) of the date on which process was served;

shall be admissible as evidence of any facts so stated.

(2) In this rule 'process' has the same meaning as in section 51(3) of the 2003 Act.

R-551 **Supply of copy of notice of request for assistance abroad**

49.3 Where a request for assistance under section 7 of the Crime (International Co-operation) Act 2003 is made by a justice of the peace or a judge exercising the jurisdiction of the Crown Court and is sent in accordance with section 8(1) of the 2003 Act, the justices' clerk or the Crown Court officer shall send a copy of the letter of request to the Secretary of State as soon as practicable after the request has been made.

R-552 **Persons entitled to appear and take part in proceedings before a nominated court, and exclusion of the public**

49.4 A court nominated under section 15(1) of the Crime (International Co-operation) Act 2003 (nominating a court to receive evidence) may—

(a) determine who may appear or take part in the proceedings under Schedule 1 to the 2003 Act before the court and whether a party to the proceedings is entitled to be legally represented; and

(b) direct that the public be excluded from those proceedings if it thinks it necessary to do so in the interests of justice.

R-553 **Record of proceedings to receive evidence before a nominated court**

49.5 (1) Where a court is nominated under section 15(1) of the Crime (International Co-operation) Act 2003 the justices' clerk or Crown Court officer shall enter in an overseas record—

(a) details of the request in respect of which the notice under section 15(1) of the 2003 Act was given;

(b) the date on which, and place at which, the proceedings under Schedule 1 to the 2003 Act in respect of that request took place;

(c) the name of any witness who gave evidence at the proceedings in question;

(d) the name of any person who took part in the proceedings as a legal representative or an interpreter;
(e) whether a witness was required to give evidence on oath or (by virtue of section 5 of the Oaths Act 1978) after making a solemn affirmation; and
(f) whether the opportunity to cross-examine any witness was refused.

(2) When the court gives the evidence received by it under paragraph 6(1) of Schedule 1 to the 2003 Act to the court or authority that made the request or to the territorial authority for forwarding to the court or authority that made the request, the justices' clerk or Crown Court officer shall send to the court, authority or territorial authority (as the case may be) a copy of an extract of so much of the overseas record as relates to the proceedings in respect of that request.

Interpreter for the purposes of proceedings involving a television or telephone link R-554

49.6 (1) This rule applies where a court is nominated under section 30(3) (hearing witnesses in the UK through television links) or section 31(4) (hearing witnesses in the UK by telephone) of the Crime (International Co-operation) Act 2003.

(2) Where it appears to the justices' clerk or the Crown Court officer that the witness to be heard in the proceedings under Part 1 or 2 of Schedule 2 to the 2003 Act ('the relevant proceedings') is likely to give evidence in a language other than English, he shall make arrangements for an interpreter to be present at the proceedings to translate what is said into English.

(3) Where it appears to the justices' clerk or the Crown Court officer that the witness to be heard in the relevant proceedings is likely to give evidence in a language other than that in which the proceedings of the court referred to in section 30(1) or, as the case may be, 31(1) of the 2003 Act ('the external court') will be conducted, he shall make arrangements for an interpreter to be present at the relevant proceedings to translate what is said into the language in which the proceedings of the external court will be conducted.

(4) Where the evidence in the relevant proceedings is either given in a language other than English or is not translated into English by an interpreter, the court shall adjourn the proceedings until such time as an interpreter can be present to provide a translation into English.

(5) Where a court in Wales understands Welsh—
(a) paragraph (2) does not apply where it appears to the justices' clerk or Crown Court officer that the witness in question is likely to give evidence in Welsh;
(b) paragraph (4) does not apply where the evidence is given in Welsh; and
(c) any translation which is provided pursuant to paragraph (2) or (4) may be into Welsh instead of English.

Record of television link hearing before a nominated court R-555

49.7 (1) This rule applies where a court is nominated under section 30(3) of the Crime (International Co-operation) Act 2003.

(2) The justices' clerk or Crown Court officer shall enter in an overseas record—
(a) details of the request in respect of which the notice under section 30(3) of the 2003 Act was given;
(b) the date on which, and place at which, the proceedings under Part 1 of Schedule 2 to that Act in respect of that request took place;
(c) the technical conditions, such as the type of equipment used, under which the proceedings took place;
(d) the name of the witness who gave evidence;
(e) the name of any person who took part in the proceedings as a legal representative or an interpreter; and
(f) the language in which the evidence was given.

(3) As soon as practicable after the proceedings under Part 1 of Schedule 2 to the 2003 Act took place, the justices' clerk or Crown Court officer shall send to the external authority that made the request a copy of an extract of so much of the overseas record as relates to the proceedings in respect of that request.

Record of telephone link hearing before a nominated court R-556

49.8 (1) This rule applies where a court is nominated under section 31(4) of the Crime (International Co-operation) Act 2003.

(2) The justices' clerk or Crown Court officer shall enter in an overseas record—
(a) details of the request in respect of which the notice under section 31(4) of the 2003 Act was given;

(b) the date, time and place at which the proceedings under Part 2 of Schedule 2 to the 2003 Act took place;
(c) the name of the witness who gave evidence;
(d) the name of any interpreter who acted at the proceedings; and
(e) the language in which the evidence was given.

R-557 **Overseas record**

49.9 (1) The overseas records of a magistrates' court shall be part of the register (within the meaning of section 150(1) of the Magistrates' Courts Act 1980).
(2) The overseas records of any court shall not be open to inspection by any person except—
(a) as authorised by the Secretary of State; or
(b) with the leave of the court.

R-558 **Overseas freezing orders**

49.10 (1) This rule applies where a court is nominated under section 21(1) of the Crime (International Co-operation) Act 2003 to give effect to an overseas freezing order.
(2) Where the Secretary of State serves a copy of such an order on the court officer—
(a) the general rule is that the court must consider the order no later than the next business day;
(b) exceptionally, the court may consider the order later than that, but not more than 5 business days after service.
(3) The court must not consider the order unless—
(a) it is satisfied that the chief officer of police for the area in which the evidence is situated has had notice of the order; and
(b) that chief officer of police has had an opportunity to make representations, at a hearing if that officer wants.
(4) The court may consider the order—
(a) without a hearing; or
(b) at a hearing, in public or in private.

R-559 **Overseas forfeiture orders**

49.11 (1) This rule applies where—
(a) the Crown Court can—
(i) make a restraint order under article 5 of the Criminal Justice (International Cooperation) Act 1990 (Enforcement of Overseas Forfeiture Orders) Order 2005, or
(ii) give effect to an external forfeiture order under article 19 of that Order;
(b) the Director of Public Prosecutions or the Director of the Serious Fraud Office receives—
(i) a request for the restraint of property to which article 3 of the 2005 Order applies, or
(ii) a request to give effect to an external forfeiture order to which article 15 of the Order applies; and
(c) the Director wants the Crown Court to—
(i) make such a restraint order, or
(ii) give effect to such a forfeiture order.
(2) The Director must—
(a) apply in writing;
(b) serve the application on the court officer; and
(c) serve the application on the defendant and on any other person affected by the order, unless the court is satisfied that—
(i) the application is urgent, or
(ii) there are reasonable grounds for believing that to give notice of the application would cause the dissipation of the property which is the subject of the application.
(3) The application must—
(a) identify the property the subject of the application;
(b) identify the person who is or who may become the subject of such a forfeiture order;
(c) explain how the requirements of the 2005 Order are satisfied, as the case may be—
(i) for making a restraint order, or
(ii) for giving effect to a forfeiture order;

(d) where the application is to give effect to a forfeiture order, include an application to appoint the Director as the enforcement authority; and
(e) propose the terms of the Crown Court order.

(4) If the court allows the application, it must—
(a) where it decides to make a restraint order—
(i) specify the property the subject of the order,
(ii) specify the person or persons who are prohibited from dealing with that property,
(iii) specify any exception to that prohibition, and
(iv) include any ancillary order that the court believes is appropriate to ensure that the restraint order is effective;
(b) where it decides to give effect to a forfeiture order, exercise its power to—
(i) direct the registration of the order as an order of the Crown Court,
(ii) give directions for notice of the order to be given to any person affected by it, and
(iii) appoint the applicant Director as the enforcement authority.

(5) Paragraph (6) applies where a person affected by an order, or the Director, wants the court to vary or discharge a restraint order or cancel the registration of a forfeiture order.

(6) Such a person must—
(a) apply in writing as soon as practicable after becoming aware of the grounds for doing so;
(b) serve the application on the court officer and, as applicable—
(i) the other party, and
(ii) any other person who will or may be affected;
(c) explain why it is appropriate, as the case may be—
(i) for the restraint order to be varied or discharged, or
(ii) for the registration of the forfeiture order to be cancelled;
(d) propose the terms of any variation; and
(e) ask for a hearing, if one is wanted, and explain why it is needed.

(7) The court may—
(a) consider an application
(i) at a hearing, which must be in private unless the court otherwise directs, or
(ii) without a hearing;
(b) allow an application to be made orally.

Overseas restraint orders **R-560**

49.12 (1) This rule applies where—
(a) the Crown Court can give effect to an overseas restraint order under regulation 10 of the Criminal Justice and Data Protection (Protocol No. 36) Regulations 2014;
(b) the Director of Public Prosecutions or the Director of the Serious Fraud Office receives a request from a court or authority in another European Union member State to give effect to such an order; and
(c) the Director serves on the Crown Court officer—
(i) the certificate which accompanied the request for enforcement of the order,
(ii) a copy of the order restraining the property to which that certificate relates, and
(iii) a copy of an order confiscating the property in respect of which the restraint order was made, or an indication of when such a confiscation order is expected.

(2) On service of those documents on the court officer—
(a) the general rule is that the Crown Court must consider the order, with a view to its registration, no later than the next business day;
(b) exceptionally, the court may consider the order later than that, but not more than 5 business days after service.

(3) The court—
(a) must not consider the order unless the Director—
(i) is present, or
(ii) has had a reasonable opportunity to make representations;
(b) subject to that, may consider the order—
(i) at a hearing, which must be in private unless the court otherwise directs, or
(ii) without a hearing.

(4) If the court decides to give effect to the order, the court must—
(a) direct its registration as an order of the Crown Court; and
(b) give directions for notice of the order to be given to any person affected by it.

(5) Paragraph (6) applies where a person affected by the order, or the Director, wants the court to cancel the registration or vary the property to which the order applies.

(6) Such a person must—

(a) apply in writing as soon as practicable after becoming aware of the grounds for doing so;

(b) serve the application on the court officer and, as applicable—

(i) the other party, and

(ii) any other person who will or may be affected;

(c) explain, as applicable—

(i) when the overseas restraint order ceased to have effect in the European Union member State in which it was made,

(ii) why continuing to give effect to that order would be impossible as a consequence of an immunity under the law of England and Wales,

(iii) why continuing to give effect to that order would be incompatible with a Convention right within the meaning of the Human Rights Act 1998,

(iv) why therefore it is appropriate for the registration to be cancelled or varied;

(d) include with the application any evidence in support;

(e) propose the terms of any variation; and

(f) ask for a hearing, if one is wanted, and explain why it is needed.

R-561 **Overseas confiscation orders**

49.13 (1) This rule applies where—

(a) the Crown Court can give effect to an overseas confiscation order under regulation 15 of the Criminal Justice and Data Protection (Protocol No. 36) Regulations 2014;

(b) the Director of Public Prosecutions or the Director of the Serious Fraud Office receives a request from a court or authority in another European Union member State to give effect to such an order; and

(c) the Director serves on the Crown Court officer—

(i) the certificate which accompanied the request for enforcement of the order, and

(ii) a copy of the confiscation order to which that certificate relates.

(2) The court—

(a) must not consider the order unless the Director—

(i) is present, or

(ii) has had a reasonable opportunity to make representations;

(b) subject to that, may consider the order—

(i) at a hearing, which must be in private unless the court otherwise directs, or

(ii) without a hearing.

(3) If the court decides to give effect to the order, the court must—

(a) direct its registration as an order of the Crown Court; and

(b) give directions for notice of the order to be given to any person affected by it.

(4) Paragraph (5) applies where a person affected by the order, or the Director, wants the court to cancel the registration or vary the property to which the order applies.

(5) Such a person must—

(a) apply in writing as soon as practicable after becoming aware of the grounds for doing so;

(b) serve the application on the court officer and, as applicable—

(i) the other party, and

(ii) any other person who will or may be affected;

(c) explain, as applicable—

(i) when the overseas confiscation order ceased to have effect in the European Union member State in which it was made,

(ii) why continuing to give effect to that order would be statute-barred, provided that the criminal conduct that gave rise to the order falls within the jurisdiction of England and Wales,

(iii) why continuing to give effect to that order would be impossible as a consequence of an immunity under the law of England and Wales,

(iv) why continuing to give effect to that order would be incompatible with a Convention right within the meaning of the Human Rights Act 1998,

(v) why therefore it is appropriate for the registration to be cancelled or varied;

(d) include with the application any evidence in support;

(e) propose the terms of any variation; and

(f) ask for a hearing, if one is wanted, and explain why it is needed.

Criminal Procedure Rules Part 50 Extradition

Section 1: general rules

When this Part applies R-562

50.1 (1) This Part applies to extradition under Part 1 or Part 2 of the Extradition Act 2003.
(2) Section 2 of this Part applies to proceedings in a magistrates' court, and in that Section—
(a) rules 50.3 to 50.7, 50.15 and 50.16 apply to extradition under Part 1 of the Act;
(b) rules 50.3, 50.4 and 50.8 to 50.16 apply to extradition under Part 2 of the Act.
(3) Section 3 of this Part applies where—
(a) a party wants to appeal to the High Court against an order by the magistrates' court or by the Secretary of State;
(b) a party to an appeal to the High Court wants to appeal further to the Supreme Court under—
(i) section 32 of the Act (appeal under Part 1 of the Act), or
(ii) section 114 of the Act (appeal under Part 2 of the Act).

Meaning of 'magistrates' court', 'presenting officer' and 'defendant' R-563

50.2 In this Part, and for the purposes of this Part in other rules—
(a) 'magistrates' court' means a District Judge (Magistrates' Courts) exercising the powers to which Section 2 of this Part applies;
(b) 'presenting officer' means an officer of the National Crime Agency, a police officer, a prosecutor or other person representing an authority or territory seeking the extradition of a defendant;
(c) 'defendant' means a person arrested under Part 1 or Part 2 of the Extradition Act 2003.

Section 2: extradition proceedings in a magistrates' court

Exercise of magistrates' court's powers R-564

50.3 (1) The general rule is that the magistrates' court must exercise its powers at a hearing in public, but that is subject to any power it has to—
(a) impose reporting restrictions;
(b) withhold information from the public; or
(c) order a hearing in private.
(2) The general rule is that the court must exercise its powers in the defendant's presence, but it may do so in the defendant's absence where—
(a) the court discharges the defendant; or
(b) the defendant is represented and the defendant's presence is impracticable by reason of his or her—
(i) ill health, or
(ii) disorderly conduct.
(3) The court may exercise its power to adjourn—
(a) if either party asks, or on its own initiative; and
(b) in particular—
(i) to allow there to be obtained information that the court requires,
(ii) following a provisional arrest under Part 1 of the Extradition Act 2003, pending receipt of the warrant,
(iii) following a provisional arrest under Part 2 of the Act, pending receipt of the extradition request,
(iv) if the court is informed that the defendant is serving a custodial sentencing in the United Kingdom,
(v) if it appears to the court that the defendant is not fit to be extradited, unless the court discharges the defendant for that reason,
(vi) where a court dealing with a warrant to which Part 1 of the Act applies is informed that another such warrant has been received in the United Kingdom, or
(vii) where a court dealing with a warrant to which Part 1 of the Act applies is informed of a request for the temporary transfer of the defendant to the territory to which the defendant's extradition is sought.
(4) The court must exercise its power to adjourn if informed that the defendant has been charged with an offence in the United Kingdom.
(5) The general rule is that, before exercising a power to which this Part applies, the court must give each party an opportunity to make representations, unless that party is absent deliberately.

R-565 Duty of magistrates' court officer

50.4 The magistrates' court officer must—
(a) as soon as practicable, serve notice of the court's decision to extradite or discharge—
(i) on the defendant,
(ii) on the designated authority which certified the arrest warrant, where Part 1 of the Extradition Act 2003 applies,
(iii) on the Secretary of State, where Part 2 of the Act applies; and
(b) give the court such assistance as it requires.

Extradition under Part 1 of the Extradition Act 2003

R-566 Preliminary hearing after arrest

50.5 (1) This rule applies where the defendant is first brought before the court after—
(a) arrest under a warrant to which Part 1 of the Extradition Act 2003 applies; or
(b) provisional arrest under Part 1 of the Act.
(2) The presenting officer must—
(a) serve on the court officer—
(i) the arrest warrant, and
(ii) a certificate, given by the authority designated by the Secretary of State, that the warrant was issued by an authority having the function of issuing such warrants in the territory to which the defendant's extradition is sought; or
(b) apply at once for an extension of time within which to serve that warrant and that certificate.
(3) An application under paragraph (2)(b) must—
(a) explain why the requirement to serve the warrant and certificate at once could not reasonably be complied with; and
(b) include—
(i) any written material in support of that explanation, and
(ii) representations about bail pending service of those documents.
(4) When the presenting officer serves the warrant and certificate, in the following sequence the court must—
(a) decide whether the defendant is the person in respect of whom the warrant was issued;
(b) explain, in terms the defendant can understand (with help, if necessary)—
(i) the allegation made in the warrant, and
(ii) that the defendant may consent to extradition, and how that may be done and with what effect;
(c) arrange for an extradition hearing to begin—
(i) no more than 21 days after the defendant's arrest, or
(ii) if either party so applies, at such a later date as the court decides is in the interests of justice;
(d) consider any ancillary application, including an application about bail pending the extradition hearing; and
(e) give any direction as is appropriate to the needs of the case about the introduction of evidence at the extradition hearing.

R-567 Extradition hearing

50.6 (1) This rule applies at the extradition hearing arranged by the court under rule 50.5.
(2) In the following sequence, the court must decide—
(a) whether the offence specified in the warrant is an extradition offence;
(b) whether a bar to extradition applies, namely—
(i) the rule against double jeopardy,
(ii) absence of prosecution decision,
(iii) extraneous considerations,
(iv) the passage of time,
(v) the defendant's age,
(vi) speciality,
(vii) earlier extradition or transfer to the United Kingdom, or
(viii) forum;
(c) where the warrant alleges that the defendant is unlawfully at large after conviction, whether conviction was in the defendant's presence and if not—
(i) whether the defendant was absent deliberately,
(ii) if the defendant was not absent deliberately, whether the defendant would be entitled to a retrial (or to a review of the conviction, amounting to a retrial);

(d) whether extradition would be—
(i) compatible with the defendant's human rights, and
(ii) proportionate;
(e) whether it would be unjust or oppressive to extradite the defendant because of his or her physical or mental condition;
(f) after deciding each of (a) to (e) above, before progressing to the next, whether to order the defendant's discharge,
(g) whether to order the temporary transfer of the defendant to the territory to which the defendant's extradition is sought.

(3) If the court discharges the defendant, the court must consider any ancillary application, including an application about—
(a) reporting restrictions; or
(b) costs.

(4) If the court does not discharge the defendant, the court must—
(a) exercise its power to order the defendant's extradition;
(b) explain, in terms the defendant can understand (with help, if necessary), that the defendant may appeal to the High Court within the next 7 days; and
(c) consider any ancillary application, including an application about—
(i) bail pending extradition,
(ii) reporting restrictions, or
(iii) costs.

(5) If the court orders the defendant's extradition, the court must order its postponement where—
(a) the defendant has been charged with an offence in the United Kingdom; or
(b) the defendant has been sentenced to imprisonment or detention in the United Kingdom.

Discharge where warrant withdrawn R-568

50.7 (1) This rule applies where the authority that certified the warrant gives the court officer notice that the warrant has been withdrawn—
(a) after the start of the hearing under rule 50.5; and
(b) before the court orders the defendant's extradition or discharge.
(2) The court must exercise its power to discharge the defendant.

Extradition under Part 2 of the Extradition Act 2003

Issue of arrest warrant R-569

50.8 (1) This rule applies where the Secretary of State serves on the court officer—
(a) an extradition request to which Part 2 of the Extradition Act 2003 applies;
(b) a certificate given by the Secretary of State that the request was received in the way approved for the request; and
(c) a copy of any Order in Council which applies to the request.
(2) In the following sequence, the court must decide—
(a) whether the offence in respect of which extradition is requested is an extradition offence; and
(b) whether there is sufficient evidence, or (where the Secretary of State has so ordered, for this purpose) information, to justify the issue of a warrant of arrest.
(3) The court may issue an arrest warrant—
(a) without giving the parties an opportunity to make representations; and
(b) without a hearing, or at a hearing in public or in private.

Preliminary hearing after arrest R-570

50.9 (1) This rule applies where a defendant is first brought before the court after arrest under a warrant to which rule 50.8 applies.
(2) In the following sequence, the court must—
(a) explain, in terms the defendant can understand (with help, if necessary)—
(i) the content of the extradition request, and
(ii) that the defendant may consent to extradition, and how that may be done and with what effect;
(b) arrange for an extradition hearing to begin—
(i) no more than 2 months later, or
(ii) if either party so applies, at such a later date as the court decides is in the interests of justice;

(c) consider any ancillary application, including an application about bail pending the extradition hearing; and
(d) give any direction as is appropriate to the needs of the case about the introduction of evidence at the extradition hearing.

R-571 Issue of provisional arrest warrant

50.10 (1) This rule applies where a presenting officer wants a justice of the peace to issue a provisional arrest warrant under Part 2 of the Extradition Act 2003, pending receipt of an extradition request.
(2) The presenting officer must—
(a) serve on the court officer an information in writing; and
(b) verify the information on oath or affirmation.
(3) In the following sequence, the justice must decide—
(a) whether the alleged offence is an extradition offence; and
(b) whether there is sufficient evidence, or (where the Secretary of State has so ordered, for this purpose) information, to justify the issue of a warrant of arrest.

R-572 Preliminary hearing after provisional arrest

50.11 (1) This rule applies where a defendant is first brought before the court after arrest under a provisional arrest warrant to which rule 50.10 applies.
(2) The court must—
(a) explain, in terms the defendant can understand (with help, if necessary)—
(i) the allegation in respect of which the warrant was issued, and
(ii) that the defendant may consent to extradition, and how that may be done and with what effect; and
(b) consider any ancillary application, including an application about bail pending receipt of the extradition request.

R-573 Arrangement of extradition hearing after provisional arrest

50.12 (1) This rule applies when the Secretary of State serves on the court officer—
(a) a request for extradition in respect of which a defendant has been arrested under a provisional arrest warrant to which rule 50.10 applies;
(b) a certificate given by the Secretary of State that the request was received in the way approved for the request; and
(c) a copy of any Order in Council which applies to the request.
(2) Unless a time limit for service of the request has expired, the court must—
(a) arrange for an extradition hearing to begin—
(i) no more than 2 months after service of the request, or
(ii) if either party so applies, at such a later date as the court decides is in the interests of justice;
(b) consider any ancillary application, including an application about bail pending the extradition hearing; and
(c) give any direction as is appropriate to the needs of the case about the introduction of evidence at the extradition hearing.

R-574 Extradition hearing

50.13 (1) This rule applies at the extradition hearing arranged by the court under rule 50.9 or rule 50.12.
(2) In the following sequence, the court must decide—
(a) whether the documents served on the court officer by the Secretary of State include—
(i) those listed in rule 50.8(1) or rule 50.12(1), as the case may be,
(ii) particulars of the person whose extradition is requested,
(iii) particulars of the offence specified in the request, and
(iv) as the case may be, a warrant for the defendant's arrest, or a certificate of the defendant's conviction and (if applicable) sentence, issued in the requesting territory;
(b) whether the defendant is the person whose extradition is requested;
(c) whether the offence specified in the request is an extradition offence;
(d) whether the documents served on the court officer by the Secretary of State have been served also on the defendant;
(e) whether a bar to extradition applies, namely—
(i) the rule against double jeopardy,
(ii) extraneous considerations,
(iii) the passage of time,
(iv) hostage-taking considerations, or
(v) forum;

(f) where the request accuses the defendant of an offence, whether there is evidence which would be sufficient to make a case requiring an answer by the defendant if the extradition proceedings were a trial (unless the Secretary of State has otherwise ordered, for this purpose);
(g) where the request accuses the defendant of being unlawfully at large after conviction, whether the defendant was—
(i) convicted in his or her presence, or
(ii) absent deliberately;
(h) where the request accuses the defendant of being unlawfully at large after conviction, and the defendant was absent but not deliberately—
(i) whether the defendant would be entitled to a retrial (or to a review of the conviction amounting to a retrial), and
(ii) if so, whether there is evidence which would be sufficient to make a case requiring an answer by the defendant if the extradition proceedings were a trial (unless the Secretary of State has otherwise ordered, for this purpose);
(i) whether extradition would be compatible with the defendant's human rights;
(j) whether it would be unjust or oppressive to extradite the defendant because of his or her physical or mental condition;
(k) after deciding each of (a) to (j) above, before progressing to the next, whether to order the defendant's discharge.

(3) If the court discharges the defendant, the court must consider any ancillary application, including an application about—
(a) reporting restrictions; or
(b) costs.

(4) If the court does not discharge the defendant, the court must—
(a) exercise its power to send the case to the Secretary of State to decide whether to extradite the defendant;
(b) explain, in terms the defendant can understand (with help, if necessary), that—
(i) the defendant may appeal to the High Court not more than 14 days after being informed of the Secretary of State's decision, and
(ii) any such appeal brought before the Secretary of State's decision has been made will not be heard until after that decision; and
(c) consider any ancillary application, including an application about—
(i) bail pending extradition,
(ii) reporting restrictions, or
(iii) costs.

(5) If the Secretary of State orders the defendant's extradition, the court must order its postponement where—
(a) the defendant has been charged with an offence in the United Kingdom; or
(b) the defendant has been sentenced to imprisonment or detention in the United Kingdom.

Discharge where extradition request withdrawn R-575

50.14 (1) This rule applies where the Secretary of State gives the court officer notice that the extradition request has been withdrawn—
(a) after the start of the hearing under rule 50.9 or 50.11; and
(b) before the court—
(i) sends the case to the Secretary of State to decide whether to extradite the defendant, or
(ii) discharges the defendant.

(2) The court must exercise its power to discharge the defendant.

Evidence at extradition hearing

Introduction of additional evidence R-576

50.15 (1) Where a party wants to introduce evidence at an extradition hearing under the law that would apply if that hearing were a trial, the relevant Part of these Rules applies with such adaptations as the court directs.

(2) If the court admits as evidence the written statement of a witness—
(a) each relevant part of the statement must be read or summarised aloud; or
(b) the court must read the statement and its gist must be summarised aloud.

(3) If a party introduces in evidence a fact admitted by another party, or the parties jointly admit a fact, a written record must be made of the admission.

Discharge after failure to comply with a time limit

R-577 Defendant's application to be discharged

50.16 (1) This rule applies where a defendant wants to be discharged—

(a) because of a failure—

(i) to give the defendant a copy of any warrant under which the defendant is arrested as soon as practicable after arrest,

(ii) to bring the defendant before the court as soon as practicable after arrest under a warrant,

(iii) to bring the defendant before the court no more than 48 hours after provisional arrest under Part 1 of the Extradition Act 2003;

(b) following the expiry of a time limit for—

(i) service of a warrant to which Part 1 of the 2003 Act applies, after provisional arrest under that Part of the Act (48 hours, under section 6 of the Act, unless the court otherwise directs),

(ii) service of an extradition request to which Part 2 of the Act applies, after provisional arrest under that Part of the Act (45 days, under section 74 of the Act, unless the Secretary of State has otherwise ordered for this purpose),

(iii) receipt of an undertaking that the defendant will be returned to complete a sentence in the United Kingdom, where the court required such an undertaking (21 days, under section 37 of the Act),

(iv) making an extradition order, after the defendant has consented to extradition under Part 1 of the Act (10 days, under section 46 of the Act),

(v) extradition, where an extradition order has been made under Part 1 of the Act and any appeal by the defendant has failed (10 days, under sections 35, 36 and 47 of the Act, unless the court otherwise directs),

(vi) extradition, where an extradition order has been made under Part 2 of the Act and any appeal by the defendant has failed (28 days, under sections 117 and 118 of the Act),

(vii) the resumption of extradition proceedings, where those proceedings were adjourned pending disposal of another extradition claim which has concluded (21 days, under section 180 of the Act),

(viii) extradition, where extradition has been deferred pending the disposal of another extradition claim which has concluded (21 days, under section 181 of the Act), or

(ix) re-extradition, where the defendant has been returned to the United Kingdom to serve a sentence before serving a sentence overseas (as soon as practicable, under section 187 of the Act); or

(c) because an extradition hearing does not begin on the date arranged by the court.

(2) Unless the court otherwise directs—

(a) such a defendant must apply in writing and serve the application on—

(i) the court officer, and

(ii) the prosecutor;

(b) the application must explain the grounds on which it is made; and

(c) the court officer must arrange a hearing as soon as practicable, and in any event no later than the second business day after an application is served.

Section 3: appeal to the High Court

R-578 Exercise of the High Court's powers

50.17 (1) The general rule is that the High Court must exercise its powers at a hearing in public, but—

(a) that is subject to any power the court has to—

(i) impose reporting restrictions,

(ii) withhold information from the public, or

(iii) order a hearing in private;

(b) despite the general rule, the court may determine without a hearing—

(i) an application for permission to appeal to the High Court (but a renewed such application must be determined at a hearing),

(ii) an application for permission to appeal from the High Court to the Supreme Court,

(iii) an application for permission to reopen a decision under rule 50.27 (Reopening the determination of an appeal), or

(iv) an application concerning bail; and

(c) despite the general rule the court may, without a hearing—
(i) give case management directions, or
(ii) reject a notice or application and, if applicable, dismiss an application for permission to appeal, where rule 50.31 (Payment of High Court fees) applies and the party who served the notice or application fails to comply with that rule.

(2) If the High Court so directs, a party may attend a hearing by live link.

(3) The general rule is that where the High Court exercises its powers at a hearing it may do so only if the defendant attends, in person or by live link, but, despite the general rule, the court may exercise its powers in the defendant's absence if—
(a) the defendant waives the right to attend;
(b) subject to any appeal to the Supreme Court, the result of the court's order would be the discharge of the defendant; or
(c) the defendant is represented and—
(i) the defendant is in custody, or
(ii) the defendant's presence is impracticable by reason of his or her ill health or disorderly conduct.

(4) If the High Court gives permission to appeal to the High Court—
(a) unless the court otherwise directs, the decision indicates that the court gives the appellant permission to appeal on each ground identified by the appeal notice;
(b) unless the court otherwise directs, the decision indicates that the court finds reasonably arguable each ground on which the court gives permission to appeal; and
(c) the court must give such directions as are required for the preparation and hearing of the appeal, including a direction as to whether the appeal must be heard by a single judge of the High Court or by a divisional court.

(5) If the High Court decides without a hearing an application for permission to appeal from the High Court to the Supreme Court, the High Court must announce its decision at a hearing in public.

(6) The High Court may—
(a) shorten a time limit or extend it (even after it has expired), unless that is inconsistent with other legislation;
(b) allow or require a party to vary or supplement a notice that that party has served;
(c) direct that a notice or application be served on any person;
(d) allow a notice or application to be in a different form to one set out in the Practice Direction, or to be presented orally.

(7) A party who wants an extension of time within which to serve a notice or make an application must—
(a) apply for that extension of time when serving that notice or making that application; and
(b) give the reasons for the application for an extension of time.

Case management in the High Court R-579

50.18 (1) The High Court and the parties have the same duties and powers as under Part 3 (Case management), subject to paragraph (3).

(2) A master of the High Court, a deputy master, or a court officer nominated for the purpose by the Lord Chief Justice—
(a) must fulfil the duty of active case management under rule 3.2, and in fulfilling that duty may exercise any of the powers of case management under—
(i) rule 3.5 (the court's general powers of case management),
(ii) rule 3.10(3) (requiring a certificate of readiness), and
(iii) rule 3.11 (requiring a party to identify intentions and anticipated requirements)
subject to the directions of a judge of the High Court; and
(b) must nominate a case progression officer under rule 3.4.

(3) Rule 3.6 (Application to vary a direction) does not apply to a decision to give or to refuse—
(a) permission to appeal; or
(b) permission to reopen a decision under rule 50.27 (Reopening the determination of an appeal).

Service of appeal notice R-580

50.19 (1) A party who wants to appeal to the High Court must serve an appeal notice on—
(a) in every case—
(i) the High Court officer,
(ii) the other party, and

Criminal Procedure Rules 2015 and Criminal Practice Directions

(iii) the Director of Public Prosecutions, unless the Director already has the conduct of the proceedings;

(b) the designated authority which certified the arrest warrant, where Part 1 of the Extradition Act 2003 applies; and

(c) the Secretary of State, where the appeal is against—

(i) an order by the Secretary of State, or

(ii) an order by the magistrates' court sending a case to the Secretary of State.

(2) A defendant who wants to appeal must serve the appeal notice—

(a) not more than 7 days after the day on which the magistrates' court makes an order for the defendant's extradition, starting with that day, where that order is under Part 1 of the Extradition Act 2003;

(b) not more than 14 days after the day on which the Secretary of State informs the defendant of the Secretary of State's decision, starting with that day, where under Part 2 of the Act—

(i) the magistrates' court sends the case to the Secretary of State for a decision whether to extradite the defendant, or

(ii) the Secretary of State orders the defendant's extradition.

(3) An authority or territory seeking the defendant's extradition which wants to appeal against an order for the defendant's discharge must serve the appeal notice—

(a) not more than 7 days after the day on which the magistrates' court makes that order, starting with that day, if the order is under Part 1 of the Extradition Act 2003;

(b) not more than 14 days after the day on which the magistrates' court makes that order, starting with that day, if the order is under Part 2 of the Act;

(c) not more than 14 days after the day on which the Secretary of State informs the territory's representative of the Secretary of State's order, starting with that day, where the order is under Part 2 of the Act.

R-581 Form of appeal notice

50.20 (1) An appeal notice constitutes—

(a) an application to the High Court for permission to appeal to that court; and

(b) an appeal to that court, if the court gives permission.

(2) An appeal notice must be in writing.

(3) In every case, the appeal notice must—

(a) specify—

(i) the date of the defendant's arrest under Part 1 or Part 2 of the Extradition Act 2003, and

(ii) the decision about which the appellant wants to appeal, including the date of that decision;

(b) identify each ground of appeal on which the appellant relies;

(c) summarise the relevant facts;

(d) identify any document or other material that the appellant thinks the court will need to decide the appeal; and

(e) include or attach a list of those on whom the appellant has served the appeal notice.

(4) If a defendant serves an appeal notice after the expiry of the time limit specified in rule 50.19 (Service of appeal notice)—

(a) the notice must explain what the defendant did to ensure that it was served as soon as it could be; and

(b) where the appeal is on human rights grounds against an order for extradition made by the Secretary of State, the notice must explain why—

(i) the appeal is necessary to avoid real injustice, and

(ii) the circumstances are exceptional and make it appropriate to consider the appeal.

(5) Unless the High Court otherwise directs, the appellant may amend the appeal notice—

(a) by serving on those listed in rule 50.19(1) the appeal notice as so amended;

(b) not more than 10 business days after service of the appeal notice.

(6) Where the appeal is against an order by the magistrates' court—

(a) if the grounds of appeal are that the magistrates' court ought to have decided differently a question of fact or law at the extradition hearing, the appeal notice must—

(i) identify that question,

(ii) explain what decision the magistrates' court should have made, and why, and

(iii) explain why the magistrates' court would have been required not to make the order under appeal, if that question had been decided differently;

(b) if the grounds of appeal are that there is an issue which was not raised at the extradition hearing, or that evidence is available which was not available at the extradition hearing, the appeal notice must—
(i) identify that issue or evidence,
(ii) explain why it was not then raised or available,
(iii) explain why that issue or evidence would have resulted in the magistrates' court deciding a question differently at the extradition hearing, and
(iv) explain why, if the court had decided that question differently, the court would have been required not to make the order it made.

(7) Where the appeal is against an order by the Secretary of State—
(a) if the grounds of appeal are that the Secretary of State ought to have decided differently a question of fact or law, the appeal notice must—
(i) identify that question,
(ii) explain what decision the Secretary of State should have made, and why, and
(iii) explain why the Secretary of State would have been required not to make the order under appeal, if that question had been decided differently;
(b) if the grounds of appeal are that there is an issue which was not raised when the case was being considered by the Secretary of State, or that information is available which was not then available, the appeal notice must—
(i) identify that issue or information,
(ii) explain why it was not then raised or available,
(iii) explain why that issue or information would have resulted in the Secretary of State deciding a question differently, and
(iv) explain why, if the Secretary of State had decided that question differently, the order under appeal would not have been made.

Respondent's notice R-582

50.21 (1) A party on whom an appellant serves an appeal notice under rule 50.19 may serve a respondent's notice, and must do so if—
(a) that party wants to make representations to the High Court; or
(b) the court so directs.
(2) Such a party must serve any such notice on—
(a) the High Court officer;
(b) the appellant;
(c) the Director of Public Prosecutions, unless the Director already has the conduct of the proceedings; and
(d) any other person on whom the appellant served the appeal notice.
(3) Such a party must serve any such notice not more than 5 business days after service on that party of, as appropriate—
(a) the appeal notice;
(b) an appellant's notice renewing an application for permission to appeal;
(c) a direction to serve a respondent's notice.
(4) A respondent's notice must—
(a) give the date or dates on which the respondent was served with, as appropriate—
(i) the appeal notice,
(ii) the appellant's notice renewing the application for permission to appeal,
(iii) the direction to serve a respondent's notice;
(b) identify each ground of opposition on which the respondent relies and the ground of appeal to which each such ground of opposition relates;
(c) summarise any relevant facts not already summarised in the appeal notice; and
(d) identify any document or other material that the respondent thinks the court will need to decide the appeal.

Renewing an application for permission to appeal R-583

50.22 (1) This rule applies where the High Court—
(a) refuses permission to appeal to the High Court; or
(b) gives permission to appeal to the High Court, but not on every ground identified by the appeal notice.
(2) Unless the court makes that decision at a hearing, the appellant may renew the application by serving notice on—
(a) the High Court officer;

(b) the respondent; and
(c) any other person on whom the appellant served the appeal notice,
not more than 5 business days after service of notice of the court's decision on the appellant.
(3) Where the court refuses permission to appeal, the renewal notice must explain the grounds for the renewal.
(4) Where the court gives permission to appeal, but not on every ground identified by the appeal notice, the renewal notice must specify the excluded ground or grounds on which the appellant wants to rely and explain the grounds for the renewal.

R-584 **Appeal hearing**

50.23 (1) Unless the High Court otherwise directs, where the appeal to the High Court is under Part 1 of the Extradition Act 2003 the hearing of the appeal must begin no more than 40 days after the defendant's arrest.
(2) Unless the High Court otherwise directs, where the appeal to the High Court is under Part 2 of the 2003 Act the hearing of the appeal must begin no more than 76 days after the later of—
(a) service of the appeal notice; or
(b) the day on which the Secretary of State informs the defendant of the Secretary of State's order, in a case in which—
(i) the appeal is by the defendant against an order by the magistrates' court sending the case to the Secretary of State, and
(ii) the appeal notice is served before the Secretary of State decides whether the defendant should be extradited.
(3) If the effect of the decision of the High Court on the appeal is that the defendant is to be extradited—
(a) the High Court must consider any ancillary application, including an application about—
(i) bail pending extradition,
(ii) reporting restrictions,
(iii) costs;
(b) the High Court is the appropriate court to order a postponement of the defendant's extradition where—
(i) the defendant has been charged with an offence in the United Kingdom, or
(ii) the defendant has been sentenced to imprisonment or detention in the United Kingdom.
(4) If the effect of the decision of the High Court on the appeal is that the defendant is discharged, the High Court must consider any ancillary application, including an application about—
(a) reporting restrictions;
(b) costs.

R-585 **Discontinuing an appeal**

50.24 (1) This rule applies where—
(a) an appellant has served an appeal notice under rule 50.19;
(b) the High Court has given permission to appeal to the High Court; and
(c) the court has not determined the appeal.
(2) If the appellant wants to discontinue the appeal, the appellant must notify—
(a) the High Court officer;
(b) the respondent;
(c) the Director of Public Prosecutions, unless the Director already has the conduct of the proceedings; and
(d) any other person on whom the appellant served the appeal notice.
(3) The parties to the appeal must serve on the High Court officer—
(a) a joint notice consenting to the dismissal of the appeal; and
(b) a joint notice of any agreement between the parties about costs.
(4) Where a defendant who is on bail pending appeal discontinues that appeal—
(a) the defendant must surrender to custody as directed by the magistrates' court officer; and
(b) any conditions of bail apply until then.

R-586 **Application for permission to appeal to the Supreme Court**

50.25 (1) This rule applies where a party to an appeal to the High Court wants to appeal to the Supreme Court.
(2) Such a party must—
(a) apply orally to the High Court for permission to appeal immediately after the court's decision; or

(b) apply in writing and serve the application on the High Court officer and every other party not more than 14 days after that decision.

(3) Such a party must—

(a) identify the point of law of general public importance that the appellant wants the High Court to certify is involved in the decision;

(b) serve on the High Court officer a written statement of that point of law; and

(c) give reasons why—

(i) that point of law ought to be considered by the Supreme Court, and

(ii) the High Court ought to give permission to appeal.

(4) As well as complying with paragraph (3), a defendant's application for permission to appeal to the Supreme Court must include or attach any application for the following, with reasons—

(a) bail pending appeal;

(b) permission to attend any hearing in the Supreme Court, if the appellant is in custody.

Determination of detention pending appeal to the Supreme Court against discharge **R-587**

50.26 On an application for permission to appeal to the Supreme Court against a decision of the High Court which, but for that appeal, would have resulted in the defendant's discharge, the High Court must—

(a) decide whether to order the detention of the defendant; and

(b) determine any application for—

(i) bail pending appeal,

(ii) permission to attend any hearing in the Supreme Court,

(iii) a representation order.

Reopening the determination of an appeal **R-588**

50.27 (1) This rule applies where a party wants the High Court to reopen a decision of that court which determines an appeal or an application for permission to appeal.

(2) Such a party must—

(a) apply in writing for permission to reopen that decision, as soon as practicable after becoming aware of the grounds for doing so; and

(b) serve the application on the High Court officer and every other party.

(3) The application must—

(a) specify the decision which the applicant wants the court to reopen; and

(b) give reasons why—

(i) it is necessary for the court to reopen that decision in order to avoid real injustice,

(ii) the circumstances are exceptional and make it appropriate to reopen the decision, and

(iii) there is no alternative effective remedy.

(4) The court must not give permission to reopen a decision unless each other party has had an opportunity to make representations.

Declaration of incompatibility with a Convention right **R-589**

50.28 (1) This rule applies where a party—

(a) wants the High Court to make a declaration of incompatibility with a Convention right under section 4 of the Human Rights Act 1998; or

(b) raises an issue that appears to the High Court may lead to the court making such a declaration.

(2) If the High Court so directs, the High Court officer must serve notice on—

(a) the relevant person named in the list published under section 17(1) of the Crown Proceedings Act 1947; or

(b) the Treasury Solicitor, if it is not clear who is the relevant person.

(3) That notice must include or attach details of—

(a) the legislation affected and the Convention right concerned;

(b) the parties to the appeal; and

(c) any other information or document that the High Court thinks relevant.

(4) A person who has a right under the 1998 Act to become a party to the appeal must—

(a) serve notice on—

(i) the High Court officer, and

(ii) the other parties,

if that person wants to exercise that right; and

(b) in that notice—

(i) indicate the conclusion that that person invites the High Court to reach on the question of incompatibility, and

(ii) identify each ground for that invitation, concisely outlining the arguments in support.

(5) The High Court must not make a declaration of incompatibility—
(a) less than 21 days after the High Court officer serves notice under paragraph (2); and
(b) without giving any person who serves a notice under paragraph (4) an opportunity to make representations at a hearing.

R-590 **Duties of court officers**

50.29 (1) The magistrates' court officer must—
(a) keep any document or object exhibited in the proceedings in the magistrates' court, or arrange for it to be kept by some other appropriate person, until—
(i) 6 weeks after the conclusion of those proceedings, or
(ii) the conclusion of any proceedings in the High Court that begin within that 6 weeks;
(b) provide the High Court with any document, object or information for which the High Court officer asks, within such period as the High Court officer may require; and
(c) arrange for the magistrates' court to hear as soon as practicable any application to that court for bail pending appeal.

(2) A person who, under arrangements made by the magistrates' court officer, keeps a document or object exhibited in the proceedings in the magistrates' court must—
(a) keep that exhibit until—
(i) 6 weeks after the conclusion of those proceedings, or
(ii) the conclusion of any proceedings in the High Court that begin within that 6 weeks,
unless the magistrates' court or the High Court otherwise directs; and
(b) provide the High Court with any such document or object for which the High Court officer asks, within such period as the High Court officer may require.

(3) The High Court officer must—
(a) give as much notice as reasonably practicable of each hearing to—
(i) the parties,
(ii) the defendant's custodian, if any, and
(iii) any other person whom the High Court requires to be notified;
(b) serve a record of each order or direction of the High Court on—
(i) the parties,
(ii) any other person whom the High Court requires to be notified;
(c) if the High Court's decision determines an appeal or application for permission to appeal, serve a record of that decision on—
(i) the defendant's custodian, if any,
(ii) the magistrates' court officer, and
(iii) the designated authority which certified the arrest warrant, where Part 1 of the Extradition Act 2003 applies;
(d) where rule 50.24 applies (Discontinuing an appeal), arrange for the High Court to consider the parties' joint notice under that rule;
(e) treat the appeal as if it had been dismissed by the High Court where—
(i) the hearing of the appeal does not begin within the period required by rule 50.23 (Appeal hearing) or ordered by the High Court, or
(ii) on an appeal by a requesting territory under section 105 of the Extradition Act 2003, the High Court directs the magistrates' court to decide a question again and the magistrates' court comes to the same conclusion as it had done before.

R-591 **Constitution of the High Court**

50.30 (1) A master of the High Court, a deputy master, or a court officer nominated for the purpose by the Lord Chief Justice, may exercise any power of the High Court to which the rules in this Section apply, except the power to—
(a) give or refuse permission to appeal;
(b) determine an appeal;
(c) reopen a decision which determines an appeal or an application for permission to appeal;
(d) grant or withhold bail; or
(e) impose or vary a condition of bail.

(2) Despite paragraph (1), such a master, deputy master or court officer may exercise one of the powers listed in paragraph (1)(b), (d) or (e) if making a decision to which the parties have agreed in writing.

(3) A renewed application for permission to appeal to the High Court may be determined by—
(a) a single judge of the High Court other than the judge who first refused permission, or
(b) a divisional court.

(4) An appeal may be determined by—
(a) a single judge of the High Court; or
(b) a divisional court.

Payment of High Court fees R-592

50.31 (1) This rule applies where a party serves on the High Court officer a notice or application in respect of which a court fee is payable under legislation that requires the payment of such a fee.

(2) Such a party must pay the fee, or satisfy the conditions for any remission of the fee, when so serving the notice or application.

(3) If such a party fails to comply with paragraph (2), then unless the High Court otherwise directs—
(a) the High Court officer must serve on that party a notice requiring payment of the fee due, or satisfaction of the conditions for any remission of that fee, within a period specified in the notice;
(b) that party must comply with such a requirement; and
(c) until the expiry of the period specified in the notice, the High Court must not exercise its power—
(i) to reject the notice or application in respect of which the fee is payable, or
(ii) to dismiss an application for permission to appeal, in consequence of rejecting an appeal notice.

Criminal Practice Directions Part 50 Extradition

CPD XI Other Proceedings 50A: Extradition: General Matters and Management of the Appeal PD-88

General matters: expedition at all times

50A.1 Compliance with these directions is essential to ensure that extradition proceedings are dealt with expeditiously. Both in accordance with the spirit of the Council Framework Decision of 13 June 2002 on the European Arrest Warrant and surrender procedures between Member States and the United Kingdom's other treaty obligations. It is of the utmost importance that orders which provide directions for the proper management and progress of cases are obeyed so that the parties can fulfil their duty to assist the Court in furthering the overriding objective and in making efficient use of judicial resources.

General guidance under s. 2(7A) Extradition Act 2003 (as amended by the Anti-Social Behaviour, Crime and Policing Act 2014)

50A.2 When proceeding under section 21A of the Act and considering under subsection (3)(a) of the Act the seriousness of the conduct alleged to constitute the extradition offence, the judge will determine the issue on the facts of each case as set out in the warrant, subject to the guidance in paragraph 50A.3 below.

50A.3 In any case where the conduct alleged to constitute the offence falls into one of the categories in the table at paragraph 50A.5 below, unless there are exceptional circumstances, the judge should generally determine that extradition would be disproportionate. It would follow under the terms of s. 21A (4) (b) of the Act that the judge must order the person's discharge.

50A.4 The exceptional circumstances referred to above in paragraph 50A.3 will include:
i. Vulnerable victim
ii. Crime committed against someone because of their disability, gender-identity, race, religion or belief, or sexual orientation
iii. Significant premeditation
iv. Multiple counts
v. Extradition also sought for another offence
vi. Previous offending history

50A.5 The table is as follows:

Category of offence	Examples
Minor **theft** — (not robbery/ burglary or theft from the person)	Where the theft is of a low monetary value and there is a low impact on the victim or indirect harm to others, for example: (a) Theft of an item of food from a supermarket (b) Theft of a small amount of scrap metal from company premises (c) Theft of a very small sum of money
Minor financial offences (**forgery, fraud** and **tax** offences)	Where the sums involved are small and there is a low impact on the victim and / or low indirect harm to others, for example: (a) Failure to file a tax return or invoices on time (b) Making a false statement in a tax return (c) Dishonestly applying for a tax refund (d) Obtaining a bank loan using a forged or falsified document (e) Non-payment of child maintenance
Minor **road traffic, driving** and related offences	Where no injury, loss or damage was incurred to any person or property, for example: (a) Driving whilst using a mobile phone (b) Use of a bicycle whilst intoxicated
Minor **public order** offences	Where there is no suggestion the person started the trouble, and the offending behaviour was for example: (a) Non-threatening verbal abuse of a law enforcement officer or government official (b) Shouting or causing a disturbance, without threats (c) Quarrelling in the street, without threats
Minor **criminal damage**, (other than by fire)	For example, breaking a window
Possession of controlled substance (other than one with a high capacity for harm such as heroin, cocaine, LSD or crystal meth)	Where it was possession of a very small quantity and intended for personal use

PD-89 **CPD XI Other Proceedings 50B Management of the Appeal**

50B.1 Applications for permission to appeal to the High Court under the Extradition Act 2003 must be started in the Administrative Court of the Queen's Bench Division at the Royal Courts of Justice in London.

50.B.2 A Lord Justice of Appeal appointed by the Lord Chief Justice will have responsibility to assist the President of the Queen's Bench Division with overall supervision of extradition appeals.

Definitions

50B.3 Where appropriate 'appeal' includes 'application for permission to appeal'.

50B.4 'EAW' means European Arrest Warrant.

50B.5 A 'nominated legal officer of the court' is a court officer assigned to the Administrative Court Office who is a barrister or solicitor and who has been nominated for the purpose by the Lord Chief Justice under CrimPR 50.18 and 50.30.

Forms

50B.6 The forms are to be used in the High Court, in accordance with the CrimPR 50.19, 50.20, 50.21 and 50.22.

50B.7 The forms may be amended or withdrawn from time to time, or new forms added, under the authority of the Lord Chief Justice.

Management of the Appeal

50B.8 Where it is not possible for the High Court to begin to hear the appeal in accordance with time limits contained in Crim PR 50.23(1) and (2), the Court may extend the time limit if it believes it to be in the interests of justice to do so and may do so even after the time limit has expired.

50B.9 The power to extend those time limits may be exercised by a Lord Justice of Appeal, a Single Judge of the High Court, a Master of the Administrative Court or a nominated legal officer of the court.

50B.10 Case Management directions setting down a timetable may be imposed upon the parties by a Lord Justice of Appeal, a Single Judge of the High Court, a Master of the Administrative Court or a nominated legal officer of the court.

Listing of Oral, Renewal Hearings and Substantive Hearings

50B.11 Arrangements for the fixing of dates for hearings will be made by a Listing Officer of the Administrative Court under the direction of the Judge with overall responsibility for supervision of extradition appeals.

50B.12 A Lord Justice of Appeal, a Single Judge of the High Court, a Master of the Administrative Court or a nominated legal officer of the court may give such directions to the Listing Officer as they deem necessary with regard to the fixing of dates, including as to whether cases in the same/related proceedings or raising the same or similar issues should be heard together or consecutively under the duty imposed by Crim PR 1.1(2)(e). Parties must alert the nominated legal officer of the court for the need for such directions.

50B.13 Save in exceptional circumstances, regard will not be given to an advocate's existing commitments. This is in accordance with the spirit of the legislation that extradition matters should be dealt with expeditiously. Extradition matters are generally not so complex that an alternative advocate cannot be instructed.

50B.14 If a party disagrees with the time estimate given by the Court, they must inform the Listing Office within 5 business days of the notification of the listing and they must provide a time estimate of their own.

Expedited appeals

50B.15 The Court may direct that the hearing of an appeal be expedited.

50B.16 The Court will deal with requests for an expedited appeal without a hearing. Requests for expedition must be made in writing, either within the appeal notice, or by application notice, clearly marked with the Administrative Court reference number, which must be lodged with the Administrative Court Office or emailed to the appropriate email address: administrativecourtoffice.crimex@hmcts.x.gsi.gov.uk and notice must be given to the other parties.

50B.17 Any requests for an expedited appeal made to an out of hours Judge must be accompanied by:

i) A detailed chronology;
ii) Reasons why the application could not be made within Court hours;
iii) Any Orders or Judgments made in the proceedings

Amendment to Notices

50B.18 Amendment to Notice of Appeal requiring permission

(i) Subject to Crim PR 50.20(5), an appeal notice may not be amended without the permission of the Court.
(ii) An application for permission to amend made before permission to appeal has been considered will be determined without a hearing.
(iii) An application for permission to amend after permission to appeal has been granted and any submissions in opposition will normally be dealt with at the hearing unless there is any risk that the hearing may have to be adjourned. If there is any risk that the application to amend may lead the other party to seek time to answer the proposed amendment, the application must be made as soon as practicable and well in advance of the hearing. A failure to make immediate applications for such an amendment is likely to result in refusal.
(iv) Legal representatives or the appellant, if acting in person, must
  a. Inform the Court at the time they make the application if the existing time estimate is affected by the proposed amendment; and
  b. Attempt to agree any revised time estimate no later than 5 business days after service of the application.

50B.19 Amendment to Respondent's Notice

(i) A respondent's notice may not be amended without the permission of the Court.
(ii) An application for permission to amend made before permission to appeal has been considered will be determined without a hearing.
(iii) An application for permission to amend after permission to appeal has been granted and any submissions in opposition will normally be dealt with at the hearing unless there is any risk

that the hearing may have to be adjourned. If there is any risk that the application to amend may require the other party to seek time to answer the proposed amendment, the application must be made as soon as practicable and well in advance of the hearing. A failure to make immediate applications for such an amendment is likely to result in refusal.

(iv) Legal representatives or the appellant, if acting in person, must
  a. Inform the Court at the time they make the application if the existing time estimate is affected by the proposed amendment; and
  b. Attempt to agree any revised time estimate no later than 5 business days after service of the application.

Use of Live-Links

50B.20 When a party acting in person is in custody, the Court office will request the institution to use live-link for attendance at any oral or renewal hearing or substantive appeal. The institution must give precedence to all such applications in the High Court over live-links to the lower courts, including the Crown Court.

Interpreters

50B.21 It is the responsibility of the Court Listing Officer to ensure the attendance of an accredited interpreter when an unrepresented party in extradition proceedings is acting in person and does not understand or speak English.

50B.22 Where a party who does not understand or speak English is legally represented it is the responsibility of his/her solicitors to instruct an interpreter if required for any hearing in extradition proceedings.

Disposing of applications and appeals by way of consent

50B.23 Any consent order to dismiss pursuant to Crim PR 50.24(3) must be approved by a Lord Justice of Appeal or Single Judge of the High Court and be pronounced in open Court.

50B.24 A consent order to allow an appeal brought under s.28 of the Extradition Act 2003 must provide—

(i) for the quashing of the decision of the District Judge in Westminster Magistrates' Court discharging the Requested Person;
(ii) for the matter to be remitted to the District Judge to hold fresh extradition proceedings;
(iii) the consent order may be approved by the Lord Justice of Appeal, Single Judge of the High Court or a Master of the High Court. The order once approved will be sent to the parties.

50B.25 A consent order to allow an appeal brought under s.110 of the Extradition Act 2003 must provide—

(i) for the quashing of the decision of the Secretary of State for the Home Department not to order extradition;
(ii) for the matter to be remitted to the Secretary of State to make a fresh decision on whether or not to order extradition;
(iii) the consent order may be approved by the Lord Justice of Appeal, Single Judge of the High Court or a Master of the High Court. The order once approved will be sent to the parties.

50B.26 Where one of the parties is a child or protected party, any disposal of an application or appeal requires the Court's approval. A draft order signed by the party's solicitors should be sent to the Court, together with an opinion from the advocate acting on behalf of the child or protected party and, in the case of a protected party, any relevant documents prepared for the Court of Protection.

Fees

50B.27 Applications to extend representation orders do not attract any fee.

50B.28 Fees are payable for all other applications in accordance with the current Fees Order SI/2014/874.

PD-90 **CPD XI Other Proceedings 50C: Extradition: Representation Orders**

50C.1 Representation orders may be granted by a Lord Justice of Appeal, a Single Judge of the High Court, a Master of the Administrative Court or a nominated legal officer of the court upon a properly completed CRM14 being lodged with the Court. A representation order will cover junior advocate and solicitors for the preparation of the Notice of Appeal to determination of the appeal.

50C.2 Applications to extend representation orders may be granted by a Lord Justice of Appeal, a Single Judge of the High Court, a Master of the Administrative Court or a nominated Court Officer who may direct a case management hearing before a Lord Justice of Appeal, a Single Judge, or a

Master. Since these applications do not attract a fee, parties may lodge them with the Court by attaching them to an email addressed to the nominated legal officer of the court.

50C.3 Applications to extend representation orders to cover the instruction of Queen's Counsel to appear either alone or with junior advocate must be made in writing, either by letter or application notice, clearly marked with the Administrative Court reference number, which must be lodged with the Administrative Court Office or emailed to the appropriate email address: administrativecourtoffice.crimex@hmcts.x.gsi.gov.uk.

The request must:

(i) identify the substantial novel or complex issues of law or fact in the case;
(ii) explain why these may only be adequately presented by a Queen's Counsel;
(iii) state whether a Queen's Counsel has been instructed on behalf of the respondent;
(iv) explain any delay in making the request;
(v) be supported by advice from junior advocate or Queen's Counsel.

50C.4 Applications for prior authority to cover the cost of obtaining expert evidence must be made in writing, either by letter, clearly marked with the Administrative Court reference number, which must be sent or emailed to the Administrative Court Office.

The request must:

(i) confirm that the evidence sought has not been considered in any previous appeals determined by the appellate courts;
(ii) explain why the evidence was not called at the extradition hearing in Westminster Magistrates' Court and what evidence can be produced to support that;
(iii) explain why the new evidence would have resulted in the District Judge deciding a question at the extradition hearing differently and whether, if so, the District Judge would have been required to make a different order as to discharge of the requested person;
(iv) explain why the evidence was not raised when the case was being considered by the Secretary of State for the Home Department or information was available that was not available at that time;
(v) explain why the new evidence would have resulted in the Secretary of State deciding a question differently, and if the question had been decided differently, the Secretary of State would not have ordered the person's extradition;
(vi) state when the need for the new evidence first became known;
(vii) explain any delay in making the request;
(viii) explain what relevant factual, as opposed to expert evidence, is being given by whom to create the factual basis for the expert's opinion;
(ix) explain why this particular area of expertise is relevant: for example why a child psychologist should be appointed as opposed to a social worker;
(x) state whether the requested person has capacity;
(xi) set out a full breakdown of all costs involved including any VAT or other tax payable, including alternative quotes or explaining why none are available;
(xii) provide a list of all previous extensions of the representation order and the approval of expenditure to date;
(xiii) provide a timetable for the production of the evidence and its anticipated effect on the time estimate and hearing date;
(xiv) set out the level of compliance to date with any directions order.

50C.5 Experts must have direct personal experience of and proven expertise in the issue on which a report is sought; it is only if they do have such experience and it is relevant, that they can give evidence of what they have observed.

50C.6 Where an order is granted to extend a representation order to obtain further evidence it will still be necessary for the party seeking to rely on the new evidence to satisfy the Court hearing the application for permission or the substantive appeal that the evidence obtained should be admitted having regard to sections 27(4) and 29(4) of the Extradition Act 2003 and the judgment in *Szombathely City Court v Fenyvesi* [2009] EWHC 231 (Admin).

50C.7 Applications to extend representation for the translation of documents must be made in writing, either by letter, clearly marked with the Administrative Court reference number, which must be sent or emailed to the appropriate email address: administrativecourtoffice.crimex@hmcts.x.gsi.gov.uk

The request should:

(i) explain the importance of the document for which a translation is being sought and the justification for obtaining it;

(ii) explain what it is believed the contents of the document is and the issues it will assist the court to address in hearing the appeal;
(iii) confirm that the evidence sought has not been considered in any previous appeals determined by the appellate courts;
(iv) confirm that the evidence sought was not called at the extradition hearing in the Westminster Magistrates' Court;
(v) explain why the evidence sought would have resulted in the District Judge deciding a question at the extradition hearing differently and whether, if so, the District Judge would have been required to make a different order as to discharge of the requested person;
(vi) confirm that the new evidence was not raised when the case was being considered by the Secretary of State for the Home Department;
(vii) explain why the new evidence sought would have resulted in the Secretary of State deciding a question differently, and if the question had been decided differently, the Secretary of State would not have ordered the person's extradition;
(viii) confirm when the need for the new evidence first became known;
(ix) explain any delay in making the request;
(x) explain fully the evidential basis for incurring the expenditure;
(xi) explain why the appellant cannot produce the evidence himself or herself in the form of a statement of truth;
(xii) set out a full breakdown of all costs involved including any VAT or other tax payable and the Legal Aid Agency contractual rates;
(xiii) provide a list of all previous extensions of the representation order and the expenditure to date.

50C.8 Where an order is made to extend representation to cover the cost of the translation of documents it will still be necessary for the party seeking to rely on the documents as evidence to satisfy the Court that it should be admitted at the hearing of the appeal having regard to sections 27(4) and 29(4) of the Extradition Act 2003 and the judgment in *Szombathely City Court v Fenyvesi* [2009] EWHC 231 (Admin).

PD-91 CPD XI Other Proceedings 50D: Extradition: Applications

Extension or abridgement of time

50D.1

(i) Any party who seeks extension or abridgment of time for the service of documents, evidence or skeleton arguments must apply to the High Court on the appropriate form and pay the appropriate fee.
(ii) Applications for extension or abridgment of time may be determined by a Lord Justice of Appeal, a Single Judge of the High Court, a Master of the Administrative Court or a nominated legal officer of the court.
(iii) Applications for extension of time must include a witness statement setting out the reasons for non-compliance with any previous order and the proposed timetable for compliance.
(iv) Any application made to an out of hours Judge must be accompanied with:
   a. A detailed chronology;
   b. Reasons why the application could not be made within Court hours;
   c. Any Orders or Judgments made in the proceedings

Application to come off record

50D.2 Any solicitor seeking to come off record as acting for a party must apply to the High Court on the appropriate form and pay the appropriate fee at least 7 business days before the hearing of the appeal. Applications may be determined by a Lord Justice of Appeal, a Single Judge of the High Court, a Master of the Administrative Court or a nominated legal officer of the court.

50D.3 The application must be supported by a statement of truth —

(i) providing proper and sufficient reasons why the solicitor wishes to come off record;
(ii) confirming that the solicitor has complied with Orders made by the High Court before the application to come off record was made or an explanation as to why there has been non-compliance;
(iii) confirming that where, the Requested Person is on bail, that person has been advised of the time and date of the appeal hearing and the need to attend in person;
(iv) confirming where the Requested Person is in custody, the institution in which he/she is being held, the person's prison number and date of birth.

Application to adjourn

50D.4 Where a hearing date has been fixed, any application to vacate the hearing must be made on the appropriate form. A fee is required for the application if it is made within 14 days of the hearing date. The application must:

(i) explain the reasons why an application is being made to vacate the hearing;
(ii) detail the views of the other parties to the appeal;
(iii) include a draft order with the application notice.

50D.5 If the parties both seek an adjournment then the application must be submitted for consideration by a Lord Justice of Appeal, a single Judge of the High Court or a Master of the Administrative Court. Exceptional circumstances must be shown if a date for the hearing has been fixed or the adjournment will result in material delay to the determination of the appeal.

50D.6 An application to adjourn following a compromise agreement must be supported by evidence justifying exceptional circumstances and why it is in compliance with the overriding objective.

Variation of directions

50D.7 Where parties are unable to comply with any order of the Court they must apply promptly to vary directions before deadlines for compliance have expired and seek further directions. An application to vary directions attracts a fee and the application notice [on the appropriate form] must:

(i) provide full and proper explanations for why the current and existing directions have not been complied with;
(ii) detail the views of the other parties to the appeal;
(iii) include a draft order setting out in full the timetable and directions as varied i.e. a superseding order which stands alone.

50D.8 A failure to make the application prior to the expiry of the date specified in the Order will generally result in the refusal of the application unless good reasons are shown.

Application to certify a point of law of general public importance

50D.9 Where an application is made under Crim PR 50.25(2)(b) the application must be made on the appropriate form accompanied by the relevant fee.

50D.10 Any response to the application must be made within 10 business days.

50D.11 Where an application to certify is granted but permission to appeal to the Supreme Court is refused, it shall be for those representing the Requested Person to apply for an extension of the Representation Order to cover proceedings in the Supreme Court, if so advised.

50D.12 The representation order may be extended by a Lord Justice of Appeal, a Single Judge of the High Court, a Master of the Administrative Court or a nominated legal officer of the court.

50D.13 The result of the application to certify a point of law of general public importance and permission to appeal to the Supreme Court may be notified in advance to the legal representatives but legal representatives must not communicate it to the Requested Person until 1 hour before the pronouncement is made in open court.

50D.14 There shall be no public announcement of the result until after it has been formally pronounced.

Application to reopen the determination of an appeal

50D.15 An application under Crim PR 50.27 to reopen an appeal must be referred to the court that determined the appeal, but may if circumstances require be considered by a Judge or Judges other than those who determined the original appeal.

Application to extend required period for removal pursuant to section 36 of the Extradition Act 2003

50D.16 Where an application is made for an extension of the required period within which to extradite a Requested Person it must be accompanied by:

(i) a witness statement explaining why it is not possible to remove the Requested Person within the required period and the proposed timetable for removal;
(ii) a draft order.

50D.17 The application to extend time may only be made within an extant required period for removal.

50D.18 Where extensions of time are sought for the same reason in respect of a number of Requested Persons who are due to be extradited at the same time, a single application may be made to the Court listing each of the Requested Persons for whom an extension is sought.

50D.19 The application may be determined by a Lord Justice of Appeal, a Single Judge of the High Court, a Master of the Administrative Court or a legal officer of the court and a single order listing those persons may be granted.

Application for a discharge pursuant to section 42 of the Extradition Act 2003

50D.20 Where an application notice is issued seeking the discharge of a Requested Person it must be accompanied by

(i) the notification by the requesting state that the EAW has been withdrawn together with a translation of the same;

(ii) a witness statement containing:

a. details of whether the withdrawn EAW is the only EAW outstanding in respect of the Requested Person

b. details of other EAWs outstanding in respect of the Requested Person and the stage which the proceedings have reached

c. whether only part of the EAW has been withdrawn

d. details of any bail conditions

e. details of any institution in which the Requested Person is being detained, the Requested Person's prison number and date of birth.

50D.21 The decision to discharge may be made by a Lord Justice of Appeal, a Single Judge of the High Court, a Master of the Administrative Court or a nominated legal officer of the court.

50D.22 It is the responsibility of the High Court to serve the approved order on the appropriate institution and Westminster Magistrates' Court.

PD-92 **CPD XI Other Proceedings 50E: Extradition: Court Papers**

Skeleton arguments

50E.1 The Court on granting permission to appeal or directing an oral hearing for permission to appeal will give directions as to the filing of skeleton arguments. Strict compliance is required with all time limits.

50E.2 A skeleton argument must:

(a) not normally exceed 25 pages (excluding front sheets and back sheets) and be concise;

(b) be printed on A4 paper in not less than 12 point font and 1.5 line spacing;

(c) define the issues in the appeal;

(d) be set out in numbered paragraphs;

(e) be cross-referenced to any relevant document in the bundle;

(f) be self-contained and not incorporate by reference material from previous skeleton arguments;

(g) not include extensive quotations from documents or authorities.

50E.3 Where it is necessary to refer to an authority, the skeleton argument must

(a) state the proposition of law the authority demonstrates; and

(b) identify but not quote the parts of the authority that support the proposition.

50E.4 If more than one authority is cited in support of a given proposition, the skeleton argument must briefly state why.

50E.5 A chronology of relevant events will be necessary in most appeals.

50E.6 Where a skeleton argument has been prepared in respect of an application for permission to appeal, the same skeleton argument may be relied upon in the appeal upon notice being given to the Court or a replacement skeleton may be lodged not less than 10 business days before the hearing of the appeal.

50E.7 At the hearing the Court may refuse to hear argument on a point not included in a skeleton argument filed within the prescribed time.

Bundles

50E.8 The bundle for the hearing should be agreed by the parties save where the Requested Person is acting in person. In those circumstances the Court expects the Requesting State to prepare the bundle.

50E.9 The bundle must be paginated and indexed.

50E.10 Subject to any order made by the Court, the following documents must be included in the appeal bundle:

(a) a copy of the appellant's notice;

(b) a copy of any respondent's notice;

(c) a copy of any appellant's or respondent's skeleton argument;

(d) a copy of the order under appeal;
(e) a copy of any order made by the Court in the exercise of its case management powers;
(f) any judgment of the Court made in a previous appeal involving the party or parties which is relevant to the present proceedings.
(g) where the bundle of papers reaches more than 200 pages, the parties should agree a core appeal bundle which must contain (a)-(f) above.

50E.11 The Bundle should only contain relevant documents and must not include duplicate documents.

50E.12 Bundles lodged with the Court will not be returned to the parties but will be destroyed in the confidential waste system at the conclusion of the proceedings and without further notification.

CPD XI Other Proceedings 50F: Extradition: Consequences of Non Compliance with Directions PD-93

50F.1 Failure to comply with these directions will lead to applications for permission and appeals being dealt with on the material available to the Court at the time when the decision is made.

50F.2 Judges dealing with extradition appeals will seek full and proper explanations for any breaches of the rules and the provisions of this Practice Direction.

50F.3 If no good explanation can be given immediately by counsel or solicitors, the senior partner or the departmental head responsible is likely to be called to court to explain any failure to comply with a court order. Where counsel or solicitors fail to obey orders of the Court and are unable to provide proper and sufficient reasons for their disobedience they may anticipate the matter being formally referred to the President of the Queen's Bench Division with a recommendation that the counsel or solicitors involved be reported to their professional bodies.

50F.4 The court may also refuse to admit any material or any evidence not filed in compliance with the order for Directions or outside a time limit specified by the court.

50F.5 A failure to comply with the time limits or other requirements for skeleton arguments will have the consequences specified in 50E.7.

Criminal Practice Directions: General Application

CPD XII General Application A: Court Dress PD-94

A.1 In magistrates' courts, advocates appear without robes or wigs. In all other courts, Queen's Counsel wear a short wig and a silk (or stuff) gown over a court coat with bands, junior counsel wear a short wig and stuff gown with bands. Solicitors and other advocates authorised under the Courts and Legal Services Act 1990 wear a black solicitor's gown with bands; they may wear short wigs in circumstances where they would be worn by Queen's Counsel or junior counsel.

A.2 High Court Judges hearing criminal cases may wear the winter criminal robe year-round. However, scarlet summer robes may be worn.

CPD XII General Application B: Modes of Address and Titles of Judges and Magistrates PD-95

Modes of Address

B.1 The following judges, when sitting in court, should be addressed as 'My Lord' or 'My Lady', as the case may be, whatever their personal status:
(a) Judges of the Court of Appeal and of the High Court;
(b) any Circuit Judge sitting as a judge of the Court of Appeal (Criminal Division) or the High Court under section 9(1) of the Senior Courts Act 1981;
(c) any judge sitting at the Central Criminal Court;
(d) any Senior Circuit Judge who is an Honorary Recorder.

B.2 Subject to the paragraph above, Circuit Judges, qualifying judge advocates, Recorders and Deputy Circuit Judges should be addressed as 'Your Honour' when sitting in court.

District Judges (Magistrates' Courts) should be addressed as 'Sir [or Madam]' or 'Judge' when sitting in Court.

Magistrates in court should be addressed through the Chairperson as 'Sir[or Madam]' or collectively as 'Your Worships'.

Description

B.3 In cause lists, forms and orders members of the judiciary should be described as follows:
(a) Circuit Judges, as 'His [or Her] Honour Judge A'.
When the judge is sitting as a judge of the High Court under section 9(1) of the Senior Courts Act 1981, the words 'sitting as a judge of the High Court' should be added;

(b) Recorders, as 'Mr [or Mrs, Ms or Miss] Recorder B'.
This style is appropriate irrespective of any honour or title which the recorder might possess, but if in any case it is desired to include an honour or title, the alternative description, 'Sir CD, Recorder' or 'The Lord D, Recorder' may be used;
(c) Deputy Circuit Judges, as 'His [or Her] Honour EF, sitting as a Deputy Circuit Judge';
(d) qualifying judges advocates, as 'His [or Her] Honour GH, sitting as a qualifying judge advocate.';
(e) District Judges (Magistrates' Courts), as 'District Judge (Magistrates' Courts) J'.

PD-96 **CPD XII General application C: Availability of Judgments given in the Court of Appeal and the High Court**

C.1 For cases in the High Court, reference should be made to Practice Direction 40E, the supplementary Practice Direction to the Civil Procedure Rules Part 40.

C.2 For cases in the Court of Appeal (Criminal Division), the following provisions apply.

Availability of reserved judgments before handing down, corrections and applications consequential on judgment

C.3 Where judgment is to be reserved the Presiding Judge may, at the conclusion of the hearing, invite the views of the parties' legal representatives as to the arrangements to be made for the handing down of the judgment.

C.4 Unless the court directs otherwise, the following provisions apply where the Presiding Judge is satisfied that the judgment will attract no special degree of confidentiality or sensitivity.

C.5 The court will provide a copy of the draft judgment to the parties' legal representatives about three working days before handing down, or at such other time as the court may direct. Every page of every judgment which is made available in this way will be marked 'Unapproved judgment: No permission is granted to copy or use in court.' The draft is supplied in confidence and on the conditions that:
(a) neither the draft judgment nor its substance will be disclosed to any other person or used in the public domain; and
(b) no action will be taken (other than internally) in response to the draft judgment, before the judgment is handed down.

C.6 Unless the parties' legal representatives are told otherwise when the draft judgment is circulated, any proposed corrections to the draft judgment should be sent to the clerk of the judge who prepared the draft (or to the associate, if the judge has no clerk) with a copy to any other party's legal representatives, by 12 noon on the day before judgment is handed down.

C.7 If, having considered the draft judgment, the prosecution will be applying to the Court for a retrial or either party wishes to make any other application consequent on the judgment, the judge's clerk should be informed with a time estimate for the application by 12 noon on the day before judgment is handed down. This will enable the court to make appropriate listing arrangements and notify advocates to attend if the court so requires. There is no fee payable to advocates who attend the hand down hearing if not required to do so by the court. If either party is considering applying to the Court to certify a point for appeal to the Supreme Court, it would assist if the judge's clerk could be informed at the same time, although this is not obligatory as under section 34 of the Criminal Appeal Act 1968, the time limit for such applications is 28 days.

Communication to the parties including the defendant or the victim

C.8 The contents are not to be communicated to the parties, including to the defendant, respondent or the victim (defined as a person entitled to receive services under the Code of Practice for Victims of Crime) until two hours before the listed time for pronouncement of judgment.

C.9 Judges may permit more information about the result of a case to be communicated on a confidential basis to the parties including to the defendant, respondent or the victim at an earlier stage if good reason is shown for making such a direction.

C.10 If, for any reason, the parties' legal representatives have special grounds for seeking a relaxation of the usual condition restricting disclosure to the parties, a request for relaxation of the condition may be made informally through the judge's clerk (or through the associate, if the judge has no clerk).

C.11 If the parties or their legal representatives are in any doubt about the persons to whom copies of the draft judgment may be distributed they should enquire of the judge or Presiding Judge.

C.12 Any breach of the obligations or restrictions in this section or failure to take reasonable steps to ensure compliance may be treated as contempt of court.

Restrictions on disclosure or reporting

C.13 Anyone who is supplied with a copy of the handed-down judgment, or who reads it in court, will be bound by any direction which the court may have given in a child case under section 39 of the Children and Young Persons Act 1933 or section 45 or 45A of the Youth Justice and Criminal Evidence Act 1999, or any other form of restriction on disclosure, or reporting, of information in the judgment.

C.14 Copies of the approved judgment can be ordered from the official shorthand writers, on payment of the appropriate fee. Judgments identified as of legal or public interest will generally be made available on the website managed by BAILLI: http://www.bailii.org/

CPD XII General Application D: Citation of Authority and Provision of Copies of Judgments to the Court **PD-97**

D.1 This Practice Direction applies to all criminal matters before the Court of Appeal (Criminal Division), the Crown Court and the magistrates' courts. In relation to those matters only, Practice Direction (Citation of Authorities) [2012] 1 WLR 780 is hereby revoked.

Citation of authority

D.2 In *R v Erskine; R v Williams* [2009] EWCA Crim 1425, [2010] 1 WLR 183, (2009) 2 Cr App R 29 the Lord Chief Justice stated:

75. The essential starting point, relevant to any appeal against conviction or sentence, is that, adapting the well known aphorism of Viscount Falkland in 1641: if it is not necessary to refer to a previous decision of the court, it is necessary not to refer to it. Similarly, if it is not necessary to include a previous decision in the bundle of authorities, it is necessary to exclude it. That approach will be rigidly enforced.

76. It follows that when the advocate is considering what authority, if any, to cite for a proposition, only an authority which establishes the principle should be cited. Reference should not be made to authorities which do no more than either (a) illustrate the principle or (b) restate it.

78. Advocates must expect to be required to justify the citation of each authority relied on or included in the bundle. The court is most unlikely to be prepared to look at an authority which does no more than illustrate or restate an established proposition.

80. . . .In particular, in sentencing appeals, where a definitive Sentencing Guidelines Council guideline is available there will rarely be any advantage in citing an authority reached before the issue of the guideline, and authorities after its issue which do not refer to it will rarely be of assistance. In any event, where the authority does no more than uphold a sentence imposed at the Crown Court, the advocate must be ready to explain how it can assist the court to decide that a sentence is manifestly excessive or wrong in principle.

D.3 Advocates should only cite cases when it is necessary to do so; when the case identifies or represents a principle or the development of a principle. In sentencing appeals, other cases are rarely helpful, providing only an illustration, and this is especially true if there is a sentencing guideline. Unreported cases should only be cited in exceptional circumstances, and the advocate must expect to explain why such a case has been cited.

D.4 Advocates should not assume that because a case cited to the court is not referred to in the judgment the court has not considered it; it is more likely that the court was not assisted by it.

D.5 When an authority is to be cited, whether in written or oral submissions, the advocate should always provide the neutral citation followed by the law report reference.

D.6 The following practice should be followed:

i) Where a judgment is reported in the Official Law Reports (A.C., Q.B., Ch., Fam.) published by the Incorporated Council of Law Reporting for England and Wales or the Criminal Appeal Reports or the Criminal Appeal Reports (Sentencing) one of those two series of reports must be cited; either is equally acceptable. However, where a judgment is reported in the Criminal Appeal Reports or the Criminal Appeal Reports (Sentencing) that reference must be given in addition to any other reference. Other series of reports and official transcripts of judgment may only be used when a case is not reported, or not yet reported, in the Official Law Reports or the Criminal Appeal Reports or the Criminal Appeal Reports (Sentencing).

ii) If a judgment is not reported in the Official Law Reports, the Criminal Appeal Reports or the Criminal Appeal Reports (Sentencing), but it is reported in an authoritative series of reports which contains a headnote and is made by individuals holding a Senior Courts qualification (for the purposes of section 115 of the Courts and Legal Services Act 1990), that report should be cited.

iii) Where a judgment is not reported in any of the reports referred to above, but is reported in other reports, they may be cited.

iv) Where a judgment has not been reported, reference may be made to the official transcript if that is available, not the handed-down text of the judgment, as this may have been subject to late revision after the text was handed down. Official transcripts may be obtained from, for instance, BAILLI (http://www.bailii.org/).

D.7 In the majority of cases, it is expected that all references will be to the Official Law Reports and the Criminal Appeal Reports or the Criminal Appeal Reports (Sentencing); it will be rare for there to be a need to refer to any other reports. An unreported case should not be cited unless it contains a relevant statement of legal principle not found in reported authority, and it is expected that this will only occur in exceptional circumstances.

Provision of copies of judgments to the Court

D.8 The paragraphs below specify whether or not copies should be provided to the court. Authorities should not be included for propositions not in dispute. If more than one authority is to be provided, the copies should be presented in paginated and tagged bundles.

D.9 If required, copies of judgments should be provided either by way of a photocopy of the published report or by way of a copy of a reproduction of the judgment in electronic form that has been authorised by the publisher of the relevant series, but in any event:

i) the report must be presented to the court in an easily legible form (a 12-point font is preferred but a 10 or 11-point font is acceptable); and

ii) the advocate presenting the report must be satisfied that it has not been reproduced in a garbled form from the data source.

In any case of doubt the court will rely on the printed text of the report (unless the editor of the report has certified that an electronic version is more accurate because it corrects an error contained in an earlier printed text of the report).

D.10 If such a copy is unavailable, a printed transcript such as from BAILLI may be included.

Provision of copies to the Court of Appeal (Criminal Division)

D.11 Advocates must provide to the Registrar of Criminal Appeals, with their appeal notice, respondent's notice or skeleton argument, a list of authorities upon which they wish to rely in their written or oral submissions. The list of authorities should contain the name of the applicant, appellant or respondent and the Criminal Appeal Office number where known. The list should include reference to the relevant paragraph numbers in each authority. An updated list can be provided if a new authority is issued, or in response to a respondent's notice or skeleton argument. From time to time, the Registrar may issue guidance as to the style or content of lists of authorities, including a suggested format; this guidance should be followed by all parties. The latest guidance is available from the Criminal Appeal Office.

D.12 If the case cited is reported in the Official Law Reports, the Criminal Appeal Reports or the Criminal Appeal Reports (Sentencing), the law report reference must be given after the neutral citation, and the relevant paragraphs listed, but copies should not be provided to the court.

D.13 If, exceptionally, reference is made to a case that is not reported in the Official Law Reports, the Criminal Appeal Reports or the Criminal Appeal Reports (Sentencing), three copies must be provided to the Registrar with the list of authorities and the relevant appeal notice or respondent's notice (or skeleton argument, if provided). The relevant passages of the authorities should be marked or sidelined.

Provision of copies to the Crown Court and the magistrates' courts

D.14 When the court is considering routine applications, it may be sufficient for the court to be referred to the applicable legislation or to one of the practitioner texts. However, it is the responsibility of the advocate to ensure that the court is provided with the material that it needs properly to consider any matter.

D.15 If it would assist the court to consider any authority, the directions at paragraphs D.2 to D.7 above relating to citation will apply and a list of authorities should be provided.

D.16 Copies should be provided by the party seeking to rely upon the authority in accordance with CrimPR 24.13. This Rule is applicable in the magistrates' courts, and in relation to the provision of authorities, should also be followed in the Crown Court since courts often do not hold library stock (see CrimPR 25.17). Advocates should comply with paragraphs D.8 to D.10 relating to the provision of copies to the court.

CPD XII General application E: Preparation of Judgments: Neutral Citation PD-98

E.1 Since 11 January 2001 every judgment of the Court of Appeal, and of the Administrative Court, and since 14 January 2002 every judgment of the High Court, has been prepared and issued as approved with single spacing, paragraph numbering (in the margins) and no page numbers. In courts with more than one judge, the paragraph numbering continues sequentially through each judgment and does not start again at the beginning of each judgment. Indented paragraphs are not numbered. A unique reference number is given to each judgment. For judgments of the Court of Appeal, this number is given by the official shorthand writers, Merrill Legal Solutions (Tel: 020 7421 4000 ext.4036). For judgments of the High Court, it is provided by the Courts Recording and Transcription Unit at the Royal Courts of Justice. Such a number will also be furnished, on request to the Courts Recording and Transcription Unit, Royal Courts of Justice, Strand, London WC2A 2LL (Tel: 020 7947 7820), (e-mail: rcj.cratu@hmcts.gsi.gov.uk) for High Court judgments delivered outside London.

E.2 Each Court of Appeal judgment starts with the year, followed by EW (for England and Wales), then CA (for Court of Appeal), followed by Civ or Crim and finally the sequential number. For example, '*Smith v Jones* [2001] EWCA Civ 10'.

E.3 In the High Court, represented by HC, the number comes before the divisional abbreviation and, unlike Court of Appeal judgments, the latter is bracketed: (Ch), (Pat), (QB), (Admin), (Comm), (Admlty), (TCC) or (Fam), as appropriate. For example, '[2002] EWHC 123 (Fam)', or '[2002] EWHC 124 (QB)', or '[2002] EWHC 125 (Ch)'.

E.4 This 'neutral citation', as it is called, is the official number attributed to the judgment and must always be used at least once when the judgment is cited in a later judgment. Once the judgment is reported, this neutral citation appears in front of the familiar citation from the law reports series. Thus: '*Smith v Jones* [2001] EWCA Civ 10; [2001] QB 124; [2001] 2 All ER 364', etc.

E.5 Paragraph numbers are referred to in square brackets. When citing a paragraph from a High Court judgment, it is unnecessary to include the descriptive word in brackets: (Admin), (QB), or whatever. When citing a paragraph from a Court of Appeal judgment, however, 'Civ' or 'Crim' is included. If it is desired to cite more than one paragraph of a judgment, each numbered paragraph should be enclosed with a square bracket. Thus paragraph 59 in *Green v White* [2002] EWHC 124 (QB) would be cited: '*Green v White* [2002] EWHC 124 at [59]'; paragraphs 30 — 35 in *Smith v Jones* would be '*Smith v Jones* [2001] EWCA Civ 10 at [30] — [35]'; similarly, where a number of paragraphs are cited: '*Smith v Jones* [2001] EWCA Civ 10 at [30], [35] and [40 — 43]'.

E.6 If a judgment is cited more than once in a later judgment, it is helpful if only one abbreviation is used, e.g., '*Smith v Jones*' or 'Smith's case', but preferably not both (in the same judgment).

CPD XII General application F: Citation of Hansard PD-99

F.1 Where any party intends to refer to the reports of Parliamentary proceedings as reported in the Official Reports of either House of Parliament ('Hansard') in support of any such argument as is permitted by the decisions in *Pepper v Hart* [1993] AC 593 and *Pickstone v Freemans PLC* [1989] AC 66, or otherwise, he must, unless the court otherwise directs, serve upon all other parties and the court copies of any such extract, together with a brief summary of the argument intended to be based upon such extract. No other report of Parliamentary proceedings may be cited.

F.2 Unless the court otherwise directs, service of the extract and summary of the argument shall be effected not less than 5 clear working days before the first day of the hearing, whether or not it has a fixed date. Advocates must keep themselves informed as to the state of the lists where no fixed date has been given. Service on the court shall be effected by sending three copies to the Registrar of Criminal Appeals, Royal Courts of Justice, Strand, London, WC2A 2LL or to the court manager of the relevant Crown Court centre, as appropriate. If any party fails to do so, the court may make such order (relating to costs or otherwise) as is, in all the circumstances, appropriate.

Criminal Practice Directions Listing

CPD XIII Listing A: Judicial Responsibility for Listing and Key Principles PD-100

Listing as a judicial responsibility and function

A.1 Listing is a judicial responsibility and function. The purpose is to ensure that all cases are brought to a hearing or trial in accordance with the interests of justice, that the resources available for criminal justice are deployed as effectively as possible, and that cases are heard by an appropriate judge or bench with the minimum of delay.

A.2 The agreement reached between the Lord Chief Justice and the Secretary of State for Constitutional Affairs and Lord Chancellor set out in a statement to the House of Lords on 26 January 2004 ('the Concordat'), states that judges, working with HMCTS, are responsible for deciding on the assignment of cases to particular courts and the listing of those cases before particular judges. Therefore:

(a) The Presiding Judges of each circuit have the overall responsibility for listing at all courts, Crown and magistrates', on their circuit;
(b) Subject to the supervision of the Presiding Judges, the Resident Judge at each Crown Court has the general responsibility within his or her court centre for the allocation of criminal judicial work, to ensure the just and efficient despatch of the business of the court or group of courts. This includes overseeing the deployment of allocated judges at the court or group, including the distribution of work between all the judges allocated to that court. A Resident Judge must appoint a deputy or deputies to exercise his or her functions when he or she is absent from his or her court centre. See also paragraph A.5: Discharge of judicial responsibilities;
(c) The listing officer in the Crown Court is responsible for carrying out the day-to-day operation of listing practice under the direction of the Resident Judge. The listing officer at each Crown Court centre has one of the most important functions at that Crown Court and makes a vital contribution to the efficient running of that Crown Court and to the efficient operation of the administration of criminal justice;
(d) In the magistrates' courts, the Judicial Business Group, subject to the supervision of the Presiding Judges of the circuit, is responsible for determining the listing practice in that area. The day-to-day operation of that listing practice is the responsibility of the justices' clerk with the assistance of the listing officer.

Key principles of listing

A.3 When setting the listing practice, the Resident Judge or the Judicial Business Group should take into account principles a-j:

(a) Ensure the timely trial of cases and resolution of other issues (such as confiscation) so that justice is not delayed. The following factors are relevant:
    i. In general, each case should be tried within as short a time of its arrival in the court as is consistent with the interests of justice, the needs of victims and witnesses, and with the proper and timely preparation by the prosecution and defence of their cases in accordance with the directions and timetable set;
    ii. Priority should be accorded to the trial of young defendants, and cases where there are vulnerable or young witnesses. In *R v Barker* [2010] EWCA Crim 4, the Lord Chief Justice highlighted 'the importance to the trial and investigative process of keeping any delay in a case involving a child complainant to an irreducible minimum';
    iii. Custody time limits (CTLs) should be observed, see CPD XIII Listing F;
    iv. Every effort must be made to avoid delay in cases in which the defendant is on bail;
(b) Ensure that in the magistrates' court unless impracticable, non-custody anticipated guilty plea cases are listed 14 days after charge, and non-custody anticipated not guilty pleas are listed 28 days after charge;
(c) Provide, when possible, for certainty and/or as much advance notice as possible, of the trial date; and take all reasonable steps to ensure that the trial date remains fixed;
(d) Ensure that a judge or bench with any necessary authorisation and of appropriate experience is available to try each case and, wherever desirable and practicable, there is judicial continuity, including in relation to post-trial hearings;
(e) Strike an appropriate balance in the use of resources, by taking account of:
    i. The efficient deployment of the judiciary in the Crown Court and the magistrates' courts taking into account relevant sitting requirements for magistrates. See CPD XIII Annex 1 for information to support judicial deployment in the magistrates' courts;
    ii. The proper use of the courtrooms available at the court;
    iii. The provision in long and/or complex cases for adequate reading time for the judiciary;
    iv. The facilities in the available courtrooms, including the security needs (such as a secure dock), size and equipment, such as video and live link facilities;
    v. The proper use of those who attend the Crown Court as jurors;
    vi. The availability of legal advisers in the magistrates' courts;
    vii. The need to return those sentenced to custody as soon as possible after the sentence is passed, and to facilitate the efficient operation of the prison escort contract;

(f) Provide where practicable:
   i. the defendant and the prosecution with the advocate of their choice where this does not result in any delay to the trial of the case; and,
   ii. for the efficient deployment of advocates, lawyers and associate prosecutors of the Crown Prosecution Service, and other prosecuting authorities, and of the resources available to the independent legal profession, for example by trying to group certain cases together;

(g) Meet the need for special security measures for category A and other high-risk defendants;

(h) Ensure that proper time (including judicial reading time) is afforded to hearings in which the court is exercising powers that impact on the rights of individuals, such as applications for investigative orders or warrants;

(i) Consider the significance of ancillary proceedings, such as confiscation hearings, and the need to deal with such hearings promptly and, where possible, for such hearings to be conducted by the trial judge;

(j) Provide for government initiatives or projects approved by the Lord Chief Justice.

A.4 Although the listing practice at each Crown Court centre and magistrates' court will take these principles into account, the listing practice adopted will vary from court to court depending particularly on the number of courtrooms and the facilities available, the location and the workload, its volume and type.

Discharge of judicial responsibilities

A.5 The Resident Judge of each court is responsible for:

i. ensuring that good practice is implemented throughout the court, such that all hearings commence on time;
ii. ensuring that the causes of trials that do not proceed on the date originally fixed are examined to see if there is any systemic issue;
iii. monitoring the general performance of the court and the listing practices;
iv. monitoring the timeliness of cases and reporting any cases of serious concern to the Presiding Judge;
v. maintaining and reviewing annually a list of Recorders, qualifying judge advocates and Deputy Circuit Judges authorised to hear appeals from the magistrates' courts unless such a list is maintained by the Presiding Judge.

A.6 The Judicial Business Group for each clerkship subject to the overall jurisdiction of the Presiding Judge is responsible for:

i. monitoring the workload and anticipated changes which may impact on listing policies;
ii. ensuring that any listing practice meets the needs of the system as a whole.

CPD XIII Listing B: Classification **PD-101**

B.1 The classification structure outlined below is solely for the purposes of trial in the Crown Court. The structure has been devised to accommodate practical administrative functions and is not intended to reflect a hierarchy of the offences therein.

Offences are classified as follows:

Class 1: A:

i. Murder;
ii. Attempted Murder;
iii. Manslaughter;
iv. Infanticide;
v. Child destruction (section 1(1) of the Infant Life (Preservation) Act 1929);
vi. Abortion (section 58 of the Offences against the Person Act 1861);
vii. Assisting a suicide;
viii. Cases including section 5 of the Domestic Violence, Crime and Victims Act 2004, as amended (if a fatality has resulted);
ix. Soliciting, inciting, encouraging or assisting, attempting or conspiring to commit any of the above offences or assisting an offender having committed such an offence.

Class 1: B:

i. Genocide;
ii. Torture, hostage-taking and offences under the War Crimes Act 1991;
iii. Offences under ss. 51 and 52 International Criminal Courts Act 2001;
iv. An offence under section 1 of the Geneva Conventions Act 1957;

v. Terrorism offences (where offence charged is indictable only and took place during an act of terrorism or for the purposes of terrorism as defined in s.1 of the Terrorism Act 2000);
vi. Piracy, under the Merchant Shipping and Maritime Security Act 1997;
vii. Treason;
viii. An offence under the Official Secrets Acts;
ix. Incitement to disaffection;
x. Soliciting, inciting, encouraging or assisting, attempting or conspiring to commit any of the above offences or assisting an offender having committed such an offence.

Class 1: C:

i. Prison mutiny, under the Prison Security Act 1992;
ii. Riot in the course of serious civil disturbance;
iii. Serious gang related crime resulting in the possession or discharge of firearms, particularly including a campaign of firebombing or extortion, especially when accompanied by allegations of drug trafficking on a commercial scale;
iv. Complex sexual offence cases in which there are many complainants (often under age, in care or otherwise particularly vulnerable) and/or many defendants who are alleged to have systematically groomed and abused them, often over a long period of time;
v. Cases involving people trafficking for sexual, labour or other exploitation and cases of human servitude;
vi. Soliciting, inciting, encouraging or assisting, attempting or conspiring to commit any of the above offences or assisting an offender having committed such an offence.

Class 1: D:

i. Causing death by dangerous driving;
ii. Causing death by careless driving;
iii. Causing death by unlicensed, disqualified or uninsured driving;
iv. Any Health and Safety case resulting in a fatality or permanent serious disability;
v. Any other case resulting in a fatality or permanent serious disability;
vi. Soliciting, inciting, encouraging or assisting, attempting or conspiring to commit any of the above offences or assisting an offender having committed such an offence.

Class 2: A

i. Arson with intent to endanger life or reckless as to whether life was endangered;
ii. Cases in which explosives, firearms or imitation firearms are used or carried or possessed;
iii. Kidnapping or false imprisonment (without intention to commit a sexual offence but charged on the same indictment as a serious offence of violence such as under section 18 or section 20 of the Offences Against the Person Act 1861);
iv. Cases in which the defendant is a police officer, member of the legal profession or a high profile or public figure;
v. Cases in which the complainant or an important witness is a high profile or public figure;
vi. Riot otherwise than in the course of serious civil disturbance;
vii. Child cruelty;
viii. Cases including section 5 of the Domestic Violence, Crime and Victims Act 2004, as amended (if no fatality has resulted);
ix. Soliciting, inciting, encouraging or assisting, attempting or conspiring to commit any of the above offences or assisting an offender having committed such an offence.

Class 2: B

i. Any sexual offence, with the exception of those included in Class 1C;
ii. Kidnapping or false imprisonment (with intention to commit a sexual offence or charged on the same indictment as a sexual offence);
iii. Soliciting, inciting, encouraging or assisting, attempting or conspiring to commit any of the above offences or assisting an offender having committed such an offence.

Class 2: C:

i. Serious, complex fraud;
ii. Serious and/or complex money laundering;
iii. Serious and/or complex bribery;
iv. Corruption;
v. Complex cases in which the defendant is a corporation (including cases for sentence as well as for trial);
vi. Any case in which the defendant is a corporation with a turnover in excess of £1bn (including cases for sentence as well as for trial);

vii. Soliciting, inciting, encouraging or assisting, attempting or conspiring to commit any of the above offences or assisting an offender having committed such an offence.

Class 3: All other offences not listed in the classes above.

Deferred Prosecution Agreements

B.2 Cases coming before the court under section 45 [of] and Schedule 17 [to] the Crime and Courts Act 2013 must be referred to the President of the Queen's Bench Division who will allocate the matter to a judge from a list of judges approved by the Lord Chief Justice. Only the allocated judge may thereafter hear any matter or make any decision in relation to that case.

Criminal Cases Review Commission

B.3 Where the CCRC refers a case upon conviction from the magistrates' courts to the Crown Court, this shall be dealt with at a Crown Court centre designated by the Senior Presiding Judge.

CPD XIII Listing C: Referral of Cases in the Crown Court to the Resident Judge and to the Presiding Judges **PD-102**

C.1 This Practice Direction specifies:

(a) cases which must be referred to a Presiding Judge for release; and

(b) cases which must be referred to the Resident Judge before being assigned to a judge, Recorder or qualifying judge advocate to hear.

It is applicable to all Crown Courts, but its application may be modified by the Senior Presiding Judge or the Presiding Judges, with the approval of the Senior Presiding Judge, through the provision of further specific guidance to Resident Judges in relation to the allocation and management of the work at their court.

C.2 This Practice Direction does not prescribe the way in which the Resident Judge gives directions as to listing policy to the listing officer; its purpose is to ensure that there is appropriate judicial control over the listing of cases. However, the Resident Judge must arrange with the listing officers a satisfactory means of ensuring that all cases listed at their court are listed before judges, Recorders or qualifying judge advocates of suitable seniority and experience, subject to the requirements of this Practice Direction. The Resident Judge should ensure that listing officers are made aware of the contents and importance of this Practice Direction, and that listing officers develop satisfactory procedures for referral of cases to him or her.

C.3 In order to assist the Resident Judge and the listing officer, all cases sent to the Crown Court should where possible include a brief case summary prepared by the prosecution. The prosecutor should ensure that any factors that make the case complex, or would lead it to be referred to the Resident Judge or a Presiding Judge are highlighted. The defence may also send submissions to the court, again highlighting any areas of complexity or any other factors that might assist in the case being allocated to an appropriate judge.

Cases in the Crown Court to be referred to the Resident Judge

C.4 All cases in Class 1A, 1B, 1C, 1D, 2A and 2C must be referred to the Resident Judge as must any case which appears to raise particularly complex, sensitive or serious issues.

C.5 Resident Judges should give guidance to the judges and staff of their respective courts as to which Class 2B cases should be referred to them following consultation with the Senior Presiding Judge. This will include any cases that may be referred to the Presiding Judge, see below. Class 2B cases to be referred to the Resident Judge are likely to be identified by the list officer, or by the judge at the first hearing in the Crown Court.

C.6 Once a case has been referred to the Resident Judge, the Resident Judge should refer the case to the Presiding Judge, following the guidance below, or allocate the case to an appropriate category of judge, and if possible to a named judge.

Cases in the Crown Court to be referred to a Presiding Judge

C.7 All cases in Class 1A, 1B and 1C must be referred by the Resident Judge to a Presiding Judge, as must a case in any class which is:

i. An usually grave or complex case or one in which a novel and important point of law is to be raised;

ii. A case where it is alleged that the defendant caused more than 1 fatality;

iii. A non-fatal case of baby shaking where serious injury resulted;

iv. A case where the defendant is a police officer, or a member of the legal profession or a high profile figure;

v. A case which for any reason is likely to attract exceptional media attention;
vi. A case where a large organisation or corporation may, if convicted, be ordered to pay a very large fine;
vii. Any case likely to last more than three months.

C.8 Resident Judges are encouraged to refer any other case if they think it is appropriate to do so.

C.9 Presiding Judges and Resident Judges should agree a system for the referral of cases to the Presiding Judge, ideally by electronic means. The system agreed should include provision for the Resident Judge to provide the Presiding Judge with a brief summary of the case, a clear recommendation by the Resident Judge about the judges available to try the case and any other comments. A written record of the decision and brief reasons for it must be made and retained.

C.10 Once a case has been referred to the Presiding Judge, the Presiding Judge may retain the case for trial by a High Court Judge, or release the case back to the Resident Judge, either for trial by a named judge, or for trial by an identified category of judges, to be allocated by the Resident Judge.

PD-103 CPD XIII Listing D: Authorisation of Judges

D.1 Judges must be authorised by the Lord Chief Justice before they may hear certain types of case.

D.2 Judges (other than High Court Judges) to hear Class 1A cases must be authorised to hear such cases. Any judge previously granted a 'Class 1' or 'murder' authorisation is authorised to hear Class 1A cases. Judges previously granted an 'attempted murder' (including soliciting, incitement or conspiracy thereof) authorisation can only deal with these cases within Class 1A.

D.3 Judges (other than High Court Judges) to hear sexual offences cases in Class 1C or any case within Class 2B must be authorised to hear such cases. Any judge previously granted a 'Class 2' or 'serious sex offences' authorisation is authorised to hear sexual offences cases in Class 1C or 2B. It is a condition of the authorisation that it does not take effect until the judge has attended the relevant Judicial College course; the Resident Judge should check in the case of newly authorised judges that they have attended the course. Judges who have been previously authorised to try such cases should make every effort to ensure their training is up-to-date and maintained by attending the Serious Sexual Offences Seminar at least once every three years. See CPD XIII Annex 2 for guidance in dealing with sexual offences in the youth court.

D.4 Cases in the magistrates' courts involving the imposition of very large fines
i. Where a defendant appears before a magistrates' court for an either way offence, to which CPD XIII Annex 3 applies the case must be dealt with by a DJ (MC) who has been authorised to deal with such cases by the Chief Magistrate.
ii. The authorised DJ (MC) must first consider whether such cases should be allocated to the Crown Court or, where the defendant pleads guilty, committed for sentence under s. 3 Powers of [Criminal] Courts (Sentenc[ing]) Act 2000, and must do so when the DJ (MC) considers the offence or combination of offences so serious that the Crown Court should deal with the defendant had they been convicted on indictment.
iii. If an authorised DJ (MC) decides not to commit such a case the reasons must be recorded in writing to be entered onto the court register.

PD-104 CPD XIII Listing E: Allocation of Business within the Crown Court

E.1 Cases in Class 1A may only be tried by:
i. a High Court Judge, or
ii. a Circuit Judge, or Deputy High Court Judge, authorised to try such cases and provided that the Presiding Judge has released the case for trial by such a judge.

E.2 Cases in Class 1B may only be tried by:
i. a High Court Judge, or
ii. a Circuit Judge, or a Deputy High Court Judge, provided that the Presiding Judge has released the case for trial by such a judge.

E.3 Cases in Class 1C may only be tried by:
i. a High Court Judge, or
ii. a Circuit Judge, or a Deputy High Court Judge, or Deputy Circuit Judge, authorised to try such cases (if the case requires the judge to be authorised to hear sexual offences cases), provided that the Presiding Judge has released the case for trial by such a judge, or, if the case is a sexual offence, the Presiding Judge has assigned the case to that named judge.

See also CPD XIII Listing C.10.

E.4 Cases in Class 1D and 2A may be tried by:
i. a High Court Judge, or

ii. a Circuit Judge, or Deputy High Court Judge, or Deputy Circuit Judge, or a Recorder or a qualifying judge advocate, provided that either the Presiding Judge has released the case or the Resident Judge has allocated the case for trial by such a judge; with the exception that Class 2A i) cases may not be tried by a Recorder or qualifying judge advocate.

E.5 Cases in Class 2B may be tried by:

i. a High Court Judge, or
ii. a Circuit Judge, or Deputy High Court Judge, or Deputy Circuit Judge, or a Recorder or a qualifying judge advocate, authorised to try such cases and provided that either the Presiding Judge has released the case or the Resident Judge has allocated the case for trial by such a judge.

E.6 Cases in Class 2C may be tried by:

i. a High Court Judge, or
ii. a Circuit Judge, or Deputy High Court Judge, or Deputy Circuit Judge, or a Recorder or a qualifying judge advocate, with suitable experience (for example, with company accounts or other financial information) and provided that either the Presiding Judge has released the case or the Resident Judge has allocated the case for trial by such a judge.

E.7 Cases in Classes 1D, 2A and 2C will usually be tried by a Circuit Judge.

E.8 Cases in Class 3 may be tried by a High Court Judge, or a Circuit Judge, a Deputy Circuit Judge, a Recorder or a qualifying judge advocate. A case in Class 3 shall not be listed for trial by a High Court Judge except with the consent of a Presiding Judge.

E.9 If a case has been allocated to a judge, Recorder or qualifying judge advocate, the preliminary hearing should be conducted by the allocated judge if practicable, and if not, if possible by a judge of at least equivalent standing. PCMHs should only be heard by Recorders or qualifying judge advocates with the approval of the Resident Judge.

E.10 For cases in Class 1A, 1B or 1C, or any case that has been referred to the Presiding Judge, the preliminary hearing and PCMH must be conducted by a High Court Judge; by a Circuit Judge; or by a judge authorised by the Presiding Judges to conduct such hearings. In the event of a guilty plea before such an authorised judge, the case will be adjourned for sentencing and will immediately be referred to the Presiding Judge who may retain the case for sentence by a High Court Judge, or release the case back to the Resident Judge, either for sentence by a named judge, or for sentence by an identified category of judges, to be allocated by the Resident Judge.

E.11 Appeals from decisions of magistrates' courts shall be heard by:

i. a Resident Judge, or
ii. a Circuit Judge, nominated by the Resident Judge, who regularly sits at the Crown Court centre, or
iii. a Recorder or qualifying judge advocate or a Deputy Circuit Judge listed by the Presiding Judge to hear such appeals; or, if there is no such list nominated by the Resident Judge to hear such appeals;
iv. and, no less than two and no more than four justices of the peace, none of whom took part in the decision under appeal;
v. where no Circuit Judge or Recorder or qualifying judge advocate satisfying the requirements above is available, by a Circuit Judge, Recorder, qualifying judge advocate or Deputy Circuit Judge selected by the Resident Judge to hear a specific case or cases listed on a specific day.

E.12 Allocation or committal for sentence following breach (such as a matter in which a community order has been made, or a suspended sentence passed), should, where possible, be listed before the judge who originally dealt with the matter or, if not, before a judge of the same or higher level.

E.13 Applications for removal of a driving disqualification should be made to the location of the Crown Court where the order of disqualification was made. Where possible, the matter should be listed before the judge who originally dealt with the matter or, if not, before a judge of the same or higher level.

CPD XIII Listing F: Listing of Trials, Custody Time Limits and Transfer of Cases **PD-105**

Estimates of trial length

F.1 Under the regime set out in the Criminal Procedure Rules, the parties will be expected to provide an accurate estimate of the length of trial at the hearing where the case is to be managed based on a detailed estimate of the time to be taken with each witness to be called, and accurate information about the availability of witnesses.

F.2 At the hearing the judge will ask the prosecution to clarify any custody time limit ('CTL') dates. The court clerk must ensure the CTL date is marked clearly on the court file or electronic file. When a case is subject to a CTL all efforts must be made at the first hearing to list the case within the CTL and the judge should seek to ensure this. Further guidance on listing CTL cases can be found below.

Cases that should usually have fixed trial dates

F.3 The cases where fixtures should be given will be set out in the listing practice applicable at the court, but should usually include the following:

i. Cases in classes 1A, 1B, 1C, 2B and 2C;
ii. Cases involving vulnerable and intimidated witnesses (including domestic violence cases), whether or not special measures have been ordered by the court;
iii. Cases where the witnesses are under 18 or have to come from overseas;
iv. Cases estimated to last more than a certain time — the period chosen will depend on the size of the centre and the available judges;
v. Cases where a previous fixed hearing has not been effective;
vi. Re-trials; and,
vii. Cases involving expert witnesses.

Custody Time Limits

F.4 Every effort must be made to list cases for trial within the CTL limits set by Parliament. The guiding principles are:

i. At the first hearing in the Crown Court, prosecution will inform the court when the CTL lapses.
ii. All efforts must be made to list the case within the CTL. The CTL may only be extended in accordance with s. 22 Prosecution of Offences Act 1985 and the Prosecution of Offences (Custody Time Limits) Regulations 1987.
iii. If suitable, given priority and listed on a date not less than 2 weeks before the CTL expires, the case may be placed in a warned list.
iv. The CTL must be kept under continual review by the parties, HMCTS and the Resident Judge.
v. If the CTL is at risk of being exceeded, an additional hearing should take place and should be listed before the Resident Judge or trial judge or other judge nominated by the Resident Judge.
vi. An application to extend the CTL in any case listed outside the CTL must be considered by the court whether or not it was listed with the express consent of the defence.
vii. Any application to extend CTLs must be considered as a matter of urgency. The reasons for needing the extension must be ascertained and fully explained to the court.
viii. Where courtroom or judge availability is an issue, the court must itself list the case to consider the extension of any CTL. The Delivery Director of the circuit must provide a statement setting out in detail what has been done to try to accommodate the case within the CTL.
ix. Where courtroom or judge availability is not in issue, but all parties and the court agree that the case will not be ready for trial before the expiration of the CTL, a date may be fixed outside the CTL. This may be done without prejudice to any application to extend the CTLs or with the express consent of the defence; this must be noted on the papers.

F.5 As legal argument may delay the swearing in of a jury, it is desirable to extend the CTL to a date later than the first day of the trial.

Re-trials ordered by the Court of Appeal

F.6 The Crown Court must comply with the directions of the Court of Appeal and cannot vary those directions without reference to the Court of Appeal.

F.7 In cases where a retrial is ordered by the Court of Appeal the CTL is 112 days starting from the date that the new indictment is preferred i.e. from the date that the indictment is delivered to the Crown Court. Court centres should check that CREST has calculated the dates correctly and that it has not used 182 days on cases that have previously been 'sent'.

Changes to the date of fixed cases

F.8 Once a trial date or window is fixed, it should not be vacated or moved without good reason. Under the Criminal Procedure Rules, parties are expected to be ready by the trial date.

F.9 The listing officer may, in circumstances determined by the Resident Judge, agree to the movement of the trial to a date to which the defence and prosecution both consent, provided the timely hearing of the case is not delayed. The prosecution will be expected to have consulted the witnesses before agreeing to any change.

F.10 In all other circumstances, requests to adjourn or vacate fixtures or trial windows must be referred to the Resident Judge for his or her personal attention; the Resident Judge may delegate the decision to a named deputy.

Transferring cases to another court

F.11 Transfer between courts on the same circuit must be agreed by the Resident Judges of each court, subject to guidance from the Presiding Judges of the circuit.

F.12 Transfer of trials between circuits must be agreed between the Presiding Judges and Delivery Directors of the respective circuits.

F.13 Transfers may be agreed either in specific cases or in accordance with general principles agreed between those cited above.

CPD XIII Listing G: Listing of Hearings other than Trials **PD-106**

G.1 In addition to trials, the court's listing practice will have to provide court time for shorter matters, such as those listed below. These hearings are important, often either for setting the necessary case management framework for the proper and efficient preparation of cases for trial, or for determining matters that affect the rights of individuals. They must be afforded the appropriate level of resource that they require to be considered properly, and this may include judicial reading time as well as an appropriate length of hearing.

G.2 The applicant is responsible for notifying the court, and the other party if appropriate, and ensuring that the papers are served in good time, including a time estimate for judicial reading time and for the hearing. The applicant must endeavour to complete the application within the time estimate provided unless there are exceptional circumstances.

G.3 Hearings other than trials include the following:

- i. Applications for search warrants and Production Orders, sufficient reading time must be provided, see G.8 below;
- ii. Bail applications;
- iii. Applications to vacate or adjourn hearings;
- iv. Applications for dismissal of charges;
- v. Preliminary hearings;
- vi. Preparatory hearings;
- vii. Plea and case management hearings;
- viii. Applications for disclosure of further unused material under section 8 of CPIA 1996;
- ix. Case progression or case management hearings;
- x. Applications in respect of sentence indications not sought at the PCMH;
- xi. Sentences;
- xii. Civil applications under the Anti-Social Behaviour, Crime and Policing Act 2014;
- xiii. Appeals from the magistrates' court: it is essential in all cases where witnesses are likely to be needed on the appeal to check availability before a date is fixed.

G.4 Short hearings should not generally be listed before a judge such that they may delay the start or continuation of a trial at the Crown Court. It is envisaged that any such short hearing will be completed by 10.30am or start after 4.30pm.

G.5 Each Crown Court equipped with a video link with a prison must have in place arrangements for the conduct of PCMHs, other pre-trial hearings and sentencing hearings by video link.

Notifying sureties of hearing dates

G.6 Where a surety has entered into a recognizance in the magistrates' court in respect of a case allocated or sent to the Crown Court and where the bail order or recognizance refers to attendance at the first hearing in the Crown Court, the defendant should be reminded by the listing officer that the surety should attend the first hearing in the Crown Court in order to provide further recognizance. If attendance is not arranged, the defendant may be remanded in custody pending the recognisance being provided.

G.7 The Court should also notify sureties of the dates of the hearing at the Crown Court at which the defendant is ordered to appear in as far in advance as possible: see the observations of Parker LJ in *R v Crown Court at Reading ex p. Bello* [1992] 3 All ER 353.

Applications for Production Orders and Search Warrants

G.8 The use of production orders and search warrants involve the use of intrusive state powers that affect the rights and liberties of individuals. It is the responsibility of the court to ensure that those powers are not abused. To do so, the court must be presented with a properly completed application, on the appropriate form, which includes a summary of the investigation to provide the context for the order, a clear explanation of how the statutory requirements are fulfilled, and full and frank disclosure of anything that might undermine the basis for the application. Further directions on the proper making and consideration of such applications will be provided by Practice Direction. However, the complexity of the application must be taken into account in listing it such that the judge is afforded appropriate reading time and the hearing is given sufficient time for the issues to be considered thoroughly, and a short judgment given.

Confiscation and Related Hearings

G.9 Applications for restraint orders should be determined by the Resident Judge, or a judge nominated by the Resident Judge, at the Crown Court location at which they are lodged.

G.10 In order to prevent possible dissipation of assets of significant value, applications under the Proceeds of Crime Act 2002 should be considered urgent when lists are being fixed. In order to prevent potential prejudice, applications for the variation and discharge of orders, for the appointment of receivers, and applications to punish alleged breaches of orders as a contempt of court should similarly be treated as urgent and listed expeditiously.

Confiscation Hearings

G.11 It is important that confiscation hearings take place in good time after the defendant is convicted or sentenced.

PD-107 **CPD XIII Annex 1: General Principles for the Deployment of the Judiciary in the Magistrates' Court**

This distils the full deployment guidance issued in November 2012. The relevant sections dealing specifically with the allocation of work within the magistrates' court have been incorporated into this Practice Direction. It does not seek to replace the guidance in its entirety.

Presumptions

1. The presumptions which follow are intended to provide an acceptable and flexible framework establishing the deployment of the DJ (MC)s and magistrates. The system must be capable of adaptation to meet particular needs, whether of locality or caseload. In any event, the presumptions which follow are illustrative not exhaustive.
2. DJ(MC)s should generally (not invariably) be deployed in accordance with the following presumptions ('the Presumptions'):
   (a) Cases involving complex points of law and evidence.
   (b) Cases involving complex procedural issues.
   (c) Long cases (included on grounds of practicality).
   (d) Interlinked cases (given the need for consistency, together with their likely complexity and novelty).
   (e) Cases for which armed police officers are required in court, such as high end firearms cases.
   (f) A share of the more routine business of the Court, including case management and pre-trial reviews, (for a variety of reasons, including the need for DJ(MC)s to have competence in all areas of work and the desirability of an equitable division of work between magistrates and DJ(MC)s, subject always to the interests of the administration of justice).
   (g) Where appropriate, in supporting the training of magistrates.
   (h) Occasionally, in mixed benches of DJ(MC)s and magistrates (with a particular view both to improving the case management skills of magistrates and to improving the culture of collegiality).
   (i) In the short term tackling of particular local backlogs ('backlog busting'), sometimes in combination with magistrates from the local or (with the SPJ's approval) adjoining benches.
3. In accordance with current arrangements certain classes of cases necessarily require DJ(MC)s and have therefore been excluded from the above presumptions; these are as follows:
   (a) Extradition;
   (b) Terrorism;
   (c) Prison Adjudications;
   (d) Sex cases in the Youth Court as per Annex 2;
   (e) Cases where the defendant is likely to be sentenced to a very large fine, see Annex 3;
   (f) The Special Jurisdiction of the Chief Magistrate.
4. In formulating the Presumptions, the following considerations have been taken into account:
   (a) The listing of cases is here, as elsewhere, a judicial function, see CPD XIII A.1. In the magistrates' courts the Judicial Business Group, subject to the supervision of the Presiding

Judges of the circuit, is responsible for determining the day to day listing practice in that area. The day-to-day operation of that listing practice is the responsibility of the justices' clerk with the assistance of the listing officer.

(b) Equally, providing the training of magistrates is a responsibility of justices' clerks.

(c) It is best not to treat 'high profile' cases as a separate category but to consider their listing in the light of the principles and presumptions. The circumstances surrounding high profile cases do not permit ready generalisation, save that they are likely to require especially sensitive handling. Listing decisions involving such cases will often benefit from good communication at a local level between the justices' clerk, the DJ (MC) and the Bench Chairman.

(d) Account must be taken of the need to maintain the competences of all members of the judiciary sitting in the magistrates' court.

CPD XIII Annex 2: Sexual Offences in the Youth Court PD-108

Introduction

1. This annex sets out the procedure to be applied in the Youth Court in all cases involving allegations of sexual offences which are capable of being sent for trial at the Crown Court under the grave crime provisions.
2. This applies to all cases involving such charges, irrespective of the gravity of the allegation, the age of the defendant and / or the antecedent history of the defendant[1].
3. This does not alter the test[2] that the Youth Court must apply when determining whether a case is a 'grave crime'.
4. In the Crown Court, cases involving allegations of sexual offences frequently involve complex and sensitive issues and only those Circuit Judges and Recorders who have been specifically authorised and who have attended the appropriate Judicial College course may try this type of work.
5. A number of District Judges (Magistrates' Courts) have now undertaken training in dealing with these difficult cases and have been specifically authorised to hear cases involving serious sexual offences which fall short of requiring to be sent to the Crown Court ('an authorised DJ(MC)'). As such, a procedure similar to that of the Crown Court will now apply to allegations of sexual offences in the Youth Court.

Procedure

6. The determination of venue in the Youth Court is governed by section 51 Crime and Disorder Act 1998, which provides that the youth must be tried summarily unless charged with such a grave crime that long term detention is a realistic possibility[3], or that one of the other exceptions to this presumption arises.
7. Wherever possible such cases should be listed before an authorised DJ(MC), to decide whether the case falls within the grave crime provisions and should therefore be sent for trial. If jurisdiction is retained and the allegation involves actual, or attempted, penetrative activity, the case must be tried by an authorised DJ(MC). In all other cases, the authorised DJ(MC) must consider whether the case is so serious and / or complex that it must be tried by an authorised DJ(MC), or whether the case can be heard by any DJ(MC) or any Youth Court Bench.
8. If it is not practicable for an authorised DJ(MC) to determine venue, any DJ(MC) or any Youth Court Bench may consider that issue. If jurisdiction is retained, appropriate directions may be given but the case papers, including a detailed case summary and a note of any representations made by the parties, must be sent to an authorised DJ(MC) to consider. As soon as possible the authorised DJ(MC) must decide whether the case must be tried by an authorised DJ(MC) or whether the case is suitable to be heard by any DJ(MC) or any Youth Court Bench; however, if the case involves actual, or alleged, penetrative activity, the trial must be heard by an authorised DJ(MC).
9. Once an authorised DJ(MC) has decided that the case is one which must be tried by an authorised DJ(MC), and in all cases involving actual or alleged penetrative activity, all further procedural hearings should, so far as practicable, be heard by an authorised DJ(MC).

[1] So, for example, every allegation of sexual touching, under s3 of the Sexual Offences Act 2003, is covered by this protocol.

[2] Set out in the Sentencing Guidelines Council's definitive guideline, entitled 'Overarching Principles — Sentencing Youths' Published by the Sentencing Guidelines Council in November 2009.

[3] Section 24(1) of the Magistrates Court Act 1980

Cases remitted for sentence

10. All cases which are remitted for sentence from the Crown Court to the Youth Court should be listed for sentence before an authorised DJ(MC).

Arrangements for an authorised DJ(MC) to be appointed

11. Where a case is to be tried by an authorised DJ(MC) but no such Judge is available, the Bench Legal Adviser should contact the Chief Magistrates Office for an authorised DJ(MC) to be assigned.

PD-109 **CPD XIII Annex 3: Cases Involving Very Large Fines in the Magistrates' Court**

1. This Annex applies when s. 85 Legal Aid, Sentencing and Punishment of Offenders Act 2012 comes into force and the magistrates' court has the power to impose a maximum fine of any amount.
2. An authorised DJ(MC) must deal with any allocation decision, trial and sentencing hearing in the following types of cases which are triable either way:
   a) Cases involving death or significant, life changing injury or a high risk of death or significant, life-changing injury;
   b) Cases involving substantial environmental damage or polluting material of a dangerous nature;
   c) Cases where major adverse effect on human health or quality of life, animal health or flora has resulted;
   d) Cases where major costs through clean up, site restoration or animal rehabilitation have been incurred;
   e) Cases where the defendant corporation has a turnover in excess of £10 million but does not exceed £250 million, and has acted in a deliberate, reckless or negligent manner;
   f) Cases where the defendant corporation has a turnover in excess of £250 million;
   g) Cases where the court will be expected to analyse complex company accounts;
   h) High profile cases or ones of an exceptionally sensitive nature.
3. The prosecution agency must notify the justices' clerk where practicable of any case of the type mentioned in paragraph 2 of this Annex, no less than 7 days before the first hearing to ensure that an authorised DJ(MC) is available at the first hearing.
4. The justices' clerk shall contact the Office of the Chief Magistrate to ensure that an authorised DJ(MC) can be assigned to deal with such a case if there is not such a person available in the courthouse. The justices' clerk shall also notify a Presiding Judge of the Circuit that such a case has been listed.
5. Where an authorised DJ(MC) is not appointed at the first hearing the court shall adjourn the case. The court shall ask the accused for an indication of his plea, but shall not allocate the case nor, if the accused indicates a guilty plea, sentence him, commit him for sentence, ask for a pre-sentence report or give any indication as to likely sentence that will be imposed. The justices' clerk shall ensure an authorised DJ(MC) is appointed for the following hearing and notify the Presiding Judge of the Circuit that the case has been listed.
6. When dealing with sentence, section 3 of the Powers of Criminal Courts (Sentenc[ing]) Act 2000 can be invoked where, despite the magistrates' court having maximum fine powers available to it, the offence or combination of offences make it so serious that the Crown Court should deal with it as though the person had been convicted on indictment.
7. An authorised DJ(MC) should consider allocating the case to the Crown Court or committing the accused for sentence.

PD-110 **CPD XIII Annex 4: Application This annex replaces the Protocol on the case management of Terrorism Cases issued in December 2006 by the President of the Queen's Bench Division**

1. This annex applies to 'terrorism cases'. For the purposes of this annex a case is a 'terrorism case' where:
   (a) one of the offences charged against any of the defendants is indictable only and it is alleged by the prosecution that there is evidence that it took place during an act of terrorism or for the purposes of terrorism as defined in s1 of the Terrorist Act 2000. This may include, but is not limited to:
      (i) murder;
      (ii) manslaughter;
      (iii) an offence under section 18 of the Offences against the Person Act 1861 (wounding with intent);
      (iv) an offence under section 23 or 24 of that Act (administering poison etc);
      (v) an offence under section 28 or 29 of that Act (explosives);

(vi) an offence under section 2, 3 or 5 of the Explosive Substances Act 1883 (causing explosions);
(vii) an offence under section 1(2) of the Criminal Damage Act 1971 (endangering life by damaging property);
(viii) an offence under section 1 of the Biological Weapons Act 1974 (biological weapons);
(ix) an offence under section 2 of the Chemical Weapons Act 1996 (chemical weapons);
(x) an offence under section 56 of the Terrorism Act 2000 (directing a terrorist organisation);
(xi) an offence under section 59 of that Act (inciting terrorism overseas);
(xii) offences under (v), (vii) and (viii) above given jurisdiction by virtue of section 62 of that Act (terrorist bombing overseas); and
(xiii) an offence under section 5 of the Terrorism Act 2006 (preparation of terrorism acts).

(b) one of the offences charged is indictable only and includes an allegation by the prosecution of serious fraud that took place during an act of terrorism or for the purposes of terrorism as defined in s1 of the Terrorist Act 2000 and the prosecutor gives a notice under section 51B of the Crime and Disorder Act 1998 (Notices in serious or complex fraud cases);
(c) one of the offences charged is indictable only, which includes an allegation that a defendant conspired, incited or attempted to commit an offence under sub paragraphs (1)(a) or (b) above; or
(d) it is a case (which can be indictable only or triable either way) that a judge of the terrorism cases list (see paragraph 2(a) below) considers should be a terrorism case. In deciding whether a case not covered by subparagraphs (1)(a), (b) or (c) above should be a terrorism case, the judge may hear representations from the Crown Prosecution Service.

The terrorism cases list

2. (a) All terrorism cases, wherever they originate in England and Wales, will be managed in a list known as the 'terrorism cases list' by such judges of the High Court as are nominated by the President of the Queen's Bench Division.
(b) Such cases will be tried, unless otherwise directed by the President of the Queen's Bench Division, by a judge of the High Court as nominated by the President of the Queen's Bench Division.

3. The judges managing the terrorism cases referred to in paragraph 2(a) will be supported by the London and South Eastern Regional Co-ordinator's Office (the 'Regional Co-ordinator's Office'). An official of that office or an individual nominated by that office will act as the case progression officer for cases in that list for the purposes of CrimPR 3.4.

Procedure after charge

4. Immediately after a person has been charged in a terrorism case, anywhere in England and Wales, a representative of the Crown Prosecution Service will notify the person on the 24 hour rota for special jurisdiction matters at Westminster Magistrates' Court of the following information:
(a) the full name of each defendant and the name of his solicitor of other legal representative, if known;
(b) the charges laid;
(c) the name and contact details of the Crown Prosecutor with responsibility for the case, if known; and
(d) confirmation that the case is a terrorism case.

5. The person on the 24-hour rota will then ensure that all terrorism cases wherever they are charged in England and Wales are listed before the Chief Magistrate or other District Judge designated under the Terrorism Act 2000. Unless the Chief Magistrate or other District Judge designated under the Terrorism Act 2000 directs otherwise, the first appearance of all defendants accused of terrorism offences will be listed at Westminster Magistrates' Court.

6. In order to comply with section 46 of the Police and Criminal Evidence Act 1984, if a defendant in a terrorism case is charged at a police station within the local justice area in which Westminster Magistrates' Court is situated, the defendant must be brought before Westminster Magistrates' Court as soon as is practicable and in any event not later than the first sitting after he is charged with the offence. If a defendant in a terrorism case is charged in a police station outside the local justice area in which Westminster Magistrates' Court is situated, unless the Chief Magistrate or other designated judge directs otherwise, the defendant must be removed to that area as soon as is practicable. He must then be brought before Westminster Magistrates' Court as soon as is practicable after his arrival in the area and in any event not later than the first sitting of Westminster Magistrates' Court after his arrival in that area.

7. As soon as is practicable after charge a representative of the Crown Prosecution Service will also provide the Regional Listing Co-ordinator's Office with the information listed in paragraph 4 above.
8. The Regional Co-ordinator's Office will then ensure that the Chief Magistrate and the Legal Aid Agency have the same information.

Cases to be sent to the Crown Court under section 51 of the Crime and Disorder Act 1998

9. The court should ordinarily direct that the plea and trial preparation hearing should take place about 14 days after charge.
10. The sending magistrates' court should contact the Regional Listing Co-ordinator's Office who will be responsible for notifying the magistrates' court as to the relevant Crown Court to which to send the case.
11. In all terrorism cases, the magistrates' court case progression form for cases sent to the Crown Court under section 51 of the Crime and Disorder Act 1998 should not be used. Instead of the automatic directions set out in that form, the magistrates' court shall make the following directions to facilitate the preliminary hearing at the Crown Court:
    (a) three days prior to the preliminary hearing in the terrorism cases list, the prosecution must serve upon each defendant and the Regional Listing co-ordinator:
        (i) a preliminary summary of the case;
        (ii) the names of those who are to represent the prosecution, if known;
        (iii) an estimate of the length of the trial;
        (iv) a suggested provisional timetable which should generally include:
            - the general nature of further enquiries being made by the prosecution,
            - the time needed for the completion of such enquiries,
            - the time required by the prosecution to review the case,
            - a timetable for the phased service of the evidence,
            - the time for the provision by the Attorney General for his consent if necessary,
            - the time for service of the detailed defence case statement,
            - the date for the case management hearing, and
            - the estimated trial date;
        (v) a preliminary statement of the possible disclosure issues setting out the nature and scale of the problem, including the amount of unused material, the manner in which the prosecution seeks to deal with these matters and a suggested timetable for discharging their statutory duty; and
        (vi) any information relating to bail and custody time limits.
    (b) one day prior to the preliminary hearing in the terrorist cases list, each defendant must serve in writing on the Regional Listing Co-ordinator and the prosecution:
        (i) the proposed representation;
        (ii) observations on the timetable; and
        (iii) an indication of plea and the general nature of the defence.

Cases to be sent to the Crown Court after the prosecutor gives notice under section 51B of the Crime and Disorder Act 1998

12. If a terrorism case is to be sent to the Crown Court after the prosecutor gives a notice under section 51B of the Crime and Disorder Act 1998 the magistrates' court should proceed as in paragraphs 9-11 above.
13. When a terrorism case is so sent or transferred the case will go into the terrorism list and be managed by a judge as described in paragraph 2(a) above.

The plea and trial preparation hearing at the Crown Court

14. At the plea and trial preparation hearing, the judge will determine whether the case is one to remain in the terrorism list and if so, give directions setting the provisional timetable.
15. The Legal Aid Agency must attend the hearing by an authorised officer to assist the court.

Use of video links

16. Unless a judge otherwise directs, all Crown Court hearings prior to the trial will be conducted by video link for all defendants in custody.

Security

17. The police service and the prison service will provide the Regional Listing Co-ordinator's Office with an initial joint assessment of the security risks associated with any court appearance by the defendants within 14 days of charge. Any subsequent changes in circumstances or the

assessment of risk which have the potential to impact upon the choice of trial venue will be notified to the Regional Listing Co-ordinator's Office immediately.

CPD XIII Annex 5: Management of cases from the organised crime division of the Crown Prosecution Service This annex replaces the guidance issued by the Senior Presiding Judge in January 2014 **PD-111**

1. The Organised Crime Division (OCD) of the CPS is responsible for prosecution of cases from the National Crime Agency (NCA). Typically, these cases involve more than one defendant, are voluminous and raise complex and specialised issues of law. It is recognised that if not closely managed, such cases have the potential to cost vast amounts of public money and take longer than necessary.
2. This annex applies to all cases handled by the OCD.

Designated court centres

3. Subject to the overriding discretion of the Presiding Judges of the circuit, OCD cases should normally be heard at Designated Court Centres (DCC). The process of designating court centres for this purpose has taken into account geographical factors and the size, security and facilities of those court centres. The designated court centres are:
   (a) Northern Circuit: Manchester, Liverpool and Preston.
   (b) North Eastern Circuit: Leeds, Newcastle and Sheffield.
   (c) Western Circuit: Bristol and Winchester.
   (d) South Eastern Circuit (not including London): Reading, Luton, Chelmsford, Ipswich, Maidstone, Lewes and Hove.
   (e) South Eastern Circuit (London only): Southwark, Blackfriars, Kingston, Woolwich, Croydon and the Central Criminal Court.
   (f) Midland Circuit: Birmingham, Leicester and Nottingham.
   (g) Wales Circuit: Cardiff, Swansea and Mold.

Selection of designated court centres

4. If arrests are made in different parts of the country and the OCD seeks to have all defendants tried by one Crown Court, the OCD will, at the earliest opportunity, write to the relevant court cluster manager with a recommendation as to the appropriate designated court centre, requesting that the decision be made by the relevant Presiding Judges. In the event that the designated court centre within one region is unable to accommodate a case, for example, as a result of a custody time limit expiry date, consideration may be given to transferring the case to a DCC in another region with the consent of the relevant Presiding Judges.
5. There will be a single point of contact person at the OCD for each HMCTS region, to assist listing co-ordinators.
6. The single contact person for each HMCTS region will be the relevant Cluster Manager, with the exception of the South Eastern Circuit, where the appropriate person will be the Regional Listing Co-ordinator.

Designation of the trial judge

7. The trial judge will be assigned by the Presiding Judge at the earliest opportunity, and in accordance with CPD XIII Listing E: Allocation of Business within the Crown Court. Where the trial judge is unable to continue with the case, all further pre-trial hearings should be by a single judge until a replacement has been assigned.

Procedure after charge

8. Within 24 hours of the laying of a charge, a representative of the OCD will notify the relevant Cluster Manager of the following information to enable an agreement to be reached between that Cluster Manager and the reviewing CPS lawyer before the first appearance as to the DCC to which the case should be sent:
   (a) the full name of each defendant and the name of his legal representatives, if known;
   (b) the charges laid; and
   (c) the name and contact details of the Crown Prosecutor with responsibility for the case.

Exceptions

9. Where it is not possible to have a case dealt with at a DCC, the OCD should liaise closely with the relevant Cluster Manager and the Presiding Judges to ensure that the cases are sent to the most appropriate court centre. This will, among other things, take into account the location of the likely source of the case, convenience of the witnesses, travelling distance for OCD staff and facilities at the court centres.

10. In the event that it is allocated to a non-designated court centre, the OCD should be permitted to make representations in writing to the Presiding Judges within 14 days as to why the venue is not suitable. The Presiding Judges will consider the reasons and, if necessary, hold a hearing. The CPS may renew their request at any stage where further reasons come to light that may affect the original decision on venue.
11. Nothing in this annex should be taken to remove the right of the defence to make representations as to the venue.

SENTENCING GUIDELINES

Sentencing Guidelines

This is an edited version of the various definitive sentencing guidelines, both those originally issued by the Sentencing Guidelines Council and those issued by the Sentencing Council for England and Wales. It contains all of the essential guideline material relevant to offences in *Blackstone's Criminal Practice*. Fuller versions are available on the Sentencing Council website via http://sentencingcouncil.judiciary.gov.uk/sentencing-guidelines.htm. By virtue of the Coroners and Justice Act 2009 (Commencement No. 4, Transitional and Saving Provisions) Order 2010 (SI 2010 No. 816), art. 7, guidelines issued by the SGC 'are to be treated as guidelines issued by the Sentencing Council'. For more on the status of guidelines and the duty of courts to follow them, see **E1.3** in the main work.

PART 1 REDUCTION IN SENTENCE FOR A GUILTY PLEA

[Introductory material and declaration that the guideline applies to all cases sentenced on or after *23 July 2007*.]

A. Statutory Provision SG-1

[Sets out the CJA 2003, ss. 144 (reduction in sentence for guilty plea: see **E1.8** in the main work) and 174(2)(d) (duty to give reasons and explain effect of sentence: see **E1.23**).]

1.1 This guideline applies whether a case is dealt with in a magistrates' court or in the Crown Court and whenever practicable in the youth court (taking into account legislative restrictions such as those relevant to the length of Detention and Training orders).

1.2 The application of this guideline to sentencers when arriving at the appropriate minimum term for the offence of murder is set out in Section F.

. . .

B. Statement of Purpose SG-2

2.1 When imposing a custodial sentence, statute requires that a court must impose the shortest term that is commensurate with the seriousness of the offence(s).[1] Similarly, when imposing a community order, the restrictions on liberty must be commensurate with the seriousness of the offence(s).[2] Once that decision is made, a court is required to give consideration to the reduction for any guilty plea. As a result, the final sentence after the reduction for a guilty plea will be less than the seriousness of the offence requires.

2.2 A reduction in sentence is appropriate because a guilty plea avoids the need for a trial (thus enabling other cases to be disposed of more expeditiously), shortens the gap between charge and sentence, saves considerable cost, and, in the case of an early plea, saves victims and witnesses from the concern about having to give evidence. The reduction principle derives from the need for the effective administration of justice and not as an aspect of mitigation.

2.3 Where a sentencer is in doubt as to whether a custodial sentence is appropriate, the reduction attributable to a guilty plea will be a relevant consideration. Where this is amongst the factors leading to the imposition of a non-custodial sentence, there will be no need to apply a further reduction on account of the guilty plea. A similar approach is appropriate where the reduction for a guilty plea is amongst the factors leading to the imposition of a financial penalty or discharge instead of a community order.

2.4 When deciding the most appropriate length of sentence, the sentencer should address separately the issue of remorse, together with any other mitigating features, before calculating the reduction for the guilty plea. Similarly, assistance to the prosecuting or enforcement authorities is a separate issue which may attract a reduction in sentence under other procedures; care will need to be taken to ensure that there is no 'double counting'.

2.5 The implications of other offences that an offender has asked to be taken into consideration should be reflected in the sentence before the reduction for guilty plea has been applied.

2.6 A reduction in sentence should only be applied to the *punitive elements* of a penalty.[3] The guilty plea reduction has no impact on sentencing decisions in relation to ancillary orders, including orders of disqualification from driving.

---

[1] Criminal Justice Act 2003, section 153(2)

[2] Criminal Justice Act 2003, section 148(2)

[3] Where a court imposes an indeterminate sentence for public protection, the reduction principle applies in the normal way to the determination of the minimum term (see para. 5.1, footnote and para. 7 below) but release from custody requires the authorisation of the Parole Board once that minimum term has been served.

SG-3 **C. Application of the Reduction Principle**

3.1 Recommended Approach

The court decides sentence for the offences taking into account other offences that have been formally admitted (TICs),

↓

The court selects the amount of the reduction by reference to the sliding scale,

↓

The court applies the reduction,

↓

When pronouncing sentence the court should usually state what the sentence would have been if there had been no reduction as a result of the guilty plea.

SG-4 **D. Determining the Level of Reduction**

4.1 The level of reduction should be *a proportion of the total sentence* imposed, with the proportion calculated by reference to the circumstances in which the guilty plea was indicated, in particular the stage in the proceedings. The greatest reduction will be given where the plea was indicated at the 'first reasonable opportunity'.

4.2 Save where section 144(2) of the 2003 Act[4] applies, the level of the reduction will be gauged on a *sliding scale* ranging from a recommended *one third* (where the guilty plea was entered at the first reasonable opportunity in relation to the offence for which sentence is being imposed), reducing to a recommended *one quarter* (where a trial date has been set) and to a recommended *one tenth* (for a guilty plea entered at the 'door of the court' or after the trial has begun). See diagram below.

4.3 The level of reduction should reflect the stage at which the offender indicated a *willingness to admit guilt* to the offence for which he is eventually sentenced:

(i) the largest recommended reduction will not normally be given unless the offender indicated willingness to admit guilt at the *first reasonable opportunity*; when this occurs will vary from case to case (*see Annex 1 for illustrative examples*);

(ii) where the admission of guilt comes later than the first reasonable opportunity, the reduction for guilty plea will be less than one third;

(iii) where the plea of guilty comes very late, it is still appropriate to give some reduction;

(iv) if after pleading guilty there is a *Newton* hearing and the offender's version of the circumstances of the offence is rejected, this should be taken into account in determining the level of reduction;

(v) if the not guilty plea was entered and maintained for tactical reasons (such as to retain privileges whilst on remand), a late guilty plea should attract very little, if any, discount.

In each category, there is a presumption that the recommended reduction will be given unless there are good reasons for a lower amount.

First reasonable opportunity	After trial date is set	Door of the court/ after trial has begun
======== |	============== |	================ |
recommended 1/3	**recommended 1/4**	**recommended 1/10**

SG-5 **E. Withholding a Reduction**

On the basis of dangerousness

5.1 Where a sentence for a 'dangerous offender' is imposed under the provisions in the Criminal Justice Act 2003, whether the sentence requires the calculation of a minimum term or is an extended sentence, the approach will be the same as for any other determinate sentence (see also section G below).[5]

---

[4] See section A above.

[5] There will be some cases arising from offences committed before the commencement of the relevant provisions of the Criminal Justice Act 2003 in which a court will determine that a longer than commensurate, extended, or indeterminate sentence is required for the protection of the public. In such a case, the minimum custodial term (but not the protection of public element of the sentence) should be reduced to reflect the plea.

Where the prosecution case is overwhelming

5.2 The purpose of giving credit is to encourage those who are guilty to plead at the earliest opportunity. Any defendant is entitled to put the prosecution to proof and so every defendant who is guilty should be encouraged to indicate that guilt at the first reasonable opportunity.

5.3 Where the prosecution case is overwhelming, it may not be appropriate to give the full reduction that would otherwise be given. Whilst there is a presumption in favour of the full reduction being given where a plea has been indicated at the first reasonable opportunity, the fact that the prosecution case is overwhelming without relying on admissions from the defendant may be a reason justifying departure from the guideline.

5.4 Where a court is satisfied that a lower reduction should be given for this reason, a recommended reduction of 20% is likely to be appropriate where the guilty plea was indicated at the first reasonable opportunity.

5.5 A Court departing from a guideline must state the reasons for doing so.[6]

Where the maximum penalty for the offence is thought to be too low

5.6 The sentencer is bound to sentence for the offence with which the offender has been charged, and to which he has pleaded guilty. The sentencer cannot remedy perceived defects (for example an inadequate charge or maximum penalty) by refusal of the appropriate discount.

Where jurisdictional issues arise

(i) Where sentencing powers are limited to 6 months imprisonment despite multiple offences

5.7 When the total sentence for both or all of the offences is 6 months imprisonment, a court may determine to impose consecutive sentences which, even allowing for a reduction for a guilty plea where appropriate on each offence, would still result in the imposition of the maximum sentence available. In such circumstances, in order to achieve the purpose for which the reduction principle has been established,[7] some modest allowance should normally be given against the total sentence for the entry of a guilty plea.

(ii) Where a maximum sentence might still be imposed

5.8 Despite a guilty plea being entered which would normally attract a reduction in sentence, a magistrates' court may impose a sentence of imprisonment of 6 months for a single either-way offence where, but for the plea, that offence would have been committed to the Crown Court for sentence.

5.9 Similarly, a detention and training order of 24 months may be imposed on an offender aged under 18 if the offence is one which would but for the plea have attracted a sentence of long-term detention in excess of 24 months under the Powers of Criminal Courts (Sentencing) Act 2000, section 91.

F. Application to Sentencing for Murder SG-6

6.1 Murder has always been regarded as the most serious criminal offence and the sentence prescribed is different from other sentences. By law, the sentence for murder is imprisonment (detention) for life and an offender will remain subject to the sentence for the rest of his/her life.

6.2 The decision whether to release the offender from custody during this sentence will be taken by the Parole Board which will consider whether it is safe to release the offender on licence. The Court that imposes the sentence is required by law to set a minimum term that has to be served before the Parole Board may start to consider whether to authorise release on licence. If an offender is released, the licence continues for the rest of the offender's life and recall to prison is possible at any time.

6.3 Uniquely, Parliament has set starting points[8] (based on the circumstances of the killing) which a Court will apply when it fixes the minimum term. Parliament has further prescribed that, having identified the appropriate starting point, the Court must then consider whether to increase or reduce it in the light of aggravating or mitigating factors, some of which are listed in statute. Finally, Parliament specifically provides[9] that the obligation to have regard to any guilty plea applies to the fixing of the minimum term, by making the same statutory provisions that apply to other offences apply to murder without limiting the courts discretion (as it did with other sentences under the Powers of Criminal Courts (Sentencing) Act 2000).

6.4 There are important differences between the usual fixed term sentence and the minimum term set following the imposition of the mandatory life sentence for murder. The most significant of these,

[6] Criminal Justice Act 2003, section 174(2)(a)
[7] See section B above.
[8] Criminal Justice Act 2003, schedule 21
[9] Criminal Justice Act 2003, schedule 1 para. 12(c)

from the sentencer's point of view, is that a reduction for a plea of guilty in the case of murder will have double the effect on time served in custody when compared with a determinate sentence. This is because a determinate sentence will provide (in most circumstances) for the release of the offender[10] on licence half way through the total sentence whereas in the case of murder a minimum term is the period in custody before consideration is given by the Parole Board to whether release is appropriate.

6.5 Given this difference, the special characteristic of the offence of murder and the unique statutory provision of starting points, careful consideration will need to be given to the extent of any reduction and to the need to ensure that the minimum term properly reflects the seriousness of the offence. Whilst the general principles continue to apply (both that a guilty plea should be encouraged and that the extent of any reduction should reduce if the indication of plea is later than the first reasonable opportunity), the process of determining the level of reduction will be different.

6.6 *Approach*

1. Where a Court determines that there should be a *whole life* minimum term, there will be no reduction for a guilty plea.
2. In other circumstances,
   a) the Court will weigh carefully the overall length of the minimum term taking into account other reductions for which offenders may be eligible so as to avoid a combination leading to an inappropriately short sentence;
   b) where it is appropriate to reduce the minimum term having regard to a plea of guilty, the reduction will not exceed one sixth and will never exceed 5 years;
   c) the sliding scale will apply so that, where it is appropriate to reduce the minimum term on account of a guilty plea, the maximum reduction (one sixth or five years whichever is the less) is only available where there has been an indication of willingness to plead guilty at the first reasonable opportunity, with a recommended 5% for a late guilty plea;
   d) the Court should then review the sentence to ensure that the minimum term accurately reflects the seriousness of the offence taking account of the statutory starting point, all aggravating and mitigating factors and any guilty plea entered.

SG-7 **G. Application to other Indeterminate Sentences**

7.1 There are other circumstances in which an indeterminate sentence will be imposed. This may be a discretionary life sentence or imprisonment for public protection.

7.2 As with the mandatory life sentence imposed following conviction for murder, the Court will be obliged to fix a minimum term to be served before the Parole Board is able to consider whether the offender can be safely released.

7.3 However, the process by which that minimum term is fixed is different from that followed in relation to the mandatory life sentence and requires the Court first to determine what the equivalent determinate sentence would have been. Accordingly, the approach to the calculation of the reduction for any guilty plea should follow the process and scale adopted in relation to determinate sentences, as set out in section D above.

SG-8

Annex 1

First Reasonable Opportunity

1. The critical time for determining the reduction for a guilty plea is the first reasonable opportunity for the defendant to have indicated a willingness to plead guilty. This opportunity will vary with a wide range of factors and the Court will need to make a judgement on the particular facts of the case before it.
2. The key principle is that the purpose of giving a reduction is to recognise the benefits that come from a guilty plea both for those directly involved in the case in question but also in enabling Courts more quickly to deal with other outstanding cases.
3. This Annex seeks to help Courts to adopt a consistent approach by giving examples of circumstances where a determination will have to be made.
   (a) the first reasonable opportunity may be the first time that a defendant appears before the court and has the opportunity to plead guilty;
   (b) but the court may consider that it would be reasonable to have expected an indication of willingness even earlier, perhaps whilst under interview;

   Note: For a) and b) to apply, the Court will need to be satisfied that the defendant (and any legal adviser) would have had sufficient information about the allegations.

[10] In accordance with the provisions of the Criminal Justice Act 2003

(c) where an offence triable either way is committed to the Crown Court for trial and the defendant pleads guilty at the first hearing in that Court, the reduction will be less than if there had been an indication of a guilty plea given to the magistrates' court (recommended reduction of one third) but more than if the plea had been entered after a trial date had been set (recommended reduction of one quarter), and is likely to be in the region of 30%;
(d) where an offence is triable only on indictment, it may well be that the first reasonable opportunity would have been during the police station stage; where that is not the case, the first reasonable opportunity is likely to be at the first hearing in the Crown Court;
(e) where a defendant is convicted after pleading guilty to an alternative (lesser) charge to that to which he/she had originally pleaded not guilty, the extent of any reduction will be determined by the stage at which the defendant first formally indicated to the court willingness to plead guilty to the lesser charge, and the reason why that lesser charge was proceeded with in preference to the original charge.

PART 2 NEW SENTENCES: CRIMINAL JUSTICE ACT 2003 SG-9

Foreword

[Introductory material which is not reproduced.]

This guideline applies only to sentences passed under the sentencing framework applicable to those aged 18 or over.

The guideline is divided into two sections:

- Section 1 covers the practical aspects of implementing the non-custodial powers namely the new community sentence and the new form of deferred sentence;
- Section 2 deals with the new custodial sentence provisions relating to suspended sentences, prison sentences of 12 months or more, and intermittent custody.[11]

The Act also contains an extensive range of provisions to protect the public from dangerous offenders. These will be dealt with separately.

...

Section 1 SG-10

Part 1—Community Sentences

A. Statutory Provisions

(i) The Thresholds for Community Sentences

1.1.1 Seriousness—Section 148 Criminal Justice Act 2003:

[Sets out the CJA 2003, s. 148(1) (restrictions on imposing community sentence: see **E8.2** in the main work).]

1.1.2 Persistent Offenders—Section 151 Criminal Justice Act 2003:

[Sets out the CJA 2003, s. 151(1) and (2) (community order for persistent offender previously fined—not yet in force: see **E8.6** in the main work).]

(ii) The Sentences Available

1.1.3 Meaning of Community Sentence—Section 147 Criminal Justice Act 2003

(1) In this Part 'community sentence' means a sentence which consists of or includes—
(a) a community order (as defined by section 177), or
(b) one or more youth community orders.

1.1.4 Offenders aged 16 or over—Section 177 Criminal Justice Act 2003:

[Sets out the CJA 2003, s. 177(1) to (4) (community order requirements: see **E8.9** *et seq.* in the main work).]

[11] References to the Probation Service reflect current roles and responsibilities. By the time these provisions come into force, some or all of those roles and responsibilities may be those of the National Offender Management Service (NOMS).

(iii) Determining Which Orders to make & Requirements to Include

1.1.5 Suitability—Section 148 Criminal Justice Act 2003:

[Sets out the CJA 2003, s. 148(2) (restrictions on imposing community sentence: see **E8.2** in the main work).]

1.1.6 Restrictions on liberty—Section 149 Criminal Justice Act 2003:

[Sets out the CJA 2003, s. 149(1) (passing of community sentence on offender remanded in custody: see **E8.3** in the main work).]

1.1.7 Compatibility—Section 177 Criminal Justice Act 2003:

[Sets out the CJA 2003, s. 177(6) (community orders requirements: see **E8.10** in the main work).]

(iv) Electronic Monitoring

1.1.8 [Sets out the CJA 2003, s. 177(3) and (4) (electronic monitoring requirements: see **E8.28** in the main work).]

SG-11 **B. Imposing a Community Sentence—The Approach**

1.1.9 In the Seriousness guideline [at **SG-26**)] the two thresholds for the imposition of a community sentence are considered. Sentencers must consider all of the disposals available (within or below the threshold passed) at the time of sentence, and reject them before reaching the provisional decision to make a community sentence, so that even where the threshold for a community sentence has been passed a financial penalty or discharge may still be an appropriate penalty. Where an offender has a low risk of reoffending, particular care needs to be taken in the light of evidence that indicates that there are circumstances where inappropriate intervention can increase the risk of re-offending rather than decrease it. In addition, recent improvements in enforcement of financial penalties make them a more viable sentence in a wider range of cases.

1.1.10 Where an offender is being sentenced for a non-imprisonable offence or offences, great care will be needed in assessing whether a community sentence is appropriate since failure to comply could result in a custodial sentence.

1.1.11 Having decided (in consultation with the Probation Service where appropriate) that a community sentence is justified, the court must decide which requirements should be included in the community order. The requirements or orders imposed will have the effect of restricting the offender's liberty, whilst providing punishment in the community, rehabilitation for the offender, and/or ensuring that the offender engages in reparative activities.

The key issues arising are:

(i) which requirements to impose;

(ii) how to make allowance for time spent on remand; and

(iii) how to deal with breaches.

(i) Requirements

1.1.12 When deciding which requirements to include, the court must be satisfied on three matters—

(i) that the *restriction on liberty is commensurate with the seriousness* of the offence(s);[12]

(ii) that the *requirements are the most suitable* for the offender;[13] and

(iii) that, where there are two or more requirements included, they are *compatible with each other*.[14]

1.1.13 Sentencers should have the possibility of breach firmly in mind when passing sentence for the original offence. If a court is to reflect the seriousness of an offence, there is little value in setting requirements as part of a community sentence that are not demanding enough for an offender. On the other hand, there is equally little value in imposing requirements that would 'set an offender up to fail' and almost inevitably lead to sanctions for a breach.

In community sentences, the guiding principles are proportionality and suitability. Once a court has decided that the offence has crossed the community sentence threshold and that a community sentence is justified, the *initial* factor in defining which requirements to include in a community sentence should be the seriousness of the offence committed.

1.1.14 This means that 'seriousness' is an important factor in deciding whether the Court chooses the low, medium or high range (see below) but, having taken that decision, selection of the content of the order within the range will be determined by a much wider range of factors.

- **Sentencing ranges must remain flexible enough to take account of the suitability of the offender, his or her ability to comply with particular requirements and their availability in the local area.**

---

[12] Criminal Justice Act 2003, section 148(2)(b)

[13] ibid section 148(2)(a)

[14] ibid section 177(6)

- **The justification for imposing a community sentence in response to persistent petty offending is the persistence of the offending behaviour rather than the seriousness of the offences being committed. The requirements imposed should ensure that the restriction on liberty is proportionate to the seriousness of the offending, to reflect the fact that the offences, of themselves, are not sufficiently serious to merit a community sentence.**

(a) Information for Sentencers

1.1.15 In many cases, a pre-sentence report[15] will be pivotal in helping a sentencer decide whether to impose a custodial sentence or whether to impose a community sentence and, if so, whether particular requirements, or combinations of requirements, are suitable for an individual offender. The court must always ensure (especially where there are multiple requirements) that the restriction on liberty placed on the offender is proportionate to the seriousness of the offence committed.[16] The court must also consider the likely effect of one requirement on another, and that they do not place conflicting demands upon the offender.[17]

1.1.16 The Council supports the approach proposed by the Panel at paragraph 78 of its Advice that, having reached the provisional view that a community sentence is the most appropriate disposal, the sentencer should request a pre-sentence report, indicating which of the three sentencing ranges is relevant and the purpose(s) of sentencing that the package of requirements is required to fulfil. Usually the most helpful way for the court to do this would be to produce a written note for the report writer, copied on the court file. If it is known that the same tribunal and defence advocate will be present at the sentencing hearing and a probation officer is present in court when the request for a report is made, it may not be necessary to commit details of the request to writing. However, events may change during the period of an adjournment and it is good practice to ensure that there is a clear record of the request for the court. These two factors will guide the Probation Service in determining the nature and combination of requirements that may be appropriate and the onerousness and intensity of those requirements. A similar procedure should apply when ordering a pre-sentence report when a custodial sentence is being considered.

1.1.17 There will be occasions when any type of report may be unnecessary despite the intention to pass a community sentence though this is likely to be infrequent. A court could consider dispensing with the need to obtain a pre-sentence report for adult offenders—

- where the offence falls within the **LOW** range of seriousness (see [below]) and
- where the sentencer was minded to impose a single requirement, such as an exclusion requirement (where the circumstances of the case mean that this would be an appropriate disposal without electronic monitoring) and
- where the sentence will not require the involvement of the Probation Service, for example an electronically monitored curfew (subject to the court being satisfied that there is an appropriate address at which the curfew can operate).

(b) Ranges of Sentence Within the Community Sentence Band

1.1.18 To enable the court to benefit from the flexibility that community sentences provide and also to meet its statutory obligations, any structure governing the use of community requirements must allow the courts to choose the most appropriate sentence for each individual offender.

1.1.19 Sentencers have a statutory obligation to pass sentences that are commensurate with the seriousness of an offence. However, within the range of sentence justified by the seriousness of the offence(s), courts will quite properly consider those factors that heighten the risk of the offender committing further offences or causing further harm with a view to lessening that risk. The extent to which requirements are imposed must be capable of being varied to ensure that the restriction on liberty is commensurate with the seriousness of the offence.

1.1.20 The Council recognises that it would be helpful for sentencers to have a framework to help them decide on the most appropriate use of the new community sentence. While there is no single guiding principle, the seriousness of the offence that has been committed is an important factor. Three sentencing ranges (low, medium and high) within the community sentence band can be identified. It is not possible to position particular types of offence at firm points within the three ranges because the seriousness level of an offence is largely dependent upon the culpability of the

[15] Under the Act, a pre-sentence report includes a full report following adjournment, a specific sentence report, a short format report or an oral report. The type of report supplied will depend on the level of information requested. Wherever it appears, the term 'pre-sentence report' includes all these types of report.

[16] Criminal Justice Act 2003, section 148(2)

[17] ibid section 177(6)

offender and this is uniquely variable. The difficulty is particularly acute in relation to the medium range where it is clear that requirements will need to be tailored across a relatively wide range of offending behaviour.

1.1.21 In general terms, the lowest range of community sentence would be for those offenders whose offence was relatively minor within the community sentence band and would include persistent petty offenders whose offences only merit a community sentence by virtue of failing to respond to the previous imposition of fines. Such offenders would merit a 'light touch' approach, for example, normally a single requirement such as a short period of unpaid work, or a curfew, or a prohibited activity requirement or an exclusion requirement (where the circumstances of the case mean that this would be an appropriate disposal without electronic monitoring).

1.1.22 The top range would be for those offenders who have only just fallen short of a custodial sentence and for those who have passed the threshold but for whom a community sentence is deemed appropriate.

1.1.23 In all three ranges there must be sufficient flexibility to allow the sentence to be varied to take account of the suitability of particular requirements for the individual offender and whether a particular requirement or package of requirements might be more effective at reducing any identified risk of re-offending. It will fall to the sentencer to ensure that the sentence strikes the right balance between proportionality and suitability.

There should be three sentencing ranges (low, medium and high) within the community sentence band based upon seriousness.

It is not intended that an offender necessarily progress from one range to the next on each sentencing occasion. The decision as to the appropriate range each time is based upon the seriousness of the new offence(s).

The decision on the nature and severity of the requirements to be included in a community sentence should be guided by:

(i) the assessment of offence seriousness (LOW, MEDIUM OR HIGH);
(ii) the purpose(s) of sentencing the court wishes to achieve;
(iii) the risk of re-offending;
(iv) the ability of the offender to comply; and
(v) the availability of requirements in the local area.

The resulting restrictions on liberty must be a proportionate response to the offence that was committed.

1.1.24 Below we set out a non-exhaustive description of examples of requirements that might be appropriate in the three sentencing ranges. These examples focus on punishment in the community, although it is recognised that not all packages will necessarily need to include a punitive requirement. There will clearly be other requirements of a rehabilitative nature, such as a treatment requirement or an accredited programme, which may be appropriate depending on the specific needs of the offender and assessment of suitability. Given the intensity of such interventions, it is expected that these would normally only be appropriate at medium and high levels of seriousness, and where assessed as having a medium or high risk of re-offending. In addition, when passing sentence in any one of the three ranges, the court should consider whether a rehabilitative intervention such as a programme requirement, or a restorative justice intervention might be suitable as an additional or alternative part of the sentence.

LOW

1.1.25 For offences only just crossing the community sentence threshold (such as persistent petty offending, some public order offences, some thefts from shops, or interference with a motor vehicle, where the seriousness of the offence or the nature of the offender's record means that a discharge or fine is inappropriate).

1.1.26 Suitable requirements might include:

- 40 to 80 hours of unpaid work or
- a curfew requirement within the lowest range (e.g. up to 12 hours per day for a few weeks) or
- an exclusion requirement (where the circumstances of the case mean that this would be an appropriate disposal without electronic monitoring) lasting a few months or
- a prohibited activity requirement or
- an attendance centre requirement (where available).

1.1.27 Since the restriction on liberty must be commensurate with the seriousness of the offence, particular care needs to be taken with this band to ensure that this obligation is complied with.

In most cases, only one requirement will be appropriate and the length may be curtailed if additional requirements are necessary.

MEDIUM

1.1.28 For offences that obviously fall within the community sentence band such as handling stolen goods worth less than £1,000 acquired for resale or somewhat more valuable goods acquired for the handlers own use, some cases of burglary in commercial premises, some cases of taking a motor vehicle without consent, or some cases of obtaining property by deception.

1.1.29 Suitable requirements might include:
- a greater number (e.g. 80 to 150) of hours of unpaid work or
- an activity requirement in the middle range (20 to 30 days) or
- a curfew requirement within the middle range (e.g. up to 12 hours for 2–3 months) or
- an exclusion requirement lasting in the region of 6 months or
- a prohibited activity requirement.

1.1.30 Since the restriction on liberty must be commensurate with the seriousness of the offence, particular care needs to be taken with this band to ensure that this obligation is complied with.

HIGH

1.1.31 For offences that only just fall below the custody threshold or where the custody threshold is crossed but a community sentence is more appropriate in all the circumstances, for example some cases displaying the features of a standard domestic burglary committed by a first-time offender.

1.1.32 More intensive sentences which combine two or more requirements may be appropriate at this level. Suitable requirements might include an unpaid work order of between 150 and 300 hours; an activity requirement up to the maximum 60 days; an exclusion order lasting in the region of 12 months; a curfew requirement of up to 12 hours a day for 4–6 months.

(c) Electronic Monitoring

1.1.33 The court must also consider whether an electronic monitoring requirement[18] should be imposed which is mandatory[19] in some circumstances.

Electronic monitoring should be used with the primary purpose of promoting and monitoring compliance with other requirements, in circumstances where the punishment of the offender and/or the need to safeguard the public and prevent re-offending are the most important concerns.

(d) Recording the Sentence Imposed

1.1.34 Under the new framework there is only one (generic) community sentence provided by statute. This does not mean that offenders who have completed a community sentence and have then re-offended should be regarded as ineligible for a second community sentence on the basis that this has been tried and failed. Further community sentences, perhaps with different requirements, may well be justified.

1.1.35 Those imposing sentence will wish to be clear about the 'purposes' that the community sentence is designed to achieve when setting the requirements. Sharing those purposes with the offender and Probation Service will enable them to be clear about the goals that are to be achieved.

1.1.36 Any future sentencer must have full information about the requirements that were inserted by the court into the previous community sentence imposed on the offender (including whether it was a low/medium/high level order) and also about the offender's response. This will enable the court to consider the merits of imposing the same or different requirements as part of another community sentence. The requirements should be recorded in such a way as to ensure that they can be made available to another court if another offence is committed.

When an offender is required to serve a community sentence, the court records should be clearly annotated to show which particular requirements have been imposed.

(ii) Time Spent on Remand

1.1.37 The court will need to consider whether to give any credit for time spent in custody on remand.[20] (For further detail from the Panel's Advice, see Annex A.)

The court should seek to give credit for time spent on remand (in custody or equivalent status) in all cases. It should make clear, when announcing sentence, whether or not credit for time on

[18] ibid section 177(3) and (4)

[19] Unless the necessary facilities are not available or, in the particular circumstances of the case, the court considers it inappropriate.

[20] Criminal Justice Act 2003, section 149

remand has been given (bearing in mind that there will be no automatic reduction in sentence once section 67 of the Criminal Justice Act 1967 is repealed) and should explain its reasons for not giving credit when it considers either that this is not justified, would not be practical, or would not be in the best interests of the offender.

1.1.38 Where an offender has spent a period of time in custody on remand, there will be occasions where a custodial sentence is warranted but the length of the sentence justified by the seriousness of the offence would mean that the offender would be released immediately. Under the present framework, it may be more appropriate to pass a community sentence since that will ensure supervision on release.

1.1.39 However, given the changes in the content of the second part of a custodial sentence of 12 months or longer, a court in this situation where the custodial sentence would be 12 months or more should, under the new framework, pass a custodial sentence in the knowledge that licence requirements will be imposed on release from custody. This will ensure that the sentence imposed properly reflects the seriousness of the offence.

1.1.40 Recommendations made by the court at the point of sentence will be of particular importance in influencing the content of the licence. This will properly reflect the gravity of the offence(s) committed.

(iii) Breaches

1.1.41 Where an offender fails, without reasonable excuse, to comply with one or more requirements, the 'responsible officer'[21] can either give a warning or initiate breach proceedings. Where the offender fails to comply without reasonable excuse for the second time within a 12-month period, the 'responsible officer' must initiate proceedings.

1.1.42 In such proceedings the court must[22] either *increase the severity of the existing sentence* (i.e. impose more onerous conditions including requirements aimed at enforcement, such as a curfew or supervision requirement) or *revoke the existing sentence and proceed as though sentencing for the original offence*. The court is required to take account of the circumstances of the breach,[23] which will inevitably have an impact on its response.

1.1.43 In certain circumstances (where an offender has wilfully and persistently failed to comply with an order made in respect of an offence that is not itself punishable by imprisonment), the court can *impose a maximum of 51 weeks custody*.[24]

1.1.44 When increasing the onerousness of requirements, the court must consider the impact on the offender's ability to comply and the possibility of precipitating a custodial sentence for further breach. For that reason, and particularly where the breach occurs towards the end of the sentence, the court should take account of compliance to date and may consider that extending the supervision or operational periods will be more sensible; in other cases it might choose to add punitive or rehabilitative requirements instead. In making these changes the court must be mindful of the legislative restrictions on the overall length of community sentences and on the supervision and operational periods allowed for each type of requirement.

1.1.45 The court dealing with breach of a community sentence should have as its primary objective ensuring that the requirements of the sentence are finished, and this is important if the court is to have regard to the statutory purposes of sentencing. A court that imposes a custodial sentence for breach without giving adequate consideration to alternatives is in danger of imposing a sentence that is not commensurate with the seriousness of the original offence and is solely a punishment for breach. This risks undermining the purposes it has identified as being important. Nonetheless, courts will need to be vigilant to ensure that there is a realistic prospect of the purposes of the order being achieved.

Having decided that a community sentence is commensurate with the seriousness of the offence, the *primary* objective when sentencing for breach of requirements is to ensure that those requirements are completed.

1.1.46 A court sentencing for breach must take account of the extent to which the offender has complied with the requirements of the community order, the reasons for breach and the point at which the breach has occurred. Where a breach takes place towards the end of the operational period and the court is satisfied that the offender's appearance before the court is likely to be sufficient in itself to ensure future compliance, then given that it is not open to the court to make no order, an

[21] Criminal Justice Act 2003 schedule 8, paragraphs 5–6
[22] ibid paragraphs 9–10
[23] ibid paragraph 9(2)
[24] ibid paragraph 9(1)(c)

approach that the court might wish to adopt could be to re-sentence in a way that enables the original order to be completed properly—for example, a differently constructed community sentence that aims to secure compliance with the purposes of the original sentence.

1.1.47 If the court decides to increase the onerousness of an order, it must give careful consideration, with advice from the Probation Service, to the offender's ability to comply. A custodial sentence should be the last resort, where all reasonable efforts to ensure that an offender completes a community sentence have failed.

- **The Act allows for a custodial sentence to be imposed in response to breach of a community sentence. Custody should be the last resort, reserved for those cases of deliberate and repeated breach where all reasonable efforts to ensure that the offender complies have failed.**
- **Before increasing the onerousness of requirements, sentencers should take account of the offender's ability to comply and should avoid precipitating further breach by overloading the offender with too many or conflicting requirements.**
- **There may be cases where the court will need to consider re-sentencing to a differently constructed community sentence in order to secure compliance with the purposes of the original sentence, perhaps where there has already been partial compliance or where events since the sentence was imposed have shown that a different course of action is likely to be effective.**

SECTION I
PART 2—DEFERRED SENTENCES

A. Statutory Provisions SG-12

1.2.1 Under the existing legislation,[25] a court can defer a sentence for up to six months, provided the offender consents and the court considers that deferring the sentence is in the interests of justice.

1.2.2 The new provisions[26] continue to require the consent of the offender and that the court be satisfied that the making of such a decision is in the interests of justice. However, it is also stated that the power to defer sentence can only be exercised where:
'the offender undertakes to comply with any requirements as to his conduct during the period of the deferment that the court considers it appropriate to impose'.[27]

1.2.3 This enables the court to impose a wide variety of conditions (including a residence requirement).[28] The Act allows the court to appoint the probation service or other responsible person to oversee the offender's conduct during this period and prepare a report for the court at the point of sentence i.e. the end of the deferment period.

1.2.4 As under the existing legislation, if the offender commits another offence during the deferment period the court may have the power to sentence for both the original and the new offence at once. Sentence cannot be deferred for more than six months and, in most circumstances, no more than one period of deferment can be granted.[29]

1.2.5 A significant change is the provision enabling a court to deal with an offender before the end of the period of deferment.[30] For example if the court is satisfied that the offender has failed to comply with one or more requirements imposed in connection with the deferment, the offender can be brought back before the court and the court can proceed to sentence.

B. Use of Deferred Sentences SG-13

1.2.6 Under the new framework, there is a wider range of sentencing options open to the courts, including the increased availability of suspended sentences, and deferred sentences are likely to be used in very limited circumstances. A deferred sentence enables the court to review the conduct of the defendant before passing sentence, having first prescribed certain requirements. It also provides several opportunities for an offender to have some influence as to the sentence passed—

a) it tests the commitment of the offender not to re-offend;

---

[25] Powers of Criminal Courts (Sentencing) Act 2000, sections 1 and 2
[26] Criminal Justice Act 2003 schedule 23 repealing and replacing sections 1 and 2 of the 2000 Act
[27] ibid new section 1(3)(b) as inserted by schedule 23 to the Criminal Justice Act 2003
[28] ibid new section 1A(1)
[29] ibid new section 1(4)
[30] ibid new section 1B

b) it gives the offender an opportunity to do something where progress can be shown within a short period;

c) it provides the offender with an opportunity to behave or refrain from behaving in a particular way that will be relevant to sentence.

1.2.7 Given the new power to require undertakings and the ability to enforce those undertakings before the end of the period of deferral, the decision to defer sentence should be predominantly for a small group of cases at either the custody threshold or the community sentence threshold where the sentencer feels that there would be particular value in giving the offender the opportunities listed because, if the offender complies with the requirements, a different sentence will be justified at the end of the deferment period. This could be a community sentence instead of a custodial sentence or a fine or discharge instead of a community sentence. It may, rarely, enable a custodial sentence to be suspended rather than imposed immediately.

The use of deferred sentences should be predominantly for a small group of cases close to a significant threshold where, should the defendant be prepared to adapt his behaviour in a way clearly specified by the sentencer, the court may be prepared to impose a lesser sentence.

1.2.8 A court may impose any conditions during the period of deferment that it considers appropriate.[31] These could be specific requirements as set out in the provisions for community sentences,[32] or requirements that are drawn more widely. These should be specific, measurable conditions so that the offender knows exactly what is required and the court can assess compliance; the restriction on liberty should be limited to ensure that the offender has a reasonable expectation of being able to comply whilst maintaining his or her social responsibilities.

1.2.9 Given the need for clarity in the mind of the offender and the possibility of sentence by another court, the court should give a clear indication (and make a written record) of the type of sentence it would be minded to impose if it had not decided to defer and ensure that the offender understands the consequences of failure to comply with the court's wishes during the deferral period.

When deferring sentence, the sentencer must make clear the consequence of not complying with any requirements and should indicate the type of sentence it would be minded to impose. Sentencers should impose specific, measurable conditions that do not involve a serious restriction on liberty.

Section 2—Custodial Sentences

Part 1—Custodial Sentences of 12 Months or More

SG-14 **A. Statutory Provisions**

2.1.1 Under existing legislation:

- an adult offender receiving a custodial sentence of at least 12 months and below 4 years will automatically be released at the halfway point and will then be supervised under licence until the three-quarter point of the sentence; [For some, the actual release date may be earlier as a result of release on Home Detention Curfew (HDC).]
- an adult offender receiving a determinate sentence of 4 years or above will be eligible for release from the halfway point and, if not released before, will automatically be released at the two-thirds point. After release, the offender will be supervised under licence until the three-quarter point of the sentence.

2.1.2 Under the new framework, the impact of a custodial sentence will be more severe since the period in custody and under supervision will be for the whole of the sentence term set by the court. Additionally, separate provisions for the protection of the public will be introduced for those offenders designated as 'dangerous' under the Act which are designed to ensure that release only occurs when it is considered safe to do so.

2.1.3 Where a prison sentence of 12 months or more is imposed on an offender who is not classified as 'dangerous', that offender will be entitled to be released from custody after completing half of the sentence. The whole of the second half of the sentence will be subject to licence requirements. These requirements will be set shortly before release by the Secretary of State (with advice from the Governor responsible for authorising the prisoner's release in consultation with the Probation Service) but a court will be able to make recommendations at the sentencing stage on the content

[31] ibid new section 1(3)(b) as inserted by schedule 23 to the Criminal Justice Act 2003

[32] Criminal Justice Act 2003, section 177

of those requirements.[33] The conditions that the Secretary of State may attach to a licence are to be prescribed by order.[34]

2.1.4 The Act requires that a custodial sentence for a fixed term should be for the shortest term that is commensurate with the seriousness of the offence.[35]

B. Imposition of Custodial Sentences of 12 Months or More

SG-15

(i) Length of Sentence

2.1.5 The requirement that the second half of a prison sentence will be served in the community subject to conditions imposed prior to release is a major new development and will require offenders to be under supervision for the full duration of the sentence prescribed by the court. The Probation Service will be able to impose a number of complementary requirements on the offender during the second half of a custodial sentence and these are expected to be more demanding and involve a greater restriction on liberty than current licence conditions.

2.1.6 As well as restricting liberty to a greater extent, the new requirements will last until the very end of the sentence, rather than to the three-quarter point as at present, potentially making a custodial sentence significantly more demanding than under existing legislation. Breach of these requirements at any stage is likely to result in the offender being returned to custody and this risk continues, therefore, for longer under the new framework than under the existing legislation.

Transitional arrangements

2.1.7 In general, a fixed term custodial sentence of 12 months or more under the new framework will increase the sentence actually served (whether in custody or in the community) since it continues to the end of the term imposed. Existing guidelines issued since 1991 have been based on a different framework and so, in order to maintain consistency between the lengths of sentence under the current and the new framework, there will need to be some adjustment to the starting points for custodial sentences contained in those guidelines (subject to the special sentences under the 2003 Act where the offender is a 'dangerous' offender).

2.1.8 This aspect of the guideline will be temporary to overcome the short-term situation where sentencing guidelines (issued since implementation of the reforms to custodial sentences introduced by the Criminal Justice Act 1991) are based on a different framework and the new framework has made those sentences more demanding. As new guidelines are issued they will take into account the new framework in providing starting points and ranges of appropriate sentence lengths for offences and an adjustment will not be necessary.

2.1.9 Since there are so many factors that will vary, it is difficult to calculate precisely how much more demanding a sentence under the new framework will be. The Council's conclusion is that the sentencer should seek to achieve the best match between a sentence under the new framework and its equivalent under the old framework so as to maintain the same level of punishment. As a guide, the Council suggests the sentence length should be reduced by in the region of 15%.

2.1.10 The changes in the nature of a custodial sentence will require changes in the way the sentence is announced. Sentencers will need to continue[36] to spell out the practical implications of the sentence being imposed so that offenders, victims and the public alike all understand that the sentence does not end when the offender is released from custody. The fact that a breach of the requirements imposed in the second half of the sentence is likely to result in a return to custody should also be made very clear at the point of sentence.

- **When imposing a fixed term custodial sentence of 12 months or more under the new provisions, courts should consider reducing the overall length of the sentence that would have been imposed under the current provisions by in the region of 15%.**
- **When announcing sentence, sentencers should explain the way in which the sentence has been calculated, how it will be served and the implications of non-compliance with licence requirements. In particular, it needs to be stated clearly that the sentence is in two parts, one in custody and one under supervision in the community.**
- **This proposal does not apply to sentences for dangerous offenders, for which separate provision has been made in the Act.**

[33] Criminal Justice Act 2003, section 238(1)
[34] ibid section 250
[35] ibid section 153(2)
[36] Having reference to the Consolidated Criminal Practice Direction [see appendix 5], Annex C, as suitably amended.

(ii) Licence conditions

2.1.11 Under the Act, a court imposing a prison sentence of 12 months or more may recommend conditions that should be imposed by the Secretary of State (with advice from the Governor responsible for authorising the prisoner's release in consultation with the Probation Service) on release from custody.[37] Recommendations do not form part of the sentence and they are not binding on the Secretary of State.[38]

2.1.12 When passing such a sentence, the court will not know with any certainty to what extent the offender's behaviour may have been addressed in custody or what the offender's health and other personal circumstances might be on release and so it will be extremely difficult, especially in the case of longer custodial sentences, for sentencers to make an informed judgement about the most appropriate licence conditions to be imposed on release. However, in most cases, it would be extremely helpful for sentencers to indicate areas of an offender's behaviour about which they have the most concern and to make suggestions about the types of intervention whether this, in practice, takes place in prison or in the community.

2.1.13 The involvement of the Probation Service at the pre-sentence stage will clearly be pivotal. A recommendation on the likely post-release requirements included in a presentence report will assist the court with the decision on overall sentence length, although any recommendation would still have to be open to review when release is being considered. A curfew, exclusion requirement or prohibited activity requirement might be suitable conditions to recommend for the licence period. A court might also wish to suggest that the offender should complete a rehabilitation programme, for example for drug abuse, anger management, or improving skills such as literacy and could recommend that this should be considered as a licence requirement if the programme has not been undertaken or completed in custody.

2.1.14 The Governor responsible for authorising the prisoner's release, in consultation with the Probation Service, is best placed to make recommendations at the point of release; this is the case at present and continues to be provided for in the Act. *Specific* court recommendations will only generally be appropriate in the context of relatively short sentences, where it would not be unreasonable for the sentencer to anticipate the relevance of particular requirements at the point of release. Making recommendations in relation to longer sentences (other than suggestions about the types of intervention that might be appropriate at some point during the sentence) would be unrealistic. The Governor and Probation Service should have due regard to any recommendations made by the sentencing court and the final recommendation to the Secretary of State on licence conditions will need to build upon any interventions during the custodial period and any other changes in the offender's circumstances.

- **A court may sensibly suggest interventions that could be useful when passing sentence, but should only make *specific* recommendations about the requirements to be imposed on licence when announcing short sentences and where it is reasonable to anticipate their relevance at the point of release. The Governor and Probation Service should have due regard to any recommendations made by the sentencing court but its decision should be contingent upon any changed circumstances during the custodial period.**
- **The court should make it clear, at the point of sentence, that the requirements to be imposed on licence will ultimately be the responsibility of the Governor and Probation Service and that they are entitled to review any recommendations made by the court in the light of any changed circumstances.**

Section 2—Custodial Sentences

Part 2—Suspended Sentences of Imprisonment

SG-16 **A. Statutory Provisions**

2.2.1 Section 189 Criminal Justice Act 2003

[Sets out the CJA 2003, s. 189(1) to (7) (suspended sentences of imprisonment: see **E6.2** to **E6.6** in the main work).]

2.2.2 Imposition of requirements—Section 190 Criminal Justice Act 2003:

[Sets out the CJA 2003, s. 190(1) to (5) (imposition of requirements by suspended sentence order: see **E6.7** in the main work).]

2.2.3 Power to provide for review—Section 191 Criminal Justice Act 2003:

37 Criminal Justice Act 2003, section 238(1)

38 ibid section 250

[Sets out the CJA 2003, s. 191(1) to (5) (power to provide for review of suspended sentence order: see **E6.10** in the main work).]

2.2.4 Periodic reviews—Section 192 Criminal Justice Act 2003:

[Sets out the CJA 2003, s. 192(1) to (8) (periodic review of suspended sentence order: see **E6.10** in the main work).]

2.2.5 Breach, revocation or amendment of orders, and effect of further conviction—Section 193 Criminal Justice Act 2003

Schedule 12 (which relates to the breach, revocation or amendment of the community requirements of suspended sentence orders, and to the effect of any further conviction) shall have effect.

B. Imposing a Suspended Sentence

SG-17

2.2.6 A suspended sentence is a sentence of imprisonment. It is subject to the same criteria as a sentence of imprisonment which is to commence immediately. In particular, this requires a court to be satisfied that the custody threshold has been passed and that the length of the term is the shortest term commensurate with the seriousness of the offence.

2.2.7 A court which passes a prison sentence of less than 12 months may suspend it for between 6 months and 2 years (the operational period).[39] During that period, the court can impose one or more requirements for the offender to undertake in the community. The requirements are identical to those available for the new community sentence.

2.2.8 The period during which the offender undertakes community requirements is 'the supervision period' when the offender will be under the supervision of a 'responsible officer'; this period may be shorter than the operational period. The court may periodically review the progress of the offender in complying with the requirements and the reviews will be informed by a report from the responsible officer.

2.2.9 If the offender fails to comply with a requirement during the supervision period, or commits a further offence during the operational period, the suspended sentence can be activated in full or in part or the terms of the supervision made more onerous. There is a presumption that the suspended sentence will be activated either in full or in part.

(i) The decision to suspend

2.2.10 There are many similarities between the suspended sentence and the community sentence. In both cases, requirements can be imposed during the supervision period and the court can respond to breach by sending the offender to custody. The crucial difference is that the suspended sentence is a prison sentence and is appropriate only for an offence that passes the custody threshold and for which imprisonment is the only option. A community sentence may also be imposed for an offence that passes the custody threshold where the court considers that to be appropriate.

2.2.11 The full decision making process for imposition of custodial sentences under the new framework (including the custody threshold test) is set out in paragraphs 1.31–1.33 of the Seriousness guideline. For the purposes of suspended sentences the relevant steps are:

(a) Has the custody threshold been passed?
(b) If so, is it unavoidable that a custodial sentence be imposed?
(c) If so, can that sentence be suspended? (sentencers should be clear that they would have imposed a custodial sentence if the power to suspend had not been available)
(d) If not, can the sentence be served intermittently?
(e) If not, impose a sentence which takes immediate effect for the term commensurate with the seriousness of the offence.

(ii) Length of sentence

2.2.12 Before making the decision to suspend sentence, the court must already have decided that a prison sentence is justified and should also have decided the length of sentence that would be the shortest term commensurate with the seriousness of the offence if it were to be imposed immediately. The decision to suspend the sentence should not lead to a longer term being imposed than if the sentence were to take effect immediately.

A prison sentence that is suspended should be for the same term that would have applied if the offender were being sentenced to immediate custody.

2.2.13 When assessing the length of the operational period of a suspended sentence, the court should have in mind the relatively short length of the sentence being suspended and the advantages to be gained by retaining the opportunity to extend the operational period at a later stage (see below).

[39] The power to suspend a sentence is expected to come into force earlier than the provisions implementing 'custody plus' and transitional provisions are expected to enable any sentence of imprisonment of under 12 months to be suspended. This guideline therefore is written in the language of the expected transitional provisions.

The operational period of a suspended sentence should reflect the length of the sentence being suspended. As an approximate guide, an operational period of up to 12 months might normally be appropriate for a suspended sentence of up to 6 months and an operational period of up to 18 months might normally be appropriate for a suspended sentence of up to 12 months.

(iii) Requirements

2.2.14 The court will set the requirements to be complied with during the supervision period. Whilst the offence for which a suspended sentence is imposed is generally likely to be more serious than one for which a community sentence is imposed, the imposition of the custodial sentence is a clear punishment and deterrent. In order to ensure that the overall terms of the sentence are commensurate with the seriousness of the offence, it is likely that the requirements to be undertaken during the supervision period would be less onerous than if a community sentence had been imposed. These requirements will need to ensure that they properly address those factors that are most likely to reduce the risk of re-offending.

Because of the very clear deterrent threat involved in a suspended sentence, requirements imposed as part of that sentence should generally be less onerous than those imposed as part of a community sentence. A court wishing to impose onerous or intensive requirements on an offender should reconsider its decision to suspend sentence and consider whether a community sentence might be more appropriate.

SG-18 C. Breaches

2.2.15 The essence of a suspended sentence is to make it abundantly clear to an offender that failure to comply with the requirements of the order or commission of another offence will almost certainly result in a custodial sentence. Where an offender has breached any of the requirements without reasonable excuse for the first time, the responsible officer must either give a warning or initiate breach proceedings.[40] Where there is a further breach within a twelve-month period, breach proceedings must be initiated.[41]

2.2.16 Where proceedings are brought the court has several options, including extending the operational period. However, the presumption (which also applies where breach is by virtue of the commission of a further offence) is that the suspended prison sentence will be activated (either with its original custodial term or a lesser term) unless the court takes the view that this would, in all the circumstances, be unjust. In reaching that decision, the court may take into account both the extent to which the offender has complied with the requirements and the facts of the new offence.[42]

2.2.17 Where a court considers that the sentence needs to be activated, it may activate it in full or with a reduced term. Again, the extent to which the requirements have been complied with will be very relevant to this decision.

2.2.18 If a court amends the order rather than activating the suspended prison sentence, it must either make the requirements more onerous, or extend the supervision or operational periods (provided that these remain within the limits defined by the Act).[43] In such cases, the court must state its reasons for not activating the prison sentence,[44] which could include the extent to which the offender has complied with requirements or the facts of the subsequent offence.

2.2.19 If an offender near the end of an operational period (having complied with the requirements imposed) commits another offence, it may be more appropriate to amend the order rather than activate it.

2.2.20 If a new offence committed is of a less serious nature than the offence for which the suspended sentence was passed, it may justify activating the sentence with a reduced term or amending the terms of the order.

2.2.21 It is expected that any activated suspended sentence will be consecutive to the sentence imposed for the new offence.

2.2.22 If the new offence is non-imprisonable, the sentencer should consider whether it is appropriate to activate the suspended sentence at all.

[40] Criminal Justice Act 2003 schedule 12, para 4
[41] ibid para. 5
[42] ibid para. 8(4)
[43] ibid section 189(3) and (4)
[44] ibid schedule 12, para. 8(3)

Where the court decides to amend a suspended sentence order rather than activate the custodial sentence, it should give serious consideration to extending the supervision or operational periods (within statutory limits) rather than making the requirements more onerous.

Section 2—Custodial Sentences SG-19

Part 3—Intermittent Custody

[The relevant guidelines on intermittent custody are not reproduced in light of the Home Office announcement of November 2006 that the provisions are not to be implemented.]

Annex A SG-20

Time Spent on Remand—Sentencing Advisory Panel's Advice

The Act makes provision for a sentencer to give credit for time spent on remand in custody where a custodial sentence is passed.[45] It also empowers the court to have regard to time spent on remand in custody when determining the restrictions on liberty to be imposed by a community order or youth community order.[46] Where an offender has spent several weeks in custody, this may affect the nature of the sentence that is passed. For example, where the court decides that a custodial sentence is justified some sentencers may decide to pass a community sentence instead, on the basis that the offender has already completed the equivalent of a punitive element in a sentence. The Panel takes the view that, given the changes in the content of the second part of a custodial sentence, in such cases it will be more appropriate to pass a custodial sentence knowing that licence requirements will be imposed on release from custody (which may be immediate). Recommendations made by the court at the point of sentence will then be of particular importance in influencing the content of the licence. This will help to ensure that the record clearly shows the assessment of seriousness of the offending behaviour.

Whereas the Act clearly states that time spent on remand is to be regarded as part of a custodial sentence unless the Court considers it unjust,[47] it states that sentencers passing a community sentence *may* have regard to time spent on remand, but no further information is given on how this discretion should be exercised. The Panel recognises that giving credit for time spent on remand is likely to be easier to apply in relation to punitive requirements rather than the rehabilitative elements of a community sentence. For example, reducing the number of unpaid work hours could be fairly easy, whereas reducing the length of a rehabilitation programme might not be appropriate as it could undermine its effectiveness. Where an offender has been kept on remand, one could take the view that this action was justified by the bail provisions and that the sentencer should not, therefore, feel obliged to adjust the terms of the community sentence. However, in principle, the Panel recommends that the court should seek to give credit for time spent on remand in all cases and should explain its reasons for not doing so when it considers either that this is not justified, would not be practical, or would not be in the best interests of the offender.

The court should seek to give credit for time spent on remand in all cases. It should make clear, when announcing sentence, whether or not credit for time on remand has been given and should explain its reasons for not giving credit when it considers either that this is not justified, would not be practical, or would not be in the best interests of the offender.

Where, following a period of time spent in custody on remand, the court decides that a custodial sentence is justified then, given the changes in the content of the second part of a custodial sentence, the court should pass a custodial sentence in the knowledge that licence requirements will be imposed on release from custody. Recommendations made by the court at the point of sentence will be of particular importance in influencing the content of the licence.[48]

[45] Criminal Justice Act 2003, section 240
[46] ibid section 149
[47] ibid section 240 (which will, at a future date, replace Criminal Justice Act 1967, section 67, by which such period is now deducted automatically).
[48] This recommendation only applies to sentences of 12 months and above pending the implementation of 'custody plus'.

SG-21 # PART 3 OVERARCHING PRINCIPLES: SERIOUSNESS

Foreword

Following the planned implementation of many of the sentencing provisions in the 2003 Act in April 2005, this guideline deals with the general concept of seriousness in the light of those provisions and considers how sentencers should determine when the respective sentencing thresholds have been crossed when applying the provisions of the Act.

This guideline applies only to sentences passed under the sentencing framework applicable to those aged 18 or over although there are some aspects that will assist courts assessing the seriousness of offences committed by those under 18.

. . .

Seriousness

SG-22 **A. Statutory provisions**

1.1 In every case where the offender is aged 18 or over at the time of conviction, the court must have regard to the five purposes of sentencing contained in section 142(1) Criminal Justice Act 2003:

(a) the punishment of offenders
(b) the reduction of crime (including its reduction by deterrence)
(c) the reform and rehabilitation of offenders
(d) the protection of the public
(e) the making of reparation by offenders to persons affected by their offence.

1.2 The Act does not indicate that any one purpose should be more important than any other and in practice they may all be relevant to a greater or lesser degree in any individual case—the sentencer has the task of determining the manner in which they apply.

1.3 The sentencer must start by considering the *seriousness* of the offence, the assessment of which will:

- determine which of the sentencing thresholds has been crossed;
- indicate whether a custodial, community or other sentence is the most appropriate;
- be the key factor in deciding the length of a custodial sentence, the onerousness of requirements to be incorporated in a community sentence and the amount of any fine imposed.

1.4 A court is required to pass a sentence that is commensurate with the seriousness of the offence. The *seriousness* of an offence is determined by two main parameters; the *culpability* of the offender and the *harm* caused or risked being caused by the offence.

1.5 Section 143(1) Criminal Justice Act 2003 provides:

'In considering the seriousness of any offence, the court must consider the offender's culpability in committing the offence and any harm which the offence caused, was intended to cause or might foreseeably have caused.'

SG-23 **B. Culpability**

1.6 Four levels of criminal culpability can be identified for sentencing purposes:

1.7 Where the offender

(i) has the *intention* to cause harm, with the highest culpability when an offence is planned. The worse the harm intended, the greater the seriousness.
(ii) is *reckless* as to whether harm is caused, that is, where the offender appreciates at least some harm would be caused but proceeds giving no thought to the consequences even though the extent of the risk would be obvious to most people.
(iii) has *knowledge* of the specific risks entailed by his actions even though he does not intend to cause the harm that results.
(iv) is guilty of *negligence.*

Note: *There are offences where liability is strict and no culpability need be proved for the purposes of obtaining a conviction, but the degree of culpability is still important when deciding sentence. The extent to which recklessness, knowledge or negligence are involved in a particular offence will vary.*

SG-24 **C. Harm**

1.8 The relevant provision is widely drafted so that it encompasses those offences where harm is caused but also those where neither individuals nor the community suffer harm but a risk of harm is present.

To Individual Victims

1.9 The types of harm caused or risked by different types of criminal activity are diverse and victims may suffer physical injury, sexual violation, financial loss, damage to health or psychological distress. There are gradations of harm within all of these categories.

1.10 The nature of harm will depend on personal characteristics and circumstances of the victim and the court's assessment of harm will be an effective and important way of taking into consideration the impact of a particular crime on the victim.

1.11 In some cases no actual harm may have resulted and the court will be concerned with assessing the relative dangerousness of the offender's conduct; it will consider the likelihood of harm occurring and the gravity of the harm that could have resulted.

To the Community

1.12 Some offences cause harm to the community at large (instead of or as well as to an individual victim) and may include economic loss, harm to public health, or interference with the administration of justice.

Other Types of Harm

1.13 There are other types of harm that are more difficult to define or categorise. For example, cruelty to animals certainly causes significant harm to the animal but there may also be a human victim who also suffers psychological distress and/or financial loss.

1.14 Some conduct is criminalised purely by reference to public feeling or social mores. In addition, public concern about the damage caused by some behaviour, both to individuals and to society as a whole, can influence public perception of the harm caused, for example, by the supply of prohibited drugs.

D. The Assessment of Culpability and Harm SG-25

1.15 Section 143(1) makes clear that the assessment of the seriousness of any individual offence must take account not only of any harm actually caused by the offence, but also of any harm that was intended to be caused or might foreseeably be caused by the offence.

1.16 Assessing seriousness is a difficult task, particularly where there is an imbalance between culpability and harm:

- sometimes the harm that actually results is greater than the harm intended by the offender;
- in other circumstances, the offender's culpability may be at a higher level than the harm resulting from the offence.

1.17 Harm must always be judged in the light of culpability. The precise level of culpability will be determined by such factors as motivation, whether the offence was planned or spontaneous or whether the offender was in a position of trust.

Culpability will be greater if:

- an offender deliberately causes more harm than is necessary for the commission of the offence; or
- where an offender targets a vulnerable victim (because of their old age or youth, disability or by virtue of the job they do).

1.18 Where unusually serious harm results and was unintended and beyond the control of the offender, culpability will be significantly influenced by the extent to which the harm could have been foreseen.

1.19 If much *more* harm, or much *less* harm has been caused by the offence than the offender intended or foresaw, the culpability of the offender, depending on the circumstances, may be regarded as carrying greater or lesser weight as appropriate.

The culpability of the offender in the particular circumstances of an individual case should be the initial factor in determining the seriousness of an offence.

(i) Aggravating factors

1.20 Sentencing guidelines for a particular offence will normally include a list of aggravating features which, if present in an individual instance of the offence, would indicate *either* a higher than usual level of culpability on the part of the offender, *or* a greater than usual degree of harm caused by the offence (or sometimes both).

1.21 The lists below bring together the most important aggravating features with potential application to more than one offence or class of offences. They include some factors (such as the vulnerability of victims or abuse of trust) which are integral features of certain offences; in such cases, the presence of the aggravating factor is already reflected in the penalty for the offence and *cannot be used as justification for increasing the sentence further*. The lists are not intended to be comprehensive and the aggravating factors are not listed in any particular order of priority. On occasions, two or more of the factors listed will describe the same feature of the offence and care needs to be taken to avoid 'doublecounting'. Those factors starred with an asterisk are statutory aggravating factors where the statutory provisions are in force. Those marked with a hash are yet to be brought into force but as factors in an individual case are still relevant and should be taken into account.

1.22 *Factors indicating higher culpability:*

- Offence committed whilst on bail for other offences*
- Failure to respond to previous sentences
- Offence was racially or religiously aggravated*
- Offence motivated by, or demonstrating, hostility to the victim based on his or her sexual orientation (or presumed sexual orientation)
- Offence motivated by, or demonstrating, hostility based on the victims disability (or presumed disability)
- Previous conviction(s), particularly where a pattern of repeat offending is disclosed
- Planning of an offence
- An intention to commit more serious harm than actually resulted from the offence
- Offenders operating in groups or gangs
- 'Professional' offending
- Commission of the offence for financial gain (where this is not inherent in the offence itself)
- High level of profit from the offence
- An attempt to conceal or dispose of evidence
- Failure to respond to warnings or concerns expressed by others about the offender's behaviour
- Offence committed whilst on licence
- Offence motivated by hostility towards a minority group, or a member or members of it
- Deliberate targeting of vulnerable victim(s)
- Commission of an offence while under the influence of alcohol or drugs
- Use of a weapon to frighten or injure victim
- Deliberate and gratuitous violence or damage to property, over and above what is needed to carry out the offence
- Abuse of power
- Abuse of a position of trust

1.23 *Factors indicating a more than usually serious degree of harm:*

- Multiple victims
- An especially serious physical or psychological effect on the victim, even if unintended
- A sustained assault or repeated assaults on the same victim
- Victim is particularly vulnerable
- Location of the offence (for example, in an isolated place)
- Offence is committed against those working in the public sector or providing a service to the public
- Presence of others e.g. relatives, especially children or partner of the victim
- Additional degradation of the victim (e.g. taking photographs of a victim as part of a sexual offence)
- In property offences, high value (including sentimental value) of property to the victim, or substantial consequential loss (e.g. where the theft of equipment causes serious disruption to a victim's life or business)

(ii) Mitigating factors

1.24 Some factors may indicate that an offender's culpability is *unusually* low, or that the harm caused by an offence is less than usually serious.

1.25 *Factors indicating significantly lower culpability:*

- A greater degree of provocation than normally expected
- Mental illness or disability
- Youth or age, where it affects the responsibility of the individual defendant
- The fact that the offender played only a minor role in the offence

(iii) Personal mitigation

1.26 Section 166(1) Criminal Justice Act 2003 makes provision for a sentencer to take account of any matters that 'in the opinion of the court, are relevant in mitigation of sentence'.

1.27 When the court has formed an initial assessment of the seriousness of the offence, then it should consider any offender mitigation. The issue of remorse should be taken into account at this point along with other mitigating features such as admissions to the police in interview.

(iv) Reduction for a guilty plea

1.28 Sentencers will normally reduce the severity of a sentence to reflect an early guilty plea. This subject is covered by a separate guideline and provides a sliding scale reduction with a normal maximum one-third reduction being given to offenders who enter a guilty plea at the first reasonable opportunity.

1.29 Credit may also be given for ready co-operation with the authorities. This will depend on the particular circumstances of the individual case.

E. The Sentencing Thresholds SG-26

1.30 Assessing the seriousness of an offence is only the first step in the process of determining the appropriate sentence in an individual case. Matching the offence to a type and level of sentence is a separate and complex exercise assisted by the application of the respective threshold tests for custodial and community sentences.

The Custody Threshold

1.31 Section 152(2) Criminal Justice Act 2003 provides:

The court must not pass a custodial sentence unless it is of the opinion that the offence, or the combination of the offence and one or more offences associated with it, was so serious that neither a fine alone nor a community sentence can be justified for the offence.'

1.32 In applying the threshold test, sentencers should note:

- the clear intention of the threshold test is to reserve prison as a punishment for the most serious offences;
- it is impossible to determine definitively which features of a particular offence make it serious enough to merit a custodial sentence;
- passing the custody threshold does *not* mean that a custodial sentence should be deemed inevitable, and custody can still be avoided in the light of personal mitigation or where there is a suitable intervention in the community which provides sufficient restriction (by way of punishment) while addressing the rehabilitation of the offender to prevent future crime. For example, a prolific offender who currently could expect a short custodial sentence (which, in advance of custody plus, would have no provision for supervision on release) might more appropriately receive a suitable community sentence.

1.33 The approach to the imposition of a custodial sentence under the new framework should be as follows:

(a) Has the custody threshold been passed?
(b) If so, is it unavoidable that a custodial sentence be imposed?
(c) If so, can that sentence be suspended? (sentencers should be clear that they would have imposed a custodial sentence if the power to suspend had not been available)
(d) If not, can the sentence be served intermittently?
(e) If not, impose a sentence which takes immediate effect for the term commensurate with the seriousness of the offence.

The Threshold for Community Sentences

1.34 Section 148(1) Criminal Justice Act 2003 provides:

'A court must not pass a community sentence on an offender unless it is of the opinion that the offence, or the combination of the offence and one or more offences associated with it, was serious enough to warrant such a sentence.'

1.35 In addition, the threshold for a community sentence can be crossed even though the seriousness criterion is not met. Section 151 Criminal Justice Act 2003 provides that, in relation to an offender aged 16 or over on whom, on 3 or more previous occasions, sentences had been passed consisting only of a fine, a community sentence may be imposed (if it is in the interests of justice) despite the fact that the seriousness of the current offence (and others associated with it) might not warrant such a sentence.

1.36 Sentencers should consider all of the disposals available (within or below the threshold passed) at the time of sentence before reaching the provisional decision to make a community sentence, so that, even where the threshold for a community sentence has been passed, a financial penalty or discharge may still be an appropriate penalty.

Summary

1.37 It would not be feasible to provide a form of words or to devise any formula that would provide a general solution to the problem of where the custody threshold lies. Factors vary too widely between offences for this to be done. It is the task of *guidelines for individual offences* to provide more detailed guidance on what features within that offence point to a custodial sentence, and also to deal with issues such as sentence length, the appropriate requirements for a community sentence or the use of appropriate ancillary orders.

Having assessed the seriousness of an individual offence, sentencers must consult the sentencing guidelines for an offence of that type for guidance on the factors that are likely to indicate whether a custodial sentence or other disposal is most likely to be appropriate.

SG-27 F. Prevalence

1.38 The seriousness of an individual case should be judged on its own dimensions of harm and culpability rather than as part of a collective social harm. It is legitimate for the overall approach to sentencing levels for particular offences to be guided by their cumulative effect. However, it would be wrong to further penalise individual offenders by increasing sentence length for committing an individual offence of that type.

1.39 There may be exceptional local circumstances that arise which may lead a court to decide that prevalence should influence sentencing levels. The pivotal issue in such cases will be the harm being caused to the community. It is essential that sentencers both have supporting evidence from an external source (for example the local Criminal Justice Board) to justify claims that a particular crime is prevalent in their area and are satisfied that there is a compelling need to treat the offence more seriously than elsewhere.

The key factor in determining whether sentencing levels should be enhanced in response to prevalence will be the level of harm being caused in the locality. Enhanced sentences should be exceptional and in response to exceptional circumstances. Sentencers must sentence within the sentencing guidelines once the prevalence has been addressed.

SG-28 PART 4 MANSLAUGHTER BY REASON OF PROVOCATION

Foreword

...This guideline stems from a reference from the Home Secretary for consideration of the issue of sentencing where provocation is argued in cases of homicide, and, in particular, domestic violence homicides. For the purpose of describing 'domestic violence', the Home Secretary adopted the Crown Prosecution Service definition.[49] The guideline applies to sentencing of an adult offender for this offence in whatever circumstances it occurs. It identifies the widely varying features of both the provocation and the act of retaliation and sets out the approach to be adopted in deciding both the sentencing range and the starting point within that range.

This guideline is for use where the conviction for manslaughter is clearly founded on provocation alone. There will be additional, different and more complicated matters to be taken into account where the other main partial defence, diminished responsibility, is a factor.

The Council's Guideline *New Sentences: Criminal Justice Act 2003* recognised the potentially more demanding nature of custodial sentences of 12 months or longer imposed under the new framework introduced by the Criminal Justice Act 2003. Consequently the sentencing ranges and starting points in this guideline take that principle into account.

...

[49] 'Any criminal offence arising out of physical, sexual, psychological, emotional or financial abuse by one person against a current or former partner in a close relationship, or against a current or former family member.' A new definition of domestic violence was agreed in 2004 (and appears in the CPS Policy on Prosecuting cases of Domestic Violence, 2005) 'any incident of threatening behaviour, violence or abuse [psychological, physical, sexual, financial or emotional] between adults who are or have been intimate partners or family members, regardless of gender or sexuality'.

Manslaughter by Reason of Provocation

A. Statutory Provision SG-29

1.1 Murder and manslaughter are common law offences and there is no complete statutory definition of either. 'Provocation' is one of the partial defences by which an offence that would otherwise be murder may be reduced to manslaughter.

1.2 Before the issue of provocation can be considered, the Crown must have proved beyond reasonable doubt that all the elements of murder were present, including the necessary intent (i.e. the offender must have intended either to kill the victim or to cause grievous bodily harm). The court must then consider section 3 of the Homicide Act 1957, which provides:

Where on a charge of murder there is evidence on which the jury can find that the person charged was provoked (whether by things done or by things said or by both together) to lose his self-control, the question whether the provocation was enough to make a reasonable man do as he did shall be left to be determined by the jury; and in determining that question the jury shall take into account everything both done and said according to the effect which, in their opinion, it would have on a reasonable man.

Although both murder and manslaughter result in death, the difference in the level of culpability creates offences of a distinctively different character. Therefore the approach to sentencing in each should start from a different basis.

B. Establishing the Basis for Sentencing SG-30

2.1 The Court of Appeal in *Attorney General's Reference (Nos. 74, 95 and 118 of 2002) (Suratan and others)*,[50] set out a number of assumptions that a judge must make in favour of an offender found not guilty of murder but guilty of manslaughter by reason of provocation. The assumptions are required in order to be faithful to the verdict and should be applied equally in all cases whether conviction follows a trial or whether the Crown has accepted a plea of guilty to manslaughter by reason of provocation:

- first, that the offender had, at the time of the killing, lost self-control; mere loss of temper or jealous rage is not sufficient
- second, that the offender was caused to lose self-control by things said or done, normally by the person killed
- third, that the offender's loss of control was reasonable in all the circumstances, even bearing in mind that people are expected to exercise reasonable control over their emotions and that, as society advances, it ought to call for a higher measure of self control
- fourth, that the circumstances were such as to make the loss of self-control sufficiently excusable to reduce the gravity of the offence from murder to manslaughter.

Bearing in mind the loss of life caused by manslaughter by reason of provocation, the starting point for sentencing should be a custodial sentence. Only in a very small number of cases involving very exceptional mitigating factors should a judge consider that a non-custodial sentence is justified.

The same general sentencing principles should apply in all cases of manslaughter by reason of provocation irrespective of whether or not the killing takes place in a domestic context.

C. Factors Influencing Sentence SG-31

3.1 A number of elements must be considered and balanced by the sentencer. Some of these are common to all types of manslaughter by reason of provocation; others have a particular relevance in cases of manslaughter in a domestic context.

3.2 *The degree of provocation as shown by its nature and duration*—An assessment of the *degree* of the provocation as shown by its nature and duration is the critical factor in the sentencing decision.

(a) *In assessing the degree of provocation, account should be taken of the following factors:*

- if the provocation (which does not have to be a wrongful act) involves gross and extreme conduct on the part of the victim, it is a more significant mitigating factor than conduct which, although significant, is not as extreme
- the fact that the victim presented a threat not only to the offender, but also to children in his or her care
- the offender's previous experiences of abuse and/or domestic violence either by the victim or by other people

[50] [2003] 2 Cr App R (S) 42

Sentencing Guidelines

- any mental condition which may affect the offender's perception of what amounts to provocation
- the nature of the conduct, the period of time over which it took place and its cumulative effect
- discovery or knowledge of the fact of infidelity on the part of a partner does not necessarily amount to *high* provocation. The gravity of such provocation depends entirely on all attendant circumstances.

(b) *Whether the provocation was suffered over a long or short period is important to the assessment of gravity. The following factors should be considered:*
- the impact of provocative behaviour on an offender can build up over a period of time
- consideration should not be limited to acts of provocation that occurred immediately before the victim was killed. For example, in domestic violence cases, cumulative provocation may eventually become intolerable, the latest incident seeming all the worse because of what went before.

(c) *When looking at the nature of the provocation the court should consider both the type of provocation and whether, in the particular case, the actions of the victim would have had a particularly marked effect on the offender:*
- actual (or anticipated) violence from the victim will generally be regarded as involving a higher degree of provocation than provocation arising from abuse, infidelity or offensive words unless that amounts to psychological bullying
- in cases involving actual or anticipated violence, the culpability of the offender will therefore generally be less than in cases involving verbal provocation
- where the offender's actions were motivated by fear or desperation, rather than by anger, frustration, resentment or a desire for revenge, the offender's culpability will generally be lower.

3.3 *The extent and timing of the retaliation*—It is implicit in the verdict of manslaughter by reason of provocation that the killing was the result of a loss of self-control because of things said and/or done. The intensity, extent and nature of that loss of control must be assessed in the context of the provocation that preceded it.

3.4 The *circumstances of the killing* itself will be relevant to the offender's culpability, and hence to the appropriate sentence:
- in general, the offender's violent response to provocation is likely to be less culpable the shorter the time gap between the provocation (or the last provocation) and the killing—as evidenced, for example, by the use of a weapon that happened to be available rather than by one that was carried for that purpose or prepared for use in advance
- conversely, it is not necessarily the case that greater culpability will be found where there has been a significant lapse of time between the provocation (or the last provocation) and the killing. Where the provocation is cumulative, and particularly in those circumstances where the offender is found to have suffered domestic violence from the victim over a significant period of time, the required loss of self-control may not be sudden as some experience a 'slow-burn' reaction and appear calm
- choosing or taking advantage of favourable circumstances for carrying out the killing (so that the victim was unable to resist, such as where the victim was not on guard, or was asleep) may well be an aggravating factor—unless this is mitigated by the circumstances of the offender, resulting in the offender being the weaker or vulnerable party.

3.5 The *context of the relationship* between the offender and the victim must be borne in mind when assessing the nature and degree of the provocation offered by the victim before the crime and the length of time over which the provocation existed. In cases where the parties were still in a relationship at the time of the killing, it will be necessary to examine the balance of power between one party and the other and to consider other family members who may have been drawn into, or been victims of, the provocative behaviour.

Although there will usually be less culpability when the retaliation to provocation is sudden, it is not always the case that greater culpability will be found where there has been a significant lapse of time between the provocation and the killing.

It is for the sentencer to consider the impact on an offender of provocative behaviour that has built up over a period of time.

An offence should be regarded as aggravated where it is committed in the presence of a child or children or other vulnerable family member, whether or not the offence takes place in a domestic setting.

3.6 *Post-offence behaviour*—The behaviour of the offender after the killing can be relevant to sentence:

- immediate and genuine remorse may be demonstrated by the summoning of medical assistance, remaining at the scene, and co-operation with the authorities
- concealment or attempts to dispose of evidence or dismemberment of the body may aggravate the offence.

Post-offence behaviour is relevant to the sentence. It may be an aggravating or mitigating factor. When sentencing, the judge should consider the motivation behind the offender's actions.

3.7 *Use of a weapon*

(a) In relation to this offence, as in relation to many different types of offence, the carrying and use of a weapon is an aggravating factor. Courts must consider the type of weapon used and, importantly, whether it was to hand or carried to the scene and who introduced it to the incident.

(b) The use or not of a weapon is a factor heavily influenced by the gender of the offender. Whereas men can and do kill using physical strength alone, women often cannot and thus resort to using a weapon. The issue of key importance is whether the weapon was to hand or carried deliberately to the scene, although the circumstances in which the weapon was brought to the scene will need to be considered carefully.

Although there will usually be less culpability when the retaliation to provocation is sudden, it is not always the case that greater culpability will be found where there has been a significant lapse of time between the provocation and the killing.

It is for the sentencer to consider the impact on an offender of provocative behaviour that has built up over a period of time.

An offence should be regarded as aggravated where it is committed in the presence of a child or children or other vulnerable family member, whether or not the offence takes place in a domestic setting.

The use of a weapon should not necessarily move a case into another sentencing bracket.

In cases of manslaughter by reason of provocation, use of a weapon may reflect the imbalance in strength between the offender and the victim and how that weapon came to hand is likely to be far more important than the use of the weapon itself.

It will be an aggravating factor where the weapon is brought to the scene in contemplation of use *before* the loss of self-control (which may occur some time before the fatal incident).

D. Sentence Ranges and Starting Points SG-32

4.1 **Manslaughter is a 'serious offence' for the purposes of the provisions in the Criminal Justice Act 2003[51] for dealing with dangerous offenders. It is possible that a court will be required to use the sentences for public protection prescribed in the Act when sentencing an offender convicted of the offence of manslaughter by reason of provocation. An alternative is a discretionary life sentence. In accordance with normal practice, when setting the minimum term to be served within an indeterminate sentence under these provisions, that term will usually be half the equivalent determinate sentence.**

4.2 *Identifying sentence ranges*—The key factor that will be relevant in every case is the nature and the duration of the provocation.

(a) The process to be followed by the court will be:
- identify the sentence range by reference to the degree of provocation
- adjust the starting point within the range by reference to the length of time over which the provocation took place
- take into consideration the circumstances of the killing (e.g. the length of time that had elapsed between the provocation and the retaliation and the circumstances in which any weapon was used).

(b) This guideline establishes that:
- there are three sentencing ranges defined by the degree of provocation—low, substantial and high
- within the three ranges, the starting point is based on provocation taking place over a short period of time
- the court will move from the starting point (based upon the degree of provocation) by considering the length of time over which the provocation has taken place, and by reference to any aggravating and mitigating factors.

[51] Sections 224–230

Sentencing Guidelines

SG-33

Manslaughter by Reason of Provocation

Factors to take into consideration

1. The sentences for public protection must be considered in all cases of manslaughter.
2. The presence of any of the general aggravating factors identified in the Council's Guideline *Overarching Principles: Seriousness* or any of the additional factors identified in this Guideline will indicate a sentence above the normal starting point.
3. This offence will not be an initial charge but will arise following a charge of murder. The Council Guideline *Reduction in Sentence for a Guilty Plea* will need to be applied with this in mind. In particular, consideration will need to be given to the time at which it was indicated that the defendant would plead guilty to manslaughter by reason of provocation.
4. An assessment of the *degree* of the provocation as shown by its nature and duration is the critical factor in the sentencing decision.
5. The intensity, extent and nature of the loss of control must be assessed in the context of the pro-vocation that preceded it.
6. Although there will usually be less culpability when the retaliation to provocation is sudden, it is not always the case that greater culpability will be found where there has been a significant lapse of time between the provocation and the killing.
7. It is for the sentencer to consider the impact on an offender of provocative behaviour that has built up over a period of time.
8. The use of a weapon should not necessarily move a case into another sentencing bracket.
9. Use of a weapon may reflect the imbalance in strength between the offender and the victim and how that weapon came to hand is likely to be far more important than the use of the weapon itself.
10. It will be an aggravating factor where the weapon is brought to the scene in contemplation of use *before* the loss of self-control (which may occur some time before the fatal incident).
11. Post-offence behaviour is relevant to the sentence. It may be an aggravating or mitigating factor. When sentencing, the judge should consider the motivation behind the offender's actions.

This is a serious offence for the purposes of section 224 of the Criminal Justice Act 2003

Maximum penalty: Life imprisonment

Type/Nature of Activity	Sentence Ranges & Starting Points
Low degree of provocation: A low degree of provocation occurring over a short period	**Sentence Range:** 10 years–life **Starting Point**—12 years' custody
Substantial degree of provocation: A substantial degree of provocation occurring over a short period	**Sentence Range:** 4–9 years **Starting Point**—8 years' custody
High degree of provocation: A high degree of provocation occurring over a short period	**Sentence Range:** if custody is necessary, up to 4 years **Starting Point**—3 years' custody

Additional aggravating factors	Additional mitigating factors
1. Concealment or attempts to dispose of evidence.* 2. Dismemberment or mutilation of the body.* 3. Offence committed in the presence of a child/children or other vulnerable family member. *subject to para 3.6 above.	1. The offender was acting to protect another. 2. Spontaneity and lack of premeditation. 3. Previous experiences of abuse and/or domestic violence. 4. Evidence that the victim presented an ongoing danger to the offender or another. 5. Actual (or reasonably anticipated) violence from the victim.

The Council Guideline New Sentences: Criminal Justice Act 2003 recognised the potentially more demanding nature of custodial sentences of 12 months or longer imposed under the new framework introduced by the Criminal Justice Act 2003. The sentencing ranges and starting points in the above guideline take account of this.

PART 5 ROBBERY SG-34

...This guideline applies to the sentencing of offenders convicted of robbery who are sentenced on or after 1 August 2006.

Part 1 of this guideline provides starting points and sentencing ranges that are applicable to three types of robbery; street robbery or 'mugging', robberies of small businesses and less sophisticated commercial robberies. For other types of robbery, relevant guidance from the Court of Appeal should be applied; this is summarised in Part 2 of this guideline.

The guideline makes clear that robbery will usually merit a custodial sentence but that exceptional circumstances may justify a non-custodial penalty for an adult and, more frequently, for a young offender. In this way it is not intended to make a significant change to current practice. Over the past ten years the majority of young offenders sentenced for robbery have been given a non-custodial sentence. This contrasts with adult offenders where the majority sentenced for robbery have been given a custodial sentence.[52]

The Council Guideline *New Sentences: Criminal Justice Act 2003* recognised the potentially more demanding nature of custodial sentences of 12 months or longer imposed under the new framework introduced by the Criminal Justice Act 2003. Consequently the sentencing ranges and starting points in this guideline take that principle into account...

A. Statutory Provision SG-35

Section 8(1) Theft Act 1968 provides:

A person is guilty of robbery if he steals, and immediately before or at the time of doing so, and in order to do so, he uses force on any person or puts or seeks to put any person in fear of being then and there subjected to force.

B. Forms of Robbery and Structure of the Guideline SG-36

For the purposes of this guideline, five categories of robbery have been identified and established from sentencing ranges and previous guidance. They are:

1. Street robbery or 'mugging'
2. Robberies of small businesses
3. Less sophisticated commercial robberies
4. Violent personal robberies in the home
5. Professionally planned commercial robberies

The guideline is divided into two parts.

Part 1—This part covers categories 1–3 above.

For each of the three categories, three levels of seriousness have been identified based on the extent of force used or threatened.

For each level of seriousness a sentencing range and a starting point within that range have been identified.

Adult and youth offenders are distinguished and the guideline provides for them as separate groups.

Part 2—No guideline is provided for categories 4 and 5. Violent personal robberies are often accompanied by other serious offences which affect sentencing decisions. For professionally planned commercial robberies, existing case authority is still valid and this is summarised in Part 2.

C. Part 1 SG-37

Street robbery or 'mugging'

Street robberies will usually involve some physical force (or threat) to steal modest sums, although in some cases there is significant intimidation or violence. The victim may or may not be physically injured.

Robberies of small businesses

This category covers robberies of businesses such as a small shop or post office, petrol station or public transport/taxi facility which may well lack the physical and electronic security devices available to banks or building societies and larger businesses.

52 In 2004 37% of youths and 87% of adults sentenced for robbery were given custodial sentences.

Less sophisticated commercial robberies

This category covers a wide range of locations, extent of planning and degree of violence including less sophisticated bank robberies or where larger commercial establishments are the target but without detailed planning or high levels of organisation.

SG-38 **D. Assessing Seriousness**

(i) Levels of Seriousness

Three levels of seriousness are identified by reference to the features or type of activity that characterise an offence at each level and the degree of force or threat present. The levels apply to all three categories of robbery but it will be very rare for robberies of small businesses or less sophisticated commercial robberies to have the features of the lowest level of seriousness.

Level 1—Threat and/or use of minimal force

The offence includes the threat or use of force and removal of property such as snatching from a person's grasp causing bruising/pain and discomfort.

The relative seriousness of a level 1 offence depends on:
(a) the nature and duration of any force, threat or intimidation
(b) the extent of injury (if any) to the victim
(c) the value of the property taken
(d) the number and degree of aggravating factors

Level 2—Use of weapon to threaten and/or use of significant force

A weapon is produced and used to threaten, and/or force is used which results in injury to the victim.

The relative seriousness of a level 2 offence depends on:
(a) the nature and duration of the threat or intimidation
(b) the extent of injury (if any) to the victim
(c) the nature of the weapon used, whether it was real and, if it was a real firearm, whether it was loaded
(d) the value of the property taken
(e) the number and degree of aggravating factors

Level 3—Use of weapon and/or significant force and serious injury caused

The victim is caused serious physical injury, such as a broken limb, stab wound or internal injury, by the use of significant force and/or use of a weapon. Offences at this level are often accompanied by the presence of additional aggravating factors such as a degree of planning or the targeting of large sums of money or valuable goods.

The relative seriousness of a level 3 offence depends on:
(a) the extent of injury (if any) to the victim
(b) the nature of the weapon used
(c) the value of the property taken
(d) the number and degree of aggravating factors

(ii) Aggravating & Mitigating Factors

The presence of one or more aggravating features will indicate a more severe sentence within the suggested range. If the aggravating feature(s) are exceptionally serious, the case may move to the next level of seriousness.

Aggravating factors particularly relevant to robbery

(a) Degree of force or violence

- Use of a particular degree of force is more serious than the threat (which is not carried into effect) to use that same degree of force.
- Depending on the facts, however, a threat to use a high degree of force might properly be regarded as more serious than actual use of a lesser degree of force.

(b) Use of a weapon

- Possession of a weapon during the course of an offence will be an aggravating factor, even if it is not used, because it indicates planning.
- Possession of a firearm which is loaded is more serious than possession of a firearm which is unloaded.
- Whether the weapon is real or imitation is not a major factor in determining sentence because the amount of fear created in the victim is likely to be the same.

- In cases of robbery in which a firearm is carried by the offender, a separate offence of possession of a firearm may be charged. In such circumstances, sentencers should consider, where appropriate, the use of consecutive sentences which properly reflect the totality of the offending.

(c) **Vulnerability of the victim**

- Targeting the elderly, the young, those with disabilities and persons performing a service to the public, especially outside normal working hours, will aggravate an offence.

(d) **Number involved in the offence and roles of offenders**

- Group offending will aggravate an offence because the level of intimidation and fear caused to the victim is likely to be greater.
- It may also indicate planning or 'gang' activity.
- The precise role of each offender will be important. Being the ringleader in a group is an aggravating factor. However, an offender may have played a peripheral role in the offence and, rather than having planned to take part, may have become involved spontaneously through the influence of others (see Mitigating Factors below).

(e) **Value of items taken**

- Property value may be more important in planned/sophisticated robberies.
- The value of the property capable of being taken should be taken into account as well as the amount/value of the property actually taken.

(f) **Offence committed at night/in hours of darkness**

- A victim is more vulnerable while in darkness than during daylight, all other things being equal.
- The degree of fear experienced by the victim is likely to be greater if an offence is committed at night or during hours of darkness.

(g) **Wearing of a disguise**

- The wearing of a disguise in order to commit an offence of robbery usually indicates a degree of planning on the part of the offender.
- The deliberate selection of a particular type of disguise in advance of the offence, for example, a balaclava or a mask, will be more serious than the improvised use of items of clothing such as a hat or hood.

Mitigating factors particularly relevant to robbery:

(a) **Unplanned/opportunistic**

- Many street robberies are unplanned or opportunistic by their nature so the extent of the mitigation in such cases may be limited.

(b) **Peripheral involvement**

- Where, as part of a group robbery, the offender has played a peripheral role in the offence this should be treated as a mitigating factor although it should be borne in mind that by participating as part of a group, even in a minor role, the offender is likely to have increased the degree of fear caused to the victim (see Aggravating Factors above).

(c) **Voluntary return of property taken**

- The point at which the property is returned will be important and, in general, the earlier the property is returned the greater the degree of mitigation the offender should receive. **The court will also take account of the presence or absence of other factors including:**
- **Personal mitigation**
- **First offence of violence**
- **Clear evidence of remorse**
- **Ready co-operation with the police**
- **Response to previous sentences**

A list of the most important general aggravating and mitigating factors can be found in the Guideline *Overarching Principles: Seriousness*.[53] These factors are reproduced at Annex A for ease of reference.

[53] Paragraphs 1.22–1.25

Young Offenders

- Young offenders may have characteristics relevant to their offending behaviour which are different from adult offenders. Also, by statute, the youth justice system has the principal aim of preventing offending by children and young persons.[54] Because of this, there may be factors which are of greater significance in cases involving young offenders including:
- Age of the offender
- Immaturity of the offender
- Group Pressure

Sentencers should recognise the varying significance of these factors for different ages.

(iii) Reduction in Sentence for Guilty Plea

Having taking account of aggravating and mitigating factors the court should consider whether the sentence should be reduced to take account of a guilty plea and by how much, in accordance with the Guideline: *Reduction in Sentence for a Guilty Plea.*

SG-39 **E. Public Protection Sentences—Dangerous Offenders**

Robbery is a serious offence for the purposes of section 225 of the Criminal Justice Act 2003 and sentencers should consider whether a life sentence or sentence for public protection should be imposed.

SG-40 **F. Ancillary Orders**

In all cases, courts should consider making the following orders:

- Restitution Order[55]—requiring the return of property
- Compensation Order[56]—for injury, loss or damage suffered.

Where a non-custodial sentence is imposed, courts may also consider making:

- Anti-social behaviour order[57]—to protect the public from behaviour causing harassment, alarm or distress. This order may be particularly appropriate where the offence of robbery forms part of a pattern of behaviour but such an order may be unnecessary if it will simply prohibit what is already criminal conduct. It may be used to prevent some offenders associating with other offenders with whom offences of robbery have been committed.

SG-41 **G. Factors to take into consideration—Adult Offenders**

1. Robbery is a serious offence for the purposes of section 225 of the Criminal Justice Act 2003 and sentencers should consider whether a life sentence or sentence for public protection should be imposed. The following guidelines apply to offenders who have not been assessed as dangerous.
2. The sentencing ranges and presumptive starting points apply to all three categories of robbery detailed above:
   - **Street robbery or 'mugging'**
   - **Robberies of small businesses**
   - **Less sophisticated commercial robberies**
3. The 'starting points' are based upon a first time offender who pleaded not guilty.
4. A reduction to the appropriate sentence, taking account of seriousness and aggravating and mitigating factors, will need to be made if an offender has pleaded guilty. The effect of applying the reduction may be that the sentence imposed for an offence at one level of seriousness may fall within the range suggested for the next lowest level of seriousness.
5. The relative seriousness of each offence will be determined by the following factors:
   - **Degree of force and/or nature and duration of threats**
   - **Degree of injury to the victim**
   - **Degree of fear experienced by the victim**
   - **Value of property taken**
6. Use of a particular degree of force is more serious than the threat (which is not carried into effect) to use that same degree of force. Depending on the facts, however, a threat to use a high degree of force might properly be regarded as more serious than actual use of a lesser degree of force.
7. If a weapon is involved in the use or threat of force, the offence will be more serious. Possession of a weapon during the course of an offence will be an aggravating factor, even if it is not used, because it

[54] Crime and Disorder Act 1998, section 37
[55] Powers of Criminal Courts (Sentencing) Act 2000, sections 148–149
[56] ibid section 130
[57] Crime and Disorder Act 1998, section 1 as amended

indicates planning. If the offence involves a real firearm it will be more serious if that firearm is loaded. Whether the weapon is real or imitation is not a major factor in determining sentence because the amount of fear created in the victim is likely to be the same.

8. The value of the property capable of being taken as well as the actual amount taken is important.
9. The presence of one or more aggravating features will indicate a more severe sentence within the suggested range and, if the aggravating feature(s) are exceptionally serious, the case will move up to the next level.
10. In all cases, courts should consider making a restitution order and/or a compensation order. Where a non-custodial sentence is imposed, the court may also consider making an anti-social behaviour order.
11. Passing the custody threshold does not mean that a custodial sentence should be deemed inevitable.[58]

Street Robbery or 'Mugging' Robberies of Small Businesses Less Sophisticated Commercial Robberies SG-42

Robbery is a serious offence for the purposes of sections 225 and 227 Criminal Justice Act 2003

Maximum Penalty: Life imprisonment

ADULT OFFENDERS

Type/nature of activity	**Starting point**	**Sentencing Range**
The offence includes the threat or use of minimal force and removal of property.	12 months' custody	Up to 3 years' custody
A weapon is produced and used to threaten, and/or force is used which results in injury to the victim.	4 years' custody	2–7 years' custody
The victim is caused serious physical injury by the use of significant force and/or use of a weapon.	8 years' custody	7–12 years' custody

Additional aggravating factors	**Additional mitigating factors**
1. More than one offender involved.	1. Unplanned/opportunistic.
2. Being the ringleader of a group of offenders.	2. Peripheral involvement.
3. Restraint, detention or additional degradation, taken.	3. Voluntary return of property of the victim.
4. Offence was pre-planned.	4. Clear evidence of remorse.
5. Wearing a disguise.	5. Ready co-operation with the police.
6. Offence committed at night.	
7. Vulnerable victim targeted.	
8. Targeting of large sums of money or valuable goods.	
9. Possession of a weapon that was not used.	

H. Factors to Take into Consideration—Young Offenders SG-43

1. A youth court cannot impose a custodial sentence on an offender aged 10 or 11. If the offender is aged 12, 13 or 14, a detention and training order can only be imposed by a youth court in the case of persistent young offenders. In the Crown Court, however, long term detention in accordance with the Powers of Criminal Courts (Sentencing) Act 2000 can be ordered on any young offender without the requirement of persistence. The Crown Court may also impose an extended sentence, detention for public protection or detention for life where the young offender meets the criteria for being a 'dangerous offender.' **The following guidelines apply to offenders who have *not* been assessed as dangerous.**

[58] Guideline *Overarching Principles: Seriousness*, para 1.32

2. If a youth court is considering sending a case to the Crown Court, the court must be of the view that it is such a serious case that detention above two years is required, or that the appropriate sentence is a custodial sentence approaching the two year limit which is normally applicable to older offenders.[59]
3. The sentencing ranges and presumptive starting points apply to all three categories of robbery detailed above:
   - **Street robbery or 'mugging'**
   - **Robberies of small businesses**
   - **Less sophisticated commercial robberies**
4. The 'starting points' are based upon a first-time offender, aged 17 years old, who pleaded not guilty. For younger offenders sentencers should consider whether a lower starting point is justified in recognition of the offender's age or immaturity.
5. Young offenders may have characteristics relevant to their offending behaviour which are different from adult offenders. Also, by statute, the youth justice system has the principal aim of preventing offending by children and young persons.[60] Because of this, there may be factors which are of greater significance in cases involving young offenders. Sentencers should recognise the varying significance of such factors for different ages.
6. A reduction to the appropriate sentence, taking account of seriousness, and aggravating and mitigating factors, will need to be made if an offender has pleaded guilty. The effect of applying the reduction may be that the sentence imposed for an offence at one level of seriousness may fall within the range suggested for the next lowest level of seriousness.
7. The relative seriousness of each offence will be determined by the following factors:
   - **Degree of force and/or nature and duration of threats**
   - **Degree of injury to the victim**
   - **Degree of fear experienced by the victim**
   - **Value of property taken**
8. Use of a particular degree of force is more serious than the threat (which is not carried into effect) to use that same degree of force. Depending on the facts, however, a threat to use a high degree of force might properly be regarded as more serious than actual use of a lesser degree of force.
9. If a weapon is involved in the use or threat of force, the offence will be more serious. Possession of a weapon during the course of an offence will be an aggravating factor, even if it is not used, because it indicates planning. If the offence involves a real firearm it will be more serious if that firearm is loaded. Whether the weapon is real or imitation is not a major factor in determining sentence because the amount of fear created in the victim is likely to be the same.
10. The value of the property capable of being taken as well as the actual amount taken is important.
11. The presence of one or more aggravating features will indicate a more severe sentence within the suggested range and, if the aggravating feature(s) are exceptionally serious, the case will move up to the next level.
12. In all cases, courts should consider making a restitution order and/or a compensation order. Where a non-custodial sentence is imposed, the court may also consider making an anti-social behaviour order.
13. Courts are required by section 44(1) of the Children and Young Persons Act 1933 to have regard to the welfare of the child, and under section 37 of the Crime and Disorder Act 1998 to have regard to the overall aim of the youth justice system of preventing re-offending.
14. Passing the custody threshold does not mean that a custodial sentence should be deemed inevitable.[61]
15. Where there is evidence that the offence has been committed to fund a drug habit and that treatment for this could help tackle the offender's offending behaviour, sentencers should consider a drug treatment requirement as part of a supervision order or action plan order.

[59] *W v Southampton Youth Court, K v Wirral Borough Magistrates' Court* [2003] 1 Cr App R (S) 87

[60] Crime and Disorder Act 1998, section 37

[61] Guideline *Overarching Principles: Seriousness*, paragraph 1.32

SG-44

Street Robbery or 'Mugging' Robberies of Small Businesses Less Sophisticated Commercial Robberies

Robbery is a serious offence for the purposes of sections 226 and 228 Criminal Justice Act 2003

YOUNG OFFENDERS*

Type/nature of activity	Starting point	Sentencing Range
The offence includes the threat or use of minimal force and removal of property.	Community Order	Community Order–12 months detention and training order
A weapon is produced and used to threaten, and/or force is used which results in injury to the victim.	3 years' detention	1–6 years' detention
The victim is caused serious physical injury by the use of significant force and/or use of a weapon.	7 years' detention	6–10 years' detention

* The 'starting points' are based upon a first-time offender aged 17 years old who pleaded not guilty. For younger offenders, sentencers should consider whether a lower starting point is justified in recognition of the offender's age or immaturity.

Maximum Penalty: Life imprisonment

Additional aggravating factors	Additional mitigating factors
1. More than one offender involved. 2. Being the ringleader of a group of offenders. 3. Restraint, detention or additional degradation, taken. 4. Offence was pre-planned. 5. Wearing a disguise. 6. Offence committed at night. 7. Vulnerable victim targeted. 8. Targeting of large sums of money or valuable goods. 9. Possession of a weapon that was not used.	1. Unplanned/opportunistic. 2. Peripheral involvement. 3. Voluntary return of property of the victim. 4. Clear evidence of remorse. 5. Ready co-operation with the police. 6. Age of the offender. 7. Immaturity of the offender. 8. Peer group pressure.

I. Part 2

Relevant guidance from the Court of Appeal (which is summarised below for ease of reference) should apply to cases falling within the final two categories of robbery.

Violent personal robberies in the home

The sentencing range for robbery in the home involving physical violence is 13–16 years for a first time offender pleading not guilty. In this type of case, the starting point reflects the high level of violence, although it is clear that longer terms will be appropriate where extreme violence is used.[62]

This category overlaps with some cases of aggravated burglary (an offence which also carries a maximum of life imprisonment) where comparable sentences are passed. Consideration will need to be given as to whether the offender is a 'dangerous offender' for the purposes of the Criminal Justice Act 2003.

[62] *O'Driscoll* (1986) 8 Cr App R (S) 121

Sentencing Guidelines

Professionally planned commercial robberies

The leading Court of Appeal decision on sentencing for robbery is the 1975 case of *Turner*.[63] This focuses on serious commercial robberies at the upper end of the sentencing range but just below the top level—planned professional robberies of banks and security vehicles, involving firearms and high value theft, but without the additional elements that characterise the most serious cases. The Court of Appeal said it had 'come to the conclusion that the normal sentence for anyone taking part in a bank robbery or in the holdup of a security or a Post Office van should be 15 years if firearms were carried and no serious injury done.'

The Court also said that 18 years should be about the maximum for crimes which are not 'wholly abnormal' (such as the Great Train Robbery).[64]

In cases involving the most serious commercial robberies the Court has imposed 20–30 years (15–20 years after a plea of guilty).

Consideration will need to be given as to whether the offender is a 'dangerous offender' for the purposes of the Criminal Justice Act 2003.

Annex A

[Annex A consists of extracts from the SGC Guideline, *Overarching Principles: Seriousness*, which is reproduced in full in **part 3**.]

SG-45

PART 6 BREACH OF A PROTECTIVE ORDER

Foreword

...This guideline applies to offenders convicted of breach of an order who are sentenced on or after 18 December 2006.

This guideline deals specifically with the sentencing of offenders who have breached either a restraining order imposed in order to prevent future conduct causing harassment or fear of violence, or a non-molestation order which prohibits a person from molesting another person.

It highlights the particular factors that courts should take into account when dealing with the criminal offence of breaching an order and includes starting points based on the different types of activity which can constitute a breach. It also identifies relevant aggravating and mitigating factors.

...

SG-46 **A. Statutory Provisions**

1.1 For the purposes of this guideline, two protective orders are considered:

(i) Restraining Order

1.2 It is an offence contrary to the Protection from Harassment Act 1997 to behave in a way which a person knows (or ought to know) causes someone else harassment (section 2) or fear of violence (section 4). When imposing sentence on an offender, a court may also impose a restraining order to prevent future conduct causing harassment or fear of violence.

1.3 An offence under these provisions may have occurred in a domestic context or may have occurred in other contexts. The Domestic Violence, Crime and Victims Act 2004 provides for such orders also to be made on conviction for any offence or following acquittal.[65]

1.4 It is an offence contrary to section 5(5) of the Act to fail to comply with the restraining order without reasonable excuse. That offence is punishable with a maximum of five years imprisonment.

(ii) Non-Molestation Order

1.5 Section 42 of the Family Law Act 1996 provides that, during family proceedings, a court may make a non-molestation order containing either or both of the following provisions:

(a) provision prohibiting a person ('the respondent') from molesting another person who is associated with the respondent;

(b) provision prohibiting the respondent from molesting a relevant child.

63 (1975) 61 Cr App R 67

64 *Wilson and others* (1964) 48 Cr App R 329

65 When in force, section 12 of the 2004 Act amends section 5 of the 1997 Act and inserts a new section 5A to that Act.

1.6 Section 1 of the Domestic Violence, Crime and Victims Act 2004[66] inserts a new section 42A into the 1996 Act. Section 42A(1) will provide that it is an offence to fail to comply with the order without reasonable excuse. That offence is punishable with a maximum of five years imprisonment.

1.7 In addition, breach of a non-molestation order may be dealt with as a contempt of court.

B. Sentencing for Breach SG-47

2.1 The facts that constitute a breach of a protective order may or may not also constitute a substantive offence. Where they do constitute a substantive offence, it is desirable that the substantive offence and the breach of the order should be charged as separate counts. Where necessary, consecutive sentences should be considered to reflect the seriousness of the counts and achieve the appropriate totality.

2.2 Sometimes, however, only the substantive offence or only the breach of the order will be charged. The basic principle is that the sentence should reflect all relevant aspects of the offence so that, provided the facts are not in issue, the result should be the same, regardless of whether one count or two has been charged. For example:

(i) **if the substantive offence only has been charged, the fact that it constitutes breach of a protective order should be treated as an aggravating factor;**

(ii) **if breach of the protective order only has been charged, the sentence should reflect the nature of the breach, namely, the conduct that amounts to the substantive offence, aggravated by the fact that it is also breach of an order.**

2.3 If breach of a protective order has been charged where no substantive offence was involved, the sentence should reflect the circumstances of the breach, including whether it was an isolated breach, or part of a course of conduct in breach of the order; whether it was planned or unpre-meditated; and any consequences of the breach, including psychiatric injury or distress to the person protected by the order.

C. Factors Influencing Sentencing SG-48

3.1 **In order to ensure that a protective order achieves the purpose it is intended for—protecting the victim from harm—it is important that the terms of the order are necessary and proportionate.**

3.2 The circumstances leading to the making of one of the protective orders will vary widely. Whilst a restraining order will be made in criminal proceedings, it will almost certainly result from offences of markedly different levels of seriousness or even acquittal. A nonmolestation order will have been made in civil proceedings and, again, may follow a wide variety of conduct by the subject of the order.

3.3 **In all cases the order will have been made to protect an individual from harm and action in response to breach should have as its primary aim the importance of ensuring that the order is complied with and that it achieves the protection that it was intended to achieve.**

3.4 **When sentencing for a breach of an order, the main aim should be to achieve future compliance with that order where that is realistic.**

The nature and context of the originating conduct or offence

3.5 The nature of the original conduct or offence is relevant in so far as it allows a judgement to be made on the level of harm caused to the victim by the breach and the extent to which that harm was intended by the offender.

3.6 If the original offence was serious, conduct which breaches the order might have a severe effect on the victim where in other contexts such conduct might appear minor. Even indirect contact, such as telephone calls, can cause significant harm or anxiety for a victim.

3.7 However, sentence following a breach is for the breach alone and must avoid punishing the offender again for the offence or conduct as a result of which the order was made.

The nature and context of the conduct that caused the breach

3.8 **The protective orders are designed to protect a victim. When dealing with a breach, a court will need to consider the extent to which the conduct amounting to breach put the victim at risk of harm.**

3.9 There may be exceptional cases where the nature of the breach is particularly serious but has not been dealt with by a separate offence being charged. In these cases, the risk posed by the offender and the nature of the breach will be particularly significant in determining the response. Where the order is breached by the use of physical violence, the starting point should normally be a custodial sentence.

---

[66] When in force.

3.10 Non-violent behaviour and/or indirect contact can also cause (or be intended to cause) a high degree of harm and anxiety. In such circumstances, it is likely that the custody threshold will have been crossed.

3.11 Where an order was made in civil proceedings, its purpose may have been to cause the subject of the order to modify behaviour rather than to imply that the conduct was especially serious. If so, it is likely to be disproportionate to impose a custodial sentence for a breach of the order if the breach did not involve threats or violence.

3.12 In some cases where a breach might result in a short custodial sentence but the court is satisfied that the offender genuinely intends to reform his or her behaviour and there is a real prospect of rehabilitation, the court may consider it appropriate to impose a sentence that will allow this. This may mean imposing a suspended sentence order or a community order (where appropriate with a requirement to attend an accredited domestic violence programme).

3.13 **Breach of a protective order will generally be more serious than breach of a conditional discharge.** Not only is a breach of a protective order an offence in its own right but it also undermines a specific prohibition imposed by the court. Breach of a conditional discharge amounts to an offender failing to take a chance that has been provided by the court.

SG-49 D. Aggravating and Mitigating Factors

4.1 Many of the aggravating factors which apply to an offence of violence in a domestic context will apply also to an offence arising from breach of a protective order.

Aggravating Factors

(i) Victim is particularly vulnerable

4.2 For cultural, religious, language, financial or any other reasons, some victims may be more vulnerable than others. This vulnerability means that the terms of a protective order are particularly important and a violation of those terms will warrant a higher penalty than usual.

4.3 Age, disability or the fact that the victim was pregnant or had recently given birth at the time of the offence may make a victim particularly vulnerable.

4.4 Any steps taken to prevent the victim reporting an incident or obtaining assistance will usually aggravate the offence.

(ii) Impact on children

4.5 If a protective order is imposed in order to protect children, either solely or in addition to another victim, then a breach of that order will generally be more serious.[67]

(iii) A proven history of violence or threats by the offender

4.6 Of necessity, a breach of a protective order will not be the first time an offender has caused fear or harassment towards a victim. However, the offence will be more serious if the breach is part of a series of prolonged violence or harassment towards the victim or the offender has a history of disobedience to court orders.

4.7 Where an offender has previously been convicted of an offence involving domestic violence, either against the same or a different person, or has been convicted for a breach of an order, this is likely to be a statutory aggravating factor.[68]

(iv) Using contact arrangements with a child to instigate an offence

4.8 An offence will be aggravated where an offender exploits contact arrangements with a child in order to commit an offence.

(v) Victim is forced to leave home

4.9 A breach will be aggravated if, as a consequence, the victim is forced to leave home.

(vi) Additional aggravating factors

4.10 In addition to the factors listed above, the following will aggravate a breach of an order:

- the offence is a further breach, following earlier breach proceedings;
- the breach was committed immediately or shortly after the order was made.

---

[67] The definition of 'harm' in section 31(9) of the Children Act 1989 as amended by section 120 of the Adoption and Children Act 2002 includes 'impairment suffered from seeing or hearing the ill-treatment of another'.

[68] Criminal Justice Act 2003, section 143(2)

Mitigating Factors

(i) Breach was committed after a long period of compliance

4.11 If the court is satisfied that the offender has complied with a protective order for a substantial period before a breach is committed, the court should take this into account when imposing sentence for the breach. The history of the relationship and the specific nature of the contact will be relevant in determining its significance as a mitigating factor.

(ii) Victim initiated contact

4.12 If the conditions of an order are breached following contact from the victim, this should be considered as mitigation. It is important to consider the history of the relationship and the specific nature of the contact in determining its significance as a mitigating factor.

4.13 Nonetheless it is important for the court to make clear that it is the responsibility of the offender and not the victim to ensure that the order is complied with.

E. Factors to take into Consideration **SG-50**

Aims of sentencing

(a) When sentencing for a breach of a protective order (which would have been imposed to protect a victim from further harm), the main aim should be to achieve future compliance with that order.

(b) A court will need to assess the level of risk posed by the offender. If the offender requires treatment or assistance for mental health or other issues, willingness to undergo treatment or accept help may influence sentence.

1. Key Factors

(a) The nature of the conduct that caused the breach of the order, in particular, whether the contact was direct or indirect, although it is important to recognise that indirect contact is capable of causing significant harm or anxiety.

(b) **There may be exceptional cases where the nature of the breach is particularly serious but has not been dealt with by a separate offence being charged. In these cases the risk posed by the offender and the nature of the breach will be particularly significant in determining the response.**

(c) The nature of the original conduct or offence is relevant to sentencing for the breach in so far as it allows a judgement to be made on the level of harm caused to the victim by the breach, and the extent to which that harm was intended by the offender.

(d) The sentence following a breach is for the breach alone and must avoid punishing the offender again for the offence or conduct as a result of which the order was made.

(e) Where violence is used to breach a restraining order or a molestation order, custody is the starting point for sentence.

(f) Non-violent conduct in breach may cross the custody threshold where a high degree of harm or anxiety has been caused to the victim.

(g) Where an order was made in civil proceedings, its purpose may have been to cause the subject of the order to modify behaviour rather than to imply that the conduct was especially serious. If so, it is likely to be disproportionate to impose a custodial sentence for a breach of the order if the breach did not involve threats or violence.

(h) In some cases where a breach might result in a short custodial sentence but the court is satisfied that the offender genuinely intends to reform his or her behaviour and there is a real prospect of rehabilitation, the court may consider it appropriate to impose a sentence that will allow this. This may mean imposing a suspended sentence order or a community order (where appropriate with a requirement to attend an accredited domestic violence programme).

(i) While, in principle, consecutive sentences may be imposed for each breach of which the offender is convicted, the overall sentence should reflect the totality principle.

2. General

(a) Breach of a protective order should be considered more serious than a breach of a conditional discharge.

(b) The principle of reduction in sentence for a guilty plea should be applied as set out in the Council guideline *Reduction in Sentence for a Guilty Plea*.

3. Non-custodial sentences

(a) It is likely that all breaches of protective orders will pass the threshold for a community sentence. The reference in the starting points to medium and low range community orders refers to the Council guideline *New Sentences: Criminal Justice Act 2003* paragraphs 1.1.18–1.1.32.

(b) In accordance with general principle, the fact that the seriousness of an offence crosses a particular threshold does not preclude the court from imposing another type of sentence of a lower level where appropriate.

BREACH OF A PROTECTIVE ORDER

Breach of a Restraining Order
Section 5(5) Protection from Harassment Act 1997
Breach of a Non-Molestation Order
*Section 42A Family Law Act 1996**

Maximum Penalty: **5 years imprisonment**

Where the conduct is particularly serious, it would normally be charged as a separate offence. These starting points are based on the premise that the activity has either been prosecuted separately as an offence or is not of a character sufficient to justify prosecution of it as an offence in its own right.

Nature of activity	**Starting points**
	Custodial Sentence
Breach (whether one or more) involving significant physical violence and significant physical or psychological harm to the victim.	More than 12 months The length of the custodial sentence imposed will depend on the nature and seriousness of the breach(es).
More than one breach involving some violence and/or significant physical or psychological harm to the victim.	26–39 weeks' custody [Medium/High Custody Plus order]**
Single breach involving some violence and/or significant physical or psychological harm to the victim.	13–26 weeks' custody [Low/Medium Custody Plus order]**
	Non-Custodial Sentence
More than one breach involving no/minimal contact or some direct contact.	MEDIUM range community order
Single breach involving no/minimal direct contact.	LOW range community order

Additional aggravating factors	**Additional mitigating factors**
1. Victim is particularly vulnerable. 2. Impact on children. 3. A proven history of violence or threats by the offender. 4. Using contact arrangements with a child to instigate an offence. 5. Victim is forced to leave home. 6. Offence is a further breach, following earlier breach proceedings. 7. Offender has a history of disobedience to court orders. 8. Breach was committed immediately or shortly after the order was made.	1. Breach occurred after a long period of compliance. 2. Victim initiated contact.

* When in force.
** When the relevant provisions of the Criminal Justice Act 2003 are in force.

SG-51 PART 7 OVERARCHING PRINCIPLES: DOMESTIC VIOLENCE

Foreword

...This guideline applies to offences sentenced on or after 18 December 2006.

This guideline stems from a reference from the Home Secretary for consideration of sentencing in cases of domestic violence. The referral suggested that 'domestic violence' should be described in terms of the Crown Prosecution Service definition (described on page 3) and this suggestion was adopted by the Council.

Consequently this guideline is for use for all cases that fall within the Crown Prosecution Service definition of domestic violence.

There is no specific offence of domestic violence. The definition covers a broad set of circumstances and allows conduct amounting to domestic violence to be covered by a wide range of offences. The guideline identifies the principles relevant to the sentencing of cases involving violence that has occurred in a domestic context and includes details of particular aggravating and mitigating factors.

This guideline makes clear that offences committed in a domestic context should be regarded as being no less serious than offences committed in a non-domestic context. Indeed, because an offence has been committed in a domestic context, there are likely to be aggravating factors present that make it more serious.

In many situations of domestic violence, the circumstances require the sentence to demonstrate clearly that the conduct is unacceptable. However, there will be some situations where all parties genuinely and realistically wish the relationship to continue as long as the violence stops. In those situations, and where the violence is towards the lower end of the scale of seriousness, it is likely to be appropriate for the court to impose a sentence that provides the support necessary.

. . .

A. Definition of Domestic Violence SG-52

1.1 There is no specific offence of domestic violence and conduct amounting to domestic violence is covered by a number of statutory provisions. For the purposes of this guideline, wherever such offending occurs, domestic violence is:

> 'Any incident of threatening behaviour, violence or abuse [psychological, physical, sexual, financial or emotional] between adults who are or have been intimate partners or family members, regardless of gender or sexuality.'[69]

1.2 Most incidents of domestic violence can be charged as one of a wide range of offences including physical assault (with or without a weapon), harassment, threats to cause injury or to kill, destroying or damaging property, false imprisonment (locking the victim in a room or preventing that person from leaving the house), and sexual offences.

1.3 This guideline covers issues which are relevant across the range of offences that might be committed in a domestic context. Under the above definition, the domestic context includes relationships involving intimate partners who are living together, intimate partners who do not live together and former intimate partners. It is also wide enough to include relationships between family members, for example between a father and a daughter, or a mother and a daughter, perhaps where the daughter is the mother's carer.

B. Assessing Seriousness SG-53

2.1 **As a starting point for sentence, offences committed in a domestic context should be regarded as being no less serious than offences committed in a non-domestic context.**

2.2 Thus, the starting point for sentencing should be the same irrespective of whether the offender and the victim are known to each other (whether by virtue of being current or former intimate partners, family members, friends or acquaintances) or unknown to each other.

2.3 A number of aggravating factors may commonly arise by virtue of the offence being committed in a domestic context and these will increase the seriousness of such offences. These are described in more detail in C below.

C. Aggravating and Mitigating Factors SG-54

3.1 Since domestic violence takes place within the context of a current or past relationship, the history of the relationship will often be relevant in assessing the gravity of the offence. Therefore, a court is entitled to take into account anything occurring within the relationship as a whole, which may reveal relevant aggravating or mitigating factors.

[69] This is the Government definition of domestic violence agreed in 2004. It is taken from Policy on Prosecuting cases of Domestic Violence, Crown Prosecution Service, 2005.

3.2 The following aggravating and mitigating factors (which are not intended to be exhaustive) are of particular relevance to offences committed in a domestic context, and should be read alongside the general factors set out in the Council guideline *Overarching Principles: Seriousness*.[70]

Aggravating Factors

(i) Abuse of trust and abuse of power

3.3 The guideline *Overarching Principles: Seriousness* identifies abuse of a position of trust and abuse of power as factors that indicate higher culpability. Within the nature of relationship required to meet the definition of domestic violence set out above, trust implies a mutual expectation of conduct that shows consideration, honesty, care and responsibility. In some such relationships, one of the parties will have the power to exert considerable control over the other.

3.4 In the context of domestic violence:

- an *abuse of trust*, whether through direct violence or emotional abuse, represents a violation of this understanding;
- an *abuse of power* in a relationship involves restricting another individual's autonomy which is sometimes a specific characteristic of domestic violence. This involves the exercise of control over an individual by means which may be psychological, physical, sexual, financial or emotional.

3.5 Where an abuse of trust or abuse of power is present, it will aggravate the seriousness of an offence. These factors are likely to exist in many offences of violence within a domestic context.

3.6 However, the breadth of the definition of domestic violence (set out in 1.1 above) encompasses offences committed by a former spouse or partner. Accordingly, there will be circumstances where the abuse of trust or abuse of power may be a very minor feature of an offence or may be deemed no longer to exist—for example, where the offender and victim have been separated for a long period of time.

(ii) Victim is particularly vulnerable

3.7 For cultural, religious, language, financial or any other reasons, some victims of domestic violence may be more vulnerable than others, not least because these issues may make it almost impossible for the victim to leave a violent relationship.

3.8 Where a perpetrator has exploited a victim's vulnerability (for instance, when the circumstances have been used by the perpetrator to prevent the victim from seeking and obtaining help), an offence will warrant a higher penalty.

3.9 Age, disability or the fact that the victim was pregnant or had recently given birth at the time of the offence may make a victim particularly vulnerable.

3.10 Any steps taken to prevent the victim reporting an incident or obtaining assistance will usually aggravate the offence.

(iii) Impact on children

3.11 Exposure of children to an offence (either directly or indirectly) is an aggravating factor.

3.12 Children are likely to be adversely affected by directly witnessing violence or other abuse and by being aware of it taking place while they are elsewhere in the home.[71]

(iv) Using contact arrangements with a child to instigate an offence

3.13 An offence will be aggravated where an offender exploits contact arrangements with a child in order to commit an offence.

(v) A proven history of violence or threats by the offender in a domestic setting

3.14 It is important that an assessment of the seriousness of an offence recognises the cumulative effect of a series of violent incidents or threats over a prolonged period, where such conduct has been proved or accepted.

3.15 Where an offender has previously been convicted of an offence involving domestic violence either against the same or a different partner, this is likely to be a statutory aggravating factor.[72]

[70] Published December 2004. The lists of aggravating factors from the guideline are reproduced at Annex A for ease of reference. See also www.sentencing-guidelines.gov.uk

[71] The definition of 'harm' in section 31(9) of the Children Act 1989 as amended by section 120 of the Adoption and Children Act 2002 includes 'impairment suffered from seeing or hearing the ill-treatment of another'.

[72] Criminal Justice Act 2003, section 143(2)

(vi) A history of disobedience to court orders

3.16 A breach of an order that has been imposed for the purpose of protecting a victim can cause significant harm or anxiety. Where an offender's history of disobedience has had this effect, it will be an aggravating factor.

3.17 Commission of the offence in breach of a non-molestation order imposed in civil proceedings, in breach of a sentence (such as a conditional discharge) imposed for similar offending, or while subject to an ancillary order, such as a restraining order, will aggravate the seriousness of the offence.

3.18 The appropriate response to breach of a civil order is dealt with in a separate guideline *Breach of a Protective Order*.

(vii) Victim forced to leave home

3.19 An offence will be aggravated if, as a consequence, the victim is forced to leave home.

Mitigating Factors

(i) Positive good character

3.20 As a general principle of sentencing, a court will take account of an offender's positive good character. However, it is recognised that one of the factors that can allow domestic violence to continue unnoticed for lengthy periods is the ability of the perpetrator to have two personae. In respect of an offence of violence in a domestic context, an offender's good character in relation to conduct outside the home should generally be of no relevance where there is a proven pattern of behaviour.

3.21 Positive good character is of greater relevance in the rare case where the court is satisfied that the offence was an isolated incident.

(ii) Provocation

3.22 It may be asserted that the offence, at least in part, has been provoked by the conduct of the victim. Such assertions need to be treated with great care, both in determining whether they have a factual basis and in considering whether in the circumstances the alleged conduct amounts to provocation sufficient to mitigate the seriousness of the offence.

3.23 For provocation to be a mitigating factor, it will usually involve actual or anticipated violence including psychological bullying. Provocation is likely to have more of an effect as mitigation if it has taken place over a significant period of time.

D. Other Factors Influencing Sentence **SG-55**

Wishes of the victim and effect of the sentence

4.1 As a matter of general principle, a sentence imposed for an offence of violence should be determined by the seriousness of the offence, not by the expressed wishes of the victim.

4.2 There are a number of reasons why it may be particularly important that this principle is observed in a case of domestic violence:

- it is undesirable that a victim should feel a responsibility for the sentence imposed;
- there is a risk that a plea for mercy made by a victim will be induced by threats made by, or by a fear of, the offender;
- the risk of such threats will be increased if it is generally believed that the severity of the sentence may be affected by the wishes of the victim.

4.3 Nonetheless, there may be circumstances in which the court can properly mitigate a sentence to give effect to the expressed wish of the victim that the relationship be permitted to continue. The court must, however, be confident that such a wish is genuine, and that giving effect to it will not expose the victim to a real risk of further violence. Critical conditions are likely to be the seriousness of the offence and the history of the relationship. It is vitally important that the court has up-to-date information in a pre-sentence report and victim personal statement.

4.4 Either the offender or the victim (or both) may ask the court to take into consideration the interests of any children and to impose a less severe sentence. The court will wish to have regard not only to the effect on the children if the relationship is disrupted but also to the likely effect on the children of any further incidents of domestic violence.

E. Factors to Take into Consideration **SG-56**

The following points of principle should be considered by a court when imposing sentence for any offence of violence committed in a domestic context.

1. Offences committed in a domestic context should be regarded as being no less serious than offences committed in a non-domestic context.

2. Many offences of violence in a domestic context are dealt with in a magistrates' court as an offence of common assault or assault occasioning actual bodily harm because the injuries sustained are relatively minor. Offences involving serious violence will warrant a custodial sentence in the majority of cases.
3. Some offences will be specified offences for the purposes of the dangerous offender provisions.[73] In such circumstances, consideration will need to be given to whether there is a significant risk of serious harm to members of the public, which include, of course, family members. If so, the court will be required to impose a life sentence, imprisonment for public protection or an extended sentence.
4. Where the custody threshold is only just crossed, so that if a custodial sentence is imposed it will be a short sentence, the court will wish to consider whether the better option is a suspended sentence order or a community order, including in either case a requirement to attend an accredited domestic violence programme. Such an option will only be appropriate where the court is satisfied that the offender genuinely intends to reform his or her behaviour and that there is a real prospect of rehabilitation being successful. Such a situation is unlikely to arise where there has been a pattern of abuse.

Annex A

Extracts from Guideline *Overarching Principles: Seriousness*

[Omitted: the relevant Guideline is set out in full in part 3.]

PART 8 SEXUAL OFFENCES

[These guidelines have effect from 1 April 2014. Part 7 of the 2007 guideline is also reproduced].

SG-57 **Applicability of guideline**

In accordance with section 120 of the Coroners and Justice Act 2009, the Sentencing Council issues this definitive guideline. It applies to all offenders aged 18 and older, who are sentenced on or after 1 April 2014.

...This guideline applies only to offenders aged 18 and older. General principles to be considered in the sentencing of youths are in the Sentencing Guidelines Council's definitive guideline, *Overarching Principles—Sentencing Youths.*

SG-58 **Structure, ranges and starting points**

For the purposes of section 125(3)–(4) of the Coroners and Justice Act 2009, the guideline specifies *offence ranges*— the range of sentences appropriate for each type of offence. Within each offence, the Council has specified different *categories* which reflect varying degrees of seriousness. The offence range is split into *category ranges* — sentences appropriate for each level of seriousness. The Council has also identified a starting point within each category.

Starting points define the position within a category range from which to start calculating the provisional sentence. **Starting points apply to all offences within the corresponding category and are applicable to all offenders, in all cases.** Once the starting point is established, the court should consider further aggravating and mitigating factors and previous convictions so as to adjust the sentence within the range. Starting points and ranges apply to all offenders, whether they have pleaded guilty or been convicted after trial. Credit for a guilty plea is taken into consideration only at step four in the decision making process, after the appropriate sentence has been identified.

Information on ancillary orders is set out at Annex A [see **SG-186**]. Information on historic offences is set out at annexes B and C on [see **SG-187** and **SG-188**].

Information on community orders and fine bands is set out at Annex D [not reproduced here but see **SG-358** and **SG-382**].

[73] Criminal Justice Act 2003, part 12, chapter 5

Rape SG-59

Sexual Offences Act 2003 (section 1)

[For rape of a child under 13, see SG-75.]
Triable only on indictment
Maximum: Life imprisonment

Offence range: 4–19 years' custody

This is a serious specified offence for the purposes of sections 224 and 225(2) (life sentence for serious offences) of the Criminal Justice Act 2003.

For offences committed on or after 3 December 2012, this is an offence listed in Part 1 of Schedule 15B for the purposes of sections 224A (life sentence for second listed offence) of the Criminal Justice Act 2003.

For convictions on or after 3 December 2012 (irrespective of the date of commission of the offence), this is a specified offence for the purposes of section 226A (extended sentence for certain violent or sexual offences) of the Criminal Justice Act 2003.

STEP ONE Determining the offence category SG-60

The court should determine which categories of harm and culpability the offence falls into by reference **only** to the tables below.

Offences may be of such severity, for example involving a campaign of rape, that sentences of 20 years and above may be appropriate.

Harm	
Category 1	• The extreme nature of one or more category 2 factors or the extreme impact caused by a combination of category 2 factors **may** elevate to category 1
Category 2	• Severe psychological or physical harm • Pregnancy or STI as a consequence of offence • Additional degradation/humiliation • Abduction • Prolonged detention/sustained incident • Violence or threats of violence (beyond that which is inherent in the offence) • Forced/uninvited entry into victim's home • Victim is particularly vulnerable due to personal circumstances*
Category 3	Factor(s) in categories 1 and 2 not present

* For children under 13 please refer to the guideline [at SG-75].

Culpability	
A	B
• Significant degree of planning • Offender acts together with others to commit the offence • Use of alcohol/drugs on victim to facilitate the offence • Abuse of trust • Previous violence against victim • Offence committed in course of burglary • Recording of the offence • Commercial exploitation and/or motivation • Offence racially or religiously aggravated • Offence motivated by, or demonstrating, hostility to the victim based on his or her sexual orientation (or presumed sexual orientation) or transgender identity (or presumed transgender identity) • Offence motivated by, or demonstrating, hostility to the victim based on his or her disability (or presumed disability)	Factor(s) in category A not present

STEP TWO Starting point and category range SG-61

Having determined the category, the court should use the corresponding starting points to reach a sentence within the category range below. The starting point applies to all offenders irrespective of plea or previous convictions. Having determined the starting point, step two allows further adjustment for aggravating or mitigating features set out below.

A case of particular gravity, reflected by multiple features of culpability or harm in step one, could merit upward adjustment from the starting point before further adjustment for aggravating or mitigating features, set out below.

	A	B
Category 1	**Starting point** 15 years' custody **Category range** 13–19 years' custody	**Starting point** 12 years' custody **Category range** 10–15 years' custody
Category 2	**Starting point** 10 years' custody **Category range** 9–13 years' custody	**Starting point** 8 years' custody **Category range** 7–9 years' custody
Category 3	**Starting point** 7 years' custody **Category range** 6–9 years' custody	**Starting point** 5 years' custody **Category range** 4–7 years' custody

The table below contains a **non-exhaustive** list of additional factual elements providing the context of the offence and factors relating to the offender. Identify whether any combination of these, or other relevant factors, should result in an upward or downward adjustment from the starting point. **In particular, relevant recent convictions are likely to result in an upward adjustment.** In some cases, having considered these factors, it may be appropriate to move outside the identified category range.

Aggravating factors
Statutory aggravating factors • Previous convictions, having regard to a) the nature of the offence to which the conviction relates and its relevance to the current offence; and b) the time that has elapsed since the conviction • Offence committed whilst on bail *Other aggravating factors* • Specific targeting of a particularly vulnerable victim • Ejaculation (where not taken into account at step one) • Blackmail or other threats made (where not taken into account at step one) • Location of offence • Timing of offence • Use of weapon or other item to frighten or injure • Victim compelled to leave their home (including victims of domestic violence) • Failure to comply with current court orders • Offence committed whilst on licence • Exploiting contact arrangements with a child to commit an offence • Presence of others, especially children • Any steps taken to prevent the victim reporting an incident, obtaining assistance and/or from assisting or supporting the prosecution • Attempts to dispose of or conceal evidence • Commission of offence whilst under the influence of alcohol or drugs

Mitigating factors
• No previous convictions **or** no relevant/recent convictions • Remorse • Previous good character and/or exemplary conduct* • Age and/or lack of maturity where it affects the responsibility of the offender • Mental disorder or learning disability, particularly where linked to the commission of the offence

* Previous good character/exemplary conduct is different from having no previous convictions. The more serious the offence, the less the weight which should normally be attributed to this factor. Where previous good character/exemplary conduct has been used to facilitate the offence, this mitigation should not normally be allowed and such conduct may constitute an aggravating factor.

In the context of this offence, previous good character/exemplary conduct should not normally be given any significant weight and will not normally justify a reduction in what would otherwise be the appropriate sentence.

STEP THREE Consider any factors which indicate a reduction, such as assistance to the prosecution **SG-62**

The court should take into account sections 73 and 74 of the Serious Organised Crime and Police Act 2005 (assistance by defendants: reduction or review of sentence) and any other rule of law by virtue of which an offender may receive a discounted sentence in consequence of assistance given (or offered) to the prosecutor or investigator.

STEP FOUR Reduction for guilty pleas

The court should take account of any potential reduction for a guilty plea in accordance with section 144 of the Criminal Justice Act 2003 and the *Guilty Plea* guideline.

STEP FIVE Dangerousness

The court should consider whether having regard to the criteria contained in Chapter 5 of Part 12 of the Criminal Justice Act 2003 it would be appropriate to award a life sentence (section 224A or section 225(2)) or an extended sentence (section 226A). When sentencing offenders to a life sentence under these provisions, the notional determinate sentence should be used as the basis for the setting of a minimum term.

STEP SIX Totality principle

If sentencing an offender for more than one offence, or where the offender is already serving a sentence, consider whether the total sentence is just and proportionate to the offending behaviour.

STEP SEVEN Ancillary orders

The court must consider whether to make any ancillary orders. The court must also consider what other requirements or provisions may *automatically* apply. Further information is included at Annex A [see **SG-186**].

STEP EIGHT Reasons

Section 174 of the Criminal Justice Act 2003 imposes a duty to give reasons for, and explain the effect of, the sentence.

STEP NINE Consideration for time spent on bail

The court must consider whether to give credit for time spent on bail in accordance with section 240A of the Criminal Justice Act 2003.

Assault by Penetration **SG-63**

Sexual Offences Act 2003 (section 2)

Triable only on indictment
Maximum: Life imprisonment

Offence range: Community order — 19 years' custody

[Repeats information as to the CJA 2003, ss. 224, 225(2), 224A and 226A which is set out at **SG-59**.]

STEP ONE Determining the offence category **SG-64**

The court should determine which categories of harm and culpability the offence falls into by reference **only** to the tables below.

Sentencing Guidelines

Harm	
Category 1	• The extreme nature of one or more category 2 factors or the extreme impact caused by a combination of category 2 factors **may** elevate to category 1
Category 2	• Severe psychological or physical harm • Penetration using large or dangerous object(s) • Additional degradation/humiliation • Abduction • Prolonged detention/sustained incident • Violence or threats of violence (beyond that which is inherent in the offence) • Forced/uninvited entry into victim's home • Victim is particularly vulnerable due to personal circumstances *
Category 3	Factor(s) in categories 1 and 2 not present

* For children under 13 please refer to the guideline [at SG-79].

Culpability	
A	**B**
• Significant degree of planning • Offender acts together with others to commit the offence • Use of alcohol/drugs on victim to facilitate the offence • Abuse of trust • Previous violence against victim • Offence committed in course of burglary • Recording of the offence • Commercial exploitation and/or motivation • Offence racially or religiously aggravated • Offence motivated by, or demonstrating, hostility to the victim based on his or her sexual orientation (or presumed sexual orientation) or transgender identity (or presumed transgender identity) • Offence motivated by, or demonstrating, hostility to the victim based on his or her disability (or presumed disability)	Factor(s) in category A not present

SG-65 STEP TWO **Starting point and category range**

Having determined the category, the court should use the corresponding starting points to reach a sentence within the category range below. The starting point applies to all offenders irrespective of plea or previous convictions.

Having determined the starting point, step two allows further adjustment for aggravating or mitigating features, set out below.

A case of particular gravity, reflected by multiple features of culpability or harm in step one, could merit upward adjustment from the starting point before further adjustment for aggravating or mitigating features, set out below.

Where there is a sufficient prospect of rehabilitation, a community order with a sex offender treatment programme requirement under section 202 of the Criminal Justice Act 2003 can be a proper alternative to a short or moderate length custodial sentence.

	A	B
Category 1	**Starting point** 15 years' custody **Category range** 13–19 years' custody	**Starting point** 12 years' custody **Category range** 10–15 years' custody
Category 2	**Starting point** 8 years' custody **Category range** 5–13 years' custody	**Starting point** 6 years' custody **Category range** 4–9 years' custody
Category 3	**Starting point** 4 years' custody **Category range** 2–6 years' custody	**Starting point** 2 years' custody **Category range** High level community order–4 years' custody

The table below contains a **non-exhaustive** list of additional factual elements providing the context of the offence and factors relating to the offender. Identify whether any combination of these, or other relevant factors, should result in an upward or downward adjustment from the starting point. **In particular, relevant recent convictions are likely to result in an upward adjustment.** In some cases, having considered these factors, it may be appropriate to move outside the identified category range.

When sentencing appropriate **category 3** offences, the court should also consider the custody threshold as follows:

- Has the custody threshold been passed?
- If so, is it unavoidable that a custodial sentence be imposed?
- If so, can that sentence be suspended?

Aggravating factors
Statutory aggravating factors • Previous convictions, having regard to a) the nature of the offence to which the conviction relates and its relevance to the current offence; and b) the time that has elapsed since the conviction • Offence committed whilst on bail *Other aggravating factors* • Specific targeting of a particularly vulnerable victim • Blackmail or other threats made (where not taken into account at step one) • Location of offence • Timing of offence • Use of weapon or other item to frighten or injure • Victim compelled to leave their home (including victims of domestic violence) • Failure to comply with current court orders • Offence committed whilst on licence • Exploiting contact arrangements with a child to commit an offence • Presence of others, especially children • Any steps taken to prevent the victim reporting an incident, obtaining assistance and/or from assisting or supporting the prosecution • Attempts to dispose of or conceal evidence • Commission of offence whilst under the influence of alcohol or drugs

Mitigating factors
• No previous convictions **or** no relevant/recent convictions • Remorse • Previous good character and/or exemplary conduct* • Age and/or lack of maturity where it affects the responsibility of the offender • Mental disorder or learning disability, particularly where linked to the commission of the offence

* [Repeats note as to distinction between previous good character/exemplary conduct and having no previous convictions and how to deal with them in respect of the offence: see **SG-61** for the full text.]

STEPS THREE to NINE **SG-66**

[These are in the same terms as those applicable to rape: see **SG-62**.]

Sexual Assault **SG-67**

Sexual Offences Act 2003 (section 3)

Triable either way
Maximum: 10 years' custody

Offence range: Community order—7 years' custody

For convictions on or after 3 December 2012 (irrespective of the date of commission of the offence), this is a specified offence for the purposes of section 226A (extended sentence for certain violent or sexual offences) of the Criminal Justice Act 2003.

STEP ONE Determining the offence category **SG-68**

The court should determine which categories of harm and culpability the offence falls into by reference **only** to the tables below.

Harm	
Category 1	• Severe psychological or physical harm • Abduction • Violence or threats of violence • Forced/uninvited entry into victim's home
Category 2	• Touching of naked genitalia or naked breasts • Prolonged detention/sustained incident • Additional degradation/humiliation • Victim is particularly vulnerable due to personal circumstances *
Category 3	Factor(s) in categories 1 and 2 not present

* For children under 13 please refer to the guideline [at **SG-83**].

Culpability	
A	B
• Significant degree of planning • Offender acts together with others to commit the offence • Use of alcohol/drugs on victim to facilitate the offence • Abuse of trust • Previous violence against victim • Offence committed in course of burglary • Recording of offence • Commercial exploitation and/or motivation • Offence racially or religiously aggravated • Offence motivated by, or demonstrating, hostility to the victim based on his or her sexual orientation (or presumed sexual orientation) or transgender identity (or presumed transgender identity) • Offence motivated by, or demonstrating, hostility to the victim based on his or her disability (or presumed disability)	Factor(s) in category A not present

SG-69 STEP TWO **Starting point and category range**

Having determined the category, the court should use the corresponding starting points to reach a sentence within the category range below. The starting point applies to all offenders irrespective of plea or previous convictions. Having determined the starting point, step two allows further adjustment for aggravating or mitigating features, set out below.

A case of particular gravity, reflected by multiple features of culpability or harm in step one, could merit upward adjustment from the starting point before further adjustment for aggravating or mitigating features, set out below.

Where there is a sufficient prospect of rehabilitation, a community order with a sex offender treatment programme requirement under section 202 of the Criminal Justice Act 2003 can be a proper alternative to a short or moderate length custodial sentence.

	A	B
Category 1	**Starting point** 4 years' custody **Category range** 3–7 years' custody	**Starting point** 2 years 6 months' custody **Category range** 2–4 years' custody
Category 2	**Starting point** 2 years' custody **Category range** 1–4 years' custody	**Starting point** 1 year's custody **Category range** High level community order–2 years' custody
Category 3	**Starting point** 26 weeks' custody **Category range** High level community order–1 year's custody	**Starting point** High level community order **Category range** Medium level community order–26 weeks' custody

The table below contains a **non-exhaustive** list of additional factual elements providing the context of the offence and factors relating to the offender. Identify whether any combination of these, or other relevant factors, should result in an upward or downward adjustment from the starting point. **In particular, relevant recent convictions are likely to result in an upward adjustment.** In some cases, having considered these factors, it may be appropriate to move outside the identified category range.

When sentencing appropriate **category 2 or 3 offences**, the court should also consider the custody threshold as follows:

- Has the custody threshold been passed?
- If so, is it unavoidable that a custodial sentence be imposed?
- If so, can that sentence be suspended?

Aggravating factors
Statutory aggravating factors • Previous convictions, having regard to a) the nature of the offence to which the conviction relates and its relevance to the current offence; and b) the time that has elapsed since the conviction • Offence committed whilst on bail *Other aggravating factors* • Specific targeting of a particularly vulnerable victim • Blackmail or other threats made (where not taken into account at step one) • Location of offence • Timing of offence • Use of weapon or other item to frighten or injure • Victim compelled to leave their home (including victims of domestic violence) • Failure to comply with current court orders • Offence committed whilst on licence • Exploiting contact arrangements with a child to commit an offence • Presence of others, especially children • Any steps taken to prevent the victim reporting an incident, obtaining assistance and/or from assisting or supporting the prosecution • Attempts to dispose of or conceal evidence • Commission of offence whilst under the influence of alcohol or drugs

Mitigating factors
• No previous convictions **or** no relevant/recent convictions • Remorse • Previous good character and/or exemplary conduct* • Age and/or lack of maturity where it affects the responsibility of the offender • Mental disorder or learning disability, particularly where linked to the commission of the offence • Demonstration of steps taken to address offending behaviour

* Previous good character/exemplary conduct is different from having no previous convictions. The more serious the offence, the less the weight which should normally be attributed to this factor. Where previous good character/exemplary conduct has been used to facilitate the offence, this mitigation should not normally be allowed and such conduct may constitute an aggravating factor.

STEP THREE Consider any factors which indicate a reduction, such as assistance to the prosecution **SG-70**

The court should take into account sections 73 and 74 of the Serious Organised Crime and Police Act 2005 (assistance by defendants: reduction or review of sentence) and any other rule of law by virtue of which an offender may receive a discounted sentence in consequence of assistance given (or offered) to the prosecutor or investigator.

STEP FOUR Reduction for guilty pleas

The court should take account of any potential reduction for a guilty plea in accordance with section 144 of the Criminal Justice Act 2003 and the *Guilty Plea* guideline.

STEP FIVE Dangerousness

The court should consider whether having regard to the criteria contained in Chapter 5 of Part 12 of the Criminal Justice Act 2003 it would be appropriate to award an extended sentence (section 226A).

STEPS SIX to NINE

[These are in the same terms as those applicable to rape: see **SG-62**.]

SG-71 CAUSING A PERSON TO ENGAGE IN SEXUAL ACTIVITY WITHOUT CONSENT

Sexual Offences Act 2003 (section 4)

Triable only on indictment (if penetration involved)

- otherwise, triable either way

Maximum: Life imprisonment (if penetration involved)

- otherwise, 10 years

Offence range: Community order — 7 years' custody (if no penetration involved) / 19 years' custody (if penetration involved)

[Repeats information as to the CJA 2003, ss. 224, 225(2), 224A and 226A which is set out at **SG-59**.]

SG-72 **STEP ONE Determining the offence category**

The court should determine which categories of harm and culpability the offence falls into by reference **only** to the tables below.

Harm	
Category 1	• The extreme nature of one or more category 2 factors or the extreme impact caused by a combination of category 2 factors **may** elevate to category 1
Category 2	• Severe psychological or physical harm • Penetration using large or dangerous object(s) • Pregnancy or STI as a consequence of offence • Additional degradation/humiliation • Abduction • Prolonged detention/sustained incident • Violence or threats of violence • Forced/uninvited entry into victim's home • Victim is particularly vulnerable due to personal circumstances *
Category 3	Factor(s) in categories 1 and 2 not present

* For children under 13 please refer to the guideline [at **SG-87**].

Culpability	
A	B
• Significant degree of planning • Offender acts together with others to commit the offence • Use of alcohol/drugs on victim to facilitate the offence • Abuse of trust • Previous violence against victim • Offence committed in course of burglary • Recording of the offence • Commercial exploitation and/or motivation • Offence racially or religiously aggravated • Offence motivated by, or demonstrating, hostility to the victim based on his or her sexual orientation (or presumed sexual orientation) or transgender identity (or presumed transgender identity) • Offence motivated by, or demonstrating, hostility to the victim based on his or her disability (or presumed disability)	Factor(s) in category A not present

STEP TWO Starting point and category range SG-73

Having determined the category, the court should use the corresponding starting points to reach a sentence within the category range below. The starting point applies to all offenders irrespective of plea or previous convictions.

Having determined the starting point, step two allows further adjustment for aggravating or mitigating features, set out below.

A case of particular gravity, reflected by multiple features of culpability or harm in step one, could merit upward adjustment from the starting point before further adjustment for aggravating or mitigating features, set out below.

Where there is a sufficient prospect of rehabilitation, a community order with a sex offender treatment programme requirement under section 202 of the Criminal Justice Act 2003 can be a proper alternative to a short or moderate length custodial sentence.

Where offence involved penetration		
	A	B
Category 1	**Starting point** 15 years' custody **Category range** 13–19 years' custody	**Starting point** 12 years' custody **Category range** 10–15 years' custody
Category 2	**Starting point** 8 years' custody **Category range** 5–13 years' custody	**Starting point** 6 years' custody **Category range** 4–9 years' custody
Category 3	**Starting point** 4 years' custody **Category range** 2–6 years' custody	**Starting point** 2 years' custody **Category range** High level community order–4 years' custody

Where offence did not involve penetration		
	A	B
Category 1	**Starting point** 4 years' custody **Category range** 3–7 years' custody	**Starting point** 2 years 6 months' custody **Category range** 2–4 years' custody
Category 2	**Starting point** 2 years' custody **Category range** 1–4 years' custody	**Starting point** 1 year's custody **Category range** High level community order–2 years' custody
Category 3	**Starting point** 26 weeks' custody **Category range** High level community order–1 year's custody	**Starting point** High level community order **Category range** Medium level community order–26 weeks' custody

The table below contains a **non-exhaustive** list of additional factual elements providing the context of the offence and factors relating to the offender. Identify whether any combination of these, or other relevant factors, should result in an upward or downward adjustment from the starting point. **In particular, relevant recent convictions are likely to result in an upward adjustment.** In some cases, having considered these factors, it may be appropriate to move outside the identified category range.

When sentencing appropriate **category 2 or 3** offences, the court should also consider the custody threshold as follows:

- Has the custody threshold been passed?
- If so, is it unavoidable that a custodial sentence be imposed?
- If so, can that sentence be suspended?

Aggravating factors

Statutory aggravating factors
- Previous convictions, having regard to a) the nature of the offence to which the conviction relates and its relevance to the current offence; and b) the time that has elapsed since the conviction
- Offence committed whilst on bail

Other aggravating factors
- Specific targeting of a particularly vulnerable victim
- Ejaculation (where not taken into account at step one)
- Blackmail or other threats made (where not taken into account at step one)
- Location of offence
- Timing of offence
- Use of weapon or other item to frighten or injure
- Victim compelled to leave their home (including victims of domestic violence)
- Failure to comply with current court orders
- Offence committed whilst on licence
- Exploiting contact arrangements with a child to commit an offence
- Presence of others, especially children
- Any steps taken to prevent the victim reporting an incident, obtaining assistance and/or from assisting or supporting the prosecution
- Attempts to dispose of or conceal evidence
- Commission of offence whilst under the influence of alcohol or drugs

Mitigating factors

- No previous convictions **or** no relevant/recent convictions
- Remorse
- Previous good character and/or exemplary conduct*
- Age and/or lack of maturity where it affects the responsibility of the offender
- Mental disorder or learning disability, particularly where linked to the commission of the offence

* [Repeats note as to distinction between previous good character/exemplary conduct and having no previous convictions and how to deal with them in respect of the offence: see **SG-61** for the full text.]

SG-74 STEPS THREE to NINE

[These are in the same terms as those applicable to rape: see **SG-62**.]

SG-75

Rape of a Child Under 13

Sexual Offences Act 2003 (section 5)

Triable only on indictment
Maximum: Life imprisonment

Offence range: 6–19 years' custody

[Repeats information as to the CJA 2003, ss. 224, 225(2), 224A and 226A, which is set out at **SG-59**.]

SG-76 STEP ONE **Determining the offence category**

The court should determine which categories of harm and culpability the offence falls into by reference **only** to the tables below.

Offences may be of such severity, for example involving a campaign of rape, that sentences of 20 years and above may be appropriate.

When dealing with the statutory offence of rape of a child under 13, the court may be faced with a wide range of offending behaviour.

Sentencers should have particular regard to the fact that these offences are not only committed through force or fear of force but may include exploitative behaviour towards a child which should be considered to indicate high culpability.

This guideline is designed to deal with the majority of offending behaviour which deserves a significant custodial sentence; the starting points and ranges reflect the fact that such offending merits such an approach. There may also be **exceptional** cases, where a lengthy community order with a requirement to participate in a sex offender treatment programme may be the best way of changing the offender's behaviour and of protecting the public by preventing any repetition of the offence. This guideline may not be appropriate where the sentencer is satisfied that on the available evidence, and in the absence of exploitation, a young or particularly immature defendant genuinely believed, on reasonable grounds, that the victim was aged 16 or over and that they were engaging in lawful sexual activity.

Sentencers are reminded that if sentencing outside the guideline they must be satisfied that it would be contrary to the interests of justice to follow the guideline.

Harm	
Category 1	• The extreme nature of one or more category 2 factors or the extreme impact caused by a combination of category 2 factors **may** elevate to category 1
Category 2	• Severe psychological or physical harm • Pregnancy or STI as a consequence of offence • Additional degradation/humiliation • Abduction • Prolonged detention /sustained incident • Violence or threats of violence • Forced/uninvited entry into victim's home • Child is particularly vulnerable due to extreme youth and/or personal circumstances
Category 3	Factor(s) in categories 1 and 2 not present

Culpability	
A	**B**
• Significant degree of planning • Offender acts together with others to commit the offence • Use of alcohol/drugs on victim to facilitate the offence • Grooming behaviour used against victim • Abuse of trust • Previous violence against victim • Offence committed in course of burglary • Sexual images of victim recorded, retained, solicited or shared • Deliberate isolation of victim • Commercial exploitation and/or motivation • Offence racially or religiously aggravated • Offence motivated by, or demonstrating, hostility to the victim based on his or her sexual orientation (or presumed sexual orientation) or transgender identity (or presumed transgender identity) • Offence motivated by, or demonstrating, hostility to the victim based on his or her disability (or presumed disability)	Factor(s) in category A not present

STEP TWO Starting point and category range SG-77

Having determined the category, the court should use the corresponding starting points to reach a sentence within the category range below. The starting point applies to all offenders irrespective of plea or previous convictions. Having determined the starting point, step two allows further adjustment for aggravating or mitigating features, set out below.

A case of particular gravity, reflected by multiple features of culpability or harm in step one, could merit upward adjustment from the starting point before further adjustment for aggravating or mitigating features, set out below.

Sentencers should also note the wording set out at step one which may be applicable in exceptional cases.

	A	B
Category 1	**Starting point** 16 years' custody **Category range** 13–19 years' custody	**Starting point** 13 years' custody **Category range** 11–17 years' custody
Category 2	**Starting point** 13 years' custody **Category range** 11–17 years' custody	**Starting point** 10 years' custody **Category range** 8–13 years' custody
Category 3	**Starting point** 10 years' custody **Category range** 8–13 years' custody	**Starting point** 8 years' custody **Category range** 6–11 years' custody

The table below contains a **non-exhaustive** list of additional factual elements providing the context of the offence and factors relating to the offender. Identify whether any combination of these, or other relevant factors, should result in an upward or downward adjustment from the starting point. **In particular, relevant recent convictions are likely to result in an upward adjustment.** In some cases, having considered these factors, it may be appropriate to move outside the identified category range.

Aggravating factors

Statutory aggravating factors

- Previous convictions, having regard to a) the nature of the offence to which the conviction relates and its relevance to the current offence; and b) the time that has elapsed since the conviction
- Offence committed whilst on bail

Other aggravating factors

- Specific targeting of a particularly vulnerable child
- Ejaculation (where not taken into account at step one)
- Blackmail or other threats made (where not taken into account at step one)
- Location of offence
- Timing of offence
- Use of weapon or other item to frighten or injure
- Victim compelled to leave their home, school, etc
- Failure to comply with current court orders
- Offence committed whilst on licence
- Exploiting contact arrangements with a child to commit an offence
- Presence of others, especially other children
- Any steps taken to prevent the victim reporting an incident, obtaining assistance and/or from assisting or supporting the prosecution
- Attempts to dispose of or conceal evidence
- Commission of offence whilst offender under the influence of alcohol or drugs
- Victim encouraged to recruit others

Mitigating factors

- No previous convictions **or** no relevant/recent convictions
- Remorse
- Previous good character and/or exemplary conduct*
- Age and/or lack of maturity where it affects the responsibility of the offender
- Mental disorder or learning disability, particularly where linked to the commission of the offence

* [Repeats note as to distinction between previous good character/exemplary conduct and having no previous convictions and how to deal with them in respect of the offence: see **SG-61** for the full text.]

STEPS THREE to NINE SG-78

[These are in the same terms as those applicable to rape: see SG-62.]

Assault of a Child Under 13 by Penetration SG-79

Sexual Offences Act 2003 (section 6)

Triable only on indictment
Maximum: Life imprisonment

Offence range: 2–19 years' custody

[Repeats information as to the CJA 2003, ss. 224, 225(2), 224A and 226A, which is set out at SG-59.]

STEP ONE Determining the offence category SG-80

The court should determine which categories of harm and culpability the offence falls into by reference **only** to the tables below.

Harm	
Category 1	The extreme nature of one or more category 2 factors or the extreme impact caused by a combination of category 2 factors **may** elevate to category 1
Category 2	• Severe psychological or physical harm • Penetration using large or dangerous object(s) • Additional degradation/humiliation • Abduction • Prolonged detention /sustained incident • Violence or threats of violence • Forced/uninvited entry into victim's home • Child is particularly vulnerable due to extreme youth and/or personal circumstances
Category 3	Factor(s) in categories 1 and 2 not present

Culpability	
A	B
• Significant degree of planning • Offender acts together with others to commit the offence • Use of alcohol/drugs on victim to facilitate the offence • Grooming behaviour used against victim • Abuse of trust • Previous violence against victim • Offence committed in course of burglary • Sexual images of victim recorded, retained, solicited or shared • Deliberate isolation of victim • Commercial exploitation and/or motivation • Offence racially or religiously aggravated • Offence motivated by, or demonstrating, hostility to the victim based on his or her sexual orientation (or presumed sexual orientation) or transgender identity (or presumed transgender identity) • Offence motivated by, or demonstrating, hostility to the victim based on his or her disability (or presumed disability)	Factor(s) in category A not present

STEP TWO Starting point and category range SG-81

Having determined the category, the court should use the corresponding starting points to reach a sentence within the category range below. The starting point applies to all offenders irrespective of plea or previous convictions. Having determined the starting point, step two allows further adjustment for aggravating or mitigating features, set out below.

A case of particular gravity, reflected by multiple features of culpability or harm in step one, could merit upward adjustment from the starting point before further adjustment for aggravating or mitigating features, set out below.

Sentencing Guidelines

	A	B
Category 1	**Starting point** 16 years' custody **Category range** 13–19 years' custody	**Starting point** 13 years' custody **Category range** 11–17 years' custody
Category 2	**Starting point** 11 years' custody **Category range** 7–15 years' custody	**Starting point** 8 years' custody **Category range** 5–13 years' custody
Category 3	**Starting point** 6 years' custody **Category range** 4–9 years' custody	**Starting point** 4 years' custody **Category range** 2–6 years' custody

The table below contains a **non-exhaustive** list of additional factual elements providing the context of the offence and factors relating to the offender. Identify whether any combination of these, or other relevant factors, should result in an upward or downward adjustment from the starting point. **In particular, relevant recent convictions are likely to result in an upward adjustment.** In some cases, having considered these factors, it may be appropriate to move outside the identified category range.

Aggravating factors
Statutory aggravating factors • Previous convictions, having regard to a) the nature of the offence to which the conviction relates and its relevance to the current offence; and b) the time that has elapsed since the conviction • Offence committed whilst on bail *Other aggravating factors* • Specific targeting of a particularly vulnerable child • Blackmail or other threats made (where not taken into account at step one) • Location of offence • Timing of offence • Use of weapon or other item to frighten or injure • Victim compelled to leave their home, school etc • Failure to comply with current court orders • Offence committed whilst on licence • Exploiting contact arrangements with a child to commit an offence • Presence of others, especially other children • Any steps taken to prevent the victim reporting an incident, obtaining assistance and/or from assisting or supporting the prosecution • Attempts to dispose of or conceal evidence • Commission of offence whilst under the influence of alcohol or drugs • Victim encouraged to recruit others

Mitigating factors
• No previous convictions **or** no relevant/recent convictions • Remorse • Previous good character and/or exemplary conduct* • Age and/or lack of maturity where it affects the responsibility of the offender • Mental disorder or learning disability, particularly where linked to the commission of the offence

* [Repeats note as to distinction between previous good character/exemplary conduct and having no previous convictions and how to deal with them in respect of the offence: see **SG-61** for the full text.]

SG-82 STEPS THREE to NINE

[These are in the same terms as those applicable to rape: see **SG-62**.]

SEXUAL ASSAULT OF A CHILD UNDER 13 SG-83

Sexual Offences Act 2003 (section 7)

Triable either way
Maximum: 14 years' custody

Offence range: Community order — 9 years' custody

For offences committed on or after 3 December 2012, this is an offence listed in Part 1 of Schedule 15B for the purposes of section 224A (life sentence for second listed offence) of the Criminal Justice Act 2003.

For convictions on or after 3 December 2012 (irrespective of the date of commission of the offence), this is a specified offence for the purposes of section 226A (extended sentence for certain violent or sexual offences) of the Criminal Justice Act 2003.

STEP ONE Determining the offence category SG-84

The court should determine which categories of harm and culpability the offence falls into by reference **only** to the tables below.

Harm	
Category 1	• Severe psychological or physical harm • Abduction • Violence or threats of violence • Forced/uninvited entry into victim's home
Category 2	• Touching of naked genitalia or naked breast area • Prolonged detention/sustained incident • Additional degradation/humiliation • Child is particularly vulnerable due to extreme youth and/or personal circumstances
Category 3	Factor(s) in categories 1 and 2 not present

Culpability	
A	B
• Significant degree of planning • Offender acts together with others to commit the offence • Use of alcohol/drugs on victim to facilitate the offence • Grooming behaviour used against victim • Abuse of trust • Previous violence against victim • Offence committed in course of burglary • Sexual images of victim recorded, retained, solicited or shared • Deliberate isolation of victim • Commercial exploitation and/or motivation • Offence racially or religiously aggravated • Offence motivated by, or demonstrating, hostility to the victim based on his or her sexual orientation (or presumed sexual orientation) or transgender identity (or presumed transgender identity) • Offence motivated by, or demonstrating, hostility to the victim based on his or her disability (or presumed disability)	Factor(s) in category A not present

STEP TWO Starting point and category range SG-85

Having determined the category, the court should use the corresponding starting points to reach a sentence within the category range below. The starting point applies to all offenders irrespective of plea or previous convictions. Having determined the starting point, step two allows further adjustment for aggravating or mitigating features, set out below.

A case of particular gravity, reflected by multiple features of culpability or harm in step one, could merit upward adjustment from the starting point before further adjustment for aggravating or mitigating features, set out below.

Where there is a sufficient prospect of rehabilitation, a community order with a sex offender treatment programme requirement under section 202 of the Criminal Justice Act 2003 can be a proper alternative to a short or moderate length custodial sentence.

	A	B
Category 1	**Starting point** 6 years' custody **Category range** 4–9 years' custody	**Starting point** 4 years' custody **Category range** 3–7 years' custody
Category 2	**Starting point** 4 years' custody **Category range** 3–7 years' custody	**Starting point** 2 years' custody **Category range** 1–4 years' custody
Category 3	**Starting point** 1 year's custody **Category range** 26 weeks'– 2 years' custody	**Starting point** 26 weeks' custody **Category range** High level community order–1 year's custody

The table below contains a **non-exhaustive** list of additional factual elements providing the context of the offence and factors relating to the offender. Identify whether any combination of these, or other relevant factors, should result in an upward or downward adjustment from the starting point. **In particular, relevant recent convictions are likely to result in an upward adjustment.** In some cases, having considered these factors, it may be appropriate to move outside the identified category range.

Aggravating factors

Statutory aggravating factors

- Previous convictions, having regard to a) the nature of the offence to which the conviction relates and its relevance to the current offence; and b) the time that has elapsed since the conviction
- Offence committed whilst on bail

Other aggravating factors

- Specific targeting of a particularly vulnerable child
- Blackmail or other threats made (where not taken into account at step one)
- Location of offence
- Timing of offence
- Use of weapon or other item to frighten or injure
- Victim compelled to leave their home, school, etc
- Failure to comply with current court orders
- Offence committed whilst on licence
- Exploiting contact arrangements with a child to commit an offence
- Presence of others, especially other children
- Any steps taken to prevent the victim reporting an incident, obtaining assistance and/or from assisting or supporting the prosecution
- Attempts to dispose of or conceal evidence
- Commission of offence whilst under the influence of alcohol or drugs
- Victim encouraged to recruit others

Mitigating factors

- No previous convictions **or** no relevant/recent convictions
- Remorse
- Previous good character and/or exemplary conduct*
- Age and/or lack of maturity where it affects the responsibility of the offender
- Mental disorder or learning disability, particularly where linked to the commission of the offence

* [Repeats note as to distinction between previous good character/exemplary conduct and having no previous convictions and how to deal with them in respect of the offence: see **SG-61** for the full text.]

STEP THREE Consider any factors which indicate a reduction, such as assistance to the prosecution SG-86

The court should take into account sections 73 and 74 of the Serious Organised Crime and Police Act 2005 (assistance by defendants: reduction or review of sentence) and any other rule of law by virtue of which an offender may receive a discounted sentence in consequence of assistance given (or offered) to the prosecutor or investigator.

STEP FOUR Reduction for guilty pleas

The court should take account of any potential reduction for a guilty plea in accordance with section 144 of the Criminal Justice Act 2003 and the *Guilty Plea* guideline.

STEP FIVE Dangerousness

The court should consider whether having regard to the criteria contained in Chapter 5 of Part 12 of the Criminal Justice Act 2003 it would be appropriate to award a life sentence (section 224A) or an extended sentence (section 226A). When sentencing offenders to a life sentence under these provisions, the notional determinate sentence should be used as the basis for the setting of a minimum term.

STEPS SIX to NINE

[These are in the same terms as those applicable to rape: see **SG-62**.]

Causing or Inciting a Child Under 13 to Engage in Sexual Activity SG-87

Sexual Offences Act 2003 (section 8)

Triable only on indictment (if penetration involved)

- otherwise, triable either way

Maximum: Life imprisonment (if penetration involved)

- otherwise, 14 years' custody

Offence range: 1–17 years' custody

[Repeats information as to the CJA 2003, ss. 224, 225(2), 224A and 226A, which is set out at **SG-59**.]

STEP ONE Determining the offence category SG-88

The court should determine which categories of harm and culpability the offence falls into by reference **only** to the tables below.

Harm	
Category 1	• The extreme nature of one or more category 2 factors or the extreme impact caused by a combination of category 2 factors **may** elevate to category 1
Category 2	• Severe psychological or physical harm • Penetration of vagina or anus (using body or object) by, or of, victim • Penile penetration of mouth by, or of, victim • Additional degradation/humiliation • Abduction • Prolonged detention/sustained incident • Violence or threats of violence • Forced/uninvited entry into victim's home • Child is particularly vulnerable due to extreme youth and/or personal circumstances
Category 3	Factor(s) in categories 1 and 2 not present

Culpability	
A	B
• Significant degree of planning • Offender acts together with others to commit the offence • Use of alcohol/drugs on victim to facilitate the offence • Grooming behaviour used against victim • Abuse of trust • Previous violence against victim • Offence committed in course of burglary • Sexual images of victim recorded, retained, solicited or shared • Deliberate isolation of victim • Commercial exploitation and/or motivation • Offence racially or religiously aggravated • Offence motivated by, or demonstrating hostility to the victim based on his or her sexual orientation (or presumed sexual orientation) or transgender identity (or presumed transgender identity) • Offence motivated by, or demonstrating, hostility to the victim based on his or her disability (or presumed disability)	Factor(s) in category A not present

SG-89 STEP TWO **Starting point and category range**

Having determined the category, the court should use the corresponding starting points to reach a sentence within the category range below. The starting point applies to all offenders irrespective of plea or previous convictions. Having determined the starting point, step two allows further adjustment for aggravating or mitigating features, set out below.

A case of particular gravity, reflected by multiple features of culpability or harm in step one, could merit upward adjustment from the starting point before further adjustment for aggravating or mitigating features, set out below.

	A	B
Category 1	**Starting point** 13 years' custody **Category range** 11–17 years' custody	**Starting point** 11 years' custody **Category range** 10–15 years' custody
Category 2	**Starting point** 8 years' custody **Category range** 5–10 years' custody	**Starting point** 6 years' custody **Category range** 3–9 years' custody
Category 3	**Starting point** 5 years' custody **Category range** 3–8 years' custody	**Starting point** 2 years' custody **Category range** 1–4 years' custody

The table below contains a **non-exhaustive** list of additional factual elements providing the context of the offence and factors relating to the offender. Identify whether any combination of these, or other relevant factors, should result in an upward or downward adjustment from the starting point. **In particular, relevant recent convictions are likely to result in an upward adjustment.** In some cases, having considered these factors, it may be appropriate to move outside the identified category range.

Aggravating factors
Statutory aggravating factors • Previous convictions, having regard to a) the nature of the offence to which the conviction relates and its relevance to the current offence; and b) the time that has elapsed since the conviction • Offence committed whilst on bail

Other aggravating factors

- Specific targeting of a particularly vulnerable child
- Ejaculation (where not taken into account at step one)
- Blackmail or other threats made (where not taken into account at step one)
- Pregnancy or STI as a consequence of offence
- Location of offence
- Timing of offence
- Use of weapon or other item to frighten or injure
- Victim compelled to leave their home, school, etc
- Failure to comply with current court orders
- Offence committed whilst on licence
- Exploiting contact arrangements with a child to commit an offence
- Presence of others, especially other children
- Any steps taken to prevent the victim reporting an incident, obtaining assistance and/or from assisting or supporting the prosecution
- Attempts to dispose of or conceal evidence
- Commission of offence whilst offender under the influence of alcohol or drugs
- Victim encouraged to recruit others

Mitigating factors

- No previous convictions **or** no relevant/recent convictions
- Remorse
- Previous good character and/or exemplary conduct*
- Age and/or lack of maturity where it affects the responsibility of the offender
- Mental disorder or learning disability, particularly where linked to the commission of the offence
- Sexual activity was incited but no activity took place because the offender voluntarily desisted or intervened to prevent it

* [Repeats note as to distinction between previous good character/exemplary conduct and having no previous convictions and how to deal with them in respect of the offence: see **SG-61** for the full text.]

STEPS THREE to NINE **SG-90**

[These are in the same terms as those applicable to rape: see **SG-62.**]

SEXUAL ACTIVITY WITH A CHILD **SG-91**

Sexual Offences Act 2003 (section 9)

CAUSING OR INCITING A CHILD TO ENGAGE IN SEXUAL ACTIVITY

Sexual Offences Act 2003 (section 10)

Triable only on indictment (if penetration involved)

- otherwise, triable either way

Maximum: 14 years' custody

Offence range: Community order — 10 years' custody

[Repeats information as to the CJA 2003, ss. 224A and 226A, which is set out at **SG-83.**]

Arranging or facilitating the commission of a child offence (section 14 of the Sexual Offences Act 2003 — [see SG-103])

The starting points and ranges in this guideline are also applicable to offences of arranging or facilitating the commission of a child offence. In such cases, the level of harm should be determined by reference to the type of activity arranged or facilitated. Sentences commensurate with the applicable starting point and range will ordinarily be appropriate. For offences involving significant commercial exploitation and/or an international element, it may, in the interests of justice, be appropriate to increase a sentence to a point above the category range. In exceptional cases, such as where a vulnerable offender performed a limited role, having been coerced or exploited by others, sentences below the starting point and range may be appropriate.

SG-92 **STEP ONE Determining the offence category**

The court should determine which categories of harm and culpability the offence falls into by reference **only** to the tables below.

This guideline also applies to offences committed remotely/online

Harm	
Category 1	• Penetration of vagina or anus (using body or object) • Penile penetration of mouth In either case by, or of, the victim
Category 2	Touching, or exposure, of naked genitalia or naked breasts by, or of, the victim
Category 3	Other sexual activity

Culpability	
A	**B**
• Significant degree of planning • Offender acts together with others to commit the offence • Use of alcohol/drugs on victim to facilitate the offence • Grooming behaviour used against victim • Abuse of trust • Use of threats (including blackmail) • Sexual images of victim recorded, retained, solicited or shared • Specific targeting of a particularly vulnerable child • Offender lied about age • Significant disparity in age • Commercial exploitation and/or motivation • Offence racially or religiously aggravated • Offence motivated by, or demonstrating, hostility to the victim based on his or her sexual orientation (or presumed sexual orientation) or transgender identity (or presumed transgender identity) • Offence motivated by, or demonstrating, hostility to the victim based on his or her disability (or presumed disability)	Factor(s) in category A not present

SG-93 **STEP TWO Starting point and category range**

Having determined the category, the court should use the corresponding starting points to reach a sentence within the category range below. The starting point applies to all offenders irrespective of plea or previous convictions. Having determined the starting point, step two allows further adjustment for aggravating or mitigating features, set out below.

A case of particular gravity, reflected by multiple features of culpability or harm in step one, could merit upward adjustment from the starting point before further adjustment for aggravating or mitigating features, set out below.

Where there is a sufficient prospect of rehabilitation, a community order with a sex offender treatment programme requirement under section 202 of the Criminal Justice Act 2003 can be a proper alternative to a short or moderate length custodial sentence.

	A	**B**
Category 1	**Starting point** 5 years' custody **Category range** 4–10 years' custody	**Starting point** 1 year's custody **Category range** High level community order–2 years' custody
Category 2	**Starting point** 3 years' custody **Category range** 2–6 years' custody	**Starting point** 26 weeks' custody **Category range** High level community order–1 year's custody
Category 3	**Starting point** 26 weeks' custody **Category range** High level community order–3 years' custody	**Starting point** Medium level community order **Category range** Low level community order–High level community order

The table below contains a **non-exhaustive** list of additional factual elements providing the context of the offence and factors relating to the offender. Identify whether any combination of these, or other relevant factors, should result in an upward or downward adjustment from the starting point. **In particular, relevant recent convictions are likely to result in an upward adjustment.** In some cases, having considered these factors, it may be appropriate to move outside the identified category range.

When sentencing appropriate **category 2 or 3 offences**, the court should also consider the custody threshold as follows:

- Has the custody threshold been passed?
- If so, is it unavoidable that a custodial sentence be imposed?
- If so, can that sentence be suspended?

Aggravating factors
Statutory aggravating factors • Previous convictions, having regard to a) the nature of the offence to which the conviction relates and its relevance to the current offence; and b) the time that has elapsed since the conviction • Offence committed whilst on bail *Other aggravating factors* • Severe psychological or physical harm • Ejaculation • Pregnancy or STI as a consequence of offence • Location of offence • Timing of offence • Victim compelled to leave their home, school, etc • Failure to comply with current court orders • Offence committed whilst on licence • Exploiting contact arrangements with a child to commit an offence • Presence of others, especially other children • Any steps taken to prevent the victim reporting an incident, obtaining assistance and/or from assisting or supporting the prosecution • Attempts to dispose of or conceal evidence • Failure of offender to respond to previous warnings • Commission of offence whilst under the influence of alcohol or drugs • Victim encouraged to recruit others • Period over which offence committed

Mitigating factors
• No previous convictions **or** no relevant/recent convictions • Remorse • Previous good character and/or exemplary conduct* • Age and/or lack of maturity where it affects the responsibility of the offender • Mental disorder or learning disability, particularly where linked to the commission of the offence • Sexual activity was incited but no activity took place because the offender voluntarily desisted or intervened to prevent it

* [Repeats note as to distinction between previous good character/exemplary conduct and having no previous convictions and how to deal with them in respect of the offence: see SG-61 for the full text.]

STEP THREE to NINE **SG-94**

[These are in the same terms as those applicable to sexual assault of a child under 13: see SG-86.]

Sentencing Guidelines

SG-95 ## Sexual Activity with a Child Family Member

Sexual Offences Act 2003 (section 25)

Inciting a Child Family Member to Engage in Sexual Activity

Sexual Offences Act 2003 (section 26)

Triable only on indictment (if penetration involved)

- otherwise, triable either way

Maximum: 14 years' custody

Offence range: Community order — 10 years' custody

[Repeats information as to the CJA 2003, ss. 224A and 226A, which is set out at **SG-83**.]

SG-96 **STEP ONE Determining the offence category**

The court should determine which categories of harm and culpability the offence falls into by reference **only** to the tables below. This offence involves those who have a family relationship with the victim and it should be assumed that the greater the abuse of trust within this relationship the more grave the offence.

Harm	
Category 1	• Penetration of vagina or anus (using body or object) • Penile penetration of mouth In either case by, or of, the victim
Category 2	Touching of naked genitalia or naked breasts by, or of, the victim
Category 3	Other sexual activity

Culpability	
A	**B**
• Significant degree of planning • Offender acts together with others to commit the offence • Use of alcohol/drugs on victim to facilitate the offence • Grooming behaviour used against victim • Use of threats (including blackmail) • Sexual images of victim recorded, retained, solicited or shared • Specific targeting of a particularly vulnerable child • Significant disparity in age • Commercial exploitation and/or motivation • Offence racially or religiously aggravated • Offence motivated by, or demonstrating, hostility to the victim based on his or her sexual orientation (or presumed sexual orientation) or transgender identity (or presumed transgender identity) • Offence motivated by, or demonstrating, hostility to the victim based on his or her disability (or presumed disability)	Factor(s) in category A not present

SG-97 **STEP TWO Starting point and category range**

Having determined the category, the court should use the corresponding starting points to reach a sentence within the category range below. The starting point applies to all offenders irrespective of plea or previous convictions. Having determined the starting point, step two allows further adjustment for aggravating or mitigating features, set out below.

A case of particular gravity, reflected by multiple features of culpability or harm in step one, could merit upward adjustment from the starting point before further adjustment for aggravating or mitigating features, set out below.

Where there is a sufficient prospect of rehabilitation, a community order with a sex offender treatment programme requirement under section 202 of the Criminal Justice Act 2003 can be a proper alternative to a short or moderate length custodial sentence.

	A	B
Category 1	**Starting point** 6 years' custody **Category range** 4–10 years' custody	**Starting point** 3 years 6 months' custody **Category range** 2 years 6 months'–5 years' custody
Category 2	**Starting point** 4 years' custody **Category range** 2–6 years' custody	**Starting point** 18 months' custody **Category range** 26 weeks'–2 years 6 months' custody
Category 3	**Starting point** 1 year's custody **Category range** High level community order–3 years' custody	**Starting point** Medium level community order **Category range** Low level community order–High level community order

The table below contains a **non-exhaustive** list of additional factual elements providing the context of the offence and factors relating to the offender. Identify whether any combination of these, or other relevant factors, should result in an upward or downward adjustment from the starting point. **In particular, relevant recent convictions are likely to result in an upward adjustment.** In some cases, having considered these factors, it may be appropriate to move outside the identified category range.

When sentencing appropriate **category 3 offences**, the court should also consider the custody threshold as follows:

- Has the custody threshold been passed?
- If so, is it unavoidable that a custodial sentence be imposed?
- If so, can that sentence be suspended?

Aggravating factors
Statutory aggravating factors • Previous convictions, having regard to a) the nature of the offence to which the conviction relates and its relevance to the current offence; and b) the time that has elapsed since the conviction • Offence committed whilst on bail
Other aggravating factors • Severe psychological or physical harm • Ejaculation • Pregnancy or STI as a consequence of offence • Location of offence • Timing of offence • Victim compelled to leave their home, school, etc • Failure to comply with current court orders • Offence committed whilst on licence • Exploiting contact arrangements with a child to commit an offence • Presence of others, especially other children • Any steps taken to prevent the victim reporting an incident, obtaining assistance and/or from assisting or supporting the prosecution • Attempts to dispose of or conceal evidence • Failure of offender to respond to previous warnings • Commission of offence whilst under the influence of alcohol or drugs • Victim encouraged to recruit others • Period over which offence committed

Mitigating factors
• No previous convictions **or** no relevant/recent convictions • Remorse • Previous good character and/or exemplary conduct* • Age and/or lack of maturity where it affects the responsibility of the offender • Mental disorder or learning disability, particularly where linked to the commission of the offence • Sexual activity was incited but no activity took place because the offender voluntarily desisted or intervened to prevent it

* [Repeats note as to distinction between previous good character/exemplary conduct and having no previous convictions and how to deal with them in respect of the offence: see **SG-61** for the full text.]

SG-98 STEPS THREE to NINE

[These are in the same terms as those applicable to sexual assault of a child under 13: see **SG-86**.]

SG-99

Engaging in Sexual Activity in the Presence of a Child

Sexual Offences Act 2003 (section 11)

Causing a Child to Watch a Sexual Act

Sexual Offences Act 2003 (section 12)

Triable either way
Maximum: 10 years' custody

Offence range: Community order — 6 years' custody

[Repeats information as to the CJA 2003, ss. 224A and 226A, which is set out at **SG-83**.]

Arranging or facilitating the commission of a child offence (section 14 of the Sexual Offences Act 2003 — guidance [at SG-103])
The starting points and ranges in this guideline are also applicable to offences of arranging or facilitating the commission of a child offence. In such cases, the level of harm should be determined by reference to the type of activity arranged or facilitated. Sentences commensurate with the applicable starting point and range will ordinarily be appropriate. For offences involving significant commercial exploitation and/or an international element, it may, in the interests of justice, be appropriate to increase a sentence to a point above the category range. In exceptional cases, such as where a vulnerable offender performed a limited role, having been coerced or exploited by others, sentences below the starting point and range may be appropriate.

SG-100 STEP ONE **Determining the offence category**

The court should determine which categories of harm and culpability the offence falls into by reference **only** to the tables below.

Harm	
Category 1	• Causing victim to view extreme pornography • Causing victim to view indecent/prohibited images of children • Engaging in, or causing a victim to view live, sexual activity involving sadism/violence/sexual activity with an animal/a child
Category 2	Engaging in, or causing a victim to view images of or view live, sexual activity involving: • penetration of vagina or anus (using body or object) • penile penetration of the mouth • masturbation
Category 3	Factor(s) in categories 1 and 2 not present

Culpability	
A	B
• Significant degree of planning • Offender acts together with others in order to commit the offence • Use of alcohol/drugs on victim to facilitate the offence • Grooming behaviour used against victim • Abuse of trust • Use of threats (including blackmail) • Specific targeting of a particularly vulnerable child • Significant disparity in age • Commercial exploitation and/or motivation • Offence racially or religiously aggravated • Offence motivated by, or demonstrating, hostility to the victim based on his or her sexual orientation (or presumed sexual orientation) or transgender identity (or presumed transgender identity) • Offence motivated by, or demonstrating, hostility to the victim based on his or her disability (or presumed disability)	Factor(s) in category A not present

SG-101

STEP TWO **Starting point and category range**

Having determined the category, the court should use the corresponding starting points to reach a sentence within the category range below. The starting point applies to all offenders irrespective of plea or previous convictions. Having determined the starting point, step two allows further adjustment for aggravating or mitigating features, set out below.

A case of particular gravity, reflected by multiple features of culpability or harm in step one, could merit upward adjustment from the starting point before further adjustment for aggravating or mitigating features, set out below.

Where there is a sufficient prospect of rehabilitation, a community order with a sex offender treatment programme requirement under section 202 of the Criminal Justice Act 2003 can be a proper alternative to a short or moderate length custodial sentence.

	A	B
Category 1	**Starting point** 4 years' custody **Category range** 3–6 years' custody	**Starting point** 2 years' custody **Category range** 1–3 years' custody
Category 2	**Starting point** 2 years' custody **Category range** 1–3 years' custody	**Starting point** 1 year's custody **Category range** High level community order–18 months' custody
Category 3	**Starting point** 26 weeks' custody **Category range** High level community order–1 year's custody	**Starting point** Medium level community order **Category range** Low level community order–Medium level community order

The table below contains a **non-exhaustive** list of additional factual elements providing the context of the offence and factors relating to the offender. Identify whether any combination of these, or other relevant factors, should result in an upward or downward adjustment from the starting point. **In particular, relevant recent convictions are likely to result in an upward adjustment.** In some cases, having considered these factors, it may be appropriate to move outside the identified category range.

When sentencing appropriate **category 2 or 3 offences**, the court should also consider the custody threshold as follows:

- has the custody threshold been passed?
- if so, is it unavoidable that a custodial sentence be imposed?
- if so, can that sentence be suspended?

Aggravating factors
Statutory aggravating factors • Previous convictions, having regard to a) the nature of the offence to which the conviction relates and its relevance to the current offence; and b) the time that has elapsed since the conviction • Offence committed whilst on bail *Other aggravating factors* • Location of offence • Timing of offence • Victim compelled to leave their home, school, etc • Failure to comply with current court orders • Offence committed whilst on licence • Exploiting contact arrangements with a child to commit an offence • Presence of others, especially other children • Any steps taken to prevent the victim reporting an incident, obtaining assistance and/or from assisting or supporting the prosecution • Attempts to dispose of or conceal evidence • Failure of offender to respond to previous warnings • Commission of offence whilst offender under the influence of alcohol or drugs • Victim encouraged to recruit others
Mitigating factors
• No previous convictions **or** no relevant/recent convictions • Remorse • Previous good character and/or exemplary conduct* • Age and/or lack of maturity where it affects the responsibility of the offender • Mental disorder or learning disability, particularly where linked to the commission of the offence • Demonstration of steps taken to address offending behaviour

* [Repeats note as to distinction between previous good character/exemplary conduct and having no previous convictions and how to deal with them in respect of the offence: see **SG-69** for the full text.]

SG-102 **STEPS THREE to NINE**

[These are in the same terms as those applicable to sexual assault of a child under 13: see **SG-86**.]

Arranging or Facilitating the Commission of a Child Sex Offence SG-103

Sexual Offences Act 2003 (section 14)

Triable either way

Maximum: 14 years' custody

[Repeats information as to the CJA 2003, ss. 224A and 226A, which is set out at **SG-83**.]

Sentencers should refer to the guideline for the applicable, substantive offence of arranging or facilitating under sections 9 to 12. See [SG-91 et seq.]. The level of harm should be determined by reference to the type of activity arranged or facilitated. Sentences commensurate with the applicable starting point and range will ordinarily be appropriate. For offences involving significant commercial exploitation and/or an international element, it may, in the interests of justice, be appropriate to increase a sentence to a point above the category range. In exceptional cases, such as where a vulnerable offender performed a limited role, having been coerced or exploited by others, sentences below the starting point and range may be appropriate.

Meeting a Child following Sexual Grooming SG-104

Sexual Offences Act 2003 (section 15)

Triable either way

Maximum: 10 years' custody

Offence range: 1–7 years' custody

[Repeats information as to the CJA 2003, ss. 224A and 226A, which is set out at **SG-83**.]

STEP ONE Determining the offence category SG-105

The court should determine the offence category using the table below.

Category 1	Raised harm **and** raised culpability
Category 2	Raised harm **or** raised culpability
Category 3	Grooming **without** raised harm or culpability factors present

The court should determine culpability and harm caused or intended, by reference **only** to the factors below, which comprise the principal factual elements of the offence. Where an offence does not fall squarely into a category, individual factors may require a degree of weighting before making an overall assessment and determining the appropriate offence category.

Factors indicating raised harm
• Continued contact despite victim's attempts to terminate contact • Sexual images exchanged • Victim exposed to extreme sexual content for example, extreme pornography • Child is particularly vulnerable due to personal circumstances

Factors indicating raised culpability
• Offender acts together with others to commit the offence • Communication indicates penetrative sexual activity is intended • Offender lied about age/persona • Use of threats (including blackmail), gifts or bribes • Abuse of trust • Specific targeting of a particularly vulnerable child • Abduction/detention • Commercial exploitation and/or motivation • Offence racially or religiously aggravated • Offence motivated by, or demonstrating, hostility to the victim based on his or her sexual orientation (or presumed sexual orientation) or transgender identity (or presumed transgender identity) • Offence motivated by, or demonstrating, hostility to the victim based on his or her disability (or presumed disability)

SG-106 **STEP TWO Starting point and category range**

Having determined the category, the court should use the corresponding starting points to reach a sentence within the category range below. The starting point applies to all offenders irrespective of plea or previous convictions. Having determined the starting point, step two allows further adjustment for aggravating or mitigating features, set out below.

A case of particular gravity, reflected by multiple features of culpability or harm in step one, could merit upward adjustment from the starting point before further adjustment for aggravating or mitigating features, set out below.

Category 1	**Starting point** 4 years' custody **Category range** 3–7 years' custody
Category 2	**Starting point** 2 years' custody **Category range** 1–4 years' custody
Category 3	**Starting point** 18 months' custody **Category range** 1 year–2 years 6 months' custody

The table below contains a **non-exhaustive** list of additional factual elements providing the context of the offence and factors relating to the offender. Identify whether any combination of these, or other relevant factors, should result in an upward or downward adjustment from the starting point. **In particular, relevant recent convictions are likely to result in an upward adjustment.** In some cases, having considered these factors, it may be appropriate to move outside the identified category range.

Aggravating factors
Statutory aggravating factors • Previous convictions, having regard to a) the nature of the offence to which the conviction relates and its relevance to the current offence; and b) the time that has elapsed since the conviction • Offence committed whilst on bail *Other aggravating factors* • Failure to comply with current court orders • Offence committed whilst on licence • Any steps taken to prevent the victim reporting an incident, obtaining assistance and/or from assisting or supporting the prosecution • Attempts to dispose of or conceal evidence • Victim encouraged to recruit others

Mitigating factors
• No previous convictions **or** no relevant/recent convictions • Remorse • Previous good character and/or exemplary conduct* • Age and/or lack of maturity where it affects the responsibility of the offender • Mental disorder or learning disability, particularly where linked to the commission of the offence • Demonstration of steps taken to address offending behaviour

* [Repeats note as to distinction between previous good character/exemplary conduct and having no previous convictions and how to deal with them in respect of the offence: see **SG-69** for the full text.]

SG-107 **STEPS THREE TO NINE**

[These are in the same terms as those applicable to sexual assault of a child under 13: see **SG-86**.]

Abuse of Position of Trust: Sexual Activity with a Child SG-108

Sexual Offences Act 2003 (section 16)

Abuse of Position of Trust: Causing or Inciting a Child to Engage in Sexual Activity

Sexual Offences Act 2003 (section 17)

Triable either way

Maximum: 5 years' custody

Offence range: Community order—2 years' custody

[Repeats information as to the CJA 2003, s. 226A which is set out at SG-67.]

STEP ONE Determining the offence category SG-109

The court should determine which categories of harm and culpability the offence falls into by reference **only** to the tables below.

This guideline also applies to offences committed remotely/online

Harm	
Category 1	• Penetration of vagina or anus (using body or object) • Penile penetration of mouth In either case by, or of, the victim
Category 2	• Touching, or exposure, of naked genitalia or naked breasts by, or of, the victim
Category 3	Factor(s) in categories 1 and 2 not present

Culpability	
A	B
• Significant degree of planning • Offender acts together with others to commit the offence • Use of alcohol/drugs on victim to facilitate the offence • Grooming behaviour used against victim • Use of threats (including blackmail) • Sexual images of victim recorded, retained, solicited or shared • Specific targeting of a particularly vulnerable child • Commercial exploitation and/or motivation • Offence racially or religiously aggravated • Offence motivated by, or demonstrating, hostility to the victim based on his or her sexual orientation (or presumed sexual orientation) or transgender identity (or presumed transgender identity) • Offence motivated by, or demonstrating, hostility to the victim based on his or her disability (or presumed disability)	Factor(s) in category A not present

STEP TWO Starting point and category range SG-110

Having determined the category, the court should use the corresponding starting points to reach a sentence within the category range below. The starting point applies to all offenders irrespective of plea or previous convictions. Having determined the starting point, step two allows further adjustment for aggravating or mitigating features, set out below.

A case of particular gravity, reflected by multiple features of culpability or harm in step one, could merit upward adjustment from the starting point before further adjustment for aggravating or mitigating features, set out below.

Where there is a sufficient prospect of rehabilitation, a community order with a sex offender treatment programme requirement under section 202 of the Criminal Justice Act 2003 can be a proper alternative to a short or moderate length custodial sentence.

	A	B
Category 1	**Starting point** 18 months' custody **Category range** 1–2 years' custody	**Starting point** 1 year's custody **Category range** 26 weeks'–18 months' custody
Category 2	**Starting point** 1 year's custody **Category range** 26 weeks'–18 months' custody	**Starting point** 26 weeks' custody **Category range** High level community order–1 year's custody
Category 3	**Starting point** 26 weeks' custody **Category range** High level community order–1 year's custody	**Starting point** Medium level community order **Category range** Low level community order–High level community order

The table below contains a **non-exhaustive** list of additional factual elements providing the context of the offence and factors relating to the offender. Identify whether any combination of these, or other relevant factors, should result in an upward or downward adjustment from the starting point. **In particular, relevant recent convictions are likely to result in an upward adjustment.** In some cases, having considered these factors, it may be appropriate to move outside the identified category range.

When sentencing appropriate **category 2 or 3 offences**, the court should also consider the custody threshold as follows:

- Has the custody threshold been passed?
- If so, is it unavoidable that a custodial sentence be imposed?
- If so, can that sentence be suspended?

Aggravating factors
Statutory aggravating factors • Previous convictions, having regard to a) the nature of the offence to which the conviction relates and its relevance to the current offence; and b) the time that has elapsed since the conviction • Offence committed whilst on bail *Other aggravating factors* • Ejaculation • Pregnancy or STI as a consequence of offence • Location of offence • Timing of offence • Victim compelled to leave their home, school, etc • Failure to comply with current court orders • Offence committed whilst on licence • Presence of others, especially other children • Any steps taken to prevent the victim reporting an incident, obtaining assistance and/or from assisting or supporting the prosecution • Attempts to dispose of or conceal evidence • Failure of offender to respond to previous warnings • Commission of offence whilst under the influence of alcohol or drugs • Victim encouraged to recruit others

Mitigating factors
• No previous convictions **or** no relevant/recent convictions • Remorse • Previous good character and/or exemplary conduct* • Age and/or lack of maturity where it affects the responsibility of the offender • Mental disorder or learning disability, particularly where linked to the commission of the offence • Sexual activity was incited but no activity took place because the offender voluntarily desisted or intervened to prevent it • Demonstration of steps taken to address offending behaviour

* [Repeats note as to distinction between previous good character/exemplary conduct and having no previous convictions and how to deal with them in respect of the offence: see **SG-69** for the full text.]

STEPS THREE TO NINE SG-111

[These are in the same terms as those applicable to sexual assault: see **SG-70**.]

Abuse of Position of Trust: Sexual Activity in the Presence of a Child SG-112

Sexual Offences Act 2003 (section 18)

Abuse of Position of Trust: Causing a Child to Watch a Sexual Act

Sexual Offences Act 2003 (section 19)

Triable either way

Maximum: 5 years' custody

Offence range: Community order—2 years' custody

[Repeats information as to the CJA 2003, s. 226A, which is set out at **SG-67**.]

STEP ONE Determining the offence category SG-113

The court should determine which categories of harm and culpability the offence falls into by reference **only** to the tables below.

Harm	
Category 1	• Causing victim to view extreme pornography • Causing victim to view indecent/prohibited images of children • Engaging in, or causing a victim to view live, sexual activity involving sadism/violence/sexual activity with an animal/a child
Category 2	Engaging in, or causing a victim to view images of or view live, sexual activity involving: • penetration of vagina or anus (using body or object) • penile penetration of mouth • masturbation
Category 3	Factor(s) in categories 1 and 2 not present

Culpability	
A	B
• Significant degree of planning • Offender acts together with others to commit the offence • Use of alcohol/drugs on victim to facilitate the offence • Grooming behaviour used against victim • Use of threats (including blackmail) • Specific targeting of a particularly vulnerable child • Commercial exploitation and/or motivation • Offence racially or religiously aggravated • Offence motivated by, or demonstrating, hostility to the victim based on his or her sexual orientation (or presumed sexual orientation) or transgender identity (or presumed transgender identity) • Offence motivated by, or demonstrating, hostility to the victim based on his or her disability (or presumed disability)	Factor(s) in category A not present

STEP TWO Starting point and category range SG-114

Having determined the category, the court should use the corresponding starting points to reach a sentence within the category range below. The starting point applies to all offenders irrespective of plea or previous convictions. Having determined the starting point, step two allows further adjustment for aggravating or mitigating features, set out below.

A case of particular gravity, reflected by multiple features of culpability or harm in step one, could merit upward adjustment from the starting point before further adjustment for aggravating or mitigating features, set out below.

Where there is a sufficient prospect of rehabilitation, a community order with a sex offender treatment programme requirement under section 202 of the Criminal Justice Act 2003 can be a proper alternative to a short or moderate length custodial sentence.

	A	B
Category 1	**Starting point** 18 months' custody **Category range** 1–2 years' custody	**Starting point** 1 year's custody **Category range** 26 weeks'–18 months' custody
Category 2	**Starting point** 1 year's custody **Category range** 26 weeks'–18 months' custody	**Starting point** 26 weeks' custody **Category range** High level community order–1 year's custody
Category 3	**Starting point** 26 weeks' custody **Category range** High level community order–1 year's custody	**Starting point** Medium level community order **Category range** Low level community order–High level community order

The table below contains a **non-exhaustive** list of additional factual elements providing the context of the offence and factors relating to the offender. Identify whether any combination of these, or other relevant factors, should result in an upward or downward adjustment from the starting point. **In particular, relevant recent convictions are likely to result in an upward adjustment.** In some cases, having considered these factors, it may be appropriate to move outside the identified category range.

When sentencing appropriate **category 2 or 3 offences**, the court should also consider the custody threshold as follows:

- Has the custody threshold been passed?
- If so, is it unavoidable that a custodial sentence be imposed?
- If so, can that sentence be suspended?

Aggravating factors
Statutory aggravating factors • Previous convictions, having regard to a) the nature of the offence to which the conviction relates and its relevance to the current offence; and b) the time that has elapsed since the conviction • Offence committed whilst on bail
Other aggravating factors • Location of offence • Timing of offence • Victim compelled to leave their home, school, etc • Failure to comply with current court orders • Offence committed whilst on licence • Presence of others, especially other children • Any steps taken to prevent the victim reporting an incident, obtaining assistance and/or from assisting or supporting the prosecution • Attempts to dispose of or conceal evidence • Failure of offender to respond to previous warnings • Commission of offence whilst under the influence of alcohol or drugs • Victim encouraged to recruit others

Mitigating factors
• No previous convictions **or** no relevant/recent convictions • Remorse • Previous good character and/or exemplary conduct* • Age and/or lack of maturity where it affects the responsibility of the offender • Mental disorder or learning disability, particularly where linked to the commission of the offence • Demonstration of steps taken to address offending behaviour

* [Repeats note as to distinction between previous good character/exemplary conduct and having no previous convictions and how to deal with them in respect of the offence: see **SG-69** for the full text.]

SG-115 STEPS THREE TO NINE

[These are in the same terms as those applicable to sexual assault: see **SG-70**.]

Possession of Indecent Photograph of Child SG-116

Criminal Justice Act 1988 (section 160)

Triable either way

Maximum: 5 years' custody

Offence range: Community order—3 years' custody

Indecent Photographs of Children

Protection of Children Act 1978 (section 1)

Triable either way

Maximum: 10 years' custody

Offence range: Community order—9 years' custody

[Repeats information as to the CJA 2003, ss. 224A and 226A, which is set out at SG-83.]

STEP ONE Determining the offence category SG-117

The court should determine the offence category using the table below.

	Possession	Distribution*	Production**
Category A	Possession of images involving penetrative sexual activity Possession of images involving sexual activity with an animal or sadism	Sharing images involving penetrative sexual activity Sharing images involving sexual activity with an animal or sadism	Creating images involving penetrative sexual activity Creating images involving sexual activity with an animal or sadism
Category B	Possession of images involving non-penetrative sexual activity	Sharing of images involving non-penetrative sexual activity	Creating images involving non-penetrative sexual activity
Category C	Possession of other indecent images not falling within categories A or B	Sharing of other indecent images not falling within categories A or B	Creating other indecent images not falling within categories A or B

* Distribution includes possession with a view to distributing or sharing images.

** Production includes the taking or making of any image at source for instance the original image.

Making an image by simple downloading should be treated as possession for the purposes of sentencing.

In most cases the intrinsic character of the most serious of the offending images will initially determine the appropriate category. If, however, the most serious images are unrepresentative of the offender's conduct a lower category may be appropriate. A lower category will not, however, be appropriate if the offender has produced or taken (for example photographed) images of a higher category.

STEP TWO Starting point and category range SG-118

Having determined the category, the court should use the corresponding starting points to reach a sentence within the category range below. The starting point applies to all offenders irrespective of plea or previous convictions. Having determined the starting point, step two allows further adjustment for aggravating or mitigating features, set out below.

Where there is a sufficient prospect of rehabilitation, a community order with a sex offender treatment programme requirement under section 202 of the Criminal Justice Act 2003 can be a proper alternative to a short or moderate length custodial sentence.

	Possession	Distribution	Production
Category A	**Starting point** 1 year's custody **Category range** 26 weeks–3 years' custody	**Starting point** 3 years' custody **Category range** 2–5 years' custody	**Starting point** 6 years' custody **Category range** 4–9 years' custody
Category B	**Starting point** 26 weeks' custody **Category range** High level community order–18 months' custody	**Starting point** 1 year's custody **Category range** 26 weeks–2 years' custody	**Starting point** 2 years' custody **Category range** 1–4 years' custody
Category C	**Starting point** High level community order **Category range** Medium level community order–26 weeks' custody	**Starting point** 13 weeks' custody **Category range** High level community order–26 weeks' custody	**Starting point** 18 months' custody **Category range** 1–3 years' custody

The table below contains a **non-exhaustive** list of additional factual elements providing the context of the offence and factors relating to the offender. Identify whether any combination of these, or other relevant factors, should result in an upward or downward adjustment from the starting point. **In particular, relevant recent convictions are likely to result in an upward adjustment.** In some cases, having considered these factors, it may be appropriate to move outside the identified category range.

When sentencing appropriate **category 2 or 3 offences**, the court should also consider the custody threshold as follows:

- Has the custody threshold been passed?
- If so, is it unavoidable that a custodial sentence be imposed?
- If so, can that sentence be suspended?

Aggravating factors
Statutory aggravating factors • Previous convictions, having regard to a) the nature of the offence to which the conviction relates and its relevance to the current offence; and b) the time that has elapsed since the conviction • Offence committed whilst on bail
Other aggravating factors • Failure to comply with current court orders • Offence committed whilst on licence • Age and/or vulnerability of the child depicted* • Discernable pain or distress suffered by child depicted • Period over which images were possessed, distributed or produced • High volume of images possessed, distributed or produced • Placing images where there is the potential for a high volume of viewers • Collection includes moving images • Attempts to dispose of or conceal evidence • Abuse of trust • Child depicted known to the offender • Active involvement in a network or process that facilitates or commissions the creation or sharing of indecent images of children • Commercial exploitation and/or motivation • Deliberate or systematic searching for images portraying young children, category A images or the portrayal of familial sexual abuse • Large number of different victims • Child depicted intoxicated or drugged

* Age and/or vulnerability of the child should be given significant weight. In cases where the actual age of the victim is difficult to determine sentencers should consider the development of the child (infant, pre-pubescent, post-pubescent)

Mitigating factors
• No previous convictions **or** no relevant/recent convictions • Remorse • Previous good character and/or exemplary conduct* • Age and/or lack of maturity where it affects the responsibility of the offender • Mental disorder or learning disability, particularly where linked to the commission of the offence • Demonstration of steps taken to address offending behaviour

* [Repeats note as to distinction between previous good character/exemplary conduct and having no previous convictions and how to deal with them in respect of the offence: see **SG-69** for the full text.]

STEPS THREE TO NINE **SG-119**

[These are in the same terms as those applicable to sexual assault of a child under 13: see **SG-86**.]

Causing or Inciting Prostitution for Gain **SG-120**

Sexual Offences Act 2003 (section 52)

Controlling Prostitution for Gain

Sexual Offences Act 2003 (section 53)

Triable either way

Maximum: 7 years' custody

Offence range: Community order—6 years' custody

[Repeats information as to the CJA 2003, s. 226A which is set out at **SG-67**.]

The terms 'prostitute' and 'prostitution' are used in this guideline in accordance with the statutory language contained in the Sexual Offences Act 2003.

STEP ONE Determining the offence category **SG-121**

The court should determine which categories of harm and culpability the offence falls into by reference **only** to the tables below.

Harm	
Category 1	• Abduction/detention • Violence or threats of violence • Sustained and systematic psychological abuse • Individual(s) forced or coerced to participate in unsafe/degrading sexual activity • Individual(s) forced or coerced into seeing many 'customers' • Individual(s) forced/coerced/deceived into prostitution
Category 2	Factor(s) in category 1 not present

Culpability		
A	B	C
• Causing, inciting or controlling prostitution on significant commercial basis • Expectation of significant financial or other gain • Abuse of trust • Exploitation of those known to be trafficked • Significant involvement in limiting the freedom of prostitute(s) • Grooming of individual(s) to enter prostitution including through cultivation of a dependency on drugs or alcohol	• Close involvement with prostitute(s) for example control of finances, choice of clients, working conditions, etc (where offender's involvement is not as a result of coercion)	• Performs limited function under direction • Close involvement but engaged by coercion/ intimidation/exploitation

SG-122 **STEP TWO Starting point and category range**

Having determined the category, the court should use the corresponding starting points to reach a sentence within the category range below. The starting point applies to all offenders irrespective of plea or previous convictions. Having determined the starting point, step two allows further adjustment for aggravating or mitigating features, set out below.

A case of particular gravity, reflected by multiple features of culpability or harm in step one, could merit upward adjustment from the starting point before further adjustment for aggravating or mitigating features, set out below.

Where there is a sufficient prospect of rehabilitation, a community order with a sex offender treatment programme requirement under section 202 of the Criminal Justice Act 2003 can be a proper alternative to a short or moderate length custodial sentence.

	A	B	C
Category 1	**Starting point** 4 years' custody **Category range** 3–6 years' custody	**Starting point** 2 years 6 months' custody **Category range** 2–4 years' custody	**Starting point** 1 year's custody **Category range** 26 weeks'–2 years' custody
Category 2	**Starting point** 2 years' 6 months' custody **Category range** 2–5 years' custody	**Starting point** 1 year's custody **Category range** High level community order–2 years' custody	**Starting point** Medium level community Order **Category range** Low level community order–High level community order

The table below contains a **non-exhaustive** list of additional factual elements providing the context of the offence and factors relating to the offender. Identify whether any combination of these, or other relevant factors, should result in an upward or downward adjustment from the starting point. **In particular, relevant recent convictions are likely to result in an upward adjustment.** In some cases, having considered these factors, it may be appropriate to move outside the identified category range.

When sentencing appropriate **category 2 offences**, the court should also consider the custody threshold as follows:

- Has the custody threshold been passed?
- If so, is it unavoidable that a custodial sentence be imposed?
- If so, can that sentence be suspended?

Aggravating factors

Statutory aggravating factors

- Previous convictions, having regard to a) the nature of the offence to which the conviction relates and its relevance to the current offence; and b) the time that has elapsed since the conviction
- Offence committed whilst on bail

Other aggravating factors

- Failure to comply with current court orders
- Offence committed whilst on licence
- Deliberate isolation of prostitute(s)
- Threats made to expose prostitute(s) to the authorities (for example, immigration or police), family/friends or others
- Harm threatened against the family/friends of prostitute(s)
- Passport/identity documents removed
- Prostitute(s) prevented from seeking medical treatment
- Food withheld
- Earnings withheld/kept by offender or evidence of excessive wage reduction or debt bondage, inflated travel or living expenses or unreasonable interest rates
- Any steps taken to prevent the reporting of an incident, obtaining assistance and/or from assisting or supporting the prosecution
- Attempts to dispose of or conceal evidence
- Prostitute(s) forced or coerced into pornography
- Timescale over which operation has been run

Mitigating factors
• No previous convictions **or** no relevant/recent convictions • Remorse • Previous good character and/or exemplary conduct* • Age and/or lack of maturity where it affects the responsibility of the offender • Mental disorder or learning disability, particularly where linked to the commission of the offence • Demonstration of steps taken to address offending behaviour

* [Repeats note as to distinction between previous good character/exemplary conduct and having no previous convictions and how to deal with them in respect of the offence: see **SG-69** for the full text.]

STEPS THREE TO NINE SG-123

[These are in the same terms as those applicable to sexual assault: see **SG-70**.]

Keeping a Brothel Used for Prostitution SG-124

Sexual Offences Act 1956 (section 33A)

Triable either way

Maximum: 7 years' custody

Offence range: Community order—6 years' custody

The terms 'prostitute' and 'prostitution' are used in this guideline in accordance with the statutory language contained in the Sexual Offences Act 2003.

STEP ONE Determining the offence category SG-125

The court should determine which categories of harm and culpability the offence falls into by reference **only** to the tables below.

Harm	
Category 1	• Under 18 year olds working in brothel • Abduction/detention • Violence or threats of violence • Sustained and systematic psychological abuse • Those working in brothel forced or coerced to participate in unsafe/degrading sexual activity • Those working in brothel forced or coerced into seeing many 'customers' • Those working in brothel forced/coerced/deceived into prostitution • Established evidence of community impact
Category 2	Factor(s) in category 1 not present

Culpability		
A	B	C
• Keeping brothel on significant commercial basis • Involvement in keeping a number of brothels • Expectation of significant financial or other gain • Abuse of trust • Exploitation of those known to be trafficked • Significant involvement in limiting freedom of those working in brothel • Grooming of a person to work in the brothel including through cultivation of a dependency on drugs or alcohol	• Keeping/managing premises • Close involvement with those working in brothel e.g. control of finances, choice of clients, working conditions, etc. (where offender's involvement is not as a result of coercion)	• Performs limited function under direction • Close involvement but engaged by coercion/intimidation/exploitation

STEP TWO Starting point and category range SG-126

Having determined the category, the court should use the corresponding starting points to reach a sentence within the category range below. The starting point applies to all offenders irrespective of plea or previous convictions. Having determined the starting point, step two allows further adjustment for aggravating or mitigating features, set out below.

A case of particular gravity, reflected by multiple features of culpability or harm in step one, could merit upward adjustment from the starting point before further adjustment for aggravating or mitigating features, set out below.

Where there is a sufficient prospect of rehabilitation, a community order with a sex offender treatment programme requirement under section 202 of the Criminal Justice Act 2003 can be a proper alternative to a short or moderate length custodial sentence.

	A	B	C
Category 1	**Starting point** 5 years' custody **Category range** 3–6 years' custody	**Starting point** 3 years' custody **Category range** 2–5 years' custody	**Starting point** 1 year's custody **Category range** High level community order–18 months' custody
Category 2	**Starting point** 3 years' custody **Category range** 2–5 years' custody	**Starting point** 12 months' custody **Category range** 26 weeks'–2 years' custody	**Starting point** Medium level community order **Category range** Low level community order–High level community order

The table below contains a **non-exhaustive** list of additional factual elements providing the context of the offence and factors relating to the offender. Identify whether any combination of these, or other relevant factors, should result in an upward or downward adjustment from the starting point. **In particular, relevant recent convictions are likely to result in an upward adjustment.** In some cases, having considered these factors, it may be appropriate to move outside the identified category range.

When sentencing appropriate **category 1 offences**, the court should also consider the custody threshold as follows:

- Has the custody threshold been passed?
- If so, is it unavoidable that a custodial sentence be imposed?
- If so, can that sentence be suspended?

Aggravating factors
Statutory aggravating factors • Previous convictions, having regard to a) the nature of the offence to which the conviction relates and its relevance to the current offence; and b) the time that has elapsed since the conviction • Offence committed whilst on bail *Other aggravating factors* • Failure to comply with current court orders • Offence committed whilst on licence • Deliberate isolation of those working in brothel • Threats made to expose those working in brothel to the authorities (for example, immigration or police), family/friends or others • Harm threatened against the family/friends of those working in brothel • Passport/identity documents removed • Those working in brothel prevented from seeking medical treatment • Food withheld • Those working in brothel passed around by offender and moved to other brothels • Earnings of those working in brothel withheld/kept by offender or evidence of excessive wage reduction or debt bondage, inflated travel or living expenses or unreasonable interest rates • Any steps taken to prevent those working in brothel reporting an incident, obtaining assistance and/or from assisting or supporting the prosecution • Attempts to dispose of or conceal evidence • Those working in brothel forced or coerced into pornography • Timescale over which operation has been run

Mitigating factors
• No previous convictions **or** no relevant/recent convictions • Remorse • Previous good character and/or exemplary conduct* • Age and/or lack of maturity where it affects the responsibility of the offender • Mental disorder or learning disability, particularly where linked to the commission of the offence • Demonstration of steps taken to address offending behaviour

* [Repeats note as to distinction between previous good character/exemplary conduct and having no previous convictions and how to deal with them in respect of the offence: see **SG-69** for the full text.]

STEPS THREE TO EIGHT **SG-127**

[These are the same as those applicable to rape (see **SG-62**) but with the omission of the step relating to dangerousness.]

Causing or Inciting Child Prostitution or Pornography **SG-128**

Sexual Offences Act 2003 (section 48)

Controlling a Child Prostitute or Child Involved in Pornography

Sexual Offences Act 2003 (section 49)

Arranging or Facilitating Child Prostitution or Pornography

Sexual Offences Act 2003 (section 50)

Triable either way

Maximum: 14 years' custody

Offence range:	Victim aged under 13	1–13 years' custody
	Victim aged 13–15	26 weeks'–11 years' custody
	Victim aged 16–17	Community order–7 years' custody

[Repeats information as to the CJA 2003, ss. 224A and 226A which is set out at **SG-83**.]

The terms 'child prostitute', 'child prostitution' and 'child involved in pornography' are used in this guideline in accordance with the statutory language contained in the Sexual Offences Act 2003.

STEP ONE **Determining the offence category** **SG-129**

The court should determine which categories of harm and culpability the offence falls into by reference **only** to the tables below.

For offences that involve wide scale commercial and/or international activity sentences above the category range may be appropriate.

Harm	
Category 1	• Victims involved in penetrative sexual activity • Abduction/detention • Violence or threats of violence • Sustained and systematic psychological abuse • Victim(s) participated in unsafe/degrading sexual activity beyond that which is inherent in the offence • Victim(s) passed around by the offender to other 'customers' and/or moved to other brothels
Category 2	Factor(s) in category 1 not present

Culpability		
A	B	C
• Directing or organising child prostitution or pornography on significant commercial basis • Expectation of significant financial or other gain • Abuse of trust • Exploitation of victim(s) known to be trafficked • Significant involvement in limiting the freedom of the victim(s) • Grooming of a victim to enter prostitution or pornography including through cultivation of a dependency on drugs or alcohol	• Close involvement with inciting, controlling, arranging or facilitating child prostitution or pornography (where offender's involvement is not as a result of coercion)	• Performs limited function under direction • Close involvement but engaged by coercion/ intimidation / exploitation

SG-130 **STEP TWO Starting point and category range**

Having determined the category, the court should use the corresponding starting points to reach a sentence within the category range below. The starting point applies to all offenders irrespective of plea or previous convictions. Having determined the starting point, step two allows further adjustment for aggravating or mitigating features, set out below.

A case of particular gravity, reflected by multiple features of culpability or harm in step one, could merit upward adjustment from the starting point before further adjustment for aggravating or mitigating features, set out below.

Where there is a sufficient prospect of rehabilitation, a community order with a sex offender treatment programme requirement under section 202 of the Criminal Justice Act 2003 can be a proper alternative to a short or moderate length custodial sentence.

		A	B	C
Category 1	U13	**Starting point** 10 years' custody **Category range** 8–13 years' custody	**Starting point** 8 years' custody **Category range** 6–11 years' custody	**Starting point** 5 years' custody **Category range** 2–6 years' custody
	13–15	**Starting point** 8 years' custody **Category range** 6–11 years' custody	**Starting point** 5 years' custody **Category range** 4–8 years' custody	**Starting point** 2 years 6 months' custody **Category range** 1–4 years' custody
	16–17	**Starting point** 4 years' custody **Category range** 3–7 years' custody	**Starting point** 2 years' custody **Category range** 1–4 years' custody	**Starting point** 1 year's custody **Category range** 26 weeks'–2 years' custody
Category 2	U13	**Starting point** 8 years' custody **Category range** 6–11 years' custody	**Starting point** 6 years' custody **Category range** 4–9 years' custody	**Starting point** 2 years' custody **Category range** 1–4 years' custody
	13–15	**Starting point** 6 years' custody **Category range** 4–9 years' custody	**Starting point** 3 years' custody **Category range** 2–5 years' custody	**Starting point** 1 year's custody **Category range** 26 weeks'–2 years' custody
	16–17	**Starting point** 3 years' custody **Category range** 2–5 years' custody	**Starting point** 1 year's custody **Category range** 26 weeks'–2 years' custody	**Starting point** 26 weeks' custody **Category range** High level community order–1 year's custody

The table below contains a **non-exhaustive** list of additional factual elements providing the context of the offence and factors relating to the offender. Identify whether any combination of these, or other relevant factors, should result in an upward or downward adjustment from the starting point. **In particular, relevant recent convictions are likely to result in an upward adjustment.** In some cases, having considered these factors, it may be appropriate to move outside the identified category range.

When sentencing appropriate **category 2 offences**, the court should also consider the custody threshold as follows:

- Has the custody threshold been passed?
- If so, is it unavoidable that a custodial sentence be imposed?
- If so, can that sentence be suspended?

Aggravating factors
Statutory aggravating factors • Previous convictions, having regard to a) the nature of the offence to which the conviction relates and its relevance to the current offence; and b) the time that has elapsed since the conviction • Offence committed whilst on bail *Other aggravating factors* • Failure to comply with current court orders • Offence committed whilst on licence • Deliberate isolation of victim(s) • Vulnerability of victim(s) • Threats made to expose victim(s) to the authorities (for example immigration or police), family/friends or others • Harm threatened against the family/friends of victim(s) • Passport/identity documents removed • Victim(s) prevented from seeking medical treatment • Victim(s) prevented from attending school • Food withheld • Earnings withheld/kept by offender or evidence of excessive wage reduction or debt bondage, inflated travel or living expenses or unreasonable interest rates • Any steps taken to prevent the victim reporting an incident, obtaining assistance and/or from assisting or supporting the prosecution • Attempts to dispose of or conceal evidence • Timescale over which the operation has been run

Mitigating factors
• No previous convictions **or** no relevant/recent convictions • Remorse • Previous good character and/or exemplary conduct* • Age and/or lack of maturity where it affects the responsibility of the offender • Mental disorder or learning disability, particularly where linked to the commission of the offence

* [Repeats note as to distinction between previous good character/exemplary conduct and having no previous convictions and how to deal with them in respect of the offence: see **SG-61** for the full text.]

STEPS THREE TO NINE SG-131

[These are in the same terms as those applicable to sexual assault of a child under 13: see **SG-86**.]

Paying for the Sexual Services of a Child SG-132

Sexual Offences Act 2003 (section 47)

Triable only on indictment (if involving penetration against victim under 16)—otherwise triable either way

Maximum:	Victim under 13 (penetrative)	Life imprisonment
	Victim under 13 (non-penetrative)	14 years' custody
	Victim aged 13–15	14 years' custody
	Victim aged 16–17	7 years' custody
Offence range:	Victim aged 16–17	Community order–5 years' custody

This guideline should only be used where the victim is aged 16 or 17 years old. If the victim is under 13 please refer to the guidelines for rape of a child under 13, assault by penetration of a child under 13, sexual assault of a child under 13 or causing or inciting a child under 13 to engage in sexual activity, depending on the activity involved in the offence.

If the victim is aged 13–15 please refer to the sexual activity with a child guideline.

[Repeats information as to the CJA 2003, s. 226A, which is set out at **SG-67**.]

SG-133 **STEP ONE Determining the offence category**

The court should determine which categories of harm and culpability the offence falls into by reference **only** to the tables below.

This guideline should only be used where the victim was aged 16 or 17 years old.

Harm	
Category 1	• Penetration of vagina or anus (using body or object) by, or of, the victim • Penile penetration of mouth by, or of, the victim • Violence or threats of violence • Victim subjected to unsafe/degrading sexual activity (beyond that which is inherent in the offence)
Category 2	• Touching of naked genitalia or naked breasts by, or of, the victim
Category 3	• Other sexual activity

Culpability	
A	B
• Abduction/detention • Sexual images of victim recorded, retained, solicited or shared • Offender acts together with others to commit the offence • Use of alcohol/drugs on victim • Abuse of trust • Previous violence against victim • Sexual images of victim recorded, retained, solicited or shared • Blackmail or other threats made (including to expose victim to the authorities, family/friends or others) • Offender aware that he has a sexually transmitted disease • Offender aware victim has been trafficked	Factor(s) in category A not present

SG-134 **STEP TWO Starting point and category range**

Having determined the category, the court should use the corresponding starting points to reach a sentence within the category range below **for victims aged 16 or 17**. The starting point applies to all offenders irrespective of plea or previous convictions. Having determined the starting point, step two allows further adjustment for aggravating or mitigating features, set out below.

A case of particular gravity, reflected by multiple features of culpability in step one, could merit upward adjustment from the starting point before further adjustment for aggravating or mitigating features, set out below.

Where there is a sufficient prospect of rehabilitation, a community order with a sex offender treatment programme requirement under section 202 of the Criminal Justice Act 2003 can be a proper alternative to a short or moderate length custodial sentence.

	A	B
Category 1	**Starting point** 4 years' custody **Category range** 2–5 years' custody	**Starting point** 2 years' custody **Category range** 1–4 years' custody
Category 2	**Starting point** 3 years' custody **Category range** 1–4 years' custody	**Starting point** 1 year's custody **Category range** 26 weeks'–2 years' custody
Category 3	**Starting point** 1 year's custody **Category range** 26 weeks'–2 years' custody	**Starting point** 26 weeks' custody **Category range** High level community order–1 year's custody

The table below contains a **non-exhaustive** list of additional factual elements providing the context of the offence and factors relating to the offender. Identify whether any combination of these, or other relevant factors, should result in an upward or downward adjustment from the starting point. **In particular, relevant recent convictions are likely to result in an upward adjustment.** In some cases, having considered these factors, it may be appropriate to move outside the identified category range.

When sentencing appropriate **category 3 offences**, the court should also consider the custody threshold as follows:

- Has the custody threshold been passed?
- If so, is it unavoidable that a custodial sentence be imposed?
- If so, can that sentence be suspended?

Aggravating factors
Statutory aggravating factors • Previous convictions, having regard to a) the nature of the offence to which the conviction relates and its relevance to the current offence; and b) the time that has elapsed since the conviction • Offence committed whilst on bail *Other aggravating factors* • Ejaculation • Failure to comply with current court orders • Offence committed whilst on licence • Any steps taken to prevent the victim reporting an incident, obtaining assistance and/or from assisting or supporting the prosecution • Attempts to dispose of or conceal evidence

Mitigating factors
• No previous convictions or no relevant/recent convictions • Remorse • Previous good character and/or exemplary conduct* • Age and/or lack of maturity where it affects the responsibility of the offender • Mental disorder or learning disability, particularly where linked to the commission of the offence • Demonstration of steps taken to address offending behaviour

* [Repeats note as to distinction between previous good character/exemplary conduct and having no previous convictions and how to deal with them in respect of the offence: see **SG-69** for the full text.]

STEPS THREE TO NINE **SG-135**

[These are in the same terms as those applicable to sexual assault: see **SG-70**.]

SG-136 TRAFFICKING PEOPLE FOR SEXUAL EXPLOITATION

Sexual Offences Act 2003 (sections 59A)

(This guideline also applies to offences, committed before 6 April 2013, of trafficking into/within/out of the UK for sexual exploitation contrary to sections 57 to 59 of the Sexual Offences Act 2003)

Triable either way

Maximum: 14 years' custody

Offence range: Community order—12 years' custody

[Repeats information as to the CJA 2003, s. 226A, which is set out at **SG-67**.]

The term 'prostitution' is used in this guideline in accordance with the statutory language contained in the Sexual Offences Act 2003.

SG-137 **STEP ONE Determining the offence category**

The court should determine which categories of harm and culpability the offence falls into by reference **only** to the tables below.

Harm	
Category 1	• Abduction/detention • Violence or threats of violence • Sustained and systematic psychological abuse • Victim(s) under 18 • Victim(s) forced or coerced to participate in unsafe/degrading sexual activity • Victim(s) forced/coerced into prostitution • Victim(s) tricked/deceived as to purpose of visit
Category 2	• Factor(s) in category 1 not present

Culpability		
A	B	C
• Directing or organising trafficking on significant commercial basis • Expectation of significant financial or other gain • Significant influence over others in trafficking organisation/hierarchy • Abuse of trust	• Operational or management function within hierarchy • Involves others in operation whether by coercion/intimidation/exploitation or reward (and offender's involvement is not as a result of coercion)	• Performs limited function under direction • Close involvement but engaged by coercion/intimidation/exploitation

SG-138 **STEP TWO Starting point and category range**

Having determined the category of harm and culpability, the court should use the corresponding starting points to reach a sentence within the category range below. The starting point applies to all offenders irrespective of plea or previous convictions. Having determined the starting point, step two allows further adjustment for aggravating or mitigating features, set out below.

A case of particular gravity, reflected by multiple features of culpability or harm in step one, could merit upward adjustment from the starting point before further adjustment for aggravating or mitigating features, set out below.

Where there is a sufficient prospect of rehabilitation, a community order with a sex offender treatment programme requirement under section 202 of the Criminal Justice Act 2003 can be a proper alternative to a short or moderate length custodial sentence.

	A	B	C
Category 1	**Starting point** 8 years' custody **Category range** 6–2 years' custody	**Starting point** 6 years' custody **Category range** 4–8 years' custody	**Starting point** 18 months' custody **Category range** 26 weeks'–2 years' custody
Category 2	**Starting point** 6 years' custody **Category range** 4–8 years' custody	**Starting point** 4 years' custody **Category range** 2–6 years' custody	**Starting point** 26 weeks' custody **Category range** High level community order–18 months' custody

The table below contains a **non-exhaustive** list of additional factual elements providing the context of the offence and factors relating to the offender. Identify whether any combination of these, or other relevant factors, should result in an upward or downward adjustment from the starting point. **In particular, relevant recent convictions are likely to result in an upward adjustment.** In some cases, having considered these factors, it may be appropriate to move outside the identified category range.

When sentencing appropriate **category 2 offences**, the court should also consider the custody threshold as follows:

- Has the custody threshold been passed?
- If so, is it unavoidable that a custodial sentence be imposed?
- If so, can that sentence be suspended?

Aggravating factors
Statutory aggravating factors • Previous convictions, having regard to a) the nature of the offence to which the conviction relates and its relevance to the current offence; and b) the time that has elapsed since the conviction • Offence committed whilst on bail *Other aggravating factors* • Failure to comply with current court orders • Offence committed whilst on licence • Deliberate isolation of victim(s) • Children of victim(s) left in home country due to trafficking • Threats made to expose victim(s) to the authorities (for example immigration or police), family/friends or others • Harm threatened against the family/friends of victim • Exploitation of victim(s) from particularly vulnerable backgrounds • Victim(s) previously trafficked/sold/passed around • Passport/identity documents removed • Victim(s) prevented from seeking medical treatment • Food withheld • Use of drugs/alcohol or other substance to secure victim's compliance • Earnings of victim(s) withheld/kept by offender or evidence of excessive wage reduction, debt bondage, inflated travel or living expenses, unreasonable interest rates • Any steps taken to prevent the victim reporting an incident, obtaining assistance and/or from assisting or supporting the prosecution • Attempts to dispose of or conceal evidence • Timescale over which operation has been run

Mitigating factors
• No previous convictions **or** no relevant/recent convictions • Remorse • Previous good character and/or exemplary conduct* • Age and/or lack of maturity where it affects the responsibility of the offender • Mental disorder or learning disability, particularly where linked to the commission of the offence

* [Repeats note as to distinction between previous good character/exemplary conduct and having no previous convictions and how to deal with them in respect of the offence: see **SG-61** for the full text.]

Sentencing Guidelines

SG-139 **STEPS THREE TO NINE**

[These are in the same terms as those applicable to sexual assault: see **SG-70**.]

SG-140 ## Sexual Activity with a person with a Mental Disorder Impeding Choice

Sexual Offences Act 2003 (section 30)

Causing or Inciting a Person, with a Mental Disorder Impeding Choice, to Engage in Sexual Activity

Sexual Offences Act 2003 (section 31)

Triable only on indictment (if penetration involved)

- otherwise, triable either way

Maximum: Life imprisonment (if penetration involved)

- otherwise, 14 years' custody

Offence range: Community order—19 years' custody

[Repeats information as to the CJA 2003, ss. 224, 225(2), 224A and 226A, which is set out at **SG-59**.]

SG-141 **STEP ONE Determining the offence category**

The court should determine which categories of harm and culpability the offence falls into by reference **only** to the tables below.

Harm	
Category 1	• The extreme nature of one or more category 2 factors or the extreme impact caused by a combination of category 2 factors **may** elevate to category 1
Category 2	• Severe psychological or physical harm • Pregnancy or STI as a consequence of offence • Additional degradation/humiliation • Abduction • Prolonged detention /sustained incident • Violence or threats of violence • Forced/uninvited entry into victim's home or residence
Category 3	Factor(s) in categories 1 and 2 not present

Culpability	
A	**B**
• Significant degree of planning • Offender acts together with others to commit the offence • Use of alcohol/drugs on victim to facilitate the offence • Grooming behaviour used against victim • Abuse of trust • Previous violence against victim • Offence committed in course of burglary • Sexual images of victim recorded, retained, solicited or shared • Deliberate isolation of victim • Commercial exploitation and/or motivation • Offence racially or religiously aggravated • Offence motivated by, or demonstrating, hostility to the victim based on his or her sexual orientation (or presumed sexual orientation) or transgender identity (or presumed transgender identity) • Offence motivated by, or demonstrating, hostility to the victim based on the victim's disability (or presumed disability)	Factor(s) in category A not present

STEP TWO Starting point and category range SG-142

Having determined the category of harm and culpability, the court should use the corresponding starting points to reach a sentence within the category range below. The starting point applies to all offenders irrespective of plea or previous convictions. Having determined the starting point, step two allows further adjustment for aggravating or mitigating features, set out below.

A case of particular gravity, reflected by multiple features of culpability or harm in step one, could merit upward adjustment from the starting point before further adjustment for aggravating or mitigating features, set out below.

Where there is a sufficient prospect of rehabilitation, a community order with a sex offender treatment programme requirement under section 202 of the Criminal Justice Act 2003 can be a proper alternative to a short or moderate length custodial sentence.

Where offence involved penetration

	A	B
Category 1	**Starting point** 16 years' custody **Category range** 13–19 years' custody	**Starting point** 13 years' custody **Category range** 11–17 years' custody
Category 2	**Starting point** 13 years' custody **Category range** 11–17 years' custody	**Starting point** 10 years' custody **Category range** 8–13 years' custody
Category 3	**Starting point** 10 years' custody **Category range** 8–13 years' custody	**Starting point** 8 years' custody **Category range** 6–11 years' custody

Where offence did not involve penetration

	A	B
Category 1	**Starting point** 6 years' custody **Category range** 4–9 years' custody	**Starting point** 4 years' custody **Category range** 3–7 years' custody
Category 2	**Starting point** 4 years' custody **Category range** 3–7 years' custody	**Starting point** 2 years' custody **Category range** 1–4 years' custody
Category 3	**Starting point** 1 year's custody **Category range** 26 weeks'– 2 years' custody	**Starting point** 26 weeks' custody **Category range** High level community order– 1 year's custody

The table below contains a **non-exhaustive** list of additional factual elements providing the context of the offence and factors relating to the offender. Identify whether any combination of these, or other relevant factors, should result in an upward or downward adjustment from the starting point. **In particular, relevant recent convictions are likely to result in an upward adjustment.** In some cases, having considered these factors, it may be appropriate to move outside the identified category range.

When appropriate, the court should also consider the custody threshold as follows:

- Has the custody threshold been passed?
- If so, is it unavoidable that a custodial sentence be imposed?
- If so, can that sentence be suspended?

Aggravating factors
Statutory aggravating factors • Previous convictions, having regard to a) the nature of the offence to which the conviction relates and its relevance to the current offence; and b) the time that has elapsed since the conviction • Offence committed whilst on bail
Other aggravating factors • Ejaculation (where not taken into account at step one) • Blackmail or other threats made (where not taken into account at step one) • Location of offence • Timing of offence • Use of weapon or other item to frighten or injure • Victim compelled to leave their home or institution (including victims of domestic violence) • Failure to comply with current court orders • Offence committed whilst on licence • Presence of others, especially children • Any steps taken to prevent the victim reporting an incident, obtaining assistance and/or from assisting or supporting the prosecution • Attempts to dispose of or conceal evidence • Commission of offence whilst under the influence of alcohol or drugs

Mitigating factors
• No previous convictions or no relevant/recent convictions • Remorse • Previous good character and/or exemplary conduct* • Age and/or lack of maturity where it affects the responsibility of the offender • Mental disorder or learning disability, particularly where linked to the commission of the offence • Sexual activity was incited but no activity took place because the offender voluntarily desisted or intervened to prevent it

* [Repeats note as to distinction between previous good character/exemplary conduct and having no previous convictions and how to deal with them in respect of the offence: see **SG-61** for the full text.]

SG-143 STEPS THREE TO NINE

[These are in the same terms as those applicable to rape: see **SG-62**.]

SG-144

Engaging in Sexual Activity in the Presence of a Person with Mental Disorder Impeding Choice

Sexual Offences Act 2003 (section 32)

Causing a Person, with Mental Disorder Impeding Choice, to Watch a Sexual Act

Sexual Offences Act 2003 (section 33)

Triable either way

Maximum: 10 years' custody

Offence range: Community order—6 years' custody

[Repeats information as to the CJA 2003, s. 226A which is set out at **SG-67**.]

SG-145 STEP ONE **Determining the offence category**

The court should determine which categories of harm and culpability the offence falls into by reference **only** to the tables below.

Harm	
Category 1	• Causing victim to view extreme pornography • Causing victim to view indecent/prohibited images of children • Engaging in, or causing a victim to view live, sexual activity involving sadism/violence/sexual activity with an animal/a child
Category 2	Engaging in, or causing a victim to view images of or view live, sexual activity involving: • penetration of vagina or anus (using body or object) • penile penetration of mouth • masturbation
Category 3	Factor(s) in categories 1 and 2 not present

Culpability	
A	B
• Significant degree of planning • Offender acts together with others in order to commit the offence • Use of alcohol/drugs on victim to facilitate the offence • Grooming behaviour used against victim • Abuse of trust • Use of threats (including blackmail) • Commercial exploitation and/or motivation • Offence racially or religiously aggravated • Offence motivated by, or demonstrating, hostility to the victim based on his or her sexual orientation (or presumed sexual orientation) or transgender identity (or presumed transgender identity) • Offence motivated by, or demonstrating, hostility to the victim based on his or her disability (or presumed disability)	Factor(s) in category A not present

STEP TWO Starting point and category range SG-146

Having determined the category of harm and culpability, the court should use the corresponding starting points to reach a sentence within the category range below. The starting point applies to all offenders irrespective of plea or previous convictions.

Having determined the starting point, step two allows further adjustment for aggravating or mitigating features, set out below.

A case of particular gravity, reflected by multiple features of culpability or harm in step one, could merit upward adjustment from the starting point before further adjustment for aggravating or mitigating features, set out below.

Where there is a sufficient prospect of rehabilitation, a community order with a sex offender treatment programme requirement under section 202 of the Criminal Justice Act 2003 can be a proper alternative to a short or moderate length custodial sentence.

	A	B
Category 1	**Starting point** 4 years' custody **Category range** 3–6 years' custody	**Starting point** 2 years' custody **Category range** 1–3 years' custody
Category 2	**Starting point** 2 years' custody **Category range** 1–3 years' custody	**Starting point** 1 year's custody **Category range** High level community order–18 months' custody
Category 3	**Starting point** 26 weeks' custody **Category range** High level community order–1 year's custody	**Starting point** Medium level community order **Category range** Low level community order–Medium level community order

The table below contains a **non-exhaustive** list of additional factual elements providing the context of the offence and factors relating to the offender. Identify whether any combination of these, or other relevant factors, should result in an upward or downward adjustment from the starting point. **In particular, relevant recent convictions are likely to result in an upward adjustment.** In some cases, having considered these factors, it may be appropriate to move outside the identified category range.

When sentencing appropriate **category 2 or 3 offences**, the court should also consider the custody threshold as follows:

- Has the custody threshold been passed?
- If so, is it unavoidable that a custodial sentence be imposed?
- If so, can that sentence be suspended?

Aggravating factors
Statutory aggravating factors • Previous convictions, having regard to a) the nature of the offence to which the conviction relates and its relevance to the current offence; and b) the time that has elapsed since the conviction • Offence committed whilst on bail
Other aggravating factors • Location of offence • Timing of offence • Failure to comply with current court orders • Offence committed whilst on licence • Any steps taken to prevent the victim reporting an incident, obtaining assistance and/or from assisting or supporting the prosecution • Attempts to dispose of or conceal evidence • Commission of offence whilst under the influence of alcohol or drugs

Mitigating factors
• No previous convictions **or** no relevant/recent convictions • Remorse • Previous good character and/or exemplary conduct* • Age and/or lack of maturity where it affects the responsibility of the offender • Mental disorder or learning disability, particularly where linked to the commission of the offence • Demonstration of steps taken to address offending behaviour

* [Repeats note as to distinction between previous good character/exemplary conduct and having no previous convictions and how to deal with them in respect of the offence: see **SG-69** for the full text.]

SG-147 STEPS THREE TO NINE

[These are in the same terms as those applicable to sexual assault: see **SG-70**.]

SG-148

Inducement, Threat or Deception to Procure Sexual Activity with a Person with a Mental Disorder

Sexual Offences Act 2003 (section 34)

Causing a Person with a Mental Disorder to Engage in or Agree to Engage in Sexual Activity by Inducement, Threat or Deception

Sexual Offences Act 2003 (section 35)

Triable only on indictment (if penetration involved); otherwise triable either way

Maximum: Life imprisonment (if penetration involved); otherwise 14 years' custody

Offence range: Community order—10 years' custody

[Repeats information as to the CJA 2003, ss. 224, 225(2), 224A and 226A, which is set out at **SG-59**.]

STEP ONE Determining the offence category SG-149

The court should determine which categories of harm and culpability the offence falls into by reference **only** to the tables below.

This guideline also applies to offences committed remotely/online.

Harm	
Category 1	• Penetration of vagina or anus (using body or object) • Penile penetration of mouth In either case by, or of, the victim
Category 2	Touching, or exposure, of naked genitalia or naked breasts by, or of, the victim
Category 3	Other sexual activity

Culpability	
A	**B**
• Significant degree of planning • Offender acts together with others to commit the offence • Use of alcohol/drugs on victim to facilitate the offence • Abuse of trust • Sexual images of victim recorded, retained, solicited or shared • Commercial exploitation and/or motivation • Offence racially or religiously aggravated • Offence motivated by, or demonstrating, hostility to the victim based on his or her sexual orientation (or presumed sexual orientation) or transgender identity (or presumed transgender identity) • Offence motivated by, or demonstrating, hostility to the victim based on his or her disability (or presumed disability)	Factor(s) in category A not present

STEP TWO Starting point and category range SG-150

Having determined the category of harm and culpability, the court should use the corresponding starting points to reach a sentence within the category range below. The starting point applies to all offenders irrespective of plea or previous convictions. Having determined the starting point, step two allows further adjustment for aggravating or mitigating features, set out below.

A case of particular gravity, reflected by multiple features of culpability or harm in step one, could merit upward adjustment from the starting point before further adjustment for aggravating or mitigating features, set out below.

Where there is a sufficient prospect of rehabilitation, a community order with a sex offender treatment programme requirement under section 202 of the Criminal Justice Act 2003 can be a proper alternative to a short or moderate length custodial sentence.

	A	**B**
Category 1	**Starting point** 5 years' custody **Category range** 4–10 years' custody	**Starting point** 1 year's custody **Category range** High level community order–2 years' custody
Category 2	**Starting point** 3 years' custody **Category range** 2–6 years' custody	**Starting point** 26 weeks' custody **Category range** High level community order–1 year's custody
Category 3	**Starting point** 26 weeks' custody **Category range** High level community order–3 years' custody	**Starting point** Medium level community order **Category range** Low level community order–High level community order

Sentencing Guidelines

The table below contains a **non-exhaustive** list of additional factual elements providing the context of the offence and factors relating to the offender. Identify whether any combination of these, or other relevant factors, should result in an upward or downward adjustment from the starting point. **In particular, relevant recent convictions are likely to result in an upward adjustment.** In some cases, having considered these factors, it may be appropriate to move outside the identified category range.

When sentencing appropriate **category 2 or 3 offences**, the court should also consider the custody threshold as follows:

- Has the custody threshold been passed?
- If so, is it unavoidable that a custodial sentence be imposed?
- If so, can that sentence be suspended?

Aggravating factors
Statutory aggravating factors • Previous convictions, having regard to a) the nature of the offence to which the conviction relates and its relevance to the current offence; and b) the time that has elapsed since the conviction • Offence committed whilst on bail *Other aggravating factors* • Severe psychological or physical harm • Ejaculation • Pregnancy or STI as a consequence of offence • Location of offence • Timing of offence • Victim compelled to leave their home or institution (including victims of domestic violence) • Failure to comply with current court orders • Offence committed whilst on licence • Any steps taken to prevent the victim reporting an incident, obtaining assistance and/or from assisting or supporting the prosecution • Attempts to dispose of or conceal evidence • Commission of offence whilst under the influence of alcohol or drugs

Mitigating factors
• No previous convictions **or** no relevant/recent convictions • Remorse • Previous good character and/or exemplary conduct* • Age and/or lack of maturity where it affects the responsibility of the offender • Mental disorder or learning disability, particularly where linked to the commission of the offence

* [Repeats note as to distinction between previous good character/exemplary conduct and having no previous convictions and how to deal with them in respect of the offence: see **SG-61** for the full text.]

SG-151 STEPS THREE TO NINE

[These are in the same terms as those applicable to rape: see **SG-62**.]

SG-152

Engaging in Sexual Activity in the Presence, Procured by Inducement, Threat or Deception, of a Person with a Mental Disorder

Sexual Offences Act 2003 (section 36)

Causing a Person with a Mental Disorder to Watch a Sexual Act by Inducement, Threat or Deception

Sexual Offences Act 2003 (section 37)

Triable either way

Maximum: 10 years' custody

Offence range: Community order—6 years' custody

[Repeats information as to the CJA 2003, s. 226A, which is set out at **SG-67**.]

STEP ONE Determining the offence category SG-153

The court should determine which categories of harm and culpability the offence falls into by reference **only** to the tables below.

Harm	
Category 1	• Causing victim to view extreme pornography • Causing victim to view indecent/prohibited images of children • Engaging in, or causing a victim to view live, sexual activity involving sadism/violence/ sexual activity with an animal/a child
Category 2	Engaging in, or causing a victim to view images of or view live, sexual activity involving: • penetration of vagina or anus (using body or object) • penile penetration of mouth • masturbation
Category 3	Factor(s) in categories 1 and 2 not present

Culpability	
A	B
• Significant degree of planning • Offender acts together with others in order to commit the offence • Use of alcohol/drugs on victim to facilitate the offence • Abuse of trust • Commercial exploitation and/or motivation • Offence racially or religiously aggravated • Offence motivated by, or demonstrating, hostility to the victim based on his or her sexual orientation (or presumed sexual orientation) or transgender identity (or presumed transgender identity) • Offence motivated by, or demonstrating, hostility to the victim based on his or her disability (or presumed disability)	Factor(s) in category A not present

STEP TWO Starting point and category range SG-154

Having determined the category of harm and culpability, the court should use the corresponding starting points to reach a sentence within the category range below. The starting point applies to all offenders irrespective of plea or previous convictions. Having determined the starting point, step two allows further adjustment for aggravating or mitigating features, set out below.

A case of particular gravity, reflected by multiple features of culpability or harm in step one, could merit upward adjustment from the starting point before further adjustment for aggravating or mitigating features, set out below.

Where there is a sufficient prospect of rehabilitation, a community order with a sex offender treatment programme requirement under section 202 of the Criminal Justice Act 2003 can be a proper alternative to a short or moderate length custodial sentence.

	A	B
Category 1	**Starting point** 4 years' custody **Category range** 3–6 years' custody	**Starting point** 2 years' custody **Category range** 1–3 years' custody
Category 2	**Starting point** 2 years' custody **Category range** 1–3 years' custody	**Starting point** 1 year's custody **Category range** High level community order–18 months' custody
Category 3	**Starting point** 26 weeks' custody **Category range** High level community order–1 year's custody	**Starting point** Medium level community order **Category range** Low level community order–Medium level community order

The table below contains a **non-exhaustive** list of additional factual elements providing the context of the offence and factors relating to the offender. Identify whether any combination of these, or other relevant factors, should result in an upward or downward adjustment from the starting point. **In particular, relevant recent convictions are likely to result in an upward adjustment.** In some cases, having considered these factors, it may be appropriate to move outside the identified category range.

When sentencing appropriate **category 2 or 3 offences**, the court should also consider the custody threshold as follows:

- Has the custody threshold been passed?
- If so, is it unavoidable that a custodial sentence be imposed?
- If so, can that sentence be suspended?

Aggravating factors
Statutory aggravating factors • Previous convictions, having regard to a) the nature of the offence to which the conviction relates and its relevance to the current offence; and b) the time that has elapsed since the conviction • Offence committed whilst on bail *Other aggravating factors* • Location of offence • Timing of offence • Failure to comply with current court orders • Offence committed whilst on licence • Any steps taken to prevent the victim reporting an incident, obtaining assistance and/or from assisting or supporting the prosecution • Attempts to dispose of or conceal evidence • Commission of offence whilst under the influence of alcohol or drugs

Mitigating factors
• No previous convictions **or** no relevant/recent convictions • Remorse • Previous good character and/or exemplary conduct* • Age and/or lack of maturity where it affects the responsibility of the offender • Mental disorder or learning disability, particularly where linked to the commission of the offence • Demonstration of steps taken to address offending behaviour

* [Repeats note as to distinction between previous good character/exemplary conduct and having no previous convictions and how to deal with them in respect of the offence: see **SG-69** for the full text.]

SG-155 STEPS THREE TO NINE

[These are in the same terms as those applicable to sexual assault: see **SG-70**.]

SG-156 CARE WORKERS: SEXUAL ACTIVITY WITH A PERSON WITH A MENTAL DISORDER

Sexual Offences Act 2003 (section 38)

CARE WORKERS: CAUSING OR INCITING SEXUAL ACTIVITY

Sexual Offences Act 2003 (section 39)

Triable only on indictment (if penetration involved); otherwise triable either way

Maximum: 14 years' custody (if penetration involved); otherwise 10 years' custody

Offence range: Community order—10 years' custody

[Repeats information as to the CJA 2003, s. 226A, which is set out at **SG-67**.]

SG-157 STEP ONE **Determining the offence category**

The court should determine which categories of harm and culpability the offence falls into by reference **only** to the tables below.

This guideline also applies to offences committed remotely/online.

Harm	
Category 1	• Penetration of vagina or anus (using body or object) • Penile penetration of mouth In either case by, or of, the victim
Category 2	• Touching, or exposure, of naked genitalia or naked breasts by, or of, the victim
Category 3	Factor(s) in categories 1 and 2 not present

Culpability	
A	B
• Significant degree of planning • Offender acts together with others to commit the offence • Use of alcohol/drugs on victim to facilitate the offence • Grooming behaviour used against victim • Use of threats (including blackmail) • Sexual images of victim recorded, retained, solicited or shared • Commercial exploitation and/or motivation • Offence racially or religiously aggravated • Offence motivated by, or demonstrating, hostility to the victim based on his or her sexual orientation (or presumed sexual orientation) or transgender identity (or presumed transgender identity) • Offence motivated by, or demonstrating, hostility to the victim based on his or her disability (or presumed disability)	Factor(s) in category A not present

STEP TWO Starting point and category range SG-158

Having determined the category of harm and culpability, the court should use the corresponding starting points to reach a sentence within the category range below. The starting point applies to all offenders irrespective of plea or previous convictions. Having determined the starting point, step two allows further adjustment for aggravating or mitigating features, set out below.

A case of particular gravity, reflected by multiple features of culpability or harm in step one, could merit upward adjustment from the starting point before further adjustment for aggravating or mitigating features, set out below.

Where there is a sufficient prospect of rehabilitation, a community order with a sex offender treatment programme requirement under section 202 of the Criminal Justice Act 2003 can be a proper alternative to a short or moderate length custodial sentence.

	A	B
Category 1	**Starting point** 5 years' custody **Category range** 4–10 years' custody	**Starting point** 18 months' custody **Category range** 1–2 years' custody
Category 2	**Starting point** 3 year's custody **Category range** 2–6 years' custody	**Starting point** 26 weeks' custody **Category range** Medium level community order–1 year's custody
Category 3	**Starting point** 26 weeks' custody **Category range** High level community order–3 years' custody	**Starting point** Medium level community order **Category range** Low level community order–High level community order

The table below contains a **non-exhaustive** list of additional factual elements providing the context of the offence and factors relating to the offender. Identify whether any combination of these, or other relevant factors, should result in an upward or downward adjustment from the starting point. **In particular, relevant recent convictions are likely to result in an upward adjustment.** In some cases, having considered these factors, it may be appropriate to move outside the identified category range.

When sentencing appropriate **category 2 or 3 offences**, the court should also consider the custody threshold as follows:

- Has the custody threshold been passed?
- If so, is it unavoidable that a custodial sentence be imposed?
- If so, can that sentence be suspended?

Aggravating factors
Statutory aggravating factors • Previous convictions, having regard to a) the nature of the offence to which the conviction relates and its relevance to the current offence; and b) the time that has elapsed since the conviction • Offence committed whilst on bail *Other aggravating factors* • Ejaculation • Pregnancy or STI as a consequence of offence • Location of offence • Timing of offence • Victim compelled to leave their home or institution (including victims of domestic violence) • Failure to comply with current court orders • Offence committed whilst on licence • Any steps taken to prevent the victim reporting an incident, obtaining assistance and/or from assisting or supporting the prosecution • Attempts to dispose of or conceal evidence • Failure of offender to respond to previous warnings • Commission of offence whilst under the influence of alcohol or drugs

Mitigating factors
• No previous convictions or no relevant/recent convictions • Remorse • Previous good character and/or exemplary conduct* • Age and/or lack of maturity where it affects the responsibility of the offender • Mental disorder or learning disability, particularly where linked to the commission of the offence • Sexual activity was incited but no activity took place because the offender voluntarily desisted or intervened to prevent it

* [Repeats note as to distinction between previous good character/exemplary conduct and having no previous convictions and how to deal with them in respect of the offence: see **SG-61** for the full text.]

SG-159 STEPS THREE TO NINE

[These are in the same terms as those applicable to sexual assault: see **SG-70**.]

SG-160

Care Workers: Sexual Activity in the Presence of a person with a Mental Disorder

Sexual Offences Act 2003 (section 40)

Care Workers: Causing a Person with a Mental Disorder to Watch a Sexual Act

Sexual Offences Act 2003 (section 41)

Triable either way

Maximum: 7 years' custody

Offence range: Community order—2 years' custody

[Repeats information as to the CJA 2003, s. 226A, which is set out at **SG-67**.]

STEP ONE Determining the offence category SG-161

The court should determine which categories of harm and culpability the offence falls into by reference only to the tables below.

Harm	
Category 1	• Causing victim to view extreme pornography • Causing victim to view indecent/prohibited images of children • Engaging in, or causing a victim to view live, sexual activity involving sadism/violence/sexual activity with an animal/a child
Category 2	Engaging in, or causing a victim to view images of or view live, sexual activity involving: • penetration of vagina or anus (using body or object) • penile penetration of mouth • masturbation
Category 3	Factor(s) in categories 1 and 2 not present

Culpability	
A	B
• Significant degree of planning • Offender acts together with others to commit the offence • Use of alcohol/drugs on victim to facilitate the offence • Grooming behaviour used against victim • Use of threats (including blackmail) • Commercial exploitation and/or motivation • Offence racially or religiously aggravated • Offence motivated by, or demonstrating, hostility to the victim based on his or her sexual orientation (or presumed sexual orientation) or transgender identity (or presumed transgender identity) • Offence motivated by, or demonstrating, hostility to the victim based on his or her disability (or presumed disability)	Factor(s) in category A not present

STEP TWO Starting point and category range SG-162

Having determined the category of harm and culpability, the court should use the corresponding starting points to reach a sentence within the category range below. The starting point applies to all offenders irrespective of plea or previous convictions. Having determined the starting point, step two allows further adjustment for aggravating or mitigating features, set out below.

A case of particular gravity, reflected by multiple features of culpability or harm in step one, could merit upward adjustment from the starting point before further adjustment for aggravating or mitigating features, set out below.

Where there is a sufficient prospect of rehabilitation, a community order with a sex offender treatment programme requirement under section 202 of the Criminal Justice Act 2003 can be a proper alternative to a short or moderate length custodial sentence.

	A	B
Category 1	**Starting point** 18 months' custody **Category range** 1–2 years' custody	**Starting point** 1 year's custody **Category range** 26 weeks'–18 months' custody
Category 2	**Starting point** 1 year's custody **Category range** 26 weeks'–18 months' custody	**Starting point** 26 weeks' custody **Category range** High level community order–1 year's custody
Category 3	**Starting point** 26 weeks' custody **Category range** High level community order–1 year's custody	**Starting point** Medium level community order **Category range** Low level community order–High level community order

The table below contains a **non-exhaustive** list of additional factual elements providing the context of the offence and factors relating to the offender. Identify whether any combination of these, or other relevant factors, should result in an upward or downward adjustment from the starting point. **In particular, relevant recent convictions are likely to result in an upward adjustment.** In some cases, having considered these factors, it may be appropriate to move outside the identified category range.

When sentencing appropriate **category 2 or 3 offences**, the court should also consider the custody threshold as follows:

- Has the custody threshold been passed?
- If so, is it unavoidable that a custodial sentence be imposed?
- If so, can that sentence be suspended?

Aggravating factors
Statutory aggravating factors • Previous convictions, having regard to a) the nature of the offence to which the conviction relates and its relevance to the current offence; and b) the time that has elapsed since the conviction • Offence committed whilst on bail *Other aggravating factors* • Location of offence • Timing of offence • Failure to comply with current court orders • Offence committed whilst on licence • Any steps taken to prevent the victim reporting an incident, obtaining assistance and/or from assisting or supporting the prosecution • Attempts to dispose of or conceal evidence • Failure of offender to respond to previous warnings • Commission of offence whilst under the influence of alcohol or drugs

Mitigating factors
• No previous convictions **or** no relevant/recent convictions • Remorse • Previous good character and/or exemplary conduct* • Age and/or lack of maturity where it affects the responsibility of the offender • Mental disorder or learning disability, particularly where linked to the commission of the offence • Demonstration of steps taken to address offending behaviour

* [Repeats note as to distinction between previous good character/exemplary conduct and having no previous convictions and how to deal with them in respect of the offence: see **SG-69** for the full text.]

SG-163 **STEPS THREE TO NINE**

[These are in the same terms as those applicable to sexual assault: see **SG-70**.]

SG-164

Exposure

Sexual Offences Act 2003 (section 66)

Triable either way

Maximum: 2 years' custody

Offence range: Fine—1 year's custody

[Repeats information as to the CJA 2003, s. 226A, which is set out at **SG-67**.]

SG-165 **STEP ONE Determining the offence category**

The court should determine the offence category using the table below.

Category 1	Raised harm **and** raised culpability
Category 2	Raised harm **or** raised culpability
Category 3	Exposure **without** raised harm or culpability factors present

The court should determine culpability and harm caused or intended, by reference **only** to the factors below, which comprise the principal factual elements of the offence. Where an offence does not fall squarely into a category, individual factors may require a degree of weighting before making an overall assessment and determining the appropriate offence category.

Factors indicating raised harm
• Victim followed/pursued • Offender masturbated

Factors indicating raised culpability
• Specific or previous targeting of a particularly vulnerable victim • Abuse of trust • Use of threats (including blackmail) • Offence racially or religiously aggravated • Offence motivated by, or demonstrating, hostility to the victim based on his or her sexual orientation (or presumed sexual orientation) or transgender identity (or presumed transgender identity) • Offence motivated by, or demonstrating, hostility to the victim based on his or her disability (or presumed disability)

STEP TWO Starting point and category range SG-166

Having determined the category, the court should use the corresponding starting points to reach a sentence within the category range below. The starting point applies to all offenders irrespective of plea or previous convictions. Having determined the starting point, step two allows further adjustment for aggravating or mitigating features, set out below.

A case of particular gravity, reflected by multiple features of culpability or harm in step one, could merit upward adjustment from the starting point before further adjustment for aggravating or mitigating features, set out below.

Where there is a sufficient prospect of rehabilitation, a community order with a sex offender treatment programme requirement under section 202 of the Criminal Justice Act 2003 can be a proper alternative to a short or moderate length custodial sentence.

Category 1	**Starting point** 26 weeks' custody **Category range** 12 weeks'–1 year's custody
Category 2	**Starting point** High level community order **Category range** Medium level community order–26 weeks' custody
Category 3	**Starting point** Medium level community order **Category range** Band A fine–High level community order

The table below contains a **non-exhaustive** list of additional factual elements providing the context of the offence and factors relating to the offender. Identify whether any combination of these, or other relevant factors, should result in an upward or downward adjustment from the starting point. **In particular, relevant recent convictions are likely to result in an upward adjustment.** In some cases, having considered these factors, it may be appropriate to move outside the identified category range.

When sentencing **category 2 offences**, the court should also consider the custody threshold as follows:

- Has the custody threshold been passed?
- If so, is it unavoidable that a custodial sentence be imposed?
- If so, can that sentence be suspended?

When sentencing **category 3 offences**, the court should also consider the community order threshold as follows:

- Has the community order threshold been passed?

Aggravating factors
Statutory aggravating factors • Previous convictions, having regard to a) the nature of the offence to which the conviction relates and its relevance to the current offence; and b) the time that has elapsed since the conviction • Offence committed whilst on bail *Other aggravating factors* • Location of the offence • Timing of the offence • Any steps taken to prevent the victim reporting an incident, obtaining assistance and/or from assisting or supporting the prosecution • Failure to comply with current court orders • Offence committed whilst on licence • Commission of offence whilst under the influence of alcohol or drugs • Presence of others, especially children

Mitigating factors
• No previous convictions **or** no relevant/recent convictions • Remorse • Previous good character and/or exemplary conduct* • Age and/or lack of maturity where it affects the responsibility of the offender • Mental disorder or learning disability, particularly where linked to the commission of the offence • Demonstration of steps taken to address offending behaviour

* [Repeats note as to distinction between previous good character/exemplary conduct and having no previous convictions and how to deal with them in respect of the offence: see **SG-69** for the full text.]

SG-167 STEPS THREE TO NINE

[These are in the same terms as those applicable to sexual assault: see **SG-70**.]

SG-168

Voyeurism

Sexual Offences Act 2003 (section 67)

Triable either way

Maximum: 2 years' custody

Offence range: Fine—18 months' custody

[Repeats information as to the CJA 2003, s. 226A, which is set out at **SG-67**.]

SG-169 STEP ONE **Determining the offence category**

The court should determine the offence category using the table below.

Category 1	Raised harm **and** raised culpability
Category 2	Raised harm **or** raised culpability
Category 3	Voyeurism **without** raised harm or culpability factors present

The court should determine culpability and harm caused or intended, by reference **only** to the factors below, which comprise the principal factual elements of the offence. Where an offence does not fall squarely into a category, individual factors may require a degree of weighting before making an overall assessment and determining the appropriate offence category.

Factors indicating raised harm
• Image(s) available to be viewed by others • Victim observed or recorded in their own home or residence

Factors indicating raised culpability
• Significant degree of planning • Image(s) recorded • Abuse of trust • Specific or previous targeting of a particularly vulnerable victim • Commercial exploitation and/or motivation • Offence racially or religiously aggravated • Offence motivated by, or demonstrating, hostility to the victim based on his or her sexual orientation (or presumed sexual orientation) or transgender identity (or presumed transgender identity) • Offence motivated by, or demonstrating, hostility to the victim based on his or her disability (or presumed disability)

STEP TWO Starting point and category range SG-170

Having determined the category, the court should use the corresponding starting points to reach a sentence within the category range below. The starting point applies to all offenders irrespective of plea or previous convictions. Having determined the starting point, step two allows further adjustment for aggravating or mitigating features, set out below.

A case of particular gravity, reflected by multiple features of culpability or harm in step one, could merit upward adjustment from the starting point before further adjustment for aggravating or mitigating features, set out below.

Where there is a sufficient prospect of rehabilitation, a community order with a sex offender treatment programme requirement under section 202 of the Criminal Justice Act 2003 can be a proper alternative to a short or moderate length custodial sentence.

Category 1	**Starting point** 26 weeks' custody **Category range** 12 weeks'–18 months' custody
Category 2	**Starting point** High level community order **Category range** Medium level community order–26 weeks' custody
Category 3	**Starting point** Medium level community order **Category range** Band A fine–High level community order

The table below contains a **non-exhaustive** list of additional factual elements providing the context of the offence and factors relating to the offender. Identify whether any combination of these, or other relevant factors, should result in an upward or downward adjustment from the starting point. **In particular, relevant recent convictions are likely to result in an upward adjustment.** In some cases, having considered these factors, it may be appropriate to move outside the identified category range.

When sentencing **category 2 offences**, the court should also consider the custody threshold as follows:

- Has the custody threshold been passed?
- If so, is it unavoidable that a custodial sentence be imposed?
- If so, can that sentence be suspended?

When sentencing **category 3 offences**, the court should also consider the community order threshold as follows:

- Has the community order threshold been passed?

Aggravating factors
Statutory aggravating factors • Previous convictions, having regard to a) the nature of the offence to which the conviction relates and its relevance to the current offence; and b) the time that has elapsed since the conviction • Offence committed whilst on bail
Other aggravating factors • Location of offence • Timing of offence • Failure to comply with current court orders • Offence committed whilst on licence • Distribution of images, whether or not for gain • Placing images where there is the potential for a high volume of viewers • Period over which victim observed • Period over which images were made or distributed • Any steps taken to prevent victim reporting an incident, obtaining assistance and/or from assisting or supporting the prosecution • Attempts to dispose of or conceal evidence

Mitigating factors
• No previous convictions **or** no relevant/recent convictions • Remorse • Previous good character and/or exemplary conduct* • Age and/or lack of maturity where it affects the responsibility of the offender • Mental disorder or learning disability, particularly where linked to the commission of the offence • Demonstration of steps taken to address offending behaviour

* [Repeats note as to distinction between previous good character/exemplary conduct and having no previous convictions and how to deal with them in respect of the offence: see **SG-69** for the full text.]

SG-171 STEPS THREE TO NINE

[These are in the same terms as those applicable to sexual assault: see **SG-70**.]

SG-172

Sex with an Adult Relative: Penetration

Sexual Offences Act 2003 (section 64)

Sex with an Adult Relative: Consenting to Penetration

Sexual Offences Act 2003 (section 65)

Triable either way

Maximum: 2 years' custody

Offence range: Fine—2 years' custody

[Repeats information as to the CJA 2003, s. 226A, which is set out at **SG-67**.]

SG-173 STEP ONE **Determining the offence category**

The court should determine the offence category using the table below.

Category 1	Raised harm **and** raised culpability
Category 2	Raised harm **or** raised culpability
Category 3	Sex with an adult relative **without** raised harm or culpability factors present

The court should determine culpability and harm caused or intended, by reference **only** to the factors below, which comprise the principal factual elements of the offence. Where an offence does not fall squarely into a category, individual factors may require a degree of weighting before making an overall assessment and determining the appropriate offence category.

Factors indicating raised harm
• Victim is particularly vulnerable due to personal circumstances • Child conceived

Factors indicating raised culpability
• Grooming behaviour used against victim • Use of threats (including blackmail)

STEP TWO Starting point and category range SG-174

Having determined the category, the court should use the corresponding starting points to reach a sentence within the category range below. The starting point applies to all offenders irrespective of plea or previous convictions. Having determined the starting point, step two allows further adjustment for aggravating or mitigating features, set out below.

A case of particular gravity, reflected by multiple features of culpability or harm in step one, could merit upward adjustment from the starting point before further adjustment for aggravating or mitigating features, set out below.

Where there is a sufficient prospect of rehabilitation, a community order with a sex offender treatment programme requirement under section 202 of the Criminal Justice Act 2003 can be a proper alternative to a short or moderate length custodial sentence.

Category 1	**Starting point** 1 year's custody **Category range** 26 weeks'–2 years' custody
Category 2	**Starting point** High level community order **Category range** Medium level community order– 1 year's custody
Category 3	**Starting point** Medium level community order **Category range** Band A fine–High level community order

The table below contains a **non-exhaustive** list of additional factual elements providing the context of the offence and factors relating to the offender. Identify whether any combination of these, or other relevant factors, should result in an upward or downward adjustment from the starting point. **In particular, relevant recent convictions are likely to result in an upward adjustment.** In some cases, having considered these factors, it may be appropriate to move outside the identified category range.

When sentencing **category 2 offences**, the court should also consider the custody threshold as follows:

- Has the custody threshold been passed?
- If so, is it unavoidable that a custodial sentence be imposed?
- If so, can that sentence be suspended?

When sentencing **category 3 offences**, the court should also consider the community order threshold as follows:

- Has the community order threshold been passed?

Aggravating factors
Statutory aggravating factors • Previous convictions, having regard to a) the nature of the offence to which the conviction relates and its relevance to the current offence; and b) the time that has elapsed since the conviction • Offence committed whilst on bail

Sentencing Guidelines

Other aggravating factors • Failure to comply with current court orders • Offence committed whilst on licence • Failure of offender to respond to previous warnings • Any steps taken to prevent reporting an incident, obtaining assistance and/or from assisting or supporting the prosecution • Attempts to dispose of or conceal evidence

Mitigating factors
• No previous convictions **or** no relevant/recent convictions • Remorse • Previous good character and/or exemplary conduct* • Age and/or lack of maturity where it affects the responsibility of the offender • Mental disorder or learning disability, particularly where linked to the commission of the offence • Demonstration of steps taken to address offending behaviour

* [Repeats note as to distinction between previous good character/exemplary conduct and having no previous convictions and how to deal with them in respect of the offence: see **SG-69** for the full text.]

SG-175 STEPS THREE TO NINE

[These are in the same terms as those applicable to sexual assault: see **SG-70**.]

SG-176

Administering a Substance with Intent

Sexual Offences Act 2003 (section 61)

Triable either way

Maximum: 10 years' custody

Offence range: 1–9 years' custody

[Repeats information as to the CJA 2003, s. 226A, which is set out at **SG-67**.]

SG-177 STEP ONE **Determining the offence category**

The court should determine the offence category using the table below.

Category 1	Raised harm **and** raised culpability
Category 2	Raised harm **or** raised culpability
Category 3	Administering a substance with intent **without** raised harm or culpability factors present

The court should determine culpability and harm caused or intended, by reference **only** to the factors below, which comprise the principal factual elements of the offence. Where an offence does not fall squarely into a category, individual factors may require a degree of weighting before making an overall assessment and determining the appropriate offence category. Where no substantive sexual offence has been committed the main consideration for the court will be the offender's conduct as a whole including, but not exclusively, the offender's intention.

Factors indicating raised harm
• Severe psychological or physical harm • Prolonged detention/sustained incident • Additional degradation/humiliation

Factors indicating raised culpability
• Significant degree of planning • Specific targeting of a particularly vulnerable victim • Intended sexual offence carries a statutory maximum of life • Abuse of trust • Recording of offence • Offender acts together with others to commit the offence • Commercial exploitation and/or motivation • Offence racially or religiously aggravated • Offence motivated by, or demonstrating, hostility to the victim based on his or her sexual orientation (or presumed sexual orientation) or transgender identity (or presumed transgender identity) • Offence motivated by, or demonstrating, hostility to the victim based on his or her disability (or presumed disability)

STEP TWO Starting point and category range SG-178

Having determined the category, the court should use the corresponding starting points to reach a sentence within the category range below. The starting point applies to all offenders irrespective of plea or previous convictions. Having determined the starting point, step two allows further adjustment for aggravating or mitigating features, set out below.

A case of particular gravity, reflected by multiple features of culpability or harm in step one, could merit upward adjustment from the starting point before further adjustment for aggravating or mitigating features, set out below.

Category 1	**Starting point** 6 years' custody **Category range** 4–9 years' custody
Category 2	**Starting point** 4 years' custody **Category range** 3–7 years' custody
Category 3	**Starting point** 2 years' custody **Category range** 1–5 years' custody

The table below contains a **non-exhaustive** list of additional factual elements providing the context of the offence and factors relating to the offender. Identify whether any combination of these, or other relevant factors, should result in an upward or downward adjustment from the starting point. **In particular, relevant recent convictions are likely to result in an upward adjustment.** In some cases, having considered these factors, it may be appropriate to move outside the identified category range.

Aggravating factors
Statutory aggravating factors • Previous convictions, having regard to a) the nature of the offence to which the conviction relates and its relevance to the current offence; and b) the time that has elapsed since the conviction • Offence committed whilst on bail *Other aggravating factors* • Location of offence • Timing of offence • Any steps taken to prevent reporting an incident, obtaining assistance and/or from assisting or supporting the prosecution • Attempts to dispose of or conceal evidence • Failure to comply with current court orders • Offence committed whilst on licence

Mitigating factors
• No previous convictions **or** no relevant/recent convictions • Remorse • Previous good character and/or exemplary conduct* • Age and/or lack of maturity where it affects the responsibility of the offender • Mental disorder or learning disability, particularly where linked to the commission of the offence • Demonstration of steps taken to address offending behaviour

* [Repeats note as to distinction between previous good character/exemplary conduct and having no previous convictions and how to deal with them in respect of the offence: see **SG-69** for the full text.]

SG-179 **STEPS THREE TO NINE**

[These are in the same terms as those applicable to sexual assault: see **SG-70**.]

SG-180

Committing an Offence with Intent to Commit a Sexual Offence

Sexual Offences Act 2003 (section 62)

Triable only on indictment (if kidnapping or false imprisonment committed)

- otherwise, triable either way

Maximum: Life imprisonment (if kidnapping or false imprisonment committed)

- otherwise, 10 years

[Repeats information as to the CJA 2003, ss. 224, 225(2), 224A and 226A which is set out at **SG-59**.]

The starting point and range should be commensurate with that for the preliminary offence actually committed, but with an enhancement to reflect the intention to commit a sexual offence.

The enhancement will vary depending on the nature and seriousness of the intended sexual offence, but 2 years is suggested as a suitable enhancement where the intent was to commit rape or assault by penetration.

SG-181

Trespass with Intent to Commit a Sexual Offence

Sexual Offences Act 2003 (section 63)

Triable either way

Maximum: 10 years' custody

Offence range: 1–9 years' custody

[Repeats information as to the CJA 2003, s. 226A, which is set out at **SG-67**.]

SG-182 **STEP ONE Determining the offence category**

The court should determine the offence category using the table below.

Category 1	Raised harm **and** raised culpability
Category 2	Raised harm **or** raised culpability
Category 3	Trespass with intent to commit a sexual offence **without** raised harm or culpability factors present

The court should determine culpability and harm caused or intended, by reference **only** to the factors below, which comprise the principal factual elements of the offence. Where an offence does not fall squarely into a category, individual factors may require a degree of weighting before making an overall assessment and determining the appropriate offence category. Where no substantive sexual offence has been committed the main consideration for the court will be the offender's conduct as a whole including, but not exclusively, the offender's intention.

Factors indicating raised harm
• Prolonged detention/sustained incident • Additional degradation/humiliation • Offence committed in victim's home

Factors indicating raised culpability
• Significant degree of planning • Specific targeting of a particularly vulnerable victim • Intended sexual offence attracts a statutory maximum of life imprisonment • Possession of weapon or other item to frighten or injure • Abuse of trust • Offender acts together with others to commit the offence • Commercial exploitation and/or motivation • Offence racially or religiously aggravated • Offence motivated by, or demonstrating, hostility to the victim based on his or her sexual orientation (or presumed sexual orientation) or transgender identity (or presumed transgender identity) • Offence motivated by, or demonstrating, hostility to the victim based on his or her disability (or presumed disability)

STEP TWO Starting point and category range SG-183

Having determined the category, the court should use the corresponding starting points to reach a sentence within the category range below. The starting point applies to all offenders irrespective of plea or previous convictions. Having determined the starting point, step two allows further adjustment for aggravating or mitigating features, set out below.

A case of particular gravity, reflected by multiple features of culpability or harm in step one, could merit upward adjustment from the starting point before further adjustment for aggravating or mitigating features, set out below.

Category 1	**Starting point** 6 years' custody **Category range** 4–9 years' custody
Category 2	**Starting point** 4 years' custody **Category range** 3–7 years' custody
Category 3	**Starting point** 2 years' custody **Category range** 1–5 years' custody

The table below contains a **non-exhaustive** list of additional factual elements providing the context of the offence and factors relating to the offender. Identify whether any combination of these, or other relevant factors, should result in an upward or downward adjustment from the starting point. **In particular, relevant recent convictions are likely to result in an upward adjustment.** In some cases, having considered these factors, it may be appropriate to move outside the identified category range.

Aggravating factors
Statutory aggravating factors • Previous convictions, having regard to a) the nature of the offence to which the conviction relates and its relevance to the current offence; and b) the time that has elapsed since the conviction • Offence committed whilst on bail *Other aggravating factors* • Location of offence • Timing of offence • Any steps taken to prevent reporting an incident, obtaining assistance and/or from assisting or supporting the prosecution • Attempts to dispose of or conceal evidence • Failure to comply with current court orders • Offence committed whilst on licence

Mitigating factors
• No previous convictions **or** no relevant/recent convictions • Remorse • Previous good character and/or exemplary conduct* • Age and/or lack of maturity where it affects the responsibility of the offender • Mental disorder or learning disability, particularly where linked to the commission of the offence • Demonstration of steps taken to address offending behaviour

* [Repeats note as to distinction between previous good character/exemplary conduct and having no previous convictions and how to deal with them in respect of the offence: see **SG-69** for the full text.]

SG-184 STEPS THREE TO NINE

[These are in the same terms as those applicable to sexual assault: see **SG-70**.]

SG-185

Child Sex Offences Committed by Children or Young Persons (Sections 9–12) (Offender Under 18)

Sexual Offences Act 2003 (section 13)

Sexual Activity with a Child Family Member (Offender Under 18)

Sexual Offences Act 2003 (section 25)

Inciting a Child Family Member to Engage in Sexual Activity (Offender Under 18)

Sexual Offences Act 2003 (section 26)

Triable either way

Maximum: 5 years' custody

These are 'grave crimes' for the purposes of section 91 of the Powers of Criminal Courts (Sentencing) Act 2000.

[Repeats information as to the CJA 2003, s. 226A which is set out at **SG-67**.]

*Definitive guidelines for the sentencing of offenders under 18 years old are **not** included.*

When sentencing offenders under 18, a court must in particular:

- *follow the definitive guideline **Overarching Principles—Sentencing Youths**; and have regard to:*
- *the principal aim of the youth justice system (to prevent offending by children and young people); and*
- *the welfare of the young offender.*

ANNEX A

SG-186

Ancillary Orders

This summary of the key provisions is correct as at the date of publication but will be subject to subsequent changes in law. If necessary, seek legal advice.

Ancillary order	Statutory reference
Compensation The court must consider making a compensation order in any case in which personal injury, loss or damage has resulted from the offence. The court must give reasons if it decides not to make an order in such cases.	Section 130 of the Powers of Criminal Courts (Sentencing) Act 2000
Confiscation A confiscation order may be made by the Crown Court in circumstances in which the offender has obtained a financial benefit as a result of, or in connection with, his criminal conduct.	Section 6 and Schedule 2 of the Proceeds of Crime Act 2002

Ancillary order	Statutory reference
Deprivation of property The court may order the offender is deprived of property used for the purpose of committing, or facilitating the commission of, any offence, or intended for that purpose.	Section 143 of the Powers of Criminal Courts (Sentencing) Act 2000
Disqualification from working with children From 17 June 2013 courts no longer have the power to disqualify offenders from working with children pursuant to the Criminal Justice and Court Services Act 2000.	Schedule 10 of the Safeguarding Vulnerable Groups Act 2006 Safeguarding Vulnerable Groups Act 2006 (Commencement No. 8 and Saving) Order 2012 (SI 2012/2231) Protection of Freedoms Act 2012 (Commencement No. 6) Order 2013 (SI 2013/1180)
Restraining order Following a conviction *or an acquittal*, a court may make a restraining order for the purpose of protecting the victim or another person from harassment or a fear of violence.	Sections 5 and 5A of the Protection from Harassment Act 1997
Serious crime prevention order (SCPO) An SCPO may be made by the Crown Court in respect of qualifying offenders, if the court is satisfied such an order would protect the public by preventing, restricting or disrupting the involvement of the offender in serious crime.	Section 19 and Schedule 1 of the Serious Crime Act 2007
Sexual offences prevention order (SOPO) A SOPO may be made against qualifying offenders if the court is satisfied such an order is necessary to protect the public or any particular member of the public from serious sexual harm from the offender. The terms of the SOPO must be proportionate to the objective of protecting the public and consistent with the sentence and other ancillary orders, conditions and requirements to which the offender is subject.	Section 104 and Schedules 3 and 5 of the Sexual Offences Act 2003

Automatic orders on conviction

The following requirements or provisions are **not** part of the sentence imposed by the court but apply automatically by operation of law. The role of the court is to inform the offender of the applicable requirements and/or prohibition.

Requirement or provision	Statutory reference
Notification requirements A relevant offender automatically becomes subject to notification requirements, obliging him to notify the police of specified information for a specified period. The court should inform the offender accordingly. *The operation of the notification requirement is not a relevant consideration in determining the sentence for the offence.*	Sections 80 to 88 and Schedule 3 of the Sexual Offences Act 2003
Protection for children and vulnerable adults A statutory scheme pursuant to which offenders *will* or *may* be barred from regulated activity relating to children or vulnerable adults, with or without the right to make representations, depending on the offence. The court should inform the offender accordingly.	Section 2 and Schedule 3 of the Safeguarding Vulnerable Groups Act 2006 Safeguarding Vulnerable Groups Act 2006 (Prescribed Criteria and Miscellaneous Provisions) Regulations 2009 (SI 2009/37) (as amended)

ANNEX B

SG-187

Approach to Sentencing of Historic Sexual Offences

Details of the principal offences are set out in the table at Annex C [at SG-188].

When sentencing sexual offences under the Sexual Offences Act 1956, or other legislation pre-dating the 2003 Act, the court should apply the following principles:[74]

1. The offender must be sentenced in accordance with the sentencing regime applicable at the *date of sentence*. Under the Criminal Justice Act 2003[75] the court must have regard to the statutory purposes of sentencing and must base the sentencing exercise on its assessment of the seriousness of the offence.
2. The sentence is limited to the maximum sentence available at the *date of the commission of the offence*. If the maximum sentence has been reduced, the lower maximum will be applicable.
3. The court should have regard to any applicable sentencing guidelines for equivalent offences under the Sexual Offences Act 2003.
4. The seriousness of the offence, assessed by the culpability of the offender and the harm caused or intended, is the main consideration for the court. The court should not seek to establish the likely sentence had the offender been convicted shortly after the date of the offence.
5. When assessing the culpability of the offender, the court should have regard to relevant culpability factors set out in any applicable guideline.
6. The court must assess carefully the harm done to the victim based on the facts available to it, having regard to relevant harm factors set out in any applicable guideline. Consideration of the circumstances which brought the offence to light will be of importance.
7. The court must consider the relevance of the passage of time carefully as it has the potential to aggravate or mitigate the seriousness of the offence. It will be an aggravating factor where the offender has continued to commit sexual offences against the victim or others or has continued to prevent the victim reporting the offence.
8. Where there is an absence of further offending over a long period of time, especially if combined with evidence of good character, this may be treated by the court as a mitigating factor. However, as with offences dealt with under the Sexual Offences Act 2003, previous good character/exemplary conduct is different from having no previous convictions. The more serious the offence, the less the weight which should normally be attributed to this factor. Where previous good character/exemplary conduct has been used to facilitate the offence, this mitigation should not normally be allowed and such conduct may constitute an aggravating factor.
9. If the offender was very young and immature at the time of the offence, depending on the circumstances of the offence, this may be regarded as personal mitigation.
10. If the offender made admissions at the time of the offence that were not investigated this is likely to be regarded as personal mitigation. Even greater mitigation is available to the offender who reported himself to the police and/or made early admissions.
11. A reduction for an early guilty plea should be made in the usual manner.

ANNEX C

SG-188

Historic Offences

Offence (Sexual Offences Act 1956 unless stated otherwise)	Effective dates	Maximum
Rape and assault offences		
Rape (section 1)	1 January 1957–30 April 2004	Life
Buggery with a person or animal (section 12)	1 January 1957–30 April 2004 (from 3 November 1994 non-consensual acts of buggery were defined as rape)	Life

[74] *R v H and others* [2011] EWCA Crim 2753

[75] Section 143

Offence (Sexual Offences Act 1956 unless stated otherwise)	Effective dates	Maximum
Indecent assault on a woman (section 14)	1 January 1957–30 April 2004	1 January 1957–1 July 1960: 2 years 2 July 1960–15 September 1985: 2 years or 5 years if victim under 13 and age stated on indictment 16 September 1985 onwards: 10 years
Indecent assault upon a man (section 15)	1 January 1957–30 April 2004	10 years
Offences against children		
Sexual intercourse with a girl under 13 (section 5)	1 January 1957–30 April 2004	Life
Incest by a male person (section 10)	1 January 1957–30 April 2004	Life if victim under 13; otherwise 7 years
Incest by a female person (section 11)	1 January 1957–30 April 2004	7 years
Indecency between men (section 13)	1 January 1957–30 April 2004	1 January 1957–2 November 1994: 2 years 3 November 1994 onwards: Male offender over 21 with male under age of consent: 5 years Otherwise: 2 years
Indecency with a child (section 1 of the Indecency with Children Act 1960)	2 July 1960–30 April 2004	1 July 1960–30 September 1997: 2 years 1 October 1997 onwards: 10 years *Note: on 11 January 2001 the age definition of a child increased from 14 to 16.*
Incitement of a girl under 16 to commit incest (section 54 of the Criminal Law Act 1977)	8 September 1977–30 April 2004	2 years
Abuse of position of trust (section 3 of the Sexual Offences (Amendment) Act 2000)	8 January 2001–30 April 2004	5 years
Indecent images		
Taking indecent photographs of a child (section 1 of the Protection of Children Act 1978)	20 August 1978–present	20 August 1978–10 January 2001: 3 years 11 January 2001 onwards: 10 years
Possession of indecent photographs of a child (section 160 of the Criminal Justice Act 1988)	29 September 1988–present	29 September 1988–10 January 2001: 6 months 11 January 2001 onwards: 5 years
Exploitation offences		
Procurement of woman by threats (section 2) Procurement by false pretences (section 3) Causing prostitution of women (section 22) Procuration of girl under 21 for unlawful sexual intercourse in any part of the world (section 23) Detention in a brothel (section 24) Permitting a defective to use premises for intercourse (section 27) Causing or encouraging prostitution (etc) of a girl under 16 (section 28) Causing or encouraging prostitution of a defective (section 29)	1 January 1957–30 April 2004	2 years
Living on earnings of prostitution (section 30) Controlling a prostitute (section 31)	1 January 1957–30 April 2004	1 January 1957–15 August 1959: 2 years 16 August 1959 onwards: 7 years

Offence (Sexual Offences Act 1956 unless stated otherwise)	Effective dates	Maximum
Trafficking into/within/out of the UK for sexual exploitation (sections 57–59 of the Sexual Offences Act 2003)	1 May 2005–5 April 2013	14 years
Offences against those with a mental disorder		
Intercourse with a defective (section 7) Procurement of a defective (section 9)	1 January 1957–30 April 2004	2 years
Sexual intercourse with patients (section 128 of the Mental Health Act 1956)	1 November 1960–30 April 2004	2 years
Other offences		
Administering drugs to obtain or facilitate intercourse (section 4)	1 January 1957–30 April 2004	2 years
Burglary with intent to commit rape (section 9 of the Theft Act 1968)	1 January 1969–30 April 2004	14 years if dwelling; otherwise 10 years

With thanks to Sweet & Maxwell, HHJ Rook QC and Robert Ward CBE for their kind permission to reproduce parts of *Sexual Offences Law & Practice*.

ANNEX D

SG-189

Fine Bands and Community Orders

[The information set out here is also set out in the Magistrates' Court Sentencing Guidelines, which includes further guidance on fines and community orders: see **SG-358** and **SG-382**.]

SG-190

Part 7: Sentencing Young Offenders—Offences with a Lower Statutory Maximum

7.1 The SOA 2003 makes special provision in respect of the maximum sentence that can be imposed for certain offences where committed by a person under the age of 18 (a young offender). The sentencing framework that applies to the sentencing of young offenders is also different.

7.2 This section deals with those offences within the context of the framework that currently applies. Many cases will be sentenced in the youth court, but a significant proportion may also be dealt with in the Crown Court. The essential elements of each offence, relevant charging standards and any other general issues pertaining to the offence are set out in the offence guidelines . . . .

7.3 The offences with which Part 7 is concerned are:
- (i) Sexual activity with a child
- (ii) Causing or inciting a child to engage in sexual activity
- (iii) Engaging in sexual activity in the presence of a child
- (iv) Causing a child to watch a sexual act
- (v) Sexual activity with a child family member
- (vi) Inciting a child family member to engage in sexual activity

7.4 In relation to each offence, the maximum sentence for an offence committed by a young offender is 5 years' custody compared with a maximum of 14 years or 10 years for an offender aged 18 or over. Offences under (i), (ii), (v) and (vi) above can be committed to the Crown Court where it is considered that sentencing powers greater than those available in a magistrates' court may be needed.[76]

7.5 The provisions relating to the sentencing of dangerous offenders apply to young offenders with some variation and, where appropriate, cases should be sent for trial or committed for sentence in the Crown Court. The offences in this section are 'serious' offences for the purposes of the provisions. Where the significant harm criterion is met, the court is required[77] to impose one of the sentences for public protection, which in the case of those under 18 are discretionary detention for life, indeterminate detention for public protection or an extended sentence.

[76] Powers of Criminal Courts (Sentencing) Act 2000, section 91
[77] Criminal Justice Act 2003, sections 226 and 228

7.6 The following guidelines are for those offences where the court considers that the facts found by the court justify the involvement of the criminal law—these findings may be different from those on which the decision to prosecute was made.

7.7 The sentencing framework that applies to young offenders is different from that for adult offenders. The significant factors are set out below.

7.8 For each offence, the circumstances that would suggest that a custodial sentence should be passed where it is available to the court and those that would suggest that a case should be dealt with in the Crown Court (as 'grave crimes') are set out. As for adult offenders, these guidelines relate to sentencing on conviction for a first-time offender after a plea of not guilty.

7.9 The principal aim for all involved in the youth justice system is to prevent offending by children and young persons.[78]

7.10 A court imposing sentence on a youth must have regard to the welfare,[79] maturity, sexual development and intelligence of the youth. These are always important factors.

7.11 Where a young offender pleads guilty to one of these offences and it is the first offence of which they are convicted, a youth court may impose an absolute discharge, a mental health disposal, a custodial sentence, or make a referral order.

7.12 Except where the dangerous offender provisions apply:

(i) Where the young offender is aged 12, 13 or 14, a custodial sentence may only be imposed if the youth is a 'persistent offender' or has committed a 'grave crime' warranting detention for a period in excess of 2 years.[80]

(ii) Where a young offender is aged 10 or 11, no custodial sentence is available in the youth court.

(iii) Where a custodial sentence is imposed in the youth court, it must be a Detention and Training Order (DTO), which can only be for 4/6/8/10/12/18 or 24 months.

(iv) Where a custodial sentence is imposed in the Crown Court, it may be a DTO or it may be detention for a period up to the maximum for the offence.

Sexual activity with a child SG-191
(when committed by a person under the age of 18)

THIS IS A SPECIFIED OFFENCE FOR THE PURPOSES OF SECTION 224 CJA 2003

Intentional sexual touching of a person under 16 (sections 9 and 13)

Maximum penalty: **5 years (14 years** if offender is 18 or over)

The starting points below are based upon a first-time offender aged 17 years old who pleaded not guilty. For younger offenders, sentencers should consider whether a lower starting point is justified in recognition of the offender's age or immaturity.

Type/nature of activity	Starting points	Sentencing ranges
Offence involving penetration where one or more aggravating factors exist or where there is a substantial age gap between the parties	**Detention and Training Order 12 months**	**Detention and Training Order 6–24 months**
CUSTODY THRESHOLD		
Any form of sexual activity that does not involve any aggravating factors	**Community order**	**An appropriate non-custodial sentence***

* 'Non-custodial sentence' in this context suggests a youth community order (as defined in the Criminal Justice Act 2003, section 147(2)) or a fine. In most instances, an offence will have crossed the threshold for a community order. However, in accordance with normal sentencing practice, a court is not precluded from imposing a financial penalty where that is determined to be the appropriate sentence.

[78] Crime and Disorder Act 1998, section 37
[79] Children and Young Persons Act 1933, section 44
[80] Powers of Criminal Courts (Sentencing) Act 2000, section 100

Aggravating factors	Mitigating factors
1. Background of intimidation or coercion 2. Use of drugs, alcohol or other substance to facilitate the offence 3. Threats to prevent victim reporting the incident 4. Abduction or detention 5. Offender aware that he or she is suffering from a sexually transmitted infection	1. Relationship of genuine affection 2. Youth and immaturity of offender

An offender convicted of this offence is automatically subject to notification requirements when sentenced to imprisonment for a term of at least 12 months.[81]

SG-192 **Causing or inciting a child to engage in sexual activity**
(when committed by a person under the age of 18)

THIS IS A SPECIFIED OFFENCE FOR THE PURPOSES OF SECTION 224 CJA 2003

Intentional causing/inciting of person under 16 to engage in sexual activity (sections 10 and 13)

Maximum penalty: **5 years** (**14 years** if offender is 18 or over)

The same starting points apply whether the activity was caused or incited and whether or not the incited activity took place.

The starting points below are based upon a first-time offender aged 17 years old who pleaded not guilty. For younger offenders, sentencers should consider whether a lower starting point is justified in recognition of the offender's age or immaturity

Type/nature of activity	Starting points	Sentencing ranges
Sexual activity involving penetration where one or more aggravating factors exist	**Detention and Training Order 12 months**	**Detention and Training Order 6–24 months**
CUSTODY THRESHOLD		
Any form of sexual activity (non-penetrative or penetrative) not involving any aggravating factors	**Community order**	**An appropriate non-custodial sentence***

* 'Non-custodial sentence' in this context suggests a youth community order (as defined in the Criminal Justice Act 2003, section 147(2)) or a fine. In most instances, an offence will have crossed the threshold for a community order. However, in accordance with normal sentencing practice, a court is not precluded from imposing a financial penalty where that is determined to be the appropriate sentence.

Aggravating factors	Mitigating factors
1. Background of intimidation or coercion 2. Use of drugs, alcohol or other substance to facilitate the offence 3. Threats to prevent victim reporting the incident 4. Abduction or detention 5. Offender aware that he or she is suffering from a sexually transmitted infection	1. Relationship of genuine affection 2. Offender intervenes to prevent incited offence from taking place 3. Youth and immaturity of offender

An offender convicted of this offence is automatically subject to notification requirements when sentenced to imprisonment for a term of at least 12 months.[82]

[81] In accordance with the SOA 2003, section 80 and schedule 3
[82] In accordance with the SOA 2003, section 80 and schedule 3

Engaging in sexual activity in the presence of a child SG-193
(when committed by a person under the age of 18)

THIS IS A SPECIFIED OFFENCE FOR THE PURPOSES OF SECTION 224 CJA 2003

Intentionally and for the purpose of obtaining sexual gratification, engaging in sexual activity in the presence of a person under 16, knowing or believing that the child is aware of the activity (sections 11 and 13)

Maximum penalty: 5 years (10 years if offender is 18 or over)

The starting points below are based upon a first-time offender aged 17 years old who pleaded not guilty. For younger offenders, sentencers should consider whether a lower starting point is justified in recognition of the offender's age or immaturity.

Type/nature of activity	Starting points	Sentencing ranges
Sexual activity involving penetration where one or more aggravating factors exist	**Detention and Training Order 12 months**	**Detention and Training Order 6–24 months**
CUSTODY THRESHOLD		
Any form of sexual activity (non-penetrative or penetrative) not involving any aggravating factors	**Community order**	**An appropriate non-custodial sentence***

* 'Non-custodial sentence' in this context suggests a youth community order (as defined in the Criminal Justice Act 2003, section 147(2)) or a fine. In most instances, an offence will have crossed the threshold for a community order. However, in accordance with normal sentencing practice, a court is not precluded from imposing a financial penalty where that is determined to be the appropriate sentence.

Aggravating factors	Mitigating factors
1. Background of intimidation or coercion 2. Use of drugs, alcohol or other substance to facilitate the offence 3. Threats to prevent victim reporting the incident 4. Abduction or detention	1. Youth and immaturity of offender

An offender convicted of this offence is automatically subject to notification requirements when sentenced to imprisonment for a term of at least 12 months.[83]

Causing a child to watch a sexual act SG-194
(when committed by a person under the age of 18)

THIS IS A SPECIFIED OFFENCE FOR THE PURPOSES OF SECTION 224 CJA 2003

Intentionally causing a person under 16 to watch sexual activity or look at a photograph or pseudo- photograph of sexual activity for the purpose of obtaining sexual gratification (sections 12 and 13)

Maximum penalty: 5 years (10 years if offender is 18 or over)

The starting points below are based upon a first-time offender aged 17 years old who pleaded not guilty. For younger offenders, sentencers should consider whether a lower starting point is justified in recognition of the offender's age or immaturity.

[83] In accordance with the SOA 2003, section 80 and schedule 3

Type/nature of activity	Starting points	Sentencing ranges
Live sexual activity	**Detention and Training Order 8 months**	**Detention and Training Order 6–12 months**
CUSTODY THRESHOLD		
Moving or still images of people engaged in sexual acts involving penetration	**Community order**	**An appropriate non-custodial sentence***
Moving or still images of people engaged in sexual acts other than penetration	**Community order**	**An appropriate non-custodial sentence***

* 'Non-custodial sentence' in this context suggests a youth community order (as defined in the Criminal Justice Act 2003, section 147(2)) or a fine. In most instances, an offence will have crossed the threshold for a community order. However, in accordance with normal sentencing practice, a court is not precluded from imposing a financial penalty where that is determined to be the appropriate sentence.

Aggravating factors	Mitigating factors
1. Background of intimidation or coercion 2. Use of drugs, alcohol or other substance to facilitate the offence 3. Threats to prevent victim reporting the incident 4. Abduction or detention 5. Images of violent activity	1. Youth and immaturity of offender

An offender convicted of this offence is automatically subject to notification requirements when sentenced to imprisonment for a term of at least 12 months.[84]

SG-195 **Sexual activity with a child family member and Inciting a child family member to engage in sexual activity**

(when committed by a person under the age of 18)

THIS IS A SERIOUS OFFENCE FOR THE PURPOSES OF SECTION 224 CJA 2003

Intentional sexual touching with a child family member (section 25)

Intentionally inciting sexual touching by a child family member (section 26)

Maximum penalty for both offences: **5 years** (**14 years** if offender is 18 or over)

The starting points below are based upon a first-time offender aged 17 years old who pleaded not guilty. For younger offenders, sentencers should consider whether a lower starting point is justified in recognition of the offender's age or immaturity.

Type/nature of activity	Starting points	Sentencing ranges
Offence involving penetration where one or more aggravating factors exist or where there is a substantial age gap between the parties	**Detention and Training Order 18 months**	**Detention and Training Order 6–24 months**
CUSTODY THRESHOLD		
Any form of sexual activity (non-penetrative or penetrative) not involving any aggravating factors	**Community order**	**An appropriate non-custodial sentence***

* 'Non-custodial sentence' in this context suggests a youth community order (as defined in the Criminal Justice Act 2003, section 147(2)) or a fine. In most instances, an offence will have crossed the threshold for a community order. However, in accordance with normal sentencing practice, a court is not precluded from imposing a financial penalty where that is determined to be the appropriate sentence.

[84] In accordance with the SOA 2003, section 80 and schedule 3

Aggravating factors	Mitigating factors
1. Background of intimidation or coercion 2. Use of drugs, alcohol or other substance 3. Threats deterring the victim from reporting the incident 4. Offender aware that he or she is suffering from a sexually transmitted infection	1. Small disparity in age between victim and offender 2. Relationship of genuine affection 3. Youth and immaturity of offender

An offender convicted of this offence is automatically subject to notification requirements when sentenced to imprisonment for a term of at least 12 months.[85]

PART 9 FAIL TO SURRENDER TO BAIL

Foreword

SG-196

This guideline applies to the sentencing of offenders convicted of failing to surrender to bail who are sentenced on or after **10 December 2007**. Bail Act offences are committed in significant numbers each year and are a major cause of disruption, delay and unnecessary cost for the criminal justice system. A prime objective of courts is to bring criminal proceedings to a conclusion as soon as practicable, and a rigorous and consistent response when offenders fail to answer bail is needed to help achieve this. This, in turn, may help to discourage future offending. Where it is not possible to dispose of the original offence, sentencing for a Bail Act offence should normally be undertaken separately and carried out as soon as appropriate in light of the circumstances of an individual case.

When a Bail Act offence has been committed, the sentence must be commensurate with the seriousness of the offence and must take into account both the reason why the offender failed to surrender and the degree of harm intended or caused. For these purposes, 'harm' is not only that caused to individual victims and witnesses but includes the consequential effect on police and court resources and the wider negative impact on public confidence in the criminal justice system.

As the considerations for offences committed by youths will differ markedly from those relevant for adult offenders, this guideline relates to the sentencing of adult offenders only.

Fail to Surrender to Bail

SG-197

A. Statutory provision

1. [Sets out the Bail Act 1976, s. 6 (see **D7.136** in the main work.)]
2. An offence under subsection (1) or (2) is punishable either on summary conviction or, in the Crown Court, as if it were a criminal contempt of court. The maximum sentence in a magistrates' court is 3 months imprisonment.[86] If the matter is committed to the Crown Court for sentence, or dealt with there, the maximum sentence is 12 months custody and the sentence is subject to the usual appellate procedures.[87]

B. Assessing Seriousness

SG-198

3. When assessing the seriousness of an offence, the court must consider the offender's culpability and any harm which the offence caused, was intended to cause or might foreseeably have caused.[88]
4. In assessing **culpability**, a court will need to consider whether the failure to surrender was intended to cause harm and, if so, what level of harm. In assessing **harm**, a court will need to consider to what extent the failure to surrender impeded the course of justice. When applied to Bail Act offences, 'harm' includes not only the harm caused to individual victims and witnesses but the consequential drain on police and court resources and the wider negative impact on public confidence in the criminal justice system.
5. The same *approach* to sentencing should be adopted whether the offence is committed contrary to section 6(1) or to section 6(2). However, the offence contrary to section 6(2) requires that there had

[85] In accordance with the SOA 2003, section 80 and schedule 3
[86] Police and Justice Act 2006, section 34 amends various sections of the Criminal Justice Act 2003 so that this maximum sentence is not affected by the general provisions relating to custodial sentences of less than 12 months when in force.
[87] Administration of Justice Act 1960, section 13
[88] Criminal Justice Act 2003, section 143(1)

Sentencing Guidelines

been a reasonable excuse not to attend on the original date and so the degree of harm arising from the failure to attend as soon as reasonably practicable after that date is likely to be less. Accordingly, the seriousness of the offence is likely to be less also.

(i) Culpability

6. The obligation on a person who is granted bail is to surrender to custody at the court or the police station as required. The assessment of culpability requires consideration of the immediate reason why the defendant failed to appear. This can range from forgetfulness (comparable to the category of culpability described as 'negligence' in the Council guideline on seriousness[89]) or fear of the outcome of the hearing through to a deliberate act. Where the failure to surrender was deliberate, it will be relevant whether it was designed to disrupt the system to the defendant's advantage or whether the defendant simply gave no thought at all to the consequences.

(ii) Harm

7. Some degree of harm, even if only a minor delay or inconvenience to the authorities, will always be caused when a defendant fails to surrender. The degree of harm *actually* caused will vary considerably depending on the particular circumstances of the offence. The harm that the offence might foreseeably have caused[90] must also be taken into account.
8. **Failure to surrender to a court** for any reason (whether bail is granted by the police or by a court) inevitably delays justice. Potentially, it will result in additional distress to victims and witnesses. It will almost always waste public money in the form of court time and the resources of the prosecution, the police and the defence.
   (a) Where a defendant fails to appear for a first court hearing but attends shortly afterwards, the only harm caused is likely to be the financial cost to the system. Procedural delays may also be caused by the prosecution, the defence or the Courts Service at various stages of the process and, where a case could not have proceeded even if the defendant had surrendered to bail, this should be taken into account when assessing the harm actually caused.
   (b) Where a defendant appears for trial on the wrong day but enters a late guilty plea enabling the case to be disposed of to some degree at least (albeit with some delay and disruption), the harm caused by the delay may be offset by the benefits stemming from the change of plea.
   (c) The most serious harm is likely to result when a defendant fails to appear for trial, especially if this results in witnesses being sent away. A lengthy aborted trial in the Crown Court will be more harmful than a short hearing in a magistrates' court though each situation has the potential to affect public confidence in the system.
   (d) Where a court decides not to proceed to trial in the absence of the defendant (see paragraphs 34–39), interference with the course of justice may be particularly acute. Memories may become less certain with the passage of time. Victims and witnesses, many of whom find the prospect of preparing for and attending court daunting, are likely to be caused distress and/or inconvenience. They may find it more difficult to attend court on the second or subsequent occasion, to the extent that they may not even appear at all. In such circumstances the harm is very high because justice will be prevented. Victims of violent or sexual offences are particularly likely to be distressed to learn that the accused is 'at large' in defiance of the court.
   (e) The level of harm is likely to be assessed as high where an offender fails to appear for sentence and is also seen to be flouting the authority of the court, such as where the avoidance of sentence results in the consequential avoidance of ancillary orders such as disqualification from driving or from working with children or vulnerable adults, the payment of compensation or registration as a sex offender. This may increase the level of harm whenever the offender continues to present a risk to public safety.
9. In general terms, the same approach to sentencing should be adopted whether the offence involves a failure to surrender to a court or to a police station since the legal obligation is the same. However, the harm that results from failure to surrender to a court will usually be greater than that resulting from failure to surrender to a police station and this will affect the assessment of the seriousness of an individual offence.
10. **Failure to surrender to a police station** results in police time being wasted and the course of justice being impeded; potentially, it can also result in victims and witnesses being distressed and concerned about their safety and the ability of the system to protect the public and deliver justice. However, the circumstances in which such bail is granted are less formal than the grant of court bail and the history

[89] *Overarching Principles: Seriousness*, page 4, www.sentencing-guidelines.gov.uk
[90] Criminal Justice Act, section 143(1)

of the individual case should be examined. There may be less culpability where bail has been enlarged on a number of occasions and less harm if *court* proceedings are not significantly delayed.

(iii) Nature and seriousness of original offence

11. Failure to surrender to custody is an offence in its own right and the sentence imposed should be proportionate to the seriousness of the offending behaviour itself. Where the Bail Act offence is sentenced in advance of the offence in relation to which bail was granted the assessment of seriousness will take place without reference to the seriousness of, or likely sentence for, the original offence.
12. However, the specific nature of the original offence may significantly affect the harm or likelihood of harm caused by the failure to surrender. Particular types of offence (such as violent or sexual offences) may have implications for public protection and safety and the offender's failure to surrender might cause fear and distress to witnesses.
13. Seriousness is not reduced automatically by subsequent acquittal of the original offence. Whilst it may seem harsh that a defendant before the court for an offence of which he is not guilty should be punished for the ancillary offence of failure to surrender during the course of the prosecution of that offence, both the culpability and the likely harm—delay, distress and inconvenience to witnesses, and additional costs—are the same. Moreover, one of the most serious effects of a Bail Act offence can be that a trial cannot take place because of the failure to surrender and it will often be invidious to expect a court to identify genuinely innocent defendants.

(iv) Aggravating and mitigating factors

14. Since 'recent and relevant' previous convictions aggravate the seriousness of an offence,[91] defendants who repeatedly fail to attend court are likely to receive more severe sentences.
15. The period of time for which a defendant absconds is also likely to influence the court when considering sentence. Whilst being absent for a long period of time will aggravate an offence, the fact that a defendant arrives at court only a few days, or even only a few hours, late, is not a factor that will necessarily mitigate sentence; in many cases, the harm will already have been done (for example, the trial may have been put back, witnesses may have been inconvenienced and there may be an increased likelihood that witnesses will fail to attend at a future hearing).
16. Leaving the jurisdiction is an aggravating factor as are other actions designed to avoid the jurisdiction of the court such as changing identity and appearance.
17. **The following aggravating factors are particularly relevant to an offence of failing to surrender to bail:**
    - repeat offending;
    - offender's absence causes a lengthy delay to the administration of justice;
    - determined attempt to avoid the jurisdiction of the court.
18. Prompt voluntary surrender might mitigate sentence where it saves police time in tracing and arresting an offender. It may also be an indication of remorse. This must be weighed against the degree of harm caused by the offence, which may still be significant. Surrender initiated by the offender merits consideration as a mitigating factor. Surrender in response to follow up action has no significance.
19. The fact that an offender has a disorganised or chaotic lifestyle, which may be due to a dependency on drugs or alcohol, does not of itself reduce the seriousness of the offence. Depending on the particular facts, it may be regarded as personal mitigation.
20. A misunderstanding (which does not amount to a defence) may be a mitigating factor but must be differentiated from a mistake on the part of the defendant, where the error must be regarded as his or her own responsibility.[92]
21. Where an offender has literacy or language difficulties, steps should normally be taken by the police or the court to address this when bail is granted. Such difficulties may be mitigation (where they do not amount to a defence but contribute to the offender failing to surrender to bail) where potential problems were not identified and/or appropriate steps were not taken to mitigate the risk in the circumstances as known at the time that bail is granted.
22. An offender's position as the sole or primary carer of dependant relatives may be personal mitigation when it is the reason why the offender has failed to surrender to custody.
23. **The following mitigating factors are particularly relevant to an offence of failing to surrender:**
    - prompt voluntary surrender;

    and, where they are not sufficient to amount to a defence:
    - misunderstanding;

[91] ibid. section 143(2)
[92] See, for example, *Laidlaw v Atkinson* Queen's Bench Division CO/275/86

- a failure to comprehend the requirements or significance of bail;
- caring responsibilities.

SG-199 C. Procedural issues

(i) When to sentence

24. The key principle is that a court should *deal* with a defendant who fails to surrender *as soon as is practicable* even if the trial or other hearing for the offence that led to the grant of bail is adjourned.[93] The following factors are relevant to the decision as to what is practicable:
    - when the proceedings in respect of which bail was granted are expected to conclude;
    - the seriousness of the offence for which the defendant is already being prosecuted;
    - the type of penalty that might be imposed for the breach of bail and for the original offence;
    - any other relevant circumstances.
25. Whether or not the defendant is guilty of a Bail Act offence should be determined as soon as possible. It will be central to the issue of whether bail should now be granted or refused. Even where the offence is denied, a trial is normally short; it should be held on the first appearance after arrest or surrender, unless an adjournment is necessary (for example, for the defence to obtain medical evidence).
26. When there is a plea or finding of guilt, sentence should be imposed *as soon as practicable*. The point at which it becomes possible to sentence an offence and the point at which it is practicable to do so will vary widely from case to case; a decision about timing is best made according to individual circumstances.
27. A key relevant circumstance is whether the substantive offence is to be adjourned, either for a pre-sentence report or for trial, and whether the remand is to be on bail or in custody.
28. Where the defendant is remanded in custody, the sentencing options for the Bail Act offence are limited.
29. Where the defendant is to regain his or her liberty, there is the possibility of a noncustodial sentence. A community order, including an electronically monitored curfew requirement and, perhaps, a supervision requirement or an activity requirement may be helpful in ensuring attendance at future court hearings.
30. In more serious cases in which the custody threshold has been passed, a suspended sentence order could serve the same purpose.
31. These factors support sentencing without delay or with a short delay for a presentence report. On the other hand, there will be occasions when it is more appropriate that all outstanding matters should be dealt with on one sentencing occasion. This may be where the totality of offending may affect sentence type (for example where two or more offences together pass the custody threshold, but individually do not) or where the harm caused by the failure to surrender cannot be assessed at an early stage (for example, where witnesses may no longer be available).
32. A magistrates' court will be constrained by the maximum sentence available. In certain circumstances, Bail Act offences that would normally be dealt with in a magistrates' court may be committed to the Crown Court to be dealt with.[94]

(ii) Consecutive and concurrent custodial sentences

33. Where a custodial sentence is imposed for the original offence and a custodial sentence is also deemed appropriate for a Bail Act offence, a court should normally impose a consecutive sentence. However, a concurrent sentence will be appropriate where otherwise the overall sentence would be disproportionate to the combined seriousness of the offences.

(iii) Conducting trials in the absence of the defendant

34. A defendant has a duty to surrender to bail and a right to be present at his or her trial. However, where a defendant is absent voluntarily, having breached the duty to surrender, a court may proceed to hear a case in the defendant's absence. In a magistrates' court this is a statutory power.[95] While some sentences may be imposed in a defendant's absence, it is not possible to impose a custodial sentence or a community order, and it is undesirable to impose a disqualification from driving.
35. The Consolidated Criminal Practice Direction[96] reinforces the encouragement to courts to proceed in absence and identifies factors to be taken into account before so doing which include:
    - the conduct of the defendant;
    - the disadvantage to the defendant;

[93] See Consolidated Criminal Practice Direction last revised April 2007—www.hmcourtsservice.gov.uk/cms/pds.htm
[94] Bail Act 1976, section 6(6)
[95] Magistrates' Courts Act 1980, section 11
[96] Last revised April 2007—www.hmcourts-service.gov.uk/cms/pds.htm

- the public interest;
- the effect of any delay; and
- whether the attendance of the defendant could be secured at a later hearing.

36. Additional factors for a magistrates' court to consider include:
    - there is less risk of either a magistrate or a district judge drawing an impermissible inference from a defendant's absence than would be the case with a jury; and
    - in a magistrates' court the finder of fact may ask questions and test the evidence of prosecution witnesses.
37. The overriding concern of the court is to ensure that a trial conducted in the absence of the defendant is as fair as circumstances permit and, in particular, that the defendant's rights under Article 6 of the European Convention on Human Rights (ECHR)[97] are not infringed.
38. Proceeding to trial in the absence of the defendant may reduce the harm arising from a Bail Act offence. When considering the degree to which this should influence sentence, it must be borne in mind that the position in a magistrates' court is different from that in the Crown Court. An appeal against conviction from a magistrates' court can result in a re-hearing, whereas that is not the case after a jury trial. There is also the discretionary power under section 142 of the Magistrates' Courts Act 1980 to set aside a conviction and order a re-hearing in a magistrates' court. If an application to set aside a conviction is successful, witnesses will be required to give evidence again at a later date. It will be relevant to an assessment of harm whether either of those provisions has been used.
39. Where it has proved possible to proceed to trial or conclude proceedings in the absence of the defendant, this should have no bearing on *culpability* for a Bail Act offence as the intention of the defendant remains unchanged. It may, however, be relevant to the assessment of *harm* as this may have been reduced or avoided because of the decision to proceed in absence.

D. Sentencing ranges and starting points SG-200

(i) This guideline applies to a first time offender who has been convicted after a trial. A first time offender is a person who does not have a conviction which, by virtue of section 143(2) of the Criminal Justice Act 2003, must be treated as an aggravating factor.

(ii) The guideline establishes levels of seriousness based upon both offender culpability and the resulting consequences. These are set out in the column headed 'nature of failure and harm'.

(iii) A court will identify the description that most nearly matches the particular facts of the offence and this will identify a starting point from which the sentencer can depart to reflect any aggravating or mitigating factors affecting the *seriousness of the offence* to reach a provisional sentence.

(iv) The sentencing range is the bracket into which the provisional sentence will normally fall. The particular circumstances may, however, make it appropriate that the provisional sentence falls outside the range.

(v) Where the offender has previous convictions which aggravate the seriousness of the current offence, that may take the provisional sentence beyond the range given particularly where there are significant other aggravating factors present.

(vi) Once the provisional sentence has been identified by reference to those factors affecting the seriousness of the offence, the court will take into account any relevant factors of personal mitigation, which may take the sentence beyond the range given.

(vii) Where there has been a guilty plea, any reduction attributable to that plea will be applied to the sentence at this stage. Again, this reduction may take the sentence below the range provided.

(viii) A court must give its reasons for imposing a sentence of a different kind or outside the range provided in the guidelines.[98]

The Decision Making Process

[Sets out the standard sequential decision making process: identify starting point, consider aggravating factors, consider mitigating factors, apply reduction for guilty plea, review in light of the totality principle and give reasons.]

E. Factors to take into consideration SG-201

1. Whilst the approach to sentencing should generally be the same whether the defendant failed to surrender to a court or to a police station and whether the offence is contrary to section 6(1) or 6(2), the court must examine all the relevant circumstances.
2. Whilst the seriousness of the original offence does not of itself aggravate or mitigate the seriousness of the offence of failing to surrender, the circumstances surrounding the original offence may be relevant in assessing the harm arising from this offence.

---

97 Right to a fair trial

98 Criminal Justice Act 2003, section 174(2)(a)

3. Where it has proved possible to conclude proceedings in the absence of the defendant, this may be relevant to the assessment of harm caused.
4. Where the failure to surrender to custody was 'deliberate':
   - at or near the bottom of the range will be cases where the defendant gave no thought at all to the consequences, or other mitigating factors are present, and the degree of delay or interference with the progress of the case was not significant in all the circumstances;
   - at or near the top of the range will be cases where any of aggravating factors 1–3 are present if there is also a significant delay and/or interference with the progress of the case.
5. Only the most common aggravating and mitigating factors specifically relevant to Bail Act offences are included in the guideline. When assessing the seriousness of an offence, the courts must always have regard to the full list of aggravating and mitigating factors in the Council guideline on Seriousness.[99]
6. A previous conviction that is likely to be 'relevant' for the purposes of this offence is one which demonstrates failure to comply with an order of a court.
7. Acquittal of the original offence does not automatically mitigate this offence.
8. The fact that an offender has a disorganised or chaotic lifestyle should not normally be treated as mitigation of the offence, but may be regarded as personal mitigation depending on the particular facts of a case.
9. Once the provisional sentence has been identified by reference to factors affecting the seriousness of the offence, the court will take into account any relevant factors of personal mitigation, and any reduction where a guilty plea was entered.[100]
10. The sentence for this offence should normally be in addition to any sentence for the original offence. Where custodial sentences are being imposed for a Bail Act offence and the original offence at the same time, the normal approach should be for the sentences to be consecutive. The length of any custodial sentence imposed must be commensurate with the seriousness of the offence(s).[101]
11. If an offence is serious enough to justify imposition of a community order, a curfew requirement with an electronic monitoring requirement may be a particularly appropriate part of such an order in any of the three sentencing ranges.
12. Power exists for magistrates' courts to impose one day's detention in appropriate cases.[102]

SG-202

BAIL ACT 1976, SS. 6(1) & 6(2)

Maximum penalty: 12 months imprisonment in the Crown Court
3 months imprisonment in a magistrates' court

The following starting points and sentencing ranges are for a first time offender aged 18 or over who pleaded not guilty. They should be applied as set out above.

Nature of failure & harm	Starting point	Sentencing range
Deliberate failure to attend causing delay and/or interference with the administration of justice. *The type and degree of harm actually caused will affect where in the range the case falls. See guidance…*	**14 days' custody**	*Crown Court* **Community order (medium)–40 weeks' custody** *Magistrates' court* **Community order (low)–10 weeks' custody**
Negligent or non-deliberate failure to attend causing delay and/or interference with the administration of justice	**Fine**	**Fine–Community order (medium)**
Surrenders late on day but case proceeds as planned	**Fine**	**Fine**

Additional aggravating factors	Additional mitigating factors
1. Lengthy absence 2. Serious attempts to evade justice 3. Determined attempt seriously to undermine the course of justice 4. Previous relevant convictions and/or repeated breach of court orders or police bail	1. Prompt voluntary surrender *When not amounting to a defence* 2. Misunderstanding 3. A failure to comprehend bail significance or requirements 4. Caring responsibilities [see para. 22 for further detail]

99 *Overarching Principles: Seriousness*, pages 6–7, published 16 December 2004, www.sentencing-guidelines.gov.uk
100 Reduction in sentence for a guilty plea (revised), published July 2007, www.sentencing-guidelines.gov.uk
101 Criminal Justice Act 2003, section 152(2)
102 Magistrates' Courts Act 1980, section 135

PART 10 ASSAULT: DEFINITIVE GUIDELINE (CROWN COURT) SG-203

[Note: This definitive guideline was the first to be issued by the Sentencing Council: see E1.2 in the main work.]

Applicability of Guideline SG-204

In accordance with section 120 of the Coroners and Justice Act 2009, the Sentencing Council issues this definitive guideline. It applies to all offenders aged 18 and older, who are sentenced on or after 13 June 2011, regardless of the date of the offence.

Section 125(1) of the Coroners and Justice Act 2009 provides that when sentencing offences committed after 6 April 2010:

'Every court—

(a) must, in sentencing an offender, follow any sentencing guideline which is relevant to the offender's case, and
(b) must, in exercising any other function relating to the sentencing of offenders, follow any sentencing guidelines which are relevant to the exercise of the function,

unless the court is satisfied that it would be contrary to the interests of justice to do so.'

This guideline applies only to offenders aged 18 and older. General principles to be considered in the sentencing of youths are in the Sentencing Guidelines Council's definitive guideline, *Overarching Principles—Sentencing Youths* [see SG-515].

Structure, ranges and starting points SG-205

For the purposes of section 125(3)–(4) of the Coroners and Justice Act 2009, the guideline specifies *offence ranges*—the range of sentences appropriate for each type of offence. Within each offence, the Council has specified three *categories* which reflect varying degrees of seriousness. The offence range is split into *category ranges*—sentences appropriate for each level of seriousness. The Council has also identified a starting point within each category.

Starting points define the position within a category range from which to start calculating the provisional sentence. **Starting points apply to all offences within the corresponding category and are applicable to all offenders in all cases irrespective of plea or previous convictions.** Once the starting point is established the court should consider further aggravating and mitigating factors and previous convictions so as to adjust the sentence within the range. Credit for a guilty plea is taken into consideration only at step 4 in the process, after the appropriate sentence has been identified.

Information on community orders and fine bands is [available at SG-382 and SG-358].

Causing Grievous Bodily Harm with Intent to do Grievous Bodily Harm/ Wounding with Intent to do Grievous Bodily Harm SG-206

Offences against the Person Act 1861 (section 18)

This is a serious specified offence for the purposes of section 224 of the Criminal Justice Act 2003

Triable only on indictment

Maximum: Life imprisonment

Offence range: 3–16 years' custody

STEP ONE Determining the offence category

The court should determine the offence category using the table below.

Category 1	Greater harm (serious injury must normally be present) **and** higher culpability
Category 2	Greater harm (serious injury must normally be present) **and** lower culpability; **or** lesser harm **and** higher culpability
Category 3	Lesser harm **and** lower culpability

The court should determine the offender's culpability and the harm caused, or intended, by reference only to the factors below (as demonstrated by the presence of one or more). These factors comprise the principal factual elements of the offence and should determine the category.

Factors indicating greater harm Injury (which includes disease transmission and/or psychological harm) which is serious in the context of the offence (must normally be present) Victim is particularly vulnerable because of personal circumstances Sustained or repeated assault on the same victim	**Factors indicating lesser harm** Injury which is less serious in the context of the offence
Factors indicating higher culpability *Statutory aggravating factors:* Offence racially or religiously aggravated Offence motivated by, or demonstrating, hostility to the victim based on his or her sexual orientation (or presumed sexual orientation) Offence motivated by, or demonstrating, hostility to the victim based on the victim's disability (or presumed disability) *Other aggravating factors:* A significant degree of premeditation Use of weapon or weapon equivalent (for example, shod foot, headbutting, use of acid, use of animal) Intention to commit more serious harm than actually resulted from the offence Deliberately causes more harm than is necessary for commission of offence Deliberate targeting of vulnerable victim Leading role in group or gang Offence motivated by, or demonstrating, hostility based on the victim's age, sex, gender identity (or presumed gender identity)	**Factors indicating lower culpability** Subordinate role in a group or gang A greater degree of provocation than normally expected Lack of premeditation Mental disorder or learning disability, where linked to commission of the offence Excessive self defence

STEP TWO Starting point and category range

Having determined the category, the court should use the corresponding starting points to reach a sentence within the category range below. The starting point applies to all offenders irrespective of plea or previous convictions. A case of particular gravity, reflected by multiple features of culpability in step one, could merit upward adjustment from the starting point before further adjustment for aggravating or mitigating features, set out below.

Offence category	Starting Point (*Applicable to all Offenders*)	Category Range (*Applicable to all Offenders*)
Category 1	12 years' custody	9–16 years' custody
Category 2	6 years' custody	5–9 years' custody
Category 3	4 years' custody	3–5 years' custody

The table below contains a non-exhaustive list of additional factual elements providing the context of the offence and factors relating to the offender. Identify whether any combination of these, or other relevant factors, should result in an upward or downward adjustment from the starting point. In some cases, having considered these factors, it may be appropriate to move outside the identified category range.

Factors increasing seriousness *Statutory aggravating factors:* Previous convictions, having regard to a) the nature of the offence to which the conviction relates and its relevance to the current offence; and b) the time that has elapsed since the conviction Offence committed whilst on bail *Other aggravating factors include:* Location of the offence Timing of the offence Ongoing effect upon the victim Offence committed against those working in the public sector or providing a service to the public Presence of others including relatives, especially children or partner of the victim Gratuitous degradation of victim	**Factors reducing seriousness or reflecting personal mitigation** No previous convictions or no relevant/recent convictions Single blow Remorse Good character and/or exemplary conduct Determination, and/or demonstration of steps taken to address addiction or offending behaviour Serious medical conditions requiring urgent, intensive or long-term treatment Isolated incident Age and/or lack of maturity where it affects the responsibility of the offender

In domestic violence cases, victim forced to leave their home Failure to comply with current court orders Offence committed whilst on licence An attempt to conceal or dispose of evidence Failure to respond to warnings or concerns expressed by others about the offender's behaviour Commission of offence whilst under the influence of alcohol or drugs Abuse of power and/or position of trust Exploiting contact arrangements with a child to commit an offence Previous violence or threats to the same victim Established evidence of community impact Any steps taken to prevent the victim reporting an incident, obtaining assistance and/or from assisting or supporting the prosecution Offences taken into consideration (TICs)	Lapse of time since the offence where this is not the fault of the offender Mental disorder or learning disability, where not linked to the commission of the offence Sole or primary carer for dependent relatives

STEP THREE Consider any other factors which indicate a reduction, such as assistance to the prosecution

The court should take into account sections 73 and 74 of the Serious Organised Crime and Police Act 2005 (assistance by defendants: reduction or review of sentence) and any other rule of law by virtue of which an offender may receive a discounted sentence in consequence of assistance given (or offered) to the prosecutor or investigator.

STEP FOUR Reduction for Guilty Pleas

The court should take account of any potential reduction for a guilty plea in accordance with section 144 of the Criminal Justice Act 2003 and the *Guilty Plea* guideline.

STEP FIVE Dangerousness

Causing grievous bodily harm with intent to do grievous bodily harm/wounding with intent to do grievous bodily harm is a serious offence within the meaning of Chapter 5 of the Criminal Justice Act 2003 and at this stage the court should consider whether having regard to the criteria contained in that Chapter it would be appropriate to award a life sentence, imprisonment for public protection or an extended sentence. Where offenders meet the dangerousness criteria, the notional determinate sentence should be used as the basis for the setting of a minimum term.

STEP SIX Totality Principle

If sentencing an offender for more than one offence, or where the offender is already serving a sentence, consider whether the total sentence is just and proportionate to the offending behaviour.

STEP SEVEN Compensation and ancillary orders

In all cases, the court should consider whether to make compensation and/or other ancillary orders.

STEP EIGHT Reasons

Section 174 of the Criminal Justice Act 2003 imposes a duty to give reasons for, and explain the effect of, the sentence.

STEP NINE Consideration for remand time

Sentencers should take into consideration any remand time served in relation to the final sentence. The court should consider whether to give credit for time spent on remand in custody or on bail in accordance with sections 240 and 240A of the Criminal Justice Act 2003.

Inflicting Grievous Bodily Harm/Unlawful Wounding SG-207

Offences against the Person Act 1861 (section 20)

Racially/Religiously Aggravated GBH/Unlawful Wounding

Crime and Disorder Act 1998 (section 29)

These are specified offences for the purposes of section 224 of the Criminal Justice Act 2003

Triable either way

Maximum (section 20): 5 years

Maximum (section 29): 7 years

Offence range: Community order—4 years' custody

STEP ONE Determining the offence category

Category 1	Greater harm (serious injury must normally be present) **and** higher culpability
Category 2	Greater harm (serious injury must normally be present) **and** lower culpability; **or** lesser harm **and** higher culpability
Category 3	Lesser harm **and** lower culpability

The court should determine the offender's culpability and the harm caused, or intended, by reference only to the factors below (as demonstrated by the presence of one or more). These factors comprise the principal factual elements of the offence and should determine the category.

Factors indicating greater harm Injury (which includes disease transmission and/or psychological harm) which is serious in the context of the offence (must normally be present) Victim is particularly vulnerable because of personal circumstances Sustained or repeated assault on the same victim	**Factors indicating lesser harm** Injury which is less serious in the context of the offence
Factors indicating higher culpability *Statutory aggravating factors:* Offence motivated by, or demonstrating, hostility to the victim based on his or her sexual orientation (or presumed sexual orientation) Offence motivated by, or demonstrating, hostility to the victim based on the victim's disability (or presumed disability) *Other aggravating factors:* A significant degree of premeditation Use of weapon or weapon equivalent (for example, shod foot, headbutting, use of acid, use of animal) Intention to commit more serious harm than actually resulted from the offence Deliberately causes more harm than is necessary for commission of offence Deliberate targeting of vulnerable victim Leading role in group or gang Offence motivated by, or demonstrating, hostility based on the victim's age, sex, gender identity (or presumed gender identity)	**Factors indicating lower culpability** Subordinate role in group or gang A greater degree of provocation than normally expected Lack of premeditation Mental disorder or learning disability, where linked to commission of the offence Excessive self defence

STEP TWO Starting Point and Category Range

Having determined the category, the court should use the corresponding starting points to reach a sentence within the category range below. The starting point applies to all offenders irrespective of plea or previous convictions. A case of particular gravity, reflected by multiple features of culpability in step one, could merit upward adjustment from the starting point before further adjustment for aggravating or mitigating features, set out below.

Offence Category	Starting Point (*Applicable to all offenders*)	Category Range (*Applicable to all offenders*)
Category 1	**3 years' custody**	**2 years 6 months'–4 years' custody**
Category 2	**1 year 6 months' custody**	**1–3 years' custody**
Category 3	**High level community order**	Low level community order–**51 weeks' custody**

The table below contains a **non-exhaustive** list of additional factual elements providing the context of the offence and factors relating to the offender. Identify whether any combination of these, or other relevant factors, should result in an upward or downward adjustment from the starting point. In some cases, having considered these factors, it may be appropriate to move outside the identified category range.

When sentencing **category 3 offences**, the court should also consider the custody threshold as follows:

- Has the custody threshold been passed?
- If so, is it unavoidable that a custodial sentence be imposed?
- If so, can that sentence be suspended?

Factors increasing seriousness	**Factors reducing seriousness or reflecting personal mitigation**
Statutory aggravating factors: Previous convictions, having regard to a) the nature of the offence to which the conviction relates and its relevance to the current offence; and b) the time that has elapsed since the conviction Offence committed whilst on bail *Other aggravating factors include:* Location of the offence Timing of the offence Ongoing effect upon the victim Offence committed against those working in the public sector or providing a service to the public Presence of others including relatives, especially children or partner of the victim Gratuitous degradation of victim In domestic violence cases, victim forced to leave their home Failure to comply with current court orders Offence committed whilst on licence An attempt to conceal or dispose of evidence Failure to respond to warnings or concerns expressed by others about the offender's behaviour Commission of offence whilst under the influence of alcohol or drugs Abuse of power and/or position of trust Exploiting contact arrangements with a child to commit an offence Previous violence or threats to the same victim Established evidence of community impact Any steps taken to prevent the victim reporting an incident, obtaining assistance and/or from assisting or supporting the prosecution Offences taken into consideration (TICs)	No previous convictions **or** no relevant/recent convictions Single blow Remorse Good character and/or exemplary conduct Determination and/or demonstration of steps taken to address addiction or offending behaviour Serious medical conditions requiring urgent, intensive or long-term treatment Isolated incident Age and/or lack of maturity where it affects the responsibility of the offender Lapse of time since the offence where this is not the fault of the offender Mental disorder or learning disability, where **not** linked to the commission of the offence Sole or primary carer for dependent relatives

Section 29 offences only: The court should determine the appropriate sentence for the offence without taking account of the element of aggravation and then make an addition to the sentence, considering the level of aggravation involved. It may be appropriate to move outside the identified category range, taking into account the increased statutory maximum.

STEP THREE Consider any other factors which indicate a reduction, such as assistance to the prosecution

The court should take into account sections 73 and 74 of the Serious Organised Crime and Police Act 2005 (assistance by defendants: reduction or review of sentence) and any other rule of law by virtue of which an offender may receive a discounted sentence in consequence of assistance given (or offered) to the prosecutor or investigator.

STEP FOUR Reduction for guilty pleas

The court should take account of any potential reduction for a guilty plea in accordance with section 144 of the Criminal Justice Act 2003 and the *Guilty Plea* guideline.

STEP FIVE Dangerousness

Inflicting grievous bodily harm/Unlawful wounding and racially/religiously aggravated GBH/Unlawful wounding are specified offences within the meaning of Chapter 5 of the Criminal Justice Act 2003 and at this stage the court should consider whether having regard to the criteria contained in that Chapter it would be appropriate to award an extended sentence.

[Steps Six to Nine are almost identical to those which apply for causing grievous bodily harm with intent: see **SG-206**.]

SG-208

Assault Occasioning Actual Bodily Harm

Offences against the Person Act 1861 (section 47)

Racially/Religiously Aggravated ABH

Crime and Disorder Act 1998 (section 29)

These are specified offences for the purposes of section 224 of the Criminal Justice Act 2003

Triable either way

Maximum (section 47): 5 years' custody

Maximum (section 29): 7 years' custody

Offence range: Fine—3 years' custody

STEP ONE Determining the offence category

The court should determine the offence category using the table below.

Category 1	Greater harm (serious injury must normally be present) **and** higher culpability
Category 2	Greater harm (serious injury must normally be present) **and** lower culpability; **or** lesser harm **and** higher culpability
Category 3	Lesser harm **and** lower culpability

The court should determine the offender's culpability and the harm caused, or intended, by reference **only** to the factors identified in the table below (as demonstrated by the presence of one or more). These factors comprise the principal factual elements of the offence and should determine the category.

Factors indicating greater harm Injury (which includes disease transmission and/or psychological harm) which is serious in the context the offence (must normally be present) Victim is particularly vulnerable because of personal circumstances Sustained or repeated assault on the same victim	**Factors indicating lesser harm** Injury which is less serious in the context of the offence
Factors indicating higher culpability *Statutory aggravating factors:* Offence motivated by, or demonstrating, hostility to the victim based on his or her sexual orientation (or presumed sexual orientation) Offence motivated by, or demonstrating, hostility to the victim based on the victim's disability (or presumed disability) *Other aggravating factors:* A significant degree of premeditation Use of weapon or weapon equivalent (for example, shod foot, headbutting, use of acid, use of animal) Intention to commit more serious harm than actually resulted from the offence Deliberately causes more harm than is necessary for commission of offence Deliberate targeting of vulnerable victim Leading role in group or gang Offence motivated by, or demonstrating, hostility based on the victim's age, sex, gender identity (or presumed gender identity)	**Factors indicating lower culpability** Subordinate role in a group or gang A greater degree of provocation than normally expected Lack of premeditation Mental disorder or learning disability, where linked to commission of the offence Excessive self defence

STEP TWO Starting Point and Category Range

Having determined the category, the court should use the corresponding starting points to reach a sentence within the category range below. The starting point applies to all offenders irrespective of plea or previous convictions. A case of particular gravity, reflected by multiple features of culpability in step one, could merit upward adjustment from the starting point before further adjustment for aggravating or mitigating features, set out below.

Offence category	Starting Point (*Applicable to all offenders*)	Category Range (*Applicable to all offenders*)
Category 1	1 year 6 months' custody	1–3 years' custody
Category 2	26 weeks' custody	Low level community order–51 weeks' custody
Category 3	Medium level community order	Band A fine–High level community order

The table below contains a **non-exhaustive** list of additional factual elements providing the context of the offence and factors relating to the offender. Identify whether any combination of these, or other relevant factors, should result in an upward or downward adjustment from the starting point. In some cases, having considered these factors, it may be appropriate to move outside the identified category range.

When sentencing **category 2** offences, the court should also consider the custody threshold as follows:

- Has the custody threshold been passed?
- If so, is it unavoidable that a custodial sentence be imposed?
- If so, can that sentence be suspended?

When sentencing **category 3** offences, the court should also consider the community order threshold as follows:

- Has the community order threshold been passed?

Factors increasing seriousness	Factors reducing seriousness or reflecting personal mitigation
Statutory aggravating factors: Previous convictions, having regard to a) the nature of the offence to which the conviction relates and its relevance to the current offence; and b) the time that has elapsed since the conviction Offence committed whilst on bail *Other aggravating factors include:* Location of the offence Timing of the offence Ongoing effect upon the victim Offence committed against those working in the public sector or providing a service to the public Presence of others including relatives, especially children or partner of the victim Gratuitous degradation of victim In domestic violence cases, victim forced to leave their home Failure to comply with current court orders Offence committed whilst on licence An attempt to conceal or dispose of evidence Failure to respond to warnings or concerns expressed by others about the offender's behaviour Commission of offence whilst under the influence of alcohol or drugs Abuse of power and/or position of trust Exploiting contact arrangements with a child to commit an offence Established evidence of community impact Any steps taken to prevent the victim reporting an incident, obtaining assistance and/or from assisting or supporting the prosecution Offences taken into consideration (TICs)	No previous convictions or no relevant/recent convictions Single blow Remorse Good character and/or exemplary conduct Determination and/or demonstration of steps taken to address addiction or offending behaviour Serious medical conditions requiring urgent, intensive or long-term treatment Isolated incident Age and/or lack of maturity where it affects the responsibility of the offender Lapse of time since the offence where this is not the fault of the offender Mental disorder or learning disability, where not linked to the commission of the offence Sole or primary carer for dependent relatives

Section 29 offences only: The court should determine the appropriate sentence for the offence without taking account of the element of aggravation and then make an addition to the sentence, considering the level of aggravation involved. It may be appropriate to move outside the identified category range, taking into account the increased statutory maximum.

[Steps Three to Nine are almost identical to those for inflicting grievous bodily harm: see **SG-206**.]

SG-209

Assault with Intent to Resist Arrest

Offences against the Person Act 1861 (section 38)

This is a specified offence for the purposes of section 224 of the Criminal Justice Act 2003

Triable either way

Maximum 2 years' custody

Offence range: Fine—51 weeks' custody

STEP ONE Determining the offence category

The court should determine the offence category using the table below.

Category 1	Greater harm **and** higher culpability
Category 2	Greater harm **and** lower culpability; **or** lesser harm **and** higher culpability
Category 3	Lesser harm **and** lower culpability

The court should determine the offender's culpability and the harm caused, or intended, by reference **only** to the factors identified in the table below (as demonstrated by the presence of one or more). These factors comprise the principal factual elements of the offence and should determine the category.

Factors indicating greater harm Sustained or repeated assault on the same victim **Factors indicating higher culpability** *Statutory aggravating factors:* Offence racially or religiously aggravated Offence motivated by, or demonstrating, hostility to the victim based on his or her sexual orientation (or presumed sexual orientation) Offence motivated by, or demonstrating, hostility to the victim based on the victim's disability (or presumed disability) *Other aggravating factors:* A significant degree of premeditation Use of weapon or weapon equivalent (for example, shod foot, headbutting, use of acid, use of animal) Intention to commit more serious harm than actually resulted from the offence Deliberately causes more harm than is necessary for commission of offence Leading role in group or gang Offence motivated by, or demonstrating, hostility based on the victim's age, sex, gender identity (or presumed gender identity)	**Factors indicating lesser harm** Injury which is less serious in the context of the offence **Factors indicating lower culpability** Subordinate role in group or gang Lack of premeditation Mental disorder or learning disability, where linked to commission of the offence

STEP TWO Starting Point and Category Range

Having determined the category, the court should use the corresponding starting points to reach a sentence within the category range below. The starting point applies to all offenders irrespective of plea or previous convictions. A case of particular gravity, reflected by multiple features of culpability in step one, could merit upward adjustment from the starting point before further adjustment for aggravating or mitigating features, set out below.

Offence Category	Starting Point (*Applicable to all offenders*)	Category Range (*Applicable to all offenders*)
Category 1	**26 weeks' custody**	**12 weeks'–51 weeks' custody**
Category 2	**Medium level community order**	**Low level community order–High level community order**
Category 3	**Band B fine**	**Band A fine–Band C fine**

The table below contains a **non-exhaustive** list of additional factual elements providing the context of the offence and factors relating to the offender. Identify whether any combination of these, or other relevant factors, should result in an upward or downward adjustment from the starting point. In some cases, having considered these factors, it may be appropriate to move outside the identified category range.

When sentencing **category 1** offences, the court should consider whether the sentence can be suspended.

Factors increasing seriousness	Factors reducing seriousness or reflecting personal mitigation
Statutory aggravating factors: Previous convictions, having regard to a) the nature of the offence to which the conviction relates and its relevance to the current offence; and b) the time that has elapsed since the conviction Offence committed whilst on bail *Other aggravating factors include:* Location of the offence Timing of the offence Ongoing effect upon the victim Gratuitous degradation of victim Failure to comply with current court orders Offence committed whilst on licence An attempt to conceal or dispose of evidence Failure to respond to warnings or concerns expressed by others about the offender's behaviour Commission of offence whilst under the influence of alcohol or drugs Established evidence of community impact Any steps taken to prevent the victim reporting an incident, obtaining assistance and/or from assisting or supporting the prosecution Offences taken into consideration (TICs)	No previous convictions **or** no relevant/recent convictions Single blow Remorse Good character and/or exemplary conduct Determination and/or demonstration of steps taken to address addiction or offending behaviour Serious medical conditions requiring urgent, intensive or long-term treatment Isolated incident Age and/or lack of maturity where it affects the responsibility of the offender Lapse of time since the offence where this is not the fault of the offender Mental disorder or learning disability, where **not** linked to the commission of the offence Sole or primary carer for dependent relatives

[Steps Three to Nine are almost identical to those for inflicting grievous bodily harm: see **SG-206**.]

ASSAULT ON A POLICE CONSTABLE IN EXECUTION OF HIS DUTY **SG-210**

Police Act 1996 (section 89)

Triable only summarily

Maximum: 26 weeks' custody

Offence range: Fine—26 weeks' custody

STEP ONE Determining the offence category

The court should determine the offence category using the table below.

Category 1	Greater harm **and** higher culpability
Category 2	Greater harm **and** lower culpability; **or** lesser harm **and** higher culpability
Category 3	Lesser harm **and** lower culpability

The court should determine the offender's culpability and the harm caused, or intended, by reference **only** to the factors below (as demonstrated by the presence of one or more). These factors comprise the principal factual elements of the offence and should determine the category.

Factors indicating greater harm	Factors indicating lesser harm
Sustained or repeated assault on the same victim	Injury which is less serious in the context of the offence
Factors indicating higher culpability *Statutory aggravating factors:* Offence racially or religiously aggravated Offence motivated by, or demonstrating, hostility to the victim based on his or her sexual orientation (or presumed sexual orientation) Offence motivated by, or demonstrating, hostility to the victim based on the victim's disability (or presumed disability) *Other aggravating factors:* A significant degree of premeditation Use of weapon or weapon equivalent (for example, shod foot, headbutting, use of acid, use of animal) Intention to commit more serious harm than actually resulted from the offence Deliberately causes more harm than is necessary for commission of offence Leading role in group or gang Offence motivated by, or demonstrating, hostility based on the victim's age, sex, gender identity (or presumed gender identity)	**Factors indicating lower culpability** Subordinate role in group or gang Lack of premeditation Mental disorder or learning disability, where linked to commission of the offence

STEP TWO Starting point and category range

Having determined the category, the court should use the corresponding starting points to reach a sentence within the category range below. The starting point applies to all offenders irrespective of plea or previous convictions. A case of particular gravity, reflected by multiple features of culpability in step one, could merit upward adjustment from the starting point before further adjustment for aggravating or mitigating features, set out below.

Offence Category	Starting Point (*Applicable to all offenders*)	Category Range (*Applicable to all offenders*)
Category 1	12 weeks' custody	Low level community order–26 weeks' custody
Category 2	Medium level community order	Low level community order–High level community order
Category 3	Band B fine	Band A fine–Band C fine

The table below contains a **non-exhaustive** list of additional factual elements providing the context of the offence and factors relating to the offender. Identify whether any combination of these, or other relevant factors, should result in an upward or downward adjustment from the starting point. In some cases, having considered these factors, it may be appropriate to move outside the identified category range.

When sentencing **category 1** offences, the court should also consider the custody threshold as follows:

- Has the custody threshold been passed?
- If so, is it unavoidable that a custodial sentence be imposed?
- If so, can that sentence be suspended?

Factors increasing seriousness	Factors reducing seriousness or reflecting personal mitigation
Statutory aggravating factors: Previous convictions, having regard to a) the nature of the offence to which the conviction relates and its relevance to the current offence; and b) the time that has elapsed since the conviction Offence committed whilst on bail *Other aggravating factors include:* Location of the offence Timing of the offence Ongoing effect upon the victim Gratuitous degradation of victim Failure to comply with current court orders Offence committed whilst on licence An attempt to conceal or dispose of evidence Failure to respond to warnings or concerns expressed by others about the offender's behaviour Commission of offence whilst under the influence of alcohol or drugs Established evidence of community impact Any steps taken to prevent the victim reporting an incident, obtaining assistance and/or from assisting or supporting the prosecution Offences taken into consideration (TICs)	No previous convictions **or** no relevant/recent convictions Single blow Remorse Good character and/or exemplary conduct Determination and/or demonstration of steps taken to address addiction or offending behaviour Serious medical conditions requiring urgent, intensive or long-term treatment Isolated incident Age and/or lack of maturity where it affects the responsibility of the defendant Mental disorder or learning disability, where **not** linked to the commission of the offence Sole or primary carer for dependent relatives

[Steps Three to Eight are almost identical to those for inflicting grievous bodily harm (see **SG-206**) but with the omission of Step Five (Dangerousness).]

Common Assault **SG-211**

Criminal Justice Act 1988 (section 39)

Racially/Religiously Aggravated Common Assault

Crime and Disorder Act 1998 (section 29)

Racially/religiously aggravated assault is a specified offence for the purposes of section 224 of the Criminal Justice Act 2003

Triable only summarily

Maximum (section 39): 26 weeks' custody

Triable either way

Maximum (section 29): 2 years' custody

Offence range: Discharge—26 weeks' custody

STEP ONE Determining the Offence Category

The court should determine the offence category using the table below.

Category 1	Greater harm (injury or fear of injury must normally be present) **and** higher culpability
Category 2	Greater harm (injury or fear of injury must normally be present) **and** lower culpability; **or** lesser harm and higher culpability
Category 3	Lesser harm **and** lower culpability

The court should determine the offender's culpability and the harm caused, or intended, by reference **only** to the factors below (as demonstrated by the presence of one or more). These factors comprise the principal factual elements of the offence and should determine the category.

Factors indicating greater harm	Factors indicating lesser harm
Injury or fear of injury which is serious in the context of the offence (must normally be present) Victim is particularly vulnerable because of personal circumstances Sustained or repeated assault on the same victim	Injury which is less serious in the context of the offence
Factors indicating higher culpability *Statutory aggravating factors:* Offence motivated by, or demonstrating, hostility to the victim based on his or her sexual orientation (or presumed sexual orientation) Offence motivated by, or demonstrating, hostility to the victim based on the victim's disability (or presumed disability) *Other aggravating factors:* A significant degree of premeditation Threatened or actual use of weapon or weapon equivalent (for example, shod foot, headbutting, use of acid, use of animal) Intention to commit more serious harm than actually resulted from the offence Deliberately causes more harm than is necessary for commission of offence Deliberate targeting of vulnerable victim Leading role in group or gang Offence motivated by, or demonstrating, hostility based on the victim's age, sex, gender identity (or presumed gender identity)	**Factors indicating lower culpability** Subordinate role in group or gang A greater degree of provocation than normally expected Lack of premeditation Mental disorder or learning disability, where linked to commission of the offence Excessive self defence

STEP TWO Starting point and category range

Having determined the category, the court should use the corresponding starting points to reach a sentence within the category range below. The starting point applies to all offenders irrespective of plea or previous convictions. A case of particular gravity, reflected by multiple features of culpability in step one, could merit upward adjustment from the starting point before further adjustment for aggravating or mitigating features, set out below.

Offence Category	Starting Point (*Applicable to all offenders*)	Category Range (*Applicable to all offenders*)
Category 1	**High level community order**	**Low level community order–26 weeks' custody**
Category 2	**Medium level community order**	**Band A fine–High level community order**
Category 3	**Band A fine**	**Discharge–Band C fine**

The table below contains a **non-exhaustive** list of additional factual elements providing the context of the offence and factors relating to the offender. Identify whether any combination of these, or other relevant factors, should result in an upward or downward adjustment from the starting point. In some cases, having considered these factors, it may be appropriate to move outside the identified category range.

When sentencing **category 1** offences, the court should also consider the custody threshold as follows:

- Has the custody threshold been passed?
- If so, is it unavoidable that a custodial sentence be imposed?
- If so, can that sentence be suspended?

When sentencing **category 2** offences, the court should also consider the community order threshold as follows:

- Has the community order threshold been passed?

Factors increasing seriousness	Factors reducing seriousness or reflecting personal mitigation
Statutory aggravating factors: Previous convictions, having regard to a) the nature of the offence to which the conviction relates and its relevance to the current offence; and b) the time that has elapsed since the conviction Offence committed whilst on bail *Other aggravating factors include:* Location of the offence Timing of the offence Ongoing effect upon the victim Offence committed against those working in the public sector or providing a service to the public Presence of others including relatives, especially children or partner of the victim Gratuitous degradation of victim In domestic violence cases, victim forced to leave their home Failure to comply with current court orders Offence committed whilst on licence An attempt to conceal or dispose of evidence Failure to respond to warnings or concerns expressed by others about the offender's behaviour Commission of offence whilst under the influence of alcohol or drugs Abuse of power and/or position of trust Exploiting contact arrangements with a child to commit an offence Established evidence of community impact Any steps taken to prevent the victim reporting an incident, obtaining assistance and/or from assisting or supporting the prosecution Offences taken into consideration (TICs)	No previous convictions **or** no relevant/recent convictions Single blow Remorse Good character and/or exemplary conduct Determination and/or demonstration of steps taken to address addiction or offending behaviour Serious medical conditions requiring urgent, intensive or long-term treatment Isolated incident Age and/or lack of maturity where it affects the responsibility of the offender Lapse of time since the offence where this is not the fault of the offender Mental disorder or learning disability, where **not** linked to the commission of the offence Sole or primary carer for dependent relatives

Section 29 offences only: The court should determine the appropriate sentence for the offence without taking account of the element of aggravation and then make an addition to the sentence, considering the level of aggravation involved. It may be appropriate to move outside the identified category range, taking into account the increased statutory maximum.

[Steps Three to Nine are almost identical to those for inflicting grievous bodily harm: see **SG-206**.]

SG-212 ANNEX: FINE BANDS AND COMMUNITY ORDERS

[The tables set out here are also set out in the Magistrates' Court Sentencing Guidelines, which includes further guidance on fines and community orders: see **SG-358** and **SG-382**.]

SG-213 PART 11 OVERARCHING PRINCIPLES: ASSAULTS ON CHILDREN AND CRUELTY TO A CHILD

FOREWORD

...This guideline applies to the sentencing of offenders on or after 3 March 2008.

In a separate guideline the Council has set out the principles and guidance relevant to the sentencing of assault offences ranging from common assault at the lowest end of the seriousness scale, up to wounding or causing grievous bodily harm with intent.

This guideline details additional relevant principles for sentencing where the assault was on a child.

In addition, this guideline defines sentencing principles, starting points and ranges for the offence of cruelty to a child which may involve a variety of types of conduct and stem from a pattern of offending behaviour against a child rather than an isolated assault....

SG-214 **Introduction and structure of the guideline**[103]

1. The Council has produced a separate guideline covering offences of assault which do not result in the death of the victim, ranging in seriousness from common assault to wounding or causing grievous bodily harm with intent. Those offences involve the infliction of permanent or temporary harm on a victim by direct action, or an intention to cause harm to a victim even if harm does not in fact result.
2. That guideline applies only to the sentencing of offenders aged 18 and older convicted of assault, primarily where the victim of the assault is aged 16 or over. It covers:
   - assessing the culpability of the offender and the harm caused;
   - relevant aggravating and mitigating factors;
   - use of a weapon and particular parts of the body;
   - aggravated assaults;
   - provocation as mitigation;
   - compensating victims, and
   - ancillary orders.
3. In **Part 1** of this guideline additional principles are set out which should be considered when the victim of an assault is a child (aged 15 years and under).
4. **Part 2** provides guidance in relation to the offence of cruelty to a child[104] which has a wide-ranging definition that can include assault but also other forms of conduct likely to cause a child under 16 years of age unnecessary suffering or injury to health.

Part 1: Assaults on children: General principles

SG-215 **A. Assessing seriousness**

5. The primary factor in considering sentence is the seriousness of the offence committed; that is determined by assessing the culpability of the offender and the harm caused, intended or reasonably foreseeable.[105] A community sentence can be imposed only if the court considers that the offence is serious enough to justify it[106] and a custodial sentence can be imposed only if the court considers that a community sentence or a fine alone cannot be justified in view of the seriousness of the offence.[107] The Council has published a definitive guideline that guides sentencers determining whether the respective thresholds have been crossed.[108]
6. In considering the seriousness of an offence committed by an offender who has one or more previous convictions, the court must consider whether it should treat any of them as an aggravating factor

103 Assault and other offences against the person; www.sentencing-guidelines.gov.uk
104 Children and Young Persons Act 1933, section 1(1)
105 Criminal Justice Act 2003, section 152(2)
106 ibid, section 148(1)
107 ibid, section 152(2)
108 *Overarching Principles: Seriousness* published on 16 December 2004; www.sentencing-guidelines.gov.uk

having regard to the nature of the offence to which each conviction relates and its relevance to the current offence, and the time that has elapsed since the conviction.[109]

7. When dealing with cases involving assaults committed by adults against children, many of which involved some of the aggravating factors described below, the Court of Appeal has given a consistent message that an assault against a child will normally merit a custodial sentence. The Council's view is that such a presumption will not always be appropriate, but in all cases, the fact that the victim is a child is likely to aggravate the seriousness of the offence where the offender is an adult.

(i) Aggravation

8. The fact that the victim of an assault is a child will often mean that the offence involves a particularly vulnerable victim.
9. For all offences of assault, where the offence has been committed by an adult offender and the victim is a child under 16 years, the most relevant aggravating factors, as listed in the Council guideline *Overarching Principles: Seriousness*, are likely to be those set out below. Many of those are most likely to be present where the defendant has caring responsibilities for the child:
   - victim is particularly vulnerable;
   - abuse of power;
   - abuse of position of trust;
   - an especially serious physical or psychological effect on the victim, even if unintended;
   - presence of others e.g. relatives, especially other children;
   - additional degradation of the victim.

   Additional aggravating factors are:
   - sadistic behaviour;
   - threats to prevent the victim reporting the offence;
   - deliberate concealment of the victim from the authorities; and
   - failure to seek medical help.
10. Many offences committed by adults against children will involve an abuse of power and many also will include an abuse of a position of trust. The Education Act 1996 abolished the right of teachers and other school staff to administer corporal punishment.[110]
11. The location of the offence, for example the fact that an offence takes place in the child's home, and the particular circumstances, such as the fact that the victim is isolated—common aggravating factors in cases of child cruelty—may also be present in relation to individual offences of assault against children.

(ii) Mitigation

12. An offender might seek to argue that any harm caused to the child amounted to lawful chastisement and a court might form the view that the offender held a genuine belief that his or her actions amounted to no more than a legitimate form of physical punishment. The defence of lawful chastisement is available only in relation to a charge of common assault. Where that defence is not available, or, in relation to a charge of common assault, such a defence has failed, sentence for the offence would normally be approached in the same way as any other assault.
13. There will be circumstances where the defendant has been charged with an assault occasioning actual bodily harm and the court finds as fact that the defendant only intended to administer lawful chastisement to the child, and the injury that was inflicted was neither intended nor foreseen by the defendant.
14. Although the defendant would have intended nothing more than lawful chastisement (as currently allowed by the law), he or she would have no defence to such a charge because an assault occasioning actual bodily harm does not require the offender to intend or even foresee that his act will result in any physical harm; it is sufficient that it did. Such a finding of fact should result in a substantial reduction in sentence and should not normally result in a custodial sentence. Where not only was the injury neither intended nor foreseen, but was not even reasonably foreseeable, then a discharge might be appropriate.

B. Other factors relevant to sentencing SG-216

(i) The adverse effect of the sentence on the victim

15. In many circumstances, an offence of assault on a child will cause the court to conclude that only a custodial sentence can be justified. Imposition of such a sentence will often protect a victim from

[109] Criminal Justice Act 2003, section 143(2)
[110] Section 548

further harm and anguish; some children will be less traumatised once they are no longer living with an abusive carer.

16. However, where imprisonment of the offender deprives a child victim of his or her sole or main carer (and may result in the child being taken into care), it may punish and re-victimise the child.
17. In view of the seriousness of the offence committed and the risk of further harm to the victim or other children, even though a child may be distressed by separation from a parent or carer, imposing a custodial sentence on the offender may be the only option. However, where sentencing options remain more open, the court should take into account the impact that a custodial sentence for the offender might have on the victim.
18. There will be cases where the child victim is the subject of concurrent care proceedings and, indeed, the child's future care arrangements may well have been determined by the time the offender is sentenced. Both the sentencing court and the Family Court need to be aware of the progress of any concurrent proceedings.
19. **In considering whether a custodial sentence is the most appropriate disposal for an offence of assault on a child the court should take into account any available information concerning the future care of the child.**

(ii) Offenders who have primary care responsibilities

20. The gender of an offender is irrelevant for sentencing purposes. The important factor for consideration is the offender's role as sole or primary carer of the victim or other children or dependants.
21. In cases where an immediate custodial sentence of less than 12 months is justified, it is possible that a suspended sentence order (where available) might be the most appropriate sentence. This could enable the offender, subject to the necessary risk assessment being made, to resume care for, or at least have regular contact with, the child and could also open up opportunities for imposing requirements to rehabilitate and support an offender in need. In practice, this principle is likely to benefit more women than men, firstly because women commit the larger proportion of offences and secondly because men are less likely to be the sole or primary carers of children but the principle is established on the grounds of carer status and not gender.
22. **Where the offender is the sole or primary carer of the victim or other dependants, this potentially should be taken into account for sentencing purposes, regardless of whether the offender is male or female. In such cases, an immediate custodial sentence may not be appropriate and, subject to a risk assessment, the offender may be able to resume care for or have contact with the victim.**

Part 2: Cruelty to a child

SG-217 **A. Statutory provision**

23. [Sets out the CYPA 1933, s. 1(1) (see **B2.137** in the main work).][111]

SG-218 **B. Forms of cruelty to a child**

24. As is clear from the definition, the offence covers a variety of types of conduct that can compendiously or separately amount to child cruelty. The four generally accepted categories are:
    (i) assault and ill-treatment;
    (ii) failure to protect;
    (iii) neglect; and
    (iv) abandonment.
25. With regard to assaults, the CPS Charging Standard[112] suggests that an assault charged as child cruelty will differ in nature from that which is generally charged as an offence against the person and notes that 'the offence is particularly relevant in cases of cruelty over a period of time.' As such, it is more likely to apply to offences where there is evidence that a child was assaulted by someone with caring responsibility during a certain period but where there is no clear evidence of any particular incidents, the extent of those incidents or the specific time of the incidents.
26. Where a serious assault has been committed, the CPS Charging Standard advises that a charge of child cruelty will not be appropriate and that the most appropriate offence against the person should be charged in such circumstances.[113]

[111] In addition to the Children and Young Persons Act 1933 the UN Convention on the Rights of the Child may be particularly relevant when dealing with this offence. Article 19 obliges States Parties to take all appropriate legislative, administrative, social and educational measures to protect the child from all forms of physical or mental violence, injury or abuse, neglect or negligent treatment, maltreatment or exploitation, including sexual abuse, while in the care of parent(s), legal guardian(s) or any other person who has the care of the child.

[112] The Charging Standard on Offences Against the Person; www.cps.gov.uk

[113] *Child Cruelty: Charging Practice*; www.cps.gov.uk/legal/section7

27. For the purposes of the offence, 'neglect' can mean physical and/or emotional neglect.

C. Assessing seriousness

SG-219

28. It is not appropriate to identify one category of child cruelty as being automatically more serious than another; there will be a multitude of scenarios, some of which will involve more than one type of cruelty, in which the seriousness of the types of cruelty judged one against another will vary markedly. A long period of neglect, for example, could, in some circumstances, be more harmful to a child than a short period of violence.
29. In order to assess properly the seriousness of an offence, the precise nature of the offence must be established before consideration is given to a range of contingent factors, including the defendants intent, the length of time over which the cruelty took place, and the degree of physical and psychological harm suffered by the victim.

(i) Culpability

30. Although the nature and degree of harm that was caused, was intended or was reasonably foreseeable will impact on the seriousness of an offence of child cruelty, the Council guideline[114] clearly establishes that culpability should be the initial factor in determining the seriousness of an offence. In child cruelty offences, where there is such a wide variation in the nature and degree of harm that can be caused to a victim, there will similarly be a considerable variation in levels of culpability.
31. Child cruelty may be the consequence of a wide range of factors including:
    - sadism
    - violence resulting from any number of causes
    - a reduced ability to protect a child in the face of aggression from an overbearing partner
    - indifference or apathy resulting from low intelligence or induced by alcohol or drug dependence
    - immaturity or social deprivation resulting in an inability to cope with the pressures of caring for children
    - psychiatric illness
32. In the short term, an offence might arise as the result of a momentary lack of control by an otherwise responsible and loving carer. The extent to which any of these factors might have contributed to the commission of an offence will be important in determining the culpability of the offender.
33. A court must strike a balance between the need to reflect the serious view which society takes of the ill-treatment of very young children and the need to protect those children, and also the pressures upon immature and inadequate parents attempting to cope with the problems of infancy.
34. The extent to which remorse should influence sentence will always have to be judged in the light of all the circumstances surrounding the case.
35. In view of the seriousness with which society as a whole regards child cruelty, the normal sentencing starting point for an offence of child cruelty should be a custodial sentence. The length of that sentence will be influenced, however, by the circumstances in which the offence took place.

(ii) Harm

36. In order to assist a court in assessing the exact nature and seriousness of an offence of child cruelty, the CPS Charging Standard[115] advises that 'it may be preferable to have two or more alternative allegations in order that conduct complained of is appropriately described' and this certainly seems to be of benefit to sentencers. Where an offender has been convicted of an offence of child cruelty and the indictment clearly states the nature of the offender's conduct—neglect for example—the sentencer can be clear about the nature of the conduct for which the offender is to be sentenced.
37. However, even if the nature of the offending behaviour can be identified, statute is silent as to the relative seriousness of the different types of child cruelty identified above, creating obvious difficulties for the sentencing court.
38. There is a significant distinction between cases of wilful ill-treatment which usually involve positive acts of abuse and physical violence, and cases of neglect which are typified by the absence of actions.
39. In some cases there will be physical injury, whether resulting directly from an assault or ill-treatment or resulting from a period of abandonment or neglect. In other cases the harm occasioned may be lack of proper care, attention or supervision or exposure to the risk of harm.
40. As to whether one form of cruelty is worse than another will depend not only on the degree to which the victim suffers as a result but also on the motivation and culpability of the offender, which can range from inadequate parenting skills and an inability to cope, or constantly prioritising the needs of the offender or the offender's partner over those of the child, through to purposeful, sadistic and systematic abuse.

114 *Overarching Principles: Seriousness*, page 5, published on 16 December 2004; www.sentencing-guidelines.gov.uk
115 The Charging Standard on Offences Against the Person; www.cps.gov.uk

(iii) Aggravating and mitigating factors

41. The *Seriousness* guideline[116] sets out aggravating and mitigating factors that are applicable to a wide range of cases. Not all will be relevant to the offence of cruelty to a child. Care needs to be taken to ensure that there is no double counting where an essential element of the offence charged might, in other circumstances, be an aggravating factor. The sentencing starting points for the offence of child cruelty have been calculated to reflect the inherent abuse of trust or power and these cannot be treated as aggravating factors.

42. The following additional factors will aggravate offences of child cruelty:
- targeting one particular child from the family
- sadistic behaviour
- threats to prevent the victim from reporting the offence
- deliberate concealment of the victim from the authorities
- failure to seek medical help

43. The following additional factor will mitigate offences of child cruelty:
- seeking medical help or bringing the situation to the notice of the authorities

SG-220 **D. Other factors relevant to sentencing**

(i) Long-term psychological harm

44. There is no immediately predictable link between a type of offending behaviour and the impact it may have on the victim, either in the immediate or long term. The innate resilience of children and the presence of protection from another adult or the wider environment are also important factors that will influence the impact of the offence upon the child.

45. However, victims of child cruelty will frequently suffer psychological as well as physical harm. The evidence of emotional and behavioural consequences of child abuse is frequently presented by the following characteristics:[117]
- impaired capacity to enjoy life—abused children often appear sad, preoccupied and listless;
- psychiatric or psychosomatic stress symptoms, for example, bed-wetting, tantrums, bizarre behaviour, eating problems etc;
- low self-esteem—children who have been abused often think they must be worthless to deserve such treatment;
- school learning problems, such as lack of concentration;
- withdrawal—many abused children withdraw from relationships with other children and become isolated and depressed;
- opposition/defiance—a generally negative, uncooperative attitude;
- hyper-vigilance—typified in the 'frozen watchfulness' expression;
- compulsivity—abused children sometimes compulsively carry out certain activities or rituals;
- pseudo-mature behaviour—a false appearance of independence or being excessively 'good' all the time or offering indiscriminate affection to any adult who takes an interest.

46. Abuse can also be evidenced by 'learned behaviour aggression' and a tendency for a victim of child cruelty to inflict violence on others. Victims may also mature into adults with poor parenting skills who perpetrate similar acts of cruelty on their own children.

47. There is an established general principle that the sentence imposed for an offence can be based both on what is known about the harm caused to an individual victim and, in some cases, what is known about the harm caused to society as a whole.

48. Whilst objective evidence about the degree of physical harm should be available at the point of sentence, psychological harm, especially that which may or may not manifest itself in the future, will be extremely difficult, and often impossible, to assess at the point of sentence. Where there is objective expert evidence about the particularly severe psychological trauma suffered by an individual victim, which indicates a more than usually serious degree of harm, this would be captured by the generic aggravating factor in the Council guideline—*An especially serious physical or psychological effect on the victim, even if unintended.*[118]

49. **The sentencing starting points for the offence of child cruelty have been calculated to reflect the likelihood of psychological harm and this cannot be treated as aggravating factors. Where there is an especially serious physical or psychological effect on the victim, even if unintended, this should increase sentence.**

---

[116] *Overarching Principles: Seriousness*, paragraphs 1.20–1.27, published on 16 December 2004; www.sentencing-guidelines.gov.uk

[117] 'The Effects of Physical Abuse and Neglect' in Wendy Stanton Rogers et al ed, *Child Abuse and Neglect*, The Open University 1992 page 206, citing a study by Martin, H.P. and Beezley P., 'Behavioural observations of abused children', *Developmental Medicine and Child Neurology*, Vol 19 (1977), pages 373–87

[118] *Overarching Principles: Seriousness*, page 7, published on 16 December 2004; www.sentencing-guidelines.gov.uk

(ii) The adverse effect of the sentence on the victim

50. Imposing a custodial sentence for an offence of child cruelty is the most appropriate outcome in most cases in that it properly reflects society's view of the seriousness of this type of offending behaviour and protects victims from further harm and anguish. In addition, it is not unreasonable to suppose that some children will be less traumatised once they are no longer living with an abusive carer.
51. However, there is a counter argument that, as the imprisonment of the offender may deprive a child victim of his or her sole or main carer and may result in the child being taken into care, a custodial sentence effectively punishes and re-victimises the child and, it is argued, should only be considered in the most serious of cases.
52. In some cases, even though a child may be distressed by separation from a parent or carer, imposing a custodial sentence on the offender may be the only option in view of the seriousness of the offence committed and the risk of further harm to the victim or other children. However, where sentencing options remain open, the court should take into account the impact that a custodial sentence for the offender might have on the victim.
53. In many cases the child victim will be the subject of concurrent care proceedings and, indeed, the child's future care arrangements may well have been determined by the time the offender is sentenced. Both the sentencing court and the Family Court need to be aware of the progress of any concurrent proceedings.
54. **In considering whether a custodial sentence is the most appropriate disposal for an offence of child cruelty, the court should take into account any available information concerning the future care of the child.**

(iii) Offenders who have primary care responsibilities

55. The gender of an offender is irrelevant for sentencing purposes. The important factor for consideration is the offender's role as sole or primary carer of the victim or other children or dependants.
56. In cases where an immediate custodial sentence of less than 12 months is justified, it is possible that a suspended sentence order might be the most appropriate sentence. This could enable the offender, subject to the necessary risk assessment being made, to resume care for, or at least have regular contact with, the child and could also open up opportunities for imposing requirements to rehabilitate and support an offender in need. In practice, this principle is likely to benefit more women than men, firstly because women commit the larger proportion of offences and secondly because men are less likely to be the sole or primary carers of children but the principle is established on the grounds of carer status and not gender.
57. **Where the offender is the sole or primary carer of the victim or other dependants, this potentially should be taken into account for sentencing purposes, regardless of whether the offender is male or female. In such cases, an immediate custodial sentence may not be appropriate and, subject to a risk assessment, the offender may be able to resume care for or have contact with the victim.**

(iv) Personal mitigation

58. There may be other factors that impact on an offender's behaviour towards children in his or her care and should legitimately influence the nature and length of the sentence passed in child cruelty cases.
59. In relation to the offence of cruelty to a child, the most relevant areas of personal mitigation are likely to be:
    - Mental illness/depression
    - Inability to cope with the pressures of parenthood
    - Lack of support
    - Sleep deprivation
    - Offender dominated by an abusive or stronger partner
    - Extreme behavioural difficulties in the child, often coupled with a lack of support
    - Inability to secure assistance or support services in spite of every effort having been made by the offender
60. It must be noted, however, that some of the factors identified above, in particular sleep deprivation, lack of support and an inability to cope could be regarded as an inherent part of caring for children, especially when a child is very young. Thus, such factors could be put forward in mitigation by most carers charged with an offence of child cruelty. It follows that, before being accepted in mitigation, there must be evidence that these factors were present to a high degree and had an identifiable and significant impact on the offender's behaviour.

E. Starting points and sentencing ranges **SG-221**

1. Typically, a guideline will apply to an offence that can be committed in a variety of circumstances with different levels of seriousness. It will apply to a first-time offender who has been convicted after a trial.

Within the guidelines, a first-time offender is a person who does not have a conviction which, by virtue of section 143(2) of the CJA 2003, must be treated as an aggravating factor.

2. As an aid to consistency of approach, the guidelines describe a number of types of activity which would fall within the broad definition of the offence. These are set out in a column headed 'Type/nature of activity'.
3. The expected approach is for a court to identify the description that most nearly matches the particular facts of the offence for which sentence is being imposed. This will identify a starting point from which the sentencer can depart to reflect aggravating or mitigating factors affecting the seriousness of the offence (beyond those contained within the column describing the type or nature of offence activity) to reach a provisional sentence.
4. The *sentencing range* is the bracket into which the provisional sentence will normally fall after having regard to factors which aggravate or mitigate the seriousness of the offence. The particular circumstances may, however, make it appropriate that the provisional sentence falls outside the range.
5. Where the offender has previous convictions which aggravate the seriousness of the current offence, that may take the provisional sentence beyond the range given, particularly where there are significant other aggravating factors present.
6. Once the provisional sentence has been identified by reference to those factors affecting the seriousness of the offence, the court will take into account any relevant factors of personal mitigation, which may take the sentence outside the range indicated in the guideline.
7. Where there has been a guilty plea, any reduction attributable to that plea will be applied to the sentence at this stage. This reduction may take the sentence below the range provided.
8. A court must give its reasons for imposing a sentence of a different kind or outside the range provided in the guidelines.[119]

SG-222 **The Decision Making Process**

The process . . . is intended to show that the sentencing approach for the offence of cruelty to a child is fluid and requires the structured exercise of discretion.

[Sets out the standard sequential decision making process: identify dangerous offenders, identify starting point, consider aggravating factors, consider mitigating factors, apply reduction for guilty plea, consider ancillary orders, review in light of the totality principle and give reasons.]

SG-223 **F. Factors to take into consideration**

1. Cruelty to a child is a specified offence for the purposes of section 224 of the Criminal Justice Act 2003 and sentencers should consider whether a sentence for public protection should be imposed. **The following guideline applies to offenders who have *not* been assessed as dangerous.**
2. The suggested starting points and sentencing ranges in the guideline are based upon a first-time adult offender convicted after a trial (see . . . above).
3. The same starting point and sentencing range is proposed for offences which might fall into the four categories (assault; ill-treatment or neglect; and abandonment). These are designed to take into account the fact that the victim is particularly vulnerable, assuming an abuse of trust or power and the likelihood of psychological harm, and designed to reflect the seriousness with which society as a whole regards these offences, is proposed for an offence in each.
4. Only additional aggravating and mitigating factors specifically relevant to this offence are included in the guideline. When assessing the seriousness of any offence, the courts must always refer to the full list of aggravating and mitigating factors in the Council guideline on Seriousness.[120]
5. Where there is an especially serious physical or psychological effect on the victim, even if unintended, this should increase sentence.
6. In considering whether a custodial sentence is the most appropriate disposal for an offence of child cruelty, the court should take into account any available information concerning the future care of the child.
7. Where the offender is the sole or primary carer of the victim or other dependants, this potentially should be taken into account for sentencing purposes, regardless of whether the offender is male or female. In such cases, an immediate custodial sentence may not be appropriate.
8. Sentencers should take into account relevant matters of personal mitigation such as those suggested at paragraph 59 above.

[119] Criminal Justice Act 2003, section 174(2)(a)

[120] *Overarching Principles: Seriousness*, published on 16 December 2004; www.sentencing-guidelines.gov.uk

Cruelty to a child SG-224

Children and Young Persons Act 1933 (section 1(1))

THIS IS A SERIOUS OFFENCE FOR THE PURPOSES OF SECTION 224 CRIMINAL JUSTICE ACT 2003.

Maximum penalty: 10 years imprisonment

Nature of failure & harm	Starting point	Sentencing range
(i) Serious cruelty over a period of time. (ii) Serious long-term neglect. (iii) Failure to protect a child from either of the above.	6 years' custody	5–9 years' custody
(i) Series of assaults (the more serious the individual assaults and the longer the period over which they are perpetrated, the more serious the offence). (ii) Protracted neglect or ill-treatment (the longer the period of ill-treatment or neglect and the longer the period over which it takes place, the more serious the offence). (iii) Failure to protect a child from either of the above.	3 years' custody	2–5 years' custody
(i) Assault(s) resulting in injuries consistent with ABH. (ii) More than one incident of neglect or ill-treatment (but not amounting to long-term behaviour). (iii) Single incident of long-term abandonment OR regular incidents of short-term abandonment (the longer the period of long-term abandonment or the greater the number of incidents of short-term abandonment) the more serious the offence). (iv) Failure to protect a child from any of the above.	36 weeks' custody	26 weeks'–2 years' custody
(i) Short-term neglect or ill-treatment. (ii) Single incident of short-term abandonment. (iii) Failure to protect a child from any of the above.	12 weeks' custody	Community Order (LOW)–26 weeks' custody

Additional aggravating factors	Additional mitigating factors
1. Targeting one particular child from the family. 2. Sadistic behaviour. 3. Threats to prevent the victim from reporting the offence. 4. Deliberate concealment of the victim from the authorities. 5. Failure to seek medical help.	1. Seeking medical help or bringing the situation to the notice of the authorities.

PART 12 MAGISTRATES' COURT SENTENCING GUIDELINES SG-225

What's included in the Magistrates' Court Sentencing Guidelines

- Overarching guidelines issued by the Sentencing Council…
- Guidelines and guidance issued by the Sentencing Guidelines Council:
  - offence guidelines…
  - motoring offence guidelines…and
  - explanatory material…
- Offence specific guidelines issued by the Sentencing Council….
- In some instances, the guidelines previously issued by the Sentencing Guidelines Council and Court of Appeal have been necessarily summarised; the original guideline or Court of Appeal judgment should be consulted for comprehensive guidance.

Following these guidelines

When sentencing offences committed after 6 April 2010, every court is under a statutory obligation to follow any relevant Council guideline unless it would be contrary to the interests of justice to do so.[121] If a court imposes a sentence outside the range indicated in an offence specific guideline, it is obliged to state its reasons for doing so.[122]

When to use these guidelines

- These guidelines apply to sentencing in a magistrates' court whatever the composition of the court. They cover offences for which sentences are frequently imposed in a magistrates' court when dealing with adult offenders.
- They also apply to allocation (mode of trial) decisions. When dealing with an either way offence for which there is no plea or an indication of a not guilty plea, these guidelines will be relevant to the allocation decision and should be consulted at this stage.

In general, either way offences should be tried summarily unless it is likely that the court's sentencing powers will be insufficient and reference should be made to the definitive offence guidelines to assess the likely sentence. Reference should be made to the allocation guideline [at **SG-590**] which replaces the relevant sections of the Mode of Trial guidelines in Part V.51 of the *Consolidated Criminal Practice Direction*.

- These guidelines apply also to the Crown Court when dealing with appeals against sentences imposed in a magistrates' court and when sentencing for summary only offences.

...

SG-226

User Guide

[The User Guide briefly explains that the Magistrates' Court Sentencing Guidelines include two structures requiring different approaches by the user. Where offence guidelines (and motoring offence guidelines) were originally issued by the Sentencing Guidelines Council, one approach is to be followed; where offence guidelines have been issued by the Sentencing Council, another must be followed. The offence guidelines are set out below in accordance with the alphabetical order originally adopted on the issue of the Magistrates' Court Sentencing Guidelines, integrating guidelines from the Sentencing Council into that format. However, it should be noted that the guidelines for assault offences, theft offences, fraud, bribery and money laundering offences, burglary offences, most drugs offences, offences relating to dangerous dogs, sexual offences and environmental offences were issued by the Sentencing Council and are thus subject to the second approach mentioned above (see **SG-233**).]

[User Guide applicable where offence guidelines issued by the Sentencing Guidelines Council]

1. Assess offence seriousness (culpability and harm)

Offence seriousness is the starting point for sentencing under the Criminal Justice Act 2003. The court's assessment of offence seriousness will:

- determine which of the sentencing thresholds has been crossed;
- indicate whether a custodial, community or other sentence is the most appropriate;
- be the key factor in deciding the length of a custodial sentence, the onerousness of requirements to be incorporated in a community sentence and the amount of any fine

When considering the seriousness of any offence, the court must consider the offender's *culpability* in committing the offence and any *harm* which the offence caused, was intended to cause, or might forseeably have caused.[123] In using these guidelines, this assessment should be approached in two stages:

SG-227 **1. Offence seriousness (culpability and harm)**

A. Identify the appropriate starting point

The guidelines set out *examples* of the nature of activity which may constitute the offence, progressing from less to more serious conduct, and provide a *starting point* based on a *first time offender pleading not guilty*. The guidelines also specify a sentencing *range for* each example of activity. Refer [below] for further guidance on the meaning of the terms 'starting point', 'range' and 'first time offender'.

---

[121] Coroners and Justice Act 2009, section 125(1)

[122] Criminal Justice Act 2003, section 174(2)(a)

[123] Criminal Justice Act 2003, section 143(1)

Sentencers should begin by considering which of the examples of offence activity corresponds most closely to the circumstances of the particular case in order to identify the appropriate *starting point:*

- where the starting point is a fine, this is indicated as band A, B or C. The approach to assessing fines is set out [below];
- where the community sentence threshold is passed, the guideline sets out whether the starting point should be a low, medium or high level community order. Refer [below] for further guidance;
- where the starting point is a custodial sentence, refer [below] for further guidance.

The Council's definitive guideline *Overarching Principles: Seriousness*, published 16 December 2004 [see SG-21], identifies four levels of culpability for sentencing purposes (intention, recklessness, knowledge and negligence). The starting points in the individual offence guidelines assume that culpability is at the highest level applicable to the offence (often, but not always, intention). *Where a lower level of culpability is present, this should be taken into account.*

1. Offence seriousness (culpability and harm) **SG-228**

B. Consider the effect of aggravating and mitigating factors

Once the starting point has been identified, the court can add to or reduce this to reflect any aggravating or mitigating factors that impact on the *culpability* of the offender and/or *harm* caused by the offence to reach a provisional sentence. Any factors contained in the description of the activity used to reach the starting point must not be counted again.

The *range* is the bracket into which the provisional sentence will normally fall after having regard to factors which aggravate or mitigate the seriousness of the offence.

However:

- the court is not precluded from going outside the range where the facts justify it;
- previous convictions which aggravate the seriousness of the current offence may take the provisional sentence beyond the range, especially where there are significant other aggravating factors present.

In addition, where an offender is being sentenced for multiple offences, the courts assessment of the totality of the offending may result in a sentence above the range indicated for the individual offences, including a sentence of a different type. Refer [below] for further guidance.

The guidelines identify aggravating and mitigating factors which may be particularly relevant to each individual offence. These include some factors drawn from the general list of aggravating and mitigating factors in the Council's definitive guideline *Overarching Principles: Seriousness.* In each case, sentencers should have regard to the full list, which includes the factors that, by statute, make an offence more serious:

- offence committed while on bail for other offences;
- offence was racially or religiously aggravated;
- offence was motivated by, or demonstrates, hostility based on the victim's sexual orientation (or presumed sexual orientation);
- offence was motivated by, or demonstrates, hostility based on the victim's disability (or presumed disability);
- offender has previous convictions that the court considers can reasonably be treated as aggravating factors having regard to their relevance to the current offence and the time that has elapsed since conviction.

While the lists…aim to identify the most common aggravating and mitigating factors, *they are not intended to be exhaustive.* Sentencers should always consider whether there are any other factors that make the offence more or less serious.

2. Form a preliminary view of the appropriate sentence, then consider offender mitigation **SG-229**

When the court has reached a provisional sentence based on its assessment of offence seriousness, it should take into account matters of offender mitigation. The Council guideline *Overarching Principles: Seriousness* states that the issue of remorse should be taken into account at this point along with other mitigating features such as admissions to the police in interview.

3. Consider a reduction for a guilty plea **SG-230**

The Council guideline *Reduction in Sentence for a Guilty Plea* [set out in full in **part 1**] states that the *punitive* elements of the sentence should be reduced to recognise an offender's guilty plea. The reduction has no impact on sentencing decisions in relation to ancillary orders, including disqualification.

The level of the reduction should reflect the stage at which the offender indicated a willingness to admit guilt and will be gauged on a sliding scale, ranging from a *recommended* one third (where the guilty plea was entered at the first reasonable opportunity), reducing to a *recommended* one quarter (where a trial date has been set) and to a *recommended* one tenth (for a guilty plea entered at the 'door of the court' or after the trial has begun). There is a presumption that the recommended reduction will be given unless there are good reasons for a lower amount.

The application of the reduction may affect the type, as well as the severity, of the sentence. It may also take the sentence below the *range* in some cases.

The court must state that it has reduced a sentence to reflect a guilty plea.[124] It should usually indicate what the sentence would have been if there had been no reduction as a result of the plea.

SG-231 **4. Consider ancillary orders, including compensation**

Ancillary orders of particular relevance to individual offences are identified in the relevant guidelines.

The court must *always* consider making a compensation order where the offending has resulted in personal injury, loss or damage.[125] The court is required to give reasons if it decides not to make such an order.[126]

SG-232 **5. Decide sentence: Give reasons**

Sentencers must state reasons for the sentence passed in every case, including for any ancillary orders imposed.[127] It is particularly important to identify any aggravating or mitigating factors, or matters of offender mitigation, that have resulted in a sentence more or less severe than the suggested starting point.

If a court imposes a sentence of a different kind or outside the *range* indicated in the guidelines, *it must state its reasons for doing so.*[128]

The court should also give its reasons for not making an order that has been canvassed before it or that it might have been expected to make.

SG-233 **[User Guide applicable where offence guidelines issued by the Sentencing Council]**

Step One: Determining the offence category

The decision making process includes a two step approach to assessing seriousness. The first step is to determine the offence category by means of an assessment of the offender's culpability and the harm caused, or intended, by reference *only* to the factors set out at step one in each guideline. The contents are tailored for each offence and comprise the principal factual elements of the offence.

Step Two: Starting point and category range

The guidelines provide a *starting point* which applies to all offenders irrespective of plea or previous convictions. The guidelines also specify a *category range* for each offence category.

The guidelines provide non-exhaustive lists of aggravating and mitigating factors relating to the context of the offence and to the offender. Sentencers should identify whether any combination of these, or other relevant factors, should result in an upward or downward adjustment from the starting point.

In some cases, it may be appropriate to move outside the identified category range when reaching a provisional sentence.

Further Steps

Having reached a provisional sentence, there are a number of further steps within the guidelines. These steps are clearly set out within each guideline and are tailored specifically for each offence in order to ensure that only the most appropriate guidance is included within each offence specific guideline.

The further steps include:

- reduction for assistance to the prosecution;
- reduction for guilty pleas (courts should refer to the *Guilty Plea* guideline [at **SG-1**]);
- where an offender is being sentenced for multiple offences — the court's assessment of the totality of the offending may result in a sentence above the range indicated for the individual offences,

124 Criminal Justice Act 2003, section 174(2)(d)
125 Powers of Criminal Courts (Sentencing) Act 2000, section 130(1)
126 ibid, section 130(3)
127 Criminal Justice Act 2003, section 174(1)
128 ibid, section 174(2)(a)

including a sentence of a different type (refer to [the Totality Guideline at **SG-578**] for further guidance);

- compensation orders and/or ancillary orders appropriate to the case; and
- reasons for, and explain the effect of, the sentence.

Allocation Guideline **SG-234**
[Not reproduced here: see **SG-590**.]

Offences Taken into Consideration Guideline **SG-235**
[Not reproduced here: see **SG-572**.]

Totality Guideline **SG-236**
[Not reproduced here: see **SG-578**.]

Offences **SG-237**

Alcohol Sale Offences

Licensing Act 2003, s. 141 (sale of alcohol to drunk person); s. 146 (sale of alcohol to children); s. 147 (allowing sale of alcohol to children)

Triable only summarily:

Examples of nature of activity	Starting point	Range
Sale to a child (i.e. person under 18)/to a drunk person	**Band B fine**	**Band A fine to band C fine**

Maximum: Level 3 fine (s.141); Level 5 fine (ss.146 and 147)

Offence seriousness (culpability and harm)

A. Identify the appropriate starting point
Starting points based on first time offender pleading not guilty

Note: refer to [below] for approach to fines for offences committed for commercial purposes

B. Consider the effect of aggravating and mitigating factors (other than those within examples above)

Common aggravating and mitigating factors are identified [elsewhere]—the following may be particularly relevant but these lists are not exhaustive

Factors indicating higher culpability	Factors indicating greater degree of harm
1. No attempt made to establish age 2. Spirits/high alcohol level of drink 3. Drunk person highly intoxicated 4. Large quantity of alcohol supplied 5. Sale intended for consumption by group of children/drunk people 6. Offender in senior or management position	1. Younger child/children 2. Drunk person causing distress to others 3. Drunk person aggressive

[Sets out the standard sequential sentencing procedure but specifies the need to consider the forfeiture or suspension of a personal liquor licence.]

Note: Section 23 of the Violent Crime Reduction Act 2006 created a new offence of persistently selling alcohol to children, which came into force on 6 April 2007. This is committed if, on three or more different occasions within a period of three consecutive months, alcohol is unlawfully sold on the same premises to a person under 18. The offence is summary only and the maximum penalty is a £10,000 fine. *Consult your legal adviser for guidance on the approach to sentencing and the court's powers in relation to liquor licences.*

Sentencing Guidelines

SG-238

Animal Cruelty

Animal Welfare Act 2006, s. 4 (unnecessary suffering); s. 8 (fighting etc.); s. 9 (breach of duty of person responsible for animal to ensure welfare)

Triable only summarily:
Maximum: £20,000 fine and/or 6 months (ss. 4 and 8) Level 5 fine and/or 6 months (s. 9)

Offence seriousness (culpability and harm)

A. Identify the appropriate starting point

Starting points based on first time offender pleading not guilty

Examples of nature of activity	Starting point	Range
One impulsive act causing little or no injury; short term neglect	Band C fine	Band B fine–medium level community order
Several incidents of deliberate ill-treatment/frightening animal(s); medium term neglect	High level community order	Medium level community order–12 weeks' custody
Attempt to kill/torture; animal baiting/conducting or permitting cock-fighting etc.; prolonged neglect	18 weeks' custody	12–26 weeks' custody

Offence seriousness (culpability and harm)

B. Consider the effect of aggravating and mitigating factors (other than those within examples above)

Common aggravating and mitigating factors are identified [elsewhere]—the following may be particularly relevant but these lists are not exhaustive

Factors indicating higher culpability	Factors indicating greater degree of harm
1. Offender in position of special responsibility 2. Adult involves children in offending 3. Animal(s) kept for livelihood 4. Use of weapon 5. Offender ignored advice/warnings 6. Offence committed for commercial gain	1. Serious injury or death 2. Several animals affected **Factors indicating lower culpability** 1. Offender induced by others 2. Ignorance of appropriate care 3. Offender with limited capacity

[Sets out the standard sequential sentencing procedure but also mentions the need to consider disqualification from ownership of animal.]

SG-239

Anti-social Behaviour Order, Breach Of

Factors to take into consideration

This guideline and accompanying notes are taken from the Sentencing Guidelines Council's definitive guideline *Breach of an Anti-Social Behaviour Order*, published 9 December 2008 [see **SG-458**].

Key factors

(a) An ASBO may be breached in a very wide range of circumstances and may involve one or more terms not being complied with. The examples given below are intended to illustrate how the scale of the conduct that led to the breach, taken as a whole, might come within the three levels of seriousness:
- No harm caused or intended—in the absence of intimidation or the causing of fear of violence, breaches involving being drunk or begging may be at this level, as may prohibited use of public

transport or entry into a prohibited area, where there is no evidence that harassment, alarm or distress was caused or intended.

- Lesser degree of harm intended or likely—examples may include lesser degrees of threats or intimidation, the use of seriously abusive language, or causing more than minor damage to property.
- Serious harm caused or intended—breach at this level of seriousness will involve the use of violence, significant threats or intimidation or the targeting of individuals or groups of people in a manner that leads to a fear of violence.

(b) The suggested starting points are based on the assumption that the offender had the highest level of culpability.

(c) In the most serious cases, involving repeat offending and a breach causing serious harassment together with the presence of several aggravating factors, such as the use of violence, a sentence beyond the highest range will be justified.

(d) When imposing a community order, the court must ensure that the requirements imposed are proportionate to the seriousness of the breach, compatible with each other, and also with the prohibitions of the ASBO if the latter is to remain in force. Even where the threshold for a custodial sentence is crossed, a custodial sentence is not inevitable.

(e) An offender may be sentenced for more than one offence of breach, which occurred on different days. While consecutive sentences may be imposed in such cases, the overall sentence should reflect the totality principle.

Crime and Disorder Act 1988, s.1(10)

Triable either way:
Maximum when tried summarily: Level 5 fine and/or 6 months
Maximum when tried on indictment: 5 years

Note: A conditional discharge is not available as a sentence for this offence

Offence seriousness (culpability and harm)

A. Identify the appropriate starting point
Starting points based on first time offender* pleading not guilty

Examples of nature of activity	Starting point	Range
Breach where no harassment, alarm or distress was caused or intended	**Low level community order**	**Band B fine–medium level community order**
Breach involving a lesser degree of actual or intended harassment, alarm or distress than in the box below, or where such harm would have been likely had the offender not been apprehended	**6 weeks' custody**	**Medium level community order–26 weeks' custody**
Breach involving serious actual or intended harassment, alarm or distress	**26 weeks' custody**	**Custody threshold–Crown Court**

* *For the purposes of this guideline a 'first time offender' is one who does not have a previous conviction for breach of an ASBO*

Offence seriousness (culpability and harm)

B. Consider the effect of aggravating and mitigating factors (other than those within examples above)

Common aggravating and mitigating factors are identified [elsewhere]—the following may be particularly relevant but these lists are not exhaustive.

Factors indicating higher culpability	Factors indicating lower culpability
1. Offender has a history of disobedience to court orders 2. Breach was committed immediately or shortly after the order was made 3. Breach was committed subsequent to earlier breach proceedings arising from the same order 4. Targeting of a person the order was made to protect or a witness in the original proceedings	1. Breach occurred after a long period of compliance 2. The prohibition(s) breached was not fully understood, especially where an interim order was made without notice

[Sets out the standard sequential sentencing procedure.]

SG-240

Arson (Criminal Damage by Fire)

Criminal Damage Act 1971, s. 1

Triable either way:
Maximum when tried summarily: Level 5 fine and/or 6 months
Maximum when tried on indictment: Life
Where offence committed in domestic context, refer [below] for guidance.

Offence seriousness (culpability and harm)

A. Identify the appropriate starting point

Starting points based on first time offender pleading not guilty

Examples of nature of activity	Starting point	Range
Minor damage by fire	High level community order	Medium level community order–12 weeks' custody
Moderate damage by fire	12 weeks' custody	6–26 weeks' custody
Significant damage by fire	Crown Court	Crown Court

Offence seriousness (culpability and harm)

B. Consider the effect of aggravating and mitigating factors (other than those within examples above)

Common aggravating and mitigating factors are identified [elsewhere]—the following may be particularly relevant but these lists are not exhaustive

Factors indicating higher culpability	Factor indicating lower culpability
1. Revenge attack **Factors indicating greater degree of harm** 1. Damage to emergency equipment 2. Damage to public amenity 3. Significant public or private fear caused e.g. in domestic context	1. Damage caused recklessly

[Sets out the standard sequential sentencing procedure.]

ASSAULT OCCASIONING ACTUAL BODILY HARM SG-241

Offences against the Person Act 1861 (section 47)

RACIALLY/RELIGIOUSLY AGGRAVATED ABH

Crime and Disorder Act 1998 (section 29)

[This guideline was published by the Sentencing Council and has effect in respect of all sentences passed after 13 June 2011 on offenders aged 18 or older. It replaces the guideline which previously applied and which continued to have effect until that date.]

These are specified offences for the purposes of section 224 of the Criminal Justice Act 2003

Triable either way

Section 47
Maximum when tried summarily: Level 5 fine and/or 26 weeks' custody
Maximum when tried on indictment: 5 years' custody

Section 29
Maximum when tried summarily: Level 5 fine and/or 26 weeks' custody
Maximum when tried on indictment: 7 years' custody

Offence range: Fine—3 years' custody

This guideline applies to all offenders aged 18 and older, who are sentenced on or after 13 June 2011. The definitions [at **SG-349**] of 'starting point' and 'first time offender' do not apply for this guideline. Starting point and category ranges apply to all offenders in all cases, irrespective of plea or previous convictions.

STEP ONE Determining the offence category

The court should determine the offence category using the table below.

Category 1	Greater harm (serious injury must normally be present) **and** higher culpability
Category 2	Greater harm (serious injury must normally be present) **and** lower culpability; **or** lesser harm and higher culpability
Category 3	Lesser harm and lower culpability

The court should determine the offender's culpability and the harm caused, or intended, by reference only to the factors identified in the table below (as demonstrated by the presence of one or more). These factors comprise the principal factual elements of the offence and should determine the category.

Factors indicating greater harm Injury (which includes disease transmission and/or psychological harm) which is serious in the context of the offence (must normally be present) Victim is particularly vulnerable because of personal circumstances Sustained or repeated assault on the same victim	**Factors indicating lesser harm** Injury which is less serious in the context of the offence
Factors indicating higher culpability *Statutory aggravating factors:* Offence motivated by, or demonstrating, hostility to the victim based on his or her sexual orientation (or presumed sexual orientation) Offence motivated by, or demonstrating, hostility to the victim based on the victim's disability (or presumed disability) *Other aggravating factors:* A significant degree of premeditation Use of weapon or weapon equivalent (for example, shod foot, headbutting, use of acid, use of animal) Intention to commit more serious harm than actually resulted from the offence Deliberately causes more harm than is necessary for commission of offence Deliberate targeting of vulnerable victim Leading role in group or gang Offence motivated by, or demonstrating, hostility based on the victim's age, sex, gender identity (or presumed gender identity)	**Factors indicating lower culpability** Subordinate role in group or gang A greater degree of provocation than normally expected Lack of premeditation Mental disorder or learning disability, where linked to commission of the offence Excessive self defence

STEP TWO Starting point and category range

Having determined the category, the court should use the corresponding starting points to reach a sentence within the category range below. The starting point applies to all offenders irrespective of plea or previous convictions. A case of particular gravity, reflected by multiple features of culpability in step one, could merit upward adjustment from the starting point before further adjustment for aggravating or mitigating features, set out below.

Offence Category	**Starting Point** (*Applicable to all offenders*)	**Category Range** (*Applicable to all offenders*)
Category 1	Crown Court	Crown Court
Category 2	26 weeks' custody	Low level community order–Crown Court (51 weeks' custody)
Category 3	Medium level community order	Band A fine–High level community order

The table below contains a **non-exhaustive** list of additional factual elements providing the context of the offence and factors relating to the offender. Identify whether any combination of these, or other relevant factors, should result in an upward or downward adjustment from the starting point. In some cases, having considered these factors, it may be appropriate to move outside the identified category range.

When sentencing **category 2** offences, the court should also consider the custody threshold as follows:

- Has the custody threshold been passed?
- If so, is it unavoidable that a custodial sentence be imposed?
- If so, can that sentence be suspended?

When sentencing **category 3** offences, the court should also consider the community order threshold as follows:

- Has the community order threshold been passed?

Factors increasing seriousness	**Factors reducing seriousness or reflecting personal mitigation**
Statutory aggravating factors: Previous convictions, having regard to a) the nature of the offence to which the conviction relates and its relevance to the current offence; and b) the time that has elapsed since the conviction Offence committed whilst on bail *Other aggravating factors include:* Location of the offence Timing of the offence Ongoing effect upon the victim Offence committed against those working in the public sector or providing a service to the public Presence of others including relatives, especially children or partner of the victim Gratuitous degradation of victim In domestic violence cases, victim forced to leave their home Failure to comply with current court orders Offence committed whilst on licence An attempt to conceal or dispose of evidence Failure to respond to warnings or concerns expressed by others about the offender's behaviour Commission of offence whilst under the influence of alcohol or drugs Abuse of power and/or position of trust Exploiting contact arrangements with a child to commit an offence Established evidence of community impact Any steps taken to prevent the victim reporting an incident, obtaining assistance and/or from assisting or supporting the prosecution Offences taken into consideration (TICs)	No previous convictions **or** no relevant/recent convictions Single blow Remorse Good character and/or exemplary conduct Determination and/or demonstration of steps taken to address addiction or offending behaviour Serious medical conditions requiring urgent, intensive or long-term treatment Isolated incident Age and/or lack of maturity where it affects the responsibility of the offender Lapse of time since the offence where this is not the fault of the offender Mental disorder or learning disability, where **not** linked to the commission of the offence Sole or primary carer for dependent relatives

Section 29 offences only: The court should determine the appropriate sentence for the offence without taking account of the element of aggravation and then make an addition to the sentence, considering the level of aggravation involved. It may be appropriate to move outside the identified category range, taking into account the increased statutory maximum.

STEP THREE Consider any other factors which indicate a reduction, such as assistance to the prosecution

The court should take into account any rule of law by virtue of which an offender may receive a discounted sentence in consequence of assistance given (or offered) to the prosecutor or investigator.

STEP FOUR Reduction for guilty pleas

The court should take account of any potential reduction for a guilty plea in accordance with section 144 of the Criminal Justice Act 2003 and the Guilty Plea guideline.

STEP FIVE Dangerousness

Inflicting grievous bodily harm/Unlawful wounding and racially/religiously aggravated GBH/Unlawful wounding are specified offences within the meaning of Chapter 5 of the Criminal Justice Act 2003 and at this stage the court should consider whether having regard to the criteria contained in that Chapter it would be appropriate to award an extended sentence.

STEP SIX Totality principle

If sentencing an offender for more than one offence, or where the offender is already serving a sentence, consider whether the total sentence is just and proportionate to the offending behaviour.

STEP SEVEN Compensation and ancillary orders

In all cases, the court should consider whether to make compensation and/or other ancillary orders.

STEP EIGHT Reasons

Section 174 of the Criminal Justice Act 2003 imposes a duty to give reasons for, and explain the effect of, the sentence.

STEP NINE Consideration for remand time

Sentencers should take into consideration any remand time served in relation to the final sentence. The court should consider whether to give credit for time spent on remand in custody or on bail in accordance with sections 240 and 240A of the Criminal Justice Act 2003.

Assault with Intent to Resist Arrest SG-242

Offences against the Person Act 1861 (section 38)

[This guideline was published by the Sentencing Council and has effect in respect of all sentences passed after 13 June 2011 on offenders aged 18 or older. It replaces the guideline which previously applied and which continued to have effect until that date.]

This is a specified offence for the purposes of section 224 of the Criminal Justice Act 2003

Triable either way
Maximum when tried summarily: Level 5 fine and/or 26 weeks' custody
Maximum when tried on indictment: 2 years' custody

Offence range: Fine—51 weeks' custody

This guideline applies to all offenders aged 18 and older, who are sentenced on or after 13 June 2011. The definitions [at **SG-349**] of 'starting point' and 'first time offender' do not apply for this guideline. Starting point and category ranges apply to all offenders in all cases, irrespective of plea or previous convictions.

STEP ONE Determining the offence category

The court should determine the offence category using the table below.

Category 1	Greater harm **and** higher culpability
Category 2	Greater harm **and** lower culpability; or lesser harm **and** higher culpability
Category 3	Lesser harm **and** lower culpability

The court should determine the offender's culpability and the harm caused, or intended, by reference only to the factors identified in the table below (as demonstrated by the presence of one or more). These factors comprise the principal factual elements of the offence and should determine the category.

Factors indicating greater harm Sustained or repeated assault on the same victim	**Factors indicating lesser harm** Injury which is less serious in the context of the offence
Factors indicating higher culpability *Statutory aggravating factors:* Offence racially or religiously aggravated Offence motivated by, or demonstrating, hostility to the victim based on his or her sexual orientation(or presumed sexual orientation) Offence motivated by, or demonstrating, hostility to the victim based on the victim's disability (or presumed disability) *Other aggravating factors:* A significant degree of premeditation Use of weapon or weapon equivalent (for example, shod foot, headbutting, use of acid, use of animal) Intention to commit more serious harm than actually resulted from the offence Deliberately causes more harm than is necessary for commission of offence Leading role in group or gang Offence motivated by, or demonstrating, hostility based on the victim's age, sex, gender identity (or presumed gender identity)	**Factors indicating lower culpability** Subordinate role in group or gang Lack of premeditation Mental disorder or learning disability, where linked to commission of the offence

STEP TWO Starting point and category range

Having determined the category, the court should use the corresponding starting points to reach a sentence within the category range below. The starting point applies to all offenders irrespective of plea or previous convictions. A case of particular gravity, reflected by multiple features of culpability in step one, could merit upward adjustment from the starting point before further adjustment for aggravating or mitigating features, set out below.

Offence Category	Starting Point (*Applicable to all offenders*)	Category Range (*Applicable to all offenders*)
Category 1	26 weeks' custody	12 weeks' custody–Crown Court (51 weeks' custody)
Category 2	Medium level community order	Low level community order–High level community order
Category 3	Band B fine	Band A fine–Band C fine

The table below contains a **non-exhaustive** list of additional factual elements providing the context of the offence and factors relating to the offender. Identify whether any combination of these, or other relevant factors, should result in an upward or downward adjustment from the starting point. In some cases, having considered these factors, it may be appropriate to move outside the identified category range.

When sentencing **category 1** offences, the court should consider whether the sentence can be suspended.

Factors increasing seriousness	**Factors reducing seriousness or reflecting personal mitigation**
Statutory aggravating factors: Previous convictions, having regard to a) the nature of the offence to which the conviction relates and its relevance to the current offence; and b) the time that has elapsed since the conviction Offence committed whilst on bail *Other aggravating factors include:* Location of the offence Timing of the offence Ongoing effect upon the victim Gratuitous degradation of victim Failure to comply with current court orders Offence committed whilst on licence An attempt to conceal or dispose of evidence Failure to respond to warnings or concerns expressed by others about the offender's behaviour Commission of offence whilst under the influence of alcohol or drugs Established evidence of community impact Any steps taken to prevent the victim reporting an incident, obtaining assistance and/or from assisting or supporting the prosecution Offences taken into consideration (TICs)	No previous convictions or no relevant/recent convictions Single blow Remorse Good character and/or exemplary conduct Determination and/or demonstration of steps taken to address addiction or offending behaviour Serious medical conditions requiring urgent, intensive or long-term treatment Isolated incident Age and/or lack of maturity where it affects the responsibility of the defendant Mental disorder or learning disability, where not linked to the commission of the offence Sole or primary carer for dependent relatives

[Steps Three to Nine are almost identical to those which apply to assault occasioning actual bodily harm: see SG-241.]

Assault on a Police Constable in Execution of his Duty SG-243

Police Act 1996 (section 89)

[This guideline was published by the Sentencing Council and has effect in respect of all sentences passed after 13 June 2011 on offenders aged 18 or older. It replaces the guideline which previously applied and which continued to have effect until that date.]

Triable only summarily
Maximum: Level 5 fine and/or 26 weeks' custody

Offence range: Fine—26 weeks' custody

This guideline applies to all offenders aged 18 and older, who are sentenced on or after 13 June 2011. The definitions [at **SG-349**] of 'starting point' and 'first time offender' do not apply for this guideline. Starting point and category ranges apply to all offenders in all cases, irrespective of plea or previous convictions.

Sentencing Guidelines

STEP ONE Determining the offence category

The court should determine the offence category using the table below.

Category 1	Greater harm **and** higher culpability
Category 2	Greater harm **and** lower culpability; or lesser harm **and** higher culpability
Category 3	Lesser harm **and** lower culpability

The court should determine the offender's culpability and the harm caused, or intended, by reference only to the factors below (as demonstrated by the presence of one or more). These factors comprise the principal factual elements of the offence and should determine the category.

Factors indicating greater harm	Factors indicating lesser harm
Sustained or repeated assault on the same victim	Injury which is less serious in the context of the offence
Factors indicating higher culpability	**Factors indicating lower culpability**
Statutory aggravating factors: Offence racially or religiously aggravated Offence motivated by, or demonstrating, hostility to the victim based on his or her sexual orientation (or presumed sexual orientation) Offence motivated by, or demonstrating, hostility to the victim based on the victim's disability (or presumed disability) *Other aggravating factors:* A significant degree of premeditation Use of weapon or weapon equivalent (for example, shod foot, headbutting, use of acid, use of animal) Intention to commit more serious harm than actually resulted from the offence Deliberately causes more harm than is necessary for commission of offence Leading role in group or gang Offence motivated by, or demonstrating, hostility based on the victim's age, sex, gender identity (or presumed gender identity)	Subordinate role in group or gang Lack of premeditation Mental disorder or learning disability, where linked to commission of the offence

STEP TWO Starting point and category range

Having determined the category, the court should use the corresponding starting points to reach a sentence within the category range below. The starting point applies to all offenders irrespective of plea or previous convictions. A case of particular gravity, reflected by multiple features of culpability in step one, could merit upward adjustment from the starting point before further adjustment for aggravating or mitigating features, set out below.

Offence Category	Starting Point (*Applicable to all offenders*)	Category Range (*Applicable to all offenders*)
Category 1	12 weeks' custody	Low level community order–26 weeks' custody
Category 2	Medium level community order	Low level community order–High level community order
Category 3	Band B fine	Band A fine–Band C fine

The table below contains a **non-exhaustive** list of additional factual elements providing the context of the offence and factors relating to the offender. Identify whether any combination of these, or other relevant factors, should result in an upward or downward adjustment from the starting point. In some cases, having considered these factors, it may be appropriate to move outside the identified category range.

When sentencing **category 1** offences, the court should also consider the custody threshold as follows:

- Has the custody threshold been passed?
- If so, is it unavoidable that a custodial sentence be imposed?
- If so, can that sentence be suspended?

Factors increasing seriousness	Factors reducing seriousness or reflecting personal mitigation
Statutory aggravating factors: Previous convictions, having regard to a) the nature of the offence to which the conviction relates and its relevance to the current offence; and b) the time that has elapsed since the conviction Offence committed whilst on bail *Other aggravating factors include:* Location of the offence Timing of the offence Ongoing effect upon the victim Gratuitous degradation of victim Failure to comply with current court orders Offence committed whilst on licence An attempt to conceal or dispose of evidence Failure to respond to warnings or concerns expressed by others about the offender's behaviour Commission of offence whilst under the influence of alcohol or drugs Established evidence of community impact Any steps taken to prevent the victim reporting an incident, obtaining assistance and/or from assisting or supporting the prosecution Offences taken into consideration (TICs)	No previous convictions or no relevant/recent convictions Single blow Remorse Good character and/or exemplary conduct Determination and/or demonstration of steps taken to address addiction or offending behaviour Serious medical conditions requiring urgent, intensive or long-term treatment Isolated incident Age and/or lack of maturity where it affects the responsibility of the offender Lapse of time since the offence where this is not the fault of the offender Mental disorder or learning disability, where not linked to the commission of the offence Sole or primary carer for dependent relatives

[Steps Three to Eight are almost identical to Steps Three to Nine which apply to assault occasioning actual bodily harm (see **SG-241**) but Step Five (Dangerousness) is omitted.]

Bail, Failure to Surrender **SG-244**

Factors to take into consideration

This guideline and accompanying notes are taken from the Sentencing Guidelines Council's definitive guideline *Fail to Surrender to Bail*, published 29 November 2007 [see **SG-196**]

Key factors

(a) Whilst the approach to sentencing should generally be the same whether the offender failed to surrender to a court or to a police station *and* whether the offence is contrary to ss. 6(1) or 6(2), the court must examine all the relevant circumstances.

(b) The following factors may be relevant when assessing the harm caused by the offence:

- Where an offender fails to appear for a first court hearing but attends shortly afterwards, the only harm caused is likely to be the financial cost to the system. Where a case could not have proceeded even if the offender had surrendered to bail, this should be taken into account.
- Where an offender appears for trial on the wrong day but enters a late guilty plea enabling the case to be disposed of to some degree at least, the harm caused by the delay may be offset by the benefits stemming from the change of plea.
- The most serious harm is likely to result when an offender fails to appear for trial, especially if this results in witnesses being sent away. Where it has been possible to conclude proceedings in the absence of the offender, this may be relevant to the assessment of harm caused.
- The level of harm is likely to be assessed as high where an offender fails to appear for sentence and is also seen to be flouting the authority of the court, such as where the avoidance of sentence results in the consequential avoidance of ancillary orders such as disqualification from driving, the payment of compensation or registration as a sex offender. This may increase the level of harm whenever the offender continues to present a risk to public safety.
- Whilst the seriousness of the original offence does not of itself aggravate or mitigate the seriousness of the offence of failing to surrender, the circumstances surrounding the original offence may be relevant in assessing the harm arising from the Bail Act offence.

- The circumstances in which bail to return to a police station is granted are less formal than the grant of court bail and the history of the individual case should be examined. There may be less culpability where bail has been enlarged on a number of occasions and less harm if court proceedings are not significantly delayed.

(c) Where the failure to surrender to custody was 'deliberate':
- at or near the bottom of the sentencing range will be cases where the offender gave no thought at all to the consequences, or other mitigating factors are present, and the degree of delay or interference with the progress of the case was not significant in all the circumstances;
- at or near the top of the range will be cases where aggravating factors 1, 2 or 4 [below] are present if there is also a significant delay and/or interference with the progress of the case.

(d) A previous conviction that is likely to be 'relevant' for the purposes of this offence is one which demonstrates failure to comply with an order of a court.

(e) Acquittal of the original offence does not automatically mitigate the Bail Act offence.

(f) The fact that an offender has a disorganised or chaotic lifestyle should not normally be treated as offence mitigation, but may be regarded as offender mitigation depending on the particular facts.

(g) A misunderstanding which does not amount to a defence may be a mitigating factor whereas a mistake on the part of the offender is his or her own responsibility.

(h) Where an offender has literacy or language difficulties, these may be mitigation (where they do not amount to a defence) where potential problems were not identified and/or appropriate steps were not taken to mitigate the risk in the circumstances as known at the time that bail was granted.

(i) An offender's position as the sole or primary carer of dependent relatives may be offender mitigation when it is the reason why the offender failed to surrender to custody.

(j) The sentence for this offence should usually be in addition to any sentence for the original offence. Where custodial sentences are being imposed for a Bail Act offence and the original offence at the same time, the normal approach should be for the sentences to be consecutive. The length of any custodial sentence imposed must be commensurate with the seriousness of the offence(s).

(k) If an offence is serious enough to justify the imposition of a community order, a curfew requirement with an electronic monitoring requirement may be particularly appropriate—see [below].

Guidelines

Bail Act 1976, ss. 6(1) and 6(2)

Triable either way:
Maximum when tried summarily: Level 5 fine and/or 3 months
Maximum when tried on indictment: 12 months

In certain circumstances, a magistrates' court may commit to the Crown Court for sentence. *Consult your legal adviser for guidance.*

Offence seriousness (culpability and harm)

A. Identify the appropriate starting point

Starting points based on first time offender pleading not guilty

Examples of nature of activity	**Starting point**	**Range**
Surrenders late on day but case proceeds as planned	Band A fine	Band A fine–Band B fine
Negligent or non-deliberate failure to attend causing delay and/or interference with the administration of justice	Band C fine	Band B fine–medium level community order
Deliberate failure to attend causing delay and/or interference with the administration of justice	14 days' custody	Low level community order–10 weeks' custody

B. Consider the effect of aggravating and mitigating factors (other than those within examples above)

Common aggravating and mitigating factors are identified [elsewhere]—the following may be particularly relevant but these lists are not exhaustive

Factors indicating higher culpability	Factors indicating lower culpability
1. Serious attempts to evade justice 2. Determined attempt seriously to undermine the course of justice 3. Previous relevant convictions and/or breach of court orders or police bail	Where not amounting to a defence: 1. Misunderstanding 2. Failure to comprehend bail significance or requirements 3. Caring responsibilities
Factor indicating greater degree of harm	**Factor indicating lesser degree of harm**
4. Lengthy absence	4. Prompt voluntary surrender

[Sets out the standard sequential sentencing procedure.]

In appropriate cases, a magistrates' court may impose one day's detention: Magistrates' Courts Act 1980, s. 135

Bladed Article/Offensive Weapon, Possession Of SG-245

Factors to take into consideration

These guidelines and accompanying notes are drawn from the Court of Appeal's decision in *R v Celaire and Poulton* [2003] 1 Cr App R (S) 116. [But see the note issued as to the effect of *Povey* [2009] 1 Cr App R (S) 228, discussed at **B12.142** in the main work.]

Key factors

(a) Concurrent sentences may be appropriate if the weapons offence is ancillary to a more serious offence; consecutive sentences may be appropriate if the offences are distinct and independent.
(b) When assessing offence seriousness, consider the offender's intention, the circumstances of the offence and the nature of the weapon involved.
(c) Some weapons are inherently more dangerous than others but the nature of the weapon is not the primary determinant of offence seriousness. A relatively less dangerous weapon, such as a billiard cue or knuckle-duster, may be used to create fear and such an offence may be at least as serious as one in which a more obviously dangerous weapon, such as a knife or an acid spray, is being carried for self-defence or no actual attempt has been made by the offender to use it.
(d) Nevertheless, the fact that the offender was carrying a weapon which is offensive per se may shed light on his or her intentions.

Guidelines

Triable either way:
Maximum when tried summarily: Level 5 fine and/or 6 months
Maximum when tried on indictment: 4 years

Offence seriousness (culpability and harm)

A. Identify the appropriate starting point

Starting points based on first time offender pleading not guilty

Examples of nature of activity	Starting point	Range
Weapon not used to threaten or cause fear	High level community order	Band C fine–12 weeks' custody
Weapon not used to threaten or cause fear but offence committed in dangerous circumstances	6 weeks' custody	High level community order–Crown Court
Weapon used to threaten or cause fear and offence committed in dangerous circumstances	Crown Court	Crown Court

B. Consider the effect of aggravating and mitigating factors (other than those within examples above)

Common aggravating and mitigating factors are identified [elsewhere]—the following may be particularly relevant but these lists are not exhaustive

Sentencing Guidelines

Factors indicating higher culpability	Factors indicating greater degree of harm
1. Particularly dangerous weapon 2. Specifically planned use of weapon to commit violence, threaten violence or intimidate 3. Offence motivated by hostility towards minority individual or group 4. Offender under influence of drink or drugs 5. Offender operating in group or gang	1. Offence committed at school, hospital or other place where vulnerable persons may be present 2. Offence committed on premises where people carrying out public services 3. Offence committed on or outside licensed premises 4. Offence committed on public transport 5. Offence committed at large public gathering, especially where there may be risk of disorder **Factors indicating lower culpability** 1. Weapon carried only on temporary basis 2. Original possession legitimate e.g. in course of trade or business

[Sets out the standard sequential sentencing procedure and mentions need to consider deprivation of property (including weapon).]

SG-246 BURGLARY: DOMESTIC BURGLARY

[The Guidelines apply to all offenders aged 18 and older, who are sentenced on or after 16 January 2012, regardless of the date of the offence.]

Theft Act 1968 (section 9)

This is a serious specified offence for the purposes of section 224 Criminal Justice Act 2003 if it was committed with intent to:

(a) inflict grievous bodily harm on a person, or
(b) do unlawful damage to a building or anything in it.

Triable either way:
Maximum when tried summarily: Level 5 fine and/or 26 weeks' custody
Maximum when tried on indictment: 14 years' custody

Offence range: Community order—6 years' custody

Where sentencing an offender for a qualifying **third domestic burglary**, the Court must apply section 111 of the Powers of the Criminal Courts (Sentencing) Act 2000 and impose a custodial term of at least three years, unless it is satisfied that there are particular circumstances which relate to any of the offences or to the offender which would make it unjust to do so.

This guideline applies to all offenders aged 18 and older, who are sentenced on or after 16 January 2012. The definitions . . . of 'starting point' and 'first time offender' do not apply for this guideline. Starting point and category ranges apply to all offenders in all cases, irrespective of plea or previous convictions.

STEP ONE Determining the offence category

The court should determine the offence category using the table below.

Category 1	Greater harm **and** higher culpability
Category 2	Greater harm **and** lower culpability or lesser harm **and** higher culpability
Category 3	Lesser harm **and** lower culpability

The court should determine culpability and harm caused or intended, by reference only to the factors below, which comprise the principal factual elements of the offence. Where an offence does not fall squarely into a category, individual factors may require a degree of weighting before making an overall assessment and determining the appropriate offence category.

Factors indicating greater harm	Factors indicating higher culpability
Theft of/damage to property causing a significant degree of loss to the victim (whether economic, commercial or personal value) Soiling, ransacking or vandalism of property Victim on the premises (or returns) while offender present Trauma to the victim, beyond the normal inevitable consequence of -intrusion and theft Violence used or threatened against victim Context of general public disorder	Premises or victim deliberately targeted (to include pharmacy or doctor's surgery and targeting due to vulnerability of victim or hostility based on disability, race, sexual orientation and so forth) A significant degree of planning or organisation Knife or other weapon carried (where not charged separately) Equipped for burglary (for example, implements carried and/or use of vehicle) Member of a group or gang
Factors indicating lesser harm	**Factors indicating lower culpability**
Nothing stolen or only property of very low value to the victim (whether economic, commercial or personal) Limited damage or disturbance to property	Offence committed on impulse, with limited intrusion into property Offender exploited by others Mental disorder or learning disability, where linked to the commission of the offence

Sentencing Guidelines

STEP TWO Starting point and category range

Having determined the category, the court should use the corresponding starting points to reach a sentence within the category range below. The starting point applies to all offenders irrespective of plea or previous convictions.

Where the defendant is dependent on or has a propensity to misuse drugs and there is sufficient prospect of success, a community order with a drug rehabilitation requirement under section 209 of the Criminal Justice Act 2003 may be a proper alternative to a short or moderate custodial sentence.

A case of particular gravity, reflected by multiple features of culpability or harm in step 1, could merit upward adjustment from the starting point before further adjustment for aggravating or mitigating features, set out [below].

Offence Category	Starting Point (*Applicable to all offenders*)	Category Range (*Applicable to all offenders*)
Category 1	Crown Court	Crown Court
Category 2	1 year's custody	High level community order–Crown Court (2 years' custody)
Category 3	High level community order	Low level community order–26 weeks' custody

The table below contains a **non-exhaustive** list of additional factual elements providing the context of the offence and factors relating to the offender. Identify whether any combination of these, or other relevant factors, should result in an upward or downward adjustment from the starting point. **In particular, relevant recent convictions are likely to result in an upward adjustment**. In some cases, having considered these factors, it may be appropriate to move outside the identified category range.

When sentencing **category 2 or 3** offences, the court should also consider the custody threshold as follows:

- Has the custody threshold been passed?
- If so, is it unavoidable that a custodial sentence be imposed?
- If so, can that sentence be suspended?

Factors increasing seriousness	Factors reducing seriousness or reflecting personal mitigation
Statutory aggravating factors Previous convictions, having regard to a) the nature of the offence to which the conviction relates and its relevance to the current offence; and b) the time that has elapsed since the conviction* Offence committed whilst on bail *Other aggravating factors include:* Child at home (or returns home) when offence committed Offence committed at night Gratuitous degradation of the victim Any steps taken to prevent the victim reporting the incident or obtaining assistance and/or from assisting or supporting the prosecution Established evidence of community impact Commission of offence whilst under the influence of alcohol or drugs Failure to comply with current court orders Offence committed whilst on licence Offences Taken Into Consideration (TICs)	Offender has made voluntary reparation to the victim Subordinate role in a group or gang No previous convictions or no relevant/recent convictions Remorse Good character and/or exemplary conduct Determination, and/or demonstration of steps taken to address addiction or offending behaviour Serious medical conditions requiring urgent, intensive or long-term treatment Age and/or lack of maturity where it affects the responsibility of the offender Lapse of time since the offence where this is not the fault of the offender Mental disorder or learning disability, where not linked to the commission of the offence Sole or primary carer for dependent relatives

* Where sentencing an offender for a qualifying third domestic burglary, the Court must apply section 111 of the Powers of the Criminal Courts (Sentencing) Act 2000 and impose a custodial term of at least three years, unless it is satisfied that there are particular circumstances which relate to any of the offences or to the offender which would make it unjust to do so.

STEP THREE Consider any factors which indicate a reduction, such as assistance to the prosecution

The court should take into account any rule of law by virtue of which an offender may receive a discounted sentence in consequence of assistance given (or offered) to the prosecutor or investigator.

STEP FOUR Reduction for guilty pleas

The court should take account of any potential reduction for a guilty plea in accordance with section 144 of the Criminal Justice Act 2003 and the *Guilty Plea* guideline.

Where a minimum mandatory sentence is imposed under section 111 Powers of Criminal Courts (Sentencing) Act, the discount for an early guilty plea must not exceed 20 per cent.

STEP FIVE Dangerousness

A burglary offence under section 9 Theft Act 1986 is a serious specified offence within the meaning of chapter 5 of the Criminal Justice Act 2003 if it was committed with the intent to (a) inflict grievous bodily harm on a person, or (b) do unlawful damage to a building or anything in it. The court should consider whether having regard to the criteria contained in that chapter it would be appropriate to award imprisonment for public protection or an extended sentence. Where offenders meet the dangerousness criteria, the notional determinate sentence should be used as the basis for the setting of a minimum term.

[Steps Six to Nine follow the standard sequential sentencing procedure: see SG-241.]

SG-247 BURGLARY: NON-DOMESTIC BURGLARY

[The Guidelines apply to all offenders aged 18 and older, who are sentenced on or after 16 January 2012, regardless of the date of the offence.]

Theft Act 1968 (section 9)

This is a serious specified offence for the purposes of section 224 Criminal Justice Act 2003 if it was committed with intent to:

(a) inflict grievous bodily harm on a person, or
(b) do unlawful damage to a building or anything in it.

Triable either way:
Maximum when tried summarily: Level 5 fine and/or 26 weeks' custody

Maximum when tried on indictment: 10 years' custody

Offence range: Fine—5 years' custody

This guideline applies to all offenders aged 18 and older, who are sentenced on or after 16 January 2012. The definitions . . . of 'starting point' and 'first time offender' do not apply for this guideline. Starting point and category ranges apply to all offenders in all cases, irrespective of plea or previous convictions.

STEP ONE Determining the offence category

The court should determine the offence category using the table below.

Category 1	Greater harm **and** higher culpability
Category 2	Greater harm **and** lower culpability or lesser harm **and** higher culpability
Category 3	Lesser harm **and** lower culpability

The court should determine culpability and harm caused or intended, by reference only to the factors below, which comprise the principal factual elements of the offence. Where an offence does not fall squarely into a category, individual factors may require a degree of weighting before making an overall assessment and determining the appropriate offence category.

Factors indicating greater harm Theft of/damage to property causing a significant degree of loss to the victim (whether economic, commercial or personal value) Soiling, ransacking or vandalism of property Victim on the premises (or returns) while offender present Trauma to the victim, beyond the normal inevitable consequence of intrusion and theft Violence used or threatened against victim Context of general public disorder	**Factors indicating higher culpability** Premises or victim deliberately targeted (to include pharmacy or doctor's surgery and targeting due to vulnerability of victim or hostility based on disability, race, sexual orientation and so forth) A significant degree of planning or organisation Knife or other weapon carried (where not charged separately) Equipped for burglary (for example, implements carried and/or use of vehicle) Member of a group or gang
Factors indicating lesser harm Nothing stolen or only property of very low value to the victim (whether economic, commercial or personal) Limited damage or disturbance to property	**Factors indicating lower culpability** Offence committed on impulse, with limited intrusion into property Offender exploited by others Mental disorder or learning disability, where linked to the commission of the offence

STEP TWO Starting point and category range

Having determined the category, the court should use the corresponding starting points to reach a sentence within the category range below. The starting point applies to all offenders irrespective of plea or previous convictions.

Where the defendant is dependent on or has a propensity to misuse drugs and there is sufficient prospect of success, a community order with a drug rehabilitation requirement under section 209 of the Criminal Justice Act 2003 may be a proper alternative to a short or moderate custodial sentence.

A case of particular gravity, reflected by multiple features of culpability or harm in step 1, could merit upward adjustment from the starting point before further adjustment for aggravating or mitigating features, set out below.

Offence Category	Starting Point (*Applicable to all offenders*)	Category Range (*Applicable to all offenders*)
Category 1	Crown Court	Crown Court
Category 2	18 weeks' custody	Low level community order–Crown Court (51 weeks' custody)
Category 3	Medium level community order	Band B fine–18 weeks' custody

The table below contains a **non-exhaustive** list of additional factual elements providing the context of the offence and factors relating to the offender. Identify whether any combination of these, or other relevant factors, should result in an upward or downward adjustment from the starting point. **In particular, relevant recent convictions are likely to result in an upward adjustment.** In some cases, having considered these factors, it may be appropriate to move outside the identified category range.

When sentencing **category 2 or 3** offences, the court should also consider the custody threshold as follows:

- Has the custody threshold been passed?
- If so, is it unavoidable that a custodial sentence be imposed?
- If so, can that sentence be suspended?

When sentencing category 3 offences, the court should also consider the community order threshold as follows:

- Has the community order threshold been passed?

Factors increasing seriousness	**Factors reducing seriousness or reflecting personal mitigation**
Statutory aggravating factors: Previous convictions, having regard to a) the nature of the offence to which the conviction relates and its relevance to the current offence; and b) the time that has elapsed since the conviction Offence committed whilst on bail *Other aggravating factors include:* Offence committed at night, particularly where staff present or likely to be present Abuse of a position of trust Gratuitous degradation of the victim Any steps taken to prevent the victim reporting the incident or obtaining assistance and/or from assisting or supporting the prosecution Established evidence of community impact Commission of offence whilst under the influence of alcohol or drugs Failure to comply with current court orders Offence committed whilst on licence Offences Taken Into Consideration (TICs)	Offender has made voluntary reparation to the victim Subordinate role in a group or gang No previous convictions **or** no relevant/recent convictions Remorse Good character and/or exemplary conduct Determination, and/or demonstration of steps taken to address addiction or offending behaviour Serious medical conditions requiring urgent, intensive or long-term treatment Age and/or lack of maturity where it affects the responsibility of the offender Lapse of time since the offence where this is not the fault of the offender Mental disorder or learning disability, where not linked to the commission of the offence Sole or primary carer for dependent relatives

STEP THREE Consider any factors which indicate a reduction, such as assistance to the prosecution

The court should take into account any rule of law by virtue of which an offender may receive a discounted sentence in consequence of assistance given (or offered) to the prosecutor or investigator.

STEP FOUR Reduction for guilty pleas

The court should take account of any potential reduction for a guilty plea in accordance with section 144 of the Criminal Justice Act 2003 and the *Guilty Plea* guideline.

[Steps Five to Nine are the same as for domestic burglary: see **SG-246**.]

SG-248

Common Assault

Criminal Justice Act 1988 (section 39)

Racially/Religiously Aggravated Common Assault

Crime and Disorder Act 1998 (section 29)

[This guideline was published by the Sentencing Council and has effect in respect of all sentences passed after 13 June 2011 on offenders aged 18 or older. It replaces the guideline which previously applied and which continued to have effect until that date.]

Racially/religiously aggravated assault is a specified offence for the purposes of section 224 of the Criminal Justice Act 2003

Section 39
Triable only summarily
Maximum when tried summarily: Level 5 fine and/or 26 weeks' custody

Section 29
Triable either way
Maximum when tried summarily: Level 5 fine and/or 26 weeks' custody
Maximum when tried on indictment: 2 years' custody

Offence range: Discharge—26 weeks' custody

This guideline applies to all offenders aged 18 and older, who are sentenced on or after 13 June 2011. The definitions [at **SG-349**] of 'starting point' and 'first time offender' do not apply for this guideline. Starting point and category ranges apply to all offenders in all cases, irrespective of plea or previous convictions.

STEP ONE Determining the offence category

The court should determine the offence category using the table below.

Category 1	Greater harm (injury or fear of injury must normally be present) **and** higher culpability
Category 2	Greater harm (injury or fear of injury must normally be present) **and** lower culpability; **or** lesser harm and higher culpability
Category 3	Lesser harm **and** lower culpability

The court should determine the offender's culpability and the harm caused, or intended, by reference only to the factors below (as demonstrated by the presence of one or more). These factors comprise the principal factual elements of the offence and should determine the category.

Factors indicating greater harm Injury or fear of injury which is serious in the context of the offence (must normally be present) Victim is particularly vulnerable because of personal circumstances Sustained or repeated assault on the same victim **Factors indicating higher culpability** *Statutory aggravating factors:* Offence motivated by, or demonstrating, hostility to the victim based on his or her sexual orientation (or presumed sexual orientation) Offence motivated by, or demonstrating, hostility to the victim based on the victim's disability (or presumed disability) *Other aggravating factors:* A significant degree of premeditation Threatened or actual use of weapon or weapon equivalent (for example, shod foot, headbutting, use of acid, use of animal) Intention to commit more serious harm than actually resulted from the offence Deliberately causes more harm than is necessary for commission of offence Deliberate targeting of vulnerable victim Leading role in group or gang Offence motivated by, or demonstrating, hostility based on the victim's age, sex, gender identity (or presumed gender identity)	**Factors indicating lesser harm** Injury which is less serious in the context of the offence **Factors indicating lower culpability** Subordinate role in group or gang A greater degree of provocation than normally expected Lack of premeditation Mental disorder or learning disability, where linked to commission of the offence Excessive self defence

STEP TWO Starting point and category range

Having determined the category, the court should use the corresponding starting points to reach a sentence within the category range below. The starting point applies to all offenders irrespective of plea or previous convictions. A case of particular gravity, reflected by multiple features of culpability in step one, could merit upward adjustment from the starting point before further adjustment for aggravating or mitigating features, set out below.

Offence Category	Starting Point (*Applicable to all offenders*)	Category Range (*Applicable to all offenders*)
Category 1	High level community order	Low level community order–26 weeks' custody
Category 2	Medium level community order	Band A fine–High level community order
Category 3	Band A fine	Discharge–Band C fine

The table below contains a **non-exhaustive** list of additional factual elements providing the context of the offence and factors relating to the offender. Identify whether any combination of these, or other relevant factors, should result in an upward or downward adjustment from the starting point. In some cases, having considered these factors, it may be appropriate to move outside the identified category range.

When sentencing **category 1** offences, the court should also consider the custody threshold as follows:

- Has the custody threshold been passed?
- If so, is it unavoidable that a custodial sentence be imposed?
- If so, can that sentence be suspended?

When sentencing **category 2** offences, the court should also consider the community order threshold as follows:

- Has the community order threshold been passed?

Factors increasing seriousness	**Factors reducing seriousness or reflecting personal mitigation**
Statutory aggravating factors: Previous convictions, having regard to a) the nature of the offence to which the conviction relates and its relevance to the current offence; and b) the time that has elapsed since the conviction Offence committed whilst on bail *Other aggravating factors include:* Location of the offence Timing of the offence Ongoing effect upon the victim Offence committed against those working in the public sector or providing a service to the public Presence of others including relatives, especially children or partner of the victim Gratuitous degradation of victim In domestic violence cases, victim forced to leave their home Failure to comply with current court orders Offence committed whilst on licence An attempt to conceal or dispose of evidence Failure to respond to warnings or concerns expressed by others about the offender's behaviour Commission of offence whilst under the influence of alcohol or drugs Abuse of power and/or position of trust Exploiting contact arrangements with a child to commit an offence Established evidence of community impact Any steps taken to prevent the victim reporting an incident, obtaining assistance and/or from assisting or supporting the prosecution Offences taken into consideration (TICs)	No previous convictions or no relevant/recent convictions Single blow Remorse Good character and/or exemplary conduct Determination and/or demonstration of steps taken to address addiction or offending behaviour Serious medical conditions requiring urgent, intensive or long-term treatment Isolated incident Age and/or lack of maturity where it affects the responsibility of the offender Lapse of time since the offence where this is not the fault of the offender Mental disorder or learning disability, where not linked to the commission of the offence Sole or primary carer for dependent relatives

Section 29 offences only: The court should determine the appropriate sentence for the offence without taking account of the element of aggravation and then make an addition to the sentence, considering the level of aggravation involved. It may be appropriate to move outside the identified category range, taking into account the increased statutory maximum.

[Steps Three to Nine are almost identical to those which apply to assault occasioning actual bodily harm: see **SG-241**.]

COMMUNICATION NETWORK OFFENCES SG-249

Communications Act 2003, ss. 127(1) and 127(2)

Triable only summarily:
Maximum: Level 5 fine and/or 6 months

Offence seriousness (culpability and harm)

A. Identify the appropriate starting point

Starting points based on first time offender pleading not guilty

Sending grossly offensive, indecent, obscene or menacing messages (s.127(1))		
Examples of nature of activity	**Starting point**	**Range**
Single offensive, indecent, obscene or menacing call of short duration, having no significant impact on receiver	Band B fine	Band A fine–band C fine
Single call where extreme language used, having only moderate impact on receiver	Medium level community order	Low level community order–high level community order
Single call where extreme language used and substantial distress or fear caused to receiver; OR One of a series of similar calls as described in box above	6 weeks' custody	High level community order–12 weeks' custody

Sending false message/persistent use of communications network for purpose of causing annoyance, inconvenience or needless anxiety (s.127(2))		
Examples of nature of activity	**Starting point**	**Range**
Persistent silent calls over short period to private individual, causing inconvenience or annoyance	Band B fine	Band A fine–band C fine
Single hoax call to public or private organisation resulting in moderate disruption or anxiety	Medium level community order	Low level community order–high level community order
Single hoax call resulting in major disruption or substantial public fear or distress; OR One of a series of similar calls as described in box above	12 weeks' custody	High level community order–18 weeks' custody

B. Consider the effect of aggravating and mitigating factors (other than those within examples above)

Common aggravating and mitigating factors are identified [elsewhere]

[Sets out the standard sequential sentencing procedure.]

COMMUNITY ORDER, BREACH OF SG-250

Criminal Justice Act 2003, sch. 8

These notes are taken from the Sentencing Guidelines Council's definitive guideline *New Sentences: Criminal Justice Act 2003*, published 16 December 2004[129] [see SG-11]

Options in breach proceedings:
When dealing with breaches of community orders for offences committed after 4 April 2005, the court must either:

- amend the terms of the original order so as to impose more onerous requirements. The court may extend the duration of particular requirements within the order, but it cannot extend the overall length of the original order; or
- revoke the original order and proceed to sentence for the original offence. Where an offender has wilfully and persistently failed to comply with an order made in respect of an offence that is not punishable by imprisonment, the court can impose up to six months' custody.

[129] Criminal Justice Act 2003, sch.8, para. 9(1)(c)

Sentencing Guidelines

Approach:
- having decided that a community order is commensurate with the seriousness of the offence, the primary objective when sentencing for breach of requirements is to ensure that those requirements are completed;
- a court sentencing for breach must take account of the extent to which the offender has complied with the requirements of the original order, the reasons for the breach, and the point at which the breach has occurred;
- if increasing the onerousness of requirements, sentencers should take account of the offender's ability to comply and should avoid precipitating further breach by overloading the offender with too many or conflicting requirements;
- there may be cases where the court will need to consider re-sentencing to a differently constructed community order in order to secure compliance with the purposes of the original sentence, perhaps where there has already been partial compliance or where events since the sentence was imposed have shown that a different course of action is likely to be effective;
- where available, custody should be the last resort, reserved for those cases of deliberate and repeated breach where all reasonable efforts to ensure that the offender complies have failed.

Where the original order was made by the Crown Court, breach proceedings must be commenced in that court unless the order provided that any failure to comply with its requirements may be dealt with in a magistrates' court.

SG-251

Criminal Damage (other than by Fire)

Racially Or Religiously Aggravated Criminal Damage

Criminal Damage Act 1971, s. 1(1)

Crime and Disorder Act 1998, s. 30

Criminal damage: triable only summarily if value involved does not exceed £5,000:
Maximum: Level 4 fine and/or 3 months
Triable either way if value involved exceeds £5,000:
Maximum when tried summarily: Level 5 fine and/or 6 months
Maximum when tried on indictment: 10 years

Racially or religiously aggravated criminal damage: triable either way
Maximum when tried summarily: Level 5 fine and/or 6 months
Maximum when tried on indictment: 14 years

Where offence committed in domestic context, refer [below] for guidance

Offence seriousness (culpability and harm)

A. Identify the appropriate starting point

Starting points based on first time offender pleading not guilty

Examples of nature of activity	Starting point	Range
Minor damage e.g. breaking small window; small amount of graffiti	Band B fine	Conditional discharge–band C fine
Moderate damage e.g. breaking large plate-glass or shop window; widespread graffiti	Low level community order	Band C fine–medium level community order
Significant damage up to £5,000 e.g. damage caused as part of a spree	High level community order	Medium level community order–12 weeks' custody
Damage between £5,000 and £10,000	12 weeks' custody	6–26 weeks' custody
Damage over £10,000	Crown Court	Crown Court

B. Consider the effect of aggravating and mitigating factors (other than those within examples above)

Common aggravating and mitigating factors are identified [elsewhere]—the following may be particularly relevant but these lists are not exhaustive

Factors indicating higher culpability	**Factors indicating lower culpability**
1. Revenge attack 2. Targeting vulnerable victim **Factors indicating greater degree of harm** 1. Damage to emergency equipment 2. Damage to public amenity 3. Significant public or private fear caused e.g. in domestic context	1. Damage caused recklessly 2. Provocation

[Sets out the standard sequential sentencing procedure. Notes that 'If offender charged and convicted of the racially or religiously aggravated offence, increase the sentence to reflect this element']

Cruelty to a Child SG-252

Factors to take into consideration

This guideline and accompanying notes are taken from the Sentencing Guidelines Council's definitive guidelines *Overarching Principles: Assaults on children and Cruelty to a child*, published 20 February 2008 [see **SG-213**]

Key factors

(a) The same starting point and sentencing range is proposed for offences which might fall into the four categories (assault; ill-treatment or neglect; abandonment; and failure to protect). These are designed to take into account the fact that the victim is particularly vulnerable, assuming an abuse of trust or power and the likelihood of psychological harm, and designed to reflect the seriousness with which society as a whole regards these offences.

(b) As noted above, the starting points have been calculated to reflect the likelihood of psychological harm and this cannot be treated as an aggravating factor. Where there is an especially serious physical or psychological effect on the victim, even if unintended, this should increase sentence.

(c) The normal sentencing starting point for an offence of child cruelty should be a custodial sentence. The length of that sentence will be influenced by the circumstances in which the offence took place.

(d) However, in considering whether a custodial sentence is the most appropriate disposal, the court should take into account any available information concerning the future care of the child.

(e) Where the offender is the sole or primary carer of the victim or other dependants, this potentially should be taken into account for sentencing purposes, regardless of whether the offender is male or female. In such cases, an immediate custodial sentence may not be appropriate.

(f) The most relevant areas of personal mitigation are likely to be:
- Mental illness/depression
- Inability to cope with the pressures of parenthood
- Lack of support
- Sleep deprivation
- Offender dominated by an abusive or stronger partner
- Extreme behavioural difficulties in the child, often coupled with a lack of support
- Inability to secure assistance or support services in spite of every effort having been made by the offender.

Some of the factors identified above, in particular sleep deprivation, lack of support and an inability to cope, could be regarded as an inherent part of caring for children, especially when a child is very young and could be put forward as mitigation by most carers charged with an offence of child cruelty. It follows that, before being accepted as mitigation, there must be evidence that these factors were present to a high degree and had an identifiable and significant impact on the offender's behaviour.

Guidelines

Children and Young Persons Act 1933, s.1(1)

Triable either way:
Maximum when tried summarily: Level 5 fine and/or 6 months
Maximum when tried on indictment: 10 years

Sentencing Guidelines

Offence seriousness (culpability and harm)

A. Identify the appropriate starting point

Starting points based on first time offender pleading not guilty

Examples of nature of activity	Starting point	Range
(i) Short term neglect or ill-treatment (ii) Single incident of short-term abandonment (iii) Failure to protect a child from any of the above	12 weeks' custody	Low level community order–26 weeks' custody
(i) Assault(s) resulting in injuries consistent with ABH (ii) More than one incident of neglect or ill-treatment (but not amounting to long-term behaviour) (iii) Single incident of long-term abandonment OR regular incidents of short-term abandonment (the longer the period of long-term abandonment or the greater the number of incidents of short-term abandonment, the more serious the offence) (iv) Failure to protect a child from any of the above	Crown Court	26 weeks' custody–Crown Court
(i) Series of assaults (ii) Protracted neglect or ill-treatment (iii) Serious cruelty over a period of time (iv) Failure to protect a child from any of the above	Crown Court	Crown Court

B. Consider the effect of aggravating and mitigating factors (other than those within examples above)

Common aggravating and mitigating factors are identified [elsewhere]—the following may be particularly relevant but these lists are not exhaustive

1. Targeting one particular child from the family 2. Sadistic behaviour 3. Threats to prevent the victim from reporting the offence 4. Deliberate concealment of the victim from the authorities 5. Failure to seek medical help	1. Seeking medical help or bringing the situation to the notice of the authorities

[Sets out the standard sequential sentencing procedure.]

SG-253 Dangerous Dogs Act Offences and Related Offences

[The guidelines for the magistrates' court are identical to the general guidelines: see **SG-595**.]

SG-254 Drugs—Class A—Fail to Attend/Remain for Initial Assessment

Drugs Act 2005, s. 12

Triable only summarily:

Maximum: Level 4 fine and/or 3 months

Offence seriousness (culpability and harm)

A. Identify the appropriate starting point

Starting points based on first time offender pleading not guilty

Examples of nature of activity	Starting point	Range
Refusal to provide sample without good cause when required by police officer	Medium level community order	Band C fine–high level community order

B. Consider the effect of aggravating and mitigating factors (other than those within examples above)

Common aggravating and mitigating factors are identified [elsewhere]—the following may be particularly relevant but these lists are not exhaustive

Factor indicating greater degree of harm	Factors indicating lower culpability
1. Threats or abuse to staff	1. Subsequent voluntary contact with drug workers 2. Subsequent compliance with testing on arrest/charge

[Sets out the standard sequential sentencing procedure.]

Drugs—Class A—Fail/Refuse to provide a Sample SG-255

Police and Criminal Evidence Act 1984, s. 63B

Triable only summarily:
Maximum: Level 4 fine and/or 3 months

Offence seriousness (culpability and harm)

A. Identify the appropriate starting point

Starting points based on first time offender pleading not guilty

Examples of nature of activity	Starting point	Range
Failure to attend at the appointed place and time	Medium level community order	Band C fine–high level community order

B. Consider the effect of aggravating and mitigating factors (other than those within examples above)

Common aggravating and mitigating factors are identified [elsewhere]—the following may be particularly relevant but these lists are not exhaustive

Factors indicating greater degree of harm	Factors indicating lower culpability
1. Threats or abuse to assessor or other staff	1. Offender turns up but at wrong place or time or fails to remain for duration of appointment 2. Subsequent voluntary contact to rearrange appointment

[Sets out the standard sequential sentencing procedure.]

Drugs—Fraudulent Evasion of a Prohibition by Bringing Into or Taking Out of the UK a Controlled Drug SG-256

Misuse of Drugs Act 1971 (section 3)

Customs and Excise Management Act 1979 (section 170(2))

Triable either way unless the defendant could receive the minimum sentence of seven years for a third drug trafficking offence under section 110 Powers of Criminal Courts (Sentencing) Act 2000 in which case the offence is triable only on indictment.

Class A

Maximum: Life imprisonment

Offence range: 3 years 6 months'—16 years' custody

A Class A offence is a drug trafficking offence for the purpose of imposing a minimum sentence under section 110 Powers of Criminal Courts (Sentencing) Act 2000

Class B

Maximum: 14 years' custody and/or unlimited fine

Offence range: 12 weeks'—10 years' custody

Class C

Maximum: 14 years' custody and/or unlimited fine

Offence range: Community order—8 years' custody

STEP ONE Determining the offence category SG-257

The court should determine the offender's culpability (role) and the harm caused (quantity) with reference to the tables below.

Sentencing Guidelines

In assessing culpability, the sentencer should weigh up all the factors of the case to determine role. Where there are characteristics present which fall under different role categories, the court should balance these characteristics to reach a fair assessment of the offender's culpability.

In assessing harm, quantity is determined by the weight of the product. Purity is not taken into account at step 1 but is dealt with at step 2.

Where the operation is on the most serious and commercial scale, involving a quantity of drugs significantly higher than category 1, sentences of 20 years and above may be appropriate, depending on the role of the offender.

Culpability demonstrated by offender's role One or more of these characteristics may demonstrate the offender's role. These lists are not exhaustive.	**Category of harm** Indicative quantity of drug concerned (upon which the starting point is based):
LEADING role: • Directing or organising buying and selling on a commercial scale; • Substantial links to, and influence on, others in a chain; • Close links to original source; • Expectation of substantial financial gain; • Uses business as cover; • Abuses a position of trust or responsibility. **SIGNIFICANT role:** • Operational or management function within a chain; • involves others in the operation whether by pressure, influence, intimidation or reward; • Motivated by financial or other advantage, whether or not operating alone; • Some awareness and understanding of scale of operation. **LESSER role:** • Performs a limited function under direction; • Engaged by pressure, coercion, intimidation; • Involvement through naivety/exploitation; • No influence on those above in a chain; • Very little, if any, awareness or understanding of the scale of operation; • If own operation, solely for own use (considering reasonableness of account in all the circumstances).	**Category 1:** • Heroin, cocaine — 5kg; • Ecstasy — 10,000 tablets; • LSD — 250,000 squares; • Amphetamine — 20kg; • Cannabis — 200kg; • Ketamine — 5kg. **Category 2:** • Heroin, cocaine — 1kg; • Ecstasy — 2,000 tablets; • LSD — 25,000 squares; • Amphetamine — 4kg; • Cannabis — 40kg; • Ketamine — 1kg; **Category 3:** • Heroin, cocaine — 150g; • Ecstasy — 300 tablets; • LSD — 2,500 squares; • Amphetamine — 750g; • Cannabis — 6kg; • Ketamine — 150g. **Category 4:** • Heroin, cocaine — 5g; • Ecstasy — 20 tablets; • LSD — 170 squares; • Amphetamine — 20g; • Cannabis — 100g; • Ketamine — 5g.

SG-258 **STEP TWO Starting point and category range**

Having determined the category, the court should use the corresponding starting point to reach a sentence within the category range below. The starting point applies to all offenders irrespective of plea or previous convictions. The court should then consider further adjustment within the category range for aggravating or mitigating features, set out [at **SG-259**]. In cases where the offender is regarded as being at the very top of the 'leading' role it may be justifiable for the court to depart from the guideline.

Where the defendant is dependent on or has a propensity to misuse drugs and there is sufficient prospect of success, a community order with a drug rehabilitation requirement under section 209 of the Criminal Justice Act 2003 can be a proper alternative to a short or moderate length custodial sentence.

For class A cases, section 110 of the Powers of Criminal Courts (Sentencing) Act 2000 provides that a court should impose a minimum sentence of at least seven years' imprisonment for a third class A trafficking offence except where the court is of the opinion that there are particular circumstances which (a) relate to any of the offences or to the offender; and (b) would make it unjust to do so in all the circumstances.

CLASS A	Leading role	Significant role	Lesser role
Category 1	**Starting point** 14 years' custody **Category range** 12–16 years' custody	**Starting point** 10 years' custody **Category range** 9–12 years' custody	**Starting point** 8 years' custody **Category range** 6–9 years' custody
Category 2	**Starting point** 11 years' custody **Category range** 9–13 years' custody	**Starting point** 8 years' custody **Category range** 6 years 6 months'–10 years' custody	**Starting point** 6 years' custody **Category range** 5–7 years' custody
Category 3	**Starting point** 8 years 6 months' custody **Category range** 6 years 6 months'–10 years' custody	**Starting point** 6 years' custody **Category range** 5–7 years' custody	**Starting point** 4 years 6 months' custody **Category range** 3 years 6 months'–5 years' custody
Category 4	Where the quantity falls below the indicative amount set out for category 4 [at **SG-257**], first identify the role for the importation offence, then refer to the starting point and ranges for possession or supply offences, depending on intent. Where the quantity is significantly larger than the indicative amounts for category 4 but below category 3 amounts, refer to the category 3 ranges above.		

CLASS B	Leading role	Significant role	Lesser role
Category 1	**Starting point** 8 years' custody **Category range** 7–10 years' custody	**Starting point** 5 years 6 months' custody **Category range** 5–7 years' custody	**Starting point** 4 years' custody **Category range** 2 years 6 months'–5 years' custody
Category 2	**Starting point** 6 years' custody **Category range** 4 years 6 months'–8 years' custody	**Starting point** 4 years' custody **Category range** 2 years 6 months'–5 years' custody	**Starting point** 2 years' custody **Category range** 18 months'–3 years' custody
Category 3	**Starting point** 4 years' custody **Category range** 2 years 6 months'–5 years' custody	**Starting point** 2 years' custody **Category range** 18 months'–3 years' custody	**Starting point** 1 year's custody **Category range** 12 weeks'–18 months' custody
Category 4	Where the quantity falls below the indicative amount set out for category 4 [at **SG-257**], first identify the role for the importation offence, then refer to the starting point and ranges for possession or supply offences, depending on intent. Where the quantity is significantly larger than the indicative amounts for category 4 but below category 3 amounts, refer to the category 3 ranges above		

CLASS C	Leading role	Significant role	Lesser role
Category 1	**Starting point** 5 years' custody **Category range** 4–8 years' custody	**Starting point** 3 years' custody **Category range** 2–5 years' custody	**Starting point** 18 months' custody **Category range** 1–3 years' custody
Category 2	**Starting point** 3 years 6 months' custody **Category range** 2 years'–5 years' custody	**Starting point** 18 months' custody **Category range** 1–3 years' custody	**Starting point** 26 weeks' custody **Category range** 12 weeks'–18 months' custody

Category 3	**Starting point** 18 months' custody **Category range** 1–3 years' custody	**Starting point** 26 weeks' custody **Category range** 12 weeks–18 months' custody	**Starting point** High level community order **Category range** Medium level community order–12 weeks' custody
Category 4	Where the quantity falls below the indicative amount set out for category 4 [at **SG-257**], first identify the role for the importation offence, then refer to the starting point and ranges for possession or supply offences, depending on intent. Where the quantity is significantly larger than the indicative amounts for category 4 but below category 3 amounts, refer to the category 3 ranges above.		

SG-259 The table below contains a **non-exhaustive** list of additional factual elements providing the context of the offence and factors relating to the offender. Identify whether any combination of these, or other relevant factors, should result in an upward or downward adjustment from the starting point. In some cases, having considered these factors, it may be appropriate to move outside the identified category range.

For appropriate **class C** ranges, consider the custody threshold as follows:

- Has the custody threshold been passed?
- If so, is it unavoidable that a custodial sentence be imposed?
- If so, can that sentence be suspended?

Factors increasing seriousness	**Factors reducing seriousness or reflecting personal mitigation**
Statutory aggravating factors: Previous convictions, having regard to a) nature of the offence to which conviction relates and relevance to current offence; and b) time elapsed since conviction (see [italicised text at **SG-258**] if third drug trafficking conviction) Offender used or permitted a person under 18 to deliver a controlled drug to a third person Offence committed on bail *Other aggravating factors include:* Sophisticated nature of concealment and/or attempts to avoid detection Attempts to conceal or dispose of evidence, where not charged separately Exposure of others to more than usual danger, for example drugs cut with harmful substances Presence of weapon, where not charged separately High purity Failure to comply with current court orders Offence committed on licence	Lack of sophistication as to nature of concealment Involvement due to pressure, intimidation or coercion falling short of duress, except where already taken into account at step 1 Mistaken belief of the offender regarding the type of drug, taking into account the reasonableness of such belief in all the circumstances Isolated incident Low purity No previous convictions or no relevant or recent convictions Offender's vulnerability was exploited Remorse Good character and/or exemplary conduct Determination and/or demonstration of steps having been taken to address addiction or offending behaviour Serious medical conditions requiring urgent, intensive or long-term treatment Age and/or lack of maturity where it affects the responsibility of the offender Mental disorder or learning disability Sole or primary carer for dependent relatives

SG-260 **STEP THREE Consider any factors which indicate a reduction, such as assistance to the prosecution**

The court should take into account sections 73 and 74 of the Serious Organised Crime and Police Act 2005 (assistance by defendants: reduction or review of sentence) and any other rule of law by virtue of which an offender may receive a discounted sentence in consequence of assistance given (or offered) to the prosecutor or investigator.

STEP FOUR Reduction for guilty pleas

The court should take account of any potential reduction for a guilty plea in accordance with section 144 of the Criminal Justice Act 2003 and the *Guilty Plea* guideline [see **SG-1**].

For class A offences, where a minimum mandatory sentence is imposed under section 110 Powers of Criminal Courts (Sentencing) Act, the discount for an early guilty plea must not exceed 20 per cent.

STEP FIVE Totality principle

If sentencing an offender for more than one offence, or where the offender is already serving a sentence, consider whether the total sentence is just and proportionate to the offending behaviour.

STEP SIX Confiscation and ancillary orders

In all cases, the court is required to consider confiscation where the Crown invokes the process or where the court considers it appropriate. It should also consider whether to make ancillary orders.

STEP SEVEN Reasons

Section 174 of the Criminal Justice Act 2003 imposes a duty to give reasons for, and explain the effect of, the sentence.

STEP EIGHT Consideration for remand time

Sentencers should take into consideration any remand time served in relation to the final sentence at this final step. The court should consider whether to give credit for time spent on remand in custody or on bail in accordance with sections 240 and 240A of the Criminal Justice Act 2003.

Drugs—Supplying or Offering to Supply a Controlled Drug SG-261

Misuse of Drugs Act 1971 (section 4(3))

Possession of a Controlled Drug with Intent to Supply it to Another

Misuse of Drugs Act 1971 (section 5(3))

Triable either way unless the defendant could receive the minimum sentence of seven years for a third drug trafficking offence under section 110 Powers of Criminal Courts (Sentencing) Act 2000 in which case the offence is triable only on indictment.

Class A

Maximum: Life imprisonment

Offence range: Community order—16 years' custody

A class A offence is a drug trafficking offence for the purpose of imposing a minimum sentence under section 110 Powers of Criminal Courts (Sentencing) Act 2000

Class B

Maximum: 14 years' custody and/or unlimited fine

Offence range: Fine—10 years' custody

Class C

Maximum: 14 years' custody and/or unlimited fine

Offence range: Fine—8 years' custody

STEP ONE Determining the offence category SG-262

The court should determine the offender's culpability (role) and the harm caused (quantity/type of offender) with reference to the tables below.

In assessing culpability, the sentencer should weigh up all the factors of the case to determine role. Where there are characteristics present which fall under different role categories, the court should balance these characteristics to reach a fair assessment of the offender's culpability.

*In assessing harm, quantity is determined by the weight of the product. Purity is not taken into account at step 1 but is dealt with at step 2. Where the offence is **street dealing or supply of drugs in prison by a prison employee**, the quantity of the product is less indicative of the harm caused and therefore **the starting point is not based on quantity**.*

Sentencing Guidelines

Where the operation is on the most serious and commercial scale, involving a quantity of drugs significantly higher than category 1, sentences of 20 years and above may be appropriate, depending on the role of the offender.

Culpability demonstrated by offender's role One or more of these characteristics may demonstrate the offender's role. These lists are not exhaustive.	**Category of harm** Indicative quantity of drug concerned (upon which the starting point is based):
LEADING role: • Directing or organising buying and selling on a commercial scale; • Substantial links to, and influence on, others in a chain; • Close links to original source; • Expectation of substantial financial gain; • Uses business as cover; • Abuses a position of trust or responsibility, for example prison employee, medical professional. **SIGNIFICANT role:** • Operational or management function within a chain; • Involves others in the operation whether by pressure, influence, intimidation or reward; • Motivated by financial or other advantage, whether or not operating alone; • Some awareness and understanding of scale of operation; • Supply, other than by a person in position of responsibility, to a prisoner for gain without coercion. **LESSER role:** • Performs a limited function under direction; • Engaged by pressure, coercion, intimidation; • Involvement through naivety/exploitation; • No influence on those above in a chain; • Very little, if any, awareness or understanding of the scale of operation; • If own operation, absence of financial gain, for example joint purchase for no profit, or sharing minimal quantity between peers on non-commercial basis.	**Category 1** • Heroin, cocaine — 5kg; • Ecstasy — 10,000 tablets; • LSD — 250,000 squares; • Amphetamine — 20kg; • Cannabis — 200kg; • Ketamine — 5kg. **Category 2** • Heroin, cocaine — 1kg; • Ecstasy — 2,000 tablets; • LSD — 25,000 squares; • Amphetamine — 4kg; • Cannabis — 40kg; • Ketamine — 1kg. **Category 3** Where the offence is selling direct to users [footnote indicates that this includes test purchase officers] ('street-dealing'), the starting point is not based on a quantity OR Where the offence is supply of drugs in prison by a prison employee, the starting point is not based on a quantity — see [italicised text above]. OR • Heroin, cocaine — 150g; • Ecstasy — 300 tablets; • LSD — 2,500 squares; • Amphetamine — 750g; • Cannabis — 6kg; • Ketamine — 150g. **Category 4** • Heroin, cocaine — 5g; • Ecstasy — 20 tablets; • LSD — 170 squares; • Amphetamine — 20g; • Cannabis — 100g; • Ketamine — 5g; OR Where the offence is selling directly to users [footnote indicates that this includes test purchase officers] ('street-dealing'), the starting point is not based on quantity — go to category 3.

SG-263 **STEP TWO Starting point and category range**

Having determined the category, the court should use the corresponding starting point to reach a sentence within the category range below. The starting point applies to all offenders irrespective of plea or previous convictions. The court should then consider further adjustment within the category range for aggravating or mitigating features, set out [at **SG-264**]. In cases where the offender is regarded as being at the very top of the 'leading' role it may be justifiable for the court to depart from the guideline.

Where the defendant is dependent on or has a propensity to misuse drugs and there is sufficient prospect of success, a community order with a drug rehabilitation requirement under section 209 of the Criminal Justice Act 2003 can be a proper alternative to a short or moderate length custodial sentence.

For class A cases, section 110 of the Powers of Criminal Courts (Sentencing) Act 2000 provides that a court should impose a minimum sentence of at least seven years' imprisonment for a third class A trafficking offence except where the court is of the opinion that there are particular circumstances which (a) relate to any of the offences or to the offender; and (b) would make it unjust to do so in all the circumstances.

CLASS A	Leading role	Significant role	Lesser role
Category 1	**Starting point** 14 years' custody	**Starting point** 10 years' custody	**Starting point** 7 years' custody
	Category range 12–16 years' custody	**Category range** 9–12 years' custody	**Category range** 6–9 years' custody
Category 2	**Starting point** 11 years' custody	**Starting point** 8 years' custody	**Starting point** 5 years' custody
	Category range 9–13 years' custody	**Category range** 6 years 6 months'–10 years' custody	**Category range** 3 years 6 months'–7 years' custody
Category 3	**Starting point** 8 years 6 months' custody	**Starting point** 4 years 6 months' custody	**Starting point** 3 years' custody
	Category range 6 years 6 months'–10 years' custody	**Category range** 3 years 6 months'–7 years' custody	**Category range** 2–4 years 6 months' custody
Category 4	**Starting point** 5 years 6 months' custody	**Starting point** 3 years 6 months' custody	**Starting point** 18 months' custody
	Category range 4 years 6 months'–7 years 6 months' custody	**Category range** 2–5 years' custody	**Category range** High level community order–3 years' custody

CLASS B	Leading role	Significant role	Lesser role
Category 1	**Starting point** 8 years' custody	**Starting point** 5 years 6 months' custody	**Starting point** 3 years' custody
	Category range 7–10 years' custody	**Category range** 5–7 years' custody	**Category range** 2 years 6 months'–5 years' custody
Category 2	**Starting point** 6 years' custody	**Starting point** 4 years' custody	**Starting point** 1 year's custody
	Category range 4 years 6 months'–8 years' custody	**Category range** 2 years 6 months'–5 years' custody	**Category range** 26 weeks'–3 years' custody
Category 3	**Starting point** 4 years' custody	**Starting point** 1 year's custody	**Starting point** High level community order
	Category range 2 years 6 months'–5 years' custody	**Category range** 26 weeks'–3 years' custody	**Category range** Low level community order–26 weeks' custody
Category 4	**Starting point** 18 months' custody	**Starting point** High level community order	**Starting point** Low level community order
	Category range 26 weeks'–3 years' custody	**Category range** Medium level community order–26 weeks' custody	**Category range** Band B fine–medium level community order

CLASS C	Leading role	Significant role	Lesser role
Category 1	**Starting point** 5 years' custody **Category range** 4–8 years' custody	**Starting point** 3 years' custody **Category range** 2–5 years' custody	**Starting point** 18 months' custody **Category range** 1–3 years' custody
Category 2	**Starting point** 3 years 6 months' custody **Category range** 2 years'–5 years' custody	**Starting point** 18 months' custody **Category range** 1–3 years' custody	**Starting point** 26 weeks' custody **Category range** 12 weeks'–18 months' custody
Category 3	**Starting point** 18 months' custody **Category range** 1–3 years' custody	**Starting point** 26 weeks' custody **Category range** 12 weeks–18 months' custody	**Starting point** High level community order **Category range** Low level community order–12 weeks' custody
Category 4	**Starting point** 26 weeks' custody **Category range** High level community order–18 months' custody	**Starting point** High level community order **Category range** Low level community order–12 weeks' custody	**Starting point** Low level community order **Category range** Band A fine–medium level community order

SG-264 The table below contains a **non-exhaustive** list of additional factual elements providing the context of the offence and factors relating to the offender. Identify whether any combination of these, or other relevant factors, should result in an upward or downward adjustment from the starting point. In some cases, having considered these factors, it may be appropriate to move outside the identified category range.

For appropriate **class B** and **C** ranges, consider the custody threshold as follows:

- Has the custody threshold been passed?
- If so, is it unavoidable that a custodial sentence be imposed?
- If so, can that sentence be suspended?

For appropriate **class B** and **C** ranges, the court should also consider the community threshold as follows:

- Has the community threshold been passed?

Factors increasing seriousness	**Factors reducing seriousness or reflecting personal mitigation**
Statutory aggravating factors: Previous convictions, having regard to a) nature of the offence to which conviction relates and relevance to current offence; and b) time elapsed since conviction (see [italicised text at **SG-263**] if third drug trafficking conviction) Offender used or permitted a person under 18 to deliver a controlled drug to a third person Offender 18 or over supplies or offers to supply a drug on, or in the vicinity of, school premises either when school in use as such or at a time between one hour before and one hour after they are to be used Offence committed on bail	Involvement due to pressure, intimidation or coercion falling short of duress, except where already taken into account at step 1 Supply only of drug to which offender addicted Mistaken belief of the offender regarding the type of drug, taking into account the reasonableness of such belief in all the circumstances Isolated incident Low purity No previous convictions **or** no relevant or recent convictions Offender's vulnerability was exploited

Other aggravating factors include: Targeting of any premises intended to locate vulnerable individuals or supply to such individuals and/or supply to those under 18 Exposure of others to more than usual danger, for example drugs cut with harmful substances Attempts to conceal or dispose of evidence, where not charged separately Presence of others, especially children and/or non-users Presence of weapon, where not charged separately Charged as importation of a very small amount High purity Failure to comply with current court orders Offence committed on licence Established evidence of community impact	Remorse Good character and/or exemplary conduct Determination and/or demonstration of steps having been taken to address addiction or offending behaviour Serious medical conditions requiring urgent, intensive or long-term treatment Age and/or lack of maturity where it affects the responsibility of the offender Mental disorder or learning disability Sole or primary carer for dependent relatives

[Steps Three to Eight are identical to those applicable to Fraudulent evasion of a prohibition by bringing into or taking out of the UK a controlled drug: see **SG-260**.] **SG-265**

Production of a Controlled Drug **SG-266**

Misuse of Drugs Act 1971 (section 4(2)(a) or (b))

Triable either way unless the defendant could receive the minimum sentence of seven years for a third drug trafficking offence under section 110 Powers of Criminal Courts (Sentencing) Act 2000 in which case the offence is triable only on indictment.

Class A

Maximum: Life imprisonment

Offence range: Community order—16 years' custody

A class A offence is a drug trafficking offence for the purpose of imposing a minimum sentence under section 110 Powers of Criminal Courts (Sentencing) Act 2000

Class B

Maximum: 14 years' custody

Offence range: Discharge—10 years' custody

Class C

Maximum: 14 years' custody

Offence range: Discharge—8 years' custody

Cultivation of Cannabis Plant **SG-267**

Misuse of Drugs Act 1971 (section 6(2))

Maximum: 14 years' custody

Offence range: Discharge—10 years' custody

STEP ONE Determining the offence category

The court should determine the offender's culpability (role) and the harm caused (output or potential output) with reference to the tables below.

In assessing culpability, the sentencer should weigh up all of the factors of the case to determine role. Where there are characteristics present which fall under different role categories, the court should balance these characteristics to reach a fair assessment of the offender's culpability.

In assessing harm, output or potential output is determined by the weight of the product or number of plants/scale of operation. For production offences, purity is not taken into account at step 1 but is dealt with at step 2.

Where the operation is on the most serious and commercial scale, involving a quantity of drugs significantly higher than category 1, sentences of 20 years and above may be appropriate, depending on the role of the offender.

Culpability demonstrated by offender's role One or more of these characteristics may demonstrate the offender's role. These lists are not exhaustive.	**Category of harm** Indicative quantity of drug concerned (upon which the starting point is based):
LEADING role: • Directing or organising buying and selling on a commercial scale; • Substantial links to, and influence on, others in a chain; • Expectation of substantial financial gain; • Uses business as cover; • Abuses a position of trust or responsibility **SIGNIFICANT role:** • Operational or management function within a chain; • Involves others in the operation whether by pressure, influence, intimidation or reward; • Motivated by financial or other advantage, whether or not operating alone; • Some awareness and understanding of scale of operation; **LESSER role:** • Performs a limited function under direction; • Engaged by pressure, coercion, intimidation; • Involvement through naivety/exploitation; • No influence on those above in a chain; • Very little, if any, awareness or understanding of the scale of operation; • If own operation, solely for own use (considering reasonableness of account in all the circumstances).	**Category 1** • Heroin, cocaine — 5kg; • Ecstasy — 10,000 tablets; • LSD — 250,000 squares; • Amphetamine — 20kg; • Cannabis—operation capable of producing industrial quantities for commercial use; • Ketamine — 5kg. **Category 2** • Heroin, cocaine — 1kg; • Ecstasy — 2,000 tablets; • LSD — 25,000 squares; • Amphetamine — 4kg; • Cannabis—operation capable of producing significant quantities for commercial use; • Ketamine — 1kg. **Category 3** • Heroin, cocaine — 150g; • Ecstasy — 300 tablets; • LSD — 2,500 squares; • Amphetamine — 750g; • Cannabis—28 plants; [footnote indicates 'With assumed yield of 40g per plant'] • Ketamine — 150g. **Category 4** • Heroin, cocaine — 5g; • Ecstasy — 20 tablets; • LSD — 170 squares; • Amphetamine — 20g; • Cannabis — 9 plants (domestic operation); [footnote indicates 'With assumed yield of 40g per plant'] • Ketamine — 5g.

STEP TWO Starting point and category range SG-268

Having determined the category, the court should use the corresponding starting point to reach a sentence within the category range below. The starting point applies to all offenders irrespective of plea or previous convictions. The court should then consider further adjustment within the category range for aggravating or mitigating features, set out [at **SG-269**]. In cases where the offender is regarded as being at the very top of the 'leading' role it may be justifiable for the court to depart from the guideline.

Where the defendant is dependent on or has a propensity to misuse drugs and there is sufficient prospect of success, a community order with a drug rehabilitation requirement under section 209 of the Criminal Justice Act 2003 can be a proper alternative to a short or moderate length custodial sentence.

*For **class A** cases, section 110 of the Powers of Criminal Courts (Sentencing) Act 2000 provides that a court should impose a minimum sentence of at least seven years' imprisonment for a third class A trafficking offence except where the court is of the opinion that there are particular circumstances which (a) relate to any of the offences or to the offender; and (b) would make it unjust to do so in all the circumstances.*

CLASS A	Leading role	Significant role	Lesser role
Category 1	**Starting point** 14 years' custody	**Starting point** 10 years' custody	**Starting point** 7 years' custody
	Category range 12–16 years' custody	**Category range** 9–12 years' custody	**Category range** 6–9 years' custody
Category 2	**Starting point** 11 years' custody	**Starting point** 8 years' custody	**Starting point** 5 years' custody
	Category range 9–13 years' custody	**Category range** 6 years 6 months'–10 years' custody	**Category range** 3 years 6 months'–7 years' custody
Category 3	**Starting point** 8 years 6 months' custody	**Starting point** 5 years 'custody	**Starting point** 3 years 6 months' custody
	Category range 6 years 6 months'–10 years' custody	**Category range** 3 years 6 months'–7 years' custody	**Category range** 2–5 years' custody
Category 4	**Starting point** 5 years 6 months' custody	**Starting point** 13 years 6 months' custody	**Starting point** 18 months' custody
	Category range 4 years 6 months'–7 years 6 months' custody	**Category range** 2–5 years' custody	**Category range** High level community order–3 years' custody

CLASS B	Leading role	Significant role	Lesser role
Category 1	**Starting point** 8 years' custody	**Starting point** 5 years 6 months' custody	**Starting point** 3 years' custody
	Category range 7–10 years' custody	**Category range** 5–7 years' custody	**Category range** 2 years 6 months'–5 years' custody
Category 2	**Starting point** 6 years' custody	**Starting point** 4 years' custody	**Starting point** 1 year's custody
	Category range 4 years 6 months'–8 years' custody	**Category range** 2 years 6 months'–5 years' custody	**Category range** 26 weeks'–3 years' custody
Category 3	**Starting point** 4 years' custody	**Starting point** 1 year's custody	**Starting point** High level community order
	Category range 2 years 6 months'–5 years' custody	**Category range** 26 weeks'–3 years' custody	**Category range** Low level community order–26 weeks' custody
Category 4	**Starting point** 1 year's custody	**Starting point** High level community order	**Starting point** Band C fine
	Category range High level community order–3 years' custody	**Category range** Medium level community order–26 weeks' custody	**Category range** Discharge–medium level community order

CLASS C	Leading role	Significant role	Lesser role
Category 1	**Starting point** 5 years' custody	**Starting point** 3 years' custody	**Starting point** 18 months' custody
	Category range 4–8 years' custody	**Category range** 2–5 years' custody	**Category range** 1–3 years' custody
Category 2	**Starting point** 3 years 6 months' custody	**Starting point** 18 months' custody	**Starting point** 26 weeks' custody
	Category range 2–5 years' custody	**Category range** 1–3 years' custody	**Category range** High level community order–18 months' custody
Category 3	**Starting point** 18 months' custody	**Starting point** 26 weeks' custody	**Starting point** High level community order
	Category range 1–3 years' custody	**Category range** High level community order–18 months' custody	**Category range** Low level community order–12 weeks' custody
Category 4	**Starting point** 26 weeks' custody	**Starting point** High level community order	**Starting point** Band C fine
	Category range High level community order–18 months' custody	**Category range** Low level community order–12 weeks' custody	**Category range** Discharge–medium level community order

SG-269 The table below contains a **non-exhaustive** list of additional factual elements providing the context of the offence and factors relating to the offender. Identify whether any combination of these, or other relevant factors, should result in an upward or downward adjustment from the starting point. In some cases, having considered these factors, it may be appropriate to move outside the identified category range.

Where appropriate, consider the custody threshold as follows:

- Has the custody threshold been passed?
- If so, is it unavoidable that a custodial sentence be imposed?
- If so, can that sentence be suspended?

Where appropriate, the court should also consider the community threshold as follows:

- Has the community threshold been passed?

Factors increasing seriousness	Factors reducing seriousness or reflecting personal mitigation
Statutory aggravating factors: Previous convictions, having regard to a) nature of the offence to which conviction relates and relevance to current offence; and b) time elapsed since conviction (see [italicised text at **SG-268**] if third drug trafficking conviction) Offence committed on bail *Other aggravating factors include:* Nature of any likely supply Level of any profit element Use of premises accompanied by unlawful access to electricity/other utility supply of others Ongoing/large scale operation as evidenced by presence and nature of specialist equipment Exposure of others to more than usual danger, for example drugs cut with harmful substances Attempts to conceal or dispose of evidence, where not charged separately Presence of others, especially children and/or non-users Presence of weapon, where not charged separately High purity or high potential yield Failure to comply with current court orders Offence committed on licence Established evidence of community impact	Involvement due to pressure, intimidation or coercion falling short of duress, except where already taken into account at step 1 Isolated incident Low purity No previous convictions **or** no relevant or recent convictions Offender's vulnerability was exploited Remorse Good character and/or exemplary conduct Determination and/or demonstration of steps having been taken to address addiction or offending behaviour Serious medical conditions requiring urgent, intensive or long-term treatment Age and/or lack of maturity where it affects the responsibility of the offender Mental disorder or learning disability Sole or primary carer for dependent relatives

[Steps Three to Eight are identical to those applicable to Fraudulent evasion of a prohibition by bringing into or taking out of the UK a controlled drug: see **SG-260**.] **SG-270**

Permitting Premises to be Used **SG-271**

Misuse of Drugs Act 1971 (section 8)

Triable either way unless the defendant could receive the minimum sentence of seven years for a third drug trafficking offence under section 110 Powers of Criminal Courts (Sentencing) Act 2000 in which case the offence is triable only on indictment.

Class A

Maximum: 14 years' custody

Offence range: Community order—4 years' custody

A class A offence is a drug trafficking offence for the purpose of imposing a minimum sentence under section 110 Powers of Criminal Courts (Sentencing) Act 2000

Class B

Maximum: 14 years' custody

Offence range: Fine—18 months' custody

Class C

Maximum: 14 years' custody

Offence range: Discharge—26 weeks' custody

STEP ONE Determining the offence category **SG-272**

The court should determine the offender's culpability and the harm caused (extent of the activity and/or the quantity of drugs) with reference to the table below.

In assessing harm, quantity is determined by the weight of the product. Purity is not taken into account at step 1 but is dealt with at step 2

Category 1	Higher culpability **and** greater harm
Category 2	Lower culpability **and** greater harm; **or** higher culpability **and** lesser harm
Category 3	Lower culpability **and** lesser harm

Factors indicating culpability (non-exhaustive)	**Factors indicating harm (non-exhaustive)**
Higher culpability: Permits premises to be used primarily for drug activity, for example crack house Permits use in expectation of substantial financial gain Uses legitimate business premises to aid and/or conceal illegal activity, for example public house or club *Lower culpability*: Permits use for limited or no financial gain No active role in any supply taking place Involvement through naivety	*Greater harm*: Regular drug-related activity Higher quantity of drugs, for example: • Heroin, cocaine — more than 5g; • Cannabis — more than 50g. *Lesser harm:* Infrequent drug-related activity Lower quantity of drugs, for example: • Heroin, cocaine — up to 5g; • Cannabis — up to 50g.

STEP TWO Starting point and category range **SG-273**

Having determined the category, the court should use the table below to identify the corresponding starting point to reach a sentence within the category range. The starting point applies to all offenders irrespective of plea or previous convictions. The court should then consider further adjustment within the category range for aggravating or mitigating features, set out [at **SG-274**].

Where the defendant is dependent on or has a propensity to misuse drugs and there is sufficient prospect of success, a community order with a drug rehabilitation requirement under section 209 of the Criminal Justice Act 2003 can be a proper alternative to a short or moderate length custodial sentence.

For class A cases, section 110 of the Powers of Criminal Courts (Sentencing) Act 2000 provides that a court should impose a minimum sentence of at least seven years' imprisonment for a third class A trafficking offence except where the court is of the opinion that there are particular circumstances which (a) relate to any of the offences or to the offender; and (b) would make it unjust to do so in all the circumstances.

Class A

Offence category	Starting point (*applicable to all offenders*)	Category range (*applicable to all offenders*)
Category 1	2 years 6 months' custody	18 months'–4 years' custody
Category 2	36 weeks' custody	High level community order–18 months' custody
Category 3	Medium level community order	Low level community order–high level community order

Class B

Offence category	Starting point (*applicable to all offenders*)	Category range (*applicable to all offenders*)
Category 1	1 year's custody	26 weeks'–18 months' custody
Category 2	High level community order	Low level community order–26 weeks' custody
Category 3	Band C fine	Band A fine–low level community order

Class C

Offence category	Starting point (*applicable to all offenders*)	Category range (*applicable to all offenders*)
Category 1	12 weeks' custody	High level community order–26 weeks' custody [footnote indicates that 'when tried summarily, the maximum penalty is 12 weeks' custody']
Category 2	Low level community order	Band C fine–high level community order
Category 3	Band A fine	Discharge–band C fine

SG-274 The table below contains a **non-exhaustive** list of additional factual elements providing the context of the offence and factors relating to the offender. Identify whether any combination of these, or other relevant factors, should result in an upward or downward adjustment from the starting point. In some cases, having considered these factors, it may be appropriate to move outside the identified category range.

Where appropriate, consider the custody threshold as follows:

- Has the custody threshold been passed?
- If so, is it unavoidable that a custodial sentence be imposed?
- If so, can that sentence be suspended?

Where appropriate, the court should also consider the community threshold as follows:

- Has the community threshold been passed?

Factors increasing seriousness	**Factors reducing seriousness or reflecting personal mitigation**
Statutory aggravating factors: Previous convictions, having regard to a) nature of the offence to which conviction relates and relevance to current offence; and b) time elapsed since conviction (see italicised text at **SG-273** if third drug trafficking conviction) Offence committed on bail *Other aggravating factors include:* Length of time over which premises used for drug activity Volume of drug activity permitted Premises adapted to facilitate drug activity Location of premises, for example proximity to school Attempts to conceal or dispose of evidence, where not charged separately Presence of others, especially children and/or non-users High purity Presence of weapons, where not charged separately Failure to comply with current court orders Offence committed on licence Established evidence of community impact	Involvement due to pressure, intimidation or coercion falling short of duress Isolated incident Low purity No previous convictions or no relevant or recent convictions Offender's vulnerability was exploited Remorse Good character and/or exemplary conduct Determination and/or demonstration of steps having been taken to address addiction or offending behaviour Serious medical conditions requiring urgent, intensive or long-term treatment Age and/or lack of maturity where it affects the responsibility of the offender Mental disorder or learning disability Sole or primary carer for dependent relatives

[Steps Three to Eight are identical to those applicable to Fraudulent evasion of a prohibition by bringing into or taking out of the UK a controlled drug: see **SG-260**.] **SG-275**

POSSESSION OF A CONTROLLED DRUG **SG-276**

Misuse of Drugs Act 1971 (section 5(2))

Triable either way

CLASS A

Maximum: 7 years' custody

Offence range: Fine—51 weeks' custody

CLASS B

Maximum: 5 years' custody
Offence range: Discharge—26 weeks' custody

CLASS C

Maximum: 2 years' custody

Offence range: Discharge—Community order

STEP ONE Determining the offence category **SG-277**

The court should identify the offence category based on the class of drug involved.

Category 1	Class A drug
Category 2	Class B drug
Category 3	Class C drug

Sentencing Guidelines

SG-278 **STEP TWO Starting point and category range**

The court should use the table below to identify the corresponding starting point. The starting point applies to all offenders irrespective of plea or previous convictions. The court should then consider further adjustment within the category range for aggravating or mitigating features, set out [at **SG-279**].

Where the defendant is dependent on or has a propensity to misuse drugs and there is sufficient prospect of success, a community order with a drug rehabilitation requirement under section 209 of the Criminal Justice Act 2003 can be a proper alternative to a short or moderate length custodial sentence.

Offence category	**Starting point** (*applicable to all offenders*)	**Category range** (*applicable to all offenders*)
Category 1 (class A)	Band C fine	Band A fine–51 weeks' custody
Category 2 (class B)	Band B fine	Discharge–26 weeks' custody
Category 3 (class C)	Band A fine	Discharge–medium level community order

SG-279 The table below contains a **non-exhaustive** list of additional factual elements providing the context of the offence and factors relating to the offender. Identify whether any combination of these, or other relevant factors, should result in an upward or downward adjustment from the starting point. **In particular, possession of drugs in prison is likely to result in an upward adjustment.** In some cases, having considered these factors, it may be appropriate to move outside the identified category range.

Where appropriate, consider the custody threshold as follows:

- Has the custody threshold been passed?
- If so, is it unavoidable that a custodial sentence be imposed?
- If so, can that sentence be suspended?

Where appropriate, the court should also consider the community threshold as follows:

- Has the community threshold been passed?

Factors increasing seriousness	**Factors reducing seriousness or reflecting personal mitigation**
Statutory aggravating factors: Previous convictions, having regard to a) nature of the offence to which conviction relates and relevance to current offence; and b) time elapsed since conviction Offence committed on bail *Other aggravating factors include:* Possession of drug in prison Presence of others, especially children and/or non-users Possession of drug in a school or licensed premises Failure to comply with current court orders Offence committed on licence Attempts to conceal or dispose of evidence, where not charged separately Charged as importation of a very small amount Established evidence of community impact	No previous convictions **or** no relevant or recent convictions Remorse Good character and/or exemplary conduct Offender is using cannabis to help with a diagnosed medical condition Determination and/or demonstration of steps having been taken to address addiction or offending behaviour Serious medical conditions requiring urgent, intensive or long-term treatment Isolated incident Age and/or lack of maturity where it affects the responsibility of the offender Mental disorder or learning disability Sole or primary carer for dependent relatives

SG-280 [Steps Three to Eight are similar to those applicable to Fraudulent evasion of a prohibition by bringing into or taking out of the UK a controlled drug (see **SG-260**) but the reference at Step Four to minimum mandatory sentences does not apply and Step Six merely states 'In all cases, the court should consider whether to make ancillary orders'.]

Drunk and Disorderly in a Public Place SG-281

Criminal Justice Act 1967, s. 91

Triable only summarily
Maximum: Level 3 fine

Offence seriousness (culpability and harm)

A. Identify the appropriate starting point

Starting points based on first time offender pleading not guilty

Examples of nature of activity	Starting point	Range
Shouting, causing disturbance for some minutes	Band A fine	Conditional discharge–band B fine
Substantial disturbance caused	Band B fine	Band A fine–band C fine

B. Consider the effect of aggravating and mitigating factors (other than those within examples above)

Common aggravating and mitigating factors are identified [elsewhere]—the following may be particularly relevant but these lists are not exhaustive

Factors indicating higher culpability	Factors indicating lower culpability
1. Offensive words or behaviour involved 2. Lengthy incident 3. Group action **Factors indicating greater degree of harm** 1. Offence committed at school, hospital or other place where vulnerable persons may be present 2. Offence committed on public transport 3. Victim providing public service	1. Minor and non-threatening 2. Stopped as soon as police arrived

[Sets out the standard sequential sentencing procedure and includes mention of need to consider football banning order.]

Electricity, Abstract/Use without Authority SG-282

[The Guidelines relating to this offence for magistrates' courts directly reproduce the Theft Offences Definitive Guideline as regards 'Abstracting electricity', which has effect in respect of all persons aged 18 or over who are sentenced on or after 1 February 2016: see SG-457G.]

Environmental Offences SG-283

[The guidelines applicable in magistrates' courts are identical to those set out in part 26 of the Sentencing Guidelines, see **SG-610**.]

Exploitation of Prostitution SG-284

[The *guidelines* set out below are applicable to adult offenders sentenced after 1 April 2014.]

Causing or Inciting Prostitution For Gain

Sexual Offences Act 2003 (section 52)

Controlling Prostitution for Gain

Sexual Offences Act 2003 (section 53)

Triable either way:
Maximum: 7 years' custody

Offence range: Community order—6 years' custody

For convictions on or after 3 December 2012 (irrespective of the date of commission of the offence), these are specified offences for the purposes of section 226A (extended sentence for certain violent or sexual offences) of the Criminal Justice Act 2003.

The terms 'prostitute' and 'prostitution' are used in this guideline in accordance with the statutory language contained in the Sexual Offences Act 2003.

STEP ONE Determining the offence category

The court should determine which categories of harm and culpability the offence falls into by reference **only** to the tables below.

HARM	
Category 1	• Abduction/detention • Violence or threats of violence • Sustained and systematic psychological abuse • Individual(s) forced or coerced to participate in unsafe/degrading sexual activity • Individual(s) forced or coerced into seeing many 'customers' • Individual(s) forced/coerced/deceived into prostitution
Category 2	Factor(s) in category 1 not present

CULPABILITY		
A	B	C
• Causing, inciting or controlling prostitution on significant commercial basis • Expectation of significant financial or other gain • Abuse of trust • Exploitation of those known to be trafficked • Significant involvement in limiting the freedom of prostitute(s) • Grooming of individual(s) to enter prostitution including through cultivation of a dependency on drugs or alcohol	• Close involvement with prostitute(s) for example control of finances, choice of clients, working conditions, etc (where offender's involvement is not as a result of coercion)	• Performs limited function under direction • Close involvement but engaged by coercion/intimidation/ exploitation

STEP TWO Starting point and category range

Having determined the category, the court should use the corresponding starting points to reach a sentence within the category range below. The starting point applies to all offenders irrespective of plea or previous convictions. Having determined the starting point, step two allows further adjustment for aggravating or mitigating features, set out [below].

A case of particular gravity, reflected by multiple features of culpability or harm in step one, could merit upward adjustment from the starting point before further adjustment for aggravating or mitigating features, set out [below].

Where there is a sufficient prospect of rehabilitation, a community order with a sex offender treatment programme requirement under section 202 of the Criminal Justice Act 2003 can be a proper alternative to a short or moderate length custodial sentence.

Category 1	**Starting point** 4 years' custody	**Starting point** 2 years 6 months' custody	**Starting point** 1 year's custody
	Category range 3–6 years' custody	**Category range** 2–4 years' custody	**Category range** 26 weeks'–2 years' custody
Category 2	**Starting point** 2 years' 6 months' custody	**Starting point** 1 year's custody	**Starting point** Medium level community Order
	Category range 2–5 years' custody	**Category range** High level community order–2 years' custody	**Category range** Low level community order–High level community order

The table below contains a **non-exhaustive** list of additional factual elements providing the context of the offence and factors relating to the offender. Identify whether any combination of these, or other relevant factors, should result in an upward or downward adjustment from the starting point. **In particular, relevant recent convictions are likely to result in an upward adjustment.** In some cases, having considered these factors, it may be appropriate to move outside the identified category range.

When sentencing appropriate **category 2 offences**, the court should also consider the custody threshold as follows:

- Has the custody threshold been passed?
- If so, is it unavoidable that a custodial sentence be imposed?
- If so, can that sentence be suspended?

Aggravating factors
Statutory aggravating factors
• Previous convictions, having regard to a) the nature of the offence to which the conviction relates and its relevance to the current offence; and b) the time that has elapsed since the conviction • Offence committed whilst on bail
Other aggravating factors
• Failure to comply with current court orders • Offence committed whilst on licence • Deliberate isolation of prostitute(s) • Threats made to expose prostitute(s) to the authorities (for example, immigration or police), family/friends or others • Harm threatened against the family/friends of prostitute(s) • Passport/identity documents removed • Prostitute(s) prevented from seeking medical treatment • Food withheld • Earnings withheld/kept by offender or evidence of excessive wage reduction or debt bondage, inflated travel or living expenses or unreasonable interest rates • Any steps taken to prevent the reporting of an incident, obtaining assistance and/or from assisting or supporting the prosecution • Attempts to dispose of or conceal evidence • Prostitute(s) forced or coerced into pornography • Timescale over which operation has been run

Mitigating factors
• No previous convictions **or** no relevant/recent convictions • Remorse • Previous good character and/or exemplary conduct* • Age and/or lack of maturity where it affects the responsibility of the offender • Mental disorder or learning disability, particularly where linked to the commission of the offence • Demonstration of steps taken to address offending behaviour

* Previous good character/exemplary conduct is different from having no previous convictions. The more serious the offence, the less the weight which should normally be attributed to this factor. Where previous good character/exemplary conduct has been used to facilitate the offence, this mitigation should not normally be allowed and such conduct may constitute an aggravating factor.

[Sets out the standard sequential sentencing procedure.]

EXPOSURE

SG-285

[The guidelines set out below are applicable to adult offenders sentenced after 1 April 2014.]

Sexual Offences Act 2003 (section 66)

Triable either way:
Maximum: 2 years' custody
Offence range: Fine—1 year's custody

For convictions on or after 3 December 2012 (irrespective of the date of commission of the offence), this is a specified offence for the purposes of section 226A (extended sentence for certain violent or sexual offences) of the Criminal Justice Act 2003.

STEP ONE Determining the offence category

The court should determine the offence category using the table below.

Category 1	Raised harm **and** raised culpability
Category 2	Raised harm **or** raised culpability
Category 3	Exposure **without** raised harm or culpability factors present

The court should determine culpability and harm caused or intended, by reference **only** to the factors below, which comprise the principal factual elements of the offence. Where an offence does not fall squarely into a category, individual factors may require a degree of weighting before making an overall assessment and determining the appropriate offence category.

Factors indicating raised harm
• Victim followed/pursued • Offender masturbated

Factors indicating raised culpability
• Specific or previous targeting of a particularly vulnerable victim • Abuse of trust • Use of threats (including blackmail) • Offence racially or religiously aggravated • Offence motivated by, or demonstrating, hostility to the victim based on his or her sexual orientation (or presumed sexual orientation) or transgender identity (or presumed transgender identity) • Offence motivated by, or demonstrating, hostility to the victim based on his or her disability (or presumed disability)

STEP TWO Starting point and category range

Having determined the category, the court should use the corresponding starting points to reach a sentence within the category range [below]. The starting point applies to all offenders irrespective of plea or previous convictions. Having determined the starting point, step two allows further adjustment for aggravating or mitigating features, set out [below].

A case of particular gravity, reflected by multiple features of culpability or harm in step one, could merit upward adjustment from the starting point before further adjustment for aggravating or mitigating features, set out [below].

Where there is a sufficient prospect of rehabilitation, a community order with a sex offender treatment programme requirement under section 202 of the Criminal Justice Act 2003 can be a proper alternative to a short or moderate length custodial sentence.

Category 1	**Starting point** 26 weeks' custody
	Category range 12 weeks'–1 year's custody
Category 2	**Starting point** High level community order
	Category range Medium level community order–26 weeks' custody
Category 3	**Starting point** Medium level community order
	Category range Band A fine–High level community order

The table below contains a **non-exhaustive** list of additional factual elements providing the context of the offence and factors relating to the offender. Identify whether any combination of these, or other relevant factors, should result in an upward or downward adjustment from the starting point. **In particular, relevant recent convictions are likely to result in an upward adjustment.** In some cases, having considered these factors, it may be appropriate to move outside the identified category range.

When sentencing **category 2 offences**, the court should also consider the custody threshold as follows:

- Has the custody threshold been passed?
- If so, is it unavoidable that a custodial sentence be imposed?
- If so, can that sentence be suspended?

When sentencing **category 3 offences**, the court should also consider the community order threshold as follows:

- Has the community order threshold been passed?

Aggravating factors
Statutory aggravating factors • Previous convictions, having regard to a) the nature of the offence to which the conviction relates and its relevance to the current offence; and b) the time that has elapsed since the conviction • Offence committed whilst on bail *Other aggravating factors* • Location of the offence • Timing of the offence • Any steps taken to prevent the victim reporting an incident, obtaining assistance and/or from assisting or supporting the prosecution • Failure to comply with current court orders • Offence committed whilst on licence • Commission of offence whilst under the influence of alcohol or drugs • Presence of others, especially children

Mitigating factors
• No previous convictions **or** no relevant/recent convictions • Remorse • Previous good character and/or exemplary conduct* • Age and/or lack of maturity where it affects the responsibility of the offender • Mental disorder or learning disability, particularly where linked to the commission of the offence • Demonstration of steps taken to address offending behaviour

* Previous good character/exemplary conduct is different from having no previous convictions. The more serious the offence, the less the weight which should normally be attributed to this factor. Where previous good character/exemplary conduct has been used to facilitate the offence, this mitigation should not normally be allowed and such conduct may constitute an aggravating factor.

[Sets out the standard sequential sentencing procedure.]

Firearm, Carrying in Public Place SG-286

Firearms Act 1968, s. 19

Triable either way (but triable only summarily if the firearm is an air weapon):
Maximum when tried summarily: Level 5 fine and/or 6 months
Maximum when tried on indictment: 7 years (12 months for imitation firearms)

Offence seriousness (culpability and harm)

A. Identify the appropriate starting point

Starting points based on first time offender pleading not guilty

Examples of nature of activity	**Starting point**	**Range**
Carrying an unloaded air weapon	Low level community order	Band B fine–medium level community order
Carrying loaded air weapon/imitation firearm/unloaded shot gun without ammunition	High level community order	Medium level community order–26 weeks' custody (air weapon) Medium level community order to Crown Court (imitation firearm, unloaded shot gun)
Carrying loaded shot gun/carrying shot gun or any other firearm together with ammunition for it	Crown Court	Crown Court

B. Consider the effect of aggravating and mitigating factors (other than those within examples above)

Common aggravating and mitigating factors are identified [elsewhere]—the following may be particularly relevant but these lists are not exhaustive

Factors indicating higher culpability	Factors indicating lower culpability
1. Brandishing the firearm 2. Carrying firearm in a busy place 3. Planned illegal use **Factors indicating greater degree of harm** 1. Person or people put in fear 2. Offender participating in violent incident	1. Firearm not in sight 2. No intention to use firearm 3. Firearm to be used for lawful purpose (not amounting to a defence)

[Sets out the standard sequential sentencing procedure, ancillary orders to be considered include compensation, forfeiture or suspension of personal liquor licence and football banning order (where appropriate).]

SG-287

Football Related Offences

Sporting Events (Control of Alcohol etc.) Act 1985: s. 2(1) (possession of alcohol whilst entering or trying to enter ground); s.2(2) (being drunk in, or whilst trying to enter, ground) Football Offences Act 1991: s. 2 (throwing missile); s. 3 (indecent or racist chanting); s. 4 (going onto prohibited areas)

Criminal Justice and Public Order Act 1994: s. 166 (unauthorised sale or attempted sale of tickets)

Triable only summarily:
Maximum: Level 2 fine (being drunk in ground) Level 3 fine (throwing missile; indecent or racist chanting; going onto prohibited areas) Level 5 fine (unauthorised sale of tickets) Level 3 fine and/or 3 months (possession of alcohol)

Offence seriousness (culpability and harm)

A. Identify the appropriate starting point

Starting points based on first time offender pleading not guilty

Examples of nature of activity	Starting point	Range
Being drunk in, or whilst trying to enter, ground	Band A fine	Conditional discharge–band B fine
Going onto playing or other prohibited area; Unauthorised sale or attempted sale of tickets	Band B fine	Band A fine–band C fine
Throwing missile; Indecent or racist chanting	Band C fine	Band C fine
Possession of alcohol whilst entering or trying to enter ground	Band C fine	Band B fine–high level community order

B. Consider the effect of aggravating and mitigating factors (other than those within examples above)

Common aggravating and mitigating factors are identified [elsewhere]—the following may be particularly relevant but these lists are not exhaustive

Factors indicating higher culpability 1. Commercial ticket operation; potential high cash value; counterfeit tickets 2. Inciting others to misbehave 3. Possession of large quantity of alcohol 4. Offensive language or behaviour (where not an element of the offence) **Factors indicating greater degree of harm** 1. Missile likely to cause serious injury e.g. coin, glass, bottle, stone

[Sets out the standard sequential sentencing procedure and mentions need to consider a football banning order.]

Fraud, Bribery and Money Laundering Offences SG-288

[The guidelines applicable in magistrates' courts are identical to those set out in part 17 of the Sentencing Guidelines, see **SG-472**].

Going Equipped, for Theft SG-289

[The Guidelines relating to going equipped for magistrates' courts directly reproduce the Theft Offences Definitive Guideline as regards 'Going equipped for theft or burglary', which has effect in respect of all persons aged 18 or over who are sentenced on or after 1 February 2016: see **SG-457C**.]

Grievous Bodily Harm/Unlawful Wounding & Racially or Religiously Aggravated Grievous Bodily Harm/Unlawful Wounding SG-290

[See 'Inflicting Grievous Bodily Harm/Unlawful Wounding' at **SG-296**, the Guideline from the Sentencing Council which has effect from 13 June 2011.]

Handling Stolen Goods SG-291

[The Guidelines relating to handling for magistrates' courts directly reproduce the Theft Offences Definitive Guideline as regards 'Handling Stolen Goods', which has effect in respect of all persons aged 18 or over who are sentenced on or after 1 February 2016: see **SG-456**.]

Harassment—Putting People in Fear of Violence Racially or Religiously Aggravated Harassment—Putting People in Fear of Violence SG-292

Protection from Harassment Act 1997, s. 4

Crime and Disorder Act 1998, s. 32

Harassment: triable either way
Maximum when tried summarily: Level 5 fine and/or 6 months

Maximum when tried on indictment: 5 years
Racially or religiously aggravated harassment: triable either way
Maximum when tried summarily: Level 5 fine and/or 6 months

Maximum when tried on indictment: 7 years
Where offence committed in domestic context, refer [below] for guidance

Offence seriousness (culpability and harm)

A. Identify the appropriate starting point

Starting points based on first time offender pleading not guilty

Examples of nature of activity	Starting point	Range
A pattern of two or more incidents of unwanted contact	6 weeks' custody	High level community order–18 weeks' custody
Deliberate threats, persistent action over a longer period; or Intention to cause fear of violence	18 weeks' custody	12 weeks' custody–Crown Court
Sexual threats, vulnerable person targeted	Crown Court	Crown Court

B. Consider the effect of aggravating and mitigating factors (other than those within examples above)

Common aggravating and mitigating factors are identified [elsewhere]—the following may be particularly relevant but these lists are not exhaustive

Factors indicating higher culpability	Factors indicating lower culpability
1. Planning 2. Offender ignores obvious distress 3. Offender involves others 4. Using contact arrangements with a child to instigate offence **Factors indicating greater degree of harm** 1. Victim needs medical help/counselling 2. Action over long period 3. Children frightened 4. Use or distribution of photographs	1. Limited understanding of effect on victim 2. Initial provocation

[Sets out the standard sequential sentencing procedure. Notes that 'If offender charged and convicted of the racially or religiously aggravated offence, increase the sentence to reflect this element'.]

SG-293

Harassment (Without Violence)

Racially or Religiously Aggravated Harassment (Non Violent)

Protection from Harassment Act 1997, s.2

Crime and Disorder Act 1998, s.32

Harassment: triable only summarily
Maximum: Level 5 fine and/or 6 months

Racially or religiously aggravated harassment: triable either way
Maximum when tried summarily: Level 5 fine and/or 6 months
Maximum when tried on indictment: 2 years

Where offence committed in domestic context, refer [below] for guidance

Offence seriousness (culpability and harm)

A. Identify the appropriate starting point

Examples of nature of activity	Starting point	Range
Small number of incidents	Medium level community order	Band C fine–high level community order
Constant contact at night, trying to come into workplace or home, involving others	6 weeks' custody	Medium level community order–12 weeks' custody
Threatening violence, taking personal photographs, sending offensive material	18 weeks' custody	12–26 weeks' custody

Starting points based on first time offender pleading not guilty

B. Consider the effect of aggravating and mitigating factors (other than those within examples above)

Common aggravating and mitigating factors are identified [elsewhere]—the following may be particularly relevant but these lists are not exhaustive

Factors indicating higher culpability	Factors indicating lower culpability
1. Planning 2. Offender ignores obvious distress 3. Offender involves others 4. Using contact arrangements with a child to instigate offence **Factors indicating greater degree of harm** 1. Victim needs medical help/counselling 2. Action over long period 3. Children frightened 4. Use or distribution of photographs	1. Limited understanding of effect on victim 2. Initial provocation

[Sets out the standard sequential sentencing procedure. Notes that 'If offender charged and convicted of the racially or religiously aggravated offence, increase the sentence to reflect this element'.]

IDENTITY DOCUMENTS—POSSESS FALSE/ANOTHER'S/IMPROPERLY OBTAINED SG-294

Identity Cards Act 2006, s. 25(5)
(possession of a false identity document (as defined in s. 26—includes a passport))

Triable either way:
Maximum when tried summarily: Level 5 fine and/or 6 months
Maximum when tried on indictment: 2 years (s.25(5))

Note: possession of a false identity document with the intention of using it is an indictable-only offence (Identity Cards Act 2006, s. 25(1)). The maximum penalty is 10 years imprisonment.

Offence seriousness (culpability and harm)

A. Identify the appropriate starting point

Starting points based on first time offender pleading not guilty

B. Consider the effect of aggravating and mitigating factors (other than those within examples above)

Examples of nature of activity	Starting point	Range
Single document possessed	Medium level community order	Band C fine–high level community order
Small number of documents, no evidence of dealing	12 weeks' custody	6 weeks' custody–Crown Court
Considerable number of documents possessed, evidence of involvement in larger operation	Crown Court	Crown Court

Common aggravating and mitigating factors are identified [elsewhere]—the following may be particularly relevant but these lists are not exhaustive

[Sets out the standard sequential sentencing procedure.]

Factors indicating higher culpability	Factor indicating lower culpability
1. Clear knowledge that documents false 2. Number of documents possessed (where not in offence descriptions above) **Factors indicating greater degree of harm** 1. Group activity 2. Potential impact of use (where not in offence descriptions above)	1. Genuine mistake or ignorance

INDECENT PHOTOGRAPHS OF CHILDREN [, POSSESSION OF] SG-295

[The guidelines set out below are applicable to adult offenders sentenced after 1 April 2014.]

Criminal Justice Act 1988 (section 160)

Triable either way:
Maximum: 5 years' custody
Offence range: Community order—3 years' custody

INDECENT PHOTOGRAPHS OF CHILDREN

Protection of Children Act 1978 (section 1)

Triable either way
Maximum: 10 years' custody
Offence range: Community order—9 years' custody

For section 1 offences committed on or after 3 December 2012, this is an offence listed in Part 1 of Schedule 15B for the purposes of section 224A (life sentence for second listed offence) of the Criminal Justice Act 2003.

For convictions on or after 3 December 2012 (irrespective of the date of commission of the offence), these are specified offences for the purposes of section 226A (extended sentence for certain violent or sexual offences) of the Criminal Justice Act 2003.

STEP ONE Determining the offence category

The court should determine the offence category using the table below.

In most cases the intrinsic character of the most serious of the offending images will initially determine the appropriate category. If, however, the most serious images are unrepresentative of the offender's conduct a lower category may be appropriate. A lower category will not, however, be appropriate if the offender has produced or taken (for example photographed) images of a higher category.

	Possession	Distribution*	Production**
Category A	Possession of images involving penetrative sexual activity Possession of images involving sexual activity with an animal or sadism	Sharing images involving penetrative sexual activity Sharing images involving sexual activity with an animal or sadism	Creating images involving penetrative sexual activity Creating images involving sexual activity with an animal or sadism
Category B	Possession of images involving non-penetrative sexual activity	Sharing of images involving non-penetrative sexual activity	Creating images involving non-penetrative sexual activity
Category C	Possession of other indecent images not falling within categories A or B	Sharing of other indecent images not falling within categories A or B	Creating other indecent images not falling within categories A or B

* Distribution includes possession with a view to distributing or sharing images.

** Production includes the taking or making of any image at source, for instance the original image. Making an image by simple downloading should be treated as possession for the purposes of sentencing.

STEP TWO Starting point and category range

Having determined the category, the court should use the corresponding starting points to reach a sentence within the category range below. The starting point applies to all offenders irrespective of plea or previous convictions. Having determined the starting point, step two allows further adjustment for aggravating or mitigating features, set out [below].

Where there is a sufficient prospect of rehabilitation, a community order with a sex offender treatment programme requirement under section 202 of the Criminal Justice Act 2003 can be a proper alternative to a short or moderate length custodial sentence.

The table below contains a **non-exhaustive** list of additional factual elements providing the context of the offence and factors relating to the offender. Identify whether any combination of these, or other relevant

	Possession	Distribution	Production
Category A	**Starting point** 1 year's custody	**Starting point** 3 years' custody	**Starting point** 6 years' custody
	Category range 26 weeks–3 years' custody	**Category range** 2–5 years' custody	**Category range** 4–9 years' custody
Category B	**Starting point** 26 weeks' custody	**Starting point** 1 year's custody	**Starting point** 2 years' custody
	Category range High level community order–18 months' custody	**Category range** 26 weeks'–2 years' custody	**Category range** 1–4 years' custody
Category C	**Starting point** High level community order	**Starting point** 13 weeks' custody	**Starting point** 18 months' custody
	Category range Medium level community order–26 weeks' custody	**Category range** High level community order–26 weeks' custody	**Category range** 1–3 years' custody

factors, should result in an upward or downward adjustment from the starting point. **In particular, relevant recent convictions are likely to result in an upward adjustment**. In some cases, having considered these factors, it may be appropriate to move outside the identified category range.

When sentencing appropriate **category 2 or 3 offences**, the court should also consider the custody threshold as follows:

- Has the custody threshold been passed?
- If so, is it unavoidable that a custodial sentence be imposed?
- If so, can that sentence be suspended?

[Sets out the standard sequential sentencing procedure.]

Aggravating factors
Statutory aggravating factors
• Previous convictions, having regard to a) the nature of the offence to which the conviction relates and its relevance to the current offence; and b) the time that has elapsed since the conviction • Offence committed whilst on bail
Other aggravating factors
• Failure to comply with current court orders • Offence committed whilst on licence • Age and/or vulnerability of the child depicted+ • Discernible pain or distress suffered by child depicted • Period over which images were possessed, distributed or produced • High volume of images possessed, distributed or produced • Placing images where there is the potential for a high volume of viewers • Collection includes moving images • Attempts to dispose of or conceal evidence • Abuse of trust • Child depicted known to the offender • Active involvement in a network or process that facilitates or commissions the creation or sharing of indecent images of children • Commercial exploitation and/or motivation • Deliberate or systematic searching for images portraying young children, category A images or the portrayal of familial sexual abuse • Large number of different victims • Child depicted intoxicated or drugged

+ Age and/or vulnerability of the child should be given significant weight. In cases where the actual age of the victim is difficult to determine sentencers should consider the development of the child (infant, pre-pubescent, post-pubescent)

Mitigating factors
• No previous convictions **or** no relevant/recent convictions • Remorse • Previous good character and/or exemplary conduct* • Age and/or lack of maturity where it affects the responsibility of the offender • Mental disorder or learning disability, particularly where linked to the commission of the offence • Demonstration of steps taken to address offending behaviour

* Previous good character/exemplary conduct is different from having no previous convictions. The more serious the offence, the less the weight which should normally be attributed to this factor. Where previous good character/exemplary conduct has been used to facilitate the offence, this mitigation should not normally be allowed and such conduct may constitute an aggravating factor.

Inflicting Grievous Bodily Harm/Unlawful Wounding SG-296

Offences against the Person Act 1861 (section 20)

Racially/Religiously Aggravated GBH/Unlawful Wounding

Crime and Disorder Act 1998 (section 29)

[This guideline was published by the Sentencing Council and has effect in respect of all sentences passed after 13 June 2011 on offenders aged 18 or older. It replaces the guideline which previously applied and which continued to have effect until that date.]

These are specified offences for the purposes of section 224 of the Criminal Justice Act 2003

Triable either way

Section 20
Maximum when tried summarily: Level 5 fine and/or 26 weeks' custody
Maximum when tried on indictment: 5 years' custody

Section 29
Maximum when tried summarily: Level 5 fine and/or 26 weeks' custody
Maximum when tried on indictment: 7 years' custody

Offence range: Community order—4 years' custody

This guideline applies to all offenders aged 18 and older, who are sentenced on or after 13 June 2011. The definitions at [**SG-349**] of 'starting point' and 'first time offender' do not apply for this guideline. Starting point and category ranges apply to all offenders in all cases, irrespective of plea or previous convictions.

STEP ONE Determining the offence category

The court should determine the offence category using the table below:

Category 1	Greater harm (serious injury must normally be present) **and** higher culpability
Category 2	Greater harm (serious injury must normally be present) **and** lower culpability; **or** lesser harm and higher culpability
Category 3	Lesser harm and lower culpability

The court should determine the offender's culpability and the harm caused, or intended, by reference only to the factors below (as demonstrated by the presence of one or more). These factors comprise the principal factual elements of the offence and should determine the category.

Factors indicating greater harm Injury (which includes disease transmission and/or psychological harm) which is serious in the context of the offence (must normally be present) Victim is particularly vulnerable because of personal circumstances Sustained or repeated assault on the same victim **Factors indicating higher culpability** *Statutory aggravating factors:* Offence motivated by, or demonstrating, hostility to the victim based on his or her sexual orientation (or presumed sexual orientation) Offence motivated by, or demonstrating, hostility to the victim based on the victim's disability (or presumed disability) *Other aggravating factors:* A significant degree of premeditation Use of weapon or weapon equivalent (for example, shod foot, headbutting, use of acid, use of animal) Intention to commit more serious harm than actually resulted from the offence Deliberately causes more harm than is necessary for commission of offence Deliberate targeting of vulnerable victim Leading role in group or gang Offence motivated by, or demonstrating, hostility based on the victim's age, sex, gender identity (or presumed gender identity)	**Factors indicating lesser harm** Injury which is less serious in the context of the offence **Factors indicating lower culpability** Subordinate role in a group or gang A greater degree of provocation than normally expected Lack of premeditation Mental disorder or learning disability, where linked to commission of the offence Excessive self defence

STEP TWO Starting point and category range

Having determined the category, the court should use the corresponding starting points to reach a sentence within the category range below. The starting point applies to all offenders irrespective of plea or previous convictions.

A case of particular gravity, reflected by multiple features of culpability in step one, could merit upward adjustment from the starting point before further adjustment for aggravating or mitigating features, set out below.

Offence Category	**Starting Point** *(Applicable to all offenders)*	**Category Range** *(Applicable to all offenders)*
Category 1	Crown Court	Crown Court
Category 2	Crown Court	Crown Court
Category 3	High level community order	Low level community order–Crown Court (51 weeks' custody)

The table below contains a **non-exhaustive** list of additional factual elements providing the context of the offence and factors relating to the offender. Identify whether any combination of these, or other relevant factors, should result in an upward or downward adjustment from the starting point. In some cases, having considered these factors, it may be appropriate to move outside the identified category range.

When sentencing **category 3** offences, the court should also consider the custody threshold as follows:

- Has the custody threshold been passed?
- If so, is it unavoidable that a custodial sentence be imposed?
- If so, can that sentence be suspended?

Factors increasing seriousness	**Factors reducing seriousness or reflecting personal mitigation**
Statutory aggravating factors: Previous convictions, having regard to a) the nature of the offence to which the conviction relates and its relevance to the current offence; and b) the time that has elapsed since the conviction Offence committed whilst on bail *Other aggravating factors include:* Location of the offence Timing of the offence Ongoing effect upon the victim Offence committed against those working in the public sector or providing a service to the public Presence of others including relatives, especially children or partner of the victim Gratuitous degradation of victim In domestic violence cases, victim forced to leave their home Failure to comply with current court orders Offence committed whilst on licence An attempt to conceal or dispose of evidence Failure to respond to warnings or concerns expressed by others about the offender's behaviour Commission of offence whilst under the influence of alcohol or drugs Abuse of power and/or position of trust Exploiting contact arrangements with a child to commit an offence Established evidence of community impact Any steps taken to prevent the victim reporting an incident, obtaining assistance and/or from assisting or supporting the prosecution Offences taken into consideration (TICs)	No previous convictions or no relevant/recent convictions Single blow Remorse Good character and/or exemplary conduct Determination and/or demonstration of steps taken to address addiction or offending behaviour Serious medical conditions requiring urgent, intensive or long-term treatment Isolated incident Age and/or lack of maturity where it affects the responsibility of the offender Lapse of time since the offence where this is not the fault of the offender Mental disorder or learning disability, where not linked to the commission of the offence Sole or primary carer for dependent relatives

Section 29 offences only: The court should determine the appropriate sentence for the offence without taking account of the element of aggravation and then make an addition to the sentence, considering the level of aggravation involved. It may be appropriate to move outside the identified category range, taking into account the increased statutory maximum.

[Steps Three to Nine are almost identical to those which apply to assault occasioning actual bodily harm: see **SG-241**.]

SG-297 Keeping a Brothel used for Prostitution

[The guidelines set out below are applicable to adult offenders sentenced after 1 April 2014.]

Sexual Offences Act 1956 (section 33A)

Triable either way
Maximum: 7 years' custody
Offence range: Community order—6 years' custody

The terms 'prostitute' and 'prostitution' are used in this guideline in accordance with the statutory language contained in the Sexual Offences Act 2003.

STEP ONE Determining the offence category

The court should determine which categories of harm and culpability the offence falls into by reference **only** to the tables below.

Harm	
Category 1	• Under 18 year olds working in brothel • Abduction/detention • Violence or threats of violence • Sustained and systematic psychological abuse • Those working in brothel forced or coerced to participate in unsafe/degrading sexual activity • Those working in brothel forced or coerced into seeing many 'customers' • Those working in brothel forced/coerced/deceived into prostitution • Established evidence of community impact
Category 2	Factor(s) in category 1 not present.

Culpability		
A	B	C
• Keeping brothel on significant commercial basis • Involvement in keeping a number of brothels • Expectation of significant financial or other gain • Abuse of trust • Exploitation of those known to be trafficked • Significant involvement in limiting freedom of those working in brothel • Grooming of a person to work in the brothel including through cultivation of a dependency on drugs or alcohol	• Keeping/managing premises • Close involvement with those working in brothel e.g. control of finances, choice of clients, working conditions, etc. (where offender's involvement is not as a result of coercion)	• Performs limited function under direction • Close involvement but engaged by coercion/ intimidation/ exploitation

STEP TWO Starting point and category range

Having determined the category, the court should use the corresponding starting points to reach a sentence within the category range [below]. The starting point applies to all offenders irrespective of plea or previous convictions. Having determined the starting point, step two allows further adjustment for aggravating or mitigating features, set out [below].

A case of particular gravity, reflected by multiple features of culpability or harm in step one, could merit upward adjustment from the starting point before further adjustment for aggravating or mitigating features, set out [below].

Where there is a sufficient prospect of rehabilitation, a community order with a sex offender treatment programme requirement under section 202 of the Criminal Justice Act 2003 can be a proper alternative to a short or moderate length custodial sentence.

	A	B	C
Category 1	**Starting point** 5 years' custody **Category range** 3–6 years' custody	**Starting point** 3 years' custody **Category range** 2–5 years' custody	**Starting point** 1 year's custody **Category range** High level community order–18 months' custody
Category 2	**Starting point** 3 years' custody **Category range** 2–5 years' custody	**Starting point** 12 months' custody **Category range** 26 weeks'–2 years' custody	**Starting point** Medium level community order **Category range** Low level community order–High level community order

The table below contains a **non-exhaustive** list of additional factual elements providing the context of the offence and factors relating to the offender. Identify whether any combination of these, or other relevant factors, should result in an upward or downward adjustment from the starting point. **In particular, relevant recent convictions are likely to result in an upward adjustment**. In some cases, having considered these factors, it may be appropriate to move outside the identified category range.

When sentencing appropriate **category 1 offences**, the court should also consider the custody threshold as follows:

- Has the custody threshold been passed?
- If so, is it unavoidable that a custodial sentence be imposed?
- If so, can that sentence be suspended?

Aggravating factors
Statutory aggravating factors • Previous convictions, having regard to a) the nature of the offence to which the conviction relates and its relevance to the current offence; and b) the time that has elapsed since the conviction • Offence committed whilst on bail
Other aggravating factors • Failure to comply with current court orders • Offence committed whilst on licence • Deliberate isolation of those working in brothel • Threats made to expose those working in brothel to the authorities (for example, immigration or police), family/friends or others • Harm threatened against the family/friends of those working in brothel • Passport/identity documents removed • Those working in brothel prevented from seeking medical treatment • Food withheld • Those working in brothel passed around by offender and moved to other brothels • Earnings of those working in brothel withheld/kept by offender or evidence of excessive wage reduction or debt bondage, inflated travel or living expenses or unreasonable interest rates • Any steps taken to prevent those working in brothel reporting an incident, obtaining assistance and/or from assisting or supporting the prosecution • Attempts to dispose of or conceal evidence • Those working in brothel forced or coerced into pornography • Timescale over which operation has been run

Mitigating factors
• No previous convictions or no relevant/recent convictions • Remorse • Previous good character and/or exemplary conduct* • Age and/or lack of maturity where it affects the responsibility of the offender • Mental disorder or learning disability, particularly where linked to the commission of the offence • Demonstration of steps taken to address offending behaviour

* Previous good character/exemplary conduct is different from having no previous convictions. The more serious the offence, the less the weight which should normally be attributed to this factor. Where previous good character/exemplary conduct has been used to facilitate the offence, this mitigation should not normally be allowed and such conduct may constitute an aggravating factor.

[Sets out the standard sequential sentencing procedure.]

SG-298 Making off Without Payment

[The Guidelines relating to making off for magistrates' courts directly reproduce the Theft Offences Definitive Guideline as regards 'Making off without payment', which has effect in respect of all persons aged 18 or over who are sentenced on or after 1 February 2016: see **SG-457K**.]

SG-299 Obstruct/Resist a Police Constable in Execution of Duty

Police Act 1996, s. 89(2)

Triable only summarily:

Maximum: Level 3 fine and/or one month

Offence seriousness (culpability and harm)

A. Identify the appropriate starting point

Starting points based on first time offender pleading not guilty

Examples of nature of activity	Starting point	Range
Failure to move when required to do so	Band A fine	Conditional discharge–band B fine
Attempt to prevent arrest or other lawful police action; or giving false details	Band B fine	Band A fine–band C fine
Several people attempting to prevent arrest or other lawful police action	Low level community order	Band C fine–medium level community order

B. Consider the effect of aggravating and mitigating factors (other than those within examples above)

Common aggravating and mitigating factors are identified [elsewhere]—the following may be particularly relevant but these lists are not exhaustive

Factors indicating higher culpability	Factors indicating lower culpability
1. Premeditated action 2. Aggressive words/threats 3. Aggressive group action	1. Genuine mistake or misjudgement 2. Brief incident

[Sets out the standard sequential sentencing procedure.]

PROTECTIVE ORDER, BREACH OF

SG-300

Factors to take into consideration

This guideline and accompanying notes are taken from the Sentencing Guidelines Council's definitive guideline *Breach of a Protective Order*, published 7 December 2006 [see **SG-45**].

Aims of sentencing

(a) The main aim of sentencing for breach of a protective order (which would have been imposed to protect a victim from future harm) should be to achieve future compliance with that order.
(b) The court will need to assess the level of risk posed by the offender. Willingness to undergo treatment or accept help may influence sentence.

Key factors

(i) The nature of the conduct that caused the breach of the order. In particular, whether the contact was direct or indirect, although it is important to recognise that indirect contact is capable of causing significant harm or anxiety.
(ii) There may be exceptional cases where the nature of the breach is particularly serious but has not been dealt with by a separate offence being charged. In these cases the risk posed by the offender and the nature of the breach will be particularly significant in determining the response.
(iii) The nature of the original conduct or offence is relevant in so far as it allows a judgement to be made on the level of harm caused to the victim by the breach, and the extent to which that harm was intended.
(iv) The sentence following a breach is for the breach alone and must avoid punishing the offender again for the offence or conduct as a result of which the order was made.
(v) It is likely that all breaches of protective orders will pass the threshold for a community sentence. Custody is the starting point where violence is used. Non-violent conduct may also cross the custody threshold where a high degree of harm or anxiety has been caused.
(vi) Where an order was made in civil proceedings, its purpose may have been to cause the subject of the order to modify behaviour rather than to imply that the conduct was especially serious. If so, it is likely to be disproportionate to impose a custodial sentence if the breach of the order did not involve threats or violence.
(vii) In some cases where a breach might result in a short custodial sentence but the court is satisfied that the offender genuinely intends to reform his or her behaviour and there is a real prospect of rehabilitation, the court may consider it appropriate to impose a sentence that will allow this. This may mean imposing a suspended sentence order or a community order (where appropriate with a requirement to attend an accredited domestic violence programme).

Guidelines

Protection from Harassment Act 1997, s. 5(5) (breach of restraining order)
Family Law Act 1996, s. 42A (breach of non-molestation order)

Triable either way:
Maximum when tried summarily: Level 5 fine and/or 6 months
Maximum when tried on indictment: 5 years

Where the conduct is particularly serious, it would normally be charged as a separate offence. These starting points are based on the premise that the activity has either been prosecuted separately as an offence or is not of a character sufficient to justify prosecution of it as an offence in its own right.

Where offence committed in domestic context, refer [below] for guidance

Offence seriousness (culpability and harm)

A. Identify the appropriate starting point

Starting points based on first time offender pleading not guilty

Examples of nature of activity	Starting point	Range
Single breach involving no/minimal direct contact	**Low level community order**	**Band C fine–medium level community order**
More than one breach involving no/minimal contact or some direct contact	**Medium level community order**	**Low level community order–high level community order**
Single breach involving some violence and/or significant physical or psychological harm to the victim	**18 weeks' custody**	**13–26 weeks' custody**
More than one breach involving some violence and/or significant physical or psychological harm to the victim	**Crown Court**	**26 weeks' custody–Crown Court**
Breach (whether one or more) involving significant physical violence and significant physical or psychological harm to the victim	**Crown Court**	**Crown Court**

B. Consider the effect of aggravating and mitigating factors (other than those within examples above)

Common aggravating and mitigating factors are identified [elsewhere]—the following may be particularly relevant but these lists are not exhaustive

Factors indicating higher culpability	Factors indicating greater degree of harm
1. Proven history of violence or threats by the offender 2. Using contact arrangements with a child to instigate offence 3. Offence is a further breach, following earlier breach proceedings 4. Offender has history of disobedience to court orders 5. Breach committed immediately or shortly after order made	1. Victim is particularly vulnerable 2. Impact on children 3. Victim is forced to leave home **Factors indicating lower culpability** 1. Breach occurred after long period of compliance 2. Victim initiated contact

[Sets out the standard sequential sentencing procedure.]

SG-301 Public Order Act, s. 2—Violent Disorder

Public Order Act 1986, s. 2

Triable either way:
Maximum when tried summarily: Level 5 fine and/or 6 months
Maximum when tried on indictment: 5 years

Offence seriousness (culpability and harm)

A. Identify the appropriate starting point

Starting points based on first time offender pleading not guilty

> *These offences should normally be dealt with in the Crown Court.* However, there may be rare cases involving minor violence or threats of violence leading to no or minor injury, with few people involved and no weapon or missiles, in which a custodial sentence within the jurisdiction of a magistrates' court may be appropriate.

SG-302 Public Order Act, s. 3—Affray

Public Order Act 1986, s. 3

Triable either way:
Maximum when tried summarily: Level 5 fine and/or 6 months
Maximum when tried on indictment: 3 years

Offence seriousness (culpability and harm)

A. Identify the appropriate starting point

Starting points based on first time offender pleading not guilty

Examples of nature of activity	Starting point	Range
Brief offence involving low-level violence, no substantial fear created	**Low level community order**	**Band C fine–medium level community order**
Degree of fighting or violence that causes substantial fear	**High level community order**	**Medium level community order–12 weeks' custody**
Fight involving a weapon/ throwing objects, or conduct causing risk of serious injury	**18 weeks' custody**	**12 weeks' custody–Crown Court**

B. Consider the effect of aggravating and mitigating factors (other than those within examples above)

Common aggravating and mitigating factors are identified [elsewhere]—the following may be particularly relevant but these lists are not exhaustive

Factors indicating higher culpability	Factors indicating lower culpability
1. Group action 2. Threats 3. Lengthy incident **Factors indicating greater degree of harm** 1. Vulnerable person(s) present 2. Injuries caused 3. Damage to property	1. Did not start the trouble 2. Provocation 3. Stopped as soon as police arrived

[Sets out the standard sequential sentencing procedure and mentions the need to consider a football banning order.]

Sentencing Guidelines

Public Order Act, s. 4—Threatening Behaviour—Fear or Provocation of Violence Racially or Religiously Aggravated Threatening Behaviour SG-303

Public Order Act 1986, s. 4

Crime and Disorder Act 1998, s. 31

Threatening behaviour: triable only summarily
Maximum: Level 5 fine and/or 6 months

Racially or religiously aggravated threatening behaviour: triable either way
Maximum when tried summarily: Level 5 fine and/or 6 months
Maximum when tried on indictment: 2 years
Where offence committed in domestic context, refer [below] for guidance

Offence seriousness (culpability and harm)

A. Identify the appropriate starting point

Starting points based on first time offender pleading not guilty

Examples of nature of activity	Starting point	Range
Fear or threat of low level immediate unlawful violence such as push, shove or spit	**Low level community order**	**Band B fine–medium level community order**
Fear or threat of medium level immediate unlawful violence such as punch	**High level community order**	**Low level community order–12 weeks' custody**
Fear or threat of high level immediate unlawful violence such as use of weapon; missile thrown; gang involvement	**12 weeks' custody**	**6–26 weeks' custody**

B. Consider the effect of aggravating and mitigating factors (other than those within examples above)

Common aggravating and mitigating factors are identified [elsewhere]—the following may be particularly relevant but these lists are not exhaustive

Factors indicating higher culpability	Factors indicating lower culpability
1. Planning 2. Offender deliberately isolates victim 3. Group action 4. Threat directed at victim because of job 5. History of antagonism towards victim **Factors indicating greater degree of harm** 1. Offence committed at school, hospital or other place where vulnerable persons may be present 2. Offence committed on enclosed premises such as public transport 3. Vulnerable victim(s) 4. Victim needs medical help/counselling	1. Impulsive action 2. Short duration 3. Provocation

[Sets out the standard sequential sentencing procedure and mentions the need to consider a football banning order. Notes that 'If offender charged and convicted of the racially or religiously aggravated offence, increase the sentence to reflect this element'.]

SG-304

Public Order Act, s. 4A—Disorderly Behaviour with Intent to Cause Harassment, Alarm or Distress

Racially Or Religiously Aggravated Disorderly Behaviour With Intent To Cause Harassment, Alarm Or Distress

Public Order Act 1986, s. 4A
Crime and Disorder Act 1998, s. 31

Disorderly behaviour with intent to cause harassment, alarm or distress: triable only summarily
Maximum: Level 5 fine and/or 6 months

Racially or religiously aggravated disorderly behaviour with intent to cause harassment etc.: triable either way

Maximum when tried summarily: Level 5 fine and/or 6 months
Maximum when tried on indictment: 2 years

Offence seriousness (culpability and harm)

A. Identify the appropriate starting point

Starting points based on first time offender pleading not guilty

Examples of nature of activity	Starting point	Range
Threats, abuse or insults made more than once but on same occasion against the same person e.g. while following down the street	**Band C fine**	**Band B fine–low level community order**
Group action or deliberately planned action against targeted victim	**Medium level community order**	**Low level community order–12 weeks' custody**
Weapon brandished or used or threats against vulnerable victim—course of conduct over longer period	**12 weeks' custody**	**High level community order–26 weeks' custody**

B. Consider the effect of aggravating and mitigating factors (other than those within examples above)

Common aggravating and mitigating factors are identified [elsewhere]—the following may be particularly relevant but these lists are not exhaustive

Factors indicating higher culpability	Factors indicating lower culpability
1. High degree of planning 2. Offender deliberately isolates victim **Factors indicating greater degree of harm** 1. Offence committed in vicinity of victim's home 2. Large number of people in vicinity 3. Actual or potential escalation into violence 4. Particularly serious impact on victim	1. Very short period 2. Provocation

[Sets out the standard sequential sentencing procedure and mentions the need to consider a football banning order. Notes that 'If offender charged and convicted of the racially or religiously aggravated offence, increase the sentence to reflect this element'.]

Public Order Act, s. 5—Disorderly Behaviour (Harassment, Alarm or Distress) Racially or Religiously Aggravated Disorderly Behaviour SG-305

Public Order Act 1986, s. 5

Crime and Disorder Act 1998, s. 31

Disorderly behaviour: triable only summarily
Maximum: Level 3 fine

Racially or religiously aggravated disorderly behaviour: triable only summarily
Maximum: Level 4 fine

Offence seriousness (culpability and harm)

A. Identify the appropriate starting point

Starting points based on first time offender pleading not guilty

Examples of nature of activity	Starting point	Range
Shouting, causing disturbance for some minutes	**Band A fine**	**Conditional discharge to band B fine**
Substantial disturbance caused	**Band B fine**	**Band A fine to band C fine**

B. Consider the effect of aggravating and mitigating factors (other than those within examples above)

Common aggravating and mitigating factors are identified [elsewhere]—the following may be particularly relevant but these lists are not exhaustive

Factors indicating higher culpability	Factors indicating lower culpability
1. Group action 2. Lengthy incident **Factors indicating greater degree of harm** 1. Vulnerable person(s) present 2. Offence committed at school, hospital or other place where vulnerable persons may be present 3. Victim providing public service	1. Stopped as soon as police arrived 2. Brief/minor incident 3. Provocation

[Sets out the standard sequential sentencing procedure and mentions the need to consider a football banning order. Notes that 'If offender charged and convicted of the racially or religiously aggravated offence, increase the sentence to reflect this element'.]

SG-306

Railway Fare Evasion

Regulation of Railways Act 1889, s. 5(3) (travelling on railway without paying fare, with intent to avoid payment); s. 5(1) (failing to produce ticket)

Triable only summarily:
Maximum: Level 3 fine or 3 months (s. 5(3)); level 2 fine (s. 5(1))

Offence seriousness (culpability and harm)

A. Identify the appropriate starting point

Starting points based on first time offender pleading not guilty

Examples of nature of activity	Starting point	Range
Failing to produce ticket or pay fare on request	**Band A fine**	**Conditional discharge–band B fine**
Travelling on railway without having paid the fare or knowingly and wilfully travelling beyond the distance paid for, with intent to avoid payment	**Band B fine**	**Band A fine–band C fine**

B. Consider the effect of aggravating and mitigating factors (other than those within examples above)

Common aggravating and mitigating factors are identified [elsewhere]—the following may be particularly relevant but these lists are not exhaustive

Factor indicating higher culpability	Factor indicating greater degree of harm
1. Offensive or intimidating language or behaviour towards railway staff	1. High level of loss caused or intended to be caused

[Sets out the standard sequential sentencing procedure.]

SG-307

School Non-attendance

Education Act 1996, s. 444(1) (parent fails to secure regular attendance at school of registered pupil); s. 444(1A) (parent knowingly fails to secure regular attendance at school of registered pupil)

Triable only summarily
Maximum: Level 3 fine (s. 444(1)); level 4 fine and/or 3 months (s. 444(1A))

Offence seriousness (culpability and harm)

A. Identify the appropriate starting point

Starting points based on first time offender pleading not guilty

Examples of nature of activity	Starting point	Range
Short period following previous good attendance (s.444(1))	**Band A fine**	**Conditional discharge–band A fine**
Erratic attendance for long period (s. 444(1))	**Band B fine**	**Band B fine–Band C fine**
Colluding in and condoning non-attendance or deliberately instigating non-attendance (s. 444(1A))	**Medium level community order**	**Low level community order–high level community order**

B. Consider the effect of aggravating and mitigating factors (other than those within examples above)

Common aggravating and mitigating factors are identified [elsewhere]—the following may be particularly relevant but these lists are not exhaustive

Factors indicating higher culpability	Factors indicating lower culpability
1. Parental collusion (s.444(1) only) 2. Lack of parental effort to ensure attendance (s.444(1) only) 3. Threats to teachers and/or officials 4. Refusal to co-operate with school and/or officials **Factors indicating greater degree of harm** 1. More than one child 2. Harmful effect on other children in family	1. Parent unaware of child's whereabouts 2. Parent tried to ensure attendance 3. Parent concerned by child's allegations of bullying/unable to get school to address bullying

[Sets out the standard sequential sentencing procedure and mentions need to consider a parenting order.]

SEX OFFENDERS REGISTER—FAIL TO COMPLY WITH NOTIFICATION REQUIREMENTS SG-308

Sexual Offences Act 2003, s. 91(1)(a) (fail to comply with notification requirements); s. 91(1)(b) (supply false information)

Triable either way:
Maximum when tried summarily: Level 5 fine and/or 6 months
Maximum when tried on indictment: 5 years

Offence seriousness (culpability and harm)

A. Identify the appropriate starting point

Starting points based on first time offender pleading not guilty

Examples of nature of activity	Starting point	Range
Negligent or inadvertent failure to comply with requirements	**Medium level community order**	**Band C fine–high level community order**
Deliberate failure to comply with requirements OR Supply of information known to be false	**6 weeks' custody**	**High level community order–26 weeks' custody**
Conduct as described in box above AND Long period of non-compliance OR Attempts to avoid detection	**18 weeks' custody**	**6 weeks' custody–Crown Court**

B. Consider the effect of aggravating and mitigating factors (other than those within examples above)

Common aggravating and mitigating factors are identified [elsewhere]—the following may be particularly relevant but these lists are not exhaustive

Factor indicating higher culpability	Factor indicating lower culpability
1. Long period of non-compliance (where not in the examples above) **Factor indicating greater degree of harm** 1. Alarm or distress caused to victim 2. Particularly serious original offence	1. Genuine misunderstanding

[Sets out the standard sequential sentencing procedure.]

Note:
An offender convicted of this offence will always have at least one relevant previous conviction for the offence that resulted in the notification requirements being imposed. The starting points and ranges take this into account; any other previous convictions should be considered in the usual way.

SG-309

Sexual Activity in a Public Lavatory

Sexual Offences Act 2003, s. 71

Triable only summarily
Maximum: Level 5 fine and/or 6 months

This guideline and accompanying notes are taken from the Sentencing Guidelines Council's definitive guideline *Sexual Offences Act 2003*, published 30 April 2007

Key factors

(a) This offence is committed where an offender intentionally engages in sexual activity in a public lavatory. It was introduced to give adults and children the freedom to use public lavatories for the purpose for which they are designed, without the fear of being an unwilling witness to overtly sexual behaviour of a kind that most people would not expect to be conducted in public. It is primarily a public order offence rather than a sexual offence.
(b) When dealing with a repeat offender, the starting point should be a low level community order with a range of Band C fine to medium level community order. The presence of aggravating factors may suggest that a sentence above the range is appropriate.
(c) This guideline may be relevant by way of analogy to conduct charged as the common law offence of outraging public decency; the offence is triable either way and has a maximum penalty of a level 5 fine and/or 6 months imprisonment when tried summarily.

Offence seriousness (culpability and harm)

A. Identify the appropriate starting point

Starting points based on first time offender pleading not guilty

Examples of nature of activity	Starting point	Range
Basic offence as defined in the Act, assuming no aggravating or mitigating factors	**Band C fine**	**Band C fine**
Offence with aggravating factors	**Low level community order**	**Band C fine–medium level community order**

B. Consider the effect of aggravating and mitigating factors (other than those within examples above)

Common aggravating and mitigating factors are identified [elsewhere]—the following may be particularly relevant but these lists are not exhaustive

Factors indicating higher culpability
1. Intimidating behaviour/threats of violence to member(s) of the public 2. Blatant behaviour

[Sets out the standard sequential sentencing procedure.]

SG-310

Sexual Assault

[The guidelines set out below are applicable to adult offenders sentenced after 1 April 2014.]

Sexual Offences Act 2003 (section 3)

Triable either way
Maximum: 10 years' custody

Offence range: Community order–7 years' custody

For convictions on or after 3 December 2012 (irrespective of the date of commission of the offence), this is a specified offence for the purposes of section 226A (extended sentence for certain violent or sexual offences) of the Criminal Justice Act 2003.

STEP ONE Determining the offence category

The court should determine which categories of harm and culpability the offence falls into by reference only to the tables below.

Harm	
Category 1	• Severe psychological or physical harm • Abduction • Violence or threats of violence • Forced/uninvited entry into victim's home
Category 2	• Touching of naked genitalia or naked breasts • Prolonged detention/sustained incident • Additional degradation/humiliation • Victim is particularly vulnerable due to personal circumstances* * for children under 13 please refer to the guideline [at SG-84]
Category 3	Factor(s) in categories 1 and 2 not present

Culpability	
A	B
• Significant degree of planning • Offender acts together with others to commit the offence • Use of alcohol/drugs on victim to facilitate the offence • Abuse of trust • Previous violence against victim • Offence committed in course of burglary • Recording of offence • Commercial exploitation and/or motivation • Offence racially or religiously aggravated • Offence motivated by, or demonstrating, hostility to the victim based on his or her sexual orientation (or presumed sexual orientation) or transgender identity (or presumed transgender identity) • Offence motivated by, or demonstrating, hostility to the victim based on his or her disability (or presumed disability)	Factor(s) in category A not present

STEP TWO Starting point and category range

Having determined the category, the court should use the corresponding starting points to reach a sentence within the category range [below]. The starting point applies to all offenders irrespective of plea or previous convictions. Having determined the starting point, step two allows further adjustment for aggravating or mitigating features, set out [below].

A case of particular gravity, reflected by multiple features of culpability or harm in step one, could merit upward adjustment from the starting point before further adjustment for aggravating or mitigating features, set out [below].

Where there is a sufficient prospect of rehabilitation, a community order with a sex offender treatment programme requirement under section 202 of the Criminal Justice Act 2003 can be a proper alternative to a short or moderate length custodial sentence.

	A	B
Category 1	**Starting point** 4 years' custody **Category range** 3–7 years' custody	**Starting point** 2 years 6 months' custody **Category range** 2–4 years' custody
Category 2	**Starting point** 2 years' custody **Category range** 1–4 years' custody	**Starting point** 1 year's custody **Category range** High level community order–2 years' custody
Category 3	**Starting point** 26 weeks' custody **Category range** High level community order–1 year's custody	**Starting point** High level community order **Category range** Medium level community order–26 weeks' custody

The table below contains a **non-exhaustive** list of additional factual elements providing the context of the offence and factors relating to the offender. Identify whether any combination of these, or other relevant factors, should result in an upward or downward adjustment from the starting point. **In particular, relevant recent convictions are likely to result in an upward adjustment**. In some cases, having considered these factors, it may be appropriate to move outside the identified category range.

When sentencing appropriate **category 2 or 3 offences**, the court should also consider the custody threshold as follows:

- has the custody threshold been passed?
- if so, is it unavoidable that a custodial sentence be imposed?
- if so, can that sentence be suspended?

Aggravating factors
Statutory aggravating factors
• Previous convictions, having regard to a) the nature of the offence to which the conviction relates and its relevance to the current offence; and b) the time that has elapsed since the conviction • Offence committed whilst on bail

Other aggravating factors
• Specific targeting of a particularly vulnerable victim • Blackmail or other threats made (where not taken into account at step one) • Location of offence • Timing of offence • Use of weapon or other item to frighten or injure • Victim compelled to leave their home (including victims of domestic violence) • Failure to comply with current court orders • Offence committed whilst on licence • Exploiting contact arrangements with a child to commit an offence • Presence of others, especially children • Any steps taken to prevent the victim reporting an incident, obtaining assistance and/or from assisting or supporting the prosecution • Attempts to dispose of or conceal evidence • Commission of offence whilst under the influence of alcohol or drugs

Mitigating factors
• No previous convictions **or** no relevant/recent convictions • Remorse • Previous good character and/or exemplary conduct* • Age and/or lack of maturity where it affects the responsibility of the offender • Mental disorder or learning disability, particularly where linked to the commission of the offence • Demonstration of steps taken to address offending behaviour

* Previous good character/exemplary conduct is different from having no previous convictions. The more serious the offence, the less the weight which should normally be attributed to this factor. Where previous good character/exemplary conduct has been used to facilitate the offence, this mitigation should not normally be allowed and such conduct may constitute an aggravating factor.

[Sets out the standard sequential sentencing procedure.]

SG-311

SEXUAL ASSAULT OF A CHILD UNDER 13

[The guidelines set out below are applicable to adult offenders sentenced after 1 April 2014.]

Sexual Offences Act 2003 (section 7)

Triable either way
Maximum: 14 years' custody

Offence range: Community order–9 years' custody

For offences committed on or after 3 December 2012, this is an offence listed in Part 1 of Schedule 15B for the purposes of section 224A (life sentence for second listed offence) of the Criminal Justice Act 2003.

For convictions on or after 3 December 2012 (irrespective of the date of commission of the offence), this is a specified offence for the purposes of section 226A (extended sentence for certain violent or sexual offences) of the Criminal Justice Act 2003.

STEP ONE Determining the offence category

The court should determine which categories of harm and culpability the offence falls into by reference **only** to the tables below.

Harm	
Category 1	• Severe psychological or physical harm • Abduction • Violence or threats of violence • Forced/uninvited entry into victim's home
Category 2	• Touching of naked genitalia or naked breast area • Prolonged detention/sustained incident • Additional degradation/humiliation • Child is particularly vulnerable due to extreme youth and/or personal circumstances
Category 3	Factor(s) in categories 1 and 2 not present

Culpability	
A	B
• Significant degree of planning • Offender acts together with others to commit the offence • Use of alcohol/drugs on victim to facilitate the offence • Grooming behaviour used against victim • Abuse of trust • Previous violence against victim • Offence committed in course of burglary • Sexual images of victim recorded, retained, solicited or shared • Deliberate isolation of victim • Commercial exploitation and/or motivation • Offence racially or religiously aggravated • Offence motivated by, or demonstrating, hostility to the victim based on his or her sexual orientation (or presumed sexual orientation) or transgender identity (or presumed transgender identity) • Offence motivated by, or demonstrating, hostility to the victim based on his or her disability (or presumed disability)	Factor(s) in category A not present

STEP TWO Starting point and category range

Having determined the category, the court should use the corresponding starting points to reach a sentence within the category range [below]. The starting point applies to all offenders irrespective of plea or previous convictions. Having determined the starting point, step two allows further adjustment for aggravating or mitigating features, set out [below].

A case of particular gravity, reflected by multiple features of culpability or harm in step one, could merit upward adjustment from the starting point before further adjustment for aggravating or mitigating features, set out [below].

Where there is a sufficient prospect of rehabilitation, a community order with a sex offender treatment programme requirement under section 202 of the Criminal Justice Act 2003 can be a proper alternative to a short or moderate length custodial sentence.

	A	B
Category 1	**Starting point** 6 years' custody **Category range** 4–9 years' custody	**Starting point** 4 years' custody **Category range** 3–7 years' custody
Category 2	**Starting point** 4 years' custody **Category range** 3–7 years' custody	**Starting point** 2 years' custody **Category range** 1–4 years' custody
Category 3	**Starting point** 1 year's custody **Category range** 26 weeks'–2 years' custody	**Starting point** 26 weeks' custody **Category range** High level community order–1 year's custody

The table below contains **a non-exhaustive** list of additional factual elements providing the context of the offence and factors relating to the offender. Identify whether any combination of these, or other relevant factors, should result in an upward or downward adjustment from the starting point. **In particular, relevant recent convictions are likely to result in an upward adjustment**. In some cases, having considered these factors, it may be appropriate to move outside the identified category range.

Aggravating factors

Statutory aggravating factors

- Previous convictions, having regard to a) the nature of the offence to which the conviction relates and its relevance to the current offence; and b) the time that has elapsed since the conviction
- Offence committed whilst on bail

Other aggravating factors

- Specific targeting of a particularly vulnerable child
- Blackmail or other threats made (where not taken into account at step one)
- Location of offence
- Timing of offence
- Use of weapon or other item to frighten or injure
- Victim compelled to leave their home, school, etc
- Failure to comply with current court orders
- Offence committed whilst on licence
- Exploiting contact arrangements with a child to commit an offence
- Presence of others, especially other children
- Any steps taken to prevent the victim reporting an incident, obtaining assistance and/or from assisting or supporting the prosecution
- Attempts to dispose of or conceal evidence
- Commission of offence whilst under the influence of alcohol or drugs
- Victim encouraged to recruit others

Mitigating factors

- No previous convictions **or** no relevant/recent convictions
- Remorse
- Previous good character and/or exemplary conduct*
- Age and/or lack of maturity where it affects the responsibility of the offender
- Mental disorder or learning disability, particularly where linked to the commission of the offence

* Previous good character/exemplary conduct is different from having no previous convictions. The more serious the offence, the less the weight which should normally be attributed to this factor. Where previous good character/exemplary conduct has been used to facilitate the offence, this mitigation should not normally be allowed and such conduct may constitute an aggravating factor.

In the context of this offence, previous good character/exemplary conduct should not normally be given any significant weight and will not normally justify a reduction in what would otherwise be the appropriate sentence.

[Sets out the standard sequential sentencing procedure.]

Taxi Touting/Soliciting for Hire SG-312

Criminal Justice and Public Order Act 1994, s. 167

Triable only summarily:
Maximum: Level 4 fine

Offence seriousness (culpability and harm)

A. Identify the appropriate starting point

Starting points based on first time offender pleading not guilty

Examples of nature of activity	Starting point	Range
Licensed taxi-driver touting for trade (i.e. making approach rather than waiting for a person to initiate hiring)	Band A fine	Conditional discharge–band A fine and consider disqualification 1–3 months
PHV licence held but touting for trade rather than being booked through an operator; an accomplice to touting	Band B fine	Band A fine–band C fine and consider disqualification 3–6 months
No PHV licence held	Band C fine	Band B fine–Band C fine and disqualification 6–12 months

Note: refer [below] for approach to fines for offences committed for commercial purposes

B. Consider the effect of aggravating and mitigating factors (other than those within examples above)

Common aggravating and mitigating factors are identified [elsewhere]—the following may be particularly relevant but these lists are not exhaustive

Factors indicating higher culpability	Factor indicating lower culpability
1. Commercial business/large scale operation 2. No insurance/invalid insurance 3. No driving licence and/or no MOT 4. Vehicle not roadworthy **Factors indicating greater degree of harm** 1. Deliberately diverting trade from taxi rank 2. PHV licence had been refused/offender ineligible for licence	1. Providing a service when no licensed taxi available

[Sets out the standard sequential sentencing procedure and mentions need to consider disqualification from driving and deprivation of property.]

Theft—General Principles SG-313

[The Guidelines relating to theft for magistrates' courts directly reproduce the Theft Offences Definitive Guideline as regards 'General Theft', which has effect in respect of all persons aged 18 or over who are sentenced on or after 1 February 2016: see **SG-448**.]

SG-314

Theft—Breach of Trust

[The Guidelines relating to theft in breach of trust for magistrates' courts are now covered in the Theft Offences Definitive Guideline under 'General Theft', which has effect in respect of all persons aged 18 or over who are sentenced on or after 1 February 2016: see **SG-448**.]

SG-315

Theft—Breach of Trust

[This Guideline is now superseded: see **SG-314**.]

SG-316

Theft—Dwelling

[The Guidelines relating to theft in a dwelling for magistrates' courts are now covered in the Theft Offences Definitive Guideline under 'General Theft', which has effect in respect of all persons aged 18 or over who are sentenced on or after 1 February 2016: see **SG-448**.]

SG-317

Theft—Person

[The Guidelines relating to theft from the person for magistrates' courts are now covered in the Theft Offences Definitive Guideline under 'General Theft', which has effect in respect of all persons aged 18 or over who are sentenced on or after 1 February 2016: see **SG-448**.]

SG-318

Theft—Shop

[The Guidelines relating to theft from a shop for magistrates' courts directly reproduce the Theft Offences Definitive Guideline as regards 'Theft from a shop or stall', which has effect in respect of all persons aged 18 or over who are sentenced on or after 1 February 2016: see **SG-452**.]

SG-319

Threats to Kill

Offences Against the Person Act 1861, s. 16

Triable either way:
Maximum when tried summarily: Level 5 fine and/or 6 months
Maximum when tried on indictment: 10 years

Where offence committed in domestic context, refer [below] for guidance

Offence seriousness (culpability and harm)

A. Identify the appropriate starting point

Starting points based on first time offender pleading not guilty

Examples of nature of activity	Starting point	Range
One threat uttered in the heat of the moment, no more than fleeting impact on victim	Medium level community order	Low level community order–high level community order
Single calculated threat or victim fears that threat will be carried out	12 weeks' custody	6–26 weeks' custody
Repeated threats or visible weapon	Crown Court	Crown Court

B. Consider the effect of aggravating and mitigating factors (other than those within examples above)

Common aggravating and mitigating factors are identified [elsewhere]—the following may be particularly relevant but these lists are not exhaustive

Factors indicating higher culpability	Factor indicating lower culpability
1. Planning 2. Offender deliberately isolates victim 3. Group action 4. Threat directed at victim because of job 5. History of antagonism towards victim **Factors indicating greater degree of harm** 1. Vulnerable victim 2. Victim needs medical help/counselling	1. Provocation

[Sets out the standard sequential sentencing procedure and mentions need to consider football banning order.]

Trade Mark, Unauthorised use of etc. SG-320

Trade Marks Act 1994, s. 92

Triable either way:
Maximum when tried summarily: Level 5 fine and/or 6 months
Maximum when tried on indictment: 10 years

Offence seriousness (culpability and harm)

A. Identify the appropriate starting point

Starting points based on first time offender pleading not guilty

Examples of nature of activity	Starting point	Range
Small number of counterfeit items	Band C fine	Band B fine–low level community order
Larger number of counterfeit items but no involvement in wider operation	Medium level community order, plus fine*	Low level community order–12 weeks' custody, plus fine*
High number of counterfeit items or involvement in wider operation e.g. manufacture or distribution	12 weeks' custody	6 weeks' custody–Crown Court
Central role in large-scale operation	Crown Court	Crown Court

* This may be an offence for which it is appropriate to combine a fine with a community order. Consult your legal adviser for further guidance.

B. Consider the effect of aggravating and mitigating factors (other than those within examples above)

Common aggravating and mitigating factors are identified [elsewhere]—the following may be particularly relevant but these lists are not exhaustive

Factors indicating higher culpability	Factor indicating lower culpability
1. High degree of professionalism 2. High level of profit **Factor indicating greater degree of harm** 1. Purchasers at risk of harm e.g. from counterfeit drugs	1. Mistake or ignorance about provenance of goods

[Sets out the standard sequential sentencing procedure and mentions need to consider ordering forfeiture and destruction of the goods.]

SG-321

TV Licence Payment Evasion

Communications Act 2003, s. 363

Triable only summarily:
Maximum: Level 3 fine

Offence seriousness (culpability and harm)

A. Identify the appropriate starting point

Starting points based on first time offender pleading not guilty

B. Consider the effect of aggravating and mitigating factors (other than those within examples above)

Examples of nature of activity	Starting point	Range
Up to 6 months unlicensed use	Band A fine	Band A fine
Over 6 months unlicensed use	Band B fine	Band A fine–band B fine

Common aggravating and mitigating factors are identified [elsewhere]—the following may be particularly relevant but these lists are not exhaustive

Factors indicating lower culpability
1. Accidental oversight or belief licence held
2. Confusion of responsibility
3. Licence immediately obtained

[Sets out the standard sequential sentencing procedure.]

SG-322

Vehicle Interference

Criminal Attempts Act 1981, s. 9

Triable only summarily:
Maximum: Level 4 fine and/or 3 months

Offence seriousness (culpability and harm)

A. Identify the appropriate starting point

Starting points based on first time offender pleading not guilty

B. Consider the effect of aggravating and mitigating factors (other than those within examples above)

Examples of nature of activity	Starting point	Range
Trying door handles; no entry gained to vehicle; no damage caused	Band C fine	Band A fine–low level community order
Entering vehicle, little or no damage caused	Medium level community order	Band C fine–high level community order
Entering vehicle, with damage caused	High level community order	Medium level community order–12 weeks' custody

Common aggravating and mitigating factors are identified [elsewhere]—the following may be particularly relevant but these lists are not exhaustive

Factor indicating higher culpability
1. Targeting vehicle in dark/isolated location

Factors indicating greater degree of harm
1. Emergency services vehicle
2. Disabled driver's vehicle
3. Part of series

[Sets out the standard sequential sentencing procedure.]

Vehicle Licence/Registration Fraud SG-323

Vehicle Excise and Registration Act 1994, s.44

Triable either way:
Maximum when tried summarily: Level 5 fine
Maximum when tried on indictment: 2 years

Offence seriousness (culpability and harm)

A. Identify the appropriate starting point

Starting points based on first time offender pleading not guilty

Examples of nature of activity	Starting point	Range
Use of unaltered licence from another vehicle	Band B fine	Band B fine
Forged licence bought for own use, or forged/altered for own use	Band C fine	Band C fine
Use of number plates from another vehicle; or Licence/ number plates forged or altered for sale to another	High level community order (in Crown Court)	Medium level community order–Crown Court (Note: community order and custody available only in Crown Court)

B. Consider the effect of aggravating and mitigating factors (other than those within examples above)

Common aggravating and mitigating factors are identified [elsewhere]—the following may be particularly relevant but these lists are not exhaustive

Factors indicating higher culpability	Factors indicating lower culpability
1. LGV, PSV, taxi etc. 2. Long-term fraudulent use **Factors indicating greater degree of harm** 1. High financial gain 2. Innocent victim deceived 3. Legitimate owner inconvenienced	1. Licence/registration mark from another vehicle owned by defendant 2. Short-term use

[Sets out the standard sequential sentencing procedure and mentions the need to consider disqualification from driving and deprivation of property (including vehicle).]

Vehicle Taking, without Consent SG-324

Theft Act 1968, s. 12

Triable only summarily:
Maximum: Level 5 fine and/or 6 months
May disqualify (no points available)

Offence seriousness (culpability and harm)

A. Identify the appropriate starting point

Starting points based on first time offender pleading not guilty

Examples of nature of activity	Starting point	Range
Exceeding authorised use of e.g. employer's or relative's vehicle; retention of hire car beyond return date	Low level community order	Band B fine–medium level community order
As above with damage caused to lock/ignition; OR Stranger's vehicle involved but no damage caused	Medium level community order	Low level community order–high level community order
Taking vehicle from private premises; OR Causing damage to e.g. lock/ignition of stranger's vehicle	High level community order	Medium level community order–26 weeks' custody

B. Consider the effect of aggravating and mitigating factors (other than those within examples above)

Common aggravating and mitigating factors are identified [elsewhere]—the following may be particularly relevant but these lists are not exhaustive

Factors indicating greater degree of harm	Factor indicating lower culpability
1. Vehicle later burnt 2. Vehicle belonging to elderly/disabled person 3. Emergency services vehicle 4. Medium to large goods vehicle 5. Passengers carried	1. Misunderstanding with owner **Factor indicating lesser degree of harm** 1. Offender voluntarily returned vehicle to owner

[Sets out the standard sequential sentencing procedure and mentions need to consider disqualification from driving.]

SG-325

Vehicle Taking (Aggravated)

Damage caused to Property other than the Vehicle in Accident or damage Caused to the Vehicle

Theft Act 1968, s. 12A(2)(c) and (d)

Triable either way (triable only summarily if damage under £5,000):
Maximum when tried summarily: Level 5 fine and/or 6 months
Maximum when tried on indictment: 2 years

- Must endorse and disqualify for at least 12 months
- Must disqualify for *at least* 2 years if offender has had two or more disqualifications for periods of 56 days or more in preceding 3 years…

If there is a delay in sentencing after conviction, consider interim disqualification

Offence seriousness (culpability and harm)

A. Identify the appropriate starting point

Starting points based on first time offender pleading not guilty

Examples of nature of activity	Starting point	Range
Exceeding authorised use of e.g. employer's or relative's vehicle; retention of hire car beyond return date; minor damage to taken vehicle	Medium level community order	Low level community order–high level community order
Greater damage to taken vehicle and/or moderate damage to another vehicle and/or property	High level community order	Medium level community order–12 weeks' custody
Vehicle taken as part of burglary or from private premises; severe damage	18 weeks' custody	12–26 weeks' custody (Crown Court if damage over £5,000)

B. Consider the effect of aggravating and mitigating factors (other than those within examples above)

Common aggravating and mitigating factors are identified [elsewhere]—the following may be particularly relevant but these lists are not exhaustive

Factors indicating higher culpability	Factors indicating lower culpability
1. Vehicle deliberately damaged/destroyed 2. Offender under influence of alcohol/drugs **Factors indicating greater degree of harm** 1. Passenger(s) carried 2. Vehicle belonging to elderly or disabled person 3. Emergency services vehicle 4. Medium to large goods vehicle 5. Damage caused in moving traffic accident	1. Misunderstanding with owner 2. Damage resulting from actions of another (where this does not provide a defence)

[Sets out the standard sequential sentencing procedure.]

VEHICLE TAKING (AGGRAVATED) SG-326

DANGEROUS DRIVING OR ACCIDENT CAUSING INJURY

Theft Act 1968, ss. 12A(2)(a) and (b)

Triable either way:
Maximum when tried summarily: Level 5 fine and/or 6 months
Maximum when tried on indictment: 2 years; 14 years if accident caused death

- Must endorse and disqualify for at least 12 months
- Must disqualify for *at least* 2 years if offender has had two or more disqualifications for periods of 56 days or more in preceding 3 years…

If there is a delay in sentencing after conviction, consider interim disqualification

Offence seriousness (culpability and harm)

A. Identify the appropriate starting point

Starting points based on first time offender pleading not guilty

Examples of nature of activity	**Starting point**	**Range**
Taken vehicle involved in single incident of bad driving where little or no damage or risk of personal injury	High level community order	Medium level community order–12 weeks' custody
Taken vehicle involved in incident(s) involving excessive speed or showing off, especially on busy roads or in built-up area	18 weeks' custody	12–26 weeks' custody
Taken vehicle involved in prolonged bad driving involving deliberate disregard for safety of others	Crown Court	Crown Court

B. Consider the effect of aggravating and mitigating factors (other than those within examples above)

Common aggravating and mitigating factors are identified [elsewhere]—the following may be particularly relevant but these lists are not exhaustive

Factors indicating higher culpability	**Factors indicating greater degree of harm**
1. Disregarding warnings of others 2. Evidence of alcohol or drugs 3. Carrying out other tasks while driving 4. Carrying passengers or heavy load 5. Tiredness 6. Trying to avoid arrest 7. Aggressive driving, such as driving much too close to vehicle in front, inappropriate attempts to overtake, or cutting in after overtaking	1. Injury to others 2. Damage to other vehicles or property

[Sets out the standard sequential sentencing procedure and mentions the need to consider ordering disqualification until appropriate driving test passed.]

VOYEURISM SG-327

[The guidelines set out below are applicable to adult offenders sentenced after 1 April 2014.]

Sexual Offences Act 2003 (section 67)

Triable either way
Maximum: 2 years' custody

Offence range: Fine–18 months' custody

For convictions on or after such date (irrespective of the date of commission of the offence), these are specified offences for the purposes of section 226A (extended sentence for certain violent or sexual offences) of the Criminal Justice Act 2003.

STEP ONE Determining the offence category

The court should determine the offence category using the table below.

Category 1	Raised harm **and** raised culpability
Category 2	Raised harm **or** raised culpability
Category 3	Voyeurism **without** raised harm or culpability factors present

The court should determine culpability and harm caused or intended, by reference only to the factors below, which comprise the principal factual elements of the offence. Where an offence does not fall squarely into a category, individual factors may require a degree of weighting before making an overall assessment and determining the appropriate offence category.

Factors indicating raised harm
• Image(s) available to be viewed by others • Victim observed or recorded in their own home or residence

Factors indicating raised culpability
• Significant degree of planning • Image(s) recorded • Abuse of trust • Specific or previous targeting of a particularly vulnerable victim • Commercial exploitation and/or motivation • Offence racially or religiously aggravated • Offence motivated by, or demonstrating, hostility to the victim based on his or her sexual orientation (or presumed sexual orientation) or transgender identity (or presumed transgender identity) • Offence motivated by, or demonstrating, hostility to the victim based on his or her disability (or presumed disability)

STEP TWO Starting point and category range

Having determined the category, the court should use the corresponding starting points to reach a sentence within the category range [below]. The starting point applies to all offenders irrespective of plea or previous convictions. Having determined the starting point, step two allows further adjustment for aggravating or mitigating features, set out [below].

A case of particular gravity, reflected by multiple features of culpability or harm in step one, could merit upward adjustment from the starting point before further adjustment for aggravating or mitigating features, set out [below].

Where there is a sufficient prospect of rehabilitation, a community order with a sex offender treatment programme requirement under section 202 of the Criminal Justice Act 2003 can be a proper alternative to a short or moderate length custodial sentence.

Category 1	**Starting point** 26 weeks' custody **Category range** 12 weeks'–18 months' custody
Category 2	**Starting point** High level community order **Category range** Medium level community order–26 weeks' custody
Category 3	**Starting point** Medium level community order **Category range** Band A fine–High level community order

The table below contains a **non-exhaustive** list of additional factual elements providing the context of the offence and factors relating to the offender. Identify whether any combination of these, or other relevant factors, should result in an upward or downward adjustment from the starting point. **In particular, relevant recent convictions are likely to result in an upward adjustment.** In some cases, having considered these factors, it may be appropriate to move outside the identified category range.

When sentencing **category 2 offences**, the court should also consider the custody threshold as follows:

- Has the custody threshold been passed?
- If so, is it unavoidable that a custodial sentence be imposed?
- If so, can that sentence be suspended?

When sentencing **category 3 offences**, the court should also consider the community order threshold as follows:

- Has the community order threshold been passed?

Aggravating factors
Statutory aggravating factors
• Previous convictions, having regard to a) the nature of the offence to which the conviction relates and its relevance to the current offence; and b) the time that has elapsed since the conviction • Offence committed whilst on bail

Other aggravating factors
• Location of offence • Timing of offence • Failure to comply with current court orders • Offence committed whilst on licence • Distribution of images, whether or not for gain • Placing images where there is the potential for a high volume of viewers • Period over which victim observed • Period over which images were made or distributed • Any steps taken to prevent victim reporting an incident, obtaining assistance and/or from assisting or supporting the prosecution • Attempts to dispose of or conceal evidence

Mitigating factors
• No previous convictions **or** no relevant/recent convictions • Remorse • Previous good character and/or exemplary conduct* • Age and/or lack of maturity where it affects the responsibility of the offender • Mental disorder or learning disability, particularly where linked to the commission of the offence • Demonstration of steps taken to address offending behaviour

* Previous good character/exemplary conduct is different from having no previous convictions. The more serious the offence, the less the weight which should normally be attributed to this factor. Where previous good character/exemplary conduct has been used to facilitate the offence, this mitigation should not normally be allowed and such conduct may constitute an aggravating factor.

[Sets out the standard sequential sentencing procedure.]

Witness Intimidation SG-328

Criminal Justice and Public Order Act 1994, s. 51

Triable either way:
Maximum when tried summarily: 6 months or level 5 fine
Maximum when tried on indictment: 5 years

Where offence committed in domestic context, refer [below] for guidance

Offence seriousness (culpability and harm)

A. Identify the appropriate starting point

Starting points based on first time offender pleading not guilty

Examples of nature of activity	Starting point	Range
Sudden outburst in chance encounter	6 weeks' custody	Medium level community order–18 weeks' custody
Conduct amounting to a threat; staring at, approaching or following witnesses; talking about the case; trying to alter or stop evidence	18 weeks' custody	12 weeks' custody–Crown Court
Threats of violence to witnesses and/or their families; deliberately seeking out witnesses	Crown Court	Crown Court

B. Consider the effect of aggravating and mitigating factors (other than those within examples above)

Common aggravating and mitigating factors are identified [elsewhere]—the following may be particularly relevant but these lists are not exhaustive

Factors indicating higher culpability
1. Breach of bail conditions
2. Offender involves others

Factors indicating greater degree of harm
1. Detrimental impact on administration of justice
2. Contact made at or in vicinity of victim's home

[Sets out the standard sequential sentencing procedure.]

SG-329

Motoring Offences

Careless Driving (Drive Without Due Care and Attention)

Road Traffic Act 1988, s. 3

Triable only summarily: Maximum: Level 5 fine
Must endorse and may disqualify. If no disqualification, impose 3–9 points

Offence seriousness (culpability and harm)

A. Identify the appropriate starting point

Starting points based on first time offender pleading not guilty

Examples of nature of activity	Starting point	Range
Momentary lapse of concentration or misjudgement at low speed	Band A fine	Band A fine 3–4 points
Loss of control due to speed, mishandling or insufficient attention to road conditions, or carelessly turning right across on-coming traffic	Band B fine	Band B fine 5–6 points
Overtaking manoeuvre at speed resulting in collision of vehicles, or driving bordering on the dangerous	Band C fine	Band C fine Consider disqualification OR 7–9 points

B. Consider the effect of aggravating and mitigating factors (other than those within examples above)

Common aggravating and mitigating factors are identified [elsewhere]—the following may be particularly relevant but these lists are not exhaustive

Factors indicating higher culpability	Factors indicating lower culpability
1. Excessive speed 2. Carrying out other tasks while driving 3. Carrying passengers or heavy load 4. Tiredness **Factors indicating greater degree of harm** 1. Injury to others 2. Damage to other vehicles or property 3. High level of traffic or pedestrians in vicinity 4. Location e.g. near school when children are likely to be present	1. Minor risk 2. Inexperience of driver 3. Sudden change in road or weather conditions

[Sets out the standard sequential sentencing procedure and mentions need to consider ordering disqualification until appropriate driving test passed.]

Causing Death by Careless or Inconsiderate Driving

SG-330

Factors to take into consideration

This guideline and accompanying notes are taken from the Sentencing Guidelines Council's definitive guideline *Causing Death by Driving*, published 15 July 2008 [see SG-437].

Key factors

(a) It is unavoidable that some cases will be on the borderline between *dangerous* and *careless* driving, or may involve a number of factors that significantly increase the seriousness of an offence. As a result, the guideline for this offence identifies three levels of seriousness, the range for the highest of which overlaps with ranges for the lower levels of seriousness for *causing death by dangerous driving*.

(b) The three levels of seriousness are defined by the degree of carelessness involved in the standard of driving:
- the most serious level for this offence is where the offender's driving fell *not that far short of dangerous*;
- the least serious group of offences relates to those cases where the level of culpability is low—for example in a case involving an offender who misjudges the speed of another vehicle, or turns without seeing an oncoming vehicle because of restricted visibility;
- other cases will fall into the intermediate level.

(c) Where the level of carelessness is low and there are no aggravating factors, even the fact that death was caused is not sufficient to justify a prison sentence.

(d) A fine is unlikely to be an appropriate sentence for this offence; where a non-custodial sentence is considered appropriate, this should be a community order. The nature of the requirements will be determined by the purpose identified by the court as of primary importance. Requirements most likely to be relevant include unpaid work requirement, activity requirement, programme requirement and curfew requirement.

(e) Offender mitigation particularly relevant to this offence includes conduct after the offence such as where the offender gave direct, positive, assistance at the scene of a collision to victim(s). It may also include remorse—whilst it can be expected that anyone who has caused a death by driving would be remorseful, this cannot undermine its importance for sentencing purposes. It is for the court to determine whether an expression of remorse is genuine.

(f) Where an offender has a good driving record, this is not a factor that automatically should be treated as mitigation, especially now that the presence of previous convictions is a statutory aggravating factor. However, any evidence to show that an offender has previously been an exemplary driver, for example having driven an ambulance, police vehicle, bus, taxi or similar vehicle conscientiously and without incident for many years, is a fact that the courts may well wish to take into account by way of offender mitigation. This is likely to have even greater effect where the driver is driving on public duty (for example, on ambulance, fire services or police duties) and was responding to an emergency.

(g) Disqualification of the offender from driving and endorsement of the offender's driving licence are mandatory, and the offence carries between 3 and 11 penalty points when the court finds special reasons for not imposing disqualification. There is a discretionary power to order an extended driving test/re-test where a person is convicted of this offence.

Guidelines

Road Traffic Act 1988, s. 2B

Triable either way:
Maximum when tried summarily: Level 5 fine and/or 6 months
Maximum when tried on indictment: 5 years

Offence seriousness (culpability and harm)

A. Identify the appropriate starting point

Starting points based on first time offender pleading not guilty

Examples of nature of activity	Starting point	Range
Careless or inconsiderate driving arising from momentary inattention with no aggravating factors	Medium level community order	Low level community order–high level community order
Other cases of careless or inconsiderate driving	Crown Court	High level community order–Crown Court
Careless or inconsiderate driving falling not far short of dangerous driving	Crown Court	Crown Court

B. Consider the effect of aggravating and mitigating factors (other than those within examples above)

Common aggravating and mitigating factors are identified [elsewhere]—the following may be particularly relevant but these lists are not exhaustive

Factors indicating higher culpability	Factors indicating lower culpability
1. Other offences committed at the same time, such as driving other than in accordance with the terms of a valid licence; driving while disqualified; driving without insurance; taking a vehicle without consent; driving a stolen vehicle 2. Previous convictions for motoring offences, particularly offences that involve bad driving 3. Irresponsible behaviour, such as failing to stop or falsely claiming that one of the victims was responsible for the collision **Factors indicating greater degree of harm** 1. More than one person was killed as a result of the offence 2. Serious injury to one or more persons in addition to the death(s)	1. Offender seriously injured in the collision 2. The victim was a close friend or relative 3. The actions of the victim or a third party contributed to the commission of the offence 4. The offender's lack of driving experience contributed significantly to the likelihood of a collision occurring and/or death resulting 5. The driving was in response to a proven and genuine emergency falling short of a defence

[Sets out the standard sequential sentencing procedure and mentions need to consider ordering disqualification and deprivation of property.]

SG-331 Causing Death by Driving: Unlicensed, Disqualified or Uninsured Drivers

Factors to take into consideration

Key factors

(a) Culpability arises from the offender driving a vehicle on a road or other public place when, by law, not allowed to do so; the offence does not involve any fault in the standard of driving.

(b) Since driving whilst disqualified is more culpable than driving whilst unlicensed or uninsured, a higher starting point is proposed when the offender was disqualified from driving at the time of the offence.

(c) Being uninsured, unlicensed or disqualified are the only determinants of seriousness for this offence, as there are no factors relating to the standard of driving. The list of aggravating factors identified is slightly different as the emphasis is on the decision to drive by an offender who is not permitted by law to do so.

(d) A fine is unlikely to be an appropriate sentence for this offence; where a non-custodial sentence is considered appropriate, this should be a community order.

(e) Where the *decision to drive was brought about by a genuine and proven emergency*, that may mitigate offence seriousness and so it is included as an additional mitigating factor.

(f) An additional mitigating factor covers those situations where an offender genuinely believed that there was valid insurance or a valid licence.

(g) Offender mitigation particularly relevant to this offence includes conduct after the offence such as where the offender gave direct, positive, assistance at the scene of a collision to victim(s). It may also include remorse—whilst it can be expected that anyone who has caused a death by driving would be remorseful, this cannot undermine its importance for sentencing purposes. It is for the court to determine whether an expression of remorse is genuine.

(h) Where an offender has a good driving record, this is not a factor that automatically should be treated as mitigation, especially now that the presence of previous convictions is a statutory aggravating factor. However, any evidence to show that an offender has previously been an exemplary driver, for example having driven an ambulance, police vehicle, bus, taxi or similar vehicle conscientiously and without incident for many years, is a fact that the courts may well wish to take into account by way of offender mitigation. This is likely to have even greater effect where the driver is driving on public duty (for example, on ambulance, fire services or police duties) and was responding to an emergency.

(i) Disqualification of the offender from driving and endorsement of the offender's driving licence are mandatory, and the offence carries between 3 and 11 penalty points when the court finds special reasons for not imposing disqualification. There is a discretionary power[130] to order an extended driving test/re-test where a person is convicted of this offence.

130 Road Traffic Offenders Act 1988, s. 36(4)

Guidelines

Road Traffic Act 1988, s. 3ZB

Triable either way:
Maximum when tried summarily: Level 5 fine and/or 6 months
Maximum when tried on indictment: 2 years

Offence seriousness (culpability and harm)

A. Identify the appropriate starting point

Starting points based on first time offender pleading not guilty

Examples of nature of activity	Starting point	Range
The offender was unlicensed or uninsured—no aggravating factors	Medium level community order	Low level community order–high level community order
The offender was unlicensed or uninsured plus at least 1 aggravating factor from the list below	26 weeks' custody	High level community order–Crown Court
The offender was disqualified from driving **OR** The offender was unlicensed or uninsured plus 2 or more aggravating factors from the list below	Crown Court	Crown Court

B. Consider the effect of aggravating and mitigating factors (other than those within examples above)

Common aggravating and mitigating factors are identified [elsewhere]—the following may be particularly relevant but these lists are not exhaustive

Factors indicating higher culpability	Factors indicating lower culpability
1. Previous convictions for motoring offences, whether involving bad driving or involving an offence of the same kind that forms part of the present conviction (i.e. unlicensed, disqualified or uninsured driving) 2. Irresponsible behaviour such as failing to stop or falsely claiming that someone else was driving **Factors indicating greater degree of harm** 1. More than one person was killed as a result of the offence 2. Serious injury to one or more persons in addition to the death(s)	1. The decision to drive was brought about by a proven and genuine emergency falling short of a defence 2. The offender genuinely believed that he or she was insured or licensed to drive 3. The offender was seriously injured as a result of the collision 4. The victim was a close friend or relative

[Sets out the standard sequential sentencing procedure and mentions need to consider ordering disqualification and deprivation of property.]

DANGEROUS DRIVING SG-332

Road Traffic Act 1988, s. 2

Triable either way:
Maximum when tried summarily: Level 5 fine and/or 6 months
Maximum when tried on indictment: 2 years

- Must endorse and disqualify for *at least* 12 months. Must order extended re-test
- Must disqualify for *at least* 2 years if offender has had two or more disqualifications for periods of 56 days or more in preceding 3 years. If there is a delay in sentencing after conviction, consider interim disqualification

Offence seriousness (culpability and harm)

A. Identify the appropriate starting point

Starting points based on first time offender pleading not guilty

Examples of nature of activity	Starting point	Range
Single incident where little or no damage or risk of personal injury	Medium level community order	Low level community order–high level community order Disqualify 12–15 months
Incident(s) involving excessive speed or showing off, especially on busy roads or in built-up area; OR Single incident where little or no damage or risk of personal injury but offender was disqualified driver	12 weeks' custody	High level community order–26 weeks' custody Disqualify 15–24 months
Prolonged bad driving involving deliberate disregard for safety of others; OR Incident(s) involving excessive speed or showing off, especially on busy roads or in built-up area, by disqualified driver; OR Driving as described in box above while being pursued by police	Crown Court	Crown Court

B. Consider the effect of aggravating and mitigating factors (other than those within examples above)

Common aggravating and mitigating factors are identified [elsewhere]—the following may be particularly relevant but these lists are not exhaustive

Factors indicating higher culpability	Factors indicating lower culpability
1. Disregarding warnings of others 2. Evidence of alcohol or drugs 3. Carrying out other tasks while driving 4. Carrying passengers or heavy load 5. Tiredness 6. Aggressive driving, such as driving much too close to vehicle in front, racing, inappropriate attempts to overtake, or cutting in after overtaking 7. Driving when knowingly suffering from a medical condition which significantly impairs the offender's driving skills 8. Driving a poorly maintained or dangerously loaded vehicle, especially where motivated by commercial concerns **Factors indicating greater degree of harm** 1. Injury to others 2. Damage to other vehicles or property	1. Genuine emergency 2. Speed not excessive 3. Offence due to inexperience rather than irresponsibility of driver

[Sets out the standard sequential sentencing procedure and mentions need to consider order for deprivation of property.]

SG-333

Drive Whilst Disqualified

Road Traffic Act 1988, s. 103

Triable only summarily: Maximum: Level 5 fine and/or 6 months

Must endorse and may disqualify. If no disqualification, impose 6 points

Offence seriousness (culpability and harm)

A. Identify the appropriate starting point

Starting points based on first time offender pleading not guilty

Examples of nature of activity	Starting point	Range
Full period expired but retest not taken	Low level community order	Band C fine–medium level community order 6 points or disqualify for 3–6 months
Lengthy period of ban already served	High level community order	Medium level community order–12 weeks' custody Lengthen disqualification for 6–12 months beyond expiry of current ban
Recently imposed ban	12 weeks' custody	High level community order–26 weeks' custody Lengthen disqualification for 12–18 months beyond expiry of current ban

B. Consider the effect of aggravating and mitigating factors (other than those within examples above)

Common aggravating and mitigating factors are identified [elsewhere]—the following may be particularly relevant but these lists are not exhaustive

Factors indicating higher culpability	Factors indicating lower culpability
1. Never passed test 2. Planned long-term evasion 3. Vehicle obtained during ban 4. Driving for remuneration **Factors indicating greater degree of harm** 1. Distance driven 2. Evidence of associated bad driving 3. Offender caused accident	1. Defendant not present when disqualification imposed and genuine reason why unaware of ban 2. Genuine emergency established

[Sets out the standard sequential sentencing procedure and mentions need to consider order for deprivation of property.]

Note: An offender convicted of this offence will always have at least one relevant previous conviction for the offence that resulted in disqualification. The starting points and ranges take this into account; any other previous convictions should be considered in the usual way…

Excess Alcohol (Drive/Attempt to Drive) SG-334

Road Traffic Act 1988, s. 5(1)(a)

Triable only summarily: Maximum: Level 5 fine and/or 6 months

- Must endorse and disqualify for at least 12 months
- Must disqualify for *at least* 2 years if offender has had two or more disqualifications for periods of 56 days or more in preceding 3 years—refer [below]…
- Must disqualify for *at least* 3 years if offender has been convicted of a relevant offence in preceding 10 years—refer [below]…

If there is a delay in sentencing after conviction, consider interim disqualification

Note: the final column below provides guidance regarding the length of disqualification that may be appropriate in cases to which the 3 year minimum applies. The period to be imposed in any individual case will depend on an assessment of all the relevant circumstances, including the length of time since the earlier ban was imposed and the gravity of the current offence.

Offence seriousness (culpability and harm)

A. Identify the appropriate starting point

Starting points based on first time offender pleading not guilty

Level of alcohol			Starting point	Range	Disqualification	Disqual. 2nd offence in 10 years—see note above
Breath (mg)	**Blood (ml)**	**Urine (ml)**				
36–59	81–137	108–183	Band C fine	Band C fine	12–16 months	36–40 months
60–89	138–206	184–274	Band C fine	Band C fine	17–22 months	36–46 months
90–119	207–275	275–366	Medium level community order	Low level community order–high level community order	23–28 months	36–52 months
120–150 and above	276–345 and above	367–459 and above	12 weeks' custody	High level community order–26 weeks' custody	29–36 months	36–60 months

Sentencing Guidelines

B. Consider the effect of aggravating and mitigating factors (other than those within examples above)

Common aggravating and mitigating factors are identified [elsewhere]—the following may be particularly relevant but these lists are not exhaustive

Factors indicating higher culpability	Factors indicating lower culpability
1. LGV, HGV, PSV etc. 2. Poor road or weather conditions 3. Carrying passengers 4. Driving for hire or reward 5. Evidence of unacceptable standard of driving **Factors indicating greater degree of harm** 1. Involved in accident 2. Location e.g. near school 3. High level of traffic or pedestrians in the vicinity	1. Genuine emergency established* 2. Spiked drinks* 3. Very short distance driven*

* Even where not amounting to special reasons.

[Sets out the standard sequential sentencing procedure and mentions need to consider offering drink/drive rehabilitation course and forfeiture or suspension of personal liquor licence.]

SG-335

Excess Alcohol (In Charge)

Road Traffic Act 1988, s. 5(1)(b)

Triable only summarily: Maximum: Level 4 fine and/or 3 months
Must endorse and may disqualify. If no disqualification, impose 10 points

Offence seriousness (culpability and harm)

A. Identify the appropriate starting point

Starting points based on first time offender pleading not guilty

B. Consider the effect of aggravating and mitigating factors (other than those within examples above)

Level of alcohol			Starting point	Range
Breath (mg)	**Blood (ml)**	**Urine (ml)**		
36–59	81–137	108–183	Band B fine	Band B fine 10 points
60–89	138–206	184–274	Band B fine	Band B fine 10 points OR consider disqualification
90–119	207–275	275–366	Band C fine	Band C fine–medium level community order Consider disqualification up to 6 months OR 10 points
120–150 and above	276–345 and above	367–459 and above	Medium level community order	Low level community order–6 weeks' custody Disqualify 6–12 months

Common aggravating and mitigating factors are identified [elsewhere]—the following may be particularly relevant but these lists are not exhaustive.

[Sets out the standard sequential sentencing procedure and mentions need to consider forfeiture or suspension of personal liquor licence.]

Factors indicating higher culpability	Factor indicating lower culpability
1. LGV, HGV, PSV etc. 2. Ability to drive seriously impaired 3. High likelihood of driving 4. Driving for hire or reward	1. Low likelihood of driving

Fail to Stop/Report Road Accident SG-336

Road Traffic Act 1988, s. 170(4)

Triable only summarily: Maximum: Level 5 fine and/or 6 months
Must endorse and may disqualify. If no disqualification, impose 5–10 points

Offence seriousness (culpability and harm)

A. Identify the appropriate starting point

Starting points based on first time offender pleading not guilty

Examples of nature of activity	Starting point	Range
Minor damage/injury or stopped at scene but failed to exchange particulars or report	Band B fine	Band B fine 5–6 points
Moderate damage/injury or failed to stop and failed to report	Band C fine	Band C fine 7–8 points Consider disqualification
Serious damage/injury and/or evidence of bad driving	High level community order	Band C fine–26 weeks' custody Disqualify 6–12 months OR 9–10 points

B. Consider the effect of aggravating and mitigating factors (other than those within examples above)

Common aggravating and mitigating factors are identified [elsewhere]—the following may be particularly relevant but these lists are not exhaustive

Factors indicating higher culpability	Factors indicating lower culpability
1. Evidence of drink or drugs/evasion of test 2. Knowledge/suspicion that personal injury caused (where not an element of the offence) 3. Leaving injured party at scene 4. Giving false details	1. Believed identity known 2. Genuine fear of retribution 3. Subsequently reported

[Sets out the standard sequential sentencing procedure.]

Fail to Provide Specimen for Analysis (Drive/Attempt to Drive) SG-337

Road Traffic Act 1988, s. 7(6)

Triable only summarily: Maximum: Level 5 fine and/or 6 months

- Must endorse and disqualify for at least 12 months
- Must disqualify for *at least* 2 years if offender has had two or more disqualifications for periods of 56 days or more in preceding 3 years—refer [below]...
- Must disqualify for *at least* 3 years if offender has been convicted of a relevant offence in preceding 10 years—refer [below]...

If there is a delay in sentencing after conviction, consider interim disqualification

Note: the final column below provides guidance regarding the length of disqualification that may be appropriate in cases to which the 3 year minimum applies. The period to be imposed in any individual case will depend on an assessment of all the relevant circumstances, including the length of time since the earlier ban was imposed and the gravity of the current offence.

Offence seriousness (culpability and harm)

A. Identify the appropriate starting point

Starting points based on first time offender pleading not guilty

Sentencing Guidelines

Examples of nature of activity	Starting point	Range	Disqualification	Disqual. 2nd offence in 10 years
Defendant refused test when had honestly held but unreasonable excuse	Band C fine	Band C fine	12–16 months	36–40 months
Deliberate refusal or deliberate failure	Low level community order	Band C fine–high level community order	17–28 months	36–52 months
Deliberate refusal or deliberate failure where evidence of serious impairment	12 weeks' custody	High level community order–26 weeks' custody	29–36 months	36–60 months

B. Consider the effect of aggravating and mitigating factors (other than those within examples above)

Common aggravating and mitigating factors are identified [elsewhere]—the following may be particularly relevant but these lists are not exhaustive

Factors indicating higher culpability	Factor indicating lower culpability
1. Evidence of unacceptable standard of driving 2. LGV, HGV, PSV etc. 3. Obvious state of intoxication 4. Driving for hire or reward **Factor indicating greater degree of harm** 1. Involved in accident	1. Genuine but unsuccessful attempt to provide specimen

[Sets out the standard sequential sentencing procedure and mentions need to consider offering drink/drive rehabilitation course.]

SG-338

Fail to Provide Specimen for Analysis (In Charge)

Road Traffic Act 1988, s. 7(6)

Triable only summarily: Maximum: Level 4 fine and/or 3 months
Must endorse and may disqualify. If no disqualification, impose 10 points

Offence seriousness (culpability and harm)

A. Identify the appropriate starting point

Starting points based on first time offender pleading not guilty

Examples of nature of activity	Starting point	Range
Defendant refused test when had honestly held but unreasonable excuse	Band B fine	Band B fine 10 points
Deliberate refusal or deliberate failure	Band C fine	Band C fine–medium level community order Consider disqualification OR 10 points
Deliberate refusal or deliberate failure where evidence of serious impairment	Medium level community order	Low level community order–6 weeks' custody Disqualify 6–12 months

B. Consider the effect of aggravating and mitigating factors (other than those within examples above)

Common aggravating and mitigating factors are identified [elsewhere]—the following may be particularly relevant but these lists are not exhaustive

Factors indicating higher culpability	Factors indicating lower culpability
1. Obvious state of intoxication 2. LGV, HGV, PSV etc. 3. High likelihood of driving 4. Driving for hire or reward	1. Genuine but unsuccessful attempt to provide specimen 2. Low likelihood of driving

[Sets out the standard sequential sentencing procedure.]

No Insurance SG-339

Road Traffic Act 1988, s. 143

Triable only summarily: Maximum: Level 5 fine
Must endorse and may disqualify. If no disqualification, impose 6–8 points—see notes below

Offence seriousness (culpability and harm)

A. Identify the appropriate starting point

Starting points based on first time offender pleading not guilty

Examples of nature of activity	Starting point	Range
Using a motor vehicle on a road or other public place without insurance	Band C fine	Band C fine 6 points–12 months' disqualification—see notes below

B. Consider the effect of aggravating and mitigating factors (other than those within examples above)

Common aggravating and mitigating factors are identified [elsewhere]—the following may be particularly relevant but these lists are not exhaustive

Factors indicating higher culpability	Factors indicating lower culpability
1. Never passed test 2. Gave false details 3. Driving LGV, HGV, PSV etc. 4. Driving for hire or reward 5. Evidence of sustained uninsured use **Factor indicating greater degree of harm** 1. Involved in accident 2. Accident resulting in injury	1. Responsibility for providing insurance rests with another 2. Genuine misunderstanding 3. Recent failure to renew or failure to transfer vehicle details where insurance was in existence 4. Vehicle not being driven

[Sets out the standard sequential sentencing procedure.]

Note: Consider range from 7 points–2 months disqualification where vehicle was being driven and no evidence that the offender has held insurance. Consider disqualification of 6–12 months if evidence of sustained uninsured use and/or involvement in accident.

Speeding SG-340

Road Traffic Regulation Act 1984, s. 89(10)

Triable only summarily: Maximum: Level 3 fine (level 4 if motorway)

Must endorse and may disqualify. If no disqualification, impose 3–6 points

Offence seriousness (culpability and harm)

A. Identify the appropriate starting point

Starting points based on first time offender pleading not guilty

Speed limit (mph)	Recorded speed (mph)		
20	21–30	31–40	41–50
30	31–40	41–50	51–60
40	41–55	56–65	66–75
50	51–65	66–75	76–85
60	61–80	81–90	91–100
70	71–90	91–100	101–110
Starting point	Band A fine	Band B fine	Band B fine
Range	Band A fine	Band B fine	Band B fine
Points/disqualification	3 points	4–6 points OR Disqualify 7–28 days	Disqualify 7–56 days OR 6 points

B. Consider the effect of aggravating and mitigating factors (other than those within examples above)

Common aggravating and mitigating factors are identified [elsewhere]—the following may be particularly relevant but these lists are not exhaustive

Factors indicating higher culpability	Factor indicating lower culpability
1. Poor road or weather conditions 2. LGV, HGV, PSV etc. 3. Towing caravan/trailer 4. Carrying passengers or heavy load 5. Driving for hire or reward 6. Evidence of unacceptable standard of driving over and above speed limit **Factors indicating greater degree of harm** 1. Location e.g. near school 2. High level of traffic or pedestrians in the vicinity	1. Genuine emergency established

[Sets out the standard sequential sentencing procedure.]

SG-341 Unfit Through Drink or Drugs (Drive/Attempt to Drive)

Road Traffic Act 1988, s. 4(1)

Triable only summarily: Maximum: Level 5 fine and/or 6 months

- Must endorse and disqualify for at least 12 months
- Must disqualify for *at least* 2 years if offender has had two or more disqualifications for periods of 56 days or more in preceding 3 years—refer [below]…
- Must disqualify for *at least* 3 years if offender has been convicted of a relevant offence in preceding 10 years—refer [below]…

If there is a delay in sentencing after conviction, consider interim disqualification

Note: the final column below provides guidance regarding the length of disqualification that may be appropriate in cases to which the 3 year minimum applies. The period to be imposed in any individual case will depend on an assessment of all the relevant circumstances, including the length of time since the earlier ban was imposed and the gravity of the current offence.

Offence seriousness (culpability and harm)

A. Identify the appropriate starting point

Starting points based on first time offender pleading not guilty

Examples of nature of activity	Starting point	Range	Disqualification	Disqual. 2nd offence in 10 years
Evidence of moderate level of impairment and no aggravating factors	Band C fine	Band C fine	12–16 months	36–40 months
Evidence of moderate level of impairment and presence of one or more aggravating factors listed below	Band C fine	Band C fine	17–22 months	36–46 months
Evidence of high level of impairment and no aggravating factors	Medium level community order	Low level community order–high level community order	23–28 months	36–52 months
Evidence of high level of impairment and presence of one or more aggravating factors listed below	12 weeks' custody	High level community order–26 weeks' custody	29–36 months	36–60 months

B. Consider the effect of aggravating and mitigating factors (other than those within examples above)

Common aggravating and mitigating factors are identified [elsewhere]—the following may be particularly relevant but these lists are not exhaustive

Factors indicating higher culpability	Factors indicating lower culpability
1. LGV, HGV, PSV etc. 2. Poor road or weather conditions 3. Carrying passengers 4. Driving for hire or reward 5. Evidence of unacceptable standard of driving **Factors indicating greater degree of harm** 1. Involved in accident 2. Location e.g. near school 3. High level of traffic or pedestrians in the vicinity	1. Genuine emergency established* 2. Spiked drinks* 3. Very short distance driven*

* Even where not amounting to special reasons.

[Sets out the standard sequential sentencing procedure and mentions need to consider offering a drink/drive rehabilitation course.]

Unfit Through Drink or Drugs (In Charge) **SG-342**

Road Traffic Act 1988, s. 4(2)

Triable only summarily: Maximum: Level 4 fine and/or 3 months
Must endorse and may disqualify. If no disqualification, impose 10 points

Offence seriousness (culpability and harm)

A. Identify the appropriate starting point

Starting points based on first time offender pleading not guilty

Examples of nature of activity	Starting point	Range
Evidence of moderate level of impairment and no aggravating factors	Band B fine	Band B fine 10 points
Evidence of moderate level of impairment and presence of one or more aggravating factors listed below	Band B fine	Band B fine 10 points or consider disqualification
Evidence of high level of impairment and no aggravating factors	Band C fine	Band C fine–medium level community order 10 points or consider disqualification
Evidence of high level of impairment and presence of one or more aggravating factors listed below	High level community order	Medium level community order–12 weeks' custody Consider disqualification OR 10 points

Sentencing Guidelines

B. Consider the effect of aggravating and mitigating factors (other than those within examples above)

Common aggravating and mitigating factors are identified [elsewhere]—the following may be particularly relevant but these lists are not exhaustive

Factors indicating higher culpability	Factor indicating lower culpability
1. LGV, HGV, PSV etc. 2. High likelihood of driving 3. Driving for hire or reward	1. Low likelihood of driving

[Sets out the standard sequential sentencing procedure and mentions need to consider offering a drink/drive rehabilitation course.]

SG-343 Offences Appropriate for Imposition of Fine or Discharge

SG-344 Part 1: Offences concerning the driver

Offence	Maximum	Points	Starting point	Special considerations
Fail to co-operate with preliminary (roadside) breath test	L3	4	B	
Fail to give information of driver's identity as required	L3	6	C	For limited companies, endorsement is not available; a fine is the only available penalty
Fail to produce insurance certificate	L4	–	A	Fine per offence, not per document
Fail to produce test certificate	L3	–	A	
Drive otherwise than in accordance with licence (where could be covered)	L3	–	A	
Drive otherwise than in accordance with licence	L3	3–6	A	Aggravating factor if no licence ever held

SG-345 Part 2: Offences concerning the vehicle

*The guidelines for some of the offences below differentiate between three types of offender when the offence is committed in the course of business: driver, owner-driver and owner-company. **For owner-driver, the starting point is the same as for driver; however, the court should consider an uplift of at least 25%.**

Offence	Maximum	Points	Starting point	Special considerations
No excise licence	**L3 or 5 times annual duty, whichever is greater**	–	**A (1–3 months unpaid) B (4–6 months unpaid) C (7–12 months unpaid)**	Add duty lost
Fail to notify change of ownership to DVLA	L3	–	A	If offence committed in course of business: A (driver) A* (owner-driver) B (owner-company)
No test certificate	L3	–	A	If offence committed in course of business: A (driver) A* (owner-driver) B (owner-company)
Brakes defective	L4	3	B	If offence committed in course of business: B (driver) B* (owner-driver) C (owner-company) L5 if goods vehicle—see Part 5 below
Steering defective	L4	3	B	If offence committed in course of business: B (driver) B* (owner-driver) C (owner- company) L5 if goods vehicle—see Part 5 below

Offence	Maximum	Points	Starting point	Special considerations
Tyres defective	L4	3	B	If offence committed in course of business: B (driver) B* (owner-driver) C (owner-company) L5 if goods vehicle—see Part 5 below Penalty per tyre
Condition of vehicle/ accessories/ Equipment involving danger of injury (Road Traffic Act 1988, s.40A)	L4	3	B	Must disqualify for at least 6 months if offender has one or more previous convictions for same offence within three years If offence committed in course of business: B (driver) B* (owner-driver) C (owner-company) L5 if goods vehicle—see Part 5 below
Exhaust defective	L3	–	A	If offence committed in course of business: A (driver) A* (owner-driver) B (owner-company)
Lights defective	L3	–	A	If offence committed in course of business: A (driver) A* (owner-driver) B (owner-company)

Part 3: Offences concerning use of vehicle SG-346

*The guidelines for some of the offences below differentiate between three types of offender when the offence is committed in the course of business: driver, owner-driver and owner-company. **For owner-driver, the starting point is the same as for driver; however, the court should consider an uplift of at least 25%.**

Offence	Maximum	Points	Starting point	Special considerations
Weight, position or distribution of load or manner in which load secured involving danger of injury (Road Traffic Act 1988, s.40A)	L4	3	B	Must disqualify for at least 6 months if offender has one or more previous convictions for same offence within three years. If offence committed in course of business: A (driver) A* (owner-driver) B (owner-company) L5 if goods vehicle—see Part 5 below
Number of passengers or way carried involving danger of injury (Road Traffic Act 1988, s.40A)	L4	3	B	If offence committed in course of business: A (driver) A* (owner-driver) B (owner-company) L5 if goods vehicle—see Part 5 below
Position or manner in which load secured (not involving danger) (Road Traffic Act 1988, s.42)	L3	–	A	L4 if goods vehicle—see Part 5 below
Overloading/exceeding axle weight	L5	–	A	Starting point caters for cases where the overload is up to and including 10%. Thereafter, 10% should be added to the penalty for each additional 1% of overload Penalty per axle If offence committed in course of business: A (driver) A* (owner-driver) B (owner-company) If goods vehicle—see Part 5 below
Dangerous parking	L3	3	A	
Pelican/zebra crossing contravention	L3	3	A	
Fail to comply with traffic sign (e.g. red traffic light, stop sign, double white lines, no entry sign)	L3	3	A	

(*Contined*)

Sentencing Guidelines

Offence	Maximum	Points	Starting point	Special considerations
Fail to comply with traffic sign (e.g. give way sign, keep left sign, temporary signs)	L3	–	A	
Fail to comply with police constable directing traffic	L3	3	A	
Fail to stop when required by police constable	L5 (mechanically propelled vehicle) L3 (cycle)	–	B	
Use of mobile telephone	L3	3	A	
Seat belt offences	L2 (adult or child in front) L2 (child in rear)	–	A	
Fail to use appropriate child car seat	L2	–	A	

SG-347 Part 4: Motorway Offences

Offence	Maximum	Points	Starting point	Special considerations
Drive in reverse or wrong way on slip road	L4	3	B	
Drive in reverse or wrong way on motorway	L4	3	C	
Drive off carriageway (central reservation or hard shoulder)	L4	3	B	
Make U turn	L4	3	C	
Learner driver or excluded vehicle	L4	3	B	
Stop on hard shoulder	L4	–	A	
Vehicle in prohibited lane	L4	3	A	
Walk on motorway, slip road or hard shoulder	L4	–	A	

SG-348 Part 5: Offences re buses/goods vehicles over 3.5 tonnes (GVW)

* The guidelines for these offences differentiate between three types of offender: driver; owner-driver; and owner-company. **For owner-driver, the starting point is the same as for driver; however, the court should consider an uplift of at least 25%.**

** In all cases, take safety, damage to roads and commercial gain into account. Refer [below] for approach to fines for 'commercially motivated' offences.

Offence	Maximum	Points	Starting point	Special considerations
No goods vehicle plating certificate	L3	–	A (driver) A* (owner-driver) B (owner-company)	
No goods vehicle test certificate	L4	–	B (driver) B* (owner-driver) C (owner-company)	
Brakes defective	L5	3	B (driver) B* (owner-driver) C (owner-company)	

Offence	Maximum	Points	Starting point	Special considerations
Steering defective	L5	3	B (driver) B* (owner-driver) C (owner-company)	
Tyres defective	L5	3	B (driver) B* (owner-driver) C (owner-company)	Penalty per tyre
Exhaust emission	L4	–	B (driver) B* (owner-driver) C (owner-company)	
Condition of vehicle/ accessories/equipment involving danger of injury (Road Traffic Act 1988, s.40A)	L5	3	B (driver) B* (owner-driver) C (owner-company)	Must disqualify for at least 6 months if offender has one or more previous convictions for same offence within three years
Number of passengers or way carried involving danger of injury (Road Traffic Act 1988, s.40A)	L5	3	B (driver) B* (owner-driver) C (owner-company)	Must disqualify for at least 6 months if offender has one or more previous convictions for same offence within three years
Weight, position or distribution of load or manner in which load secured involving danger of injury (Road Traffic Act 1988, s.40A)	L5	3	B (driver) B* (owner-driver) C (owner-company)	Must disqualify for at least 6 months if offender has one or more previous convictions for same offence within three years
Position or manner in which load secured (not involving danger) (Road Traffic Act 1988, s.42)	L4	–	B (driver) B* (owner-driver) C (owner-company)	
Overloading/ exceeding axle weight	L5	–	B (driver) B* (owner-driver) C (owner-company)	Starting points cater for cases where the overload is up to and including 10%. Thereafter, 10% should be added to the penalty for each additional 1% of overload Penalty per axle
No operator's licence	L4	–	B (driver) B* (owner-driver) C (owner-company)	
Speed limiter not used or incorrectly calibrated	L4	–	B (driver) B* (owner-driver) C (owner-company)	
Tachograph not used/ not working	L5	–	B (driver) B* (owner-driver) C (owner-company)	
Exceed permitted driving time/periods of duty	L4	–	B (driver) B* (owner-driver) C (owner-company)	
Fail to keep/return written record sheets	L4	–	B (driver) B* (owner-driver) C (owner-company)	
Falsify or alter records with intent to deceive	L5/2 years	–	B (driver) B* (owner-driver) C (owner-company)	Either way offence

Explanatory Material

SG-349 [The relevant explanatory material on 'range', 'starting point' and 'first-time offender' was omitted in the revision of the Explanatory material which had effect in August 2015.]

SG-350 [The relevant explanatory material was omitted in the revision of the Explanatory material which had effect in August 2015.]

SG-351 [The relevant explanatory material was omitted in the revision of the Explanatory material which had effect in August 2015.]

SG-352 [The relevant explanatory material was omitted in the revision of the Explanatory material which had effect in August 2015.]

SG-353 [The relevant explanatory material was omitted in the revision of the Explanatory material which had effect in August 2015.]

SG-354 [The relevant explanatory material was omitted in the revision of the Explanatory material which had effect in August 2015.]

SG-355 [The relevant explanatory material was omitted in the revision of the Explanatory material which had effect in August 2015.]

SG-356

Approach to the Assessment of Fines

SG-357 **Introduction**

1. The amount of a fine must reflect the *seriousness* of the offence.[131]
2. The court must also take into account the *financial circumstances* of the offender; this applies whether it has the effect of increasing or reducing the fine.[132]
3. The aim is for the fine to have an equal impact on offenders with different financial circumstances; it should be a hardship but should not force the offender below a reasonable 'subsistence' level. Normally a fine should be of an amount that is capable of being paid within 12 months though there may be exceptions to this.
4. The guidance below aims to establish a clear, consistent and principled approach to the assessment of fines that will apply fairly in the majority of cases. However, it is impossible to anticipate every situation that may be encountered and in each case the court will need to exercise its judgement to ensure that the fine properly reflects the *seriousness of the offence* and takes into account the *financial circumstances* of the offender.

SG-358 **Fine bands**

5. For the purpose of the offence guidelines, a fine is based on one of three bands (A, B or C). The selection of the relevant fine band, and the position of the individual offence within that band, is determined by the seriousness of the offence. In some cases fine bands D–F may be used even where the community or custody threshold have been passed.

	Starting point	**Range**
Fine Band A	50% of relevant weekly income	25–75% of relevant weekly income
Fine Band B	100% of relevant weekly income	75–125% of relevant weekly income
Fine Band C	150% of relevant weekly income	125–175% of relevant weekly income
Fine Band D	250% of relevant weekly income	200–300% of relevant weekly income
Fine Band E	400% of relevant weekly income	300–500% of relevant weekly income
Fine Band F	600% of relevant weekly income	500–700% of relevant weekly income

6. For an explanation of the meaning of starting point and range, both generally and in relation to fines, see [SG-233].

[131] Criminal Justice Act 2003, section 164(2)
[132] ibid, sections 164(1) and 164(4)

Definition of relevant weekly income SG-359

7. The *seriousness* of an offence determines the choice of fine band and the position of the offence within the range for that band. The offender's *financial circumstances* are taken into account by expressing that position as a proportion of the offender's *relevant weekly income.*
8. Where
   - an offender is in receipt of income from employment or is self-employed *and*
   - that income is *more than £120 per week* after deduction of tax and national insurance (or equivalent where the offender is self-employed),

the actual income is the *relevant weekly income.*

9. Where
   - an offender's only source of income is state benefit (including where there is relatively low additional income as permitted by the benefit regulations) *or*
   - the offender is in receipt of income from employment or is self-employed but the amount of income after deduction of tax and national insurance is *£120 or less,*

the *relevant weekly income is deemed to be £110.*

Additional information about the basis for this approach is set out [at **SG-367A**].

10. In calculating relevant weekly income, no account should be taken of tax credits, housing benefit, child benefit or similar.

No reliable information SG-360

11. Where an offender has failed to provide information, or the court is not satisfied that it has been given sufficient reliable information, it is entitled to make such determination as it thinks fit regarding the financial circumstances of the offender.[133] Any determination should be clearly stated on the court records for use in any subsequent variation or enforcement proceedings. In such cases, a record should also be made of the applicable fine band and the court's assessment of the position of the offence within that band based on the seriousness of the offence.
12. Where there is no information on which a determination can be made, the court should proceed on the basis of an *assumed relevant weekly income of £440.* This is derived from national median pre-tax earnings; a gross figure is used as, in the absence of financial information from the offender, it is not possible to calculate appropriate deductions.[134]
13. Where there is some information that tends to suggest a significantly lower or higher income than the recommended £440 default sum, the court should make a determination based on that information.
14. A court is empowered to remit a fine in whole or part if the offender subsequently provides information as to means.[135] The assessment of offence seriousness and, therefore, the appropriate fine band and the position of the offence within that band is not affected by the provision of this information.

Assessment of financial circumstances SG-361

15. While the initial consideration for the assessment of a fine is the offender's relevant weekly income, the court is required to take account of the offender's *financial circumstances* including assets more broadly. Guidance on important parts of this assessment is set out below.
16. An offender's financial circumstances may have the effect of increasing or reducing the amount of the fine; however, they are not relevant to the assessment of offence seriousness. They should be considered separately from the selection of the appropriate fine band and the court's assessment of the position of the offence within the range for that band.

Out of the ordinary expenses SG-362

17. In deciding the proportions of relevant weekly income that are the starting points and ranges for each fine band, account has been taken of reasonable living expenses. Accordingly, no further allowance should normally be made for these. In addition, no allowance should normally be made where the offender has dependants.

[133] Criminal Justice Act 2003, s. 164(5)

[134] This figure is a projected estimate based upon the 2012–13 Survey of Personal Incomes using economic assumptions consistent with the Office for Budget Responsibility's March 2015 economic and fiscal outlook. The latest actual figure is for 2012–13, when median pre-tax income was £404 per week (https://www.gov.uk/government/statistics/shares-of-total-income-before-and-after-tax-and-income-tax-for-percentile-groups).

[135] Criminal Justice Act 2003, s. 165(2)

18. Outgoings will be relevant to the amount of the fine only where the expenditure is *out of the ordinary* and *substantially* reduces the ability to pay a financial penalty so that the requirement to pay a fine based on the standard approach would lead to *undue* hardship.

SG-363 Unusually low outgoings

19. Where the offender's living expenses are substantially lower than would normally be expected, it may be appropriate to adjust the amount of the fine to reflect this. This may apply, for example, where an offender does not make any financial contribution towards his or her living costs.

SG-364 Savings

20. Where an offender has savings these will not normally be relevant to the assessment of the amount of a fine although they may influence the decision on time to pay.
21. However, where an offender has little or no income but has substantial savings, the court may consider it appropriate to adjust the amount of the fine to reflect this.

SG-365 Household has more than one source of income

22. Where the household of which the offender is a part has more than one source of income, the fine should normally be based on the income of the offender alone.
23. However, where the offender's part of the income is very small (or the offender is wholly dependent on the income of another), the court may have regard to the extent of the household's income and assets which will be available to meet any fine imposed on the offender.[136]

SG-366 Potential earning capacity

24. Where there is reason to believe that an offender's potential earning capacity is greater than his or her current income, the court may wish to adjust the amount of the fine to reflect this.[137] This may apply, for example, where an unemployed offender states an expectation to gain paid employment within a short time. The basis for the calculation of fine should be recorded in order to ensure that there is a clear record for use in variation or enforcement proceedings.

SG-367 High income offenders

25. Where the offender is in receipt of very high income, a fine based on a proportion of relevant weekly income may be disproportionately high when compared with the seriousness of the offence. In such cases, the court should adjust the fine to an appropriate level; as a general indication, in most cases the fine for a first time offender pleading not guilty should not exceed 75% of the maximum fine. In the case of fines which are unlimited the court should decide the appropriate level with the guidance of the legal adviser.

SG-367A Approach to offenders on low income

26. An offender whose primary source of income is state benefit will generally receive a base level of benefit (e.g. job seekers' allowance, a relevant disability benefit or income support) and may also be eligible for supplementary benefits depending on his or her individual circumstances (such as child tax credits, housing benefit, council tax benefit and similar). In some cases these benefits may have been replaced by Universal Credit.
27. If relevant weekly income were defined as the amount of benefit received, this would usually result in higher fines being imposed on offenders with a higher level of need; in most circumstances that would not properly balance the seriousness of the offence with the financial circumstances of the offender. While it might be possible to exclude from the calculation any allowance above the basic entitlement of a single person, that could be complicated and time consuming.
28. Similar issues can arise where an offender is in receipt of a low earned income since this may trigger eligibility for means related benefits such as working tax credits and housing benefit depending on the particular circumstances. It will not always be possible to determine with any confidence whether such a person's financial circumstances are significantly different from those of a person whose primary source of income is state benefit.
29. For these reasons, a simpler and fairer approach to cases involving offenders in receipt of low income (whether primarily earned or as a result of benefit) is to identify an amount that is deemed to represent the offender's relevant weekly income.
30. While a precise calculation is neither possible nor desirable, it is considered that an amount that is approximately half-way between the base rate for job seekers' allowance and the net weekly income

---

[136] *R v Engen* [2004] EWCA Crim 1536 (CA)
[137] *R v Little* (unreported) 14 April 1976 (CA)

of an adult earning the minimum wage for 30 hours per week represents a starting point that is both realistic and appropriate; this is currently £120.[138] The calculation is based on a 30 hour working week in recognition of the fact that many of those on minimum wage do not work a full 37 hour week and that lower minimum wage rates apply to younger people.

31. It is expected that this figure will remain in use until 31 March 2015. Future revisions of the guideline will update the amount in accordance with current benefit and minimum wage levels.

Offence committed for 'commercial' purposes **SG-368**

32. Some offences are committed with the intention of gaining a significant commercial benefit. These often occur where, in order to carry out an activity lawfully, a person has to comply with certain processes which may be expensive. They include, for example, 'taxi-touting' (where unauthorised persons seek to operate as taxi drivers) and 'fly-tipping' (where the cost of lawful disposal is considerable).
33. In some of these cases, a fine based on the standard approach set out above may not reflect the level of financial gain achieved or sought through the offending. Accordingly:
    a. where the offender has generated income or avoided expenditure to a level that can be calculated or estimated, the court may wish to consider that amount when determining the financial penalty;
    b. where it is not possible to calculate or estimate that amount, the court may wish to draw on information from the enforcing authorities about the general costs of operating within the law.

Offence committed by an organisation **SG-368A**

34. Where an offence is committed by an organisation, guidance on fines can be found in the environmental offences guideline [see **SG-610**].
35. See the Criminal Practice Direction CPD XIII Listing Annex 3 [see **PD-109**] for directions on dealing with cases involving very large fines in the magistrates' court.

Reduction for a guilty plea **SG-369**

36. Where a guilty plea has been entered, the amount of the fine should be reduced by the appropriate proportion. Courts should refer to the Guilty Plea guidelines [at **SG-1**].

Other considerations **SG-370**

Maximum fines

37. A fine must not exceed the statutory limit. Where this is expressed in terms of a 'level', the maxima are:

Level 1	£200
Level 2	£500
Level 3	£1,000
Level 4	£2,500
Level 5	unlimited[139]

See the Criminal Practice Direction XIII Listing Annex 3 [at **PD-109**] for directions on dealing with cases involving very large fines in the magistrates' court.

Multiple offences

38. Where an offender is to be fined for two or more offences that arose out of the same incident, it will often be appropriate to impose on the most serious offence a fine which reflects the totality of the offending where this can be achieved within the maximum penalty for that offence. 'No separate penalty' should be imposed for the other offences.
39. Where compensation is being ordered, that will need to be attributed to the relevant offence as will any necessary ancillary orders.

[138] With effect from 1 October 2014, the minimum wage is £6.50 per hour for an adult aged 21 or over. Based on a 30 hour week, this equates to approximately £189 after deductions for tax and national insurance. To ensure equivalence of approach, the level of job seekers' allowance for a single person aged 18 to 24 has been used for the purpose of calculating the mid point; this is currently £57.90.

[139] For offences committed after 13 March 2015. For offences committed before that date the level 5 maximum is £5,000.

Imposition of fines with custodial sentences

40. A fine and a custodial sentence may be imposed for the same offence although there will be few circumstances in which this is appropriate, particularly where the custodial sentence is to be served immediately. One example might be where an offender has profited financially from an offence but there is no obvious victim to whom compensation can be awarded. Combining these sentences is most likely to be appropriate only where the custodial sentence is short and/or the offender clearly has, or will have, the means to pay.
41. Care must be taken to ensure that the overall sentence is proportionate to the seriousness of the offence and that better off offenders are not able to 'buy themselves out of custody'.
42. Consult your legal adviser if considering lodging fines or costs on the imposition of a custodial sentence.

Consult your legal adviser in any case in which you are considering combining a fine with a custodial sentence.

Payment

43. A fine is payable in full on the day on which it is imposed. The offender should always be asked for immediate payment when present in court and some payment on the day should be required wherever possible.
44. Where that is not possible, the court may, in certain circumstances,[140] require the offender to be detained. More commonly, a court will allow payments to be made over a period set by the court:
    a. if periodic payments are allowed, the fine should normally be payable within a maximum of 12 months;
    b. compensation should normally be payable within 12 months. However, in exceptional circumstances it may be appropriate to allow it to be paid over a period of up to 3 years.
45. Where fine bands D, E and F apply (see paragraph 5 above), it may be appropriate for the fine to be of an amount that is larger than can be repaid within 12 months. In such cases, the fine should normally be payable within a maximum of 18 months (band D) or 2 years (bands E and F).
46. When allowing payment by *instalments payments should be set at a realistic rate taking into account the offender's disposable* income. The following approach may be useful.

Net weekly income	Starting point for weekly payment
£60	£5
£120	£10
£200	£25
£250	£30
£300	£50
£400	£80

If the offender has dependants or larger than usual commitments, the weekly payment is likely to be decreased.

47. The payment terms must be included in any collection order made in respect of the amount imposed; see below.

SG-370A **Collection orders**

48. The Courts Act 2003 created a fines collection scheme which provides for greater administrative enforcement of fines. Consult your legal adviser for further guidance.

Attachment of earnings orders/applications for benefit deductions

49. Unless it would be impracticable or inappropriate to do so, the court must make an attachment of earnings or (AEO) or application for benefit deductions (ABD) whenever:
    - compensation is imposed;[141] or
    - the court concludes that the offender is an existing defaulter and that the existing default cannot be disregarded.[142]

[140] See section 82 of the Magistrates' Court Act for restrictions on the power to impose imprisonment on default.
[141] Courts Act 2003, sch. 5, para. 7A
[142] ibid, para. 8

50. In other cases, the court may make an AEO or ABD with the offender's consent.[143]
The court must make a collection order in every case in which a fine or compensation order is imposed unless this would be impracticable or inappropriate.[144] The collection order must state:

- the amount of the sum due, including the amount of any fine, compensation order or other sum;
- whether the court considers the offender to be an existing defaulter;
- whether an AEO or ABD has been made and information about the effect of the order;
- if the court has not made an AEO or ABD, the payment terms;
- if an AEO or ABD has been made, the reserve terms (i.e. the payment terms that will apply if the AEO or ABD fails). It will often be appropriate to set a reserve term of payment in full within 14 days.

Compensation SG-370B

1. The court *must* consider making a compensation order in any case where personal injury, loss or damage has resulted from the offence. It can either be a sentence in its own right or an ancillary order. The court must give reasons if it decides not to order compensation.[145]
2. There is no statutory limit on the amount of compensation that may be imposed in respect of offences for an offender aged 18 or over. Compensation may also be ordered in respect of offences taken into consideration.[146]
3. Where the personal injury, loss or damage arises from a road accident, a compensation order may be made only if there is a conviction for an offence under the Theft Act 1968, or the offender is uninsured and the Motor Insurers' Bureau will not cover the loss.
4. Subject to consideration of the victim's views (see paragraph 6 below), the court must order compensation wherever possible and should not have regard to the availability of other sources such as civil litigation or the Criminal Injuries Compensation Scheme. Any amount paid by an offender under a compensation order will generally be deducted from a subsequent civil award or payment under the Scheme to avoid double compensation.
5. Compensation may be ordered for such amount as the court considers appropriate having regard to any evidence and any representations made by the offender or prosecutor. The court must also take into account the offender's means (see also paragraphs 9–11 below).
6. Compensation should benefit, not inflict further harm on, the victim. Any financial recompense from the offender may cause distress. A victim may or may not want compensation from the offender and assumptions should not be made either way. The victim's views are properly obtained through sensitive discussion by the police or witness care unit, when it can be explained that the offender's ability to pay will ultimately determine whether, and how much, compensation is ordered and whether the compensation will be paid in one lump sum or by instalments. If the victim does not want compensation, this should be made known to the court and respected.
7. In cases where it is difficult to ascertain the full amount of the loss suffered by the victim, consideration should be given to making a compensation order for an amount representing the agreed or likely loss. Where relevant information is not immediately available, it may be appropriate to grant an adjournment for it to be obtained.
8. The court should consider two types of loss:
    - financial loss sustained as a result of the offence such as the cost of repairing damage or, in case of injury, any loss of earnings or medical expenses;
    - pain and suffering caused by the injury (including terror, shock or distress) and any loss of facility. This should be assessed in light of all factors that appear to the court to be relevant, including any medical evidence, the victim's age and personal circumstances.
9. Once the court has formed a preliminary view of the appropriate level of compensation, it must have regard to the means of the offender so far as they are known. Where the offender has little money, the order may have to be scaled down or additional time allowed to pay; the court may allow compensation to be paid over a period of up to three years in appropriate cases.

[143] ibid, para. 9
[144] ibid, para.12
[145] Powers of Criminal Courts (Sentencing) Act 2000, s. 130
[146] ibid, s. 131

10. The fact that a custodial sentence is imposed does not, in itself, make it inappropriate to order compensation; however, it may be relevant to whether the offender has the means to satisfy the order. *Consult your legal adviser in any case where you are considering combining compensation with a custodial sentence.*
11. Where the court considers that it would be appropriate to impose a fine and a compensation order but the offender has insufficient means to pay both, priority should be given to compensation. Compensation also takes priority over the victim surcharge where the offender's means are an issue.

SG-370C **Suggested starting points for physical and mental injuries**

12. The tables below suggest starting points for compensating physical and mental injuries commonly encountered in a magistrates' court. They have been developed to be consistent with the approach in the Criminal Injuries Compensation Authority tariff (revised 2012). The CICA tariff makes no award for minor injuries which result in short term disability; the suggested starting points for these injuries are adapted from an earlier tariff.

Type of injury	Description	Suggested Starting point
Graze	Depending on size	Up to £75
Bruise	Depending on size	Up to £100
Cut: no permanent scar	Depending on size and whether stitched	£100–300
Black eye		£125
Eye	Blurred or double vision lasting up to 6 weeks Blurred or double vision lasting for 6 to 13 weeks Blurred or double vision lasting for more than 13 weeks (recovery expected)	£500 £1,000 £1,500
Brain	Concussion lasting one week	£1,500
Nose	Undisplaced fracture of nasal bone Displaced fracture requiring manipulation Deviated nasal septum requiring septoplasty	£1,000 £2,000 £2,000
Loss of non-front tooth Loss of front tooth	Depending on cosmetic effect	£750 per tooth £1,500 per tooth
Facial scar	Minor disfigurement (permanent)	£1,000
Arm	Fractured humerus, radius, ulna (substantial recovery)	£1,500
Shoulder	Dislocated (substantial recovery)	£900
Wrist	Dislocated/fractured—including scaphoid fracture (substantial recovery) Fractured—colles type (substantial recovery)	£2,400 £2,400
Sprained wrist, ankle	Disabling for up to 6 weeks Disabling for 6 to 13 weeks Disabling for more than 13 weeks	£500 £800 £1,000
Finger	Fractured finger other than index finger (substantial recovery) Fractured index finger (substantial recovery) Fractured thumb (substantial recovery)	£300 £1,200 £1,750
Leg	Fractured fibula (substantial recovery) Fractured femur, tibia (substantial recovery)	£1,000 £1,800
Abdomen	Injury requiring laparotomy	£1,800
Temporary mental anxiety (including terror, shock, distress), not medically verified		£500
Disabling mental anxiety, lasting more than 6 weeks, medically verified*		£1,000
Disability mental illness, lasting up to 28 weeks, confirmed by psychiatric diagnosis*		£1,500

* mental injury is disabling if it has a substantial adverse effect on a person's ability to carry out normal day-to-day activities for the time specified (e.g. impaired work or school performance or effects on social relationships or sexual dysfunction).

13. The following table, which is also based on the Criminal Injuries Compensation Authority tariff, sets out suggested starting points for compensating physical and sexual abuse. It will be rare for cases involving this type of harm to be dealt with in a magistrates' court and it will be important to *consult your legal adviser for guidance in these situations.*

Type of injury	Description	Suggested starting point
Physical abuse of adult	Intermittent physical assaults resulting in accumulation of healed wounds, burns or scalds, but with no appreciable disfigurement	£2,000
Physical abuse of child	Isolated or intermittent assault(s) resulting in weals, hair pulled from scalp etc. Intermittent physical assaults resulting in accumulation of healed wounds, burns or scalds, but with no appreciable disfigurement	£1,000 £1,000
Sexual abuse of adult	Non-penetrative indecent physical acts over clothing Non-penetrative indecent act(s) under clothing	£1,000 £2,000
Sexual abuse of child (under 18)	Non-penetrative indecent physical act(s) over clothing Non-penetrative frequent assaults over clothing or non-penetrative indecent act under clothing Repetitive indecent acts under clothing	£1,000 £1,500 or 2,000 £3,300

PROSECUTION COSTS

SG-370D

Where an offender is convicted of an offence, the court has discretion to make such order as to costs as it considers just and reasonable.[147]

The Court of Appeal has given the following guidance:[148]

i) an order for costs should never exceed the sum which, having regard to the offender's means and any other financial order imposed, he or she is able to pay and which it is reasonable to order him or her to pay;
ii) an order for costs should never exceed the sum which the prosecutor actually and reasonably incurred;
iii) the purpose of the order is to compensate the prosecutor. Where the conduct of the defence has put the prosecutor to avoidable expense, the offender may be ordered to pay some or all of that sum to the prosecutor but the offender must not be punished for exercising the right to defend himself or herself;
iv) the costs ordered to be paid should not be grossly disproportionate to any fine imposed for the offence. This principle was affirmed in *BPS Advertising Limited v London Borough of Barnet*[149] in which the Court held that, while there is no question of an arithmetical relationship, the question of costs should be viewed in the context of the maximum penalty considered by Parliament to be appropriate for the seriousness of the offence;
v) if the combined total of the proposed fine and the costs sought by the prosecutor exceeds the sum which the offender could reasonably be ordered to pay, the costs order should be reduced rather than the fine;
vi) it is for the offender to provide details of his or her financial position so as to enable the court to assess what he or she can reasonably afford to pay. If the offender fails to do so, the court is entitled to draw reasonable inferences as to means from all the circumstances of the case;
vii) if the court proposes to make any financial order against the offender, it must give him or her fair opportunity to adduce any relevant financial information and to make appropriate submissions.

Where the prosecutor is the Crown Prosecution Service, prosecution costs exclude the costs of the investigation, which are met by the police. In non-CPS cases where the costs of the investigation are incurred by the prosecutor a costs award may cover the costs of investigation as well as prosecution.[150] However, where the investigation was carried out as part of a council officer's routine duties, for which he or she would have been paid in the normal way, this is a relevant factor to be taken into account when deciding the appropriate amount of any costs order.[151]

[147] Prosecution of Offences Act 1985, s. 18
[148] *R v Northallerton Magistrates' Court, ex parte Dove* [2000] 1 Cr App R (S) 136 (CA)
[149] [2006] EWCA 3335 (Admin) QBD
[150] Further guidance is provided in the Criminal Costs Practice Direction and the Criminal Procedure Rules Part 76 see https://www.justice.gov.uk/courts/procedure-rules/criminal/rulesmenu
[151] ibid

Where the court wishes to impose costs in addition to a fine, compensation and/or the victim surcharge but the offender has insufficient resources to pay the total amount, the order of priority is:

i) compensation;
ii) victim surcharge;
iii) fine;
iv) costs.

SG-370E **Victim Surcharge**

1. When sentencing for offences committed on or after 1 October 2012 a court must order the Victim Surcharge in the following ways:[152]

Offenders aged 18 and older at the date of the offence

Disposal type	Victim Surcharge
Conditional discharge	£15
Fine	At 10% of the fine value with a £20 minimum and a £120 maximum *(rounded up or down to the nearest pound)*
Community order	£60
Suspended sentence order	£80 (six months or less)
Immediate custody [153]	*£80 (six months or less)

Offenders aged under 18 at the date of the offence

Disposal type	Victim Surcharge
Conditional discharge	£10
Fine, Youth Rehabilitation Order or Referral Order	£15
Immediate custody	N/A*

* When sentencing an offender to immediate custody for a single offence committed before 1 September 2014 or more than one offence, at least one of which was committed before 1 September 2014, no surcharge is payable.

Person who is not an individual (for example, a company or other legal person)

Disposal type	Victim Surcharge
Conditional discharge	£15
Fine	At 10% of the fine value with a £20 minimum and a £120 maximum *(Surcharge should be rounded up or down to the nearest pound)*

2. Where the court dealing with an offender imposes more than one disposal, for example, a fine in conjunction with a community order, the surcharge amount should be whichever amount payable is greatest.
3. When sentencing an offender to immediate custody for a single offence committed before 1 September 2014 or more than one offence, at least one of which was committed before 1 September 2014, no surcharge is payable.[154]
4. Where the offender has the means to pay the financial impositions of the court, there should be no reduction in compensation or fines whenever the surcharge is ordered. However, when the court:

---

[152] Criminal Justice Act 2003, s. 161A; Criminal Justice Act 2003 (Surcharge) Order 2012
[153] The Criminal Justice Act (2003) Surcharge Order 2014
[154] Criminal Justice Act 2003 (Surcharge) Order 2012, art. 5(3)

- orders the offender to pay both a surcharge and compensation, but the offender is unable to pay both, the court must reduce the amount of the Surcharge (if necessary to nil);[155] or
- orders the offender to pay both a fine and a Surcharge, the court may only reduce the fine to the extent that the offender is unable to pay both.[156]

5. Where the offender does not have sufficient means to pay the total financial penalty considered appropriate by the court, the order of priority is compensation, surcharge, fine, costs.
6. When sentencing for one or more offences any one of which was committed *after 1 April 2007 but before 1 October 2012*, a surcharge is payable only if the offender is dealt with by way of a fine at a flat rate of £15.[157]

Criminal Courts Charge **SG-370F**

1. The charge is payable as part of sentence and is in addition to any other penalty (e.g. costs, victim surcharge etc). It applies only to offenders *aged 18 or over* when the offence was committed.[158]
2. The court *must* order the criminal courts charge when dealing with an offender following conviction of a criminal offence or for failing to comply with a community requirement, suspended sentence order or supervision requirement, but the court *must not* take into account the criminal courts charge when sentencing the offender.[159]
3. The charge is not payable where the offender is absolutely discharged, or is made subject to a hospital order or guardianship.[160]
4. Where an offender might otherwise be subject to more than one charge (for example where he pleads guilty to one offence but is convicted after trial of another) the higher of the applicable charges applies.
5. A summary trial is deemed to have commenced when the prosecution opens its case. Where a trial has commenced and the offender then changes his plea, the amount payable is in respect to a trial.

Applicable charges:

Conviction by a magistrates' court in proceedings conducted in accordance with section 16A of the Magistrates' Courts Act 1980 (trial by single justice on the papers)	£150
Conviction by a magistrates' court for a summary offence on a guilty plea	£150
Conviction by a magistrates' court at a trial of a summary offence where (a) the defendant did not enter a plea; (b) the trial proceeded in the absence of the defendant; and (c) the court dealt with the case on the papers without reliance on any oral evidence	£150
Conviction by a magistrates' court for an offence triable either-way on a guilty plea	£180
Conviction by a magistrates' court at a trial of a summary offence	£520
Conviction by a magistrates' court at a trial of an offence triable either way	£1000
Magistrates' court when dealing with a person under section 21B(1)(b), (c) or (d) of the POA 1985 (breach of CO, SSO or supervision requirement)	£100

Community Orders **SG-382**

1. Community orders have the effect of restricting the offender's liberty while providing punishment in the community, rehabilitation for the offender, and/or ensuring that the offender engages in reparative activities.
2. A community order must not be imposed unless the offence is 'serious enough to warrant such a sentence'.[161]
   - sentencers must consider all available disposals at the time of sentence; even where the threshold for a community sentence has been passed, a fine or discharge may be an appropriate penalty;

[155] Criminal Justice Act 2003, s. 161A(3)
[156] Criminal Justice Act 2003, s. 164(4A)
[157] Criminal Justice Act 2003 (Surcharge) Order 2012, art. 7(2)
[158] Prosecution of Offences Act 1985, s. 21A(2)
[159] ibid, s. 21A(4)
[160] The Prosecutions of Offences Act 1985 (Criminal Courts Charge) Regulations 2015, reg. 2
[161] Criminal Justice Act 2003, s. 148

- where an offender is being sentenced for a non-imprisonable offence, the court may not make a community order.[162]

3. Community orders consist of one or more of the following requirements:
   - rehabilitation activity requirement;
   - unpaid work requirement;
   - programme requirement;
   - prohibited activity requirement;
   - curfew requirement;
   - exclusion requirement;
   - residence requirement;
   - foreign travel prohibition requirement (when in force);[163]
   - mental health treatment requirement;
   - drug rehabilitation requirement;
   - alcohol treatment requirement;
   - alcohol abstinence and monitoring requirement (in pilot areas);[164]
   - in a case where the offender is aged under 25, attendance centre requirement (where available).
4. Where a court makes a community order it must include at least one requirement imposed for the purpose of punishment and/or impose a fine in addition to the community order.[165] Which requirements amount to punishment is a matter for the court to decide in each case.
5. The court must ensure that the restriction on the offender's liberty is commensurate with the seriousness of the offence and that the requirements are the most suitable for the offender.[166] Where two or more requirements are included, they must be compatible with each other.[167]

Community order ranges

6. The seriousness of the offence should be the *initial* factor in determining which requirements to include in a community order. Offence guidelines refer to three sentencing ranges within the community order band based on offence seriousness (low, medium and high). See below for non-exhaustive examples of requirements that might be appropriate in each. The examples focus on punishment in the community; other requirements of a rehabilitative nature may be more appropriate in some cases.

Low	Medium	High
Offences only just cross community order threshold, where the seriousness of the offence or the nature of the offender's record means that a discharge or fine is inappropriate	Offences that obviously fall within the community order band	Offences only just fall below the custody threshold or the custody threshold is crossed but a community order is more appropriate in the circumstances
In general, only one requirement will be appropriate and the length may be curtailed if additional requirements are necessary		More intensive sentences which combine two or more requirements may be appropriate
Suitable requirements might include: • 40–80 hours unpaid work • Curfew requirement within the lowest range (e.g. up to 16 hours per day for a few weeks) • Exclusion requirement, without electronic monitoring, for a few months • Prohibited activity requirement • Attendance centre requirement (where available)	Suitable requirements might include: • Greater number of hours of unpaid work (e.g. 80–150 hours) • Curfew requirement within the middle range (e.g. up to 16 hours for 2–3 months) • Exclusion requirement lasting in the region of 6 months • Prohibited activity requirement	Suitable requirements might include: • 150–300 hours unpaid work • Curfew requirement up to 16 hours per day for 4–12 months • Exclusion order lasting in the region of 12 months

[162] ibid, s. 150A(1) as amended by the Criminal Justice and Immigration Act 2008, s. 11(1)
[163] ibid, s. 206A as amended by the Legal Aid, Sentencing and Punishment of Offenders Act 2012, s. 72
[164] Legal Aid, Sentencing and Punishment of Offenders Act 2012, s. 77
[165] Criminal Justice Act 2003, s.177(2A) as added by the Crime and Courts Act 2013 sch. 16(1) para. 2 (applies to offences committed on or after 11 December 2013)
[166] Criminal Justice Act 2003, ss. 148(2)(a) and 148(2)(b)
[167] ibid, s. 177(6)

7. The particular requirements imposed within the range must be suitable for the individual offender and will be influenced by a wide range of factors including the stated purpose(s) of the sentence, the risk of re-offending, the ability of the offender to comply, and the availability of the requirements in the local area. Sentencers must ensure that the sentence strikes the right balance between proportionality and suitability. The resulting restriction on liberty must be a proportionate response to the offence that was committed.

Pre-sentence reports

8. In many cases, a pre-sentence report will be pivotal in helping the court decide whether to impose a community order and, if so, whether particular requirements or combinations of requirements are suitable for an individual offender. Whenever the court reaches the provisional view that a community order may be appropriate, it should usually request a pre-sentence report. It will be helpful to indicate the court's preliminary opinion as to which of the three sentencing ranges is relevant and the purpose(s) of sentencing that the package of requirements is expected to fulfil. Ideally this should be provided to the Probation Service in written form[168] and, if the sentence is to be adjourned to a future date, a copy retained on the court file for the benefit of the sentencing bench.

Electronic monitoring **SG-383**

9. Subject to limited exceptions, the court must impose an electronic monitoring requirement where it makes a community order with a curfew or exclusion requirement, and may do so in all other cases.[169] Electronic monitoring should be used with the primary purpose of promoting and monitoring compliance with other requirements, in circumstances where the punishment of the offender and/or the need to safeguard the public and prevent re-offending are the most important concerns.

Breach of Community Order **SG-384**

10. Refer to [SG-250] for guidance on the approach to sentencing for breaches of community orders.

Custodial Sentences **SG-385**

1. A custodial sentence must not be imposed unless the offence 'was so serious that neither a fine alone nor a community sentence can be justified for the offence'.[170] Guidance regarding this threshold and the approach to the imposition of custodial sentences is set out in the Sentencing Guidelines Council's definitive guideline *Overarching Principles*: *Seriousness*, published 16 December 2004 [see **SG-21**].
2. The guideline emphasises that:
   - the clear intention of the threshold test is to reserve prison as a punishment for the most serious offences;
   - passing the custody threshold does not mean that a custodial sentence should be deemed inevitable; custody can still be avoided in light of offender mitigation or where there is a suitable intervention in the community which provides sufficient restriction (by way of punishment) while addressing the rehabilitation of the offender to prevent future crime.
   - however, when dealing with either way offences, where the offending is so serious that the court is of the opinion that the Crown Court should have the power to deal with the offender the case should be committed to the Crown Court for sentence[171] notwithstanding that a community order may be the appropriate sentence (this will allow the Crown Court to deal with any breach of a community order, if that is the sentence passed);
   - the approach to the imposition of a custodial sentence should be as follows:
     (a) Has the custody threshold been passed?
     (b) If so, is it unavoidable that a custodial sentence be imposed?
     (c) If so, can that sentence be suspended? (Sentencers should be clear that they would have imposed a custodial sentence if the power to suspend had not been available.)
     (d) If not, impose a sentence which takes immediate effect for the shortest term commensurate with the seriousness of the offence.[172]

[168] This may be in electronic form
[169] Criminal Justice Act 2003, ss. 177(3) and 177(4)
[170] Criminal Justice Act 2003, s. 152(2)
[171] Powers of Criminal Courts Sentencing Act 2000, s. 3
[172] [Criminal Justice Act 2003], s. 153(2)

Pre-sentence report

3. Before deciding whether:
   - the custody threshold has been passed; and, if so
   - [the] length of imprisonment which represents the shortest term commensurate with the seriousness of the offence;

   the court should obtain a pre-sentence report, unless the court considers a report to be unnecessary.[173] *Consult your legal adviser before deciding to sentence to custody without a pre-sentence report.*

Suspended sentences

4. The approach to imposing a suspended sentence order is as follows:
   (a) Has the custody threshold been passed? If not, a suspended sentence *cannot* be passed.
   (b) If so, is it unavoidable that a custodial sentence be imposed?
   (c) If so, can that sentence be suspended? (Sentencers should be clear that they would have imposed a custodial sentence if the power to suspend had not been available.)
5. The requirement to obtain a pre-sentence report at paragraph 3 above, applies to suspended sentence orders.
6. If the court imposes a term of imprisonment between 14 days and six months,[174] it may suspend the sentence for between six months and two years (the 'operational period').
7. Where the court imposes two or more sentences to be served consecutively, the court may suspend the sentence where the aggregate of the terms is between 14 days and 12 months.[175]
8. When the court suspends a sentence, it may impose one or more requirements for the offender to undertake in the community.[176] The requirements are identical to those available for community orders.
9. If considering imposing a suspended sentence order the court should take account of the following:
   - a custodial sentence that is suspended should be for the same term that would have applied if the sentence was to be served immediately;
   - the time for which a sentence is suspended should reflect the length of the sentence; up to 12 months might normally be appropriate for a suspended sentence of up to six months;
   - the imposition of a custodial sentence is both punishment and a deterrent; to ensure that the overall terms of the sentence are commensurate with offence seriousness, requirements imposed as part of the sentence should generally be less onerous than if a community order had been imposed;
   - a court wishing to impose onerous or intensive requirements should reconsider whether a community sentence might be more appropriate (see [SG-382]);
   - where an offender has breached a suspended sentence, there is a presumption that the suspended prison term will be activated in full or in part (see further below).
10. When the court imposes a suspended sentence with community requirements, it may also order that the sentence be reviewed periodically at a review hearing.[177] *Please consult your legal adviser before doing so.*

Breach of a Suspended Sentence Order

11. If the offender fails to comply with a community requirement or commits a further offence during the operational period of a suspended sentence order imposed in a magistrates' court, the court must activate the suspended sentence in full or in part unless it would be unjust in all the circumstances to do so. Relevant considerations will include the extent to which (if any) the offender complied with the requirements, and, where a subsequent offence has been committed, the facts of that offence. Where the court does not activate the sentence it must state its reasons.[178] If the order was imposed by the Crown Court the court must commit for sentence or notify the Crown Court; *consult your legal adviser if dealing with a breach of a Crown Court order.*

---

[173] Criminal Justice Act 2003 ss. 156(3) and 156(4)
[174] ibid., s. 189(1) as amended by art. 2(2)(a) of the Criminal Justice Act 2003 (Sentencing) (Transitory Provisions) Order 2005
[175] ibid, s. 189(2) as amended by the Legal Aid, Sentencing and Punishment of Offenders Act 2012, s. 68(2)
[176] ibid., s.189(1A) as amended by the Legal Aid, Sentencing and Punishment of Offenders Act 2012, s.68(1)
[177] ibid, s. 191
[178] ibid, sch. 12

12. If the court does not activate the sentence in whole or in part it *must* amend the order so as to:
    (a) order the offender to pay a fine of up to £2,500;
    OR one or more of:
    (b) (where community requirements were imposed) make the community requirements more onerous;
    (c) (where community requirements were imposed) extend the supervision period;
    (d) extend the operational period (but not beyond two years from the date when the original order was made).

Compensation SG-386

[See now **SG-370B**.]

Victim Surcharge SG-390

[See now **SG-370E**.]

Ancillary Orders SG-393

There are several ancillary orders available in a magistrates' court which should be considered in appropriate cases. Annex A lists the offences in respect of which certain orders are available [not reproduced]. The individual offence guidelines above also identify ancillary orders particularly likely to be relevant to the offence. In all cases, consult your legal adviser regarding available orders and their specific requirements and effects.

Ancillary orders should be taken into account when assessing whether the overall penalty is commensurate with offence seriousness.

Anti-social behaviour orders SG-394

These have now been replaced by Criminal Behaviour Orders (see below)

Binding over orders SG-395

The court has the power to bind an individual over to keep the peace.[179]

The order is designed to prevent future misconduct and requires the individual to promise to pay a specified sum if the terms of the order are breached. Exercise of the power does not depend upon conviction.

Guidance on the making of binding over orders is set out in [CPD VII, Sentencing J: see PD-69]. Key principles include:

(1) before imposing the order, the court must be satisfied so that it is sure that a breach of the peace involving violence or an imminent threat of violence has occurred, or that there is a real risk of violence in the future. The court should hear evidence and the parties before making any order;
(2) the court should state its reasons for making the order;
(3) the order should identify the specific conduct or activity from which the individual must refrain, the length of the order and the amount of the recognisance;
(4) the length of the order should be proportionate to the harm sought to be avoided and should not generally exceed 12 months;
(5) when fixing the amount of the recognisance, the court should have regard to the individual's financial resources.

Confiscation orders SG-396

Confiscation orders under the Proceeds of Crime Act 2002 may only be made by the Crown Court.

An offender convicted of an offence in a magistrates' court must be committed to the Crown Court where this is requested by the prosecution with a view to a confiscation order being considered.[180]

If the committal is made in respect of an either way offence, the court must state whether it would have committed the offender to the Crown Court for sentencing had the issue of a confiscation order not arisen.

[179] Justices of the Peace Act 1361, Magistrates Court Act 1980, s. 115
[180] Proceeds of Crime Act 2002, s. 70

SG-396A **Criminal Behaviour Orders**

A Criminal Behaviour Order (CBO) is an order which is available on conviction for any criminal offence by any criminal court, introduced by the Anti-social Behaviour, Crime and Policing Act 2014[181] with effect from 20 October 2014. It replaces the former powers of the court to make orders such as an ASBO or a drinking banning order on conviction.

A CBO is an order designed to tackle the most serious and persistent anti-social individuals where their behaviour has brought them before a criminal court. The anti-social behaviour to be addressed does not need to be connected to the criminal behaviour, or activity which led to the conviction. However, if there is no link the court will need to reflect on the reasons for making the order.

A CBO can deal with a wide range of anti-social behaviours following the offender's conviction, for example threatening violence against others in the community, or persistently being drunk and aggressive in public. However, the order should not be designed to stop reasonable, trivial or benign behaviours that have not caused, or are not likely to cause anti-social behaviour.

Any application will be made by the prosecution.[182] The majority of applications will therefore be made by the CPS, either at their own initiative, or at the request of the police. However, it may also be applied for by local councils, providing they are the prosecuting authority in the case. *The court cannot make a CBO of its own volition.*

A CBO may only be made against an offender when they have been sentenced to at least a conditional discharge for the substantive offence.[183] *A CBO cannot be made where the offender has been given an absolute discharge.*

The court may only make a CBO if it is satisfied that two conditions are met:[184]

1. The court must be satisfied, beyond reasonable doubt, that the offender has engaged in behaviour that caused, or was likely to cause, harassment, alarm or distress to one or more persons,[185] and
2. That making the order will help in preventing the offender from engaging in such behaviour.[186]

For the first condition, the burden of proof on the prosecution is to the criminal standard, beyond reasonable doubt. (There is no test of necessity as with ASBOs.)

A CBO may:

1. Prohibit the offender from doing anything described in the order ('a prohibition'), and/or
2. Require the offender to do anything described in the order ('a requirement').[187]

However, any prohibitions and/or requirements must, so far as practicable, avoid any interference with times an offender would normally work, attend school or other educational establishment and any conflict with any other court order or injunction.[188]

If the order requires the offender to do anything, then the order must specify the individual or organisation that is responsible for supervising compliance with the requirement[189] and must hear from them about both the suitability and enforceability of a requirement, before including it in the CBO.[190]

The order must be proportionate and reasonable. It will be for the court to decide the measures which are most appropriate and available to tackle the underlying cause of the anti-social behaviour. The order should be tailored to the specific needs of each perpetrator.

When deciding whether or not to make a CBO, the court is entitled to consider evidence submitted by the prosecution and by the offender.[191] It does not matter whether the evidence would have been admissible, or has been heard as part of the criminal proceedings in which the offender was convicted,[192] but it should

181 Anti-social Behaviour, Crime and Policing Act 2014, s. 22
182 ibid, s. 22(7)
183 ibid, s. 22(8)
184 ibid, s. 22(2)
185 ibid, s. 22(3)
186 ibid, s. 22(4)
187 ibid, s. 22(5)
188 ibid, s. 22(9)
189 ibid, s. 24(2)
190 ibid, s. 24(3)
191 ibid, s. 23(1)
192 ibid, s. 23(2)

be relevant to the test to be applied to the making of the order (i.e. that the offender has engaged in behaviour that caused, or was likely to cause, harassment, alarm or distress to any person, and that the court considers that making the order will assist in preventing the offender from engaging in such behaviour). This evidence could include hearsay or bad character evidence. Special measures are available for witnesses who are vulnerable and intimidated witnesses in accordance with Section 16 and 17 Youth Justice and Criminal Evidence Act 1999.[193]

A CBO takes effect on the day it is made,[194] unless the offender is already subject to an existing CBO, in which case it may take effect on the day in which the previous order expires.[195] The order must specify the period for which it has effect.[196] In the case of an adult, the order must be for a fixed period of not less than two years or it may be an indefinite period, so that it is made until further order.[197] An order may specify different periods for which particular prohibitions or requirements have effect within the order.[198]

The court can impose an *interim order* in cases where the offender is convicted but the court is adjourning the hearing of the application for a CBO,[199] before or after sentence for the offence. The offender need not be sentenced to be made subject to an interim order.[200] The court can make an interim order if the court thinks it is just to do so. An interim order can be made until final hearing or further order.[201] When making an interim order the court has the same powers as if it were making a final order.[202]

It is likely that the hearing for a CBO will take place at the same time as the sentencing for the criminal case. For adult offenders, there is no formal consultation requirement. However, in order to ensure that applications are made appropriately and efficiently, there is an expectation that any relevant agencies will have been consulted so that the prosecution have the relevant information to decide whether to make an order or not and if so, in what terms. The prosecution should be prepared to deal with an application on the date of hearing.

The court may deal with the application for a CBO at the same time as it imposes sentence for the offence. Alternatively, the court may sentence the offender for the criminal offence and adjourn the application for a CBO to a later date.[203] However, the court cannot hear an application once sentence has taken place, unless the application was made by the prosecution before sentence was concluded, as an application cannot be made retrospectively.

If the offender does not appear at an adjourned hearing for a CBO, the court may further adjourn the proceedings, issue a warrant for the offender's arrest, or hear the proceedings in the offender's absence.[204] To issue a warrant for the offender's arrest, the court must be satisfied that the offender has been given adequate notice of the time and place for the hearing.[205] To proceed in the offender's absence, the court must be satisfied that the offender has been given adequate notice of the time and place for the hearing and been told if they do not attend, the court may hear the application in their absence.[206]

Further guidance is provided by the Home Office in *Anti-social Behaviour, Crime and Policing Act 2014: Reform of anti-social behaviour powers; Statutory guidance for frontline professionals.* July 2014.[207]

Deprivation orders SG-397

The court has the power to deprive an offender of property used for the purpose of committing or facilitating the commission of an offence, whether or not it deals with the offender in any other way.[208]

Sentencing Guidelines

193 ibid, s. 31
194 ibid, s. 25(1)
195 ibid, s. 25(2)
196 ibid, s. 25(3)
197 ibid, s. 25(5)
198 ibid, s. 25(6)
199 ibid, s. 26(1)
200 ibid, s. 26(3)
201 ibid, s. 26(2)
202 ibid, s. 26(4)
203 ibid, s. 26(3)
204 ibid, s. 23(4)
205 ibid, s. 23(5)
206 ibid, s. 23(6)
207 www.gov.uk/government/uploads/system/uploads/attachment_data/file/332839/StatutoryGuidanceFrontline.pdf
208 Powers of Criminal Courts (Sentencing) Act 2000, s. 143

Before making the order, the court must have regard to the value of the property and the likely financial and other effects on the offender.

Without limiting the circumstances in which the court may exercise the power, a vehicle is deemed to have been used for the purpose of committing the offence where the offence is punishable by imprisonment and consists of:

(1) driving, attempting to drive, or being in charge of a motor vehicle;
(2) failing to provide a specimen; or
(3) failing to stop and/or report an accident.[209]

SG-398 Deprivation of ownership of animal

Where an offender convicted of one of the following offences under the Animal Welfare Act 2006 is the owner of an animal in relation to which the offence is committed, the court may make an order depriving him or her of ownership of the animal and for its disposal:[210]

(1) causing unnecessary suffering (s. 4);
(2) mutilation (s. 5);
(3) docking of dogs' tails (ss. 6(1) and 6(2));
(4) fighting etc. (s. 8);
(5) breach of duty to ensure welfare (s. 9);
(6) breach of disqualification order (s. 36(9)).

The court is required to give reasons if it decides not to make such an order.

Deprivation of ownership may be ordered instead of or in addition to dealing with the offender in any other way.

SG-398A Destruction orders and contingent destruction orders for dogs

See the Dangerous Dogs Guideline at [**SG-595**] (however note that this guideline is due to be updated — consult your legal adviser).

SG-399 Disqualification from ownership of animals

Where an offender is convicted of one of the following offences under the Animal Welfare Act 2006, the court may disqualify him or her from owning or keeping animals, dealing in animals, and/or transporting animals:[211]

(1) causing unnecessary suffering (s. 4);
(2) mutilation (s. 5);
(3) docking of dogs' tails (ss. 6(1) and 6(2));
(4) administration of poisons etc. (s. 7);
(5) fighting etc. (s. 8);
(6) breach of duty to ensure welfare (s. 9);
(7) breach of licensing or registration requirements (s. 13(6));
(8) breach of disqualification order (s. 36(9)).

The court is required to give reasons if it decides not to make such an order.

The court may specify a period during which an offender may not apply for termination of the order under section 43 of the Animal Welfare Act 2006; if no period is specified, an offender may not apply for termination of the order until one year after the order was made.

Disqualification may be imposed instead of or in addition to dealing with the offender in any other way.

SG-400 Disqualification from driving — general power

The court may disqualify any person convicted of an offence from driving for such period as it thinks fit.[212] This may be instead of or in addition to dealing with the offender in any other way.

---

209 ibid, ss. 143(6) and 143(7)
210 Animal Welfare Act 2006, s. 33
211 ibid, s. 34
212 Powers of Criminal Courts (Sentencing) Act 2000, s. 146

The section does not require the offence to be connected to the use of a vehicle. The Court of Appeal has held that the power is available as part of the overall punitive element of a sentence, and the only restrictions on the exercise of the power are those in the statutory provision.[213]

Disqualification of company directors SG-401

The Company Directors Disqualification Act 1986 empowers the court to disqualify an offender from being a director or taking part in the promotion, formation or management of a company for up to five years.

An order may be made in two situations:

(1) where an offender has been convicted of an indictable offence in connection with the promotion, formation, management, liquidation or striking off of a company;[214] or
(2) where an offender has been convicted of an offence involving a failure to file documents with, or give notice to, the registrar of companies. If the offence is triable only summarily, disqualification can be ordered only where the offender has been the subject of three default orders or convictions in the preceding five years.[215]

Drinking banning orders SG-402

These have now been replaced by Criminal Behaviour Orders (see [SG-396A]).

Exclusion orders SG-403

The court may make an exclusion order where an offender has been convicted of an offence committed on licensed premises involving the use or threat of violence.

The order prohibits the offender from entering *specified* licensed premises without the consent of the licensee. The term of the order must be between three months and two years.

Football banning orders SG-404

The court must make a football banning order where an offender has been convicted of a relevant offence and it is satisfied that there are reasonable grounds to believe that making a banning order would help to prevent violence or disorder.[216] If the court is not so satisfied, it must state that fact and give its reasons.

Relevant offences are those set out in schedule 1 [to] the Football Spectators Act 1989…

The order requires the offender to report to a police station within five days, may require the offender to surrender his or her passport, and may impose requirements on the offender in relation to any regulated football matches.

Where the order is imposed in addition to a sentence of immediate imprisonment, the term of the order must be between six and ten years. In other cases, the term of the order must be between three and five years.

Forfeiture and destruction of drugs SG-405

Where an offender is convicted of an offence under the Misuse of Drugs Act 1971, the court may order forfeiture and destruction of anything shown to the satisfaction of the court to relate to the offence.[217]

Forfeiture and destruction of weapons orders SG-405A

A court convicting a person of possession of an offensive weapon may make an order for the forfeiture or disposal of the weapon (Prevention of Crime Act 1953, s1(2))

See also deprivation orders [at SG-397].

213 *R v Cliff* [2004] EWCA Crim 3139
214 Company Directors Disqualification Act 1988, s. 2
215 ibid, s. 5
216 Football Spectators Act 1989, s. 14A
217 Misuse of Drugs Act 1971, s. 27(1)

SG-406 **Forfeiture and destruction of goods bearing unauthorised trade mark**

Where the court is satisfied that an offence under section 92 of the Trade Marks Act 1994 has been committed, it must (on the application of a person who has come into possession of the goods in connection with the investigation or prosecution of the offence) order forfeiture of the goods.[218]

If it considers it appropriate, instead of ordering destruction of the goods, the court may direct that they be released to a specified person on condition that the offending sign is erased, removed or obliterated.

SG-407 **Forfeiture or suspension of liquor licence**

Where an offender who holds a personal licence to supply alcohol is charged with a 'relevant offence', he or she is required to produce the licence to the court, or inform the court of its existence, no later than his or her first appearance.[219]

'Relevant offences' are listed in schedule 4 [to] the Licensing Act 2003…

Where the offender is convicted, the court may order forfeiture of the licence or suspend it for up to six months.[220] When deciding whether to order forfeiture or suspension, the court may take account of the offender's previous convictions for 'relevant offences'.[221]

Whether or not forfeiture or suspension is ordered, the court is required to notify the licensing authority of the offender's conviction and the sentence imposed.

SG-408 **Parenting orders**

The court may make a parenting order where an offender has been convicted of an offence under section 444 of the Education Act 1996 (failing to secure regular attendance at school) and the court is satisfied that the order would be desirable in the interests of preventing the commission of any further offence under that section.[222]

The order may impose such requirements that the court considers desirable in the interests of preventing the commission of a further offence under section 444.

A requirement to attend a counselling or guidance programme may be included only if the offender has been the subject of a parenting order on a previous occasion.

The term of the order must not exceed 12 months.

SG-409 **Restitution orders**

Where goods have been stolen and an offender is convicted of any offence with reference to theft of those goods, the court may make a restitution order.[223]

The court may:

(1) order anyone in possession or control of the stolen goods to restore them to the victim;
(2) on the application of the victim, order that goods directly or indirectly representing the stolen goods (as being the proceeds of any disposal or realisation of the stolen goods) be transferred to the victim; or
(3) order that a sum not exceeding the value of the stolen goods be paid to the victim out of any money taken out of the offender's possession on his or her apprehension.

SG-410 **Restraining orders**

Where an offender is convicted of any offence, the court may make a restraining order.[224]

The order may prohibit the offender from doing anything for the purpose of protecting the victim of the offence, or any other person mentioned in the order, from further conduct which amounts to harassment or will cause a fear of violence.

The order may have effect for a specified period or until further order.

218 Trade Marks Act 1994, s. 97
219 Licensing Act 2003, s. 128(1)
220 ibid, s. 129(2)
221 ibid, s. 129(3)
222 Crime and Disorder Act 1998, s. 8
223 Powers of Criminal Courts (Sentencing) Act 2000, s. 148
224 Protection from Harassment Act 1997, s. 5

A court before which a person is *acquitted* of an offence may make a restraining order if the court considers that it is necessary to protect a person from harassment by the defendant.[225] *Consult your legal adviser for guidance.*

Sexual harm prevention orders **SG-410A**

Orders can be made in relation to a person who has been convicted, found not guilty by reason of insanity or found to be under a disability and to have done the act charged, or cautioned etc. for an offence listed in either Schedule 3 or Schedule 5 to the Sexual Offences Act 2003 either in the UK or overseas (see Annex A [not reproduced]). This includes offenders whose convictions etc. pre-date the commencement of the 2003 Act.

No application is necessary for the court to make a SHPO at the point of sentence although the prosecutor may wish to invite the court to consider making an order in appropriate cases. The court may ask pre-sentence report writers to consider the suitability of a SHPO on a non-prejudicial basis.

In order to make a SHPO, the court must be satisfied that the offender presents a risk of sexual harm to the public (or particular members of the public) and that an order is necessary to protect against this risk. The details of the offence are likely to be a key factor in the court's decision, together with the offender's previous convictions and the assessment of risk presented by the national probation service in any pre-sentence report. The court may take into consideration the range of other options available to it in respect of protecting the public. The court may want to consider:

1. would an order minimise the risk of harm to the public or to any particular members of the public?
2. is it proportionate?
3. can it be policed effectively?

The only prohibitions which can be imposed by a SHPO are those which are necessary for the purpose of protecting the public from sexual harm from the defendant. These can, however, be wide ranging. An order may, for example, prohibit someone from undertaking certain forms of employment such as acting as a home tutor to children. It may also prohibit the offender from engaging in particular activities on the internet. The decision of the Court of Appeal in *R v Smith and Others* [2011] EWCA Crim 1772 reinforces the need for the terms of a SHPO to be tailored to the exact requirements of the case. SHPOs may be used to limit and manage internet use by an offender, where it is considered proportionate and necessary to do so. The behaviour prohibited by the order might well be considered unproblematic if exhibited by another member of the public — it is the offender's previous offending behaviour and subsequent demonstration that they may pose a risk of further such behaviour, which will make them eligible for an order.

The order may include only negative prohibitions; there is no power to impose positive obligations. The order may have effect for a fixed period (not less than five years) or until further order. *Consult your legal adviser for guidance.*

Sexual offences prevention orders **SG-411**

These have now been replaced by Sexual Harm Prevention Orders. A Sexual Offences Prevention Order may only be made if the order was applied for before 8 March 2015. *Consult your legal adviser for guidance.*

Costs **SG-412**

[See now **SG-370D**.]

Deferred Sentences **SG-413**

The court is empowered to defer passing sentence for up to six months.[226] The court may impose any conditions during the period of deferment that it considers appropriate. These could be specific requirements as set out in the provisions for community sentences, restorative justice activities[227] or requirements

[225] ibid, s. 5A

[226] Powers of Criminal Courts (Sentencing) Act 2000, s. 1 as amended by Criminal Justice Act 2003, s. 278 and sch. 23, para. 1

[227] ibid. s. 1ZA as inserted by the Crime and Courts Act 2013, s. 44, sch. 16, Pt 2, para. 5

that are drawn more widely. The purpose of deferment is to enable the court to have regard to the offender's conduct after conviction or any change in his or her circumstances, including the extent to which the offender has complied with any requirements imposed by the court.

Three conditions must be satisfied before sentence can be deferred:

1) the offender must consent (and in the case of restorative justice activities the other participants must consent);[228]
2) the offender must undertake to comply with requirements imposed by the court; and
3) the court must be satisfied that deferment is in the interests of justice.

Deferred sentences will be appropriate in very limited circumstances:

- deferred sentences will be appropriate in very limited circumstances;
- deferred sentences are likely to be relevant predominantly in a small group of cases close to either the community or custodial sentence threshold where, should the offender be prepared to adapt his behaviour in a way clearly specified by the sentencer, the court may be prepared to impose a lesser sentence;
- sentencers should impose specific and measurable conditions that do not involve a serious restriction on liberty;
- the court should give a clear indication of the type of sentence it would have imposed if it had decided not to defer;
- the court should also ensure that the offender understands the consequences of failure to comply with the court's wishes during the deferment period.

If the offender fails to comply with any requirement imposed in connection with the deferment, or commits another offence, he or she can be brought back to court before the end of the deferment period and the court can proceed to sentence.

SG-414 Offences Committed in a Domestic Context[229]

1. Domestic violence is defined as:
   Any incident or pattern of incidents of controlling, coercive or threatening behaviour, violence or abuse between those aged 16 or over who are or have been intimate partners or family members regardless of gender or sexuality. This can encompass but is not limited to the following types of abuse:
   - psychological
   - physical
   - sexual
   - financial
   - emotional.

   Controlling behaviour is: a range of acts designed to make a person subordinate and/or dependent by isolating them from sources of support, exploiting their resources and capacities for personal gain, depriving them of the means needed for independence, resistance and escape and regulating their everyday behaviour.
   Coercive behaviour is: an act or a pattern of acts of assault, threats, humiliation and intimidation or other abuse that is used to harm, punish, or frighten the victim.
   This definition includes so called 'honour' based violence, female genital mutilation (FGM) and forced marriage. Victims of domestic violence are not confined to one gender or ethnic group.
2. When sentencing an offence committed in a domestic context, refer to the Sentencing Guidelines Council's definitive guideline *Overarching Principles: Domestic Violence*, published 7 December 2006 [see **SG-51**]. The guideline emphasises that:
   - as a starting point for sentence, offences committed in a domestic context should be regarded as no less serious than offences committed in a non-domestic context;

[228] ibid. s.1ZA(3)

[229] In respect of the guidance in paragraphs 5–9 below, courts must treat transgender identity as an aggravating factor under section 146 of the Criminal Justice Act 2003 only upon implementation of section 65 of the Legal Aid, Sentencing and Punishment of Offenders Act 2012

- many offences of violence in a domestic context are dealt with in a magistrates' court as an offence of common assault or assault occasioning actual bodily harm because the injuries sustained are relatively minor. Offences involving serious violence will warrant a custodial sentence in the majority of cases;
- a number of aggravating factors may commonly arise by virtue of the offence being committed in a domestic context (see list below);
- since domestic violence takes place within the context of a current or past relationship, the history of the relationship will often be relevant in assessing the gravity of the offence. A court is entitled to take into account anything occurring within the relationship as a whole, which may reveal relevant aggravating or mitigating factors;
- in respect of an offence of violence in a domestic context, an offender's good character in relation to conduct outside the home should generally be of no relevance where there is a proven pattern of behaviour;
- assertions that the offence has been provoked by conduct of the victim need to be treated with great care, both in determining whether they have a factual basis and in considering whether the circumstances of the alleged conduct amounts to provocation sufficient to mitigate the seriousness of the offence;
- where the custody threshold is only just crossed, so that if a custodial sentence is imposed it will be a short sentence, the court will wish to consider whether the better option is a suspended sentence order or a community order, including in either case a requirement to attend an accredited domestic violence programme. Such an option will only be appropriate where the court is satisfied that the offender genuinely intends to reform his or her behaviour and that there is a real prospect of rehabilitation being successful. A pre-sentence report should be requested to assess the suitability of such an option.

Refer to paragraphs 4.1 to 4.4 of the Council guideline [at SG-55] for guidance regarding the relevance of the victim's wishes as to sentence.

Aggravating factors SG-415

3. The following aggravating factors may be of particular relevance to offences committed in a domestic context and should be read alongside the general factors set out [elsewhere]:

Factors indicating higher culpability	**Factors indicating a greater degree of harm**
1. Abuse of trust and abuse of power 2. Using contact arrangements with a child to instigate an offence 3. Proven history of violence or threats by the offender in a domestic setting 4. History of disobedience to court orders	1. Victim is particularly vulnerable 2. Impact on children

Hate Crime

Racial or religious aggravation—statutory provisions SG-416

1. Sections 29 to 32 of the Crime and Disorder Act 1998 create specific racially or religiously aggravated offences, which have higher maximum penalties than the non-aggravated versions of those offences. The individual offence guidelines indicate whether there is a specifically aggravated form of the offence.
2. An offence is racially or religiously aggravated for the purposes of sections 29–32 of the Act if the offender demonstrates hostility towards the victim based on his or her membership (or presumed membership) of a racial or religious group, or if the offence is racially or religiously motivated.
3. For all other offences, section 145 of the Criminal Justice Act 2003 provides that the court must regard racial or religious aggravation as an aggravating factor.
4. The court should not treat an offence as racially or religiously aggravated for the purposes of section 145 where a racially or religiously aggravated form of the offence was charged but resulted in an acquittal. The court should not normally treat an offence as racially or religiously aggravated if a racially or religiously aggravated form of the offence was available but was not charged. *Consult your legal adviser for further guidance in these situations.*

Sentencing Guidelines

SG-417 Aggravation related to disability, sexual orientation or transgender identity—statutory provisions

5. Under section 146 of the Criminal Justice Act 2003, the court must treat as an aggravating factor the fact that:
   - an offender demonstrated hostility towards the victim based on his or her disability, sexual orientation or transgender identity (or presumed disability, sexual orientation or transgender identity); or
   - the offence was motivated by hostility towards persons who have a particular disability, who are of a particular sexual orientation or who are transgender.

SG-418 Approach to sentencing

6. A court should not conclude that offending involved aggravation related to race, religion, disability, sexual orientation or transgender identity without first putting the offender on notice and allowing him or her to challenge the allegation.
7. When sentencing any offence where such aggravation is found to be present, the following approach should be followed. This applies both to the specific racially or religiously aggravated offences under the Crime and Disorder Act 1998 and to offences which are regarded as aggravated under section 145 or 146 of the Criminal Justice Act 2003:
   - sentencers should first determine the appropriate sentence, leaving aside the element of aggravation related to race, religion, disability, sexual orientation or transgender identity but taking into account all other aggravating or mitigating factors;
   - the sentence should then be increased to take account of the aggravation related to race, religion, disability, sexual orientation or transgender identity;
   - the increase may mean that a more onerous penalty of the same type is appropriate, or that the threshold for a more severe type of sentence is passed;
   - the sentencer must state in open court that the offence was aggravated by reason of race, religion, disability, sexual orientation or transgender identity;
   - the sentencer should state what the sentence would have been without that element of aggravation.
8. The extent to which the sentence is increased will depend on the seriousness of the aggravation. The following factors could be taken as indicating a high level of aggravation:

SG-419 Offender's intention

- The element of aggravation based on race, religion, disability, sexual orientation or transgender identity was planned
- The offence was part of a pattern of offending by the offender
- The offender was a member of, or was associated with, a group promoting hostility based on race, religion, disability, sexual orientation or transgender identity
- The incident was deliberately set up to be offensive or humiliating to the victim or to the group of which the victim is a member

SG-420 Impact on the victim or others

- The offence was committed in the victim's home
- The victim was providing a service to the public
- The timing or location of the offence was calculated to maximise the harm or distress it caused
- The expressions of hostility were repeated or prolonged
- The offence caused fear and distress throughout a local community or more widely
- The offence caused particular distress to the victim and/or the victim's family.

9. At the lower end of the scale, the aggravation may be regarded as less serious if:
   - It was limited in scope or duration
   - The offence was not motivated by hostility on the basis of race, religion, disability, sexual orientation or transgender identity, and the element of hostility or abuse was minor or incidental
10. In these guidelines, the specific racially or religiously aggravated offences under the Crime and Disorder Act 1998 are addressed on the same page as the 'basic offence'; the starting points and ranges indicated on the guideline relate to the 'basic' (i.e. non-aggravated) offence. The increase for the element of racial or religious aggravation may result in a sentence above the range; *this will not constitute a departure from the guideline for which reasons must be given.*

Environmental/Health and Safety Offences SG-421

[Omitted.]

Road Traffic Offences SG-422

Disqualification SG-423

Obligatory disqualification

1. Some offences carry obligatory disqualification for a minimum of 12 months.[230] The minimum period is automatically increased where there have been certain previous convictions and disqualifications.
2. An offender must be disqualified for at least two years if he or she has been disqualified two or more times for a period of at least 56 days in the three years preceding the commission of the offence.[231] The following disqualifications are to be disregarded for the purposes of this provision:
   - interim disqualification;
   - disqualification where vehicle used for the purpose of crime;
   - disqualification for stealing or taking a vehicle or going equipped to steal or take a vehicle.
3. An offender must be disqualified for at least three years if he or she is convicted of one of the following offences *and* has within the ten years preceding the commission of the offence been convicted of any of these offences:[232]
   - causing death by careless driving when under the influence of drink or drugs;
   - driving or attempting to drive while unfit;
   - driving or attempting to drive with excess alcohol;
   - failing to provide a specimen (drive/attempting to drive).
4. The individual offence guidelines above indicate whether disqualification is mandatory for the offence and the applicable minimum period. Consult your legal adviser for further guidance.

Special Reasons

5. The period of disqualification may be reduced or avoided if there are special reasons.[233] These must relate to the offence; circumstances peculiar to the offender cannot constitute special reasons.[234] The Court of Appeal has established that, to constitute a special reason, a matter must:[235]
   - be a mitigating or extenuating circumstance;
   - not amount in law to a defence to the charge;
   - be directly connected with the commission of the offence;
   - be one which the court ought properly to take into consideration when imposing sentence.

Consult your legal adviser for further guidance on special reasons applications.

'Totting up' disqualification

6. Disqualification for a minimum of six months must be ordered if an offender incurs 12 penalty points or more within a three-year period.[236] The minimum period may be automatically increased if the offender has been disqualified within the preceding three years. Totting up disqualifications, unlike other disqualifications, erase all penalty points.
7. The period of a totting up disqualification can be reduced or avoided for exceptional hardship or other mitigating circumstances. No account is to be taken of hardship that is not exceptional hardship or circumstances alleged to make the offence not serious. Any circumstances taken into account in the preceding three years to reduce or avoid a totting disqualification must be disregarded.[237]
8. *Consult your legal adviser for further guidance on exceptional hardship applications.*

Discretionary disqualification

9. Whenever an offender is convicted of an endorsable offence or of taking a vehicle without consent, the court has a discretionary power to disqualify instead of imposing penalty points. The individual offence guidelines above indicate whether the offence is endorsable and the number or range of penalty points it carries.

---

230 Road Traffic Offenders Act 1988, s. 34
231 ibid, s. 34(4)
232 ibid, s. 34(3)
233 ibid, s. 34(1)
234 *Whittal v Kirby* [1946] 2 All ER 552 (CA)
235 *R v Wickens* (1958) 42 Cr App R 436 (CA)
236 Road Traffic Offenders Act 1988, s. 35
237 ibid

10. The number of variable points or the period of disqualification should reflect the seriousness of the offence. Some of the individual offence guidelines above include penalty points and/or periods of disqualification in the sentence starting points and ranges; however, the court is not precluded from sentencing outside the range where the facts justify it. Where a disqualification is for less than 56 days, there are some differences in effect compared with disqualification for a longer period; in particular, the licence will automatically come back into effect at the end of the disqualification period (instead of requiring application by the driver) and the disqualification is not taken into account for the purpose of increasing subsequent obligatory periods of disqualification.[238]
11. In some cases in which the court is considering discretionary disqualification the offender may already have sufficient penalty points on his or her licence that he or she would be liable to a 'totting up' disqualification if further points were imposed. In these circumstances, the court should impose penalty points rather than discretionary disqualification so that the minimum totting up disqualification period applies (see paragraph 6 above).

Disqualification until a test is passed

12. Where an offender is convicted of dangerous driving, the court must order disqualification until an extended driving test is passed.
13. The court has discretion to disqualify until a test is passed where an offender is convicted of any endorsable offence.[239] Where disqualification is obligatory, the extended test applies. In other cases, it will be the ordinary test.
14. An offender disqualified as a 'totter' under the penalty points provisions may also be ordered to re-take a driving test; in this case, the extended test applies.
15. The discretion to order a re-test is likely to be exercised where there is evidence of inexperience, incompetence or infirmity, or the disqualification period is lengthy (that is, the offender is going to be 'off the road' for a considerable time).

Reduced period of disqualification for completion of rehabilitation course

16. Where an offender is disqualified for 12 months or more in respect of an alcohol-related driving offence, the court may order that the period of disqualification will be reduced if the offender satisfactorily completes an approved rehabilitation course.[240]
17. Before offering an offender the opportunity to attend a course, the court must be satisfied that an approved course is available and must inform the offender of the effect of the order, the fees that the offender is required to pay, and when he or she must pay them.
18. The court should also explain that the offender may be required to satisfy the Secretary of State that he or she does not have a drink problem and is fit to drive before the offender's licence will be returned at the end of the disqualification period.[241]
19. In general, a court should consider offering the opportunity to attend a course to all offenders convicted of a relevant offence for the first time. The court should be willing to consider offering an offender the opportunity to attend a second course where it considers there are good reasons. It will not usually be appropriate to give an offender the opportunity to attend a third course.
20. The reduction must be at least three months but cannot be more than one quarter of the total period of disqualification:
    - a period of 12 months disqualification must be reduced to nine months;
    - in other cases, a reduction of one week should be made for every month of the disqualification so that, for example, a disqualification of 24 months will be reduced by 24 weeks.
21. When it makes the order, the court must specify a date for completion of the course which is at least two months before the end of the reduced period of disqualification.

Disqualification in the offender's absence

22. When considering disqualification in absence the starting point should be that disqualification in absence should be imposed if there is no reason to believe the defendant is not aware of the proceedings, and after the statutory notice has been served pursuant to section 11(4) of the Magistrates' Courts Act 1980 where appropriate. Disqualification should not be imposed in absence where there

---

238 ibid, ss. 34(4), 35(2), 37(1A)
239 ibid, s. 36(4)
240 Road Traffic Offenders Act 1988, s. 34A
241 Road Traffic Act 1988

is evidence that the defendant has an acceptable reason for not attending or where there are reasons to believe it would be contrary to the interests of justice to do so.

New drivers **SG-424**

23. Drivers who incur six points or more during the two-year probationary period after passing the driving test will have their licence revoked automatically by the Secretary of State; they will be able to drive only after application for a provisional licence pending the passing of a further test.[242]
24. An offender liable for an endorsement which will cause the licence to be revoked under the new drivers' provisions may ask the court to disqualify rather than impose points. This will avoid the requirement to take a further test. Generally, this would be inappropriate since it would circumvent the clear intention of Parliament.

[Material on dangerous offenders — no longer included in the Guideline.] **SG-425**

Out of Court Disposals **SG-426**

1. There are several alternatives to formal charges available to police and CPS when dealing with adults, including cannabis and khat warnings, penalty notices for disorder, community resolution, simple cautions and conditional cautions.

Cannabis or khat warning

2. A cannabis or khat warning may be given where the offender is found in possession of a small amount of cannabis or khat consistent with personal use and the offender admits the elements of the offence. The drug is confiscated and a record of the warning will be made on local systems. The warning is not a conviction and should not be regarded as an aggravating factor when sentencing for subsequent offences.

Simple caution

3. A simple caution may be issued where there is evidence that the offender has committed an offence, the offender admits to the offence, and the offender agrees to being given the caution.
4. When sentencing an offender who has received a simple caution on a previous occasion:
   - the simple caution is not a previous conviction and, therefore, is not a statutory aggravating factor;
   - however, the caution will form part of the offender's criminal record and if the caution is recent and is relevant to the current offence it may be considered to be an aggravating factor.

Conditional caution **SG-427**

5. A conditional caution[243] requires an offender to comply with conditions, as an alternative to prosecution. The conditions that can be attached must be rehabilitative, reparative and/or a financial penalty. (If the offender is a 'relevant foreign offender' — that is someone without permission to enter or stay in the UK, conditions can be offered that have the object of effecting departure from and preventing return to the UK.) Before the caution can be given, the offender must admit the offence and consent to the conditions.
6. When sentencing an offender who has received a conditional caution in respect of an earlier offence:
   - a conditional caution is not a previous conviction and, therefore, is not a statutory aggravating factor;
   - however, if the conditional caution is recent and is relevant to the current offence it may be considered to be an aggravating factor;
   - the offender's response to the caution may properly influence the court's assessment of the offender's suitability for a particular sentence, so long as it remains within the limits established by the seriousness of the current offence.

Approach to sentencing for offence for which offender was cautioned but failed to comply with conditions

7. If the offender fails, without reasonable cause, to comply with the conditional caution, he or she may be prosecuted for the original offence. When sentencing in such a case:
   - the offender's non-compliance with the conditional caution does not increase the seriousness of the original offence and must not be regarded as an aggravating factor;

[242] Road Traffic (New Drivers) Act 1995
[243] Criminal Justice Act 2003, s. 22

Sentencing Guidelines

- the offender's non-compliance may be relevant to selection of the type of sentence. For example, it may indicate that it is inappropriate to include certain requirements as part of a community order. The circumstances of the offender's failure to satisfy the conditions, and any partial compliance, will be relevant to this assessment.

SG-428 *Penalty notices—fixed penalty notices and penalty notices for disorder*

8. Penalty notices may be issued as an alternative to prosecution in respect of a range of offences. Unlike conditional cautions, an admission of guilt is not a prerequisite to issuing a penalty notice.
9. An offender who is issued with a penalty notice may nevertheless be prosecuted for the offence if he or she:
   - asks to be tried for the offence;
   - fails to pay the penalty within the period stipulated in the notice and the prosecutor decides to proceed with charges.[244]
10. When sentencing in cases in which a penalty notice was available:
    - the fact that the offender did not take advantage of the penalty (whether that was by requesting a hearing or failing to pay within the specified timeframe) does not increase the seriousness of the offence and must not be regarded as an aggravating factor. The appropriate sentence must be determined in accordance with the sentencing principles set out above (including the amount of any fine, which must take an offender's financial circumstances into account), disregarding the availability of the penalty;
    - where a penalty notice was not offered or taken up for reasons unconnected with the offence itself, such as administrative difficulties outside the control of the offender, the starting point should be a fine equivalent to the amount of the penalty and no order of costs should be imposed. The offender should not be disadvantaged by the unavailability of the penalty notice in these circumstances. A list of offences for which penalty notices are available, and the amount of the penalty, is set out in Annex B.
11. Where an offender has had previous penalty notice(s), the fact that an offender has previously been issued with a penalty notice does not increase the seriousness of the current offence and must not be regarded as an aggravating factor. It may, however, properly influence the court's assessment of the offender's suitability for a particular sentence, so long as it remains within the limits established by the seriousness of the current offence.

SG-429 *Community Resolution*

12. Community resolution is an informal non-statutory disposal used for dealing with less serious crime and anti-social behaviour where the offender accepts responsibility. The views of the victim (where there is one) are taken into account in reaching an informal agreement between the parties which can involve restorative justice techniques.
13. When sentencing an offender who has received a community resolution for an earlier offence:
    - A community resolution is not a conviction and is therefore not a statutory aggravating factor, but if recent and relevant to the offence it may be considered to be an aggravating factor.

SG-432 VICTIM PERSONAL STATEMENTS

A victim personal statement (VPS) gives victims a formal opportunity to say how a crime has affected them. Where the victim has chosen to make such a statement, a court should consider and take it into account prior to passing sentence.

[CPD VII, Sentencing F: see **PD-65**] emphasises that:

- evidence of the effects of an offence on the victim must be in the form of a witness statement under section 9 of the Criminal Justice Act 1967 or an expert's report;
- the statement must be served on the defence prior to sentence;
- except where inferences can properly be drawn from the nature of or circumstances surrounding the offence, the court must not make assumptions unsupported by evidence about the effects of an offence on the victim;
- at the discretion of the court the VPS may also be read aloud in whole or in part or it may be summarised. If it is to be read aloud the court should also determine who should do so. In making these decisions the court should take into account the victim's preferences, and follow them unless there is

[244] In some cases of non-payment, the penalty is automatically registered and enforceable as a fine without need for recourse to the courts. This procedure applies to penalty notices for disorder and fixed penalty notices issued in respect of certain road traffic offences but not to fixed penalty notices issued for most other criminal offences

a good reason not to do so (for example, inadmissible or potentially harmful content). Court hearings should not be adjourned solely to allow the victim to attend court to read the VPS;

- the court must pass what it judges to be the appropriate sentence having regard to the circumstances of the offence and the offender, taking into account, so far as the court considers it appropriate, the consequences to the victim;
- the opinions of the victim or the victim's close relatives as to what the sentence should be are not relevant.

See also the guidance [at **SG-370B**] particularly with reference to the victim's views as to any compensation order that may be imposed.

Prevalence and community impact statements SG-432A

Taken from the Sentencing Guidelines Council's definitive guideline *Overarching Principles: Seriousness*.

The seriousness of an individual case should be judged on its own dimensions of harm and culpability rather than as part of a collective social harm.

However, there may be exceptional local circumstances that arise which may lead a court to decide that prevalence should influence sentencing levels. The pivotal issue in such cases will be the harm being caused to the community. It is essential that sentencers both have supporting evidence from an external source (for example a community impact statement compiled by the police) to justify claims that a particular crime is prevalent in their area and are satisfied that there is a compelling need to treat the offence more seriously than elsewhere. A community impact statement is a document providing information to the court about the impact of offences on the community.

The key factor in determining whether sentencing levels should be enhanced in response to prevalence will be the level of harm being caused in the locality. Enhanced sentences should be exceptional and in response to exceptional circumstances. Sentencers must sentence within the sentencing guidelines once the prevalence has been addressed.

Annex A: Availability of Ancillary Orders SG-433

[Annex A consists of a list of offences covered in the MCSG for which particular ancillary orders are available and is omitted. For guidance on the various available ancillary orders, see the relevant material in the main work.]

Annex B [Offences for which Penalty Notices are Available] SG-434

Penalty notices for disorder SG-435

Offence	Legislation	Amount
Criminal damage (where damage under £500 in value, and not normally where damage over £300)	Criminal Damage Act 1971, s.1	£90
Disorderly behaviour	Public Order Act 1986, s.5	£90
Drunk and disorderly	Criminal Justice Act 1967, s.91	£90
Sale of alcohol to drunk person on relevant premises (not including off-licenses)	Licensing Act 2003, s.141	£90
Sale of alcohol to person under 18 (staff only; licensees should be subject of a summons)	Licensing Act 2003, s.146	£90
Theft from a shop (where goods under £200 in value, and not normally where goods over £100)	Theft Act 1968, s.1	£90

SG-436 **Fixed penalty notices**

Offence	Legislation	Amount	Penalty points
Careless driving	Road Traffic Act 1988, s. 3	£100	3
Brakes, steering or tyres defective	Road Traffic Act 1988, s.41A	£200	3
Breach of other construction and use requirements	Road Traffic Act 1988, s.42	£100 or £200	3
Driving other than in accordance with licence	Road Traffic Act 1988, s.87(1)	£100	3
Failing to comply with police officer signal	Road Traffic Act 1988, s.35	£100	3
Failing to comply with traffic sign	Road Traffic Act 1988, s.36	£100	3
Failing to supply details of driver's identity	Road Traffic Act 1988, s.172	£200	6
No insurance	Road Traffic Act 1988, s.143	£300	6
No test certificate	Road Traffic Act 1988, s.47	£100	–
Overloading/exceeding axle weight	Road Traffic Act 1988, s.41B	£100 to £300	–
Pelican/zebra crossing contravention	Road Traffic Regulation Act 1984, s.25(5)	£100	3
Railway fare evasion (where penalty notice scheme in operation by train operator)	Railways (Penalty Fares) Regulations 1994	£20 or twice the full single fare to next stop, whichever is greater	–
Seat belt offences	Road Traffic Act 1988, s.14 and s. 15(2) or 15(4)	£100	–
School non-attendance	Education Act 1996, s.444(1)	£60 if paid within 21 days; £120 if paid within 28 days	–
Speeding	Road Traffic Regulation Act 1984, s.89(1)	£100	3
Using hand-held mobile phone while driving	Road Traffic Act 1988, s.41D	£100	3
Using vehicle in dangerous condition	Road Traffic Act 1988, s.40A	£100	3

PART 13 CAUSING DEATH BY DRIVING

SG-437

Foreword

...This guideline applies to the sentencing of offenders convicted of any of the offences dealt with herein who are sentenced on or after **4 August 2008**.

This guideline applies only to the sentencing of offenders aged 18 and older. The legislative provisions relating to the sentencing of youths are different; the younger the age, the greater the difference. A separate guideline setting out general principles relating to the sentencing of youths is planned.

...

SG-438 **Introduction**

1. This guideline applies to the four offences of *causing death by dangerous driving, causing death by driving under the influence of alcohol or drugs, causing death by careless driving and causing death by driving: unlicensed, disqualified or uninsured drivers.*
2. The Crown Prosecution Service's *Policy for Prosecuting Cases of Bad Driving* sets out the approach for prosecutors when considering the appropriate charge based on an assessment of the standard of the offender's driving. This has been taken into account when formulating this guideline. Annex A sets out the statutory definitions for dangerous, careless and inconsiderate driving together with examples of the types of driving behaviour likely to result in the charge of one offence rather than another.

3. Because the principal harm done by these offences (the death of a person) is an element of the offence, the factor that primarily determines the starting point for sentence is the culpability of the offender. Accordingly, for all offences other than *causing death by driving: unlicensed, disqualified or uninsured drivers,* the central feature should be an evaluation of the quality of the driving involved and the degree of danger that it foreseeably created. These guidelines draw a distinction between those factors of an offence that are intrinsic to the quality of driving (referred to as 'determinants of seriousness') and those which, while they aggravate the offence, are not.
4. The levels of seriousness in the guidelines for those offences based on dangerous or careless driving alone have been determined by reference *only* to determinants of seriousness. Aggravating factors will have the effect of either increasing the starting point within the sentencing range provided or, in certain circumstances, of moving the offence up to the next sentencing range. The outcome will depend on both the number of aggravating factors present and the potency of those factors. Thus, the same outcome could follow from the presence of one particularly bad aggravating factor or two or more less serious factors.
5. The determinants of seriousness likely to be relevant in relation to *causing death by careless driving under the influence* are both the degree of carelessness and the level of intoxication. The guideline sets out an approach to assessing both those aspects but giving greater weight to the degree of intoxication since Parliament has provided for a maximum of 14 years imprisonment rather than the maximum of 5 years where the death is caused by careless driving only.
6. Since there will be no allegation of bad driving, the guideline for *causing death by driving; unlicensed, disqualified or uninsured drivers* links the assessment of offender culpability to the nature of the prohibition on the offender's driving and includes a list of factors that may aggravate an offence.
7. The degree to which an aggravating factor is present (and its interaction with any other aggravating and mitigating factors) will be immensely variable and the court is best placed to judge the appropriate impact on sentence. Clear identification of those factors relating to the standard of driving as the initial determinants of offence seriousness is intended to assist the adoption of a common approach.

A. Assessing seriousness **SG-439**

(i) Determinants of seriousness

8. There are five factors that may be regarded as determinants of offence seriousness, each of which can be demonstrated in a number of ways. Common examples of each of the determinants are set out below and key issues are discussed in the text that follows…

Examples of the determinants are:

- *Awareness of risk*
  (a) a prolonged, persistent and deliberate course of very bad driving
- *Effect of alcohol or drugs*
  (b) consumption of alcohol above the legal limit
  (c) consumption of alcohol at or below the legal limit where this impaired the offender's ability to drive
  (d) failure to supply a specimen for analysis
  (e) consumption of illegal drugs, where this impaired the offender's ability to drive
  (f) consumption of legal drugs or medication where this impaired the offender's ability to drive (including legal medication known to cause drowsiness) where the driver knew, or should have known, about the likelihood of impairment
- *Inappropriate speed of vehicle*
  (g) greatly excessive speed; racing; competitive driving against another vehicle
  (h) driving above the speed limit
  (i) driving at a speed that is inappropriate for the prevailing road or weather conditions
  (j) driving a PSV, HGV or other goods vehicle at a speed that is inappropriate either because of the nature of the vehicle or its load, especially when carrying passengers
- *Seriously culpable behaviour of offender*
  (k) aggressive driving (such as driving much too close to the vehicle in front, persistent inappropriate attempts to overtake, or cutting in after overtaking)
  (l) driving while using a hand-held mobile phone
  (m) driving whilst the driver's attention is avoidably distracted, for example by reading or adjusting the controls of electronic equipment such as a radio, hands-free mobile phone or satellite navigation equipment
  (n) driving when knowingly suffering from a medical or physical condition that significantly impairs the offender's driving skills, including failure to take prescribed medication

(o) driving when knowingly deprived of adequate sleep or rest, especially where commercial concerns had a bearing on the commission of the offence
(p) driving a poorly maintained or dangerously loaded vehicle, especially where commercial concerns had a bearing on the commission of the offence

- *Victim*

(q) failing to have proper regard to vulnerable road users

9. Issues relating to the determinants of seriousness are considered below.

(a) Alcohol/drugs

10. For those offences where the presence of alcohol or drugs is not an element of the offence, where there is sufficient evidence of driving impairment attributable to alcohol or drugs, the consumption of alcohol or drugs prior to driving will make an offence more serious. Where the drugs were legally purchased or prescribed, the offence will only be regarded as more serious if the offender knew or should have known that the drugs were likely to impair driving ability.
11. Unless inherent in the offence or charged separately, failure to provide a specimen for analysis (or to allow a blood specimen taken without consent to be analysed) should be regarded as a determinant of offence seriousness.
12. Where it is established to the satisfaction of the court that an offender had consumed alcohol or drugs unwittingly before driving, that may be regarded as a mitigating factor. However, consideration should be given to the circumstances in which the offender decided to drive or continue to drive when driving ability was impaired.

(b) Avoidable distractions

13. A distinction has been drawn between **ordinary** avoidable distractions and those that are more significant because they divert the attention of the driver for longer periods or to a greater extent; in this guideline these are referred to as a **gross** avoidable distraction. The guideline for causing *death by dangerous driving* provides for a gross avoidable distraction to place the offence in a higher level of seriousness.
14. Any avoidable distraction will make an offence more serious but the degree to which an offender's driving will be impaired will vary. Where the reaction to the distraction is significant, it may be the factor that determines whether the offence is based on *dangerous* driving or on *careless* driving; in those circumstances, care must be taken to avoid 'double counting'.
15. Using a hand-held mobile phone when driving is, in itself, an unlawful act; the fact that an offender was avoidably distracted by using a hand-held mobile phone when a causing death by driving offence was committed will always make an offence more serious. Reading or composing text messages *over a period of time will be a gross* avoidable distraction and is likely to result in an offence of causing death by dangerous driving being in a higher level of seriousness.
16. Where it is proved that an offender was briefly distracted by reading a text message or adjusting a hands-free set or its controls at the time of the collision, this would be on a par with consulting a map or adjusting a radio or satellite navigation equipment, activities that would be considered an avoidable distraction.

(c) Vulnerable road users

17. Cyclists, motorbike riders, horse riders, pedestrians and those working in the road are vulnerable road users and a driver is expected to take extra care when driving near them. Driving too close to a bike or horse; allowing a vehicle to mount the pavement; driving into a cycle lane; and driving without the care needed in the vicinity of a pedestrian crossing, hospital, school or residential home, are all examples of factors that should be taken into account when determining the seriousness of an offence. See paragraph 24 below for the approach where the actions of another person contributed to the collision.
18. The fact that the victim of a causing death by driving offence was a particularly vulnerable road user is a factor that should be taken into account when determining the seriousness of an offence.

(ii) Aggravating and mitigating factors

(a) More than one person killed

19. The seriousness of any offence included in these guidelines will generally be greater where more than one person is killed since it is inevitable that the degree of harm will be greater. In relation to the assessment of culpability, whilst there will be circumstances in which a driver could reasonably anticipate the possible death of more than one person (for example, the driver of a vehicle with passengers (whether that is a bus, taxi or private car) or a person driving badly in an area where there are many people), there will be many circumstances where the driver could not anticipate the number of people who would be killed.

20. The greater obligation on those responsible for driving other people is not an element essential to the quality of the driving and so has not been included amongst the determinants of seriousness that affect the choice of sentencing range. In practical terms, separate charges are likely to be brought in relation to each death caused. Although concurrent sentences are likely to be imposed (in recognition of the fact that the charges relate to one episode of offending behaviour), each individual sentence is likely to be higher because the offence is aggravated by the fact that more than one death has been caused.
21. Where more than one person is killed, that will aggravate the seriousness of the offence because of the increase in harm. Where the number of people killed is high *and* that was reasonably foreseeable, the number of deaths is likely to provide sufficient justification for moving an offence into the next highest sentencing band.

(b) Effect on offender

22. Injury to the offender may be a mitigating factor when the offender has suffered very serious injuries. In most circumstances, the weighting it is given will be dictated by the circumstances of the offence and the effect should bear a direct relationship to the extent to which the offender's driving was at fault—the greater the fault, the less the effect on mitigation; this distinction will be of particular relevance where an offence did not involve any fault in the offender's standard of driving.
23. Where one or more of the victims was in a close personal or family relationship with the offender, this may be a mitigating factor. In line with the approach where the offender is very seriously injured, the degree to which the relationship influences the sentence should be linked to offender culpability in relation to the commission of the offence; mitigation for this reason is likely to have less effect where the culpability of the driver is particularly high.

(c) Actions of others

24. Where the actions of the victim or a third party contributed to the commission of an offence, this should be acknowledged and taken into account as a mitigating factor.

(d) Offender's age/lack of driving experience

25. The Council guideline *Overarching Principles: Seriousness* [see **SG-21**] includes a generic mitigating factor '*youth or age, where it affects the responsibility of the individual defendant*'. There is a great deal of difference between recklessness or irresponsibility—which may be due to youth—and inexperience in dealing with prevailing conditions or an unexpected or unusual situation that presents itself—which may be present regardless of the age of the offender. The fact that an offender's lack of driving experience contributed to the commission of an offence should be treated as a mitigating factor; in this regard, the age of the offender is not relevant.

(iii) Personal mitigation

(a) Good driving record

26. This is not a factor that automatically should be treated as a mitigating factor, especially now that the presence of previous convictions is a statutory aggravating factor. However, any evidence to show that an offender has previously been an exemplary driver, for example having driven an ambulance, police vehicle, bus, taxi or similar vehicle conscientiously and without incident for many years, is a fact that the courts may well wish to take into account by way of personal mitigation. This is likely to have even greater effect where the driver is driving on public duty (for example, on ambulance, fire services or police duties) and was responding to an emergency.

(b) Conduct after the offence

—Giving assistance at the scene

27. There may be many reasons why an offender does not offer help to the victims at the scene—the offender may be injured, traumatised by shock, afraid of causing further injury or simply have no idea what action to take—and it would be inappropriate to assess the offence as more serious on this ground (and so increase the level of sentence). However, where an offender gave direct, positive, assistance to victim(s) at the scene of a collision, this should be regarded as personal mitigation.

—Remorse

28. Whilst it can be expected that anyone who has caused death by driving would be expected to feel remorseful, this cannot undermine its importance for sentencing purposes. Remorse is identified as personal mitigation in [*Overarching Principles: Seriousness*: see **SG-21**] and the Council can see no reason for it to be treated differently for this group of offences. It is for the court to determine whether an expression of remorse is genuine; where it is, this should be taken into account as personal mitigation.

(c) Summary

29. Evidence that an offender is normally a careful and conscientious driver, giving direct, positive assistance to a victim and genuine remorse may be taken into account as personal mitigation and may justify a reduction in sentence.

SG-440 **B. Ancillary orders**

(i) Disqualification for driving

30. For each offence, disqualification is a mandatory part of the sentence (subject to the usual (very limited) exceptions), and therefore an important element of the overall punishment for the offence. In addition, an order that the disqualification continues until the offender passes an extended driving test order is compulsory[245] for those convicted of causing death by dangerous driving or by careless driving when under the influence, and discretionary[246] in relation to the two other offences.

31. Any disqualification is effective from the date on which it is imposed. When ordering disqualification from driving, the duration of the order should allow for the length of any custodial period in order to ensure that the disqualification has the desired impact. In principle, the minimum period of disqualification should either equate to the length of the custodial sentence imposed (in the knowledge that the offender is likely to be released having served half of that term), or the relevant statutory minimum disqualification period, whichever results in the longer period of disqualification.

(ii) Deprivation order

32. A general sentencing power exists which enables courts to deprive an offender of property used for the purposes of committing an offence.[247] A vehicle used to commit an offence included in this guideline can be regarded as being used for the purposes of committing the offence.

SG-441 **C. Sentencing ranges and starting points**

1. Typically, a guideline will apply to an offence that can be committed in a variety of circumstances with different levels of seriousness. It will apply to a first-time offender who has been convicted after a trial. Within the guidelines, a first-time offender is a person who does not have a conviction which, by virtue of section 143(2) of the CJA 2003, must be treated as an aggravating factor.
2. As an aid to consistency of approach, the guidelines describe a number of types of activity which would fall within the broad definition of the offence. These are set out in a column headed 'Type/nature of activity'.
3. The expected approach is for a court to identify the description that most nearly matches the particular facts of the offence for which sentence is being imposed. This will identify a starting point from which the sentencer can depart to reflect aggravating or mitigating factors affecting the seriousness of the offence (beyond those contained within the column describing the type or nature of offence activity) to reach a provisional sentence.
4. The *sentencing range* is the bracket into which the provisional sentence will normally fall after having regard to factors which aggravate or mitigate the seriousness of the offence. The particular circumstances may, however, make it appropriate that the provisional sentence falls outside the range.
5. Where the offender has previous convictions which aggravate the seriousness of the current offence, that may take the provisional sentence beyond the range given, particularly where there are significant other aggravating factors present.
6. Once the provisional sentence has been identified by reference to those factors affecting the seriousness of the offence, the court will take into account any relevant factors of personal mitigation, which may take the sentence outside the range indicated in the guideline.
7. Where there has been a guilty plea, any reduction attributable to that plea will be applied to the sentence at this stage. This reduction may take the sentence below the range provided.
8. A court must give its reasons for imposing a sentence of a different kind or outside the range provided in the guidelines.[248]

The decision making process

The process set out below is intended to show that the sentencing approach for offences of causing death by driving is fluid and requires the structured exercise of discretion.

245 Road Traffic Offenders Act 1988, section 36(1)
246 ibid, section 36(4)
247 Powers of Criminal Courts (Sentencing) Act 2000, section 143
248 Criminal Justice Act 2003, section 174(2)(a)

[Sets out the standard decision making process: identify dangerous offenders, identify starting point, consider aggravating factors, consider mitigating factors, apply reduction for guilty plea, consider ancillary orders, review in light of totality principle and give reasons.]

D. Offence guidelines **SG-442**

Causing death by dangerous driving
Factors to take into consideration

1. The following guideline applies to a 'first-time offender' aged 18 or over convicted after trial (see. . .above), who has not been assessed as a dangerous offender requiring a sentence under ss. 224–228 Criminal Justice Act 2003 (as amended).
2. When assessing the seriousness of any offence, the court must always refer to the full list of aggravating and mitigating factors in the Council guideline on Seriousness[249] as well as those set out in the adjacent table as being particularly relevant to this type of offending behaviour.

3. Levels of seriousness

The 3 levels are distinguished by factors related predominantly to the standard of driving; the general description of the degree of risk is complemented by examples of the type of bad driving arising. The presence of aggravating factors or combinations of a small number of determinants of seriousness will increase the starting point within the range. Where there is a larger group of determinants of seriousness and/or aggravating factors, this may justify moving the starting point to the next level.

Level 1—The most serious offences encompassing driving that involved a deliberate decision to ignore (or a flagrant disregard for) the rules of the road and an apparent disregard for the great danger being caused to others. Such offences are likely to be characterised by:

- *A prolonged, persistent and deliberate course of very bad driving AND/OR*
- *Consumption of substantial amounts of alcohol or drugs leading to gross impairment AND/OR*
- *A group of determinants of seriousness which in isolation or smaller number would place the offence in level 2*

Level 1 is that for which the increase in maximum penalty was aimed primarily. Where an offence involves both of the determinants of seriousness identified, particularly if accompanied by aggravating factors such as multiple deaths or injuries, or a very bad driving record, this may move an offence towards the top of the sentencing range.

Level 2—This is driving that created a substantial risk of danger and is likely to be characterised by:

- *Greatly excessive speed, racing or competitive driving against another driver OR*
- *Gross avoidable distraction such as reading or composing text messages over a period of time OR*
- *Driving whilst ability to drive is impaired as a result of consumption of alcohol or drugs, failing to take prescribed medication or as a result of a known medical condition OR*
- *A group of determinants of seriousness which in isolation or smaller number would place the offence in level 3*

Level 3—This is driving that created a significant risk of danger and is likely to be characterised by:

- *Driving above the speed limit/at a speed that is inappropriate for the prevailing conditions OR*
- *Driving when knowingly deprived of adequate sleep or rest or knowing that the vehicle has a dangerous defect or is poorly maintained or is dangerously loaded OR*
- *A brief but obvious danger arising from a seriously dangerous manoeuvre OR*
- *Driving whilst avoidably distracted OR*
- *Failing to have proper regard to vulnerable road users*

The starting point and range overlap with Level 2 is to allow the breadth of discretion necessary to accommodate circumstances where there are significant aggravating factors.

4. Sentencers should take into account relevant matters of personal mitigation; see in particular guidance on **good driving record, giving assistance at the scene** and **remorse**. . .above.

Causing Death by Dangerous Driving

Road Traffic Act 1988 (section 1)

This is a serious offence for the purposes of section 224 Criminal Justice Act 2003

Maximum penalty: 14 years imprisonment;
minimum disqualification of 2 years with compulsory extended re-test

[249] *Overarching Principles: Seriousness*, published 16 December 2004, www.sentencing-guidelines.gov.uk

Sentencing Guidelines

Nature of offence	Starting point	Sentencing range
Level 1 The most serious offences encompassing driving that involved a deliberate decision to ignore (or a flagrant disregard for) the rules of the road and an apparent disregard for the great danger being caused to others	8 years' custody	7–14 years' custody
Level 2 Driving that created a *substantial* risk of danger	5 years' custody	4–7 years' custody
Level 3 Driving that created a *significant* risk of danger *[Where the driving is markedly less culpable than for this level, reference should be made to the starting point and range for the most serious level of causing death by careless driving]*	3 years' custody	2–5 years' custody

Additional aggravating factors	Additional mitigating factors
1. Previous convictions for motoring offences, particularly offences that involve bad driving or the consumption of excessive alcohol or drugs before driving 2. More than one person killed as a result of the offence 3. Serious injury to one or more victims, in addition to the death(s) 4. Disregard of warnings 5. Other offences committed at the same time, such as driving other than in accordance with the terms of a valid licence; driving while disqualified; driving without insurance; taking a vehicle without consent; driving a stolen vehicle 6. The offender's irresponsible behaviour such as failing to stop, falsely claiming that one of the victims was responsible for the collision, or trying to throw the victim off the car by swerving in order to escape 7. Driving off in an attempt to avoid detection or apprehension	1. Alcohol or drugs consumed unwittingly 2. Offender was seriously injured in the collision 3. The victim was a close friend or relative 4. Actions of the victim or a third party contributed significantly to the likelihood of a collision occurring and/or death resulting 5. The offender's lack of driving experience contributed to the commission of the offence 6. The driving was in response to a proven and genuine emergency falling short of a defence

SG-443 **Causing death by careless driving when under the influence of drink or drugs or having failed without reasonable excuse either to provide a specimen for analysis or to permit the analysis of a blood sample**

Factors to take into consideration

1. The following guideline applies to a 'first-time offender' aged 18 or over convicted after trial (see…above), who has not been assessed as a dangerous offender requiring a sentence under ss. 224–228 Criminal Justice Act 2003 (as amended).
2. When assessing the seriousness of any offence, the court must always refer to the full list of aggravating and mitigating factors in the Council guideline on Seriousness[250] as well as those set out in the adjacent table as being particularly relevant to this type of offending behaviour.
3. This offence can be committed through:
   (i) being unfit to drive through drink or drugs;
   (ii) having consumed so much alcohol as to be over the prescribed limit;
   (iii) failing without reasonable excuse to provide a specimen for analysis within the timescale allowed; or
   (iv) failing without reasonable excuse to permit the analysis of a blood sample taken when incapable of giving consent.

[250] *Overarching Principles: Seriousness*, published 16 December 2004, www.sentencing-guidelines.gov.uk

4. In comparison with *causing death by dangerous driving*, the level of culpability in the actual manner of driving is lower but that culpability is increased in all cases by the fact that the offender has driven after consuming drugs or an excessive amount of alcohol. Accordingly, there is considerable parity in the levels of seriousness with the deliberate decision to drive after consuming alcohol or drugs aggravating the *careless* standard of driving onto a par with *dangerous* driving.
5. The fact that the offender was under the influence of drink or drugs is an inherent element of this offence. For discussion on the significance of driving after having consumed drink or drugs, see...above.
6. The guideline is based both on the level of alcohol or drug consumption and on the degree of carelessness.
7. The increase in sentence is more marked where there is an increase in the level of intoxication than where there is an increase in the degree of carelessness reflecting the 14 year imprisonment maximum for this offence compared with a 5 year maximum for causing death by careless or inconsiderate driving alone.
8. A refusal to supply a specimen for analysis may be a calculated step by an offender to avoid prosecution for driving when having consumed in excess of the prescribed amount of alcohol, with a view to seeking to persuade the court that the amount consumed was relatively small. A court is entitled to draw adverse inferences from a refusal to supply a specimen without reasonable excuse and should treat with caution any attempt to persuade the court that only a limited amount of alcohol had been consumed.[251] The three levels of seriousness where the offence has been committed in this way derive from the classification in the Magistrates' Court Sentencing Guidelines.
9. Sentencers should take into account relevant matters of personal mitigation; see in particular guidance on **good driving record, giving assistance at the scene** and **remorse**...above.

Causing Death by Careless Driving when Under the Influence of Drink or Drugs or having Failed either to Provide a Specimen for Analysis or to Permit Analysis of a Blood Sample

Road Traffic Act 1988 (section 3A)

This is a serious offence for the purposes of section 224 Criminal Justice Act 2003

Maximum penalty: 14 years imprisonment;
minimum disqualification of 2 years with compulsory extended re-test

The legal limit of alcohol is 35 µg breath (80 mg in blood and 107 mg in urine)	**Careless/inconsiderate driving arising from momentary inattention with no aggravating factors**	**Other cases of careless/ inconsiderate driving**	**Careless/inconsiderate driving falling not far short of dangerousness**
71 µ or above of alcohol/high quantity of drugs OR deliberate non-provision of specimen where evidence of serious impairment	**Starting point:** 6 years' custody **Sentencing range:** 5–10 years' custody	**Starting point:** 7 years' custody **Sentencing range:** 6–12 years' custody	**Starting point:** 8 years' custody **Sentencing range:** 7–14 years' custody
51–70 µg of alcohol/moderate quantity of drugs OR deliberate non-provision of specimen	**Starting point:** 4 years' custody **Sentencing range:** 3–7 years' custody	**Starting point:** 5 years' custody **Sentencing range:** 4–8 years' custody	**Starting point:** 6 years' custody **Sentencing range:** 5–9 years' custody
35–50 µg of alcohol/minimum quantity of drugs OR test refused because of honestly held but unreasonable belief	**Starting point:** 18 months' custody **Sentencing range:** 26 weeks'–4 years' custody	**Starting point:** 3 years' custody **Sentencing range:** 2–5 years' custody	**Starting point:** 4 years' custody **Sentencing range:** 3–6 years' custody

[251] *Attorney-General's Reference No. 21 of 2000* [2001] 1 Cr App R (S) 173

Additional aggravating factors	Additional mitigating factors
1. Other offences committed at the same time, such as driving other than in accordance with the terms of a valid licence; driving while disqualified; driving without insurance; taking a vehicle without consent; driving a stolen vehicle 2. Previous convictions for motoring offences, particularly offences that involve bad driving or the consumption of excessive alcohol before driving 3. More than one person was killed as a result of the offence 4. Serious injury to one or more persons in addition to the death(s) 5. Irresponsible behaviour such as failing to stop or falsely claiming that one of the victims was responsible for the collision	1. Alcohol or drugs consumed unwittingly 2. Offender was seriously injured in the collision 3. The victim was a close friend or relative 4. The actions of the victim or a third party contributed significantly to the likelihood of a collision occurring and/or death resulting 5. The driving was in response to a proven and genuine emergency falling short of a defence

SG-444 **Causing death by careless or inconsiderate driving**

Factors to take into consideration

1. The following guideline applies to a 'first-time offender' aged 18 or over convicted after trial (see...above), who has not been assessed as a dangerous offender requiring a sentence under ss. 224–228 Criminal Justice Act 2003 (as amended).
2. When assessing the seriousness of any offence, the court must always refer to the full list of aggravating and mitigating factors in the Council guideline on Seriousness[252] as well as those set out in the adjacent table as being particularly relevant to this type of offending behaviour.
3. The maximum penalty on indictment is 5 years imprisonment. The offence is triable either way and, in a magistrates' court, statute provides that the maximum sentence is 12 months imprisonment; this will be revised to 6 months imprisonment until such time as the statutory provisions increasing the sentencing powers of a magistrates' court are implemented.[253]
4. Disqualification of the offender from driving and endorsement of the offender's driving licence are mandatory, and the offence carries between 3 and 11 penalty points when the court finds special reasons for not imposing disqualification. There is a discretionary power[254] to order an extended driving test where a person is convicted of this offence.
5. Since the maximum sentence has been set at 5 years imprisonment, the sentence ranges are generally lower for this offence than for the offences of *causing death by dangerous driving* or *causing death by careless driving under the influence*, for which the maximum sentence is 14 years imprisonment. However, it is unavoidable that some cases will be on the borderline between *dangerous* and *careless* driving, or may involve a number of factors that significantly increase the seriousness of an offence. As a result, the guideline for this offence identifies three levels of seriousness, the range for the highest of which overlaps with ranges for the lowest level of seriousness for *causing death by dangerous driving*.
6. The three levels of seriousness are defined by the degree of carelessness involved in the standard of driving. The most serious level for this offence is where the offender's driving fell *not that far short of dangerous*. The least serious group of offences relates to those cases where the level of culpability is low—for example in a case involving an offender who misjudges the speed of another vehicle, or turns without seeing an oncoming vehicle because of restricted visibility. Other cases will fall into the intermediate level.
7. The starting point for the most serious offence of *causing death by careless driving* is lower than that for the least serious offence of *causing death by dangerous driving* in recognition of the different standards of driving behaviour. However, the range still leaves scope, within the 5 year maximum, to impose longer sentences where the case is particularly serious.
8. Where the level of carelessness is low and there are no aggravating factors, even the fact that death was caused is not sufficient to justify a prison sentence.
9. A fine is unlikely to be an appropriate sentence for this offence; where a non-custodial sentence is considered appropriate, this should be a community order. The nature of the requirements will be determined by the purpose[255] identified by the court as of primary importance. Requirements most likely to be relevant include unpaid work requirement, activity requirement, programme requirement and curfew requirement.

---

252 *Overarching Principles: Seriousness*, published 16 December 2004, www.sentencing-guidelines.gov.uk

253 Criminal Justice Act 2003, sections 154(1) and 282; Road Safety Act 2006, section 61(5)

254 Road Traffic Offenders Act 1988, section 36(4)

255 Criminal Justice Act 2003, section 142(1)

10. Sentencers should take into account relevant matters of personal mitigation; see in particular guidance on **good driving record, giving assistance at the scene** and **remorse**...above.

Causing Death by Careless or Inconsiderate Driving

Road Traffic Act 1988 (section 2B)

Maximum penalty: 5 years' imprisonment;
minimum disqualification of 12 months, discretionary re-test

Nature of offence	Starting point	Sentencing range
Careless or inconsiderate driving falling not far short of dangerous driving	15 months' custody	36 weeks'–3 years' custody
Other cases of careless or inconsiderate driving	36 weeks' custody	Community order (HIGH)–2 years' custody
Careless or inconsiderate driving arising from momentary inattention with no aggravating factors	Community order (MEDIUM)	Community order (LOW)–Community order (HIGH)

Additional aggravating factors	Additional mitigating factors
1. Other offences committed at the same time, such as driving other than in accordance with the terms of a valid licence; driving while disqualified; driving without insurance; taking a vehicle without consent; driving a stolen vehicle 2. Previous convictions for motoring offences, particularly offences that involve bad driving 3. More than one person was killed as a result of the offence 4. Serious injury to one or more persons in addition to the death(s) 5. Irresponsible behaviour, such as failing to stop or falsely claiming that one of the victims was responsible for the collision	1. Offender was seriously injured in the collision 2. The victim was a close friend or relative 3. The actions of the victim or a third party contributed to the commission of the offence 4. The offender's lack of driving experience contributed significantly to the likelihood of a collision occurring and/or death resulting 5. The driving was in response to a proven and genuine emergency falling short of a defence

Causing death by driving: unlicensed, disqualified or uninsured drivers SG-445

Factors to take into consideration

1. The following guideline applies to a 'first-time offender' aged 18 or over convicted after trial (see...above), who has not been assessed as a dangerous offender requiring a sentence under ss. 224–228 Criminal Justice Act 2003 (as amended).
2. When assessing the seriousness of any offence, the court must always refer to the full list of aggravating and mitigating factors in the Council guideline on Seriousness[256] as well as those set out in the adjacent table as being particularly relevant to this type of offending behaviour.
3. This offence has a maximum penalty of 2 years imprisonment and is triable either way. In a magistrates' court, statute provides that the maximum sentence is 12 months imprisonment; this will be revised to 6 months imprisonment until such time as the statutory provisions increasing the sentencing powers of a magistrates' court are implemented.[257]
4. Disqualification of the offender from driving and endorsement of the offender's driving licence are mandatory, and the offence carries between 3 and 11 penalty points when the court finds special reasons for not imposing disqualification. There is a discretionary power[258] to order an extended driving test where a person is convicted of this offence.
5. Culpability arises from the offender driving a vehicle on a road or other public place when, by law, not allowed to do so; the offence does not require proof of any fault in the standard of driving.
6. Because of the significantly lower maximum penalty, the sentencing ranges are considerably lower than for the other three offences covered in this guideline; many cases may be sentenced in a magistrates' court, particularly where there is an early guilty plea.

[256] *Overarching Principles: Seriousness*, published 16 December 2004, www.sentencing-guidelines.gov.uk
[257] Criminal Justice Act 2003, sections 154(1) and 282; Road Safety Act 2006, section 61(5)
[258] Road Traffic Offenders Act 1988, section 36(4)

7. A fine is unlikely to be an appropriate sentence for this offence; where a noncustodial sentence is considered appropriate, this should be a community order.
8. Since driving whilst disqualified is more culpable than driving whilst unlicensed or uninsured, a higher starting point is proposed when the offender was disqualified from driving at the time of the offence.
9. Being uninsured, unlicensed or disqualified are the only determinants of seriousness for this offence, as there are no factors relating to the standard of driving. The list of aggravating factors identified is slightly different as the emphasis is on the decision to drive by an offender who is not permitted by law to do so.
10. In some cases, the extreme circumstances that led an offender to drive whilst unlicensed, disqualified or uninsured may result in a successful defence of 'duress of circumstances'.[259] In less extreme circumstances, where the *decision to drive was brought about by a genuine and proven emergency*, that may mitigate offence seriousness and so it is included as an additional mitigating factor.
11. A driver may hold a reasonable belief in relation to the validity of insurance (for example having just missed a renewal date or relied on a third party to make an application) and also the validity of a licence (for example incorrectly believing that a licence covered a particular category of vehicle). In light of this, an additional mitigating factor covers those situations where an offender genuinely believed that there was valid insurance or a valid licence.
12. Sentencers should take into account relevant matters of personal mitigation; see in particular guidance on **good driving record, giving assistance at the scene** and **remorse**. . .above.

Causing Death by Driving: Unlicensed, Disqualified or Uninsured Drivers

Road Traffic Act 1988 (section 3ZB)

Maximum penalty: 2 years imprisonment;
minimum disqualification of 12 months, discretionary re-test

Nature of offence	Starting point	Sentencing range
The offender was disqualified from driving **OR** The offender was unlicensed or uninsured plus 2 or more aggravating factors from the list below	12 months' custody	36 weeks'–2 years' custody
The offender was unlicensed or uninsured plus at least 1 aggravating factor from the list below	26 weeks' custody	Community order (HIGH)–36 weeks' custody
The offender was unlicensed or uninsured—no aggravating factors	Community order (MEDIUM)	Community order (LOW)–Community order (HIGH)

Additional aggravating factors	Additional mitigating factors
1. Previous convictions for motoring offences, whether involving bad driving or involving an offence of the same kind that forms part of the present conviction (i.e. unlicensed, disqualified or uninsured driving) 2. More than one person was killed as a result of the offence 3. Serious injury to one or more persons in addition to the death(s) 4. Irresponsible behaviour such as failing to stop or falsely claiming that someone else was driving	1. The decision to drive was brought about by a proven and genuine emergency falling short of a defence 2. The offender genuinely believed that he or she was insured or licensed to drive 3. The offender was seriously injured as a result of the collision 4. The victim was a close friend or relative

[259] In *DPP v Mullally* [2006] EWHC 3448 (Admin) the Divisional Court held that the defence of necessity must be strictly controlled and that it must be proved that the actions of the defendant were reasonable in the given circumstances. See also *Hasan* [2005] UKHL 22

Annex A: Dangerous and Careless Driving SG-446

Statutory definitions and examples

[Omitted—see the relevant material in part C]

PART 14 THEFT SG-447

Definitive Guideline

Applicability of Guideline

[Omitted: See **SG-539** for identical text save that this guideline has effect from 1 February 2016.]

Structure, ranges and starting points

[Omitted: See **SG-540** for identical text.]

General Theft SG-448

Theft Act 1968 (section 1)

Including:
Theft from the person
Theft in a dwelling
Theft in breach of trust
Theft from a motor vehicle
Theft of a motor vehicle
Theft of a pedal bicycle
and all other section 1 Theft Act 1968 offences, excluding theft from a shop or stall

Triable either way
Maximum: 7 years' custody
Offence range: Discharge — 6 years' custody

STEP ONE Determining the offence category SG-449

The court should determine the offence category with reference **only** to the factors identified in the following tables. In order to determine the category the court should assess **culpability** and **harm.**

The level of culpability is determined by weighing up all the factors of the case to determine the offender's role and the extent to which the offending was **planned** and the **sophistication** with which it was carried out.

CULPABILITY demonstrated by one or more of the following:
A — High culpability
A leading role where offending is part of a group activity
Involvement of others through coercion, intimidation or exploitation
Breach of a high degree of trust or responsibility
Sophisticated nature of offence/significant planning
Theft involving intimidation or the use or threat of force
Deliberately targeting victim on basis of vulnerability
B — Medium culpability
A significant role where offending is part of a group activity
Some degree of planning involved
Breach of some degree of trust or responsibility
All other cases where characteristics for categories A or C are not present
C — Lesser culpability
Performed limited function under direction
Involved through coercion, intimidation or exploitation
Little or no planning
Limited awareness or understanding of offence

CULPABILITY demonstrated by one or more of the following:

Where there are characteristics present which fall under different levels of culpability, the court should balance these characteristics to reach a fair assessment of the offender's culpability.

HARM
Harm is assessed by reference to the **financial loss** that results from the theft **and any significant additional harm** suffered by the victim or others — examples of significant additional harm may include **but are not limited to:**

Items stolen were of substantial value to the loser — regardless of monetary worth
High level of inconvenience caused to the victim or others
Consequential financial harm to victim or others
Emotional distress
Fear/loss of confidence caused by the crime
Risk of or actual injury to persons or damage to property
Impact of theft on a business
Damage to heritage assets
Disruption caused to infrastructure

Intended loss should be used where actual loss has been prevented.

Category 1	Very high value goods stolen (above £100,000) **or** High value with significant additional harm to the victim or others
Category 2	High value goods stolen (£10,000 to £100,000) and no significant additional harm **or** Medium value with significant additional harm to the victim or others
Category 3	Medium value goods stolen (£500 to £10,000) **and** no significant additional harm **or** Low value with significant additional harm to the victim or others
Category 4	Low value goods stolen (up to £500) **and** Little or no significant additional harm to the victim or others

SG-450 STEP TWO **Starting point and category range**

Having determined the category at step one, the court should use the starting point to reach a sentence within the appropriate category range in the table below.

The starting point applies to all offenders irrespective of plea or previous convictions.

Harm	**Culpability**		
	A	B	C
Category 1 Adjustment should be made for any significant additional harm factors where very high value goods are stolen.	**Starting point** 3 years 6 months' custody	**Starting point** 2 years' custody	**Starting point** 1 year's custody
	Category range 2 years 6 months' — 6 years' custody	**Category range** 1 — 3 years - 6 months' custody	**Category range** 26 weeks' — 2 years' custody
Category 2	**Starting point** 2 years' custody	**Starting point** 1 year's custody	**Starting point** High level community order
	Category range 1 — 3 years 6 months' custody	**Category range** 26 weeks' — 2 years' custody	**Category range** Low level community order — 36 weeks' custody

Harm	Culpability		
Category 3	**Starting point** 1 year's custody	**Starting point** High level community order	**Starting point** Band C fine
	Category range 26 weeks' — 2 years' custody	**Category range** Low level community order — 36 weeks' custody	**Category range** Band B fine — Low level community order
Category 4	**Starting point** High level community order	**Starting point** Low level community order	**Starting point** Band B fine
	Category range Medium level community order — 36 weeks' custody	**Category range** Band C fine — Medium level community order	**Category range** Discharge — Band C fine

The table above refers to single offences. Where there are multiple offences, consecutive sentences may be appropriate: please refer to the *Offences Taken Into Consideration* and *Totality guideline* [see **SG-572** and **SG-578**].

Where multiple offences are committed in circumstances which justify consecutive sentences, and the total amount stolen is in excess of £1 million, then an aggregate sentence in excess of 7 years may be appropriate.

> Where the offender is dependent on or has a propensity to misuse drugs or alcohol and there is sufficient prospect of success, a community order with a drug rehabilitation requirement under section 209, or an alcohol treatment requirement under section 212 of the Criminal Justice Act 2003 may be a proper alternative to a short or moderate custodial sentence.
>
> Where the offender suffers from a medical condition that is susceptible to treatment but does not warrant detention under a hospital order, a community order with a mental health treatment requirement under section 207 of the Criminal Justice Act 2003 may be a proper alternative to a short or moderate custodial sentence.

The court should then consider further adjustment for any aggravating or mitigating factors. The following is a **non-exhaustive** list of additional factual elements providing the context of the offence and factors relating to the offender. Identify whether any combination of these, or other relevant factors, should result in an upward or downward adjustment from the sentence arrived at so far.

Factors increasing seriousness	Factors reducing seriousness or reflecting personal mitigation
Statutory aggravating factors: Previous convictions, having regard to a) the **nature** of the offence to which the conviction relates and its **relevance** to the current offence; and b) the **time** that has elapsed since the conviction Offence committed whilst on bail Offence motivated by, or demonstrating hostility based on any of the following characteristics or presumed characteristics of the victim: religion, race, disability, sexual orientation or transgender identity	No previous convictions **or** no relevant/ recent convictions Remorse, particularly where evidenced by voluntary reparation to the victim Good character and/or exemplary conduct Serious medical condition requiring urgent, intensive or long-term treatment Age and/or lack of maturity where it affects the responsibility of the offender

Other aggravating factors: Stealing goods to order Steps taken to prevent the victim reporting or obtaining assistance and/or from assisting or supporting the prosecution Offender motivated by intention to cause harm or out of revenge Offence committed over sustained period of time Attempts to conceal/dispose of evidence Failure to comply with current court orders Offence committed on licence Offences taken into consideration Blame wrongly placed on others Established evidence of community/wider impact (for issues other than prevalence) Prevalence — see below	Mental disorder or learning disability Sole or primary carer for dependent relatives Determination and/or demonstration of steps having been taken to address addiction or offending behaviour Inappropriate degree of trust or responsibility

Prevalence

There may be exceptional local circumstances that arise which may lead a court to decide that prevalence should influence sentencing levels. The pivotal issue in such cases will be the harm caused to the community.

It is essential that the court before taking account of prevalence:

- has supporting evidence from an external source, for example, Community Impact Statements, to justify claims that a particular crime is prevalent in their area, and is causing particular harm in that community, and
- is satisfied that there is a compelling need to treat the offence more seriously than elsewhere.

SG-451 **STEP THREE Consider any factors which indicate a reduction, such as assistance to the prosecution**

The court should take into account sections 73 and 74 of the Serious Organised Crime and Police Act 2005 (assistance by defendants: reduction or review of sentence) and any other rule of law by virtue of which an offender may receive a discounted sentence in consequence of assistance given (or offered) to the prosecutor or investigator.

STEP FOUR Reduction for guilty pleas

The court should take account of any potential reduction for a guilty plea in accordance with section 144 of the Criminal Justice Act 2003 and the Guilty Plea guideline [see **SG-1**].

STEP FIVE Totality principle

If sentencing an offender for more than one offence, or where the offender is already serving a sentence, consider whether the total sentence is just and proportionate to the overall offending behaviour in accordance with the *Offences Taken into Consideration* and *Totality* guideline [see **SG-572** and **SG-578**].

STEP SIX Confiscation, compensation and ancillary orders

The court must proceed with a view to making a confiscation order if it is asked to do so by the prosecutor or if the court believes it is appropriate for it to do so.

Where the offence has resulted in loss or damage the court must consider whether to make a compensation order.

If the court makes both a confiscation order and an order for compensation and the court believes the offender will not have sufficient means to satisfy both orders in full, the court must direct that the compensation be paid out of sums recovered under the confiscation order (section 13 of the Proceeds of Crime Act 2002).

The court may also consider whether to make ancillary orders. These may include a deprivation order, or a restitution order.

STEP SEVEN Reasons

Section 174 of the Criminal Justice Act 2003 imposes a duty to give reasons for, and explain the effect of, the sentence.

STEP EIGHT Consideration for time spent on bail

The court must consider whether to give credit for time spent on bail in accordance with section 240A of the Criminal Justice Act 2003.

Theft from a Shop or Stall SG-452

Theft Act 1968 (section 1)

Triable either way

Maximum: 7 years' custody

(except for an offence of low-value shoplifting which is treated as a summary only offence in accordance with section 22A of the Magistrates' Courts Act 1980 where the maximum is 6 months' custody).

Offence range: Discharge — 3 years' custody

STEP ONE Determining the offence category SG-453

The court should determine the offence category with reference **only** to the factors identified in the following tables. In order to determine the category the court should assess **culpability** and **harm**.

The level of culpability is determined by weighing up all the factors of the case to determine the offender's role and the extent to which the offending was **planned** and the **sophistication** with which it was carried out.

CULPABILITY demonstrated by one or more of the following:
A — High culpability
A leading role where offending is part of a group activity
Involvement of others through coercion, intimidation or exploitation
Sophisticated nature of offence/significant planning
Significant use or threat of force
Offender subject to a banning order from the relevant store
Child accompanying offender is actively used to **facilitate** the offence (not merely present when offence is committed)
B — Medium culpability
A significant role where offending is part of a group activity
Some degree of planning involved
Limited use or threat of force
All other cases where characteristics for categories A or C are not present
C — Lesser culpability
Performed limited function under direction
Involved through coercion, intimidation or exploitation
Little or no planning
Mental disorder/learning disability where linked to commission of the offence

Where there are characteristics present which fall under different levels of culpability, the court should balance these characteristics to reach a fair assessment of the offender's culpability.

HARM

Harm is assessed by reference to the **financial loss** that results from the theft **and any significant additional harm** suffered by the victim — examples of significant additional harm may include **but are not limited to:**

Emotional distress
Damage to property
Effect on business
A greater impact on the victim due to the size or type of their business
A particularly vulnerable victim

Intended loss should be used where actual loss has been prevented.

Category 1	High value goods stolen (above £1,000) **or** Medium value with significant additional harm to the victim
Category 2	Medium value goods stolen (£200 to £1,000) **and** no significant additional harm **or** Low value with significant additional harm to the victim
Category 3	Low value goods stolen (up to £200) **and** Little or no significant additional harm to the victim

SG-454 **STEP TWO Starting point and category range**

Having determined the category at step one, the court should use the starting point to reach a sentence within the appropriate category range in the table below.

The starting point applies to all offenders irrespective of plea or previous convictions.

Harm	**Culpability**		
	A	**B**	**C**
Category 1 Where the value greatly exceeds £1,000 it may be appropriate to move outside the identified range. Adjustment should be made for any significant additional harm where high value goods are stolen.	**Starting point** 26 weeks' custody	**Starting point** Medium level community order	**Starting point** Band C fine
	Category range 12 weeks' — 3 years' custody	**Category range** Low level community order — 26 weeks' custody	**Category range** Band B fine — Low level community order
Category 2	**Starting point** 12 weeks' custody	**Starting point** Low level community order	**Starting point** Band B fine
	Category range High level community order — 26 weeks' custody	**Category range** Band C fine — Medium level community order	**Category range** Band A fine — Band C fine
Category 3	**Starting point** High level community order	**Starting point** Band C fine	**Starting point** Band A fine
	Category range Low level community order — 12 weeks' custody	**Category range** Band B fine — Low level community order	**Category range** Discharge — Band B fine

Consecutive sentences for multiple offences may be appropriate — please refer to the *Offences Taken Into Consideration* and *Totality* guideline [see **SG-572** and **SG-578**].

Previous diversionary work with an offender does not preclude the court from considering this type of sentencing option again if appropriate.

Where the offender is dependent on or has a propensity to misuse drugs or alcohol and there is sufficient prospect of success, a community order with a drug rehabilitation requirement under section 209, or an alcohol treatment requirement under section 212 of the Criminal Justice Act 2003 may be a proper alternative to a short or moderate custodial sentence. Where the offender suffers from a medical condition that is susceptible to treatment but does not warrant detention under a hospital order, a community order with a mental health treatment requirement under section 207 of the Criminal Justice Act 2003 may be a proper alternative to a short or moderate custodial sentence.

The court should then consider further adjustment for any aggravating or mitigating factors. The following is a **non-exhaustive** list of additional factual elements providing the context of the offence and factors relating to the offender. Identify whether any combination of these, or other relevant factors, should result in an upward or downward adjustment from the sentence arrived at so far.

Factors increasing seriousness	**Factors reducing seriousness or reflecting personal mitigation**
Statutory aggravating factors: Previous convictions, having regard to a) the **nature** of the offence to which the conviction relates and its **relevance** to the current offence; and b) the time that has elapsed since the conviction Relevant recent convictions **may** justify an upward adjustment, including outside the category range. In cases involving significant persistent offending, the community and custodial thresholds may be crossed even though the offence otherwise warrants a lesser sentence. Any custodial sentence must be kept to the necessary minimum Offence committed whilst on bail Offence motivated by, or demonstrating hostility based on any of the following characteristics or presumed characteristics of the victim: religion, race, disability, sexual orientation or transgender identity *Other aggravating factors:* Stealing goods to order Steps taken to prevent the victim reporting or obtaining assistance and/or from assisting or supporting the prosecution Attempts to conceal/dispose of evidence Offender motivated by intention to cause harm or out of revenge Failure to comply with current court orders Offence committed on licence Offences taken into consideration Established evidence of community/wider impact (for issues other than prevalence) Prevalence — see below	No previous convictions **or** no relevant/recent convictions Remorse, particularly where evidenced by voluntary reparation to the victim Good character and/or exemplary conduct Serious medical condition requiring urgent, intensive or long-term treatment Age and/or lack of maturity where it affects the responsibility of the offender Mental disorder or learning disability (where not linked to the commission of the offence) Sole or primary carer for dependent relatives Determination and/or demonstration of steps having been taken to address addiction or offending behaviour Offender experiencing **exceptional** financial hardship

Prevalence
There may be exceptional local circumstances that arise which may lead a court to decide that prevalence should influence sentencing levels. The pivotal issue in such cases will be the harm caused to the community.
It is essential that the court before taking account of prevalence:
• has supporting evidence from an external source, for example, Community Impact Statements, to justify claims that a particular crime is prevalent in their area, and is causing particular harm in that community, and
• is satisfied that there is a compelling need to treat the offence more seriously than elsewhere.

SG-455 [Steps Three to Eight are identical to those applicable to General Theft: see **SG-451**.]

SG-456 HANDLING STOLEN GOODS

Theft Act 1968 (section 22)

Triable either way
Maximum: 14 years' custody
Offence range: Discharge — 8 years' custody

SG-457 STEP ONE **Determining the offence category**

The court should determine the offence category with reference **only** to the factors identified in the following tables. In order to determine the category the court should assess **culpability** and **harm.**

The level of culpability is determined by weighing up all the factors of the case to determine the offender's role and the extent to which the offending was **planned** and the **sophistication** with which it was carried out.

CULPABILITY demonstrated by one or more of the following:
A — High culpability
A leading role where offending is part of a group activity
Involvement of others through coercion, intimidation or exploitation
Abuse of position of power or trust or responsibility
Professional and sophisticated offence
Advance knowledge of the primary offence
Possession of very recently stolen goods from a domestic burglary or robbery
B — Medium culpability
A significant role where offending is part of a group activity
Offender acquires goods for resale
All other cases where characteristics for categories A or C are not present
C — Lesser culpability
Performed limited function under direction
Involved through coercion, intimidation or exploitation
Little or no planning
Limited awareness or understanding of offence
Goods acquired for offender's personal use

Where there are characteristics present which fall under different levels of culpability, the court should balance these characteristics to reach a fair assessment of the offender's culpability.

HARM

Harm is assessed by reference to the **financial value** (to the loser) of the handled goods **and any significant additional harm** associated with the underlying offence on the victim or others — examples of additional harm may include **but are not limited to:**

Property stolen from a domestic burglary or a robbery (unless this has already been taken into account in assessing culpability)
Items stolen were of substantial value to the loser, regardless of monetary worth
Metal theft causing disruption to infrastructure
Damage to heritage assets

Category 1	Very high value goods stolen (above £100,000) **or** High value with significant additional harm to the victim or others
Category 2	High value goods stolen (£10,000 to £100,000) and no significant additional harm **or** Medium value with significant additional harm to the victim or others
Category 3	Medium value goods stolen (£1,000 to £10,000) and no significant additional harm **or** Low value with significant additional harm to the victim or others
Category 4	Low value goods stolen (up to £1,000) **and** Little or no significant additional harm to the victim or others

STEP TWO Starting point and category range **SG-457A**

Having determined the category at step one, the court should use the starting point to reach a sentence within the appropriate category range in the table below.

The starting point applies to all offenders irrespective of plea or previous convictions.

Harm	**Culpability**		
	A	B	C
Category 1 Where the value greatly exceeds £100,000, it may be appropriate to move outside the identified range. Adjustment should be made for any significant additional harm where very high value stolen goods are handled	**Starting point** 5 years' custody	**Starting point** 3 years' custody	**Starting point** 1 year's custody
	Category range 3 — 8 years' custody	**Category range** 1 year 6 months' — 4 years' custody	**Category range** 26 weeks' — 1 year 6 months' custody
Category 2	**Starting point** 3 years' custody	**Starting point** 1 year's custody	**Starting point** High level community order
	Category range 1 year 6 months' — 4 years' custody	**Category range** 26 weeks' — 1 year 6 months' custody	**Category range** Low level community order — 26 weeks' custody
Category 3	**Starting point** 1 year's custody	**Starting point** High level community order	**Starting point** Band C fine
	Category range 26 weeks' — 2 years' custody	**Category range** Low level community order — 26 weeks' custody	**Category range** Band B fine — Low level community order
Category 4	**Starting point** High level community order	**Starting point** Low level community order	**Starting point** Band B fine
	Category range Medium level community order — 26 weeks' custody	**Category range** Band C fine — High level community order	**Category range** Discharge — Band C fine

Sentencing Guidelines

Consecutive sentences for multiple offences may be appropriate — please refer to the *Offences Taken Into Consideration* and *Totality* guideline [see **SG-572** and **SG-578**].

The court should then consider further adjustment for any aggravating or mitigating factors. The following is a **non-exhaustive** list of additional factual elements providing the context of the offence and factors relating to the offender. Identify whether any combination of these, or other relevant factors, should result in an upward or downward adjustment from the starting point.

Factors increasing seriousness	**Factors reducing seriousness or reflecting personal mitigation**
Statutory aggravating factors: Previous convictions, having regard to a) the **nature** of the offence to which the conviction relates and its **relevance** to the current offence; and b) the **time** that has elapsed since the conviction Offence committed whilst on bail *Other aggravating factors:* Seriousness of the underlying offence, for example, armed robbery Deliberate destruction, disposal or defacing of stolen property Damage to a third party Failure to comply with current court orders Offence committed on licence Offences taken into consideration Established evidence of community/wider impact	No previous convictions **or** no relevant/recent convictions Good character and/or exemplary conduct Serious medical condition requiring urgent, intensive or long-term treatment Age and/or lack of maturity where it affects the responsibility of the offender Mental disorder or learning disability Sole or primary carer for dependent relatives Determination and/or demonstration of steps having been taken to address addiction or offending behaviour

SG-457B [Steps Three to Eight are identical to those applicable to General Theft: see **SG-451**.]

SG-457C

Going Equipped for Theft or Burglary

Theft Act 1968 (section 25)

Triable either way
Maximum: 3 years' custody
Offence range: Discharge — 18 months' custody

SG-457D **STEP ONE Determining the offence category**

The court should determine the offence category with reference **only** to the factors identified in the following tables. In order to determine the category the court should assess **culpability** and **harm**.

The level of culpability is determined by weighing up all the factors of the case to determine the offender's role and the extent to which the offending was **planned** and the **sophistication** with which it was carried out.

CULPABILITY demonstrated by one or more of the following
A — High culpability
A leading role where offending is part of a group activity Involvement of others through coercion, intimidation or exploitation Significant steps taken to conceal identity and/or avoid detection Sophisticated nature of offence/significant planning Offender equipped for robbery or domestic burglary
B — Medium culpability
A significant role where offending is part of a group activity All other cases where characteristics for categories A or C are not present
C — Lesser culpability
Involved through coercion, intimidation or exploitation Limited awareness or understanding of offence Little or no planning

CULPABILITY demonstrated by one or more of the following:

Where there are characteristics present which fall under different levels of culpability, the court should balance these characteristics to reach a fair assessment of the offender's culpability.

HARM

This guideline refers to preparatory offences where no theft has been committed. The level of harm is determined by weighing up all the factors of the case to determine the harm that would be caused if the item(s) were used to commit a substantive offence.

Greater harm

Possession of item(s) which have the potential to facilitate an offence affecting a large number of victims Possession of item(s) which have the potential to facilitate an offence involving high value items

Lesser harm

All other cases

STEP TWO Starting point and category range **SG-457E**

Having determined the category at step one, the court should use the starting point to reach a sentence within the appropriate category range in the table below.

The starting point applies to all offenders irrespective of plea or previous convictions.

Harm	Culpability		
	A	B	C
Greater	**Starting point** 1 year's custody	**Starting point** 18 weeks' custody	**Starting point** Medium level community order
	Category range 26 weeks' — 1 year 6 months' custody	**Category range** High level community order — 36 weeks' custody	**Category range** Low level community order — High level community order
Lesser	**Starting point** 26 weeks' custody	**Starting point** High level community order	**Starting point** Band C fine
	Category range 12 weeks' — 36 weeks' custody	**Category range** Medium level community order — 12 weeks' custody	**Category range** Discharge — Medium level community order

Consecutive sentences for multiple offences may be appropriate — please refer to the *Offences Taken Into Consideration* and *Totality* guideline [see SG-572 and SG-578].

The court should then consider further adjustment for any aggravating or mitigating factors. The following is a **non-exhaustive** list of additional factual elements providing the context of the offence and factors relating to the offender. Identify whether any combination of these, or other relevant factors, should result in an upward or downward adjustment from the starting point.

Factors increasing seriousness	**Factors reducing seriousness or reflecting personal mitigation**
Statutory aggravating factors: Previous convictions, having regard to a) the **nature** of the offence to which the conviction relates and its **relevance** to the current offence; and b) the **time** that has elapsed since the conviction Offence committed whilst on bail *Other aggravating factors:* Attempts to conceal/dispose of evidence Established evidence of community/wider impact Failure to comply with current court orders Offence committed on licence Offences taken into consideration	No previous convictions **or** no relevant/recent convictions Good character and/or exemplary conduct Serious medical condition requiring urgent, intensive or long-term treatment Age and/or lack of maturity where it affects the responsibility of the offender Mental disorder or learning disability Sole or primary carer for dependent relatives Determination and/or demonstration of steps having been taken to address addiction or offending behaviour

SG-457F [Steps Three to Eight are identical to those applicable to General Theft: see **SG-451**.]

SG-457G

Abstracting Electricity

Theft Act 1968 (section 13)

Triable either way
Maximum: 5 years' custody
Offence range: Discharge — 1 year's custody

SG-457H **STEP ONE Determining the offence category**

The court should determine the offence category with reference **only** to the factors identified in the following tables. In order to determine the category the court should assess **culpability** and **harm.**

The level of culpability is determined by weighing up all the factors of the case to determine the offender's role and the extent to which the offending was **planned** and the **sophistication** with which it was carried out.

CULPABILITY demonstrated by one or more of the following:
A — High culpability
A leading role where offending is part of a group activity Involvement of others through coercion, intimidation or exploitation Sophisticated nature of offence/significant planning Abuse of position of power or trust or responsibility Commission of offence in association with or to further other criminal activity
B — Medium culpability
A significant role where offending is part of a group activity All other cases where characteristics for categories A or C are not present
C — Lesser culpability
Performed limited function under direction Involved through coercion, intimidation or exploitation Limited awareness or understanding of offence

CULPABILITY demonstrated by one or more of the following:

Where there are characteristics present which fall under different levels of culpability, the court should balance these characteristics to reach a fair assessment of the offender's culpability.

HARM

The level of harm is assessed by weighing up all the factors of the case to determine the level of harm caused.

Greater harm

A significant risk of, or actual injury to persons or damage to property Significant volume of electricity extracted as evidenced by length of time of offending and/or advanced type of illegal process used

Lesser harm

All other cases

STEP TWO Starting point and category range SG-457I

Having determined the category at step one, the court should use the starting point to reach a sentence within the appropriate category range in the table below.

The starting point applies to all offenders irrespective of plea or previous convictions.

Harm	Culpability		
	A	B	C
Greater	**Starting point** 12 weeks' custody	**Starting point** Medium level community order	**Starting point** Band C fine
	Category range High level community order — 1 year's custody	**Category range** Low level community order — 12 weeks' custody	**Category range** Band B fine — Low level community order
Lesser	**Starting point** High level community order	**Starting point** Low level community order	**Starting point** Band A fine
	Category range Medium level community order — 12 weeks' custody	**Category range** Band C fine — Medium level community order	**Category range** Discharge — Band C fine

The court should then consider further adjustment for any aggravating or mitigating factors. The table below contains a **non-exhaustive** list of additional factual elements providing the context of the offence and factors relating to the offender.

Identify whether any combination of these, or other relevant factors, should result in an upward or downward adjustment from the starting point.

Factors increasing seriousness	**Factors reducing seriousness or reflecting personal mitigation**
Statutory aggravating factors: Previous convictions, having regard to a) the **nature** of the offence to which the conviction relates and its **relevance** to the current offence; and b) the **time** that has elapsed since the conviction Offence committed whilst on bail *Other aggravating factors:* Electricity abstracted from another person's property Attempts to conceal/dispose of evidence Failure to comply with current court orders Offence committed on licence Offences taken into consideration Blame wrongly placed on others Established evidence of community/wider impact	No previous convictions **or** no relevant/recent convictions Good character and/or exemplary conduct Serious medical condition requiring urgent, intensive or long-term treatment Age and/or lack of maturity where it affects the responsibility of the offender Mental disorder or learning disability Sole or primary carer for dependent relatives Determination and/or demonstration of steps having been taken to address addiction or offending behaviour

SG-457J [Steps Three to Eight are identical to those applicable to General Theft: see **SG-451**.]

SG-457K

Making Off without Payment

Theft Act 1978 (section 3)

Triable either way
Maximum: 2 years' custody
Offence range: Discharge — 36 weeks' custody

SG-457L **STEP ONE Determining the offence category**

The court should determine the offence category with reference **only** to the factors identified in the following tables. In order to determine the category the court should assess **culpability** and **harm**.

The level of culpability is determined by weighing up all the factors of the case to determine the offender's role and the extent to which the offending was **planned** and the **sophistication** with which it was carried out.

CULPABILITY demonstrated by one or more of the following
A — High culpability
A leading role where offending is part of a group activity
Involvement of others through coercion, intimidation or exploitation
Sophisticated nature of offence/significant planning
Offence involving intimidation or the use or threat of force
Deliberately targeting victim on basis of vulnerability

B — Medium culpability
A significant role where offending is part of a group activity Some degree of planning involved
All other cases where characteristics for categories A or C are not present
C — Lesser culpability
Performed limited function under direction
Involved through coercion, intimidation or exploitation
Little or no planning Limited awareness or understanding of offence

Where there are characteristics present which fall under different levels of culpability, the court should balance these characteristics to reach a fair assessment of the offender's culpability.

HARM

Harm is assessed by reference to the **actual loss** that results from the offence **and any significant additional harm** suffered by the victim — examples of additional harm may include **but are not limited to:**

A high level of inconvenience caused to the victim
Emotional distress
Fear/loss of confidence caused by the crime
A greater impact on the victim due to the size or type of their business

Category 1	Goods or services obtained above £200 or Goods/services up to £200 with significant additional harm to the victim
Category 2	Goods or services obtained up to £200 and Little or no significant additional harm to the victim

Sentencing Guidelines

STEP TWO **Starting point and category range** **SG-457M**

Having determined the category at step one, the court should use the starting point to reach a sentence within the appropriate category range in the table below.

The starting point applies to all offenders irrespective of plea or previous convictions.

Harm	**Culpability**		
	A	**B**	**C**
Category 1 Where the value greatly exceeds £200, it may be appropriate to move outside the identified range. Adjustment should be made for any significant additional harm for offences above £200.	**Starting point** 12 weeks' custody	**Starting point** Low level community order	**Starting point** Band B fine
	Category range High level community order — 36 weeks' custody	**Category range** Band C fine — High level community order	**Category range** Band A fine — Low level community order
Category 2	**Starting point** Medium level community order	**Starting point** Band C fine	**Starting point** Band A fine
	Category range Low level community order — 12 weeks' custody	**Category range** Band B fine — Low level community order	**Category range** Discharge — Band B fine

Consecutive sentences for multiple offences may be appropriate — please refer to the *Offences Taken Into Consideration* and *Totality* guideline [see **SG-572** and **SG-578**].

The court should then consider further adjustment for any aggravating or mitigating factors. The following list is a **non-exhaustive** list of additional factual elements providing the context of the offence and factors relating to the offender.

Identify whether any combination of these, or other relevant factors, should result in an upward or downward adjustment from the starting point.

Factors increasing seriousness	**Factors reducing seriousness or reflecting personal mitigation**
Statutory aggravating factors: Previous convictions, having regard to a) the **nature** of the offence to which the conviction relates and its **relevance** to the current offence; and b) the **time** that has elapsed since the conviction Offence committed whilst on bail Offence motivated by, or demonstrating hostility based on any of the following characteristics or presumed characteristics of the victim: religion, race, disability, sexual orientation or transgender identity *Other aggravating factors:* Steps taken to prevent the victim reporting or obtaining assistance and/or from assisting or supporting the prosecution Attempts to conceal/dispose of evidence Failure to comply with current court orders Offence committed on licence Offences taken into consideration Established evidence of community/wider impact	No previous convictions **or** no relevant/recent convictions Remorse, particularly where evidenced by voluntary reparation to the victim Good character and/or exemplary conduct Serious medical condition requiring urgent, intensive or long-term treatment Age and/or lack of maturity where it affects the responsibility of the offender Mental disorder or learning disability Sole or primary carer for dependent relatives Determination and/or demonstration of steps having been taken to address addiction or offending behaviour

SG-457N [Steps Three to Eight are identical to those applicable to General Theft: see **SG-451**.]

SG-457O

Annex

[The tables set out here are also set out in the Magistrates' Court Sentencing Guidelines, which includes further guidance on fines and community orders: see **SG-358** and **SG-382**.]

PART 15 BREACH OF AN ANTI-SOCIAL BEHAVIOUR ORDER SG-458

...This guideline applies to the sentencing of offenders convicted of breaching an anti-social behaviour order (ASBO) who are sentenced on or after 5 January 2009.

The Council has previously set out the approach to dealing with breaches of orders in its guidelines on New Sentences: Criminal Justice Act 2003 and Breach of Protective Orders. The main aim of sentencing for breach of a court order is to achieve the purpose of the order; in the case of an ASBO that is to protect the public from behaviour that is likely to cause harassment, alarm or distress.

Any perception that the courts do not treat seriously a failure to comply with a court order can undermine public confidence and is therefore an important additional consideration.

Since the ability of a court to deal appropriately with an order that has been breached depends on how it was made, Annex A to the guideline summarises the key principles and considerations applicable to the making of an ASBO.

This guideline applies to the sentencing of adult and young offenders. It is recognised that a large proportion of orders are imposed on persons under 18 years of age. Although the sentencing framework for youths is very different from that for adults, and a guideline for sentencing young offenders will follow in due course, the Council considered that sentencers would find it helpful to have guiding principles for sentencing young offenders for breach of an ASBO...

A. Statutory provision SG-459

1. [Sets out the CDA 1998, s. 1(10).]
2. Where a person is convicted of an offence of breach of an anti-social behaviour order (ASBO), it is not open to the court to make an order discharging the offender conditionally.[260]

B. Introduction SG-460

3. An ASBO is a preventative order that can be made in either civil or criminal proceedings; its aim is to protect the public from behaviour that causes, or is likely to cause, harassment, alarm or distress. An order may be made on application to a magistrates' court, on conviction, or in conjunction with other proceedings in the County Court.
4. Since the ability of a court to deal appropriately with an order that has been breached depends on how it was made, Annex A summarises the key principles and considerations applicable to the making of an ASBO.
5. This guideline relates to the sentencing of both adult and young offenders. As the sentencing framework that applies to offenders aged under 18 is significantly different from that for older offenders, the guidance for young offenders is in the form of principles particularly regarding the circumstances in which a custodial sentence might be justified. The maximum penalty in the case of a young offender is detention for 24 months.
6. Breach of this type of order is different from breach of a community order or failure to surrender to custody because it has the potential to affect a community or the public at large in a way that causes direct harm.

The main aim of sentencing for breach of a court order is to achieve the purpose of the order. Therefore, the sentence for breach of an ASBO should primarily reflect the harassment, alarm or distress involved; the fact that it constituted breach of a court order is a secondary consideration.

C. Assessing seriousness SG-461

7. The sentence for breach of an ASBO must be commensurate with the seriousness of the offence; that is determined by assessing the culpability of the offender and any harm which the offence caused, was intended to cause or might foreseeably have caused.[261]
8. A community sentence can be imposed only if a court considers that the offence is serious enough to justify it,[262] and a custodial sentence can be imposed only if a court considers that a community sentence or a fine alone cannot be justified in view of the seriousness of the offence.[263] The Council has

[260] Crime and Disorder Act 1998, section 1(11)
[261] Criminal Justice Act 2003, section 143(1)
[262] Criminal Justice Act 2003, section 148(1)
[263] ibid, section 152(2)

published a definitive guideline on seriousness that guides sentencers through the process of determining whether the respective sentencing thresholds have been crossed.[264]

9. A wide range of prohibitions can be attached to an order; consequently the degree of harm resulting from a breach will vary greatly and may be experienced by the wider community as well as by individuals.
10. In order properly to assess the seriousness of a breach of an ASBO, a court needs to be aware of the purpose of the order and the context in which it was made. A breach may be of one or more prohibitions in an order; the approach to sentencing is based on an assessment of the seriousness of the harm arising from the breach (or intended by the offender) rather than the number of prohibitions not complied with.

(i) Culpability and harm

11. When a court is considering the seriousness of breach of an order such as an ASBO, it will need to consider two aspects of culpability:
    (a) **The degree to which the offender intended to breach the order.**
    Culpability is variable and an offender may have:
    - intended the breach;
    - been reckless as to whether the order was breached;
    - been aware of the risk of breach; or
    - been unaware of this risk due to an incomplete understanding of the terms of the order.

    (b) **The degree to which the offender intended to cause the harm that resulted (or could have resulted).**
    Culpability will be higher where the offender foresaw the harm likely to be caused by the breach and will be at its highest where such harm was intended.
12. There are also two dimensions to the harm involved in breach of an ASBO:
    (a) the breach may itself cause harassment, alarm or distress, which can reduce the quality of life in a community.
    (b) breach of an ASBO contravenes an order of the court, and this can undermine public confidence in the effective administration of justice.
13. The assessment of the seriousness of an individual offence must take into account not only the harm actually caused by an offence but also any harm that was intended or might foreseeably have been caused.[265]
14. The test of foreseeability is objective[266] but as the prohibitions imposed must have been considered by a court to be necessary to prevent anti-social behaviour, some degree of harm must always be foreseeable whenever an order is breached. Where a breach causes harm that was not readily foreseeable, the level of culpability should carry more weight than harm when assessing offence seriousness.[267]

(ii) Relevance of the originating conduct

15. The **original conduct** that led to the making of an order is a relevant consideration in so far as it indicates the level of harm caused and whether this was intended.[268]
16. High culpability and/or harm may be indicated if the breach continues a pattern of behaviour against an identifiable victim. Conversely, where there is little connection between the breach and the behaviour that the order was aimed at, this may indicate a less serious offence.
17. The court should examine the prohibitions of the order itself (particularly those in older orders which may have been made without the benefit of the guidance summarised in Annex A), their necessity and reasonableness in all the circumstances.[269]

[264] *Overarching Principles: Seriousness*, published 16 December 2004, www.sentencing-guidelines.gov.uk
[265] Criminal Justice Act 2003, section 143(1)
[266] Harm must have been foreseeable by 'a reasonable person'
[267] *Overarching Principles: Seriousness*, published 16 December 2004, www.sentencing-guidelines.gov.uk
[268] *Breach of a Protective Order*, published 7 December 2006, www.sentencing-guidelines.gov.uk
[269] Where appropriate, an application may be made separately for the order to be varied: Crime and Disorder Act 1998, sections 1(8) or 1CA. See also the Magistrates' Courts (Anti-Social Behaviour Orders) Rules 2002. Where the subject/offender is aged under 18, Practice Direction (Magistrates' Courts: Anti-Social Behaviour Orders: Composition of Benches) [2006] 1 AER 886 provides for the constitution of the court.

(iii) Breach of an interim order

18. Breach of an interim order or a final order is equally serious and the same approach to sentencing should be taken.
19. Sentence for a breach of an interim order should be imposed as soon as possible. If the hearing regarding the final order can be brought forward, this should be done so that the two issues can be considered together. However, sentencing for the breach of the interim order should not be delayed for this purpose.
20. Where an interim order is breached the court should consider the extent to which an urgent need for specific interim prohibitions was demonstrated, or if the interim order was sought principally to obtain additional time to prepare a case for the full hearing.[270]
21. Where an interim order has been made without notice to the subject, the order does not take effect until it has been served. If doubts arise about the extent to which the subject has understood the prohibitions but the defence of reasonable excuse is not made out, a lack of understanding of the terms of the order may still mitigate the seriousness of the offence through reducing culpability.

(iv) A breach that also constitutes another criminal offence

22. Whether one offence or two has been charged, the sentence should reflect all relevant aspects of the offence so that, provided the facts are not in issue, the result should be the same.[271]
    (a) if the substantive offence only has been charged, the fact that it constitutes breach of an ASBO should be treated as an aggravating factor;
    (b) if breach of the order only has been charged, the sentence should reflect the full circumstances of the breach, which will include the conduct that could have been charged as a substantive offence.
23. Where breach of an ASBO also constitutes another offence with a lower maximum penalty than that for breach of the order, this penalty is an element to be considered in the interests of proportionality, although the court is not limited by it when sentencing an adult or youth for breach.

(v) Aggravating and mitigating factors

24. The Council guideline *Overarching Principles: Seriousness* identifies a number of factors that might increase or mitigate the seriousness of an offence. For ease of reference, the factors are set out in Annex B.

(vi) Personal mitigation

25. Offender mitigation is particularly relevant to breach of an ASBO as compliance with the order depends on the ability to understand its terms and make rational decisions in relation to these. Sentence may be mitigated where:
    - the offender has a lower level of understanding due to mental health issues or learning difficulties;
    - the offender was acting under the influence of an older or more experienced offender; or
    - there has been compliance with an Individual Support Order or Intervention Order imposed when the ASBO was made.

D. Sentencing guideline—Adult offenders SG-462

Sentencing ranges and starting points

1. This guideline applies to a *'first time offender'* who has been **convicted after a trial**. In common with other proceedings based on breach of a court order,[272] it is likely that an offender in breach of an ASBO will have previous convictions. That has been taken into account in determining the starting points and ranges. Therefore, within this guideline, a 'first time offender' is a person who does not have a conviction for breach of an ASBO rather than the usual approach which is based on the existence of any conviction which, by virtue of section 143(2) of the Criminal Justice Act 2003, must be treated as an aggravating factor.

---

270 A report commissioned by the YJB concluded that there may be grounds for interim ASBOs only where there is an urgent need for specific prohibitions: Aikta-Reena Solanki, Tim Bateman, Gwyneth Boswell and Emily Hill, Anti-social Behaviour Orders, YJB (2006).

271 *Breach of a Protective Order*, published 7 December 2006, www.sentencing-guidelines.gov.uk

272 For example, failing to surrender to bail

2. As an aid to consistency of approach, the guideline describes a number of types of activity which would fall within the broad definition of the offence. These are set out in a column headed 'Nature of failure & harm'.
3. The expected approach is for a court to identify the description that most nearly matches the particular facts of the offence for which sentence is being imposed. This will identify a starting point from which the sentencer can depart to reflect aggravating or mitigating factors affecting the seriousness of the offence (beyond those contained within the column describing the nature of the failure or of the harm) to reach a **provisional sentence**.
4. The **sentencing range** is the bracket into which the provisional sentence will normally fall after having regard to factors which aggravate or mitigate the seriousness of the offence. The particular circumstances may, however, make it appropriate that the provisional sentence falls outside the range.
5. Where the offender has previous convictions which aggravate the seriousness of the current offence, that may take the provisional sentence beyond the range given particularly where there are significant other aggravating factors present.
6. Once the provisional sentence has been identified by reference to those factors affecting the seriousness of the offence, the court will take into account any relevant factors of personal mitigation, which may take the sentence beyond the range given.
7. Where there has been a guilty plea, any reduction attributable to that plea will be applied to the sentence at this stage. Again, this reduction may take the sentence below the range provided.
8. A court must give its reasons for imposing a sentence of a different kind or outside the range provided in the guidelines.[273]

The decision making process

[Sets out the standard sequential decision making process: identify starting point, consider aggravating factors, consider mitigating factors, apply reduction for guilty plea, consider ancillary orders, review in light of the totality principle and give reasons.]

Factors to take into consideration

1. The starting points and sentencing ranges are for a *'first time offender'* who pleaded not guilty. In this guideline, a *'first time offender'* is one who does not have a previous conviction for breach of an ASBO.
2. Where a court determines that there are other convictions which it is reasonable to treat as a factor aggravating the seriousness of the breach,[274] that factor will be taken into account at stage 2 of the sentencing process set out on page 7.
3. An ASBO may be breached in a wide range of circumstances and may involve one or more prohibitions not being complied with. The examples given below are intended to illustrate how the scale of the conduct that led to the breach, taken as a whole, might come within the three levels of seriousness:
   - Serious harm caused or intended—breach at this level of seriousness will involve the use of violence, significant threats or intimidation or the targeting of individuals or groups of people in a manner that leads to a fear of violence.
   - Lesser degree of harm intended or likely—examples may include lesser degrees of threats or intimidation, the use of seriously abusive language, or causing more than minor damage to property.
   - No harm caused or intended—in the absence of intimidation or the causing of fear of violence, breaches involving being drunk or begging may be at this level, as may prohibited use of public transport or entry into a prohibited area, where there is no evidence that harassment, alarm or distress was caused or intended.
4. The suggested starting points are based on the assumption that the offender had the highest level of culpability.
5. Aggravating and mitigating factors specifically relevant to sentencing for breach of an ASBO are included in the guideline. Care needs to be taken to ensure that there is no double counting where an element of the breach determines the level of seriousness where it might in other circumstances be an aggravating factor. When assessing the seriousness of an offence, the court must always refer to the full list of aggravating and mitigating factors in the Council guideline on Seriousness (see Annex B).[275]

---

273 Criminal Justice Act 2003, section 174(2)(a)
274 In accordance with Criminal Justice Act 2003, section 143(2)
275 *Overarching Principles: Seriousness*, published 16 December 2004, www.sentencing-guidelines.gov.uk

6. In the most serious cases, involving repeat offending and a breach causing serious harassment together with the presence of several aggravating factors, such as the use of violence, a sentence beyond the highest range will be justified.
7. Once the provisional sentence has been identified by reference to factors affecting the seriousness of the offence, the court will take into account any relevant factors of personal mitigation (see paragraph 25 above), and, in accordance with the Council guideline[276] consider reducing the sentence where a guilty plea was entered.
8. When imposing a community order, the court must ensure that the requirements imposed are proportionate to the seriousness of the breach, compatible with each other,[277] and also with the prohibitions of the ASBO if the latter is to remain in force. Even where the threshold for a custodial sentence is crossed, a custodial sentence is not inevitable.[278]
9. An offender may be sentenced for more than one offence of breach, which occurred on different days. While consecutive sentences may be imposed in such cases, the overall sentence should reflect the totality principle.

Breach of an Anti-Social Behaviour Order

Crime and Disorder Act 1998 (section 1(10))

Maximum Penalty: 5 years' imprisonment

Note: A conditional discharge is not available as a sentence for this offence

Nature of failure & harm	Starting point	Sentencing range
Serious harassment, alarm or distress has been caused or where such harm was intended	26 weeks' custody	Custody threshold–2 years' custody
Lesser degree of harassment, alarm or distress, where such harm was intended, or where it would have been likely if the offender had not been apprehended	6 weeks' custody	Community Order (MEDIUM)–26 weeks' custody
No harassment, alarm or distress was actually caused by the breach and none was intended by the offender	Community Order (LOW)	Fine Band B–Community Order (MEDIUM)

Aggravating factors	Mitigating factors
1. Offender has a history of disobedience to court orders. 2. Breach was committed immediately or shortly after the order was made. 3. Breach was committed subsequent to earlier breach proceedings arising from the same order. 4. Targeting of a person the order was made to protect or a witness in the original proceedings.	1. Breach occurred after a long period of compliance. 2. The prohibition(s) breached was not fully understood, especially where an interim order was made without notice.

E. Sentencing principles: Young Offenders SG-463

1. The approach to assessing the seriousness of a breach outlined above at paragraphs 7 to 25 applies equally to youths. A court must impose a community or custodial sentence only if such a sentence is warranted by the seriousness of the offence and no lesser sentence can be justified.
2. When sentencing a young offender, the normal approach is for the penalty to reflect both the reduction in culpability (for example, due to a lesser ability to foresee the consequences of actions) and the more onerous effects of punishments on education and personal development in comparison with an adult offender.
3. The sentencing framework that applies to offenders aged under 18 is significantly different from that for adult offenders and key principles are set out in Annex C. The maximum penalty for this offence when committed by a young offender is a 24 month detention and training order (DTO). With the

276 *Reduction in Sentence for a Guilty Plea*, published 20 July 2007, www.sentencing-guidelines.gov.uk
277 *New Sentences: Criminal Justice Act 2003*, published 16 December 2004, www.sentencing-guidelines.gov.uk
278 ibid

exception of a conditional discharge,[279] the full range of disposals of the youth court is available, and these are also outlined in Annex C.[280]

4. In most cases of breach by a young offender convicted after a trial, the appropriate sentence will be a community sentence.[281] Within the sentence(s) available, a range of requirements can be attached; the court will consider the seriousness of the breach, which requirement(s) will best prevent further offending and the individual circumstances of the offender.
5. The court must ensure that the requirements imposed are compatible both with each other and with the prohibitions of the ASBO if the latter is to remain in force, and that the combination of both is not so onerous as to make further breaches likely.
6. The particular stage of intellectual or emotional maturity of the individual (which may not correspond with actual age) will also influence sentence. A young offender is likely to perceive a particular time period as being longer in comparison with an adult, and this may be of relevance when considering how much time has elapsed between imposition and breach of the order.
7. The principles to be followed when sentencing a youth for breach of an ASBO are as follows:

'First time offender'[282] pleading guilty: the court[283] must make a referral order unless it imposes an absolute discharge, a custodial sentence or a hospital order;

In all other cases:

(i) in some less serious cases, such as where the breach has not involved any harassment, alarm or distress, a fine may be appropriate if it will be paid by the offender, or otherwise a reparation order;
(ii) in most cases, the appropriate sentence will be a community sentence;
(iii) the custody threshold should be set at a significantly higher level than the threshold applicable to adult offenders;
(iv) the custody threshold usually will not be crossed unless the breach involved serious harassment, alarm or distress through either the use of violence, threats or intimidation or the targeting of individuals/groups in a manner that led to a fear of violence;
(v) exceptionally, the custody threshold may also be crossed where a youth is being sentenced for more than one offence of breach (committed on separate occasions within a short period) involving a lesser but substantial degree of harassment, alarm or distress;
(vi) even where the custody threshold is crossed, the court should normally impose a community sentence in preference to a DTO, as custody should be used only as a measure of last resort; and
(vii) where the court considers a custodial sentence to be unavoidable, the starting point for sentencing should be 4 months detention, with a range of up to 12 months. Where a youth is being sentenced for more than one breach involving serious harassment, alarm or distress, sentence may go beyond that range.

Aggravating and mitigating factors

8. As with adult offenders, factors that are likely to aggravate an offence of breach of an anti-social behaviour order are:
   - history of disobedience of court orders;
   - the breach was committed immediately or shortly after the order was made;
   - the breach was committed subsequent to earlier breach proceedings arising from the same order;
   - targeting of a person the order was made to protect or of a witness in the original proceedings.
9. Factors that are likely to mitigate the seriousness of the breach are:
   - the breach occurred after a long period of compliance;
   - the prohibition(s) breached was not fully understood, especially where an interim order was made without notice.

Personal mitigation

10. Offender mitigation is particularly relevant to breach of an ASBO as compliance with the order depends on the ability to understand its terms and make rational decisions in relation to these. Sentence may be mitigated where:

[279] Crime and Disorder Act 1998, section 1(11) and section 1C(9)

[280] If the young offender has also been charged with a grave crime under section 91 Powers of Criminal Courts (Sentencing) Act 2000, the case may be committed to the Crown Court. Similarly, where the young offender is committed to the Crown Court for sentence under the dangerous offender provisions.

[281] Though see paragraph 7 below

[282] For the purpose of this requirement, a 'first time offender' is an offender who has never been convicted by or before a court in the United Kingdom of any offence other than the offence and any connected offence, or been bound over in criminal proceedings; Powers of Criminal Court (Sentencing) Act 2000, section 17(1)(b) and (c)

[283] A referral order may be made by a youth court or other magistrates' court; Powers of Criminal Courts (Sentencing) Act 2000, section 16(1)

- the offender has a lower level of understanding due to mental health issues or learning difficulties;
- the offender was acting under the influence of an older or more experienced offender; or
- there has been compliance with an Individual Support Order or Intervention Order imposed when the ASBO was made.

11. Other offender mitigating factors that may be particularly relevant to young offenders include peer pressure and a lack of parental support.

PART 16 ATTEMPTED MURDER SG-464

...This guideline applies to the sentencing of offenders convicted of any of the offences dealt with herein who are sentenced on or after 27 July 2009.

This guideline applies only to the sentencing of offenders aged 18 and older. The legislative provisions relating to the sentencing of youths are different; the younger the age, the greater the difference. A separate guideline setting out general principles relating to the sentencing of youths is planned.

...

Introduction SG-465

1. This guideline covers the single offence of attempted murder. The Council has published a separate definitive guideline for offences of assault which do not result in the death of the victim.[284]
2. There are critical differences between murder and attempted murder; not only is the intended result not achieved but also, for attempted murder, there must have been an intention to kill whereas a charge of murder may arise where the intention was to inflict grievous bodily harm. These differences are reflected in the approach set out below which supersedes previous guidance from the Court of Appeal in *Ford*[285] and other judgments.

A. Assessing seriousness SG-466

(i) Culpability and harm

3. The culpability of the offender is the initial factor in determining the seriousness of an offence. It is an essential element of the offence of attempted murder that the offender had an intention to kill; accordingly an offender convicted of this offence will have demonstrated a high level of culpability. Even so, the precise level of culpability will vary in line with the circumstances of the offence and whether the offence was planned or spontaneous. The use of a weapon may influence this assessment.
4. In common with all offences against the person, this offence has the potential to contain an imbalance between culpability and harm.[286]
5. Where the degree of harm actually caused to the victim of an attempted murder is negligible, it is inevitable that this will impact on the overall assessment of offence seriousness.
6. However, although the degree of (or lack of) physical or psychological harm suffered by a victim may generally influence sentence, the statutory definition of harm encompasses not only the harm actually caused by an offence but also any harm that the offence was intended to cause or might foreseeably have caused; since the offence can only be committed where there is an intention to kill, an offence of attempted murder will always involve, in principle, the most serious level of harm.

(ii) Aggravating and mitigating factors

7. The most serious offences of attempted murder will include those which encompass the factors set out in schedule 21 to the Criminal Justice Act 2003, paragraphs 4 and 5 that, had the offence been murder, would make the seriousness of the offence 'exceptionally high' or 'particularly high'. [See E3.2 in the main work.]
8. The particular facts of the offence will identify the appropriate level. In all cases, the aggravating and mitigating factors that will influence the identification of the provisional sentence within the range follow those set out in schedule 21 with suitable adjustments. These factors are included in the guideline [below].
9. The *Seriousness* guideline[287] sets out aggravating and mitigating factors that are applicable to a wide range of cases; [see **SG-21**]. Some are already reflected in the factors referred to above. Care needs to be taken to ensure that there is no double counting where an essential element of the offence charged

[284] *Assault and other offences against the person*, published 20 February 2008, www.sentencing-guidelines.gov.uk
[285] [2005] EWCA Crim 1358
[286] See *Overarching Principles: Seriousness*, para. 1.17, published 16 December 2004, www.sentencing-guidelines.gov.uk
[287] *Overarching Principles: Seriousness*, paras. 1.20–1.27 published on 16 December 2004; www.sentencing-guidelines.gov.uk

might, in other circumstances, be an aggravating factor. An additional statutory aggravating factor has been introduced by the Counter-Terrorism Act 2008 for prescribed offences which include attempted murder.[288]

10. This guideline is not intended to provide for an offence found to be based on a genuine belief that the murder would have been an act of mercy. Whilst the approach to assessing the seriousness of the offence may be similar, there are likely to be other factors present (relating to the offence and the offender) that would have to be taken into account and reflected in the sentence.

SG-467 **B. Ancillary orders**

Compensation orders

11. A court must consider making a compensation order in respect of any personal injury, loss or damage occasioned. There is no limit to the amount of compensation that may be awarded in the Crown Court.

SG-468 **C. Sentencing ranges and starting points**

12. Typically, a guideline will apply to an offence that can be committed in a variety of circumstances with different levels of seriousness. The starting points and ranges are based upon an adult '*first time offender*' who has been **convicted after a trial**. Within the guidelines, a '*first time offender*' is a person who does not have a conviction which, by virtue of section 143(2) of the Criminal Justice Act 2003, must be treated as an aggravating factor.
13. As an aid to consistency of approach, the guideline describes a number of levels or types of activity which would fall within the broad definition of the offence.
14. The expected approach is for a court to identify the description that most nearly matches the particular facts of the offence for which sentence is being imposed. This will identify a **starting point** from which the sentencer can depart to reflect aggravating or mitigating factors affecting the seriousness of the offence (beyond those contained within the column describing the nature of the offence) to reach a **provisional sentence**.
15. The **sentencing range** is the bracket into which the provisional sentence will normally fall after having regard to factors which aggravate or mitigate the seriousness of the offence. The particular circumstances may, however, make it appropriate that the provisional sentence falls outside the range.
16. Where the offender has previous convictions which aggravate the seriousness of the current offence, that may take the provisional sentence beyond the range given particularly where there are significant other aggravating factors present.
17. Once the provisional sentence has been identified by reference to those factors affecting the seriousness of the offence, the court will take into account any relevant factors of personal mitigation, which may take the sentence below the range given.
18. Where there has been a guilty plea, any reduction attributable to that plea will be applied to the sentence at this stage. This reduction may take the sentence below the range provided.
19. A court must give its reasons for imposing a sentence of a different kind or outside the range provided in the guidelines.

SG-469 **D. Factors to take into consideration**

1. Attempted murder is a serious offence for the purposes of the provisions in the Criminal Justice Act 2003[289] for dealing with dangerous offenders. When sentencing an offender convicted of this offence, in many circumstances a court may need to consider imposing a discretionary life sentence or one of the sentences for public protection prescribed in the Act.
2. The starting points and ranges are based upon a first time adult offender convicted after a trial (see paragraphs 12–19 above). They will be relevant when imposing a determinate sentence and when fixing any minimum term that may be necessary. When setting the minimum term to be served within an indeterminate sentence, in accordance with normal practice that term will usually be half the equivalent determinate sentence.[290]
3. Attempted murder requires an intention to kill. Accordingly, an offender convicted of this offence will have demonstrated a high level of culpability. Even so, the precise level of culpability will vary in line with the circumstances of the offence and whether the offence was planned or spontaneous. The use of a weapon may influence this assessment.

---

[288] Section 30 and schedule 2. If a court determines that the offence has a terrorist connection, it must treat that as an aggravating factor, and state in open court that the offence was so aggravated.

[289] Sections 224–230 as amended

[290] *R v Szczerba* [2002] 2 Cr App R (S) 86

4. The level of injury or harm sustained by the victim as well as any harm that the offence was intended to cause or might foreseeably have caused, must be taken into account and reflected in the sentence imposed.
5. The degree of harm will vary greatly. Where there is low harm and high culpability, culpability is more significant.[291] Even in cases where a low level of injury (or no injury) has been caused, an offence of attempted murder will be extremely serious.
6. The most serious offences will include those which encompass the factors set out in schedule 21 to the Criminal Justice Act 2003, paragraphs 4 and 5 that, had the offence been murder, would make the seriousness of the offence 'exceptionally high' or 'particularly high': see [E3.2 in the main work].
7. The particular facts of the offence will identify the appropriate level. In all cases, the aggravating and mitigating factors that will influence the identification of the provisional sentence within the range follow those set out in schedule 21 with suitable adjustments. This guideline is not intended to provide for an offence found to be based on a genuine belief that the murder would have been an act of mercy.
8. When assessing the seriousness of an offence, the court should also refer to the list of general aggravating and mitigating factors in the Council guideline on *Seriousness* (see [SG-21]). Care should be taken to ensure there is no double counting where an essential element of the offence charged might, in other circumstances, be an aggravating factor.

ATTEMPTED MURDER SG-470

Criminal Attempts Act 1981 (section 1(1))

THIS IS A SERIOUS OFFENCE FOR THE PURPOSES OF SECTION 224 CRIMINAL JUSTICE ACT 2003

Maximum penalty: Life imprisonment

Nature of offence	Starting point	Sentencing range
Level 1 *The most serious offences including those which (if the charge had been murder) would come within para. 4 or para. 5 of schedule 21 to the Criminal Justice Act 2003*		
• Serious and long term physical or psychological harm	30 years' custody	27–35 years' custody
• Some physical or psychological harm	20 years' custody	17–25 years' custody
• Little or no physical or psychological harm	15 years' custody	12–20 years' custody
Level 2 *Other planned attempt to kill*		
• Serious and long term physical or psychological harm	20 years' custody	17–25 years' custody
• Some physical or psychological harm	15 years' custody	12–20 years' custody
• Little or no physical or psychological harm	10 years' custody	7–15 years' custody
Level 3 *Other spontaneous attempt to kill*		
• Serious and long term physical or psychological harm	15 years' custody	12–20 years' custody
• Some physical or psychological harm	12 years' custody	9–17 years' custody
• Little or no physical or psychological harm	9 years' custody	6–14 years' custody

Specific aggravating factors	Specific mitigating factors
(a) the fact that the victim was particularly vulnerable, for example, because of age or disability (b) mental or physical suffering inflicted on the victim (c) the abuse of a position of trust (d) the use of duress or threats against another person to facilitate the commission of the offence (e) the fact that the victim was providing a public service or performing a public duty	(a) the fact that the offender suffered from any mental disorder or mental disability which lowered his degree of culpability (b) the fact that the offender was provoked (for example, by prolonged stress) (c) the fact that the offender acted to any extent in self-defence (d) the age of the offender

[291] *Overarching Principles: Seriousness*, para. 1.19, published on 16 December 2004; www.sentencing.guidelines.gov.uk

The presence of one or more aggravating features will indicate a more severe sentence within the suggested range and, if the aggravating feature(s) are exceptionally serious, the case will move up to the next level.

SG-471 [Annex A is an extract from the CJA 2003, sch. 21. It is not reproduced here. For the relevant text, see E3.4 in the main work.

Annex B reproduces the elements indicating higher culpability, a more than usually serious degree of harm and lower culpability and factors which may be relevant personal mitigation from the Council guideline *Overarching Principles: Seriousness*. See SG-21 for the full guideline.]

PART 17 FRAUD, BRIBERY, AND MONEY LAUNDERING OFFENCES

SG-472

Definitive Guideline

Effective from 1 October 2014

SG-473 **Applicability of Guideline**

[Omitted: See SG-539]

SG-474 **Structure, ranges and starting points**

[Omitted: See SG-540]

SG-475

Fraud

Fraud by false representation, fraud by failing to disclose information, fraud by abuse of position
Fraud Act 2006 (section 1)
Triable either way

Conspiracy to defraud
Common law
Triable on indictment only

Maximum: 10 years' custody
Offence range: Discharge — 8 years' custody

False accounting
Theft Act 1968 (section 17)
Triable either way

Maximum: 7 years' custody
Offence range: Discharge — 6 years and 6 months' custody

SG-476 STEP ONE **Determining the offence category**

The court should determine the offence category with reference to the tables below. In order to determine the category the court should assess **culpability** and **harm**.

The level of **culpability** is determined by weighing up all the factors of the case to determine the offender's role and the extent to which the offending was planned and the sophistication with which it was carried out.

Culpability demonstrated by one or more of the following:
A — High culpability
A leading role where offending is part of a group activity Involvement of others through pressure, influence Abuse of position of power or trust or responsibility Sophisticated nature of offence/significant planning Fraudulent activity conducted over sustained period of time Large number of victims Deliberately targeting victim on basis of vulnerability
B — Medium culpability
Other cases where characteristics for categories A or C are not present A significant role where offending is part of a group activity
C — Lesser culpability
Involved through coercion, intimidation or exploitation Not motivated by personal gain Peripheral role in organised fraud Opportunistic 'one-off' offence; very little or no planning Limited awareness or understanding of the extent of fraudulent activity

Where there are characteristics present which fall under different levels of culpability, the court should balance these characteristics to reach a fair assessment of the offender's culpability.

Harm is initially assessed by the actual, intended or risked loss as may arise from the offence.

The values in the table below are to be used for **actual** or **intended** loss only.

Intended loss relates to offences where circumstances prevent the actual loss that is intended to be caused by the fraudulent activity.

Risk of loss (for instance in mortgage frauds) involves consideration of both the likelihood of harm occurring and the extent of it if it does. Risk of loss is less serious than actual or intended loss. Where the offence has caused risk of loss but no (or much less) actual loss the normal approach is to move down to the corresponding point in the next category. This may not be appropriate if either the likelihood or extent of risked loss is particularly high.

Harm A — Loss caused or intended		
Category 1	£500,000 or more	Starting point based on £1 million
Category 2	£100,000–£500,000 **or** Risk of category 1 harm	Starting point based on £300,000
Category 3	£20,000–£100,000 **or** Risk of category 2 harm	Starting point based on £50,000
Category 4	£5,000–£20,000 **or** Risk of category 3 harm	Starting point based on £12,500
Category 5	Less than £5,000 **or** Risk of category 4 harm	Starting point based on £2,500
Risk of category 5 harm, move down the range within the category		

Harm B — Victim impact demonstrated by one or more of the following:
The court should then take into account the level of harm caused to the victim(s) or others to determine whether it warrants the sentence being moved up to the corresponding point in the next category or further up the range of the initial category.
High impact — move up a category; if in category 1 move up the range
Serious detrimental effect on the victim whether financial or otherwise, for example substantial damage to credit rating
Victim particularly vulnerable (due to factors including but not limited to their age, financial circumstances, mental capacity)
Medium impact — move upwards within the category range
Considerable detrimental effect on the victim whether financial or otherwise
Lesser impact — no adjustment
Some detrimental impact on victim, whether financial or otherwise

SG-477 **STEP TWO Starting point and category range**

Having determined the category at step one, the court should use the appropriate starting point (as adjusted in accordance with step one above) to reach a sentence within the category range in the table below. The starting point applies to all offenders irrespective of plea or previous convictions.

Where the value is larger or smaller than the amount on which the starting point is based, this should lead to upward or downward adjustment as appropriate.

Where the value greatly exceeds the amount of the starting point in category 1, it may be appropriate to move outside the identified range.

TABLE 1 Section 1 Fraud Act 2006 conspiracy to defraud

Maximum: 10 years' custody

	Culpability		
Harm	**A**	**B**	**C**
Category 1 £500,000 or more Starting point based on £1 million	**Starting point** 7 years' custody **Category range** 5–8 years' custody	**Starting point** 5 years' custody **Category range** 3–6 years' custody	**Starting point** 3 years' custody **Category range** 18 months'–4 years' custody
Category 2 £100,000–£500,000 Starting point based on £300,000	**Starting point** 5 years' custody **Category range** 3–6 years' custody	**Starting point** 3 years' custody **Category range** 18 months'–4 years' custody	**Starting point** 18 months' custody **Category range** 26 weeks'–3 years' custody
Category 3 £20,000–£100,000 Starting point based on £50,000	**Starting point** 3 years' custody **Category range** 18 months'–4 years' custody	**Starting point** 18 months' custody **Category range** 26 weeks'–3 years' custody	**Starting point** 26 weeks' custody **Category range** Medium level community order–1 year's custody
Category 4 £5,000–£20,000 Starting point based on £12,500	**Starting point** 18 months' custody **Category range** 26 weeks'–3 years' custody	**Starting point** 26 weeks' custody **Category range** Medium level community order –1 year's custody	**Starting point** Medium level community order **Category range** Band B fine–High level community order
Category 5 Less than £5,000 Starting point based on £2,500	**Starting point** 36 weeks' custody **Category range** High level community order–1 year's custody	**Starting point** Medium level community order **Category range** Band B fine–26 weeks' custody	**Starting point** Band B fine **Category range** Discharge–Medium level community order

TABLE 2 Section 17 Theft Act 1968: false accounting

Maximum: 7 years' custody

	Culpability		
Harm	**A**	**B**	**C**
Category 1 £500,000 or more Starting point based on £1 million	**Starting point** 5 years 6 months' custody **Category range** 4 years'–6 years 6 months' custody	**Starting point** 4 years' custody **Category range** 2 years 6 months'–5 years' custody	**Starting point** 2 years 6 months' custody **Category range** 15 months'–3 years 6 months' custody
Category 2 £100,000–£500,000 Starting point based on £300,000	**Starting point** 4 years' custody **Category range** 2 years 6 months'–5 years' custody	**Starting point** 2 years 6 months' custody **Category range** 15 months'–3 years 6 months' custody	**Starting point** 15 months' custody **Category range** 26 weeks'–2 years 6 months' custody
Category 3 £20,000–£100,000 Starting point based on £50,000	**Starting point** 2 years 6 months' custody **Category range** 15 months'–3 years 6 months' custody	**Starting point** 15 months' custody **Category range** High level community order–2 years 6 months' custody	**Starting point** High level community order **Category range** Low level community order–36 weeks' custody
Category 4 £5,000–£20,000 Starting point based on £12,500	**Starting point** 15 months' custody **Category range** High level community order–2 years 6 months' custody	**Starting point** High level community order **Category range** Low level community order–36 weeks' custody	**Starting point** Low level community order **Category range** Band B fine–Medium level community order
Category 5 Less than £5,000 Starting point based on £2,500	**Starting point** 26 weeks' custody **Category range** Medium level community order–36 weeks' custody	**Starting point** Low level community order **Category range** Band B fine–Medium level community order	**Starting point** Band B fine **Category range** Discharge–Low level community order

The table below contains a non-exhaustive list of additional factual elements providing the context of the offence and factors relating to the offender.

Identify whether any combination of these or other relevant factors should result in an upward or downward adjustment from the sentence arrived at so far.

Consecutive sentences for multiple offences may be appropriate where large sums are involved.

Factors increasing seriousness	**Factors reducing seriousness or reflecting personal mitigation**
Statutory aggravating factors: Previous convictions, having regard to a) the nature of the offence to which the conviction relates and its relevance to the current offence; and b) the time that has elapsed since the conviction Offence committed whilst on bail *Other aggravating factors:* Steps taken to prevent the victim reporting or obtaining assistance and/or from assisting or supporting the prosecution	No previous convictions or no relevant/recent convictions Remorse Good character and/or exemplary conduct Little or no prospect of success Serious medical conditions requiring urgent, intensive or long-term treatment Age and/or lack of maturity where it affects the responsibility of the offender

Attempts to conceal/dispose of evidence Established evidence of community/wider impact Failure to comply with current court orders Offence committed on licence Offences taken into consideration Failure to respond to warnings about behaviour Offences committed across borders Blame wrongly placed on others	Lapse of time since apprehension where this does not arise from the conduct of the offender Mental disorder or learning disability Sole or primary carer for dependent relatives Offender co-operated with investigation, made early admissions and/or voluntarily reported offending Determination and/or demonstration of steps having been taken to address addiction or offending behaviour Activity originally legitimate

SG-478 STEP THREE **Consider any factors which indicate a reduction, such as assistance to the prosecution**

The court should take into account sections 73 and 74 of the Serious Organised Crime and Police Act 2005 (assistance by defendants: reduction or review of sentence) and any other rule of law by virtue of which an offender may receive a discounted sentence in consequence of assistance given (or offered) to the prosecutor or investigator.

SG-479 STEP FOUR **Reduction for guilty pleas**

The court should take account of any potential reduction for a guilty plea in accordance with section 144 of the Criminal Justice Act 2003 and the *Guilty Plea* guideline.

SG-480 STEP FIVE **Totality principle**

If sentencing an offender for more than one offence, or where the offender is already serving a sentence, consider whether the total sentence is just and proportionate to the overall offending behaviour.

SG-481 STEP SIX **Confiscation, compensation and ancillary orders**

The court must proceed with a view to making a confiscation order if it is asked to do so by the prosecutor or if the court believes it is appropriate for it to do so.

Where the offence has resulted in loss or damage the court must consider whether to make a compensation order.

If the court makes both a confiscation order and an order for compensation and the court believes the offender will not have sufficient means to satisfy both orders in full, the court must direct that the compensation be paid out of sums recovered under the confiscation order (section 13 of the Proceeds of Crime Act 2002).

The court may also consider whether to make ancillary orders. These may include a deprivation order, a financial reporting order, a serious crime prevention order and disqualification from acting as a company director.

SG-482 STEP SEVEN **Reasons**

Section 174 of the Criminal Justice Act 2003 imposes a duty to give reasons for, and explain the effect of, the sentence.

SG-483 STEP EIGHT **Consideration for time spent on bail**

The court must consider whether to give credit for time spent on bail in accordance with section 240A of the Criminal Justice Act 2003.

Possessing, Making or Supplying Articles for Use in Fraud SG-484

Possession of articles for use in frauds
Fraud Act 2006 (section 6)
Triable either way
Maximum: 5 years' custody
Offence range: Band A fine — 3 years' custody

Making or supplying articles for use in frauds
Fraud Act 2006 (section 7)
Triable either way
Maximum: 10 years' custody
Offence range: Band C fine — 7 years' custody

STEP ONE Determining the offence category SG-485

The court should determine the offence category with reference to the tables below. In order to determine the category the court should assess **culpability** and **harm**.

The level of **culpability** is determined by weighing up all the factors of the case to determine the offender's role and the extent to which the offending was planned and the sophistication with which it was carried out.

Culpability demonstrated by one or more of the following:
A — High culpability
A leading role where offending is part of a group activity
Involvement of others through pressure, influence
Abuse of position of power or trust or responsibility
Sophisticated nature of offence/significant planning
Fraudulent activity conducted over sustained period of time
Articles deliberately designed to target victims on basis of vulnerability
B — Medium culpability
Other cases where characteristics for categories A or C are not present
A significant role where offending is part of a group activity
C — Lesser culpability
Performed limited function under direction
Involved through coercion, intimidation or exploitation
Not motivated by personal gain
Opportunistic 'one-off' offence; very little or no planning
Limited awareness or understanding of extent of fraudulent activity

Where there are characteristics present which fall under different levels of culpability, the court should balance these characteristics to reach a fair assessment of the offender's culpability.

Harm
This guideline refers to preparatory offences where no substantive fraud has been committed. The level of harm is determined by weighing up all the factors of the case to determine the harm that would be caused if the article(s) were used to commit a substantive offence.
Greater harm
Large number of articles created/supplied/in possession Article(s) have potential to facilitate fraudulent acts affecting large number of victims Article(s) have potential to facilitate fraudulent acts involving significant sums Use of third party identities Offender making considerable gain as result of the offence
Lesser harm
All other offences

SG-486 **STEP TWO Starting point and category range**
Having determined the category at step one, the court should use the appropriate starting point to reach a sentence within the category range in the table below. The starting point applies to all offenders irrespective of plea or previous convictions.

Section 6 Fraud Act 2006: Possessing articles for use in fraud

Maximum: 5 years' custody

	Culpability		
Harm	**A**	**B**	**C**
Greater	**Starting point** 18 months' custody	**Starting point** 36 weeks' custody	**Starting point** High level community order
	Category range 36 weeks' custody–3 years' custody	**Category range** High level community order–2 years' custody	**Category range** Medium level community order–26 weeks' custody
Lesser	**Starting point** 26 weeks' custody	**Starting point** Medium level community order	**Starting point** Band B fine
	Category range High level community order–18 months' custody	**Category range** Low level community order–26 weeks' custody	**Category range** Band A fine–Medium level community order

Section 7 Fraud Act 2006: Making or adapting or supplying articles for use in fraud

Maximum: 10 years' custody

	Culpability		
Harm	**A**	**B**	**C**
Greater	**Starting point** 4 years 6 months' custody	**Starting point** 2 years 6 months' custody	**Starting point** 1 year's custody
	Category range 3–7 years' custody	**Category range** 18 months'–5 years' custody	**Category range** High level community order–3 years' custody
Lesser	**Starting point** 2 years' custody	**Starting point** 36 weeks' custody	**Starting point** Medium level community order
	Category range 26 weeks'–4 years' custody	**Category range** Low level community order–2 years' custody	**Category range** Band C fine–26 weeks' custody

The table below contains a non-exhaustive list of additional factual elements providing the context of the offence and factors relating to the offender.

Identify whether any combination of these or other relevant factors should result in an upward or downward adjustment from the starting point

Consecutive sentences for multiple offences may be appropriate where large sums are involved.

Factors increasing seriousness	**Factors reducing seriousness or reflecting personal mitigation**
Statutory aggravating factors: Previous convictions, having regard to a) the nature of the offence to which the conviction relates and its relevance to the current offence; and b) the time that has elapsed since the conviction Offence committed whilst on bail *Other aggravating factors:* Steps taken to prevent the victim reporting or obtaining assistance and/or from assisting or supporting the prosecution Attempts to conceal/dispose of evidence Established evidence of community/wider impact Failure to comply with current court orders Offence committed on licence Offences taken into consideration Failure to respond to warnings about behaviour Offences committed across borders Blame wrongly placed on others	No previous convictions **or** no relevant/recent convictions Remorse Good character and/or exemplary conduct Little or no prospect of success Serious medical conditions requiring urgent, intensive or long-term treatment Age and/or lack of maturity where it affects the responsibility of the offender Lapse of time since apprehension where this does not arise from the conduct of the offender Mental disorder or learning disability Sole or primary carer for dependent relatives Offender co-operated with investigation, made early admissions and/or voluntarily reported offending Determination and/or demonstration of steps having been taken to address addiction or offending behaviour Activity originally legitimate

STEPS THREE to EIGHT **SG-487**

[These are identical to those set out at SG-479 *et seq.*]

Revenue Fraud **SG-488**

Fraud

Conspiracy to defraud (common law)
Triable on indictment only
Fraud Act 2006 (section 1)
Triable either way

Maximum: 10 years' custody
Offence range: Low level community order — 8 years' custody

False accounting

Theft Act 1968 (section 17)

Fraudulent evasion of VAT; False statement for VAT purposes; Conduct amounting to an offence

Value Added Tax Act 1994 (section 72)

Fraudulent evasion of income tax

Taxes Management Act 1970 (section 106A)

Fraudulent evasion of excise duty; Improper importation of goods

Customs and Excise Management Act 1979 (sections 50, 170 and 170B)

Triable either way
Maximum: 7 years' custody
Offence range: Band C fine — 6 years and 6 months' custody

Fraud

Cheat the public revenue (common law)
Triable on indictment only
Maximum: Life imprisonment
Offence range: 3 — 17 years' custody

SG-489 STEP ONE Determining the offence category

The court should determine the offence category with reference to the tables below. In order to determine the category the court should assess **culpability** and **harm.**

The level of **culpability** is determined by weighing up all the factors of the case to determine the offender's role and the extent to which the offending was planned and the sophistication with which it was carried out.	Harm — Gain/intended gain to offender or loss/ intended loss to HMRC
Culpability demonstrated by one or more of the following:	**Category 1** £50 million or more Starting point based on £80 million
A — **High culpability**	**Category 2** £10 million–£50 million Starting point based on £30 million
A leading role where offending is part of a group activity	**Category 3** £2 million–£10 million Starting point based on £5 million
Involvement of others through pressure/influence	**Category 4** £500,000–£2 million Starting point based on £1 million
Abuse of position of power or trust or responsibility	**Category 5** £100,000–£500,000 Starting point based on £300,000
Sophisticated nature of offence/significant planning	**Category 6** £20,000–£100,000 Starting point based on £50,000
Fraudulent activity conducted over sustained period of time	**Category 7** Less than £20,000 Starting point based on £12,500
B — Medium culpability	
Other cases where characteristics for categories A or C are not present	
A significant role where offending is part of a group activity	
C — Lesser culpability	
Involved through coercion, intimidation or exploitation	
Not motivated by personal gain	
Opportunistic 'one-off' offence; very little or no planning	
Performed limited function under direction	
Limited awareness or understanding of extent of fraudulent activity	

Where there are characteristics present which fall under different levels of culpability, the court should balance these characteristics to reach a fair assessment of the offender's culpability

STEP TWO **Starting point and category range** SG-490

Having determined the category at step one, the court should use the appropriate starting point to reach a sentence within the category range in the table below. The starting point applies to all offenders irrespective of plea or previous convictions.

Where the value is larger or smaller than the amount on which the starting point is based, this should lead to upward or downward adjustment as appropriate.

Where the value greatly exceeds the amount of the starting point in category 1, it may be appropriate to move outside the identified range.

TABLE 1 Section 1 Fraud Act 2006: Conspiracy to defraud (common law)

Maximum: 10 years' custody

For offences where the value of the fraud is over £2 million refer to the corresponding category in Table 3 subject to the maximum sentence of 10 years for this offence.

	Culpability		
Harm	**A**	**B**	**C**
Category 4 £500,000–£2 million Starting point based on £1 million	**Starting point** 7 years' custody **Category range** 5–8 years' custody	**Starting point** 5 years' custody **Category range** 3–6 years' custody	**Starting point** 3 years' custody **Category range** 18 months'–4 years' custody
Category 5 £100,000–£500,000 Starting point based on £300,000	**Starting point** 5 years' custody **Category range** 3–6 years' custody	**Starting point** 3 years' custody **Category range** 18 months'–4 years' custody	**Starting point** 18 months' custody **Category range** 26 weeks'–3 years' custody
Category 6 £20,000–£100,000 Starting point based on £50,000	**Starting point** 3 years' custody **Category range** 18 months'–4 years' custody	**Starting point** 18 months' custody **Category range** 26 weeks'–3 years' custody	**Starting point** 26 weeks' custody **Category range** Medium level community order–1 year's custody
Category 7 Less than £20,000 Starting point based on £12,500	**Starting point** 18 months' custody **Category range** 36 weeks'–3 years' custody	**Starting point** 36 weeks' custody **Category range** Medium level community order–18 months' custody	**Starting point** Medium level community order **Category range** Low level community order– High level community order

TABLE 2 Section 17 Theft Act 1968: False Accounting

Section 72(1) Value Added Tax Act 1994: Fraudulent evasion of VAT

Section 72(3) Valued Added Tax Act 1994: False statement for VAT purposes

Section 72(8) Value Added Tax Act 1994: Conduct amounting to an offence

Section 106(a) Taxes Management Act 1970: Fraudulent evasion of income tax

Section 170(1)(a)(i), (ii), (b), 170(2)(a), 170B Customs and Excise Management Act 1979: Fraudulent evasion of excise duty

Section 50(1)(a), (2) Customs and Excise Management Act 1979: Improper importation of goods

Maximum: 7 years' custody

	Culpability		
Harm	**A**	**B**	**C**
Category 4 £500,000–£2 million	**Starting point** 5 years 6 months' custody	**Starting point** 4 years' custody	**Starting point** 2 years 6 months' custody
Starting point based on £1 million	**Category range** 4 years'–6 years 6 months' custody	**Category range** 2 years 6 months'–5 years' custody	**Category range** 15 months'–3 years 6 months' custody
Category 5 £100,000–£500,000	**Starting point** 4 years' custody	**Starting point** 2 years 6 months' custody	**Starting point** 15 months' custody
Starting point based on £300,000	**Category range** 2 years 6 months'–5 years' custody	**Category range** 15 months'–3 years 6 months' custody	**Category range** 26 weeks'–2 years 6 months' custody
Category 6 £20,000–£100,000	**Starting point** 2 years 6 months' custody	**Starting point** 15 months' custody	**Starting point** High level community order
Starting point based on £50,000	**Category range** 15 months'–3 years 6 months' custody	**Category range** High level community order–2 years 6 months' custody	**Category range** Low level community order–36 weeks' custody
Category 7 Less than £20,000	**Starting point** 15 months' custody	**Starting point** 26 weeks' custody	**Starting point** Medium level community order
Starting point based on £12,500	**Category range** 26 weeks'–2 years 6 months' custody	**Category range** Medium level community order–15 months' custody	**Category range** Band C fine–High level community order

TABLE 3 Cheat the Revenue (common law)

Maximum: Life imprisonment

Where the offending is on the most serious scale, involving sums significantly higher than the starting point in category 1, sentences of 15 years and above may be appropriate depending on the role of the offender. In cases involving sums below £2 million the court should refer to Table 1.

	Culpability		
Harm	**A**	**B**	**C**
Category 1 £50 million or more Starting point based on £80 million	**Starting point** 12 years' custody **Category range** 10–17 years' custody	**Starting point** 8 years' custody **Category range** 7–12 years' custody	**Starting point** 6 years' custody **Category range** 4–8 years' custody
Category 2 £10 million–£50 million Starting point based on £30 million	**Starting point** 10 years' custody **Category range** 8–13 years' custody	**Starting point** 7 years' custody **Category range** 5–9 years' custody	**Starting point** 5 years' custody **Category range** 3–6 years' custody
Category 3 £2 million–£10 million Starting point based on £5 million	**Starting point** 8 years' custody **Category range** 6–10 years' custody	**Starting point** 6 years' custody **Category range** 4–7 years' custody	**Starting point** 4 years' custody **Category range** 3–5 years' custody

The table below contains a non-exhaustive list of additional factual elements providing the context of the offence and factors relating to the offender.

Identify whether any combination of these or other relevant factors should result in any further upward or downward adjustment from the starting point.

Consecutive sentences for multiple offences may be appropriate where large sums are involved.

Factors increasing seriousness	**Factors reducing seriousness or reflecting personal mitigation**
Statutory aggravating factors: Previous convictions, having regard to a) the nature of the offence to which the conviction relates and its relevance to the current offence; and b) the time that has elapsed since the conviction Offence committed whilst on bail *Other aggravating factors:* Involves multiple frauds Number of false declarations Attempts to conceal/dispose of evidence Failure to comply with current court orders Offence committed on licence	No previous convictions **or** no relevant/recent convictions Remorse Good character and/or exemplary conduct Little or no prospect of success Serious medical condition requiring urgent, intensive or long term treatment Age and/or lack of maturity where it affects the responsibility of the offender Lapse of time since apprehension where this does not arise from the conduct of the offender Mental disorder or learning disability Sole or primary carer for dependent relatives

Offences taken into consideration Failure to respond to warnings about behaviour Blame wrongly placed on others Damage to third party (for example as a result of identity theft) Dealing with goods with an additional health risk Disposing of goods to under age purchasers	Offender co-operated with investigation, made early admissions and/or voluntarily reported offending Determination and/or demonstration of steps having been taken to address addiction or offending behaviour Activity originally legitimate

SG-491 STEPS THREE to EIGHT

[These are identical to those set out at SG-478 *et seq.*]

SG-492

Benefit Fraud

Dishonest representations for obtaining benefit etc

Social Security Administration Act 1992 (section 111A)

Tax Credit fraud

Tax Credits Act 2002 (section 35)

False accounting

Theft Act 1968 (section 17)

Triable either way
Maximum: 7 years' custody
Offence range: Discharge — 6 years 6 months' custody

False representations for obtaining benefit etc

Social Security Administration Act 1992 (section 112)

Triable summarily only
Maximum: Level 5 fine and/or 3 months' custody
Offence range: Discharge — 12 weeks' custody

Fraud by false representation, fraud by failing to disclose information, fraud by abuse of position

Fraud Act 2006 (section 1)
Triable either way

Conspiracy to defraud

Common law
Triable on indictment only

Maximum: 10 years' custody
Offence range: Discharge — 8 years' custody

STEP ONE Determining the offence category SG-493

The court should determine the offence category with reference to the tables below. In order to determine the category the court should assess **culpability** and **harm.**

The level of **culpability** is determined by weighing up all the factors of the case to determine the offender's role and the extent to which the offending was planned and the sophistication with which it was carried out.	**Harm — Amount obtained or intended to be obtained**
Culpability demonstrated by one or more of the following:	**Category 1** £500,000–£2 million Starting point based on £1 million
A — High culpability	**Category 2** £100,000–£500,000 Starting point based on £300,000
A leading role where offending is part of a group activity	**Category 3** £50,000–£100,000 Starting point based on £75,000
Involvement of others through pressure/influence	**Category 4** £10,000–£50,000 Starting point based on £30,000
Abuse of position of power or trust or responsibility	**Category 5** £2,500–£10,000 Starting point based on £5,000
Sophisticated nature of offence/significant planning	**Category 6** Less than £2,500 Starting point based on £1,000
B — Medium culpability	
Other cases where characteristics for categories A or C are not present	
Claim not fraudulent from the outset	
A significant role where offending is part of a group activity	
C — Lesser culpability	
Involved through coercion, intimidation or exploitation	
Performed limited function under direction	

Where there are characteristics present which fall under different levels of culpability, the court should balance these characteristics to reach a fair assessment of the offender's culpability.

STEP TWO Starting point and category range SG-494

Having determined the category at step one, the court should use the appropriate starting point to reach a sentence within the category range in the table below. The starting point applies to all offenders irrespective of plea or previous convictions.

Where the value is larger or smaller than the amount on which the starting point is based, this should lead to upward or downward adjustment as appropriate.

Where the value greatly exceeds the amount of the starting point in category 1, it may be appropriate to move outside the identified range.

TABLE 1 Section 111A Social Security Administration Act 1992: Dishonest representations to obtain benefit etc

Section 35 Tax Credits Act 2002: Tax Credit fraud

Section 17 Theft Act 1968: False accounting

Maximum: 7 years' custody

	Culpability		
Harm	**A**	**B**	**C**
Category 1 £500,000 or more	**Starting point** 5 years 6 months' custody	**Starting point** 4 years' custody	**Starting point** 2 years 6 months' custody
Starting point based on £1 million	**Category range** 4 years'–6 years 6 months' custody	**Category range** 2 years 6 months'–5 years' custody	**Category range** 15 months'–3 years 6 months' custody
Category 2 £100,000–£500,000	**Starting point** 4 years' custody	**Starting point** 2 years 6 months' custody	**Starting point** 1 year's custody
Starting point based on £300,000	**Category range** 2 years 6 months'–5 years' custody	**Category range** 15 months'–3 years 6 months' custody	**Category range** 26 weeks'–2 years 6 months' custody
Category 3 £50,000–£100,000	**Starting point** 2 years 6 months' custody	**Starting point** 1 year's custody	**Starting point** 26 weeks' custody
Starting point based on £75,000	**Category range** 2 years'–3 years 6 months' custody	**Category range** 26 weeks'–2 years 6 months' custody	**Category range** High level community order–36 weeks' custody
Category 4 £10,000–£50,000	**Starting point** 18 months' custody	**Starting point** 36 weeks' custody	**Starting point** Medium level community order
Starting point based on £30,000	**Category range** 36 weeks'–2 years 6 months' custody	**Category range** Medium level community order–21 months' custody	**Category range** Low level community order–26 weeks' custody
Category 5 £2,500–£10,000	**Starting point** 36 weeks' custody	**Starting point** Medium level community order	**Starting point** Low level community order
Starting point based on £5,000	**Category range** Medium level community order–18 months' custody	**Category range** Low level community order–26 weeks' custody	**Category range** Band B fine–Medium level community order
Category 6 Less than £2,500	**Starting point** Medium level community order	**Starting point** Low level community order	**Starting point** Band A fine
Starting point based on £1,000	**Category range** Low level community order–26 weeks' custody	**Category range** Band A fine–Medium level community order	**Category range** Discharge–Band B fine

TABLE 2 Section 112 Social Security Administration Act 1992: False representations for obtaining benefit etc

Maximum: Level 5 fine and/or 3 months' custody

	Culpability		
Harm	**A**	**B**	**C**
Category 5 Above £2,500	**Starting point** High level community order	**Starting point** Medium level community order	**Starting point** Low level community order
Starting point based on £5,000	**Category range** Medium level community order–12 weeks' custody	**Category range** Band B fine–High level community order	**Category range** Band A fine–Medium level community order
Category 6 Less than £2,500	**Starting point** Medium level community order	**Starting point** Band B fine	**Starting point** Band A fine
Starting point based on £1,000	**Category range** Low level community order–High level community order	**Category range** Band A fine–Band C fine	**Category range** Discharge–Band B fine

TABLE 3 Section 1 Fraud Act 2006
Conspiracy to defraud (common law)

Maximum: 10 years' custody

	Culpability		
Harm	**A**	**B**	**C**
Category 1 £500,000 or more	**Starting point** 7 years' custody	**Starting point** 5 years' custody	**Starting point** 3 years' custody
Starting point based on £1 million	**Category range** 5–8 years' custody	**Category range** 3–6 years' custody	**Category range** 18 months'–4 years' custody
Category 2 £100,000–£500,000	**Starting point** 5 years' custody	**Starting point** 3 years' custody	**Starting point** 15 months' custody
Starting point based on £300,000	**Category range** 3–6 years' custody	**Category range** 18 months'–4 years' custody	**Category range** 26 weeks'–3 years' custody
Category 3 £50,000–£100,000	**Starting point** 3 years' custody	**Starting point** 15 months' custody	**Starting point** 36 weeks' custody
Starting point based on £75,000	**Category range** 2 years 6 months'–4 years' custody	**Category range** 36 weeks'–3 years' custody	**Category range** 26 weeks'–1 year's custody
Category 4 £10,000–£50,000	**Starting point** 21 months' custody	**Starting point** 1 year's custody	**Starting point** High level community order
Starting point based on £30,000	**Category range** 1 year's–3 years' custody	**Category range** High level community order–2 years' custody	**Category range** Low level community order–26 weeks' custody
Category 5 £2,500–£10,000	**Starting point** 1 year's custody	**Starting point** High level community order	**Starting point** Medium level community order

	Culpability		
Harm	**A**	**B**	**C**
Starting point based on £5,000	**Category range** High level community order–2 years' custody	**Category range** Low level community order–26 weeks' custody	**Category range** Band C fine–High level community order
Category 6 Less than £2,500	**Starting point** High level community order	**Starting point** Low level community order	**Starting point** Band B fine
Starting point based on £1,000	**Category range** Low level community order–26 weeks' custody	**Category range** Band B fine–Medium level community order	**Category range** Discharge–Band C fine

The table below contains a non-exhaustive list of additional factual elements providing the context of the offence and factors relating to the offender.

Identify whether any combination of these or other relevant factors should result in any further upward or downward adjustment from the starting point.

Consecutive sentences for multiple offences may be appropriate where large sums are involved.

Factors increasing seriousness	**Factors reducing seriousness or reflecting personal mitigation**
Statutory aggravating factors: Previous convictions, having regard to a) the nature of the offence to which the conviction relates and its relevance to the current offence; and b) the time that has elapsed since the conviction Offence committed whilst on bail *Other aggravating factors:* Claim fraudulent from the outset Proceeds of fraud funded lavish lifestyle Length of time over which the offending was committed Number of false declarations Attempts to conceal/dispose of evidence Failure to comply with current court orders Offence committed on licence Offences taken into consideration Failure to respond to warnings about behaviour Blame wrongly placed on others Damage to third party (for example as a result of identity theft)	No previous convictions **or** no relevant/recent convictions Remorse Good character and/or exemplary conduct Serious medical condition requiring urgent, intensive or long term treatment Legitimate entitlement to benefits not claimed Little or no prospect of success Age and/or lack of maturity where it affects the responsibility of the offender Lapse of time since apprehension where this does not arise from the conduct of the offender Mental disorder or learning disability Sole or primary carer for dependent relatives Offender co-operated with investigation, made early admissions and/or voluntarily reported offending Determination and/or demonstration of steps having been taken to address addiction or offending behaviour Offender experiencing significant financial hardship or pressure at time fraud was committed due to **exceptional** circumstances

STEPS THREE to EIGHT SG-495

[These are identical to those set out at SG-478 *et seq.*]

Money Laundering SG-496

Concealing/disguising/converting/transferring/removing criminal property from England & Wales
Proceeds of Crime Act 2002 (section 327)

Entering into arrangements concerning criminal property
Proceeds of Crime Act 2002 (section 328)

Acquisition, use and possession of criminal property
Proceeds of Crime Act 2002 (section 329)

Triable either way
Maximum: 14 years' custody
Offence range: Band B fine — 13 years' imprisonment

STEP ONE Determining the offence category SG-497

The court should determine the offence category with reference to the tables below. In order to determine the category the court should assess **culpability** and **harm.**

The level of **culpability** is determined by weighing up all the factors of the case to determine the offender's role and the extent to which the offending was planned and the sophistication with which it was carried out.	**Harm A**
Culpability demonstrated by one or more of the following:	**Harm is initially assessed by the value of the money laundered.**
A — High culpability	**Category 1** £10 million or more Starting point based on £30 million
A leading role where offending is part of a group activity	**Category 2** £2 million–£10 million Starting point based on £5 million
Involvement of others through pressure, influence	**Category 3** £500,000–£2 million Starting point based on £1 million
Abuse of position of power or trust or responsibility	**Category 4** £100,000–£500,000 Starting point based on £300,000
Sophisticated nature of offence/significant planning	**Category 5** £10,000–£100,000 Starting point based on £50,000
Criminal activity conducted over sustained period of time	**Category 6** Less than £10,000 Starting point based on £5,000
B — Medium culpability	**Harm B** Money laundering is an integral component of much serious criminality. **To complete the assessment of harm, the court should take into account the level of harm associated with the underlying offence to determine whether it warrants upward adjustment of the starting point within the range, or in appropriate cases, outside the range.** Where it is possible to identify the underlying offence, regard should be given to the relevant sentencing levels for that offence.
Other cases where characteristics for categories A or C are not present	
A significant role where offending is part of a group activity	
C — Lesser culpability	
Performed limited function under direction	
Involved through coercion, intimidation or exploitation	
Not motivated by personal gain	
Opportunistic 'one-off' offence; very little or no planning	
Limited awareness or understanding of extent of criminal activity	

Where there are characteristics present which fall under different levels of culpability, the court should balance these characteristics to reach a fair assessment of the offender's culpability.

SG-498 **STEP TWO Starting point and category range**

Having determined the category at step one, the court should use the appropriate starting point (as adjusted in accordance with step one above) to reach a sentence within the category range in the table below. The starting point applies to all offenders irrespective of plea or previous convictions.

Where the value is larger or smaller than the amount on which the starting point is based, this should lead to upward or downward adjustment as appropriate.

Where the value greatly exceeds the amount of the starting point in category 1, it may be appropriate to move outside the identified range.

Section 327 Proceeds of Crime Act 2002: Concealing/disguising/converting/transferring/removing criminal property from England & Wales

Section 328 Proceeds of Crime Act 2002: Entering into arrangements concerning criminal property

Section 329 Proceeds of Crime Act 2002: Acquisition, use and possession of criminal property

Maximum: 14 years' custody

	Culpability		
Harm	**A**	**B**	**C**
Category 1 £10 million or more Starting point based on £30 million	**Starting point** 10 years' custody **Category range** 8–13 years' custody	**Starting point** 7 years' custody **Category range** 5–10 years' custody	**Starting point** 4 years' custody **Category range** 3–6 years' custody
Category 2 £2 million–£10 million Starting point based on £5 million	**Starting point** 8 years' custody **Category range** 6–9 years' custody	**Starting point** 5 years' custody **Category range** 3 years 6 months'–7 years' custody	**Starting point** 3 years 6 months' custody **Category range** 2–5 years' custody
Category 3 £500,000–£2 million Starting point based on £1 million	**Starting point** 7 years' custody **Category range** 5–8 years' custody	**Starting point** 5 years' custody **Category range** 3–6 years' custody	**Starting point** 3 years' custody **Category range** 18 months'–4 years' custody
Category 4 £100,000–£500,000 Starting point based on £300,000	**Starting point** 5 years' custody **Category range** 3–6 years' custody	**Starting point** 3 years' custody **Category range** 18 months'–4 years' custody	**Starting point** 18 months' custody **Category range** 26 weeks'–3 years' custody
Category 5 £10,000–£100,000 Starting point based on £50,000	**Starting point** 3 years' custody **Category range** 18 months'–4 years' custody	**Starting point** 18 months' custody **Category range** 26 weeks'–3 years' custody	**Starting point** 26 weeks' custody **Category range** Medium level community order–1 year's custody
Category 6 Less than £10,000 Starting point based on £5,000	**Starting point** 1 year's custody **Category range** 26 weeks'–2 years' custody	**Starting point** High level community order **Category range** Low level community order–1 year's custody	**Starting point** Low level community order **Category range** Band B fine–Medium level community order

The table below contains a non-exhaustive list of additional factual elements providing the context of the offence and factors relating to the offender.

Identify whether any combination of these or other relevant factors should result in an upward or downward adjustment of the sentence arrived at thus far.

Consecutive sentences for multiple offences may be appropriate where large sums are involved.

Factors increasing seriousness	Factors reducing seriousness or reflecting personal mitigation
Statutory aggravating factors: Previous convictions, having regard to a) the nature of the offence to which the conviction relates and its relevance to the current offence; and b) the time that has elapsed since the conviction Offence committed whilst on bail *Other aggravating factors:* Attempts to conceal/dispose of evidence Established evidence of community/wider impact Failure to comply with current court orders Offence committed on licence Offences taken into consideration Failure to respond to warnings about behaviour Offences committed across borders Blame wrongly placed on others Damage to third party for example loss of employment to legitimate employees	No previous convictions **or** no relevant/recent convictions Remorse Little or no prospect of success Good character and/or exemplary conduct Serious medical conditions requiring urgent, intensive or long-term treatment Age and/or lack of maturity where it affects the responsibility of the offender Lapse of time since apprehension where this does not arise from the conduct of the offender Mental disorder or learning disability Sole or primary carer for dependent relatives Offender co-operated with investigation, made early admissions and/or voluntarily reported offending Determination and/or demonstration of steps having been taken to address addiction or offending behaviour Activity originally legitimate

STEPS THREE to EIGHT **SG-499**

[These are identical to those set out at SG-478 *et seq*.]

BRIBERY **SG-500**

Bribing another person
Bribery Act 2010 (section 1)

Being bribed
Bribery Act 2010 (section 2)

Bribery of foreign public officials
Bribery Act 2010 (section 6)

Triable either way
Maximum: 10 years' custody
Offence range: Discharge — 8 years' custody

SG-501 STEP ONE **Determining the offence category**

The court should determine the offence category with reference to the tables below. In order to determine the category the court should assess **culpability** and **harm.**

The level of **culpability** is determined by weighing up all the factors of the case to determine the offender's role and the extent to which the offending was planned and the sophistication with which it was carried out.	**Harm** is assessed in relation to any impact caused by the offending (whether to identifiable victims or in a wider context) and the actual or intended gain to the offender.	
Culpability demonstrated by one or more of the following:	Harm demonstrated by one or more of the following factors:	
A — High culpability	**Category 1**	• Serious detrimental effect on individuals (for example by provision of substandard goods or services resulting from the corrupt behaviour) • Serious environmental impact • Serious undermining of the proper function of local or national government, business or public services • Substantial actual or intended financial gain to offender or another or loss caused to others
A leading role where offending is part of a group activity	**Category 2**	• Significant detrimental effect on individuals • Significant environmental impact • Significant undermining of the proper function of local or national government, business or public services • Significant actual or intended financial gain to offender or another or loss caused to others • Risk of category 1 harm
Involvement of others through pressure, influence	**Category 3**	• Limited detrimental impact on individuals, the environment, government, business or public services • Risk of category 2 harm
Abuse of position of significant power or trust or responsibility	**Category 4**	• Risk of category 3 harm
Intended corruption (directly or indirectly) of a senior official performing a public function	**Risk of harm** involves consideration of both the likelihood of harm occurring and the extent of it if it does. Risk of harm is less serious than the same actual harm. Where the offence has caused risk of harm but no (or much less) actual harm, the normal approach is to move to the next category of harm down. This may not be appropriate if either the likelihood or extent of potential harm is particularly high.	
Intended corruption (directly or indirectly) of a law enforcement officer		
Sophisticated nature of offence/significant planning		
Offending conducted over sustained period of time		
Motivated by expectation of substantial financial, commercial or political gain		

B — Medium culpability
All other cases where characteristics for categories A or C are not present
A significant role where offending is part of a group activity
C — Lesser culpability
Involved through coercion, intimidation or exploitation
Not motivated by personal gain
Peripheral role in organised activity
Opportunistic 'one-off' offence; very little or no planning
Limited awareness or understanding of extent of corrupt activity

Where there are characteristics present which fall under different levels of culpability, the court should balance these characteristics to reach a fair assessment of the offender's culpability.

STEP TWO Starting point and category range **SG-502**

Having determined the category at step one, the court should use the corresponding starting point to reach a sentence within the category range below. The starting point applies to all offenders irrespective of plea or previous convictions.

Section 1 Bribery Act 2010: Bribing another person

Section 2 Bribery Act 2010: Being bribed

Section 6 Bribery Act 2010: Bribery of foreign public officials

Maximum: 10 years' custody

	Culpability		
Harm	**A**	**B**	**C**
Category 1	**Starting point** 7 years' custody	**Starting point** 5 years' custody	**Starting point** 3 years' custody
	Category range 5–8 years' custody	**Category range** 3–6 years' custody	**Category range** 18 months'–4 years' custody
Category 2	**Starting point** 5 years' custody	**Starting point** 3 years' custody	**Starting point** 18 months' custody
	Category range 3–6 years' custody	**Category range** 18 months'–4 years' custody	**Category range** 26 weeks'–3 years' custody
Category 3	**Starting point** 3 years' custody	**Starting point** 18 months' custody	**Starting point** 26 weeks' custody
	Category range 18 months'–4 years' custody	**Category range** 26 weeks'–3 years' custody	**Category range** Medium level community order–1 year's custody
Category 4	**Starting point** 18 months' custody	**Starting point** 26 weeks' custody	**Starting point** Medium level community order
	Category range 26 weeks'–3 years' custody	**Category range** Medium level community order–1 year's custody	**Category range** Band B fine–High level community order

The table below contains a non-exhaustive list of additional factual elements providing the context of the offence and factors relating to the offender.

Identify whether any combination of these or other relevant factors should result in an upward or downward adjustment from the starting point.

Consecutive sentences for multiple offences may be appropriate where large sums are involved.

Factors increasing seriousness	**Factors reducing seriousness or reflecting personal mitigation**
Statutory aggravating factors: Previous convictions, having regard to a) the nature of the offence to which the conviction relates and its relevance to the current offence; and b) the time that has elapsed since the conviction Offence committed whilst on bail *Other aggravating factors:* Steps taken to prevent victims reporting or obtaining assistance and/or from assisting or supporting the prosecution Attempts to conceal/dispose of evidence Established evidence of community/wider impact Failure to comply with current court orders Offence committed on licence Offences taken into consideration Failure to respond to warnings about behaviour Offences committed across borders Blame wrongly placed on others Pressure exerted on another party Offence committed to facilitate other criminal activity	No previous convictions **or** no relevant/recent convictions Remorse Good character and/or exemplary conduct Little or no prospect of success Serious medical conditions requiring urgent, intensive or long-term treatment Age and/or lack of maturity where it affects the responsibility of the offender Lapse of time since apprehension where this does not arise from the conduct of the offender Mental disorder or learning disability Sole or primary carer for dependent relatives Offender co-operated with investigation, made early admissions and/or voluntarily reported offending

SG-503 STEPS THREE to EIGHT

[These are identical to those set out at **SG-478** *et seq.*]

SG-504 CORPORATE OFFENDERS: FRAUD, BRIBERY, AND MONEY LAUNDERING

Fraud

Conspiracy to defraud (common law)
Cheat the public revenue (common law)
Triable only on indictment

Fraud Act 2006 (sections 1, 6 and 7)
Theft Act 1968 (section 17)
Value Added Tax Act 1994 (section 72)
Customs and Excise Management Act 1979 (section 170)
Triable either way

Bribery

Bribery Act 2010 (sections 1, 2, 6 and 7)
Triable either way

Money laundering
Proceeds of Crime Act 2002 (sections 327, 328 and 329)
Triable either way
Maximum: Unlimited fine

Most cases of corporate offending in this area are likely to merit allocation for trial to the Crown Court.

Committal for sentence is mandatory if confiscation (see step two) is to be considered. (Proceeds of Crime Act 2002 section 70).

STEP ONE Compensation SG-505

The court must consider making a compensation order requiring the offender to pay compensation for any personal injury, loss or damage resulting from the offence in such an amount as the court considers appropriate, having regard to the evidence and to the means of the offender.

Where the means of the offender are limited, priority should be given to the payment of compensation over payment of any other financial penalty.

Reasons should be given if a compensation order is not made.

(See section 130 Powers of Criminal Courts (Sentencing) Act 2000)

STEP TWO Confiscation SG-506

Confiscation must be considered if either the Crown asks for it or the court thinks that it may be appropriate.

Confiscation must be dealt with before, and taken into account when assessing, any other fine or financial order (except compensation).

(See Proceeds of Crime Act 2002 sections 6 and 13)

STEP THREE Determining the offence category SG-507

Culpability	Harm	
The sentencer should weigh up all the factors of the case to determine culpability. **Where there are characteristics present which fall under different categories, the court should balance these characteristics to reach a fair assessment of the offender's culpability.** **Culpability** demonstrated by the offending corporation's role and motivation. May be demonstrated by one or more of the following **non-exhaustive** characteristics.	Harm is represented by a financial sum calculated by reference to the table below **Amount obtained or intended to be obtained (or loss avoided or intended to be avoided)**	
A— High culpability	**Fraud**	For offences of fraud, conspiracy to defraud, cheating the Revenue and fraudulent evasion of duty or VAT, harm will normally be the actual or intended gross gain to the offender.
Corporation plays a leading role in organised, planned unlawful activity (whether acting alone or with others)	**Bribery**	For offences under the Bribery Act the appropriate figure will normally be the gross profit from the contract obtained, retained or sought as a result of the offending. An alternative measure for offences under section 7 may be the likely cost avoided by failing to put in place appropriate measures to prevent bribery.
Wilful obstruction of detection (for example destruction of evidence, misleading investigators, suborning employees)	**Money laundering**	For offences of money laundering the appropriate figure will normally be the amount laundered or, alternatively, the likely cost avoided by failing to put in place an effective anti-money laundering programme if this is higher.

Culpability	Harm
Involving others through pressure or coercion (for example employees or suppliers)	**General** Where the actual or intended gain cannot be established, the appropriate measure will be the amount that the court considers was likely to be achieved in all the circumstances. In the absence of sufficient evidence of the amount that was likely to be obtained, 10–20 per cent of the relevant revenue (for instance between 10 and 20 per cent of the worldwide revenue derived from the product or business area to which the offence relates for the period of the offending) **may** be an appropriate measure. There may be large cases of fraud or bribery in which the true harm is to commerce or markets generally. That may justify adopting a harm figure beyond the normal measures here set out.
Targeting of vulnerable victims or a large number of victims	
Corruption of local or national government officials or ministers	
Corruption of officials performing a law enforcement role	
Abuse of dominant market position or position of trust or responsibility	
Offending committed over a sustained period of time	
Culture of wilful disregard of commission of offences by employees or agents with no effort to put effective systems in place (section 7 Bribery Act only)	
B — Medium culpability	
Corporation plays a significant role in unlawful activity organised by others	
Activity not unlawful from the outset	
Corporation reckless in making false statement (section 72 VAT Act 1994)	
All other cases where characteristics for categories A or C are not present	
C — Lesser culpability	
Corporation plays a minor, peripheral role in unlawful activity organised by others	
Some effort made to put bribery prevention measures in place but insufficient to amount to a defence (section 7 Bribery Act only)	
Involvement through coercion, intimidation or exploitation	

SG-508 **STEP FOUR Starting point and category range**

Having determined the culpability level at step three, the court should use the table below to determine the starting point within the category range below. The starting point applies to all offenders irrespective of plea or previous convictions.

The harm figure at step three is multiplied by the relevant percentage figure representing culpability.

	Culpability Level		
	A	**B**	**C**
Harm figure multiplier	**Starting point** 300%	**Starting point** 200%	**Starting point** 100%
	Category range 250% to 400%	**Category range** 100% to 300%	**Category range** 20% to 150%

Having determined the appropriate starting point, the court should then consider adjustment within the category range for aggravating or mitigating features. In some cases, having considered these factors, it may be appropriate to move outside the identified category range. (See below for a **non-exhaustive** list of aggravating and mitigating factors.)

Factors increasing seriousness	**Factors reducing seriousness or reflecting mitigation**
Previous relevant convictions or subject to previous relevant civil or regulatory enforcement action Corporation or subsidiary set up to commit fraudulent activity Fraudulent activity endemic within corporation Attempts made to conceal misconduct Substantial harm (whether financial or otherwise) suffered by victims of offending or by third parties affected by offending Risk of harm greater than actual or intended harm (for example in banking/credit fraud) Substantial harm caused to integrity or confidence of markets Substantial harm caused to integrity of local or national governments Serious nature of underlying criminal activity (money laundering offences) Offence committed across borders or jurisdictions	No previous relevant convictions or previous relevant civil or regulatory enforcement action Victims voluntarily reimbursed/compensated No actual loss to victims Corporation co-operated with investigation, made early admissions and/or voluntarily reported offending Offending committed under previous director(s)/ manager(s) Little or no actual gain to corporation from offending

General principles to follow in setting a fine

The court should determine the appropriate level of fine in accordance with section 164 of the Criminal Justice Act 2003, which requires that the fine must reflect the seriousness of the offence and requires the court to take into account the financial circumstances of the offender.

Obtaining financial information

Companies and bodies delivering public or charitable services

Where the offender is a company or a body which delivers a public or charitable service, it is expected to provide comprehensive accounts for the last three years, to enable the court to make an accurate assessment of its financial status. In the absence of such disclosure, or where the court is not satisfied that it has been given sufficient reliable information, the court will be entitled to draw reasonable inferences as to the offender's means from evidence it has heard and from all the circumstances of the case.

1. *For companies*: annual accounts. Particular attention should be paid to turnover; profit before tax; directors' remuneration, loan accounts and pension provision; and assets as disclosed by the balance sheet. Most companies are required to file audited accounts at Companies House. Failure to produce relevant recent accounts on request may properly lead to the conclusion that the company can pay any appropriate fine.
2. *For partnerships*: annual accounts. Particular attention should be paid to turnover; profit before tax; partners' drawings, loan accounts and pension provision; assets as above. Limited liability partnerships (LLPs) may be required to file audited accounts with Companies House. If adequate accounts are not produced on request, see paragraph 1.
3. *For local authorities, fire authorities and similar public bodies*: the Annual Revenue Budget ('ARB') is the equivalent of turnover and the best indication of the size of the defendant organisation. It is unlikely to be necessary to analyse specific expenditure or reserves unless inappropriate expenditure is suggested.

4. *For health trusts*: the independent regulator of NHS Foundation Trusts is Monitor. It publishes quarterly reports and annual figures for the financial strength and stability of trusts from which the annual income can be seen, available via www.monitor-nhsft.gov.uk. Detailed analysis of expenditure or reserves is unlikely to be called for.
5. *For charities*: it will be appropriate to inspect annual audited accounts. Detailed analysis of expenditure or reserves is unlikely to be called for unless there is a suggestion of unusual or unnecessary expenditure.

SG-509 STEP FIVE **Adjustment of fine**

Having arrived at a fine level, the court should consider whether there are any further factors which indicate an adjustment in the level of the fine. The court should 'step back' and consider the overall effect of its orders. The combination of orders made, compensation, confiscation and fine ought to achieve:

- the removal of all gain
- appropriate additional punishment, and
- deterrence

The fine may be adjusted to ensure that these objectives are met in a fair way. The court should consider any further factors relevant to the setting of the level of the fine to ensure that the fine is proportionate, having regard to the size and financial position of the offending organisation and the seriousness of the offence.

The fine must be substantial enough to have a real economic impact which will bring home to both management and shareholders the need to operate within the law. Whether the fine will have the effect of putting the offender out of business will be relevant; in some bad cases this may be an acceptable consequence.

In considering the ability of the offending organisation to pay any financial penalty the court can take into account the power to allow time for payment or to order that the amount be paid in instalments.

The court should consider whether the level of fine would otherwise cause unacceptable harm to third parties. In doing so the court should bear in mind that the payment of any compensation determined at step one should take priority over the payment of any fine.

The table below contains a **non-exhaustive** list of additional factual elements for the court to consider.

Factors to consider in adjusting the level of fine
Fine fulfils the objectives of punishment, deterrence and removal of gain
The value, worth or available means of the offender
Fine impairs offender's ability to make restitution to victims
Impact of fine on offender's ability to implement effective compliance programmes
Impact of fine on employment of staff, service users, customers and local economy (but not shareholders)
Impact of fine on performance of public or charitable function

The Court should identify whether any combination of these, or other relevant factors, should result in a proportionate increase or reduction in the level of fine.

SG-510 STEP SIX **Consider any factors which would indicate a reduction, such as assistance to the prosecution**

The court should take into account sections 73 and 74 of the Serious Organised Crime and Police Act 2005 (assistance by defendants: reduction or review of sentence) and any other rule of law by virtue of which an offender may receive a discounted sentence in consequence of assistance given (or offered) to the prosecutor or investigator.

SG-511 STEP SEVEN **Reduction for guilty pleas**

The court should take into account any potential reduction for a guilty plea in accordance with section 144 of the Criminal Justice Act 2003 and the Guilty Plea guideline.

SG-512 STEP EIGHT **Ancillary Orders**

In all cases the court must consider whether to make any ancillary orders.

STEP NINE Totality principle SG-513

If sentencing an offender for more than one offence, consider whether the total sentence is just and proportionate to the offending behaviour.

STEP TEN Reasons SG-514

Section 174 of the Criminal Justice Act 2003 imposes a duty to give reasons for, and explain the effect of, the sentence.

PART 18 OVERARCHING PRINCIPLES—SENTENCING YOUTHS SG-515

FOREWORD

. . .This guideline applies to the sentencing of offenders on or after **30 November 2009**.

Generally, the Sentencing Guidelines Council has not produced offence specific guidelines for those under the age of 18 years. However, guidelines have been produced for those offences under the Sexual Offences Act 2003 which have a lower maximum penalty when committed by a person under 18 and for Robbery. These continue to provide the relevant starting points and ranges for all youths convicted of those offences and are not superseded by this guideline.

Overarching Principles—Sentencing Youths SG-516

General Approach

1. **Statutory provisions**

1.1 Offence seriousness is the starting point for sentencing. In considering the seriousness of any offence, the court must consider the offender's culpability in committing the offence and any harm which the offence caused, was intended to cause or might foreseeably have caused.[292] In imposing sentence, the restrictions on liberty must be commensurate with the seriousness of the offence.

1.2 When sentencing an offender aged under 18, a court must[293] have regard to:

a) the principal aim of the youth justice system (to prevent offending by children and young persons);[294] and

b) the welfare of the offender.[295]

1.3 In addition to the statutory provisions,[296] a court sentencing a young offender must be aware of obligations under a range of international conventions which emphasise the importance of avoiding 'criminalisation' of young people whilst ensuring that they are held responsible for their actions and, where possible, take part in repairing the damage that they have caused. This includes recognition of the damage caused to the victims and understanding by the young person that the deed was not acceptable. Within a system that provides for both the acknowledgement of guilt and sanctions which rehabilitate, the intention is to establish responsibility and, at the same time, to promote re-integration rather than to impose retribution.

2. **Sentencing principles** SG-517

2.1 **The approach to sentence will be individualistic.**

2.2 The youth of the offender is widely recognised as requiring a different approach from that which would be adopted in relation to an adult. Even within the category of 'youth', the response to an offence is likely to be very different depending on whether the offender is at the lower end of the age bracket, in the middle or towards the top end; in many instances, the maturity of the offender will be at least as important as the chronological age.

[292] Criminal Justice Act 2003, section 143(1)

[293] This section does not apply when imposing a mandatory life sentence, when imposing a statutory minimum custodial sentence, when imposing detention for life under the dangerous offender provisions or when making certain orders under the Mental Health Act 1983.

[294] Crime and Disorder Act 1998, section 37(1), see para. 2.6 below

[295] Children and Young Persons Act 1933, section 44(1), see para. 2.7

[296] Criminal Justice and Immigration Act 2008, section 9 (inserting section 142A into the Criminal Justice Act 2003) has not been brought into force.

2.3 However, the sentence must remain proportionate to the seriousness of the present offence (except in the rare circumstances where the criteria for a sentence under the dangerous offender provisions are met) and should not impose greater restrictions on liberty than the seriousness of the offence justifies simply to deal with the risk of re-offending. Particular care will need to be taken where a young person has committed a relatively less serious offence but there is a high risk of re-offending.

2.4 Whilst a court is required to aggravate the seriousness of an offence where there are previous convictions (if the court considers that to be reasonable taking account both of the offence and the time that had elapsed since the previous conviction[297]), **a sentence that follows re-offending does not need to be more severe than the previous sentence solely because there had been a previous conviction.**

(i) Approach to determining sentence

2.5 When determining sentence, the court will:

(1) **Assess the culpability of the offender and the harm caused (or intended or foreseeable) taking into account aggravating and mitigating factors relating to the offence.**

The assessment of offence seriousness will fix the most severe penalty that can be imposed and will determine whether an offence has crossed the necessary threshold to enable the court to impose a community or custodial sentence.

Even where the custody threshold has been crossed, a court is not required to impose a custodial sentence; similarly with the community sentence threshold.[298]

Harm may be to individual victims or to the community or society at large. Of the four levels of culpability for sentencing purposes, intention is the highest followed by recklessness, knowledge and negligence. Even within those levels there will be gradations of seriousness.

Statutory aggravating factors (including previous convictions) will be relevant in assessing the seriousness of an offence.

(2) **Consider any mitigating factors that apply to the offender and any reduction for a guilty plea.**

When considering the maturity of the offender and its relevance to the sentence, it will only be in the most exceptional case that this will require more information than is available to the court through the representations of the advocates and any pre-sentence report.

(3) **Having taken account of all these factors, a court must then determine sentence including any relevant ancillary orders.**

The overall impact of the sentence and the ancillary orders must be considered to ensure that the restrictions on liberty are no more than is commensurate with the seriousness of the offence.

(ii) The principal aim of the youth justice system

2.6 By section 37 of the Crime and Disorder Act 1998, the principal aim of the youth justice system is to prevent offending by children and young people. For the offender, it incorporates the need to demonstrate that such conduct is not acceptable in a way that makes an impact on the offender whilst also identifying and seeking to address any other factors that make offending more likely. For any victim of the offence and society as a whole, it incorporates the need to demonstrate that the law is being effectively enforced and to sustain confidence in the rule of law.

(iii) The welfare of the offender

2.7 By section 44 of the Children and Young Persons Act 1933, 'Every court in dealing with a child or young person who is brought before it, either as an offender or otherwise, shall have regard to the *welfare* of the child or young person, and shall in a proper case take steps for removing him from undesirable surroundings, and for securing that proper provision is made for his education and training'.

2.8 In other requirements or obligations, different terminology—*best interests, well-being* or *welfare*—may be used. Generally, although there are shades of difference between the meanings, it is unlikely that different decisions will arise solely from those differences.

2.9 Accordingly, since 'welfare' is the term used in the legislation applicable to England and Wales, that is the term used in this guideline. Welfare includes the obligation to secure proper provision for education and training,[299] where appropriate to remove from undesirable surroundings[300] and the

---

297 Criminal Justice Act 2003, section 174(2)
298 ibid, section 148(5)
299 Children and Young Persons Act 1933, section 44
300 ibid

need to choose the best option for the young person taking account of the circumstances of the offence.

In having regard to the 'welfare' of the young person, a court should ensure that it is alert to:

- **the high incidence of mental health problems amongst young people in the criminal justice system;**
- **the high incidence of those with learning difficulties or learning disabilities amongst young people in the criminal justice system;**
- **the effect that speech and language difficulties might have on the ability of the young person (or any adult with them) to communicate with the court, to understand the sanction imposed or to fulfil the obligations resulting from that sanction;**
- **the extent to which young people anticipate that they will be discriminated against by those in authority and the effect that it has on the way that they conduct themselves during court proceedings;**
- **the vulnerability of young people to self harm, particularly within a custodial environment;**
- **the extent to which changes taking place during adolescence can lead to experimentation;**
- **the effect on young people of experiences of loss or of abuse.**

2.10 In the light of the high incidence of these impairments amongst young people in custody or subject to a community sentence, and taking account of the fact that the principal aim of the youth justice system is preventing offending, a court should always seek to ensure that it has access to information about how best to identify and respond to those impairments and, where necessary, that a proper assessment has taken place in order to enable the most appropriate sentence to be imposed.

(iv) The purpose of sentencing

2.11 As set out in paragraph 1 above, a court sentencing a person under the age of 18 is obliged to have regard to the principal aim of the youth justice system (to prevent offending by children and young persons) and to the welfare of the offender. As the principal aim of the youth justice system[301] is the prevention of offending by children and young people, the emphasis should be on approaches that seem most likely to be effective with young people.

3. Effect on sentence of the offender being a young person SG-518

3.1 In addition to the distinctive range of penalties available for youths, there is an expectation that, generally, a young person will be dealt with less severely than an adult offender, although this distinction diminishes as the offender approaches age 18 (subject to an assessment of maturity and criminal sophistication). In part, this is because young people are unlikely to have the same experience and capacity as an adult to realise the effect of their actions on other people or to appreciate the pain and distress caused and because a young person is likely to be less able to resist temptation, especially where peer pressure is exerted.

3.2 Additionally, in most cases a young person is likely to benefit from being given greater opportunity to learn from mistakes without undue penalisation or stigma, especially as a court sanction might have a significant effect on the prospects and opportunities of the young person, and, therefore, on the likelihood of effective integration into society.

3.3 When sentencing a young offender whose offence involves sexual activity but there is no evidence of a coercive or abusive relationship or of anything other than consensual activity, a court will need to be aware that a desire to explore gender identity or sexual orientation may result in offending behaviour. Depending on the seriousness of the offending behaviour, offender mitigation may arise where that behaviour stems from sexual immaturity or confusion.[302]

3.4 Individual sanctions are likely to have a greater impact on a youth than on an adult, especially lengths of time spent in a custodial establishment, not least because of the exposure to influences likely to entrench criminal conduct (to which a young person may be more susceptible than an adult) and the greater risk of self harm than exists in relation to an adult.

3.5 It is also important to consider whether the young offender lacks the maturity fully to appreciate the consequences of his conduct and the extent to which the offender has been acting on an impulsive basis and the offender's conduct has been affected by inexperience, emotional volatility or negative influences.

Sentencing Guidelines

---

[301] See para. 2.6 above

[302] The Sentencing Advisory Panel has previously stated that Crown Prosecutors and the court should take account of an offender's immaturity and normal juvenile experimentation: *Sexual Offences Act 2003 – the Panel's Advice to the Council –* page 4, para. 21, www.sentencing-guidelines.gov.uk

3.6 Factors regularly present in the background of those juveniles who commit offences include: low family income, poor housing, poor employment records, low educational attainment, early experience of offending by other family members or of violence or abuse (often accompanied by harsh and erratic discipline within the home) and the misuse of drugs.[303] There is also evidence that those young people who are 'looked after' have been more at risk of being drawn into the criminal justice system than other young people acting *in similar ways*.[304]

3.7 It is clear that these factors do not cause delinquency (since many who have experienced them do not commit crime); nonetheless, there is a strong association and any response to criminal activity amongst young people will need to recognise the presence of such factors if it is to be effective.

The following factors have led to a different approach to the sentencing of young people who offend (compared with the approach for adult offenders) and will affect the sentence imposed in an individual case:

- **offending by a young person is frequently a phase which passes fairly rapidly and therefore the reaction to it needs to be kept well balanced in order to avoid alienating the young person from society;**
- **a criminal conviction at this stage of a person's life may have a disproportionate impact on the ability of the young person to gain meaningful employment and play a worthwhile role in society;**
- **the impact of punishment is felt more heavily by young people in the sense that any sentence will seem to be far longer in comparison with their relative age compared with adult offenders;**
- **young people may be more receptive to changing the way they conduct themselves and be able to respond more quickly to interventions;**
- **young people should be given greater opportunity to learn from their mistakes;**
- **young people will be no less vulnerable than adults to the contaminating influences that can be expected within a custodial context and probably more so.**

SG-519 **4. The relevant considerations**

4.1 This guideline sets out a process that will enable the various obligations and requirements to be applied consistently. It is, however, only a framework and is intended to apply to the generality of cases.

In determining the sentence, the key elements are:

- the age of the offender (chronological and emotional),
- the seriousness of the offence,
- the likelihood of further offences being committed, and
- the extent of harm likely to result from those further offences.

The approach to sentence will be individualistic.

Proper regard should be had to the mental health and capability of the young person, and to any learning disability, learning difficulty, speech and language difficulty or other disorder, any of which is likely to affect the likelihood of those purposes being achieved.

4.2 The younger an offender (taking account of maturity and not just chronological age) the more likely it is that considering the welfare of the young person will be of greater significance. Since many young people 'grow out of' crime, the obligation to have regard to the welfare of a young person who has offended might in some circumstances be best manifested by protecting that person from the adverse effects of intervention in his or her life rather than by providing for some positive action.

4.3 The requirement to have regard to the welfare of a young person is subject to the obligation to impose only those restrictions on liberty that are commensurate with the seriousness of the offence; accordingly, a court should not impose greater restrictions because of other factors in the young person's life.

4.4 In relation to custodial sentences, the reconviction rate is high and there are concerns about the effect on vulnerable young people of being in closed conditions. Risks commonly found are those of self harm and suicide and, in relation to female offenders, the additional impact on the offender herself and on the child if the offender is the primary carer of a child or is pregnant.[305] Since a court is obliged to have regard to the welfare of the young person, it must have regard to these issues when considering sentence.

303 See, for example, the range of approaches in the *Youth Crime Action Plan 2008* Chapter 5: www.homeoffice.gov.uk

304 See, for example, *Care experience and criminalisation* The Adolescent and Childcare Trust, September 2008 www.tactcare.org.uk *Sentencing Guidelines Council*

305 *The Corston Report — a review of women with particular vulnerabilities in the Criminal Justice System*, March 2007, www.homeoffice.gov.uk

4.5 Particular care should be taken where an offender has mental health problems, learning disabilities, learning difficulties or other disabilities. Research shows that there is a high incidence of these issues in young people in the youth justice system and, in particular, in custody.

4.6 These issues are not always able to be identified at an early stage in the proceedings leading to sentence. As a result, a court needs to be alert to the possibility that the conduct of the young person (and that of any adult accompanying them in court) might be affected by issues relating to mental health, learning or communication, or some other form of disability that has not previously been identified.

4.7 In such circumstances, care needs to be taken in ensuring that the young person is able to take a proper part in the court proceedings, is able to understand what the court requires as a result of the sentence imposed and that that sentence properly takes account of difficulties in compliance that may arise from those issues.

4.8 Some young people may attend court believing that they will be discriminated against or otherwise unfairly treated; this might be for any of a wide range of reasons including ethnicity and sexuality. However unjustified that belief is, a court will need to be alert to the fact that the young person's behaviour in court might be affected by it.

4.9 The obligations to treat the prevention of offending by children and young persons as the principal aim of sentencing and to have regard to their welfare both require a court to consider the impairments and life experiences noted above, not only in determining the sentence to be imposed, but also in determining the length or content of that sentence.

The proper approach for the Crown Court, a magistrates' court or a youth court when sentencing a young offender is for the court, within a sentence that is no more restrictive on liberty than is proportionate to the seriousness of the offence(s), to seek to impose a sentence that takes proper account of the matters to which the court must have regard (see paragraph 1 above) by:

- confronting the young offender with the consequences of the offending and helping the young offender to develop a sense of personal responsibility—these consequences may be experienced by the offender himself or herself, by the family of the offender, by the victim(s) of the offence and/or by the community;
- tackling the particular factors (personal, family, social, educational or health) that put the young person at risk of offending;
- strengthening those factors that reduce the risk that the young person will continue to offend;
- encouraging reparation to victims;
- defining, agreeing and reinforcing the responsibilities of parents.

5. Crossing a significant age threshold between commission of an offence and sentence SG-520

5.1 There will be occasions when an increase in the age of an offender[306] will result in the maximum sentence on the date of *conviction* being greater than that available on the date on which the offence was *committed*.

5.2 In such circumstances, the approach should be:

- where an offender crosses a relevant age threshold between the date on which the offence was committed and the date of conviction or sentence, a court should take as its starting point the sentence likely to have been imposed on the date on which the offence was committed;
- where an offender attains the age of 18 after committing the offence but before conviction, section 142 of the Criminal Justice Act 2003 applies (whilst section 37 of the 1998 Act and section 44 of the 1933 Act (see 2.6–2.10 above) apply to those aged under 18) and the sentencing disposal has to take account of the matters set out in that section;[307]
- it will be rare for a court to have to consider passing a sentence more severe than the maximum it would have had jurisdiction to pass at the time the offence was committed even where an offender has subsequently attained the age of 18;
- however, a sentence at or close to that maximum may be appropriate, especially where a serious offence was committed by an offender close to the age threshold.

6. Persistent offenders SG-521

6.1 Certain sentences are available only where the offender is a 'persistent offender' — in particular, a youth rehabilitation order with intensive supervision and surveillance or with fostering in relation to an

[306] Primarily attaining the age of 12, 15 or 18.

[307] Accordingly, when sentencing those convicted when aged 18 and above who have committed an offence whilst under that age, more general public policy considerations may play a greater part.

offender aged between 10 and 14[308] and a detention and training order in relation to an offender aged between 12 and 14.[309] This criterion does not have to be met before the Crown Court imposes long term detention (see paragraph 12 below) or detention for life.

6.2 Similarly, additional powers may be available to a court where a youth rehabilitation order has been breached 'wilfully and persistently'.

6.3 'Persistent offender' is not defined in legislation but has been considered by the Court of Appeal on a number of occasions. However, following the implementation of the 2008 Act, the sentencing framework is different from that when the definition was judicially developed, particularly the greater emphasis on the requirement to use a custodial sentence as 'a measure of last resort'.

6.4 A dictionary definition of 'persistent offender' is 'persisting or having a tendency to persist'; 'persist' is defined as 'to continue firmly or obstinately in a course of action in spite of difficulty or opposition'.

6.5 In determining whether an offender is a persistent offender for these purposes, a court should consider the simple test of whether the young person is one who persists in offending:

i) in most circumstances, the normal expectation is that the offender will have had some contact with authority in which the offending conduct was challenged before being classed as 'persistent'; a finding of persistence in offending may be derived from information about previous convictions but may also arise from orders which require an admission or finding of guilt — these include reprimands, final warnings, restorative justice disposals and conditional cautions; since they do not require such an admission, penalty notices for disorder are unlikely to be sufficiently reliable;

ii) a young offender is certainly likely to be found to be persistent (and, in relation to a custodial sentence, the test of being a measure of last resort is most likely to be satisfied) where the offender has been convicted of, or made subject to a pre-court disposal that involves an admission or finding of guilt in relation to, imprisonable offences on at least 3 occasions in the past 12 months.

6.6 Even where a young person is found to be a persistent offender, a court is not obliged to impose the custodial sentence or youth rehabilitation order with intensive supervision and surveillance or fostering that becomes available as a result of that finding. The other tests continue to apply and it is clear that Parliament expects custodial sentences to be imposed only rarely on those aged 14 or less.

SG-522 **7. Enforcing the responsibilities of parents and guardians**

7.1 A significant difference arising from the procedures for dealing with young people who commit criminal offences is the importance attached to the presence of a parent, carer or appropriate adult at key stages, especially when sentence is imposed. In addition, specific provisions exist to enable a court to reinforce the responsibilities of a parent or guardian.

7.2 The statutory framework clearly envisages the attendance of an adult with a degree of responsibility for the young person; this obligation reflects the principal aim of reducing offending, recognising that that is unlikely to be achieved by the young person alone. A court must be aware of a risk that a young person will seek to avoid this requirement either by urging the court to proceed in the absence of an adult or in arranging for a person to come to court who purports to have (but in reality does not have) the necessary degree of responsibility.

7.3 Insistence on attendance may produce a delay in the case before the court; however, it is important that this obligation is maintained and that it is widely recognised that a court will require such attendance, especially when imposing sentence. If a court proceeds in the absence of a responsible adult, it should ensure that the outcome of the hearing is properly communicated.

7.4 Where a person under the age of 18 is convicted of an offence, the court is under a duty to **bind over a parent or guardian** if satisfied that such a course of action would be desirable in the interest of preventing the commission of further offences.[310] Such an order may not be made where the court imposes a referral order. Similarly, the court has the power to make a **parenting order** where it would be desirable in the interest of preventing the commission of any further offence.[311] Where the offender is aged 16 or less and the court considers that a parenting order would be desirable,

[308] Criminal Justice and Immigration Act 2008, section 1(4)(c)
[309] Powers of Criminal Courts (Sentencing) Act 2000, section 100(2)
[310] Powers of Criminal Courts (Sentencing) Act 2000, section 150
[311] Crime and Disorder Act 1998, section 8(6)

there is a presumption in favour of the order being made and reasons must be given if it is not made.[312] In most circumstances where an order is necessary, it is more likely that a parenting order will be appropriate.

7.5 When considering whether to impose a parenting order, the court should give careful consideration to the strength of the familial relationships and to any diversity issues that might impact on the achievement of the purposes of the order. Such factors and issues arising may be documented in a pre-sentence report.

7.6 Particular issues may arise in relation to an offender who is, or who runs the risk of, experiencing familial abuse or rejection on the grounds of sexual orientation. In considering such factors, which may be documented in a pre-sentence report the court must take care not to disclose facts about an offender's sexual orientation without his or her consent. Similar issues might arise in a family where racial tensions exist.

Sentences **SG-523**

8. Referral orders

8.1 Where an offender is being sentenced in a youth court or a magistrates' court, a referral order is a mandatory sentence in many circumstances in which a young person is to be sentenced for the first time and is discretionary in a wider range of situations. In particular, it is possible to make an order on a second conviction where a referral order was not made following the first conviction.

8.2 When an order is made, the court determines the length of the order (between 3 months and 12 months) but the action taken during that order is decided by a Youth Offender Panel consisting of members of the community supported by a member of a Youth Offending Team. Any victim of the offence may be invited to attend the meeting of the Panel at which the terms are agreed.

8.3 When determining the length of an order, although the needs of the offender are a factor, the primary consideration in most circumstances is the relative seriousness of the offence. Given the mandatory nature of the order in many circumstances, it is less likely that the needs of the offender will be considered in a pre-sentence report. This consideration is more likely to take place once the order has been made and in preparation for the Panel meeting since, within the period of the order, the Youth Offender Panel will agree what needs to be undertaken by the young person both in the light of the nature of the offence and of the young person's needs.

8.4 **A court should be prepared to use the whole range of periods allowed; in general, orders of 10–12 months should be made only for the more serious offences.**

8.5 Typically, the length of an order should be between 3–5 months for offences where the court assesses seriousness to be relatively low, between 5–7 months for an offence of medium level seriousness and between 7–9 months for an offence where the court considers seriousness to be relatively high. In determining which level applies, a court may find assistance in Section 2 of the Youth Court Bench Book issued by the Judicial Studies Board which provides indications of the level of seriousness of an average offence of the types described.[313]

9. Financial orders **SG-524**

9.1 A court may impose a fine for any offence. In accordance with statutory requirements, where financial orders are being considered, priority must be given to compensation orders and, where an order for costs is to be made alongside a fine, the amount of the costs must not exceed the amount of the fine.

9.2 In practice, many young people who offend have few financial resources. Where a young person is in receipt of the *Education Maintenance Allowance* or a similar provision which is related to the means of the offender or those with whom the offender lives, a court will need to consider the extent to which making a deduction from the allowance would prejudice the access of the young person to education or training.

9.3 **As a general rule, it will rarely be appropriate to take the allowance into account as a resource from which a financial penalty may be paid, especially where the recipient is a young person who is living independently or as part of a household primarily dependent on state benefit.**

---

312 ibid, section 9(1)

313 www.jsboard.co.uk/downloads/ycbb/ycbb_section2.pdf

Sentencing Guidelines

SG-525 **10. Youth Rehabilitation Orders**

10.1 The Criminal Justice and Immigration Act 2008 provides for a single community sentence (the youth rehabilitation order) within which a court may include one or more requirements variously designed to provide for punishment, for protection of the public, for reducing reoffending and for reparation.

10.2 A youth rehabilitation order with intensive supervision and surveillance or with fostering is also provided but may be imposed only where a custodial sentence otherwise would have been appropriate (see 10.23 below).[314]

(i) Threshold and availability

10.3 In order for a court to be able to impose a youth rehabilitation order, it must be satisfied that the offence is 'serious enough'.[315] Even where an offence crosses this threshold, a court is not obliged to make a youth rehabilitation order.[316]

10.4 In determining the content and length of an order, the guiding principles are proportionality and suitability since statute provides that the restrictions on liberty within such an order must be commensurate with the seriousness of the offence[317] and that, taken together, the requirements within the order are the most suitable for the offender.[318]

10.5 In contrast to the provisions relating to adult offenders, a court may impose a youth rehabilitation order (other than one with intensive supervision and surveillance or fostering[319]) for an offence that is not imprisonable.

10.6 A youth rehabilitation order is not an available sentence where the 'compulsory referral conditions' are found to exist; accordingly, the order will not be available in a youth court or other magistrates' court for a first time offender who has pleaded guilty to an imprisonable offence.

(ii) Effect of a guilty plea

10.7 Where a court is considering sentence for an offence for which a custodial sentence is justified, a guilty plea may be one of the factors that persuades a court that it can properly impose a youth rehabilitation order instead and no further adjustment to the sentence needs to be made to fulfil the obligation to give credit for that plea.

10.8 Where the provisional sentence is already a youth rehabilitation order, the necessary reduction for a guilty plea should apply to those requirements within the order that are primarily punitive rather than to those which are primarily rehabilitative.

(iii) Approach to determining nature and extent of requirements

10.9 In determining the nature and extent of requirements to be included within an order and the length of that order, the key factors are the assessment of the seriousness of the offence, the objective(s) the court wishes to achieve, the risk of re-offending, the ability of the offender to comply, and the availability of requirements in the local area.

10.10 Since a court must determine that the offence (or combination of offences) is 'serious enough' to justify such an order, a court will be able to determine the nature and extent of the requirements within the order primarily by reference to the likelihood of the young person re-offending and to the risk of the young person causing serious harm. This is in accordance with the principal aim of the youth justice system and the welfare principle.

10.11 Before making an order a court will consider a pre-sentence report. In preparing that report, (following national standards and practice guidance) the Youth Offending Team (YOT) will be seeking to identify an appropriate balance between the seriousness of the offence, the risk of harm in the future from any further offences the young person might commit and the needs of the young person.

10.12 In most cases, the assessment by the YOT will be undertaken by use of *Asset*[320] supported by professional judgement. An initial assessment will calculate the risk of re-offending; where necessary, an additional assessment will assess the risk of serious harm likely to be involved in further offending.

---

314 Criminal Justice and Immigration Act 2008, sections 1(3) and 1(4); Criminal Justice Act 2003, section 174(2)(ca) and (cb) as inserted by Criminal Justice and Immigration Act 2008, sched. 4, para. 80(2); however, it may be imposed in other circumstances following 'wilful and persistent' breach of a youth rehabilitation order: see para. 10.41 below

315 Criminal Justice Act 2003, section 148(1)

316 ibid, section 148(5)

317 ibid, section 148(3)(b)

318 ibid, section 148(3)(a)

319 Such an order may be imposed following wilful and persistent failure to comply with a youth rehabilitation order imposed for a non-imprisonable offence: Criminal Justice and Immigration Act 2008, sched. 2, para. 6(13) and para. 8(12)

320 A 'common, structured framework for the assessment of all young people involved in the criminal justice system' which is designed to 'identify a multitude of factors and circumstances. . .which may have contributed' to the offending behaviour: see www.yjb.gov.uk

10.13 Those assessments will be reviewed by the YOT in the context of all other available information and the report will identify a level of intervention for the court to consider. There are three intervention levels:

- **Standard level** — for those who show a low likelihood of reoffending and a low risk of serious harm; in those circumstances, the order primarily will seek to repair the harm caused by the offence — typically, this will involve interventions to meet the requirements of the order and the engagement of parents in those interventions and/or in supporting the young person;
- **Enhanced level** — for those who show a medium likelihood of reoffending or a medium risk of serious harm; in those circumstances, the order will, in addition, seek to enable help or change as appropriate — typically, this will involve greater activity in motivating the young person and in addressing the reasons for non-compliance with the law and may involve external interventions;
- **Intensive level** — for those with a high likelihood of reoffending or a high or very high risk of serious harm; in those circumstances, the order will, in addition, seek to ensure control of the young person as necessary to minimise the risk of further offending or of serious harm—typically this will involve additional controls, restrictions and monitoring.[321]

10.14 For the broad generality of offences where a youth rehabilitation order is to be imposed, this approach will enable the writer of a pre-sentence report to make proposals that match the obligations on the court to balance the various statutory obligations that apply.

10.15 Where a young person is assessed as presenting a **high risk of re-offending or of causing serious harm** despite having committed a relatively less serious offence, the emphasis is likely to be on requirements that are primarily rehabilitative or for the protection of the public. Care will need to be taken to ensure both that the requirements are 'those most suitable for the offender' and that the restrictions on liberty are commensurate with the seriousness of the offence.

10.16 Where a young person is assessed as presenting a **low risk despite having committed a relatively high seriousness offence**, the emphasis is likely to be on requirements that are primarily punitive, again ensuring that restrictions on liberty are commensurate with the seriousness of the offence. In relation to young offenders, the primary purpose of punitive sanctions is to achieve acknowledgement by the young person of responsibility for his or her actions and, where possible, to take a proper part in repairing the damage caused.

(iv) Length of order

10.17 When imposing a youth rehabilitation order, the court must fix a period within which the requirements of the order are to be completed; this must not be more than 3 years from the date on which the order comes into effect.[322] Where the order contains two or more requirements, the order may specify an earlier date for any of those requirements.[323]

10.18 The period specified as the overall period for the order will normally commence on the day the order is made but, where the young person is already subject to a detention and training order, the court may specify that the youth rehabilitation order will take effect either on the day that supervision begins in relation to the detention and training order or on the expiry of the term of that order.[324]

10.19 It is not possible to make a youth rehabilitation order when the young person is already subject to another youth rehabilitation order or to a reparation order unless the court revokes those orders.[325]

10.20 The overall length of an order has three main consequences:

- where a supervision requirement is included, the obligation to attend appointments as directed by the responsible officer continues for the whole period;
- where a young person is in breach of a youth rehabilitation order, one of the sanctions available to a court is to amend the order by including within it any requirement that it would have had power to include when the order was made;[326] however, that new requirement must be capable of being complied with before the expiry of the overall period;[327]
- a young person is liable to re-sentence for the offence(s) for which the order was made if convicted of another offence whilst the order is in force.[328]

10.21 In determining the length of an order, a court should allow sufficient time for the order as a whole to be complied with, recognising that the young person is at risk of further sanction throughout

321 YOUTH JUSTICE: The Scaled Approach, YJB 2009 www.yjb.gov.uk/scaledapproach
322 Criminal Justice and Immigration Act 2008, sched. 1, para. 32(1)
323 ibid, para. 32(2)
324 ibid, para. 30
325 ibid, para. 30(4)
326 Criminal Justice and Immigration Act 2008, sched. 2, para. 6(2) (magistrates' court) and para. 8(2) (Crown Court)
327 ibid, para. 6(6) and para. 8(6)
328 ibid, para. 18 and para. 19

the whole of the period, but allowing sufficient flexibility should a sanction need to be imposed for breach of the order. Where appropriate, an application for early discharge may be made.

(v) Determining the requirements and the length of an order—summary

10.22 As set out in paragraph 2.1 above, the approach to the sentencing of a youth will be individualistic. Where a court is satisfied that an offence has crossed the community sentence threshold and that such a sentence is necessary or has crossed the custody threshold but is an offence for which a youth rehabilitation order is nonetheless considered to be appropriate, taking account of the assessment in the pre-sentence report, the consideration process that the court should follow is:

i) ***what requirements are most suitable for the offender?***
ii) ***what overall period is necessary to ensure that all requirements may be satisfactorily completed?***
iii) ***are the restrictions on liberty that result from those requirements commensurate with the seriousness of the offence?***

(vi) Orders with intensive supervision and surveillance or with fostering

10.23 Such orders may be made where:[329]

- the court is dealing with a young person for an offence punishable with imprisonment;
- that offence (or combination of offences) crosses the custody threshold; and
- custody would be an appropriate sentence.

If the offender was under 15 at the time of conviction, such an order may be imposed only where the offender is a 'persistent offender'.

10.24 When imposing such an order, the court must give its reasons for concluding that the offence(s) cross(es) the community sentence threshold and that the requirements set out above have been met.[330]

(a) With intensive supervision and surveillance

10.25 A youth rehabilitation order with intensive supervision and surveillance is an order that contains an 'extended activity requirement', that is, an activity requirement with a maximum of 180 days. As a result, there are further obligations to include a supervision requirement[331] and a curfew requirement.[332]

10.26 Where appropriate, a youth rehabilitation order with intensive supervision and surveillance may also include additional requirements, although the order as a whole must comply with the obligation that the requirements must be those most suitable for the offender and that any restrictions on liberty must be commensurate with the seriousness of the offence.

10.27 When imposing such an order, a court must ensure that the requirements are not so onerous as to make the likelihood of breach almost inevitable.

(b) With fostering

10.28 Where a fostering requirement is included within a youth rehabilitation order, it will require the offender to reside with a local authority foster parent for a specified period; that period must not exceed 12 months.[333] The court must be satisfied that a significant factor in the offence was the circumstances in which the young person was living and that the imposition of a fostering requirement would assist in the rehabilitation of the young person. It is likely that other rights will be engaged (such as those under Article 8 of the European Convention on Human Rights[334]) and any interference with such rights must be proportionate.

10.29 Before including this requirement, the court must consult both the young person's parent or guardian (unless impracticable) and the local authority; it cannot be included unless the offender was legally represented in court when the court was considering whether or not to impose the requirement or, having had the opportunity to be represented, the offender has not applied for representation or that right was withdrawn because of the offender's conduct.[335] This requirement

[329] Though see the additional powers where an offender has 'wilfully and persistently' failed to comply with a youth rehabilitation order; para. 10.41 below

[330] Criminal Justice Act 2003, section 174(2)(ca) and (cb)

[331] A requirement to attend appointments with the responsible officer (or any other person determined by the responsible officer): Criminal Justice and Immigration Act 2008, sched. 1, para. 9

[332] A minimum of 2 hours and a maximum of 12 hours on any one day which must fall within the period of 6 months from the day on which the requirement first takes effect: ibid, para. 14; it is likely that this curfew will be electronically monitored: ibid, para. 3(4)(b) and para. 2

[333] Criminal Justice and Immigration Act 2008, sched. 1, para. 18

[334] Right to respect for family and private life

[335] Criminal Justice and Immigration Act 2008, sched. 1, para. 19

may be included only where the court has been notified that arrangements are available in the area of the relevant local authority.

10.30 A fostering requirement cannot be included with intensive supervision and surveillance and it cannot be included in a youth rehabilitation order unless the higher criteria described above have been met. Where appropriate, a youth rehabilitation order with fostering may also include other requirements (and must include supervision) although the order as a whole must comply with the obligation that the requirements must be those most suitable for the offender and that any restrictions on liberty must be commensurate with the seriousness of the offence.

10.31 It is unlikely that the statutory criteria will be met in many cases; where they are met and the court is considering making an order, care should be taken to ensure that there is a well developed plan for the care and support of the young person throughout the period of the order and following conclusion of the order. A court will need to be provided with sufficient information, including proposals for education and training during the order and plans for the offender on completion of the order.

(vii) Breaches

10.32 Where a young person fails to comply with a youth rehabilitation order, the 'responsible officer' must consider whether there was a reasonable excuse. If the officer considers that there was no reasonable excuse and this is the first failure to comply with the order without reasonable excuse, the officer must issue a 'warning'.[336]

10.33 The warning will describe the circumstances of the failure to comply, a statement that the failure is not acceptable and a warning that a further failure to comply may lead to the order being referred back to the court. In most circumstances, two warnings will be permitted within a 12 month period before the matter is referred back to court.

10.34 There is a presumption in favour of referring the matter back to court after a third failure to comply and a discretionary power to do so after the second failure to comply.[337]

10.35 Breach of an order brought before a court may arise from a failure to keep an appointment or otherwise co-operate with the responsible officer or may arise from a failure to comply with one or more of the other requirements of the order.

10.36 Even where a breach has been proved, a court is not obliged to make any order but may allow the youth rehabilitation order to continue as imposed. In contrast with the powers in relation to an adult offender, there is no obligation on the court to make an order more onerous. Where a court determines that a sanction is necessary, it has the power to:

- impose a fine (in which case the order continues in its original form);
- amend the terms of the order; or
- revoke the order and re-sentence the offender.[338]

10.37 If amending the terms of the order, the court may impose any requirement that it could have imposed when making the order and this may be in addition to, or in substitution for, any requirements contained in the order. If the youth rehabilitation order did not contain an unpaid work requirement and the court includes such a requirement using this power, the minimum period of unpaid work is 20 hours; this will give greater flexibility when responding to less serious breaches or where there are significant other requirements to be complied with.[339]

10.38 A court may not amend the terms of a youth rehabilitation order that did not include an extended activity requirement or a fostering requirement by inserting them at this stage; should these requirements be considered appropriate following breach, the offender must be re-sentenced and the original youth rehabilitation order revoked.[340]

10.39 Before imposing a custodial sentence as a result of re-sentencing following breach, a court should be satisfied that the YOT and other local authority services have taken all steps necessary to ensure that the young person has been given appropriate opportunity and support necessary for compliance.[341]

10.40 Where the failure arises primarily from non-compliance with reporting or other similar obligations and a sanction is necessary, the most appropriate response is likely to be the inclusion of

[336] Criminal Justice and Immigration Act 2008, sched. 2, para. 3

[337] ibid, para. 4; where a young person has attained the age of 18 since the order was made, except where the order was made in the Crown Court and no direction was made permitting breach proceedings to be dealt with in the youth court or a magistrates' court, breach proceedings will be dealt with in a magistrates' court other than a youth court: ibid, para. 5(3); however, the powers of a magistrates' court are the same as those of a youth court: ibid, para. 6

[338] ibid, para. 6 and para. 8

[339] Criminal Justice and Immigration Act 2008, sched. 2, para. 6(7) and para. 8(7)

[340] ibid, para. 6(8) and para. 8(8)

[341] cp Education and Skills Act 2008, s.45(5)

(or increase in) a primarily punitive requirement such as the curfew requirement, unpaid work, the exclusion requirement and the prohibited activity requirement or...the imposition of a fine. However, continuing failure to comply with the order is likely to lead to revocation of the order and re-sentencing for the original offence.

10.41 Where the offender has 'wilfully and persistently' failed to comply with the order, and the court proposes to sentence again for the offence(s) in respect of which the order was made, additional powers are available.[342] These additional powers include:

- the making of a youth rehabilitation order with intensive supervision and surveillance even though the offence is not imprisonable or a custodial sentence would not have been imposed if the order had not been available;
- even though the offence is not imprisonable, the imposition of a detention and training order for 4 months for breach of a youth rehabilitation order with intensive supervision and surveillance imposed following wilful and persistent breach of an order made for a non-imprisonable offence.

10.42 In considering whether the failure to comply is 'persistent', account should be taken of the principles set out in paragraph 6 above.

The primary objective when sentencing for breach of a youth rehabilitation order is to ensure that the young person completes the requirements imposed by the court.

Where the failure arises primarily from non-compliance with reporting or other similar obligations, where a sanction is necessary, the most appropriate is likely to be the inclusion of (or increase in) a primarily punitive requirement.

A court must ensure that it has sufficient information to enable it to understand why the order has been breached and that all steps have been taken by the YOT and other local authority services to give the young person appropriate opportunity and support. This will be particularly important if the court is considering imposing a custodial sentence as a result of the breach.

Where a court is determining whether the young person has 'wilfully and persistently breached an order, it should apply the same approach as when determining whether an offender is a 'persistent offender'. In particular, almost certainly a young person will have 'persistently breached a youth rehabilitation order where there have been three breaches (each resulting in an appearance before a court) demonstrating a lack of willingness to comply with the order.

SG-526 11. Custodial sentences

11.1 There is a statutory presumption that a person aged under 18 will be dealt with summarily, usually in a youth court; in such circumstances, the maximum custodial sentence will be a detention and training order of no more than 24 months. Such an order may be made only for the periods prescribed—4, 6, 8, 10, 12, 18 or 24 months.[343]

11.2 The custodial sentences available in the Crown Court are:

- detention and training order of up to 24 months;
- long term detention—in relation to a young person convicted[344] in the Crown Court, under section 91 of the Powers of Criminal Courts (Sentencing) Act 2000;
- extended sentence of detention or detention for public protection — where a young person is sent for trial or committed for sentence to the Crown Court to be dealt with under the dangerous offender provisions; in each case, the minimum period to be spent in custody under the sentence must be two years;
- detention at Her Majesty's pleasure—for offences of murder.

11.3 A detention and training order may not be imposed on an offender aged 10 or 11 years at the time of conviction; an order may be imposed in relation to an offender aged between 12 and 14 at the time of conviction only if the offender is a 'persistent offender' (see paragraph 6 above).[345] However, the persistent offender criterion does not have to be met before the Crown Court imposes long term detention or detention for life in relation to offenders who are under 15 years of age.

11.4 A pre-sentence report must be considered before a custodial sentence is imposed.

[342] In accordance with para. 6 and para. 8 of sched. 2 to the Criminal Justice and Immigration Act 2008

[343] Although consecutive sentences may lead to different periods being imposed in total.

[344] On the implementation of provisions contained in Criminal Justice Act 2003, sched. 3, this sentence is likely to be able to be imposed following conviction in a youth court also subsequent to an indication to plead guilty.

[345] Powers of Criminal Courts (Sentencing) Act 2000, section 100(2)

(i) **Threshold and approach**

11.5 Under both domestic law and international convention, a custodial sentence must be imposed only as a 'measure of last resort'; statute provides that such a sentence may be imposed only where an offence is 'so serious that neither a community sentence nor a fine alone can be justified'.[346]

11.6 For a first time offender who has pleaded guilty to an imprisonable offence, in most circumstances a referral order will be the most appropriate sentence.

11.7 Since the minimum length of a custodial sentence in the youth court is 4 months (significantly in excess of the minimum available in relation to an adult offender) and since the term of a custodial sentence must be the shortest commensurate with the seriousness of the offence, it is inevitable that the custody threshold is higher in the case of a young person than in the case of an adult—any case that warrants a detention and training order of less than four months must result in a non-custodial sentence.

11.8 In relation to a person under the age of 18, in determining whether an offence has crossed the custody threshold a court will need to consider whether the offence has resulted (or could reasonably have resulted) in serious harm. In determining whether a custodial sentence is unavoidable, generally, a court will need to take account both of the seriousness of the offence (particularly the extent to which it caused (or was likely to cause) serious harm) and of the risk of serious harm in the future. A custodial sentence is most likely to be unavoidable where it is necessary to protect the public from serious harm.

11.9 In addition, a court must take account of:

i) the requirement to have regard to the principal aim of the youth justice system;[347]
ii) the requirement to have regard to the welfare of the offender and the evidence that the risks associated with young offenders in a custodial setting are high.[348]

11.10 Even where the threshold is crossed, a court is not required to impose a custodial sentence.

11.11 Before deciding to impose a custodial sentence on a young offender, the court must ensure that all the statutory tests are satisfied—namely:

i) that the offender cannot properly be dealt with by a fine alone or by a youth rehabilitation order,
ii) that a youth rehabilitation order with intensive supervision and surveillance or with fostering cannot be justified, and
iii) that custody is the last resort and in doing so should take account of the circumstances, age and maturity of the young offender.

11.12 When a custodial sentence is imposed, a court must state its reasons for being satisfied that the offence(s) is (are) so serious that no other sanction is appropriate and, in particular, why a youth rehabilitation order with intensive supervision and surveillance or with fostering cannot be justified.[349] This justification will need to be based on the principles set out in the statutory framework.

Where the offence(s) has crossed the custody threshold, the statutory tests are likely to be satisfied only where a custodial sentence will be more effective in preventing offending by children and young persons. The obligation to have regard to the welfare of the offender will require a court to take account of a wide range of issues including those relating to mental health, capability and maturity.

(ii) **Length of sentence**

11.13 A court imposing a custodial sentence is required to set the shortest term commensurate with the seriousness of the offence(s).[350] Offence specific guidelines do not generally provide starting points or ranges for offenders aged under 18 because of the wide range of issues that are likely to arise and the marked differences in the sentencing framework depending on the age of the offender. Where they are provided,[351] they are for offenders aged 17 with a provision that, for younger offenders, a court should consider whether a lower starting point is justified in recognition of the offender's age and maturity.

[346] Criminal Justice Act 2003, section 152(2)
[347] The prevention of offending; see para. 2.6 above
[348] See para. 2 above
[349] Criminal Justice Act 2003, section 174(4B) as inserted by Criminal Justice and Immigration Act 2008, sched. 4, para. 80(3)
[350] Criminal Justice Act 2003, section 153(2)
[351] Robbery pages 12–14; *Sexual Offences Act 2003* pages 133–139; *Breach of an Anti-Social Behaviour Order* pages 10–12: www.sentencing-guidelines.gov.uk

11.14 Any approach needs to take account of the general sentencing rules that apply where there is more than one offence or more than one defendant. Where the offence has been committed by offender(s) aged 18 or over and by offender(s) aged under 18, the court will need to consider the role of each offender and the number of offenders involved.

11.15 Where the primary offender is under the age of 18, a court is likely to determine sentence for that offender first giving proper weight to the offender's age and maturity; that will provide a framework within which sentence for the offender(s) over 18 can be determined. Where the primary offender is over 18, a court is likely to determine sentence for that offender first; that will provide a framework within which sentence for the offender(s) under 18 can be determined giving proper weight to age and maturity.

11.16 Where an offence crosses the custodial threshold and the court determines that a custodial sentence is unavoidable:

- **where the offender is aged 15, 16 or 17, the court will need to consider the maturity of the offender as well as chronological age. Where there is no offence specific guideline, it may be appropriate, depending on maturity, to consider a starting point from half to three quarters of that which would have been identified for an adult offender.**

  It will be particularly important to consider maturity when the court has to sentence more than one offender. When the offenders are of different ages, including when one or more is over 18, the court will also need to have proper regard to parity between their sentences.

  The closer an offender was to age 18 when the offence was committed and the greater the maturity of the offender or the sophistication of the offence, the closer the starting point is likely to be to that appropriate for an adult. Some offenders will be extremely mature, more so than some offenders who are over 18, whilst others will be significantly less mature.

  For younger offenders, greater flexibility will be required to reflect the potentially wide range of culpability.

  Where an offence shows considerable planning or sophistication, a court may need to adjust the approach upwards.

  Where the offender is particularly immature, the court may need to adjust the approach downwards.
- **where the offender is aged 14 or less**, sentence should normally be imposed in a youth court (except in cases of homicide or where the young person comes within the 'dangerous offender' criteria); the length of a custodial sentence will normally be shorter than for an offender aged 15–17 convicted of the same offence.
- **an offender aged 14 years or less** should be sentenced to long term detention[352] only where that is necessary for the protection of the public either because of the risk of serious harm from future offending or because of the persistence of offending behaviour; exceptionally, such a sentence may be appropriate where an offender aged 14 years or less has committed a very serious offence but is not a persistent offender and there is no risk of serious harm from future offending.

11.17 In determining the term of a detention and training order, the court must take account of any period for which the offender has been remanded in custody or on bail subject to a qualifying curfew condition and electronic monitoring.[353] As the available terms are specified, the proper approach in taking a remand period into account is to reduce, if possible, the sentence otherwise appropriate to reflect that period.[354] Where a short custodial sentence was being considered, the court might conclude that a non-custodial sentence was appropriate.

11.18 On the implementation of the relevant parts of schedule 3 to the Criminal Justice Act 2003, a 'plea before venue' procedure will be introduced for offenders under the age of 18 and will include a general power to commit for sentence where a court accepts jurisdiction following indication of a guilty plea. As with adult offenders, where a young person could have been dealt with in the Crown Court but the youth court has retained jurisdiction, where appropriate the maximum period of 24 months may be imposed following a guilty plea at the first reasonable opportunity where that plea was a factor in retaining a case for sentence in the youth court.

---

352 Powers of Criminal Courts (Sentencing) Act 2000, section 91

353 Powers of Criminal Courts (Sentencing) Act 2000, section 101(8) and (9); for these purpose, 'remanded in custody' includes periods held in police detention and certain remands or committals to local authority accommodation: ibid, section 101(11)

354 Such a period must be set against the part of the sentence that is to be served in custody, not the whole sentence: *Eagles* [2006] EWCA Crim 2368; *Joyce* [2007] EWCA Crim 3374

12. Trial and Sentencing of Cases in the Crown Court

SG-527

12.1 There is a clear principle (established both in statute and in domestic and European case law) that cases involving young offenders should be tried and sentenced in the youth court wherever possible. This section summarises the relevant statutory provisions and case law.[355]

12.2 It has long been recognised that the Crown Court should be reserved for the most serious cases, noting the greater formality of the proceedings and the increased number of people likely to be present.[356] These factors present additional obstacles in ensuring that proceedings in the Crown Court involving young offenders are conducted in accordance with international obligations.[357]

12.3 Accordingly, it is rare for a young offender to be tried or sentenced in the Crown Court and for a sentence beyond the powers of the youth court to be imposed, except where that sentence is substantially beyond those powers.

12.4 A youth will appear in the Crown Court for trial and sentence only:

i) when charged with 'homicide';
ii) when subject to a minimum statutory sentence;
iii) when charged with a 'grave crime' and a youth court has determined that, if convicted, a sentence beyond its powers should be available; or
iv) when charged together with an adult offender who has been sent to the Crown Court and it has been determined that the cases should be kept together.

12.5 Where a sentence under the 'dangerous offender' provisions is likely to be needed the youth may be committed for trial or for sentence.

(i) Homicide

12.6 An exception to the presumption that a person aged under 18 should be tried summarily arises where the young person is charged with an offence of 'homicide'. For a case falling within this description, there is no discretion and it must be sent to the Crown Court for trial. The meaning of 'homicide' is not defined in statute.

(ii) Statutory minimum sentences

12.7 A further exception to the presumption in favour of summary trial arises where a young person is charged with an offence which has a statutory minimum custodial sentence and the criteria for that sentence would be likely to be satisfied if the young person were convicted.[358] A sentence of long term detention[359] may be imposed following committal where these mandatory sentence provisions apply; before there can be a departure from the minimum sentence prescribed, a court must find that there are 'exceptional circumstances'.

(iii) 'Grave crimes'

12.8 A further exception to the statutory presumption in favour of summary trial arises where a young person is charged with a 'grave crime' and a youth court has determined that, if convicted, a sentence beyond its powers should be available. In such circumstances, a young person may be sentenced by the Crown Court to long term detention under section 91 of the Powers of Criminal Courts (Sentencing) Act 2000. At present, such a sentence may be imposed only by the Crown Court and only where the offender was convicted in the Crown Court, and that court considers that neither a community order nor a detention and training order is suitable.

12.9 An offence comes within section 91 where:

- it is punishable with 14 years imprisonment or more for an adult (but is not a sentence fixed by law), or
- is an offence contrary to sections 3, 13, 25 or 26 of the Sexual Offences Act 2003,[360] or
- is one of a number of specified offences in relation to firearms, ammunition and weapons which are subject to a minimum term but in respect of which a court has found exceptional circumstances justifying a lesser sentence.

12.10 This general power should be used rarely since:

i) it is the general policy of Parliament that those under 18 should be tried in the youth court wherever possible;

---

355 See in particular *R (H, A, and O) v Southampton Youth Court* [2004] EWHC 2912 (Admin)
356 ibid, [33]
357 See, for example, *S.C. v United Kingdom* (2005) 40 EHRR 10
358 Magistrates' Courts Act 1980, section 24
359 Under Powers of Criminal Courts (Sentencing) Act 2000, section 91
360 Sexual assault, child sex offences committed by a child or young person, sexual activity with a child family member, inciting a child family member to engage in sexual activity

ii) trial in the Crown Court under this provision should be reserved for the most serious cases, recognising the greater formality of the proceedings and the greatly increased number of people involved;
iii) offenders aged under 15 will rarely attract a period of detention under this provision and those under 12 even more rarely.[361]

12.11 Accordingly,
i) a young person aged 10 or 11 (or aged 12–14 but not a persistent offender) should be committed to the Crown Court under this provision only where charged with an offence of such gravity that, despite the normal prohibition on a custodial sentence for a person of that age, a sentence exceeding two years is a realistic possibility[362]
ii) a young person aged 12–17 (for which a detention and training order could be imposed) should be committed to the Crown Court under this provision only where charged with an offence of such gravity that a sentence substantially beyond the 2 year maximum for a detention and training order is a realistic possibility[363]

(iv) Dangerous offenders

12.12 There are rigorous statutory tests which must be satisfied before a court may conclude that a youth is a 'dangerous offender' and requires sentence under the dangerous offender provisions in the Criminal Justice Act 2003 (as amended).[364] Such a sentence may be imposed only where an equivalent determinate sentence of at least 4 years would have been imposed. Criteria relating to future offending and the risk of serious harm must be assessed in the light of the maturity of the offender, the possibility of change in a much shorter time than would apply for an adult and the wider circumstances of the young person.

12.13 At present, the provisions by which a potentially 'dangerous' young offender reaches the Crown Court are overlapping to some extent as a result of the only partial implementation of the provisions of the Criminal Justice Act 2003, which introduce a new section 51A to the Crime and Disorder Act 1998. This new section requires a young offender to be sent for trial where it appears that the criteria for imposition of a sentence under the dangerous offender provisions will be met on conviction. However, the power to commit for sentence following conviction in a youth court or magistrates' court is preserved.[365]

12.14 The nature of the offence is likely to be very significant in determining both whether the offender meets the risk and harm criteria and, even if so, whether a sentence under the provisions is necessary (given that there is now wide discretion).
Since a young offender should normally be dealt with in a youth court, where a young person charged with a specified offence would not otherwise be committed or sent to the Crown Court for trial, generally it is preferable for the decision whether to commit under these provisions to be made after conviction.[366]

(v) Jointly charged with an adult

12.15 A further exception to the presumption in favour of summary trial arises where a young person is charged jointly with a person aged 18 or over; if the court considers it necessary to commit them both for trial it will have the power to commit the young person to the Crown Court for trial.[367]

12.16 Any presumption in favour of sending a youth to the Crown Court to be tried jointly with an adult must be balanced with the general presumption that young offenders should be dealt with in a youth court.

12.17 When deciding whether to separate the youth and adult defendants, a court must consider:
- the young age of the offender, particularly where the age gap between the adult and youth is substantial,

---

[361] See footnote [402]; those who meet the criteria for 'dangerous offenders' will be dealt with under separate provisions: see below
[362] See *R(D) v Manchester City Youth Court* [2001] EWHC Admin 860
[363] See *C & D v Sheffield Youth Court* [2003] EWHC Admin 35 confirming the relevance of undisputed personal mitigation
[364] See the review of statutory provisions and case law authority in *Dangerous Offenders: A Guide for Sentencers and Practitioners* at p.18 www.sentencing-guidelines.gov.uk
[365] Powers of Criminal Courts (Sentencing) Act 2000, s.3C; where an offence falls within section 91 (see para. 12.9) and, following committal under this section, the Crown Court does not impose a sentence under the dangerous offender provisions, it may impose a sentence of long term detention: ibid, section 5A
[366] See, for example, the statement that there is a strong presumption against sending young offenders to the Crown Court unless clearly required: *R(W) v Southampton Youth Court* [2002] EWHC 1640 per Lord Woolf CJ
[367] The procedures around the transfer to the Crown Court of a young person charged with an offence will change on the implementation of the relevant provisions in the Criminal Justice Act 2003, sched. 3

- the immaturity and intellect of the youth,
- the relative culpability of the youth compared with the adult and whether or not the role played by the youth was minor, and
- any lack of previous convictions on the part of the youth compared with the adult offender.

12.18 A very significant factor will be whether the trial of the adult and youth could be severed without inconvenience to witnesses or injustice to the case as a whole, including whether there are benefits in the same tribunal sentencing all offenders. In most circumstances, a single trial of all issues is likely to be most in the interests of justice.

(vi) Remittal from the Crown Court

12.19 Where a young person is convicted before the Crown Court of an offence other than homicide, there is an obligation to remit the young person to a youth court for sentence unless that is 'undesirable'.[368] In considering whether remittal is 'undesirable', a court should balance the need for expertise in the sentencing of young offenders with the benefits of sentence being imposed by the court which had determined guilt.

12.20 Particular attention should be given to the presumption where a young person appears before the Crown Court only because he or she is jointly charged with an adult offender. A referral order is not available in the Crown Court for a first-time offender and such orders may now be made following a second conviction in certain circumstances.

PART 19 CORPORATE MANSLAUGHTER SG-528

Definitive Guideline

[This is an excerpt from the definitive guideline 'Health and Safety Offences, Corporate Manslaughter and Food Safety and Hygiene Offences'.]

Applicability of guidelines

[Omitted: See **SG-539** for identical text save that this guideline has effect from 1 February 2016.]

Corporate Manslaughter SG-529

Corporate Manslaughter and Corporate Homicide Act 2007 (section 1)

Triable only on indictment

Maximum: unlimited fine

Offence range: £180,000 fine — £20 million fine

STEP ONE Determining the seriousness of the offence SG-530

By definition, the **harm** and **culpability** involved in corporate manslaughter will be very serious. Every case will involve death and corporate fault at a high level. The court should assess factors affecting the seriousness of the offence within this context by asking:

(a) How foreseeable was serious injury?

Usually, the more foreseeable a serious injury was, the graver the offence. Failure to heed warnings or advice from the authorities, employees or others or to respond appropriately to 'near misses' arising in similar circumstances may be factors indicating greater foreseeability of serious injury.

(b) How far short of the appropriate standard did the offender fall?

Where an offender falls far short of the appropriate standard, the level of culpability is likely to be high. Lack of adherence to recognised standards in the industry or the inadequacy of training, supervision and reporting arrangements may be relevant factors to consider.

(c) How common is this kind of breach in this organisation?

How widespread was the non-compliance? Was it isolated in extent or, for example, indicative of a systematic departure from good practice across the offender's operations or representative of systemic failings? Widespread non-compliance is likely to indicate a more serious offence.

[368] Powers of Criminal Courts (Sentencing) Act 2000, section 8(2)

(d) Was there more than one death, or a high risk of further deaths, or serious personal injury in addition to death?

The greater the number of deaths, very serious personal injuries or people put at high risk of death, the more serious the offence.

Offence Category A: Where answers to questions (a)–(d) indicate a high level of harm or culpability within the context of offence.

Offence Category B: Where answers to questions (a)–(d) indicate a lower level of culpability.

SG-531 STEP TWO **Starting point and category range**

Having determined the offence category, the court should identify the relevant table for the offender [below]. There are tables for different sized organisations.

At step two, the court is required to focus on the organisation's annual turnover or equivalent to reach a starting point for a fine. The court should then consider further adjustment within the category range for aggravating and mitigating features.

At step three, the court may be required to refer to other financial factors listed below to ensure that the proposed fine is proportionate.

Obtaining financial information

The offender is expected to provide comprehensive accounts for the last three years, to enable the court to make an accurate assessment of its financial status. In the absence of such disclosure, or where the court is not satisfied that it has been given sufficient reliable information, the court will be entitled to draw reasonable inferences as to the offender's means from evidence it has heard and from all the circumstances of the case, **which may include the inference that the offender can pay any fine.**

Normally, only information relating to the organisation before the court will be relevant, unless it is demonstrated to the court that the resources of a linked organisation are available and can properly be taken into account.

1. *For companies*: annual accounts. Particular attention should be paid to turnover; profit before tax; directors' remuneration, loan accounts and pension provision; and assets as disclosed by the balance sheet. Most companies are required to file audited accounts at Companies House. **Failure to produce relevant recent accounts on request may properly lead to the conclusion that the company can pay any appropriate fine.**
2. *For partnerships*: annual accounts. Particular attention should be paid to turnover; profit before tax; partners' drawings, loan accounts and pension provision; assets as above. Limited liability partnerships (LLPs) may be required to file audited accounts with Companies House. **If adequate accounts are not produced on request, see paragraph 1.**
3. *For local authorities, fire authorities and similar public bodies*: the Annual Revenue Budget ('ARB') is the equivalent of turnover and the best indication of the size of the organisation. It is unlikely to be necessary to analyse specific expenditure or reserves (where relevant) unless inappropriate expenditure is suggested.
4. *For health trusts*: the independent regulator of NHS Foundation Trusts is Monitor. It publishes quarterly reports and annual figures for the financial strength and stability of trusts from which the annual income can be seen, available via **www.monitor-nhsft.gov.uk.** Detailed analysis of expenditure or reserves is unlikely to be called for.
5. *For charities*: it will be appropriate to inspect annual audited accounts. Detailed analysis of expenditure or reserves is unlikely to be called for unless there is a suggestion of unusual or unnecessary expenditure.

Very large organisation
Where an offending organisation's turnover or equivalent very greatly exceeds the threshold for large organisations, it may be necessary to move outside the suggested range to achieve a proportionate sentence.

Large organisation — Turnover more than £50 million

Offence category	Starting point	Category range
A	£7,500,000	£4,800,000 — £20,000,000
B	£5,000,000	£3,000,000 — £12,500,000

Medium organisation — Turnover £10 million to £50 million

Offence category	Starting point	Category range
A	£3,000,000	£1,800,000 — £7,500,000
B	£2,000,000	£1,200,000 — £5,000,000

Small organisation — Turnover £10 million to £50 million

Offence category	Starting point	Category range
A	£800,000	£540,000 — £2,800,000
B	£540,000	£350,000 — £2,000,000

Micro organisation — Turnover up to £2 million

Offence category	Starting point	Category range
A	£450,000	£270,000 — £800,000
B	£300,000	£180,000 — £540,000

The table below contains a **non-exhaustive** list of factual elements providing the context of the offence and factors relating to the offender. Identify whether any combination of these, or other relevant factors, should result in an upward or downward adjustment from the starting point.

Factors increasing seriousness	Factors reducing seriousness or reflecting mitigation
Statutory aggravating factor: Previous convictions, having regard to a) the nature of the offence to which the conviction relates and its relevance to the current offence; and b) the time that has elapsed since the conviction *Other aggravating factors include*: Cost-cutting at the expense of safety Deliberate concealment of illegal nature of activity Breach of any court order Obstruction of justice Poor health and safety record Falsification of documentation or licences Deliberate failure to obtain or comply with relevant licences in order to avoid scrutiny by authorities Offender exploited vulnerable victims	No previous convictions **or** no relevant/recent convictions Evidence of steps taken to remedy problem High level of co-operation with the investigation, beyond that which will always be expected Good health and safety record Effective health and safety procedures in place Self-reporting, co-operation and acceptance of responsibility Other events beyond the responsibility of the offender contributed to the death (**however**, actions of victims are unlikely to be considered contributory events. Offenders are required to protect workers or others who are neglectful of their own safety in a way which is reasonably foreseeable)

Sentencing Guidelines

SG-532 **STEPS THREE AND FOUR**

The court should 'step back', review and, if necessary, adjust the initial fine based on turnover to **ensure that it fulfils the objectives of sentencing** for these offences. The court may adjust the fine upwards or downwards, including outside the range.

SG-533 **STEP THREE Check whether the proposed fine based on turnover is proportionate to the overall means of the offender**

General principles to follow in setting a fine

The court should finalise the appropriate level of fine in accordance with section 164 of the Criminal Justice Act 2003, which requires that the fine must reflect the seriousness of the offence and requires the court to take into account the financial circumstances of the offender.

Fines cannot and do not attempt to value a human life in money. The fine should meet the objectives of punishment, the reduction of offending through deterrence and removal of gain derived through the commission of the offence. The fine **must be sufficiently substantial to have a real economic impact which will bring home to management and shareholders the need to achieve a safe environment for workers and members of the public affected by their activities.**

Review of the fine based on turnover

The court should 'step back', review and, if necessary, adjust the initial fine reached at step two to **ensure that it fulfils the general principles** set out above. The court may adjust the fine upwards or downwards including outside of the range.

The court should examine the financial circumstances of the offender in the round to assess the economic realities of the organisation and the most efficacious way of giving effect to the purposes of sentencing.

In finalising the sentence, the court should have regard to the following factors:

- The profitability of an organisation will be a relevant factor. If an organisation has a small profit margin relative to its turnover, downward adjustment may be needed. If it has a large profit margin, upward adjustment may be needed.
- Any quantifiable economic benefit derived from the offence, including through avoided costs or operating savings, should normally be added to the fine arrived at in step two. Where this is not readily available, the court may draw on information available from enforcing authorities and others about general costs of operating within the law.
- Whether the fine will have the effect of putting the offender out of business will be relevant; in some cases this may be an acceptable consequence.

In considering the ability of the offending organisation to pay any financial penalty, the court can take into account the **power to allow time for payment or to order that the amount be paid in instalments**, if necessary over a number of years.

SG-534 **STEP FOUR Consider other factors that may warrant adjustment of the proposed fine**

The court should consider any wider impacts of the fine within the organisation or on innocent third parties; such as (but not limited to):

- impact of the fine on offender's ability to improve conditions in the organisation to comply with the law;
- impact of the fine on employment of staff, service users, customers and local economy (but not shareholders or directors).

Where the fine will fall on public or charitable bodies, the fine should normally be substantially reduced if the offending organisation is able to demonstrate the proposed fine would have a significant impact on the provision of their services.

SG-535 **STEP FIVE Consider any factors which indicate a reduction, such as assistance to the prosecution**

The court should take into account sections 73 and 74 of the Serious Organised Crime and Police Act 2005 (assistance by defendants: reduction or review of sentence) and any other rule of law by virtue of which an offender may receive a discounted sentence in consequence of assistance given (or offered) to the prosecutor or investigator.

SG-536 **STEP SIX Reduction for guilty pleas**

The court should take account of any potential reduction for a guilty plea in accordance with section 144 of the Criminal Justice Act 2003 and the *Guilty Plea* guideline.

SG-537 **STEP SEVEN Compensation and ancillary orders**

In all cases, the court must consider whether to make ancillary orders. These may include:

Publicity Orders
(Section 10 Corporate Manslaughter and Corporate Homicide Act 2007)

A publicity order should ordinarily be imposed in a case of corporate manslaughter. It may require publication in a specified manner of:

a) the fact of conviction;

b) specified particulars of the offence;

c) the amount of any fine;

d) the terms of any remedial order.

The object of a publicity order is deterrence and punishment.

(i) The order should specify with particularity the matters to be published in accordance with section 10(1). Special care should be taken with the terms of the particulars of the offence committed.
(ii) The order should normally specify the place where public announcement is to be made, and consideration should be given to indicating the size of any notice or advertisement required. It should ordinarily contain a provision designed to ensure that the conviction becomes known to shareholders in the case of companies and local people in the case of public bodies. Consideration should be given to requiring a statement on the offender's website. A newspaper announcement may be unnecessary if the proceedings are certain to receive news coverage in any event, but if an order requires publication in a newspaper it should specify the paper, the form of announcement to be made and the number of insertions required.
(iii) The prosecution should provide the court in advance of the sentencing hearing, and should serve on the offender, a draft of the form of order suggested and the judge should personally endorse the final form of the order.
(iv) Consideration should be given to stipulating in the order that any comment placed by the offender alongside the required announcement should be separated from it and clearly identified as such.

A publicity order is part of the penalty. Any exceptional cost of compliance should be considered in fixing the fine. It is not, however, necessary to fix the fine first and then deduct the cost of compliance.

Remediation
(Section 9 Corporate Manslaughter and Corporate Homicide Act 2007)

An offender ought by the time of sentencing to have remedied any specific failings involved in the offence and if it has not, will be deprived of significant mitigation.

If, however, it has not, a remedial order should be considered if it can be made sufficiently specific to be enforceable. The prosecution is required by section 9(2) Corporate Manslaughter and Corporate Homicide Act 2007 to give notice of the form of any such order sought, which can only be made on its application. The judge should personally endorse the final form of such an order.

The cost of compliance with such an order should not ordinarily be taken into account in fixing the fine; the order requires only what should already have been done.

Compensation

Where the offence has resulted in loss or damage, the court must consider whether to make a compensation order. The assessment of compensation in cases involving death or serious injury will usually be complex and will ordinarily be covered by insurance. In the great majority of cases the court should conclude that compensation should be dealt with in the civil courts, and should say that no order is made for that reason.

If compensation is awarded, priority should be given to the payment of compensation over payment of any other financial penalty where the means of the offender are limited.

Where the offender does not have sufficient means to pay the total financial penalty considered appropriate by the court, compensation and fine take priority over prosecution costs.

STEP EIGHT Totality principle **SG-538**

If sentencing an offender for more than one offence, consider whether the total sentence is just and proportionate to the offending behaviour in accordance with the *Offences Taken into Consideration* and *Totality* guideline.

STEP NINE Reasons **SG-538A**

Section 174 of the Criminal Justice Act 2003 imposes a duty to give reasons for, and explain the effect of, the sentence.

PART 20 BURGLARY OFFENCES

SG-539 Definitive Guideline

Applicability of Guideline

In accordance with section 120 of the Coroners and Justice Act 2009, the Sentencing Council issues this definitive guideline. It applies to all offenders aged 18 and older, who are sentenced on or after 16 January 2012, regardless of the date of the offence.

Section 125(1) of the Coroners and Justice Act 2009 provides that when sentencing offences committed after 6 April 2010:

Every court—

(a) must, in sentencing an offender, follow any sentencing guideline which is relevant to the offender's case, and

(b) must, in exercising any other function relating to the sentencing of offenders, follow any sentencing guidelines which are relevant to the exercise of the function,

unless the court is satisfied that it would be contrary to the interests of justice to do so.

This guideline applies only to offenders aged 18 and older. General principles to be considered in the sentencing of youths are in the Sentencing Guidelines Council's definitive guideline, *Overarching Principles—Sentencing Youths* [see **SG-515**].

SG-540 **Structure, ranges and starting points**

For the purposes of section 125(3)–(4) Coroners and Justice Act 2009, the guideline specifies offence ranges—the range of sentences appropriate for each type of offence. Within each offence, the Council has specified three categories which reflect varying degrees of seriousness. The offence range is split into category ranges—sentences appropriate for each level of seriousness. The Council has also identified a starting point within each category.

Starting points define the position within a category range from which to start calculating the provisional sentence. As in the Sentencing Council's Assault Definitive Guideline, this guideline adopts an offence based starting point. **Starting points apply to all offences within the corresponding category and are applicable to all offenders, in all cases.** Once the starting point is established, the court should consider further aggravating and mitigating factors and previous convictions so as to adjust the sentence within the range. Starting points and ranges apply to all offenders, whether they have pleaded guilty or been convicted after trial. Credit for a guilty plea is taken into consideration only at step four in the decision making process, after the appropriate sentence has been identified.

Information on community orders and fine bands is set out in the annex [not reproduced: see **SG-356** and **SG-382**].

SG-541 Aggravated Burglary

Theft Act 1968 (section 10)

This is a serious specified offence for the purposes of section 224 of the Criminal Justice Act 2003

Triable only on indictment
Maximum: Life imprisonment
Offence range: 1–13 years' custody

STEP ONE Determining the offence category

Category 1	Greater harm **and** higher culpability
Category 2	Greater harm **and** lower culpability **or** lesser harm **and** higher culpability
Category 3	Lesser harm **and** lower culpability

The court should determine the offence category using the table below.

The court should determine culpability and harm caused or intended, by reference only to the factors below, which comprise the principal factual elements of the offence. Where an offence does not fall squarely into a category, individual factors may require a degree of weighting before making an overall assessment and determining the appropriate offence category.

Factors indicating greater harm	Factors indicating higher culpability
Theft of/damage to property causing a significant degree of loss to the victim (whether economic, commercial, sentimental or personal value) Soiling, ransacking or vandalism of property Victim at home or on the premises (or returns) while offender present Significant physical or psychological injury or other significant trauma to the victim Violence used or threatened against victim, particularly involving a weapon Context of general public disorder **Factors indicating lesser harm** No physical or psychological injury or other significant trauma to the victim No violence used or threatened and a weapon is not produced	Victim or premises deliberately targeted (for example, due to vulnerability or hostility based on disability, race, sexual orientation) A significant degree of planning or organisation Equipped for burglary (for example, implements carried and/or use of vehicle) Weapon present on entry Member of a group or gang **Factors indicating lower culpability** Offender exploited by others Mental disorder or learning disability, where linked to the commission of the offence

STEP TWO Starting point and category range

Having determined the category, the court should use the corresponding starting points to reach a sentence within the category range below. The starting point applies to all offenders irrespective of plea or previous convictions. A case of particular gravity, reflected by multiple features of culpability or harm in step 1, could merit upward adjustment from the starting point before further adjustment for aggravating or mitigating features, set out below.

Offence Category	Starting Point (*Applicable to all offenders*)	Category Range (*Applicable to all offenders*)
Category 1	10 years' custody	9–13 years' custody
Category 2	6 years' custody	4–9 years' custody
Category 3	2 years' custody	1–4 years' custody

The table below contains a **non-exhaustive** list of additional factual elements providing the context of the offence and factors relating to the offender. Identify whether any combination of these, or other relevant factors, should result in an upward or downward adjustment from the starting point. **In particular, relevant recent convictions are likely to result in an upward adjustment**. In some cases, having considered these factors, it may be appropriate to move outside the identified category range.

Factors increasing seriousness	Factors reducing seriousness or reflecting personal mitigation
Statutory aggravating factors: Previous convictions, having regard to a) the nature of the offence to which the conviction relates and its relevance to the current offence; and b) the time that has elapsed since the conviction Offence committed whilst on bail *Other aggravating factors include:* Child at home (or returns home) when offence committed Offence committed at night Abuse of power and/or position of trust Gratuitous degradation of victim Any steps taken to prevent the victim reporting the incident or obtaining assistance and/or from assisting or supporting the prosecution Victim compelled to leave their home (in particular victims of domestic violence) Established evidence of community impact Commission of offence whilst under the influence of alcohol or drugs Failure to comply with current court orders Offence committed whilst on licence Offences Taken Into Consideration (TICs)	Subordinate role in a group or gang Injuries caused recklessly Nothing stolen or only property of very low value to the victim (whether economic, commercial, sentimental or personal) Offender has made voluntary reparation to the victim No previous convictions or no relevant/recent convictions Remorse Good character and/or exemplary conduct Determination, and/or demonstration of steps taken to address addiction or offending behaviour Serious medical conditions requiring urgent, intensive or long-term treatment Age and/or lack of maturity where it affects the responsibility of the offender Lapse of time since the offence where this is not the fault of the offender Mental disorder or learning disability, where not linked to the commission of the offence Sole or primary carer for dependent relatives

STEP THREE Consider any factors which indicate a reduction, such as assistance to the prosecution

The court should take into account sections 73 and 74 of the Serious Organised Crime and Police Act 2005 (assistance by defendants: reduction or review of sentence) and any other rule of law by virtue of which an offender may receive a discounted sentence in consequence of assistance given (or offered) to the prosecutor or investigator.

STEP FOUR Reduction for guilty pleas

The court should take account of any potential reduction for a guilty plea in accordance with section 144 of the Criminal Justice Act 2003 and the Guilty Plea guideline.

STEP FIVE Dangerousness

An aggravated burglary is a serious specified offence within the meaning of chapter 5 of the Criminal Justice Act 2003 and at this stage the court should consider whether having regard to the criteria contained in that chapter it would be appropriate to award a life sentence, imprisonment for public protection or an extended sentence. Where offenders meet the dangerousness criteria, the notional determinate sentence should be used as the basis for the setting of a minimum term.

STEP SIX Totality principle

If sentencing an offender for more than one offence, or where the offender is already serving a sentence, consider whether the total sentence is just and proportionate to the offending behaviour.

STEP SEVEN Compensation and ancillary orders

In all cases, courts should consider whether to make compensation and/or other ancillary orders.

STEP EIGHT Reasons

Section 174 of the Criminal Justice Act 2003 imposes a duty to give reasons for, and explain the effect of, the sentence.

STEP NINE Consideration for remand time

Sentencers should take into consideration any remand time served in relation to the final sentence at this final step. The court should consider whether to give credit for time spent on remand in custody or on bail in accordance with sections 240 and 240A of the Criminal Justice Act 2003.

SG-542 DOMESTIC BURGLARY

Theft Act 1968 (section 9)

This is a serious specified offence for the purposes of section 224 Criminal Justice Act 2003 if it was committed with intent to:

(a) inflict grievous bodily harm on a person, or
(b) do unlawful damage to a building or anything in it.

Triable either way

Maximum when tried summarily: Level 5 fine and/or 26 weeks' custody
Maximum when tried on indictment: 14 years' custody

Offence range: Community order — 6 years' custody

Where sentencing an offender for a qualifying third domestic burglary, the court must apply Section 111 of the Powers of the Criminal Courts (Sentencing) Act 2000 and impose a custodial term of at least three years, unless it is satisfied that there are particular circumstances which relate to any of the offences or to the offender which would make it unjust to do so.

STEP ONE Determining the offence category

The court should determine the offence category using the table below.

Category 1	Greater harm **and** higher culpability
Category 2	Greater harm **and** lower culpability **or** lesser harm **and** higher culpability
Category 3	Lesser harm **and** lower culpability

The court should determine culpability and harm caused or intended, by reference **only** to the factors below, which comprise the principal factual elements of the offence. Where an offence does not fall squarely into a category, individual factors may require a degree of weighting before making an overall assessment and determining the appropriate offence category.

Factors indicating greater harm Theft of/damage to property causing a significant degree of loss to the victim (whether economic, sentimental or personal value) Soiling, ransacking or vandalism of property Occupier at home (or returns home) while offender present Trauma to the victim, beyond the normal inevitable consequence of intrusion and theft Violence used or threatened against victim Context of general public disorder **Factors indicating lesser harm** Nothing stolen or only property of very low value to the victim (whether economic, sentimental or personal) Limited damage or disturbance to property	**Factors indicating higher culpability** Victim or premises deliberately targeted (for example, due to vulnerability or hostility based on disability, race, sexual orientation) A significant degree of planning or organisation Knife or other weapon carried (where not charged separately) Equipped for burglary (for example, implements carried and/or use of vehicle) Member of a group or gang **Factors indicating lower culpability** Offence committed on impulse, with limited intrusion into property Offender exploited by others Mental disorder or learning disability, where linked to the commission of the offence

STEP TWO Starting point and category range

Having determined the category, the court should use the corresponding starting points to reach a sentence within the category range below. The starting point applies to all offenders irrespective of plea or previous convictions.

Where the defendant is dependent on or has a propensity to misuse drugs and there is sufficient prospect of success, a community order with a drug rehabilitation requirement under section 209 of the Criminal Justice Act 2003 may be a proper alternative to a short or moderate custodial sentence.

Offence Category	**Starting Point** (*Applicable to all offenders*)	**Category Range** (*Applicable to all offenders*)
Category 1	3 years' custody	2–6 years' custody
Category 2	1 year's custody	High level community order–2 years' custody
Category 3	High level Community Order	Low level community order–26 weeks' custody

A case of particular gravity, reflected by multiple features of culpability or harm in step 1, could merit upward adjustment from the starting point before further adjustment for aggravating or mitigating features, set out below.

The table below contains a non-exhaustive list of additional factual elements providing the context of the offence and factors relating to the offender. Identify whether any combination of these, or other relevant factors, should result in an upward or downward adjustment from the starting point. **In particular, relevant recent convictions are likely to result in an upward adjustment.** In some cases, having considered these factors, it may be appropriate to move outside the identified category range.

When sentencing **category 2 or 3** offences, the court should also consider the custody threshold as follows:

- Has the custody threshold been passed?
- If so, is it unavoidable that a custodial sentence be imposed?
- If so, can that sentence be suspended?

Factors increasing seriousness	Factors reducing seriousness or reflecting personal mitigation
Statutory aggravating factors: Previous convictions, having regard to a) the nature of the offence to which the conviction relates and its relevance to the current offence; and b) the time that has elapsed since the conviction* Offence committed whilst on bail *Other aggravating factors include*: Child at home (or returns home) when offence committed Offence committed at night Gratuitous degradation of the victim Any steps taken to prevent the victim reporting the incident or obtaining assistance and/or from assisting or supporting the prosecution Victim compelled to leave their home (in particular victims of domestic violence) Established evidence of community impact Commission of offence whilst under the influence of alcohol or drugs Failure to comply with current court orders Offence committed whilst on licence Offences Taken Into Consideration (TICs)	Offender has made voluntary reparation to the victim Subordinate role in a group or gang No previous convictions or no relevant/recent convictions Remorse Good character and/or exemplary conduct Determination, and/or demonstration of steps taken to address addiction or offending behaviour Serious medical conditions requiring urgent, intensive or long-term treatment Age and/or lack of maturity where it affects the responsibility of the offender Lapse of time since the offence where this is not the fault of the offender Mental disorder or learning disability, where not linked to the commission of the offence Sole or primary carer for dependent relatives

* Where sentencing an offender for a qualifying **third domestic burglary**, the court must apply section 111 of the Powers of the Criminal Courts (Sentencing) Act 2000 and impose a custodial term of at least three years, unless it is satisfied that there are particular circumstances which relate to any of the offences or to the offender which would make it unjust to do so.

STEP THREE Consider any factors which indicate a reduction, such as assistance to the prosecution

The court should take into account sections 73 and 74 of the Serious Organised Crime and Police Act 2005 (assistance by defendants: reduction or review of sentence) and any other rule of law by virtue of which an offender may receive a discounted sentence in consequence of assistance given (or offered) to the prosecutor or investigator.

STEP FOUR Reduction for guilty pleas

The court should take account of any potential reduction for a guilty plea in accordance with section 144 of the Criminal Justice Act 2003 and the Guilty Plea guideline.

Where a minimum mandatory sentence is imposed under section 111 Powers of Criminal Courts (Sentencing) Act, the discount for an early guilty plea must not exceed 20 per cent.

[Steps Five to Nine are identical to those for aggravated burglary: see **SG-541**.]

SG-543

Non-domestic Burglary

Theft Act 1968 (section 9)

This is a serious specified offence for the purposes of section 224 Criminal Justice Act 2003 if it was committed with intent to:

(a) inflict grievous bodily harm on a person, or
(b) do unlawful damage to a building or anything in it.

Triable either way

Maximum when tried summarily: Level 5 fine and/or 26 weeks' custody
Maximum when tried on indictment: 10 years' custody

Offence range: Fine — 5 years' custody

STEP ONE Determining the offence category

The court should determine the offence category using the table below.

Category 1	Greater harm **and** higher culpability
Category 2	Greater harm **and** lower culpability **or** lesser harm **and** higher culpability
Category 3	Lesser harm **and** lower culpability

The court should determine culpability and harm caused or intended, by reference only to the factors below, which comprise the principal factual elements of the offence. Where an offence does not fall squarely into a category, individual factors may require a degree of weighting before making an overall assessment and determining the appropriate offence category.

Factors indicating greater harm Theft of/damage to property causing a significant degree of loss to the victim (whether economic, commercial or personal value) Soiling, ransacking or vandalism of property Victim on the premises (or returns) while offender present Trauma to the victim, beyond the normal inevitable consequence of intrusion and theft Violence used or threatened against victim Context of general public disorder	**Factors indicating higher culpability** Premises or victim deliberately targeted (to include pharmacy or doctor's surgery and targeting due to vulnerability of victim or hostility based on disability, race, sexual orientation and so forth) A significant degree of planning or organisation Knife or other weapon carried (where not charged separately) Equipped for burglary (for example, implements carried and/or use of vehicle) Member of a group or gang
Factors indicating lesser harm Nothing stolen or only property of very low value to the victim (whether economic, commercial or personal) Limited damage or disturbance to property	**Factors indicating lower culpability** Offence committed on impulse, with limited intrusion into property Offender exploited by others Mental disorder or learning disability, where linked to the commission of the offence

STEP TWO Starting point and category range

Having determined the category, the court should use the corresponding starting points to reach a sentence within the category range below. The starting point applies to all offenders irrespective of plea or previous convictions.

Where the defendant is dependent on or has a propensity to misuse drugs and there is sufficient prospect of success, a community order with a drug rehabilitation requirement under section 209 of the Criminal Justice Act 2003 may be a proper alternative to a short or moderate custodial sentence.

A case of particular gravity, reflected by multiple features of culpability or harm in step 1, could merit upward adjustment from the starting point before further adjustment for aggravating or mitigating features, set out [below].

Offence Category	Starting Point (*Applicable to all offenders*)	Category Range (*Applicable to all offenders*)
Category 1	2 years' custody	1–5 years' custody
Category 2	18 weeks' custody	Low level community order–51 weeks' custody
Category 3	Medium level community order	Band B fine–18 weeks' custody

The table below contains a non-exhaustive list of additional factual elements providing the context of the offence and factors relating to the offender. Identify whether any combination of these, or other relevant factors, should result in an upward or downward adjustment from the starting point. **In particular, relevant recent convictions are likely to result in an upward adjustment.** In some cases, having considered these factors, it may be appropriate to move outside the identified category range.

When sentencing **category 2 or 3** offences, the court should also consider the custody threshold as follows:

- Has the custody threshold been passed?
- If so, is it unavoidable that a custodial sentence be imposed?
- If so, can that sentence be suspended?

Sentencing Guidelines

When sentencing **category** 3 offences, the court should also consider the community order threshold as follows:

- Has the community order threshold been passed?

Factors increasing seriousness	Factors reducing seriousness or reflecting personal mitigation
Statutory aggravating factors: Previous convictions, having regard to a) the nature of the offence to which the conviction relates and its relevance to the current offence; and b) the time that has elapsed since the conviction Offence committed whilst on bail *Other aggravating factors include*: Offence committed at night, particularly where staff present or likely to be present Abuse of a position of trust Gratuitous degradation of the victim Any steps taken to prevent the victim reporting the incident or obtaining assistance and/or from assisting or supporting the prosecution Established evidence of community impact Commission of offence whilst under the influence of alcohol or drugs Failure to comply with current court orders Offence committed whilst on licence Offences Taken Into Consideration (TICs)	Offender has made voluntary reparation to the victim Subordinate role in a group or gang No previous convictions or no relevant/recent convictions Remorse Good character and/or exemplary conduct Determination, and/or demonstration of steps taken to address addiction or offending behaviour Serious medical conditions requiring urgent, intensive or long-term treatment Age and/or lack of maturity where it affects the responsibility of the offender Lapse of time since the offence where this is not the fault of the offender Mental disorder or learning disability, where not linked to the commission of the offence Sole or primary carer for dependent relatives

[Steps Three to Nine are identical to those for domestic burglary: see **SG-542**.]

SG-544 Annex: Fine Bands and Community Orders

[The tables set out here are also set out in the Magistrates' Court Sentencing Guidelines, which includes further guidance on fines and community orders: see **SG-358** and **SG-382**.]

SG-545

PART 21 DRUGS OFFENCES

Definitive Guideline

Applicability of Guideline

[Omitted: See **SG-539** for identical text save that this guideline has effect from 27 February 2012.]

Structure, ranges and starting points

[Omitted: See **SG-540** for identical text.]

SG-546

Fraudulent Evasion of a Prohibition by Bringing Into or Taking Out of the UK a Controlled Drug

Misuse of Drugs Act 1971 (section 3)

Customs and Excise Management Act 1979 (section 170(2))

Triable either way unless the defendant could receive the minimum sentence of seven years for a third drug trafficking offence under section 110 Powers of Criminal Courts (Sentencing) Act 2000 in which case the offence is triable only on indictment.

Class A

Maximum: Life imprisonment

Offence range: 3 years 6 months' — 16 years' custody

A Class A offence is a drug trafficking offence for the purpose of imposing a minimum sentence under section 110 Powers of Criminal Courts (Sentencing) Act 2000

Class B

Maximum: 14 years' custody and/or unlimited fine

Offence range: 12 weeks' — 10 years' custody

Class C

Maximum: 14 years' custody and/or unlimited fine

Offence range: Community order — 8 years' custody

STEP ONE Determining the offence category **SG-547**

The court should determine the offender's culpability (role) and the harm caused (quantity) with reference to the tables below.

In assessing culpability, the sentencer should weigh up all the factors of the case to determine role. Where there are characteristics present which fall under different role categories, the court should balance these characteristics to reach a fair assessment of the offender's culpability.

In assessing harm, quantity is determined by the weight of the product. Purity is not taken into account at step 1 but is dealt with at step 2.

Where the operation is on the most serious and commercial scale, involving a quantity of drugs significantly higher than category 1, sentences of 20 years and above may be appropriate, depending on the role of the offender.

Culpability demonstrated by offender's role One or more of these characteristics may demonstrate the offender's role. These lists are not exhaustive.	**Category of harm** Indicative quantity of drug concerned (upon which the starting point is based):
LEADING role: • Directing or organising buying and selling on a commercial scale; • Substantial links to, and influence on, others in a chain; • Close links to original source; • Expectation of substantial financial gain; • Uses business as cover; • Abuses a position of trust or responsibility.	**Category 1:** • Heroin, cocaine — 5kg; • Ecstasy — 10,000 tablets; • LSD — 250,000 squares; • Amphetamine — 20kg; • Cannabis — 200kg; • Ketamine — 5kg. **Category 2:** • Heroin, cocaine — 1kg; • Ecstasy — 2,000 tablets; • LSD — 25,000 squares; • Amphetamine — 4kg; • Cannabis — 40kg; • Ketamine — 1kg;
SIGNIFICANT role: • Operational or management function within a chain; • Involves others in the operation whether by pressure, influence, intimidation or reward; • Motivated by financial or other advantage, whether or not operating alone; • Some awareness and understanding of scale of operation. **LESSER role:** • Performs a limited function under direction; • Engaged by pressure, coercion, intimidation; • Involvement through naivety/exploitation; • No influence on those above in a chain; • Very little, if any, awareness or understanding of the scale of operation; • If own operation, solely for own use (considering reasonableness of account in all the circumstances).	**Category 3:** • Heroin, cocaine — 150g; • Ecstasy — 300 tablets; • LSD — 2,500 squares; • Amphetamine — 750g; • Cannabis — 6kg; • Ketamine — 150g. **Category 4:** • Heroin, cocaine — 5g; • Ecstasy — 20 tablets; • LSD — 170 squares; • Amphetamine — 20g; • Cannabis — 100g; • Ketamine — 5g.

SG-548 **STEP TWO Starting point and category range**

Having determined the category, the court should use the corresponding starting point to reach a sentence within the category range below. The starting point applies to all offenders irrespective of plea or previous convictions. The court should then consider further adjustment within the category range for aggravating or mitigating features, set out [at **SG-549**]. In cases where the offender is regarded as being at the very top of the 'leading' role it may be justifiable for the court to depart from the guideline.

Where the defendant is dependent on or has a propensity to misuse drugs and there is sufficient prospect of success, a community order with a drug rehabilitation requirement under section 209 of the Criminal Justice Act 2003 can be a proper alternative to a short or moderate length custodial sentence.

For class A cases, section 110 of the Powers of Criminal Courts (Sentencing) Act 2000 provides that a court should impose a minimum sentence of at least seven years' imprisonment for a third class A trafficking offence except where the court is of the opinion that there are particular circumstances which (a) relate to any of the offences or to the offender; and (b) would make it unjust to do so in all the circumstances.

CLASS A	Leading role	Significant role	Lesser role
Category 1	**Starting point** 14 years' custody	**Starting point** 10 years' custody	**Starting point** 8 years' custody
	Category range 12–16 years' custody	**Category range** 9–12 years' custody	**Category range** 6–9 years' custody
Category 2	**Starting point** 11 years' custody	**Starting point** 8 years' custody	**Starting point** 6 years' custody
	Category range 9–13 years' custody	**Category range** 6 years 6 months'–10 years' custody	**Category range** 5–7 years' custody
Category 3	**Starting point** 8 years 6 months' custody	**Starting point** 6 years' custody	**Starting point** 4 years 6 months' custody
	Category range 6 years 6 months'–10 years' custody	**Category range** 5–7 years' custody	**Category range** 3 years 6 months'–5 years' custody
Category 4	Where the quantity falls below the indicative amount set out for category 4 [at **SG-547**], first identify the role for the importation offence, then refer to the starting point and ranges for possession or supply offences, depending on intent. Where the quantity is significantly larger than the indicative amounts for category 4 but below category 3 amounts, refer to the category 3 ranges above.		

CLASS B	Leading role	Significant role	Lesser role
Category 1	**Starting point** 8 years' custody	**Starting point** 5 years 6 months' custody	**Starting point** 4 years' custody
	Category range 7–10 years' custody	**Category range** 5–7 years' custody	**Category range** 2 years 6 months'–5 years' custody
Category 2	**Starting point** 6 years' custody	**Starting point** 4 years' custody	**Starting point** 2 years' custody
	Category range 4 years 6 months'–8 years' custody	**Category range** 2 years 6 months'–5 years' custody	**Category range** 18 months'–3 years' custody
Category 3	**Starting point** 4 years' custody	**Starting point** 2 years' custody	**Starting point** 1 years' custody
	Category range 2 years 6 months'–5 years' custody	**Category range** 18 months'–3 years' custody	**Category range** 12 weeks'–18 months' custody
Category 4	Where the quantity falls below the indicative amount set out for category 4 [at **SG-547**], first identify the role for the importation offence, then refer to the starting point and ranges for possession or supply offences, depending on intent. Where the quantity is significantly larger than the indicative amounts for category 4 but below category 3 amounts, refer to the category 3 ranges above.		

CLASS C	Leading role	Significant role	Lesser role
Category 1	**Starting point** 5 years' custody	**Starting point** 3 years' custody	**Starting point** 18 months' custody
	Category range 4–8 years' custody	**Category range** 2–5 years' custody	**Category range** 1–3 years' custody
Category 2	**Starting point** 3 years 6 months' custody	**Starting point** 18 months' custody	**Starting point** 26 weeks' custody
	Category range 2 years'–5 years' custody	**Category range** 1–3 years' custody	**Category range** 12 weeks'–18 months' custody
Category 3	**Starting point** 18 months' custody	**Starting point** 26 weeks' custody	**Starting point** High level community order
	Category range 1–3 years' custody	**Category range** 12 weeks'–18 months' custody	**Category range** Medium level community order–12 weeks' custody
Category 4	Where the quantity falls below the indicative amount set out for category 4 [at SG-547], first identify the role for the importation offence, then refer to the starting point and ranges for possession or supply offences, depending on intent. Where the quantity is significantly larger than the indicative amounts for category 4 but below category 3 amounts, refer to the category 3 ranges above.		

The table below contains a **non-exhaustive** list of additional factual elements providing the context of the offence and factors relating to the offender. Identify whether any combination of these, or other relevant factors, should result in an upward or downward adjustment from the starting point. In some cases, having considered these factors, it may be appropriate to move outside the identified category range. **SG-549**

For appropriate **class C** ranges, consider the custody threshold as follows:

- Has the custody threshold been passed?
- If so, is it unavoidable that a custodial sentence be imposed?
- If so, can that sentence be suspended?

Factors increasing seriousness	Factors reducing seriousness or reflecting personal mitigation
Statutory aggravating factors: Previous convictions, having regard to a) nature of the offence to which conviction relates and relevance to current offence; and b) time elapsed since conviction (see [italicised text at SG-548] if third drug trafficking conviction) Offender used or permitted a person under 18 to deliver a controlled drug to a third person Offence committed on bail *Other aggravating factors include:* Sophisticated nature of concealment and/or attempts to avoid detection Attempts to conceal or dispose of evidence, where not charged separately Exposure of others to more than usual danger, for example drugs cut with harmful substances Presence of weapon, where not charged separately High purity Failure to comply with current court orders Offence committed on licence	Lack of sophistication as to nature of concealment Involvement due to pressure, intimidation or coercion falling short of duress, except where already taken into account at step 1 Mistaken belief of the offender regarding the type of drug, taking into account the reasonableness of such belief in all the circumstances Isolated incident Low purity No previous convictions or no relevant or recent convictions Offender's vulnerability was exploited Remorse Good character and/or exemplary conduct Determination and/or demonstration of steps having been taken to address addiction or offending behaviour Serious medical conditions requiring urgent, intensive or long-term treatment Age and/or lack of maturity where it affects the responsibility of the offender Mental disorder or learning disability Sole or primary carer for dependent relatives

SG-550 **STEP THREE Consider any factors which indicate a reduction, such as assistance to the prosecution**

The court should take into account sections 73 and 74 of the Serious Organised Crime and Police Act 2005 (assistance by defendants: reduction or review of sentence) and any other rule of law by virtue of which an offender may receive a discounted sentence in consequence of assistance given (or offered) to the prosecutor or investigator.

STEP FOUR Reduction for guilty pleas

The court should take account of any potential reduction for a guilty plea in accordance with section 144 of the Criminal Justice Act 2003 and the *Guilty Plea* guideline [see **SG-1**].

For class A offences, where a minimum mandatory sentence is imposed under section 110 Powers of Criminal Courts (Sentencing) Act, the discount for an early guilty plea must not exceed 20 per cent.

STEP FIVE Totality principle

If sentencing an offender for more than one offence, or where the offender is already serving a sentence, consider whether the total sentence is just and proportionate to the offending behaviour.

STEP SIX Confiscation and ancillary orders

In all cases, the court is required to consider confiscation where the Crown invokes the process or where the court considers it appropriate. It should also consider whether to make ancillary orders.

STEP SEVEN Reasons

Section 174 of the Criminal Justice Act 2003 imposes a duty to give reasons for, and explain the effect of, the sentence.

STEP EIGHT Consideration for remand time

Sentencers should take into consideration any remand time served in relation to the final sentence at this final step. The court should consider whether to give credit for time spent on remand in custody or on bail in accordance with sections 240 and 240A of the Criminal Justice Act 2003.

SG-551

Supplying or Offering to Supply a Controlled Drug

Misuse of Drugs Act 1971 (section 4(3))

Possession of a Controlled Drug with Intent to Supply it to Another

Misuse of Drugs Act 1971 (section 5(3))

Triable either way unless the defendant could receive the minimum sentence of seven years for a third drug trafficking offence under section 110 Powers of Criminal Courts (Sentencing) Act 2000 in which case the offence is triable only on indictment.

Class A

Maximum: Life imprisonment

Offence range: Community order — 16 years' custody

A class A offence is a drug trafficking offence for the purpose of imposing a minimum sentence under section 110 Powers of Criminal Courts (Sentencing) Act 2000

Class B

Maximum: 14 years' custody and/or unlimited fine

Offence range: Fine — 10 years' custody

SG-552

Class C

Maximum: 14 years' custody and/or unlimited fine

Offence range: Fine — 8 years' custody

STEP ONE Determining the offence category

The court should determine the offender's culpability (role) and the harm caused (quantity/type of offender) with reference to the tables below.

In assessing culpability, the sentencer should weigh up all the factors of the case to determine role. Where there are characteristics present which fall under different role categories, the court should balance these characteristics to reach a fair assessment of the offender's culpability.

In assessing harm, quantity is determined by the weight of the product. Purity is not taken into account at step 1 but is dealt with at step 2. Where the offence is street dealing or supply of drugs in prison by a prison employee, the quantity of the product is less indicative of the harm caused and therefore the starting point is not based on quantity.

Where the operation is on the most serious and commercial scale, involving a quantity of drugs significantly higher than category 1, sentences of 20 years and above may be appropriate, depending on the role of the offender.

Culpability demonstrated by offender's role One or more of these characteristics may demonstrate the offender's role. These lists are not exhaustive.	**Category of harm** Indicative quantity of drug concerned (upon which the starting point is based):
LEADING role: • Directing or organising buying and selling on a commercial scale; • Substantial links to, and influence on, others in a chain; • Close links to original source; • Expectation of substantial financial gain; • Uses business as cover; • Abuses a position of trust or responsibility, for example prison employee, medical professional.	**Category 1** • Heroin, cocaine — 5kg; • Ecstasy — 10,000 tablets; • LSD — 250,000 squares; • Amphetamine — 20kg; • Cannabis — 200kg; • Ketamine — 5kg. **Category 2** • Heroin, cocaine — 1kg; • Ecstasy — 2,000 tablets; • LSD — 25,000 squares; • Amphetamine — 4kg; • Cannabis — 40kg; • Ketamine — 1kg.
SIGNIFICANT role: • Operational or management function within a chain; • Involves others in the operation whether by pressure, influence, intimidation or reward; • Motivated by financial or other advantage, whether or not operating alone; • Some awareness and understanding of scale of operation; • Supply, other than by a person in position of responsibility, to a prisoner for gain without coercion. **LESSER role:** • Performs a limited function under direction; • Engaged by pressure, coercion, intimidation; • Involvement through naivety/exploitation; • No influence on those above in a chain; • Very little, if any, awareness or understanding of the scale of operation; • If own operation, absence of financial gain, for example joint purchase for no profit, or sharing minimal quantity between peers on non-commercial basis.	**Category 3** Where the offence is selling direct to users [footnote indicates that this includes test purchase officers] ('street-dealing'), the starting point is not based on a quantity OR Where the offence is supply of drugs in prison by a prison employee, the starting point is not based on a quantity — see [italicised text above]. OR • Heroin, cocaine — 150g; • Ecstasy — 300 tablets; • LSD — 2,500 squares; • Amphetamine — 750g; • Cannabis — 6kg; • Ketamine — 150g. **Category 4** • Heroin, cocaine — 5g; • Ecstasy — 20 tablets; • LSD — 170 squares; • Amphetamine — 20g; • Cannabis — 100g; • Ketamine — 5g; OR Where the offence is selling directly to users [footnote indicates that this includes test purchase officers] ('street-dealing'), the starting point is not based on quantity — go to category 3.

SG-553 **STEP TWO Starting point and category range**

Having determined the category, the court should use the corresponding starting point to reach a sentence within the category range below. The starting point applies to all offenders irrespective of plea or previous convictions. The court should then consider further adjustment within the category range for aggravating or mitigating features, set out [at SG-554]. In cases where the offender is regarded as being at the very top of the 'leading' role it may be justifiable for the court to depart from the guideline.

Where the defendant is dependent on or has a propensity to misuse drugs and there is sufficient prospect of success, a community order with a drug rehabilitation requirement under section 209 of the Criminal Justice Act 2003 can be a proper alternative to a short or moderate length custodial sentence.

For class A cases, section 110 of the Powers of Criminal Courts (Sentencing) Act 2000 provides that a court should impose a minimum sentence of at least seven years' imprisonment for a third class A trafficking offence except where the court is of the opinion that there are particular circumstances which (a) relate to any of the offences or to the offender; and (b) would make it unjust to do so in all the circumstances.

CLASS A	Leading role	Significant role	Lesser role
Category 1	**Starting point** 14 years' custody	**Starting point** 10 years' custody	**Starting point** 7 years' custody
	Category range 12–16 years' custody	**Category range** 9–12 years' custody	**Category range** 6–9 years' custody
Category 2	**Starting point** 11 years' custody	**Starting point** 8 years' custody	**Starting point** 5 years' custody
	Category range 9–13 years' custody	**Category range** 6 years 6 months'–10 years' custody	**Category range** 3 years 6 months'–7 years' custody
Category 3	**Starting point** 8 years 6 months' custody	**Starting point** 4 years 6 months' custody	**Starting point** 3 years' custody
	Category range 6 years 6 months'–10 years' custody	**Category range** 3 years 6 months'–7 years' custody	**Category range** 2–4 years 6 months' custody
Category 4	**Starting point** 5 years 6 months' custody	**Starting point** 3 years 6 months' custody	**Starting point** 18 months' custody
	Category range 4 years 6 months'–7 years 6 months' custody	**Category range** 2–5 years' custody	**Category range** High level community order–3 years' custody

CLASS B	Leading role	Significant role	Lesser role
Category 1	**Starting point** 8 years' custody	**Starting point** 5 years 6 months' custody	**Starting point** 3 years' custody
	Category range 7–10 years' custody	**Category range** 5–7 years' custody	**Category range** 2 years 6 months'–5 years' custody
Category 2	**Starting point** 6 years' custody	**Starting point** 4 years' custody	**Starting point** 1 years' custody
	Category range 4 years 6 months'–8 years' custody	**Category range** 2 years 6 months'–5 years' custody	**Category range** 26 weeks'–3 years' custody
Category 3	**Starting point** 4 years' custody	**Starting point** 1 year's custody	**Starting point** High level community order
	Category range 2 years 6 months'–5 years' custody	**Category range** 26 weeks'–3 years' custody	**Category range** Low level community order–26 weeks' custody

CLASS B	Leading role	Significant role	Lesser role
Category 4	**Starting point** 18 months' custody	**Starting point** High level community order	**Starting point** Low level community order
	Category range 26 weeks'–3 years' custody	**Category range** Medium level community order–26 weeks' custody	**Category range** Band B fine–medium level community order

CLASS C	Leading role	Significant role	Lesser role
Category 1	**Starting point** 5 years' custody	**Starting point** 3 years' custody	**Starting point** 18 months' custody
	Category range 4–8 years' custody	**Category range** 2–5 years' custody	**Category range** 1–3 years' custody
Category 2	**Starting point** 3 years 6 months' custody	**Starting point** 18 months' custody	**Starting point** 26 weeks' custody
	Category range 2 years'–5 years' custody	**Category range** 1–3 years' custody	**Category range** 12 weeks–18 months' custody
Category 3	**Starting point** 18 months' custody	**Starting point** 26 weeks' custody	**Starting point** High level community order
	Category range 1–3 years' custody	**Category range** 12 weeks'–18 months' custody	**Category range** Low level community order–12 weeks' custody
Category 4	**Starting point** 26 weeks' custody	**Starting point** High level community order	**Starting point** Low level community order
	Category range High level community order–18 months' custody	**Category range** Low level community order–12 weeks' custody	**Category range** Band A fine–medium level community order

The table below contains a **non-exhaustive** list of additional factual elements providing the context of the offence and factors relating to the offender. Identify whether any combination of these, or other relevant factors, should result in an upward or downward adjustment from the starting point. In some cases, having considered these factors, it may be appropriate to move outside the identified category range. **SG-554**

For appropriate **class B** and C ranges, consider the custody threshold as follows:

- Has the custody threshold been passed?
- If so, is it unavoidable that a custodial sentence be imposed?
- If so, can that sentence be suspended?

For appropriate **class B** and **C** ranges, the court should also consider the community threshold as follows:

- Has the community threshold been passed?

Factors increasing seriousness	Factors reducing seriousness or reflecting personal mitigation
Statutory aggravating factors: Previous convictions, having regard to a) nature of the offence to which conviction relates and relevance to current offence; and b) time elapsed since conviction (see [italicised text at SG-553] if third drug trafficking conviction) Offender used or permitted a person under 18 to deliver a controlled drug to a third person Offender 18 or over supplies or offers to supply a drug on, or in the vicinity of, school premises either when school in use as such or at a time between one hour before and one hour after they are to be used Offence committed on bail *Other aggravating factors include:* Targeting of any premises intended to locate vulnerable individuals or supply to such individuals and/or supply to those under 18 Exposure of others to more than usual danger, for example drugs cut with harmful substances Attempts to conceal or dispose of evidence, where not charged separately Presence of others, especially children and/or non-users Presence of weapon, where not charged separately Charged as importation of a very small amount High purity Failure to comply with current court orders Offence committed on licence Established evidence of community impact	Involvement due to pressure, intimidation or coercion falling short of duress, except where already taken into account at step 1 Supply only of drug to which offender addicted Mistaken belief of the offender regarding the type of drug, taking into account the reasonableness of such belief in all the circumstances Isolated incident Low purity No previous convictions **or** no relevant or recent convictions Offender's vulnerability was exploited Remorse Good character and/or exemplary conduct Determination and/or demonstration of steps having been taken to address addiction or offending behaviour Serious medical conditions requiring urgent, intensive or long-term treatment Age and/or lack of maturity where it affects the responsibility of the offender Mental disorder or learning disability Sole or primary carer for dependent relatives

SG-555 [Steps Three to Eight are identical to those applicable to Fraudulent evasion of a prohibition by bringing into or taking out of the UK a controlled drug: see **SG-550**.]

SG-556

Production of a Controlled Drug

Misuse of Drugs Act 1971 (section 4(2)(a) or (b))

Triable either way unless the defendant could receive the minimum sentence of seven years for a third drug trafficking offence under section 110 Powers of Criminal Courts (Sentencing) Act 2000 in which case the offence is triable only on indictment.

Class A

Maximum: Life imprisonment

Offence range: Community order — 16 years' custody

A class A offence is a drug trafficking offence for the purpose of imposing a minimum sentence under section 110 Powers of Criminal Courts (Sentencing) Act 2000

Class B

Maximum: 14 years' custody

Offence range: Discharge — 10 years' custody

Class C

Maximum: 14 years' custody

Offence range: Discharge — 8 years' custody

Cultivation of Cannabis Plant SG-557

Misuse of Drugs Act 1971 (section 6(2))

Maximum: 14 years' custody

Offence range: Discharge — 10 years' custody

STEP ONE Determining the offence category

The court should determine the offender's culpability (role) and the harm caused (output or potential output) with reference to the tables below.

In assessing culpability, the sentencer should weigh up all of the factors of the case to determine role. Where there are characteristics present which fall under different role categories, the court should balance these characteristics to reach a fair assessment of the offender's culpability.

In assessing harm, output or potential output is determined by the weight of the product or number of plants/scale of operation. For production offences, purity is not taken into account at step 1 but is dealt with at step 2.

Where the operation is on the most serious and commercial scale, involving a quantity of drugs significantly higher than category 1, sentences of 20 years and above may be appropriate, depending on the role of the offender.

Culpability demonstrated by offender's role One or more of these characteristics may demonstrate the offender's role. These lists are not exhaustive.	**Category of harm** Indicative quantity of drug concerned (upon which the starting point is based):
LEADING role: • Directing or organising buying and selling on a commercial scale; • Substantial links to, and influence on, others in a chain; • Expectation of substantial financial gain; • Uses business as cover; • Abuses a position of trust or responsibility	**Category 1** • Heroin, cocaine — 5kg; • Ecstasy — 10,000 tablets; • LSD — 250,000 squares; • Amphetamine — 20kg; • Cannabis — operation capable of producing industrial quantities for commercial use; • Ketamine — 5kg.
SIGNIFICANT role: • Operational or management function within a chain; • Involves others in the operation whether by pressure, influence, intimidation or reward; • Motivated by financial or other advantage, whether or not operating alone; • Some awareness and understanding of scale of operation;	**Category 2** • Heroin, cocaine — 1kg; • Ecstasy — 2,000 tablets; • LSD — 25,000 squares; • Amphetamine — 4kg; • Cannabis — operation capable of producing significant quantities for commercial use; • Ketamine — 1kg.
LESSER role: • Performs a limited function under direction; • Engaged by pressure, coercion, intimidation; • Involvement through naivety/exploitation; • No influence on those above in a chain; • Very little, if any, awareness or understanding of the scale of operation; • If own operation, solely for own use (considering reasonableness of account in all the circumstances).	**Category 3** • Heroin, cocaine — 150g; • Ecstasy — 300 tablets; • LSD — 2,500 squares; • Amphetamine — 750g; • Cannabis — 28 plants; [footnote indicates 'With assumed yield of 40g per plant'] • Ketamine — 150g.
	Category 4 • Heroin, cocaine — 5g; • Ecstasy — 20 tablets; • LSD — 170 squares; • Amphetamine — 20g; • Cannabis — 9 plants (domestic operation); [footnote indicates 'With assumed yield of 40g per plant'] • Ketamine — 5g.

SG-558 **STEP TWO Starting point and category range**

Having determined the category, the court should use the corresponding starting point to reach a sentence within the category range below. The starting point applies to all offenders irrespective of plea or previous convictions. The court should then consider further adjustment within the category range for aggravating or mitigating features, set out [at **SG-559**]. In cases where the offender is regarded as being at the very top of the 'leading' role it may be justifiable for the court to depart from the guideline.

Where the defendant is dependent on or has a propensity to misuse drugs and there is sufficient prospect of success, a community order with a drug rehabilitation requirement under section 209 of the Criminal Justice Act 2003 can be a proper alternative to a short or moderate length custodial sentence.

For class A cases, section 110 of the Powers of Criminal Courts (Sentencing) Act 2000 provides that a court should impose a minimum sentence of at least seven years' imprisonment for a third class A trafficking offence except where the court is of the opinion that there are particular circumstances which (a) relate to any of the offences or to the offender; and (b) would make it unjust to do so in all the circumstances.

CLASS A	Leading role	Significant role	Lesser role
Category 1	**Starting point** 14 years' custody	**Starting point** 10 years' custody	**Starting point** 7 years' custody
	Category range 12–16 years' custody	**Category range** 9–12 years' custody	**Category range** 6–9 years' custody
Category 2	**Starting point** 11 years' custody	**Starting point** 8 years' custody	**Starting point** 5 years' custody
	Category range 9–13 years' custody	**Category range** 6 years 6 months'–10 years' custody	**Category range** 3 years 6 months'–7 years' custody
Category 3	**Starting point** 8 years 6 months' custody	**Starting point** 5 years' custody	**Starting point** 3 years 6 months' custody
	Category range 6 years 6 months'–10 years' custody	**Category range** 3 years 6 months'–7 years' custody	**Category range** 2–5 years' custody
Category 4	**Starting point** 5 years 6 months' custody	**Starting point** 3 years 6 months' custody	**Starting point** 18 months' custody
	Category range 4 years 6 months'–7 years 6 months' custody	**Category range** 2–5 years' custody	**Category range** High level community order–3 years' custody

CLASS B	Leading role	Significant role	Lesser role
Category 1	**Starting point** 8 years' custody	**Starting point** 5 years 6 months' custody	**Starting point** 3 years' custody
	Category range 7–10 years' custody	**Category range** 5–7 years' custody	**Category range** 2 years 6 months'–5 years' custody
Category 2	**Starting point** 6 years' custody	**Starting point** 4 years' custody	**Starting point** 1 years' custody
	Category range 4 years 6 months'–8 years' custody	**Category range** 2 years 6 months'–5 years' custody	**Category range** 26 weeks'–3 years' custody

CLASS B	Leading role	Significant role	Lesser role
Category 3	**Starting point** 4 years' custody	**Starting point** 1 year's custody	**Starting point** High level community order
	Category range 2 years 6 months'–5 years' custody	**Category range** 26 weeks'–3 years' custody	**Category range** Low level community order–26 weeks' custody
Category 4	**Starting point** 1 years' custody	**Starting point** High level community order	**Starting point** Band C fine
	Category range High level community order–3 years' custody	**Category range** Medium level community order–26 weeks' custody	**Category range** Discharge–medium level community order

CLASS C	Leading role	Significant role	Lesser role
Category 1	**Starting point** 5 years' custody	**Starting point** 3 years' custody	**Starting point** 18 months' custody
	Category range 4–8 years' custody	**Category range** 2–5 years' custody	**Category range** 1–3 years' custody
Category 2	**Starting point** 3 years 6 months' custody	**Starting point** 18 months' custody	**Starting point** 26 weeks' custody
	Category range 2–5 years' custody	**Category range** 1–3 years' custody	**Category range** High level community order–18 months' custody
Category 3	**Starting point** 18 months' custody	**Starting point** 26 weeks' custody	**Starting point** High level community order
	Category range 1–3 years' custody	**Category range** High level community order–18 months' custody	**Category range** Low level community order–12 weeks' custody
Category 4	**Starting point** 26 weeks' custody	**Starting point** High level community order	**Starting point** Band C fine
	Category range High level community order–18 months' custody	**Category range** Low level community order–12 weeks' custody	**Category range** Discharge–medium level community order

The table below contains a **non-exhaustive** list of additional factual elements providing the context of the offence and factors relating to the offender. Identify whether any combination of these, or other relevant factors, should result in an upward or downward adjustment from the starting point. In some cases, having considered these factors, it may be appropriate to move outside the identified category range. **SG-559**

Where appropriate, consider the custody threshold as follows:

- Has the custody threshold been passed?
- If so, is it unavoidable that a custodial sentence be imposed?
- If so, can that sentence be suspended?

Where appropriate, the court should also consider the community threshold as follows:

- Has the community threshold been passed?

Factors increasing seriousness	Factors reducing seriousness or reflecting personal mitigation
Statutory aggravating factors: Previous convictions, having regard to a) nature of the offence to which conviction relates and relevance to current offence; and b) time elapsed since conviction (see [italicised text at **SG-558**] if third drug trafficking conviction) Offence committed on bail *Other aggravating factors include:* Nature of any likely supply Level of any profit element Use of premises accompanied by unlawful access to electricity/other utility supply of others Ongoing/large scale operation as evidenced by presence and nature of specialist equipment Exposure of others to more than usual danger, for example drugs cut with harmful substances Attempts to conceal or dispose of evidence, where not charged separately Presence of others, especially children and/or non-users Presence of weapon, where not charged separately High purity or high potential yield Failure to comply with current court orders Offence committed on licence Established evidence of community impact	Involvement due to pressure, intimidation or coercion falling short of duress, except where already taken into account at step 1 Isolated incident Low purity No previous convictions **or** no relevant or recent convictions Offender's vulnerability was exploited Remorse Good character and/or exemplary conduct Determination and/or demonstration of steps having been taken to address addiction or offending behaviour Serious medical conditions requiring urgent, intensive or long-term treatment Age and/or lack of maturity where it affects the responsibility of the offender Mental disorder or learning disability Sole or primary carer for dependent relatives

SG-560 [Steps Three to Eight are identical to those applicable to Fraudulent evasion of a prohibition by bringing into or taking out of the UK a controlled drug: see **SG-550**.]

SG-561

Permitting Premises to be Used

Misuse of Drugs Act 1971 (section 8)

Triable either way unless the defendant could receive the minimum sentence of seven years for a third drug trafficking offence under section 110 Powers of Criminal Courts (Sentencing) Act 2000 in which case the offence is triable only on indictment.

Class A

Maximum: 14 years' custody

Offence range: Community order — 4 years' custody

A class A offence is a drug trafficking offence for the purpose of imposing a minimum sentence under section 110 Powers of Criminal Courts (Sentencing) Act 2000

Class B

Maximum: 14 years' custody

Offence range: Fine — 18 months' custody

Class C

Maximum: 14 years' custody

Offence range: Discharge — 26 weeks' custody

SG-562 **STEP ONE Determining the offence category**

The court should determine the offender's culpability and the harm caused (extent of the activity and/or the quantity of drugs) with reference to the table below.

In assessing harm, quantity is determined by the weight of the product. Purity is not taken into account at step 1 but is dealt with at step 2

Category 1	**Higher culpability and greater harm**
Category 2	Lower culpability **and** greater harm; **or** higher culpability **and** lesser harm
Category 3	Lower culpability **and** lesser harm

Factors indicating culpability (non-exhaustive)	**Factors indicating harm (non-exhaustive)**
Higher culpability: Permits premises to be used primarily for drug activity, for example crack house Permits use in expectation of substantial financial gain Uses legitimate business premises to aid and/or conceal illegal activity, for example public house or club *Lower culpability*: Permits use for limited or no financial gain No active role in any supply taking place Involvement through naivety	*Greater harm*: Regular drug-related activity Higher quantity of drugs, for example: Heroin, cocaine — more than 5g; Cannabis — more than 50g. *Lesser harm:* Infrequent drug-related activity Lower quantity of drugs, for example: Heroin, cocaine — up to 5g; Cannabis — up to 50g.

STEP TWO Starting point and category range **SG-563**

Having determined the category, the court should use the table below to identify the corresponding starting point to reach a sentence within the category range. The starting point applies to all offenders irrespective of plea or previous convictions. The court should then consider further adjustment within the category range for aggravating or mitigating features, set out [at SG-564].

Where the defendant is dependent on or has a propensity to misuse drugs and there is sufficient prospect of success, a community order with a drug rehabilitation requirement under section 209 of the Criminal Justice Act 2003 can be a proper alternative to a short or moderate length custodial sentence.

For class A cases, section 110 of the Powers of Criminal Courts (Sentencing) Act 2000 provides that a court should impose a minimum sentence of at least seven years' imprisonment for a third class A trafficking offence except where the court is of the opinion that there are particular circumstances which (a) relate to any of the offences or to the offender; and (b) would make it unjust to do so in all the circumstances.

Class A

Offence category	**Starting point** (*applicable to all offenders*)	**Category range** (*applicable to all offenders*)
Category 1	2 years 6 months' custody	18 months'–4 years' custody
Category 2	36 weeks' custody	High level community order–18 months' custody
Category 3	Medium level community order	Low level community order–high level community order

Class B

Offence category	**Starting point** (*applicable to all offenders*)	**Category range** (*applicable to all offenders*)
Category 1	1 year's custody	26 weeks'–18 months' custody
Category 2	High level community order	Low level community order–26 weeks' custody
Category 3	Band C fine	Band A fine–low level community order

Class C

Offence category	Starting point (*applicable to all offenders*)	Category range (*applicable to all offenders*)
Category 1	12 weeks' custody	High level community order–26 weeks' custody [footnote indicates that 'when tried summarily, the maximum penalty is 12 weeks' custody']
Category 2	Low level community order	Band C fine–high level community order
Category 3	Band A fine	Discharge–Band C fine

SG-564 The table below contains a **non-exhaustive** list of additional factual elements providing the context of the offence and factors relating to the offender. Identify whether any combination of these, or other relevant factors, should result in an upward or downward adjustment from the starting point. In some cases, having considered these factors, it may be appropriate to move outside the identified category range.

Where appropriate, consider the custody threshold as follows:

- Has the custody threshold been passed?
- If so, is it unavoidable that a custodial sentence be imposed?
- If so, can that sentence be suspended?

Where appropriate, the court should also consider the community threshold as follows:

- Has the community threshold been passed?

Factors increasing seriousness	Factors reducing seriousness or reflecting personal mitigation
Statutory aggravating factors: Previous convictions, having regard to a) nature of the offence to which conviction relates and relevance to current offence; and b) time elapsed since conviction (see [italicised text at **SG-563**] if third drug trafficking conviction) Offence committed on bail *Other aggravating factors include:* Length of time over which premises used for drug activity Volume of drug activity permitted Premises adapted to facilitate drug activity Location of premises, for example proximity to school Attempts to conceal or dispose of evidence, where not charged separately Presence of others, especially children and/or non-users High purity Presence of weapons, where not charged separately Failure to comply with current court orders Offence committed on licence Established evidence of community impact	Involvement due to pressure, intimidation or coercion falling short of duress Isolated incident Low purity No previous convictions **or** no relevant or recent convictions Offender's vulnerability was exploited Remorse Good character and/or exemplary conduct Determination and/or demonstration of steps having been taken to address addiction or offending behaviour Serious medical conditions requiring urgent, intensive or long-term treatment Age and/or lack of maturity where it affects the responsibility of the offender Mental disorder or learning disability Sole or primary carer for dependent relatives

SG-565 [Steps Three to Eight are identical to those applicable to Fraudulent evasion of a prohibition by bringing into or taking out of the UK a controlled drug: see **SG-550**.]

SG-566

Possession of a Controlled Drug

Misuse of Drugs Act 1971 (section 5(2))

Triable either way

Class A

Maximum: 7 years' custody

Offence range: Fine — 51 weeks' custody

Class B

Maximum: 5 years' custody

Offence range: Discharge — 26 weeks' custody

Class C

Maximum: 2 years' custody

Offence range: Discharge — Community order

STEP ONE Determining the offence category SG-567

The court should identify the offence category based on the class of drug involved.

Category 1	Class A drug
Category 2	Class B drug
Category 3	Class C drug

STEP TWO Starting point and category range SG-568

The court should use the table below to identify the corresponding starting point. The starting point applies to all offenders irrespective of plea or previous convictions. The court should then consider further adjustment within the category range for aggravating or mitigating features, set out [at **SG-569**].

Where the defendant is dependent on or has a propensity to misuse drugs and there is sufficient prospect of success, a community order with a drug rehabilitation requirement under section 209 of the Criminal Justice Act 2003 can be a proper alternative to a short or moderate length custodial sentence.

Offence category	**Starting point** (*applicable to all offenders*)	**Category range** (*applicable to all offenders*)
Category 1 (class A)	Band C fine	Band A fine–51 weeks' custody
Category 2 (class B)	Band B fine	Discharge–26 weeks' custody
Category 3 (class C)	Band A fine	Discharge–medium level community order

The table below contains a **non-exhaustive** list of additional factual elements providing the context of the offence and factors relating to the offender. Identify whether any combination of these, or other relevant factors, should result in an upward or downward adjustment from the starting point. **In particular, possession of drugs in prison is likely to result in an upward adjustment.** In some cases, having considered these factors, it may be appropriate to move outside the identified category range. SG-569

Where appropriate, consider the custody threshold as follows:

- Has the custody threshold been passed?
- If so, is it unavoidable that a custodial sentence be imposed?
- If so, can that sentence be suspended?

Where appropriate, the court should also consider the community threshold as follows:

- Has the community threshold been passed?

Factors increasing seriousness	Factors reducing seriousness or reflecting personal mitigation
Statutory aggravating factors: Previous convictions, having regard to a) nature of the offence to which conviction relates and relevance to current offence; and b) time elapsed since conviction Offence committed on bail *Other aggravating factors include:* Possession of drug in prison Presence of others, especially children and/or non-users Possession of drug in a school or licensed premises Failure to comply with current court orders Offence committed on licence Attempts to conceal or dispose of evidence, where not charged separately Charged as importation of a very small amount Established evidence of community impact	No previous convictions **or** no relevant or recent convictions Remorse Good character and/or exemplary conduct Offender is using cannabis to help with a diagnosed medical condition Determination and/or demonstration of steps having been taken to address addiction or offending behaviour Serious medical conditions requiring urgent, intensive or long-term treatment Isolated incident Age and/or lack of maturity where it affects the responsibility of the offender Mental disorder or learning disability Sole or primary carer for dependent relatives

SG-570 [Steps Three to Eight are similar to those applicable to Fraudulent evasion of a prohibition by bringing into or taking out of the UK a controlled drug (see **SG-550**) but the reference at Step Four to minimum mandatory sentences does not apply and Step Six merely states 'In all cases, the court should consider whether to make ancillary orders'.]

SG-571 ANNEX: FINE BANDS AND COMMUNITY ORDERS

[The tables set out here are also set out in the Magistrates' Court Sentencing Guidelines, which includes further guidance on fines and community orders: see **SG-358** and **SG-382**.]

SG-572 PART 22 OFFENCES TAKEN INTO CONSIDERATION

DEFINITIVE GUIDELINE

Applicability of guideline

In accordance with section 120 of the Coroners and Justice Act 2009, the Sentencing Council issues this definitive guideline. It applies to all offenders whose cases are dealt with on or after 11 June 2012.

[Sets out the CAJA 2009, s. 125(1): see **SG-539**.]

This guideline applies where an offender admits the commission of other offences in the course of sentencing proceedings and requests those other offences to be taken into consideration.[369]

SG-573 General principles

When sentencing an offender who requests offences to be taken into consideration (TICs), courts should pass a total sentence which reflects *all* the offending behaviour. The sentence must be just and proportionate and must not exceed the statutory maximum for the conviction offence.

SG-574 Offences to be Taken Into Consideration

The court has discretion as to whether or not to take TICs into account. In exercising its discretion the court should take into account that TICs are capable of reflecting the offender's overall criminality. The court is likely to consider that the fact that the offender has assisted the police (particularly if the offences would not otherwise have been detected) and avoided the need for further proceedings demonstrates a genuine determination by the offender to 'wipe the slate clean'.[370]

[369] Section 305 Criminal Justice Act 2003 and section 161(1) Powers of Criminal Courts (Sentencing) Act 2000

[370] Per Lord Chief Justice, *R v Miles* [2006] EWCA Crim 256

It is generally **undesirable** for TICs to be accepted in the following circumstances:

- where the TIC is likely to attract a greater sentence than the conviction offence;
- where it is in the public interest that the TIC should be the subject of a separate charge;
- where the offender would avoid a prohibition, ancillary order or similar consequence which it would have been desirable to impose on conviction. For example:
- where the TIC attracts mandatory disqualification or endorsement and the offence(s) for which the defendant is to be sentenced do not;
- where the TIC constitutes a breach of an earlier sentence;[371]
- where the TIC is a specified offence for the purposes of section 224 of the Criminal Justice Act 2003, but the conviction offence is non-specified; or
- where the TIC is not founded on the same facts or evidence or part of a series of offences of the same or similar character (unless the court is satisfied that it is in the interests of justice to do so).

Jurisdiction **SG-575**

The magistrates' court cannot take into consideration an indictable only offence.

The Crown Court can take into account summary only offences provided the TICs are founded on the same facts or evidence as the indictable charge, or are part of a series of offences of the same or similar character as the indictable conviction offence.[372]

Procedural safeguards **SG-576**

A court should generally only take offences into consideration if the following procedural provisions have been satisfied:

- the police or prosecuting authorities have prepared a schedule of offences (TIC schedule) that they consider suitable to be taken into consideration. The TIC schedule should set out the nature of each offence, the date of the offence(s), relevant detail about the offence(s) (including, for example, monetary values of items) and any other brief details that the court should be aware of;
- a copy of the TIC schedule must be provided to the defendant and his representative (if he has one) before the sentence hearing. The defendant should sign the TIC schedule to provisionally admit the offences;
- at the sentence hearing, the court should ask the defendant in open court whether he admits each of the offences on the TIC schedule and whether he wishes to have them taken into consideration;[373]
- if there is any doubt about the admission of a particular offence, it should not be accepted as a TIC. Special care should be taken with vulnerable and/or unrepresented defendants;
- if the defendant is committed to the Crown Court for sentence, this procedure must take place again at the Crown Court even if the defendant has agreed to the schedule in the magistrates' court.

Application **SG-577**

The sentence imposed on an offender should, in most circumstances, be increased to reflect the fact that other offences have been taken into consideration. The court should:

1. Determine the sentencing starting point for the conviction offence, referring to the relevant definitive sentencing guidelines. No regard should be had to the presence of TICs at this stage.
2. Consider whether there are any aggravating or mitigating factors that justify an upward or downward adjustment from the starting point.

The presence of TICs should generally be treated as an aggravating feature that justifies an upward adjustment from the starting point. Where there is a large number of TICs, it may be appropriate to move outside the category range, although this must be considered in the context of the case and subject to the principle of totality. The court is limited to the statutory maximum for the conviction offence.

3. Continue through the sentencing process including:
    - consider whether the frank admission of a number of offences is an indication of a defendant's remorse or determination and/or demonstration of steps taken to address addiction or offending behaviour;
    - any reduction for a guilty plea should be applied to the overall sentence;
    - the principle of totality;

[371] *R v Webb* (1953) 37 Cr App 82
[372] Section 40 Criminal Justice Act 1988
[373] *Anderson v DPP* [1978] AC 964

- when considering ancillary orders these can be considered in relation to any or all of the TICs, specifically:
- compensation orders[374]- in the magistrate[s'] court the total compensation cannot exceed the limit for the conviction offence;
- restitution orders.[375]

SG-578
PART 23 TOTALITY

Definitive Guideline

Applicability of guideline
In accordance with section 120 of the Coroners and Justice Act 2009, the Sentencing Council issues this definitive guideline. It applies to all offenders whose cases are dealt with on or after 11 June 2012.

[Sets out the CAJA 2009, s. 125(1): see **SG-539**.]

This guideline applies when sentencing an offender for multiple offences or when sentencing an offender who is already serving an existing sentence. In these situations, the courts should apply the principle of totality.

SG-579 **General principles**

The principle of totality comprises two elements:

1. All courts, when sentencing for more than a single offence, should pass a total sentence which reflects *all* the offending behaviour before it and is just and proportionate. This is so whether the sentences are structured as concurrent or consecutive. Therefore, concurrent sentences will ordinarily be longer than a single sentence for a single offence.
2. It is usually impossible to arrive at a just and proportionate sentence for multiple offending simply by adding together notional single sentences. It is necessary to address the offending behaviour, together with the factors personal to the offender as a whole.

SG-580 **Concurrent/consecutive sentences**

There is no inflexible rule governing whether sentences should be structured as concurrent or consecutive components. The overriding principle is that the overall sentence must be just and proportionate.

SG-581 **General approach (as applied to Determinate Custodial Sentences)**

1. **Consider the sentence for each individual offence, referring to the relevant sentencing guidelines.**
2. **Determine whether the case calls for concurrent or consecutive sentences.**

Concurrent Sentences will ordinarily be appropriate where:

a) offences arise out of the same incident or facts.

Examples include:

- a single incident of dangerous driving resulting in injuries to multiple victims;[376]
- robbery with a weapon where the weapon offence is ancillary to the robbery and is not distinct and independent of it;[377]
- fraud and associated forgery;
- separate counts of supplying different types of drugs of the same class as part of the same transaction.

b) there is a series of offences of the same or similar kind, especially when committed against the same person.

Examples include:

- repetitive small thefts from the *same* person, such as by an employee;
- repetitive benefit frauds of the same kind, committed in each payment period.

---

[374] Section 131(2) Powers of Criminal Courts (Sentencing) Act 2000
[375] Section 148 ibid
[376] *R v Lawrence* (1989) 11 Cr App R (S) 580
[377] *R v Poulton and Celaire* [2002] EWCA Crim 2487; *Attorney General's Reference No 21 & 22 of 2003* [2003] EWCA Crim 3089

Where concurrent sentences are to be passed the sentence should reflect the overall criminality involved. The sentence should be appropriately aggravated by the presence of the associated offences.

Examples include:

- a single incident of dangerous driving resulting in injuries to multiple victims where there are separate charges relating to each victim. The sentences should generally be passed concurrently, but each sentence should be aggravated to take into account the harm caused;
- repetitive fraud or theft, where charged as a series of small frauds/thefts, would be properly considered in relation to the total amount of money obtained and the period of time over which the offending took place. The sentences should generally be passed concurrently, each one reflecting the overall seriousness;
- robbery with a weapon where the weapon offence is ancillary to the robbery and is not distinct and independent of it. The principal sentence for the robbery should properly reflect the presence of the weapon. The court must avoid double-counting and may deem it preferable for the possession of the weapon's offence to run concurrently to avoid the appearance of under-sentencing in respect of the robbery.[378]

Consecutive sentences will ordinarily be appropriate where:

a) offences arise out of unrelated facts or incidents.

Examples include:

- where the offender commits a theft on one occasion and a common assault against a different victim on a separate occasion;
- an attempt to pervert the course of justice in respect of another offence also charged;[379]
- a Bail Act offence;[380]
- any offence committed within the prison context;
- offences that are unrelated because whilst they were committed simultaneously they are distinct and there is an aggravating element that requires separate recognition, for example:
  - an assault on a constable committed to try to evade arrest for another offence also charged;[381]
  - where the defendant is convicted of drug dealing and possession of a firearm offence. The firearm offence is not the essence or the intrinsic part of the drugs offence and requires separate recognition;[382]
  - where the defendant is convicted of threats to kill in the context of an indecent assault on the same occasion, the threats to kill could be distinguished as a separate element.[383]

b) offences that are of the same or similar kind but where the overall criminality will not sufficiently be reflected by concurrent sentences.

Examples include:

- where offences committed against *different* people, such as repeated thefts involving attacks on several different shop assistants;[384]
- where offences of domestic violence or sexual offences are committed against the *same* individual.

c) one of more offence (s) qualifies for a statutory minimum sentence and concurrent sentences would improperly undermine that minimum[385]

However it is not permissible to impose consecutive sentences for offences committed at the same time in order to evade the statutory maximum penalty.[386]

Where consecutive sentences are to be passed add up the sentences for each offence and consider if the aggregate length is just and appropriate.

If the aggregate length is not just and proportionate the court should consider how to reach a just and proportionate sentence. There are a number of ways in which this could be achieved.

---

[378] *Attorney General's Reference Nos 21 & 22 of 2003*
[379] *Attorney General's Reference No 1 of 1990* (1990) 12 Cr App R (S) 245
[380] *R v Millen* (1980) 2 Cr App R (S) 357
[381] *R v Kastercum* (1972) 56 Cr App R 298
[382] *R v Poulton and Celaire* [2002] EWCA Crim 2487; *Attorney General's Reference Nos 21 & 22 of 2003* [2003] EWCA Crim 3089
[383] *R v Fletcher* [2002] 2 CAR (S) 127
[384] *R v Jamieson & Jamieson* [2008] EWCA Crim 2761
[385] *R v Raza* (2010) 1 Cr App R (S) 56
[386] *R v Ralphs* [2009] EWCA Crim 2555

Examples include:

- when sentencing for similar offence types or offences of a similar level of severity the court can consider:
  - whether all of the offences can be proportionately reduced (with particular reference to the category ranges within the sentencing guidelines) and passed consecutively;
  - whether, despite their similarity, a most serious principal offence can be identified and the other sentences can all be proportionately reduced (with particular reference to the category ranges within sentencing guidelines) and passed consecutively in order that the sentence for the lead offence can be clearly identified.
- when sentencing for two or more offences of differing levels of seriousness the court can consider:
  - whether some offences are of such low seriousness in the context of the most serious offence(s) that they can be recorded as 'no separate penalty' (for example technical breaches or minor driving offences not involving mandatory disqualification);
  - whether some of the offences are of lesser seriousness and are unrelated to the most serious offence(s), that they can be ordered to run concurrently so that the sentence for the most serious offence(s) can be clearly identified.

3. **Test the overall sentence(s) against the requirement that they be just and proportionate.**
4. **Consider whether the sentence is structured in a way that will be best understood by all concerned with it.**

SG-582 Specific applications — Custodial sentences

EXISTING DETERMINATE SENTENCE, WHERE DETERMINATE SENTENCE TO BE PASSED

Circumstance	Approach
Offender serving a determinate sentence (offence(s) committed before original sentence imposed)	Consider what the sentence length would have been if the court had dealt with the offences at the same time and ensure that the totality of the sentence is just and proportionate in all the circumstances. If it is not, an adjustment should be made to the sentence imposed for the latest offence.
Offender serving a determinate sentence (offence(s) committed after original sentence imposed)	Generally the sentence will be consecutive as it will have arisen out of an unrelated incident. The court must have regard to the totality of the offender's criminality when passing the second sentence, to ensure that the total sentence to be served is just and proportionate. Where a prisoner commits acts of violence in prison, any reduction for totality is likely to be minimal.[387]
Offender serving a determinate sentence but released from custody	The new sentence should start on the day it is imposed: s.265 Criminal Justice Act 2003 prohibits a sentence of imprisonment running consecutively to a sentence from which a prisoner has been released. The sentence for the new offence will take into account the aggravating feature that it was committed on licence. However, it must be commensurate with the new offence and cannot be artificially inflated with a view to ensuring that the offender serves a period in custody additional to the recall period (which will be an unknown quantity in most cases);[388] this is so even if the new sentence will, in consequence, add nothing to the period actually served.

[387] *R v Ali* (1998) 2 Cr App R 123
[388] *R v Costello* [2010] EWCA Crim 371

Circumstance	Approach
Offender subject to a s.116 return to custody The powers under s.116 Powers of Criminal Court (Sentencing) Act 2000 remain available where the offender: • has been released from a sentence of less than 12 months;[389] • committed his offence before 4 April 2005 and is released from a sentence of less than 4 years;[390] • committed his offence before 4 April 2005 and is released from a sentence of over 4 years following a Parole Board recommendation, or after serving two-thirds of his sentence under section 33(b) Criminal Justice Act 1991.[391]	The period of return under s.116 can either be ordered to be served before or concurrently with the sentence for the new offence. In either case the period of return shall be disregarded in determining the appropriate length of the new sentence.
Offender sentenced to a determinate term and subject to an existing suspended sentence order	Where an offender commits an additional offence during the operational period of a suspended sentence and the court orders the suspended sentence to be activated, the additional sentence will generally be consecutive to the activated suspended sentence, as it will arise out of unrelated facts.

EXTENDED SENTENCES FOR PUBLIC PROTECTION

SG-583

Circumstance	Approach
Extended sentences — using multiple offences to calculate the requisite determinate term	In the case of extended sentences imposed under the Criminal Justice Act 2003, providing there is at least one specified offence, the threshold requirement under s.227(2B) Criminal Justice Act 2003 is reached if the total determinate sentence for all offences (specified or not) would be four years or more. The extended sentence should be passed either for one specified offence or concurrently on a number of them. Ordinarily either a concurrent determinate sentence or no separate penalty will be appropriate to the remaining offences.[392] The extension period is such as the court considers necessary for the purpose of protecting members of the public from serious harm caused by the offender committing further specified offences.[393] The extension period must not exceed five years (or eight for a sexual offence). The whole aggregate term must not exceed the statutory maximum. The custodial period must be adjusted for totality in the same way as determinate sentences would be. The extension period is measured by the need for protection and therefore does not require adjustment.

Sentencing Guidelines

389 Section 116 of the Powers of Criminal Courts (Sentencing) Act 2000 was repealed by section 332 of the Criminal Justice Act 2003 and Part 7 of Schedule 37. However, the effect of the saving in paragraph 29 of Schedule 2 to the Commencement No.8 and Transitional and Savings Provisions Order 2005 was that section 116 continued to apply where the earlier sentence was imposed for an offence committed before 4 April 2005, or was for a term of less than 12 months.

390 ibid

391 ibid. The Criminal Justice & Immigration Act 2008 contains a further transitional provision. Paragraph 4 of Schedule 26 inserts an exclusion into s.116 which prevents prisoners released under section 33(1A) of the 1991 Act (i.e. eligible discretionary conditional release prisoners, who are released automatically at ½ point of their sentence, rather than on a recommendation from the Parole Board) from being returned to prison under section 116.

392 *R v Pinnell* [2010] EWCA Crim 2848

393 *R v Cornelius* [2002] EWCA Crim 138

SG-584

INDETERMINATE SENTENCES

Circumstance	Approach
Imposing multiple indeterminate sentences on the same occasion and using multiple offences to calculate the minimum term for an indeterminate sentence	Indeterminate sentences should start on the date of their imposition and so should generally be ordered to run concurrently. If any offence is a serious and specified one and it appears that the defendant is dangerous within the meaning of the dangerousness provisions of the Criminal Justice Act 2003 then: a) first assess the notional determinate term for all offences (serious, specified or otherwise), adjusting for totality in the usual way;[394] b) ascertain whether the total determinate term would be four years or more, or the offender has previously been convicted of a Schedule 15A offence; if so an indeterminate sentence may be passed; and c) the indeterminate sentence should generally be passed concurrently on all serious specific offences, but there may be some circumstances in which it suffices to pass it on a single such offence.
Indeterminate sentence (where the offender is already serving an existing determinate sentence)	It is generally undesirable to order an indeterminate sentence to be served consecutively to any other period of imprisonment on the basis that indeterminate sentences should start on their imposition.[395] The court should instead order the sentence to run concurrently but can adjust the minimum term for the new offence to reflect half of any period still remaining to be served under the existing sentence (to take account of the early release provisions for determinate sentences). The court should then review the minimum term to ensure that the total sentence is just and proportionate.
Indeterminate sentence (where the offender is already serving an existing indeterminate sentence)	It is generally undesirable to order an indeterminate sentence to be served consecutively to any other period of imprisonment on the basis that indeterminate sentences should start on their imposition. However, where necessary the court can order an indeterminate sentence to run consecutively to an indeterminate sentence passed on an earlier occasion.[396] The second sentence will commence on the expiration of the minimum term of the original sentence and the offender will become eligible for a parole review after serving both minimum terms.[397] The court should consider the length of the aggregate minimum terms that must be served before the offender will be eligible for consideration by the Parole Board. If this is not just and proportionate, the court can adjust the minimum term.
Ordering a determinate sentence to run consecutively to an indeterminate sentence	The court can order a determinate sentence to run consecutively to an indeterminate sentence. The determinate sentence will commence on the expiry of the minimum term of the indeterminate sentence and the offender will become eligible for a parole review after serving half of the determinate sentence.[398] The court should consider the total sentence that the offender will serve before becoming eligible for consideration for release. If this is not just and proportionate, the court can reduce the length of the determinate sentence, or alternatively, can order the second sentence to be served concurrently.

394 *R v Rahuel Delucca* [2010] EWCA Crim 710
395 *R v O'Brien* [2006] EWCA Crim 1741
396 *R v Hills* [2008] EWCA Crim 1871; *R v Ashes* [2007] EWCA Crim 1848
397 Section 28(1B) Crime (Sentences) Act 1997
398 Section 28 ibid.

Specific applications — Non-custodial sentences

SG-585

MULTIPLE FINES FOR NON-IMPRISONABLE OFFENCES

Circumstance	Approach
Offender convicted of more than one offence where a fine is appropriate	The total fine is inevitably cumulative. The court should determine the fine for each individual offence based on the seriousness of the offence[399] and taking into account the circumstances of the case including the financial circumstances of the offender so far as they are known, or appear, to the court.[400] The court should add up the fines for each offence and consider if they are just and proportionate. If the aggregate total is not just and proportionate the court should consider how to reach a just and proportionate fine. There are a number of ways in which this can be achieved. *For example:* • where an offender is to be fined for two or more offences that arose out of the same incident or where there are multiple offences of a repetitive kind, especially when committed against the same person, it will often be appropriate to impose for the most serious offence a fine which reflects the totality of the offending where this can be achieved within the maximum penalty for that offence. No separate penalty should be imposed for the other offences; • where an offender is to be fined for two or more offences that arose out of different incidents, it will often be appropriate to impose a separate fine for each of the offences. The court should add up the fines for each offence and consider if they are just and proportionate. If the aggregate amount is not just and proportionate the court should consider whether all of the fines can be proportionately reduced. Separate fines should then be passed. Where separate fines are passed, the court must be careful to ensure that there is no double-counting.[401] Where compensation is being ordered, that will need to be attributed to the relevant offence as will any necessary ancillary orders.
Multiple offences attracting fines — crossing the community threshold	If the offences being dealt with are all imprisonable, then the community threshold can be crossed by reason of multiple offending, when it would not be crossed for a single offence.[402] However, if the offences are non-imprisonable (e.g. driving without insurance) the threshold cannot be crossed.[403]

Sentencing Guidelines

[399] Section 164(2) Criminal Justice Act 2003
[400] Section 164(3) ibid.
[401] *R v Pointon* [2008] EWCA Crim 513
[402] Section 148(1) Criminal Justice Act 2003
[403] Section 150A ibid. (in force since 14 July 2008) restricts the power to make a community order by limiting it to cases where the offence is punishable with imprisonment

SG-586 FINES IN COMBINATION WITH OTHER SENTENCES

Circumstance	Approach
A fine may be imposed in addition to any other penalty for the same offence except:	• a hospital order;[404] • a discharge;[405] • a sentence fixed by law[406] (minimum sentences, EPP, IPP); • a minimum term imposed under s.110(2) or s.111(2) of the Powers of Criminal Courts (Sentencing) Act 2000;[407] • a life sentence imposed under s.225(2) Criminal Justice Act 2003 or a sentence of detention for life for an offender under 18 under s.226(2) Criminal Justice Act 2003.[408]
Fines and determinate custodial sentences	A fine should not generally be imposed in combination with a custodial sentence because of the effect of imprisonment on the means of the defendant. However, exceptionally, it may be appropriate to impose a fine in addition to a custodial sentence where: • the sentence is suspended; • a confiscation order is not contemplated; **and** • there is no obvious victim to whom compensation can be awarded; **and** • the offender has, or will have, resources from which a fine can be paid.[409]

SG-587 COMMUNITY ORDERS

Circumstance	Approach
Multiple offences attracting community orders — crossing the custody threshold	If the offences are all imprisonable and none of the individual sentences merit a custodial sentence, the custody threshold can be crossed by reason of multiple offending.[410] If the custody threshold has been passed, the court should refer to the offence ranges in sentencing guidelines for the offences and to the general principles.
Multiple offences, where one offence would merit immediate custody and one offence would merit a community order	A community order should not be ordered to run consecutively to or concurrently with a custodial sentence. Instead the court should generally impose one custodial sentence that is aggravated appropriately by the presence of the associated offence(s). The alternative option is to impose no separate penalty for the offence of lesser seriousness.
Offender convicted of more than one offence where a community order is appropriate	A community order is a composite package rather than an accumulation of sentences attached to individual counts. The court should generally impose a single community order that reflects the overall criminality of the offending behaviour. Where it is necessary to impose more than one community order, these should be ordered to run concurrently and for ease of administration, each of the orders should be identical.

404 Section 37(8) Mental Health Act 1983
405 *R v McClelland* [1951] 1 All ER 557
406 Section 163 Criminal Justice Act 2003
407 ibid
408 ibid
409 [This footnote refers to guidance that has been superseded.]
410 Section 148(1) Criminal Justice Act 2003

Circumstance	Approach
Offender convicted of an offence while serving a community order	The power to deal with the offender depends on his being convicted whilst the order is still in force;[411] it does not arise where the order has expired, even if the additional offence was committed whilst it was still current. If an offender, in respect of whom a community order made by a magistrates' court is in force, is convicted by a magistrates' court of an additional offence, the magistrates' court should ordinarily revoke the previous community order and sentence afresh for both the original and the additional offence. Where an offender, in respect of whom a community order made by a Crown Court is in force, is convicted by a magistrates' court, the magistrates' court may, and ordinarily should, commit the offender to the Crown Court, in order to allow the Crown Court to re-sentence for the original offence and the additional offence. The sentencing court should consider the overall seriousness of the offending behaviour taking into account the additional offence and the original offence. The court should consider whether the combination of associated offences is sufficiently serious to justify a custodial sentence. If the court does not consider that custody is necessary, it should impose a single community order that reflects the overall totality of criminality. The court must take into account the extent to which the offender complied with the requirements of the previous order.

DISQUALIFICATIONS FROM DRIVING SG-588

Circumstance	Approach
Offender convicted of two or more obligatory disqualification offences (s.34(1) Road Traffic Offender Act 1988)	The court must impose an order of disqualification for each offence unless for special reasons it does not disqualify the offender.[412] All orders of disqualification imposed by the court on the same date take effect immediately and cannot be ordered to run consecutively to one another. The court should take into account all offences when determining the disqualification periods and should generally impose like periods for each offence.
Offender convicted of two or more offences involving either: a) discretionary disqualification and obligatory endorsement from driving; or b) obligatory disqualification but the court for special reasons does not disqualify the offender and the penalty points to be taken into account number 12 or more (s.28 and 35 Road Traffic Offender Act 1988)	Where an offender is convicted on the same occasion of more than one offence to which s.35(1) Road Traffic Offender Act 1988 applies, only one disqualification shall be imposed on him.[413] However, the court must take into account all offences when determining the disqualification period. For the purposes of appeal, any disqualification imposed shall be treated as an order made on conviction of each of the offences.[414]
Other combinations involving two or more offences involving discretionary disqualification	As orders of disqualification take effect immediately, it is generally desirable for the court to impose a single disqualification order that reflects the overall criminality of the offending behaviour.

411 Paragraphs 21–23 of Schedule 8 Criminal Justice Act 2003
412 Section 34(1) Road Traffic Offender Act 1988
413 Section 34(3) ibid
414 ibid

SG-589

COMPENSATION ORDERS

Circumstance	Approach
Global compensation orders	The court should not fix a global compensation figure unless the offences were committed against the same victim.[415] Where there are competing claims for limited funds, the total compensation available should normally be apportioned on a pro rata basis.[416]

The court may combine a compensation order with any other form of order.

Compensation orders and fines	Priority is given to the imposition of a compensation order over a fine.[417] This does not affect sentences other than fines. This means that the fine should be reduced or, if necessary, dispensed with altogether, to enable the compensation to be paid.
Compensation orders and confiscation orders	A compensation order can be combined with a confiscation order where the amount that may be realised is sufficient. If such an order is made, priority should be given to compensation.[418]
Compensation orders and community orders	A compensation order can be combined with a community order.
Compensation orders and suspended sentence orders	A compensation order can be combined with a suspended sentence order.[419]
Compensation orders and custody	A compensation order can be combined with a sentence of immediate custody where the offender is clearly able to pay or has good prospects of employment on his release from custody.

SG-590

PART 24 ALLOCATION

Definitive Guideline

Applicability of guideline

In accordance with section 122(2) of the Coroners and Justice Act 2009, the Sentencing Council issues this definitive guideline. It applies to all defendants in the magistrates' court (including youths jointly charged with adults) whose cases are dealt with on or after 11 June 2012. It will not be applicable in the youth court where a separate statutory procedure applies.

[Sets out the CAJA 2009, s. 125(1): see **SG-539**.]

SG-591 **Statutory framework**

In accordance with section 19 of the Magistrates' Courts Act 1980, where a defendant pleads not guilty or has not indicated an intention to plead guilty to an offence triable either way, a magistrates' court must decide whether the offence should be sent to the Crown Court for trial.

When deciding whether an either way offence is more suitable for summary trial or trial on indictment, section 19 of the Magistrates' Courts Act 1980 provides that the court shall give the prosecutor and the accused the opportunity to make representations as to which court is more suitable for the conduct of the trial.[420]

415 Section 130(12) Powers of Criminal Courts (Sentencing) Act 2000
416 *R v Mitchell* [2001] Crim LR 239
417 Section 118(5) Powers of Criminal Courts (Sentencing) Act 2000
418 *R v Warton* [1976] Crim LR 520
419 *R v Miller* [1976] Crim LR 694
420 Section 19(2) Magistrates' Courts Act 1980

The court must also have regard to:

a) the nature of the case;
b) whether the circumstances make the offence one of a serious character;
c) whether the punishment which a magistrates' court would have the power to inflict for the offence would be adequate; and
d) any other circumstances which appear to the court to make the offence more suitable for it to be tried in one way rather than the other.[421]

Guidance SG-592

It is important to ensure that all cases are tried at the appropriate level. **In general, either way offences should be tried summarily unless it is likely that the court's sentencing powers will be insufficient.** Its powers will generally be insufficient if the outcome is likely to result in a sentence in excess of six months' imprisonment for a single offence.

The court should assess the likely sentence in the light of the facts alleged by the prosecution case, taking into account all aspects of the case including those advanced by the defence.

The court should refer to definitive guidelines to assess the likely sentence for the offence.

Committal for sentence SG-593

There is ordinarily no statutory restriction on committing an either way case for sentence following conviction. The general power of the magistrates' court to commit to the Crown Court for sentence after a finding that a case is suitable for summary trial and/or conviction continues to be available where the court is of the opinion that the offence (and any associated offences) is so serious that greater punishment should be inflicted than the court has power to impose.[422] Where the court decides that the case is suitable to be dealt with in the magistrates' court, it should remind the defendant that all sentencing options remain open, including committal to the Crown Court for sentence at the time it informs the defendant of this decision.

However, where the court proceeds to the summary trial of certain offences relating to criminal damage, upon conviction there is no power to commit to Crown Court for sentence.[423]

Linked cases SG-594

Where a youth and an adult are jointly charged, the youth must be tried summarily unless the court considers it to be in the interests of justice for both the youth and the adult to be committed to the Crown Court for trial. Examples of factors that should be considered when deciding whether to separate the youth and adult defendants include:

- whether separate trials can take place without causing undue inconvenience to witnesses or injustice to the case as a whole;
- the young age of the defendant, particularly where the age gap between the adult and youth offender is substantial;
- the immaturity of the youth;
- the relative culpability of the youth compared with the adult and whether or not the role played by the youth was minor; and
- the lack of previous convictions on the part of the youth.

PART 25 DANGEROUS DOG OFFENCES SG-595

Definitive Guideline

Applicability of guideline

[Omitted: See **SG-539** for identical text save that this guideline has effect from 20 August 2012.]

Structure, ranges and starting points SG-596

[Omitted: See **SG-540** for identical text.]

421 Section 19(1) and (3) ibid
422 Section 3 Powers of Criminal Courts (Sentencing) Act 2000
423 Sections 2 and 33 Magistrates' Courts Act 1980

SG-597 OWNER OR PERSON IN CHARGE OF A DOG DANGEROUSLY OUT OF CONTROL IN A PUBLIC PLACE, INJURING ANY PERSON

Dangerous Dogs Act 1991 (section 3(1))

OWNER OR PERSON IN CHARGE ALLOWING A DOG TO BE IN A PRIVATE PLACE WHERE THE DOG IS NOT PERMITTED TO BE, INJURING ANY PERSON

Dangerous Dogs Act 1991 (section 3(3)(a))

Triable either way
Maximum: 2 years' custody

Offence range: Discharge — 18 months' custody

SG-598 **STEP ONE Determining the offence category**
The court should determine the offence category using the table below.

Category 1	Greater harm and higher culpability
Category 2	Greater harm **and** lower culpability; **or** lesser harm **and** higher culpability
Category 3	Lesser harm **and** lower culpability

The court should determine culpability and harm caused or intended, by reference only to the factors below, which comprise the principal factual elements of the offence. Where an offence does not fall squarely into a category, individual factors may require a degree of weighting before making an overall assessment and determining the appropriate offence category.

Factors indicating greater harm Serious injury (which includes disease transmission and/or psychological harm) Sustained or repeated attack Victim is a child or otherwise vulnerable because of personal circumstances **Factor indicating lesser harm** Minor injury **Factors indicating higher culpability** *Statutory aggravating factors:* Offence racially or religiously aggravated Offence motivated by, or demonstrating, hostility to the victim based on his or her sexual orientation (or presumed sexual orientation) Offence motivated by, or demonstrating, hostility to the victim based on the victim's disability (or presumed disability) *Other aggravating factors:* Failure to respond to warnings or concerns expressed by others about the dog's behaviour Goading, or allowing goading, of dog Dog used as weapon or to intimidate victim Offence motivated by, or demonstrating, hostility based on the victim's age, sex, gender identity (or presumed gender identity)	Factors indicating lower culpability Attempts made to regain control of dog and/or intervene Provocation of dog without fault of the offender Evidence of safety or control measures having been taken Mental disorder or learning disability, where linked to the commission of the offence

SG-599 **STEP TWO Starting point and category range**

Having determined the category, the court should use the corresponding starting points to reach a sentence within the category range below. The starting point applies to all offenders irrespective of plea or previous convictions. A case of particular gravity, reflected by multiple features of culpability or harm in step 1, could merit upward adjustment from the starting point before further adjustment for aggravating or mitigating features, set out [below].

Offence Category	Starting Point (*Applicable to all offenders*)	Category Range (*Applicable to all offenders*)
Category 1	6 months' custody	Medium level community order–18 months' custody
Category 2	Medium level community order	Band B fine–6 months' custody
Category 3	Band B fine	Discharge–Band C fine

The table below contains a **non-exhaustive** list of additional factual elements providing the context of the offence and factors relating to the offender. Identify whether any combination of these, or other relevant factors, should result in an upward or downward adjustment from the starting point. In some cases, having considered these factors, it may be appropriate to move outside the identified category range.

When sentencing **category 1 or 2** offences, the court should also consider the custody threshold as follows:

- Has the custody threshold been passed?
- If so, is it unavoidable that a custodial sentence be imposed?
- If so, can that sentence be suspended?

When sentencing **category 2** offences, the court should also consider the community order threshold as follows:

- Has the community order threshold been passed?

Factors increasing seriousness	Factors reducing seriousness or reflecting personal mitigation
Statutory aggravating factors: Previous convictions, having regard to a) the nature of the offence to which the conviction relates and its relevance to the current offence; and b) the time that has elapsed since the conviction Offence committed whilst on bail *Other aggravating factors include:* Injury to another animal(s) Location of the offence Ongoing effect upon the victim and/or others Failure to take adequate precautions to prevent dog escaping Allowing person insufficiently experienced or trained, to be in charge of dog Ill treatment or failure to ensure welfare needs of dog, where not charged separately Dog known to be prohibited Lack or loss of control of dog due to influence of alcohol or drugs Offence committed against those working in the public sector or providing a service to the public Established evidence of community impact Failure to comply with current court orders Offence committed whilst on licence	No previous convictions or no relevant/recent convictions Isolated incident No previous complaints against, or incidents involving, the dog Remorse Good character and/or exemplary conduct Evidence of responsible ownership Determination and/or demonstration of steps taken to address addiction or offending behaviour Serious medical conditions requiring urgent, intensive or long-term treatment Age and/or lack of maturity where it affects the responsibility of the offender Mental disorder or learning disability, where not linked to the commission of the offence Sole or primary carer for dependent relatives

STEP THREE Consider any factors which indicate a reduction, such as assistance to the prosecution **SG-600**

The court should take into account sections 73 and 74 of the Serious Organised Crime and Police Act 2005 (assistance by defendants: reduction or review of sentence) and any other rule of law by virtue of which an offender may receive a discounted sentence in consequence of assistance given (or offered) to the prosecutor or investigator.

STEP FOUR Reduction for guilty pleas

The court should take account of any potential reduction for a guilty plea in accordance with section 144 of the Criminal Justice Act 2003 and the *Guilty Plea* guideline.

STEP FIVE Compensation and ancillary orders

In all cases, the court should consider whether to make a compensation order and/or other ancillary orders.

Compensation order

The court should consider compensation orders in all cases where personal injury, loss or damage has resulted from the offence.[424] The court must give reasons if it decides not to award compensation in such cases.

Other ancillary orders available include:

Disqualification from having custody of a dog

The court may disqualify the offender from having custody of a dog.[425] The test the court should consider is whether the offender is a fit and proper person to have custody of a dog.

Destruction order/contingent destruction order

In any case where the offender is not the owner of the dog, the owner must be given an opportunity to be present and make representations to the court.

The court **shall** make a destruction order unless the court is satisfied that the dog would not constitute a danger to public safety.[426]

In reaching a decision, the court should consider the relevant circumstances which include:

- the incident — what degree of harm was caused by the dog's behaviour?
- past behaviour of the dog — is this an isolated incident or have there been previous warnings or incidents? and
- owner's character — is the owner a fit and proper person to own this particular dog?

If the court is satisfied that the dog would not constitute a danger to public safety, it shall make a contingent destruction order imposing certain available conditions.[427] A contingent destruction order should specify the measures to be taken by the owner for keeping the dog under proper control, which include:

- muzzling;
- keeping on a lead;
- neutering in appropriate cases; and
- excluding it from a specified place.[428]

Where the court makes a destruction order, it may order the offender to pay what it determines to be the reasonable expenses of destroying the dog and of keeping it pending its destruction.[429]

STEP SIX Totality principle

If sentencing an offender for more than one offence, or where the offender is already serving a sentence, consider whether the total sentence is just and proportionate to the offending behaviour.

STEP SEVEN Reasons

Section 174 of the Criminal Justice Act 2003 imposes a duty to give reasons for, and explain the effect of, the sentence.

STEP EIGHT Consideration for remand time

Sentencers should take into consideration any remand time served in relation to the final sentence at this final step. The court should consider whether to give credit for time spent on remand in custody or on bail in accordance with sections 240 and 240A of the Criminal Justice Act 2003.

SG-601 OWNER OR PERSON IN CHARGE OF A DOG DANGEROUSLY OUT OF CONTROL IN A PUBLIC PLACE

Dangerous Dogs Act 1991 (section 3(1))

424 Section 130 Powers of Criminal Courts (Sentencing) Act 2000
425 Section 4(1)(b) Dangerous Dogs Act 1991
426 Section 4(1)(a) ibid
427 Section 4A(4) Dangerous Dogs Act 1991
428 Section 4A(5) ibid
429 Section 4(4)(b) ibid

Owner or Person in Charge Allowing a Dog to be in a Private Place where the Dog is Not Permitted to Be, which Makes a Person Fear Injury

Dangerous Dogs Act 1991 (section 3(3)(b))

Triable summarily only

Maximum: 6 months' custody

Offence range: Discharge — 6 months' custody

STEP ONE Determining the offence category SG-602

The court should determine the offence category using the table below.

Category 1	Greater harm and higher culpability
Category 2	Greater harm **and** lower culpability; **or** lesser harm **and** higher culpability
Category 3	Lesser harm **and** lower culpability

The court should determine culpability and harm caused or intended, by reference **only** to the factors below, which comprise the principal factual elements of the offence. Where an offence does not fall squarely into a category, individual factors may require a degree of weighting before making an overall assessment and determining the appropriate offence category.

Factors indicating greater harm Presence of children or others who are vulnerable because of personal circumstances Injury to another animal(s) **Factors indicating higher culpability** *Statutory aggravating factors:* Offence racially or religiously aggravated Offence motivated by, or demonstrating, hostility to the victim based on his or her sexual orientation (or presumed sexual orientation) Offence motivated by, or demonstrating, hostility to the victim based on the victim's disability (or presumed disability) *Other aggravating factors*: Failure to respond to warnings or concerns expressed by others about the dog's behaviour Goading, or allowing goading, of dog Dog used as weapon or to intimidate victim Offence motivated by, or demonstrating, hostility based on the victim's age, sex, gender identity (or presumed gender identity)	**Factors indicating lesser harm** Low risk to the public **Factors indicating lower culpability** Attempts made to regain control of dog and/or intervene Provocation of dog without fault of the offender Evidence of safety or control measures having been taken Mental disorder or learning disability, where linked to the commission of the offence

STEP TWO Starting point and category range SG-603

Having determined the category, the court should use the corresponding starting points to reach a sentence within the category range below. The starting point applies to all offenders irrespective of plea or previous convictions. A case of particular gravity, reflected by multiple features of culpability or harm in step 1, could merit upward adjustment from the starting point before further adjustment for aggravating or mitigating features, set out [below].

Offence Category	Starting Point (*Applicable to all offenders*)	Category Range (*Applicable to all offenders*)
Category 1	Medium level community order	Band C fine–6 months' custody
Category 2	Band B fine	Band A fine–Low level community order
Category 3	Band A fine	Discharge–Band B fine

The table below contains a **non-exhaustive** list of additional factual elements providing the context of the offence and factors relating to the offender. Identify whether any combination of these, or other relevant factors, should result in an upward or downward adjustment from the starting point. In some cases, having considered these factors, it may be appropriate to move outside the identified category range.

When sentencing **category 1** offences, the court should also consider the custody threshold as follows:

- Has the custody threshold been passed?
- If so, is it unavoidable that a custodial sentence be imposed?
- If so, can that sentence be suspended?

When sentencing **category 1 or 2** offences, the court should also consider the community order threshold as follows:

- Has the community order threshold been passed?

Factors increasing seriousness	**Factors reducing seriousness or reflecting personal mitigation**
Statutory aggravating factors: Previous convictions, having regard to a) the nature of the offence to which the conviction relates and its relevance to the current offence; and b) the time that has elapsed since the conviction Offence committed whilst on bail *Other aggravating factors include:* Location of the offence Ongoing effect upon the victim and/or others Failure to take adequate precautions to prevent dog escaping Allowing person insufficiently experienced or trained, to be in charge of dog Ill treatment or failure to ensure welfare needs of dog, where not charged separately Dog known to be prohibited Lack or loss of control of dog due to the influence of alcohol or drugs Offence committed against those working in the public sector or providing a service to the public Established evidence of community impact Failure to comply with current court orders Offence committed whilst on licence	No previous convictions or no relevant/recent convictions Isolated incident No previous complaints against, or incidents involving, the dog Remorse Good character and/or exemplary conduct Evidence of responsible ownership Determination and/or demonstration of steps taken to address addiction or offending behaviour Serious medical conditions requiring urgent, intensive or long-term treatment Age and/or lack of maturity where it affects the responsibility of the offender Mental disorder or learning disability, where not linked to the commission of the offence Sole or primary carer for dependent relatives

SG-604 [Steps Three to Eight are almost identical to those applicable to Owner or person in charge of a dog dangerously out of control in a public place, injuring any person (see **SG-600**), but differ in relation to Destruction order/contingent destruction order. That aspect of Step 5 is set out below.]

Destruction order/contingent destruction order

In any case where the offender is not the owner of the dog, the owner must be given an opportunity to be present and make representations to the court.

The court **may** make a destruction order.[430] Alternatively, it **may** make a contingent destruction order imposing certain available conditions.[431] A contingent destruction order should specify the measures to be taken by the owner for keeping the dog under proper control, which include:

- muzzling;
- keeping on a lead;
- neutering in appropriate cases; and
- excluding it from a specified place.[432]

In reaching a decision, the court should consider the relevant circumstances which include:

- the incident — what degree of harm was caused by the dog's behaviour?

[430] Section 4(1)(a) ibid
[431] Section 4A(4) ibid
[432] Section 4A(5) ibid

- past behaviour of the dog — is this an isolated incident or have there been previous warnings or incidents? and
- owner's character — is the owner a fit and proper person to own this particular dog?

Where the court makes a destruction order, it **may** order the offender to pay what it determines to be the reasonable expenses of destroying the dog and of keeping it pending its destruction.[433]

Possession of a Prohibited Dog SG-605

Dangerous Dogs Act 1991 (section 1(3))

Breeding, Selling, Exchanging or Advertising a Prohibited Dog

Dangerous Dogs Act 1991 (section 1(2))

Triable only summarily

Maximum: 6 months' custody

Offence range: Discharge — 6 months' custody

STEP ONE Determining the offence category SG-606

The court should determine the offence category using the table below.

Category 1	Greater harm and higher culpability
Category 2	Greater harm **or** higher culpability
Category 3	**Neither** greater harm **nor** higher culpability

The court should determine culpability and harm caused or intended, by reference **only** to the factors below, which comprise the principal factual elements of the offence. Where an offence does not fall squarely into a category, individual factors may require a degree of weighting before making an overall assessment and determining the appropriate offence category.

Factors indicating greater harm	**Factors indicating higher culpability**
Injury to person Injury to another animal(s)	Possessing a dog known to be prohibited Breeding from a dog known to be prohibited Selling, exchanging or advertising a dog known to be prohibited Offence committed for gain Dog used to threaten or intimidate Permitting fighting Training and/or possession of paraphernalia for dog fighting

STEP TWO Starting point and category range SG-607

Having determined the category, the court should use the corresponding starting points to reach a sentence within the category range below. The starting point applies to all offenders irrespective of plea or previous convictions. A case of particular gravity, reflected by multiple features of culpability or harm in step 1, could merit upward adjustment from the starting point before further adjustment for aggravating or mitigating features, set out [below].

Offence Category	Starting Point (*Applicable to all offenders*)	Category Range (*Applicable to all offenders*)
Category 1	Medium level community order	Band C fine–6 months' custody*
Category 2	Band C fine	Band A fine–Medium level community order
Category 3	Band A fine	Discharge–Band B fine

* Imprisonment is not available if the provisions of s.1(7) Dangerous Dogs Act 1991 apply

433 Section 4(4)(b) ibid

The table below contains a **non-exhaustive** list of additional factual elements providing the context of the offence and factors relating to the offender. Identify whether any combination of these, or other relevant factors, should result in an upward or downward adjustment from the starting point. In some cases, having considered these factors, it may be appropriate to move outside the identified category range.

When sentencing **category 1** offences, the court should also consider the custody threshold as follows:

- Has the custody threshold been passed?
- If so, is it unavoidable that a custodial sentence be imposed?
- If so, can that sentence be suspended?

When sentencing **category 1 or 2** offences, the court should also consider the community order threshold as follows:

- Has the community order threshold been passed?

Factors increasing seriousness	**Factors reducing seriousness or reflecting personal mitigation**
Statutory aggravating factors: Previous convictions, having regard to a) the nature of the offence to which the conviction relates and its relevance to the current offence; and b) the time that has elapsed since the conviction Offence committed whilst on bail *Other aggravating factors include:* Presence of children or others who are vulnerable because of personal circumstances Ill treatment or failure to ensure welfare needs of dog, where not charged separately Established evidence of community impact Failure to comply with current court orders Offence committed whilst on licence	No previous convictions **or** no relevant/recent convictions Unaware that dog was prohibited type despite reasonable efforts to identify type Evidence of safety or control measures having been taken by owner Prosecution results from owner notification Remorse Good character and/or exemplary conduct Evidence of responsible ownership Determination and/or demonstration of steps taken to address addiction or offending behaviour Serious medical conditions requiring urgent, intensive or long-term treatment Age and/or lack of maturity where it affects the responsibility of the offender Lapse of time since the offence where this is not the fault of the offender Mental disorder or learning disability Sole or primary carer for dependent relatives

SG-608 [Steps Three to Eight are almost identical to those applicable to Owner or person in charge of a dog dangerously out of control in a public place, injuring any person (see **SG-600**), but differ in relation to Destruction order/contingent destruction order. That aspect of Step 5 is set out below.]

Destruction order/contingent destruction order

The court **shall** make a destruction order unless the court is satisfied that the dog would not constitute a danger to public safety.[434]

In reaching a decision, the court should consider the relevant circumstances which include:

- danger to the public — what is the potential risk of harm posed by the dog?
- behaviour of the dog — have there been any warnings or incidents involving the dog? and
- owner's character — is the owner a fit and proper person to own this particular dog?

If the court does not make a destruction order, the court **shall** make a contingent destruction order providing that unless the dog is exempted from the prohibition within two months it shall be destroyed.[435] Statutory procedures and conditions automatically apply to exempted dogs and no other conditions can be imposed.[436] Where the offender is the owner of the dog, it would not normally be appropriate to make a contingent destruction order in conjunction with a disqualification order.

434 Section 4(1)(a) ibid
435 Section 4A(1) ibid
436 The Dangerous Dogs Compensation and Exemption Schemes Order 1991 SI No. 1744 (as amended by The Dangerous Dogs Compensation and Exemption Schemes (Amendment) Order 1991 SI No. 2297)

Furthermore, the court **must not** transfer ownership of the dog to another.[437]

Where the court makes a destruction order, it **may** order the offender to pay what it determines to be the reasonable expenses of destroying the dog and of keeping it pending its destruction.[438]

ANNEX: FINE BANDS AND COMMUNITY ORDERS SG-609

[The tables set out here are also set out in the Magistrates' Court Sentencing Guidelines, which includes further guidance on fines and community orders: see **SG-358** and **SG-382**.]

PART 26 ENVIRONMENTAL OFFENCES SG-610

DEFINITIVE GUIDELINE

Applicability of guideline

[Omitted: See **SG-539** for identical text save that this guideline has effect from 1 July 2014.]

This guideline applies only to individual offenders aged 18 and older or organisations. General principles to be considered in the sentencing of youths are in the Sentencing Guidelines Council's definitive guideline, *Overarching Principles — Sentencing Youths.*

Structure, ranges and starting points

[Omitted: See **SG-540**]

ORGANISATIONS SG-611

Unauthorised or harmful deposit, treatment or disposal etc. of waste

Illegal discharges to air, land and water

Environmental Protection Act 1990 (section 33)

Environmental Permitting (England and Wales) Regulations 2010 (regulations 12 and 38(1), (2) and (3))

Also relevant, with adjustments, to certain related offences (see [**SG-621**])

Triable either way

Maximum: when tried on indictment: unlimited fine
when tried summarily: £50,000 fine

Offence range: £100 fine — £3 million fine

Use this guideline when the offender is an organisation. If the offender is an individual, please refer to the guideline for individuals.

> **Confiscation**
>
> **Committal to the Crown Court for sentence is mandatory if confiscation (see step two) is to be considered: Proceeds of Crime Act 2002 section 70. In such cases magistrates should state whether they would otherwise have committed for sentence.**
>
> **Financial orders must be considered in this order: (1) compensation, (2) confiscation, and (3) fine (see Proceeds of Crime Act 2002 section 13).**

STEP ONE Compensation SG-612

The court must consider making a compensation order requiring the offender to pay compensation for any personal injury, loss or damage resulting from the offence in such an amount as the court considers appropriate, having regard to the evidence and to the means of the offender.

Where the means of the offender are limited, priority should be given to the payment of compensation over payment of any other financial penalty.

Reasons should be given if a compensation order is not made.

(See section 130 Powers of Criminal Courts (Sentencing) Act 2000)

[437] Section 1(2)(b) Dangerous Dogs Act 1991
[438] Section 4(4)(b) ibid

SG-613 **STEP TWO Confiscation (Crown Court only)**

Confiscation must be considered if either the Crown asks for it or the court thinks that it may be appropriate. Confiscation must be dealt with before any other fine or financial order (except compensation).

(See sections 6 and 13 Proceeds of Crime Act 2002)

SG-614 **STEP THREE Determining the offence category**

The court should determine the offence category using only the culpability and harm factors in the tables below. The culpability and harm categories are on a sliding scale; there is inevitable overlap between the factors described in adjacent categories. Where an offence does not fall squarely into a category, individual factors may require a degree of weighting before making an overall assessment and determining the appropriate offence category.

SG-615 Dealing with a **risk of harm** involves consideration of both the likelihood of harm occurring and the extent of it if it does. Risk of harm is less serious than the same actual harm. Where the offence has caused risk of harm but no (or less) actual harm the normal approach is to move down to the next category of harm. This may not be appropriate if either the likelihood or extent of potential harm is particularly high.

Culpability	Harm	
Deliberate Intentional breach of or flagrant disregard for the law by person(s) whose position of responsibility in the organisation is such that their acts/omissions can properly be attributed to the organisation; **OR** deliberate failure by organisation to put in place and to enforce such systems as could reasonably be expected in all the circumstances to avoid commission of the offence.	**Category 1**	• Polluting material of a dangerous nature, for example, hazardous chemicals or sharp objects • Major adverse effect or damage to air or water quality, amenity value, or property • Polluting material was noxious, widespread or pervasive with long-lasting effects on human health or quality of life, animal health or flora • Major costs incurred through clean-up, site restoration or animal rehabilitation • Major interference with, prevention or undermining of other lawful activities or regulatory regime due to offence
Reckless Actual foresight of, or wilful blindness to, risk of offending but risk nevertheless taken by person(s) whose position of responsibility in the organisation is such that their acts/omissions can properly be attributed to the organisation; **OR** reckless failure by organisation to put in place and to enforce such systems as could reasonably be expected in all the circumstances to avoid commission of the offence.	**Category 2**	• Significant adverse effect or damage to air or water quality, amenity value, or property • Significant adverse effect on human health or quality of life, animal health or flora • Significant costs incurred through clean-up, site restoration or animal rehabilitation • Significant interference with or undermining of other lawful activities or regulatory regime due to offence • Risk of category 1 harm
Negligent Failure by the organisation as a whole to take reasonable care to put in place and enforce proper systems for avoiding commission of the offence.	**Category 3**	• Minor, localised adverse effect or damage to air or water quality, amenity value, or property • Minor adverse effect on human health or quality of life, animal health or flora • Low costs incurred through clean-up, site restoration or animal rehabilitation • Limited interference with or undermining of other lawful activities or regulatory regime due to offence • Risk of category 2 harm
Low or no culpability Offence committed with little or no fault on the part of the organisation as a whole, for example by accident or the act of a rogue employee and despite the presence and due enforcement of all reasonably required preventive measures, or where such proper preventive measures were unforeseeably overcome by exceptional events.	**Category 4**	• Risk of category 3 harm

STEP FOUR Starting point and category range

Having determined the category, the court should refer to the tables [below]. There are four tables of starting points and ranges: one for large organisations, one for medium organisations, one for small organisations and one for micro-organisations. The court should refer to the table that relates to the size of the offending organisation.

The court should use the corresponding starting point to reach a sentence within the category range. The court should then consider further adjustment within the category range for aggravating and mitigating features, set out [below].

General principles to follow in setting a fine

The court should determine the appropriate level of fine in accordance with section 164 of the Criminal Justice Act 2003, which requires that the fine must reflect the seriousness of the offence and the court to take into account the financial circumstances of the offender.

The level of fine should reflect the extent to which the offender fell below the required standard. The fine should meet, in a fair and proportionate way, the objectives of punishment, deterrence and the removal of gain derived through the commission of the offence; it should not be cheaper to offend than to take the appropriate precautions.

Obtaining financial information

Offenders which are companies, partnerships or bodies delivering a public or charitable service, are expected to provide comprehensive accounts for the last three years, to enable the court to make an accurate assessment of its financial status. In the absence of such disclosure, or where the court is not satisfied that it has been given sufficient reliable information, the court will be entitled to draw reasonable inferences as to the offender's means from evidence it has heard and from all the circumstances of the case.

Normally, only information relating to the organisation before the court will be relevant, unless it is demonstrated to the court that the resources of a linked organisation are available and can properly be taken into account.

1. *For companies*: annual accounts. Particular attention should be paid to turnover; profit before tax; directors' remuneration, loan accounts and pension provision; and assets as disclosed by the balance sheet. Most companies are required to file audited accounts at Companies House. **Failure to produce relevant recent accounts on request may properly lead to the conclusion that the company can pay any appropriate fine.**
2. *For partnerships*: annual accounts. Particular attention should be paid to turnover; profit before tax; partners' drawings, loan accounts and pension provision; assets as above. Limited Liability Partnerships (LLPs) may be required to file audited accounts with Companies House. **If adequate accounts are not produced on request, see paragraph 1.**
3. *For local authorities, fire authorities and similar public bodies*: the Annual Revenue Budget ('ARB') is the equivalent of turnover and the best indication of the size of the defendant organisation. It is unlikely to be necessary to analyse specific expenditure or reserves (where relevant) unless inappropriate expenditure is suggested.
4. *For health trusts*: the independent regulator of NHS Foundation Trusts is Monitor. It publishes quarterly reports and annual figures for the financial strength and stability of trusts from which the annual income can be seen, available via **www.monitor-nhsft.gov.uk**. Detailed analysis of expenditure or reserves is unlikely to be called for.
5. *For charities*: it will be appropriate to inspect annual audited accounts. Detailed analysis of expenditure or reserves is unlikely to be called for unless there is a suggestion of unusual or unnecessary expenditure.

At step four, the court will be required to focus on the organisation's annual turnover or equivalent to reach a starting point for a fine. At step six, the court may be required to refer to the other financial factors listed above to ensure that the proposed fine is proportionate.

Very large organisations
Where a defendant company's turnover or equivalent very greatly exceeds the threshold for large companies, it may be necessary to move outside the suggested range to achieve a proportionate sentence.

Large — Turnover or equivalent: £50 million and over.

Large	Starting Point	Range
Deliberate		
Category 1	£1,000,000	£450,000 — £3,000,000
Category 2	£500,000	£180,000 — £1,250,000
Category 3	£180,000	£100,000 — £450,000
Category 4	£100,000	£55,000 — £250,000
Reckless		
Category 1	£550,000	£250,000 — £1,500,000
Category 2	£250,000	£100,000 — £650,000
Category 3	£100,000	£60,000 — £250,000
Category 4	£60,000	£35,000 — £160,000
Negligent		
Category 1	£300,000	£140,000 — £750,000
Category 2	£140,000	£60,000 — £350,000
Category 3	£60,000	£35,000 — £150,000
Category 4	£35,000	£22,000 — £100,000
Low / No culpability		
Category 1	£50,000	£25,000 — £130,000
Category 2	£25,000	£14,000 — £70,000
Category 3	£14,000	£10,000 — £40,000
Category 4	£10,000	£7,000 — £25,000

Medium — Turnover or equivalent: between £10 million and £50 million.

Medium	Starting Point	Range
Deliberate		
Category 1	£400,000	£170,000 — £1,000,000
Category 2	£170,000	£70,000 — £450,000
Category 3	£70,000	£40,000 — £180,000
Category 4	£40,000	£22,000 — £100,000
Reckless		
Category 1	£220,000	£100,000 — £500,000
Category 2	£100,000	£40,000 — £250,000
Category 3	£40,000	£24,000 — £100,000
Category 4	£24,000	£14,000 — £60,000
Negligent		
Category 1	£120,000	£55,000 — £300,000
Category 2	£55,000	£25,000 — £140,000
Category 3	£25,000	£14,000 — £60,000
Category 4	£14,000	£8,000 — £35,000

Medium	Starting Point	Range
Low / No culpability		
Category 1	£20,000	£10,000 — £50,000
Category 2	£10,000	£5,500 — £25,000
Category 3	£5,000	£3,500 — £14,000
Category 4	£3,000	£2,500 — £10,000

Small — Turnover or equivalent: between £2 million and £10 million.

Small	Starting Point	Range
Deliberate		
Category 1	£100,000	£45,000 — £400,000
Category 2	£45,000	£17,000 — £170,000
Category 3	£17,000	£10,000 — £70,000
Category 4	£10,000	£5,000 — £40,000
Reckless		
Category 1	£55,000	£24,000 — £220,000
Category 2	£24,000	£10,000 — £100,000
Category 3	£10,000	£5,000 — £40,000
Category 4	£5,000	£3,000 — £24,000
Negligent		
Category 1	£30,000	£13,000 — £120,000
Category 2	£13,000	£6,000 — £55,000
Category 3	£6,000	£3,000 — £23,000
Category 4	£3,000	£1,500 — £14,000
Low / No culpability		
Category 1	£5,000	£2,500 — £20,000
Category 2	£2,500	£1,000 — £10,000
Category 3	£1,000	£700 — £5,000
Category 4	£700	£400 — £3,500

Micro — Turnover or equivalent: not more than £2 million.

Micro	Starting Point	Range
Deliberate		
Category 1	£50,000	£9,000 — £95,000
Category 2	£22,000	£3,000 — £45,000
Category 3	£9,000	£2,000 — £17,000
Category 4	£5,000	£1,000 — £10,000
Reckless		
Category 1	£30,000	£3,000 — £55,000
Category 2	£12,000	£1,500 — £24,000
Category 3	£5,000	£1,000 — £10,000
Category 4	£3,000	£500 — £5,500

Micro	Starting Point	Range
Negligent		
Category 1	£15,000	£1,500 — £30,000
Category 2	£6,500	£1,000 — £13,000
Category 3	£2,500	£500 — £5,500
Category 4	£1,400	£350 — £3,000
Low / No culpability		
Category 1	£2,500	£500 — £5,000
Category 2	£1,000	£350 — £2,400
Category 3	£400	£175 — £1,000
Category 4	£200	£100 — £700

The table below contains a **non-exhaustive** list of factual elements providing the context of the offence and factors relating to the offender. Identify whether any combination of these, or other relevant factors, should result in an upward or downward adjustment from the starting point. **In particular, relevant recent convictions and/or a history of non-compliance are likely to result in a substantial upward adjustment.** In some cases, having considered these factors, it may be appropriate to move outside the identified category range.

Factors increasing seriousness	Factors reducing seriousness or reflecting mitigation
Statutory aggravating factors: Previous convictions, having regard to a) the nature of the offence to which the conviction relates and its relevance to the current offence; and b) the time that has elapsed since the conviction *Other aggravating factors include:* History of non-compliance with warnings by regulator Location of the offence, for example, near housing, schools, livestock or environmentally sensitive sites Repeated incidents of offending or offending over an extended period of time, where not charged separately Deliberate concealment of illegal nature of activity Ignoring risks identified by employees or others Established evidence of wider/community impact Breach of any order Offence committed for financial gain Obstruction of justice	No previous convictions **or** no relevant/recent convictions Evidence of steps taken to remedy problem Remorse Compensation paid voluntarily to remedy harm caused One-off event not commercially motivated Little or no financial gain Effective compliance and ethics programme Self-reporting, co-operation and acceptance of responsibility Good character and/or exemplary conduct

SG-616 STEPS FIVE TO SEVEN

The court should now 'step back' and, using the factors set out in steps five, six and seven, review whether the sentence as a whole meets, in a fair way, the objectives of punishment, deterrence and removal of gain derived through the commission of the offence. At steps five to seven, the court may increase or reduce the proposed fine reached at step four, if necessary moving outside the range.

SG-617 STEP FIVE **Ensure that the combination of financial orders (compensation, confiscation if appropriate, and fine) removes any economic benefit derived from the offending**

The court should remove any economic benefit the offender has derived through the commission of the offence including:

- avoided costs;
- operating savings;
- any gain made as a direct result of the offence.

Where the offender is fined, the amount of economic benefit derived from the offence should normally be added to the fine arrived at in step four. If a confiscation order is made, in considering economic benefit, the court should avoid double recovery.

Economic benefit will not always be an identifiable feature of a case. For example, in some water pollution cases there may be strict liability but very little obvious gain. However, even in these cases there may be some avoidance of cost, for example alarms not installed and maintained, inadequate funding or security measures not installed. Any costs avoided will be considered as economic benefit.

Where it is not possible to calculate or estimate the economic benefit, the court may wish to draw on information from the enforcing authorities about the general costs of operating within the law.

STEP SIX Check whether the proposed fine based on turnover is proportionate to the means of the offender SG-618

The combination of financial orders must be sufficiently substantial to have a real economic impact which will bring home to both management and shareholders the need to improve regulatory compliance. Whether the fine will have the effect of putting the offender out of business will be relevant; in some bad cases this may be an acceptable consequence.

It will be necessary to examine the financial circumstances of the organisation in the round. If an organisation has a small profit margin relative to its turnover, downward adjustment may be needed. If it has a large profit margin, upward adjustment may be needed.

In considering the ability of the offending organisation to pay any financial penalty, the court can take into account the power to allow time for payment or to order that the amount be paid in instalments.

STEP SEVEN Consider other factors that may warrant adjustment of the proposed fine SG-619

The court should consider any further factors that are relevant to ensuring that the proposed fine is proportionate having regard to the means of the offender and the seriousness of the offence.

Where the fine will fall on public or charitable bodies, the fine should normally be substantially reduced if the offending organisation is able to demonstrate the proposed fine would have a significant impact on the provision of their services.

The non-exhaustive list below contains additional factual elements the court should consider in deciding whether an increase or reduction to the proposed fine is required:

- fine impairs offender's ability to make restitution to victims;
- impact of fine on offender's ability to improve conditions in the organisation to comply with the law;
- impact of fine on employment of staff, service users, customers and local economy.

STEP EIGHT Consider any factors which indicate a reduction, such as assistance to the prosecution SG-620

The court should take into account sections 73 and 74 of the Serious Organised Crime and Police Act 2005 (assistance by defendants: reduction or review of sentence) and any other rule of law by virtue of which an offender may receive a discounted sentence in consequence of assistance given (or offered) to the prosecutor or investigator.

STEP NINE Reduction for guilty pleas

The court should take account of any potential reduction for a guilty plea in accordance with section 144 of the Criminal Justice Act 2003 and the Guilty Plea guideline.

STEP TEN Ancillary orders

In all cases, the court must consider whether to make ancillary orders. These may include:

Forfeiture of vehicle

The court may order the forfeiture of a vehicle used in or for the purposes of the commission of the offence in accordance with section 33C of the Environmental Protection Act 1990.

Deprivation of property

Where section 33C of the Environmental Protection Act 1990 does not apply, the court may order the offender be deprived of property used to commit crime or intended for that purpose in accordance with section 143 of the Powers of Criminal Courts (Sentencing) Act 2000. In considering whether to make an order under section 143, the court must have regard to the value of the property and the likely effects on the offender of making the order taken together with any other order the court makes.

Remediation

Where an offender is convicted of an offence under regulation 38(1), (2) or (3) of the Environmental Permitting (England and Wales) Regulations 2010, a court may order the offender to take steps to remedy the cause of the offence within a specified period in accordance with regulation 44 of the Environmental Permitting (England and Wales) Regulations 2010.

STEP ELEVEN Totality principle

If sentencing an offender for more than one offence, or where the offender is already serving a sentence, consider whether the total sentence is just and proportionate to the offending behaviour.

STEP TWELVE Reasons

Section 174 of the Criminal Justice Act 2003 imposes a duty to give reasons for, and explain the effect of, the sentence.

SG-621 **Other environmental offences**

In sentencing other relevant and analogous environmental offences, the court should refer to the sentencing approach in steps one to three and five to seven of the guideline, **adjusting the starting points and ranges bearing in mind the statutory maxima** for those offences. An indicative list of such offences is set out below.

Offence	Mode of trial	Statutory maxima
Section 1 Control of Pollution (Amendment) Act 1989 — transporting controlled waste without registering	Triable summarily only	• level 5 fine
Section 34 Environmental Protection Act 1990 — breach of duty of care	Triable either way	• when tried on indictment: unlimited fine • when tried summarily: level 5 fine
Section 80 Environmental Protection Act 1990 — breach of an abatement notice	Triable summarily only	• where the offence is committed on industrial, trade or business premises: £20,000 fine • where the offence is committed on non-industrial etc. premises: level 5 fine with a further fine of an amount equal to one-tenth of that level for each day on which the offence continues after the conviction
Section 111 Water Industry Act 1991 — restrictions on use of public sewers	Triable either way	• when tried on indictment: imprisonment for a term not exceeding two years or a fine or both • when tried summarily: a fine not exceeding the statutory maximum and a further fine not exceeding £50 for each day on which the offence continues after conviction
Offences under the Transfrontier Shipment of Waste Regulations 2007	Triable either way	• when tried on indictment: a fine or two years' imprisonment or both • when tried summarily: a fine not exceeding the statutory maximum or three months' imprisonment or both

INDIVIDUALS SG-622

Unauthorised or harmful deposit, treatment or disposal etc. of waste

Illegal discharges to air, land and water

Environmental Protection Act 1990 (section 33)

Environmental Permitting (England and Wales) Regulations 2010 (regulations 12 and 38(1), (2) and (3))

Also relevant, with adjustments, to certain related offences (see [SG-621])

Triable either way

Maximum: when tried on indictment: unlimited fine and/or 5 years' custody
when tried summarily: £50,000 fine and/or 6 months' custody

Offence range: conditional discharge — 3 years' custody

Use this guideline when the offender is an individual. If the offender is an organisation, please refer to the guideline for organisations.

Confiscation
Committal to the Crown Court for sentence is mandatory if confiscation (see step two) is to be considered: Proceeds of Crime Act 2002 section 70. In such cases magistrates should state whether they would otherwise have committed for sentence.
If a fine is imposed, the financial orders must be considered in this order: (1) compensation, (2) confiscation, and (3) fine (see Proceeds of Crime Act 2002 section 13).

STEP ONE Compensation SG-623

The court must consider making a compensation order requiring the offender to pay compensation for any personal injury, loss or damage resulting from the offence in such an amount as the court considers appropriate, having regard to the evidence and to the means of the offender.

Where the means of the offender are limited, priority should be given to the payment of compensation over payment of any other financial penalty.

Reasons should be given if a compensation order is not made.

(See section 130 Powers of Criminal Courts (Sentencing) Act 2000)

STEP TWO Confiscation (Crown Court only) SG-624

Confiscation must be considered if either the Crown asks for it or the court thinks that it may be appropriate. Confiscation must be dealt with before any other fine or financial order (except compensation).

(See sections 6 and 13 Proceeds of Crime Act 2002)

STEP THREE Determining the offence category SG-625

The court should determine the offence category using only the culpability and harm factors in the tables below. The culpability and harm categories are on a sliding scale; there is inevitable overlap between the factors described in adjacent categories. Where an offence does not fall squarely into a category, individual factors may require a degree of weighting before making an overall assessment and determining the appropriate offence category.

Dealing with a **risk of harm** involves consideration of both the likelihood of harm occurring and the extent of it if it does. Risk of harm is less serious than the same actual harm. Where the offence has caused risk of harm but no (or less) actual harm the normal approach is to move down to the next category of harm. This may not be appropriate if either the likelihood or extent of potential harm is particularly high.

Culpability	Harm	
Deliberate Where the offender intentionally breached, or flagrantly disregarded, the law **Reckless** Actual foresight of, or wilful blindness to, risk of offending but risk nevertheless taken **Negligent** Offence committed through act or omission which a person exercising reasonable care would not commit **Low or no culpability** Offence committed with little or no fault, for example by genuine accident despite the presence of proper preventive measures, or where such proper preventive measures were unforeseeably overcome by exceptional events	Category 1	• Polluting material of a dangerous nature, for example, hazardous chemicals or sharp objects • Major adverse effect or damage to air or water quality, amenity value, or property • Polluting material was noxious, widespread or pervasive with long-lasting effects on human health or quality of life, animal health, or flora • Major costs incurred through clean-up, site restoration or animal rehabilitation • Major interference with, prevention or undermining of other lawful activities or regulatory regime due to offence
	Category 2	• Significant adverse effect or damage to air or water quality, amenity value, or property • Significant adverse effect on human health or quality of life, animal health or flora • Significant costs incurred through clean-up, site restoration or animal rehabilitation • Significant interference with or undermining of other lawful activities or regulatory regime due to offence • Risk of category 1 harm
	Category 3	• Minor, localised adverse effect or damage to air or water quality, amenity value, or property • Minor adverse effect on human health or quality of life, animal health or flora • Low costs incurred through clean-up, site restoration or animal rehabilitation • Limited interference with or undermining of other lawful activities or regulatory regime due to offence • Risk of category 2 harm
	Category 4	• Risk of category 3 harm

SG-626 STEP FOUR Starting point and category range

Having determined the category, the court should refer to the starting points [not reproduced here] to reach a sentence within the category range. The court should then consider further adjustment within the category range for aggravating and mitigating features, [not reproduced here].

General principles to follow in setting a fine

The court should determine the appropriate level of fine in accordance with section 164 of the Criminal Justice Act 2003, which requires that the fine must reflect the seriousness of the offence and the court to take into account the financial circumstances of the offender.

The level of fine should reflect the extent to which the offender fell below the required standard. The fine should meet, in a fair and proportionate way, the objectives of punishment, deterrence and the removal of gain derived through the commission of the offence; it should not be cheaper to offend than to take the appropriate precautions.

Obtaining financial information

In setting a fine, the court may conclude that the offender is able to pay any fine imposed unless the offender has supplied any financial information to the contrary. It is for the offender to disclose to the court such data relevant to their financial position as will enable it to assess what they can reasonably afford to pay. If necessary, the court may compel the disclosure of an individual offender's financial circumstances pursuant to section 162 of the Criminal Justice Act 2003. **In the absence of such disclosure, or where the court is not satisfied that it has been given sufficient reliable information, the court will be entitled to draw reasonable inferences as to the offender's means from evidence it has heard and from all the circumstances of the case.**

Starting points and ranges

Where the range includes a potential sentence of custody, the court should consider the custody threshold as follows:

- Has the custody threshold been passed?
- If so, is it unavoidable that a custodial sentence be imposed?
- If so, can that sentence be suspended?

Where the range includes a potential sentence of a community order, the court should consider the community order threshold as follows:

- Has the community order threshold been passed?

However, even where the community order threshold has been passed, a fine will normally be the most appropriate disposal. Where confiscation is not applied for, consider, if wishing to remove any economic benefit derived through the commission of the offence, combining a fine with a community order.

Offence category	Starting Point	Range
Deliberate		
Category 1	18 months' custody	1–3 years' custody
Category 2	1 year's custody	26 weeks'–18 months' custody
Category 3	Band F fine	Band E fine or medium level community order–26 weeks' custody
Category 4	Band E fine	Band D fine or low level community order–B and E fine
Reckless		
Category 1	26 weeks' custody	Band F fine or high level community order–12 months' custody
Category 2	Band F fine	Band E fine or medium level community order–26 weeks' custody
Category 3	Band E fine	Band D fine or low level community order–Band E fine
Category 4	Band D fine	Band C fine–Band D fine
Negligent		
Category 1	Band F fine	Band E fine or medium level community order–26 weeks' custody
Category 2	Band E fine	Band D fine or low level community order–Band E fine
Category 3	Band D fine	Band C fine–Band D fine
Category 4	Band C fine	Band B fine–Band C fine
Low / No culpability		
Category 1	Band D fine	Band C fine–Band D fine
Category 2	Band C fine	Band B fine–Band C fine
Category 3	Band B fine	Band A fine–Band B fine
Category 4	Band A fine	Conditional discharge–Band A fine

The table below contains a **non-exhaustive** list of factual elements providing the context of the offence and factors relating to the offender. Identify whether any combination of these, or other relevant factors, should result in an upward or downward adjustment from the starting point. **In particular, relevant recent convictions and/or a history of non-compliance are likely to result in a substantial upward adjustment**. In some cases, having considered these factors, it may be appropriate to move outside the identified category range.

Factors increasing seriousness	Factors reducing seriousness or reflecting mitigation
Statutory aggravating factors: Previous convictions, having regard to a) the nature of the offence to which the conviction relates and its relevance to the current offence; and b) the time that has elapsed since the conviction Offence committed whilst on bail *Other aggravating factors include:* History of non-compliance with warnings by regulator Location of the offence, for example, near housing, schools, livestock or environmentally sensitive sites Repeated incidents of offending or offending over an extended period of time, where not charged separately Deliberate concealment of illegal nature of activity Ignoring risks identified by employees or others Established evidence of wider/community impact Breach of any order Offence committed for financial gain Obstruction of justice Offence committed whilst on licence	No previous convictions **or** no relevant/recent convictions Remorse Compensation paid voluntarily to remedy harm caused Evidence of steps taken to remedy problem One-off event not commercially motivated Little or no financial gain Self-reporting, co-operation and acceptance of responsibility Good character and/or exemplary conduct Mental disorder or learning disability, where linked to the commission of the offence Serious medical conditions requiring urgent, intensive or long-term treatment Age and/or lack of maturity where it affects the responsibility of the offender Sole or primary carer for dependent relatives

SG-627 STEPS FIVE AND SIX

Where the sentence is or includes a fine, the court should 'step back' and, using the factors set out in steps five and six, **review whether the sentence as a whole meets, in a fair way, the objectives of punishment, deterrence and removal of gain derived through the commission of the offence**. At steps five and six, the court may increase or reduce the proposed fine reached at step four, if necessary moving outside the range.

SG-628 STEP FIVE **Ensure that the combination of financial orders (compensation, confiscation if appropriate, and fine) removes any economic benefit derived from the offending**

The court should remove any economic benefit the offender has derived through the commission of the offence including:

- avoided costs;
- operating savings;
- any gain made as a direct result of the offence.

Where the offender is fined, the amount of economic benefit derived from the offence should normally be added to the fine arrived at in step four. If a confiscation order is made, in considering economic benefit, the court should avoid double recovery.

Economic benefit will not always be an identifiable feature of a case. For example, in some water pollution cases there may be strict liability but very little obvious gain. However, even in these cases there may be some avoidance of cost, for example alarms not installed and maintained, inadequate funding or security measures not installed. Any costs avoided will be considered as economic benefit.

Where it is not possible to calculate or estimate the economic benefit derived from the offence, the court may wish to draw on information from the enforcing authorities about the general costs of operating within the law.

SG-629 STEP SIX **Consider other factors that may warrant adjustment of the proposed fine**

The court should consider any further factors that are relevant to ensuring that the proposed fine is proportionate having regard to the means of the offender and the seriousness of the offence.

The **non-exhaustive** list below contains additional factual elements the court should consider in deciding whether an increase or reduction to the proposed fine is required:

- fine impairs offender's ability to make restitution to victims;
- impact of fine on offender's ability to improve conditions to comply with the law;
- impact of fine on employment of staff, service users, customers and local economy.

STEP SEVEN Consider any factors which indicate a reduction, such as assistance to the prosecution

The court should take into account sections 73 and 74 of the Serious Organised Crime and Police Act 2005 (assistance by defendants: reduction or review of sentence) and any other rule of law by virtue of which an offender may receive a discounted sentence in consequence of assistance given (or offered) to the prosecutor or investigator.

STEP EIGHT Reduction for guilty pleas

The court should take account of any potential reduction for a guilty plea in accordance with section 144 of the Criminal Justice Act 2003 and the Guilty Plea guideline.

STEP NINE Ancillary orders **SG-630**

In all cases, the court must consider whether to make ancillary orders. These may include:

Disqualification of director

An offender may be disqualified from being a director of a company in accordance with section 2 of the Company Directors Disqualification Act 1986. The maximum period of disqualification is 15 years (Crown Court) or 5 years (magistrates' court).

Disqualification from driving

The court may order disqualification from driving where a vehicle has been used in connection with the commission of the offence (section 147 of the Powers of Criminal Courts (Sentencing) Act 2000).

The court may disqualify an offender from driving on conviction for any offence either in addition to any other sentence or instead of any other sentence (section 146 of the Powers of Criminal Courts (Sentencing) Act 2000).

The court should inform the offender of its intention to disqualify and hear representations.

Forfeiture of vehicle

The court may order the forfeiture of a vehicle used in or for the purposes of the commission of the offence in accordance with section 33C of the Environmental Protection Act 1990.

Deprivation of property

Where section 33C of the Environmental Protection Act 1990 does not apply, the court may order the offender to be deprived of property used to commit crime or intended for that purpose in accordance with section 143 of the Powers of Criminal Courts (Sentencing) Act 2000. In considering whether to make an order under section 143, the court must have regard to the value of the property and the likely effects on the offender of making the order taken together with any other order the court makes.

Remediation

Where an offender is convicted of an offence under regulation 38(1), (2) or (3) of the Environmental Permitting (England and Wales) Regulations 2010, a court may order the offender to take steps to remedy the cause of the offence within a specified period in accordance with regulation 44 of the Environmental Permitting (England and Wales) Regulations 2010.

STEP TEN Totality principle

If sentencing an offender for more than one offence, or where the offender is already serving a sentence, consider whether the total sentence is just and proportionate to the offending behaviour.

STEP ELEVEN Reasons

Section 174 of the Criminal Justice Act 2003 imposes a duty to give reasons for, and explain the effect of, the sentence.

STEP TWELVE Consideration for time spent on bail

The court must consider whether to give credit for time spent on bail in accordance with section 240A of the Criminal Justice Act 2003.

SG-631 Other environmental offences

In sentencing other relevant and analogous environmental offences, the court should refer to the sentencing approach in steps one to three and five and six of the guideline, **adjusting the starting points and ranges bearing in mind the statutory maxima** for those offences. An indicative list of such offences is set out [at SG-621 **— the list is identical for organisations and individuals**].

SG-632 Annex: Fine Bands and Community Orders

[The tables set out here are also set out in the Magistrates' Court Sentencing Guidelines, which includes further guidance on fines and community orders: see **SG-358** and **SG-382**.]

Index